The Ohio Paralegal

Essential Rules, Documents, and Resources

The Ohio Paralegal

Essential Rules, Documents, and Resources

INCLUDES

- A Comprehensive Legal Dictionary
- Ohio Rules of Professional Conduct
- Paralegal Ethics
- Paralegal Certification
- Employment Resources
- Court Opinions on Paralegals
- CLE for Paralegals
- Employment Law Governing Paralegals
- Timelines
- Sample Documents
- State Research and Citation

By

William P. Statsky

Kathleen Mercer Reed

Bradene L. Moore

THOMSON
DELMAR LEARNING

Australia Canada Mexico Singapore South Africa Spain United Kingdom United States

WEST LEGAL STUDIES

THE OHIO PARALEGAL: Essential Rules, Documents, and Resources
William P. Statsky, Kathleen Mercer Reed, and Bradene L. Moore

Career Education Strategic Business Unit:
Vice President:
Dawn Gerrain

Director of Learning Solutions:
John Fedor

Managing Editor:
Robert L. Serenka, Jr.

Acquisitions Editor:
Shelley Esposito

Senior Product Manager:
Melissa Riveglia

Editorial Assistant:
Melissa ZaZa

Director of Production:
Wendy A. Troeger

Senior Content Project Manager:
Betty L. Dickson

Art Director:
Joy Kocsis

Director of Marketing:
Wendy Mapstone

Marketing Manager:
Gerard McAvey

Marketing Coordinator:
Jonathan Sheehan

Printed In the United States
1 2 3 4 5 XXX 11 10 09 08 07

For more information contact
Thomson Delmar Learning
5 Maxwell Drive, P.O. Box 8007
Clifton Park, New York 12065

Or find us on the World Wide Web at
http://www.westlegalstudies.com

Library of Congress Cataloging-in-Publication Data

Statsky, William P.
The Ohio paralegal: essential rules, documents, and resources/by William P. Statsky, Kathleen Mercer Reed, Bradene L. Moore. -- 1st ed.
p. cm.
"Includes: A Comprehensive Legal Dictionary; The Ohio Code of Professional Responsibility & Ohio Rules of Professional Conduct; Paralegal Ethics; Court Opinions on Paralegals; A Sample Appellate Brief, A Memorandum of Law, and Pleadings; State Research and Citation."

ISBN-13: 978-1-4180-1298-4
1. Law—Ohio. 2. Legal assistants—Ohio.
I. Reed, Kathleen Mercer.
II. Moore, Bradene L. III. Title.
KFO80.S73 2007
340.023'771—dc22
2007020436

Preface

What does it take to be an outstanding paralegal in Ohio? Three key ingredients in your success are your paralegal education, native intelligence, and determination. This book seeks to complement all three by bringing together in one volume a vast amount of material that is either essential for all paralegals or useful for many.

Our focus is on the state of Ohio—state resources, state laws, and state associations. Some federal laws and institutions will also be included when they are directly relevant to the state, e.g., federal government jobs for paralegals in federal agencies located in the state.

The book has eight parts:

Part 1. Paralegal Profession
Part 2. Paralegal Employment
Part 3. Ethics, Paralegals, and Attorneys
Part 4. Legal System
Part 5. Legal Research and Records Research
Part 6. Procedure: Some Basics
Part 7. Sample Documents
Part 8. A Comprehensive Legal Dictionary

The last part contains a comprehensive legal dictionary with selected definitions specifically keyed to Ohio law.

Within each of the first seven parts of the book, the sections will often include the following features:

Introduction: an overview of what is in the section and why it was included in the book.

Table of Contents: an alphabetical list of the main topics or areas covered in the section.

Abbreviations Used in the Section

Materials and Resources: the heart of the section.

More Information: leads to further materials, usually on the Internet.

Something to Check: questions that will help you expand and build on the material in the section.

In addition, there is an online page that will provide updates and related material. To use the page, go to www.westlegalstudies.com

Contents

Acknowledgments

Many people graciously provided assistance in the preparation of this book. In particular, we would like to thank Rebecca Cain, Katharine Essex, Michelle Gossett, Linda Hamann, Michael Hyrne, Kathy McGranahan, Magistrate Alan Mutchler, Denise Schmidt, Cheryl Skolmowski, and Michael Stevenson. In addition the assistance of the following associations is gratefully acknowledged: Cincinnati Paralegal Association (CPA), Cleveland Association of Paralegals (CAP), Greater Dayton Paralegal Association (GDPA), Paralegal Association of Central Ohio (PACO), and Paralegal Association of Northwest Ohio (PANO).

The Ohio Paralegal Reviewers

Laura Barnard
Lakeland Community College

Catherine Barnes
Senior Paralegal

John Benintendi
Mt. St. Joseph

Nancy Cooper
Edison Community College

Mary Mitchell
Professional Paralegal

Tina Murray
EHOVE Ghrist Adult Career Center

Kathleen Sasala
Cleveland Law Librarian

Donna Schoebel
Capitol University of Law

Bonnie Shane
Sinclair Community College

Georgana Taggart
College of Mount Saint Joseph

Janis Walter
University of Cincinnati

PART

1

Paralegal Profession

A. Introduction

In the United States, a paralegal (sometimes called a legal assistant) is a person with substantive legal skills whose authority to use those skills is based on attorney supervision or special authorization from the government. By substantive skills, we mean skills that (a) are obtained through sophisticated training and (b) are significantly more advanced than those possessed by clerical personnel in most law offices.

The Ohio State Bar Association defines a paralegal as follows:

> A paralegal is a person, qualified by education, training or work experience who is employed or retained by a lawyer, law office, corporation, governmental agency or other entity and who performs substantive legal work for which a lawyer is responsible. (*www.ohiobar.org/join/?articleid=273*)

This is also the definition the Bar uses in the certification program that it launched in 2007 (*downloads.ohiobar.org/pub/PCS.pdf*).

This is a fascinating time to be a paralegal in Ohio. Paralegals, working in a wide variety of settings, have made major contributions in the delivery of legal services. The state has a rich paralegal history. Our objective in this book is to give you the perspective of this history and to provide resources that will help you:

- find paralegal employment,
- understand the unique features of our state government,
- find the laws that are the foundation of paralegal work,
- examine some of the major documents that paralegals prepare or help prepare on behalf of clients,
- define all or most of the legal terms that give the legal system its unique character,
- abide by the ethics code, and
- participate in organized efforts to continue the growth of the paralegal profession.

B. Paralegals in the Twenty-First Century

Highlights

- About seven out of ten paralegals in the country work for law firms; others work for corporate legal departments, government agencies, legal aid/legal service offices, and special interest organizations.
- Employment is projected to grow much faster than average, as employers try to reduce costs by hiring paralegals to perform tasks that attorneys would otherwise have to perform.
- Formally trained paralegals have the best employment opportunities as competition for jobs increases. (*www.bls.gov/oco/ocos114.htm*)

Work Settings

Paralegals are found in all types of organizations, but most are employed by law firms, corporate legal departments, and various government offices. In these organizations, they can work in many different areas of the law, including litigation, personal injury, corporate law, criminal law, employee benefits, intellectual property, labor law, bankruptcy, immigration, family law, and real estate. As the law has become more complex, paralegals have responded by becoming more specialized. Within specialties, functions often are broken down further so that paralegals may deal with a specific area. For example, paralegals specializing in labor law may concentrate exclusively on employee benefits. The United States Department of Labor has estimated that there are 224,000 paralegal jobs in the country. Bureau of Labor Statistics, U.S. Department of Labor, *Occupational Outlook Handbook*, 2006–07 Edition (*www.bls.gov/oco/ocos114.htm*).

A small number of paralegals own their own businesses and work as freelance paralegals, contracting their services to attorneys or corporate legal departments. Finally, some paralegals offer limited law-related services directly to the public without attorney supervision.

Paralegal Work

While attorneys assume ultimate responsibility for legal work, they often delegate tasks to paralegals. In fact, paralegals are continuing to assume a growing range of tasks in the nation's legal offices and perform some of the same tasks as attorneys. Nevertheless, paralegals cannot give legal advice, set fees, represent clients in court, or engage in other categories of activities that constitute the practice of law. (For more on these restrictions, see sections 3.1 and 3.2.)

One of the most important tasks of a paralegal is helping attorneys prepare for hearings, trials, real estate closings, and corporate meetings. Paralegals investigate the facts of cases and help ensure that all relevant information is considered. They can also perform preliminary legal research. After analyzing and organizing the factual and legal information, paralegals may prepare written reports that attorneys use in determining how cases should be handled. If attorneys file lawsuits on behalf of clients, paralegals can help prepare pleadings and motions to be filed in court, perform further factual and legal research, and assist attorneys during trial. Paralegals also organize and track files of case documents so that they can be easily accessible to attorneys.

In addition, paralegals perform a number of other vital functions. For example, they help draft contracts, mortgages, separation agreements, and instruments of trust. They also may assist in preparing tax returns and estate plans. Some paralegals coordinate and supervise the activities of other law office employees (many of these paralegal supervisors have joined their own association, the International Paralegal Management Association, found at *www.paralegalmanagement.org*). The variety and complexity of paralegal tasks depend on the kind of law practiced in the office, the competence and initiative of the paralegal, and the willingness of attorneys to delegate.

Paralegals who work for corporations often assist attorneys with employee contracts, shareholder agreements, stock-option plans, employee benefit plans, and other transactional documents. They may help prepare and file annual financial reports, maintain corporate minutes, record resolutions, and prepare forms to secure loans for the corporation. Paralegals often perform compliance work by monitoring and reviewing government regulations to ensure that the corporation is aware of new requirements and is operating within the law. Increasingly, experienced paralegals are assuming additional supervisory responsibilities such as overseeing team projects and serving as a communications link between the legal team and the corporation. When the corporation retains outside counsel, the corporate paralegal has additional liaison responsibilities.

The duties of paralegals who work in the public sector usually vary within each agency. In general, they analyze legal material for internal use, maintain office files, conduct factual and legal research for attorneys, and collect and analyze evidence for agency hearings. They may prepare informative or explanatory material on laws, agency regulations, and agency policy for general use by the agency and the public. Paralegals employed in legal aid/legal service offices in the community help the poor, the aged, and others in need of legal assistance. They file forms, conduct research, prepare documents, and, when authorized by law, may represent clients at administrative hearings.

Paralegals in small and medium-size law firms often perform a variety of duties that require a general knowledge of the law. Those employed by large law firms, government agencies, and corporations, however, are more likely to specialize in one area of the law.

Familiarity with computers in the law has become essential to paralegal work. Computer software packages and the Internet are used to search legal literature stored in computer databases and on CD-ROM. In litigation involving many supporting documents, paralegals usually use computer databases to retrieve, organize, and index various materials. Imaging software allows paralegals to scan documents directly into a database, while billing programs help them track hours billed to clients. Computer software packages are also used to perform tax computations and explore the consequences of various tax strategies for clients.

National Job Outlook According to the U.S. Department of Labor

Employment for paralegals and legal assistants is projected to grow much faster than average for all occupations through 2014. Employers are trying to reduce costs and increase the availability and efficiency of legal services by hiring paralegals to perform tasks formerly carried out by attorneys. Besides new jobs created by employment growth, additional job openings will arise as people retire and leave the field. Despite projections of rapid employment growth, competition for jobs should continue as many people seek to go into this profession. Experienced, formally trained paralegals often have the best employment opportunities.

Private law firms will continue to be the largest employers of paralegals, but a growing array of other organizations, such as corporate legal departments, insurance companies, real estate and title insurance firms, and banks hire paralegals. Corporations in particular are boosting their in-house legal departments to cut costs. Demand for paralegals is expected to grow as an expanding population increasingly requires legal services, especially in areas such as intellectual property, health care, elder law issues, criminal law, environmental law, and the global economy. Paralegals who specialize in areas such as real estate, bankruptcy, medical malpractice, and product liability are often in demand. The growth of prepaid legal plans should also contribute to the demand for legal services. (A prepaid plan is like health insurance in which a person pays an ongoing fee or premium for legal service needs that might arise in the future.) A growing number of experienced paralegals are expected to establish their own businesses as independent paralegals.

Job opportunities for paralegals will expand in the public sector as well. Community legal aid/legal service programs, which provide assistance to the poor, elderly, minorities, and middle-income families, will employ additional paralegals to minimize expenses and serve the most people. Federal, state, and local government agencies, consumer organizations, and the courts also should continue to hire paralegals in increasing numbers.

To a limited extent, paralegal jobs are affected by the business cycle. During recessions, demand declines for some discretionary legal services, such as estate planning, drafting wills, and handling real estate transactions. Corporations may be less inclined to initiate certain types of litigation when falling sales and profits lead to fiscal belt tightening. As a result, full-time paralegals employed in offices adversely affected by a recession may be laid off or have their work hours reduced. However, during recessions, corporations and individuals are more likely to face other problems that require legal assistance, such as bankruptcies, foreclosures, and divorces. Bureau of Labor Statistics, U.S. Department of Labor, *Occupational Outlook Handbook, 2006–07 Edition (www.bls.gov/oco/ocos114.htm).*

Career Videos on Paralegals

To watch a video on the paralegal career:

- go to *www.acinet.org/acinet*; look for video links on this page
- also type "paralegal" in the search box
- or, go directly to the list of all the career videos at: *www.acinet.org/acinet/videos_by_occupation.asp?id=27,* (scroll down to "paralegals and legal assistants").

C. Statistics on Paralegal Employment in Ohio

Exhibit 1.1A presents an overview of paralegal employment in Ohio based on data collected by the state and federal governments. Exhibit 1.1B compares the projected growth of paralegals with that of lawyers and other legal occupations.

EXHIBIT 1.1A Occupational Profile for Ohio Paralegals and Legal Assistants (SOC Code: 23-2011)

Occupational Title	Occupational Description
Paralegals and Legal Assistants	Assist lawyers by researching legal precedent, investigating facts, or preparing legal documents. Conduct research to support a legal proceeding, to formulate a defense, or to initiate legal action.

Ohio Employment Projections
Paralegals and Legal Assistants

2002 Annual Employment	2012 Projected Employment	Change in Employment 2002-2012	Percent Change 2002-2012	Total Annual Openings
5,240	6,600	1,360	26	178

Source: Ohio Job and Family Services, Office of Workforce Development, Labor Market Info Classic (lmi.state.oh.us/asp/CareerEd/CareerDisplay.asp?SOC=23-2011&SOCTitleOut=Paralegals%20and%20Legal%20Assistants)

EXHIBIT 1.1B Employment Growth of Paralegals Compared with other Legal Occupations in the Nation and in Ohio

Trends: Paralegals and legal assistants

Location	Employment		Percent Change	Job Openings [1]
	2004	2014		
United States	224,000	290,600	+ 30 %	8,460
Ohio	5,460	7,000	+ 28 %	200

Trends: Lawyers

Location	Employment		Percent Change	Job Openings [1]
	2002	2012		
United States	695,200	813,100	+ 17 %	20,720
Ohio	21,690	25,410	+ 17 %	650

Trends: Title examiners, abstractors, and searchers

Location	Employment		Percent Change	Job Openings [1]
	2002	2012		
United States	54,700	53,200	-3 %	600
Ohio	1,670	1,640	-2 %	20

Trends: Court reporters

Location	Employment		Percent Change	Job Openings [1]
	2002	2012		
United States	17,800	20,100	+ 13 %	420
Ohio	620	690	+ 11 %	10

Trends: All other legal and related workers

Location	Employment		Percent Change	Job Openings [1]
	2002	2012		
United States	100,800	108,500	+ 8 %	1,870
Ohio	5,090	5,840	+ 15 %	130

[1] Job Openings refers to the average annual job openings due to growth and net replacement.

Source: Career InfoNet; Bureau of Labor Statistics, Office of Occupational Statistics and Employment Projections; Ohio Labor Market Information (www.acinet.org) (click "Occupation Information." then "Employment Trends by Occupation," then "Ohio," then "Legal," then "Paralegal" plus other legal occupations)

Earnings

Earnings of paralegals vary greatly. Salaries depend on education, training, experience, the type and size of employer, and the geographic location of the job. In general, paralegals who work for large law firms or in large metropolitan areas earn more than those who work for smaller firms or in less populated regions. In addition to earning a salary, many paralegals receive bonuses. In May 2004, full-time wage and salary paralegals had median annual earnings, including bonuses, of $39,130. The middle 50 percent earned between $31,040 and $49,950. The top 10 percent earned more than $61,390, while the bottom 10 percent earned less than $25,360. Median annual earnings in the industries employing the largest numbers of paralegals in May 2004 were as follows:

- Federal Government: $59,370
- Local Government: $38,260
- Legal Aid/Legal Service Offices: $37,870
- State Government: $34,910

Exhibit 1.1C compares paralegal wages in major Ohio metropolitan areas.

EXHIBIT 1.1C Paralegal Wages in Major Ohio Metropolitan Areas

Location	Pay Period	2005				
		10%	25%	Median	75%	90%
United States	Hourly	$12.63	$15.61	$19.79	$25.22	$31.41
	Yearly	$26,300	$32,500	$41,200	$52,500	$65,300
Akron, OH	Hourly	$11.73	$13.38	$15.82	$19.69	$25.21
	Yearly	$24,400	$27,800	$32,900	$41,000	$52,400
Canton-Massillon, OH	Hourly	$14.27	$15.49	$17.42	$21.28	$25.45
	Yearly	$29,700	$32,200	$36,200	$44,300	$52,900
Cincinnati-Middletown, OH-KY-IN	Hourly	$11.80	$14.60	$18.18	$23.74	$29.34
	Yearly	$24,500	$30,400	$37,800	$49,400	$61,000
Cleveland-Elyria-Mentor, OH	Hourly	$14.52	$17.19	$22.64	$25.95	$28.15
	Yearly	$30,200	$35,800	$47,100	$54,000	$58,600
Columbus, OH	Hourly	$13.17	$16.61	$19.74	$23.76	$28.16
	Yearly	$27,400	$34,500	$41,100	$49,400	$58,600
Dayton-OH	Hourly	$12.41	$16.42	$20.74	$24.49	$27.43
	Yearly	$25,800	$34,200	$43,100	$50,900	$57,100
Huntington-Ashland, WV-KY-OH	Hourly	$11.23	$11.95	$13.16	$16.08	$20.01
	Yearly	$23,400	$24,900	$27,400	$33,400	$41,600
Springfield, OH	Hourly	$15.97	$17.39	$18.65	$20.12	$21.00
	Yearly	$33,200	$36,200	$38,800	$41,800	$43,700
Toledo, OH	Hourly	$12.40	$14.87	$18.79	$23.32	$25.98
	Yearly	$25,800	$30,900	$39,100	$48,500	$54,000
Youngstown-Warren, Boardman, OH-PA	Hourly	$8.03	$9.91	$12.62	$16.43	$20.58
	Yearly	$16,700	$20,600	$26,200	$34,200	$42,800

Source: Career InfoNet; Bureau of Labor Statistics, Occupational Employment Statistics Survey; the Labor Market Information Office within the State Employment Security Agency (www.acinet.org) (click "Occupational Information", then "Compare Metro Wages, then "Legal", then "Paralegal", then the cities desired)

EXHIBIT 1.1D Paralegal Salaries in Different Regions of Ohio Based on Years of Experience

PERCENT DISTRIBUTIONS OF 2004 SALARY LEVELS OF LEGAL ASSISTANTS BY LEVEL OF EXPERIENCE AND SIZE OF FIRM

Legal Assistant Salary Categories	Firm Size (Number of Attorneys) 1	2	3-6	7-20	21+	All
No Experience						
<$28k	67.9	82.4	83.3	51.5	30.8	60.9
$28-30K	3.6	5.9	16.7	24.2	19.2	14.8
$31-33K	17.9	11.8		18.2	15.4	13.3
$34-36K	10.7			3.0	15.4	6.3
$37-39K				3.0	3.8	1.6
$40-42K					11.5	2.3
$43-45K					3.8	0.8
Total	**100%**	**100%**	**100%**	**100%**	**100%**	**100%**

Legal Assistant Salary Categories	1	2	3-6	7-20	21+	All
3 Years Experience						
<$28k	38.5	50.0	27.3	14.7	3.4	23.6
$28-30K	26.9	6.3	50.0	41.2	13.8	29.1
$31-33K	7.7	18.8	4.5	17.6	24.1	15.0
$34-36K	11.5	12.5	9.1	5.9	17.2	11.0
$37-39K	7.7	6.3	4.5	8.8	20.7	10.2
$40-42K	7.7	6.3	4.5	8.8	6.9	7.1
$43-45K					6.9	1.6
$46-48K				2.9	3.4	1.6
$49-51K					3.4	0.8
Total	**100%**	**100%**	**100%**	**100%**	**100%**	**100%**

Legal Assistant Salary Categories	1	2	3-6	7-20	21+	All
5 Years Experience						
<$28k	10.5	13.3	23.8	5.3		8.9
$28-30K	26.3	26.7	28.6	13.2	10.0	18.7
$31-33K	31.6	13.3	23.8	31.6	16.7	24.4
$34-36K	15.8	26.7	14.3	7.9	16.7	14.6
$37-39K	5.3	6.7	4.8	13.2	20.0	11.4
$40-42K	10.5		4.8	21.1	20.0	13.8
$43-45K		6.7		7.9	3.3	4.1
$46-48K					10.0	2.4
$49-51K					3.3	0.8
>$51K		6.7				0.8
Total	**100%**	**100%**	**100%**	**100%**	**100%**	**100%**

Legal Assistant Salary Categories	1	2	3-6	7-20	21+	All
10 Years Experience						
<$28k	16.0	5.0	7.1	2.3		5.5
$28-30K		20.0	10.7	9.3	3.4	8.3
$31-33K	28.0	15.0	7.1	9.3		11.0
$34-36K	24.0	15.0	25.0	18.6	10.3	18.6
$37-39K	16.0	5.0	14.3	11.6	10.3	11.7
$40-42K	4.0	5.0	7.1	16.3	17.2	11.0
$43-45K	4.0	5.0	7.1	9.3	13.8	8.3
$46-48K	4.0		3.6	14.0	20.7	9.7
$49-51K		5.0	10.7	4.7	6.9	5.5
>$51K	4.0	25.0	7.1	4.7	17.2	10.3
Total	**100%**	**100%**	**100%**	**100%**	**100%**	**100%**

Source: © Ohio State Bar Association. The chart first appeared in Economics of Law Practice in Ohio (Survey 2004), Exhibit 38 (downloads.ohiobar.org/conventions/convention2005/session508%20Economics%20of%20Law.pdf)

Additional Information on Paralegal Salaries

National Federation of Paralegal Associations
www.paralegals.org
(click "Legal Resources" then "Salary Information")

National Association of Legal Assistants
www.nala.org/Survey_Table.htm
www.nala.org
(Under "General Information" click "The Paralegal Profession" then "Current Survey Info")

Legal Assistant Today
www.legalassistanttoday.com
(type "salary" in the search box)

Economics Survey of the Bar

The Ohio State Bar Association has sponsored a comprehensive survey of the economics of the practice of law in the state. The data collected included information on paralegal salaries and billing rates in different regions of the state. See Exhibits 1.1D and 1.1E.

D. Traditional Paralegal Positions in Ohio: Some Examples

Paralegals in Ohio perform a rich variety of tasks in many different settings. There is no single job description that encompasses them all. One way to understand this diversity is to look at selected paralegal profiles in Ohio law offices. The paralegals we have selected are not representative of all or most paralegals in the state, but they do demonstrate the high level of confidence their employers place in them. The primary focus of these profiles is on paralegals in the private sector. For paralegals in government, see sections 2.2 and 2.3. For work settings where paralegals work for legal aid/legal service offices, see section 2.4.

Most attorneys specialize in one or more areas of practice. As you might imagine, the same is often true of the paralegals that they employ. The exception is the solo attorney in general practice. He or she provides a broad array of legal services in many areas of law. Similarly, paralegals who work for such attorneys often provide assistance in the variety of areas covered by their

EXHIBIT 1.1E Paralegal Billing Rates in Different Regions of Ohio Based on Years of Experience

DISTRIBUTIONS OF 2004 HOURLY BILLING RATES FOR LEGAL ASSISTANTS BY FIRM SIZE AND EXPERIENCE

	Firm Size (Number of Attorneys)				
Legal Assistant Billing Rate Category	2	3-6	7-20	21+	All Firms
No Experience					
$50 or less	40.0	60.0	50.0	20.0	41.0
$51-60	30.0	20.0	20.0	17.1	20.0
$61-70	10.0	4.0	10.0	5.7	7.0
$71-80	20.0	8.0	10.0	25.7	16.0
$81-90		4.0	10.0	8.6	7.0
$91-100		4.0		17.1	7.0
$101-110				5.7	2.0
Total	**100%**	**100%**	**100%**	**100%**	**100%**
3 Years Experience					
$50 or less	12.5	25.0	13.3	2.8	11.7
$51-60	62.5	35.0	23.3	11.1	24.5
$61-70		20.0	26.7	22.2	21.3
$71-80		10.0	13.3	11.1	10.6
$81-90	12.5	5.0	10.0	22.2	13.8
$91-100	12.5		10.0	8.3	7.4
$101-110		5.0	3.3	8.3	5.3
$111-120				11.1	4.3
>$120				2.8	1.1
Total	**100%**	**100%**	**100%**	**100%**	**100%**
5 Years Experience					
$50 or less	16.7	4.5	8.6	2.9	6.2
$51-60		27.3	17.1	5.9	14.4
$61-70	66.7	22.7	11.4	14.7	18.6
$71-80	16.7	31.8	34.3	11.8	24.7
$81-90		4.5	14.3	11.8	10.3
$91-100			11.4	17.6	10.3
$101-110		9.1		11.8	6.2
$111-120				11.8	4.1
>$120			2.9	11.8	5.2
Total	**100%**	**100%**	**100%**	**100%**	**100%**
10 Years Experience					
$50 or less	20.0		2.7	3.0	3.9
$51-60	20.0	9.1	18.9	3.0	11.8
$61-70		13.6	13.5	12.1	11.8
$71-80	30.0	40.9	18.9	6.1	20.6
$81-90	10.0	18.2	21.6	6.1	14.7
$91-100		13.6	16.2	18.2	14.7
$101-110		4.5		12.1	4.9
$111-120	20.0		5.4	18.2	9.8
>$120			2.7	21.2	7.8
Total	**100%**	**100%**	**100%**	**100%**	**100%**

Source: © Ohio State Bar Association. The chart first appeared in Economics of Law Practice in Ohio (Survey 2004), Exhibit 25 (downloads.ohiobar.org/conventions/convention2005/session508%20 Economics%20of%20Law.pdf)

employers. In the main, most of the paralegals in the following profiles have specializations because they work in offices where their attorney supervisors specialize.

Becky Weber

Becky is a corporate paralegal responsible for all aspects of corporate formation and organization of limited liability companies and limited partnerships. She also performs online research, completes entity-related IRS filings, drafts business related agreements, and maintains corporate and limited liability company records for several entities.

Stephanie Altieri

Stephanie is a litigation paralegal. Her duties include drafting pleadings, preparing and reviewing discovery, helping with trial preparation, and maintaining client/court contact. She also devotes much of her efforts to assisting attorneys in the creditors' rights practice section. This involves drafting collection complaints, garnishments, attachments, and other post-judgment collection remedies. Stephanie is also a notary pubic.

April Elliott

April is a litigation paralegal who provides assistance in all facets of the litigation process from the initial client contact through the conclusion of a case. She focuses primarily on assisting with insurance defense, personal injury, collection, criminal, and construction litigation cases.

Cynthia B. Nolte

Cynthia is an elder law paralegal and a Geriatric Care Manager (G.C.M.) with membership in the National Association of Professional Geriatric Care Managers. She is committed to maximizing the independence and autonomy of seniors while striving to ensure that the highest-quality and most cost-effective health and human services are used. She assists clients by making health, safety, and wellness visits to nursing homes, assisted living facilities, and clients living independently. She also attends nursing home evaluation and plan-of-care meetings, aids clients in nursing home selection and other appropriate living accommodations, and teaches patient advocacy to their families. She is an active speaker at seminars on topics such as communicating effectively with healthcare professionals, nursing home residents' rights, nursing home resident advocacy, and the pitfalls of neglecting to plan for long-term care.

Jenny Wesley

Jenny is a real estate paralegal. She is responsible for preparing agreements, affidavits, deeds, mortgages, promissory notes, and other documents for her firm's real estate section. Jenny assists with both commercial and residential closings.

Cindy Morris

Cindy is a probate paralegal. She is involved in virtually every step of the estate administration process, and has a wide range of experience in dealing both with multi-million dollar estates as well as releases from administration. Her responsibilities include meeting with clients, drafting the initial probate documents, notifying heirs, devisees, and creditors of the probate proceedings, drafting correspondence, reviewing the decedent's records, and assisting the executor in collecting other death benefits such as insurance and social security benefits. She also collects information and assets for preparation of inventory and appraisal, determines the titling of assets, drafts the estate inventory, maintains financial records of the estate, obtains tax releases, drafts the Ohio and federal estate tax returns and fiduciary income tax returns, prepares accountings for probate and trusts, assists in the audit of estate tax returns, and makes final distribution of assets.

Bonnie J. Yeaman

Bonnie is an employee benefits paralegal. She assists in administration for approximately forty qualified plans, including profit sharing, 401(k), money purchase pension, and fringe benefit plans. Some of her duties as a third-party administrator involve annual testing for each plan, such as nondiscrimination testing and top heavy testing. In addition, for each plan she is in charge of preparing Internal Revenue Service Forms 5500, Summary Annual Reports, and Quarterly or Annual Participant Statements. It is also her responsibility to prepare and distribute election/waiver forms for terminated participants, to allocate plan forfeitures, and to prepare and process forms necessary for hardship withdrawals and loan requests.

Connie J. Russell

Connie is a workers' compensation paralegal. Her duties include assisting employers in the defense of workers' compensation claims. She maintains personal contact with clients and their third party administrators to provide support in the daily management of their workers' compensation claims. In addition, she is responsible for establishing, docketing and managing pertinent due dates; drafting pleadings, independent medical examination letters, violation of specific safety requirement answers; and preparing files for hearing and/or trial by using available resources such as electronic research, and medical records reviews.

Pamela Johnson

Pamela is a bankruptcy paralegal responsible for assisting the firm's three bankruptcy trustees and bankruptcy attorneys with the management of their ever-growing caseload through the use of technology. She draws on her more than 23 years of legal experience in bankruptcy estate administration, malpractice, insurance defense litigation, family law, housing and health care funding issues, and pension plan administration.

Sandra Nappi

Sandra is a medical malpractice and personal injury paralegal. As a former practicing nurse, she brings a wealth of knowledge gained from years of working directly with patients in the health care field. Sandra applies her practical knowledge of medicine in the firm's litigation department by helping trial attorneys with the management of medical malpractice and personal injury cases. She assists with all aspects of case preparation, including conducting interviews, communicating with clients, evaluating the case, reviewing medical records, conducting medical literature searches, scheduling depositions, and providing assistance for final trial preparation.

Amy B. Cesar

Amy is a paralegal in a corporate law department. She points out that working for a corporation is quite different from her prior work in law firms. "First of all," your client is the company for which you work. "For me, personally, the drawback of working at a large company is the many policies and rules which govern your work and behavior. The upside is that . . . you are not simply thought of as a 'paralegal.' If you demonstrate competencies beyond what are 'typical' paralegal responsibilities, you will be encouraged" to use them. "The most important skill that a paralegal in my position needs is flexibility. One never knows what the day will bring in the . . . Law Department. What is important to our in-house lawyers on any given day is what your priority becomes."

E. Nontraditional Paralegal Positions in Ohio: Some Examples

One of the major advantages of paralegal education and experience is the wide range of alternative employment settings where paralegal skills are valued by employers. Here are some examples in Ohio.

Judicial Assistant/Courtroom Deputy/Bailiff

This individual might perform a variety of duties such as helping to maintain a judge's calendar, keep order in the courtroom, and oversee custody over the jury.

Law Librarian

The librarian and librarian assistant maintain library collections such as by keeping them current. He or she also helps answer legal research/reference questions.

Lexis/Nexis

LexisNexis employs individuals with paralegal training. They assist attorneys who handle reference requests and inquiries on the vast online libraries of LexisNexis.

Title Companies

Individuals employed by title companies research tax records, judicial records, and other public documents affecting titles.

Risk Managers

Organizations such as hospitals and large businesses often have risk managers who investigate actual claims and potential risks in order to help design prevention strategies. They identify, investigate, and manage claims, maintain claims files, and coordinate defense preparation activities.

Insurance Companies

Individuals employed by insurance companies investigate claims to determine their validity. They also process claims after review. The following comments provide a more detailed picture of what this kind of work entails.

Becky Cain

Becky is a Senior Casualty Claims Representative with a national insurance company. "I am a claims adjuster who handles third-party claims of injured parties, as well as uninsured and underinsured claims of our policyholders. Now you might be thinking how exactly does a paralegal fit into this job? Well, as a claims adjuster I use all of my paralegal skills, and then some!"

Claims adjusters have many job responsibilities that paralegals also perform. Some of those responsibilities are as follows:

- determine proper policy coverages and determine how they apply to the claim at hand;
- investigate, evaluate, and negotiate bodily injury claims in accordance with certain guidelines to bring them to an equitable settlement;
- establish and authorize reserves and claim payments within your particular delegated authority;
- maintain current knowledge of liability and bodily injury coverages and of court decisions which may impact the claims function;
- maintain current knowledge of policy changes and modifications;
- initiate and conduct follow-ups;
- evaluate medical records and bills (e.g., demand packages);
- assist or prepare files for suit, trial, or subrogation;
- attend depositions and mediations; and
- submit administrative reports.

"I work directly under the supervision of a claims manager. However, we do have 'claims legal counsel.' These are attorneys who work with claims adjusters to respond to any and all legal questions and legal aspects of a claim. If litigation is filed on a claim, the claim would then be assigned to defense legal counsel to handle the litigation process, while I as the claims adjuster, work on trying to negotiate and settle the claim prior to trial. I would also assist defense counsel in litigation, attend depositions and mediations, and be present at all court hearings."

(Note: The offices at which these paralegals work include Krugliak Wilkins Griffiths & Doughterty Co., L.P.A.; Luper Neidenthal & Logan; Owens Corning, Inc. and Nationwide Mutual Insurance Company.)

F. Certification

Ohio paralegals have a number of options when seeking certification. Keep in mind, however, that certification programs are not mandatory. You can be a paralegal in Ohio and continue calling yourself a paralegal without taking and passing a certification examination. Certification is voluntary. Yet some paralegals feel that certification is an extra credential that can enhance their professionalism and commitment to the paralegal career.

Here is an overview of the major certification programs that are available:

National Certification

- CLA/CP certification of the National Association of Legal Assistants (NALA). Passing an exam and fulfilling the other requirements of NALA entitle you to be called a Certified Legal Assistant (CLA) or a Certified Paralegal (CP) (*www.nala.org*).
- PACE certification of the National Federation of Paralegal Associations (NFPA). Passing an exam and fulfilling the other requirements of NFPA entitle you to be called a Registered Paralegal (RP) or a PACE Registered Paralegal (*www.paralegals.org*).
- PP certification of NALS the Association for Legal Professionals. Passing an exam and fulfilling the other requirements of NALS entitle you to be called a Professional Paralegal (PP) (*www.nals.org*).
- AACP certification of the American Alliance of Paralegals Inc. (AAPI). Fulfilling the requirements of AAPI (which does not include an exam) entitles you to be called an American Alliance Certified Paralegal (AACP) (*www.aapipara.org*).

Ohio Certification: OSBA Certified Paralegal

The Ohio State Bar Association (OSBA) has established a voluntary credentialing program that leads to certification as an OSBA Certified Paralegal. The OSBA says it created this credential because it "believes that a program which provides objective standards to evaluate the skills, education, and character of paralegals will be of great benefit to the legal profession and the public." Certification is "for experienced paralegals that requires a high level of substantial involvement in the profession." The program is administered by a Paralegal Certification Board consisting of members appointed by the president of the OSBA. The Board will determine eligibility for certification, administer the written exam, and set passage rates. This program is patterned after the legal specialization program that the OSBA administers for attorneys.

Summary of Requirements

1. Fit within the definition of a paralegal as "a person, qualified by education, training or work experience, who is employed or retained by a lawyer, law office, corporation, governmental agency or other entity and who performs substantive legal work for which a lawyer is responsible."
2. Meet specified education/experience requirements.
3. Attend 12 credit hours of approved continuing legal or paralegal education prior to taking the examination.
4. Submit three professional references.
5. Pass the written examination.

Education/Experience

The education/experience requirements are as follows:

1. A bachelor's degree in any discipline and satisfactory completion of a paralegal studies program consisting of at least 20 semester hours (or equivalent clock hours) and a minimum of 1 year of full time experience as a practicing paralegal (or its equivalent 2,000 hours); OR
2. A bachelor's degree in paralegal studies consisting of least 124 semester hours (or equivalent clock hours) and a minimum of 1 year of full time experience as a practicing paralegal (or its equivalent of 2,000 hours); OR
3. An associate's degree in paralegal studies consisting of at least 60 semester hours (or equivalent clock hours) with a minimum of 5 years of full time experience as a practicing paralegal (or its equivalent of 10,000 hours), OR
4. A high school diploma or equivalent plus 7 years of full time experience as a practicing paralegal (or its equivalent of 14,000 hours). (To be eligible under this fourth option, you must have been employed as a paralegal before December 31, 2006.)

Continuing Legal or Paralegal Education

In the three years immediately prior to taking the examination, you must have attended at least 12 credit hours of approved continuing legal or paralegal education. A minimum of two and one half of these credit hours must be in legal ethics, professionalism, and substance abuse. Education qualifies if it is:

- approved by Ohio Supreme Court Commission on CLE,
- approved by National Association of Legal Assistants (NALA), or
- approved by National Federation of Paralegal Associations (NFPA)

Professional References

At least three "professional references" must be submitted. Two must be from Ohio attorneys in good standing "who have direct knowledge of the applicant's skills and work as a paralegal." The third reference can be from a judge, magistrate, hearing officer, mediator, arbitrator, or educator who has "direct knowledge of the applicant's skills and work as a paralegal." You must not be related to any person who provides a reference.

Written Examination

There will be a 4-hour written exam covering skills ("competencies") and specific topics. The exam will consist of multiple choice and brief answer questions. Testing sites are expected to be in Columbus, Cincinnati, Cleveland, and Toledo. Here is an overview of the skills and topics that can be tested:

Skills ("Competencies") Tested: Critical and analytical thinking, communication (both oral and written), and computer skills.

Areas Tested:

- Legal Research and Writing (10 percent of the exam)
- Legal Ethics and Professional Conduct (20 percent of the exam)
- Communication (15 percent of the exam)
- Computer Knowledge (5 percent of the exam)
- Law Office Management (5 percent of the exam)
- Four Substantive and Procedural Law Topics: (1) American Legal System, (2) Civil Rules and Procedure, and (3) (4) the applicant's choice of any two of the following seven areas: Administrative Law, Bankruptcy, Contracts, Business Organizations, Criminal Law, Probate and Estate Planning, and Real Estate (substantive law will be 20 percent of the exam; procedural law will be 25 percent of the exam)

Recertification

Once you complete the requirements, you remain certified for 4 years, after which you may seek recertification by fulfilling all of the eligibility requirements for initial certification except for the written examination.

Biennial Reporting

Every 2 years you must file a report with the Paralegal Certification Board stating that there has been no material change in the information submitted in the application for certification.

Fees

	Members	Nonmembers
Application	$150	$200
Examination Fee	$100	$150
Biennial Report	$100	$150
Recertification	$150	$200

Contacts
Ohio State Bar Association
Specialization Certification
P.O. Box 16562
Columbus, OH 43216-6562
800-282-6556; 614-487-2050
downloads.ohiobar.org/ParalegalCert/CertifiedParalegal.pdf
www.ohiobar.org/join/?articleid=763

Kalpana Yalmanchili
Director of Bar Services
Ohio State Bar Association
614-487-4433
kyalamanchili@ohiobar.org

G. More Information

Paralegal Associations in Ohio
See section 1.2 for information on every paralegal and related association in Ohio.

Ohio's Paralegal Certification Program
downloads.ohiobar.org/ParalegalCert/CertifiedParalegal.pdf
www.lawcrossing.com/article/index.php?id=1786

OSBA Establishes Paralegal Credentialing Program
www.ohiobar.org/pubs/newsletters/?op=view&type=paralegal&VolumeID=&IssueID=29&ArticleID=224

Frequently Asked Questions About the Paralegal Certification Program
www.ohiobar.org/join/?articleid=763

Guide to Paralegals in Greater Cincinnati
www.cincinnatiparalegals.org/GuidetoParalegalsinGreaterCincinnati2005.pdf

Paralegal Salary Survey (Columbus Bar Association and Paralegal Association of Central Ohio)
www.cbalaw.org/formsdocuments/documents/2005FinalParalegalSalaryStudyReport.pdf

United States Department of Labor, Paralegals, and Legal Assistants
www.bls.gov/oco/ocos114.htm

American Bar Association Standing Committee on Paralegals (SCOP)
www.abanet.org/legalservices/paralegals

National Federation of Paralegal Associations (NFPA)
www.paralegals.org

National Association of Legal Assistants (NALA)
www.nala.org

NALS: The Association for Legal Professionals
www.nals.org

International Paralegal Management Association
www.paralegalmanagement.org/ipma

Law Firms in Ohio
www.hg.org/northam-firms.html
www.hg.org/firms-ohio.html
lawyers.findlaw.com
www.findlaw.com/11stategov/oh/index.html

Economics Survey (Columbus Bar Association)(2003)
www.cbalaw.org/projects/2003economicsurvey.php

America's Largest Law Firms
www.ilrg.com/nlj250

National Association of Legal Employers (NALP)
www.nalpdirectory.com

Law Firm Salaries
www.infirmation.com/shared/insider/payscale.tcl
(click "Ohio")

American Association for Paralegal Education(AAfPE)
www.aafpe.org

H. Something to Check

1. Watch the video mentioned in this section (just before Exhibit 1.1A). What is your evaluation of the video?
2. The Ohio State Bar Association's definition of a paralegal is presented at the beginning of section A. Compare this definition to the definitions of a paralegal found on the Web sites of NFPA, NALA, NALS, and ABA's SCOP. (See their Internet addresses immediately above.) List the similarities and differences among the definitions.
3. Pick an area of practice that interests you. Find and compare three law firm descriptions of that area online. In what ways are the descriptions similar and different? To find law firms online, go to google (*www.google.com*) or any general search engine, type "Ohio law firm" and the area of law you are checking. For example:

   "Ohio law firm" "criminal law"
   "Ohio law firm" "adoption law"
   "Ohio law firm" "estate planning"

4. Pick any two cities not listed in Exhibit 1.1C. Using the instructions under Exhibit 1.1C, find the hourly and yearly wages of paralegals for these cities.

1.2 Paralegal Associations and Related Groups in Ohio

A. Introduction

There are many vibrant paralegal associations in the state that have had a major impact on the development of the field. Associations can be very helpful in finding employment and in continuing your legal education while employed. One of the best networking opportunities available to you will be the various meetings regularly held by the associations. The essence of networking is locating other paralegals and exchanging ideas, resources, leads, and business cards. Such exchanges can be important even if the subject matter of a particular meeting does not interest you. Furthermore, your involvement in a paralegal association will help strengthen the association and the profession itself.

This section presents an overview of all Ohio associations, including their Web address and related contact information. When you go to the Web site of an association, examine its services and membership categories. Find out when and where the next meeting will be held. A popular feature of some associations is a job bank that lists current paralegal openings.

The following list also includes (a) attorney associations that allow paralegal membership on committees or as associate/affiliate members of the association itself and (b) other nonattorney associations that have a close relationship to the practice of law.

For more on the involvement of paralegals and paralegal associations in Ohio bar associations, see section 3.4.

B. Ohio Paralegal Associations and Bar Associations with Paralegal Membership Categories

Akron	Cuyahoga County
Cincinnati	Dayton
Cleveland	Stark County
Columbus	Toledo

Akron

Akron Bar Association (ABA)

Associate Membership for Paralegals
330-253-5007
www.akronbar.org
Dues: $80

Legal Career Center
akronbar.legalstaff.com
("Comprehensive job listings for attorneys and support staff")

Cincinnati

Cincinnati Paralegal Association (CPA)

Cincinnati Paralegal Association
P.O. Box 1515
Cincinnati, OH 45201
513-244-1266
www.cincinnatiparalegals.org
cincinnati@cincinnatiparalegals.org

Background: CPA was founded in 1982. Its mission is to:

(a) Promote the paralegal profession.

(b) Provide seminars for continuing legal education.

(c) Act as a forum for the exchange of information.

(d) Promote and support professional standards.

(e) Communicate with the legal community and the general public.

(f) Participate in local and national issues that affect the profession.

(g) Engage in projects, solicitations, and other activities the Board of Directors deems necessary or desirable.

Membership: The major membership categories of CPA are:

1. Active: is currently employed as a paralegal (dues $60)
2. Associate: has been formally trained as a paralegal, but is currently unemployed (dues $60)
3. Student: is currently enrolled in a paralegal school (dues $35)
4. Sustaining: is a person or entity that supports CPA (dues $150)

Number of Members: 290
National Affiliation: None (formerly affiliated with the National Federation of Paralegal Associations)

Publications:
- *The Paralegal Resource* (newsletter)
- Press Releases (see "News" link) (*www.cincinnatiparalegals.org/news.htm*)
- "Paralegals Today" (regular column in Cincinnati Bar Association journal, *CBA Report*) (*www.cincybar.org/member/cbareport.asp*)
- Guide to Paralegals in Greater Cincinnati *www.cincinnatiparalegals.org/GuidetoParalegalsinGreaterCincinnati2005.pdf*

Ethics: Code of Ethics and Professional Responsibility of the Cincinnati Paralegal Association

Services Offered:
- Pro bono activities (e.g., Wills for Heroes)
- Job Bank in newsletter

- Continuing legal education seminars (CLE) (e.g., "Family Law in Ohio")
- Scholarships toward the cost of national certification

Cincinnati Bar Association (CBA)

Affiliate Membership for Paralegals
513-381-8213
www.cincybar.org/pdfs/cbaMembershipApplication.pdf
www.cincybar.org/pdfs/cbaInformationKit.pdf
Dues: $50
("Affiliate members must be sponsored by an attorney member of the" Cincinnati Bar Association.")
(Membership statement in a CBA brochure: "Current membership of more than 4,500, including attorneys, paralegals, and other legal professionals.")

Legal Career Center
cincybar.legalstaff.com
("Comprehensive job listings for attorneys and support staff")

Cleveland

Cleveland Association of Paralegals (CAP)

Cleveland Association of Paralegals
P.O. Box 14517
Cleveland, OH 44114-0517
216-556-5437
www.capohio.org

Background: CAP was founded in 1975. Its mission has been to be "instrumental in allowing paralegals to keep abreast with rapid growth and technological changes in various legal sectors while advancing continuing education and the individual role of the paralegal in executing legal services." (*www.capohio.org/~newcap*)

Membership: The major membership categories of CAP are:

1. *Voting:* has a degree with paralegal studies component; or has a minimum of 3 years of experience as a paralegal performing and currently employed performing at least 51 percent paralegal work (dues: $105).
2. *Associate:* is a graduate of a paralegal program but not currently practicing as a paralegal (dues: $85).
3. *Student:* is currently enrolled in an accredited paralegal training program (dues: $50).
4. *Sustaining:* is a person or entity that supports CAP (dues: $210).
5. *Educator:* is an educational institution that supports CAP (dues: $75).

To join CAP, you must be sponsored by an attorney member of the Cleveland Bar Association (CBA). ("If you do not know an attorney who is a member of the CBA, please contact CAP's Director of Membership.") Student members must be sponsored by the dean of their paralegal school.
www.capohio.org
(click "Membership")

Number of Members: 221

National Affiliation: National Federation of Paralegal Associations (NFPA) (*www.paralegals.org*)

Bar Association Affiliation:
Cleveland Bar Association
216-696-3525
www.clevelandbar.org
Affiliate Member Application
www.clevelandbar.org/join.asp
(click "Paralegal")

Publications:
NewsCAPsule (newsletter)
Compensation and benefit surveys and reports

Ethics: CAP's Code of Ethics and Professional Responsibility
www.capohio.org
(click "Documents" then "Cap Code of Ethics" in the drop-down menu)

Services Offered:
Job bank
(*www.capohio.org*)
(click "Job Bank")
Continuing legal education (CLE)
Scholarships
Student mentor program

Listserv for Cleveland Paralegals
groups.yahoo.com/group/clevelandassociationofparalegals

Cleveland Bar Association

Affiliate Membership for Paralegals
216-696-3525
www.clevelandbar.org/join.asp
(click "Paralegal")

Membership: The major membership categories of CBA are:

1. *Voting*: must have received degree with paralegal studies component; or a minimum 3 years' experience as a practicing paralegal and currently employed performing 51 percent paralegal work.
2. *Associate*: not eligible to be voting member, graduate of paralegal program but not currently practicing, former voting member, does not meet requirements of a practicing paralegal, or is an allied legal professional paralegal manager who does not meet the requirements of a practicing paralegal, or is an allied legal professional.
3. *Student*: currently enrolled in accredited paralegal training program and attending, either part-time or full-time, courses in paralegal studies at an institutionally accredited school.

(4) Cleveland Association of Paralegals-Cleveland Bar Association (CAP-CBA) members must be sponsored by an attorney member of the Cleveland Bar Association or one of its associated Bar Associations. Paralegal students must be sponsored by Dean of Paralegal School.

www.clevelandbar.org/join.asp
www.clevelandbar.org/CAP_application.html

Cleveland Bar Association—Legal Career Center
clevelandbar.legalstaff.com
("Comprehensive job listings for attorneys and support staff")

Columbus

Paralegal Association of Central Ohio (PACO)

Paralegal Association of Central Ohio
P.O. Box 15182
Columbus, OH 43215-0182
614-470-2000
www.pacoparalegals.org
info@pacoparalegals.org

Background: PACO, formerly Legal Assistants of Central Ohio, was formed in 1973. Its purpose is to promote the interests of paralegals, foster relationships with the legal community, serve the public, advocate the Code of Ethics and Professional Responsibility, and endorse the individual missions of PACO and the Columbus Bar Association. PACO actively promotes the paralegal profession. For example, it sells sweatshirts with the following language blazoned across the front:

> "Behind Every Successful Attorney Is an Exhausted Paralegal"

Membership: The major membership categories of PACO are:

1. *Active*: employed in a paralegal/legal assistant capacity under the supervision of an attorney (dues: $120).
2. *Associate*: not currently employed as a paralegal/legal assistant or not designated as such by their employer, or employ.ed in an allied profession (dues: $120).
3. *Student*: enrolled in a paralegal/legal assistant course of study provided by an accredited or approved institution or using an equivalent curriculum (dues: $60).
4. *Sustaining*: is a person or entity that supports PACO (dues: $150) (*www.pacoparalegals.org/membership.htm*).

Paralegals must be sponsored by an attorney member of the Columbus Bar Association. "If you . . . do not know a Columbus Bar Association member attorney, simply enclose your check for the fee and forward to the Columbus Bar. The Columbus Bar Liaison can sponsor you for membership." (*www.pacoparalegals.org/q_a.htm*)

Number of Members: 400+

National Affiliation: National Federation of Paralegal Associations (NFPA)
www.paralegals.org
www.pacoparalegals.org/national.htm

Bar Association Affiliation:
Members of PACO automatically become associate members of the Columbus Bar Association
(*www.cbalaw.org*)
(*www.pacoparalegals.org/membership.htm*)

Publications:

- *Citator* (newsletter)
(*www.pacoparalegals.org/Citator/spring2005citator.pdf*)
- *Newsflash*
- *Paralegal Salary Survey* (Columbus Bar Association and Paralegal Association of Central Ohio)
www.cbalaw.org/formsdocuments/documents/2005FinalParalegalSalaryStudyReport.pdf

Ethics: Canons
(*www.pacoparalegals.org/about_us.htm*)

Services Offered:

- Continuing legal education (CLE)
- Job bank
(*www.pacoparalegals.org/job_bank.htm*)
- Pro bono coordination
- Scholarships

Columbus Bar Association (CBA)

Nonattorney Associate Membership

Nonattorney Associate: "Any person who has never been admitted to the Bar of any U.S. jurisdiction but who is . . . a paralegal, legal assistant, court reporter or law librarian may apply to the Board of Governors for acceptance as an associate member of the Association. Each such applicant must be sponsored initially by a voting member of the Association. Associate members shall not be eligible to vote or to hold office in the Association."
614-221-4112
www.cbalaw.org/members

Ohio State Bar Association (OSBA)

Paralegal/Legal Assistant Associate Membership
614-487-2050; 800-232-7124 (Membership)
www.ohiobar.org/join/?articleid=273
(click "membership application")
Dues: $70.

Paralegal/legal assistant membership is open to any person sponsored by an attorney member of the OSBA in good standing. The bar defines a paralegal as "a person, qualified by education, training, or work experience who is employed or retained by a lawyer, law office, corporation, governmental agency, or other entity and who performs substantive legal work for which a lawyer is responsible." Membership benefits include free access to Casemaker (a legal research site) and three free continuing legal education (CLE) courses per year.

Paralegal/Legal Assistant News

All paralegal/legal assistant associate members receive the *Paralegal/Legal Assistant News* newsletter. "Published three times per year, it contains information pertinent to your job responsibilities, as well as other news about your profession and the OSBA."

OSBA Paralegal Certification

(See section 1.1)
www.ohiobar.org/pub/?articleid=785

Ohio Lawyer; OSBA Report Online

Paralegal/legal assistant associate members also receive the *Ohio Lawyer* magazine as well as the *OSBA Report Online* weekly via e-mail.

Cuyahoga County

Cuyahoga County Bar Association (CCBA)

Paralegal Membership
Dues: $45
216-621-5112
www.cuybar.org/membership-application.shtml

Legal Career Center
cuybar.legalstaff.com/cobrand_jobseekers_main.asp
("comprehensive job listings for attorneys and support staff")

Dayton

Greater Dayton Paralegal Association (GDPA)

Greater Dayton Paralegal Association
P.O. Box 10515
Mid-City Station
Dayton, OH 45402
www.gdpa.org
paralegals.org/associations/2270/files/home188.html

Background: GDPA was formed in 1984. Its purpose is to establish good fellowship among association members and members of the legal community; to encourage a higher level of ethical and professional attainment; to further education and training among members of the profession; and to cooperate and foster working relationships with local bar associations and other professional associations.

Membership: The major membership categories of GDPA are:

1. *Active*: is employed as a paralegal (dues: $60).
2. *Associate*: is a graduate of a paralegal training program, not currently employed as a paralegal (dues: $45).
3. *Associate student*: is enrolled in a formal paralegal training program and not currently employed as a paralegal, or is a student presently participating in an internship program (dues: $45).
4. *Sustaining*: is a person or entity that supports GDPA (dues: $75).

National Affiliation: National Federation of Paralegal Associations (NFPA)
(*www.paralegals.org*)

Publications:
The Paralegal News (newsletter)

Services Offered:
- Continuing legal education seminars (CLE)
- Job bank listings

Dayton Bar Association

Associate Paralegal Membership
937-222-7902
www.daybar.org/pdfs/membership_app_nonattorney.pdf
Dues: $130

> "Any person who, although not admitted to practice law before the Bar of Ohio or another state or territory of the United States, is employed or retained by a lawyer, law firm, or governmental agency as a paralegal (or legal assistant), or is employed in a capacity which involves the performance of legal services under the direction and supervision of an attorney may be sponsored for associate membership by a regular member of the Association who certifies as to the above."

Stark County

Stark County Bar Association

Associate Membership for Paralegals

(Associate membership includes paralegals, sponsored by a regular member of the bar association.)
330-453-0685 (Canton)

Todedo

Paralegal Association of Northwest Ohio (PANO)

Paralegal Association of Northwest Ohio
P.O. Box 1322
Toledo, OH 43606
www.panonet.org

Background: PANO, formerly the Toledo Association of Legal Assistants, was formed in 1977. The original purpose of PANO was to provide a network for local paralegals to share information concerning areas of practice.

Membership: The major membership categories of PANO are:

1. *Active*: is currently employed as a paralegal and meets minimum educational requirements or is a Certified Legal Assistant/Certified Paralegal of the National Association of Legal Assistants (dues: $50).

2. *Associate*: is not currently employed as a paralegal and does not meet the requirements of active or student membership (dues: $50)
3. *Student*: is a paralegal student in good standing in any institutionally accredited school (dues: $20)
4. *Sustaining*: is a person or entity that supports the paralegal profession (dues: $106) (*www.panonet.org/New%20Member%20Application.pdf*)

National Affiliation: National Association of Legal Assistants (NALA)
(*www.nala.org*)

Publications:
PANO Newsletter

Ethics: PANO has adopted the Code of Ethics and Professional Responsibility of the National Association of Legal Assistants.
(*www.panonet.org/Ethics.htm*)
(*www.nala.org/98model.htm*)

Services Offered:

- Continuing legal education seminars (CLE)
- Job bank
- Scholarships

Toledo Bar Association

Associate Membership For Paralegals
419-242-9363
www.toledobar.org

C. National Paralegal Associations

There are a number of national paralegal associations that Ohio paralegals have joined either directly or through one of their affiliates:

National Association of Legal Assistants (NALA)

National Federation of Paralegal Associations (NFPA)

NALS the Association of Legal Professionals (NALS)

American Alliance of Paralegals, Inc. (AAPI)

National Association of Legal Assistants (NALA)

Web Address: *www.nala.org*
Certification Awarded: Certified Legal Assistant (CLA); Certified Paralegal (CP); Advanced Certified Paralegal (ACP)
Certification Requirements: (*www.nala.org/cert.htm*) (*www.nala.org/apcweb/index.html*)
Ethics Code: (*www.nala.org/benefits-code.htm*) (*www.nala.org/98model.htm*)
Newsletter: *Facts and Findings* (*www.nala.org/Facts_Findings.htm*)
Continuing Legal Education: *www.nalacampus.com*
Affiliated Associations: *www.nala.org/Affiliated_Associations_Info.HTM*

National Federation of Paralegal Associations (NFPA)

Web Address: *www.paralegals.org*
Certification Awarded: PACE Registered Paralegal (RP)
Certification Requirements: *www.paralegals.org* (click "PACE/RP")
Ethics Code: *www.paralegals.org* (click "Positions & Issues")
Newsletter: *National Paralegal Reporter* *www.paralegals.org*
Continuing Legal Education: *www.paralegals.org* (click "CLE")
Career Center: *www.paralegals.org* (click "NFPA Career Center")
Affiliated Associations: *www.paralegals.org* (click "About NFPA" then "Local Member Associations")

Nals–The Association for Legal Professionals

Web Address: *www.nals.org*
Certification Awarded: Professional Paralegal (PP)
Certification Requirements: *www.nals.org/certification*
Ethics Code: *www.nals.org/aboutnals/Code*
Newsletter: *@Law* (*www.nals.org/newsletters/index.html*)
Continuing Legal Education: *www.aapipara.org/Calendar.htm*
Career Center: *www.nals.org/careercenter/index.html*
Affiliated Associations: *www.nals.org/membership/states/index.html*

American Alliance of Paralegals (AAPI)

Web Address: *www.aapipara.org*
Certification Awarded: American Alliance Certified Paralegal (AACP)
Certification Requirements: *www.aapipara.org/Certification.htm*
Ethics Code: *www.aapipara.org/Ethicalstandards.htm*
Newsletter: *Alliance Echo* (*www.aapipara.org/Newsletter.htm*)
Job Bank: *www.aapipara.org/Jobbank.htm*

D. Other Law-Related Groups

American Association of Legal Nurse Consultants—Cleveland Chapter
www.aalnc-neocleveland.org

Association of Legal Administrators—Cleveland Chapter
www.alacleveland.org

Association of Legal Administrators—Columbus Chapter
www.alacolumbus.org

Association of Legal Administrators—Northwest Ohio Chapter
www.alanwohio.org

Medina County Association for Legal Professionals
www.medinalegalprofessionals.org

NALS (Association for Legal Professionals) of Ohio
www.nalsofohio.org
www.nals.org/membership/States
(click "Ohio")

NALS (Association for Legal Professionals) of Central Ohio
www.geocities.com/nalsofco/home.html

Northeast Ohio Legal Marketing Association (LMA)
www.lmaneohio.org

Ohio Association of Security and Investigation Services
www.ohoasis.com/mc/page.do

Ohio Mediation Association
www.mediateohio.org

Ohio Regional Association of Law Libraries
www.orall.org

Ohio State Society of Enrolled Agents
www.ossea.org

Ohio Court Reporters Association
ocraonline.com

E. Something to Check

For each of the following three topics, which paralegal association has the most comprehensive links: (a) Ohio law, (b) paralegal employment, and (c) litigation services.

1.3 Sources of CLE for Paralegals

A. Introduction
B. CLE Options
C. Something to Check

A. Introduction

CLE (continuing legal education) is training in the law (often short term) that one receives after completing formal legal training. The training usually takes place at a rented hotel facility. Increasingly, however, you can take CLE offerings online from any location and at any time.

There are three reasons CLE is important for Ohio paralegals:

- First, CLE allows paralegals to keep current on changing laws, new developments in law office management, and the dynamics of the practice of law.
- Second, CLE programs can be an excellent way to network with paralegals and other professionals in the field of law.
- Third, CLE is required if you have received voluntary certification from the Ohio bar (see section 1.1) or from any of the following national certification programs:
- National Association of Legal Assistants (*www.nala. org*) for being a Certified Legal Assistant/Certified Paralegal;
- National Federation of Paralegal Associations (*www.paralegals.org*) for being a PACE Registered Paralegal;
- American Alliance of Paralegals (*www.aapipara.org*) for being an American Alliance Certified Paralegal;
- NALS—the Association for Legal Professionals (*www.nals.org*) for being a Professional Paralegal.

If you move to a state like California that has mandatory/minimum continuing legal education (MCLE) requirements, you may be able to argue that the CLE you took in Ohio will satisfy some of the CLE requirements of that state. (For California's requirements, see *www.caparalegal.org/defins.html.*)

Keep careful records of your attendance at CLE courses and events even if you do not need to do so for certification. CLE helps demonstrate your expertise and can be a marketing tool when seeking a raise or other employment.

On the tax deductibility of CLE, see Appendix A in Part 2.

B. CLE Options

Your Local Paralegal Association

Go to the Web site of your paralegal association (see section 1.2). On the site, look for links that might be labeled "Education," "Continuing Legal Education," "CLE," or "Professional Development," "Career Center," "Events," etc. Click these links to find out if the association sponsors or links to CLE programs. If there is a search box on the site, type in these terms. If there is an e-mail link to the association, send a message inquiring about CLE opportunities.

Also check the Web sites of related associations in Ohio, such as chapters of the Association of Legal Administrators (see the links listed at the end of section 1.2). They may lead you to additional CLE options you should consider.

Online Continuing Education Programs for Paralegals
Columbus Bar Association
www.cbalaw.org/cle
(click "Support Staff Training")

Ohio State Bar Association CLE Paralegal Associate Membership Benefit
www.ohiobar.org/join/?articleid=273

As a benefit of associate membership in the Ohio State Bar Association (OSBA), ". . . paralegal/legal assistants can attend three OSBA continuing legal education (CLE) courses per year free of charge (not valid for OSBA annual convention). This access to the substantial legal curriculum offered by the OSBA CLE Institute provides associate members and the attorneys for whom they work a greater ability to serve their clients."

Ohio State Bar Association Attorney CLE
www.ohiobar.org
(click "CLE")

Many paralegals take some of the same CLE programs offered to attorneys. Ohio attorneys are required to attend 24 hours of CLE every 2 years, including 2 hours of ethics, 1 hour of professionalism based in part on "A Lawyer's Creed" and "A Lawyer's Aspirational Ideals," and 30 minutes of substance abuse education that includes a discussion of prevention, detection, causes, and treatment alternatives.
www.ohiobar.org/cle/?articleid=179
www.abanet.org/cle/mcleview.html

Ohio CLE Institute
www.law.csuohio.edu/lawlibrary/lawpubs/OhioCLE.html

> "The Institute sponsors more than 300 CLE seminars annually on a variety of topics at locations throughout Ohio."

Ohio Commission on Continuing Legal Education
www.sconet.state.oh.us/ccle

Your Local Bar Association

Go to the Web site of your local bar association (see section 3.4). Click "Education," "CLE," "Continuing Legal Education," or "Professional Development" to find out what is suggested or offered by the local bar.

Examples:
Columbus Bar Association
www.cbalaw.org/cle (click "Support Staff Training")
Cleveland Bar Association
www.clevelandbar.org/affiliated_cle.asp?id=189
For Affiliated Professionals, Paralegal Resources, Continuing Legal Education

("The Cleveland Bar Association's Continuing Legal Education Programs offer a wide variety of live classes and online programs to meet your professional education needs. The Supreme Court of Ohio Commission on Continuing Legal Education has approved all courses. If you have any questions regarding a specific program please call the Cleveland Bar Education Center at (216) 696-2404.")

Law Library Association CLE Links

Go to the law library sites in your area (see section 5.8) and find out if they have any CLE links. Here is an example:
Cincinnati Law Library Association
www.hamilton-co.org/cinlawlib

West Legal Education Center
westlegaledcenter.com
(In the CLE pull-down menus, find Ohio programs. Type "ohio" in the search box.)

Taecan
www.taecan.com
(click "OH" in the pull-down menu)

Findlaw CLE
www.findlaw.com/07cle/list.html

International Paralegal Management Association
paralegalmanagement.org
(click "Events" then "Webinar")

Estrin LegalEd
www.estrinlegaled.com

Career Coach International
www.careercoachesinternational.com

American Bar Association CLE
www.abanet.org/cle/clenow

General Search Engines
www.google.com; *www.yahoo.com*; *search.msn.com*
(type "ohio cle")

C. Something to Check

Pick an area of Ohio law and practice. For that area, find five different CLE courses or offerings from different CLE providers. Describe and compare the five.

APPENDIX A

Paralegals in Court Opinions

A. Introduction

One sign of the prominence of paralegals is the extent to which paralegal issues have been discussed in court opinions. This section demonstrates this prominence by presenting excerpts from a wide range of these opinions. Some of the opinions raise ethical issues, although most of the opinions cover broader themes such as the award of paralegal fees, paralegals as jurors, the adequacy of paralegal supervision, the consequences of paralegal mistakes, and inmates as paralegals. Of course, even these themes have ethical implications, but a more comprehensive treatment of ethics will come later in sections 3.2 and 3.3.

To compile the material for this section, we did a search on Westlaw (WL) that asked for every case that mentions paralegals or legal assistants or that involved nonattorney representation.

Westlaw Query:

paralegal "legal assistant" (nonattorney nonlawyer/ 5 represent!)

This query finds every case that mentions the terms "paralegal" or "legal assistant," or that uses the words "nonattorney" or "nonlawyer" within five words of any variation of the word "represent" (e.g., representation, representing, represented). The Westlaw database selected to run this query was OH-CS-ALL. It contains all published and unpublished cases from the following courts:

Ohio state courts
United States Court of Appeals for the 6th Circuit
United States District Courts in Ohio
United States Bankruptcy Courts in Ohio

The query produced almost 600 "hits" from which excerpts have been selected for this section. We have included summaries of opinions that will be (or have been) published in traditional reporters such as Ohio Reports, Ohio Appellate Reports, North Eastern Reporter, Bankruptcy Reporter (B.C.), etc. We have also included excerpts from those unpublished opinions (i.e., opinions that have not been certified for publication) whenever they say anything of interest to the paralegal community. If you wish further information about any of the cases, e.g., whether any of the cases have been reversed or otherwise modified on appeal, check the citations in citators such as KeyCite and Shepard's. (For information on citators on Ohio law, see the chart in section 5.1.)

You can run a similar query on LexisNexis, yielding a comparable response.

B. Abbreviations

Bkrtcy.N.D.Ohio: United States Bankruptcy Court, Northern District, Ohio
B.R.: Bankruptcy Reporter
C.A.Ohio (also **C.A.6**): United States Court of Appeals for the 6th Circuit (case arising out of Ohio)
D.C.Ohio: United States District Court in Ohio
Dist.: District Court of Appeals of Ohio
F.R.D.: Federal Rules Decisions
F.Supp.: Federal Supplement Reporter
N.D.Ohio: United States District Court for the Northern District
Ohio: Supreme Court of Ohio [or] Ohio Reports
OhioApp.: Court of Appeals of Ohio
Ohio Bd.Unauth.Prac.: Ohio Board of Commissioners on the Unauthorized Practice of Law
Ohio Com.Pl.: Court of Common Pleas of Ohio
OhioMisc.: Ohio Miscellaneous Reporter
OhioSt.: Ohio State Reports
SCt: Supreme Court Reporter
S.D.Ohio: United States District Court for the Southern District
US: United States Supreme Court
WL: Westlaw

Westlaw citations are provided by year and document number. For example, 2003 WL 365353 refers to document number 365353 for the year 2002 in the Westlaw system.

C. Case Summaries

Here are the major categories of issues covered by these courts when they mentioned paralegals, legal assistants, or other nonattorneys involved in the delivery of legal services:

Paralegal fees: introduction
Paralegal fees: attorneys performing paralegal tasks

Paralegal fees: recordkeeping/documentation needed
Paralegal fees: overstaffing/excessive time/excessive fees
Improper fee sharing
Mistakes and wrongdoing
Adequacy of paralegal supervision
Conflict of interest: switching sides
Unauthorized practice of law
Miscellaneous cases involving paralegals

Paralegal Fees: Introduction

• Paralegal fees are recoverable

Paralegal fees are compensable as an element of attorney fees. *Specht v. Finnegan*, 149 Ohio App.3d 201 (Ohio App. 2002).

• Paralegal fees are recoverable at market rates

It is beyond dispute that a reasonable attorney's fee includes compensation for the work of paralegals. Counsel contends that reimbursement for paralegal time must be limited to the amount actually paid to the paralegals. This is incorrect. Paralegal time, like attorney time, is measured in comparison to the market rate, if the prevailing practice in the area is to bill paralegal time separately at market rates. *Missouri v. Jenkins*, 491 US 274 (1989) Here, evidence has established that such was the prevailing practice in the Cleveland area, and that the rates claimed are at or below the market rates for similar work. *Cleveland Area Bd. of Realtors v. City of Euclid*, 965 F.Supp. 1017, 1019 (N.D.Ohio 1997).

• The use of paralegals is "eminently reasonable"

Furthermore, it is eminently reasonable that a law firm use paralegals and law clerks to perform work that otherwise would have to be done by an attorney and charged for at significantly higher rates. *National Trust for Historic Preservation v. Corps of Engineers*, 570 F.Supp. 465, 469 (D.C.Ohio 1983).

• Assigning tasks to paralegals that they are competent to perform is a "reasonable allocation of resources"

The court notes that the majority of the time spent litigating this case up to several months before trial was incurred by associates and paralegals whose hourly rates are far lower than that of plaintiff's lead trial attorney. This represents a reasonable allocation of resources that prevents attorneys with high hourly rates from performing litigation tasks that may be performed competently by less senior attorneys or paralegals. *Jorling v. Habilitation Services, Inc.*, 2005 WL 1657060, (S.D.Ohio 2005).

• Fees for "professional functions" of a paralegal

Defendant argues that some of the work performed by plaintiff's counsel, including her attendance at mediation and the due process hearing, did not require the professional training of a paralegal. Plaintiff, however, notes that the paralegal performed several professional functions at the mediation and hearing, including tracking witness testimony, recording documentary evidence, managing exhibits, and taking trial notes. Additionally, plaintiff asserts that the paralegal assisted plaintiff's counsel with researching and writing responsibilities. These are all activities for which a paralegal is eminently suited and properly employed. Plaintiff's request for fees for work performed by the paralegal is reasonable. See *People Who Care v. Rockford Bd. of Educ.*, 90 F.3d 1307, 1315 (7th Cir. 1996) ("The only inquiry for requested paralegal fees should be whether the work was sufficiently complex to justify the efforts of a paralegal, as opposed to an employee at the next rung lower on the pay-scale ladder."). *Gross ex rel. Gross v. Perrysburg Exempted Village School Dist.*, 306 F. Supp. 2d 726 (2004), 736 (N.D.Ohio, 2004).

• The difference between secretarial costs and paralegal fees

In cases where legal services are contracted for at an hourly rate, an attorney's secretarial costs, except in unusual circumstances and then only when clearly agreed to, are part of overhead and should be reflected in the hourly rate. If an attorney charges separately for a legal assistant, the legal assistant's hourly charges should be stated and agreed to in writing. *Columbus Bar Assn. v. Brooks*, 87 Ohio St.3d 344 (Ohio 1999).

• When "properly employed and supervised," legal assistants can decrease litigation expenses

Today, modern electronic accounting methods allow attorneys to submit detailed and specialized billing for their services. Many attorneys now charge lower hourly rates and bill clients directly for paralegal time and for other legal expenses. Where expenses can be clearly and directly traced to the costs associated with a particular matter, those expenses are not properly considered part of an attorney's "overhead." Moreover, when properly employed and supervised, legal assistants may decrease litigation expenses, and their use should not be discouraged. *Ron Scheiderer & Associates v. City of London*, 1996 WL 435312 (OhioApp. 1996). This view was cited with approval in *All Climate Heating and Cooling, Inc. v. Zee Properties, Inc.*, 2002 WL 722968 (OhioApp. 2002).

- **Fees will not be allowed if the paralegal is engaged in the unauthorized practice of law at the law firm**

Paralegal fees are not compensable when paralegals or other nonlawyers (for example, law students) performed work that would constitute the unauthorized practice of law under state law. In Ohio, § 4705.01 of the Revised Code prohibits the practice of law by any person "unless the person has been admitted to the bar by order of the supreme court in compliance with its prescribed and published rules." *Gross ex rel. Gross v. Perrysburg Exempted Village School Dist.*, 306 F. Supp. 2d 726 (N.D.Ohio 2004).

Paralegal Fees: Attorneys Performing Paralegal Tasks

- **An attorney cannot bill for tasks that should have been delegated**

The record indicates that tasks that could easily have been done by a secretary or paralegal were sometimes billed to attorneys. Among the instances of such billing are the following:

- Distributing copies of ordinances, previous memos, and research
- Setting up litigation files
- Attending to summary of depositions
- Phoning Judge Aldrich's Bailiff regarding Case Management
- Faxing supplemental trial brief; proofreading this brief
- Phoning law clerk regarding schedule
- Phoning court clerk regarding status of transcripts
- Filing and serving notices of appearance
- Obtaining a copy of docket and motion of City
- Miscellaneous filing, file organization, and upkeep

The Court deducts 2 percent from the amount of the trial level fee request attributable to hours billed at attorney rates. *Cleveland Area Bd. of Realtors v. City of Euclid*, 965 F. Supp. 1017 (N.D.Ohio 1997).

- **Court deducts 10 percent of counsel's reported hours for failing to delegate tasks to his paralegal**

The court deducts 10 percent of counsel's reported hours for his performance of tasks that could have been performed by a paralegal (including the making of numerous telephone calls and arranging schedules). By his own acknowledgment, the attorney performed a number of duties that were paralegal in nature. The court calculates that he performed 75.25 hours of attorney work, for which he should be compensated at the attorney rate, and 253.5 hours of paralegal work (e.g., "attention to files"), for which he should be compensated at a paralegal rate. *Alexander v. Local 496, Laborers' Intern. Union of North America*, 2000 WL 1751297 (N.D.Ohio 2000).

- **An attorney who should have delegated tasks to a paralegal will have fees reduced even if that attorney had no paralegals in the office**

The court notes that counsel billed full hourly rates for such tasks as obtaining hearing dates, filing pleadings, copying, exhibit preparation, forwarding documents, preparing a certificate of service and ordering a transcript. When questioned about this by the court at the hearing, counsel explained that his office employs no associates, paralegals, or support personnel other than secretaries. Due to the shortage of staff on certain occasions, counsel felt it more efficient to accomplish some of these tasks themselves rather than take a secretary away from office duties. In evaluating counsel's defense of this practice, the court concludes that it is actually beside the point as to what individual performed the services. Our focus is on whether the services were actual and necessary, and what is reasonable compensation based on the type, extent, and value of those services. The appropriate distinction is between (a) legal work, in the strict sense, and (b) investigation, clerical work, compilation of facts and statistics and other work, which can often be accomplished by nonlawyers. While the court acknowledges counsel's attempts to conserve time and personnel, the fact remains that it clearly cannot approve billings of $150 to $200 per hour for tasks which could be performed by a paralegal or office staff. *In re Oakes*, 135 B.R. 511 (Bkrtcy.N.D.Ohio 1991).

- **Inefficient use of an attorney's time should not be compensated for at an attorney's rate**

The trial court should assess the time spent for specified services and determine whether any of the necessary services performed by attorneys could reasonably have been performed by less expensive personnel (i.e. law clerks or paralegals). Inefficient use of an attorney's time should not be compensated for at an attorney's rate but at a law clerk's or paralegal's rate. *Stewart v. Rhodes*, 656 F.2d 1216 (C.A.Ohio 1981).

- Defendant objects to 16.80 hours of time (at $250 per hour) spent by the plaintiff's attorney preparing exhibit books, drafting "to do" lists and case plans, indexing depositions, and preparing for trial. Defendant argues that a legal assistant or law clerk could have performed these tasks, so instead of the attorney's $250/hour rate, recovery should be limited to $75/hour (the paralegal rate) for these hours. However, in its reply, plaintiffs explain that much of that work was done immediately before trial, when only the attorney was available to do it, and, furthermore, that those tasks are properly performed by an attorney, not a paralegal or law clerk. An attorney should choose which exhibits to use for trial. An attorney possesses the knowledge to prepare case plans and formulate "to do" lists, and an attorney prepares for cross-examination of a witness. These 16.80 hours, then, were reasonably performed by the attorney and will be calculated in her portion of the lodestar determination at $250/hour. *Women's Medical Professional Corporation v. Baird, M.D.*, 2003 WL 23777732 (S.D.Ohio 2003).

Paralegal Fees: Recordkeeping/Documentation Needed

• Claim for paralegal fees too nebulous?

The trial court disallowed the remainder of appellee's claim for paralegal fees as too "nebulous." An attorney who is suing for compensation has the burden of proving the nature, extent, and value of his services. In its final decision with regard to this case, the trial court stated the following, regarding the paralegal fees sought to be recovered: "This latter amount includes some rather extensive payments to paralegal personnel, whose roles in the case are rather nebulous, and whose necessity to the proper carrying out of plaintiff's duties to defendant . . . seems far from proven and may not be provable at all. We are disinclined to allow these claimed payments as expenses chargeable to the defendant. These disallowed charges are shown to be $6,202." After an independent review of the itemized bills for the paralegals, we agree with the trial court's assessment. *Affeldt v. Threet*, 1986 WL 4006 (OhioApp. 1986).

• Application for paralegal fees must have sufficient specificity

There is a more fundamental problem with the application for fees presently under consideration. The application fails to inform the Court with sufficient specificity what each lawyer or paralegal did and when he or she did it. Without this specific information, it is difficult for the court to assess the amount of reasonable compensation to which the petitioners are entitled. The petitioners have included time spent by the paralegal in this case without a separate breakdown of that time. *Blumberg v. Jacob*, 624 F. Supp. 669 (S.D.Ohio 1985).

• Attorney and paralegal time should be recorded contemporaneously

The court questions the accuracy of the recording of attorney and paralegal time, since it appears that counsel did not consistently record time, contemporaneously with the expenditure of hours on behalf of the plaintiffs. *Tinch v. City of Dayton*, 199 F.Supp.2d 758, 764 (S.D.Ohio 2002).

• The fee request fails to tell us what a "case clerk" is

The court now turns to the problematic areas of the fee application. Complicating the court's review of the hourly rates billed for professional services is the lack of context inherent in portions of the fee application. For example, the billing statements submitted include work performed by individuals such as Kelly L. Jeric, who is identified simply as "Case Clerk." But neither the statements nor the related affidavits explain what a "case clerk" is. Absent such context, the court can hardly ascertain whether the hourly rate charge for this individual's services is reasonable. Ohio law demands greater specificity. *Chicago Title Ins. Corp. v. Magnuson*, 2005 WL 2373430 (S.D.Ohio 2005).

• Does "legal assistant" mean secretary?

A legal assistant billed at $165 per hour for 4.75 hours, and another legal assistant billed at $115 per hour for 1 hour. The record before us does not divulge who these legal assistants are. From our review of the record, legal assistant could mean secretary. If these persons were paralegals or law clerks to the firm, then the firm had the burden to state this on the record. The fees for secretarial staff are typically considered a cost of doing business and are implicit in the hourly rate charged by an attorney. Additionally, there is no indication what these individuals contributed. There was no evidence as to the work they performed, what a legal assistant is to the firm, or how $165 or $115 is reasonable in this locality. *B-Right Trucking Co. v. Interstate Plaza Consulting*, 154 Ohio App. 3d 545 (OhioApp. 2003).

• Fee documentation here is "extremely sparse"

Our review of plaintiffs' time records is complicated by the fact that documentation is extremely sparse; frequent references to "legal research" and "trial preparation" and "conference with [co-counsel/paralegal]" without further explanation leave us with no guidance as to the reasonableness of the time expended. *Davis v. Mutual Life Ins. Co. of New York*, 1990 WL 375612 (S.D.Ohio 1990).

Paralegal Fees: Overstaffing/Excessive Time/Excessive Fees

• Awarding fees at $225 an hour is an abuse of discretion

The trial court abused its discretion in awarding in excess of $100,000 in attorney's fees and paralegal time at $225 per hour. *Hokes v. Ford Motor Co.*, 2005 WL 2995112 (OhioApp. 2005).

- **Excessive and duplicative billing of attorneys and paralegals**

The real estate agents who prevailed in this civil rights action have filed a motion for attorney fees and costs. After a detailed review of the billing records, the court finds numerous instances of excessive and duplicative billing by their attorneys and paralegals. For example:

> - on 12/22/92, the paralegal billed 16.00 hours for "attend[ing] to preparation for filing of complaint, motion for preliminary injunction and restraining order, discovery requests and other pleadings," and
>
> - on 12/23/92, this paralegal billed 3.00 hours for "attend[ing] to filing of complaint, motion for preliminary injunction and restraining order and discovery requests."

Due to these and other instances of excessive and duplicative work, the Court deducts 10 percent across-the-board from the fee request. *Cleveland Area Bd. of Realtors v. City of Euclid*, 965 F. Supp. 1017 (N.D.Ohio 1997).

- **Why were five professionals (three attorneys and two paralegals) used on a relatively simple task?**

The defendant seeks to recover fees for three attorneys and two paralegals to prepare and file its Motion for Sanctions and its reply in support thereof, to wit: attorney Ireland 2.00 hours, attorney Wiseman 4.00 hours, attorney Parilo 33.25 hours, paralegal Sandy Kreitzer 6.50 hours, and paralegal Beth O'Connor 2.25 hours. The plaintiff argues that the defendant is seeking an excessive amount to prepare and to brief its request for sanctions. This court agrees. To expend 48 hours briefing a relatively simple request for sanctions is excessive. Moreover, to devote the energies of five professionals to that task can lead to redundancies and inefficiencies. *Watkins & Son Pet Supplies v. Iams Co.*, 197 F.Supp.2d 1030 (S.D.Ohio 2002).

- **Why were three paralegals used?**

After an independent review of the itemized bills for the paralegals, we agree with the trial court's assessment. There were three paralegals whose time was included in the billing. Some of their tasks seemed to be a duplication of each other's efforts in addition to being unclear as to the nature of their contribution to the case. We therefore hold that the trial court did not err in disallowing recovery of the paralegal fees. *Affeldt v. Threet*, 1986 WL 4006 (OhioApp. 1986).

- **It appears that counsel and paralegal engaged in duplication of effort**

A reduction by 30 percent of the number of hours expended on the wife's request for attorney fees was warranted in the wife's action against the city after her husband was shot and killed by a police officer. The plaintiffs seek compensation for a number of duplicative hours. Brannon and Knapp (attorneys) and Walters (a paralegal) all recorded a significant number of hours in the months preceding the trial, as well as during the trial itself. It appears from the documentation supplied by the plaintiffs, as well as from the court's observation of the trial (i.e., three people attending the trial every day with only attorney Brannon actively participating), that their counsel and paralegal engaged in duplication of effort. The plaintiffs have failed to explain adequately the tasks that Brannon, Knapp and Walters performed. Numerous entries indicate that one of the three spent ten or more hours on a particular day in "trial preparation," without a detailed explanation of the tasks accomplished during those hours. *Tinch v. City of Dayton*, 199 F. Supp. 2d 758 (S.D.Ohio 2002).

Improper Fee Sharing

- **Sharing fees with a nonattorney**

An *offer* made by an attorney to a nonlawyer to share fees was not a violation of the rule prohibiting sharing of fees, when no agreement was reached and no fees were shared with a nonlawyer. DR 3-102(A) provides that "[a] lawyer or law firm shall not share legal fees with a nonlawyer. . . ." The attorney here did not *actually* share legal fees with Stafford, a nurse on his staff, but had *entered into an agreement* to share legal fees. Entering into an agreement to share legal fees with a nonlawyer does not in and of itself constitute a violation of DR 3-102(A). Even if respondent had entered an agreement to share legal fees with Stafford, such an agreement in and of itself is not sufficient to establish a violation of DR 3-102(A). DR 3-102(A) explicitly prohibits a *sharing* of legal fees; it does not prohibit an *agreement* to share legal fees. Having said that, we hasten to add that we are not suggesting that it is proper to enter into such an agreement. Canon 9 of the Code of Professional Responsibility provides that lawyers should avoid even the appearance of impropriety. EC 9-6. Thus, offering to share a fee with a nonlawyer and/or entering an agreement to share a fee with a nonlawyer should be avoided. *Columbus Bar Assn. v. Plymale*, 91 Ohio St.3d 367 (Ohio 2001).

Mistakes and Wrongdoing

- **Paralegal checks the wrong set of local rules and client suffers summary judgment**

The attorney's paralegal was allowed to determine when motions were due to the court on behalf of the attorney's clients. According to the paralegal's affidavit, she looked to the Local Rules of the Cuyahoga County Court of Common Pleas rather than the Local Rules of the Lorain County Court of Common Pleas to determine the due date of the client's motion. This was in error. Consequently, the paralegal miscalculated the due date of appellant's motion and, as a result, the attorney failed to file the motion in time. The trial court subsequently granted the opponent's motion for summary judgment. This court does not dispute the contention that the attorney made an honest mistake in the instant matter when he, by way of his paralegal, looked to the wrong local rules and miscalculated the date his client's motion was due. While we certainly sympathize the attorney's client in that our decision today will most likely forever preclude her from having her day in court regarding her claim, vacating the summary judgment of the common pleas court at this late date would unfairly penalize those parties that have been diligently abiding by the procedural rule as well as set an ominous precedent. *Blair v. Boye-Doe*, 157 Ohio App. 3d 17 (OhioApp. 2004).

• Paralegal tries to explain the failure to obtain summons ("I do not do a lot of federal filings")

At the time Wise's complaint was filed, no summonses were issued by the Clerk of Courts. The legal assistant left the Clerk's office wrongly believing that every step had been taken to effect service. Consequently, defendants were properly served about a month after the deadline. In an affidavit, the legal assistant avers that she filed the December 15, 1997 complaint at the direction of Linda Stukey, who is counsel of record for Wise. In an effort to explain the lack of summonses issued by the Clerk of Courts, the legal assistant states in relevant part: "Mrs. Stukey was absent from the office due to surgery, illness, and complications. . . . I do not do a lot of federal filings for Mrs. Stukey. In her absence, with help of other attorneys and clerks, I tried to follow all the technical steps for service of Summons and Complaint. I personally took the complaint (exceeding 20 pages), several copies of the complaint and original summons with several copies to the Clerk of Court to file. . . . I had no doubt that the clerk who waited on me knew what was to be certified and gave no thought to it, except to note that she was a relatively new clerk at that time. With the multiple pleadings on two separate cases (97-550 and 97-551), I thought the Clerk stamped a signature on the summons to be served and had sealed the original summons for the Clerk, and gave me back my copies to serve." Regardless of this legal assistant's mistaken belief, the Court's docket sheet indicates that the Clerk of Courts did not issue any summonses for service. Although Wise's counsel bears the ultimate responsibility for the actions of her legal assistant, the court finds counsel's illness and the good-faith attempts made by her assistant to be relevant considerations. The court also notes that Wise's counsel and her assistant did make some effort to resolve the service-of-process issue by contacting the United States Postal Service. *Wise v. Department of Defense*, 196 F.R.D. 52 (S.D.Ohio 1999).

• Misfiling leads to default judgment

An attorney's client suffers a default judgment when the complaint and all other pleadings were mistakenly placed in the wrong file by the attorney's legal assistant. The file was placed in storage. It was not until after the default judgment was entered that the attorney learned of the mistaken placement of the client documents. *Acevedo v. Dan Motors*, 1998 WL 382697 (C.A.6 (Ohio) 1998).

• Attorney should not have relied on a legal secretary to determine an answering date

- Allstate Insurance Company's decision to rely on a legal secretary to determine the answer date is a complete disregard for the judicial system. The determination of the date an answer is due is a legal decision that should be made by an attorney. In fact, Allstate Insurance Company had received a copy of the complaint from appellant which would indicate to someone with a legal education that appellant had already been served with a copy of the complaint. Further, the miscommunication in this case did not occur between persons with legal training, i.e. attorneys and paralegals, but rather a secretary and an employee of the clerk's office. *Gillmore v. Tirbovich*, 2001 WL 1230536 (OhioApp. 2001).
- Respondent attorney was bedridden for several months in 2002 and relied during those months on a paralegal at his office to help him manage his law practice. Respondent instructed that paralegal to prepare a draft answer, counterclaim, and motion for a restraining order for respondent's client, Richard Zahner, in a divorce case, and deliver the documents to respondent for his review and signature. Instead, the paralegal signed respondent's name to the pleadings and filed them in November 2002 without respondent's consent. The motion for a restraining order in the case included an affidavit purportedly signed by Zahner and notarized by respondent. Respondent had not in fact seen Zahner sign the affidavit and had not notarized the signature. The paralegal had improperly notarized the affidavit and signed respondent's name on it as the notary. In December 2002, the paralegal drafted a letter to Zahner and signed respondent's name to it without indicating that respondent himself had not written, reviewed, or signed the letter. Zahner believed that respondent had written and

signed it. In January 2003, respondent instructed the paralegal to prepare written objections to a magistrate's order in Zahner's case. Again, the paralegal was to deliver the draft objections to respondent for his review and signature before they were filed. The paralegal did not do so, and respondent never reviewed the objections before the paralegal signed respondent's name on the document and filed it with the court. Respondent admitted and the board found that he had violated DR 3-101(A) (barring an attorney from aiding a nonlawyer in the unauthorized practice of law), and 6-101(A)(3) (barring an attorney from neglecting an entrusted legal matter). *Columbus Bar Assn. v. Watson*, 106 Ohio St.3d 298 (Ohio 2005).

- **Paralegal is sued under the Fair Debt Collection Act**

Lee incurred a debt to a company called Retinal Consultants. Thomas & Thomas, a Cincinnati law firm representing Retinal Consultants, sent the Lee a two-sentence letter that was eventually to precipitate the filing of this lawsuit. Prepared on the Thomas & Thomas letterhead (and prefaced with a reference to Retinal Consultants, the amount of the debt, and a file number) the letter read as follows: "Per our recent phone conversation, we had expected your check by now. Since it has not arrived as yet, we are enclosing a self-addressed envelope for your remittance." The letter was signed for Thomas & Thomas by an individual identified as "Timothy K. Gibson, Legal Assistant." Under § 807 of the Fair Debt Collection Practices Act, a debt collector such as Thomas & Thomas "may not use any false, deceptive, or misleading representation or means in connection with the collection of any debt." The section goes on to list a number of different types of conduct falling within this prohibition. Among them is the failure to disclose clearly in all communications made to collect a debt (or to obtain information about a consumer) that the debt collector is attempting to collect a debt and that any information obtained will be used for that purpose. For violating this provision, the debtor sued Thomas & Thomas and its legal assistant, Timothy K. Gibson. *Lee v. Thomas & Thomas*, 109 F.3d 302 (C.A.6 (Ohio) 1997).

- **Attorney pressures paralegal into falsifying an affidavit**

To avoid discipline, an attorney induced a former legal assistant to execute a false affidavit claiming that her law office had prepared a client's file for retrieval. The attorney's conduct in the deposition of the former legal assistant, including implying that the attorney had recorded conversations with the legal assistant that could impeach and personally embarrass her, violated the rule prohibiting attorneys from engaging in conduct involving fraud, deceit, dishonesty, or misrepresentation. The attorney's deceitful tactic petrified the legal assistant by creating a false impression that the attorney possessed compromising personal information that she could offer as evidence. *Cincinnati Bar Assn. v. Statzer*, 101 Ohio St.3d 14 (Ohio 2003).

- **Paralegal notarizes two blank affidavits**

The conduct of the attorney in causing a client to sign blank affidavits warranted a public reprimand. The attorney caused a client to sign two blank affidavits, which were then, at the attorney's direction, notarized by a paralegal in the attorney's office. *Columbus Bar Assn. v. Battisti*, 90 Ohio St.3d 452 (Ohio 2000).

Other cases involving wrongdoing

- Paralegal is convicted by the Montgomery County Court of Common Pleas of one count of grand theft, a violation of R.C. 2913.02(A)(1). A jury found that she had, while working as a paralegal for the attorney who was handling her uncle's probate estate, removed some $53,000 of estate assets and converted it to her own use. She was sentenced to serve 18 months in the Ohio State Reformatory for Women. *State v. Stevens*, 1994 WL 672534 (Ohio-App. 1994).
- During respondent's employment as an attorney for a minor's guardianship, her paralegal misappropriated funds belonging to the guardianship. *Dayton Bar Assn. v. Jessup*, 66 Ohio St.3d 5 (Ohio 1993).
- The attorney failed to supervise nonlawyers in his law office. The attorney's inattention created an office environment that allowed the attorney's nonlawyer secretary to place false information on documents regarding the date of execution of an affidavit, the date of execution of a marital separation agreement, and the date of a marriage dissolution petition. The attorney also allowed a secretary or another nonlawyer in his office evidently to forge the attorney's signature on and falsely notarize at least one document. It is a lawyer's duty to establish a system of office procedure that ensures delegated legal duties are completed properly. *The Restatement of the Law 3d, The Law Governing Lawyers* (2000), Section 11, states: "With respect to a nonlawyer employee of a law firm, the lawyer is subject to professional discipline if . . . (a) the lawyer fails to make reasonable efforts to ensure: (i) that the firm in which the lawyer practices has in effect measures giving reasonable assurance that the nonlawyer's conduct is compatible with the professional obligations of the lawyer; and (ii) that conduct of a nonlawyer over whom the lawyer has direct supervisory authority is compatible with the professional obligations of the lawyer." Comment c to

Section 11 adds: "Lack of awareness of misconduct by another person, either lawyer or nonlawyer, under a lawyer's supervision does not excuse a violation of this Section." Comment f states: "The fact that a lawyer is busy or distracted in other critically important work, such as the work of providing legal services to clients or generating a high percentage of the firm's fee revenue, does not excuse neglecting supervisory responsibilities or ignoring in appropriate conduct on the part of a supervised nonlawyer." We have long adhered to the standards described in the *Restatement*, which are echoed in Model Rule 5.3 of the American Bar Association's Model Rules of Professional Conduct. We cited and quoted from those Model Rules more than ten years ago in *Disciplinary Counsel v. Ball*, 67 Ohio St.3d 401 (1993) (holding that an attorney's failure to supervise his secretary who misappropriated client funds over a ten-year period warranted a six-month suspension). More recent decisions from this and other courts have similarly admonished lawyers for failing to supervise nonlawyer assistants with care. See, e.g., *Lorain Cty. Bar Assn v. Noll*, 105 Ohio St.3d 6 (2004) (imposing a two-year suspension, with 18 months stayed, on a lawyer who failed to adequately supervise a legal assistant and committed other violations). In the case before us, the attorney's conduct fell below the standards described in the *Restatement* and in ABA Model Rule 5.3. He at best chose to remain oblivious to the improper actions of the persons he hired, thereby violating the trust that his clients and others placed in him and his office staff. *Mahoning Cty. Bar Assn. v. Lavelle*, 107 Ohio St.3d 92 (Ohio 2005).

- An attorney forges the signature of a former paralegal, a purported witness, nine times on a quitclaim deed. *Disciplinary Counsel v. Jones*, 103 Ohio St.3d 590 (Ohio 2004).

Adequacy of Paralegal Supervision

- **Inadequate supervision of legal assistant by attorney**

The attorney's failure to adequately supervise his legal assistant, which resulted in client files being lost or destroyed, violated the disciplinary rule barring attorneys from engaging in actions that adversely reflect on the lawyer's fitness to practice law. The attorney admitted that he was oblivious to his assistant's shoddy work, and his inattentive and inadequate oversight of that assistant led him to neglect the legal needs of his clients. From the early 1990s until May 2003, his legal assistant paid bills for the law office, answered telephone calls, opened mail, maintained his appointment calendar, scheduled client appointments, and drafted pleadings and correspondence for his review. When faced with disciplinary charges, the attorney explained that the assistant had misplaced or destroyed files in his office, thereby preventing him from properly attending to his clients' interests. He also claimed that the assistant failed to follow his instructions and failed to tell him about the status of court cases filed by his office. He said that he found "piles and piles and piles" of important papers hidden in his law office in May 2003 after the assistant's departure. The attorney failed to devote the necessary time and attention to the legal needs of his clients. He allowed their files to be lost or destroyed by his legal assistant. His failure to adequately supervise his legal assistant led to many of his problems, and that failure adversely reflects on his fitness to practice law. "[I]t is a lawyer's duty to establish a system of office procedure that ensures delegated legal duties are completed properly." *Disciplinary Counsel v. Ball*, 67 Ohio St.3d 401, 404 (1993). Whatever safeguards the attorney may have established to ensure that the legal assistant performed her assigned duties properly were clearly inadequate. *Lorain Cty. Bar Assn. v. Noll*, 105 Ohio St.3d 6 (Ohio 2004).

- Haggerty essentially served as a legal assistant or paraprofessional to attorney Ball as well as a bookkeeper, where she was given authority to sign checks for disbursements from the office account and client's trust accounts. Her workload intensified and she became delinquent in filing the necessary documents and papers in probate and guardianship matters. To conceal her inactivity on these matters and others assigned to her, Haggerty diverted office mail from Ball that had reference to the uncompleted work. Although Haggerty diverted and concealed information from Ball, it appears she never destroyed letters from the court or clients which would indicate any delay. On the contrary, she appropriately placed into the office files all documents that passed through her desk. Ball has denied any knowledge of these delinquencies. He also argues that, under ABA Model Rules 5.1 and 5.3, a lawyer's vicarious responsibility in a disciplinary proceeding is limited to those situations where the lawyer orders or with knowledge ratifies, or fails to take reasonable remedial action upon learning of, the employee's wrongful acts. We disagree. The Model Rules do not condone Ball's conduct. In fact, Model Rules 5.3(a) and (b) ("Responsibilities Regarding Nonlawyer Assistants") clearly indicate that it is a lawyer's duty to establish a system of office procedure that ensures delegated legal duties are completed properly. The facts of this case do not reveal an elaborate scheme by Haggerty to secrete funds and conceal her conduct from attorney Ball. Haggerty was totally conspicuous in her criminal conduct. Ball needed only to review his files, his trust accounts, his campaign account, or heed the warnings by the court concerning the neglect of numerous files in order to be alerted to the misconduct of his secretary. Ball cannot rely on the high degree of competence Haggerty displayed over the years and the trust he developed in her to excuse his failure to provide competent counsel to his clients and guard funds over which he was a fiduciary. Ball's nonfeasance over a ten-year period was the necessary element which facilitated Haggerty's criminal acts. As such, the lack of any semblance of supervisory control over the work delegated by Ball to Haggerty constitutes neglect of legal duties entrusted to Ball in ten separate legal matters in violation of DR 6-101(A)(3). Therefore, this court concurs in the board's finding and in its recommendation, and orders that Ball be suspended from the practice of law in this state for a period of six months. *Disciplinary Counsel v. Ball,* 67 Ohio St.3d 401 (Ohio 1993).

- The attorney further violated disciplinary rules by failing to properly supervise a paralegal who provided bankruptcy-related services to clients. The attorney, who primarily practiced in Cincinnati, also maintained a law office in Norwood, Ohio, staffed by Wayne E. West, a nonlawyer. West, who identified himself as a paralegal, interviewed clients, obtained information, prepared documents, and secured signings of Chapter 13 bankruptcy petitions and other legal documents. From time to time the attorney would visit the Norwood office, interview clients, and oversee the signing of documents. However, he exercised little supervision over West, who controlled the office bank accounts, but did not keep a detailed record of disbursements. *Cincinnati Bar Assn. v. Bertsche,* 84 Ohio St.3d 170 (Ohio 1998).
- The attorney admitted to not properly supervising his paralegal employee, Leo Tomeu. *Disciplinary Counsel v. Furth,* 93 Ohio St.3d 173, 754 N.E.2d 219 (Ohio, 2001).

Conflict of Interest: Switching Sides

- An attorney's secretary once worked for the attorney representing an opposing party on a current case. "In ruling on a motion to disqualify a lawyer based on that lawyer's employment of a nonattorney once employed by the lawyer representing an opposing party, a court must use the following analysis: (1) Is there a substantial relationship between the matter at issue and the matter of the nonattorney employee's former firm's representation? (2) Did the moving party present credible evidence that the nonattorney employee was exposed to confidential information in his or her former employment relating to the matter at issue? (3) If such evidence was presented, did the challenged attorney rebut the resulting presumption of disclosure with evidence either that (a) the employee had no contact with or knowledge of the related matter or (b) the new law firm erected and followed adequate and timely screens to rebut the evidence presented in prong (2) so as to avoid disqualification?" *Green v. Toledo Hosp.,* 94 Ohio St.3d 480 (Ohio 2002).
- A nonlawyer cannot be allowed to work on one side of a case at one firm and on the other side of the same case at the opposing party's firm. Under the following two circumstances, a law firm must be disqualified from representing a client because of a nonlawyer the firm has hired:
  1. where information relating to the representation of an adverse party gained by the nonlawyer while employed in another firm has been revealed to lawyers or other personnel in the new firm; or
  2. where screening would be ineffective or the nonlawyer necessarily would be required to work on the other side of the same or a substantially related matter on which the nonlawyer worked or respecting which the nonlawyer has gained information relating to the representation of the opponent while in the former employment. *Latson v. Blanchard,* 1998 WL 683769 (OhioApp. 1998).

Unauthorized Practice of Law

Cases involving the unauthorized practice of law will be examined in section 3.1, which defines the practice of law in Ohio.

Miscellaneous Cases Involving Paralegals

• Requiring a paralegal to be deposed "may lead to a slippery slope"

A nurse paralegal must give testimony at a deposition even though "allowing a paralegal to be deposed may lead to a slippery slope." The rule that protects attorney work-product is not compromised if the deposition of the nurse paralegal is limited to the issue of how reports of the estate's experts were generated. Unfettered access to the nurse paralegal to discover thoughts and strategies for trial would violate the rule prohibiting discovery of attorney work-product. *Stanton v. Univ. Hosps. Health Sys., Inc.,* 853 N.E.2d 343 (Ohio App. 8 Dist., 2006).

• Court says paralegal "presents a clear and succinct legal argument"

The record before us includes a letter from a paralegal employed by the Legal Aid Society of Columbus, which requested that the letter be treated as a supplement to appellant's application to appeal her claim. The letter is a part of the file that was considered by the Board of Review and presents a clear and succinct legal argument in her behalf. *Caldwell v. Ranco, Inc.*, 8 Ohio App.3d 35 (OhioApp. 1982).

- **Duties of an estate paralegal**

This is an action for payment of long-term disability benefits. Plaintiff Christine Foreman's position as a legal assistant at Thompson Hine & Flory involved meeting with various individuals to determine assets for estate planning purposes, valuing assets manually or by computer, maintaining estate accounts on behalf of fiduciaries, contacting courts for processing filings, maintaining contact with trustees, reviewing and preparing accountings, and drafting tax returns, estate plan documents and court filings. *Foreman v. Fortis Benefits Ins. Co.*, 2005 WL 1917448 (S.D.Ohio 2005).

- **Paralegals serving on juries**

Defendant now argues that his attorney should have challenged Barth as a juror because she had taken paralegal classes taught by the prosecutor, Charles Coulson. We find the contention meritless. Barth testified that her past affiliation with Coulson's paralegal course would not impair her ability to render a fair and impartial verdict. *State v. Treesh*, 90 Ohio St.3d 460 (Ohio 2001).

- During voir dire, juror Hillman stated that she had worked as a paralegal in the probate department at the same law firm representing Parma Community General Hospital in this case. She stated that she did not work with the lawyer representing the hospital. At the time of trial, she worked at a different firm. Hillman stated that it would not be difficult for her to find against the hospital. She stated repeatedly that she would be able to keep an open mind and be fair to everyone. Allowing her to remain as a juror was not in error. *Kosmos v. Cleveland Elec. Illuminating Co.*, 1991 WL 281035 (OhioApp. 1991).
- An unfavorable verdict could not be impeached because a juror, who was paralegal, allegedly told other jurors during deliberations that he had researched similar cases. He denied having any predispositions that would disqualify him from being impartial on the case. Counsel failed to challenge this juror at the appropriate time. *Crawford v. Sylvania Marketplace Co.*, 72 Ohio Misc.2d 3 (Ohio Com.Pl. 1995).

- **Trial judge once hired paralegal of one of the attorneys**

Appellant moved for a recusal during the trial because the trial judge temporarily employed a paralegal who at one time worked for appellee's attorney. The judge denied the recusal because of lack of prejudice, and because 2 days of trial had already taken place. On appeal, the court ruled that the trial court acted properly in not recusing itself, because the circumstances were not such that the court was biased or prejudiced to the extent that it was unable to exercise its functions impartially. *Carson v. Weiss*, 1993 WL 367088 (Ohio App. 1993).

- **Inappropriate question asked of applicant for a paralegal job**

During an interview for a paralegal position, the attorney asks the applicant, "So tell me, are you a virgin?" In a disciplinary action against the attorney for this and related conduct, the attorney received a 2-year suspension from the practice of law. *Cincinnati Bar Assn. v. Young*, 89 Ohio St.3d 306 (Ohio 2000).

- **Prison is not required to provide inmates with paralegal assistance**

Plaintiff, an inmate, contends that defendants are required to provide a clerk, a paralegal, or some assistance to inmates to facilitate their use of the law library. The United States Supreme Court has determined that the fundamental constitutional right of access to the courts requires prison authorities to assist inmates in the preparation and filing of meaningful legal papers by providing prisoners with adequate law libraries or adequate assistance from persons trained in the law. Thus, a prisoner's constitutionally guaranteed right of access to the courts is protected when a state provides a prisoner with either the legal tools necessary to defend himself, e.g., a state provided law library, or the assistance of legally trained personnel. In this case, plaintiff was given the former. Although many states provide some degree of professional or quasi-professional legal assistance to prisoners under programs that may have a number of advantages over libraries alone, a legal access program need not include any particular element of this kind. *Lewis v. Ohio Dept. of Rehabilitation and Correction*, 1993 WL 524925 (OhioApp. 1993).

- **Additional cases on paralegals for inmates in Ohio institutions**

Taylor v. Perini, 413 F.Supp. 189 (D.C. Ohio 1976)

Knecht v. Collins, 903 F.Supp. 1193 (1995) (S.D. Ohio 1995)

Knecht v. Collins, 187 F.3d 636, 1999 WL 427173 (6th Cir. 1999)

D. Something to Check

Go to the online sources that provide free access to state court opinions in Ohio. (See chart in section 5.1). Do a search for the terms paralegal or "legal assistant." Summarize (briefly) one of the cases you find.

APPENDIX B

Becoming an Attorney in Ohio

A. Introduction

Some paralegals decide to become attorneys. If you look at the résumés of Ohio attorneys posted on their law firm Web site, you will occasionally see references to their prior employment as paralegals before they attended law school. Some attorneys worked part-time as paralegals while they were in law school. In this section, we explore what is involved in becoming an attorney in Ohio.

B. Requirements for Becoming an Ohio Attorney

Admission to the practice of law in Ohio is regulated by the Supreme Court of Ohio:

Office of Bar Admissions
Supreme Court of Ohio
65 South Front Street, 5th Floor
Columbus, Ohio 43215-3431
614-387-9340; 800-826-9010
www.sconet.state.oh.us/Admissions

To be admitted to the practice of law in Ohio, an applicant shall:

(a) be at least 21 years of age;

(b) earn a bachelor's degree from an accredited college or university;

(c) earn a J.D. or an L.L.B. degree from a law school that was approved by the American Bar Association at the time the degree was earned;

(d) demonstrate (prior to taking the Ohio bar examination) the requisite character, fitness, and moral qualifications for admission to the practice of law;

(e) pass both the Ohio bar examination and the Multistate Professional Responsibility Examination;

(f) take the oath of office *(www.sconet.state.oh.us/Rules/govbar/#rulei)*

Fees

Application to register as candidate for admission: $60

Application to take bar exam: $275
MPRE fee (see below): $55
(*www.sconet.state.oh.us/Admissions/fees*)

Bar Exam Structure

The main bar exam lasts two and a half days. There are three parts to the exam: essays, the Multistate Bar Exam (MBE), and the Multistate Performance Test (MPT). In addition, applicants must take the Multistate Professional Responsibility Examination (MPRE).

Essays

The essay portion of the Ohio bar examination tests on the following 11 subjects: business associations, civil procedure, commercial transactions, constitutional law, contracts, criminal law, evidence, legal ethics, property, torts, and wills.
(*www.sconet.state.oh.us/Admissions/PDF/essay_subjects.pdf*)

Multistate Bar Exam (MBE)

The MBE is a six-hour, two-hundred question multiple-choice examination covering contracts, torts, constitutional law, criminal law, evidence, and real property.
(*www.ncbex.org/tests.htm*)
(*www.ncbex.org/tests/Test%20Booklets/MBE_IB2003.pdf*)

Multistate Performance Test (MPT)

The MPT consists of three 90-minute skills questions covering legal analysis, fact analysis, problem solving, resolution of ethical dilemmas, organization and management of a lawyering task, and communication.
(*www.ncbex.org/tests/Test%20Booklets/MPT_IB2003.pdf*)

Multistate Professional Responsibility Examination (MPRE)

The MPRE is a sixty-question, two-hour, multiple-choice legal ethics examination administered three times a year. The test is based primarily on the ABA Model Rules of Professional Conduct. Applicants often take this exam before graduating from law school.
(*www.ncbex.org/tests.htm*)
(*www.ncbex.org/tests/Test%20Booklets/MPRE_IB2002.pdf*)

C. Law Schools in Ohio

University of Akron Law School
www.uakron.edu/law

Capital University Law School
www.law.capital.edu

Case Western Reserve University
lawwww.cwru.edu

University of Cincinnati College of Law
www.law.uc.edu

Cleveland-Marshall College of Law
www.law.csuohio.edu

University of Dayton School of Law
www.law.udayton.edu

Ohio Northern University College of Law
www.law.onu.edu

Ohio State University College of Law
moritzlaw.osu.edu

University of Toledo College of Law
law.utoledo.edu

D. More Information

Office of Bar Admissions
www.sconet.state.oh.us/Admissions

Ohio State Bar Association
www.ohiobar.org

Bar Admission in All States
www.abanet.org/legaled/baradmissions/basicoverview.html

National Conference of Bar Examiners
www.ncbex.org

Multistate Bar Exam Study Aids
www.ncbex.org/multistate-tests/mbe

Bar Review Courses
www.micromashbar.com
www.thebarexam.com/ohiobar.htm
www.supremebarreview.com/coursematerial.cfm
stu.findlaw.com/thebar/barreview.html

Financial Aid for Law School
www.lsac.org/LSAC.asp?url=lsac/financial-aid-introduction.asp
studentaid.ed.gov

The Cost of Law School: Some Examples
law.utoledo.edu/admissions/index.htm
(click "Tuition & Fees")
lawwww.cwru.edu
(click "For Prospective Students" then "Cost")

Should I Go to Law School?
www.transformingpractices.com/lc/lc4.html
chronicle.com/jobs/2004/01/2004012301c.htm
www.csun.edu/blaw/Pre-Law%20Advisement.pdf
www.wiu.edu/users/miuhon/pre_law_advisor/files/should.html

E. Something to Check

Law School library Web sites often have excellent legal research guides. Select any three law schools listed in section C above. At the Web sites of these law schools, click their law library link. At these law library sites, compare the information provided (including further links) on Ohio legal research. Describe what you are led to. Which law library leads you to the most comprehensive links?

PART 2

Paralegal Employment

2.1 Resources for Finding Employment in Ohio

A. Introduction

B. General Strategies for Finding Employment

C. Specific Resources

D. More Information

E. Something to Check

A. Introduction

How do new paralegals find their first job? How do experienced paralegals interested in a job change find opportunities that build on their experience? In this section, we present ideas and resources that can be helpful in answering these questions for full-time and part-time work. In addition to general strategies, you will find specific Internet sites that should be checked. Some of the sites cover the entire state, while others focus on specific areas of the state.

Most of the leads will be to traditional employment agencies that match employers with applicants. Staffing agencies are included. A staffing agency is an employment agency that pays the salaries of the part-time employees that it places. A business using these workers will pay the staffing agency, which in turn pays the workers. Many employment and staffing agencies do not charge job applicants for their services. (Of course, you should confirm that this is true before deciding to work with any agency.)

B. General Strategies for Finding Employment

The starting point in your job search should be the school where you received your paralegal education. The program director will be your best guide on what is available. Here are some additional strategies:

- **Paralegal Associations.** Section 1.2 lists every paralegal association in the state. It also gives you related groups such as legal administrator associations. Go to the Web site of every association near the cities or towns where you want to work. Find out if any job leads are available on these sites. Some associations list current openings that nonmembers can access. If the newsletter of an association is online, look through recent issues. They may list job openings that are not found elsewhere on the association's Web site. Send an e-mail message to the association asking for leads to employment and staffing agencies in the area. If there is a search box on the site, type in search words such as "employment", "job bank", "paralegal work", and "legal assistant employment."
- **Attorney Job Search Resources.** There are many resources in the state that focus on the search for attorney employment. (Some are listed below.) Don't be reluctant to check out Web sites for attorney employment. Many of the sites have pages or links on paralegal employment. If not, call them or send them an e-mail asking for leads on paralegal employment in the area. In the search box on the site, type in search words such as "paralegal" and "legal assistant."
- **Bar Associations.** Bar associations sometimes have employment services for their members. Some of this information might be available to the general public. (The list of bar associations in the state is in section 3.4.) Go to the Web sites of the associations to find out if any leads are available on paralegal employment. Consider sending the bar association an e-mail asking about paralegal employment and staffing agencies in the area.
- **General Circulation and Legal Newspapers.** General circulation newspapers often have want ads for paralegals. These newspapers are worth checking, particularly their online editions. Also find out what the legal newspaper is for your area—both hard copy and online. It may have want ads for paralegals.

  Ohio Newspapers Online
  www.usnpl.com/ohnews.html
  newslink.org/ohnews.html
  www.ohionews.org/members.html

- **General and Legal Search Engines.** Go to general search engines such as Google (*www.google.com*). Try searches for paralegal employment that include the name of the city where you want to work (e.g., "paralegal employment" Cleveland). In addition, go to legal search engines such as:
  - the "Legal Employment" page of Lawguru (*www.lawguru.com*)
  - the "For Legal Professionals" page of Findlaw (*www.findlaw.com*); click "Career Center" under Practice Tools
  - the "careers" pages of Detod (*www.detod.com*)
- **Google Legal Employment Directory.** *directory.google.com/Top/Society/Law/Employment*
- **Networking.** Many paralegals find employment through the networking contacts they make with attorneys, paralegals, or legal secretaries whom they meet at school, paralegal associations, social clubs, church, synagogue, etc. "Who do you know who might be looking for paralegals?" There is not a more powerful question that could be asked of anyone with any connection to the practice of law.
- **Legal Assistant Today Job Bank.** *www.legalassistanttoday.com/jobbank*
- **Paralegal Jobs in the Public Sector.** If you are seeking employment in the public sector:
  - see section 2.2 for employment in state government
  - see section 2.3 for employment in federal agencies located in Ohio

- see section 4.2 for links to employment in Ohio state courts and 4.3 for links to employment in federal courts in the state
- see section 2.4 for the links to legal aid/legal services offices and other public sector offices in Ohio
- National Legal Aid & Defender Association

www.nlada.org/Jobs
(select "Ohio")

- **Paralegal Jobs in Corporations.** Check the Web site of the Association of Corporate Counsel:
  - go to *www.acc.com*
  - click "Career Development" and "Find a Job"
  - click "Advanced Search"
  - for "Locations," select this state
  - type "paralegal" or "legal assistant" in the search box
  - or click "Other" for "Job Level"
- **Law Firm Websites.** Most law firms have a Web site and the largest ones invariably have a job section, often under the caption "careers" or "employment". Look for links to "legal support", "staff & support", "careers", "professional legal staff", "legal assistants", "paralegals" and the like. These sections usually include a description of the firm, specific jobs available, and instructions on how to apply for a job. For lists of some Ohio law offices, check:
  lawyers.findlaw.com/lawyer/state/ohio
  www.lawresearchservices.com/firms/ohio.htm
  www.washlaw.edu/links/index.php?viewCat=7
  www.nalpdirectory.com
  www.hg.org/northam-firms.html

C. Specific Resources

Statewide

Ohio State Bar Association Legal Career Center: Job Searching for Attorneys and Paralegals
ohiobar.legalstaff.com

Leads to Job Opportunities in Ohio Legal Aid, Legal Service, and Public Defender Offices
www.oslsa.org/OSLSA/PrivateWeb
(click "Job Opportunities")
opd.ohio.gov/human/Hr_Human2.htm
(click "County Public Defenders")
www.aardvarc.org/dv/states/ohdv.shtml
(This site contains an extensive list of legal aid/legal services offices in the counties of the state. Although the focus of the site is domestic violence, the links to the offices can be used to inquire about public sector job opportunities in general.)

Offices Seeking Pro Bono Help that May Have Paid Positions
See Web links in section 2.4.

Career Builder
www.careerbuilder.com
(type "paralegal" and an Ohio city)

Paralegal Gateway
paralegalgateway.com

FindLaw Careers - Ohio
careers.findlaw.com
(scroll down to Ohio)

HierosGamos - Legal Jobs in Ohio
www.hierosgamos.org/hg/legal_jobs_ohio.asp

IntJobs
intjobs.org/law/paralegal.html

JobsNet
www.jobs.net
legal.jobs.net/ohio.htm

Law Crossing
www.lawcrossing.com/lclegalstaff.php
(type "paralegal" as a keyword; in Location, scroll down to "Ohio")

Legal Staff
800-659-5589
www.legalstaff.com

Monster - Ohio
www.monster.com
jobsearch.monster.com

NFPA/Legal Staff
www.paralegals.org
(click "CLE" then "Career Center")
paralegals.org/displaycommon.cfm?an=1&subarticlenbr=839
paralegals.legalstaff.com/Common/HomePage.aspx?abbr=PARALEGALS

NALS—The Association for Legal Professionals
nals.legalstaff.com

Association of Legal Administrators
www.alanet.org/jobs/current.asp
(for "Ohio" type "paralegal")

Robert Half Legal
800-870-8367
www.roberthalflegal.com

Vault
www.vault.com
(click "Find A Job", "Law Job Board", then "Ohio" and type "paralegal")

Smart Hunt
smarthunt.com
(type "paralegal" and a city in Ohio)

Yahoo Hotjobs - Legaljobs, OH
hotjobs.yahoo.com/jobs/OH/legal-jobs
hotjobs.yahoo.com/jobs/OH/All/Legal-jobs

Detod.com
detod.legalstaff.com

Craigslist
www.craigslist.org
(click on "Ohio" then a city then "legal/paralegal")

Legal Resource Center
www.thelccn.com/lrc/shop
(click "Paralegal")

Nation Job Network
www.nationjob.com/legal

Selected Cities

Akron

Akron Bar Association - Legal Career Center
www.akronbar.org
akronbar.legalstaff.com

Career Builder - Akron
jobs.careerbuilder.com/al.ic/Ohio_Akron_Legal.htm

Employment Guide - Akron/Canton
akron.employmentguide.com
(click "legal")

JobsNet - Akron
legal.jobs.net/Ohio-Akron.htm

JobSearch - Akron
legal.jobsearch.com/Ohio-Akron.htm

Canton

JobSearch - Canton
legal.jobsearch.com/Ohio-Canton.htm

Cincinnati

Cincinnati Bar Association - Online Career Center
("the definitive employment resource for your attorney and support staff needs")
www.cincybar.org/member/jobs.asp

Cincinnati Paralegal Association
513-244-1266
www.cincinnatiparalegals.org

Job Bank in its newsletter
Example:
www.cincinnatiparalegals.org/RSVP052005.pdf

Craigslist - Cincinnati
cincinnati.craigslist.org/lgl

Cleveland

Cleveland Association of Paralegals
216-556-5437
www.capohio.org
(click "Job bank")

Cleveland Bar Association
("comprehensive job listings for attorneys and support staff")
clevelandbar.legalstaff.com

Craigslist - Cleveland
cleveland.craigslist.org/lgl

Cuyahoga County Bar Association Legal Career Center
("comprehensive job listings for attorneys and support staff")
cuybar.legalstaff.com/Common/HomePage.aspx?abbr=CUYBAR

JobsNet - Cleveland
legal.jobs.net/Ohio-Cleveland.htm

JobSearch - Cleveland
legal.jobsearch.com/Ohio-Cleveland.htm

Major Legal Services
216-579-9782
www.majorlegalservices.com

Oodle - Cleveland
cleveland.oodle.com/job/legal

Columbus

Career Builder - Columbus
jobs.careerbuilder.com/al.ic/Ohio_Columbus_Legal.htm

Career Builder - Government Jobs - Columbus
gov.careerbuilder.com/gv.ic/Ohio
(type "paralegal" as a keyword and "Columbus")

Columbus Bar Placement Services, Job Postings: Paralegals
www.cbalaw.org/members/placement/index.php

Columbus Career Ohio
ohio.columbuscareer.com

Craigslist - Columbus
columbus.craigslist.org/lgl

Legal Employment Solutions
www.legalemployment.net

Dayton

Dayton Bar Association Personnel Placement Service
("The Personnel Placement Service (PPS)... can help you begin or advance your career in legal support. We place qualified applicants in a wide variety of law-related positions including legal assistants and paralegals.")
www.daybar.org/html/pps/pps.htm

Greater Dayton Paralegal Association
(GDPA "provides...job placement opportunities")
www.gdpa.org
gdpa.legalstaff.com
paralegals.org/associations/2270/files/home188.html

Oodle - Dayton
dayton.oodle.com/job/legal

JobSearch - Dayton
legal.jobsearch.com/Ohio-Dayton.htm

Craigslist - Dayton
dayton.craigslist.org/lgl

Toledo

Job Search
legal.jobsearch.com/Ohio.htm
(click "Toledo")

Paralegal Association of Northwest Ohio
www.panonet.org
(For Members: Job Bank)

D. More Information

U.S. Department of Labor
Paralegals and Legal Assistants
www.bls.gov/oco/ocos114.htm

E. Something to Check

1. List and compare the services of two paralegal employment sites that allow you to submit your resume online.
2. What potentially useful employment information can you obtain at any of the legal administrator or legal secretary association sites in the state? (See the sites listed at the end of section 1.2.)

2.2 Sample Paralegal Job Descriptions in State Government

A. Introduction
B. Paralegal/Legal Assistant 1 & 2
C. More Information
D. Something to Check

A. Introduction

The main job category for paralegals in state government is the position of paralegal/legal Assistant. In this section, we present examples of this position. After these examples, see "More Information" for steps to take on finding openings for such positions and applying for them.

B. Paralegal/Legal Assistant 1 & 2

Classification Series: Paralegal/Legal Assistant
Series No. 6381
Major Agencies: All Agencies

SERIES PURPOSE (examples)

The purpose of the paralegal/assistant legal occupation is to assist departmental attorneys.

- At the first level, incumbents conduct research of federal &/or state statutes, recorded judicial decisions & other legal sources & reference materials in order to review corporate filings or student loan bankruptcies or prepare responses to inquiries, complaints, claims or legal/administrative procedural issues to assist departmental attorneys or the office of attorney general.
- At the second level, in the Office of the Ohio Public Defender or State Medical Board, incumbents assist attorneys in analyzing & identifying legal findings & independently write legal memoranda to support findings, assist attorneys in defining & drafting potential issues in cases, locate & review cases & statutory laws & assist attorneys in making merit decisions regarding complex issues of law (i.e., make evaluations regarding casework).

Class Title: Paralegal/Legal Assistant 1
Class Number: 63810
Salary: $29,453–$34,611 per year
Class Concept: The developmental level class works under general supervision & requires working knowledge of legal research & analysis & laws & rules applicable to assigned department's operations in order to review corporate filings or student loan bankruptcies or prepare responses to inquiries, complaints, claims or legal/administrative procedural issues, & prepare various legal & related materials for review, approval, signature &/or use by licensed attorney.
Class Title: Paralegal/Legal Assistant 2
Class Number: 63811
Salary: $32,469–$41,038
Class Concept: The full performance level class works under general supervision & requires considerable knowledge of legal research & analysis & laws & rules applicable to Office of Ohio Public Defender or State Medical Board in order to analyze & identify legal findings & independently write legal memoranda to support findings, assist attorneys in defining & drafting potential issues in cases, locate & review cases & statutory laws & assist attorneys in making merit decisions regarding complex issues of law (i.e., make evaluations regarding casework).

JOB DUTIES IN ORDER OF IMPORTANCE

(These duties are illustrative only. Incumbents may perform some or all of these duties or other job-related duties as assigned.)

Paralegal/Legal Assistant 1 (example)

1. Researches federal &/or state statutes, recorded judicial decisions & other legal sources & reference materials in order to review corporate filings or student loan bankruptcies or prepare responses to inquiries, complaints, claims or legal/administrative procedural issues to assist departmental attorney.
2. Drafts legal briefs & memoranda, contracts, pleadings, motions, affidavits, legislation, rules &/or regulations &/or prepares case summaries, legal documents & reports for review, approval & signature of &/or use by licensed attorney.
3. Reviews leases &/or contracts.
4. Negotiates settlements.
5. Files legal documents with court on behalf of attorney.
6. Responds to general inquiries.
7. Disseminates information on promulgation of administrative rules.
8. Schedules hearings pursuant to chapter 119 of revised code.

Paralegal/Legal Assistant 2 (example)

1. In Office of Ohio Public Defender or State Medical Board, assists attorneys in analyzing & identifying legal findings & independently writes legal memoranda to support findings, assists attorneys in defining & drafting potential issues in cases, locates & reviews cases & statutory laws & assists attorneys in making merit decisions regarding complex issues of law (i.e., makes evaluations regarding casework).
2. Conducts legal research for assistant public defenders by utilizing such reference tools as case law reporters, law review articles, digests & other legal & nonlegal reference & resource works; operates personal computer to conduct legal research using reference tools such as Westlaw, Westmate, Premise, Brief Bank, Internet, Westcheck, Access, CD-ROM & PC docs; shepardizes cases; reviews various legal documents (e.g., suppression motions; search & seizure; change of venue).
3. Provides assistance to assistant public defenders & assists in preparation of briefs & other pleadings for trial & appellate cases in all state & federal courts; prepares correspondence (e.g., to clients &/or court personnel).
4. Conducts fact investigations by reviewing court transcripts, other legal documents & contacting witnesses; gathers case information (e.g., travels to appropriate county, prosecutors office, client, prison, supreme court law library &/or other law libraries; contacts attorneys, prosecutors, clerks, witnesses, court reporters, judges, client's families &/or prison personnel by telephone or through correspondence).
5. Prepares appropriate legal documents based on research.
6. Compiles & produces appendix material for briefs according to various court rules.
7. Monitors cases.
8. Maintains files.
9. Makes photocopies; collates, binds & staples briefs.
10. Serves on committees & staff meetings.
11. Operates personal computer to edit, enter &/or verify data & to produce documents.

MAJOR WORKER CHARACTERISTICS:

Paralegal/Legal Assistant 1 & 2

1. Knowledge of legislative/administrative rule processes; legal research; legal terminology; legal issue recognition; case & statutory interpretation; legal analysis; law; state &/or federal laws & rules applicable to assigned department; court filing procedures; legal communication; rules of evidence.
2. Skill in use of typewriter, photocopier, video display terminal & other office equipment.
3. Ability to use proper research methods in gathering data; deal with many variables & determine recommended specific course of action; prepare legal/procedural materials & related information for review, approval & signature &/or use by licensed attorney; handle sensitive & routine inquiries from & contacts with public, legal personnel, business officials &/or clients.

MINIMUM CLASS QUALIFICATION FOR EMPLOYMENT:

Paralegal/Legal Assistant 1

1. Successful completion of certification program for paralegal or legal assistant.
2. *Or* 12 mos. law school training.
3. *Or* equivalent of Minimum Class Qualification for Employment noted above. See the chart containing a Minimum Qualification Conversion Table (*das.ohio.gov/hrd/ccmqconversion.html*).

Paralegal/Legal Assistant 2

1. Successful completion of certification program for paralegal or legal assistant; 2 yrs. exp. in legal research & writing.
2. *Or* 24 mos. law school training.
3. *Or* 36 mos. exp. as Paralegal/Legal Assistant 1 (63810).
4. *Or* equivalent of Minimum Class Qualifications for Employment noted above. See the chart containing a Minimum Qualification Conversion Table (*das.ohio.gov/hrd/ccmqconversion.html*).

C. More Information

Instructions for Job Applicants: How to Apply for a Position
www.state.oh.us/das/dhr/applinfo.html
das.ohio.gov/hrd/applinfo.html

How to Apply for a State of Ohio Job
Workshop on how to apply for state jobs. Conducted the first and third Thursday of each month from 11:30 AM to 12:30 PM at 30 E. Broad St., 29th floor, Rm. 2921, Columbus, Ohio. Reservations are not required.

Paralegal/Legal Assistant Classification Standards
das.ohio.gov/hrd/cspecs/classp.html
(Requirements: see specifications above for 63810 and 63811)

Paralegal/Certified Paralegal Position for Office of Secretary of State
das.ohio.gov/hrd/cspecs/classpdf/6381s.pdf
(Requirements for Paralegal Position: [1] 4 years experience in the public or private sector with experience in processing &/or preparation of business and corporate filings as filed with the secretary of state. OR [2] 24 months experience as a paid legal assistant or paralegal. OR [3] equivalent of minimum class qualifications for employment.)
(Requirements for Certified Paralegal Position: [1] Successful completion of certification program which is approved by the American Bar Association for paralegal or legal assistant. OR [2] 4-year degree from an accredited college or university and currently enrolled in a postgraduate law school program. OR [3] Holds a legal intern certificate from the Ohio Supreme Court. OR [4] Equivalent of minimum class qualifications for employment noted above.

Paralegal/Legal Assistant Position for Office of Attorney General
das.ohio.gov/hrd/cspecs/classpdf/6381AG.pdf

Employment in the Office of the Ohio Public Defender
opd.ohio.gov/human/Hr_Human2.htm

Hearing Assistant
("The purpose of the hearing assistant occupation is to review case folders to verify that all necessary information is present & properly completed or to ascertain ancillary issues or disposition of issues & their legal effects.")
das.ohio.gov/hrd/cspecs/classpdf/6382.pdf

Benefits for Government Employees
das.ohio.gov/hrd/empbenes.html

State Personnel Board of Review
(handles disputes involving state employees)
pbr.ohio.gov

Links to Human Resources/Personnel Offices of State Agencies
das.ohio.gov/phone/agency

Ohio's Job Bank
www.ajb.org/oh

Ohio Career Resources
www.careers.org/reg/crusa-oh-jobs-and-careers-in-ohio.html

Search for Ohio Jobs
(OLEAP: Online Employment Application Process)
statejobs.ohio.gov/applicant/index.asp

D. Something to Check

1. Use the links in section C to try to find an example of a current job opening for a paralegal/legal assistant in state government.
2. Use the links provided in sections 4.2, 4.3, and 4.5 to try to find information about any paralegal working in any state court (4.2), any federal court sitting in Ohio (4.3), and in the government of any city or county in the state (4.6).

2.3 Sample Paralegal Job Description in a Federal Agency Located in Ohio

A. Introduction

The federal government is the largest employer of paralegals in the United States. Its paralegal position is the Paralegal Specialist. This position can be somewhat different from what exists in the private sector. A Paralegal Specialist can be a document examiner, an investigator, or a law clerk, among other descriptions. He or she may work independently in the federal government, and does not always work directly for or under the supervision of an attorney.

In order to make listings of federal job vacancies accessible, an official, centralized Web site called USAJobs has been created (*www.usajobs.opm.gov*). It is managed by the Office of Personnel Management (OPM), the agency responsible for federal personnel matters. Vacancies from all federal agencies may be posted at USAJobs.
Using USAJobs
www.usajobs.opm.gov

1. Click "Job Search" and type "paralegal" in the search box.
2. Select "Legal and Claims Examining" in "Job Category Search."

The government identification code for the Paralegal Specialist is GS-950. The positions range from GS-5 to GS-11 on the federal General Schedule (GS) pay scale. (See salary link below.) The pay levels include yearly cost of living increases passed by Congress, as well as locality pay.

In addition to the USAJobs Web site, many agencies advertise their employment openings in local newspapers and other local employment agency publications. Calling local federal agencies directly can also lead to potential employment opportunities, as well as contacting individuals who may be currently employed in a federal agency. Check standard telephone directories for a list of U.S. Government offices in your area.

For a list of federal agencies and additional leads to finding a federal job, see "More Information" at the end of this section.

Elsewhere in this book you will find information on the following areas of employment:

- in state government agencies (section 2.2)
- in private law firms (section 2.1)
- in corporations (section 2.1)
- in legal service offices (sections 2.1 and 2.4)

B. Sample Job Description

The following job description is for a paralegal position in a federal government agency located in Ohio. It is an example only. The position may no longer be open. We present it here solely to give you an idea of the kinds of positions available in the federal government for Ohio paralegals. Note that the listing also includes the equivalent of interview questions ("Sample Questions Used in Evaluating Applicants"). You should consider preparing answers to such questions when applying for any paralegal job.

Title: Paralegal Specialist
Series, Grade: GS-0950-07
Salary Range: $34,920 to $45,397

Promotion Potential: To GS-11
Vacancy Announcement Number: ATR-05-17
Duty Location: U.S. Dept. of Justice Antitrust Division, Cleveland, OH
Number of Vacancies: 1 vacancy
Level: This is an entry-level, trainee position.
Appointment: Two-year appointment, which may be renewable up to a total of 4 years, subject to a 1-year trial period in accordance with 5 CFR § 316.304. Full-time, competitive position.
Who May Apply: Open to all qualified persons. Eligible displaced/surplus Department of Justice and federal employees in the local commuting area may apply. This position offers career mobility opportunities.

DUTIES

This position is located in the Cleveland Field Office of the Antitrust Division. The incumbent performs legal and factual research and closely related duties of a complex nature in support of attorneys engaged in antitrust cases and matters.

Representative duties:

- Performs research using files, library reference materials, corporate records, private and governmental studies, computer databases, and other pertinent sources, to supply needed factual information for inclusion in memoranda, briefs, and similar documents.
- Performs preliminary screening of substantive materials prior to review by attorneys.
- Maintains an accounting system for all materials to be used as exhibits in grand jury proceedings and trials.
- Prepares and organizes charts, graphs, and other material used as exhibits in court.
- Prepares tables of contents, indexes, and tables of authorities for legal briefs, memoranda, and other such documents, reviewing and researching citations, footnotes, textual references, and other entries for accuracy.
- Assists attorneys in conducting interviews with investigative sources and prospective witnesses.
- Travels to the site of trial, grand jury, discovery, etc. and there provides similar paralegal duties as described above.

QUALIFICATIONS

To qualify for this position, you must satisfy *one* of the requirements described below.

Graduate Education You must have at least one full academic year of graduate level education that demonstrates you possess the knowledge, skills, and abilities necessary to satisfactorily perform the work.

OR

Specialized Experience You must have 1 year of specialized experience equivalent to at least the GS-5 grade level during which you performed technical assignments that involved developing, authorizing or examining claims or applications that required resolving conflicting data and interpreting a body of laws, rules, regulations and policies; or preparing or reviewing contracts or other legal instruments for legal adequacy and conformance with applicable laws; or selecting and analyzing information to determine the intent of statutes, treaties, and executive orders or legal decisions, opinions, and rulings; or investigating and analyzing evidence of alleged or suspected violations of laws or regulations.

OR

Combination of Graduate Education and Specialized Experience If you have some, but not all, of the graduate education AND specialized experience described above, you may still qualify by combining the amount of creditable education and experience that you do have. To do so, first calculate the percentage of qualifying education you have as a percentage of the education required. Next, calculate the percentage of specialized experience you have as a percentage of the experience required. Then, add the two percentages.

OR

Undergraduate Degree and Superior Academic Achievement You have successfully completed, or will complete a full four-year course of study in any field leading to an undergraduate degree from an accredited college or university, or you possess or expect to possess an undergraduate degree in any field from an accredited college or university, AND you meet one of the following Superior Academic Achievement provisions:

(a) Ranked in the upper third of your college class or major subdivision at the time you apply; or

(b) Earned election to a national scholastic honor society that meets the requirements of the Association of College Honor Societies other than freshman honor societies; or

(c) Earned a grade point average (GPA) of 3.0 or higher on a 4.0 scale based on four years of undergraduate courses, or all undergraduate classes completed during the final 2 years; or

(d) Earned a GPA of 3.5 or higher on a 4.0 scale based on all completed undergraduate courses in your major, or all undergraduate courses in your major completed during the final 2 years.

BASIS FOR RATING

Your rating will be based on an evaluation of your experience, education, training, and responses to the Supplemental Qualifications Statement (SQS) items.

Your qualifications will be evaluated on the basis of your competencies in the following areas:

- ability to interpret and analyze material and make well-justified decisions from the analysis; skill in writing that reflects organization of subject matter and support for your position and conclusions;

- ability to effectively communicate orally;

- ability to effectively work with others in a team environment; and ability to determine priorities and successfully balance conflicting demands.

HOW TO APPLY

Your application will consist of three components. The first component is of the occupational questionnaire that you must complete. The second component is your resume, Optional Application for Federal Employment (OF-612), or Application for Federal Employment (SF-171). The final component of your application consists of "other" application materials. Examples of these other materials include your college transcripts and documentation of veteran status.

SAMPLE QUESTIONS USED IN EVALUATING APPLICANTS

(Note: Your responses are subject to verification through background checks, job interviews, or any other information obtained during the application process.)

- In the past 3 years, how many different paying jobs have you held for more than 2 weeks?

- On your present or most recent job, how did your supervisor rate you: outstanding; above average; average; below average; not employed or received no rating?

- How many civic or social organizations (which have regular meetings and a defined membership) have you belonged to?

- Have you successfully done work where your primary responsibility was to help others work out their problems?

- Have you successfully done work that constantly required you to work under difficult time constraints?

- Have you successfully planned an event such as a conference, fundraiser, etc.?

- Have you successfully learned a hobby or leisure activity requiring extensive study or use of complex directions?

- Have you effectively served on a problem-solving, planning, or goal-setting committee or team?

- Have you successfully completed a long-term project outside of work where you were solely responsible for doing the work?

- Have you successfully done work that required extensive on-the-job training?

- Have you worked on several major assignments or projects at the same time with minimal supervision and completed the work on time or ahead of schedule?

- Have you often been asked to proofread or edit the writing of others for content, punctuation, spelling, and grammar?

- Have you suggested or made changes to products or procedures that resulted in better meeting customer needs?

- Have you successfully done work that required you to interact with people at many levels in an organization?

- Have you successfully done work that regularly involved composing letters or writing reports containing several short paragraphs, such as investigation reports, accident reports, performance evaluations, etc.?

- Have you successfully done work that regularly involved answering questions, gathering nonsensitive information, or providing assistance to others, either in person or by telephone?

- Have you successfully done work where you had to coordinate vacation schedules, lunch breaks, etc., with other workers?

- Have you designed or developed something, on your own initiative, to help you or other employees better complete assignments?

- Have you successfully done work that regularly involved being on duty by yourself, or completing nonroutine assignments with minimal or no close supervision?

- Have you taught yourself skills that improved your performance in school or at work (for example, taught yourself typing, computer skills, a foreign language, etc.)?

- Have you successfully completed a complex research project that included collecting and analyzing information, and reporting conclusions or recommendations?

- Have you successfully done work where your supervisor regularly relied on you to make decisions while he or she was in meetings or out of the office?

- Have you taken the initiative to learn new skills or acquire additional knowledge that improved your performance at work, school, or in leisure activities?

- Have you participated in training classes, workshops, or seminars outside of school that helped you improve your teamwork skills?

- Have you been given additional responsibilities because of your ability to organize and complete your regular work more quickly than expected?

C. More Information

Finding a Federal Job

Federal Job Search
www.federaljobsearch.com
(In Career Field, click "Legal"; in Location, click "Ohio")

Federal Jobs Digest
www.jobsfed.com
(click Ohio on the map)

Office of Personnel Management Career Opportunities
www.opm.gov
(click "Job Seekers")
www.usajobs.opm.gov

USA Jobs
jobsearch.usajobs.opm.gov/a9opm.asp

FedWorld
www.fedworld.gov/jobs/jobsearch.html

Yahoo HotJobs/Government
hotjobs.yahoo.com/governmentjobs

Lists of U.S. Government Departments and Agencies
www.firstgov.gov
(click "A-Z Agency Index")
www.congress.org
(click "Federal Agencies")

Federal Salaries
www.opm.gov/oca/05tables/index.asp

Qualification Standards for General Schedule (GS) Positions
www.opm.gov/qualifications/SEC-IV/A/gs-admin.asp

D. Something to Check

1. Use the links in section C to find three examples of federal job openings for paralegals in agencies located in Ohio.
2. Go to a list of the Web sites of United States senators (*www.senate.gov*) and United States representatives (*www.house.gov*) in Congress for Ohio. Give examples of information on these sites that might be helpful for someone looking for work as a paralegal in the federal government.

2.4 Pro Bono Opportunities for Paralegals

A. Introduction

In this section you will learn a great deal about working in the public sector as we explore pro bono opportunities for paralegals. Pro bono (or pro bono publico) means for the public good. It refers to work performed without fee or compensation for the benefit of society. Certain kinds of law offices often welcome volunteer or pro bono help. Here are some examples:

- legal aid societies that provide free legal services to the poor
- public interest law offices (e.g., American Civil Liberties Union) that focus on test cases that raise broad issues of social justice
- government offices (e.g., the domestic violence unit of the local district attorney)

Paralegals with full-time jobs might devote one evening a month or two Saturday afternoons each month to pro bono work. Some employers occasionally give their paralegals time off during the week to do such work.

Paralegals perform a great range of tasks in these settings. They might interview clients to help screen applicants for the services that the office provides. They might perform factual research or draft pleadings, particularly in high-volume categories of cases such as divorce or eviction. In addition to substantive tasks such as these, pro bono paralegals might be asked to perform administrative and clerical tasks such as photocopying documents or entering data in a computer database.

Why do paralegals engage in pro bono work? The primary reason is the personal satisfaction derived by working for organizations engaged in socially worthy ventures. Many paralegals feel a professional responsibility to help ensure that disadvantaged individuals have greater access to our justice system. In addition, paralegals can gain practical experience in areas of the law outside their primary expertise. Even if their pro bono work is more administrative or clerical than legal, they may gain valuable insights and networking contacts by interacting with the staffs of these offices.

Unemployed paralegals, particularly those just out of school, have an added incentive to do pro bono work. Anything you can say on your resume about real-world law office experience might help distinguish your resume from that of someone without such experience.

Before outlining some of the major ways to explore pro bono opportunities, two ethical cautions should be covered: confidentiality and conflict of interest.

Everything you learn about a client when working pro bono should be kept confidential. The fact that some of these clients do not pay for their services is irrelevant. A poor person seeking an uncontested divorce in a legal aid office has the same right of confidentiality as a Fortune 500 company involved in complex litigation.

As you know from your course in ethics, prior client work by an attorney or paralegal could create a conflict of interest for another client in another office. One of the ways this can occur is when the prior work was on behalf of a client who has an adverse interest with a current client in a different office.

> **Example:** Jim works on behalf of a client named Smith while Jim is doing pro bono volunteering at the ABC law office. Later, Jim applies for work at the XYZ law office. One of the clients of this firm is Jones who is now suing Smith in a case that is different from (but yet related to) the case Smith had at the ABC office. If XYZ hires Jim, there may be a conflict of interest because of Jim's prior work on behalf of Smith. Hiring Jim might eventually disqualify XYZ from continuing to represent Jones.

It is unlikely that pro bono work will create such conflicts of interest, but the cautious paralegal needs to be alert to the possibility. Keep a personal journal in which you note the names of all the parties involved in cases on which you work in *any* law office. The journal should be private since it contains confidential information. (Client names, for example, are confidential.) Yet when applying for a job, one of the ways an office can determine whether you pose conflict-of-interest risks is to find out what cases you have worked on in the past. It is ethically permissible for you to reveal this information when you are in serious discussions about a new position.

B. Finding Pro Bono Opportunities

To learn about pro bono opportunities for paralegals in your area, start by asking paralegals you know (from school, at the office, at a paralegal association meeting) if they have done any pro bono work, and, if not, whether they know of others who have. Networking with other paralegals in this way can be very productive. Also ask attorneys you know where they or other attorneys do pro bono work. As pointed out later, paralegals often do pro bono work in the same offices where attorneys do such work.

1. **Paralegal Associations**
   Check with the local paralegal associations near you (see the postal and online addresses of all Ohio associations in section 1.2). Follow these steps:
   (a) Find out if the association's Web site lists pro bono opportunities or a pro bono coordinator for the association.
   (b) Check the titles of board members and officers of the association to see if anyone on the list covers pro bono matters.

(c) If the newsletter of the association is online, find out if there are any leads in it on offices that use pro bono help.
(d) E-mail the president of the association or the association's general information e-mail address to inquire about leads to pro bono work.
(e) If there is a search box on the site, type in "pro bono".
(f) Click the e-mail address name of any paralegal on the site. Introduce yourself, state that you are trying to learn about pro bono opportunities in the area, and ask if this person has any leads. Often all you need to get started is the name of one paralegal doing pro bono work. Such a person will be able to tell you if additional volunteers are needed where he or she does such work or to give you the name of others who would know.

2. Attorney Pro Bono as Leads to Paralegal Pro Bono
As indicated, a law office that accepts pro bono volunteer work by attorneys frequently accepts (or would be willing to consider) pro bono volunteer work by paralegals as well. Hence you need to check offices in Ohio that welcome pro bono work by attorneys. Call or e-mail such offices to ask if they accept pro bono work by paralegals. Here are steps to take to find out where attorneys do pro bono work:
(a) Go to the Web site of the bar associations in your area (see the addresses in section 3.4). Look for committees, sections, or special programs on pro bono. Type "pro bono" in the association's search box. Send an e-mail to the information office at the association and say, "I'm looking for leads to law offices that accept pro bono work by paralegals and would appreciate any help you can provide."
(b) Go to the ABA pro bono site:
www.abanet.org/legalservices/probono
Click "Directory of Local Pro Bono Programs." Then click Ohio on the map. These steps should lead you to a site that lists pro bono programs throughout the state:
www.abanet.org/legalservices/probono/directory/ohio.html
(c) In Google, run a search that contains the name of your city or county, the phrase "pro bono," and the word "~attorney." (The tilde (~) means you want to include synonyms of attorney such as lawyer and counsel.) Here are examples of such queries (add the word "Ohio" if you obtain many non-Ohio hits):
Cleveland "pro bono" ~attorney
Columbus "pro bono" ~attorney
"Hamilton county" ohio "pro bono" ~attorney
(d) Do the following search in Google or any search engine:
"volunteer lawyers" ohio
"Volunteer lawyers" is a term used in many communities to describe organizations that recruit pro bono legal help for specific cases and groups.
(e) Law firms often boast about the pro bono contributions of their attorneys. If you have the Web site of any Ohio law firms, particularly large ones, type "pro bono" in the search box of the site. You will often be given the names of specific organizations in the state where attorneys at that firm have volunteered.
(f) Go to the site, Ohio Legal Services (OLS), run by the Ohio State Legal Services Foundation:
www.ohiolegalservices.org
OLS is an organization dedicated to "providing legal services to low income Ohioians. Click "for pro bono" to get to its main pro bono page:
www.oslsa.org/OSLSA/ProBonoWeb
The site will give you many leads to pro bono opportunities in the state. Visit the site's Job Opportunities page, where you will find openings for paralegals and other legal workers in offices that serve the needy of the state:
www.oslsa.org/OSLSA/PrivateWeb/Jobs
You may not be looking for work, but organizations seeking to hire paralegals (or attorneys) may be interested in pro bono help. You can also call the Ohio Legal Services to inquire about such opportunities for paralegals in your area:
866-LAW OHIO
(g) Go to the Legal Services Corporation, the federal government agency that funds legal service programs:
www.lsc.gov
Click Ohio on the map or type "ohio" in the search box. You will be led to a list of all of the legal service programs in the state, many of which welcome pro bono assistance.

Examples:

Akron
Community Legal Aid Services
866–584-2350
www.communitylegalaid.org

Cincinnati
Legal Aid Society of Greater Cincinnati
800-582-2682
www.lascinti.org

Cleveland
Legal Aid Society of Cleveland
216-687-1900
www.lasclev.org

Columbus
Legal Aid Society of Columbus
614-224-8374
www.columbuslegalaid.org

Toledo
Legal Aid of Western Ohio
877-894-4599
www.lawolaw.org

(h) Check the Statewide Pro Bono Directory linked by the Ohio Legal Assistance Foundation:
www.olaf.org/probonoresources/Probonodir.shtml
www.oslsa.org/OSLSA/PublicWeb/LegalSvcs

(i) Go to the site on domestic violence in Ohio: *www.aardvarc.org/dv/states/ohdv.shtml*
The site contains an extensive list of legal aid/legal services offices in the counties of the state. These offices can be contacted not only about the need for pro bono help in domestic violence cases, but also in other areas of the law practiced by these offices.

(j) Go to Volunteer Match (*www.volunteermatch.org*). Type in your ZIP Code and click "Justice & Legal" in the interest area. You will be led to organizations seeking people who can provide direct or indirect legal help.

(k) At the Web site of the Ohio State Bar Foundation (*www.osbf.net*), click the "contact OSBF" to send a message inquiring about pro bono leads.

(l) To find a lead to an organization that covers an area of justice or human rights in which you have an interest, type a phrase relevant to that area plus the word "ohio" in Google or any other search engine. You may be led to individuals or articles that could provide leads. Here are some examples of queries:

"abortion rights" ohio
ACLU Ohio
"civil rights" ohio
"consumer rights" ohio
"death penalty" ohio
"disability rights" ohio
"environmental rights" ohio
"first amendment" ohio
"freedom of religion" ohio
"gay rights" ohio
"homelessness" ohio
"immigration rights" ohio
"labor rights" ohio
"migrant worker rights" ohio
"minority rights" ohio
"prison reform" ohio
"reproductive rights" ohio
"seniors rights" ohio
"tenants rights" ohio
"victims rights" ohio
"women's rights" ohio

(m) Look for leads on the Ohio Community Service Council site:
www.serve.ohio.gov/links.htm

3. CASA: Court Appointed Special Advocate
GAL: Guardian ad Litem
800-891-6446; 614-224-2272.
www.ohiocasa.org

CASA means "Court Appointed Special Advocate." GAL means "Guardian ad Litem." When a court must intervene to help a child, CASA/GAL volunteers (who do not have to be attorneys) are there to tell the child's story and to help protect the child's future. Volunteers do not work under attorney supervision, but are given training to serve as an informed, independent, and objective voice in court for abused and neglected children. "The volunteer focuses on, and advocates for, the child's best interests and … need for a safe, permanent home" (*www.ohiocasa.org/Volunteer.asp*). Volunteers work as fact finders, interviewers, and investigators. They gather pertinent information relative to the child's case and report on these findings in court. Their goal is to gather as much information as possible to help the court make the best decision regarding the child's future. They also monitor the case to ensure the child's needs are being met.

C. More Information

How to Use Legal Assistants in Pro Bono Publico Programs
www.abanet.org/legalservices/paralegals/probonobrochure.html
www.abanet.org/legalservices/paralegals/downloads/probonobrochure.pdf

Directory of Pro Bono Children's Law programs
www.abanet.org/litigation/committees/childrights/docs/publications_directory.pdf

Corporate Pro Bono
www.corporateprobono.org

Pro Bono Institute
www.probonoinst.org

National Association of Pro Bono Professionals
www.abanet.org/legalservices/probono/napbpro/home.html

Miscellaneous Pro Bono Links
www.ptla.org/ptlasite/probono.htm
www.abanet.org/legalservices/probono
(click "Projects"; also click "Volunteering")

Legal Aid/Legal Service Programs
www.rin.lsc.gov/scripts/LSC/PD/PDList7.asp

International Pro Bono
www.abanet.org/legalservices/probono/international.html

D. Something to Check

1. Find an office in Ohio that accepts pro bono help for adopted children who are seeking information and possible contact with their birth parents.

2. Pick any other area of the law. Find three offices in Ohio that accept pro bono help for those areas of the law.

2.5 Becoming a Notary Public

A. Introduction

Very often, law offices work with documents that must be notarized. This is particularly true in offices that do a fair amount of transactional work, e.g., incorporating a company, transferring real estate, probating an estate. If someone is not available in the office to notarize documents involved in such transactions, outside notary services must be used.

> "A notary is a public officer appointed by the Ohio Secretary of State. Administering oaths, certifying affidavits, taking acknowledgement, taking depositions and recording notarial protests are among the official duties of a notary public. An Acknowledgement is a formal declaration by a person executing a document, made to a Notary Public, [that] the person signing the document is doing so freely and voluntarily for the purpose set forth in the document. Certain documents such as deeds, mortgages, liens, powers of attorneys, and certain other instruments, must be acknowledged in the presence of a Notary Public (notarized) to be legally sufficient. However, certain documents are not required to be acknowledged or notarized, but are done so merely to insure their authenticity." (*www.akronbar.org/contentindex.asp?ID=48*)

Paralegals should consider becoming notary publics. It can be valuable even if this credential is used only occasionally as a backup when others are not readily available to notarize documents.

Caution, however, is needed when performing notary services. Attorney supervisors have been known to pressure their employees to notarize documents improperly, such as by asking them to notarize a signature that the employee did not personally observe being placed on the document involved. In fact, when paralegals are named as defendants in a suit, the most common reason is false notarization of a signature.

For a nonattorney to receive a notary public commission, you must:

1. be at least 18 years old,
2. be a citizen of the state, and
3. obtain a certificate from an Ohio judge or justice (of the court of common pleas, court of appeals, or supreme court) stating:
   a. that you are of good moral character,
   b. that you are a citizen of the county in which you reside, and
   c. that you possess the qualifications necessary to discharge the duties of a notary public or have passed an examination under rules prescribed by the judge.

Note: Many judges have adopted application procedures that involve the clerk of the court or local bar association. Therefore, you should contact the clerk of court for the court of appeals or common pleas of the county in which you reside or the local bar association. For court Web sites, see section 4.2; for bar association Web sites, see section 3.4. Once the judge signs a certificate of qualifications attesting that you have met the requirements, you give the certificate to the notary commission clerk of the Ohio Public Notary Commission within the Ohio Secretary of State's office. The fee charged by the clerk to process the application is $15. Additional fees may by charged to cover whatever method used by judges to process the applications.

The appointment as a notary is for 5 years unless the commission is revoked earlier for misconduct or incapacity.

The Ohio Notary Public Commission (within the office of the Secretary of State) maintains records of all registered notaries in the state.

Ohio Notary Public Commission
P.O. Box 1658
Columbus, OH 43216
614-644-4559

Street Address:
180 E. Broad St., 15th Floor
Columbus, OH 43215

www.sos.state.oh.us/sos/info/notaryCommission.aspx

B. Laws Governing Notaries

Recording the Commission

A notary public must present his or her commission to the clerk of the court of common pleas of the county in which the notary public resides. The clerk will record the commission and add it to the index of all recorded commissions.

Seal

You must obtain the seal of a notary public that meets state requirements. For example, it must contain the coat of arms of the state that is inked or embossed on documents that are notarized. The name of the notary public may, instead of appearing on the seal, be printed, typewritten, or stamped in legible, printed letters near the notary public's signature on each document signed by the notary public.

Official Register

A notary public must maintain an official register in which to record a copy of every certificate of protest and copy of note, which seal and record shall be exempt from execution. Upon the death or termination of appointment, the notary public's official register must be deposited in the office of the county recorder of the county in which the notary public resides.

Powers

A notary public may:

- administer oaths required or authorized by law,
- take and certify depositions,
- take and certify acknowledgments of deeds, mortgages, liens, powers of attorney, and other instruments of writing, and
- receive, make, and record notarial protests.

In taking depositions, the notary public shall have the power that is by law vested in judges of county courts to compel the attendance of witnesses and punish them for refusing to testify. Sheriffs and constables are required to serve and return all process issued by notaries public in the taking of depositions.

Oath or Affirmation

A notary public must not certify the affidavit of a person without administering the appropriate oath or affirmation to the person. A notary public who violates this section shall be removed from office by the court of common pleas of the county in which a conviction for such a violation occurs.

Protests

The instrument of protest of a notary public accompanying a bill of exchange or promissory note, that has been protested by such notary public for nonacceptance or for nonpayment, constitutes prima-facie evidence of the facts therein certified. Such instrument may be contradicted by other evidence.

Negligence as a Matter of Law

When notarizing a document, the individual involved must personally appear before the notary and show proper identification. A court has held that the failure of a notary public to obtain some evidence of identification independent of a stranger's representation is negligence as a matter of law.
(www.cbalaw.org/notary/notaryFaqs.asp)

Fees

A notary public is entitled to the following fees:

- For the protest of a bill of exchange or promissory note: $1

- For recording an instrument required to be recorded by a notary public: 10¢ for each one hundred words

- For taking and certifying an affidavit: $1.50

- For taking and certifying acknowledgments of deeds, mortgages, liens, powers of attorney, and other instruments of writing, and for taking and certifying depositions, administering oaths, and other official services, the same fees as are allowed by section 2319.27 of the Revised Code or by law to clerks of the courts of common pleas for like services.

C. More Information

Overview of Ohio Notaries Public
www.sos.state.oh.us/LawsNT/Read.aspx?ID=1

Notary Handbook
www.peoplesbar.org/notary
www.cbalaw.org/marketplace/index.php?c=3&i=9

Search for Ohio Notaries Public
www1.sos.state.oh.us/pls/portal/PORTAL_CF.NOT_QRY_NOTARYV2.SHOW_PARMS

Frequently Asked Questions about Notaries
www.peoplesbar.org/notary/faq.php

National Notary Organizations and Resources
www.americannotaryexchange.com
www.notaries.org
www.nationalnotary.org
www.nanotary.com
www.enotary.org

D. Something to Check

1. Go to the Ohio Revised Code:
   a. *onlinedocs.andersonpublishing.com*
   b. Click "Revised Code"
   c. Find § 147.02. What are the requirements for an attorney to be a notary public in the state?
2. On Google (*www.google.com*), run the following search: "ohio notary public." Summarize the categories of information found with this search.

2.6 An Employee or an Independent Contractor?

A. Introduction

B. Standards

C. Something to Check

A. Introduction

Most paralegals are employees of law firms, corporations, or other groups where they work in full-time or part-time positions. There are, however, a fair number of paralegals who have left the security of a regular paycheck in order to open their own business. They have become independent contractors (sometimes called freelance paralegals or independent paralegals) who offer services to more than one law office, usually charging the office an hourly rate or a per-project flat fee. We are not referring to individuals who offer their services directly to the public without attorney supervision. Our focus is the independent who works under the supervision of an attorney. Yet this person is not on the traditional payroll of a single law office.

Paralegals as independent contractors provide a variety of services to law firms. For example, they might:

- digest the transcript of depositions or other litigation documents
- encode or enter documents into a computer database
- collect and help interpret medical records
- prepare a 706 federal estate tax return
- prepare all the documents needed to probate an estate
- prepare trial exhibits
- conduct an asset search
- compile a chain-of-title report on real property

Such work is performed in the paralegal's office (often in his or her home) or at the law firms that have retained the paralegal.

The problem is that Ohio and the federal government (particularly the Internal Revenue Service) may conclude that these independent paralegals are not independent enough. They might be considered *employees* regardless of their title or where they do their work.

For its *employees,* a law office is required to withhold federal and state income taxes, withhold and pay social security and Medicare taxes, pay unemployment tax on wages, pay overtime compensation, provide workers' compensation coverage, etc. In general, however, none of these are required for *independent contractors* the office hires. In light of this disparity of treatment, offices are occasionally charged with improperly classifying workers as independent contractors in order to avoid their tax withholding and other employee-related obligations.

This raises the basic question: What is an employee? The answer to this question is not always clear.

- The sole test is *not* whether you are on the payroll.
- The sole test is *not* your title.
- The sole test is *not* whether you work full-time or part-time.
- The sole test is *not* whether the law office considers you an independent contractor nor whether you consider yourself to be one.
- The sole test is *not* whether you have signed an agreement with the law office specifying that you are an independent contractor rather than an employee.

It is quite possible for everyone to consider a worker to be an independent contractor—*except the government*! The Ohio state government and/or the federal government may take the position that the "independent contractor" is in fact an employee in disguise. When such a conclusion is reached, back employment taxes must be paid and penalties are possible. The law office may not be trying to avoid its tax and other responsibilities. It may simply have been mistaken in its definition of an employee. This is not uncommon. Many business have been told that workers being paid as independent contractors should have been classified as employees.

Sometimes the issue arises through tort law. For example:

> The ABC law firm hires Mary as an "independent contractor." One of Mary's tasks for the firm is to file pleadings in court. While driving to court one day in her own car, Mary has an accident. The other driver now wants to sue Mary and the ABC law firm as her employer.

Whether the driver can also sue ABC depends, in part, on whether Mary is an employee of ABC.

B. Standards

Under both Ohio and federal law, the key to determining whether someone is an independent contractor is the amount of control that exists over what he or she does and how he or she does it. Related factors are also considered, but control is key. Exhibit 2.6A summarizes the test.

No two independent paralegals operate exactly alike. Different paralegals have different relationships with their attorney clients. Some are given much more independence than others. Hence there is no one answer to the question of whether workers are employees or independent contractors. Each case must be examined separately.

Exhibit 2.6A Independent Contractor or Employee?

General Guidelines for Determining Who is an Independent Contractor and Who is an Employee

- An individual is an independent contractor if the person for whom the services are performed:
  - has the right to control or direct only the result of the work
  - does not have the right to control or direct the means and methods of accomplishing the result.
- Anyone who performs services for an office is an employee if the office can control what will be done *and* how it will be done through instructions, training, or other means. This is so even when the office gives the worker freedom of action. What matters is that the office has the *right* to control the details of how the services are performed.
- Here is how one court explained the test: "If the alleged employer retains the right to control the manner and means by which the results are to be accomplished, the individual who performs the service is an employee. If only the results are controlled, the individual performing the service is an independent contractor." *National Heritage Enterprises, Inc. v. Division of Employment Sec.* 164 S.W.3d 160, 166 (Mo.App. W.D., 2005).

There is Ohio and federal law on when a worker is an employee as opposed to an independent contractor. Ohio applies its own law on state issues such as whether a worker must be covered by workers' compensation. The federal government applies its law when the issue is whether federal income and social security taxes must be withheld. There is substantial similarity between Ohio and federal law on the question. The right of control is central under both laws.

Factors Considered under Ohio Law

Whether a worker is an employee or independent contractor depends upon a number of factors, all of which must be considered, and none of which is controlling by itself. Ohio courts apply a "multi-factor" test as outlined in *Bostic v. Connor* (1988), 37 Ohio St.3d 144, 146, 524 N.E.2d 881. In applying this test, the most significant factor to be considered is whether the office for whom the service is rendered has control or the right to control the worker both as to the work done and the manner and means in which it is performed. Here is an overview of the factors considered:

(1) who controls the details and quality of work,
(2) who controls the hours worked,
(3) who selects the materials, tools, and personnel used,
(4) who selects the routes traveled (if travel is involved),
(5) the length of time work is provided,
(6) the type of business involved,
(7) the method of payment, and
(8) any pertinent agreements or contracts.

Whether the parties believe they are creating an employer-employee relationship may have some bearing on the question, but, like the other factors listed above, this is not determinative. The existence of a written agreement purporting to establish an independent contractor relationship is not determinative and the fact that a worker is issued a 1099 form rather than a W-2 form is also not determinative with respect to independent contractor status.

Even where there is an absence of control over work details, an employer-employee relationship will be found if (1) the office hiring the worker retains pervasive control over the operation as a whole, (2) the worker's duties are an integral part of the operation, and (3) the nature of the work makes detailed control unnecessary.

Factors Considered under Federal Law

Federal law reaches substantially the same conclusion, but uses different terminology in describing the factors involved. Under federal law, three categories of evidence on control and independence are considered: (1) behavioral control, (2) financial control, and (3) type of relationship. Evidence in these categories are factors to be weighed; they are not absolute guidelines or definitions.

(1) Behavioral Control

Does the office have the right to direct and control *how* the worker does the task for which he or she is hired? Two behavioral facts that help answer this question are the type and degree of instructions received and the training provided.

- Instructions the office gives the worker. In general, employees \are subject to instructions about when, where, and how to work. Here are examples of the kinds of instructions an office could give on how work should be done:

  - when and where to do the work
  - what tools or equipment to use
  - what other workers to use to assist with the work
  - where to purchase supplies and services
  - what work must be performed by a specified individual
  - what order or sequence to follow

The amount of instruction needed varies among different jobs. Even if no instructions are given, sufficient behavioral control may exist if the office has the *right* to control how the work results are achieved. An office may lack the knowledge to instruct some highly specialized professionals; in other cases, the task may require little or no instruction. The key consideration is whether the office has retained the right to control the details of a worker's performance or has given up this right.

- Training the office gives the worker. An employee may be given training on performing the services in a particular manner. Independent contractors, on the other hand, ordinarily use their own methods.

(2) Financial Control

Factors that show whether the office has a right to control the business aspects of the worker's job include:

- The extent to which the worker has unreimbursed business expenses. Independent contractors are more likely to have unreimbursed expenses than are employees. Fixed ongoing costs that are incurred regardless of whether work is currently being performed are especially important. Note, however, that it is possible for employees to incur unreimbursed expenses in connection with the services they perform for their office.
- The extent of the worker's investment. An independent contractor (unlike an employee) often has a significant investment in the facilities he or she uses in performing services for someone else. This is not to say, however, that a significant investment is required for independent contractor status.
- The extent to which the worker makes services available to the relevant market. An independent contractor is generally free to seek out business opportunities. Independent contractors often advertise, maintain a visible business location, and are available to work in the relevant market.
- How the office pays the worker. Assume that a worker is guaranteed a regular wage amount for an hourly, weekly, or other period of time. This usually indicates that he or she is an employee, even when the wage or salary is supplemented by a commission. An independent contractor is usually paid by a flat fee for the job. In some professions, however, such as law, independent contractors are often paid hourly.
- The extent to which the worker can realize a profit or loss. An independent contractor can make a profit or suffer a loss.

(3) Type of Relationship

Facts that show the parties' type of relationship include:

- Written contracts describing the relationship the parties intended to create. Employees often do not have such contracts.
- Whether the office provides the worker with employee-type benefits, such as insurance, a pension plan, vacation pay, or sick pay. Independent contractors are seldom given such benefits.
- The permanency of the relationship. If the office engages a worker with the expectation that the relationship will continue indefinitely, rather than for a specific project or period, this is generally considered evidence that the intent of the office was to create an employer-employee relationship.
- The extent to which services performed by the worker are a key aspect of the regular business of the office. If a worker provides services that are a key aspect of the office's regular business activity, it is more likely that it will have the right to direct and control his or her activities and, therefore, this factor indicates an employer-employee relationship.

Conclusion

When the status of a paralegal is challenged, the various factors under Ohio or federal law will be weighed one by one. The evidence may conflict. Some aspects of what a paralegal does may clearly indicate an independent contractor status, while others may point to an employee-employer relationship. A court will examine the factors to determine where, on balance, a particular worker fits.

C. Something to Check

1. Using any general search engine (e.g., *www.google.com*) or legal search engine (e.g., *www.findlaw.com*), find and summarize a court opinion from any court in which the issue was whether a worker was an employee or independent contractor.
2. Interview an independent or freelance paralegal with his or her own office in Ohio. Find out how they typically provide their services to law offices. Then apply the three categories of factors (behavioral control, financial control, and type of relationship) to identify evidence of both independent contractor and employee status.

2.7 Overtime Pay under Federal and State Law

A. Introduction

Overtime law in this state is found in the following Ohio statute:

> An employer shall pay an employee for overtime at a wage rate of one and one-half times the employee's wage rate for hours worked in excess of

> forty hours in one workweek, in the manner and methods provided in and subject to the exemptions of ... the "Fair Labor Standards Act of 1938".... Rev. Code § 4111.03(A).

The Fair Labor Standards Act (FLSA) referred to in this statute is a *federal* act of Congress. Hence, Ohio follows federal law on overtime requirements, including the identification of those workers who are exempt from the requirements. If there was a conflict between federal and state overtime law, the law providing greater benefits to the employee would apply. (See More Information below for the link to the text of the FLSA.)

Eligibility for overtime depends on job duties, not on job titles. Regardless of what an employee is called, his or her right to overtime compensation will depend on a close analysis of the nature of the actual work performed by individual employees.

If an employee is eligible for overtime, he or she cannot be asked to waive this entitlement as a condition of obtaining or maintaining employment. Some paralegals would prefer *not* to receive overtime compensation even if they are entitled to it. They would rather have their extra work hours rewarded by bonuses and other perks, similar to the way attorneys are rewarded. Yet even these paralegals should know the law in the event that they may one day need to use it, particularly when leaving a position.

In general, as you will see in the following discussion, many paralegal supervisors are not eligible for overtime compensation, but most line paralegals are. The discussion assumes that a paralegal at a particular job site is *not* covered by a union contract, which can provide greater wage benefits than either federal or state law.

B. The Three Exemptions

Workers are entitled to overtime compensation if they are paid on a salary basis and earn under $455 a week ($23,660 a year). Most paralegals earn over this amount. Are they also entitled to overtime compensation? In general, the answer is yes *unless they are exempt.*

There are three main categories of exempt employees under federal law: executive, professional, or administrative. (They are referred to as the "white collar" exemptions.) Do paralegals fit within any of them? The answer depends on their primary duties, meaning the main or most important tasks they perform. It does not depend on their title, which can vary from employer to employer. Furthermore, because paralegals perform a wide variety of tasks in many different settings, the question of whether they are exempt must be determined on a person-by-person basis, one paralegal at a time. It is possible for a paralegal in an office to be exempt while another paralegal in the same office is nonexempt.

Here is an overview of the three exemptions and how they might apply to paralegals.

Executive Exemption

The employee (1) manages an enterprise such as a department or subdivision that has a permanent status or function in the office; (2) customarily and regularly directs the work of two or more employees; and (3) either has the authority to hire, promote, or fire other employees or can recommend such action and the recommendation is given particular weight.

Many paralegal *supervisors* meet all three tests of the executive exemption. They often manage the paralegal unit of the firm, supervise more than two employees, and have great influence on who is hired, promoted, or fired in their department. This is not so, however, for line paralegals. Hence they are not exempt under the executive exemption, but many paralegal supervisors would be.

Professional Exemption

The employee performs work that requires advanced knowledge that is customarily acquired by a prolonged course of specialized intellectual instruction. (Advanced knowledge means work that is predominantly intellectual in character and includes work requiring the consistent exercise of discretion and judgment.) There are two categories of exempt professional employees: learned professionals (whose specialized academic training is a standard prerequisite for entrance into the profession) and creative professionals (who work mainly in the creative arts).

Paralegals do not fit within the professional exemption. They are not "creative professionals" because law is not in the same category as music, theater, or one of the other creative arts. Nor are they "learned professionals" because prolonged specialized instruction is not a standard prerequisite to entering the field. A bachelor's degree, for example, is not a prerequisite to becoming a paralegal.

According to the U.S, Department of Labor, "while some 2 and 4-year colleges offer coursework and certification in paralegal studies, no minimum education or training requirements are established that a person must satisfy before using the occupational title 'paralegal.' This indicates that the occupation lacks a requirement of 'knowledge of an advanced type . . . customarily acquired by a prolonged course of specialized intellectual instruction' as required under 29 C.F.R. § 541.300(a)(2)." (*www.dol.gov/esa/whd/opinion/FLSA/2005/2005_12_16_54_FLSA.htm*)

Administrative Exemption

The employee (1) performs office work that is directly related to the management or general business operations of the employer or of the employer's customers and (2) exercises discretion and independent judgment with respect to matters of significance.

The question of whether the administrative exemption applies to paralegals is less clear. The first test under the administrative exemption is that the employees perform office work that is "directly related to the management or general business operations of the employer or of the employer's customers." This means "assisting with the running or servicing of the business" such as working on budgets, purchasing equipment, or administering the office's computer database. Such tasks, however, are not the primary duties of most paralegals, although they may help out in these areas. In the main, paralegals spend most of their time working on individual cases and hence do not meet the first test.

The second test (which also must be met for the administrative exemption to apply) is that the employees exercise "discretion and independent judgment with respect to matters of significance." The phrase "discretion and independent judgment" involves (a) comparing and evaluating possible courses of conduct and (b) acting or making a decision after the various possibilities have been considered. The phrase implies that the employee has authority to make an independent choice, "free from immediate direction or supervision." An employee does *not* exercise discretion and independent judgment if he or she merely uses skills in applying well-established techniques, procedures, or standards described in manuals or other sources.

Do paralegals meet the second test of exercising "discretion and independent judgment with respect to matters of significance"? They certainly work on "matters of significance." Yet it is not clear whether they exercise "discretion and independent judgment." Paralegals are often given some leeway in the performance of their work. Yet if they operate "within closely prescribed limits," they are not exercising discretion and independent judgment. Furthermore, federal officials often take the position that paralegals do not have the kind of independence this exemption requires because of the attorney supervision and approval their work must be given under the rules of ethics. If paralegals make independent choices on client matters, they run the risk of being charged with engaging in the unauthorized practice of law.

According to the U.S, Department of Labor, paralegals usually fit "into that category of employees who apply particular skills and knowledge in preparing assignments. Employees who apply such skills and knowledge generally are not exercising independent judgment, even if they have some leeway in reaching a conclusion. In addition, most jurisdictions have strict prohibitions against the unauthorized practice of law by laypersons. Under the American Bar Association's Code of Professional Responsibility, a delegation of legal tasks to a lay person is proper only if the lawyer maintains a direct relationship with the client, supervises the delegated work, and has complete professional responsibility for the work produced. The implication of such strictures is that the paralegal employees ... would not have the amount of authority to exercise independent judgments with regard to legal matters necessary to bring them within the administrative exemption." (*www.dol.gov/esa/whd/opinion/FLSA/2005/2005_12_16_54_FLSA.htm*)

To summarize:

- most paralegals are not exempt under the executive exemption (therefore, they are entitled to overtime pay)
- many paralegal supervisors are exempt under the executive exemption (hence they receive no overtime pay)
- most paralegals are not exempt under the professional exemption
- most paralegals are probably not exempt under the administrative exemption

C. Filing a Complaint

The federal and state agencies primarily responsible for enforcing wage laws are as follows:

U.S. Department of Labor
Employment Standards Administration
Wage and Hour Division
200 Constitution Avenue, NW
Washington, DC 20210
866-4-USWAGE
www.dol.gov/esa/whd

Ohio Department of Commerce
Labor and Worker Safety Division
50 West Broad Street, Ste 2800
Columbus, OH 43215-5916
614-644-2239
www.com.state.oh.us
(click "Labor & Worker Safety")

For information about filing a complaint for the failure to receive overtime compensation, contact one of the following district offices of the Wage and Hour Division of the U.S. Department of Labor:

Cincinnati Area Office
US Dept. of Labor
ESA Wage & Hour Division
550 Main St. Room 10-409
Cincinnati, OH 45202-5208
866-4-USWAGE

Cleveland District Office
US Dept. of Labor
ESA Wage & Hour Division
1240 E. 9th St., Room 817
Cleveland, OH 44199-2054
866-4-USWAGE

Columbus District Office
US Dept. of Labor
ESA Wage & Hour Division
200 N. High St., Room 646
Columbus, OH 43215-2408
866-4-USWAGE

For overtime claims, there is a 2-year statute of limitations (3 years for willful violations). Failure to file a federal claim within this period may mean that the claim is lost.

D. More Information

A Primer on Federal and State Requirements
www.lsc.state.oh.us/membersonly/123min-wage.pdf
www.jacksonlewis.com/legalupdates/article.cfm?aid=699

Federal Overtime Law: Fair Labor Standards Act (FLSA)
www.dol.gov
www.dol.gov/esa/regs/compliance/whd/fairpay/main.htm

Opinion of Wage and Hour Division of the U.S. Department of Labor on Paralegal Entitlement to Overtime Compensation
www.dol.gov/esa/whd/opinion/FLSA/2005/2005_12_16_54_FLSA.htm

Ohio Wage Law
wagehour.com.state.oh.us

Ohio Wage & Hour Bureau
www.com.state.oh.us
(click "Labor & Worker Safety")

Ohio Revised Code
www.findlaw.com/11stategov/oh/laws.html
(click "Ohio Revised Code")

United States Code (including the Fair Labor Standards Act)
www.gpoaccess.gov/uscode
(type "fair labor standards act" in the search box)

E. Something to Check

Go to the Ohio Revised Code (see Web site address under "More Information").

1) What is the definition of "employer" under Ohio's Minimum Fair Wage Standards?
2) Find the main statute on Ohio overtime law, § 4111.03(A). What is the citation to the federal Fair Labor Standards Act (FLSA) referred to in § 4111.03?
3) Go to the FLSA in the United States Code (see Web site address under "More Information"). Quote any sentence in the FSLA that mentions any of the exemptions from overtime laws.

2.8 Laid-Off Paralegals and Unemployment Compensation

A. Introduction

It can happen. You're working as a paralegal and suddenly find yourself out of work with no immediate prospects for new employment. One resource to consider while continuing to look for work is unemployment insurance (UI), which provides weekly unemployment insurance payments ("partial wage replacement") for workers who lose their job through no fault of their own. Even if you are still able to work part-time, you may be eligible for UI benefits. Approximately 700,000 individuals in Ohio receive over $1 billion in UI benefits per year.

Another reason paralegals should know about UI is that you do not have to be an attorney to represent clients in UI proceedings:

> Any individual claiming benefits or any employer may represent themselves personally or be represented by a person admitted to the practice of law *or by a person not admitted to the practice of law* in any proceeding under this chapter before the director of job and family services, or, before the commission or a hearing officer; but no such counsel or agent representing an individual claiming benefits shall either charge or receive for such services more than an amount approved by the commission. Revised Code § 4141.07(B) (emphasis added)

We will examine this authorization again in section 3.1.

B. Eligibility for UI Benefits

The Office of Unemployment Compensation is administered within the Ohio Department of Job and Family Services:

Ohio Department of Job and Family Services
Office of Unemployment Compensation
P.O. Box 182404
Columbus, OH 43218-2404
877-644-6562

jfs.ohio.gov
jfs.ohio.gov/ouc

UI benefits are supported through employer payroll taxes. You are eligible for UI if you:

(1) have worked long enough and earned sufficient wages in "covered" employment during the "base period" of your claim
(2) have lost your job through no fault of your own
(3) are available for work
(4) are actively seeking work

Covered Employment

Employment is "covered" if your employer was subject to the UI payroll tax for your wages.

Base Period

The regular base period is the first four of the last five completed calendar quarters, before your claim begins.

Minimum Earnings

You must have earned the average weekly wage during the base period before taxes or other deductions. For 2007, the average weekly wage is at least $200.

Length of Time Worked

You must have worked in a minimum of 20 weeks in covered employment during the base period.

Just Cause

- If you quit your job when the option of remaining employed existed, you will be considered to have caused your own unemployment. If you were laid off due to a lack of work (for example, your job was abolished or the office closed), you will be considered as unemployed through no fault of your own. Your employer will be asked to verify the reason for your unemployment. You are not at fault, however, if you had "just cause" to quit, such as the failure of your employer to pay you or being asked to do something unsafe, illegal, or immoral. The legal standard under Ohio law that determines whether quitting was for "just cause" is whether the action you took was one that would be taken by an ordinarily prudent person under similar circumstances.
- If your employer dismissed you from your job, you may not be eligible for benefits if the employer can establish that your discharge was for just cause. Examples of just cause include your violating office rules, neglecting your duties, or performing poor quality work.

Able to Work

You must be physically and mentally able to perform work in your occupation. If you are ill and unable to work during one or more days of your normal work week, you may be considered unable to work and not entitled to benefits for that week. If you are not physically able to work in your occupation, you may receive benefits only if you furnish medical evidence that you can do other types of work.

Available for Work

You must be ready and willing to work any shift of any occupation that is consistent with your prior training and experience. You may not be paid for weeks in which your own restrictions on hours, wages, or conditions of employment limit your chances of obtaining work.

C. UI Procedures

Application

There are three ways to file an application for UI benefits:

- at one of the local UC offices (*jfs.ohio.gov/localservices*)
- by phone (877-OHIOJOB)
- online (*unemployment.ohio.gov*)

Different levels of appeal exist if you are denied UI benefits:

Appeal from an Initial Determination

If you disagree with an initial determination, you may file a written appeal with the Ohio Department of Jobs and Family Services (ODJFS) within 21 calendar days of the date the determination was issued. The appeal can be filed:

- at any ODJFS Claims Processing Center (*www.odjfs.state.oh.us/forms/pdf/55213.pdf*)
- by mail (ODJFS Director, Bureau of UC Benefits, PO Box 182292 Columbus, OH 43218-2292)
- by fax: (614-752-4810)
- online (*unemployment.ohio.gov*)

ODJFS has 21 calendar days from the date your appeal is received to either issue a redetermination or refer the appeal to the Unemployment Compensation Review Commission (UCRC).

Unemployment Compensation Review Commission (UCRC)

UCRC will either schedule a hearing on the appeal or transfer the appeal to ODJFS for processing of a Redetermination. If you disagree with the redetermination, you may file a written appeal to the UCRC within

21 calendar days of the date the redetermination was issued. The appeal can be filed:

- at any ODJFS Claims Processing Center (*www.odjfs.state.oh.us/forms/pdf/55213.pdf*)
- by mail (ODJFS Director, Bureau of UC Benefits, PO Box 182863 Columbus, OH 43218-2863)
- by fax: (614-728-8838)
- online (*unemployment.ohio.gov*)

If accepted by the UCRC as an appeal, your case will be scheduled for either an in-person or telephone hearing before a hearing officer. If a telephone hearing is scheduled, but you prefer an in-person hearing, you must notify the UCRC within 10 days of the notice that an appeal has been filed. You must then agree to travel to a hearing site close to the location of the other parties. The hearing officer will issue a determination on the information contained in your file and presented at the hearing.

Request for Review

If you disagree with the UCRC hearing officer's decision, you request a review by the UCRC within 21 calendar days of the mailing date of the hearing officer's decision. If your request for review is allowed, the UCRC may issue a decision based on the record of the earlier hearing or hold a further hearing.

Appeal to Common Pleas Court

If you disagree with the UCRC decision, you may file a notice of appeal with the common pleas court of the county in Ohio where you reside or were last employed. Appeals must be filed within 30 calendar days of the mailing date of the UCRC decision.

D. More Information

Guide to Unemployment Compensation
www.jfs.ohio.gov/ouc/ucBen/index.stm
www.jfs.ohio.gov/ouc/index.stm

Unemployment Compensation Law: Self-Help
www.ohiolegalservices.org/OSLSA/PublicWeb/Library/Index/1710000
(click "unemployment compensation")

Employer Obligations
jfs.ohio.gov/ouc/0001employers.stm

Critique of Ohio UI System
www.policymattersohio.org/uiintro.html

U.S Department of Labor: About Unemployment Insurance
workforcesecurity.doleta.gov/unemploy/aboutui.asp

Taxation of Unemployment Compensation Benefits
www.irs.gov/taxtopics/tc418.html

E. Something to Check

1. Go to the Ohio statutory code online: *www.legislature.state.oh.us/laws.cfm* (click "ohio revised code") In the search box, type "unemployment compensation".
   (a) What section covers nonlawyer representatives at UI proceedings? Summarize this section.
   (b) What section covers administrative appeals of UI decisions? Summarize any two steps in the administrative appeals process.

2.9 Injured Paralegals and Workers' Compensation

A. Introduction

There are two main reasons Ohio paralegals should know about workers' compensation law in the state: (1) understanding your rights when injured on the job, (2) being aware of one of the major state agencies in which paralegals are allowed to represent clients at administrative hearings.

What happens if you are injured on your paralegal job? Although paralegal work certainly does not qualify as inherently dangerous work, accidents can occur. Examples:

- you have an accident while driving to the court clerk's office to file a pleading
- you slip in the hallway on the way back from your supervisor's office
- you drop a laptop on your toe

The primary system covering such mishaps is workers' compensation. In this section, we will provide an overview of your rights and practical steps you should take when injured on the job. Workers' compensation is a no-fault system, meaning that injured employees need not prove the injury was someone else's fault in order to receive workers' compensation benefits. The primary requirement for receiving benefits is that you sustain an injury arising out of and in the course of your employment.

There is another reason to learn about workers' compensation in Ohio. Paralegals can represent claimants before units of the Bureau of Workers' Compensation (BWC), the agency that administers the system. As the Supreme Court of Ohio recently noted, "lay representation has been a feature of Ohio's workers' compensation system since its inception." *Cleveland Bar Assn. v. CompManagement, Inc.*, 104 Ohio St.3d 168, 171, 818 N.E.2d 1181, 1185 (2004). We will examine this authorization in section 3.1.

B. Overview

Over 200,000 claims for work-related injuries and occupational diseases are filed each year in Ohio, with over $2 billion paid out in benefits. The workers' compensation system has two major components: (1) the Bureau of Workers' Compensation (BWC), with a central office in Columbus and sixteen customer service offices throughout the state; and (2) the Industrial Commission (IC), the adjudicatory body that hears and decides contested claims.

Ohio employers are either state-fund or self insured. State-fund employers pay an insurance premium to BWC, which then pays benefits to injured employees. Self-insured employers do not have insurance; they pay benefits directly to their injured employees.

When you file a claim, medical services are managed by a Managed Care Organization (MCO). Each state-fund employer has an MCO. (Self-insured employers can use their own managed care system.) Your MCO works with your doctor in obtaining appropriate medical care. In addition to paying medical bills, BWC makes payments to cover lost wages if you lose eight or more days from work due to the injury.

C. Steps to Take

1. Seek medical attention.
2. Report the injury to the employer promptly. The failure to do so could jeopardize the receipt of benefits.
3. Find out the name of your MCO by asking your employer, by calling BWC (800-OHIOBWC), or by checking online at *www.ohiobwc.com* (click "medical providers" then "employer/MCO lookup").
4. You can see any doctor for your first visit. After that, you must choose a BWC-certified provider for treatment. If you choose a noncertified provider, you may have to pay the medical bills involved (except in an emergency).
5. Tell your doctor or emergency room worker the name of your MCO. Your pharmacist should also be told that your medication is part of a workers' compensation case.
6. The application used to initiate a workers' compensation claim is the FROI (First Report of Injury, Occupational Disease or Death). The employer should give you a copy of this form. It is also available online (*www.ohiobwc.com*) and by contacting the BWC Customer Service Office nearest you (see "Contracts" below).
7. Complete as much of the FROI as possible. If you fill it out at the doctor's office, the doctor can provide the treatment information for the FROI.
8. Make a copy of the completed FROI for your records. Hand deliver the original or mail it (certified mail, return receipt requested) to your employer or your employer's MCO. You can also give the form to your local BWC Customer Service Office (see list below) or submit it online.
9. You will receive an information packet, including a BWC identification card. The card contains your claim number, the name of your claims service specialist (CSS), his or her phone number, and your MCO's name and phone number. If you have not received this packet within 2 weeks of the injury, call the local BWC customer service number to verify that a claim has been filed.
10. Within 28 days, BWC makes an initial decision in a written order that will be sent to you, your attorney or other authorized representative, and your employer and his or her authorized representative. The order will specify whether BWC has allowed or denied your claim. If allowed, the order will also state whether you are entitled to compensation due to the injury.
11. If you or your employer disagrees with the order, either of you may file a Notice of Appeal with the Industrial Commission (IC). The time frame for filing an appeal is generally 14 days after you receive the order.
12. The IC will hold a hearing at the Customer Service Office nearest your home. IC sends all parties a notice of the time and place of the hearing. Once the hearing takes place, the parties receive the IC's decision.
13. If still dissatisfied after completing (exhausting) this administrative process, a party can seek judicial review in a state court of common pleas.
14. It is illegal for an employer to punish or fire (retaliate against) an employee for filing a claim or testifying in another employee's workers' compensation case.

D. Contacts

Bureau of Workers' Compensation
30 W. Spring St.
Columbus, Ohio 43215-2256
800-OHIOBWC
www.ohiobwc.com

Industrial Commission
30 W. Spring St.
Columbus, Ohio 43215-2233
800-521-2691
www.ic.state.oh.us

Ombudsman (Ombuds)

(for additional help in obtaining answers to workers' compensation questions)
800-335-0996

Locating your Local Customer Service Office

ohiobwc.com
(click "injured worker" then "automatic office locator" and type in your Zip Code)

BWC Customer Service Offices

Ashtabula 440-964-8505	Governor's Hill 513-583-4400
Bridgeport 740-635-1163	Hamilton 513-785-4500
Cambridge 740-435-4200	Lima 888-419-3127
Canton 800-713-0991	Logan 800-385-5607
Cincinnati 513-852-3341	Mansfield 419-747-4090
Cleveland 800-821-7075	Portsmouth 740-353-2187
Columbus 614-728-5416	Springfield 937-327-1425
Dayton 937-264-5000	Toledo 419-245-2700
Garfield Heights 800-224-6446	Youngstown 800-551-6446

E. More Information

An Ohio Paralegal Specializing in Workers' Compensation
www.cincinnatiparalegals.org/paralegal5.PDF

Workers' Compensation Statutes and Regulations
www.ohiobwc.com/basics/infostation/default.asp
(click "Ohio Administrative Code")

Overview of Ohio Workers' Compensation
www.ohiobwc.com/basics/guidedtour/default.asp

Filing a Claim
www.ohiobwc.com/bwccommon/forms/froi/default.asp

Filing an Appeal
www.ic.state.oh.us/forms/forms.html#appeal
www.ic.state.oh.us/appeals/appeals.html
www.ohiobwc.com/worker/programs/claiminfo/CIAppealRights.asp

Injured Workers4Change
www.injuredworkers4change.org/states_links.htm
(click "Ohio")

Workerscompensation.com
www.workerscompensation.com
(click "Ohio")

U.S. Occupational Safety & Health Administration (OSHA)
www.osha.gov

F. Something to Check

1. Find the Ohio Administrative Code online. Go to *www.legislature.state.oh.us* (click "Laws, Acts, and Legislation" and then "Ohio Administrative Code"). Scroll down to and click § 4121 on the left. This will lead you to § 4121-2. Click this section to get to § 4121-2-01. Read this section. What are the requirements for being an attorney or nonattorney representative of a workers' compensation claimant?
2. Go to the Ohio Constitution online (*www.legislature.state.oh.us/constitution.cfm*). In the search box, type "workmen's compensation". Summarize what the Constitution says about workers' compensation.
3. Find three Ohio law firms online that represent clients in workers' compensation cases. Compare their descriptions of the services they offer.

APPENDIX A

Deductibility of Paralegal Education or Training

A. Introduction

Paralegals can incur education and training expenses (a) before they obtain their first job, (b) while employed, and (c) while looking for a new position after leaving an old one. Are any of these expenses deductible on their federal income tax return as a business expense? In this section, we examine the tax law governing this question.

The cost of obtaining a paralegal education by way of a bachelor's degree, associate degree, or certificate can be significant. In addition, there are the costs of earning the credits required to maintain one's credentials in voluntary certification programs such as that of the Ohio bar (Ohio Certified Paralegal) discussed in section 1.1. Finally, there are the costs of attending continuing legal education (CLE) sessions to keep current in one's field of the law. When paralegals spend their own money for any of these purposes, are they deductible?

B. Qualifying Work-Related Education that is Deductible (QWRE)

You can deduct education costs as a business expense if the education can be classified as qualifying work-related education (QWRE). What is QWRE? The following three principles apply:

1. The education must fit within either (a) or (b):
   - **(a)** The education is required by your employer or by the law to keep your present salary, status, or job, and this required education serves a bona fide business purpose of the employer.
   - **(b)** The education is used to maintain or improve skills that are needed in your present work.
2. Education that meets the minimum educational requirements of your present trade or business is *not* a QWRE.
3. Education that is part of a program of study to qualify you for a new trade or business is *not* a QWRE.

Exhibit A summarizes these principles.

Ohio paralegals often purchase continuing legal education (CLE) courses offered by associations, schools, or institutes. (See section 1.3 on CLE for paralegals.) Although CLE is not required for you to be a paralegal in the state, it certainly helps you maintain or improve your paralegal skills. Indeed, skill maintenance or improvement is a major purpose of CLE. Consequently, when you pay for such CLE yourself, the cost would constitute deductible QWRE.

Of course, your largest education expense will probably be for your *initial* paralegal training. Can this be QWRE? For most students the answer is *no* because it is a program of study to qualify you for a "new trade or business."

Suppose, however, that you are a legal secretary paying your own way to go to paralegal school part-time or during an extended break from work. Can the cost of this education be QWRE? This is a more difficult question to answer. If as a secretary you were performing some paralegal tasks (even though you were not called a paralegal), an argument can be made that you are not trying to enter a "new trade or business." You are simply expanding (improving) what you already do. It's not clear whether the IRS would accept this argument. If it does, the cost of the paralegal education would be QWRE.

Suppose that you are an experienced paralegal who wants to become an attorney. Can your law school education be QWRE? Since the requirements for being an attorney are substantially different from what is required to be a paralegal, the IRS would probably take the position that going from paralegal to attorney is entering a "new trade of business." In an example provided by the IRS, if an accountant decides to become an attorney, his or her law school education would not be QWRE even if the employer requires the accountant to obtain a law degree. According to the IRS, going from accountant to attorney qualifies the accountant for a "new trade or business."

C. More Information

Federal Tax Benefits for Education
www.irs.gov/pub/irs-pdf/p970.pdf
www.irs.gov/publications/p970/ch12.html
taxguide.completetax.com/text/Q04_5120.asp
www.unclefed.com/TaxHelpArchives/2002/HTML/p508toc.html

Ohio Department of Taxation
www.tax.ohio.gov

EXHIBIT A

When Does Your Education or Training Constitute Qualified Work-Related Education (QWRE)?

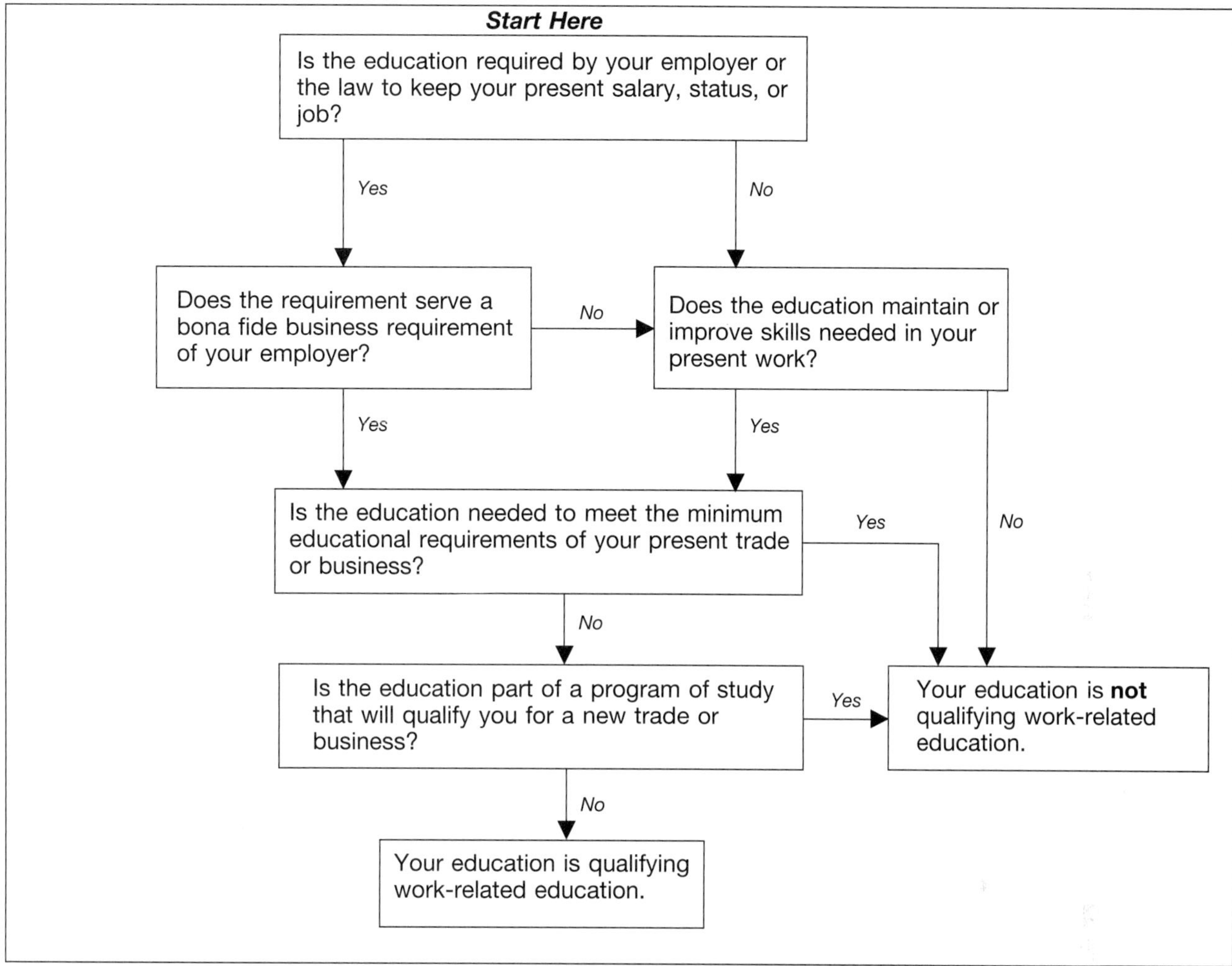

Source: Internal Revenue Service, Tax Benefits for Education, *60, Figure 12-1 (2005) (www.irs.gov/pub/irs-pdf/p970.pdf)*

D. Something to Check

Go to the Internal Revenue Service site (*www.irs.gov*). Use its search boxes to try to find material relevant to the following case. Mary is a legal investigator who works for an Ohio law firm. She wants to take an evidence course at a local paralegal school. If she pays for the course herself, under what circumstances, if any, can she deduct the cost as QWRE?

PART

3

Ethics, Paralegals, and Attorneys

A. Introduction

There is no statute in Ohio that defines the practice of law, and therefore there is no clear statutory definition of what constitutes the unauthorized practice of law (UPL). There are statutes saying who is allowed to practice law and what the legal consequences are for engaging in the unauthorized practice of law. Most of the definitional law comes from court opinions, which are our major focus here.

In section 3.2, you will find the text of the *Ohio Rules of Professional Conduct.* There are provisions in the Rules pertaining to the unauthorized practice of law, some of which are referred to here. See also the following related sections:

- Part 1, Appendix A. Paralegals in Court Opinions
- Part 1, Appendix B. Becoming an Attorney in Ohio
- Part 3, Appendix A. A Timeline: Disciplinary Proceedings Against an Attorney

B. Themes Covered

Who can practice law?
Deciding who can practice law
Criminal penalties for UPL
Civil remedies for UPL
Defining the practice of law
Paralegals charged with UPL
Lay representation in small claims court
Lay representation in administrative agencies
Workers' compensation
Unemployment compensation
Other Ohio agencies
Law-related occupations and the UPL (estate planning, banks and trust companies, real estate agents and brokers, insurance adjusters)
Bankruptcy petition preparers
Social Security
Occupational Safety and Health Review Commission
Miscellaneous

C. Applicable Laws

Who can practice law?

- No person shall be permitted to practice as an attorney and counselor at law, or to commence, conduct, or defend any action or proceeding in which the person is not a party concerned, either by using or subscribing the person's own name, or the name of another person, unless the person has been admitted to the bar by order of the supreme court in compliance with its prescribed and published rules. (R.C. § 4705.01)
- No person who is not licensed to practice law in this state shall do any of the following:
  (1) Hold that person out in any manner as an attorney at law;
  (2) Represent that person orally or in writing, directly or indirectly, as being authorized to practice law;
  (3) Commit any act that is prohibited by the supreme court as being the unauthorized practice of law. (R.C. § 4705.07(A))

Who decides who can practice law? The courts or the legislature?

- The Ohio Constitution gives the Supreme Court of Ohio original jurisdiction over admission "to the practice of law, the discipline of persons so admitted, and all other matters relating to the practice of law." (Section 2(B)(1)(g), Article IV, Ohio Constitution)
- The state constitution also states that the Supreme Court "shall make rules governing the admission to the practice of law and discipline of persons so admitted." (Section 5(B), Article IV, Ohio Constitution)
- The Ohio Supreme Court has commented that the legislature accepts the Court's role in this area. "We note that the legislature has acknowledged our authority in regulating the practice of law." (*Cleveland Bar Assn. v. Pearlman*, 106 Ohio St.3d 136 (Ohio 2005)) "Our authority to define the practice of law is inherent . . . and the legislative branch has no right to limit the inherent powers of the judicial branch of the government." (*Cleveland Bar Assn. v. Picklo*, 772 N.E.2d 1187 (Ohio 2002)) "This court [the Supreme Court of Ohio] has exclusive power to regulate, control, and define the practice of law in Ohio and, therefore, is the ultimate "authority to determine the qualifications of persons engaged in the practice of law." (*Cleveland Bar Assn. v. CompManagement, Inc.*, 818 N.E.2d 1181 (Ohio 2004))

Criminal law consequences for engaging in the unauthorized practice of law

- It is a misdemeanor in the first degree for a person "who is not licensed to practice law" in Ohio to do either of the following: (1) Hold that person out in any manner as an attorney at law; or (2) Represent that person orally or in writing, directly or indirectly, as being authorized to practice law. (R.C. §§ 4705.07; 4705.99)

Civil recourse for someone harmed by the unauthorized practice of law

- Any person who is damaged by another person who commits [an act prohibited by the supreme court as being the unauthorized practice of law] may commence a civil action to recover actual damages from the person who commits the violation. (R.C. § 4705.07 (C)(2)) Courts also have the authority to issue injunctions against the unauthorized practice of law.

What is the practice of law?

- The unauthorized practice of law is the rendering of legal services for another by any person not admitted to practice in Ohio. (Rules for the Government of the Bar of Ohio, Rule VII(2)(A)). The term "rendering of legal services" has been defined further: "The practice of law is not limited to the conduct of cases in court. It embraces the preparation of pleadings and other papers incident to actions and special proceedings and the management of such actions and proceedings on behalf of clients before judges and courts, and in addition conveyancing, the preparation of legal instruments of all kinds, and in general all advice to clients and all action taken for them in matters connected with the law." (*Cleveland Bar Assn. v. Pearlman,* 832 N.E.2d 1193 (Ohio 2005) citing *Land Title,* 193 N.E. 650 (Ohio 1934))
- In the seminal case regarding the unauthorized practice of law (*Land Title Abstract & Trust Co. v. Dworken,* 193 N.E. 650 (Ohio 1934), we held, "The practice of law is, 'as generally understood, the doing or performing services in a court of justice, in any matter depending therein, throughout its various stages, and in conformity with the adopted rules of procedure. But in a larger sense it includes legal advice and counsel, and the preparation of legal instruments and contracts by which legal rights are secured, although such matter may or may not be depending in a court.' " *Ohio State Bar Assn. v. Burdzinski, Brinkman, Czarzasty & Landwehr, Inc.,* 858 N.E.2d 372 (Ohio, 2006)
- The practice of law generally involves three principal types of professional activity. These types are legal advice and instructions to clients to inform them of their rights and obligations; preparation for clients of documents and papers requiring knowledge of legal principles which is not possessed by an ordinary layman; and appearance for clients before public tribunals, which possess the power and authority to determine rights of life, liberty and property according to law, in order to assist in the proper interpretation and enforcement of law. (*McMillen v. McCahan,* 167 N.E.2d 541 (Ohio Com.Pl. 1960))
- It is neither necessary nor desirable to attempt the formulation of a single, specific definition of what constitutes the practice of law. Functionally, the practice of law relates to the rendition of services for others that call for the professional judgment of a lawyer. The essence of the professional judgment of the lawyer is his educated ability to relate the general body and philosophy of law to a specific legal problem of a client; and thus, the public interest will be better served if only lawyers are permitted to act in matters involving professional judgment. Where this professional judgment is not involved, non-lawyers, such as court clerks, police officers, abstracters, and many governmental employees, may engage in occupations that require a special knowledge of law in certain areas. But the services of a lawyer are essential in the public interest whenever the exercise of professional legal judgment is required. (*Ohio Code of Professional Responsibility,* EC-3-5) (*www.sconet.state.oh.us/Rules/professional/#c3*)

Paralegals in law firms engage in the unauthorized practice of law when they act without attorney supervision

- Legal assistant's conduct in preparing legal documents for the attorney's clients without the assistance or oversight of the attorney, and filing those documents before they had been reviewed and approved by the attorney constituted the unauthorized practice of law. R.C. § 4705.01; Government of the Bar Rule VII(2)(A). Although laypersons may assist lawyers in preparing legal papers to be filed in court and managing pending claims, those activities must be carefully supervised and approved by a licensed practitioner to avoid unauthorized practice of law. *Columbus Bar Assn. v. Thomas,* 109 Ohio St.3d 89, 846 N.E.2d 31 (Ohio, 2006)
- It is not the unauthorized practice of law for a nonlawyer to represent another in union-election matters or in the negotiation of a collective-bargaining agreement when the activities of the nonlawyer are

confined to providing advice and services that do not require legal analysis, legal conclusions, or legal training. It is the unauthorized practice of law for a nonlawyer to draft or write a contract or other legal instrument on behalf of another that is intended to create a legally binding relationship between an employer and a union, even if the contract is copied from a form book or was previously prepared by a lawyer. *Ohio State Bar Assn. v. Burdzinski, Brinkman, Czarzasty & Landwehr, Inc.*, 858 N.E.2d 372 (Ohio, 2006)

Examples of paralegals charged with the unauthorized practice of law

- In this case, a person who identified himself as a paralegal, was enjoined from engaging in the following activities involving the practice of law: "the counseling of persons with respect to their legal rights, the preparation of legal instruments and documents to secure legal rights of any person, the preparation, signing, or filing of pleadings or other papers on behalf of persons incident to actions in courts or other tribunals in the state of Ohio, and the appearance . . . on behalf of any other persons in any court or tribunal in the state of Ohio." (*Akron Bar Assn. v. Greene*, 673 N.E.2d 1307 (Ohio 1997))
- In the case before us, Para-Legals, Inc. and LeVert engaged in the unauthorized practice of law by attempting to represent another in municipal court through the sham authority of a power of attorney. And as an employee of Para-Legals, Inc., Hampton also engaged in the unauthorized practice of law by preparing legal documents for another for filing in the domestic relations court without a licensed lawyer's oversight. The Ohio Constitution confers on the Ohio Supreme Court original jurisdiction regarding admission to the practice of law, the discipline of persons so admitted, and all other matters relating to the practice of law. And with few exceptions, the unauthorized practice of law occurs when a layperson renders legal services for another, including the management of actions and proceedings on behalf of clients before courts of law. The unauthorized practice of law also includes the preparation for another of legal pleadings and other papers by a layperson without the supervision of a licensed attorney. (*Cleveland Bar Assn. v. Para-Legals, Inc.*, 835 N.E.2d 1240 (Ohio 2005))
- Elwood L. Cromwell III of Cincinnati, Ohio, although not licensed to practice law, is charged with engaging in the unauthorized practice of law. The matter was submitted to the Board of Commissioners on the Unauthorized Practice of Law of the Supreme Court of Ohio ("board") on stipulated facts. Respondent, a resident of Cincinnati, had never received a license to practice law in any jurisdiction and is not registered as an attorney with the Supreme Court of Ohio. He conducted a business under the name Paralegal Service Group, which operated without the supervision of an attorney. In May 1994, Dawn Brown engaged respondent and paid him a retainer of $50, with an additional $200 to be paid upon settlement, to pursue her claim against an insurance company arising out of an automobile accident. Respondent then wrote to State Farm Insurance Company, stating that he had been retained to negotiate a settlement for Brown and that he hoped it would not be necessary to turn the case over to an attorney for further legal action. He also wrote to Sports Therapy, Inc., presumably a creditor of Brown, to advise it that he was negotiating a settlement for Brown, and in September 1994, he drafted a settlement agreement with respect to the matter. Then Brown fired respondent and he refunded her retainer. In January 1995, Calvin Ward engaged respondent to represent him with respect to a motor vehicle accident and paid him a retainer of $50. On Ward's behalf, respondent contacted the Windsor Group, an insurance company, with respect to a settlement. Respondent also received referrals from other individuals to retain him as their representative with respect to personal injury claims, and to review correspondence related to divorce. The board concluded that respondent's actions, including communicating with insurance companies on behalf of Brown and Ward, and communicating with a creditor and preparing a settlement agreement on Brown's behalf, constituted the unauthorized practice of law in Ohio. The board recommended that respondent be prohibited from engaging in such practices in the future. We adopt the findings and conclusions of the board. As the board correctly noted, the practice of law includes representing others with regard to their causes of action for personal injury, communicating with insurance companies about claims, making representations to creditors on behalf of third parties, and advising persons of their rights, and the terms and conditions of settlement. Not having been registered to practice law in Ohio, respondent, by his actions, was engaged in the unauthorized practice of law in Ohio. Respondent is hereby enjoined from engaging in any further activities that might constitute the unauthorized practice of law. Costs taxed to respondent. (*Cincinnati Bar Assn. v. Cromwell*, 695 N.E.2d 243 (Ohio 1998))
- Respondent, a nonattorney, conducted business at DocuPrep USA, part of a nationwide chain advertised as independently operated paralegal offices. For his particular operation, respondent advertised

that he would help customers "prepare and file the important documents of [their] life without the services and expense of a lawyer." More specifically, he offered to prepare wills and living trusts, as well as the documents necessary for divorces, name changes, stepparent adoptions, evictions, immigration, and bankruptcies, and to establish corporations, among "other uncontested legal procedures." On numerous occasions, he drafted and completed documents, including several wills, a dissolution pleading and related orders, and many bankruptcy petitions, all of which affected or determined others' legal rights. He also gave advice and counsel to people about their legal rights, all the while charging for his services. Respondent testified that when customers came to him, they did not know what type of legal document was required to accomplish their objective, and he would choose for them by using official forms and software programs. By selecting the causes of action and legal instruments he thought might protect his customers' interests, however, respondent was engaged in the unlicensed practice of law; he just did not realize it. In fact, although he did know that his customers were relying on the documents he prepared to protect their legal rights in court and elsewhere, respondent described himself as merely a document preparer. The unauthorized practice of law consists of rendering legal services and includes the preparation of legal pleadings and other papers for another without the supervision of an attorney licensed in Ohio. Respondent is therefore enjoined from preparing legal documents for others and from any other conduct constituting the unauthorized practice of law. (*Ohio State Bar Association v. Cohen*, 836 N.E.2d 1219 (Ohio 2005))

- While doing business as Your Legal Assistant, respondent gave legal advice on several occasions to Kenneth Williams and Marselle Williams, separately and collectively, on the difference between a divorce and a dissolution. Respondent also gathered information from the Williamses that he used to draft their court pleadings and other documents for filing in the domestic relations court. These pleadings were captioned In re Marriage of Williams, case No. D282513 in the Cuyahoga County Common Pleas Court, Division of Domestic Relations. Respondent's legal advice and preparation of legal documents constitute the unauthorized practice of law. Respondent is hereby enjoined from further actions constituting the unauthorized practice of law. (*Cleveland Bar Assn. v. Washington*, 836 N.E.2d 1212 (Ohio 2005))

- On two occasions Andra Coats, d.b.a. Paramount Paralegal Services, assisted others in their claims before the Ohio Bureau of Employment Services and appeared as their representative. He has also drafted divorce complaints and judgment entries for filing on behalf of pro se litigants. Coats has a college degree with a major in paralegal studies; however, he has never been licensed to practice law in Ohio, and he did not provide this representation under a licensed attorney's supervision. The Cleveland Bar Association filed a complaint charging him with having engaged in the unauthorized practice of law and sought to permanently enjoin this conduct. Coats was served with the complaint but did not answer. The Board of Commissioners on the Unauthorized Practice of Law found that his filings, appearances, and preparation of documents, all of which were completed without a licensed attorney's supervision, constituted the unauthorized practice of law. As the board explained, "The unauthorized practice of law consists of rendering legal services for another by any person not admitted to practice in Ohio." Moreover, the practice of law includes conducting cases in court, preparing and filing legal pleadings and other papers, appearing in court cases, and managing actions and proceedings on behalf of clients before judges, whether before courts or administrative agencies. The board recommended that we find that respondent engaged in the unauthorized practice of law and that we enjoin such conduct. We adopt, in the main, the board's findings and its recommendation. Accordingly, Coats is hereby enjoined from all further conduct on another's behalf, whether it involves preparing a legal document, filing, or appearing before a tribunal, that constitutes the unauthorized practice of law. (*Cleveland Bar Assn. v. Coats*, 786 N.E.2d 449 (Ohio 2003))

Probate paralegal violates paralegal registration requirements and engages in the unauthorized practice of law

- Paralegal registration. There is a special registration for paralegals in the probate division of the Franklin County Court of Common Pleas

(*www.franklincountyohio.gov/probate/PDF/LocalRules.pdf*):

Local Rule 75.8 Registration of Paralegals

(A) Paralegals performing services in matters before this Court must be registered with the Court under Case No. 461,100. The Court recognizes two (2) categories of paralegals: "employee paralegals," paralegals employed exclusively by and performing services for one law firm as an employee of that firm; and "independent paralegals," paralegals operating as freelance/independent contract paralegals or offering services to more than one law firm. Registration shall be on the forms prescribed by the Court.

(1) Employee paralegals need only be registered once, identifying the law firm and stating the paralegal services will be supervised by the attorney(s) of that law firm. An attorney from the firm and the paralegal shall sign the registration certifying that the paralegal is qualified through education, training, or work experience to assist an attorney in matters which will be filed in this Court and that an attorney from the law firm will supervise and be responsible for all services of the paralegal. In fee statements filed with the Court, services of the paralegal must be itemized separately from services performed by an attorney. The law firm shall notify the Court when the paralegal registered with the Court leaves the exclusive employment of the law firm.

(2) Independent paralegals shall be registered for each case in which the independent paralegal is performing services, identifying the case name, case number, and supervising attorney. The supervising attorney and the independent paralegal shall sign the registration certifying that the independent paralegal is qualified through education, training, or work experience to assist the supervising attorney in matters that will be filed in this Court and, as supervising attorney, he or she will supervise and be responsible for all services of the independent paralegal. In fee statements filed with the Court, services of the independent paralegal must be itemized separately from services performed by an attorney. Attorney fees reported in the account shall include a disclosure of the independent paralegal fees on the Receipts and Disbursements form.

(B) In conjunction with Civ. R. 11, a paralegal may not sign any document for the fiduciary, applicant, or supervising attorney.

(C) For purposes of this rule, the Court acknowledges the definition of "paralegal" adopted by the Columbus Bar Association. Registration with the Court does not constitute certification by the Court as to the qualifications of the paralegal.

(D) Failure to comply with this rule may result in the disallowance of the fees and such other action as the Court may deem appropriate.

A Franklin County paralegal, who without supervision of an attorney, advised and represented a minor claimant in a personal injury matter in the probate court, was found to have engaged in the "unauthorized practice of law." Local Rule 75.8(A)(2) of the Probate Division of the Common Pleas Court of Franklin County requires that an independent paralegal "shall be registered for each case in which the independent paralegal is performing services," identifying, *inter alia,* a supervising attorney. That attorney must sign the registration, certifying that the independent paralegal is qualified to perform the services and that the supervising attorney will supervise and be responsible for all services of the paralegal. On September 22, 1999, respondent, Dellwin Purnell, filed an independent paralegal registration in the probate court in connection with the personal injury claim of a minor, Kyle Petersen. The form was not signed by a supervising attorney. On September 24, 1999, respondent filed an "Application to Settle a Minor's Claim" in the probate court, striking the words "attorney" and "attorney's" from the form language "reasonable attorney fee for the attorney's services" and substituting therefor the phrase "reasonable paralegal fee for the services." The application indicated that the fee would be $3,500 and that a fee agreement between respondent and the minor's parent was attached to the application. In a letter to Liberty Mutual Insurance Company, dated October 16, 1998, respondent had indicated that he was engaged to "represent Kyle Petersen in a claim for personal injuries." On January 24, 2000, the probate judge found respondent in contempt for representing himself as a paralegal without a supervising attorney. On September 13, 2000, the Columbus Bar Association filed a complaint charging respondent with the unauthorized practice of law. Respondent failed to answer, and on December 4, 2000, the bar filed a motion for default. The matter was referred to the Board of Commissioners on the Unauthorized Practice of Law ("board"), which granted the motion. The board found the facts as stated and concluded that respondent's conduct constituted rendering legal services for another by a person not admitted to the practice of law in Ohio. The board recommended that respondent be prohibited from engaging in the unauthorized practice of law in the future. On review of the record, we adopt the findings, conclusion, and recommendation of the board. A paralegal who, without the supervision of an attorney, advises and represents a claimant in a personal injury matter is engaged in the unauthorized practice of law. Respondent is hereby enjoined from any further activities that might constitute the unauthorized practice of law. Costs are taxed to respondent. (*Columbus Bar Assn. v. Purnell,* 760 N.E.2d 817 (Ohio 2002))

Lay representation of companies in small claims court

The legislature enacted R.C. § 1925.17, which allows a nonattorney employee of a corporation to represent the corporation in small claims court. This statute was challenged in the *Pearlman* case. Here is the text of the statute and excerpts from *Pearlman*:

- *R.C. § 1925.17*: A corporation may "through any bona fide officer or salaried employee, file and present its claim or defense in any action in a small claims division arising from a claim based on a contract to which the corporation is an original party or any other claim to which the corporation is an original claimant, provided such corporation does not, in the absence of representation by an attorney at law, engage in cross-examination, argument, or other acts of advocacy."
- *Pearlman*: In this case a layperson used the authorization of R.C. § 1925.17 to represent his limited liability company in small claims court. His right to do so was challenged. The Ohio Supreme Court rejected the challenge and ruled in his favor. "A layperson who presents a claim or defense and appears in small claims court on behalf of a limited liability company as a company officer does not engage in the unauthorized practice of law, provided that the individual does not engage in cross-examination, argument, or other acts of advocacy." Hearings in small claims court "are simplified, as neither the Ohio Rules of Evidence nor the Ohio Rules of Civil Procedure apply. Thus, by design, proceedings in small claims courts are informal and geared to allowing individuals to resolve uncomplicated disputes quickly and inexpensively. Pro se activity is assumed and encouraged. The process is an alternative to full-blown judicial dispute resolution." We recognize an exception, albeit a narrow one to the general rule that corporations may be represented only by licensed attorneys. R.C. § 1925.17 limits what a corporate representative may do. The layman in this case observed these limitations. The public is not harmed by his actions. In small claims cases, where no special legal skill is needed, and where proceedings are factual, nonadversarial, and expected to move quickly, attorneys are not necessary. We decline to require corporations to hire attorneys to represent them in small claims courts. (*Cleveland Bar Assn. v. Pearlman*, 832 N.E.2d 1193 (Ohio 2005))

But a corporate officer cannot represent his corporation in a county court

- The Ohio Attorney General filed a complaint against Adventure Novelty in the county court of Belmont County, Ohio, seeking to enforce the state minimum-wage law. Respondent, a nonattorney corporate officer of Adventure Novelty filed two motions to dismiss the complaint, purportedly acting on Adventure Novelty's behalf as "Attorney or Agent." The county court rejected the motion to dismiss because it had been filed by a nonattorney. A nonattorney may not practice law in county court in defense of a corporate entity merely because he holds some official corporate position. (*Disciplinary Counsel v. Givens*, 832 N.E.2d 1200 (Ohio 2005))

Lay representation in administrative agencies

Although lay representation in court is limited, lay representation in administrative agencies is somewhat broader.

- "Lawyers have no exclusive right to appear before nonadjudicative bodies, as they do before a court." Comment on Rule 3.9. Ohio Rules of Professional Conduct.
- **Administrative Procedure Act.** "At any hearing conducted under sections 119.01 to 119.13 of the Revised Code, a party or an affected person may be represented by an attorney or by such other representative as is lawfully permitted to practice before the agency in question, but, except for hearings held before the state personnel board of review under section 124.03 of the Revised Code, only an attorney at law may represent a party or an affected person at a hearing at which a record is taken which may be the basis of an appeal to court." (R.C. § 119.13)
- **Workers' compensation.** This case challenges the right of nonattorneys (e.g., union representatives, employees of employers, and actuarial firms) to represent parties in administrative agencies in workers' compensation cases. One of the main objectives in the workers' compensation system is to provide a speedy, simple, and inexpensive method to compensate workers for work-related injuries and to do away with vexatious, protracted, and costly litigation. "Accordingly, lay representation has been a feature of Ohio's workers' compensation system since its inception." The "sophistication and presence of nonlawyer representatives in the system have steadily increased." The state of Ohio estimates that nonlawyers represent at least one party in approximately 95 percent of the hearings held each year and that "in almost half of all Industrial Commission hearings (47 percent or 89,300 total hearings) [held each year], the employer's only representative is an actuary." This court has exclusive power to regulate, control, and define the practice of law in Ohio and, therefore, the ultimate authority to determine the qualifications of persons engaged in the practice of law before the Industrial Commission. However, while this court unquestionably has the power to prohibit lay representation before an administrative agency, it is not always necessary or desirable for

the court to exercise that power to its full extent. The power to regulate includes the authority to grant as well as the authority to deny, and in certain limited settings, *the public interest is better served by authorizing laypersons to engage in conduct that might be viewed as the practice of law.* Limiting the practice of law to licensed attorneys is generally necessary to protect the public against incompetence, divided loyalties, and other attendant evils that are often associated with unskilled representation. But *not all representation requires the level of training and experience that only attorneys can provide.* In the vast majority of instances, no special skill is required in the preparation and presentation of claims. Ordinarily they consist of statements and affidavits submitted by the employer, the employee, or the latter's dependents, and by others having knowledge of the facts, accompanied by the reports of attending physicians or surgeons, on forms prepared and furnished by the commission. In light of the informal setting of workers' compensation proceedings, nonattorneys can help someone file or respond to a claim at an agency hearing, but they cannot examine and cross-examine witnesses, give legal interpretations of laws or testimony, give legal advice to workers or employers, provide stand-alone representation at a hearing by charging a fee specifically associated with such hearing representation without providing other services. Nonattorneys who appear and practice in a representative capacity before the Industrial Commission and Bureau of Workers' Compensation within these restrictions are not engaged in the unauthorized practice of law. (*Cleveland Bar Assn. v. CompManagement, Inc.*, 818 N.E.2d 1181 (Ohio 2004)) (emphasis added)

- The industrial commission shall adopt rules . . . designed to prevent the solicitation of employment in the prosecution or defense of claims and make and adopt reasonable rules designed to promote the orderly and expeditious submission, hearing, and determination of claims and may inquire into the amounts of fees charged employers or claimants by attorneys, agents, or representatives for services in matters before the commission. The commission shall set reasonable standards for those attorneys, agents, or representatives who practice before the bureau, district or staff hearing officers, or the commission. (R.C. § 4123.06)

- *Standards of Conduct of Non-Attorneys before the Industrial Commission and the Bureau of Workers' Compensation.* In recognition that no person may practice law in Ohio who has not been admitted to the Bar by the Supreme Court of Ohio, and further recognizing that the practice of law is defined by the Ohio Supreme Court, non-lawyers may not properly perform the following functions before the Industrial Commission or the Bureau of Workers' Compensation:

  1. Examine or cross-examine the claimant or any witness, directly or indirectly;
  2. Cite, file, or interpret statutory or administrative provisions, administrative rulings or case law;
  3. Make and give legal interpretations with respect to testimony, affidavits, medical evidence in the form of reports or testimony, or file any brief, memorandum, reconsideration or other pleading beyond the forms actually provided by the Commission or the Bureau;
  4. Comment upon or give opinions with respect to the evidence, credibility of witnesses, the nature and weight of the evidence, or the legal significance of the contents of the claims file;
  5. Provide legal advice to injured workers and employers;
  6. Give or render legal opinions, or cite case law or statutes to injured workers and employers before, at, or after the time when claims are initially certified or denied certification as valid claims by the employer upon the presentation of claim applications by employees;
  7. Provide stand-alone representation at hearing by charging a fee specifically associated with such hearing representation without providing other services. (Industrial Commission Resolution R04-1-01) (*www.ic.state.oh.us/resolutions/r4101.html*)

- Chiropractor (Chiofalo) engages in the unauthorized practice of law before the Industrial Commission. By arguing statutory provisions and case law, construing the text to advance his patient's case, and interpreting the weight, significance, and credibility of evidence presented, Chiofalo acted well beyond the standards for nonlawyer representation during the underlying IC proceeding. The board therefore found that Chiofalo had engaged in the unauthorized practice of law and recommended that both be enjoined from this conduct in the future. *Ohio State Bar Assn. v. Chiofalo*, 112 Ohio St.3d 113, 858 N.E.2d 378, (Ohio, 2006)

Unemployment compensation

- (A) The unemployment compensation review commission, by rule, may authorize persons other than ones who are admitted to the practice of law also to appear before the commission in any kind of proceeding as representatives of employers or claimants. The commission may prescribe in any rule so adopted the minimum qualifications for such agents and such minimum standards of practice as are appropriate. . . .

(B) . . . Any individual claiming benefits or any employer may represent themselves personally or be represented by a person admitted to the practice of law or by a person not admitted to the practice of law in any proceeding under this chapter before the director of job and family services, or, before the commission or a hearing officer; but no such counsel or agent representing an individual claiming benefits shall either charge or receive for such services more than an amount approved by the commission. (R.C. § 4141.07)

- At any proceeding before a hearing officer or review commission, any interested party may appear in person, by counsel, or an authorized representative. (Ohio Administrative Code § 4146-19-01)
- Claimants at unemployment compensation hearings are often accompanied by friends, coworkers, family, and union representatives, or are assisted by legal aid societies which may provide paralegals without charge to assist the worker in the presentation of the claim. Similarly, employers have usually relied on their own personnel staff or self-representation to contest the right of the claimant to participate. Over the years, an increasing number of employers have utilized service companies to provide management support of various payroll, tax, and employee benefit operations. Economy of scale and the technical expertise provided by such companies in the area of unemployment compensation have enabled employers, both large and small, to utilize the assistance of unemployment service specialists to manage their benefit programs. As an incidental portion of such service, agents are provided to attend board hearings as representatives of the employer. These agents are there to assure that the board has the appropriate personnel records, staff, and other documents present at the hearing and to assist in the fact-finding process during the referee's claim review. The role of such lay participants, as we perceive it, is not to render legal advice, nor to otherwise practice law by providing interpretations of board orders. Rather, the purpose of their participation is to facilitate the hearing process by serving as an adjunct to the claimant or employer in the sharing of their respective versions of the circumstances attendant to the claim. Attorneys are not often used. In part this is due to fee limitations (fees are limited to 10% of the benefits recovered). But also, "attorneys are simply not required in most of these claim reviews. This is because of the informality of the proceedings coupled with the recognition that, in most instances, a formal presentation of legal argument is not needed. Instead, the hearing is designed to be an administrative information gathering tool serving as an alternative to judicial resolution of every contested claim. The public certainly has an interest in maintaining a claims system that works well at a reasonable cost. In fact, prohibition of non-attorney representation by union representatives and legal aid employees in these cases could seriously impair meaningful access to the system on the part of claimants and undermine their right to a fair hearing. *Lay representation does not pose a hazard to the public in this limited setting.* Our conclusion is further bolstered by the clear recognition that lay representation has been the practice since the inception of Ohio's unemployment compensation program in 1936. Our decision today does not reach nor permit the rendering of legal advice regarding unemployment compensation laws or board orders. Rather, our narrow holding merely permits lay representation of parties to assist in the preparation and presentation of their cause in order to facilitate the hearing process. We believe board hearings should not be turned into adversarial proceedings since they are legislatively designed to function as an informal mechanism through which the referee, in a participatory capacity, ascertains the facts involved. (*Henize v. Giles*, 490 N.E.2d 585–590 (Ohio 1986)) (emphasis added)

Other agencies

- Ohio Ethics Commission. "Representative" means any person whom the commission has authorized to appear or act on its behalf, or any person whom the complainant, respondent, or a witness has authorized to appear or act, on his or her behalf, as counsel before the commission. (Ohio Administrative Code § 102-1-01(K))
- Department of Aging. Definition of "representative" within the Ohio Department of Aging's programs for nursing homes and other long-term care. "Representative" means a person acting on behalf of an individual seeking a long-term care consultation, applying for admission to a nursing facility, or residing in a nursing facility. A representative may be a family member, attorney, hospital social worker, or any other person chosen to act on behalf of the individual. (R.C. § 173.42(5))
- Liquor Control Commission. A complaint was filed alleging that a nonattorney engaged in unauthorized practice of law by representing liquor permit holders before the Liquor Control Commission. The Board of Commissioners on the Unauthorized Practice of Law held that nonattorney's conduct in acting as "spokesperson" for liquor permit holders before Liquor Control Commission was the rendering of "legal services," and thus was the unauthorized practice of law. (*Office of Disciplinary Counsel v. Molnar*, 567 N.E.2d 1355 (Ohio Bd.Unauth.Prac. 1990))
- Board of Revision. The preparation and filing of a valuation complaint by a nonattorney corporate

officer before the Board of Revision constitutes the unauthorized practice of law (*Sharon Village, Ltd. v. Licking Cty. Bd. of Revision,* 678 N.E.2d 932 (1997); *Rubbermaid, Inc. v. Wayne Cty. Aud.*, 767 N.E.2d 1159 (Ohio 2002)). An amendment to R.C. § 5715.19(A) providing to the contrary allows nonattorneys to practice law. This violates the separation of powers between the judicial and legislative branches of government. (*C.R. Truman, L.P. v. Cuyahoga County Bd. of Revision,* 2000 WL 1038184 (Ohio App., 2000))

Law-related occupations and UPL

- Estate plan preparers. Nonattorneys marketed and sold living trusts and estate plans, explained the legal consequences of specific decisions relating to living trusts or estate plans, and prepared legal documents related to living trusts or estate plans. These activities constitute the unauthorized practice of law. Respondents argue that the use of review attorneys to supervise the estate or trust-document preparation immunizes them from a UPL charge. The evidence reveals, however, that the review attorneys were only tangentially involved in the transactions. In most cases, they did nothing more than enter a customer's information into a computer program, and they rarely came into contact with customers. Further, approval by the review attorney was not required by the purchase agreement. (*Cleveland Bar Assn. v. Sharp Estate Serv., Inc.,* 837 N.E.2d 1183 (Ohio 2005))
- Banks and trust companies. A bank or trust company that provides specific legal information in relation to the specific facts of a particular person's estate for the purpose of obtaining a more beneficial estate condition in relation to tax and other legal consequences of death is giving legal advice. One who repeatedly gives legal advice to others with the expectation of being compensated therefor is thereby engaging in the practice of law even if he or she does not draft any legal documents based on this advice and even if he or she constantly advises those to whom the advice is given to consult their attorneys. However, the bank or trust company does not engage in the practice of law by fully discussing with counsel for a client, who is a customer or a prospective customer of the bank, any and all legal problems involved in the planning or administration of such client's estate. (*Green v. Huntington Nat. Bank,* 212 N.E.2d 585 (Ohio 1965))
- Real estate agents and brokers. A real estate broker is not involved in the practice of law by merely filling pre-printed blank forms for the purchase of real estate. Supplying simple factual material such as the date, the price, the name of the purchaser, the location of the property, the date of giving possession, and the duration of the offer, does not require skill peculiar to one trained and experienced in the law and thus does not involve the practice of law. Similarly, furnishing a certification or memorandum containing a statement of the substance of documents or facts appearing on public records that affect the title to real estate, without expressing any opinion as to the legal significance of what is found or as to the validity of the title, is not the practice of law. Likewise, providing real property appraisals and property reports, even if legal terms of art are used, does not constitute the practice of law. However, preparing legal documents and offering legal advice and consultation on matters pertaining to leasing real property, and deriving fees for such services, without a license to practice law, is the unauthorized practice of law. Statements or "remarks" relating to contingencies and obligations affecting the parties on a single page printed form real estate purchase and sale contract drawn by the broker's saleswoman would go far beyond mere scrivening and constituted an unauthorized practice of law. (*Ralph R. Greer & Co. v. McGinnis,* 217 N.E.2d 890 (Ohio Mun., 1965))
- Insurance adjusters. An insurance adjuster cannot give legal advice or represent claimants. The conduct of a licensed insurance adjuster in preparing a contract or agreement for the settlement or compromise of a claim made against insurance companies would constitute improper practice of law. (*Bar Ass'n of Greater Cleveland v. Brunson,* 304 N.E.2d 250, 256 (Ohio Com.Pl., 1973))
- Insurance adjusters. Insurance adjusters must hold a "a certificate of authority to act as a public insurance adjuster." (R.C. § 3951.08) "No holder of a certificate of authority shall make any misrepresentations of facts or advise any insured or insurer on any question of law or perform any service constituting the practice of law, nor shall any such holder of a certificate of authority in handling a claim, advise any insured or insurer to refrain from retaining counsel to protect his or its interest." (R.C. § 3951.08)

Bankruptcy petition preparer (BPP)

- The federal Bankruptcy Code recognizes the reality that pro se debtors [debtors representing themselves] often turn to non-lawyers for assistance in filing bankruptcy. Rather than prohibiting such assistance and, as a realistic matter, watching it flourish more dangerously underground, Congress chose to force it into the light by defining persons who provide such assistance and regulating their conduct. Congress enacted 11 U.S.C. § 110 in 1994 to "address the growing problem of bankruptcy [petition] preparers who abuse the system in the course of preparing documents for the debtors to file." (*In re Alexander*, 284 Bankruptcy Reporter 626 (Bkrtcy.N.D. Ohio 2002))

- 11 United States Code § 110. In this section, "bankruptcy petition preparer" means a person, other than an attorney for the debtor or an employee of such attorney under the direct supervision of such attorney, who prepares for compensation a document for filing; and "document for filing" means a petition or any other document prepared for filing by a debtor in a United States bankruptcy court or a United States district court in connection with a case under this title.
- Restrictions on BPPs:

  - Before preparing any document for filing or accepting any fees from a debtor, the BPP shall provide to the debtor a written notice informing the debtor in simple language that a bankruptcy petition preparer is not an attorney and may not practice law or give legal advice.

  - A BPP shall not advise a debtor whether to file a bankruptcy petition; which chapter of bankruptcy to use; whether the debtor's debts will be discharged; whether the debtor will be able to retain the debtor's home, car, or other property after commencing bankruptcy; what the tax consequences of bankruptcy are; how to characterize the nature of the debtor's interests in property; what the bankruptcy procedures are; or what the debtor's bankruptcy rights are.

  -The BPP who prepares a document for filing shall place on the document, after the preparer's signature, an identifying number that shall be the Social Security account number of each individual who prepared the document or assisted in its preparation.

  - A BPP shall not execute any document on behalf of a debtor.

  - A BPP shall not use the word "legal" or any similar term in any advertisements, or advertise under any category that includes the word "legal" or any similar term.

  - The Supreme Court may promulgate rules for setting a maximum allowable fee chargeable by a BPP. A BPP shall notify the debtor of any such maximum amount before preparing any document for filing for a debtor or accepting any fee from the debtor.

  - If a BPP violates this section or commits any act that the court finds to be fraudulent, unfair, or deceptive, the court shall order the bankruptcy petition preparer to pay to the debtor the debtor's actual damages; the greater of $2,000; or twice the amount paid by the debtor to the BPP; and reasonable attorneys' fees and costs in moving for damages under this subsection.

Social Security

- You can choose an attorney or other qualified person to represent you in social security hearings. (*www.ssa.gov/pubs/10075.html*)

Occupational Safety and Health Review Commission

- Occupational Safety and Health Review Commission Hearing Representatives. (a) Representation. Any party or intervenor may appear in person, through an attorney, or through another representative who is not an attorney. A representative must file an appearance in accordance with § 2200.23. In the absence of an appearance by a representative, a party or intervenor will be deemed to appear for himself. A corporation or unincorporated association may be represented by an authorized officer or agent. (29 CFR § 2200.22 (a))

Miscellaneous

- Attorney licensed in another state should stay within bounds of paralegal work while in Ohio. An attorney, licensed in another state but not in Ohio, failed to limit himself to paralegal activities within Ohio under the supervision of an Ohio attorney and, therefore, engaged in the unauthorized practice of law. (*Cleveland Bar Assn. v. Moore*, 722 N.E.2d 514 (Ohio 2000))
- Nonattorney judges. Areas of the state that do not have municipal courts may have a mayor's court in which the mayor acts as judge, usually on misdemeanor and traffic cases. "The mayor is not required to be a licensed attorney, but must complete special legal courses prescribed by the Supreme Court of Ohio." (*www.ohiobar.org/pub/lawfacts/index.asp?articleid=5*) (See R.C. 1905.03) If, however, the mayor appoints a magistrate to hear cases, the magistrate must be a licensed Ohio attorney.

D. Filing a UPL Complaint

Someone who wants to charge another with engaging in the unauthorized practice of law has several options:

1. Contact:
   Office of Disciplinary Counsel
   250 Civic Center Drive, Suite 325
   Columbus OH 43215
   800-589-5256; 614-461-0256
   www.sconet.state.oh.us/UPL/faq/uplfaq.asp

2. Contact your local bar association's unauthorized practice of law committee. (See section 3.4.)
3. Send information regarding the alleged unauthorized practice of law to: Secretary of the Board on the Unauthorized Practice of Law 65 South Front Street, 5th Floor Columbus, OH 43215-3431.

The secretary will refer this information to either the Office of Disciplinary Counsel or a local bar association's unauthorized practice of law committee for investigation.

E. More Information

Ohio Board on the Unauthorized Practice of Law
www.sconet.state.oh.us/UPL

Advisory Opinions of the Board Ohio on the Unauthorized Practice of Law
www.sconet.state.oh.us/UPL/advisory_opinions/default.asp

Federal Trade Commission Opposes Banning Nonattorney Representation in Workers' Compensation Cases
www.ftc.gov/opa/2004/08/ohioupl.htm
www.ftc.gov/os/2004/08/040803amicusbriefclevbar.pdf

Ohio State Bar Association
www.ohiobar.org
(in the search box, type "unauthorized practice of law")

American Legal Ethics Library
www.law.cornell.edu/ethics
(click "Listing by jurisdiction" then "Ohio")

Ohio Ethics
www.law.cornell.edu/ethics/oh/narr/OH_NARR_5.HTM
www.law.cornell.edu/ethics/ohio.html
www.ll.georgetown.edu/states/ethics/ohio.cfm

Distinguishing Between Legal Advice and Legal Information
www.courtinfo.ca.gov/programs/access/documents/mayihelpyou.pdf

F. Something to Check

1. Run the following search ("unauthorized practice of law" ohio) in any three general search engines (e.g., *www.google.com; www.yahoo.com; www.search.msn.com; www.ask.com*). Prepare a report on the categories of Web sites to which each search engine leads you. Cluster the same kinds of sites you find into categories, e.g., sites giving you cases on UPL in Ohio, sites giving you bar associations in Ohio that have UPL resources, sites that give you attorneys that represent clients suing other attorneys for UPL, etc. Give a brief description of each category with examples of Web sites under each category. After you finish the report for the three general search engines, comment on which engine was the most productive and why.
2. Pick any three legal search engines (e.g., *www.findlaw.com; www.catalaw.com; www.washlaw.edu; www.lawguru.com; www.romingerlegal.com*). How effective is each in leading you to material about the unauthorized practice of law in Ohio? Describe what you are able to find.
3. Read the dissenting opinion of Justice O'Donnell in *Cleveland Bar Association v. Pearlman*, 106 Ohio St.3d 136, 832 N.E.2d 1193, 2005-Ohio-4107 (2005). (See section 5.1 on finding this opinion online.) Why does Justice O'Donnell disagree with the majority that the Ohio legislature can authorize nonattorney representation in small claims court?

3.2 Ohio Rules of Professional Conduct (ORPC)

A. Introduction

Ohio's new ethics code became effective on February 1, 2007. The Ohio Rules of Professional Conduct (ORPC) is based on the American Bar Association's Model Rules of Professional Conduct, as modified by the Ohio Supreme Court. The new code replaces the Ohio Code of Professional Responsibility.

In this section, the major provisions of the ORPC are presented, with particular emphasis on sections relevant to Ohio paralegals.

For other material on or related to ethics, see also:

- Part 1, Appendix A. Paralegals in Court Opinions (some of the court opinions summarized in this section cover ethical issues)
- Section 3.1. Defining the Practice of Law and the Unauthorized Practice of Law
- Section 3.3. Ethical Opinions of the Board Of Commissioners on Grievances and Discipline Involving Paralegals and Other Nonattorneys
- Part 3, Appendix A. Disciplinary Proceedings against an Attorney

B. Rules and Comments in the ORPC of Particular Relevance to Paralegals and Other Nonattorneys

While all of the provisions in the ORPC are important, the following rules and official comments are of particular relevance to paralegals and other nonattorneys:

- **1.0 Comment 9** (duties of paralegals and other law firm personnel when screening is imposed in conflict cases)
- **1.4 Comment 4** (a lawyer's staff should be used to acknowledge receipt of requests for information from clients)
- **1.6 Comment 16** (a lawyer must act to prevent inadvertent disclosure of confidential information by his or her employees)
- **1.8(c)** (a lawyer shall not prepare on behalf of a client an instrument giving the lawyer or the lawyer's paralegal a gift)
- **1.10 Comment 4** (paralegals and imputed disqualification)
- **1.10 Comment 4** (a nonlawyer's duty to protect confidential information)
- **3.9 Comment 2** ("Lawyers have no exclusive right to appear before nonadjudicative bodies, as they do before a court.")
- **5.3(a)** (managers must take reasonable efforts to ensure that measures are in place that give reasonable assurance that paralegals and other nonlawyer assistants will comply with ethical rules)
- **5.3(b)** (supervisors must take reasonable efforts to ensure that paralegals and other nonlawyer assistants will comply with ethical rules)
- **5.3(c)** (lawyers who order or ratify ethical misconduct by paralegals and other nonlawyer assistants; failure to take remedial action)
- **5.3 Comment 1** (paraprofessionals)
- **5.3 Comment 1** (lawyers must give paralegals and other nonlawyer assistants appropriate instruction and supervision concerning the ethical aspects of their employment, particularly regarding the obligation not to disclose information relating to representation of the client, and should be responsible for their work product.)
- **5.4(a)** (lawyers shall not share legal fees with a nonlawyer)
- **5.4(a)(3)** (lawyers may include nonlawyer employees in a compensation or retirement plan)
- **5.4(b)** (lawyers may not form a partnership with a nonlawyer if any part of it consists of the practice of law)
- **5.4(d)(1)** (nonlawyers cannot own an interest in a law practice)
- **5.4(d)(2)** (nonlawyers cannot be directors or officers of a law practice)
- **5.4(d)(3)** (nonlawyers cannot have the right to direct or control the professional judgment of a lawyer)
- **5.5 Comment 2** (lawyers can employ the services of paraprofessionals and delegate functions to them, so long as the lawyers supervise the delegated work and retain responsibility for their work)
- **5.5 Comment 3** (lawyers may provide professional advice and instruction to nonlawyers whose employment requires knowledge of the law, e.g., claims adjusters)
- **5.5 Comment 3** (lawyers also may assist independent nonlawyers, such as paraprofessionals, who are authorized by the law of a jurisdiction to provide particular law-related services)
- **5.5 Comment 3** (lawyers may counsel nonlawyers who wish to proceed *pro se*)
- **5.5 Comment 13** (lawyers admitted in other jurisdictions providing services in Ohio that nonlawyers may perform but that are considered the practice of law when performed by lawyers)
- **7.2(b)** (lawyers shall not give anything of value to someone for recommending the lawyer's services)
- **7.2 Comment 5** (reciprocal referral agreements between a lawyer and a nonlawyer are prohibited)
- **7.2 Comment 5A** (nonlawyers who prepare advertising and other marketing material for lawyers)
- **7.5 Comment 1** (it is misleading to include the name of a nonlawyer in the name of a law firm)
- **7.5 Comment 4** (a legal clinic cannot be owned by, and profits or losses cannot be shared with, nonlawyers)
- **8.4 Comment 1** (misconduct when a lawyer requests or instructs an agent to engage in misconduct on the lawyer's behalf)

C. Table of Contents of the ORPC

Table of Contents

Maintaining the Integrity of the Profession

Rule 8.1 Bar Admission and Disciplinary Matters

Rule 8.2 Judicial Officials

Rule 8.3 Reporting Professional Misconduct

Rule 8.4 Misconduct

Rule 8.5 Disciplinary Authority; Choice of Law

D. Index to the ORPC

Index to the ORPC

E. Text of the ORPC

Preamble: A Lawyer's Responsibilities; Scope

[1] As an officer of the court, a lawyer not only represents clients but has a special responsibility for the quality of justice.

Lawyer as Advisor, Advocate, Negotiator, Evaluator, and Third-Party Neutral

[2] In representing clients, a lawyer performs various functions. As advisor, a lawyer provides a client with an informed understanding of the client's legal rights and obligations and explains their practical implications. As advocate, a lawyer asserts the client's position under the rules of the adversary system. As negotiator, a lawyer seeks a result advantageous to the client and consistent with requirements of honest dealings with others. As an evaluator, a lawyer examines a client's legal affairs and reports about them to the client or to others.

[3] In addition to these representational functions, a lawyer may serve as a third-party neutral, a nonrepresentational role helping the parties to resolve a dispute or other matter. See, *e.g.*, Rules 1.12 and 2.4. In addition, there are rules that apply to lawyers who are not active in the practice of law or to practicing lawyers even when they are acting in a nonprofessional capacity. For example, a lawyer who commits fraud in the conduct of a business is subject to discipline for engaging in conduct involving dishonesty, fraud, deceit, or misrepresentation. See Rule 8.4.

[4] In all professional functions a lawyer should be competent, prompt, diligent, and loyal. A lawyer should maintain communication with a client concerning the representation. A lawyer should keep in confidence information relating to representation of a client except so far as disclosure is required or permitted by the Ohio Rules of Professional Conduct or other law.

Respect for the Legal System

[5] Lawyers play a vital role in the preservation of society. A lawyer's conduct should conform to the requirements of the law, both in professional service to clients and in the lawyer's business and personal affairs. A lawyer should use the law's procedures only for legitimate purposes and not to harass or intimidate others. A lawyer should demonstrate respect for the legal system and for those who serve it, including judges, other lawyers, and public officials. Adjudicatory officials, not being wholly free to defend themselves, are entitled to receive the support of the bar against unjustified criticism. Although a lawyer, as a citizen, has a right to criticize such officials, the lawyer should do so with restraint and avoid intemperate statements that tend to lessen public confidence in the legal system. While it is a lawyer's duty, when necessary, to challenge the rectitude of official action, it is also a lawyer's duty to uphold legal process.

Helping Those Who Cannot Afford Legal Services

[6] A lawyer should seek improvement of the law, ensure access to the legal system, advance the administration of justice, and exemplify the quality of service rendered by the legal

profession. As a member of a learned profession, a lawyer should cultivate knowledge of the law beyond its use for clients, employ that knowledge in reform of the law, and work to strengthen legal education. In addition, a lawyer should further the public's understanding of and confidence in the rule of law and the justice system because legal institutions in a constitutional democracy depend on popular participation and support to maintain their authority. A lawyer should be mindful of deficiencies in the administration of justice and of the fact that the poor, and sometimes persons who are not poor, cannot afford adequate legal assistance. Therefore, all lawyers should devote professional time and resources and use civic influence to ensure equal access to our system of justice for all those who because of economic or social barriers cannot afford or secure adequate legal counsel. A lawyer should aid the legal profession in pursuing these objectives and should help the bar regulate itself in the public interest. . . .

[9] The Ohio Rules of Professional Conduct often prescribe rules for a lawyer's conduct. Within the framework of these rules, however, many difficult issues of professional discretion can arise. These issues must be resolved through the exercise of sensitive professional and moral judgment guided by the basic principles underlying the rules. . . .

Moral Judgment

[11] The legal profession is self-governing in that the Ohio Constitution vests in the Supreme Court of Ohio the ultimate authority to regulate the profession. To the extent that lawyers meet the obligations of their professional calling, the occasion for government regulation is obviated. Self-regulation also helps maintain the legal profession's independence from government domination. An independent legal profession is an important force in preserving government under law, for abuse of legal authority is more readily challenged by a profession whose members are not dependent on government for the right to practice. . . .

Role of the Supreme Court

Scope

[14] The Ohio Rules of Professional Conduct are rules of reason. They should be interpreted with reference to the purposes of legal representation and of the law itself. Some of the rules are imperatives, cast in the terms "shall" or "shall not." These define proper conduct for purposes of professional discipline. Others, generally cast in the term "may," are permissive and define areas under the rules in which the lawyer has discretion to exercise professional judgment. No disciplinary action should be taken when the lawyer chooses not to act or acts within the bounds of such discretion. Other rules define the nature of relationships between the lawyer and others. The rules are thus partly obligatory and disciplinary and partly constitutive and descriptive in that they define a lawyer's professional role. Many of the comments use the term "should." Comments do not add obligations to the rules but provide guidance for practicing in compliance with the rules.

Permissive vs. Obligatory Rules

[15] The rules presuppose a larger legal context shaping the lawyer's role. That context includes court rules relating to matters of licensure, laws defining specific obligations of lawyers, and substantive and procedural law in general. The comments are sometimes used to alert lawyers to their responsibilities under such other law. . . .

[17] Furthermore, for purposes of determining the lawyer's authority and responsibility, principles of substantive law external to these rules determine whether a client-lawyer relationship exists. Most of the duties flowing from the client-lawyer relationship attach only after the client has requested the lawyer to render legal services and the lawyer has agreed to do so. But there are some duties, such as that of confidentiality under Rule 1.6, that attach when the lawyer agrees to consider whether a client-lawyer relationship shall be established. See Rule 1.18. Whether a client-lawyer relationship exists for any specific purpose can depend on the circumstances and may be a question of fact. . . .

Confidentiality Prior to Forming an Attorney-Client Relationship

[19] Failure to comply with an obligation or prohibition imposed by a rule is a basis for invoking the disciplinary process. The rules presuppose that disciplinary assessment of a lawyer's conduct will be made on the basis of the facts and circumstances as they existed at the time of the conduct in question and in recognition of the fact that a lawyer often has to act upon uncertain or incomplete evidence of the situation. Moreover, the rules presuppose that whether or not discipline should be imposed for a violation, and the severity of a sanction, depend on all the circumstances, such as the willfulness and seriousness of the violation, extenuating factors, and whether there have been previous violations.

Factors Influencing When a Lawyer Will be Disciplined

[20] Violation of a rule should not itself give rise to a cause of action against a lawyer nor should it create any presumption in such a case that a legal duty has been breached. In addition, violation of a rule does not necessarily warrant any other nondisciplinary remedy, such as disqualification of a lawyer in pending litigation. The rules are designed to provide guidance to lawyers and to provide a structure for regulating conduct through disciplinary agencies. They are not designed to be a basis for civil liability. Furthermore, the purpose of the rules can be

Ethics Violations and a Lawyer's Civil Liability

subverted when they are invoked by opposing parties as procedural weapons. The fact that a rule is a just basis for a lawyer's self-assessment, or for sanctioning a lawyer under the administration of a disciplinary authority, does not imply that an antagonist in a collateral proceeding or transaction has standing to seek enforcement of the rule. Nevertheless, since the rules do establish standards of conduct by lawyers, a lawyer's violation of a rule may be evidence of breach of the applicable standard of conduct.

[21] The comment accompanying each rule explains and illustrates the meaning and purpose of the rule. The Preamble and this note on Scope provide general orientation. The comments are intended as guides to interpretation, but the text of each rule is authoritative.

Rule 1.0: Terminology

Defining Key Terms in the ORPC

As used in these rules:

(a) "Belief" or "believes" denotes that the person involved actually supposed the fact in question to be true. A person's belief may be inferred from circumstances.

(b) "Confirmed in writing," when used in reference to the informed consent of a person, denotes informed consent that is given in writing by the person or a writing that a lawyer promptly transmits to the person confirming an oral informed consent. See division (f) for the definition of "informed consent." If it is not feasible to obtain or transmit the writing at the time the person gives informed consent, then the lawyer must obtain or transmit it within a reasonable time thereafter.

(c) "Firm" or "law firm" denotes a lawyer or lawyers in a law partnership, professional corporation, sole proprietorship, or other association authorized to practice law; or lawyers employed in a private or public legal aid or public defender organization, a legal services organization, or the legal department of a corporation or other organization.

(d) "Fraud" or "fraudulent" denotes conduct that has an intent to deceive and is either of the following:

Fraud

(1) an actual or implied misrepresentation of a material fact that is made either with knowledge of its falsity or with such utter disregard and recklessness about its falsity that knowledge may be inferred;

(2) a knowing concealment of a material fact where there is a duty to disclose the material fact.

(e) "Illegal" denotes criminal conduct or a violation of an applicable statute or administrative regulation.

(f) "Informed consent" denotes the agreement by a person to a proposed course of conduct after the lawyer has communicated adequate information and explanation about the material risks of and reasonably available alternatives to the proposed course of conduct.

(g) "Knowingly," "known," or "knows" denotes actual knowledge of the fact in question. A person's knowledge may be inferred from circumstances.

(h) "Partner" denotes a member of a partnership, a shareholder in a law firm organized as a professional corporation, or a member of an association authorized to practice law.

(i) "Reasonable" or "reasonably" when used in relation to conduct by a lawyer denotes the conduct of a reasonably prudent and competent lawyer.

(j) "Reasonable belief" or "reasonably believes" when used in reference to a lawyer denotes that the lawyer believes the matter in question and that the circumstances are such that the belief is reasonable.

(k) "Reasonably should know" when used in reference to a lawyer denotes that a lawyer of reasonable prudence and competence would ascertain the matter in question.

(l) "Screened" denotes the isolation of a lawyer from any participation in a matter through the timely imposition of procedures within a firm that are reasonably adequate under the circumstances to protect information that the isolated lawyer is obligated to protect under these rules or other law.

Screening in Conflict Cases

(m) "Substantial" when used in reference to degree or extent denotes a matter of real importance or great consequence.

(n) "Substantially related matter" denotes one that involves the same transaction or legal dispute or one in which there is a substantial risk that confidential factual information that would normally have been obtained in the prior representation of a client would materially advance the position of another client in a subsequent matter.

(o) "Tribunal" denotes a court, an arbitrator in a binding arbitration proceeding, or a legislative body, administrative agency, or other body acting in an adjudicative capacity. A legislative body, administrative agency, or other body acts in an adjudicative capacity when a neutral official, after the presentation of evidence or legal argument by a party or parties, will render a binding legal judgment directly affecting a party's interests in a particular matter.

(p) "Writing" or "written" denotes a tangible or electronic record of a communication or representation, including handwriting, typewriting, printing, photostating, photography, audio or videorecording, and e-mail. A "signed" writing includes an electronic sound, symbol, or process attached to or logically associated with a writing and executed or adopted by a person with the intent to sign the writing.

Comment on Rule 1.0

Confirmed in Writing (1.0)

[1] If it is not feasible to obtain or transmit a written confirmation at the time the client gives informed consent, then the lawyer must obtain or transmit it within a reasonable time thereafter. If a lawyer has obtained a client's informed consent, the lawyer may act in reliance on that consent so long as it is confirmed in writing within a reasonable time thereafter.

Firm

[2] Whether two or more lawyers constitute a firm within division (c) can depend on the specific facts. For example, a lawyer in an of-counsel relationship with a law firm will be treated as part of that firm. On the other hand, two practitioners who share office space and occasionally consult or assist each other ordinarily would not be regarded as constituting a firm for purposes of fee division in Rule 1.5(e). The terms of any agreement between associated lawyers are relevant in determining whether they are a firm, as is the fact that they have mutual access to information concerning the clients they serve. Furthermore, it is relevant in doubtful cases to consider the underlying purpose of the rule that is involved.

Lawyers Sharing Office Space

[3] With respect to the law department of an organization, there is ordinarily no question that the members of the department constitute a firm within the meaning of the Ohio Rules of Professional Conduct. There can be uncertainty, however, as to the identity of the client. For example, it may not be clear whether the law department of a corporation represents a subsidiary or an affiliated corporation, as well as the corporation by which the members of the department are directly employed. A similar question can arise concerning an unincorporated association and its local affiliates.

[4] Similar questions can also arise with respect to lawyers in legal aid and legal services organizations. Depending upon the structure of the organization, the entire organization or different components of it may constitute a firm or firms for purposes of these rules. . . .

Fraud (1.0)

[5] The terms "fraud" or "fraudulent" incorporate the primary elements of common law fraud. The terms do not include negligent misrepresentation or negligent failure to apprise another of relevant information. For purposes of these rules, it is not necessary that anyone has suffered damages or relied on the misrepresentation or failure to inform. Under division (d)(2), the duty to disclose a material fact may arise under these rules or other Ohio law.

Informed Consent (1.0)

[6] Many of the Ohio Rules of Professional Conduct require the lawyer to obtain the informed consent of a client or other person (*e.g.*, a former client or, under certain circumstances, a prospective client) before accepting or continuing representation or pursuing a course of conduct. See, *e.g.*, Rules 1.6(a) and 1.7(b). The communication necessary to obtain such consent will vary according to the rule involved and the circumstances giving rise to the need to obtain informed consent. The lawyer must make reasonable efforts to ensure that the client or other person possesses information reasonably adequate to make an informed decision. Ordinarily, this will require communication that includes a disclosure of the facts and circumstances giving rise to the situation, any explanation reasonably necessary to inform the client or other person of the material advantages and disadvantages of the proposed course of conduct and a discussion of the client's or other person's options and alternatives. In some circumstances it may be appropriate for a lawyer to advise a client or other person to seek the advice of other counsel. A lawyer need not inform a client or other person of facts or implications already known to the client or other person; nevertheless, a lawyer who does not personally inform the client or other person assumes the risk that the client or other person is inadequately informed and the consent is invalid. In determining whether the information and explanation provided are reasonably adequate, relevant factors include whether the client or other person is experienced in legal matters generally and in making decisions of the type involved, and whether the client or other person is independently represented by other counsel in giving the consent. Normally, such persons need less information and explanation than others, and generally a client or other person who is independently represented by other counsel in giving the consent should be assumed to have given informed consent.

Informed Consent

[7] Obtaining informed consent will usually require an affirmative response by the client or other person. In general, a lawyer may not assume consent from a client's or other person's silence. Consent may be inferred, however, from the conduct of a client or other person who has reasonably adequate information about the matter. . . .

Screened (1.0)

[8] This definition applies to situations where screening of a personally disqualified lawyer is permitted to remove imputation of a conflict of interest under Rules 1.10, 1.11, 1.12, or 1.18.

[9] The purpose of screening is to assure the affected parties that confidential information known by the personally disqualified lawyer remains protected. The personally disqualified lawyer should acknowledge the obligation not to communicate with any of the other lawyers in the firm with respect to the matter. Similarly, other lawyers in the firm who are working on the matter should be informed that the screening is in place and that they may not communicate with the personally disqualified lawyer with respect to the matter. Additional screening measures that are appropriate for the particular matter will depend on the circumstances. To implement, reinforce, and remind all affected lawyers of the presence of the screening, it may be appropriate for the firm to undertake such procedures as a written undertaking by the screened lawyer to avoid any *communication with other firm personnel* and any contact with any firm files or other materials relating to the matter, written notice and instructions to all other firm personnel forbidding any communication with the screened lawyer relating to the matter, denial of access by the screened lawyer to firm files or other materials relating to the matter, and *periodic reminders of the screen to the screened lawyer and all other firm personnel.* [emphasis added]

Screening in Conflict Cases

[10] In order to be effective, screening measures must be implemented as soon as practical after a lawyer or law firm knows or reasonably should know that there is a need for screening. . . .

I. Client-Lawyer Relationship

Rule 1.1: Competence

A lawyer shall provide competent representation to a client. Competent representation requires the legal knowledge, skill, thoroughness, and preparation reasonably necessary for the representation.

Defining Competence

Comment on Rule 1.1

Legal Knowledge and Skill (1.1)

[1] In determining whether a lawyer employs the requisite knowledge and skill in a particular matter, relevant factors include the relative complexity and specialized nature of the matter, the lawyer's general experience, the lawyer's training and experience in the field in question, the preparation and study the lawyer is able to give the matter and whether it is feasible to refer the matter to, or associate or consult with, a lawyer of established competence in the field in question. In many instances, the required proficiency is that of a general practitioner. Expertise in a particular field of law may be required in some circumstances.

How a Lawyer Becomes Competent

[2] A lawyer need not necessarily have special training or prior experience to handle legal problems of a type with which the lawyer is unfamiliar. A newly admitted lawyer can be as competent as a practitioner with long experience. Some important legal skills, such as the analysis of precedent, the evaluation of evidence and legal drafting, are required in all legal problems. Perhaps the most fundamental legal skill consists of determining what kind of legal problems a situation may involve, a skill that necessarily transcends any particular specialized knowledge. A lawyer can provide adequate representation in a wholly novel field through necessary study. Competent representation can also be provided through the association of a lawyer of established competence in the field in question. . . .

[4] A lawyer may accept representation where the requisite level of competence can be achieved through study and investigation, as long as such additional work would not result in unreasonable delay or expense to the client. This applies as well to a lawyer who is appointed as counsel for an unrepresented person. See also Rule 6.2.

Thoroughness and Preparation (1.1)

[5] Competent handling of a particular matter includes inquiry into and analysis of the factual and legal elements of the problem, and use of methods and procedures meeting the standards of competent practitioners. It also includes adequate preparation. The required attention and preparation are determined in part by what is at stake; major litigation and complex transactions ordinarily require more extensive treatment than matters of lesser complexity and consequence. An agreement between the lawyer and the client regarding the scope of the representation may limit the matters for which the lawyer is responsible. See Rule 1.2(c). The lawyer should consult with the client about the degree of thoroughness and the level of preparation required, as well as the estimated costs involved under the circumstances.

Estimating the Costs of Legal Services

Maintaining Competence (1.1)

[6] To maintain the requisite knowledge and skill, a lawyer should keep abreast of changes in the law and its practice, engage in continuing study and education and comply with all continuing legal education requirements to which the lawyer is subject.

Rule 1.2: Scope of representation and allocation of authority between client and lawyer

(a) Subject to divisions (c), (d), and (e) of this rule, a lawyer shall abide by a client's decisions concerning the objectives of representation and, as required by Rule 1.4, shall consult with the client as to the means by which they are to be pursued. A lawyer may take action on behalf of the client as is impliedly authorized to carry out the representation. A lawyer does not violate this rule by acceding to requests of opposing counsel that do not prejudice the rights of the client, being punctual in fulfilling all professional commitments, avoiding offensive tactics, and treating with courtesy and consideration all persons involved in the legal process. A lawyer shall abide by a client's decision whether to settle a matter. In a criminal case, the lawycr shall abide by the client's decision as to a plea to be entered, whether to waive a jury trial, and whether the client will testify. . . .

Decisions to be Made by a Client

(c) A lawyer may limit the scope of a new or existing representation if the limitation is reasonable under the circumstances and communicated to the client, preferably in writing.

(d) A lawyer shall not counsel a client to engage, or assist a client, in conduct that the lawyer knows is illegal or fraudulent. A lawyer may discuss the legal consequences of any proposed course of conduct with a client and may counsel or assist a client in making a good faith effort to determine the validity, scope, meaning, or application of the law.

Conduct that Is Knowingly Illegal or Fraudulent

(e) Unless otherwise required by law, a lawyer shall not present, participate in presenting, or threaten to present criminal charges or professional misconduct allegations solely to obtain an advantage in a civil matter.

Threats

Comment on Rule 1.2

Allocation of Authority: Between Client and Lawyer (1.2)

[1] Division (a) confers upon the client the ultimate authority to determine the purposes to be served by legal representation, within the limits imposed by law and the lawyer's professional obligations. The decisions specified in division (a), such as whether to settle a civil matter, must also be made by the client. See Rule 1.4(a)(1) for the lawyer's duty to communicate with the client about such decisions. With respect to the means by which the client's objectives are to be pursued, the lawyer shall consult with the client as required by Rule 1.4(a)(2) and may take such action as is impliedly authorized to carry out the representation.

[2] On occasion, however, a lawyer and a client may disagree about the means to be used to accomplish the client's objectives. Clients normally defer to the special knowledge and skill of their lawyer with respect to the means to be used to accomplish their objectives, particularly with respect to technical, legal, and tactical matters. Conversely, lawyers usually defer to the client regarding such questions as the expense to be incurred and concern for third persons who might be adversely affected. Because of the varied nature of the matters about which a lawyer and client might disagree and because the actions in question may implicate the interests of a tribunal or other persons, this rule does not prescribe how such disagreements are to be resolved. Other law, however, may be applicable and should be consulted by the lawyer. The lawyer should also consult with the client and seek a mutually acceptable resolution of the disagreement. If such efforts are unavailing and the lawyer has a fundamental disagreement with the client, the lawyer may withdraw from the representation. See Rule 1.16(b)(4). Conversely, the client may resolve the disagreement by discharging the lawyer. See Rule 1.16(a)(3).

Disagreements Between Lawyer and Client

[3] At the outset of a representation, the client may authorize the lawyer to take specific action on the client's behalf without further consultation. Absent a material change in circumstances and subject to Rule 1.4, a lawyer may rely on such an advance authorization. The client may, however, revoke such authority at any time.

[4] In a case in which the client appears to be suffering diminished capacity, the lawyer's duty to abide by the client's decisions is guided by reference to Rule 1.14.

[4A] Division (a) makes it clear that regardless of the nature of the representation the lawyer does not breach a duty owed to the client by maintaining a professional and civil attitude toward all persons involved in the legal process. Specifically, punctuality, the avoidance of offensive tactics, and the treating of all persons with courtesy are viewed as essential components of professionalism and civility, and their breach may not be required by the client as part of the representation.

Independence from Client's Views or Activities (1.2)

[5] A lawyer's representation of a client, including representation by appointment, does not constitute an endorsement of the client's political, economic, social, or moral views or activities. Legal representation should not be denied to people who are unable to afford legal services or whose cause is controversial or the subject of popular disapproval. By the

Representing Unpopular Clients

same token, representing a client does not constitute approval of the client's views or activities.

Agreements Limiting Scope of Representation (1.2)

[7] Although division (c) affords the lawyer and client substantial latitude in defining the scope of the representation, any limitation must be reasonable under the circumstances. If, for example, a client's objective is limited to securing general information about the law that the client needs in order to handle a common and typically uncomplicated legal problem, the lawyer and client may agree that the lawyer's services will be limited to a brief telephone consultation. Such a limitation would not be reasonable if the time allotted was not sufficient to yield advice upon which the client could rely. In addition, the terms upon which representation is undertaken may exclude specific means that might otherwise be used to accomplish the client's objectives. Such limitations may exclude actions that the client thinks are too costly or that the lawyer regards as repugnant or imprudent. Although an agreement for a limited representation does not exempt a lawyer from the duty to provide competent representation, the limitation is a factor to be considered when determining the legal knowledge, skill, thoroughness, and preparation reasonably necessary for the representation. See Rule 1.1.

Limited Representation

[7A] Written confirmation of a limitation of a new or existing representation is preferred and may be any writing that is presented to the client that reflects the limitation, such as a letter or electronic transmission addressed to the client or a court order. A lawyer may create a form or checklist that specifies the scope of the client-lawyer relationship and the fees to be charged. An order of a court appointing a lawyer to represent a client is sufficient to confirm the scope of that representation. . . .

Illegal, Fraudulent, & Prohibited Transactions (1.2)

[9] Division (d) prohibits a lawyer from knowingly counseling or assisting a client to commit an illegal act or fraud. This prohibition, however, does not preclude the lawyer from giving an honest opinion about the actual consequences that appear likely to result from a client's conduct. Nor does the fact that a client uses advice in a course of action that is illegal or fraudulent of itself make a lawyer a party to the course of action. There is a critical distinction between presenting an analysis of legal aspects of questionable conduct and recommending the means by which an illegal act or fraud might be committed with impunity.

Recommending a Way to Commit Fraud

[10] When the client's course of action has already begun and is continuing, the lawyer's responsibility is especially delicate. The lawyer is required to avoid assisting the client, for example, by drafting or delivering documents that the lawyer knows are fraudulent or by suggesting how the wrongdoing might be concealed. A lawyer may not continue assisting a client in conduct that the lawyer originally supposed was legally permissible but then discovers is improper. See Rules 3.3(b) and 4.1(b).

[11] Where the client is a fiduciary, the lawyer may be charged with special obligations in dealings with a beneficiary.

[12] Division (d) applies whether or not the defrauded party is a party to the transaction. Hence, a lawyer must not participate in a transaction to effectuate illegal or fraudulent avoidance of tax liability. Division (d) does not preclude undertaking a criminal defense incident to a general retainer for legal services to a lawful enterprise. The last clause of division (d) recognizes that determining the validity or interpretation of a statute or regulation may require a course of action involving disobedience of the statute or regulation or of the interpretation placed upon it by governmental authorities.

Helping a Client Fraudulently Avoid Taxes

[13] If a lawyer comes to know or reasonably should know that a client expects assistance not permitted by the Ohio Rules of Professional Conduct or other law or if the lawyer intends to act contrary to the client's instructions, the lawyer must consult with the client regarding the limitations on the lawyer's conduct. See Rule 1.4(a)(5).

Rule 1.3: Diligence

A lawyer shall act with reasonable diligence and promptness in representing a client.

Duty of Diligence and Promptness

Comment on Rule 1.3

[1] A lawyer should pursue a matter on behalf of a client despite opposition, obstruction, or personal inconvenience to the lawyer. A lawyer also must act with commitment and dedication to the interests of the client.

[2] A lawyer must control the lawyer's work load so that each matter can be handled competently.

[3] Delay and neglect are inconsistent with a lawyer's duty of diligence, undermine public confidence, and may prejudice a client's cause. Reasonable diligence and promptness are expected of a lawyer in handling all client matters and will be evaluated in light of all relevant circumstances. The lawyer disciplinary process is particularly concerned with lawyers who consistently fail to carry out obligations to clients or consciously disregard a duty owed to a client.

[4] A lawyer should carry through to conclusion all matters undertaken for a client, unless the client-lawyer relationship is terminated as provided in Rule 1.16. Doubt about whether a client-lawyer relationship still exists should be clarified by the lawyer, preferably in writing, so that the client will not mistakenly suppose the lawyer is looking after the client's affairs when the lawyer has ceased to do so. For example, if a lawyer has handled a judicial or administrative proceeding that produced a result adverse to the client and the lawyer and the client have not agreed that the lawyer will handle the matter on appeal, the lawyer must consult with the client about post-trial alternatives including the possibility of appeal before relinquishing responsibility for the matter. See Rule 1.4(a)(2). Whether the lawyer is obligated to pursue those alternatives or prosecute the appeal for the client depends on the scope of the representation the lawyer has agreed to provide to the client. See Rules 1.2(c) and 1.5(b).

Confusion on Whether a Lawyer is Providing Representation

[5] To prevent neglect of client matters in the event of a sole practitioner's death or disability, the duty of diligence may require that each sole practitioner prepare a plan, in conformity with applicable rules, that designates another competent lawyer to review client files, notify each client of the lawyer's death or disability, and determine whether there is a need for immediate protective action. *Cf.* Rule V, Section 8(F) of the Supreme Court Rules for the Government of the Bar of Ohio.

Rule 1.4: Communication

(a) A lawyer shall do all of the following:

Keeping a Client Reasonably Informed

(1) promptly inform the client of any decision or circumstance with respect to which the client's informed consent is required by these rules;
(2) reasonably consult with the client about the means by which the client's objectives are to be accomplished;
(3) keep the client reasonably informed about the status of the matter;
(4) comply as soon as practicable with reasonable requests for information from the client;
(5) consult with the client about any relevant limitation on the lawyer's conduct when the lawyer knows that the client expects assistance not permitted by the Ohio Rules of Professional Conduct or other law.

(b) A lawyer shall explain a matter to the extent reasonably necessary to permit the client to make informed decisions regarding the representation.

(c) A lawyer shall inform a client at the time of the client's engagement of the lawyer or at any time subsequent to the engagement if the lawyer does not maintain professional liability insurance in the amounts of at least one hundred thousand dollars per occurrence and three hundred thousand dollars in the aggregate or if the lawyer's professional liability insurance is terminated. The notice shall be provided to the client on a separate form set forth following this rule and shall be signed by the client.

Informing a Client that the Lawyer does not have at least $100,000 in Liability Insurance

(1) A lawyer shall maintain a copy of the notice signed by the client for five years after termination of representation of the client.
(2) A lawyer who is involved in the division of fees pursuant to Rule 1.5 (e) shall inform the client as required by division (c) of this rule before the client is asked to agree to the division of fees. . . .

Notice To Client (1.4)

Pursuant to Rule 1.4 of the Ohio Rules of Professional Conduct, I am required to notify you that I do not maintain professional liability (malpractice) insurance of at least $100,000 per occurrence and $300,000 in the aggregate.

____
Attorney's Signature

Client Acknowledgement (1.4)

I acknowledge receipt of the notice required by Rule 1.4 of the Ohio Rules of Professional Conduct that [insert attorney's name] does not maintain professional liability (malpractice) insurance of at least $100,000 per occurrence and $300,000 in the aggregate.

____________________ ____________________
Client's Signature Date

Comment on Rule 1.4

[1] Reasonable communication between the lawyer and the client is necessary for the client to participate effectively in the representation.

Communicating with Client (1.4)

[2] If these rules require that a particular decision about the representation be made by the client, division (a)(1) requires that the lawyer promptly consult with and secure the client's consent prior to taking action unless prior discussions with the client have resolved what action the client wants the lawyer to take. For example, a lawyer who receives from opposing counsel an offer of settlement in a civil controversy or a proffered plea bargain in a criminal case must promptly inform the client of its substance unless the client has previously indicated that the proposal will be acceptable or unacceptable or has authorized the lawyer to accept or to reject the offer. See Rule 1.2(a).

[3] Division (a)(2) requires the lawyer to reasonably consult with the client about the means to be used to accomplish the client's objectives. In some situations, depending on both the importance of the action under consideration and the feasibility of consulting with the client, this duty will require consultation prior to taking action. In other circumstances, such as during a trial when an immediate decision must be made, the exigency of the situation may require the lawyer to act without prior consultation. In such cases the lawyer must nonetheless act reasonably to inform the client of actions the lawyer has taken on the client's behalf. Additionally, division (a)(3) requires that the lawyer keep the client reasonably informed about the status of the matter, such as significant developments affecting the timing or the substance of the representation and the fees and costs incurred to date.

[4] A lawyer's regular communication with clients will minimize the occasions on which a client will need to request information concerning the representation. When a client makes a reasonable request for information, however, division (a)(4) requires prompt compliance with the request, or if a prompt response is not feasible, that the lawyer, *or a member of the lawyer's staff*, acknowledge receipt of the request and advise the client when a response may be expected. Client telephone calls should be promptly returned or acknowledged. [emphasis added]

Using a Lawyer's Staff to Acknowledge Receipt of a Client's Request for Information

Explaining Matters (1.4)

[5] The client should have sufficient information to participate intelligently in decisions concerning the objectives of the representation and the means by which they are to be pursued, to the extent the client is willing and able to do so. Adequacy of communication depends in part on the kind of advice or assistance that is involved. For example, when there is time to explain a proposal made in a negotiation, the lawyer should review all important provisions with the client before proceeding to an agreement. In litigation a lawyer should explain the general strategy and prospects of success and ordinarily should consult the client on tactics that are likely to result in significant expense or to injure or coerce others. On the other hand, a lawyer ordinarily will not be expected to describe trial or negotiation strategy in detail. The guiding principle is that the lawyer should fulfill reasonable client expectations for information consistent with the duty to act in the client's best interests, and the client's overall requirements as to the character of representation.

Explaining the Prospects of Success to a Client

[6] Ordinarily, the information to be provided is that appropriate for a client who is a comprehending and responsible adult. However, fully informing the client according to this standard may be impracticable, for example, where the client is a child or suffers from diminished capacity. See Rule 1.14. When the client is an organization or group, it is often impossible or inappropriate to inform every one of its members about its legal affairs; ordinarily, the lawyer should address communications to the appropriate officials of the organization. See Rule 1.13. Where many routine matters are involved, a system of limited or occasional reporting may be arranged with the client.

Withholding Information (1.4)

[7] In some circumstances, a lawyer may be justified in delaying transmission of information when the client would be likely to react imprudently to an immediate communication. Thus, a lawyer might withhold a psychiatric diagnosis of a client when the examining psychiatrist indicates that disclosure would harm the client. A lawyer may not withhold information to serve the lawyer's own interest or convenience or the interests or convenience of another person. Rules or court orders governing litigation may provide that information supplied to a lawyer may not be disclosed to the client. Rule 3.4(c) directs compliance with such rules or orders.

Withholding Information from a Client

Professional Liability Insurance (1.4)

[8] Although it is in the best interest of the lawyer and the client that the lawyer maintain professional liability insurance or another form of adequate financial responsibility, it is not required in any circumstance other than when the lawyer practices as part of a legal professional association, corporation, legal clinic, limited liability company, or registered partnership.

[9] The client may not be aware that maintaining professional liability insurance is not mandatory and may well assume that the practice of law requires that some minimum financial responsibility be carried in the event of malpractice. Therefore, a lawyer who does not maintain certain minimum professional liability insurance shall promptly inform a prospective client or client.

Rule 1.5: Fees and expenses

(a) A lawyer shall not make an agreement for, charge, or collect an illegal or clearly excessive fee. A fee is clearly excessive when, after a review of the facts, a lawyer of ordinary prudence would be left with

Clearly Excessive Fees

a definite and firm conviction that the fee is in excess of a reasonable fee. The factors to be considered in determining the reasonableness of a fee include the following:

(1) the time and labor required, the novelty and difficulty of the questions involved, and the skill requisite to perform the legal service properly;
(2) the likelihood, if apparent to the client, that the acceptance of the particular employment will preclude other employment by the lawyer;
(3) the fee customarily charged in the locality for similar legal services;
(4) the amount involved and the results obtained;
(5) the time limitations imposed by the client or by the circumstances;
(6) the nature and length of the professional relationship with the client;
(7) the experience, reputation, and ability of the lawyer or lawyers performing the services;
(8) whether the fee is fixed or contingent.

(b) The nature and scope of the representation and the basis or rate of the fee and expenses for which the client will be responsible shall be communicated to the client, preferably in writing, before or within a reasonable time after commencing the representation, unless the lawyer will charge a client whom the lawyer has regularly represented on the same basis as previously charged. Any change in the basis or rate of the fee or expenses is subject to division (a) of this rule and shall promptly be communicated to the client, preferably in writing.

(c) A fee may be contingent on the outcome of the matter for which the service is rendered, except in a matter in which a contingent fee is prohibited by division (d) of this rule or other law.

Contingent Fee Agreement

(1) Each contingent fee agreement shall be in a writing signed by the client and the lawyer and shall state the method by which the fee is to be determined, including the percentage or percentages that shall accrue to the lawyer in the event of settlement, trial, or appeal; litigation and other expenses to be deducted from the recovery; and whether such expenses are to be deducted before or after the contingent fee is calculated. The agreement shall clearly notify the client of any expenses for which the client will be liable whether or not the client is the prevailing party.

Closing Statement

(2) If the lawyer becomes entitled to compensation under the contingent fee agreement and the lawyer will be disbursing funds, the lawyer shall prepare a closing statement and shall provide the client with that statement at the time of or prior to the receipt of compensation under the agreement. The closing statement shall specify the manner in which the compensation was determined under the agreement, any costs and expenses deducted by the lawyer from the judgment or settlement involved, and, if applicable, the actual division of the lawyer's fees with a lawyer not in the same firm, as required in division (e)(3) of this rule. The closing statement shall be signed by the client and lawyer.

Prohibited Contingent Fees

(d) A lawyer shall not enter into an arrangement for, charge, or collect any of the following:

(1) any fee in a domestic relations matter, the payment or amount of which is contingent upon the securing of a divorce or upon the amount of spousal or child support, or property settlement in lieu thereof;
(2) a contingent fee for representing a defendant in a criminal case;
(3) a fee denominated as "earned upon receipt," "nonrefundable," or in any similar terms, unless the client is simultaneously advised in writing that if the lawyer does not complete the representation for any reason, the client may be entitled to a refund of all or part of the fee based upon the value of the representation pursuant to division (a) of this rule.

Dividing a Fee

(e) Lawyers who are not in the same firm may divide fees only if all of the following apply:

(1) the division of fees is in proportion to the services performed by each lawyer or each lawyer assumes joint responsibility for the representation and agrees to be available for consultation with the client;
(2) the client has given written consent after full disclosure of the identity of each lawyer, that the fees will be divided, and that the division of fees will be in proportion to the services to be performed by each lawyer or that each lawyer will assume joint responsibility for the representation;
(3) except where court approval of the fee division is obtained, the written closing statement in a case involving a contingent fee shall be signed by the client and each lawyer and shall comply with the terms of division (c)(2) of this rule;
(4) the total fee is reasonable.

Mediation and Arbitration

(f) In cases of a dispute between lawyers arising under this rule, fees shall be divided in accordance with the mediation or arbitration provided by a local bar association. When a local bar association is not available or does not have procedures to resolve fee disputes between lawyers, the dispute shall be referred to the Ohio State Bar Association for mediation or arbitration.

Comment on Rule 1.5

Reasonableness of Fee (1.5)

[1] Division (a) requires that lawyers charge fees that are reasonable under the circumstances. The factors specified in divisions (a)(1) through (8) are not exclusive. Nor will each factor be relevant in each instance.

Nature and Scope of Representation; Basis or Rate of Fee and Expenses

[2] The detail and specificity of the communication required by division (b) will depend on the nature of the client-lawyer relationship, the work to be performed, and the basis of the rate or fee. A writing that confirms the nature and scope of the client-lawyer relationship and the fees to be charged is the preferred means of communicating this information to the client and can clarify the relationship and reduce the possibility of a misunderstanding. When the lawyer has regularly represented a client, they ordinarily will have evolved an understanding concerning the basis or rate of the fee and the expenses for which the client will be responsible. In a new client-lawyer relationship, however, an understanding as to fees and expenses must be established promptly. Unless the situation involves a regularly represented client, the lawyer should furnish the client with at least a simple memorandum or copy of the lawyer's customary fee arrangements that states the general nature of the legal services to be provided, the basis, rate or total amount of the fee, and whether and to what extent the client will be responsible for any costs, expenses, or disbursements in the course of the representation. So long as the client agrees in advance, a lawyer may seek reimbursement for the reasonable cost of services performed in-house, such as copying.

Customary Fee Arrangements

[3] Contingent fees, like any other fees, are subject to the reasonableness standard of division (a) of this rule. In determining whether a particular contingent fee is reasonable, or whether it is reasonable to charge any form of contingent fee, a lawyer must consider the factors that are relevant under the circumstances. Applicable law may impose limitations on contingent fees, such as a ceiling on the percentage allowable, or may require a lawyer to offer clients an alternative basis for the fee. Applicable law also may apply to situations other than a contingent fee, for example, government regulations regarding fees in certain tax matters.

Contingent Fees

Terms of Payment (1.5)

[4] A lawyer may require advance payment of a fee, but is obliged to return any unearned portion. See Rule 1.16(e). A lawyer may accept property in payment for services, such as an ownership interest in an enterprise, providing this does not involve acquisition of a proprietary interest in the cause of action or subject matter of the litigation contrary to Rule 1.8 (i). However, a fee paid in property instead of money may be subject to the requirements of Rule 1.8(a) because such fees often have the essential qualities of a business transaction with the client.

[5] An agreement may not be made whose terms might induce the lawyer improperly to curtail services for the client or perform them in a way contrary to the client's interest. For example, a lawyer should not enter into an agreement whereby services are to be provided only up to a stated amount when it is foreseeable that more extensive services probably will be required, unless the situation is adequately explained to the client. Otherwise, the client might have to bargain for further assistance in the midst of a proceeding or transaction. However, it is proper to define the extent of services in light of the client's ability to pay. A lawyer should not exploit a fee arrangement based primarily on hourly charges by using wasteful procedures.

Padding: Charging by the Hour for Wasteful Procedures

[5A] If all funds held by the lawyer are not disbursed at the time the closing statement required by division (c)(2) is prepared, the lawyer's obligation with regard to those funds is governed by Rule 1.15.

Prohibited Contingent Fees (1.5)

[6] Division (d) prohibits a lawyer from charging a contingent fee in a domestic relations matter when payment is contingent upon the securing of a divorce or upon the amount of spousal or child support or property settlement to be obtained. This provision does not preclude a contract for a contingent fee for legal representation in connection with the recovery of post-judgment balances due under support or other financial orders because such contracts do not implicate the same policy concerns.

Retainer (1.5)

[6A] Advance fee payments are of at least four types. The "true" or "classic" retainer is a fee paid in advance solely to ensure the lawyer's availability to represent the client and precludes the lawyer from taking adverse representation. What is often called a retainer is in fact an advance payment to ensure that fees are paid when they are subsequently earned, on either a flat fee or hourly fee basis. A flat fee is a fee of a set amount for performance of agreed work, which may or may not be paid in advance but is not deemed earned until the work is performed. An earned upon

Four Kinds of Advance Fee Payments

receipt fee is a flat fee paid in advance that is deemed earned upon payment regardless of the amount of future work performed. When a fee is earned affects whether it must be placed in the attorney's trust account, see Rule 1.15, and may have significance under other laws such as tax and bankruptcy. The reasonableness requirement and the application of the factors in division (a) may mean that a client is entitled to a refund of an advance fee payment even though it has been denominated "nonrefundable," "earned upon receipt," or in similar terms that imply the client would never receive a refund. So that a client is not misled by the use of such terms, division (d)(3) requires certain minimum disclosures that must be included in the written fee agreement. This does not mean the client will always be entitled to a refund upon early termination of the representation [*e.g.*, factor (a)(2) might justify the entire fee], nor does it determine how any refund should be calculated (e.g., hours worked times a reasonable hourly rate, quantum meruit, percentage of the work completed, etc.), but merely requires that the client be advised of the possibility of a refund based upon application of the factors set forth in division (a). In order to be able to demonstrate the reasonableness of the fee in the event of early termination of the representation, it is advisable that lawyers maintain contemporaneous time records for any representation undertaken on a flat fee basis.

Division of Fee (1.5)

Dividing a Fee

[7] A division of fee is a single billing to a client covering the fee of two or more lawyers who are not in the same firm. A division of fee facilitates association of more than one lawyer in a matter in which neither alone could serve the client as well, and most often is used when the fee is contingent and the division is between a referring lawyer and a trial lawyer. Division (e) permits the lawyers to divide a fee either on the basis of the proportion of services they render or if each lawyer assumes responsibility for the representation as a whole. Within a reasonable time after disclosure of the identity of each lawyer, the client must give written approval that the fee will be divided and that the division of fees is in proportion to the services performed by each lawyer or that each lawyer assumes joint responsibility for the representation. Except where court approval of the fee division is obtained, closing statements must be in a writing signed by the client and each lawyer and must otherwise comply with division (c) of this rule. Joint responsibility for the representation entails financial and ethical responsibility for the representation as if the lawyers were associated in a partnership. A lawyer should only refer a matter to a lawyer whom the referring lawyer reasonably believes is competent to handle the matter. See Rules 1.1 and 1.17.

[8] Division (e) does not prohibit or regulate division of fees to be received in the future for work done when lawyers were previously associated in a law firm.

Disputes over Fees (1.5)

Mediation and Arbitration

[9] If a procedure has been established for resolution of fee disputes between a client and a lawyer, such as an arbitration or mediation procedure established by a local bar association, the Ohio State Bar Association, or the Supreme Court of Ohio, the lawyer must comply with the procedure when it is mandatory, and, even when it is voluntary, the lawyer should conscientiously consider submitting to it. Law may prescribe a procedure for determining a lawyer's fee, for example, in representation of an executor or administrator, a class or a person entitled to a reasonable fee as part of the measure of damages. The lawyer entitled to such a fee and a lawyer representing another party concerned with the fee should comply with the prescribed procedure.

[10] A procedure has been established for resolution of fee disputes between lawyers who are sharing a fee pursuant to division (e) of this rule. This involves use of an arbitration or mediation procedure established by a local bar association or the Ohio State Bar Association. The lawyer must comply with the procedure. A dispute between lawyers who are splitting a fee shall not delay disbursement to the client. See Rule 1.15.

Rule 1.6: Confidentiality of information

Confidentiality: Information Relating to the Representation

(a) A lawyer shall not reveal information relating to the representation of a client, including information protected by the attorney-client privilege under applicable law, unless the client gives informed consent, the disclosure is impliedly authorized in order to carry out the representation, or the disclosure is permitted by division (b) or required by division (c) of this rule.

When the Confidentiality Rule Does Not Apply

(b) A lawyer may reveal information relating to the representation of a client, including information protected by the attorney-client privilege under applicable law, to the extent the lawyer reasonably believes necessary for any of the following purposes:

(1) to prevent reasonably certain death or substantial bodily harm;

Future-Crime Exception

(2) to prevent the commission of a crime by the client or other person;

(3) to mitigate substantial injury to the financial interests or property of another that has resulted from the client's commission of an illegal or fraudulent

act, in furtherance of which the client has used the lawyer's services;

(4) to secure legal advice about the lawyer's compliance with these rules;

(5) to establish a claim or defense on behalf of the lawyer in a controversy between the lawyer and the client, to establish a defense to a criminal charge or civil claim against the lawyer based upon conduct in which the client was involved, or to respond to allegations in any proceeding, including any disciplinary matter, concerning the lawyer's representation of the client;

(6) to comply with other law or a court order.

(c) A lawyer shall reveal information relating to the representation of a client, including information protected by the attorney-client privilege under applicable law, to the extent the lawyer reasonably believes necessary to comply with Rule 3.3 or 4.1.

Comment on Rule 1.6

[1] This rule governs the disclosure by a lawyer of information relating to the representation of a client during the lawyer's representation of the client. See Rule 1.18 for the lawyer's duties with respect to information provided to the lawyer by a prospective client, Rule 1.9(c)(2) for the lawyer's duty not to reveal information relating to the lawyer's prior representation of a former client, and Rules 1.8(b) and 1.9(c)(1) for the lawyer's duties with respect to the use of such information to the disadvantage of clients and former clients.

[2] A fundamental principle in the client-lawyer relationship is that, in the absence of the client's informed consent, the lawyer must not reveal information relating to the representation. See Rule 1.0(f) for the definition of informed consent. This contributes to the trust that is the hallmark of the client-lawyer relationship. The client is thereby encouraged to seek legal assistance and to communicate fully and frankly with the lawyer even as to embarrassing or legally damaging subject matter. The lawyer needs this information to represent the client effectively and, if necessary, to advise the client to refrain from wrongful conduct. Almost without exception, clients come to lawyers in order to determine their rights and what is, in the complex of laws and regulations, deemed to be legal and correct.

Attorney-Client Privilege, Work-Product, and Confidentiality

[3] The principle of client-lawyer confidentiality is given effect by related bodies of law: the attorney-client privilege, the work-product doctrine, and the rule of confidentiality established in professional ethics. The attorney-client privilege and work-product doctrine apply in judicial and other proceedings in which a lawyer may be called as a witness or otherwise required to produce evidence concerning a client. The rule of client-lawyer confidentiality applies in situations other than those where evidence is sought from the lawyer through compulsion of law. The confidentiality rule, for example, applies not only to matters communicated in confidence by the client but also to all information relating to the representation, whatever its source. A lawyer may not disclose such information except as authorized or required by the Ohio Rules of Professional Conduct or other law. See also Scope.

Revealing a Client's Identity

[4] Division (a) prohibits a lawyer from revealing information relating to the representation of a client. This prohibition also applies to disclosures by a lawyer that do not in themselves reveal protected information but could reasonably lead to the discovery of such information by a third person. A lawyer's use of a hypothetical to discuss issues relating to the representation is permissible so long as there is no reasonable likelihood that the listener will be able to ascertain the identity of the client or the situation involved.

Authorized Disclosure (1.6)

[5] Except to the extent that the client's instructions or special circumstances limit that authority, a lawyer is impliedly authorized to make disclosures about a client when appropriate in carrying out the representation. In some situations, for example, a lawyer may be impliedly authorized to admit a fact that cannot properly be disputed or to make a disclosure that facilitates a satisfactory conclusion to a matter. Lawyers in a firm may, in the course of the firm's practice, disclose to each other information relating to a client of the firm, unless the client has instructed that particular information be confined to specified lawyers.

Disclosure Adverse to Client (1.6)

Authorized Disclosure of Client Information

[6] Permitting lawyers to reveal information relating to the representation of clients may create a chilling effect on the client-lawyer relationship, and discourage clients from revealing confidential information to their lawyers at a time when the clients should be making a full disclosure. Although the public interest is usually best served by a strict rule requiring lawyers to preserve the confidentiality of information relating to the representation of their clients, the confidentiality rule is subject to limited exceptions. Division (b)(1) recognizes the overriding value of life and physical integrity and permits disclosure reasonably necessary to prevent reasonably certain death or substantial bodily harm. Such harm is reasonably certain to occur if it will be suffered imminently or if there is a present and substantial threat that a person will suffer such harm at a later date if the lawyer fails to take action necessary to eliminate the

threat. Thus, a lawyer who knows that a client has discharged toxic waste into a town's water supply may reveal this information to the authorities if there is a present and substantial risk that a person who drinks the water will contract a life-threatening or debilitating disease and the lawyer's disclosure is necessary to eliminate the threat or reduce the number of victims.

[7] Division (b)(2) recognizes the traditional "future crime" exception, which permits lawyers to reveal the information necessary to prevent the commission of the crime by a client or a third party.

Future-Crime Exception

[8] Division (b)(3) addresses the situation in which the lawyer does not learn of the illegal or fraudulent act of a client until after the client has used the lawyer's services to further it. Although the client no longer has the option of preventing disclosure by refraining from the wrongful conduct [see Rule 4.1], there will be situations in which the loss suffered by the affected person can be mitigated. In such situations, the lawyer may disclose information relating to the representation to the extent necessary to enable the affected persons to mitigate or recoup their losses. Division (b)(3) does not apply when a person is accused of or has committed an illegal or fraudulent act and thereafter employs a lawyer for representation concerning that conduct. In addition, division (b)(3) does not apply to a lawyer who has been engaged by an organizational client to investigate an alleged violation of law by the client or a constituent of the client.

Using a Lawyer's Services to Commit an Illegal Act

[9] A lawyer's confidentiality obligations do not preclude a lawyer from securing confidential legal advice about the lawyer's personal responsibility to comply with these rules. In most situations, disclosing information to secure such advice will be impliedly authorized for the lawyer to carry out the representation. Even when the disclosure is not impliedly authorized, division (b)(4) permits such disclosure because of the importance of a lawyer's compliance with the Ohio Rules of Professional Conduct.

[10] Where a legal claim or disciplinary charge alleges complicity of the lawyer in the conduct of a client or a former client or other misconduct of the lawyer involving representation of the client or a former client, the lawyer may respond to the extent the lawyer reasonably believes necessary to establish a defense. Such a charge can arise in a civil, criminal, disciplinary, or other proceeding and can be based on a wrong allegedly committed by the lawyer against the client or on a wrong alleged by a third person, for example, a person claiming to have been defrauded by the lawyer and client acting together. The lawyer's right to respond arises when an assertion of such complicity has been made. Division (b)(5) does not require the lawyer to await the commencement of an action or proceeding that charges such complicity, so that the defense may be established by responding directly to a third party who has made such an assertion. The right to defend also applies, of course, where a proceeding has been commenced.

The Right of a Lawyer to Defend Him/Herself by Disclosure

[11] A lawyer entitled to a fee is permitted by division (b)(5) to prove the services rendered in an action to collect it. This aspect of the rule expresses the principle that the beneficiary of a fiduciary relationship may not exploit it to the detriment of the fiduciary.

[12] Other law may require that a lawyer disclose information about a client. Whether such a law supersedes Rule 1.6 is a question of law beyond the scope of these rules. When disclosure of information relating to the representation appears to be required by other law, the lawyer must discuss the matter with the client to the extent required by Rule 1.4. If, however, the other law supersedes this rule and requires disclosure, division (b)(6) permits the lawyer to make such disclosures as are necessary to comply with the law.

[13] A lawyer may be ordered to reveal information relating to the representation of a client by a court or by another tribunal or governmental entity claiming authority pursuant to other law to compel the disclosure. Absent informed consent of the client to do otherwise, the lawyer should assert on behalf of the client all nonfrivolous claims that the order is not authorized by other law or that the information sought is protected against disclosure by the attorney-client privilege or other applicable law. In the event of an adverse ruling, the lawyer must consult with the client about the possibility of appeal to the extent required by Rule 1.4. Unless review is sought, however, division (b)(6) permits the lawyer to comply with the court's order.

[14] Division (b) permits disclosure only to the extent the lawyer reasonably believes the disclosure is necessary to accomplish one of the purposes specified. Where practicable, the lawyer should first seek to persuade the client to take suitable action to obviate the need for disclosure. A disclosure adverse to the client's interest should be no greater than the lawyer reasonably believes necessary to accomplish the purpose. If the disclosure will be made in connection with a judicial proceeding, the disclosure should be made in a manner that limits access to the information to the tribunal or other persons having a need to know it and appropriate protective orders or other arrangements should be sought by the lawyer to the fullest extent practicable. Before making a disclosure under division (b)(1), (2), or (3), a lawyer for an organization should ordinarily bring the

Climbing the Chain of Command in an Organization

issue of taking suitable action to higher authority within the organization, including, if warranted by the circumstances, to the highest authority that can act on behalf of the organization as determined by applicable law.

[15] Division (b) permits but does not require the disclosure of information relating to a client's representation to accomplish the purposes specified in divisions (b)(1) through (b)(6). In exercising the discretion conferred by this rule, the lawyer may consider such factors as the nature of the lawyer's relationship with the client and with those who might be injured by the client, the lawyer's own involvement in the transaction, and factors that may extenuate the conduct in question. A lawyer's decision not to disclose as permitted by division (b) does not violate this rule. Disclosure may be required, however, by other rules. Some rules require disclosure only if such disclosure would be permitted by division (b). See Rules 4.1(b), 8.1 and 8.3. Rule 3.3, on the other hand, requires disclosure in some circumstances regardless of whether such disclosure is permitted by this rule.

Acting Competently to Preserve Confidentiality (1.6)

[16] A lawyer must act competently to safeguard information relating to the representation of a client against inadvertent or unauthorized disclosure by the lawyer *or other persons who are participating in the representation of the client* or who are subject to the lawyer's supervision. See Rules 1.1, 5.1, and 5.3. [emphasis added]

Inadvertent Disclosure

[17] When transmitting a communication that includes information relating to the representation of a client, the lawyer must take reasonable precautions to prevent the information from coming into the hands of unintended recipients. This duty, however, does not require that the lawyer use special security measures if the method of communication affords a reasonable expectation of privacy. Special circumstances, however, may warrant special precautions. Factors to be considered in determining the reasonableness of the lawyer's expectation of confidentiality include the sensitivity of the information and the extent to which the privacy of the communication is protected by law or by a confidentiality agreement. A client may require the lawyer to implement special security measures not required by this rule or may give informed consent to the use of a means of communication that would otherwise be prohibited by this rule.

Reasonable Expectation of Privacy

Former Client (1.6)

[18] The duty of confidentiality continues after the client-lawyer relationship has terminated. See Rule 1.9(c)(2). See Rule 1.9(c)(1) for the prohibition against using such information to the disadvantage of the former client.

Duty of Confidentiality Outlasts the Attorney-Client Relationship

Rule 1.7: Conflict of interest: current clients

(a) A lawyer's acceptance or continuation of representation of a client creates a conflict of interest if either of the following applies:

(1) the representation of that client will be directly adverse to another current client;

(2) there is a substantial risk that the lawyer's ability to consider, recommend, or carry out an appropriate course of action for that client will be materially limited by the lawyer's responsibilities to another client, a former client, or a third person or by the lawyer's own personal interests.

Loyalty and Independent Judgment: Conflict of Interest with Current Clients

(b) A lawyer shall not accept or continue the representation of a client if a conflict of interest would be created pursuant to division (a) of this rule, unless all of the following apply:

(1) the lawyer will be able to provide competent and diligent representation to each affected client;

(2) each affected client gives informed consent, confirmed in writing;

(3) the representation is not precluded by division (c) of this rule.

Accepting or Continuing the Representation Despite the Conflict of Interest

(c) Even if each affected client consents, the lawyer shall not accept or continue the representation if either of the following applies:

(1) the representation is prohibited by law;

(2) the representation would involve the assertion of a claim by one client against another client represented by the lawyer in the same proceeding.

Comment on Rule 1.7

General Principles (1.7)

[1] The principles of loyalty and independent judgment are fundamental to the attorney-client relationship and underlie the conflict of interest provisions of these rules. Neither the lawyer's personal interest, the interests of other clients, nor the desires of third persons should be permitted to dilute the lawyer's loyalty to the client. All potential conflicts of interest involving a new or current client must be analyzed under this rule. In addition, a lawyer must consider whether any of the specific rules in Rule 1.8, regarding certain conflicts of interest involving current

clients, applies. For former clients, see Rule 1.9; for conflicts involving those who have consulted a lawyer about representation but did not retain that lawyer, see Rule 1.18.

[2] In order to analyze and resolve a conflict of interest problem under this rule, a lawyer must: (1) clearly identify the client or clients; (2) determine whether a conflict of interest exists; (3) decide whether the representation is barred by either criteria of division (c); (4) evaluate, under division (b)(1), whether the lawyer can competently and diligently represent all clients affected by the conflict of interest; and (5) if representation is otherwise permissible, consult with the clients affected by the conflict and obtain the informed consent of each of them, confirmed in writing.

Procedures for Resolving a Conflict

[3] To determine whether a conflict of interest would be created by accepting or continuing a representation, a lawyer should adopt reasonable procedures, appropriate for the size and type of firm and practice, for collecting and reviewing information about the persons and issues in all matters handled by the lawyer. See also Comment to Rule 5.1. Ignorance caused by a failure to institute or follow such procedures will not excuse a lawyer's violation of this rule.

[4] A lawyer must decline a new representation that would create a conflict of interest, unless representation is permitted under division (b).

[5] If unforeseeable developments, such as changes in corporate and other organizational affiliations or the addition or realignment of parties in litigation, create a conflict of interest during a representation, the lawyer must withdraw from representation unless continued representation is permissible under divisions (b)(1) and (c) and the lawyer obtains informed consent, confirmed in writing, of each affected client under the conditions of division (b)(2). See Rule 1.16.

[6] Just as conflicts can emerge in the course of a representation, the nature of a known conflict of interest can change in the course of a representation. For example, the proposed joint representation of a driver and her passenger to sue a person believed to have caused a traffic accident may initially present only a material limitation conflict, as to which the proposed clients may give informed consent. However, if the lawyer's investigation suggests that the driver may be at fault, the interests of the driver and the passenger are then directly adverse, and the joint representation cannot be continued. A lawyer must be alert to the possibility that newly acquired information requires reevaluating of a conflict of interest, and taking different steps to resolve it.

Joint Representation

[7] When a lawyer withdraws from representation in order to avoid a conflict, the lawyer must seek court approval where necessary and take steps to minimize harm to the clients. See Rule 1.16. The lawyer must also continue to protect the confidences of the client from whose representation the lawyer has withdrawn. See Rule 1.9(c).

[8] When a conflict arises from a lawyer's representation of more than one client, whether the lawyer must withdraw from representing all affected clients or may continue to represent one or more of them depends upon whether: (1) the lawyer can both satisfy the duties owed to the former client and adequately represent the remaining client or clients, given the lawyer's duties to the former client (see Rule 1.9); and (2) any necessary client consent is obtained.

Identifying the Client (1.7)

[9] In large part, principles of substantive law outside these rules determine whether a client-lawyer relationship exists or is continuing. See Scope [17]. These rules, including Rules 1.2, 1.8(f)(2), 1.13, and 6.5, must also be considered.

Identifying Conflicts of Interest: Directly Adverse Representation (1.7)

[10] The concurrent representation of clients whose interests are directly adverse always creates a conflict of interest. A directly adverse conflict can occur in a litigation or transactional setting.

Concurrent Representation

[11] *In litigation.* The representation of one client is directly adverse to another in litigation when one of the lawyer's clients is asserting a claim against another client of the lawyer. A directly adverse conflict also may arise when effective representation of a client who is a party in a lawsuit requires a lawyer to cross-examine another client, represented in a different matter, who appears as a witness in the suit. A lawyer may not represent, in the same proceeding, clients who are directly adverse in that proceeding. See Rule 1.7(c)(2). Further, absent consent, a lawyer may not act as an advocate in one proceeding against a person the lawyer represents in some other matter, even when the matters are wholly unrelated.

Adverse Interests

[12] *Class-action conflicts.* When a lawyer represents or seeks to represent a class of plaintiffs or defendants in a class-action lawsuit, unnamed members of the class are ordinarily not considered to be clients of the lawyer for purposes of applying division (a)(1) of this rule. Thus, the lawyer does not typically need to get the consent of an unnamed class member before

Class-Action Conflicts

representing a client suing the person in an unrelated matter. Similarly, a lawyer seeking to represent an opponent in a class action does not typically need the consent of an unnamed member of the class whom the lawyer represents in an unrelated matter.

[13] *In transactional and counseling practice.* The representation of one client can be directly adverse to another in a transactional matter. For example, a buyer and a seller or a borrower and a lender are directly adverse with respect to the negotiation of the terms of the sale or loan. [*Stark County Bar Assn v. Ergazos* (1982), 2 Ohio St. 3d 59; *Columbus Bar v. Ewing* (1992), 63 Ohio St. 3d 377]. If a lawyer is asked to represent the seller of a business in negotiations with a buyer whom the lawyer represents in another, unrelated matter, the lawyer cannot undertake the new representation without the informed, written consent of each client.

Conflicts in Transactional Representation

Identifying Conflicts of Interest: Material Limitation Conflicts (1.7)

[14] Even where clients are not directly adverse, a conflict of interest exists if there is a substantial risk that a lawyer's ability to consider, recommend, or carry out an appropriate course of action for the client will be materially limited as a result of the lawyer's other responsibilities or interests. The mere possibility of subsequent harm does not, itself, require disclosure and consent. The critical questions are: (1) whether a difference in interests between the client and lawyer or between two clients exists or is likely to arise; and (2) if it does, whether this difference in interests will materially interfere with the lawyer's independent professional judgment in considering alternatives or foreclose courses of action that reasonably should be pursued on behalf of any affected client. [analogous to Model Rule Comment 8]

Material Interference with Independent Professional Judgment

Lawyer's Responsibility to Current Clients-Same Matter (1.7)

[15] *In litigation.* A "material limitation" conflict exists when a lawyer represents co-plaintiffs or co-defendants in litigation and there is a substantial discrepancy in the clients' testimony, incompatible positions in relation to another party, potential cross-claims, or substantially different possibilities of settlement of the claims or liabilities in question. Such conflicts can arise in criminal cases as well as civil. The potential for conflict of interest in representing multiple defendants in a criminal matter is so grave that ordinarily a lawyer should decline to represent more than one co-defendant. On the other hand, common representation of persons having similar interests in civil litigation is proper if the requirements of division (b) are met.

Common or Multiple Representation

[16] *In transactional practice.* In transactional and counseling practice, the potential also exists for material limitation conflicts in representing multiple clients in regard to one matter. Depending upon the circumstances, a material limitation conflict of interest may be present. Relevant factors in determining whether there is a material limitation conflict include the nature of the clients' respective interests in the matter, the relative duration and intimacy of the lawyer's relationship with each client involved, the functions being performed by the lawyer, the likelihood that disagreements will arise, and the likely prejudice to each client from the conflict. These factors and others will also be relevant to the lawyer's analysis of whether the lawyer can competently and diligently represent all clients in the matter, and whether the lawyer can make the disclosures to each client necessary to secure each client's informed consent. See Comments 24–30.

Conflicts in Transactional Representation

Lawyer's Responsibility to Current Client-Different Matters (1.7)

[17] A material limitation conflict between the interests of current clients can sometimes arise when the lawyer represents each client in different matters. Simultaneous representation, in unrelated matters, of clients whose business or personal interests are only generally adverse, such as competing enterprises, does not present a material limitation conflict. Furthermore, a lawyer may ordinarily take inconsistent legal positions at different times on behalf of different clients. However, a material limitation conflict of interest exists, for example, if there is a substantial risk that a lawyer's action on behalf of one client in one case will materially limit the lawyer's effectiveness in concurrently representing another client in a different case. For example, there is a material limitation conflict if a decision for which the lawyer must advocate on behalf of one client in one case will create a precedent likely to seriously weaken the position taken on behalf of another client in another case. Factors relevant in determining whether there is a material limitation of which the clients must be advised and for which consent must be obtained include: (1) where the cases are pending; (2) whether the issue is substantive or procedural; (3) the temporal relationship between the matters; (4) the significance of the issue to the immediate and long-term interests of the clients involved; and (5) the clients' reasonable expectations in retaining the lawyer.

Other Material-Limitation Conflicts

Lawyer's Responsibilities to Former Clients and Other Third Persons (1.7)

[18] A lawyer's duties of loyalty and independence may be materially limited by responsibilities to former clients under Rule 1.9 or by the lawyer's responsibilities to other persons, such as family members or persons to whom the lawyer, in the capacity of a trustee, executor, or corporate director, owes fiduciary duties.

[19] If a lawyer for a corporation or other organization serves as a member of its board of directors, the dual roles may present a "material limitation" conflict. For example, a lawyer's ability to assure the corporate client that its communications with counsel are privileged may be compromised if the lawyer is also a board member. Alternatively, in order to participate fully as a board member, a lawyer may have to decline to advise or represent the corporation in a matter. Before starting to serve as a director of an organization, a lawyer must take the steps specified in division (b), considering whether the lawyer can adequately represent the organization if the lawyer serves as a director and, if so, reviewing the implications of the dual role with the board and obtaining its consent. Even with consent to the lawyer's acceptance of a dual role, if there is a material risk in a given situation that the dual role will compromise the lawyer's independent judgment or ability to consider, recommend, or carry out an appropriate course of action, the lawyer should abstain from participating as a director or withdraw as the corporation's lawyer as to that matter.

Conflicts in Representation within a Corporation

Personal Interest Conflicts (1.7)

[20] *Types of personal interest.* The lawyer's own interests should not be permitted to have an adverse effect on representation of a client. For example, if the probity of a lawyer's own conduct in a transaction is in serious question, the lawyer may have difficulty or be unable to give a client detached advice in regard to the same manner. Similarly, when a lawyer has discussions concerning possible employment with an opponent of the lawyer's client, or with a law firm representing the opponent, such discussions could materially limit the lawyer's representation of the client. A lawyer should not allow related business interests to affect representation, for example, by referring clients to an enterprise in which the lawyer has an undisclosed financial interest. See Rule 1.8 for specific rules pertaining to certain personal interest conflicts, including business transactions with clients. See also Rule 1.10 (personal interest conflicts under Rule 1.7 ordinarily are not imputed to other lawyers in a law firm).

Personal-Interest Conflicts

[21] *Related lawyers.* When lawyers who are closely related by blood or marriage represent different clients in the same matter or in substantially related matters, there may be a substantial risk that client confidences will be revealed and that the lawyer's family relationship will interfere with both loyalty and independent professional judgment. As a result, each client is entitled to know of the existence and implications of the relationship between the lawyers before the lawyer agrees to undertake the representation. Thus, a lawyer related to another lawyer, e.g., as parent, child, sibling, or spouse, ordinarily may not represent a client in a matter where the related lawyer represents another party, unless each client gives informed, written consent. The disqualification arising from a close family relationship is personal and ordinarily is not imputed to members of firms with whom the lawyers are associated. See Rule 1.10.

Conflicts Due to Family Ties

[22] *Sexual activity with clients.* A lawyer is prohibited from engaging in sexual activity with a current client unless the sexual relationship predates the formation of the client-lawyer relationship. See Rule 1.8(j).

Sex Between Lawyer and Client

Interest of Person Paying for Lawyer's Service (1.7)

[23] A lawyer may be paid from a source other than the client, including a co-client, if the client is informed of that fact and consents and the arrangement does not compromise the lawyer's duty of loyalty or independent judgment to the client. See Rule 1.8(f), and the special notice requirement for clients of insurance defense counsel in Rule 1.8(f)(4). If acceptance of the payment from any other source presents a substantial risk that the lawyer's representation of the client will be materially limited by the lawyer's own interest in accommodating the person paying the lawyer's fee or by the lawyer's responsibilities to a payer who is also a co-client, then the lawyer must comply with the requirements of division (b) before accepting the representation.

Conflicts when Someone other than the Client Pays a Lawyer's Fees

Adequacy When Burdened by a Conflict (1.7)

[24] After a lawyer determines that accepting or continuing a representation entails a conflict of interest, the lawyer must assess whether the lawyer can provide competent and diligent representation to each affected client consistent with the lawyer's duties of loyalty and independent judgment. When the lawyer is representing more than one client, the question of adequacy of representation must be resolved as to each client.

Considerations in Common Representation (1.7)

[25] In considering whether to represent multiple clients in the same matter, a lawyer should be mindful that if the common representation fails because the potentially adverse interests cannot be reconciled, the result can be additional cost, embarrassment, and recrimination. Ordinarily, the lawyer will be forced to withdraw from representing all of the clients if the common representation fails. In some situations, the risk of failure is so great that multiple representation is plainly impossible. For example, a lawyer cannot undertakc common representation of clients where contentious litigation or negotiations between them are imminent or contemplated. Moreover, because the lawyer is required to be impartial between commonly represented clients, representation of multiple clients is improper when it is unlikely that impartiality can be maintained. Generally, if the relationship between the parties is antagonistic, the possibility that the clients' interests can be adequately served by common representation is low. Other relevant factors are whether the lawyer subsequently will represent both parties on a continuing basis and whether the situation involves creating or terminating a relationship between the parties.

Impartiality in Common Representation

[26] Particularly important factors in determining the appropriateness of common representation are the effect on client-lawyer confidentiality and the attorney-client privilege. With regard to the attorney-client privilege, the prevailing rule is that, as between commonly represented clients, the privilege does not attach. Hence, it must be assumed that if litigation does later occur between the clients, the privilege will not protect communications made on the subject of the joint representation, while it is in effect, and the clients should be so advised.

[27] As to the duty of confidentiality, continued common representation will almost certainly be inadequate if one client asks the lawyer not to disclose to the other client information relevant to the common representation. This is so because the lawyer has an equal duty of loyalty to each client, and each client has the right to be informed of anything bearing on the representation that might affect the client's interests and the right to expect that the lawyer will use that information to that client's benefit. See Rule 1.4. The lawyer should, at the outset of the common representation and as part of the process of obtaining each client's informed consent, advise each client that information will be shared and that the lawyer will have to withdraw if one client decides that some matter material to the representation should be kept from the other. In limited circumstances, it may be appropriate for the lawyer to proceed with the representation when the clients have agreed, after being properly informed, that the lawyer will keep certain information confidential. For example, the lawyer may reasonably conclude that failure to disclose one client's trade secrets to another client will not adversely affect representation on behalf of a joint venture between the clients and agree to keep that information confidential with the informed consent of both clients.

[28] Any limitations on the scope of the representation made necessary as a result of the common representation must be fully explained to the clients at the outset of the representation and communicated to the client, preferably in writing. See Rule 1.2(c). Subject to such limitations, each client in a common representation has the right to loyal and diligent representation and to the protection of Rule 1.9 concerning the obligations to a former client. Each client also has the right to discharge the lawyer as stated in Rule 1.16.

Informed Consent (1.7)

[29] Informed consent requires that each affected client be aware of the relevant circumstances and of the material and reasonably foreseeable ways that a conflict could have adverse effects on the interests of that client. See Rule 1.0(f). The information required depends on the nature of the conflict and the nature of the risks involved. When representation of multiple clients in a single matter is undertaken, the information must include the advantages and risks of the common representation, including possible effects on loyalty, confidentiality, and the attorney-client privilege.

Explaining the Advantages and Risks of Common Representation

[30] Under some circumstances it may be impossible to make the disclosure necessary to obtain consent. For example, when the lawyer represents different clients in related matters and one of the clients refuses to consent to the disclosure necessary to permit the other client to make an informed decision, the lawyer cannot properly ask the latter to consent.

Consent Confirmed in Writing (1.7)

[31] Division (b)(2) requires the lawyer to obtain the informed consent of the client, confirmed in writing. Such a writing may consist of a document signed by the client or one that the lawyer promptly records and transmits to the client following an oral consent. See Rule 1.0(b) and (p) (writing includes electronic transmission). If it is not feasible to obtain or transmit the writing at the time the client gives informed consent, then the lawyer must obtain or transmit it within a reasonable time thereafter. See Rule 1.0(b). Written confirmation of consent does not supplant the need, in most cases, for the lawyer to talk with the client: (1) to explain the risks and advantages, if any, of representation

burdened with a conflict of interest, as well as reasonably available alternatives; and (2) to afford the client a reasonable opportunity to consider the risks and alternatives and to raise questions and concerns. The writing is required in order to impress upon clients the seriousness of the decision the client is being asked to make and to avoid disputes or ambiguities that might later occur in the absence of written consent.

Revoking Consent (1.7)

Revoking Consent

[32] A client who has given consent to a conflict may revoke the consent and, like any other client, may terminate the lawyer's representation at any time. Whether revoking consent to the client's own representation precludes the lawyer from continuing to represent other clients depends on the circumstances, including the nature of the conflict, whether the client revoked consent because of a material change in circumstances, the reasonable expectations of the other clients and whether material detriment to the other clients or the lawyer would result.

Consent to Future Conflict (1.7)

[33] Whether a lawyer may properly request a client to waive conflicts that might arise in the future is subject to the test of division (b). The effectiveness of such waivers is generally determined by the extent to which the client reasonably understands the material risks that the waiver entails. The more comprehensive the explanation of representations that might arise and the actual and reasonably foreseeable adverse consequences of those representations, the greater the likelihood that the client will have the requisite understanding. Thus, if the client agrees to consent to a particular type of conflict with which the client is already familiar, then the consent ordinarily will be effective with regard to that type of conflict. If the consent is general and open-ended, then the consent ordinarily will be ineffective, except when it is reasonably likely that the client will have understood the material risks involved. Such exceptional circumstances might be presented if the client is an experienced user of the legal services involved and is reasonably informed regarding the risk that a conflict may arise, particularly if the client is independently represented by other counsel in giving consent and the consent is limited to future conflicts unrelated to the subject of the representation. In any case, advance consent cannot be effective if the circumstances that materialize in the future are such as would make a waiver prohibited under division (b).

Prohibited Representations (1.7)

Nonconsentable/ Nonwaivable Conflicts

[34] Often, clients may be asked to consent to representation notwithstanding a conflict. However, as indicated in divisions (c)(1) and (2) some conflicts cannot be waived as a matter of law, and the lawyer involved cannot properly ask for such agreement or provide representation on the basis of the client's consent.

[35] Before requesting a conflict waiver from one or more clients in regard to a matter, a lawyer must determine whether either division (c)(1) or (2) bars the representation, regardless of waiver.

Conflicts in Marital Separation Agreements

[36] As provided by division (c)(1), certain conflicts cannot be waived as a matter of law. For example, the Supreme Court of Ohio has ruled that regardless of client consent, a lawyer may not represent both husband and wife in the preparation of a separation agreement. [*Columbus Bar Assn v. Grelle* (1968), 14 Ohio St.2d 208] Similarly, federal criminal statutes prohibit certain representations by a former government lawyer, despite the informed consent of the former client.

[37] Division (c)(2) bars representation, in the same proceeding, of clients who are directly adverse because of the institutional interest in vigorous development of each client's position. A lawyer may not represent both a claimant and the party against whom the claim is asserted whether in proceedings before a tribunal or in negotiations or mediation of a claim pending before a tribunal.

[38] Division (c)(2) does not address all nonconsentable conflicts. Some conflicts are nonconsentable because a lawyer cannot represent both clients competently and diligently or both clients cannot give informed consent. For example, a lawyer may not represent multiple parties to a negotiation whose interests are fundamentally antagonistic, regardless of their consent.

Rule 1.8: Conflict of interest: current clients: specific rules

Lawyers Entering Business Transactions with Clients

(a) A lawyer shall not enter into a business transaction with a client or knowingly acquire an ownership, possessory, security, or other pecuniary interest adverse to a client unless all of the following apply:

(1) the transaction and terms on which the lawyer acquires the interest are fair and reasonable to the client and are fully disclosed to the client in writing in a manner that can be reasonably understood by the client;

(2) the client is advised in writing of the desirability of seeking and is given a reasonable opportunity to seek the advice of independent legal counsel on the transaction;

(3) the client gives informed consent, in a writing signed by the client, to the essential terms of the transaction and the lawyer's role in the transaction, including whether the lawyer is representing the client in the transaction.

(b) Except as permitted or required by these rules, a lawyer shall not use information relating to representation of a client to the disadvantage of the client unless the client gives informed consent.

(c) A lawyer shall not solicit any substantial gift from a client. A lawyer shall not prepare on behalf of a client an instrument giving the lawyer, the lawyer's partner, associate, paralegal, law clerk, or other employee of the lawyer's firm, a lawyer acting "of counsel" in the lawyer's firm, or a person related to the lawyer any gift unless the lawyer or other recipient of the gift is related to the client. For purposes of division (c) of this rule:

Gifts from a Client to a Lawyer or Paralegal

(1) "person related to the lawyer" includes a spouse, child, grandchild, parent, grandparent, sibling, or other relative or individual with whom the lawyer or the client maintains a close, familial relationship;
(2) "gift" includes a testamentary gift. [emphasis added]

(d) Prior to the conclusion of representation of a client, a lawyer shall not make or negotiate an agreement giving the lawyer literary or media rights to a portrayal or account based in substantial part on information relating to the representation.

Media Rights to a Client's Story

(e) A lawyer shall not provide financial assistance to a client in connection with pending or contemplated litigation, except that a lawyer may do either of the following:

Advancing Court Costs and Expenses of Litigation to a Client

(1) a lawyer may advance court costs and expenses of litigation, the repayment of which may be contingent on the outcome of the matter;
(2) a lawyer representing an indigent client may pay court costs and expenses of litigation on behalf of the client.

(f) A lawyer shall not accept compensation for representing a client from someone other than the client unless divisions (f)(1) to (3) and, if applicable, division (f)(4) apply:

(1) the client gives informed consent;
(2) there is no interference with the lawyer's independence of professional judgment or with the client-lawyer relationship;
(3) information relating to representation of a client is protected as required by Rule 1.6;
(4) if the lawyer is compensated by an insurer to represent an insured, the lawyer delivers a copy of the following Statement of Insured Client's Rights to the client in person at the first meeting or by mail within ten days after the lawyer receives notice of retention by the insurer:

Lawyer Retained by an Insurance Company to Represent a Client

Statement of Insured Client's Rights (1.8)

An insurance company has retained a lawyer to defend a lawsuit or claim against you. This Statement of Insured Client's Rights is being given to you to assure that you are aware of your rights regarding your legal representation.

1. Your Lawyer: Your lawyer has been retained by the insurance company under the terms of your policy. If you have questions about the selection of the lawyer, you should discuss the matter with the insurance company or the lawyer.

2. Directing the Lawyer: Your policy may provide that the insurance company can reasonably control the defense of the lawsuit. In addition, your insurance company may establish guidelines governing how lawyers are to proceed in defending you—guidelines that you are entitled to know. However, the lawyer cannot act on the insurance company's instructions when they are contrary to your interest.

3. Communications: Your lawyer should keep you informed about your case and respond to your reasonable requests for information.

4. Confidentiality: Lawyers have a duty to keep secret the confidential information a client provides, subject to limited exceptions. However, the lawyer chosen to represent you also may have duty to share with the insurance company information relating to the defense or settlement of the claim. Whenever a waiver of lawyer-client confidentiality is needed, your lawyer has a duty to consult with you and obtain your informed consent.

5. Release of Information for Audits: Some insurance companies retain auditing companies to review the billing and files of the lawyers they hire to represent policyholders. If the lawyer believes an audit, bill review, or other action initiated by the insurance company may release confidential information in a manner that may be contrary to your interest, the lawyer must advise you regarding the matter and provide an explanation of the purpose of the audit and the procedure involved. Your written consent must be given in order for an audit to be conducted. If you withhold your consent, the audit shall not be conducted.

Audit of a Lawyer's Bill

6. Conflicts of Interest: The lawyer is responsible for identifying conflicts of interest and advising you of them. If at any time you have a concern about a conflict of interest in your case, you should discuss your concern with the lawyer. If a conflict of interest exists that cannot be resolved, the insurance company may be required to provide you with another lawyer.

7. Settlement: Many insurance policies state that the insurance company alone may make a decision regarding settlement of a claim. Some policies, however, require your consent. You should discuss with your lawyer your rights under the policy regarding settlement. No settlement requiring you to pay money in excess of your policy limits can be reached without your agreement.

8. Fees and Costs: As provided in your insurance policy, the insurance company usually pays all of the fees and costs of defending the claim. If you are responsible for paying the lawyer any fees and costs, your lawyer must promptly inform you of that.

9. Hiring your own Lawyer: The lawyer hired by the insurance company is only representing you in defending the claim brought against you. If you desire to pursue a claim against someone, you will need to hire your own lawyer. You may also wish to hire your own lawyer if there is a risk that there might be a judgment entered against you for more than the amount of your insurance. Your lawyer has a duty to inform you of this risk and other reasonably foreseeable adverse results.

Settlements Involving Multiple Clients

(g) A lawyer who represents two or more clients shall not participate in making an aggregate settlement of the claims of or against the clients, or in a criminal case an aggregated agreement as to guilty or nolo contendere pleas, unless the settlement or agreement is subject to court approval or each client gives informed consent, in a writing signed by the client. The lawyer's disclosure shall include the existence and nature of all the claims or pleas involved and of the participation of each person in the settlement or agreement.

A Lawyer's Attempt to Limit His or Her Own Malpractice Liability

(h) A lawyer shall not do any of the following:

(1) make an agreement prospectively limiting the lawyer's liability to a client for malpractice or requiring arbitration of a claim against the lawyer unless the client is independently represented in making the agreement;

(2) settle a claim or potential claim for such liability unless all of the following apply:

Settlement Agreements

(i) the settlement is not unconscionable, inequitable, or unfair;

(ii) the client or former client is advised in writing of the desirability of seeking and is given a reasonable opportunity to seek the advice of independent legal counsel in connection therewith;

(iii) the client or former client gives informed consent.

(i) A lawyer shall not acquire a proprietary interest in the cause of action or subject matter of litigation the lawyer is conducting for a client, except that the lawyer may do either of the following:

Lien to Secure Payment of Fees

(1) acquire a lien authorized by law to secure the lawyer's fee or expenses;

(2) contract with a client for a reasonable contingent fee in a civil case.

Sex Between Lawyer and Client

(j) A lawyer shall not solicit or engage in sexual activity with a client unless a consensual sexual relationship existed between them when the client-lawyer relationship commenced.

(k) While lawyers are associated in a firm, a prohibition in divisions (a) to (i) of this rule that applies to any one of them shall apply to all of them.

Comment on Rule 1.8

Business Transactions: Client and Lawyer (1.8)

Lawyers Entering Business Transactions with Clients

[1] A lawyer's legal skill and training, together with the relationship of trust and confidence between lawyer and client, create the possibility of overreaching when the lawyer participates in a business, property or financial transaction with a client, for example, a loan or sales transaction or a lawyer investment on behalf of a client. The requirements of division (a) must be met even when the transaction is not closely related to the subject matter of the representation, as when a lawyer drafting a will for a client learns that the client needs money for unrelated expenses and offers to make a loan to the client. The rule applies to lawyers engaged in the sale of goods or services related to the practice of law, for example, the sale of title insurance or investment services to existing clients of the lawyer's legal practice. See Rule 5.7. It also applies to lawyers purchasing property from estates they represent. It does not apply to ordinary fee arrangements between client and lawyer, which are governed by Rule 1.5, although its requirements must be met when the lawyer accepts an interest in the client's business or other nonmonetary property as payment of all or part of a fee. In addition, the rule does not apply to standard commercial transactions between the lawyer and the client for products or services that the client generally markets to others, for example,

banking or brokerage services, medical services, products manufactured or distributed by the client, and utilities' services. In such transactions, the lawyer has no advantage in dealing with the client, and the restrictions in division (a) are unnecessary and impracticable.

[2] Division (a)(1) requires that the transaction itself be fair to the client and that its essential terms be communicated to the client, in writing, in a manner that can be reasonably understood. Division (a)(2) requires that the client also be advised, in writing, of the desirability of seeking the advice of independent legal counsel. It also requires that the client be given a reasonable opportunity to obtain such advice. Division (a)(3) requires that the lawyer obtain the client's informed consent, in a writing signed by the client, both to the essential terms of the transaction and to the lawyer's role. When necessary, the lawyer should discuss both the material risks of the proposed transaction, including any risk presented by the lawyer's involvement, and the existence of reasonably available alternatives and should explain why the advice of independent legal counsel is desirable. See Rule 1.0(f) (definition of informed consent).

Seeking the Advice of Independent Legal Counsel

[3] The risk to a client is greatest when the client expects the lawyer to represent the client in the transaction itself or when the lawyer's financial interest otherwise poses a significant risk that the lawyer's representation of the client will be materially limited by the lawyer's financial interest in the transaction. Here the lawyer's role requires that the lawyer must comply, not only with the requirements of division (a), but also with the requirements of Rule 1.7. Under that rule, the lawyer must disclose the risks associated with the lawyer's dual role as both legal adviser and participant in the transaction, such as the risk that the lawyer will structure the transaction or give legal advice in a way that favors the lawyer's interests at the expense of the client. Moreover, the lawyer must obtain the client's informed consent. In some cases, the lawyer's interest may be such that Rule 1.7 will preclude the lawyer from seeking the client's consent to the transaction.

[4] If the client is independently represented in the transaction, division (a)(2) of this rule is inapplicable, and the division (a)(1) requirement for full disclosure is satisfied either by a written disclosure by the lawyer involved in the transaction or by the client's independent counsel. The fact that the client was independently represented in the transaction is relevant in determining whether the agreement was fair and reasonable to the client as division (a)(1) further requires.

Use of Information Related to Representation (1.8)

[5] Use of information relating to the representation to the disadvantage of the client violates the lawyer's duty of loyalty. See also Rule 1.9(b). Division (b) applies whether or not the information is used to benefit either the lawyer or a third person, such as another client or business associate of the lawyer. For example, if a lawyer learns that a client intends to purchase and develop several parcels of land, the lawyer may not use that information to purchase one of the parcels in competition with the client or to recommend that another client make such a purchase. The rule does not prohibit uses that do not disadvantage the client. For example, a lawyer who learns a government agency's interpretation of a land-use regulation during the representation of one client may properly use that information to benefit other clients. Division (b) prohibits disadvantageous use of client information unless the client gives informed consent, except as permitted or required by these rules. See Rules 1.2(d), 1.6, 1.9(c), 3.3, 4.1(b), 8.1, and 8.3.

Using Client Information for the Lawyer's Personal Benefit

Gifts to Lawyers (1.8)

[6] A lawyer may accept a gift from a client, if the transaction meets general standards of fairness. For example, a simple gift such as a present given at a holiday or as a token of appreciation is permitted. If a client offers the lawyer a more substantial gift, division (c) does not prohibit the lawyer from accepting it, although such a gift may be voidable by the client under the doctrine of undue influence, which treats client gifts as presumptively fraudulent. In any event, due to concerns about overreaching and imposition on clients, a lawyer may not suggest that a substantial gift be made to the lawyer or for the lawyer's benefit, except where the lawyer is related to the client as set forth in division (c).

[7] If effectuation of a gift requires preparing a legal instrument such as a will or conveyance the client should have the detached advice that another lawyer can provide. The sole exception to this rule is where the client is a relative of the donee.

[8] This rule does not prohibit a lawyer from seeking to have the lawyer or a partner or associate of the lawyer named as executor of the client's estate or to another potentially lucrative fiduciary position. Nevertheless, such appointments will be subject to the general conflict of interest provision in Rule 1.7 when there is a significant risk that the lawyer's interest in obtaining the appointment will materially limit the lawyer's independent professional judgment in advising the client concerning the choice of an executor or other fiduciary. In obtaining the client's informed consent to the conflict, the lawyer should advise the client concerning the nature and extent of the lawyer's

Lawyer as Executor

financial interest in the appointment, as well as the availability of alternative candidates for the position.

Literary Rights (1.8)

[9] An agreement by which a lawyer acquires literary or media rights concerning the conduct of the representation creates a conflict between the interests of the client and the personal interests of the lawyer. Measures suitable in the representation of the client may detract from the publication value of an account of the representation. Division (d) does not prohibit a lawyer representing a client in a transaction concerning literary property from agreeing that the lawyer's fee shall consist of a share in ownership in the property, if the arrangement conforms to Rule 1.5 and divisions (a) and (i).

Media Rights to a Client's Story

Financial Assistance (1.8)

[10] Lawyers may not subsidize lawsuits or administrative proceedings brought on behalf of their clients, including making or guaranteeing loans to their clients for living expenses, because to do so would encourage clients to pursue lawsuits that might not otherwise be brought and because such assistance gives lawyers too great a financial stake in the litigation. These dangers do not warrant a prohibition on a lawyer lending a client court costs and litigation expenses, including the expenses of medical examination and the costs of obtaining and presenting evidence, because these advances are virtually indistinguishable from contingent fees and help ensure access to the courts. Similarly, an exception allowing lawyers representing indigent clients to pay court costs and litigation expenses regardless of whether these funds will be repaid is warranted.

Advancing Court Costs and Expenses of Litigation to a Client

Person Paying for a Lawyer's Services (1.8)

[11] Lawyers are frequently asked to represent a client under circumstances in which a third person will compensate the lawyer, in whole or in part. The third person might be a relative or friend, an indemnitor (such as a liability insurance company) or a co-client (such as a corporation sued along with one or more of its employees). Because third-party payers frequently have interests that differ from those of the client, including interests in minimizing the amount spent on the representation and in learning how the representation is progressing, lawyers are prohibited from accepting or continuing such representations unless the lawyer determines that there will be no interference with the lawyer's independent professional judgment and there is informed consent from the client. See also Rule 5.4(c) (prohibiting interference with a lawyer's professional judgment by one who recommends, employs, or pays the lawyer to render legal services for another).

Lawyer Retained by an Insurance Company to Represent a Client

[12] Sometimes, it will be sufficient for the lawyer to obtain the client's informed consent regarding the fact of the payment and the identity of the third-party payer. If, however, the fee arrangement creates a conflict of interest for the lawyer, then the lawyer must comply with Rule 1.7. The lawyer must also conform to the requirements of Rule 1.6 concerning confidentiality. Under Rule 1.7(a), a conflict of interest exists if there is substantial risk that the lawyer's representation of the client will be materially limited by the lawyer's own interest in the fee arrangement or by the lawyer's responsibilities to the third-party payer (for example, when the third-party payer is a co-client). Under Rule 1.7(b), the lawyer may accept or continue the representation with the informed consent of each affected client, unless the conflict is nonconsentable under that paragraph. Under Rule 1.7(b), the informed consent must be confirmed in writing.

Third-Party Payers of Fees

[12A] Divisions (f)(1) to (f)(3) apply to insurance defense counsel compensated by an insurer to defend an insured, subject to the unique aspects of that relationship. Whether employed or retained by an insurance company, insurance defense counsel owes the insured the same duties to avoid conflicts, keep confidences, exercise independent judgment, and communicate as a lawyer owes any other client. These duties are subject only to the rights of the insurer, if any, pursuant to the policy contract with its insured, to control the defense, receive information relating to the defense or settlement of the claim, and settle the case. Insurance defense counsel may not permit an insurer's right to control the defense to compromise the lawyer's independent judgment, for example, regarding the legal research or factual investigation necessary to support the defense. The lawyer may not permit an insurer's right to receive information to result in the disclosure to the insurer, or its agent, of confidences of the insured. The insured's consent to the insurer's payment of defense counsel, required by Rule 1.8(f)(1), can be inferred from the policy contract. Nevertheless, an insured may not understand how defense counsel's relationship with and duties to the insurer will affect the representation. Therefore, to ensure that such consent is informed, these rules require a lawyer who undertakes defense of an insured at the expense of an insurer to provide to the client insured, at the commencement of representation, the "Statement of Insured Client's Rights."

Insurance Company Interference

Aggregate Settlements (1.8)

[13] Differences in willingness to make or accept an offer of settlement are among the risks of common representation of multiple clients by a single lawyer. Under Rule 1.7, this is one of the risks that should be discussed before undertaking the representation, as part of the process of obtaining the clients' informed consent. In addition, Rule 1.2(a) protects each client's right to have the final say in deciding whether to accept or reject an offer of settlement and in deciding whether to enter a guilty or nolo contendere plea in a criminal case. The rule stated in this paragraph is a corollary of both these rules and provides that, before any settlement offer or plea bargain is made or accepted on behalf of multiple clients, the lawyer must inform each of them about all the material terms of the settlement, including what the other clients will receive or pay if the settlement or plea offer is accepted. See also Rule 1.0(f) (definition of informed consent). Alternatively, where a settlement is subject to court approval, as in a class action, the interests of multiple clients are protected when the lawyer complies with applicable rules of civil procedure and orders of the court concerning review of the settlement.

Settlements Involving Multiple Clients

Limiting Liability: Settling Malpractice Claims (1.8)

[14] Agreements prospectively limiting a lawyer's liability for malpractice are prohibited unless the client is independently represented in making the agreement because they are likely to undermine competent and diligent representation. Also, many clients are unable to evaluate the desirability of making such an agreement before a dispute has arisen, particularly if they are then represented by the lawyer seeking the agreement. Division (h)(1) also prohibits a lawyer from prospectively entering into an agreement with the client to arbitrate any claim unless the client is independently represented. This division, however, does not limit the ability of lawyers to practice in the form of a limited-liability entity, where permitted by law, provided that each lawyer remains personally liable to the client for his or her own conduct and the firm complies with any conditions required by law, such as provisions requiring client notification or maintenance of adequate liability insurance. Nor does it prohibit an agreement in accordance with Rule 1.2 that defines the scope of the representation, although a definition of scope that makes the obligations of representation illusory will amount to an attempt to limit liability.

A Lawyer's Attempt to Limit His or Her own Malpractice Liability

[15] Agreements settling a claim or a potential claim for malpractice are not prohibited by this rule. However, the settlement may not be unconscionable, inequitable, or unfair, and, in view of the danger that a lawyer will take unfair advantage of an unrepresented client or former client, the lawyer must first advise such a person in writing of the appropriateness of independent representation in connection with such a settlement. In addition, the lawyer must give the client or former client a reasonable opportunity to find and consult independent counsel.

Acquiring Proprietary Interest in Litigation (1.8)

[16] Division (i) states the traditional general rule that lawyers are prohibited from acquiring a proprietary interest in litigation. Like division (e), the general rule has its basis in common law champerty and maintenance and is designed to avoid giving the lawyer too great an interest in the representation. In addition, when the lawyer acquires an ownership interest in the subject of the representation, it will be more difficult for a client to discharge the lawyer if the client so desires. The rule is subject to specific exceptions developed in decisional law and continued in these rules. The exception for certain advances of the costs of litigation is set forth in division (e). In addition, division (i) sets forth exceptions for liens authorized by law to secure the lawyer's fees or expenses and contracts for reasonable contingent fees. The law of each jurisdiction determines which liens are authorized by law. These may include liens granted by statute, liens originating in common law and liens acquired by contract with the client. When a lawyer acquires by contract a security interest in property other than that recovered through the lawyer's efforts in the litigation, such an acquisition is a business or financial transaction with a client and is governed by the requirements of division (a). Contracts for contingent fees in civil cases are governed by Rule 1.5.

Champerty and Maintenance

Client-Lawyer Sexual Relationships (1.8)

[17] The relationship between lawyer and client is a fiduciary one in which the lawyer occupies the highest position of trust and confidence. The relationship is almost always unequal; thus, a sexual relationship between lawyer and client can involve unfair exploitation of the lawyer's fiduciary role, in violation of the lawyer's basic ethical obligation not to use the trust of the client to the client's disadvantage. In addition, such a relationship presents a significant danger that, because of the lawyer's emotional involvement, the lawyer will be unable to represent the client without impairment of the exercise of independent professional judgment. Moreover, a blurred line between the professional and personal relationships may make it difficult to predict to what extent client confidences

Sex Between Lawyer and Client

will be protected by the attorney-client evidentiary privilege, since client confidences are protected by privilege only when they are imparted in the context of the client-lawyer relationship. Because of the significant danger of harm to client interests and because the client's own emotional involvement renders it unlikely that the client could give adequate informed consent, this rule prohibits the lawyer from engaging in sexual activity with a client regardless of whether the relationship is consensual and regardless of the absence of prejudice to the client, unless the sexual relationship predates the client-lawyer relationship. A lawyer also is prohibited from soliciting a sexual relationship with a client.

[18] Sexual relationships that predate the client-lawyer relationship are not prohibited. Issues relating to the exploitation of the fiduciary relationship and client dependency are diminished when the sexual relationship existed prior to the commencement of the client-lawyer relationship. However, before proceeding with the representation in these circumstances, the lawyer should consider whether the lawyer's ability to represent the client will be materially limited by the relationship. See Rule 1.7(a)(2).

[19] When the client is an organization, division (j) of this rule prohibits a lawyer for the organization (whether inside counsel or outside counsel) from having a sexual relationship with a constituent of the organization who supervises, directs, or regularly consults with that lawyer concerning the organization's legal matters.

Imputation of Prohibitions (1.8)

[20] Under division (k), a prohibition on conduct by an individual lawyer in divisions (a) to (i) also applies to all lawyers associated in a firm with the personally prohibited lawyer. For example, one lawyer in a firm may not enter into a business transaction with a client of another member of the firm without complying with division (a), even if the first lawyer is not personally involved in the representation of the client. The prohibition set forth in division (j) is personal and is not applied to associated lawyers.

Prohibitions Imputed to All Members of the Law Firm

Rule 1.9: Duties to former clients

(a) Unless the former client gives informed consent, confirmed in writing, a lawyer who has formerly represented a client in a matter shall not thereafter represent another person in the same or a substantially related matter in which that person's interests are materially adverse to the interests of the former client.

Former Clients and Substantially Related Matters

(b) Unless the former client gives informed consent, confirmed in writing, a lawyer shall not knowingly represent a person in the same or a substantially related matter in which a firm with which the lawyer formerly was associated had previously represented a client where both of the following apply:

Materially Adverse Interests

(1) the interests of the client are materially adverse to that person;
(2) the lawyer had acquired information about the client that is protected by Rules 1.6 and 1.9(c) and material to the matter.

(c) A lawyer who has formerly represented a client in a matter or whose present or former firm has formerly represented a client in a matter shall not thereafter do either of the following:

(1) use information relating to the representation to the disadvantage of the former client except as these rules would permit or require with respect to a client or when the information has become generally known;
(2) reveal information relating to the representation except as these rules would permit or require with respect to a client.

Using Information to the Disadvantage of a Former Client

Comment on Rule 1.9

[1] After termination of a client-lawyer relationship, a lawyer has certain continuing duties with respect to confidentiality and conflicts of interest and thus may not represent another client except in conformity with this rule. Under this rule, for example, a lawyer could not properly seek to rescind on behalf of a new client a contract drafted on behalf of the former client. So also a lawyer who has prosecuted an accused person could not properly represent the accused in a subsequent civil action against the government concerning the same transaction. Nor could a lawyer who has represented multiple clients in a matter represent one of the clients against the others in the same or a substantially related matter after a dispute arose among the clients in that matter, unless all affected clients give informed consent, confirmed in writing. See Comment [9]. Current and former government lawyers must comply with this rule to the extent required by Rule 1.11.

[2] The scope of a "matter" for purposes of this rule depends on the facts of a particular situation or transaction. The lawyer's involvement in a matter can also be a question of degree. When a lawyer has been directly involved in a specific transaction, subsequent representation of other clients with materially adverse interests in that transaction clearly is prohibited. On the other hand, a lawyer who recurrently handled a type of problem for a former client is not precluded from later representing another client in a factually

distinct problem of that type even though the subsequent representation involves a position adverse to the prior client. Similar considerations can apply to the reassignment of military lawyers between defense and prosecution functions within the same military jurisdictions. The underlying question is whether the lawyer was so involved in the matter that the subsequent representation can be justly regarded as a changing of sides in the matter in question. For a former government lawyer, "matter" is defined in Rule 1.11(e).

Changing Sides

[3] See Rule 1.0(n) for a definition of "substantially related matter." For example, a lawyer who has represented a businessperson and learned extensive private financial information about that person may not then represent that person's spouse in seeking a divorce. Similarly, a lawyer who has previously represented a client in securing environmental permits to build a shopping center would be precluded from representing neighbors seeking to oppose rezoning of the property on the basis of environmental considerations; however, the lawyer would not be precluded, on the grounds of substantial relationship, from defending a tenant of the completed shopping center in resisting eviction for nonpayment of rent. Information that has been disclosed to the public or to other parties adverse to the former client ordinarily will not be disqualifying. Information acquired in a prior representation may have been rendered obsolete by the passage of time, a circumstance that may be relevant in determining whether two representations are substantially related. In the case of an organizational client, general knowledge of the client's policies and practices ordinarily will not preclude a subsequent representation; on the other hand, knowledge of specific facts gained in a prior representation that are relevant to the matter in question ordinarily will preclude such a representation. A former client is not required to reveal the confidential information learned by the lawyer in order to establish a substantial risk that the lawyer has confidential information to use in the subsequent matter. A conclusion about the possession of such information may be based on the nature of the services the lawyer provided the former client and information that would in ordinary practice be learned by a lawyer providing such services.

Former Client Does not have to Reveal the Specific Information to Show the Risk

Lawyers Moving Between Firms (1.9)

[4] When lawyers have been associated within a firm but then end their association, the question of whether a lawyer should undertake representation is more complicated. There are several competing considerations. First, the client previously represented by the former firm must be reasonably assured that the principle of loyalty to the client is not compromised. Second, the rule should not be so broadly cast as to preclude other persons from having reasonable choice of legal counsel. Third, the rule should not unreasonably hamper lawyers from forming new associations and taking on new clients after having left a previous association. In this connection, it should be recognized that today many lawyers practice in firms, that many lawyers to some degree limit their practice to one field or another, and that many move from one association to another several times in their careers. If the concept of imputation were applied with unqualified rigor, the result would be radical curtailment of the opportunity of lawyers to move from one practice setting to another and of the opportunity of clients to change counsel.

Switching Jobs and Conflicts of Interest

[5] Division (b) operates to disqualify the lawyer only when the lawyer involved has actual knowledge of information protected by Rules 1.6 and 1.9(c). Thus, if a lawyer while with one firm acquired no knowledge or information relating to a particular client of the firm, and that lawyer later joined another firm, neither the lawyer individually nor the second firm is disqualified from representing another client in the same or a related matter even though the interests of the two clients conflict. See Rule 1.10(b) for the restrictions on a firm once a lawyer has terminated association with the firm.

Requirement of Actual Knowledge

[6] Application of division (b) depends on a situation's particular facts, aided by inferences, deductions, or working presumptions that reasonably may be made about the way in which lawyers work together. A lawyer may have general access to files of all clients of a law firm and may regularly participate in discussions of their affairs; it should be inferred that such a lawyer in fact is privy to all information about all the firm's clients. In contrast, another lawyer may have access to the files of only a limited number of clients and participate in discussions of the affairs of no other clients; in the absence of information to the contrary, it should be inferred that such a lawyer in fact is privy to information about the clients actually served but not those of other clients. In such an inquiry, the burden of proof should rest upon the lawyer whose disqualification is sought.

Access to All Files vs Access to Limited Files

[7] Independent of the question of disqualification of a firm, a lawyer changing professional association has a continuing duty to preserve confidentiality of information about a client formerly represented. See Rules 1.6 and 1.9(c).

The Continuing Duty of Confidentiality

[8] Division (c) provides that information acquired by the lawyer in the course of representing a client may not

subsequently be used or revealed by the lawyer to the disadvantage of the client. However, the fact that a lawyer has once served a client does not preclude the lawyer from using generally known information about that client when later representing another client.

Generally Known Information

[9] The provisions of this rule are for the protection of former clients and can be waived if the client gives informed consent, which consent must be confirmed in writing under divisions (a) and (b). See Rule 1.0(f). With regard to the effectiveness of an advance waiver, see Comment [33] to Rule 1.7. With regard to disqualification of a firm with which a lawyer is or was formerly associated, see Rule 1.10.

Rule 1.10: Imputation of conflicts of interest: general rule

(a) While lawyers are associated in a firm, none of them shall represent a client when the lawyer knows or reasonably should know that any one of them practicing alone would be prohibited from doing so by Rule 1.7 or 1.9, unless the prohibition is based on a personal interest of the prohibited lawyer and does not present a significant risk of materially limiting the representation of the client by the remaining lawyers in the firm.

Imputed Disqualification

(b) When a lawyer is no longer associated with a firm, no lawyer in that firm shall thereafter represent a person with interests materially adverse to those of a client represented by the formerly associated lawyer and not currently represented by the firm, if the lawyer knows or reasonably should know that either of the following applies:

Significant Risk of Materially Limiting the Representation

(1) the formerly associated lawyer represented the client in the same or a substantially related matter;

The Same or Substantially Related Matter

(2) any lawyer remaining in the firm has information protected by Rules 1.6 and 1.9(c) that is material to the matter.

(c) When a lawyer has had substantial responsibility in a matter for a former client and becomes associated with a new firm, no lawyer in the new firm shall knowingly represent, in the same matter, a person whose interests are materially adverse to the interests of the former client.

(d) In circumstances other than those covered by Rule 1.10(c), when a lawyer becomes associated with a new firm, no lawyer in the new firm shall knowingly represent a person in a matter in which the lawyer is personally disqualified under Rule 1.9 unless both of the following apply:

(1) the new firm timely screens the personally disqualified lawyer from any participation in the matter and that lawyer is apportioned no part of the fee from that matter;

Screening to Avoid Disqualification

(2) written notice is given as soon as practicable to any affected former client.

(e) A disqualification required by this rule may be waived by the affected client under the conditions stated in Rule 1.7.

(f) The disqualification of lawyers associated in a firm with former or current government lawyers is governed by Rule 1.11.

Comment on Rule 1.10

Definition of "Firm" (1.10)

[1] For purposes of the Ohio Rules of Professional Conduct, the term "firm" denotes lawyers associated in a law partnership, professional corporation, sole proprietorship, or other association authorized to practice law; or lawyers employed in a legal services organization or the legal department of a corporation or other organization. See Rule 1.0(c). Whether two or more lawyers constitute a firm within this definition can depend on the specific facts. See Rule 1.0, Comments [2] – [4A].

Definition of a Firm in Disqualification Cases

Principles of Imputed Disqualification (1.10)

[2] The rule of imputed disqualification stated in division (a) gives effect to the principle of loyalty to the client as it applies to lawyers who practice in a law firm. Such situations can be considered from the premise that a firm of lawyers is essentially one lawyer for purposes of the rules governing loyalty to the client, or from the premise that each lawyer is vicariously bound by the obligation of loyalty owed by each lawyer with whom the lawyer is associated. Division (a) operates only among the lawyers currently associated in a firm. When a lawyer moves from one firm to another, imputation of that lawyer's conflict to the lawyers remaining in the firm is governed by Rules 1.9(b) and 1.10(b).

Imputed Disqualification

[3] The rule in division (a) does not prohibit representation where neither questions of client loyalty nor protection of confidential information are presented. Where the usual concerns justifying imputation are not present, the rule eliminates imputation in the case of conflicts between the interests of a client and a lawyer's own personal interest. Note that the specific personal conflicts governed by Rule 1.8 are imputed to the firm by Rule 1.8(k). Where one lawyer in a firm could not effectively represent a given client because of strong political beliefs,

A Lawyer's Political Beliefs and Disqualification

for example, but that lawyer will do no work on the case and the personal beliefs of the lawyer will not materially limit the representation by others in the firm, the firm should not be disqualified. On the other hand, if an opposing party in a case were owned by a lawyer in the law firm, and others in the firm would be materially limited in pursuing the matter because of loyalty to that lawyer, the personal disqualification of the lawyer would be imputed to all others in the firm.

[4] *The rule in division (a) also does not prohibit representation by others in the law firm where the person prohibited from involvement in a matter is a nonlawyer, such as a paralegal* or legal secretary. Nor does division (a) prohibit representation if the lawyer is prohibited from acting because of events before the person became a lawyer, for example, work that the person did while a law student. Such persons, however, ordinarily must be screened from any personal participation in the matter to avoid communication to others in the firm of confidential information that both the nonlawyers and the firm have a legal duty to protect. See Rules 1.0(l) and 5.3. [emphasis added]

Paralegals and Conflicts of Interest

Nonlawyer's Duty to Protect Confidential Information

[5] Rule 1.10(b) prohibits lawyers in a law firm from representing a person with interests directly adverse to those of a client represented by a lawyer who formerly was associated with the firm where the matter is the same or substantially related to that in which the formerly associated lawyer represented the client or any other lawyer currently in the firm has material information protected by Rule 1.6 or 1.9(c). "Substantially related matter" is defined in Rule 1.0(n), and examples are given in Rule 1.9, Comment [3].

Removing Imputation (1.10)

[5A] Divisions (c) and (d) address imputation to lawyers in a new firm when a personally disqualified lawyer moves from one law firm to another. Division (c) imputes the conflict of a lawyer who has had substantial responsibility in a matter to all lawyers in a law firm to which the lawyer moves and prohibits the new law firm from assuming or continuing the representation of a client in the same matter if the client's interests are materially adverse to those of the former client. Division (d) provides for removal of imputation of a former client conflict of one lawyer to a new firm in all other instances in which a personally disqualified lawyer moves from one firm to another, provided that the personally disqualified lawyer is properly screened from participation in the matter and the former client or client's counsel is given notice.

[5B] Screening is not effective to avoid imputed disqualification of other lawyers in the firm if the personally disqualified lawyer had substantial responsibility for representing the former client in the same matter in which the lawyer's new firm represents an adversary of the former client. A lawyer who was sole or lead counsel for a former client in a matter had substantial responsibility for the matter. Determining whether a lawyer's role in representing the former client was substantial in other circumstances involves consideration of such factors as the lawyer's level of responsibility in the matter, the duration of the lawyer's participation, the extent to which the lawyer advised or had personal contact with the former client and the former client's personnel, and the extent to which the lawyer was exposed to confidential information of the former client likely to be material in the matter.

Screening and Consent

[5C] Requirements for effective screening procedures are stated in Rule 1.0(l). Division (d) does not prohibit the screened lawyer from receiving compensation established by prior independent agreement, but that lawyer may not receive compensation directly related to the matter in which the lawyer is disqualified.

[5D] Notice of the screened lawyer's prior representation and that screening procedures have been employed, generally should be given as soon as practicable after the need for screening becomes apparent. When disclosure is likely to significantly injure the current client, a reasonable delay may be justified.

When Notice of Screening is Required

[5E] Screening will not remove imputation where screening is not timely undertaken, or where the circumstances provide insufficient assurance that confidential information known by the personally disqualified lawyer will remain protected. Factors to be considered in deciding whether an effective screen has been created are the size and structure of the firm, the likelihood of contact between the disqualified lawyer and lawyers involved in the current representation, and the existence of safeguards or procedures that prevent the disqualified lawyer from access to information relevant to the current representation.

Factors Determining the Effectiveness of a Screen

[6] Rule 1.10(e) removes imputation with the informed consent of the affected client or former client under the conditions stated in Rule 1.7. The conditions stated in Rule 1.7 require the lawyer to determine that the lawyer can represent all affected clients competently, diligently, and loyally, that the representation is not prohibited by Rule 1.7(c), and that each affected client or former client has given informed consent to the representation, confirmed in writing. In some cases, the risk may be so severe that the conflict may not be cured by client consent. For a discussion of

Curing the Conflict by Client Consent

the effectiveness of client waivers of conflicts that might arise in the future, see Rule 1.7, Comment [33]. For a definition of informed consent, see Rule 1.0(f).

[7] Where a lawyer has joined a private firm after having represented the government, imputation is governed by Rule 1.11(b) and (c), not this rule. Under Rule 1.11(d), where a lawyer represents the government after having served clients in private practice, nongovernmental employment or in another government agency, former-client conflicts are not imputed to government lawyers associated with the individually disqualified lawyer.

[8] Where a lawyer is prohibited from engaging in certain transactions under Rule 1.8, division (k) of that rule, and not this rule, determines whether that prohibition also applies to other lawyers associated in a firm with the personally prohibited lawyer.

Rule 1.11: Special conflicts of interest for former and current government officers and employees. . . .

Rule 1.12: Former judge, arbitrator, mediator, or other third-party neutral. . . .

Rule 1.13: Organization as client

(a) A lawyer employed or retained by an organization represents the organization acting through its constituents. A lawyer employed or retained by an organization owes allegiance to the organization and not to any constituent or other person connected with the organization. The constituents of an organization include its owners and its duly authorized officers, directors, trustees, and employees.

Corporations and Other Organizations as Clients

(b) If a lawyer for an organization knows or reasonably should know that its constituent's action, intended action, or refusal to act (1) violates a legal obligation to the organization, or (2) is a violation of law that reasonably might be imputed to the organization and that is likely to result in substantial injury to the organization, then the lawyer shall proceed as is necessary in the best interest of the organization. When it is necessary to enable the organization to address the matter in a timely and appropriate manner, the lawyer shall refer the matter to higher authority, including, if warranted by the circumstances, the highest authority that can act on behalf of the organization under applicable law.

Reporting Matters Up the Chain of Command within the Organization

(c) The discretion or duty of a lawyer for an organization to reveal information relating to the representation outside the organization is governed by Rule 1.6 (b) and (c).

(d) In dealing with an organization's directors, officers, employees, members, shareholders, or other constituents, a lawyer shall explain the identity of the client when the lawyer knows or reasonably should know that the organization's interests are adverse to those of the constituents with whom the lawyer is dealing.

(e) A lawyer representing an organization may also represent any of its directors, officers, employees, members, shareholders, or other constituents, subject to the provisions of Rule 1.7. If the organization's written consent to the dual representation is required by Rule 1.7, the consent shall be given by an appropriate official of the organization, other than the individual who is to be represented, or by the shareholders.

Comment on Rule 1.13

The Entity as the Client (1.13)

[1] An organizational client is a legal entity, but it cannot act except through its officers, directors, employees, shareholders, and other constituents. "Other constituents" as used in this rule and comment means the positions equivalent to officers, directors, employees, and shareholders held by persons acting for organizational clients that are not corporations. The duties defined in this rule apply equally to unincorporated associations.

[2] When one of the constituents of an organizational client communicates with the organization's lawyer in that person's organizational capacity, the lawyer must keep the communication confidential as to persons other than the organizational client as required by Rule 1.6. Thus, by way of example, if an organizational client requests its lawyer to investigate allegations of wrongdoing, interviews made in the course of that investigation between the lawyer and the client's employees or other constituents are covered by Rule 1.6. This does not mean, however, that constituents of an organizational client are the clients of the lawyer. The lawyer may disclose to the organizational client a communication related to the representation that a constituent made to the lawyer, but the lawyer may not disclose such information to others except for disclosures explicitly or impliedly authorized by the organizational client in order to carry out the representation or as otherwise permitted by Rule 1.6.

Confidentiality within a Corporation or Other Organization

[3] Division (b) explains when a lawyer may have an obligation to report "up the ladder" within an organization as part of discharging the lawyer's duty to communicate with the organizational client. When constituents of the organization make decisions for it, their decisions ordinarily must be accepted by the lawyer

Reporting Matters Up the Chain of Command within the Organization

even if their utility or prudence is doubtful. Decisions concerning policy and operations, including ones entailing serious risk, are not as such in the lawyer's province. Division (b) makes clear, however, that when the lawyer knows or reasonably should know that the organization is likely to be substantially injured by action of an officer or other constituent that violates a legal obligation to the organization or is a violation of law that might be imputed to the organization, the lawyer must proceed as is reasonably necessary in the best interest of the organization. As defined in Rule 1.0(g), knowledge can be inferred from circumstances, and a lawyer cannot ignore the obvious.

[4] In determining whether "up-the-ladder" reporting is required under division (b), the lawyer should give due consideration to the seriousness of the violation and its consequences, the responsibility in the organization and the apparent motivation of the person involved, the policies of the organization concerning such matters, and any other relevant considerations. In some circumstances, referral to a higher authority may be unnecessary; for example, if the circumstances involve a constituent's innocent misunderstanding of the law and subsequent acceptance of the lawyer's advice. In contrast, if a constituent persists in conduct contrary to the lawyer's advice, or if the matter is of sufficient seriousness and importance or urgency to the organization, whether or not the lawyer has not communicated with the constituent, it will be necessary for the lawyer to take steps to have the matter reviewed by a higher authority in the organization. Any measures taken should, to the extent practicable, minimize the risk of revealing information relating to the representation to persons outside the organization. Even in circumstances where a lawyer is not obligated by Rule 1.13 to proceed, a lawyer may bring to the attention of an organizational client, including its highest authority, matters that the lawyer reasonably believes to be of sufficient importance to warrant doing so in the best interests of the organization.

Reporting Matters to the Board of Directors

[5] Division (b) also makes clear that, if warranted by the circumstances, a lawyer must refer a matter to the highest authority that can act on behalf of the organization under applicable law. The organization's highest authority to whom a matter may be referred ordinarily will be the board of directors or similar governing body. However, applicable law may prescribe that under certain conditions the highest authority reposes elsewhere, for example, in the independent directors of a corporation.

Relation to Other Rules (1.13)

[6] Division (c) makes clear that a lawyer for an organization has the same discretion and obligation to reveal information relating to the representation to persons outside the client as any other lawyer, as provided in Rule 1.6(b) and (c) (which incorporates Rules 3.3 and 4.1 by reference). As stated in Comment [14] to Rule 1.6, where practicable, before revealing information, the lawyer should first seek to persuade the client to take suitable action to obviate the need for disclosure. Even where such consultation is not practicable, the lawyer should consider whether giving notice to a higher authority within the organization of the lawyer's intent to disclose confidential information pursuant to Rule 1.6(b) or Rule 1.6(c) would advance or interfere with the purpose of the disclosure.

Government Agency (1.13)

[9] The duty to "report up the ladder" defined in this rule also applies to lawyers for governmental organizations. Defining precisely the identity of the client and prescribing the resulting obligations of such lawyers may be more difficult in the government context and is a matter beyond the scope of these rules. . . .

Clarifying the Lawyer's Role (1.13)

Conflict of Interest with a Constituent of the Organization

[10] There are times when the organization's interest may be or become adverse to those of one or more of its constituents. In such circumstances the lawyer should advise any constituent, whose interest the lawyer finds adverse to that of the organization, of the conflict or potential conflict of interest, that the lawyer cannot represent such constituent, and that such person may wish to obtain independent representation. Care must be taken to ensure that the individual understands that, when there is such adversity of interest, the lawyer for the organization cannot provide legal representation for that constituent individual, and that discussions between the lawyer for the organization and the individual may not be privileged.

[11] Whether such a warning should be given by the lawyer for the organization to any constituent individual may turn on the facts of each case.

Dual Representation (1.13)

[12] Division (e) recognizes that a lawyer for an organization may also represent one or more constituents of an organization, if the conditions of Rule 1.7 are satisfied.

Derivative Actions (1.13)

Conflict of Interest Involving a Shareholder's Derivative Suit

[13] Under generally prevailing law, the shareholders or members of a corporation may bring suit to compel the directors to

perform their legal obligations in the supervision of the organization. Members of unincorporated associations have essentially the same right. Such an action may be brought nominally by the organization, but usually is, in fact, a legal controversy over management of the organization.

[14] The question can arise whether counsel for the organization may defend such an action. The proposition that the organization is the lawyer's client does not alone resolve the issue. Most derivative actions are a normal incident of an organization's affairs, to be defended by the organization's lawyer like any other suit. However, if the claim involves serious charges of wrongdoing by those in control of the organization, a conflict may arise between the lawyer's duty to the organization and the lawyer's relationship with the board. In those circumstances, Rule 1.7 governs who should represent the directors and the organization.

Rule 1.14: Client with diminished capacity

(a) When a client's capacity to make adequately considered decisions in connection with a representation is diminished, whether because of minority, mental impairment or for some other reason, the lawyer shall, as far as reasonably possible, maintain a normal client-lawyer relationship with the client.

Clients who are Minors or who Suffer from Diminished Mental Capacity

(b) When the lawyer reasonably believes that the client has diminished capacity, is at risk of substantial physical, financial, or other harm unless action is taken, and cannot adequately act in the client's own interest, the lawyer may take reasonably necessary protective action, including consulting with individuals or entities that have the ability to take action to protect the client and, in appropriate cases, seeking the appointment of a guardian *ad litem,* conservator, or guardian.

(c) Information relating to the representation of a client with diminished capacity is protected by Rule 1.6. When taking protective action pursuant to division (b), the lawyer is impliedly authorized under Rule 1.6 (a) to reveal information about the client, but only to the extent reasonably necessary to protect the client's interests.

Comment on Rule 1.14

[1] The normal client-lawyer relationship is based on the assumption that the client, when properly advised and assisted, is capable of making decisions about important matters. When the client is a minor or suffers from a diminished mental capacity, however, maintaining the ordinary client-lawyer relationship may not be possible in all respects. In particular, a severely incapacitated person may have no power to make legally binding decisions. Nevertheless, a client with diminished capacity often has the ability to understand, deliberate upon, and reach conclusions about matters affecting the client's own well-being. For example, children as young as five or six years of age, and certainly those of ten or twelve, are regarded as having opinions that are entitled to weight in legal proceedings concerning their custody. So also, it is recognized that some persons of advanced age can be quite capable of handling routine financial matters while needing special legal protection concerning major transactions.

Representing Clients who May be Under a Disability

[2] The fact that a client suffers a disability does not diminish the lawyer's obligation to treat the client with attention and respect. Even if the person has a legal representative, the lawyer should as far as possible accord the represented person the status of client, particularly in maintaining communication.

[3] The client may wish to have family members or other persons participate in discussions with the lawyer. When necessary to assist in the representation, the presence of such persons generally does not affect the applicability of the attorney-client evidentiary privilege. Nevertheless, the lawyer must keep the client's interests foremost and, except for protective action authorized under division (b), must look to the client, and not family members, to make decisions on the client's behalf.

Attorney-Client Privilege

[4] If a legal representative has already been appointed for the client, the lawyer should ordinarily look to the representative for decisions on behalf of the client. In matters involving a minor, whether the lawyer should look to the parents as natural guardians may depend on the type of proceeding or matter in which the lawyer is representing the minor. If the lawyer represents the guardian as distinct from the ward, and is aware that the guardian is acting adversely to the ward's interest, the lawyer may have an obligation to prevent or rectify the guardian's misconduct. See Rule 1.2(d).

Taking Protective Action (1.14)

[5] If a lawyer reasonably believes that a client is at risk of substantial physical, financial, or other harm unless action is taken, and that a normal client-lawyer relationship cannot be maintained as provided in division (a) because the client lacks sufficient capacity to communicate or to make adequately considered decisions in connection with the representation, then division (b) permits the lawyer to take protective measures deemed necessary. Such measures could include: consulting with family members; using a reconsideration period to permit clarification or improvement

Taking Special Measures to Protect a Client under a Disability

of circumstances; using voluntary surrogate decision-making tools such as durable powers of attorney; or consulting with support groups professional services, adult-protective agencies, or other individuals or entities that have the ability to protect the client. In taking any protective action, the lawyer should be guided by such factors as the wishes and values of the client to the extent known, the client's best interests, and the goals of intruding into the client's decision-making autonomy to the least extent feasible, maximizing client capacities and respecting the client's family and social connections.

[6] In determining the extent of the client's diminished capacity, the lawyer should consider and balance such factors as: the client's ability to articulate reasoning leading to a decision; variability of state of mind and ability to appreciate consequences of a decision; the substantive fairness of a decision; and the consistency of a decision with the known long-term commitments and values of the client. In appropriate circumstances, the lawyer may seek guidance from an appropriate diagnostician.

[7] If a legal representative has not been appointed, the lawyer should consider whether appointment of a guardian *ad litem,* conservator, or guardian is necessary to protect the client's interests. Thus, if a client with diminished capacity has substantial property that should be sold for the client's benefit, effective completion of the transaction may require appointment of a legal representative. In addition, rules of procedure in litigation sometimes provide that minors or persons with diminished capacity must be represented by a guardian or next friend if they do not have a general guardian. In many circumstances, however, appointment of a legal representative may be more expensive or traumatic for the client than circumstances in fact require. Evaluation of such circumstances is a matter entrusted to the professional judgment of the lawyer. In considering alternatives, however, the lawyer should be aware of any law that requires the lawyer to advocate the least restrictive action on behalf of the client.

Disclosure of the Client's Condition (1.14)

[8] Disclosure of the client's diminished capacity could adversely affect the client's interests. For example, raising the question of diminished capacity could, in some circumstances, lead to proceedings for involuntary commitment. Information relating to the representation is protected by Rule 1.6. Therefore, unless authorized to do so, the lawyer may not disclose such information. When taking protective action pursuant to division (b), the lawyer is impliedly authorized to make the necessary disclosures, even when the client directs the lawyer to the contrary. Nevertheless, given the risks of disclosure, division (c) limits what the lawyer may disclose in consulting with other individuals or entities or seeking the appointment of a legal representative. At the very least, the lawyer should determine whether it is likely that the person or entity consulted with will act adversely to the client's interests before discussing matters related to the client. The lawyer's position in such cases is an unavoidably difficult one.

Revealing Confidential Information when a Client is Under a Disability

Emergency Legal Assistance (1.14)

[9] In an emergency where the health, safety, or a financial interest of a person with seriously diminished capacity is threatened with imminent and irreparable harm, a lawyer may take legal action on behalf of such a person even though the person is unable to establish a client-lawyer relationship or to make or express considered judgments about the matter, when the person or another acting in good faith on that person's behalf has consulted with the lawyer. Even in such an emergency, however, the lawyer should not act unless the lawyer reasonably believes that the person has no other lawyer, agent, or other representative available. The lawyer should take legal action on behalf of the person only to the extent reasonably necessary to maintain the status quo or otherwise avoid imminent and irreparable harm. A lawyer who undertakes to represent a person in such an exigent situation has the same duties under these rules as the lawyer would with respect to a client.

Legal Action to Prevent Imminent and Irreparable Harm

[10] A lawyer who acts on behalf of a person with seriously diminished capacity in an emergency should keep the confidences of the person as if dealing with a client, disclosing them only to the extent necessary to accomplish the intended protective action. The lawyer should disclose to any tribunal involved and to any other counsel involved the nature of his or her relationship with the person. The lawyer should take steps to regularize the relationship or implement other protective solutions as soon as possible. Normally, a lawyer would not seek compensation for such emergency actions taken.

Rule 1.15: Safekeeping funds and property

(a) A lawyer shall hold property of clients or third persons that is in a lawyer's possession in connection with a representation separate from the lawyer's own property. Funds shall be kept in a separate interest-bearing account in a financial institution authorized to do business in Ohio and maintained in the state where the lawyer's office is situated. The account shall be designated as a "client trust account," "IOLTA

Commingling Funds Prohibited

account," or with a clearly identifiable fiduciary title. Other property shall be identified as such and appropriately safeguarded. Records of such account funds and other property shall be kept by the lawyer and shall be preserved for a period of seven years after termination of the representation or the appropriate disbursement of such funds or property, whichever comes first. For other property, the lawyer shall maintain a record that identifies the property, the date received, the person on whose behalf the property was held, and the date of distribution. For funds, the lawyer shall do all of the following:

Seven-Year Rule on Preserving Client Records

(1) maintain a copy of the fee agreement with each client;

(2) maintain a record for each client on whose behalf funds are held that sets forth all of the following:

Record-Keeping Procedures on Client Property

(i) the name of the client;

(ii) the date, amount, and source of all funds received on behalf of such client;

(iii) the date, amount, payee, and purpose of each disbursement made on behalf of such client;

(iv) the current balance for such client.

(3) maintain a record for each bank account that sets forth all of the following:

(i) the name of such account;

(ii) the date, amount, and client affected by each credit and debit;

(iii) the balance in the account.

(4) maintain all bank statements, deposit slips, and cancelled checks, if provided by the bank, for each bank account;

(5) perform and retain a monthly reconciliation of the items contained in divisions (a)(2), (3), and (4) of this rule.

(b) A lawyer may deposit the lawyer's own funds in a client trust account for the sole purpose of paying or obtaining a waiver of bank service charges on that account, but only in an amount necessary for that purpose.

(c) A lawyer shall deposit into a client trust account legal fees and expenses that have been paid in advance, to be withdrawn by the lawyer only as fees are earned or expenses incurred.

When Legal Fees Must Go into a Client Trust Account

(d) Upon receiving funds or other property in which a client or third person has an interest, a lawyer shall promptly notify the client or third person. Except as stated in this rule or otherwise permitted by law or by agreement with the client or a third person, confirmed in writing, a lawyer shall promptly deliver to the client or third person any funds or other property that the client or third person is entitled to receive. Upon request by the client or third person, the lawyer shall promptly render a full accounting regarding such funds or other property.

Notifying a Client when Property is Received

(e) When in the course of representation a lawyer is in possession of funds or other property in which two or more persons, one of whom may be the lawyer, claim interests, the lawyer shall hold the funds or other property pursuant to division (a) of this rule until the dispute is resolved. The lawyer shall promptly distribute all portions of the funds or other property as to which the interests are not in dispute. . . .

(h) A lawyer, a lawyer in the lawyer's firm, or a firm that owns an interest in a business that provides a law-related service shall:

Businesses that Provide Law-Related Services

(1) maintain funds of clients or third persons that cannot earn any net income for the clients or third persons in an interest-bearing trust account that is established in an eligible depository institution as required by sections 3953.231, 4705.09, and 4705.10 of the Revised Code or any rules adopted by the Ohio Legal Assistance Foundation pursuant to section 120.52 of the Revised Code.

(2) notify the Ohio Legal Assistance Foundation, in a manner required by rules adopted by the Ohio Legal Assistance Foundation pursuant to section 120.52 of the Revised Code, of the existence of an interest-bearing trust account;

Notifying the Ohio Legal Assistance Foundation of an Interest-Bearing Trust Account

(3) comply with the reporting requirement contained in Gov. Bar R. VI, Section 1(F).

Comment on Rule 1.15

[1] A lawyer should hold property of others with the care required of a professional fiduciary. Securities should be kept in a safe deposit box, except when some other form of safekeeping is warranted by special circumstances. All property that is the property of clients or third persons, including prospective clients, must be kept separate from the lawyer's business and personal property and, if moneys, in one or more trust accounts. A lawyer should maintain separate trust accounts when administering estate moneys. A lawyer must maintain the records listed in division (a)(1) to (5) of this rule to effectively safeguard client funds and fulfill the role of professional fiduciary. The records required by this rule may be maintained electronically.

Care Required of a Professional Fiduciary

[2] While normally it is impermissible to commingle the lawyer's own funds with client funds, division (b) provides that it is permissible when necessary to pay or obtain a waiver of bank service charges on that account. . . . Accurate records must be kept regarding which part of the funds are the lawyer's.

Permissible Commingling

[3] Lawyers often receive funds from which the lawyer's fee will be paid. The lawyer is not required to remit to the client funds that the lawyer reasonably believes represent fees owed. However, a lawyer may not hold funds to coerce a client into accepting the lawyer's contention. The disputed portion of the funds must be kept in a trust account and the lawyer should suggest means for prompt resolution of the dispute, such as arbitration. The undisputed portion of the funds shall be promptly distributed.

A Lawyer shall not hold a Client's Funds to Coerce Action by the Client

[3A] Client funds shall be deposited in a lawyer's or law firm's IOLTA account unless the lawyer determines the funds can otherwise earn income for the client in excess of the costs incurred to secure such income (*i.e.*, net income). In determining whether a client's funds can earn income in excess of costs, the lawyer or law firm should consider the following factors: (1) the amount of the funds to be deposited; (2) the expected duration of the deposit, including the likelihood of delay in the matter for which the funds are held; (3) the rates of interest or yield at the financial institutions where the funds are to be deposited; (4) the cost of establishing and administering non-IOLTA accounts for the client's benefit, including service charges, the costs of the lawyer's services, and the costs of preparing any tax reports required for income accruing to the client's benefit; (5) the capability of financial institutions, lawyers or law firms to calculate and pay income to individual clients; (6) any other circumstances that affect the ability of the client's funds to earn a net return for the client. The lawyer or law firm should review its IOLTA account at reasonable intervals to determine whether changed circumstances require action with respect to the funds of any client.

IOLTA Requirements

[4] Division (e) also recognizes that third parties may have lawful claims against specific funds or other property in a lawyer's custody, such as a client's creditor who has a lien on funds recovered in a personal injury action. A lawyer may have a duty under applicable law to protect such third-party claims against wrongful interference by the client. In such cases, when the third-party claim is not frivolous under applicable law, the lawyer must refuse to surrender the property to the client until the claims are resolved. A lawyer should not unilaterally assume to arbitrate a dispute between the client and the third party, but, when there are substantial grounds for dispute as to the person entitled to the funds, the lawyer may file an action to have a court resolve the dispute. . . .

Disputes Over Entitlement to Funds

Rule 1.16: Declining or terminating representation

(a) Subject to divisions (c), (d), and (e) of this rule, a lawyer shall not represent a client or, where representation has commenced, shall withdraw from the representation of a client if any of the following applies:

Refusing to Represent Someone; Withdrawing from Representation

(1) the representation will result in violation of the Ohio Rules of Professional Conduct or other law;
(2) the lawyer's physical or mental condition materially impairs the lawyer's ability to represent the client;
(3) the lawyer is discharged.

A Lawyer's Physical or Mental Impairment

(b) Subject to divisions (c), (d), and (e) of this rule, a lawyer may withdraw from the representation of a client if any of the following applies:

(1) withdrawal can be accomplished without material adverse effect on the interests of the client;
(2) the client persists in a course of action involving the lawyer's services that the lawyer reasonably believes is illegal or fraudulent;
(3) the client has used the lawyer's services to perpetrate a crime or fraud;
(4) the client insists upon taking action that the lawyer considers repugnant or with which the lawyer has a fundamental disagreement;
(5) the client fails substantially to fulfill an obligation, financial or otherwise, to the lawyer regarding the lawyer's services and has been given reasonable warning that the lawyer will withdraw unless the obligation is fulfilled;
(6) the representation will result in an unreasonable financial burden on the lawyer or has been rendered unreasonably difficult by the client;
(7) the client gives informed consent to termination of the representation;
(8) the lawyer sells the law practice in accordance with Rule 1.17;
(9) other good cause for withdrawal exists.

Client Seeks Something Illegal or Fraudulent

(c) If permission for withdrawal from employment is required by the rules of a tribunal, a lawyer shall not withdraw from employment in a proceeding before that tribunal without its permission.

(d) As part of the termination of representation, a lawyer shall take steps, to the extent reasonably practicable, to protect a client's interest. The steps include giving due notice to the client, allowing reasonable time for employment of other counsel, delivering to the client all papers and property to which the client is entitled, and complying with applicable laws and rules. Client papers and property shall be promptly delivered to the client. "Client papers and property" may include correspondence, pleadings, deposition transcripts, exhibits, physical evidence, expert reports, and other items reasonably necessary to the client's representation.

Turning Over Client Papers and Property

(e) A lawyer who withdraws from employment shall refund promptly any part of a fee paid in advance that has not been earned, except when withdrawal is pursuant to Rule 1.17.

Comment on Rule 1.16

[1] A lawyer shall not accept representation in a matter unless it can be performed competently, promptly, without improper conflict of interest, and to completion. Ordinarily, a representation in a matter is completed when the agreed-upon assistance has been concluded. See Rules 1.2(c) and 6.5. See also Rule 1.3, Comment [4].

Mandatory Withdrawal (1.16)

[2] A lawyer ordinarily must decline or withdraw from representation if the client demands that the lawyer engage in conduct that is illegal or violates the Ohio Rules of Professional Conduct or other law. The lawyer is not obliged to decline or withdraw simply because the client suggests such a course of conduct; a client may make such a suggestion in the hope that a lawyer will not be constrained by a professional obligation.

Mandatory Withdrawal

[3] When a lawyer has been appointed to represent a client, withdrawal ordinarily requires approval of the appointing authority. See also Rule 6.2. Similarly, court approval or notice to the court is often required by applicable law before a lawyer withdraws from pending litigation. Difficulty may be encountered if withdrawal is based on the client's demand that the lawyer engage in unprofessional conduct. The court may request an explanation for the withdrawal, while the lawyer may be bound to keep confidential the facts that would constitute such an explanation. The lawyer's statement that professional considerations require termination of the representation ordinarily should be accepted as sufficient. Lawyers should be mindful of their obligations to both clients and the court under Rules 1.6 and 3.3.

Court Permission to Withdraw

Discharge (1.16)

[4] A client has a right to discharge a lawyer at any time, with or without cause, subject to liability for payment for the lawyer's services. Where future dispute about the discharge may be anticipated, it may be advisable to prepare a written statement reciting the circumstances.

Firing a Lawyer

[5] Whether a client can discharge appointed counsel may depend on applicable law. A client seeking to do so should be given a full explanation of the consequences. These consequences may include a decision by the appointing authority that appointment of successor counsel is unjustified, thus requiring self-representation by the client.

[6] If the client has severely diminished capacity, the client may lack the legal capacity to discharge the lawyer, and in any event the discharge may be seriously adverse to the client's interests. The lawyer should make special effort to help the client consider the consequences and may take reasonably necessary protective action as provided in Rule 1.14.

Optional Withdrawal (1.16)

[7] A lawyer may withdraw from representation in some circumstances. The lawyer has the option to withdraw if it can be accomplished without material adverse effect on the client's interests. Withdrawal is also justified if the client persists in a course of action that the lawyer reasonably believes is illegal or fraudulent, for a lawyer is not required to be associated with such conduct even if the lawyer does not further it. Withdrawal is also permitted if the lawyer's services were misused in the past even if that would materially prejudice the client. The lawyer may also withdraw where the client insists on taking action that the lawyer considers repugnant or with which the lawyer has a fundamental disagreement.

Optional Withdrawal

[8] A lawyer may withdraw if the client refuses to abide by the terms of an agreement relating to the representation, such as an agreement concerning fees or court costs or an agreement limiting the objectives of the representation.

Assisting the Client upon Withdrawal (1.16)

[8A] A decision by a lawyer to withdraw should be made only on the basis of compelling circumstances, and in a matter pending before a tribunal he must comply with the rules of the tribunal regarding withdrawal. A lawyer should not withdraw without considering carefully and endeavoring to minimize the possible adverse effect on the rights of the client and the possibility of prejudice to the client as a result of the withdrawal. Even when the lawyer justifiably withdraws, a lawyer should protect the

Minimizing the Adverse Effects of Withdrawal

welfare of the client by giving due notice of the withdrawal, suggesting employment of other counsel, delivering to the client all papers and property to which the client is entitled, cooperating with counsel subsequently employed, and otherwise endeavoring to minimize the possibility of harm. Clients receive no benefit from a lawyer keeping a copy of the file and therefore can not be charged for any copying costs. Further, the lawyer should refund to the client any compensation not earned during the employment.

[9] Even if the lawyer has been unfairly discharged by the client, a lawyer must take all reasonable steps to mitigate the consequences to the client.

Rule 1.17: Sale of law practice....

Rule 1.18: Duties to prospective client

(a) A person who discusses with a lawyer the possibility of forming a client-lawyer relationship with respect to a matter is a prospective client.

(b) Even when no client-lawyer relationship ensues, a lawyer who has had discussions with a prospective client shall not use or reveal information learned in the consultation, except as Rule 1.9 would permit with respect to information of a former client.

Duty of Confidentiality to Prospective Clients

(c) A lawyer subject to division (b) shall not represent a client with interests materially adverse to those of a prospective client in the same or a substantially related matter if the lawyer received information from the prospective client that could be significantly harmful to that person in the matter, except as provided in division (d). If a lawyer is disqualified from representation under this paragraph, no lawyer in a firm with which that lawyer is associated may knowingly undertake or continue representation in such a matter, except as provided in division (d).

(d) When the lawyer has received disqualifying information as defined in division (c), representation is permissible if either of the following applies:

(1) both the affected client and the prospective client have given informed consent, confirmed in writing;

(2) the lawyer who received the information took reasonable measures to avoid exposure to more disqualifying information than was reasonably necessary to determine whether to represent the prospective client, and both of the following apply:

(i) the disqualified lawyer is timely screened from any participation in the matter and is apportioned no part of the fee therefrom;

Screening in Conflict Cases

(ii) written notice is promptly given to the prospective client.

Comment on Rule 1.18

[1] Prospective clients, like clients, may disclose information to a lawyer, place documents or other property in the lawyer's custody, or rely on the lawyer's advice. A lawyer's discussions with a prospective client usually are limited in time and depth and leave both the prospective client and the lawyer free (and sometimes required) to proceed no further. Hence, prospective clients should receive some but not all of the protection afforded clients.

[2] Not all persons who communicate information to a lawyer are entitled to protection under this rule. A person who communicates information unilaterally to a lawyer, without any reasonable expectation that the lawyer is willing to discuss the possibility of forming a client-lawyer relationship, is not a "prospective client" within the meaning of division (a).

Limitations on Who is a Prospective Client

[3] It is often necessary for a prospective client to reveal information to the lawyer during an initial consultation prior to the decision about formation of a client-lawyer relationship. The lawyer often must learn such information to determine whether there is a conflict of interest with an existing client and whether the matter is one that the lawyer is willing to undertake. Division (b) prohibits the lawyer from using or revealing that information, except as permitted by Rule 1.9, even if the client or lawyer decides not to proceed with the representation. The duty exists regardless of how brief the initial conference may be.

[4] In order to avoid acquiring disqualifying information from a prospective client, a lawyer considering whether or not to undertake a new matter should limit the initial interview to only such information as reasonably appears necessary for that purpose. Where the information indicates that a conflict of interest or other reason for nonrepresentation exists, the lawyer should so inform the prospective client or decline the representation. If the prospective client wishes to retain the lawyer, and if consent is possible under Rule 1.7, then consent from all affected present or former clients must be obtained before accepting the representation....

[6] Under division (c), the lawyer is not prohibited from representing a client with interests adverse to those of the prospective client in the same or a substantially related matter unless the lawyer has received from the prospective client information that could be significantly harmful if used in the matter.

Same or Substantially Related Matter

[7] Under division (c), the prohibition in this rule is imputed to other lawyers as provided in Rule 1.10, but, under division (d)(1), imputation may be avoided if the lawyer obtains the informed consent, confirmed in

writing, of both the prospective and affected clients. In the alternative, imputation may be avoided if the conditions of division (d)(2) are met and all disqualified lawyers are timely screened and written notice is promptly given to the prospective client. See Rule 1.0(l) (requirements for screening procedures). Division (d)(2)(i) does not prohibit the screened lawyer from receiving a salary or partnership share established by prior independent agreement, but that lawyer may not receive compensation directly related to the matter in which the lawyer is disqualified.

Imputed Disqualification

[8] Notice, including a general description of the subject matter about which the lawyer was consulted and of the screening procedures employed, generally should be given as soon as practicable after the need for screening becomes apparent.

[9] For the duty of competence of a lawyer who gives assistance on the merits of a matter to a prospective client, see Rule 1.1. For a lawyer's duties when a prospective client entrusts valuables or papers to the lawyer's care, see Rule 1.15.

II. Counselor

Rule 2.1: Advisor

In representing a client, a lawyer shall exercise independent professional judgment and render candid advice. In rendering advice, a lawyer may refer not only to law but to other considerations, such as moral, economic, social, and political factors, that may be relevant to the client's situation.

Legal Advice: Independent Professional Judgment

Comment on Rule 2.1

Scope of Advice (2.1)

[1] A client is entitled to straightforward advice expressing the lawyer's honest assessment. Legal advice often involves unpleasant facts and alternatives that a client may be disinclined to confront. In presenting advice, a lawyer endeavors to sustain the client's morale and may put advice in as acceptable a form as honesty permits. However, a lawyer should not be deterred from giving candid advice by the prospect that the advice will be unpalatable to the client.

The Need for Straightforward Advice

[2] Advice couched in narrow legal terms may be of little value to a client, especially where practical considerations, such as cost or effects on other people, are predominant. Purely technical legal advice, therefore, can sometimes be inadequate. It is proper for a lawyer to refer to relevant moral and ethical considerations in giving advice. Although a lawyer is not a moral advisor as such, moral and ethical considerations impinge upon most legal questions and may decisively influence how the law will be applied.

Moral Considerations in Giving Advice

[3] A client may expressly or impliedly ask the lawyer for purely technical advice. When such a request is made by a client experienced in legal matters, the lawyer may accept it at face value. When such a request is made by a client inexperienced in legal matters, however, the lawyer's responsibility as advisor may include indicating that more may be involved than strictly legal considerations.

[4] Matters that go beyond strictly legal questions may also be in the domain of another profession. Family matters can involve problems within the professional competence of psychiatry, clinical psychology, or social work; business matters can involve problems within the competence of the accounting profession or of financial specialists. Where consultation with a professional in another field is itself something a competent lawyer would recommend, the lawyer should make such a recommendation. At the same time, a lawyer's advice at its best often consists of recommending a course of action in the face of conflicting recommendations of experts.

Recommending Other Professional Help

Offering Advice (2.1)

[5] In general, a lawyer is not expected to give advice until asked by the client. However, when a lawyer knows that a client proposes a course of action that is likely to result in substantial adverse legal consequences to the client, the lawyer's duty to the client under Rule 1.4 may require that the lawyer offer advice if the client's course of action is related to the representation. Similarly, when a matter is likely to involve litigation, it may be necessary under Rule 1.4 to inform the client of forms of dispute resolution that might constitute reasonable alternatives to litigation. A lawyer ordinarily has no duty to initiate investigation of a client's affairs or to give advice that the client has indicated is unwanted, but a lawyer may initiate advice to a client when doing so appears to be in the client's interest.

Giving Legal Advice that is not Asked for

Rule 2.3: Evaluation for use by third persons

(a) A lawyer may agree to provide an evaluation of a matter affecting a client for the use of someone other than the client if the lawyer reasonably believes that making the evaluation is compatible with other aspects of the lawyer's relationship with the client.

A Client's Request to Provide an Evaluation for Use by Third Parties

(b) When the lawyer knows or reasonably should know that the evaluation is likely to affect the client's interests materially and adversely, the lawyer shall not provide the evaluation unless the client gives *informed* consent.

(c) Except as disclosure is authorized in connection with a report of an evaluation, information relating to the evaluation is otherwise protected by Rule 1.6.

Comment on Rule 2.3

Definition (2.3)

[1] An evaluation may be performed at the client's direction or when impliedly authorized in order to carry out the representation. See Rule 1.2. Such an evaluation may be for the primary purpose of establishing information for the benefit of third parties; for example, an opinion concerning the title of property rendered at the behest of a vendor for the information of a prospective purchaser, or at the behest of a borrower for the information of a prospective lender. In some situations, the evaluation may be required by a government agency; for example, an opinion concerning the legality of the securities registered for sale under the securities laws. In other instances, the evaluation may be required by a third person, such as a purchaser of a business. . . .

Rule 2.4: Lawyer serving as arbitrator, mediator, or third-party neutral

(a) A lawyer serves as a third-party neutral when the lawyer assists two or more persons who are not clients of the lawyer to reach a resolution of a dispute or other matter that has arisen between them. Service as a third-party neutral may include service as an arbitrator, a mediator, or in such other capacity as will enable the lawyer to assist the parties to resolve the matter.

Lawyer as Arbitrator or Mediator

(b) A lawyer serving as a third-party neutral shall inform unrepresented parties that the lawyer is not representing them. When the lawyer knows or reasonably should know that a party does not understand the lawyer's role in the matter, the lawyer shall explain the difference between the lawyer's role as a third-party neutral and a lawyer's role as one who represents a client. . . .

III. Advocate

Rule 3.1: Meritorious claims and contentions

A lawyer shall not bring or defend a proceeding, or assert or controvert an issue in a proceeding, unless there is a basis in law and fact for doing so that is not frivolous, which includes a good faith argument for an extension, modification, or reversal of existing law. A lawyer for the defendant in a criminal proceeding, or the respondent in a proceeding that could result in incarceration, may nevertheless so defend the proceeding as to require that every element of the case be established.

Frivolous Claims and Contentions

Comment on Rule 3.1

[1] The advocate has a duty to use legal procedure for the fullest benefit of the client's cause, but also a duty not to abuse legal procedure. The law, both procedural and substantive, establishes the limits within which an advocate may proceed. However, the law is not always clear and never is static. Accordingly, in determining the proper scope of advocacy, account must be taken of the law's ambiguities and potential for change.

Abusing Legal Procedures

[2] The filing of an action or defense or similar action taken for a client is not frivolous merely because the facts have not first been fully substantiated or because the lawyer expects to develop vital evidence only by discovery. What is required of lawyers, however, is that they inform themselves about the facts of their clients' cases and the applicable law and determine that they can make good faith arguments in support of their clients' positions. Such action is not frivolous even though the lawyer believes that the client's position ultimately will not prevail. The action is frivolous, however, if the lawyer is unable either to make a good faith argument on the merits of the action taken or to support the action taken by a good faith argument for an extension, modification, or reversal of existing law.

Good Faith Arguments for Positions the Lawyer Believes will Fail

[3] The lawyer's obligations under this rule are subordinate to federal or state constitutional law that entitles a defendant in a criminal matter to the assistance of counsel in presenting a claim or contention that otherwise would be prohibited by this rule.

Rule 3.2: Expediting litigation

NOTE: ABA Model Rule 3.2 is not adopted in Ohio. The substance of Model Rule 3.2 is addressed by other provisions of the Ohio Rules of Professional Conduct, including Rules 1.3 [Diligence], 3.1 [Meritorious Claims and Contentions], and 4.4(a) [Respect for Rights of Third Persons].

Rule 3.3: Candor toward the tribunal

(a) A lawyer shall not knowingly do any of the following:

(1) make a false statement of fact or law to a tribunal or fail to correct a false statement of material fact or law previously made to the tribunal by the lawyer;

Making False Statements of Material Fact or Law

(2) fail to disclose to the tribunal legal authority in the controlling jurisdiction known to the lawyer to be directly adverse to the position of the client and not disclosed by opposing counsel;

Failing to Disclose Directly Adverse Legal Authority

(3) offer evidence that the lawyer knows to be false. If a lawyer, the lawyer's client, or a witness called by the lawyer has offered material evidence and the lawyer comes to *know* of its falsity, the lawyer shall take reasonable measures to remedy the situation, including, if necessary, disclosure to the tribunal. A lawyer may refuse to offer evidence, other than the testimony of a defendant in a criminal matter, that the lawyer reasonably believes is false.

Offering False Evidence

(b) A lawyer who represents a client in an adjudicative proceeding and who knows that a person, including the client, intends to engage, is engaging, or has engaged in criminal or fraudulent conduct related to the proceeding shall take reasonable measures to remedy the situation, including, if necessary, disclosure to the tribunal.

Disclosing a Client's Fraud

(c) The duties stated in divisions (a) and (b) of this rule continue until the issue to which the duty relates is determined by the highest tribunal that may consider the issue, or the time has expired for such determination, and apply even if compliance requires disclosure of information otherwise protected by Rule 1.6.

(d) In an *ex parte* proceeding, a lawyer shall inform the tribunal of all material facts known to the lawyer that will enable the tribunal to make an informed decision, whether or not the facts are adverse.

Comment on Rule 3.3

[1] This rule governs the conduct of a lawyer who is representing a client in the proceedings of a tribunal. See Rule 1.0(o) for the definition of "tribunal." It also applies when the lawyer is representing a client in an ancillary proceeding conducted pursuant to the tribunal's adjudicative authority, such as a deposition. Thus, for example, division (a)(3) requires a lawyer to take reasonable remedial measures if the lawyer comes to know that a client who is testifying in a deposition has offered evidence that is false.

False Evidence During a Deposition

[2] This rule sets forth the special duties of lawyers as officers of the court to avoid conduct that undermines the integrity of the adjudicative process. A lawyer acting as an advocate in an adjudicative proceeding has an obligation to present the client's case with persuasive force. Performance of that duty while maintaining confidences of the client, however, is qualified by the advocate's duty of candor to the tribunal. Consequently, although a lawyer in an adversary proceeding is not required to present an impartial exposition of the law or to vouch for the evidence submitted in a cause, the lawyer must not allow the tribunal to be misled by false statements of law or fact or evidence that the lawyer knows to be false.

Duty of Candor to the Court

Representations by a Lawyer (3.3)

[3] An advocate is responsible for pleadings and other documents prepared for litigation, but is usually not required to have personal knowledge of matters asserted therein, for litigation documents ordinarily present assertions by the client, or by someone on the client's behalf, and not assertions by the lawyer. Compare Rule 3.1. However, an assertion purporting to be on the lawyer's own knowledge, as in an affidavit by the lawyer or in a statement in open court, may properly be made only when the lawyer knows the assertion is true or believes it to be true on the basis of a reasonably diligent inquiry. There are circumstances where failure to make a disclosure is the equivalent of an affirmative misrepresentation. The obligation prescribed in Rule 1.2(d) not to counsel a client to commit or assist the client in committing a fraud applies in litigation. Regarding compliance with Rule 1.2(d), see the Comment to that rule. See also the Comment to Rule 8.4(b).

The Requirement of a Reasonably Diligent Inquiry

Legal Argument (3.3)

[4] Legal argument based on a knowingly false representation of law constitutes dishonesty toward the tribunal. A lawyer is not required to make a disinterested exposition of the law, but must recognize the existence of pertinent legal authorities. Furthermore, as stated in division (a)(2), an advocate has a duty to disclose directly adverse authority in the controlling jurisdiction that has not been disclosed by the opposing party. The underlying concept is that legal argument is a discussion seeking to determine the legal premises properly applicable to the case.

Failing to Disclose Directly Adverse Legal Authority

Offering Evidence (3.3)

[5] Division (a)(3) requires that the lawyer refuse to offer evidence that the lawyer knows to be false, regardless of the client's wishes. This duty is premised on the lawyer's obligation as an officer of the court to prevent the trier of fact from being misled by false evidence. A lawyer does not violate this rule if the lawyer offers the evidence for the purpose of establishing its falsity.

Lawyer as Officer of the Court

[6] If a lawyer knows that the client intends to testify falsely or wants the lawyer to introduce false evidence, the lawyer should seek to persuade the client that the evidence should not be offered. If the persuasion is ineffective and the lawyer continues to represent the client, the lawyer must refuse to offer the false evidence. If only a portion of a witness's testimony will be false, the lawyer may call the witness to testify but may not elicit or otherwise permit the witness to present the testimony that the lawyer knows is false.

Persuading a Client not to Offer False Evidence

[8] The prohibition against offering false evidence only applies if the lawyer knows that the evidence is false. A lawyer's reasonable belief that evidence is false does not preclude its presentation to the trier of fact. A lawyer's knowledge that evidence is false, however, can be inferred from the circumstances. See Rule 1.0(g). Thus, although a lawyer should resolve doubts about the veracity of testimony or other evidence in favor of the client, the lawyer cannot ignore an obvious falsehood.

Ignoring Obvious Falsehoods

Remedial Measures (3.3)

[10] Having offered material evidence in the belief that it was true, a lawyer may subsequently come to know that the evidence is false. Or, a lawyer may be surprised when the lawyer's client, or another witness called by the lawyer, offers testimony the lawyer knows to be false, either during the lawyer's direct examination or in response to cross-examination by the opposing lawyer. In such situations or if the lawyer knows of the falsity of testimony elicited from the client during a deposition, the lawyer must take reasonable remedial measures. In such situations, the advocate's proper course is to remonstrate with the client confidentially, advise the client of the lawyer's duty of candor to the tribunal, and seek the client's cooperation with respect to the withdrawal or correction of the false statements or evidence. If that fails, the advocate must take further remedial action including making such disclosure to the tribunal as is reasonably necessary to remedy the situation, even if doing so requires the lawyer to reveal information that otherwise would be protected by Rule 1.6. It is for the tribunal then to determine what should be done.

Withdrawing or Correcting False Evidence that has been Offered

[11] The disclosure of a client's false testimony can result in grave consequences to the client, including not only a sense of betrayal but also loss of the case and perhaps a prosecution for perjury. But the alternative is that the lawyer cooperate in deceiving the court, thereby subverting the truth-finding process which the adversary system is designed to implement. See Rule 1.2(d). Furthermore, unless it is clearly understood that the lawyer will act upon the duty to disclose the existence of false evidence, the client can simply reject the lawyer's advice to reveal the false evidence and insist that the lawyer keep silent. Thus the client could in effect coerce the lawyer into being a party to fraud on the court.

Coercing a Lawyer into Committing Fraud

Preserving Integrity of Adjudicative Process (3.3)

[12] Lawyers have a special obligation to protect a tribunal against criminal or fraudulent conduct that undermines the integrity of the adjudicative process, such as bribing, intimidating, or otherwise unlawfully communicating with a witness, juror, court official, or other participant in the proceeding, unlawfully destroying or concealing documents or other evidence, or failing to disclose information to the tribunal when required by law to do so. Thus, division (b) requires a lawyer to take reasonable remedial measures, including disclosure if necessary, whenever the lawyer knows that a person, including the lawyer's client, intends to engage, is engaging, or has engaged in criminal or fraudulent conduct related to the proceeding.

Destroying or Concealing Evidence

Duration of Obligation (3.3)

[13] A practical time limit on the obligation to rectify false evidence or false statements of law or fact must be established. A final determination of the issue to which the duty relates by the highest tribunal that may consider the issue, or the expiration of the time for such consideration, is a reasonably definite point for the termination of the obligation. Division (c) modifies the rule set forth in *Disciplinary Counsel v. Heffernan* (1991), 58 Ohio St.3d 260 to the extent that *Heffernan* imposed an obligation to disclose false evidence or statements that is unlimited in time.

Ex Parte Proceedings (3.3)

[14] Ordinarily, an advocate has the limited responsibility of presenting one side of the matters that a tribunal should consider in reaching a decision; the conflicting position is expected to be presented by the opposing party. However, in any *ex parte* proceeding, such as an application for a temporary restraining order, there is no balance of presentation by opposing advocates. The object of an *ex parte* proceeding is nevertheless to yield a substantially just result. The judge has an affirmative responsibility to accord the absent party just consideration. The lawyer for the represented party has the correlative duty to make disclosures of material facts known to the lawyer and that the lawyer reasonably believes are necessary to an informed decision.

Disclosures During *Ex Parte* Proceedings

Withdrawal (3.3)

[15] Normally, a lawyer's compliance with the duty of candor imposed by this rule does not require that the lawyer withdraw from the representation of a client whose interests will be or have been adversely affected by the lawyer's disclosure. The lawyer may, however, be required by Rule 1.16(c) to seek permission of the tribunal to withdraw if the lawyer's compliance with this rule's duty of candor results in such an extreme deterioration of the client-lawyer relationship that the lawyer can no longer competently represent the client. Also see Rule 1.16(b) for the circumstances in which a lawyer will be permitted to seek a tribunal's permission to withdraw. In connection with a request for permission to withdraw that is premised on a client's misconduct, a lawyer may reveal information relating to the representation only to the extent reasonably necessary to comply with this rule or as otherwise permitted by Rule 1.6.

Deterioration of the Attorney-Client Relationship

Rule 3.4: Fairness to opposing party and counsel

A lawyer shall not do any of the following:

(a) unlawfully obstruct another party's access to evidence; unlawfully alter, destroy, or conceal a document or other material having potential evidentiary value; or counsel or assist another person to do any such act;

Obstructing, Altering, Blocking, or Falsifying Evidence

(b) falsify evidence, counsel or assist a witness to testify falsely, or offer an inducement to a witness that is prohibited by law;

(c) knowingly disobey an obligation under the rules of a tribunal, except for an open refusal based on a good faith assertion that no valid obligation exists;

(d) in pretrial procedure, intentionally or habitually make a frivolous motion or discovery request or fail to make reasonably diligent effort to comply with a legally proper discovery request by an opposing party;

Frivolous Motions; Improper Discovery Requests

(e) in trial, allude to any matter that the lawyer does not reasonably believe is relevant or that will not be supported by admissible evidence or by a good-faith belief that such evidence may exist, assert personal *knowledge* of facts in issue except when testifying as a witness, or state a personal opinion as to the justness of a cause, the credibility of a witness, the culpability of a civil litigant, or the guilt or innocence of an accused;

Improper Personal Opinions of a Lawyer

(g) advise or cause a person to hide or to leave the jurisdiction of a tribunal for the purpose of becoming unavailable as a witness.

Comment on Rule 3.4

[1] The procedure of the adversary system contemplates that the evidence in a case is to be marshaled competitively by the contending parties. Fair competition in the adversary system is secured by prohibitions against destruction or concealment of evidence, improperly influencing witnesses, obstructive tactics in discovery procedure, and the like. However, a lawyer representing an organization, in accordance with law, may request an employee of the client to refrain from giving information to another party. See Rule 4.2, Comment [7].

Obstructing Our Adversary System

[2] Division (a) applies to all evidence, whether testimonial, physical, or documentary. Subject to evidentiary privileges, the right of an opposing party, including the government, to obtain evidence through discovery or subpoena is an important procedural right. The exercise of that right can be frustrated if relevant material is altered, concealed, or destroyed, or if the testimony of a person with knowledge is unavailable, incomplete, or false. Applicable law in many jurisdictions makes it an offense to destroy material for the purpose of impairing its availability in a pending proceeding or one whose commencement can be foreseen. Falsifying evidence is also generally a criminal offense. A lawyer is permitted to take temporary possession of physical evidence of client crimes for the purpose of conducting a limited examination that will not alter or destroy material characteristics of the evidence. In such a case, the lawyer is required to turn the evidence over to the police or other prosecuting authority, depending on the circumstances. Applicable law also prohibits the use of force, intimidation, or deception to delay, hinder, or prevent a person from attending or testifying in a proceeding.

Turning Over Evidence to Proper Authorities

[3] With regard to division (b), it is not improper to pay a witness's expenses or to compensate an expert witness on terms permitted by law. It is improper to pay an occurrence witness any fee for testifying and it is improper to pay an expert witness a contingent fee.

Proper and Improper Witness Fees

[3A] Division (e) does not prohibit a lawyer from arguing, based on the lawyer's analysis of the evidence, for any position or conclusion with respect to matters referenced in that division.

Rule 3.5: Impartiality and decorum of the tribunal

(a) A lawyer shall not do any of the following:

(1) seek to influence a judicial officer, juror, prospective juror, or other official by means prohibited by law;

Seeking Improper Influence of Jurors or Judicial Officers

(2) lend anything of value or give anything of more than *de minimis* value to a judicial officer, official, or employee of a tribunal;

Improper Ex Parte Communications

(3) communicate *ex parte* with either of the following:

(i) a judicial officer or other official as to the merits of the case during the proceeding unless authorized to do so by law or court order;

(ii) a juror or prospective juror during the proceeding unless otherwise authorized to do so by law or court order.

(4) communicate with a juror or prospective juror after discharge of the jury if any of the following applies:

(i) the communication is prohibited by law or court order;

(ii) the juror has made known to the lawyer a desire not to communicate;

(iii) the communication involves misrepresentation, coercion, duress, or harassment;

(5) engage in conduct intended to disrupt a tribunal;

(6) engage in undignified or discourteous conduct that is degrading to a tribunal.

(b) A lawyer shall reveal promptly to the tribunal improper conduct by a juror or prospective juror, or by another toward a juror, prospective juror, or family member of a juror or prospective juror, of which the lawyer has *knowledge*.

Comment on Rule 3.5

[1] Many forms of improper influence upon a tribunal are proscribed by criminal law. Others are specified in the Ohio Code of Judicial Conduct, with which an advocate should be familiar. A lawyer is required to avoid contributing to a violation of such provisions. As used in division (a)(2), "*de minimis*" means an insignificant item or interest that could not raise a reasonable question as to the impartiality of a judicial officer, official, or employee of a tribunal.

[2] During a proceeding a lawyer may not communicate *ex parte* with persons serving in an official capacity in the proceeding, such as judges, masters, magistrates, or jurors, unless authorized to do so by law, court order, or these rules.

[3] A lawyer may on occasion want to communicate with a juror or prospective juror after the jury has been discharged. The lawyer may do so unless the communication is prohibited by law or a court order but must respect the desire of the juror not to talk with the lawyer. The lawyer may not engage in improper conduct during the communication.

[4] The advocate's function is to present evidence and argument so that the cause may be decided according to law. Refraining from abusive or obstreperous conduct is a corollary of the advocate's right to speak on behalf of litigants. A lawyer may stand firm against abuse by a judge but should avoid reciprocation; the judge's default is no justification for similar dereliction by an advocate. An advocate can present the cause, protect the record for subsequent review, and preserve professional integrity by patient firmness no less effectively than by belligerence or theatrics.

Responding to Abuse by a Judge; Avoiding Belligerence or Theatrics

[5] The duty to refrain from disruptive, undignified, or discourteous conduct applies to any proceeding of a tribunal, including a deposition. See Rule 1.0(o).

Rule 3.6: Trial publicity

(a) A lawyer who is participating or has participated in the investigation or litigation of a matter shall not make an extrajudicial statement that the lawyer knows or reasonably should know will be disseminated by means of public communication and will have a substantial likelihood of materially prejudicing an adjudicative proceeding in the matter.

Proper and Improper Extrajudicial Statements

(b) Notwithstanding division (a) of this rule and if permitted by Rule 1.6, a lawyer may state any of the following:

(1) the claim, offense, or defense involved and, except when prohibited by law, the identity of the persons involved;

(2) information contained in a public record;

(3) that an investigation of a matter is in progress;

(4) the scheduling or result of any step in litigation;

(5) a request for assistance in obtaining evidence and information necessary thereto;

(6) a warning of danger concerning the behavior of a person involved when there is reason to believe that there exists the likelihood of substantial harm to an individual or to the public interest;

Warning of Danger

(7) in a criminal case, in addition to divisions (b)(1) to (6) of this rule, any of the following:

(i) the identity, residence, occupation, and family status of the accused;

(ii) if the accused has not been apprehended, information necessary to aid in apprehension of that person;

(iii) the fact, time, and place of arrest;

(iv) the identity of investigating and arresting officers or agencies and the length of the investigation.

(c) Notwithstanding division (a) of this rule, a lawyer may make a statement that a reasonable lawyer would believe is required to protect a client from the substantial undue prejudicial effect of recent publicity not initiated by the lawyer or the lawyer's client. A statement made pursuant to this division shall be limited to information necessary to mitigate the recent adverse publicity.

(d) No lawyer associated in a firm or government agency with a lawyer subject to division (a) of this rule shall make a statement prohibited by division (a) of this rule.

Comment on Rule 3.6

[1] It is difficult to strike a balance between protecting the right to a fair trial and safeguarding the right of free expression. Preserving the right to a fair trial necessarily entails some curtailment of the information that may be disseminated about a party prior to trial, particularly where trial by jury is involved. If there were no such limits, the result would be the practical nullification of the protective effect of the rules of forensic decorum and the exclusionary rules of evidence. On the other hand, there are vital social interests served by the free dissemination of information about events having legal consequences and about legal proceedings themselves. The public has a right to know about threats to its safety and measures aimed at assuring its security. It also has a legitimate interest in the conduct of judicial proceedings, particularly in matters of general public concern. Furthermore, the subject matter of legal proceedings is often of direct significance in debate and deliberation over questions of public policy.

The Public's Right to Know

[2] Special rules of confidentiality may validly govern proceedings in juvenile, domestic relations, disciplinary, and mental disability proceedings, and perhaps other types of litigation. Rule 3.4(c) requires compliance with such rules. The provisions of this rule do not supersede the confidentiality provisions of Rule 1.6.

[3] The rule sets forth a basic general prohibition against a lawyer's making statements that the lawyer knows or should know will have a substantial likelihood of materially prejudicing an adjudicative proceeding. Recognizing that the public value of informed commentary is great and the likelihood of prejudice to a proceeding by the commentary of a lawyer who is not involved in the proceeding is small, the rule applies only to lawyers who are, or who have been involved in the investigation or litigation of a case, and their associates.

[4] Division (b) identifies specific matters about which a lawyer's statements would not ordinarily be considered to present a substantial likelihood of material prejudice, and should not in any event be considered prohibited by the general prohibition of division (a). Division (b) is not intended to be an exhaustive listing of the subjects upon which a lawyer may make a statement, but statements on other matters may be subject to division (a).

[5] There are, on the other hand, certain subjects that are more likely than not to have a material prejudicial effect on a proceeding, particularly when they refer to a civil matter triable to a jury, a criminal matter, or any other proceeding that could result in incarceration. These subjects relate to:

Sensitive Topics Requiring Greater Care in Extrajudicial Comments by a Lawyer

(1) the character, credibility, reputation, or criminal record of a party, suspect in a criminal investigation or witness, or the identity of a witness, or the expected testimony of a party or witness;
(2) in a criminal case or proceeding that could result in incarceration, the possibility of a plea of guilty to the offense or the existence or contents of any confession, admission, or statement given by a defendant or suspect or that person's refusal or failure to make a statement;
(3) the performance or results of any examination or test or the refusal or failure of a person to submit to an examination or test, or the identity or nature of physical evidence expected to be presented;
(4) any opinion as to the guilt or innocence of a defendant or suspect in a criminal case or proceeding that could result in incarceration;
(5) information that the lawyer knows or reasonably should know is likely to be inadmissible as evidence in a trial and that would, if disclosed, create a substantial risk of prejudicing an impartial trial;
(6) the fact that a defendant has been charged with a crime, unless there is included therein a statement explaining that the charge is merely an accusation and that the defendant is presumed innocent until and unless proven guilty.

[6] Another relevant factor in determining prejudice is the nature of the proceeding involved. Criminal jury trials will be most sensitive to extrajudicial speech. Civil trials may be less sensitive. Nonjury hearings and arbitration proceedings may be even less affected. The rule will still place limitations on prejudicial comments in these cases, but the likelihood of prejudice may be different depending on the type of proceeding.

[7] Finally, extrajudicial statements that might otherwise raise a question under this rule may be permissible when they are made in response to statements made publicly by another party, another party's lawyer, or third persons, where a reasonable lawyer would believe a public response is required in order to avoid prejudice to the lawyer's client. When prejudicial statements have been publicly made by others, responsive statements

may have the salutary effect of lessening any resulting adverse impact on the adjudicative proceeding. Such responsive statements should be limited to contain only such information as is necessary to mitigate undue prejudice created by the statements made by others.

Rule 3.7: Lawyer as witness

(a) A lawyer shall not act as an advocate at a trial in which the lawyer is likely to be a necessary witness unless one or more of the following applies:

A Lawyer's Inconsistent Role as Advocate and Witness

(1) the testimony relates to an uncontested issue;
(2) the testimony relates to the nature and value of legal services rendered in the case;
(3) the disqualification of the lawyer would work substantial hardship on the client.

(b) A lawyer may act as an advocate in a trial in which another lawyer in the lawyer's firm is likely to be called as a witness unless precluded from doing so by Rule 1.7 or 1.9.

(c) A government lawyer participating in a case shall not testify or offer the testimony of another lawyer in the same government agency, except where division (a) applies or where permitted by law.

Comment on Rule 3.7

[1] Combining the roles of advocate and witness can prejudice the tribunal and the opposing party and can also involve a conflict of interest between the lawyer and client.

Advocate-Witness Rule (3.7)

[2] The tribunal has proper objection when the trier of fact may be confused or misled by a lawyer serving as both advocate and witness. The opposing party has proper objection where the combination of roles may prejudice that party's rights in the litigation. A witness is required to testify on the basis of personal knowledge, while an advocate is expected to explain and comment on evidence given by others. It may not be clear whether a statement by an advocate-witness should be taken as proof or as an analysis of the proof. . . .

Rule 3.8: Special responsibilities of a prosecutor

The prosecutor in a criminal case shall not do any of the following:

A Prosecutor's Duty to Disclose Evidence

(a) pursue or prosecute a charge that the prosecutor knows is not supported by probable cause;

(d) fail to make timely disclosure to the defense of all evidence or information *known* to the prosecutor that tends to negate the guilt of the accused or mitigates the offense, and, in connection with sentencing, fail to disclose to the defense all unprivileged mitigating information known to the prosecutor, except when the prosecutor is relieved of this responsibility by an order of the tribunal;

(e) subpoena a lawyer in a grand jury or other criminal proceeding to present evidence about a past or present client unless the prosecutor reasonably believes all of the following apply:

(1) the information sought is not protected from disclosure by any applicable privilege;
(2) the evidence sought is essential to the successful completion of an ongoing investigation or prosecution;
(3) there is no other feasible alternative to obtain the information.

Comment on Rule 3.8

[1] A prosecutor has the responsibility of a minister of justice and not simply that of an advocate. This responsibility carries with it specific obligations to see that the defendant is accorded justice and that guilt is decided upon the basis of sufficient evidence. Applicable law may require other measures by the prosecutor and knowing disregard of those obligations or a systematic abuse of prosecutorial discretion could constitute a violation of Rule 8.4. A prosecutor also is subject to other applicable rules such as Rules 3.6, 4.2, 4.3, 5.1, and 5.3. . . .

Rule 3.9: Advocate in nonadjudicative proceedings

A lawyer representing a client before a legislative body or administrative agency in a nonadjudicative proceeding shall disclose that the appearance is in a representative capacity and shall conform to the provisions of Rules 3.3 (a) to (c), 3.4 (a) to (c), and 3.5.

Appearances before Legislatures, Agencies, and Other Noncourts

Comment on Rule 3.9

[1] In representation before bodies such as legislatures, municipal councils, and executive and administrative agencies acting in a rule-making or policy-making capacity, lawyers present facts, formulate issues, and advance argument in the matters under consideration. The decision-making body, like a court, should be able to rely on the integrity of the submissions made to it. A lawyer appearing before such a body must deal with it honestly and in conformity with applicable rules of procedure. See Rules 3.3(a) to (c), 3.4(a) to (c), and 3.5.

[2] *Lawyers have no exclusive right to appear before nonadjudicative bodies, as they do before a court.* The requirements of this rule therefore may subject lawyers to regulations inapplicable to advocates who are not lawyers. However, legislative bodies and

"Lawyers have no exclusive right to appear before nonadjudicative bodies"

administrative agencies have a right to expect lawyers to deal with them as they deal with courts. [emphasis added]

[3] This rule applies only when a lawyer represents a client in connection with an official hearing or meeting of a governmental agency or a legislative body to which the lawyer or the lawyer's client is presenting evidence or argument. It does not apply to representation of a client in a negotiation or other bilateral transaction with a governmental agency or in connection with an application for a license or other privilege or the client's compliance with generally applicable reporting requirements, such as the filing of income tax returns. Nor does it apply to the representation of a client in connection with an investigation or examination of the client's affairs conducted by government investigators or examiners. Representation in such matters is governed by Rules 4.1 to 4.4.

IV. Transactions With Persons Other Than Clients

Rule 4.1: Truthfulness in statements to others

In the course of representing a client a lawyer shall not knowingly do either of the following: (a) make a false statement of material fact or law to a third person; (b) fail to disclose a material fact when disclosure is necessary to avoid assisting an illegal or fraudulent act by a client.

False Statements of Material Fact

Comment on Rule 4.1

Misrepresentation (4.1)

[1] A lawyer is required to be truthful when dealing with others on a client's behalf. A misrepresentation can occur if the lawyer incorporates or affirms a statement of another person that the lawyer knows is false. Misrepresentations can also occur by partially true but misleading statements or omissions that are the equivalent of affirmative false statements. For dishonest conduct that does not amount to a false statement or for misrepresentations by a lawyer other than in the course of representing a client, see Rule 8.4.

False and Misleading Statements

Statements of Fact (4.1)

[2] This rule refers to statements of fact. Whether a particular statement should be regarded as one of fact can depend on the circumstances. Under generally accepted conventions in negotiation, certain types of statements ordinarily are not taken as statements of material fact. Estimates of price or value placed on the subject of a transaction and a party's intentions as to an acceptable settlement of a claim are ordinarily in this category, and so is the existence of an undisclosed principal except where nondisclosure of the principal would constitute fraud. Lawyers should be mindful of their obligations under applicable law to avoid criminal and tortious misrepresentation.

Disclosure to Prevent Illegal or Fraudulent Client Acts (4.1)

[3] Under Rule 1.2(d), a lawyer is prohibited from counseling or assisting a client in conduct that the lawyer knows is illegal or fraudulent. Rule 4.1(b) requires a lawyer to disclose a material fact, including one that may be protected by the attorney-client privilege, when the disclosure is necessary to avoid the lawyer's assistance in the client's illegal or fraudulent act. See also Rule 8.4(c). The client can, of course, prevent such disclosure by refraining from the wrongful conduct. If the client persists, the lawyer usually can avoid assisting the client's illegal or fraudulent act by withdrawing from the representation. If withdrawal is not sufficient to avoid such assistance, division (b) of the rule requires disclosure of material facts necessary to prevent the assistance of the client's illegal or fraudulent act. Such disclosure may include disaffirming an opinion, document, affirmation, or the like, or may require further disclosure to avoid being deemed to have assisted the client's illegal or fraudulent act. Disclosure is not required unless the lawyer is unable to withdraw or the client is using the lawyer's work product to assist the client's illegal or fraudulent act.

Assisting a Client in Conduct Known to be Illegal or Fraudulent

[4] Division (b) of this rule addresses only ongoing or future illegal or fraudulent acts of a client. With respect to past illegal or fraudulent client acts of which the lawyer later becomes aware, Rule 1.6(b)(3) permits, but does not require, a lawyer to reveal information reasonably necessary to mitigate substantial injury to the financial or property interests of another that has resulted from the client's commission of an illegal or fraudulent act, in furtherance of which the client has used the lawyer's services.

Mitigating the Financial Impact of Prior Illegal or Fraudulent Conduct

Rule 4.2: Communication with person represented by counsel

In representing a client, a lawyer shall not communicate about the subject of the representation with a person the lawyer knows to be represented by another lawyer in the matter, unless the lawyer has the consent of the other lawyer or is authorized to do so by law or a court order.

Noncontact Rule: Represented Persons

Comment on Rule 4.2

[1] This rule contributes to the proper functioning of the legal system by protecting a person who has chosen

to be represented by a lawyer in a matter against possible overreaching by other lawyers who are participating in the matter, interference by those lawyers with the client-lawyer relationship, and the uncounselled disclosure of information relating to the representation.

Overreaching by Lawyers

[2] This rule applies to communications with any person who is represented by counsel concerning the matter to which the communication relates.

[3] The rule applies even though the represented person initiates or consents to the communication. A lawyer must immediately terminate communication with a person if, after commencing communication, the lawyer learns that the person is one with whom communication is not permitted by this rule.

[4] This rule does not prohibit communication with a represented person, or an employee or agent of such a person, concerning matters outside the representation. For example, the existence of a controversy between a government agency and a private party, or between two organizations, does not prohibit a lawyer for either from communicating with nonlawyer representatives of the other regarding a separate matter. Nor does this rule preclude communication with a represented person who is seeking advice from a lawyer who is not otherwise representing a client in the matter. A lawyer may not make a communication prohibited by this rule through the acts of another. See Rule 8.4(a). Parties to a matter may communicate directly with each other, and a lawyer is not prohibited from advising a client concerning a communication that the client is legally entitled to make. Also, a lawyer having independent justification or legal authorization for communicating with a represented person is permitted to do so.

Allowable Communication with a Represented Party

[5] Communications authorized by law may include communications by a lawyer on behalf of a client who is exercising a constitutional or other legal right to communicate with the government. Communications authorized by law may also include investigative activities of lawyers representing governmental entities, directly or through investigative agents, prior to the commencement of criminal or civil enforcement proceedings. When communicating with the accused in a criminal matter, a government lawyer must comply with this rule in addition to honoring the constitutional rights of the accused. The fact that a communication does not violate a state or federal constitutional right is insufficient to establish that the communication is permissible under this rule.

Communications by Government Attorneys

[6] A lawyer who is uncertain whether a communication with a represented person is permissible may seek a court order. A lawyer may also seek a court order in exceptional circumstances to authorize a communication that would otherwise be prohibited by this rule, for example, where communication with a person represented by counsel is necessary to avoid reasonably certain injury.

Avoiding Reasonably Certain Injury

[7] In the case of a represented organization, this rule prohibits communications with a constituent of the organization who supervises, directs, or regularly consults with the organization's lawyer concerning the matter or has authority to obligate the organization with respect to the matter or whose act or omission in connection with the matter may be imputed to the organization for purposes of civil or criminal liability. Consent of the organization's lawyer is not required for communication with a former constituent. If a constituent of the organization is represented in the matter by his or her own counsel, the consent by that counsel to a communication will be sufficient for purposes of this rule. In communicating with a current or former constituent of an organization, a lawyer must not use methods of obtaining evidence that violate the legal rights of the organization.

Corporations and Other Organizations

[8] The prohibition on communications with a represented person applies only in circumstances where the lawyer knows that the person is in fact represented in the matter to be discussed. This means that the lawyer has actual knowledge of the fact of the representation; but such actual knowledge may be inferred from the circumstances. See Rule 1.0(g). Thus, the lawyer cannot evade the requirement of obtaining the consent of counsel by closing eyes to the obvious.

[9] In the event the person with whom the lawyer communicates is not known to be represented by counsel in the matter, the lawyer's communications are subject to Rule 4.3.

Rule 4.3: Dealing with unrepresented person

In dealing on behalf of a client with a person who is not represented by counsel, a lawyer shall not state or imply that the lawyer is disinterested. When the lawyer knows or reasonably should know that the unrepresented person misunderstands the lawyer's role in the matter, the lawyer shall make reasonable efforts to correct the misunderstanding. The lawyer shall not give legal advice to an unrepresented person, other than the advice to secure counsel, if the lawyer knows or reasonably should know that the interests of such a person are or have a reasonable possibility of being in conflict with the interests of the client.

Contacts with Unrepresented Persons

Comments on Rule 4.3

[1] An unrepresented person, particularly one not experienced in dealing with legal matters, might assume that a lawyer is disinterested in loyalties or is a disinterested authority on the law even when the lawyer represents a client. In order to avoid a misunderstanding, a lawyer will typically need to identify the lawyer's client and, where necessary, explain that the client has interests opposed to those of the unrepresented person. For misunderstandings that sometimes arise when a lawyer for an organization deals with an unrepresented constituent, see Rule 1.13(d).

Disclosing the Lack of Neutrality

[2] The rule distinguishes between situations involving unrepresented persons whose interests may be adverse to those of the lawyer's client and those in which the person's interests are not in conflict with the client's. In the former situation, the possibility that the lawyer will compromise the unrepresented person's interests is so great that the rule prohibits the giving of any advice, apart from the advice to obtain counsel. Whether a lawyer is giving impermissible advice may depend on the experience and sophistication of the unrepresented person, as well as the setting in which the behavior and comments occur. This rule does not prohibit a lawyer from negotiating the terms of a transaction or settling a dispute with an unrepresented person. So long as the lawyer has explained that the lawyer represents an adverse party and is not representing the person, the lawyer may inform the person of the terms on which the lawyer's client will enter into an agreement or settle a matter, prepare documents that require the person's signature, and explain the lawyer's own view of the meaning of the document or the lawyer's view of the underlying legal obligations.

Permissible Communications with Unrepresented Persons

Rule 4.4: Respect for rights of third persons

(a) In representing a client, a lawyer shall not use means that have no substantial purpose other than to embarrass, harass, delay, or burden a third person, or use methods of obtaining evidence that violate the legal rights of such a person.

Embarrassment and Harassment

(b) A lawyer who receives a document relating to the representation of the lawyer's client and knows or reasonably should know that the document was inadvertently sent shall promptly notify the sender.

Inadvertent Receipt of Documents

Comment on Rule 4.4

[1] Responsibility to a client requires a lawyer to subordinate the interests of others to those of the client, but that responsibility does not imply that a lawyer may disregard the rights of third persons. It is impractical to catalogue all such rights, but they include legal restrictions on methods of obtaining evidence from third persons and unwarranted intrusions into privileged relationships, such as the client-lawyer relationship.

[2] Division (b) recognizes that lawyers sometimes receive documents that were mistakenly sent or produced by opposing parties or their lawyers. If a lawyer knows or reasonably should know that such a document was sent inadvertently, then this rule requires the lawyer to promptly notify the sender. For purposes of this rule, "document" includes e-mail or other electronic modes of transmission subject to being read or put into readable form.

E-Mail and Other Electronic Modes of Transmission

[3] Some lawyers may choose to return a document unread, for example, when the lawyer learns before receiving the document that it was sent inadvertently to the wrong address. Where a lawyer is not required by applicable law to do so, the decision to voluntarily return such a document is a matter of professional judgment ordinarily reserved to the lawyer. See Rules 1.2 and 1.4.

V. Law Firms and Associations

Rule 5.1: Responsibilities of partners, managers, and supervisory lawyers

(c) A lawyer shall be responsible for another lawyer's violation of the Ohio Rules of Professional Conduct if either of the following applies:

(1) the lawyer orders or, with *knowledge* of the specific conduct, ratifies the conduct involved;

(2) the lawyer is a partner or has comparable managerial authority in the law firm or government agency in which the other lawyer practices, or has direct supervisory authority over the other lawyer, and knows of the conduct at a time when its consequences can be avoided or mitigated but fails to take reasonable remedial action.

Responsibilities of Lawyers with Managerial Responsibilities

Comment on Rule 5.1

[2] Lawyers with managerial authority within a firm or government agency should make reasonable efforts to establish internal policies and procedures designed to provide reasonable assurance that all lawyers in the firm or government agency will conform to the Ohio Rules of Professional Conduct. Such policies and procedures could include those designed to detect and resolve conflicts of interest, identify dates by which actions must be taken in pending matters, account for client funds and property, and ensure that inexperienced lawyers are properly supervised.

[3] Other measures may be advisable depending on the firm's structure and the nature of its practice. In a small firm of experienced lawyers, informal supervision and periodic review of compliance with the firm's policies may be appropriate. In a large firm, or in practice situations in which difficult ethical problems frequently arise, more elaborate measures may be prudent. Some firms, for example, have a procedure whereby junior lawyers can make confidential referral of ethical problems directly to a designated senior partner or special committee. See Rule 5.2. In any event, the ethical atmosphere of a firm can influence the conduct of all its members, and lawyers with managerial authority should not assume that all lawyers associated with the firm will inevitably conform to the rules. These principles apply to lawyers practicing in government agencies.

The Ethical Atmosphere of a Law Firm

[4] Division (c) expresses a general principle of personal responsibility for acts of another. See also Rule 8.4(a).

[5] Division (c)(2) defines the duty of a partner or other lawyer having comparable managerial authority in a law firm or government agency, as well as a lawyer who has direct supervisory authority over performance of specific legal work by another lawyer. Whether a lawyer has supervisory authority in particular circumstances is a question of fact. Lawyers with managerial authority have at least indirect responsibility for all work being done by the firm or government agency, while a partner or manager in charge of a particular matter ordinarily also has supervisory responsibility for the work of other firm or government agency lawyers engaged in the matter. Appropriate remedial action by a partner or managing lawyer would depend on the immediacy of that lawyer's involvement and the seriousness of the misconduct. A supervisor is required to intervene to prevent avoidable consequences of misconduct if the supervisor knows that the misconduct occurred. Thus, if a supervising lawyer knows that a subordinate misrepresented a matter to an opposing party in negotiation, the supervisor as well as the subordinate has a duty to correct the resulting misapprehension.

Duties of Supervisors

[6] Professional misconduct by a lawyer under supervision could reveal a violation of division (b) on the part of the supervisory lawyer even though it does not entail a violation of division (c) because there was no direction, ratification, or knowledge of the violation.

[7] Apart from this rule and Rule 8.4(a), a lawyer does not have disciplinary liability for the conduct of a partner, associate, or subordinate. Whether a lawyer may be liable civilly or criminally for another lawyer's conduct is a question of law beyond the scope of these rules.

[8] The duties imposed by this rule on managing and supervising lawyers do not alter the personal duty of each lawyer in a firm or government agency to abide by the Ohio Rules of Professional Conduct. See Rule 5.2(a).

Rule 5.2: Responsibilities of a subordinate lawyer

(a) A lawyer is bound by the Ohio Rules of Professional Conduct notwithstanding that the lawyer acted at the direction of another person.

Ethical Violations by Subordinate Lawyers

(b) A subordinate lawyer does not violate the Ohio Rules of Professional Conduct if that lawyer acts in accordance with a supervisory lawyer's reasonable resolution of a question of professional duty.

Comment on Rule 5.2

[1] Although a lawyer is not relieved of responsibility for a violation by the fact that the lawyer acted at the direction of a supervisor, that fact may be relevant in determining whether a lawyer had the knowledge required to render conduct a violation of the rules. For example, if a subordinate filed a frivolous pleading at the direction of a supervisor, the subordinate would not be guilty of a professional violation unless the subordinate knew of the document's frivolous character.

[2] When lawyers in a supervisor-subordinate relationship encounter a matter involving professional judgment as to ethical duty, the supervisor may assume responsibility for making the judgment. Otherwise a consistent course of action or position could not be taken. If the question can reasonably be answered only one way, the duty of both lawyers is clear and they are equally responsible for fulfilling it. However, if the resolution is unclear, someone has to decide upon the course of action. That authority ordinarily reposes in the supervisor, and a subordinate may be guided accordingly. For example, if a question arises whether the interests of two clients conflict under Rule 1.7, the supervisor's reasonable resolution of the question should protect the subordinate professionally if the resolution is subsequently challenged.

Ethical Violations by Supervisors, but not of their Subordinates

Rule 5.3: Responsibilities regarding nonlawyer assistants

With respect to a nonlawyer employed by, retained by, or associated with a lawyer, all of the following apply:

(a) a lawyer who individually or together with other lawyers possesses managerial authority in a law firm or government agency shall make reasonable efforts to ensure that the firm or government agency

Paralegals and Their Managerial Superiors

has in effect measures giving reasonable assurance that the person's conduct is compatible with the professional obligations of the lawyer;

(b) a lawyer having direct supervisory authority over the nonlawyer shall make reasonable efforts to ensure that the person's conduct is compatible with the professional obligations of the lawyer;

A Paralegal Supervisor's Duty

(c) a lawyer shall be responsible for conduct of such a person that would be a violation of the Ohio Rules of Professional Conduct if engaged in by a lawyer if either of the following applies:

Ordering or Ratifying Ethical Misconduct by Paralegals and Other Nonlawyer Assistants

(1) the lawyer orders or, with the knowledge of the specific conduct, ratifies the conduct involved;
(2) the lawyer has managerial authority in the law firm or government agency in which the person is employed, or has direct supervisory authority over the person, and knows of the conduct at a time when its consequences can be avoided or mitigated but fails to take reasonable remedial action.

Comment on Rule 5.3

[1] Lawyers generally employ assistants in their practice, including secretaries, investigators, law student interns, and paraprofessionals. Such assistants, whether employees or independent contractors, act for the lawyer in rendition of the lawyer's professional services. *A lawyer must give such assistants appropriate instruction and supervision concerning the ethical aspects of their employment, particularly regarding the obligation not to disclose information relating to representation of the client, and should be responsible for their work product.* The measures employed in supervising nonlawyers should take account of the fact that they do not have legal training and are not subject to professional discipline. [emphasis added]

Secretaries, Investigators, Interns, and Independent Contractors;

Duty to Provide Instruction and Supervision on Ethics

[2] Division (a) requires lawyers with managerial authority within a law firm or government agency to make reasonable efforts to establish internal policies and procedures designed to provide reasonable assurance that nonlawyers in the firm or government agency will act in a way compatible with the Ohio Rules of Professional Conduct. Division (b) applies to lawyers who have supervisory authority over the work of a nonlawyer. Division (c) specifies the circumstances in which a lawyer is responsible for conduct of a nonlawyer that would be a violation of the Ohio Rules of Professional Conduct if engaged in by a lawyer. [The Supreme Court of Ohio cited Model Rule 5.3 with approval as establishing a lawyer's duty to maintain a system of office procedure that ensures delegated legal duties are completed properly. See *Disciplinary Counsel v. Ball* (1993), 67 Ohio St.3d 401 and *Mahoning Cty. Bar Assn v. Lavelle,* 107 Ohio St.3d 92, 2005-Ohio-5976.]

Internal Policies and Procedures on Ethics and Nonlawyer Assistants;

Disciplinary Counsel v. Ball* and *Mahoning Cty. Bar Assn v. Lavelle

Rule 5.4: Professional independence of a lawyer

(a) *A lawyer or law firm shall not share legal fees with a nonlawyer,* except in any of the following circumstances:

Sharing Legal Fees with a Nonlawyer

(1) an agreement by a lawyer with the lawyer's firm, partner, or associate may provide for the payment of money, over a reasonable period of time after the lawyer's death, to the lawyer's estate or to one or more specified persons;
(2) a lawyer who purchases the practice of a deceased, disabled, or disappeared lawyer may, pursuant to the provisions of Rule 1.17, pay to the estate or other representative of that lawyer the agreed-upon purchase price;
(3) a lawyer or law firm may include nonlawyer employees in a compensation or retirement plan, even though the plan is based in whole or in part on a profit-sharing arrangement;
(4) a lawyer may share court-awarded legal fees with a nonprofit organization that employed or retained the lawyer in the matter;
(5) a lawyer may share legal fees with a nonprofit organization that recommended employment of the lawyer in the matter, if the nonprofit organization complies with Rule XVI of the Supreme Court Rules for the Government of the Bar of Ohio.

Including Paralegals and other Nonlawyer Assistants in Compensation and Retirement Plans

(b) *A lawyer shall not form a partnership with a nonlawyer if any of the activities of the partnership consist of the practice of law.* [emphasis added]

Forming a Partnership with a Nonlawyer

(c) A lawyer shall not permit a person who recommends, employs, or pays the lawyer to render legal services for another to direct or regulate the lawyer's professional judgment in rendering such legal services.

Interference by a Third Party Payor of Legal Services

(d) A lawyer shall not practice with or in the form of a professional corporation or association authorized to practice law for a profit, if any of the following applies:

(1) a nonlawyer owns any interest therein, except that a fiduciary representative of the estate of a lawyer may hold the stock or interest of the lawyer for a reasonable time during administration;

Nonlawyers as Directors, Officers, Owners of a Law Practice

(2) a nonlawyer is a corporate director or officer thereof or occupies the position of similar responsibility in any form of association other than a corporation;

(3) a nonlawyer has the right to direct or control the professional judgment of a lawyer.

Comment on Rule 5.4

Protecting a Lawyer's Professional Independence of Judgment

[1] The provisions of this rule express traditional limitations on sharing fees. These limitations are to protect the lawyer's professional independence of judgment. Where someone other than the client pays the lawyer's fee or salary, or recommends employment of the lawyer, that arrangement does not modify the lawyer's obligation to the client. As stated in division (c), such arrangements should not interfere with the lawyer's professional judgment.

[2] This rule also expresses traditional limitations on permitting a third party to direct or regulate the lawyer's professional judgment in rendering legal services to another. See also Rule 1.8(f) (lawyer may accept compensation from a third party as long as there is no interference with the lawyer's independent professional judgment and the client gives informed consent).

Rule 5.5: Unauthorized practice of law; multijurisdictional practice of law

Lawyers in Ohio but Licensed Elsewhere

(a) A lawyer shall not practice law in a jurisdiction in violation of the regulation of the legal profession in that jurisdiction, or assist another in doing so.

(b) A lawyer who is not admitted to practice in this jurisdiction shall not do either of the following:

(1) except as authorized by these rules or other law, establish an office or other systematic and continuous presence in this jurisdiction for the practice of law;

(2) hold out to the public or otherwise represent that the lawyer is admitted to practice law in this jurisdiction.

(c) A lawyer who is admitted in another United States jurisdiction, is in good standing in the jurisdiction in which the lawyer is admitted, and regularly practices law may provide legal services on a temporary basis in this jurisdiction if one or more of the following apply:

(1) the services are undertaken in association with a lawyer who is admitted to practice in this jurisdiction and who actively participates in the matter;

(2) the services are reasonably related to a pending or potential proceeding before a tribunal in this or another jurisdiction, if the lawyer, or a person the lawyer is assisting, is authorized by law or order to appear in such proceeding or reasonably expects to be so authorized;

Pro Hac Vice Admission

(3) the services are reasonably related to a pending or potential arbitration, mediation, or other alternative dispute resolution proceeding in this or another jurisdiction, if the services arise out of or are reasonably related to the lawyer's practice in a jurisdiction in which the lawyer is admitted to practice and are not services for which the forum requires *pro hac vice* admission;

(4) the lawyer engages in negotiations, investigations, or other nonlitigation activities that arise out of or are reasonably related to the lawyer's practice in a jurisdiction in which the lawyer is admitted to practice.

(d) A lawyer admitted and in good standing in another United States jurisdiction may provide legal services in this jurisdiction in either of the following circumstances:

(1) the lawyer is registered in compliance with Gov. Bar R. VI, Section 4 and is providing services to the employer or its organizational affiliates for which the permission of a tribunal to appear *pro hac vice* is not required;

(2) the lawyer is providing services that the lawyer is authorized to provide by federal or Ohio law.

Comment on Rule 5.5

[1] A lawyer may practice law only in a jurisdiction in which the lawyer is authorized to practice. A lawyer may be admitted to practice law in a jurisdiction on a regular basis or may be authorized by court rule or order or by law to practice for a limited purpose or on a restricted basis. Division (a) applies to unauthorized practice of law by a lawyer, whether through the lawyer's direct action or by the lawyer assisting another person.

Employing Paraprofessionals and Delegating Tasks to Them

[2] The definition of the practice of law is established by law and varies from one jurisdiction to another. Whatever the definition, limiting the practice of law to members of the bar protects the public against rendition of legal services by unqualified persons. *This rule does not prohibit a lawyer from employing the services of paraprofessionals and delegating functions to them, so long as the lawyer supervises the delegated work and retains responsibility for their work.* See Rule 5.3. [emphasis added]

[3] *A lawyer may provide professional advice and instruction to nonlawyers whose employment requires knowledge of the law; for example, claims adjusters, employees of financial or commercial institutions, social workers, accountants, and persons employed in government agencies. Lawyers also may assist independent nonlawyers, such as paraprofessionals, who are authorized by the law of a jurisdiction to provide particular law-related services. In addition, a lawyer may counsel nonlawyers who wish to proceed* pro se. . . . [emphasis added]

Instructions to Nonlawyers in Other Fields

Providing Assistance to Independent Nonlawyers Who Provide Law-Related Services

[13] Division (c)(4) permits a lawyer admitted in another jurisdiction to provide certain legal services on a temporary basis in this jurisdiction that arise out of or are reasonably related to the lawyer's practice in a jurisdiction in which the lawyer is admitted but are not within divisions (c)(2) or (c)(3). *These services include both legal services and services that nonlawyers may perform but that are considered the practice of law when performed by lawyers.* . . . [emphasis added]

Rule 5.6: Restrictions on right to practice

Restrictive Agreements and the Right to Practice Law After Leaving an Office

A lawyer shall not participate in offering or making either of the following:

(a) a partnership, shareholders, operating, employment, or other similar type of agreement that restricts the right of a lawyer to practice after termination of the relationship, except an agreement concerning benefits upon retirement;

(b) an agreement in which a restriction on the lawyer's right to practice is part of the settlement of a claim or controversy.

Comment on Rule 5.6

[1] An agreement restricting the right of lawyers to practice after leaving a firm not only limits their professional autonomy but also limits the freedom of clients to choose a lawyer. Division (a) prohibits such agreements except for restrictions incident to provisions concerning retirement benefits for service with the firm.

[2] Division (b) prohibits a lawyer from agreeing not to represent other persons in connection with settling a claim or controversy. . . .

Rule 5.7: Responsibilities regarding law-related services

Lawyers Who have Ancillary Businesses

(a) A lawyer shall be subject to the Ohio Rules of Professional Conduct with respect to the provision of law-related services, as defined in division (e) of this rule, if the law related services are provided in either of the following circumstances:

(1) by the lawyer in circumstances that are not distinct from the lawyer's provision of legal services to clients;

(2) in other circumstances by an entity controlled or owned by the lawyer individually or with others, unless the lawyer takes reasonable measures to ensure that a person obtaining the law-related services knows that the services are not legal services and that the protections of the client-lawyer relationship do not exist. . . .

(e) The term "law-related services" denotes services that might reasonably be performed in conjunction with the provision of legal services and that are not prohibited as unauthorized practice of law when provided by a nonlawyer.

Comment on Rule 5.7

[1] When a lawyer performs law-related services, sometimes referred to as "ancillary business," or controls an organization that does so, there exists the potential for ethical problems. Principal among these is the possibility that the person for whom the law-related services are performed fails to understand that the services may not carry with them the protections normally afforded as part of the client-lawyer relationship. The recipient of the law-related services may expect, for example, that the protection of client confidences, prohibitions against representation of persons with conflicting interests, and obligations of a lawyer to maintain professional independence apply to the provision of law-related services when that may not be the case. . . .

VI. Public Service

Rule 6.1: Voluntary pro bono publico service

The Supreme Court of Ohio has deferred consideration of Model Rule 6.1 in light of recommendations contained in the final report of the Supreme Court Task Force on Pro Se and Indigent Representation and recommendations from the Ohio Legal Assistance Foundation.

Pro Bono Publico Service

Rule 6.2: Accepting appointments

A lawyer shall not seek to avoid appointment by a court to represent a person except for good cause, such as either of the following:

Declining an Appointment to Represent Someone

(a) representing the client is likely to result in violation of the Ohio Rules of Professional Conduct or other law;

(b) representing the client is likely to result in an unreasonable financial burden on the lawyer.

Comment on Rule 6.2

[1] A lawyer ordinarily is not obliged to accept a client whose character or cause the lawyer regards as repugnant. The lawyer's freedom to select clients is, however, qualified. All lawyers have a responsibility to assist in providing *pro bono publico* service. An individual lawyer fulfills this responsibility by accepting a fair share of unpopular matters or indigent or unpopular clients. A lawyer may also be subject to appointment by a court to serve unpopular clients or persons unable to afford legal services.

Accepting a Fair Share of Unpopular Clients

Appointed Counsel (6.2)

[2] For good cause a lawyer may seek to decline an appointment to represent a person who cannot afford to retain counsel or whose cause is unpopular. Good cause exists if the lawyer could not handle the matter competently, see Rule 1.1, or if undertaking the representation would result in an improper conflict of interest, for example, when the client or the cause is so repugnant to the lawyer as to be likely to impair the client-lawyer relationship or the lawyer's ability to represent the client. A lawyer may also seek to decline an appointment if acceptance would be unreasonably burdensome, for example, when it would impose a financial sacrifice so great as to be unjust.

A Cause that is Repugnant to a Lawyer

[3] An appointed lawyer has the same obligations to the client as retained counsel, including the obligations of loyalty and confidentiality, and is subject to the same limitations on the client-lawyer relationship, such as the obligation to refrain from assisting the client in violation of the rules.

Rule 6.3: Membership in legal services organization

ABA Model Rule 6.3 is not adopted in Ohio. The substance of Model Rule 6.3 is addressed by other provisions of the Ohio Rules of Professional Conduct that address conflicts of interest, including Rule 1.7(a) [Conflicts of Interest: Current Clients].

Rule 6.4: Law reform activities affecting client interests

ABA Model Rule 6.4 is not adopted in Ohio. The substance of Model Rule 6.4 is addressed by other provisions of the Ohio Rules of Professional Conduct that address conflicts of interest.

Rule 6.5: Nonprofit and court-annexed limited legal services programs

Short-Term Legal Services

(a) A lawyer who, under the auspices of a program sponsored by a nonprofit organization or court, provides short-term limited legal services to a client without expectation by either the lawyer or the client that the lawyer will provide continuing representation in the matter is subject to both of the following:

(1) Rules 1.7 and 1.9 (a) only if the lawyer knows that the representation of the client involves a conflict of interest;

(2) Rule 1.10 only if the lawyer knows that another lawyer associated with the lawyer in a law firm is disqualified by Rule 1.7 or 1.9 (a) with respect to the matter.

(b) Except as provided in division (a)(2) of this rule, Rule 1.10 is inapplicable to a representation governed by this rule.

Comment on Rule 6.5

[1] Legal services organizations, courts, and various nonprofit organizations have established programs through which lawyers provide short-term limited legal services—such as advice or the completion of legal forms—that will assist persons to address their legal problems without further representation by a lawyer. In these programs, such as legal-advice hotlines, advice-only clinics, or *pro se* counseling programs, a client-lawyer relationship is established, but there is no expectation that the lawyer's representation of the client will continue beyond the limited consultation. Such programs are normally operated under circumstances in which it is not feasible for a lawyer to systematically screen for conflicts of interest as is generally required before undertaking a representation. See *e.g.*, Rules 1.7, 1.9, and 1.10.

Legal-Advice Hotlines, Advice-Only Clinics, Pro Se Counseling

[2] A lawyer who provides short-term limited legal services pursuant to this rule must communicate with the client, preferably in writing, regarding the limited scope of the representation. See Rule 1.2(c). If a short-term limited representation would not be reasonable under the circumstances, the lawyer may offer advice to the client but must also advise the client of the need for further assistance of counsel. Except as provided in this rule, the Ohio Rules of Professional Conduct, including Rules 1.6 and 1.9(c), are applicable to the limited representation.

[3] Because a lawyer who is representing a client in the circumstances addressed by this rule ordinarily is not able to check systematically for conflicts of interest, division (a) requires compliance with Rules 1.7 or 1.9(a) only if the lawyer knows that the representation presents a conflict of interest for the lawyer, and with Rule 1.10 only if the lawyer knows that another lawyer in the lawyer's firm is disqualified by Rules 1.7 or 1.9(a) in the matter. . . .

VII. Information About Legal Services

Rule 7.1: Communications concerning a lawyer's services

A lawyer shall not make or use a false, misleading, or nonverifiable communication about the lawyer or the lawyer's services. A communication is false or misleading if it contains a material misrepresentation of fact or law or omits a fact necessary to make the statement considered as a whole not materially misleading.

False, Misleading, or Unverifiable Statements

Comment on Rule 7.1

[1] This rule governs all communications about a lawyer's services, including advertising permitted by Rule 7.2. Whatever means are used to make known a lawyer's services, statements about them must be truthful.

[2] Truthful statements that are misleading are also prohibited by this rule. A truthful statement is misleading if it omits a fact necessary to make the lawyer's communication considered as a whole not materially misleading. A truthful statement is also misleading if there is a substantial likelihood that it will lead a reasonable person to formulate a specific conclusion about the lawyer or the lawyer's services for which there is no reasonable factual foundation.

When a Truthful Statement can be Misleading

[3] An advertisement that truthfully reports a lawyer's achievements on behalf of clients or former clients may be misleading if presented so as to lead a reasonable person to form an unjustified expectation that the same results could be obtained for other clients in similar matters without reference to the specific factual and legal circumstances of each client's case. Similarly, an unsubstantiated comparison of the lawyer's services or fees with the services or fees of other lawyers may be misleading if presented with such specificity as would lead a reasonable person to conclude that the comparison can be substantiated. The inclusion of an appropriate disclaimer or qualifying language may preclude a finding that a statement is likely to create unjustified expectations or otherwise mislead a prospective client.

Lawyer Advertising; Unsubstantiated Statements

[4] Characterization of rates or fees chargeable by the lawyer or law firm such as "cut-rate," "lowest," "giveaway," "below cost," "discount," or "special" is misleading.

Cut-Rate, Discount, Special Fees

[5] See also Rule 8.4(e) for the prohibition against stating or implying an ability to influence improperly a government agency or official or to achieve results by means that violate the Ohio Rules of Professional Conduct or other law.

Rule 7.2: Advertising and recommendation of professional employment

(a) Subject to the requirements of Rules 7.1 and 7.3, a lawyer may advertise services through written, recorded, or electronic communication, including public media.

(b) A lawyer shall not give anything of value to a person for recommending the lawyer's services except that a lawyer may pay any of the following:

Giving Something of Value for Recommending the Lawyer's Services

(1) the reasonable costs of advertisements or communications permitted by this rule;

(2) the usual charges of a legal service plan;

(3) the usual charges for a nonprofit or lawyer referral service that complies with Rule XVI of the Supreme Court Rules for the Government of the Bar of Ohio;

(4) for a law practice in accordance with Rule 1.17.

(c) Any communication made pursuant to this rule shall include the name and office address of at least one lawyer or law firm responsible for its content.

(d) A lawyer shall not seek employment in connection with a matter in which the lawyer or law firm does not intend to participate actively in the representation, but that the lawyer or law firm intends to refer to other counsel. This provision shall not apply to organizations listed in Rules 7.2(b)(2) or (3) or if the advertisement is in furtherance of a transaction permitted by Rule 1.17.

Comment on Rule 7.2

[1] To assist the public in obtaining legal services, lawyers should be allowed to make known their services not only through reputation but also through organized information campaigns in the form of advertising. Advertising involves an active quest for clients, contrary to the tradition that a lawyer should not seek clientele. However, the public's need to know about legal services can be fulfilled in part through advertising. This need is particularly acute in the case of persons of moderate means who have not made extensive use of legal services. The interest in expanding public information about legal services ought to prevail over considerations of tradition. Nevertheless, advertising by lawyers entails the risk of practices that are misleading or overreaching.

The Value of Advertising

[2] This rule permits public dissemination of information concerning a lawyer's name or firm name, address,

and telephone number; the kinds of services the lawyer will undertake; the basis on which the lawyer's fees are determined, including prices for specific services and payment and credit arrangements; a lawyer's foreign language ability; names of references and, with their consent, names of clients regularly represented; and other information that might invite the attention of those seeking legal assistance.

Specifics That may be Included in Advertising

[3] Questions of effectiveness and taste in advertising are matters of speculation and subjective judgment. Some jurisdictions have had extensive prohibitions against television advertising, against advertising going beyond specified facts about a lawyer, or against "undignified" advertising. Television is now one of the most powerful media for getting information to the public, particularly persons of low and moderate income; prohibiting television advertising, therefore, would impede the flow of information about legal services to many sectors of the public. Limiting the information that may be advertised has a similar effect and assumes that the bar can accurately forecast the kind of information that the public would regard as relevant. Similarly, electronic media, such as the Internet, can be an important source of information about legal services, and lawful communication by electronic mail is permitted by this rule. But see Rule 7.3(a) for the prohibition against the solicitation of a prospective client through a real-time electronic exchange that is not initiated by the prospective client.

Television and Internet Advertising

[4] Neither this rule nor Rule 7.3 prohibits communications authorized by law, such as notice to members of a class in class action litigation.

Paying Others to Recommend a Lawyer (7.2)

[5] Except as provided by these rules, lawyers are not permitted to give anything of value to another for channeling professional work. *A reciprocal referral agreement between lawyers, or between a lawyer and a nonlawyer, is prohibited.* Cf. Rule 1.5. [emphasis added]

Reciprocal Referral Agreement Between a Lawyer and a Nonlawyer

[5A] Division (b)(1) allows a lawyer to pay for advertising and communications permitted by this rule, including the costs of print directory listings, on-line directory listings, newspaper ads, television and radio airtime, domain-name registrations, sponsorship fees, banner ads, and group advertising. A lawyer may compensate employees, agents, and vendors who are engaged to provide marketing or client-development services, such as publicists, public-relations personnel, business-development staff and Web site designers. See Rule 5.3 for the duties of lawyers and law firms with respect to the conduct of *nonlawyers who prepare marketing materials for them.* [emphasis added]

Nonlawyers who Prepare Marketing Material for Lawyers

[6] A lawyer may pay the usual charges of a legal service plan or a nonprofit or qualified lawyer referral service. A legal service plan is a prepaid or group legal service plan or a similar delivery system that assists prospective clients to secure legal representation. A lawyer referral service, on the other hand, is any organization that holds itself out to the public as a lawyer referral service. Such referral services are understood by laypersons to be consumer-oriented organizations that provide unbiased referrals to lawyers with appropriate experience in the subject matter of the representation and afford other client protections, such as complaint procedures or malpractice insurance requirements. Consequently, this rule only permits a lawyer to pay the usual charges of a nonprofit or qualified lawyer referral service. A qualified lawyer referral service is one that is approved pursuant to Rule XVI of the Supreme Court Rules for the Government of the Bar of Ohio. Relative to fee sharing, see Rule 5.4(a)(5).

Lawyer Referral Service

[7] A lawyer who accepts assignments or referrals from a legal service plan or referrals from a lawyer referral service must act reasonably to assure that the activities of the plan or service are compatible with the lawyer's professional obligations. See Rule 5.3. Legal service plans and lawyer referral services may communicate with prospective clients, but such communication must be in conformity with these rules. Thus, advertising must not be false or misleading, as would be the case if the communications of a group advertising program or a group legal services plan would mislead prospective clients to think that it was a lawyer referral service sponsored by a state agency or bar association. Nor could the lawyer allow in-person, telephonic, or real-time contacts that would violate Rule 7.3.

Rule 7.3: Direct contact with prospective clients

(a) A lawyer shall not by in-person, live telephone, or real-time electronic contact solicit professional employment from a prospective client when a significant motive for the lawyer's doing so is the lawyer's pecuniary gain, unless either of the following applies:

In-Person, Live, or Real-Time Solicitation

(1) the person contacted is a lawyer;

(2) the person contacted has a family, close personal, or prior professional relationship with the lawyer.

(b) A lawyer shall not solicit professional employment from a prospective client by written, recorded, or electronic communication or by in-person, telephone, or real-time electronic contact even when not otherwise prohibited by division (a), if either of the following applies:

(1) the prospective client has made known to the lawyer a desire not to be solicited by the lawyer;

Coercion, Duress, or Harassment

(2) the solicitation involves coercion, duress, or harassment.

(c) Unless the recipient of the communication is a person specified in division (a)(1) or (2) of this rule, every written, recorded, or electronic communication from a lawyer soliciting professional employment from a prospective client whom the lawyer reasonably believes to be in need of legal services in a particular matter shall comply with all of the following:

Required Contents of Soliciting Communication

(1) Disclose accurately and fully the manner in which the lawyer or law firm became aware of the identity and specific legal need of the addressee;

(2) Disclaim or refrain from expressing any predetermined evaluation of the merits of the addressee's case;

(3) Conspicuously include in its text and on the outside envelope, if any, and at the beginning and ending of any recorded or electronic communication the recital—"ADVERTISING MATERIAL" or "ADVERTISEMENT ONLY."

(d) Prior to making a communication soliciting professional employment from a prospective client pursuant to division (c) of this rule to a party who has been named as a defendant in a civil action, a lawyer or law firm shall verify that the party has been served with notice of the action filed against that party. Service shall be verified by consulting the docket of the court in which the action was filed to determine whether mail, personal, or residence service has been perfected or whether service by publication has been completed. Division (d) of this rule shall not apply to the solicitation of a debtor regarding representation of the debtor in a potential or actual bankruptcy action.

Required Verification When Soliciting Named Defendants

(e) If a communication soliciting professional employment from a prospective client or a relative of a prospective client is sent within thirty days of an accident or disaster that gives rise to a potential claim for personal injury or wrongful death, the following "Understanding Your Rights" shall be included with the communication.

Understanding Your Rights* (7.3)

Required Disclosure: Understanding Your Rights

If you have been in an accident, or a family member has been injured or killed in a crash or some other incident, you have many important decisions to make. It is important for you to consider the following:

1. Make and keep records—If your situation involves a motor vehicle crash, regardless of who may be at fault, it is helpful to obtain a copy of the police report, learn the identity of any witnesses, and obtain photographs of the scene, vehicles, and any visible injuries. Keep copies of receipts of all your expenses and medical care related to the incident.

2. You do not have to sign anything—You may not want to give an interview or recorded statement without first consulting with an attorney, because the statement can be used against you. If you may be at fault or have been charged with a traffic or other offense, it may be advisable to consult an attorney right away. However, if you have insurance, your insurance policy probably requires you to cooperate with your insurance company and to provide a statement to the company. If you fail to cooperate with your insurance company, it may void your coverage.

3. Your interests versus interests of insurance company—Your interests and those of the other person's insurance company are in conflict. Your interests may also be in conflict with your own insurance company. Even if you are not sure who is at fault, you should contact your own insurance company and advise the company of the incident to protect your insurance coverage.

4. There is a time limit to file an insurance claim—Legal rights, including filing a lawsuit, are subject to time limits. You should ask what time limits apply to your claim. You may need to act immediately to protect your rights.

5. Get it in writing—You may want to request that any offer of settlement from anyone be put in writing, including a written explanation of the type of damages which they are willing to cover.

6. Legal assistance may be appropriate—You may consult with an attorney before you sign any document or release of claims. A release may cut off all future rights against others, obligate you to repay past medical bills or disability benefits, or jeopardize future benefits. If your interests conflict with your own insurance company, you always have the right to discuss the matter with an attorney of your choice, which may be at your own expense.

7. How to find an attorney—If you need professional advice about a legal problem but do not know an attorney, you may wish to check with relatives, friends, neighbors, your employer, or co-workers who may be able to recommend an attorney. Your local bar association may have a lawyer referral service that can be found in the Yellow Pages or on the Internet.

8. Check a lawyer's qualifications—Before hiring any lawyer, you have the right to know the lawyer's background, training, and experience in dealing with cases similar to yours.

9. How much will it cost? In deciding whether to hire a particular lawyer, you should discuss, and the lawyer's written fee agreement should reflect:

a. How is the lawyer to be paid? If you already have a settlement offer, how will that affect a contingent fee arrangement?

b. How are the expenses involved in your case, such as telephone calls, deposition costs, and fees for expert witnesses, to be paid? Will these costs be advanced by the lawyer or charged to you as they are incurred? Since you are obligated to pay all expenses even if you lose your case, how will payment be arranged?

c. Who will handle your case? If the case goes to trial, who will be the trial attorney?

This information is not intended as a complete description of your legal rights, but as a checklist of some of the important issues you should consider.

*THE SUPREME COURT OF OHIO, WHICH GOVERNS THE CONDUCT OF LAWYERS IN THE STATE OF OHIO, NEITHER PROMOTES NOR PROHIBITS THE DIRECT SOLICITATION OF PERSONAL INJURY VICTIMS. THE COURT DOES REQUIRE THAT, IF SUCH A SOLICITATION IS MADE, IT MUST INCLUDE THE ABOVE DISCLOSURE.

Prepaid or Group Legal Service Plans

(f) Notwithstanding the prohibitions in division (a) of this rule, a lawyer may participate with a prepaid or group legal service plan operated by an organization not owned or directed by the lawyer that uses in-person or telephone contact to solicit memberships or subscriptions for the plan from persons who are not known to need legal services in a particular matter covered by the plan.

Comment on Rule 7.3

[1] There is a potential for abuse inherent in direct in-person, live telephone, or real-time electronic contact by a lawyer with a prospective client known to need legal services. These forms of contact between a lawyer and a prospective client subject the layperson to the private importuning of the trained advocate in a direct interpersonal encounter. The prospective client, who may already feel overwhelmed by the circumstances giving rise to the need for legal services, may find it difficult fully to evaluate all available alternatives with reasoned judgment and appropriate self-interest in the face of the lawyer's presence and insistence upon being retained immediately. The situation is fraught with the possibility of undue influence, intimidation, and overreaching.

Solicitation Abuse

[2] This potential for abuse inherent in direct in-person, live telephone, or real-time electronic solicitation of prospective clients justifies its prohibition, particularly since lawyer advertising and written and recorded communication permitted under Rule 7.2 offer alternative means of conveying necessary information to those who may be in need of legal services. Advertising and written and recorded communications that may be mailed or autodialed make it possible for a prospective client to be informed about the need for legal services, and about the qualifications of available lawyers and law firms, without subjecting the prospective client to direct in-person, telephone, or real-time electronic persuasion that may overwhelm the prospective client's judgment. In using any telephone communication, a lawyer remains subject to applicable requirements of the "Do Not Call" provisions of federal telemarketing sales regulations.

Overwhelming a Prospective Client Through Solicitation

[3] The use of general advertising and written, recorded, or electronic communications to transmit information from lawyer to prospective client, rather than direct in-person, live telephone, or real-time electronic contact, will help to ensure that the information flows cleanly as well as freely. The contents of advertisements and communications permitted under Rule 7.2 can be permanently recorded so that they cannot be disputed and may be shared with others who know the lawyer. This potential for informal review is itself likely to help guard against statements and claims that might constitute false and misleading communications, in violation of Rule 7.1. The contents of direct in-person, live telephone, or real-time electronic conversations between a lawyer and a prospective client can be disputed and may not be subject to third-party scrutiny. Consequently, they are much more likely to approach, and occasionally cross, the dividing line between accurate representations and those that are false and misleading.

[4] There is far less likelihood that a lawyer would engage in abusive practices against an individual who is a former client, or with whom the lawyer has close personal or family relationship, or in situations in which the lawyer is motivated by considerations other than the lawyer's pecuniary gain. Nor is there a serious potential for abuse when the person contacted is a lawyer. Consequently, the general prohibition in Rule 7.3(a) and the requirements of Rule 7.3(c) are not applicable in those situations. Also, division (a) is not intended to prohibit a lawyer from participating in constitutionally protected activities of public or charitable legal service organizations or bona fide political, social, civic, fraternal, employee, or trade organizations whose purposes include providing or recommending legal services to its members or beneficiaries.

Soliciting Former Clients, Friends, and Family Members

[5] But even permitted forms of solicitation can be abused. Thus, any solicitation that contains information that is false or misleading within the meaning of

Rule 7.1, that involves coercion, duress, or harassment within the meaning of Rule 7.3(b)(2), or that involves contact with a prospective client who has made known to the lawyer a desire not to be solicited by the lawyer within the meaning of Rule 7.3(b)(1) is prohibited. Moreover, if after sending a letter or other communication to a prospective client as permitted by Rule 7.2 the lawyer receives no response, any further effort to communicate with the prospective client may violate the provisions of Rule 7.3(b).

[6] This rule is not intended to prohibit a lawyer from contacting representatives of organizations or groups that may be interested in establishing a group or prepaid legal plan for their members, insureds, beneficiaries, or other third parties for the purpose of informing such entities of the availability of and details concerning the plan or arrangement that the lawyer or lawyer's firm is willing to offer. This form of communication is not directed to a prospective client. Rather, it is usually addressed to an individual acting in a fiduciary capacity seeking a supplier of legal services for others who may, if they choose, become prospective clients of the lawyer. Under these circumstances, the activity that the lawyer undertakes in communicating with such representatives and the type of information transmitted to the individual are functionally similar to and serve the same purpose as advertising permitted under Rule 7.2.

Prepaid or Group Legal Service Plans

[7] None of the requirements of Rule 7.3 applies to communications sent in response to requests from clients or prospective clients. General announcements by lawyers, including changes in personnel or office location, do not constitute communications soliciting professional employment from a client known to be in need of legal services within the meaning of this rule.

[7A] The use of written, recorded, and electronic communications to solicit prospective clients who have suffered personal injuries or the loss of a loved one can potentially be offensive. Nonetheless, it is recognized that such communications assist potential clients in not only making a meaningful determination about representation, but also can aid potential clients in recognizing issues that may be foreign to them. Accordingly, the information contained in division (e) must be communicated to the prospective client or a relative of a prospective client when the solicitation occurs within thirty days of an accident or disaster that gives rise to a potential claim for personal injury or wrongful death.

[8] Division (f) of this rule permits a lawyer to participate with an organization that uses personal contact to solicit members for its group or prepaid legal service plan, provided that the personal contact is not undertaken by any lawyer who would be a provider of legal services through the plan. The organization must not be owned or directed, whether as manager or otherwise, by any lawyer or law firm that participates in the plan. For example, division (f) would not permit a lawyer to create an organization controlled directly or indirectly by the lawyer and use the organization for the in-person or telephone solicitation of legal employment of the lawyer through memberships in the plan or otherwise. The communication permitted by these organizations also must not be directed to a person known to need legal services in a particular matter, but is to be designed to inform potential plan members generally of another means of affordable legal services. Lawyers who participate in a legal service plan must reasonably ensure that the plan sponsors are in compliance with Rules 7.1, 7.2, and 7.3(b). See Rule 8.4(a).

Rule 7.4: Communication of fields of practice and specialization

(a) A lawyer may communicate the fact that the lawyer does or does not practice in particular fields of law or limits his or her practice to or concentrates in particular fields of law.

Lawyers Engaged in Specialties

(b) A lawyer admitted to engage in patent practice before the United States Patent and Trademark Office may use the designation "Patent Attorney" or a substantially similar designation.

(c) A lawyer engaged in trademark practice may use the designation "Trademarks," "Trademark Attorney," or a substantially similar designation.

(d) A lawyer engaged in Admiralty practice may use the designation "Admiralty," "Proctor in Admiralty," or a substantially similar designation.

(e) A lawyer shall not state or imply that a lawyer is certified as a specialist in a particular field of law, unless both of the following apply:

When a Lawyer can be Called Certified

(1) the lawyer has been certified as a specialist by an organization approved by the Supreme Court Commission on Certification of Attorneys as Specialists;

(2) the name of the certifying organization is clearly identified in the communication.

Comment on Rule 7.4

[1] Division (a) of this rule permits a lawyer to indicate areas of practice in communications about the lawyer's services. If a lawyer practices only in certain fields, or will not accept matters except in a specified field or fields, the lawyer is permitted to so indicate. A lawyer is generally permitted to state that the lawyer is a "specialist," practices a "specialty," or "specializes in" particular fields, but such communications are subject to the "false and misleading" standard applied in Rule 7.1 to communications concerning a lawyer's services.

[2] Divisions (b) and (c) recognize the long-established policy of the Patent and Trademark Office for the designation of lawyers practicing before the office. Division (d) recognizes that designation of Admiralty practice has a long historical tradition associated with maritime commerce and the federal courts.

[3] Division (e) permits a lawyer to state that the lawyer is certified as a specialist in a field of law if such certification is granted by an organization approved by the Supreme Court Commission on Certification of Attorneys as Specialists. Certification signifies that an objective entity has recognized an advanced degree of knowledge and experience in the specialty area greater than is suggested by general licensure to practice law. Certifying organizations may be expected to apply standards of experience, knowledge, and proficiency to ensure that a lawyer's recognition as a specialist is meaningful and reliable. In order to ensure that consumers can obtain access to useful information about an organization granting certification, the name of the certifying organization must be included in any communication regarding the certification.

Commission on Certification of Attorneys as Specialists

Rule 7.5: Firm names and letterheads

(a) A lawyer shall not use a firm name, letterhead or other professional designation that violates Rule 7.1. A lawyer in private practice shall not practice under a trade name, a name that is misleading as to the identity of the lawyer or lawyers practicing under the name, or a firm name containing names other than those of one or more of the lawyers in the firm, except that the name of a professional corporation or association, legal clinic, limited liability company, or registered partnership shall contain symbols indicating the nature of the organization as required by Gov. Bar R. III. If otherwise lawful, a firm may use as, or continue to include in, its name the name or names of one or more deceased or retired members of the firm or of a predecessor firm in a continuing line of succession.

Law Firm Names and Letterhead Designations

(b) A law firm with offices in more than one jurisdiction that lists attorneys associated with the firm shall indicate the jurisdictional limitations on those not licensed to practice in Ohio.

(c) The name of a lawyer holding a public office shall not be used in the name of a law firm, or in communications on its behalf, during any substantial period in which the lawyer is not actively and regularly practicing with the firm.

(d) Lawyers may state or imply that they practice in a partnership or other organization only when that is the fact.

Comment on Rule 7.5

[1] A firm may be designated by the names of all or some of its members or by the names of deceased members where there has been a continuing succession in the firm's identity. The letterhead of a law firm may give the names and dates of predecessor firms in a continuing line of succession. A lawyer or law firm may also be designated by a distinctive Web site address or comparable professional designation. It may be observed that any firm name including the name of a deceased partner is, strictly speaking, a trade name. The use of such names to designate law firms has proven a useful means of identification. However, it is misleading to use the name of a lawyer not associated with the firm or a predecessor of the firm *or the name of a nonlawyer.* [emphasis added]

Web Address of a Law Firm

Misleading to use the Name of a Nonlawyer in a Law Firm Name

[2] With regard to division (d), lawyers sharing office facilities, but who are not in fact associated with each other in a law firm, may not denominate themselves as, for example, "Smith and Jones," for that title suggests that they are practicing law together in a firm. The use of a disclaimer such as "not a partnership" or "an association of sole practitioners" does not render the name or designation permissible.

Lawyers Sharing Office Space

[3] A lawyer may be designated "Of Counsel" if the lawyer has a continuing relationship with a lawyer or law firm, other than as a partner or associate.

[4] A legal clinic operated by one or more lawyers may be organized by the lawyer or lawyers for the purpose of providing standardized and multiple legal services. The name of the law office shall consist only of the names of one or more of the active lawyers in the organization, and may include the phrase "legal clinic" or words of similar import. The use of a trade name or geographical or other type of identification or description is prohibited. The name of any active lawyer in the clinic may be retained in the name of the legal clinic after the lawyer's death, retirement, or inactivity because of age or disability, and the name must otherwise conform to other provisions of the Ohio Rules of Professional Conduct and the Supreme Court Rules for the Government of the Bar of Ohio. *The legal clinic cannot be owned by, and profits or losses cannot be shared with, nonlawyers* or lawyers who are not actively engaged in the practice of law in the organization. [emphasis added]

Legal Clinics Providing Standardized Legal Services

Nonlawyers Cannot Own Legal Clinics

Rule 7.6: Political contributions to obtain government legal engagements or appointments by judges

ABA Model Rule 7.6 is not adopted in Ohio. The substance of Model Rule 7.6 is addressed by provisions of the Ohio Ethics Law, particularly R.C. 102.03(F) and (G), and other criminal prohibitions relative to bribery and attempts to influence the conduct of elected officials. A lawyer or law firm that violates these statutory prohibitions would be in violation of other provisions of the Ohio Rules of Professional Conduct, such as Rule 8.4.

VII. Maintaining The Integrity Of The Profession

Rule 8.1: Bar admission and disciplinary matters

Candor in Procedures to Admit Lawyers to Practice and to Discipline Them

In connection with a bar admission application or in connection with a disciplinary matter, a lawyer shall not do any of the following:

(a) knowingly make a false statement of material fact;

(b) in response to a demand for information from an admissions or disciplinary authority, fail to disclose a material fact or knowingly fail to respond, except that this rule does not require disclosure of information otherwise protected by Rule 1.6.

Comment on Rule 8.1

[1] The duty imposed by this rule applies to a lawyer's own admission or discipline as well as that of others. Thus, it is a separate professional offense for a lawyer to knowingly make a misrepresentation or omit a material fact in connection with a disciplinary investigation of the lawyer's own conduct. Rule I of the Supreme Court Rules for the Government of the Bar of Ohio addresses the obligations of applicants for admission to the bar.

[2] This rule is subject to the provisions of the Fifth Amendment of the United States Constitution and Article I, Section 10 of the Ohio Constitution. A person relying on such a provision in response to a question, however, should do so openly and not use the right of nondisclosure as a justification for failure to comply with this rule.

[3] A lawyer representing an applicant for admission to the bar, or representing a lawyer who is the subject of a disciplinary inquiry or proceeding, is governed by the rules applicable to the client-lawyer relationship, including Rule 1.6 and, in some cases, Rule 3.3.

Rule 8.2: Judicial officials

False and Reckless Statements About Judges

(a) A lawyer shall not make a statement that the lawyer knows to be false or with reckless disregard as to its truth or falsity concerning the qualifications or integrity of a judicial officer, or candidate for election or appointment to judicial office.

(b) A lawyer who is a candidate for judicial office shall not violate the provisions of the Ohio Code of Judicial Conduct applicable to judicial candidates.

Comment on Rule 8.2

[1] Assessments by lawyers are relied on in evaluating the professional or personal fitness of persons being considered for election or appointment to judicial office. Expressing honest and candid opinions on such matters contributes to improving the administration of justice. Conversely, false statements by a lawyer can unfairly undermine public confidence in the administration of justice.

[3] To maintain the fair and independent administration of justice, lawyers are encouraged to continue traditional efforts to defend judges and courts unjustly criticized.

Rule 8.3: Reporting professional misconduct

Reporting Another Lawyer's Dishonesty, Untrustworthiness, or Unfitness

(a) A lawyer who possesses unprivileged knowledge of a violation of the Ohio Rules of Professional Conduct that raises a question as to any lawyer's honesty, trustworthiness, or fitness as a lawyer in other respects, shall inform a disciplinary authority empowered to investigate or act upon such a violation.

Reporting a Judge

(b) A lawyer who possesses unprivileged knowledge that a judge has committed a violation of the Ohio Rules of Professional Conduct or applicable rules of judicial conduct shall inform the appropriate authority.

(c) Any information obtained by a member of a committee or subcommittee of a bar association, or by a member, employee, or agent of a nonprofit corporation established by a bar association, designed to assist lawyers with substance abuse or mental health problems, provided the information was obtained while the member, employee, or agent was performing duties as a member, employee, or agent of the committee, subcommittee, or nonprofit corporation, shall be privileged for all purposes under this rule.

Comment on Rule 8.3

Misconduct by Lawyers and Judges

[1] Self-regulation of the legal profession requires that a member of the profession initiate disciplinary investigation when the lawyer knows of a violation of the Ohio Rules of Professional Conduct involving that lawyer or another lawyer. A lawyer has a similar obligation with respect to judicial misconduct. An

apparently isolated violation may indicate a pattern of misconduct that only a disciplinary investigation can uncover. Reporting a violation is especially important where the victim is unlikely to discover the offense.

[2] A report about misconduct is not required where it would involve the disclosure of privileged information. However, a lawyer should encourage a client to consent to disclosure where it would not substantially prejudice the client's interests.

[4] The duty to report professional misconduct does not apply to a lawyer retained to represent a lawyer whose professional conduct is in question. Such a situation is governed by the rules applicable to the client-lawyer relationship. See Rule 1.6.

[5] Information about a lawyer's or judge's misconduct or fitness may be received by a lawyer in the course of that lawyer's participation in an approved lawyers or judges assistance program. In that circumstance, providing for an exception to the reporting requirements of divisions (a) and (b) of this rule encourages lawyers and judges to seek treatment through such a program. Conversely, without such an exception, lawyers and judges may hesitate to seek assistance from these programs, which may then result in additional harm to their professional careers and additional injury to the welfare of clients and the public.

Rule 8.4: Misconduct

Professional Misconduct: Dishonesty, Fraud, etc.

It is professional misconduct for a lawyer to do any of the following:

(a) violate or attempt to violate the Ohio Rules of Professional Conduct, knowingly assist or induce another to do so, or do so through the acts of another;

(b) commit an illegal act that reflects adversely on the lawyer's honesty or trustworthiness;

(c) engage in conduct involving dishonesty, fraud, deceit, or misrepresentation;

(d) engage in conduct that is prejudicial to the administration of justice;

(e) state or imply an ability to influence improperly a government agency or official or to achieve results by means that violate the Ohio Rules of Professional Conduct or other law;

(f) knowingly assist a judge or judicial officer in conduct that is a violation of the Ohio Rules of Professional Conduct, the applicable rules of judicial conduct, or other law;

Racial, Sexual, Disability, and Other Discrimination

(g) engage, in a professional capacity, in conduct involving discrimination prohibited by law because of race, color, religion, age, gender, sexual orientation, national origin, marital status, or disability;

(h) engage in any other conduct that adversely reflects on the lawyer's fitness to practice law.

Comment on Rule 8.4

Instructing a Lawyer's Agent to Engage in Misconduct

[1] Lawyers are subject to discipline when they violate or attempt to violate the Ohio Rules of Professional Conduct, knowingly assist or induce another to do so, or do so through the acts of another, as when they *request or instruct an agent to do so on the lawyer's behalf.* Division (a), however, does not prohibit a lawyer from advising a client concerning action the client is legally entitled to take. [emphasis added]

Categories of Offenses that are Evidence of Unfitness

[2] Many kinds of illegal conduct reflect adversely on fitness to practice law, such as offenses involving fraud and the offense of willful failure to file an income tax return. However, some kinds of offenses carry no such implication. Traditionally, the distinction was drawn in terms of offenses involving "moral turpitude." That concept can be construed to include offenses concerning some matters of personal morality, such as adultery and comparable offenses, that have no specific connection to fitness for the practice of law. Although a lawyer is personally answerable to the entire criminal law, a lawyer should be professionally answerable only for offenses that indicate lack of those characteristics relevant to law practice. Offenses involving violence, dishonesty, breach of trust, or serious interference with the administration of justice are in that category. A pattern of repeated offenses, even ones of minor significance when considered separately, can indicate indifference to legal obligation.

[2A] Division (c) does not prohibit a lawyer from supervising or advising about lawful covert activity in the investigation of criminal activity or violations of constitutional or civil rights when authorized by law.

[3] Division (g) does not apply to a lawyer's confidential communication to a client or preclude legitimate advocacy where race, color, religion, age, gender, sexual orientation, national origin, marital status, or disability is relevant to the proceeding where the advocacy is made.

Good Faith Challenges to the Law

[4] A lawyer may refuse to comply with an obligation imposed by law upon a good faith belief that no valid obligation exists. The provisions of Rule 1.2(d) concerning a good faith challenge to the validity, scope, meaning, or application of the law apply to challenges of legal regulation of the practice of law.

[5] Lawyers holding public office assume legal responsibilities going beyond those of other citizens. A

lawyer's abuse of public office can suggest an inability to fulfill the professional role of lawyers. The same is true of abuse of positions of private trust such as trustee, executor, administrator, guardian, agent, and officer, director, or manager of a corporation or other organization.

Rule 8.5: Disciplinary authority; choice of law

Disciplining a Lawyer

(a) Disciplinary Authority. A lawyer admitted to practice in Ohio is subject to the disciplinary authority of Ohio, regardless of where the lawyer's conduct occurs. A lawyer not admitted in Ohio is also subject to the disciplinary authority of Ohio if the lawyer provides or offers to provide any legal services in Ohio. A lawyer may be subject to the disciplinary authority of both Ohio and another jurisdiction for the same conduct.

(b) Choice of Law. In any exercise of the disciplinary authority of Ohio, the rules of professional conduct to be applied shall be as follows:

(1) for conduct in connection with a matter pending before a tribunal, the rules of the jurisdiction in which the tribunal sits, unless the rules of the tribunal provide otherwise;

(2) for any other conduct, the rules of the jurisdiction in which the lawyer's conduct occurred, or, if the predominant effect of the conduct is in a different jurisdiction, the rules of that jurisdiction shall be applied to the conduct. A lawyer shall not be subject to discipline if the lawyer's conduct conforms to the rules of a jurisdiction in which the lawyer reasonably believes the predominant effect of the lawyer's conduct will occur.

Comment on Rule 8.5

Disciplinary Authority

Power to Regulate the Practice of Law

[1A] A lawyer admitted in another state, but not Ohio, may seek permission from a tribunal to appear *pro hac vice*. The decision of whether to permit representation by an out-of-state lawyer before an Ohio tribunal is a matter within the discretion of the trial court. Once *pro hac vice* status is extended, the tribunal retains the authority to revoke the status as part of its inherent power to regulate the practice before the tribunal and protect the integrity of its proceedings. Revocation of *pro hac vice* status and disciplinary proceedings are separate methods of addressing lawyer misconduct, and a lawyer may be subject to disciplinary proceedings for the same conduct that led to revocation of *pro hac vice* status. . . .

Form Of Citation, Effective Date, Application

(a) These rules shall be known as the Ohio Rules of Professional Conduct and cited as "Prof. Cond. Rule _____."

(b) The Ohio Rules of Professional Conduct shall take effect February 1, 2007, at which time the Ohio Rules of Professional Conduct shall supersede and replace the Ohio Code of Professional Responsibility to govern the conduct of lawyers occurring on or after that effective date. The Ohio Code of Professional Responsibility shall continue to apply to govern conduct occurring prior to February 1, 2007 and shall apply to all disciplinary investigations and prosecutions relating to conduct that occurred prior to February 1, 2007.

F. More Information

Ohio Rules of Professional Conduct (ORPC)
www.sconet.state.oh.us/Atty-Svcs/ProfConduct

ORPC Rules and Comments Correlated to the Old Code
www.sconet.state.oh.us/Atty-Svcs/ProfConduct/rules/correlation_table.pdf

Summary of Revisions Made in the ORPC
www.sconet.state.oh.us/Atty-Svcs/ProfConduct/default.asp

Ohio Code of Professional Responsibility (old code)
www.sconet.state.oh.us/Rules/professional

Ohio State Bar Association
www.ohiobar.org
(in the search box, type "unauthorized practice of law")

Professionalism Codes
www.abanet.org/cpr/professionalism/profcodes.html
(scroll down to "Ohio")

American Legal Ethics Library
www.law.cornell.edu/ethics
(click "Listing by jurisdiction" then "Ohio")

Ohio Ethics
www.law.cornell.edu/ethics/oh/narr/OH_NARR_5.HTM
www.law.cornell.edu/ethics/ohio.html
www.ll.georgetown.edu/states/ethics/ohio.cfm

American Bar Association Model Rules of Professional Conduct
www.abanet.org/cpr/mrpc/model_rules.html
www.abanet.org/cpr/mrpc/home.html
www.abanet.org/cpr/mrpc/mrpc_toc.html

Ethics in General
www.abanet.org/cpr/links.html
www.abanet.org/cpr/ethicsearch/resource.html
www.legalethics.com

G. Something to Check

At the beginning of this section, there is a list called "Rules and Comments in the ORPC of Particular Relevance to Paralegals and Other Nonattorneys." Prepare a similar list of DRs (Disciplinary Rules) and ECs (Ethical Considerations) for the code that the ORPC replaced, the Ohio Code of Professional Responsibility (*www.sconet.state.oh.us/Rules/professional*).

3.3 Ethical Opinions of the Board of Commissioners on Grievances and Discipline Involving Paralegals and Other Nonattorneys

A. Introduction
B. Issues Covered
C. Advisory Opinions
D. More Information
E. Something to Check

A. Introduction

The text of the ethical rules governing attorneys is found in section 3.2. Here we will cover some of the relevant ethical opinions of the Board of Commissioners on Grievances and Discipline. The opinions are on the Ohio Code of Professional Responsibility. No opinions exist yet on the recently adopted Ohio Rules of Professional Conduct.

Board of Commissioners on Grievances and Discipline
65 South Front St., 5th Floor
Columbus, Ohio 43215-3431
614-387-9370
www.sconet.state.oh.us/boc

The Board is a twenty-eight member commission appointed by the Ohio Supreme Court. It prepares recommendations to the Supreme Court on formal disciplinary charges against Ohio's lawyers and judges. It also writes advisory ethics opinions, some of which are excerpted or summarized here.

The Board's opinions are called "advisory" because final decisions on all ethical matters are made by the Supreme Court of Ohio. The Board inserts the following notification in its opinions: "Advisory Opinions of the Board of Commissioners on Grievances and Discipline are informal, nonbinding opinions in response to prospective or hypothetical questions regarding the application of the Supreme Court Rules for the Government of the Bar of Ohio, the Supreme Court Rules for the Government of the Judiciary, the Code of Professional Responsibility, the Code of Judicial Conduct, and the Attorney's Oath of Office. Pursuant to Section 102.08 of the Ohio Revised Code, the requester of the opinion may reasonably rely on the opinion as it applies to Ohio Ethics Law and related statutes."

B. Issues Covered

Issues Covered in Advisory Opinions That Are Relevant to Paralegals and Other Nonattorneys

ABA Model Rule 5.3 (1991-9)
Assisting in the unauthorized practice of law (2002-4)
Associates (1995-1)
Attorney acting as paralegal (1992-4)
Attorney supervision of paralegals (1991-9; 2002-4)
Business cards (1989-16)
Complaint drafting (1990-10)
Computer files (1991-9)
Confidentiality (1991-9)
Contingency fee (1994-8)
Delegation of tasks to paralegals (2000-3; 2002-4)
Deposition by paralegal (2002-4)
Disclosing a paralegal's status (1989-11)
Ethics training (1991-9)
Fee splitting (1994-8)
Filing systems (1991-9)
Group, meaning of (2006-2)
Inactive attorney as paralegal (1992-4)
Insurance company guidelines on paralegal use (2000-3)
Interference with professional judgment (2000-3)
Interviewing (1990-10)
Law firm letterhead (1989-11; 1989-16)
Law firm name (1995-1; 2006-2)
Law group (2006-2)
Legal advice (1990-10)
Legal Aid Society (1990-10)
Letterhead (1989-11; 1989-16)
Paralegal name and law firm name (1995-1; 2006-2)
Paralegal status, disclosing (1989-11)
Paralegal taking a deposition (2002-4)
Paralegal use, insurance guidelines on (2000-3)
Paralegal, decision on when to use a (2000-3)
Paternity complaints (1990-10)
Practice of law defined (2002-4)
Professional judgment (2000-3)
Retired Attorney as paralegal (1992-4)
Secrets, preserving client (1991-9)
Sharing nonattorney staff (1991-9)
Staff sharing (1991-9)
Stationery (1989-11; 1989-16)
Supervision by attorney (1990-10; 1991-9; 2002-4)
Unauthorized practice of law defined (1990-10; 2002-4)
UPL (1990-10; 2002-4)

Table of Advisory Opinions Included

(the opinions included in this section are examined in the following order)

C. Advisory Opinions

▸ A paralegal cannot conduct a deposition

Opinion Number 2002-4

Supreme Court of Ohio
Board of Commissioners on Grievances and Discipline
(June 14, 2002)
(*www.sconet.state.oh.us/BOC/Advisory_Opinions/2002//op%2002-004.doc*)

Can an attorney delegate the task of taking a deposition to a paralegal?

It is improper under DR 3-101(A) of the Ohio Code of Professional Responsibility for an attorney to delegate the taking of a deposition to a paralegal. An attorney who instructs a paralegal to take a deposition, prepares deposition questions for a paralegal to use, supervises a paralegal in taking a deposition, or instructs a paralegal to represent a deponent at deposition is assisting in the unauthorized practice of law.

The Ohio Code of Professional Responsibility prohibits lawyers from aiding a non-lawyer in the unauthorized practice of law. DR 3-101(A). The Supreme Court of Ohio defines the unauthorized practice of law (in the Supreme Court Rules for the Government of the Bar of Ohio) as follows: The rendering of legal services for another by any person:

- not admitted to practice in Ohio under Rule I [admission to the practice of law] and

- not granted active status under Rule VI [registration of attorneys], or

- not certified under Rule II [limited practice of law by a legal intern],

- not certified under Rule IX [temporary certification for practice in legal services, public defender, and law school programs], or

- not certified under Rule XI [limited practice of law by foreign legal consultants] [Gov.Bar R. VII § (2)(A)].

The Supreme Court of Ohio defines the practice of law as follows: "The practice of law is not limited to the conduct of cases in court. It embraces the preparation of pleadings and other papers incident to actions and special proceedings and the management of such actions and proceedings on behalf of clients before judges and courts, and in addition, conveyancing, the preparation of legal instruments of all kinds, and in general all advice to clients and all action taken for them in matters connected with the law." *Land Title & Trust Co. v. Dworken*, 129 Ohio St. 23 (1934).

The Ohio Revised Code prohibits the practice of law by persons not admitted to practice. "No person shall be permitted to practice as an attorney and counselor at law, or to commence, conduct, or defend any action or proceeding in which the person is not a party concerned, either by using or subscribing the person's own name, or the name of another person, unless the person has been admitted to the bar by order of the supreme court in compliance with its prescribed and published rules." Ohio Rev. Code Ann. § 4705.01 (West 1998).

A deposition is: 1. A witness's out-of-court testimony that is reduced to writing (usually by a court reporter) for later use in court or for discovery purposes. 2. The session at which such testimony is recorded. *Black's Law Dictionary*, 451 (7th ed. 1999). Depositions are taken under oath and may be used as evidence in a court proceeding. See Ohio Civ R. 28 and 32.

Taking a deposition or representing a deponent at a deposition is the rendering of legal services. The Board of Commissioners on the Unauthorized Practice of Law of the Supreme Court of Ohio determined that a non-attorney corporate officer's conduct at a deposition, inter alia, objecting several times to questions made by opposing counsel and instructing the deponent not to answer, constituted the unauthorized practice of law. *Mahoning County Bar Ass'n v. Rector*, 62 Ohio Misc. 2d 564, 569 (Ohio Bd. Unauth. Prac., Sept. 10, 1992).

Outside Ohio, the Florida First District Court of Appeal, held that "the taking of a deposition constitutes the practice of law under 454.23, Florida Statutes." *State v. Foster*, 674 So. 2d 747, 749 (Fla. Dist. Ct. App. 1996). The Florida court stated that "[a] deposition is an important, formal, recorded proceeding in which lawyers must observe the Florida rules of court and must rely on their legal training and skills to question witnesses effectively. The activities and services involved in participating in a deposition often implicate ethical questions and strategic considerations of the utmost importance. The effectiveness of the person deposing a witness can have a significant impact on whether objectionable information is identified and addressed or waived, whether a case is made, and how the evidence therefrom is used in any subsequent legal proceeding. Depositions are transcribed by a court reporter for possible use later in court . . . . Without a doubt, the process of directly examining or cross-examining a witness can affect important rights under the law." *State v. Foster*, 674 So. 2d 747, 752–53 (Fla. Dist. Ct. App. 1996).

Even if a predetermined set of questions is approved by a lawyer, a paralegal may not take a deposition. Pennsylvania Bar Ass'n, Op. 87-127 (1987). Even if supervised by a licensed attorney at a discovery deposition, a paralegal may not take or defend a deposition. See Iowa Sup. Ct, Bd of Professional Ethics and Conduct, Op. 96-3 (1996). See also, *State v. Foster*, 674 So. 2d 747, 754, (Fla. Dist. Ct. App. 1996).

In conclusion, the Board advises it is improper under DR 3-101(A) of the Ohio Code of Professional Responsibility for an attorney to delegate the taking of a deposition to a paralegal. An attorney who instructs a paralegal to take a deposition, prepares deposition questions for a paralegal to use, supervises a paralegal in taking a deposition, or instructs a paralegal to represent a deponent at deposition is assisting in the unauthorized practice of law.

Also, law school graduates who reside in Ohio while awaiting admission have no authority to practice law. Law school graduates not yet admitted to the practice of law should not take depositions, for they are not authorized to practice law.

▸ Intake and the unauthorized practice of law

Opinion Number 1990-10

Supreme Court of Ohio
Board of Commissioners on Grievances and Discipline
(June 15, 1990)
(*www.sconet.state.oh.us/boc/Advisory_Opinions/1990/op%2090-010.doc*)

Are child support enforcement caseworkers engaged in the unauthorized practice of law when they conduct initial interviews of parents seeking child support, prepare paternity complaints, and perform related tasks?

At the Child Support Enforcement Agency, all client intake and initial interviews are performed by non-lawyers who are trained as enforcement personnel. These enforcement caseworkers fill out pre-printed forms for contempt actions, petitions for support, paternity complaints and wage withholding orders. Once these initial pleadings are filled out, the case file, interview notes, employment verification, and financial documentation are forwarded to the legal department for review. A staff attorney reviews the case file and, when properly prepared, it is approved and signed for filing with the proper tribunal. The enforcement department personnel are cautioned against giving legal advice and must refer any legal questions to the legal department.

In our view, this activity would not constitute the unauthorized practice of law. We held in a prior opinion that intake workers at the legal aid society may do the initial screening for their organizations. Board of Commissioners Op. 89-25 (1989). One other state has held that it is not the unauthorized practice of law for a non-lawyer social worker to interview non-custodial parents, arrange agreements and prepare form and case summaries. Alabama St. Bar Op. 87-142 (1987).

The non-lawyer enforcement personnel's work must be approved by an attorney. The staff attorneys must also continue to be available for questions from enforcement personnel or the general public. These employees must frequently be reminded of the restriction on giving any type of legal advice.

▸ Nonattorney names printed on letterhead and business cards

Opinion Number 1989-16

Supreme Court of Ohio
Board of Commissioners on Grievances and Discipline
(June 16, 1989)
(*www.sconet.state.oh.us/BOC/Advisory_Opinions/1989/op%2089-016.doc*)

May a law firm list the name of a non-lawyer office administrator on its letterhead, provided that his name is isolated from those of the attorneys practicing in the firm, and an appropriate title reflecting his administrative function appears next to his name?

May a law firm permit a non-lawyer office administrator to use a business card bearing the firm name, provided an appropriate title reflecting his administrative function appears next to his name, and the business card is used primarily with individuals concerned with the firm's business operation?

Disciplinary Rule 2-102(A)(4) does not provide for the listing of non-lawyer employees on a law firm's letterhead. In our view, therefore, non-lawyer employees may not be listed on a law firm's letterhead. Office managers and other non-lawyer employees may have business cards designating their title and identifying them as employed by the firm.

The ABA recently issued an opinion which permits listing non-lawyers on a law firm's letterhead. ABA Committee on Ethics and Professional Responsibility, Informal Op. 1527 (1989). However, the ABA opinion interprets the Model Rules, which [as of 1989] have not been adopted in Ohio.

Disciplinary Rule 2-102(A)(4) of the Code of Professional Responsibility allows an attorney to include on his or her letterhead the name of the law firm, names of members and associates, and the names and dates relating to deceased and retired partners. In our view, the information which this rule specifically permits a lawyer to include on his or her letterhead is an exhaustive list. Hence, the rule, on its face, does not specifically permit the listing of non-lawyers.

Moreover, the listing of a non-lawyer employee may tend to mislead the public which is a violation of DR 2-101(A). Therefore, we are of the opinion that listing an office administrator on a law firm's letterhead would be a violation of the Code of Professional Responsibility.

In regard to an office administrator having a business card, we believe that it is permissible for non-lawyer employees, such as office managers, investigators and legal assistants, to have a business card. ABA Committee on Ethics and Professional Responsibility Informal Op. 1185 (1971); Informal Op. 1367 (1976). The business card may include the name, address and phone number of the firm and should clearly designate the title of the non-lawyer employee and indicate "non-lawyer."

In conclusion, it is our opinion and you are so advised that a non-lawyer employee may not be listed on a law firm's letterhead. A non-lawyer employee may have a business card which includes the firm's name and the employee's title.

▸ Paralegal signature on law firm stationery

Opinion Number 1989-11

Supreme Court of Ohio
Board of Commissioners on Grievances and Discipline
(April 14, 1989)
(*www.sconet.state.oh.us/BOC/Advisory_Opinions/1989/op%2089-011.doc*)

Can a paralegal sign his or her own name on law firm stationery?

A legal assistant employee of a law firm may sign letters using her employer's law firm letterhead, provided that she is sufficiently identified as a legal assistant so as not to mislead the receiver of the correspondence. The legal assistant should be clearly identified so as not to give the impression that the person is admitted to the practice of law. ABA Committee on Ethics and Professional Responsibility, Informal Op. 1367 (1976).

▸ Splitting a fee with a legal investigator

Opinion Number 1994-8

Supreme Court of Ohio
Board of Commissioners on Grievances and Discipline
(June 17, 1994)
(*www.sconet.state.oh.us/boc/Advisory_Opinions/1994/op%2094-008.doc*)

Can an attorney split a contingency fee with a nonattorney private investigator as compensation for the investigator's work?

The splitting of a legal fee with a non-lawyer is expressly prohibited under Disciplinary Rule 3-102(A) of the Ohio Code of Professional Responsibility: "A lawyer or law firm shall not share legal fees with a non-lawyer." The rule contains narrow exceptions not applicable here.

The policy behind the Disciplinary Rule 3-102(A) prohibition on sharing legal fees with non-lawyers is to protect clients. Fee-splitting:

- encourages non-lawyers to engage in the unauthorized practice of law—a violation of Disciplinary Rule 3-101(A);
- enhances the possibility that a non-lawyer will interfere with a lawyer's independent professional judgment—a violation of Disciplinary Rule 5-101(A);
- increases the likelihood that legal fees will be increased excessively—a violation of Disciplinary Rule 2-106(A), and
- could (in the case of sharing a fee with a private investigator) be construed as an offer to pay a witness contingent upon the content of his or her testimony or the outcome of the case in violation of Disciplinary Rule 7-109(C) ("[a] lawyer shall not pay, offer to pay, or acquiesce in the payment of compensation to a witness contingent upon the content of his [her] testimony or the outcome of the case").

In Ohio, a lawyer was indefinitely suspended for violations that included splitting a fee with a non-lawyer fire loss adjuster. See *Bar Ass'n of Greater Cleveland v. Protus*, 53 Ohio St. 2d 43 (1978). In New Mexico, a lawyer was indefinitely suspended for multiple violations of their Code including agreeing to split a legal fee with a non-lawyer as compensation for investigative work. See *In re Quintana*, 104 NM 511, 724 P2d 220 (1986). In New York, an ethics committee advised that a lawyer may not hire an investigator on a contingent fee basis. *Ass'n of the Bar of the City of New York*, Formal Op. 1993-2 (1993).

It is this Board's view that a lawyer violates Disciplinary Rule 3-102(A) by agreeing to pay a non-lawyer a percentage of a recovery in a case in exchange for the non-lawyer's services in the matter.

▸ An insurer cannot tell an attorney when to use a paralegal

Opinion Number 2000-3

Supreme Court of Ohio
Board of Commissioners on Grievances and Discipline
(January 1, 2000)
(*www.sconet.state.oh.us/BOC/Advisory_Opinions/2000/op%2000-003.doc*)

Can an insurance defense attorney abide by an insurance company's litigation management guidelines in the representation of an insured, including guidelines on when to use a paralegal?

It is improper under DR 5-107(B) for an insurance defense attorney to abide by an insurance company's litigation management guidelines in the representation of an insured when the guidelines directly interfere with the professional judgment of the attorney. Attorneys must not yield professional control of their legal work to an insurer. Guidelines that dictate how work is to be allocated among defense team members by designating what tasks are to be performed by a paralegal, associate, or senior attorney are an interference with an attorney's professional judgment. Under the facts and circumstances of a particular case, an attorney may deem it necessary or more expedient to perform a research task or other task, rather than designate the task to a paralegal. This is not a decision for others to make. The attorney is professionally responsible for the legal services. Attorneys must be able to exercise professional judgment and discretion.

▸ Paralegals and other nonattorneys should not be referred to as associates

Opinion Number 1995-1

Supreme Court of Ohio
Board of Commissioners on Grievances and Discipline
(February 3, 1995)
(*www.sconet.state.oh.us/BOC/Advisory_Opinions/1995/op%2095-001.doc*)

Can an attorney in solo practice use the phrase "and Associates" in the law firm name to indicate that the attorney employs non-attorney support staff?

DR 2-101(B) of the Code of Professional Responsibility provides that "A lawyer in private practice shall not practice under a . . . name that is misleading . . . [or under] a firm name containing names other than those of one or more of the lawyers in the firm. . . ." The phrase "and associates" is not mentioned within the disciplinary rule governing firm names. Yet, it appears in firm names across the state. The question raised to this Board indicates that there may be ambiguity as to its meaning. For example, is the term "associate" a proper reference to an office sharing attorney, to a co-counsel, or to a non-lawyer employee? Or, does the word "associate" indicate an attorney partner, attorney shareholder, or attorney employee? If the latter is the proper interpretation, then it would be misleading for an attorney with no partners, shareholders, or attorney employees to use the term "and Associates" in a firm name.

This Board adopts the view that the phrase "and Associates" in a firm name indicates that an attorney employs other attorneys. It is improper for an attorney who is a sole shareholder in a legal professional association to use the phrase "X and Associates" in the firm name, when there are no attorney employees.

▸ "Group" or "Law Group" cannot be used to refer to paralegals

Opinion Number 2006-2

Supreme Court of Ohio
Board of Commissioners on Grievances and Discipline(February 10, 2006)
(*www.sconet.state.oh.us/BOC/Advisory_Opinions/2006//op%2006-002.doc*)

Can the words "Group" or "Law Group" be used in a law firm name to refer to paralegal?

Although "Group" and "Law Group" are general terms, the words are not considered misleading or a trade name when used in the name of a law firm comprised of more than one attorney. When more than one attorney practices in a law firm, "Group" or "Law Group" in the firm name is appropriate because there actually is a "group" of attorneys.

But, when there is only one attorney in a law firm, the words "Group" or "Law Group" are not proper in a law firm name. "Group" or "Law Group" should not be used in a law firm name to refer to paralegals or other non-attorney personnel. DR 2-102 does not authorize references to or inclusion of names of non-attorneys in a law firm name. "Group" or Law Group" should not be used in a law firm name to refer to office sharing attorneys. Office sharing attorneys are not in the same firm and should not be included in a firm name. "Group" or "Law Group" should not be used in a law firm name to refer to "of counsel" attorneys. "Of counsel" attorneys have a continuing, close, regular, and personal relationship with a law firm, but the relationship is other than as a partner or associate. See Bd Comm'rs on Grievances & Discipline, Op. 2004-11 (2004).

Thus, the Board advises as follows. It is proper for a solo practitioner to name his or her law firm "The X Law Group" when "X" is the solo practitioner's surname and "X" employs one or more attorney as associates. "Group" and "Law Group" are not considered misleading or a trade name when used in naming a law firm comprised of more than one attorney. "Group" or "Law Group" should not be used in a law firm name to refer to paralegals, other non-attorney personnel, office sharing attorneys, or "of counsel" attorneys.

▸ Confidentiality problems when separate attorneys share nonattorney staff

Opinion Number 1991-9

Supreme Court of Ohio
Board of Commissioners on Grievances and Discipline
(April 12, 1991)
(*www.sconet.state.oh.us/BOC/Advisory_Opinions/1991/op%2091-009.doc*)

Can attorneys who share office space (but do not practice together) share non-lawyer staff?

The Code does not specifically prohibit the sharing of office space, equipment, personnel, or expenses among lawyers. However, under DR 4-101, which governs the preservation of client confidences and secrets, the attorney has an affirmative duty not to reveal or use a confidence or secret of his client, except when permitted by the rule. DR 4-101(A)(B)(C). The lawyer also has the affirmative duty to exercise reasonable care to prevent employees, associates, and others from disclosing or using confidences of a client. EC 4-2, DR 4-101(D).

Attorneys who maintain separate law practices within the same building must maintain filing systems that are separate from and inaccessible to each other and to each other's staffs. Computer access to client files must be limited to the client's attorney and staff in the absence of full disclosure to and consent of the client.

A more flexible rule applies to the sharing of non-lawyer staff services. DR 4-101(D) places a duty of reasonable care to prevent non-lawyer personnel from violating the preservation of client confidences and secrets: "A lawyer shall exercise reasonable care to prevent his employees, associates, and others whose services are utilized by him from disclosing or using confidences or secrets of a client, except that a lawyer may reveal the information allowed by DR 4-101(C) through an employee." Code of Professional Responsibility DR 4-101(D).

The Code acknowledges that the normal operation of a law office exposes confidential professional information to non-lawyer employees and that this obligates a lawyer to select and train his employees carefully in order to preserve the sanctity of client confidences and secrets. EC 4-2. DR 7-107(J) places a related duty upon a lawyer to prevent employees from making extrajudicial statements on confidential matters.

ABA Model Rule 5.3(a) regarding non-lawyer assistants, suggests that a partner in a firm must make reasonable efforts "to ensure that the firm has in effect measures giving reasonable assurance that the person's conduct is compatible with the professional obligations of the lawyer." Under Model Rule 5.3(b), reasonable efforts must also be made by a lawyer with supervisory authority over a non-lawyer "to ensure that the person's conduct is compatible with the professional obligations of the lawyer." The rule also deems a lawyer responsible for the conduct of the non-lawyer assistant under certain circumstances. Model Rule 5.3(c). The Comment to Model Rule 5.3 advises that the lawyer should give instruction and supervision to assistants regarding ethical aspects of employment, particularly the obligation not to disclose information relating to representation of the client.

It is the opinion of this Board that it is proper for attorneys who maintain separate practices to share non-lawyer personnel provided that each attorney exercise reasonable care to prevent his employees from disclosing or using confidences or secrets of a client as required by DR 4-101. The Board suggests that in an effort to avoid potential conflicts, the lawyers disclose to their clients that non-lawyer personnel are shared by lawyers with separate law practices.

▸ Inactive or retired attorneys cannot act as paralegals

Opinion Number 1992-4

The Supreme Court of Ohio
Board of Commissioners on Grievances and Discipline
(February 14, 1992)
(*www.sconet.state.oh.us/boc/advisory_opinions/1992/op%2092-004.doc*)

May a retired or inactive attorney perform the duties as a paralegal or student law clerk in a law firm?

Governing Bar Rule VI Sections 2 and 3 unequivocally states that attorneys with "inactive" or "retired" registration status shall not be entitled to "render *any* legal service for an attorney granted active status." (Emphasis added). This restrictive language became effective September 1, 1991. Prior to September 1, 1991, "inactive" status attorneys were governed by former Governing Bar Rule VI (8) stating that "such inactive attorney shall not be entitled to practice law nor hold himself out as authorized to practice law nor hold judicial office in this State until such time as he requests and is granted reinstatement of active status." The former rule did not contain the language "render any legal service for an attorney granted active status." There was no category for "retired" status prior to September 1, 1991.

The language of the current rule sweeps broadly with a restrictive intent. Although Rule VI underwent amendment in January 1, 1992, the prohibitions regarding rendering any legal service remains intact. Therefore, the Board advises that attorneys with "inactive" or "retired" registration status may not perform the duties of a paralegal or student law clerk because of the express requirement of the Supreme Court of Ohio that these attorneys may not "render any legal service for an attorney granted active status." Gov.Bar R. VI §§ 2 and 3.

The Board acknowledges that in Opinion 88-18 it advised that providing legal research and writing services exclusively for lawyers and law firms is not considered engaging in the practice of law. Ohio Sup. Ct, Bd. of Comm'rs on Grievances and Discipline, Op. 88-18 (1988). However, in light of the current language of Governing Bar Rule VI Sections 2 and 3, Opinion 88-18 should not be interpreted as authorization for attorneys with "inactive" or "retired" registration status to perform the services of a paralegal or law clerk.

D. More Information

Supreme Court of Ohio Board of Commissioners on Grievances and Discipline
www.sconet.state.oh.us/BOC

Advisory Opinions of the Supreme Court of Ohio Board of Commissioners on Grievances and Discipline
www.sconet.state.oh.us/BOC/Advisory_Opinions

Ohio Board on the Unauthorized Practice of Law
www.sconet.state.oh.us/UPL

Advisory Opinions of the Board Ohio on the Unauthorized Practice of Law
www.sconet.state.oh.us/UPL/advisory_opinions/default.asp

Ohio State Bar Association
www.ohiobar.org
(in the search box, type "unauthorized practice of law")

American Legal Ethics Library
www.law.cornell.edu/ethics
(click "Listing by jurisdiction" then "Ohio")

Ohio Ethics
www.law.cornell.edu/ethics/oh/narr/OH_NARR_5.HTM
www.law.cornell.edu/ethics/ohio.html
www.ll.georgetown.edu/states/ethics/ohio.cfm

Ethics in General
www.abanet.org/cpr/links.html
www.abanet.org/cpr/ethicsearch/resource.html
www.legalethics.com

E. Something to Check

Go to the Web site containing ethical opinions of the Board of Commissioners on Grievances and Discipline (*www.sconet.state.oh.us/BOC/Advisory_Opinions*). Click "Search Advisory Opinions". Run the following searches and summarize one opinion located by each search:

1. "attorney advertising"
2. "in-person solicitation"

3.4 Ohio Bar Associations and Related Attorney Organizations

A. Introduction

This section identifies every major bar association in the state. Many of the Web sites for these groups have search boxes. To find out what the group has said about paralegals, type "paralegal" or "legal assistant" in the search box. You could be led to news, committee or section activities, or ethical material pertaining to paralegals and related nonattorneys.

For additional material on Ohio attorneys, see:

- Part 1, Appendix A (Becoming an Attorney in Ohio)
- Part 3, Appendix A (Disciplinary Proceedings against an Attorney)

Before examining these associations, here is an overview of the world of Ohio attorneys.

B. Attorneys in Ohio: A Snapshot

Totals
Attorneys licensed in Ohio (2004)........................52,566
Number engaged in the active practice of law.......39,984

Bar Exam (2005)
Number taking exam for the first time...................1,444
Number of repeat takers..461
Pass Rate of first time takers....................................80%
Pass Rate of repeat takers...43%

Where Ohio Attorneys Practice
Private practice...73%
Government...15%
Businesses (house counsel)..8%
Legal aid/legal services..4%

Percentages of Women
Associates in private practice 41%
Government...45%
Businesses (house counsel)..33%
Legal aid/legal services...71%

Percentages in Private Practice Who Work Part-Time
Men 4.3%
Women 11.5%
All Ohio attorneys 5.4%

Net Income (2003)
Median all attorneys $80,000
Median private practice full-time $100,000
Median full-time males $94,500
Median full-time females $70,000
Mean (average) all attorneys $108,466

Gender Gap
Cents on the dollar earned by full-time female attorneys (2003) .... 74 cents
Cents on the dollar earned by full-time female attorneys (2000) .... 65 cents

Average Hourly Billing Rate (2004)
All private practitioners $175
Full-time males $175
Full-time females $160

Total Hours in Workweek (2004)
All attorneys 50
Full-time males 50
Full-time females 45

Sources: Economics in Law Practice in Ohio (Ohio State Bar Association, 2005). See also "Statistics on Ohio Attorneys" listed under More Information at the end of this section.

C. Ohio State Bar Association (OSBA)

Ohio State Bar Association

1700 Lake Shore Drive
P.O. Box 16562
Columbus, OH 43216-6562
614-487-2050; 800-232-7124 (membership)
www.ohiobar.org

The Ohio State Bar Association (OSBA) identifies itself as "a voluntary association of attorneys, law students and paralegals/legal assistants in the state of Ohio." OSBA does not license attorneys. The licensing body in the state is the Ohio Supreme Court.

The state bar operates a voluntary specialization program that allows attorneys to become certified as specialists in the following areas of practice: estates and probate, family law, federal tax law, labor and employment law, real property-business law, real property-residential law, and workers' compensation.

Here are some state bar services and entities that are relevant to paralegals:

OSBA Paralegal/Legal Assistant Associate Membership
www.ohiobar.org/join/?articleid=273
(Paralegal/legal assistant membership is open to any person sponsored by an attorney member of the OSBA in good standing. Dues are $70 a year. The bar defines a paralegal as "a person, qualified by education, training or work experience who is employed or retained by a lawyer, law office, corporation, governmental agency or other entity and who performs substantive legal work for which a lawyer is responsible." Membership benefits include free access to Casemaker (a legal research site) and three free CLE courses per year.

OSBA Paralegal/Legal Assistant Associate Membership Application
www.ohiobar.org/join/?articleid=273
(click "Download the Paralegal Membership Application")

OSBA Paralegal Member Benefits
downloads.ohiobar.org/applications/2005-03-brochure-paralegal.pdf

OSBA's Paralegal Certification Program
downloads.ohiobar.org/ParalegalCert/CertifiedParalegal.pdf

OSBA Paralegals/Legal Assistants Committee
(Paralegal/legal assistant members are added to the roster of the state bar's Paralegals/Legal Assistants Committee and can join over 50 other committees and sections.)
www.ohiobar.org/join/?articleid=273

OSBA Other Committees of Interest to Paralegals
Law Office Automation & Technology
Unauthorized Practice of Law

OSBA Paralegal/Legal Assistant News
www.ohiobar.org/join/?articleid=273
(All members receive the *Paralegal/Legal Assistant News*, a newsletter published three times per year.)

OSBA Guide to Paralegal Education in Ohio
downloads.ohiobar.org/products/Paralegal_Education_Guide_2003.pdf

OSBA Legal Career Center: Job Searching for Attorneys and Paralegals
ohiobar.legalstaff.com
ohiobar.legalstaff.com/JobSeeker/JobSearch.aspx?abbr=OHIOBAR
(under "Job type" select "Paralegal")

D. Other Statewide and Regional Bar Associations

Ohio Academy of Trial Attorneys
800-334-2471; 614-341-6800
www.oatlaw.org/oh

Ohio Association of Civil Trial Attorneys
614/221-1900
secure.codewriters.com/asites/main-pub.cfm?usr=oacta

Ohio Association of Criminal Defense Lawyers
614-418-1824; 800-443-2626
www.oacdl.org

Ohio Women's Bar Association
www.owba.biz

Ohio Human Rights Association (OHBA)
Columbus, OH 43201
614-443-5150

Association of Corporate Counsel (Central Ohio)
www.acca.com/php/chapters/index.php?chapter=centoh

Federal Bar Association (Ohio)
www.fedbar.org/chapters.html

E. Local Bar Associations

There are local bar associations in every county and in many large cities. This section identifies the largest ones, particularly those that can be reached online.

Some of the bar associations do not have permanent addresses. They may operate out of the personal law office of an individual member of the association. For information on contacting such associations:

- check the Web site of the courts in the area (see section 4.2); they may link to local bar associations.
- phone your neighborhood public library; its research desk may be able to give you contact information.
- do a "bar association" search in Google (or in any major search engine) by typing the name of the county (or large city) plus the phrase "bar association" followed by the word Ohio. For example: "adams county bar association" ohio "stark county bar association" ohio

You may be given links that will lead you to current addresses.

AKRON

Akron Bar Association
330-253-5007
www.akronbar.org

Akron Bar Association Associate Membership for Paralegals
(Dues: $80)
www.akronbar.org

Akron Bar Association—Legal Career Center
akronbar.legalstaff.com

ASHTABULA

Ashtabula County Bar Association
www.ashtabulacountybar.com

ATHENS COUNTY

Athens County Bar Association
www.athenscountybarassociation.com

BOWLING GREEN

Wood County Bar Association
419-352-6529
www.woodcobarassociation.org

BUTLER COUNTY

Butler County Bar Association
513-896-6671
www.butlercountybar.org

Collaborative Family Law Association of Butler County
www.collaborativefamilylawassoc.com/pages/1/index.htm

CINCINNATI

Cincinnati Bar Association
513-381-8213
www.cincybar.org

Cincinnati Bar Association Affiliate Membership for Paralegals
(Dues: $50. Affiliate members must be sponsored by an attorney member of the Cincinnati Bar Association.)
www.cincybar.org/pdfs/cbaMembershipApplication.pdf
www.cincybar.org/pdfs/cbaInformationKit.pdf

Cincinnati Bar Association Online Career Center
("the definitive employment resource for your attorney and support staff needs")
www.cincybar.org/member/jobs.asp

Black Lawyers Association of Cincinnati
www.cincinnatiblac.org

Federal Bar Association Cincinnati Chapter
www.fedbar.org/cincinnati.html

Greater Cincinnati Minority Counsel Program
www.gcmcp.org

CLERMONT COUNTY

Clermont County Bar Association
513-732-7109
www.clermontlawlibrary.com/ccba/Welcome.html

CLEVELAND

Cleveland Bar Association
216-696-3525
www.clevelandbar.org

Cleveland Bar Association Affiliate Membership for Paralegals

Dues: $85. Membership categories:

- **Voting**—must have received degree with paralegal studies component; or a minimum 3 years experience as a practicing paralegal and currently employed performing 51 percent paralegal work
- **Associate**—not eligible to be voting member, graduate of paralegal program but not currently practicing, former voting member, does not meet requirements of a practicing paralegal, or is an Allied Legal Professional paralegal manager who does not meet the requirements of a practicing paralegal, or is an Allied Legal Professional
- **Student**—currently enrolled in accredited paralegal training program and attending either part-time or full-time, courses in paralegal studies at an institutionally accredited school.
- Cleveland Association of Paralegals-Cleveland Bar Association (CAP-CBA) members must be sponsored by an attorney member of the Cleveland Bar Association or one of its associated Bar Associations; Paralegal students must be sponsored by the Dean of the Paralegal School.
  www.clevelandbar.org/CAP_application.html
  www.clevelandbar.org/affiliated.asp?id=203
  www.capohio.org
  (click "Membership")

Cleveland Bar Association Unauthorized Practice of Law Committee
("The Unauthorized Practice of Law Committee investigates confidential allegations that persons not admitted to the practice of law are in fact practicing law and files complaints against such persons with the Board of Commissioners on the Unauthorized Practice of Law of the Ohio Supreme Court seeking an injunction and potential fine for such conduct.")
www.clevelandbar.org/lawyers_committees.asp?id=65&did=65

Federal Bar Association Northern District of Ohio Chapter
www.fedbar.org/ndohio.html

COLUMBUS

Columbus Bar Association
614-221-4112
www.cbalaw.org

Columbus Bar Association Non-Attorney Associate Membership
(Non-Attorney Associate. "Any person who has never been admitted to the Bar of any U. S. jurisdiction but who is . . . a paralegal, legal assistant, court reporter or law librarian . . . may apply to the Board of Governors for acceptance as an associate member of the Association. Each such applicant must be sponsored initially by a voting member of the Association. Associate members shall not be eligible to vote or to hold office in the Association.")
www.cbalaw.org/members/documents/MembershipRules.pdf
www.cbalaw.org/members/applications/CBA-PACO application.pdf

Columbus Bar Placement Services, Job Postings: Paralegals
www.cbalaw.org/members/placement

Columbus Bar Association Unauthorized Practice of Law Committee
("Mission: To enforce the unauthorized practice of law rules and protect the integrity of the practice of law.")
www.cbalaw.org/committees/advisory/UPL.php

Federal Bar Association Columbus Chapter
www.fedbar.org/columbus.html

Franklin County Trial Lawyers Association
614-228-1017
www.fctla.org

John Mercer Langston Bar Association
www.jmlba.org

Ohio Association of Civil Trial Attorneys
614/221-1900
secure.codewriters.com/asites/main-pub.cfm?usr=oacta

Ohio Association of Criminal Defense Lawyers
614-418-1824; 800-443-2626
www.oacdl.org

Women Lawyers of Franklin County
www.wlfc.ws

Ohio Human Rights Association (OHBA)
Columbus, OH 43201
614-443-5150

CUYAHOGA COUNTY

Cuyahoga County Bar Association
216-621-5112
www.cuybar.org

Cuyahoga County Bar Association Paralegal Membership
(Dues: $45)
www.cuybar.org/membership-application.shtml

Cuyahoga County Bar Association Paralegal Committee
cuybar.org/committee.shtml

Cuyahoga County Bar Association Legal Career Center
("comprehensive job listings for attorneys and support staff")
www.cuybar.org
(click "Legal Career Center")

DAYTON

Dayton Bar Association
937-222-7902
www.daybar.org

Dayton Bar Association Associate Paralegal Membership
(Dues: $130. "Any person who, although not admitted to practice law before the Bar of Ohio or another state or territory of the United States, is employed or retained by a lawyer, law firm, or governmental agency as a paralegal (or legal assistant), or is employed in a capacity which involves the performance of legal services under the direction and supervision of an attorney may be sponsored for associate membership by a regular member of the Association who certifies as to the above.")
www.daybar.org/pdfs/membership_app_nonattorney.pdf

Dayton Bar Association Personnel Placement Service
("The Personnel Placement Service (PPS) . . . can help you begin or advance your career in legal support. We place qualified applicants in a wide variety of law-related positions including: legal assistants and paralegals")
www.daybar.org/html/pps/pps.htm

Dayton Bar Association Unauthorized Practice of Law Committee
("Responsible for investigating any matter referred to the committee or which comes to its attention, and may cause a complaint to be filed where the unauthorized practice of law is found.)
www.daybar.org/html/committees/committees.htm

Federal Bar Association Dayton Chapter
www.fedbar.org/dayton.html

ERIE COUNTY

Erie County Bar Association
www.eriecountybar.com

FAIRFIELD COUNTY

Fairfield County Bar Association
www.fairfieldcountybar.org

FRANKLIN COUNTY

Franklin County Trial Lawyers Association
614-228-1017
www.fctla.org

Women Lawyers of Franklin County
www.wlfc.ws

GEAUGA COUNTY

Geauga County Bar Association
440-286-7160
www.co.geauga.oh.us/departments/bar.htm

LAKE COUNTY

Lake County Bar Association
www.lcba-ohio.org

LORAIN

Lorain County Bar Association
440-323-8416
www.loraincountybar.org

Lorain County Bar Association Associate Membership for Paralegals
www.loraincountybar.org/Membership/Application.htm
(click "Paralegal Membership")

LUCAS COUNTY

Lucas County Bar Association
419-243-7720

MAHONING COUNTY

Mahoning County Bar Association
330-746-2933
www.mahoningbar.org

RICHLAND COUNTY

Richland County Bar Association
419-774-5595

STARK COUNTY

Stark County Bar Association
330-453-0685

Stark County Bar Association Associate Membership for Paralegals
(Associate membership includes paralegals, sponsored by a regular member of the bar association)

TOLEDO

Toledo Bar Association
419-242-9363
www.toledobar.org

Toledo Bar Association Associate Membership for Paralegals
(Associate membership includes paralegals)

Toledo Bar Association Continuing Legal Education
("paralegals . . . are welcome to attend CLE seminars")
www.toledobar.org/i4a/pages/index.cfm?pageid=3299

Association of Corporate Counsel (Toledo)
www.acca.com/php/chapters/index.php?chapter=centoh

TRUMBULL COUNTY

Trumbull County Bar Association
330-675-2415
www.tcba.net

WARREN COUNTY

Warren County Bar Association
513-695-1309
www.warrenbar.org

WOOD COUNTY

Wood County Bar Association
419-352-6529
www.woodcobarassociation.org

YOUNGSTOWN

Mahoning County Bar Association
330-746-2933

F. More Information

Bar Associations in Ohio
abanet.org/barserv/stlobar.html
www.chesslaw.com/ohiolaw.htm
www.cincybar.org/intus/links/legallinks.asp
www.law.csuohio.edu/lawlibrary/Legal_Practice_and_Professionalism.htm

Directory of Ohio Attorneys
www.sconet.state.oh.us/Atty_Reg/Public_Attorney Information.asp

Statistics on Ohio Attorneys
www.abanet.org/marketresearch/2005nbroflawyersbystate.pdf
www.sconet.state.oh.us/annualreport2005.pdf
www.sconet.state.oh.us/annualreport2004.pdf
www.sconet.state.oh.us/Admissions/asp
downloads.ohiobar.org/conventions/convention2005/session508%20Economics%20of%20Law.pdf

G. Something to Check

1. Which bar sites have the most comprehensive links to Ohio law?
2. Which bar sites have the best information on the area of law in which you work or hope to work?

APPENDIX A

Timeline: Disciplinary Proceedings Against an Attorney

A. Introduction

In this section, we will outline the steps involved in bringing a complaint against an Ohio attorney for violating one or more of the rules of the Model Rules of Professional Conduct presented earlier in section 3.2.

There are four major categories of discipline that can be imposed on Ohio attorneys:

- **Disbarment**—a permanent revocation of the right to practice law with no possibility of reinstatement.
- **Indefinite suspension**—suspension of the right to practice law for an unstated period of time. Reinstatement is a possibility. A reinstatement application cannot be filed for 2 years after the indefinite suspension begins.
- **Definite suspension**—suspension of the right to practice for a specified time, e.g., 6 months to 2 years.
- **Public reprimand**—a public censure.

A period of probation may be required for attorneys subject to a definite suspension. Some attorneys charged with misconduct resign their right to practice law rather than face discipline. Such attorneys cannot be reinstated. Ohio State Bar Association, *The Law and You,* 192 (12th ed. 2002).

The most recent statistics on discipline in Ohio are as follows:

Discipline in Ohio

Number of complaints received by disciplinary agency 6,526
Number of complaints pending from prior years 381
Number of complaints summarily dismissed for lack of jurisdiction 4,284
Number of complaints investigated 2,242
Number of complaints dismissed after investigation 1,043
Number of attorneys charged after probable cause determination 106
Number of private sanctions 0
Number of public sanctions 93
Number of disbarments 6
Number of disbarments on consent 9
Number of suspensions 44
Number of public reprimands/censures 8
Total attorney discipline system budget $4,523,539
Staff of disciplinary agency:
Number of attorneys 8
Number of paralegals 2
Number of investigators 2
Average caseload per attorney 88
Average time from receipt of complaint to the filing of formal charges .... 150+ days
Average time from receipt of complaint to the imposition of public sanction .... 2 years

Source: ABA Center for Professional Responsibility, Survey on Lawyer Discipline Systems (2005) (www.abanet.org/cpr/discipline/sold/home.html).

B. Timeline

The main participants in the disciplinary process include a Certified Grievance Committee of a local bar association, the Office of Disciplinary Counsel, the Board of Commissioners on Grievances and Discipline, and the Ohio Supreme Court.

1. Filing a complaint

A complaint against an attorney can be filed with the Office of Disciplinary Counsel (ODC) or with a certified grievance committee of a local bar association.

Office of Disciplinary Counsel (ODC)
Supreme Court of Ohio
250 Civic Center Drive, Ste. 325
Columbus, OH 43215-7411
800-589-5256; 614-461-0256
www.sconet.state.oh.us/odc/default.asp

For the complaint form used by the ODC, see Exhibit A. The certified grievance committee of a local bar association may use its own complaint form. See the local bar Web sites in section 3.3. Here, for example, is information on the certified grievance committees of Cincinnati and Cleveland:
www.cincybar.org/public/concerns.asp
www.clevelandbar.org/committees.asp?id=41&did=41

EXHIBIT A Attorney Grievance Form

OFFICE OF DISCIPLINARY COUNSEL
THE SUPREME COURT OF OHIO
JONATHAN E. COUGHLAN, Disciplinary Counsel
250 Civic Center Drive, Suite 325
Columbus, Ohio 43215-7411
(614) 461-0256 1-800-589-5256 (614) 461-7205 FAX
****

INSTRUCTIONS

The Office of Disciplinary Counsel investigates allegations of ethical misconduct against attorneys and judges. Disciplinary Counsel also investigates grievances regarding the unauthorized practice of law. Please understand that this office has no jurisdiction over and will not become involved in the legal merits of any case. The attorney disciplinary process will not affect or change court decisions made in your case. In addition, Disciplinary Counsel may not give you legal advice. This form will assist you in filing your grievance. After you **have legibly completed the form and signed and dated the form**, please return it in the envelope provided. You may attach additional sheets of paper, if necessary, in order to complete the "Facts of the Grievance" portion of the form. If you wish to file a grievance against more than one attorney or judge, please use one form per attorney or judge. You may make additional copies of the form. You may enclose all forms in one envelope. If you include documentation with your grievance, send **copies only**. **PLEASE DO NOT SEND ORIGINALS.**

The Rules of the Supreme Court of Ohio require that investigations be confidential. You are requested to keep confidential the fact that you are submitting this grievance. Only the attorney or judge you are filing your grievance against may waive confidentiality. In filing a grievance against your attorney, you are waiving your attorney/client privilege. The attorney or judge you are filing your grievance against will receive notice of your grievance. Those individuals are also entitled to receive a copy of your grievance and **may** be asked to respond to your allegations. Your grievance may result in your attorney withdrawing from your case. Disciplinary Counsel cannot prevent an attorney from withdrawing from representation. Once received, it may take up to sixty (60) days for us to review and respond to your grievance. However, our office will notify you of the disposition of your grievance by mail within that time period. You may or may not be contacted by mail or telephone to provide additional information. **ALL UNSIGNED GRIEVANCES WILL BE RETURNED TO THE SENDER.**

A grievance is confidential until the Board certifies it as a formal complaint. A grievance or complaint can be dismissed at any point in the process.

Grievance Form

YOUR NAME:____

Last **First** **MI** **Phone No.**

ADDRESS:____

(Please circle) ATTORNEY or JUDGE

NAME:____

Last **First** **MI** **Phone No.**

ADDRESS:____

GRIEVANCE FILED WITH OTHER AGENCIES:

Have you filed this grievance with any other agency or bar ass'n? ____Yes ____No

If yes, name of that agency:______________________________

When filed?:____

What happened?:______________________________________

COURT ACTION:

Does this grievance involve a case that is still pending before a court? ____ Yes ___No

Have you brought civil or criminal court action against this attorney or judge? ____Yes ____No

If yes, name of that court:______________________________

Result of court action: ______________________________

Name, address, and phone number of attorney currently representing you,
if different than above: ______________________________

WITNESSES:

List the name, address, and daytime telephone number of persons who can provide information, IF NECESSARY, in support of your grievance.

NAME **ADDRESS** **PHONE NO.**

____
____
____

FACTS OF THE GRIEVANCE

Briefly explain the facts of your grievance in chronological order, including dates. Include a description of the illegal or unethical conduct committed by this legal professional. Attach COPIES (DO NOT SEND ORIGINALS) of any correspondence and documents that support your grievance.

The Rules of the Supreme Court of Ohio require that investigations be confidential. Please keep confidential the fact that you are submitting this grievance. The party(ies) you are filing your grievance against will receive notice of your grievance and may receive a copy of your grievance and be asked to respond to your allegations.

________________________ ________________________

Signature **Date**

Source: Office of Disciplinary Council (www.sconet.state.oh.us/odc/odcform.pdf).

2. Investigation

The Office of Disciplinary Counsel (ODC) or the local bar's certified grievance committee will conduct an investigation of the matter. If it determines that substantial, credible evidence exists that a violation of the Model Rules of Professional Conduct has occurred, it will file a formal complaint with the Board of Commissioners on Grievances and Discipline.

The complaint will be dismissed if the ODC or the certified grievance committee does not find sufficient evidence that the attorney has violated the Model Rules of Professional Conduct. If a certified grievance committee performed the investigation, the client can appeal the dismissal to the Board of Commissioners on Grievances and Discipline of the Supreme Court of Ohio. There is no appeal from a decision of the ODC.

Some local bar associations have programs to arbitrate fee disputes or to mediate conflicts between attorneys and clients that do not involve serious misconduct.

3. Board of Commissioners on Grievances and Discipline

If the case is referred to the Board of Commissioners on Grievances and Discipline of the Ohio Supreme Court, a three-member panel of the Board will review the complaint and determine whether probable cause exists to certify it.

Board of Commissioners on Grievances and Discipline
65 South Front St., 5th Floor
Columbus, OH 43215-3431
614-387-9370
www.sconet.state.oh.us/BOC

If the complaint is certified by the Board, a disciplinary hearing is held before a different three-member panel of the Board. The panel considers the evidence and makes a recommendation to the full Board of Commissioners. The full Board then makes a recommendation to the Supreme Court of Ohio.

4. Supreme Court of Ohio

After the Supreme Court receives the Board's report, it will issue an order to the accused attorney to show cause why the report of the Board should not be confirmed and a disciplinary order entered. Objections can then be filed to the order. After a hearing on objections, or if none are filed, the Supreme Court will issue its final order. Only the Supreme Court may discipline an attorney for professional misconduct.

In addition, aggrieved clients can bring independent legal malpractice suits against their attorney and may be able to file a claim under the Client Security Fund.

C. Client Security Fund

The Client Security Fund is an agency of the Supreme Court of Ohio. The Fund provides compensation (up to $75,000) to clients who have suffered financial losses due to the dishonest conduct of a licensed Ohio attorney acting in a fiduciary or legal capacity. The dishonesty must be in the nature of theft or embezzlement. In 2005, the Fund awarded $1,494,200 to 101 eligible claimants involving the dishonest conduct of 42 Ohio attorneys. Since its inception in 1985, the Fund has awarded $10.8 million to 1,347 claimants.

Client Security Fund
65 South Front Street, 5th Floor
Columbus, Ohio 43215-3431
800-231-1680; 614-387-9390
www.sconet.state.oh.us/Client_Security

D. Grading the Ohio Disciplinary System

HALT—An Organization of Americans for Legal Reform (*www.halt.org*) grades the disciplinary system of every state by issuing its Lawyer Discipline Report Card.

Exhibit B Grading the Ohio Disciplinary System

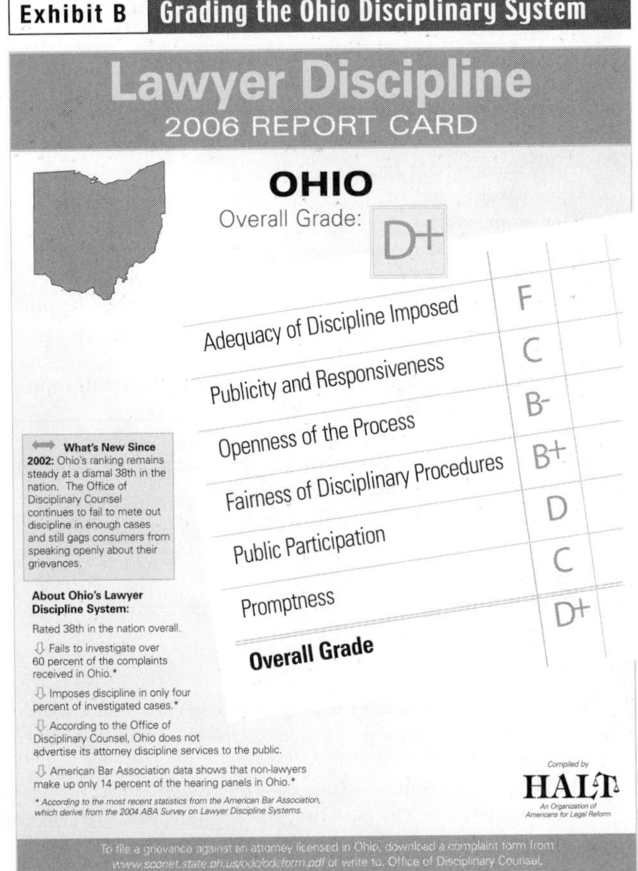

Source: HALT (http://www.halt.org/reform_projects/lawyer_accountability/report_card_2006/).

HALT gave Ohio a "D+" in both 2006 (See Exhibit B) and 2002.

Here is an explanation of the seven individual letter grades given to Ohio in Exhibit B (the number after each category below is the percent of the overall grade comprised of that category):

Adequacy of Discipline Imposed [35%]

What percentage of grievances does the agency investigate?
A = 90% or more B = 75–89% C = 50–74%
D = 20–49% F = less than 20%

What percentage of investigations result in public sanctions and what percentage lead to private sanctions?
A = 33% or more B = 25–32% C = 15–24%
D = 5–14% F = less than 5%

Publicity and Responsiveness [15%]

Does the disciplinary agency publicize itself sufficiently?
A = advertises in yellow pages, in at least one local newspaper, through flyers in courthouses, and on the Internet
B = 3 of the above C = 2 of the above D = 1 of the above
F = does not advertise its services to the public

Does the agency meet HALT's criteria for a comprehensive, clear, and consumer-friendly Web site and telephone system?
A = at least 95% of criteria
B = 85% C = 75% D = 65% or less
F = no Web site, no telephone system, or no brochure

Openness of the Process [15%]

Can a grievant attend hearings?
A = yes C = not unless a witness F = never

Can the general public attend hearings?
A = yes C = only if case reaches public sanctions stage
F = never

Where does the agency publish names of publicly sanctioned lawyers?
A = agency's Web site ***and*** at least one local newspaper
B = agency's Web site ***or*** at least one local newspaper
C = only in publications distributed to lawyers
D = only in the agency's annual report
F = nowhere

Can a consumer find out whether a grievance has ever been filed against her attorney?
A = yes—information about a grievance can be provided
B = no—but information is available once the case reaches the formal charges stage
C = no—but information is available once the case reaches the informal or formal sanctions stage
D = no—but information is available once the case reaches the formal sanctions stage
F = no—information about a disciplinary case may be released

Fairness of Disciplinary Procedures [15%]

Does the state have a "gag rule"?
A = no
C = yes, the agency requests that individuals keep their grievances confidential
F = yes, grievants will be held in contempt of court if they speak about grievance

Are grievants granted civil immunity?
A = yes C = qualified immunity F = no

What is the standard of proof in discipline hearings?
A = "preponderance of the evidence" or its equivalent
C = "clear and convincing evidence" or its equivalent
F = "beyond a reasonable doubt"

Public Participation [15%]

What percentage of nonlawyers serve on hearing panels?
A = majority nonlawyers B = 50% nonlawyers
C = 33–49% nonlawyers D = less than 33% nonlawyers
F = no nonlawyers

Promptness [5%]

On average, how long does it take before the agency brings formal charges against an attorney?
A = less than 3 months B = 3–5 months
C = 6–8 months D = 9 months – 1 year
F = more than 1 year

On average, how long does it take before the agency imposes sanctions on an attorney?
A = less than 6 months B = 6 months – 1 year
C = 1 year – 1–1/2 years D = 1–1/2 years – 2 years
F = more than 2 years

E. More Information

Overview
www.sconet.state.oh.us/BOC/faq/default.asp
www.ohiobar.org/pub/lawfacts/index.asp?articleid=9

Certified Grievance Committees in Ohio
www.ohiobar.org/pub/lawfacts/index.asp?articleid=9

Ohio Supreme Court Annual Report (covers attorney discipline)
www.sconet.state.oh.us/annualreport2005.pdf

Report Card on Effectiveness of Ohio's System of Disciplining Attorneys (2006)
www.halt.org/reform_projects/lawyer_accountability/report_card_2006

Report Card on Effectiveness of Ohio's System of Disciplining Attorneys (2002)
www.halt.org/reform_projects/lawyer_accountability/report_card

ABA Survey on Lawyer Disciplinary Systems
www.abanet.org/cpr/discipline/sold/home.html
www.abanet.org/cpr/discipline/sold/toc_2004.html

F. Something to Check

Go to the Advisory Opinions of the Board of Commissioners on Grievances and Discipline. Find and summarize three opinions: one involving paralegals, one involving the marketing of legal forms by a business, and one involving the sale of client files and lists. To find these opinions, click "Search Advisory Opinions" at the Board's site (*www.sconet.state.oh.us/BOC/Advisory_Opinions*).

PART 4

LEGAL SYSTEM

A. Introduction

In this section, we present an overview of Ohio state government. More detailed information about the major components of the government can be found in:

- section 4.2 on state courts
- section 4.4 on the state legislature
- section 4.5 on administrative agencies in the executive branch
- section 4.6 on county and city government

B. Overview

The Ohio Constitution divides the powers of government into three branches: executive, legislative, and judicial. Exhibit 4.1A presents an overview of the major units of Ohio state government.

EXECUTIVE BRANCH

Governor

Under the Ohio Constitution, the "supreme executive power of this state" is vested in the governor, whose duty is to "see that the laws are faithfully executed" (sections 3.05, 3.06, Article III, Ohio Constitution). The governor carries out the laws of the state by supervising a large bureaucracy, such as by appointing department directors and members of many boards and commissions. (See Exhibit 4.1B.) For contact information on these agencies, see section 4.5.

Through the power to sign or veto bills passed by the General Assembly, the governor also has a major role in the enactment of legislation. For a description of this role, see section 4.4.

EXHIBIT 4.1A Overview of Ohio State Government

EXECUTIVE BRANCH	LEGISLATIVE BRANCH	JUDICIAL BRANCH
Governor Lieutenant Governor Attorney General Secretary of State Treasurer of State Auditor of State State Board of Education Adjutant General	State Senate State House of Representatives Legislative Service Commission Joint Legislative Ethics Committee/ Office of the Legislative Inspector General	Ohio Supreme Court Ohio District Courts of Appeals Court of Claims Courts of Common Pleas Municipal and County Courts Small Claims Courts Mayors Courts

Governor's Office
77 South High Street,
Columbus, OH 43215
614-644-HELP
614-466-3555
governor.ohio.gov

Governor's Cabinet
(At the governor's site, place the cursor over the word "Cabinet")
ohio.gov/contacts.stm

Lieutenant Governor

614-466-3396
ltgovernor.ohio.gov

The major function of the lieutenant governor is to run the state if the Governor is unable to do so. According to Article 3 of the Ohio Constitution, "In the case of the death, conviction on impeachment, resignation, or removal, of the Governor, the Lieutenant Governor shall succeed to the office of Governor." Further, "When the Governor is unable to discharge the duties of office by reason of disability, the Lieutenant Governor shall serve as governor until the Governor's disability terminates." (section 3.15, Article III, Ohio Constitution) In addition, the lieutenant governor carries out other duties assigned by the governor.

Attorney General

614-466-4320
www.ag.state.oh.us

As the state's chief law officer, the attorney general serves as legal counsel to all statewide elected officials, the Ohio General Assembly, and all state departments, agencies, boards, and commissions. The attorney general is also charged with rule-making authority in the areas of charitable law, consumer protection, crime victim's services, criminal record checks, environmental background investigation, and peace officer training.

Secretary of State

614-466-2655
www.sos.state.oh.us

The four major functions of the secretary of state are to oversee elections, authorize corporations to do business in Ohio, document secured commercial transactions, and provide public access to documents.

Treasurer of State

614-466-2160; 800-648-7827
www.treasurer.state.oh.us

The role of the treasurer of state is to oversee all public funds collected, disbursed, and invested by the Ohio Treasury. He or she must manage such funds to achieve the goals of safety, liquidity, and maximum yield.

Auditor of State

800-282-0370; 614-466-4514
www.auditor.state.oh.us

The auditor of state is responsible for auditing all public offices in Ohio, including cities; villages; schools; universities; counties; townships; and state agencies, boards, and commissions. His or her mandate is to ensure that public funds are spent in accordance with state and local law.

State Agencies, Departments, and Commissions

For a list of the major state agencies, departments, and commissions, see section 4.5 and Exhibit 4.1B. See also:

www.megalaw.com/oh/ohgov.php
ohio.gov/contacts_phone.stm
ohio.gov/GovState.stm
www.govengine.com/stategov/ohio.html
governor.ohio.gov/
ohio.gov/contacts.stm
ohio.gov/pressroom.stm

LEGISLATIVE BRANCH

For an overview of how a bill becomes a law in Ohio, see section 4.4.

Under the Ohio Constitution, the "legislative power of the state shall be vested in a general assembly consisting of a senate and house of representatives." This power is subject to the right of the people "to propose to the general assembly laws and amendments to the constitution, and to adopt or reject the same at the polls on a referendum vote." (section 2.01, Article II, Ohio Constitution)

House of Representatives

614-466-3357
www.house.state.oh.us
www.legislature.state.oh.us/house.cfm

Individual Representatives

www.house.state.oh.us/jsps/Representatives.jsp

EXHIBIT 4.1B Ohio State Government—The Executive Branch

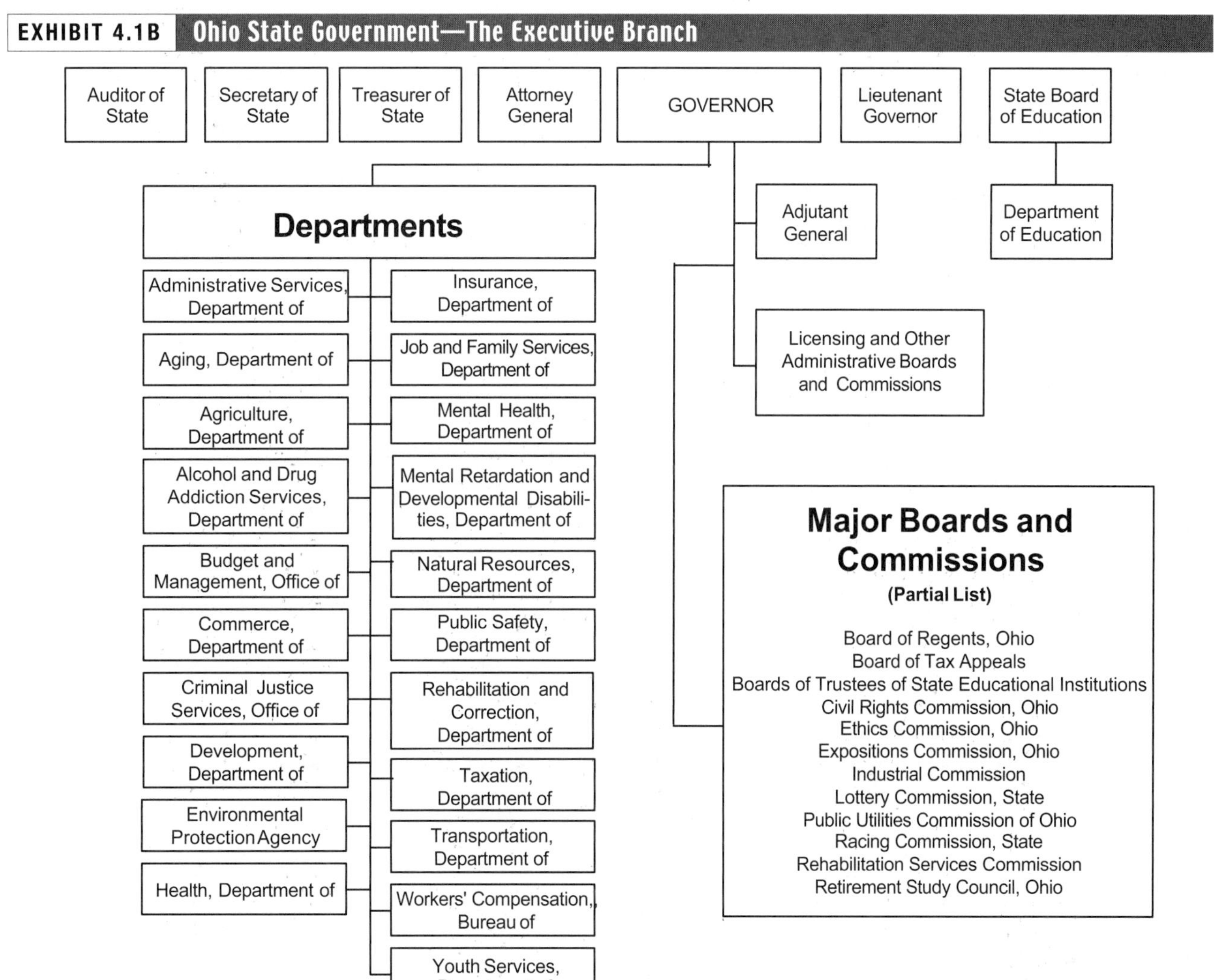

Source: Ohio Legislative Service Commission, A Guidebook for Ohio Legislators 111 (9th ed. 2005–2006) (www.lsc.state.oh.us/guidebook/chapter11.pdf).

House Committees

www.house.state.oh.us/jsps/Committee.jsp

Senate

614-466-4900
www.senate.state.oh.us
www.legislature.state.oh.us/senate.cfm

Individual Senators

www.senate.state.oh.us/senators

Senate Committees

www.senate.state.oh.us/committees

Bills, Revised Code, and Other Legislative Information

www.legislature.state.oh.us/search.cfm
www.legislature.state.oh.us/acts.cfm
www.legislature.state.oh.us

Legislative Service Commission (LSC)

614-466-3615
www.lsc.state.oh.us

The Ohio Legislative Service Commission (LSC) provides technical and research services to members of the General Assembly. LSC drafts bills; performs bill analysis; and provides research, training, and other technical services to the General Assembly. It also maintains the *Register of Ohio* (*www.registerofohio.state.oh.us*), which provides Internet access to proposed agency rules. The Fiscal Staff of the LSC prepares state revenue and expenditure estimates and provides fiscal notes, local impact statements, and general information about government fiscal issues.

Joint Legislative Ethics Committee/Office of the Legislative Inspector General (JLEC-OLIG)

614-728-5100
www.jlec-olig.state.oh.us

The Joint Legislative Ethics Committee (JLEC) monitors compliance with Ohio's ethics law applicable to the legislative branch. It also administers the state's lobbying laws. The Office of the Legislative Inspector General (OLIG) is accountable to the Joint Legislative Ethics Committee and is responsible for the actual implementation of the provisions of the ethics and lobbying laws.

Joint Committee on Agency Rule Review

614-466-4086
www.jcarr.state.oh.us

Legislative Office of Education Oversight

614-752-9686
www.loeo.state.oh.us

Correctional Institution Inspection Committee

614-466-6649
www.ciic.state.oh.us

Legislative Information Systems

614-728-0711
www.lis.state.oh.us

Statehouse News Bureau

614-221-1811
statenews.org

JUDICIAL BRANCH

The major state courts created by the Ohio Constitution are the Ohio Supreme Court, the Ohio Courts of Appeals, and the Ohio Courts of Common Pleas. (sections 2.01, 4.03, and 4.04, Article IV, Ohio Constitution) See section 4.2 for an overview of the jurisdiction of these and other state courts in Ohio. Federal courts in Ohio are covered in section 4.3.

Supreme Court of Ohio

800-826-9010; 614-387-9000
www.sconet.state.oh.us

Ohio District Courts of Appeals

www.sconet.state.oh.us/District_Courts

Courts of Common Pleas

www.sconet.state.oh.us/Web_Sites/courts
www.govengine.com/stategov/ohio.html
www.fcmcclerk.com/links/clerks/clerks.htm

Court of Claims

800-824-8263; 614-387-9800
www.cco.state.oh.us

County and Municipal Courts

www.sconet.state.oh.us/Web_Sites/courts
opd.ohio.gov/resource/lr_courts.htm
www.govengine.com/stategov/ohio.html
www.megalaw.com/oh/ohcourts.php
www.oamcc.com/directry.htm
www.oamcc.com/links.htm
www.ohiojudges.org
(click "Links")

Mayor's Courts

www.ohiomayorscourtclerks.org
www.ncsconline.org/D_KIS/info_court_web_sites.html
(click "Ohio")

Ohio Judicial Center

www.ohiojudicialcenter.gov

Ohio Judicial Conference

614-387-9750
www.ohiojudges.org

Court Opinions and Rules

See sections 4.2 and 5.1.

C. More Information

Overview of State Government
www.lsc.state.oh.us/guidebook/index.html
www.legislature.state.oh.us/about.cfm

Overview of Federal Government
www.usa.gov
www.fedworld.gov

Overview of State Courts
www.lsc.state.oh.us/guidebook/index.html

Overview of State Legislature
www.lsc.state.oh.us/guidebook/index.html
www.legislature.state.oh.us/agencies.cfm

State Constitution
www.legislature.state.oh.us/constitution.cfm

D. Something to Check

1. Use the online recourses in this section to determine the current state government deficit (or surplus) in Ohio's budget.
2. Identify any problem that you think exists in your community. Use the online sites in this section to identify government entities or persons in the executive and legislative branches that would probably have authority to solve or address this problem.

4.2 State Courts in Ohio

A. Introduction

In this section, we cover the major Ohio state courts. For related material, see:

- section 4.1 (introduction to the state government of Ohio)
- section 4.3 (federal courts in Ohio)
- section 5.1 (finding court opinions and other Ohio laws)

The main Ohio state courts are:

Supreme Court of Ohio
Courts of Appeals
Court of Claims
Courts of Common Pleas
Municipal and County Courts
Small Claims Courts
Mayors Courts

Approximately 3,100,000 cases were filed in Ohio courts in 2005: 2,444 in the Supreme Court of Ohio; 11,477 in the courts of appeals; 229,352 in the courts of common pleas, general division; 77,888 in the domestic relations courts; 93,708 in the probate courts; 253,245 in the juvenile courts; 2,265,931 in the municipal courts; 204,019 in the county courts; and 1,138 in the Ohio Court of Claims.

Exhibit 4.2A summarizes the jurisdiction and lines of appeal among these courts.

B. Ohio State Courts

Supreme Court of Ohio

The court of last resort in the state is the Supreme Court of Ohio, consisting of a chief justice and six associate justices. They are elected to 6-year terms, as are all Ohio judges. Most of the court's cases consist of appeals from the twelve district courts of appeals. It hears appeals in all death penalty cases. Here is what the state constitution says about the jurisdiction or powers of the court:

> **Art. IV, § 2 Supreme Court** (Constitution of Ohio)
> (A) The supreme court shall, until otherwise provided by law, consist of seven judges, who shall be known as the chief justice and justices. . . .
> (B) (1) The supreme court shall have original jurisdiction in the following: (a) Quo warranto; (b) Mandamus; (c) Habeas corpus; (d) Prohibition; (e) Procedendo; (f) In any cause on review as may be necessary to its complete determination; (g) Admission to the practice of law, the discipline of persons so admitted, and all other matters relating to the practice of law.

EXHIBIT 4.2A Structure of the Ohio Judicial System

OHIO JUDICIAL STRUCTURE

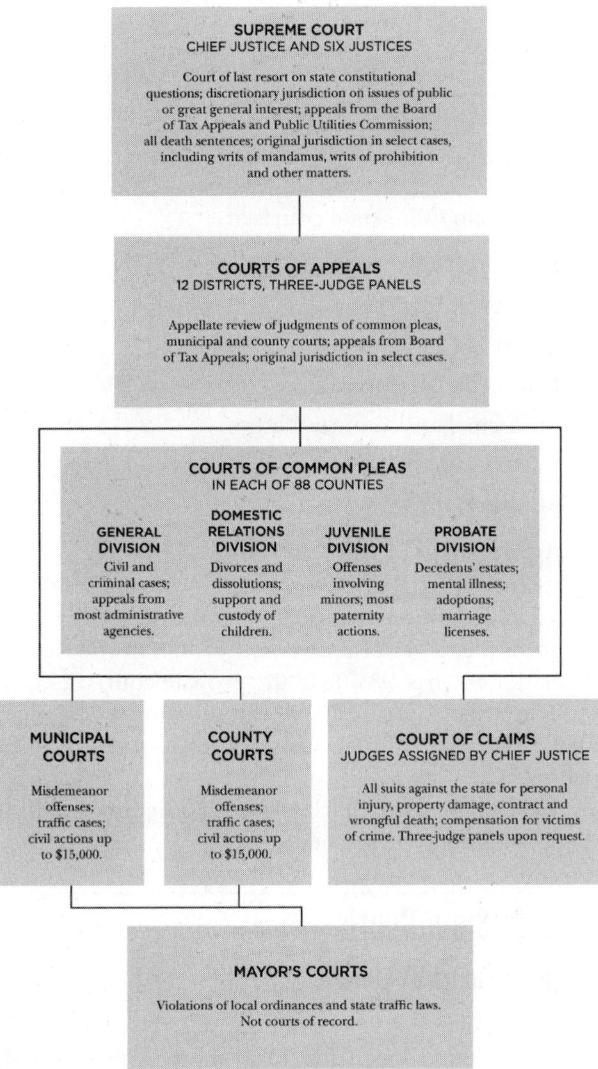

SUPREME COURT
CHIEF JUSTICE AND SIX JUSTICES
Court of last resort on state constitutional questions; discretionary jurisdiction on issues of public or great general interest; appeals from the Board of Tax Appeals and Public Utilities Commission; all death sentences; original jurisdiction in select cases, including writs of mandamus, writs of prohibition and other matters.
COURTS OF APPEALS
12 DISTRICTS, THREE-JUDGE PANELS
Appellate review of judgments of common pleas, municipal and county courts; appeals from Board of Tax Appeals; original jurisdiction in select cases.
COURTS OF COMMON PLEAS
IN EACH OF 88 COUNTIES
GENERAL DIVISION
Civil and criminal cases; appeals from most administrative agencies.
DOMESTIC RELATIONS DIVISION
Divorces and dissolutions; support and custody of children.
JUVENILE DIVISION
Offenses involving minors; most paternity actions.
PROBATE DIVISION
Decedents' estates; mental illness; adoptions; marriage licenses.
MUNICIPAL COURTS
Misdemeanor offenses; traffic cases; civil actions up to $15,000.
COUNTY COURTS
Misdemeanor offenses; traffic cases; civil actions up to $15,000.
COURT OF CLAIMS
JUDGES ASSIGNED BY CHIEF JUSTICE
All suits against the state for personal injury, property damage, contract and wrongful death; compensation for victims of crime. Three-judge panels upon request.
MAYOR'S COURTS
Violations of local ordinances and state traffic laws. Not courts of record.

Source: Supreme Court of Ohio (www.supremecourtofohio.gov/introduction/structure/structure.pdf).

> (2) The supreme court shall have appellate jurisdiction as follows: (a) In appeals from the courts of appeals as a matter of right in the following: (i) Cases originating in the courts of appeals; (ii) Cases involving questions arising under the constitution of the United States or of this state. (b) In appeals from the courts of appeals in cases of felony on leave first obtained, (c) In direct appeals from the courts of common pleas or other courts of record inferior to the court of appeals as a matter of right in cases in which the death penalty has been imposed; (d) Such revisory jurisdiction of the proceedings of administrative officers or agencies as may be conferred by law; (e) In cases of public or great general interest, the supreme court may direct any court of appeals to certify its record to the supreme court, and may review and affirm, modify, or reverse the judgment of the court of appeals. . . .
>
> (C) The decisions in all cases in the supreme court shall be reported, together with the reasons therefor.

Under these provisions of the constitution, the Supreme Court of Ohio has exclusive authority to regulate admission to the practice of law, attorney discipline, and the unauthorized practice of law.

Address

Supreme Court of Ohio
65 South Front Street
Columbus, Ohio 43215-3431
800-826-9010; 614-387-9000
www.sconet.state.oh.us

Biographies of the Justices

www.sconet.state.oh.us/Justices
www.sconet.state.oh.us/annualreport2004.pdf

Office of the Clerk

614-387-9530
www.sconet.state.oh.us/Clerk_of_Court

Opinions of the Court

www.sconet.state.oh.us/rod/newpdf
www.sconet.state.oh.us/Communications_Office/summaries/2005/1214
www.findlaw.com/11stategov/oh/courts.html

Online Case Docket

www.supremecourtofohio.gov/docket
www.sconet.state.oh.us/clerk_of_court/ecms

Supreme Court Rules of Practice and Procedure

www.sconet.state.oh.us/Rules
www.sconet.state.oh.us/Rules/practice

Oral Argument Guidelines

www.sconet.state.oh.us/Clerk_of_Court/guide_for_counsel.pdf

Statistics on Cases Filed

www.sconet.state.oh.us/annualreport2005.pdf
www.sconet.state.oh.us/annualreport2004.pdf

Filing Requirements

- All documents filed in the Supreme Court must be on white, letter-size paper with a white cover page. Plastic covers are prohibited, and documents may not be enclosed in notebooks or binders. See the

Rules of Practice for the requirements on type size and margins.

- Documents submitted for filing must be firmly stapled or bound on the left margin. The *Rules of Practice* do not require a specific binding method. However, attorneys are encouraged to use a method that will secure the document while still permitting occasional disassembly for duplication. Ideally, the bindings of copies filed with the original document should not interfere with or preclude recycling of the copies after the case has been terminated. Any document that is thicker than 2 inches must be bound in two or more numbered volumes.
- The *Rules of Practice* impose page limitations on some documents, and these limitations are strictly enforced. For example, most jurisdictional memoranda are limited to 15 pages in length, and most merit briefs are limited to 50 pages. Attorneys should consult the Rules of Practice for specific information on page restrictions before submitting their documents for filing.
- Original documents tendered for filing must be accompanied by an appropriate number of copies.
- When an attorney files a document, except a complaint filed to institute an original action, the attorney must also serve a copy of the document on all other parties to the case. Each document presented for filing with the Clerk must contain a proof of this service signed by the attorney. The Clerk is required to reject for filing any document that requires but is missing a proof of service.

Law Library

www.sconet.state.oh.us/LawLibrary

Employment Opportunities

www.sconet.state.oh.us/Employment_Opportunities

COURTS OF APPEALS

Twelve District Courts of Appeals are the intermediate appellate courts in the state. Their primary function is to hear appeals from common pleas, municipal, and county courts. The number of judges in each district varies from four to twelve.

All cases before a court of appeals are heard and decided by a three-judge panel. Here is what the state constitution says about the jurisdiction or powers of the courts of appeals:

> **Art. IV, § 3 Courts of Appeals** (Constitution of Ohio)
> (A) The state shall be divided by law into compact appellate districts in each of which there shall be a court of appeals consisting of three judges. Laws may be passed increasing the number of judges in any district wherein the volume of business may require such additional judge or judges. . . .
> (B) (1) The courts of appeals shall have original jurisdiction in the following: (a) Quo warranto; (b) Mandamus; (c) Habeas corpus; (d) Prohibition; (e) Procedendo; (f) In any cause on review as may be necessary to its complete determination. (2) Courts of appeals shall have such jurisdiction as may be provided by law to review and affirm, modify, or reverse judgments or final orders of the courts of record inferior to the court of appeals within the district, except that courts of appeals shall not have jurisdiction to review on direct appeal a judgment that imposes a sentence of death. Courts of appeals shall have such appellate jurisdiction as may be provided by law to review and affirm, modify, or reverse final orders or actions of administrative officers or agencies.
> (3) A majority of the judges hearing the cause shall be necessary to render a judgment. . . . No judgment resulting from a trial by jury shall be reversed on the weight of the evidence except by the concurrence of all three judges hearing the cause. . . .

FIRST DISTRICT COURT OF APPEALS (Cincinnati)

513-946-3500 (Cincinnati)
www.hamilton-co.org/appealscourt
www.sconet.state.oh.us/District_Courts/Districts/dc01.asp

Opinions

www.sconet.state.oh.us/rod/newpdf/?source=1
www.hamilton-co.org/appealscourt/RpSearch.asp?ct=Decisions

Rules

www.hamilton-co.org/appealscourt/rules.html

Forms

www.hamilton-co.org/appealscourt/forms.html

SECOND DISTRICT COURT OF APPEALS

937-225-4464 (Dayton)
937-328-2653 (Springfield)
www.sconet.state.oh.us/District_Courts/Districts/dc02.asp

Opinions

www.sconet.state.oh.us/rod/newpdf/?source=2

THIRD DISTRICT COURT OF APPEALS

419-223-1861 (Lima)
www.third.courts.state.oh.us
www.sconet.state.oh.us/District_Courts/Districts/dc03.asp

Opinions

www.sconet.state.oh.us/rod/newpdf/?source=3

Rules

www.third.courts.state.oh.us/rules.htm

Forms

www.third.courts.state.oh.us/forms.htm

FOURTH DISTRICT COURT OF APPEALS

740-779-6662 (Chillicothe)
740-592-3247 (Athens)
740-474-7841 (Circleville)
740-353-9497 (Portsmouth)
www.fourth.courts.state.oh.us
www.fourth.courts.state.oh.us/clerks.doc
www.sconet.state.oh.us/District_Courts/Districts/dc04.asp

Opinions

www.sconet.state.oh.us/rod/newpdf/?source=4

Rules

www.fourth.courts.state.oh.us

FIFTH DISTRICT COURT OF APPEALS

330-451-7765 (Canton)
www.fifthdist.org
www.sconet.state.oh.us/District_Courts/Districts/dc05.asp

Schedule of Cases

www.fifthdist.org/schedule.htm

Opinions

www.sconet.state.oh.us/rod/newpdf/?source=5

Rules

www.fifthdist.org/rules.htm

SIXTH DISTRICT COURT OF APPEALS

419-213-4755 (Toledo)
www.co.lucas.oh.us/Appeals
www.sconet.state.oh.us/District_Courts/Districts/dc06.asp

Opinions

www.sconet.state.oh.us/rod/newpdf/?source=6
www.co.lucas.oh.us/Appeals/Decisions.asp?SearchOrder=DecisionDate

Rules

www.co.lucas.oh.us/Appeals/SupplementalRules.asp

SEVENTH DISTRICT COURT OF APPEALS

330-740-2180 (Youngstown)
www.seventh.courts.state.oh.us
www.sconet.state.oh.us/District_Courts/Districts/dc07.asp

Opinions

www.sconet.state.oh.us/rod/newpdf/?source=7

Rules

www.seventh.courts.state.oh.us/rules.html
www.sconet.state.oh.us/District_Courts/Districts/Local_rules/7thRULES-02.pdf

EIGHTH DISTRICT COURT OF APPEALS

216-443-6350 (Cleveland)
appeals.cuyahogacounty.us
www.sconet.state.oh.us/District_Courts/Districts/dc08.asp

Opinions

www.sconet.state.oh.us/rod/newpdf/?source=8
appeals.cuyahogacounty.us/opinions.htm

Rules

appeals.cuyahogacounty.us/rules.htm

Forms

appeals.cuyahogacounty.us/forms.htm

NINTH DISTRICT COURT OF APPEALS

330-643-2250 (Akron)
www.ninth.courts.state.oh.us
www.sconet.state.oh.us/District_Courts/Districts/dc09.asp

Opinions

www.sconet.state.oh.us/rod/newpdf/?source=9

Rules

www.ninth.courts.state.oh.us/localrules.htm

Forms

www.ninth.courts.state.oh.us/FormsSamples.htm

TENTH DISTRICT COURT OF APPEALS

614-462-3580 (Columbus)
www.franklincountyohio.gov/appeals
www.sconet.state.oh.us/District_Courts/Districts/dc10.asp

Opinions

www.sconet.state.oh.us/rod/newpdf/?source=10

Rules

www.franklincountyohio.gov/appeals/formspdf/LOCALRUL.pdf

Forms

www.franklincountyohio.gov/appeals/forms.shtml

ELEVENTH DISTRICT COURT OF APPEALS

330-675-2650 (Warren)
www.11thcourt.co.trumbull.oh.us

Opinions

www.sconet.state.oh.us/rod/newpdf/?source=11

Rules

www.11thcourt.co.trumbull.oh.us/courtrules.htm
www.sconet.state.oh.us/District_Courts/Districts/dc11.asp

Forms

www.11thcourt.co.trumbull.oh.us/forms.htm

TWELFTH DISTRICT COURT OF APPEALS

513-425-6609 (Middletown)
www.twelfth.courts.state.oh.us
www.sconet.state.oh.us/District_Courts/Districts/dc12.asp

Opinions

www.sconet.state.oh.us/rod/newpdf/?source=12

Rules

www.twelfth.courts.state.oh.us/default.asp?page=rules

Forms

www.twelfth.courts.state.oh.us/default.asp?page=forms

COURT OF CLAIMS

The Court of Claims resolves all civil actions filed against the State of Ohio and its agencies. Examples of claims involve contract disputes, property damage, personal injury, discrimination, and wrongful imprisonment. The court also hears appeals from decisions made by the attorney general on claims allowed under the Victims of Crime Act. Most cases asserting claims for over $2,500 are heard by a single judge. Claims for $2,500 or less are resolved by a clerk of the court as "administrative determinations" on the basis of the case file alone. Judges on the Court of Claims consist of retired or incumbent justices or judges of other Ohio state courts.

Address

Ohio Court of Claims
65 South Front Street, 3d Floor
Columbus, OH 43215
800-824-8263; 614-387-9800
www.cco.state.oh.us/home.htm

Victims of Crime Panel
800-824-8263; 614-387-9859
www.cco.state.oh.us/cco2005/victim_appeals.htm
www.cco.state.oh.us/cco2005/rules_and_procedures.htm

Forms

www.cco.state.oh.us/cco2005/court_forms.htm

Practice Overview ("Road to the Courthouse")

www.cco.state.oh.us/cco2005/practicing.htm

COURTS OF COMMON PLEAS

In each county, the main trial court of general jurisdiction is called the Court of Common Pleas. Here is what the state constitution says about the jurisdiction or powers of such courts:

> **Art. IV, § 3 Courts of Common Pleas** (Constitution of Ohio)
> (A) There shall be a court of common pleas and such divisions thereof as may be established by law serving each county of the state. . . .
> (B) The courts of common pleas and divisions thereof shall have such original jurisdiction over all justiciable matters and such powers of review of proceedings of administrative officers and agencies as may be provided by law.
> (C) Unless otherwise provided by law, there shall be a probate division and such other divisions of the courts of common pleas as may be provided by law. . . .

Not all Courts of Common Pleas are organized the same way or have the same authority. In many of the larger counties, the work of these courts is divided into four divisions:

- *General Division*: civil and criminal cases; appeals from some administrative agencies
- *Domestic Relations Division*: family-related cases such as divorce, child custody, and spousal support
- *Juvenile Division* (sometimes called Juvenile Court): cases involving minors such as juvenile delinquency and child neglect
- *Probate Division* (sometimes called Probate Court): wills and estate, guardianships, institutionalization of the mentally ill

Web Sites of Courts of Common Pleas

www.sconet.state.oh.us/Web_Sites/courts
www.ncsconline.org/D_KIS/CourtWebSites/CtWeb_OHcommonplea.htm
www.ohiojudges.org/index.cfm?PageID=64C16230-2FAD-4EE3-99C37E40B578079B
www.govengine.com/stategov/ohio.html
www.fcmcclerk.com/links/clerks/clerks.htm

MUNICIPAL AND COUNTY COURTS

Counties and municipalities may have a municipal court, a county court, or both. A municipal court may have jurisdiction in one or more municipalities, in adjacent townships, or throughout the entire county. When municipal courts exercise countywide jurisdiction, no county court exists. A county court is used if an area of a county is not served by a municipal court. The jurisdiction of municipal and county courts is nearly identical. Both municipal and county courts have the authority to conduct preliminary hearings in felony cases, and both have jurisdiction over traffic and nontraffic misdemeanors. These courts also have limited civil jurisdiction. They may hear civil cases in which the amount of money in dispute does not exceed $15,000. (For cases in the housing division or environmental division of a municipal court, there is no dollar limit.) Ohio Legislative Service Commission, *A Guidebook for Ohio Legislators*, 126 (2005–2006).

Web Sites of Municipal and County Courts

www.sconet.state.oh.us/Web_Sites/courts
opd.ohio.gov/resource/lr_courts.htm
www.govengine.com/stategov/ohio.html
www.megalaw.com/oh/ohcourts.php
www.oamcc.com/directry.htm
www.oamcc.com/links.htm
opd.ohio.gov/resource/lr_courts.htm#Ohio%20County%20Courts

SMALL CLAIMS COURTS

Small Claims Courts can resolve civil cases in which the amount of money in controversy does not exceed $3,000. Small Claims Courts are divisions of municipal or county courts.

MAYOR'S COURTS

Areas of the state that do not have municipal courts may have a mayor's court in which the mayor acts as judge, usually on misdemeanor and traffic cases. "The mayor is not required to be a licensed attorney, but must complete special legal courses prescribed by the Supreme Court of Ohio." (*www.ohiobar.org/pub/lawfacts/index.asp?articleid=5*) (See R.C. 1905.03) If the mayor appoints a magistrate to hear cases, the magistrate must be a licensed Ohio attorney.

Mayor's Courts

www.supremecourtofohio.gov/Judicial_and_Court_Services/casemng/mayors/mayorscopy.asp

Web Sites and Clerk Addresses of Mayor's Courts

www.ohiomayorscourtclerks.org
www.ncsconline.org/D_KIS/info_court_web_sites.html
(click "Ohio")

C. More Information

Overview and Guides to Ohio Courts
www.sconet.state.oh.us/introduction
www.ncsconline.org/D_Research/Ct_Struct/OH.htm
www.sconet.state.oh.us/publications/annrep/05OCS/default.asp
www.cincybar.org/pdfs/cbaGuideToTheCourtsArticle.pdf
ohiocrts.photobooks.com
www.oamcc.com/object.htm

Links to Ohio Courts
www.ohiomagistrates.org/links.html
www.sconet.state.oh.us/District_Courts
www.legaltrek.com/HELPSITE/States/State_Contents/Ohio.htm
www.lucas-co-probate-ct.org/ProbateCounties.htm
www.probatect.org/ohioprobatecourts/courtlinks.htm
www.ohiojudges.org
(click "Links" "Ohio Courts")

Court Rules in Ohio Courts
www.llrx.com/courtrules-gen/state-Ohio.html

Ohio Judicial Conference
www.ohiojudges.org/index.cfm

Ohio Association of Court Administration
www.ohiocourtadministration.org

Ohio Magistrates
www.ohiomagistrates.org
www.ohiobar.org/pub/lycu/index.asp?articleid=421

Ohio Clerk of Courts
www.occaohio.com
www.occaohio.com/clerkphonedir.htm
www.fcmcclerk.com/links/clerks/clerks.htm
www.oamcc.com/directry.htm

Ohio Association of Municipal/County Court Clerks
www.oamcc.com

Ohio Bailiffs and Court Officers Association
www.ohiobailiffs.com

Ohio Mediation Association
www.mediate.com/ohio

Alternative Dispute Resolution (ADR)
www.ohiobar.org/pub/index.asp?articleid=74

Ohio Supreme Court Board of Commissioners on Grievances & Discipline
www.sconet.state.oh.us/BOC

D. Something to Check

1. Go to the sites that give you online access to court opinions of the Supreme Court of Ohio. Use the search features of the sites to find an opinion on any broad legal topic, e.g., capital punishment, adoption. Summarize what the opinion says about your topic.
2. Go to the Web sites of any three courts mentioned in this section. For the same general kind of litigant filing (e.g., a complaint, an amendment to a prior filing) state the filing fee in each of the three courts.
3. Go to one of the twelve Courts of Appeals that provide biographies of the justices. Pick one justice. Identify a prior job of this justice that might indicate a possible conservative or liberal philosophy of deciding cases. Explain your answer.

4.3 Federal Courts in Ohio

- A. Introduction
- B. Federal Courts
- C. PACER
- D. More Information
- E. Something to Check

A. Introduction

There are four federal courts sitting in Ohio:

United States Court of Appeals for the Sixth Circuit

United States District Courts

United States Bankruptcy Courts

Bankruptcy Appellate Panel

United States Immigration Court

In this section, we present an overview of these courts, how they operate, and the major recourses that are available when working with them.

B. Federal Courts

United States Court of Appeals for the Sixth Circuit

The United States is divided geographically into eleven numbered federal judicial circuits (also called regional circuits). Each circuit has a court of appeals, e.g., the United States Court of Appeals for the First Circuit, the United States Court of Appeals for the Second Circuit, etc. These federal courts of appeals are intermediate appellate courts just below the United States Supreme Court. In addition to the eleven numbered circuits, there are two other circuits: the District of Columbia Circuit and the Federal Circuit, both located in Washington D.C. (The Federal Circuit is a separate and unique court of appeals that has nationwide jurisdiction in specialized cases.)

Each of the fifty states (plus the territories of Guam, Puerto Rico, and the U.S. Virgin Islands) is assigned to one of the eleven numbered circuits. The states of Ohio, Kentucky, Tennessee, and Michigan are in the sixth circuit. The court of appeals for our circuit is the United States Court of Appeals for the Sixth Circuit, sometimes abbreviated as CA6 or 6th Cir.

The United States Court of Appeals for the Sixth Circuit hears appeals (1) from the United States district courts in Ohio, Kentucky, Tennessee, and Michigan, and (2) from the United States Tax Court and from certain federal administrative agencies where the nongovernmental parties are from one of the four states that make up the Sixth Circuit. The other regional circuits do the same for their circuits. Decisions of the United States courts of appeals are final except as they are subject to review on writ of certiorari by the United States Supreme Court. Judges on the court of appeals have lifetime tenure; they are nominated by the president and confirmed by the U.S. Senate.

Address

U.S. Court of Appeals, Sixth Circuit
540 Potter Stewart U.S. Courthouse
100 East Fifth Street
Cincinnati, Ohio 45202
513-564-7000

Web Site

www.ca6.uscourts.gov

Opinions

www.ca6.uscourts.gov/internet/opinions/opinions.php
www.findlaw.com/casecode/courts/6th.html
www.law.cornell.edu/federal/opinions.html

Judges

www.ca6.uscourts.gov/internet/court_of_appeals/courtappeals_judges.htm

PACER login

800-676-6856
pacer.login.uscourts.gov/cgi-bin/login.pl?court_id=06ca

Calendar

www.ca6.uscourts.gov/internet/court_calendars/courtcalendars.htm

Rules

- Federal Rules of Appellate Procedure (FRAP)
  www.access.gpo.gov/uscode/title28a/28a_3_.html
  judiciary.house.gov/media/pdfs/printers/108th/appel2004.pdf
- Sixth Circuit Rules; 6th Circuit Internal Operating Procedures
  www.ca6.uscourts.gov/internet/rules_and_procedures/rulesproc.htm
  www.ca6.uscourts.gov/internet/rules_and_procedures/pdf/rules2004.pdf

Forms

www.ca6.uscourts.gov/internet/forms/forms.htm

Petition for Writ of Certiorari Instructions

www.ca6.uscourts.gov/internet/forms/certiorari/petition.pdf

Checklist for Appellate Briefs

www.ca6.uscourts.gov/internet/forms/briefs/checklistforbriefs.htm

Common Fees:

For docketing a case: $250.00

Search (and certification) of court records: $26

Reproducing records: 50¢ per page

Opinions: 50¢ per page

Attorney Admission to 6th Circuit Bar: $200

Pro Se Appellate Brief

www.ca6.uscourts.gov/internet/forms/briefs_appendices/prose_brief.pdf

6th Circuit Law Library (Cincinnati)

513-564-7321
www.ca6.uscourts.gov/internet/library/library.htm
("Although the Cincinnati library is open to the public, materials from the collection cannot be checked out by the public.")

UNITED STATES DISTRICT COURTS

United States district courts exist within the judicial districts that are part of the regional circuits. In the 50 states, there are 89 district courts. Each state has at least one district court; Ohio has two: Southern District and Northern District. In addition to a district court for the District of Columbia, the Commonwealth of Puerto Rico has a district court with jurisdiction corresponding to that of district courts in the various states. Finally district courts also exist in the territories of the Virgin Islands, Guam, and the Northern Mariana Islands for a total of 94 district courts in the federal judicial system.

United States district courts are the trial courts of general federal jurisdiction. Within limits set by Congress and the Constitution, they can hear nearly all categories of federal cases, including both civil and criminal matters. Typically, federal courts hear civil cases in which the United States is a party or those involving the United States Constitution, laws enacted by Congress, treaties, and laws relating to navigable waters. Examples include bankruptcy and violations of federal environmental laws. Another large source of civil cases in district courts are those involving disputes between citizens of different states (diversity of citizenship) if the amount in dispute exceeds $75,000. Federal criminal cases in district courts are filed by the United States attorney who represents the United States. Examples of federal crimes prosecuted in district court include illegal importation of drugs and certain categories of bank fraud.

At present, each district court has from 2 to 28 federal district judgeships, depending upon the amount of judicial work within its boundaries. Only one judge is usually required to hear and decide a case in a district court, but in limited cases, three judges are called together to comprise the court. Judges of district courts have lifetime tenure; they are nominated by the president and confirmed by the U.S. Senate.

Each district court has one or more magistrate judge and bankruptcy judge, a clerk, a United States attorney, a United States marshal, probation officers, and court reporters. Cases from a district court are reviewable on appeal by the United States court of appeals in the circuit where the district court sits.

As indicated, there are two United States district courts sitting in Ohio:

United States District Court, Southern District of Ohio
United States District Court, Northern District of Ohio

UNITED STATES DISTRICT COURT, SOUTHERN DISTRICT OF OHIO

Addresses

U.S. District Court
Southern District of Ohio
Office of the Clerk
Western Division
Potter Stewart U.S. Courthouse, Room 103
100 East Fifth Street
Cincinnati, Ohio 45202
513-564-7500

U.S. District Court
Southern District of Ohio
Office of the Clerk
Western Division
Federal Building, Room 712
200 West Second Street
Dayton, Ohio 45402
937-512-1400

U.S. DistrictCourt
Southern District of Ohio
Eastern Division Office of the Clerk
Joseph P. Kenneary U.S. Courthouse, Room 260
85 Marconi Boulevard
Columbus, Ohio 43215
614-719-3000

Web Site

www.ohsd.uscourts.gov
www.ohsd.uscourts.gov/map.htm
www.law.cornell.edu/federal/districts.html#circuit

Judges

www.ohsd.uscourts.gov/judges.htm

Opinions

www.ohsd.uscourts.gov/opinions.htm

Local Rules and Court Orders

www.ohsd.uscourts.gov/locrules.htm

Federal Rules of Civil Procedure (FRCP)

www.law.cornell.edu/rules/frcp
www.access.gpo.gov/uscode/title28a/28a_4_.html
judiciary.house.gov/media/pdfs/printers/108th/civil2004.pdf

Federal Rules of Criminal Procedure

www.law.cornell.edu/rules/frcrmp
judiciary.house.gov/media/pdfs/printers/108th/civil2004.pdf

Electronic Case Filing (CM/ECF)

www.ohsd.uscourts.gov/cmecf.htm

ECF/Pacer Login

ecf.ohsd.uscourts.gov/cgi-bin/login.pl

Forms

www.ohsd.uscourts.gov/forms.htm

Fees

www.ohsd.uscourts.gov/feesch.htm

Employment Opportunities

www.ohsd.uscourts.gov/employme.asp

UNITED STATES DISTRICT COURT, NORTHERN DISTRICT OF OHIO

Addresses

U.S. District Court
Northern District of Ohio
Eastern Division
Carl B. Stokes United States Court House
801 West Superior Avenue
Cleveland, OH 44113
216-357-7000

U.S. District Court
Northern District of Ohio
Eastern Division
2 South Main Street
Akron, Ohio 44308
330-375-5705

U.S. District Court
Northern District of Ohio
Eastern Division
125 Market Street
Youngstown, Ohio 44503
330-746-1906

U.S. District Court
Northern District of Ohio
Western Division
1716 Spielbusch Avenue
Toledo, Ohio 43624
419-259-6412

Web Site

www.ohnd.uscourts.gov
www.ohnd.uscourts.gov/Links/Site_Map/site_map.html
www.law.cornell.edu/federal/districts.html#circuit

Judges

www.ohnd.uscourts.gov/Judges/index.html

Calendar

www.ohnd.uscourts.gov
(click "Courtroom Calendars")

Opinions

www.ohnd.uscourts.gov/Opinions/opinions.html

Local Rules

www.ohnd.uscourts.gov/Clerk_s_Office/Local_Rules/local_rules.html

Federal Rules of Civil Procedure (FRCP)

www.law.cornell.edu/rules/frcp
www.access.gpo.gov/uscode/title28a/28a_4_.html
judiciary.house.gov/media/pdfs/printers/108th/civil2004.pdf

Federal Rules of Criminal Procedure

www.law.cornell.edu/rules/frcrmp
judiciary.house.gov/media/pdfs/printers/108th/civil2004.pdf

Electronic Case Filing (CM/ECF)

www.ohnd.uscourts.gov/Electronic_Filing/electronic_filing.html

Forms

www.ohnd.uscourts.gov/Online_Forms/online_forms.html

Fees

www.ohnd.uscourts.gov/Clerk_s_Office/Fee_Schedule/fee_schedule.html

Employment Opportunities

www.ohnd.uscourts.gov
(click "Employment Opportunities")

UNITED STATES BANKRUPTCY COURTS

Federal courts have exclusive jurisdiction over bankruptcy cases. Such cases cannot be filed in state court. Although United States district courts have jurisdiction over all bankruptcy matters (28 U.S.C. § 1334), they have the authority (28 U.S.C. § 157) to delegate or refer bankruptcy cases to the United States bankruptcy courts. There is a bankruptcy court in each of the 94 federal judicial districts. A United States bankruptcy judge is a judicial officer of the United States district court and is appointed for a 14-year term by the majority of judges of the United States court of appeals in the circuit.

The primary purposes of bankruptcy law are: (1) to give an honest debtor a "fresh start" in life by relieving the debtor of most debts; and (2) to repay creditors in an orderly manner to the extent that the debtor has property available for payment. The bankruptcy courts are usually in the same physical location as the United States district courts. However, in some areas, based on local space availability, the bankruptcy court may be located in space other than the United States courthouse where the district court is situated.

Kinds of Bankruptcy

www.uscourts.gov/bankruptcycourts/bankruptcybasics.html

Bankruptcy Basics

www.uscourts.gov/bankruptcycourts/bankruptcybasics/process.html
www.uscourts.gov/bankruptcycourts/BB101705final2column.pdf

Bankruptcy Forms

www.uscourts.gov/bkforms

United States Code: Title 11 (Bankruptcy)

uscode.house.gov/download/title_11.shtml
www.law.cornell.edu/uscode/html/uscode11/usc_sup_01_11.html

Federal Rules of Bankruptcy Procedure

www.law.cornell.edu/rules/frbp
www.access.gpo.gov/uscode/title11a/11a_1_.html

UNITED STATES BANKRUPTCY COURT, SOUTHERN DISTRICT OF OHIO

Address

U.S. Bankruptcy Court
Southern District of Ohio
Cincinnati Divisional Office
221 E. Fourth Street
Atrium Two Suite 800
Cincinnati, Ohio 45202
513-684-2572

U.S. Bankruptcy Court
Southern District of Ohio
Columbus Divisional Office
170 North High Street
Columbus, Ohio 43215
614-469-6638

U.S. Bankruptcy Court
Southern District of Ohio
Dayton Office
120 West Third Street
Dayton, Ohio 45402
937-225-2516

Web Site

www.ohsb.uscourts.gov

Opinions

www.ohsb.uscourts.gov/OHSB/OpNet/search.aspx

Judges

www.ohsb.uscourts.gov/Judges/Judges_staff/Judgepage.htm

CM/ECF

www.ohsb.uscourts.gov/ecf_home/faq.htm

Calendar

www.ohsb.uscourts.gov/default.asp
(click "Case Information")

Rules

www.casb.uscourts.gov/PDF&Downloads/lrules.pdf

Forms

www.ohsb.uscourts.gov/default.asp
(click "Rules & Forms")

Fees

www.ohsb.uscourts.gov/GeneralInformation/filingfees.htm

Employment Opportunities

www.ohsb.uscourts.gov
(click "General Information" then "Employment Opportunities")

UNITED STATES BANKRUPTCY COURT, NORTHERN DISTRICT OF OHIO

Address

Northern District of Ohio
Howard M. Metzenbaum U.S. Courthouse
201 Superior Avenue
Cleveland, Ohio 44114
216-615-4300

U.S. Bankruptcy Court
Northern District of Ohio
455 U.S. Courthouse
2 South Main St.
Akron, Ohio 44308
330-375-5840

U.S. Bankruptcy Court
Northern District of Ohio
Nathaniel R. Jones Federal Building
10 East Commerce Street
Youngstown, Ohio 44503
330-746-7027

U.S. Bankruptcy Court
Northern District of Ohio
411 U.S. Courthouse
1716 Spielbusch Avenue
Toledo, Ohio 43624
419-259-6440

U.S. Bankruptcy Court
Northern District of Ohio
Frank T. Bow Federal Bldg.
201 Cleveland Avenue,
S.W. Canton, Ohio 44702
330-489-4426

Web Site

www.ohnb.uscourts.gov

Opinions

www.ohnb.uscourts.gov
(click "Judges' Information" then "Judicial Postings")

CM/ECF

www.ohnb.uscourts.gov
(click "Electronic Case Filing")

Calendar

www.ohnb.uscourts.gov
(click "Case Information")

Rules

www.ohnb.uscourts.gov
(click "Research and Forms" then "Code & Rules")

Forms

www.ohnb.uscourts.gov
(click "Research and Forms" then " Bankruptcy Forms")

Fees

www.ohnb.uscourts.gov
(click "Fees")

Employment Opportunities

www.ohnb.uscourts.gov
(Click "Announcements" then "Job Vacancies")

BANKRUPTCY APPELLATE PANEL (BAP)

The Bankruptcy Appellate Panel (BAP) hears appeals of a judgment or order of a bankruptcy judge in a district that has authorized appeals to the BAP. Currently the district court for the Northern District of Ohio has made such an authorization.

Web Site

www.ca6.uscourts.gov/internet/bap/bap.htm

6th Circuit BAP Practice Manual

www.ca6.uscourts.gov/internet/bap/pdf/bap_practice_manual.pdf

UNITED STATES IMMIGRATION COURT

The Executive Office for Immigration Review (EOIR) (*www.usdoj.gov/eoir*) adjudicates matters brought under various immigration statutes to its three administrative tribunals: the Board of Immigration Appeals, the Office of the Chief Immigration Judge, and the Office of the Chief Administrative Hearing Officer.

The Board of Immigration Appeals has nationwide jurisdiction to hear appeals from certain decisions made by immigration judges and by district directors of the Department of Homeland Security (DHS). The Office of the Chief Immigration Judge provides overall direction for more than 200 immigration judges located in 53 immigration courts throughout the nation. Immigration judges are responsible for conducting formal administrative proceedings and act independently in their decision-making capacity. Their decisions are administratively final, unless appealed or certified to the Board.

Ohio Immigration Court Location (Cleveland)

www.usdoj.gov/eoir/sibpages/ICadr.htm
www.usdoj.gov/eoir/sibpages/ICadr.htm#OH

C. PACER

Public Access to Court Electronic Records (PACER) is an electronic public access service that allows users to obtain case and docket information from federal appellate, district and bankruptcy courts, and from the U.S. Party/Case Index. PACER is a service of the United States judiciary. The PACER Service Center is operated by the Administrative Office of the United States Courts (*pacer.psc.uscourts.gov*).

Currently most courts are available on the Internet. Links to these courts are provided at the PACER site (*pacer.psc.uscourts.gov/cgi-bin/links.pl*). However, a few systems are not available on the Internet and must be dialed directly using communication software (such as ProComm Plus, pcAnywhere, or Hyperterminal) and a modem. Electronic access is available for most courts by registering with the PACER Service Center, the judiciary's centralized registration, billing, and technical support center. You can register online or by phone at (800-676-6856; 210-301-6440).

Each court maintains its own databases with case information. Because PACER database systems are maintained within each court, each jurisdiction will have a different URL or modem number. Accessing and querying information from each service is comparable. The format and content of information provided, however, may differ slightly. Lists of local and toll-free PACER modem numbers are available at the PACER court directory (*pacer.psc.uscourts.gov/cgi-bin/modem.pl*).

D. More Information

Federal Judiciary Overview
www.uscourts.gov
www.firstgov.gov/Agencies/Federal/Judicial.shtml

Guide to the Federal Courts
www.uscourts.gov/journalistguide/welcome.html
www.uscourts.gov/understand02

Federal Court Links
www.uscourts.gov/links.html

Federal Judicial Center
www.fjc.gov

Employment Opportunities in the Federal Courts
www.uscourts.gov/employment/vacancies.html#

Wikipedia on Federal Courts in Ohio
en.wikipedia.org/wiki/United_States_Court_of_Appeals_for_the_Sixth_Circuit

Overview of Federal Government
www.usa.gov
www.fedworld.gov

E. Something to Check

1. Go to the sites that give you online access to court opinions of the 6th Circuit. Use the search features of the sites to find an opinion on any broad legal topic, e.g., capital punishment, adoption. Summarize what the opinion says about your topic.
2. For one of the two district courts in Ohio, find the calendar of any judge on the court you select. Name one case on the calendar of that judge.

4.4 State Legislation: How a Bill Becomes an Ohio Statute

A. Introduction

In this section, we provide an overview of the legislative process in Ohio, and, more specifically, how a bill becomes a law. For related information, see:

- section 4.1 (introduction to the state government of Ohio, including the major units of the state legislature)
- section 5.1 (doing legal research in Ohio law, including finding state statutes online and on the shelves)

B. How a Bill Becomes an Ohio Statute

The Ohio state legislature is a two-house (bicameral) legislature consisting of the Ohio Senate and the Ohio House of Representatives.

Senate	House of Representatives
614-466-4900	614-466-3357
www.senate.state.oh.us	*www.house.state.oh.us*
www.legislature.state.oh.us/senate.cfm	*www.legislature.state.oh.us/house.cfm*

There are 33 senators and 99 representatives representing the people of the state. Together, these bodies are referred to as the General Assembly. The legislative process takes place during biennial sessions, each session consisting of a two-year period.

Idea for a Bill

A *bill* is a document in which a legislator seeks to enact a new law or to amend or repeal an existing law. The term "bill" refers to the document from the time it is drafted until it is considered and approved by both the House and the Senate. After passing both houses, a bill becomes an *act* and must be presented to the Governor for acceptance or rejection. If accepted, it becomes a *law*.

Ideas for bills can come from many sources: individual legislators, the governor, administrative agencies, lobbyists, businesses, community groups, and private citizens. The first step is to have a legislator (a senator or representative) sponsor or author the bill.

Drafting

The legislator will send the idea for the bill to the nonpartisan Legislative Service Commission (LSC), where it will be drafted into bill form. Once the bill is drafted, it is returned to the legislator for review. If he or she is satisfied with the draft, the bill is ready for the next step: formal introduction in the Senate (if the legislator is a senator) or in the House (if he or she is a representative).

First Consideration: Introducing the Bill

The Ohio Constitution requires that each bill receive consideration at least three times by each house before enactment. (A two-thirds vote can suspend this requirement.) The first consideration of a bill consists of its introduction by a reading of the bill's title by the appropriate clerk on the day of introduction. Once introduced, the bill receives a consecutive number based on when it was introduced. For example, the 13th bill introduced in the House of Representatives during a session will be known for the remainder of that session as H.B. 13; the 60th bill introduced in the Senate will be S.B. 60.

Second Consideration: Assignment to Standing Committee

After introduction, a bill goes to the Rules and Reference Committee of the House (if introduced in the House) or to the Senate Reference Committee (if introduced in the Senate), where it recommends assignment to the appropriate standing committee. Bills are assigned to policy committees according to subject area. This recommendation is the bill's second consideration.

Committee Action

The committee may hold a hearing during which testimony may be heard in support of or opposition to the bill. There are several different actions a committee may take on the bill. It may report a bill favorably with no changes; adopt amendments and report the bill as an amended bill; redraft the bill or adopt numerous or lengthy amendments and report it as a substitute bill; combine two or more bills into one amended or substitute bill; indefinitely postpone the bill, thereby defeating it; or take no action at all.

If the chairperson of a committee decides that a bill should be considered by a subcommittee, he or she will designate several members of the committee to serve on a subcommittee to consider the bill while the full committee goes ahead with other business. A subcommittee proceeds in much the same manner as the full committee. It may hold subcommittee hearings on the bill and decide to report it back to the full committee without changes, amend it, prepare a substitute bill, or recommend its defeat.

For bills accepted by the full committee, the next step is consideration of possible floor action by the Senate Rules Committee or by the House Rules and Reference Committee.

Bill Analysis

The Legislative Service Commission prepares a detailed narrative description of each bill that is scheduled for a hearing in committee. This bill analysis is updated as the bill moves through the legislative process. Each analysis contains: (1) a heading consisting of the bill number, the version of the bill being analyzed, and the bill's sponsors, (2) brief statements summarizing the bill, (3) a content and operation section that describes the bill in more detail, and (4) the bill's legislative history.

Third Consideration: Floor Action

The Senate Rules Committee and the House Rules and Reference Committee select from the many bills reported by the standing committees those that will be scheduled for floor debate and a vote by the full Senate or House. When the Rules Committee or the Rules and Reference Committee schedules a bill for floor debate and a vote, it places the bill on the Calendar above a black line. The point in the legislative process at which the full membership of the House or Senate votes on a bill is the third consideration, also known as "floor action."

Repeat Process in Other House

When a bill is passed by the first house after debate on the floor, it is forwarded to the second house where it undergoes essentially the same process of introduction, referral to committee, committee hearings, and floor action. The second house may pass the measure without change, amend it, prepare a substitute bill, indefinitely postpone it, or defeat it just as with bills originating in that house.

Resolution of Differences

If a bill is amended in the second house, it must go back to the house of origin for concurrence, meaning agreement on those amendments. If the house of origin does not concur in those amendments, the bill is referred to a two-house conference committee to resolve the differences. Generally, the conference

EXHIBIT 4.4A **The Life Cycle of State Legislation—From Idea into Law**

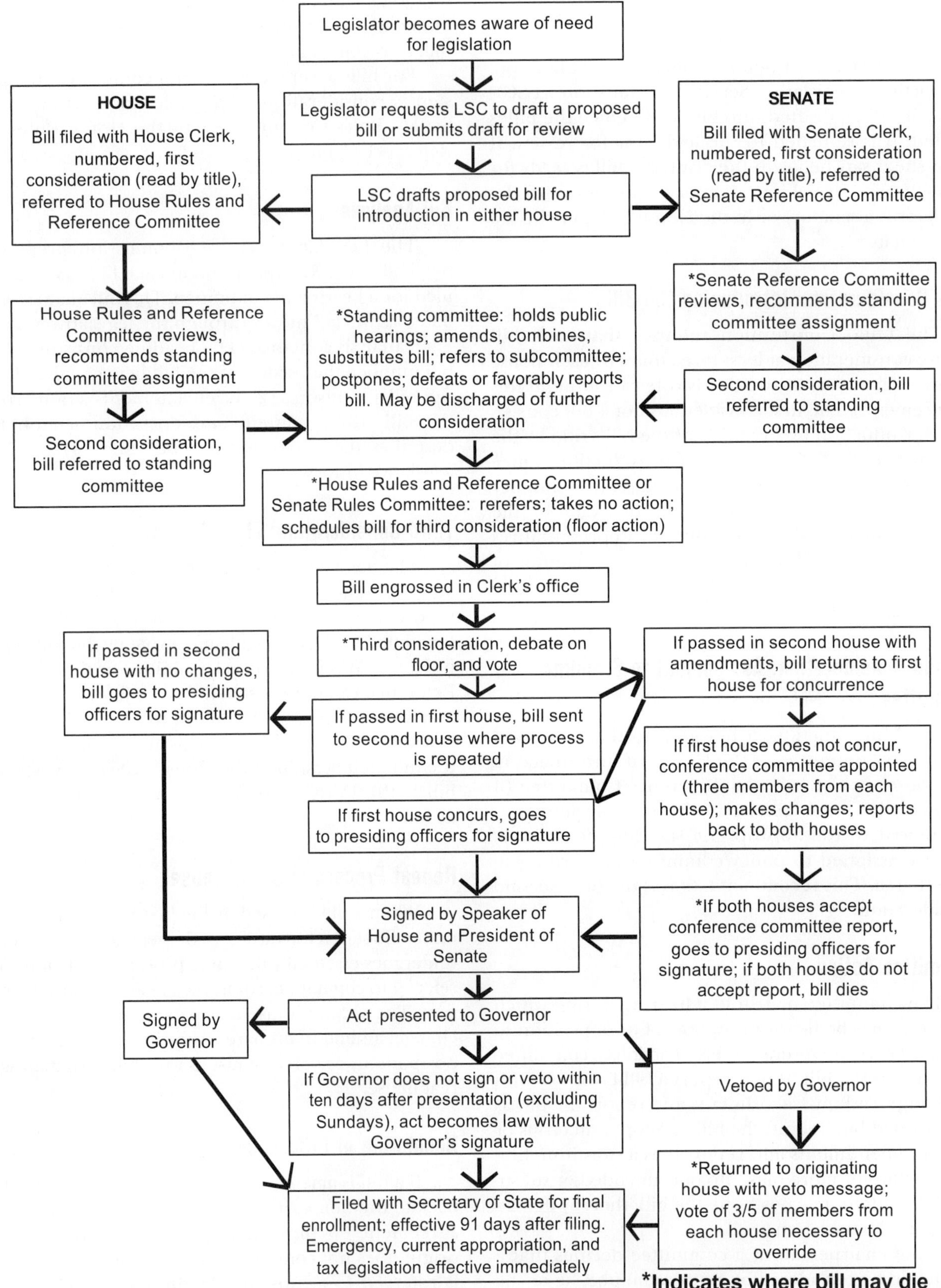

Source: Ohio Legislative Service Commission, A Guidebook for Legislators 61 (9th ed. 2005–2006) (www.lsc.state.oh.us/guidebook/chapter5.pdf).

committee includes three members from the Senate and three from the Assembly. If a compromise is reached, the bill is returned to both houses for a vote.

Governor

If both houses approve a bill, it goes to the governor. The Governor has three choices:

(a) sign the bill into law,
(b) allow it to become law without his or her signature by not acting on it within ten days of receiving it, or
(c) veto it.

A governor's veto can be overridden by a three-fifths vote in both houses.

Revised Code and Laws of Ohio

Once enacted into law, the act is filed with the secretary of state who assigns it a chapter number. These chaptered acts are statutes, and ordinarily become part of the *Ohio Revised Code.* The *Revised Code* is a comprehensive collection of statutes organized by subject matter. In addition, at the end of each biennial session of the General Assembly, the secretary of state publishes the *Laws of Ohio* in paper and electronic format. It is a compilation of all acts passed by that General Assembly. The acts appear in numerical order as they were enacted. The *Laws of Ohio* is the only official publication of the enactments of the General Assembly. The *Revised Code* is a commercial version of the code, published privately.

The legislative process just described is outlined in Exhibit 4.4A. LSC in the chart refers to the Legislative Service Commission.

C. More Information

General Assembly
www.legislature.state.oh.us

Overview of Legislative Process
www.legislature.state.oh.us/process.cfm
www.lsc.state.oh.us/guidebook/chapter5.pdf
www.legislature.state.oh.us/site_index.cfm

Legislative Information Sources Available to the Public
www.lsc.state.oh.us/research/leginfo.pdf

Current Bills of the General Assembly
www.legislature.state.oh.us/search.cfm

Revised Code of Ohio
www.legislature.state.oh.us/search.cfm#orconlinedocs.
andorsonpublishing.com/oh/lpExt.dll?f=templates&fn=main-h.htm&cp=PORC

Ohio Acts
www.legislature.state.oh.us/acts.cfm
www.legislature.state.oh.us

Ohio Legislative Service Commission
www.lsc.state.oh.us

Bill Analysis
www.lsc.state.oh.us/billdocuments.html

Legislative Agencies
www.legislature.state.oh.us/agencies.cfm

Broadcasting Legislative Sessions
www.ohiochannel.org

Legislative Information Systems
www.lis.state.oh.us

Governor
governor.ohio.gov

Secretary of State
www.sos.state.oh.us

Glossary of Legislative Terms
www.lsc.state.oh.us/guidebook/glossary.pdf
www.legislature.state.oh.us/glossary.cfm

D. Something to Check

1. Find a bill currently before the legislature on any:
   a. family law topic
   b. criminal law topic
2. Cite one bill or statute that was introduced, authored, or sponsored:
   a. by your state senator
   b. by your state representative
3. Locate any pending bill regarding health care.

4.5 State Agencies, Offices, and Boards

A. Introduction

This section covers the major state agencies and commissions in Ohio. See also:

- section 4.1 for an overview of state government
- section 4.2 on the state courts

- section 4.4 on the state legislature
- section 4.6 on county and city governments

For legal research leads on issues pertaining to many of these agencies and commissions, see the starter cites in section 5.5.

MAIN INFORMATION NUMBER FOR OHIO GOVERNMENT 614-466-2000

B. Topics

Accountants
Addiction
Administration
African Americans
Aging
Agriculture and Food
Air
Alcohol
Architects
Arts
Athletics
Attorney General
Auditor
Banks
Budget
Building and Construction
Business
Chemical Dependency
Chiropractors
Civil Rights
College
Commerce
Community Service
Conflict Resolution
Conservation
Construction
Consumers
Corporations
Corrections
Cosmetology
Counseling
Crime
Dentists
Development
Dietitians
Disabilities
Drugs
Education
Elections
Employment
Energy
Engineering
Environment
Ethics
Expo
Family Services
Financial Institutions
Funeral Directors
Governor
Health and Medicine
Hispanics
History
House of Representatives
Housing
Information Technology
Inspector General
Insurance
Job and Family Services
Labor Relations
Lake Erie
Law Enforcement
Legislature
Library
Lieutenant Governor
Liquor
Lottery
Mediation
Medicine
Mental Health
Military
National Guard
Natural Resources
Nursing
Occupational Safety/Health
Pharmacy
Prison
Public Defender
Public Safety
Public Television
Public Utilities Racing
Real Estate
Sanitarian
Savings and Loan
Schools
Secretary of State
Securities
Senate
Sports
Taxation
Television
Tobacco
Tourism
Transportation
Treasurer
Unclaimed Funds
Unemployment Compensation
Veterans
Veterinary
Victim Compensation
Whistleblowing
Workers' Compensation

ACCOUNTANTS

Accountancy Board
614-466-4135
www.acc.ohio.gov

ADDICTION

(see also Counseling)

Alcohol and Drug Addiction Services
614-466-3445
www.odadas.state.oh.us

Ohio Chemical Dependency Professionals Board
614-387-1110
ocdp.ohio.gov

ADMINISTRATION

(see also Courts, Governor, Legislature)

State Government
614-466-2000
myohio.gov
www.ohio.gov

Office of Administrative Knowledge System
614-387-2000
www.oaks.ohio.gov/oaks

Administrative Services
614-466-6511
www.das.ohio.gov

General Services: Surplus
614-466-1584
www.gsd.das.state.oh.us/Surplus/SFSUR.html

Human Resources Division
www.das.ohio.gov/hrd

Office of Information Technology
614-644-6446
oit.ohio.gov

Office of the Inspector General
614-644-9110
watchdog.ohio.gov

Ohio Office of Budget and Management
614-466-4034
www.obm.ohio.gov

State of Ohio Personnel Board of Review
614-466-7046
pbr.ohio.gov

AFRICAN AMERICANS

Commission of African American Males
800-370-4566
caam.ohio.gov

AGING

Department of Aging
614-466-5500
www.goldenbuckeye.com

AGRICULTURE AND FOOD

Ohio Board of Dietetics
614-466-3291
dietetics.ohio.gov

Department of Agriculture
800-282-1955
www.ohioagriculture.gov

AIR

(see Environment)

ALCOHOL

(see Addiction, Liquor)

ARCHITECTS

Board of Examiners of Architects
614-466-2316
www.arc.ohio.gov

Board of Landscape Architect Examiners
614-466-2316
arc.ohio.gov/lae

Office of the State Architect
614-466-4761
das.ohio.gov/gsd/sao/sao.html

ARTS

(see also Tourism)

Cultural Facilities Commission
614-752-2770
www.culture.ohio.gov

Ohio Arts Council
614-466-2613
www.oac.state.oh.us

ATHLETICS

Cultural Facilities Commission
614-752-2770
www.culture.ohio.gov

Ohio Athletics Commission
330-797-2556
aco.ohio.gov

Ohio State Racing Commission
614-466-2757
www.racing.ohio.gov

ATTORNEY GENERAL

(see also Courts, Law Enforcement)

Ohio Attorney General
614-466-4320
www.ag.state.oh.us

AUDITOR

Ohio Auditor of State
800-282-0370; 614-466-4514
www.auditor.state.oh.us

BANKS

(see Financial Institutions)

BARBERS

Ohio State Barber Board
614-466-5003
barber.ohio.gov

BUDGET

(see Administration)

BUILDING AND CONSTRUCTION

Board of Building Appeals
614-644-2616
www.com.state.oh.us/ODOC/dic/dicbba.htm

Board of Building Standards
614-644-2613
www.com.state.oh.us/ODOC/dic/dicbbs.htm

Bureau of Building Code Compliance
614-644-2622
www.com.state.oh.us/ODOC/dic/diccont.htm

Capitol Square Review and Advisory Board
614-752-9777
www.das.ohio.gov/phone/agency/csr.asp

Construction Industry Licensing Board
614-644-3493
www.com.state.oh.us/dic/dicocilb.htm

Division of Industrial Compliance
614-644-2223
www.com.state.oh.us/ODOC/dic

Ohio Building Authority
614-466-5959
oba.ohio.gov

Ohio Public Works Commission
614-466-0880
www.pwc.state.oh.us

BUSINESS

Ohio Business Portal
www.business.ohio.gov

Department of Commerce
614-466-3636
www.com.state.oh.us/ODOC

Department of Development
800-848-1300
www.odod.state.oh.us

E-Commerce Center
614-995-4918
das.ohio.gov/ITSD/ESS/ECC/Index.htm

International Trade Division
www.odod.state.oh.us/itd

Regional Economic Development Offices
614-995-1895
www.odod.state.oh.us/Regionals.htm

Securities Division
614-644-7381
www.securities.state.oh.us

CHEMICAL DEPENDENCY

(see Addiction)

CHILD SUPPORT

(see also Family)

Office of Child Support
614-752-6561
jfs.ohio.gov/OCS

CHIROPRACTORS

State Chiropractic Board
888-772-1384
chirobd.ohio.gov

CIVIL RIGHTS

Ohio Civil Rights Commission
888-278-7101
crc.ohio.gov

Ohio Legal Rights Service
800-282-9181
olrs.ohio.gov

COLLEGE

(see Education)

COMMERCE

(see Business)

COMMUNITY SERVICE

Community Service Council
888-767-OHIO
www.serve.ohio.gov

CONFLICT RESOLUTION

(see also Courts, Employment)

Ohio Commission on Dispute Resolution & Conflict Management
614-752-9595
disputeresolution.ohio.gov/index.htm

CONSERVATION

(see Energy, Environment, Natural Resources)

CONSTRUCTION

(see Building and Construction)

CONSUMERS

(see Financial Institutions)

Ohio Consumers' Counsel
877-742-5622
www.pickocc.org

CORPORATIONS

(see Business)

CORRECTIONS

(see also Law Enforcement)

Correctional Institution Inspection Committee
614-466-6649
www.ciic.state.oh.us

Department of Rehabilitation and Corrections
614-752-1159
www.drc.state.oh.us

Department of Youth Services
614-466-4314
www.dys.ohio.gov

COSMETOLOGY

State Board of Cosmetology
614-466-3834
www.cos.ohio.gov

COUNSELING

(see also Addiction, Health)

Counselor, Social Worker, and Marriage & Family Therapist Board
614-466-0912
www.cswmft.ohio.gov

COURTS

(see also Public Defender; and sections 4.2 and 4.3)

Court of Claims
800-824-8263
www.cco.state.oh.us

County and Municipal Courts
www.ohiojudges.org
(click "Links")

Ohio Judicial Conference
614-387-9750
www.ohiojudges.org

Supreme Court of Ohio
800-826-9010
www.sconet.state.oh.us

CRIME

(see Law Enforcement, Victim Compensation)

DENTISTS

(see also Health)

State Dental Board
614-466-2580
www.dental.ohio.gov

DEVELOPMENT

(see Business)

DIETITIANS

(see Agriculture and Food)

DISABILITIES

(see Health)

DRUGS

(see Addiction)

EDUCATION

College Advantage
614-752-9400
www.collegeadvantage.com

Department of Education
877-644-6338; 614-995-1545
www.ode.state.oh.us

Legislative Office of Education Oversight
614-752-9686
www.loeo.state.oh.us

Ohio Board of Regents
614-466-6000
regents.ohio.gov

Ohio Learning Network
614-995-3240
www.oln.org

Ohio School Facilities Commission
614-466-6290
www.osfc.state.oh.us

School for the Deaf
614-728-1422
www.ohioschoolforthedeaf.org

SchoolNet
614-728-8324
www.etech.ohio.gov

State Board of Career Colleges and Schools
614-466-2752
scr.ohio.gov

ELECTIONS

County Boards of Election
www.sos.state.oh.us/sos/ElectionsVoter/OhioElections.aspx?Section=boeDir

Office of the Legislative Inspector General
614-728-5100
www.jlec-olig.state.oh.us

Ohio Elections Commission
614-466-3205
elc.ohio.gov

Ohio Ethics Commission
614-466-7090
www.ethics.ohio.gov

EMERGENCY

(see Health, Law Enforcement, Public Safety)

EMPLOYMENT

(see also Health, Job and Family Services, Labor Relations, Unemployment Compensation)

Apprenticeship Council
614-644-2469
jfs.ohio.gov/apprenticeship

Labor and Worker Safety
614-644-2239
198.234.41.214/w3/webpo2.nsf?Opendatabase

Labor Market Information
lmi.state.oh.us

State of Ohio Personnel Board of Review
614-466-7046
pbr.ohio.gov

Wage and Hour Bureau
614-644-2239
198.234.41.198/w3/webwh.nsf?Opendatabase

ENERGY

(see also Environment, Natural Resources)

Office of Energy Efficiency
614-466-6797
www.odod.state.oh.us/cdd/oee

Ohio Power Siting Board
866-270-OPSB; 614-466-2871
www.opsb.ohio.gov

ENGINEERING

(see also Building)

State Board of Registration for Professional Engineers and Surveyors
877-644-6364; 614-466-3650
www.ohiopeps.org

ENVIRONMENT

(see also Agriculture, Energy, Natural Resources)

Air Quality Development Authority
614-224-3383
www.ohioairquality.org

Clean Air Resource Center
800-225-5051
www.ohioairquality.org/small_business/carc_fact_sheet.shtml

Clean Ohio Fund
www.clean.ohio.gov

Environmental Review Appeals
614-466-8950

Ohio Environmental Protection Agency
614-644-3020; 800-282-9378 (emergencies)
www.epa.state.oh.us

Petroleum Underground Storage Tank Release Compensation Board
614-752-8963
www.petroboard.com

State Board of Sanitarian Registration
614-466-1772
sanitarian.ohio.gov

ETHICS

(see Elections; for attorney ethics, see section 3.2)

EXPO

(see also Tourism)

Expo Center & State Fair
888-OHO-EXPO
www.ohioexpocenter.com

Family Services
(see also Job and Family Services)

Office of Child Support
614-752-6561
jfs.ohio.gov/OCS

Ohio Family and Children First
614-752-4044
www.ohiofcf.org

FINANCIAL INSTITUTIONS

(see also Business, Housing)

Division of Financial Institutions
866-278-0003; 614-728-8400
www.com.state.oh.us/ODOC/dfi

FUNERAL DIRECTORS

Board of Embalmers and Funeral Directors
614-466-4252
www.funeral.ohio.gov

GOVERNOR

Office of the Governor
614-466-3555
governor.ohio.gov

Statehouse News Bureau
614-221-1811
statenews.org

Health and Medicine
(see also Chiropractors, Dentists, Veterinary)

Bureau of Occupational Safety and Health
614-644-2239
198.234.41.214/w3/webpo2.nsf?Opendatabase

Commission on Minority Health
614-466-4000
mih.ohio.gov

Emergency Medical Services
800-233-0785
www.ems.ohio.gov/ems.asp

Department of Health
614-466-3543
www.odh.ohio.gov

Department of Mental Health
877-275-6364
www.mh.state.oh.us

Department of Mental Retardation and Developmental Disabilities
614-466-5214
odmrdd.state.oh.us

Governor's Council on People with Disabilities
614-438-1391
www.gcpd.ohio.gov

Medical Board
614-466-3934
www.med.ohio.gov

Occupational Therapy, Physical Therapy, and Athletic Trainers Board
614-466-3774
otptat.ohio.gov

Ohio Board of Nursing
614-466-3947
www.nursing.ohio.gov

Ohio Board of Speech-Language Pathology and Audiology
614-466-3145
slpaud.ohio.gov

Ohio Developmental Disabilities Council
614-644-5530
www.ddc.ohio.gov
olrs.ohio.gov (Ohio Legal Rights Service)

Ohio Medical Transportation Board
614-466-9451
oal.ohio.gov

Ohio Optical Dispensers Board
614-466-9709
optical.ohio.gov

Ohio Pharmacy Board
614-446-4143
www.pharmacy.ohio.gov

Ohio Respiratory Care Board
614-752-9218
respiratorycare.ohio.gov

Ohio State Board of Optometry
888-565-3044; 614-466-5115
optometry.ohio.gov

Rehabilitation Services Commission
614-438-1200
rsc.ohio.gov

School for the Deaf
614-728-1422
www.ohioschoolforthedeaf.org

State Board of Orthotics, Prosthetics, & Pedorthics
614-466-1157
www.opp.ohio.gov

State Board of Psychology
614-466-8808
www.psychology.ohio.gov

HISPANICS

Commission on Hispanic/Latino Affairs
614-466-8333
ochla.ohio.gov

HISTORY

Ohio Historical Society
614-297-2300
www.ohiohistory.org

HOUSE OF REPRESENTATIVES

(see Legislature)

HOUSING

Manufactured Homes Commission
614-734-8454
www.omhc.ohio.gov

Ohio Housing Finance Agency
888-362-6432
www.ohiohome.org

Real Estate and Professional Licensing Division
614-466-4100
www.com.state.oh.us/ODOC/real

INFORMATION TECHNOLOGY

(see Administration)

INSPECTOR GENERAL

Office of the Inspector General
614-644-9110
watchdog.ohio.gov

Office of the Legislative Inspector General
614-728-5100
www.jlec-olig.state.oh.us

INSURANCE

Department of Insurance
800-686-1526; 800-686-1527
www.ohioinsurance.gov

JOB AND FAMILY SERVICES

(see also Employment)

Department of Job and Family Services
614-466-6282
jfs.ohio.gov

Ohio Family and Children First
614-752-4044
www.ohiofcf.org

JUDICIARY

(see Courts)

LABOR RELATIONS

(see also Employment)

State Employment Relations Board
614-644-8573
www.serb.state.oh.us

LAKE ERIE

(see Natural Resources)

LAW ENFORCEMENT

(see Attorney General, Courts, Public Defender, Public Safety, Victim Compensation)

Department of Public Safety
614-466-2550
www.publicsafety.ohio.gov/odps.asp

Office of Criminal Justice Services
888-448-4842; 614-466-7782
www.publicsafety.ohio.gov/ocjs/ocjs_home.asp

Ohio Investigative Unit
614-644-2415
www.investigativeunit.ohio.gov/liquor.asp

Ohio State Highway Patrol
877-7-PATROL
www.statepatrol.ohio.gov

LEGISLATURE

House of Representatives
614-466-3357
www.house.state.oh.us

Joint Committee on Agency Rule Review
614-466-4086
www.jcarr.state.oh.us

Legislative Office of Education Oversight
614-752-9686
www.loeo.state.oh.us

Legislative Service Commission
614-466-3615
www.lsc.state.oh.us

Office of the Legislative Inspector General
614-728-5100
www.jlec-olig.state.oh.us

Senate
614-466-4900
www.senate.state.oh.us

Statehouse News Bureau
614-221-1811
statenews.org

LIBRARY

(see also section 5.8 on law libraries)

Ohio Public Library Information Network (OPLIN)
614-466-3831
www.oplin.org

State Library of Ohio
614-644-7061
winslo.state.oh.us

LIEUTENANT GOVERNOR

Office of the Lieutenant Governor
ltgovernor.ohio.gov

LIQUOR

(see also Addiction, Law Enforcement)

Division of Liquor Control
614-644-2360
www.liquorcontrol.ohio.gov/liquor.htm

Liquor Control Commission
614-466-3132
lcc.ohio.gov

LOTTERY

Ohio Lottery
800-686-4208; 216-787-3200
www.ohiolottery.com

MEDIATION

(see Conflict Resolution, Courts)

MEDICINE

(see Health and Medicine)

MENTAL HEALTH

(see Health)

MILITARY

Adjutant General's Department
800-646-3864
www.das.ohio.gov/phone/agency/adj.asp

National Guard
614-336-6000
www.ohionationalguard.com

Office of Veteran's Affairs
614-644-0898
veteransaffairs.ohio.gov

Ohio Military Reserve
614-336-6000
ohmr.ohio.gov

Veterans Home Agency
419-625-2454
www.ohioveteranshome.gov

MOTOR VEHICLES

(see also Transportation)

Bureau of Motor Vehicles
614-752-7500
ohiobmv.com

Ohio Board of Motor Vehicle Collision Repair Registration (license verification)
614-995-0714
www.collisionboard.ohio.gov

Ohio State Highway Patrol
877-7-PATROL
www.statepatrol.ohio.gov

NATIONAL GUARD

(see Military)

NATURAL RESOURCES

(see also Environment)

Clean Ohio Fund
www.clean.ohio.gov

Department of Natural Resources
614-265-6565
www.dnr.state.oh.us

Lake Erie Commission
419-245-2514
www.epa.state.oh.us/oleo

Ohio State Parks
www.dnr.state.oh.us/parks

Water Development Authority
www.owda.org

NURSING

(see Health)

OCCUPATIONAL SAFETY/HEALTH

(see Health, Workers' Compensation)

PHARMACY

Ohio Pharmacy Board
614-446-4143
www.pharmacy.ohio.gov

PRISON

(see Corrections)

PUBLIC DEFENDER

Office of the Ohio Public Defender
800-686-1573; 614-466-5394
www.opd.ohio.gov/index.htm

PUBLIC SAFETY

(see also Health, Law Enforcement)

Department of Public Safety
614-466-2550
www.publicsafety.ohio.gov/odps.asp

Emergency Management Agency
614-889-7150
www.ema.ohio.gov/ema.asp

Ohio Homeland Security
614-387-6171
www.homelandsecurity.ohio.gov/hls.asp

State Fire Marshall
614-752-8200
www.com.state.oh.us/sfm

Utility Radiology Safety Board
www.ursb.ohio.gov

PUBLIC TELEVISION

Ohio Educational Telecommunications Network
614-485-6000
www.oet.edu

PUBLIC UTILITIES

(see also Environment)

Public Utilities Commission of Ohio
800-686-PUCO
www.puco.ohio.gov

Ohio Consumers' Counsel
877-742-5622
www.pickocc.org

RACING

(see Athletics)

REAL ESTATE

(see Housing)

SANITARIAN

State Board of Sanitarian Registration
614-466-1772
sanitarian.ohio.gov

SAVINGS AND LOAN

(see Financial Institutions)

SCHOOLS

(see Education)

SECRETARY OF STATE

Ohio Secretary of State
614-466-2655
www.sos.state.oh.us

SECURITIES

(see Business)

SENATE

(see Legislature)

SPORTS

(see Athletics)

TAXATION

Board of Tax Appeals
614-466-6700
www.bta.ohio.gov

Department of Taxation
800- 282-1780; 614-466-2166
www.tax.ohio.gov

TELEVISION

(see Public Television)

TOBACCO

(see also Agriculture)

Ohio Tobacco Program
614-728-2303
www.ohioagriculture.gov/pubs/contacts.stm

Tobacco Litigation
Ohio Attorney General
www.ag.state.oh.us/web_applications/tobacco/default.asp

TOURISM

(see also Arts)

Division of Travel and Tourism
800-BUCKEYE
www.odod.state.oh.us/Travel.htm

Expo Center & State Fair
888-OHO-EXPO
www.ohioexpocenter.com

TRANSPORTATION

(see also Motor Vehicles)

Department of Transportation
614-466-7170
www.dot.state.oh.us

Ohio Turnpike Commission
888-876-7453; 440-234-2081
www.ohioturnpike.org

Rail Development Commission
614-644-0306
www.dot.state.oh.us/ohiorail

TREASURER

Ohio Treasurer of State
614-466-2160; 800-648-7827
www.treasurer.state.oh.us

UNCLAIMED FUNDS

Division of Unclaimed Funds
614-466-4433
www.unclaimedfundstreasurehunt.ohio.gov

Unemployment Compensation
(see also section 1.9)

Office of Unemployment Compensation
877-644-6562
jfs.ohio.gov/ouc

Unemployment Compensation Review Commission
614-466-6768
www.web.ucrc.state.oh.us

VETERANS

(see Military)

VETERINARY

(see also Health)

Veterinary Medical Licensing Board
614-644-5281
ovmlb.ohio.gov

VICTIM COMPENSATION

(see also Law Enforcement)

Ohio Attorney General
www.ag.state.oh.us
(click "Victim's Services")

WATER

(see Natural Resources)

WHISTLEBLOWING

(see Inspector General)

WORKERS' COMPENSATION

(see also section 1.10)

Bureau of Occupational Safety and Health
614-644-2239
198.234.41.214/w3/webpo2.nsf?Opendatabase

Bureau of Workers' Compensation
800-644-6292
www.ohiobwc.com

Industrial Commission of Ohio
800-521-2691
www.ohioic.com

C. More Information

ohio.gov/contacts.stm
www.ohio.gov/government.stm
das.ohio.gov/phone/agency
www.statelocalgov.net/state-oh.cfm

D. Something to Check

1. Find the Web sites of three Ohio agencies, offices, or boards that refer to the paralegals they employ.
2. Identify the Ohio agencies, offices, or boards that would have relevant information on (a) abortion, (b) the plight of an insolvent business, and (c) police misconduct?

4.6 Counties and Cities: Some Useful Law-Related Sites

A. Information

This section presents contact information on the following major county and city law-related sites:

- main government site
- local courts
- clerk of courts
- child support enforcement agency
- recorder
- prosecutor
- public defender
- sheriff/police

For similar information about:

- state government, see section 4.1
- state courts, see section 4.2
- public records, see section 5.7
- law libraries, see section 5.8
- federal courts in Ohio, see section 4.3
- bar associations, see section 3.4
- paralegal associations, see section 1.2

B. Table of Contents

Morgan County
Morrow County
Muskingum County
Noble County
Ottawa County
Parma, City of
Paulding County
Perry County
Pickaway County
Pike County
Portage County
Preble County
Putnam County
Richland County
Ross County
Sandusky County
Scioto County
Seneca County
Shelby County
Stark County
Summit County
Toledo, City of
Trumbull County
Tuscarawas County
Union County
Van Wert County
Vinton County
Warren County
Washington County
Wayne County
Williams County
Wood County
Wyandot County

ADAMS COUNTY

Adams: County Government
937-544-3286
www.conway.com/oh/adams/adams.htm
www.adamscountyoh.com

Adams: Court of Common Pleas
937-544-2344

Adams: Child Support Enforcement
800-544-5711; 937-544-2371

Adams: Sheriff
welcome.to/acso

AKRON, CITY OF

Akron: City Government
330-375-2345
www.ci.akron.oh.us
ci.akron.oh.us/depts.html

Akron Municipal Court
330-375-2120
courts.ci.akron.oh.us

Akron: Law Department
330-375-2030
ci.akron.oh.us/law.html

Akron: City Police
330-375-2552
publicsafety.ci.akron.oh.us/police

ALLEN COUNTY

Allen: County Government
419-228-3700
www.co.allen.oh.us
www.co.allen.oh.us/com.php

Allen Court of Common Pleas
419-223-8513
www.co.allen.oh.us/ccom.php

Allen: Domestic Relations Court
419-223-8511
www.co.allen.oh.us/cdom.php

Allen: Juvenile Court
419-227-5531
www.co.allen.oh.us/cjuv.php

Allen: Probate Court
419-223-8501
www.co.allen.oh.us/cpro.php

Allen: Lima Municipal Court
419-221-5275
www.limamunicipalcourt.org

Allen: Clerk of Courts
419-223-8513; 419-223-8529
www.co.allen.oh.us/cle.php

Allen: Child Support Enforcement
800-224-7133; 419-224-7133
www.co.allen.oh.us/chi.php

Allen: Recorder
419-223-8517
www.co.allen.oh.us/rec.php

Allen: Prosecutor
419-228-3700
www.co.allen.oh.us/pro.php

Allen: Public Defender
(court appointed; no PD office)
opd.ohio.gov/pub/pub_cty.htm

Allen: Sheriff
419-227-3535
www.co.allen.oh.us/she.php

ASHLAND COUNTY

Ashland: County Government
419-289-0000
www.ashlandcounty.org
www.ashlandcounty.org/directory.cfm

Ashland: Court of Common Pleas
419-282-4242

Ashland: Municipal Court
419-289-8137
www.ashlandohio.com/municipalcourt/index.htm

Ashland: Clerk of Courts
419-282-4242
www.ashlandcounty.org/clerkofcourts/index.htm

Ashland: Child Support Enforcement
800-589-8141; 419-289-8141

Ashland: Recorder
419-282-4238
www.ashlandcounty.org/recorder/index.htm

Ashland: Prosecutor
419-289-8857
www.ashlandcounty.org/prosecutor

Ashland: Public Defender
(court appointed; no PD office)
opd.ohio.gov/pub/pub_cty.htm

Ashland: Sheriff
419-289-3911
www.ashlandcounty.org/sheriff

ASHTABULA COUNTY

Ashtabula: County Government
440-576-3750
www.co.ashtabula.oh.us

Ashtabula: Courts
www.co.ashtabula.oh.us
(click "Court System")

Ashtabula: Clerk of Courts
440-576-3637
www.co.ashtabula.oh.us
(click "Court System")

Ashtabula: Child Support Enforcement
800-935-0242; 440-998-1110

Ashtabula: Recorder
440-576-3762
www.co.ashtabula.oh.us
(click "Offices")

Ashtabula: Prosecutor
440-576-3662
www.co.ashtabula.oh.us
(click "Offices")

Ashtabula: Public Defender
440-998-2628
opd.ohio.gov/pub/pub_cty.htm

Ashtabula: Sheriff
www.ashtabulacountysheriff.org

ATHENS COUNTY

Athens: County Government
740-592-3219
www.athenscountygovernment.com
www.athenscountygovernment.com/boc

Athens: Court of Common Pleas
740-592-3238; 740-592-3591
www.athenscountygovernment.com/cpc

Athens: Municipal Court
740-592-3328
www.athensmunicipalcourt.com

Athens: Clerk of Courts
740-592-3242
www.athenscountygovernment.com/coc

Athens: Child Support Enforcement
800-436-8933; 740-593-5046
csea.athenscountygovernment.com/csea.htm

Athens: Recorder
740-592-3228
www.athenscountygovernment.com/ro

Athens: Prosecutor
740-592-3208
www.athenscountygovernment.com/pa

Athens: Public Defender
740-593-6400
opd.ohio.gov/pub/pub_cty.htm

Athens: Sheriff
740-593-6633
www.athenscountygovernment.com/sd

AUGLAIZE COUNTY

Auglaize: County Government
419-739-6710
www.auglaizecounty.org

Auglaize: Court of Common Pleas
419-739-6770
www.auglaizecounty.org/cpcourt.htm

Auglaize: Courts (other)
www.auglaizecounty.org/domestic.htm
www.auglaizecounty.org/probatect.htm
www.auglaizecounty.org/jvct.htm
www.auglaizecounty.org/munict.htm
www.auglaizecounty.org

Auglaize: Clerk of Courts
419-739-6765
www.auglaizecounty.org/clerk.htm

Auglaize: Child Support Enforcement
419-739-6510
www.auglaizecounty.org/childsupt.htm

Auglaize: Clerk-Recorder
419-739-6735
www.auglaizecounty.org/recorder.htm

Auglaize: Prosecutor
419-738-9688
www.auglaizecounty.org/pros.htm

Auglaize: Public Defender
419-738-7111
www.auglaizecounty.org/defender.htm

Auglaize: Sheriff
419-738-2147
www.auglaizecounty.org/sheriff

BELMONT COUNTY

Belmont: County Government
740-699-2155
www.belmontcountyohio.org

Belmont: Court of Common Pleas
740-699-2137
www.belmontcountyohio.org/common_pleas.htm

Belmont: Juvenile Court
740-695-2141
www.belmontcountyjuvenilecourt.com/index2.php

Belmont: Probate Court
740-699-2144
www.belmontcountyprobatecourt.com/index3.php

Belmont: Clerk of Courts
740-699-2169
www.belmontcountycoc.com

Belmont: Child Support Enforcement
800-494-1616; 740-695-1074

Belmont: Recorder
740-695-2121
www.belmontcountyohio.org/recorder/index.html

Belmont: Prosecutor
740-699-2771
www.bcprosatty.com

Belmont: Public Defender
740-695-5263
opd.ohio.gov/pub/pub_cty.htm

Belmont: Sheriff
740-695-7933
www.belmontsheriff.com

BROWN COUNTY

Brown: County Government
937-378-3956
www.county.brown.oh.us

Brown: Municipal Court
937-738-6358
www.browncountycourt.org

Brown: Clerk of Courts
937-378-3100
www.occaohio.com/County/brown.htm

Brown: Recorder
937-378-6478
www.ohiorecorders.com/brown.html

Brown: Prosecutor
937-378-4151
www.browncountyprosecutorsoffice.org

BUTLER COUNTY

Butler: County Government
513-887-3247
www.butlercountyohio.org

Butler: Court of Common Pleas
513-785-6550
www.butlercountyohio.org/commonpleas

Butler: Courts (other)
www.butlercountyohio.org/probate
www.butlercountyohio.org/drcourt/pages/main_page.htm
www.butlercountyohio.org/juvenilejusticecenter/index.cfm?page=home
www.fairfield-city.org/court/index.cfm
www.hamiltonmunicipalcourt.org
www.ci.middletown.oh.us/depts/court/default.aspx
www.butlercountyohio.org/areacourts

Butler: Clerk of Courts
513-887-3278
www.butlercountyclerk.org

Butler: Child Support Enforcement
513-887-3362
www.butlercountyohio.org/csea

Butler: Recorder
513-887-3192
66.117.197.5/recorder

Butler: Prosecutor
513-887-3474
www.butlercountyprosecutor.org

Butler: Public Defender
(court appointed; no PD office)
opd.ohio.gov/pub/pub_cty.htm

Butler: Sheriff
800-553-1497; 513-785-1000
www.butlersheriff.org

CANTON, CITY OF

Canton: City Government
330-489-3283
www.cityofcanton.com

Canton Municipal Court
330-489-3205
www.cantoncourt.org/index.html

Canton: Law Department
330-489-3251
www.cityofcanton.com/citygov/lawdept/index.html

Canton: City Police
330-649-5800
www.cityofcanton.com/safetyservice/police/index.html

CARROLL COUNTY

Carroll: County Government
330-627-4869
www.carrollcountyohio.net
pages.eohio.net/carrcomm

Carroll: Clerk of Courts
330-627-4886
www.occaohio.com/County/carroll.htm

Carroll: Child Support Enforcement
800-567-5357; 330-627-5357

Carroll: Prosecutor
330-627-4555
www.carrollcountyohio.net/prosecutor/index.htm

Carroll: Public Defender
330-364-5595

Carroll: Police
330-627-2858
www.villageofcarrollton.com/policedept.htm

CHAMPAIGN COUNTY

Champaign: County Government
937-484-1611
www.co.champaign.oh.us

Champaign: Municipal Court
937-653-7376
www.urbanaohio.org/Court/court.htm

Champaign: Clerk of Courts
937-484-1047
www.occaohio.com/County/champaign.htm

Champaign: Child Support Enforcement
800-652-1606; 937-484-1586

Champaign: Recorder
937-484-1630
www.ohiorecorders.com/champaig.html

Champaign: Prosecutor
937-652-1555

Champaign: Public Defender
(court appointed; no PD office)
opd.ohio.gov/pub/pub_cty.htm

Champaign: Sheriff
937-652-1311
www.usacops.com/oh/s43078

CINCINNATI, CITY OF

Cincinnati: City Government
513-352-3243
www.cincinnati-oh.gov/cmgr/pages/-3046-/
www.cincinnati-oh.gov/departments.html

Cincinnati: Law Department
www.cincinnati-oh.gov/citylaw/pages/-6518-/

Cincinnati: City Police
513-352-3536
www.cincinnati-oh.gov/police/pages/-3039-/

CLARK COUNTY

Clark: County Government
937-328-2405
www.clarkcountyohio.gov

Clark: Court of Common Pleas
www.clarkcountyohio.gov/courts/index.htm

Clark: Probate Court
937-328-2435
www.probate.clarkcountyohio.gov

Clark: Municipal Court
800-544-1694
www.clerkofcourts.municipal.co.clark.oh.us

Clark: Clerk of Courts
http://12.150.181.49

Clark: Child Support Enforcement
800-516-3463; 937-327-3662

Clark: Recorder
www.landaccess.com/sites/oh/disclaimer.php?county=clark

Clark: Prosecutor
937-328-2574
www.clarkcountyohio.gov/courts/prosecutor/index.htm

Clark: Public Defender
937-328-2560
www.clarkcountyohio.gov/courts/pubdef/index.htm

Clark: Sheriff
937-238-2560
www.clarkcountysheriff.com

CLERMONT COUNTY

Clermont: County Government
513-732-7300
www.co.clermont.oh.us

Clermont: Court of Common Pleas
www.clermontclerk.org/CPleas.htm

Clermont: Court: Domestic Relations
513-732-7327
www.domesticcourt.org

Clermont: Municipal Court
www.clermontclerk.org/Muni.htm

Clermont: Clerk of Courts
www.clermontclerk.org

Clermont: Child Support Enforcement
800-571-0943; 513-732-7326

Clermont: Recorder
513-732-7236

Clermont: Prosecutor
513-732-7313

Clermont: Public Defender
513-732-7223

Clermont: Sheriff
513-732-7500
www.clermontsheriff.org

CLEVELAND, CITY OF

Cleveland: City Government
www.city.cleveland.oh.us

Cleveland Municipal Court
216-664-4870
clevelandmunicipalcourt.org

Cleveland: Law Department
216-664-2800
www.city.cleveland.oh.us
(click "government" "departments")

Cleveland: City Police
216-623-5000
www.city.cleveland.oh.us
(click "Government" "Departments" "Public Safety")

CLINTON COUNTY

Clinton: County Government
937-382-2103
co.clinton.oh.us
co.clinton.oh.us/county_offices

Clinton: Courts
co.clinton.oh.us/county_offices

Clinton: Clerk of Courts
937-382–2316
co.clinton.oh.us/clerk_of_courts

Clinton: Child Support Enforcement
937-382-5726
co.clinton.oh.us/child_support

Clinton: Clerk-Recorder
937-382-2067
co.clinton.oh.us/recorder

Clinton: Prosecutor
937-382-4559
co.clinton.oh.us/prosecuting

Clinton: Public Defender
937-382-1316
co.clinton.oh.us/public_defender

Clermont: Sheriff
937-382-1611
www.clintonsheriff.com

COLUMBIANA COUNTY

Columbiana: County Government
330-424-9511
www.columbianacounty.org

Columbiana: Courts
www.ccclerk.org/the_courts.htm

Columbiana: Clerk of Courts
330-424-777
www.ccclerk.org

Columbiana: Child Support Enforcement
800-353-0125; 330-424-7781

Columbiana: Recorder
330-424-9517 x1351
www.columbianacounty.org/recorder_index.htm

Columbiana: Public Defender
330-337-9578
opd.ohio.gov/pub/pub_cty.htm

Columbiana: Sheriff
330-424-1104
www.colcountysheriff.com

COLUMBUS: CITY OF

Columbus: City Government
614-645-7671
www.cityofcolumbus.org

Columbus: City Attorney
614-645-7385
www.columbuscityattorney.org

Columbus: City Police
614-645-4545
www.columbuspolice.org/default.htm

COSHOCTON COUNTY

Coshocton: County Government
740-622-1753
www.co.coshocton.oh.us

Coshocton: Court of Common Pleas
740-622-1595
www.co.coshocton.oh.us/courts.htm

Coshocton: Clerk of Courts
740-622-1456
www.co.coshocton.oh.us/clerk.htm

Coshocton: Child Support Enforcement

Coshocton: Recorder
740-622-2817
www.co.coshocton.oh.us/recorder.htm

Coshocton: Prosecutor
740-622-3566
www.co.coshocton.oh.us/prosecutor.htm

Coshocton: Public Defender
740-623-0800
opd.ohio.gov/pub/pub_cty.htm

Coshocton: Sheriff
740-622-2411
www.coshoctonsheriff.com

CRAWFORD COUNTY

Crawford: County Government
419-562-5876
www.crawford-co.org

Crawford: Court of Common Pleas
www.crawfordcocpcourt.org

Crawford: Clerk of Courts
419-562-2766
www.crawford-co.org/Clerk/default.html

Crawford: Child Support Enforcement
800-761-0773; 419-562-0773

Crawford: Recorder
419-562-6961
www.ohiorecorders.com/crawford.html

Crawford: Sheriff
419-562-7906
www.crawfordcountysheriffohio.com

CUYAHOGA COUNTY

Cuyahoga: County Government
216-443-7000
www.cuyahogacounty.us

Cuyahoga: Courts (other)
www.cuyahogacounty.us
(click "more Legal & Judicial" under "Legal Resources")

Cuyahoga: Clerk of Courts
www.cuyahogacounty.us

Cuyahoga: Child Support Enforcement
216-443-5100
www.cuyahogacounty.us/CSEA

Cuyahoga: Recorder
216-443-5898
recorder.cuyahogacounty.us

Cuyahoga: Prosecutor
216-443-7800
prosecutor.cuyahogacounty.us

Cuyahoga: Public Defender
216-443-7223
publicdefender.cuyahogacounty.us

Cuyahoga: Sheriff
216-443-6000
www.cuyahogacounty.us/sheriff

DARKE COUNTY

Darke: County Government
937-547-7370; 937-547-7300
www.co.darke.oh.us

Darke: Courts
co.darke.oh.us/elected.htm

Darke: Clerk of Courts
937-547-7336
co.darke.oh.us/elected.htm

Darke: Child Support Enforcement
800-501-5635; 937-548-4132

Darke: Clerk-Recorder
937-547-7390
co.darke.oh.us/elected.htm

Darke: Prosecutor
937-547-7380
co.darke.oh.us/elected.htm

Darke: Sheriff
937-548-3399
co.darke.oh.us/elected.htm

DAYTON, CITY OF

Dayton: City Government
www.ci.dayton.oh.us

Dayton Municipal Court
www.daytonmunicipalcourt.org

Dayton: City Police
737-333-COPS
www.ci.dayton.oh.us/police

DEFIANCE COUNTY

Defiance: County Government
419-782-4761
www.defiance-county.com

Defiance: Courts
www.defiance-county.com
(click "court" entries)

Defiance: Clerk of Courts
419-782-1936
www.defiance-county.com/clerkofcourts.html

Defiance: Child Support Enforcement
800-569-8003; 419-784-2123
www.defiance-county.com/csea.html

Defiance: Recorder
419-782-4741
www.defiance-county.com/recorder.html

Defiance: Prosecutor
419-784-3700
www.defiance-county.com/prosecutor.html

Defiance: Sheriff
419-784-1155
www.defiance-county.com/somain.htm

DELAWARE COUNTY

Delaware: County Government
740-833-2100
www.co.delaware.oh.us

Delaware: Court of Common Pleas
www.co.delaware.oh.us/court

Delaware: Clerk of Courts
740-833-2500
www.co.delaware.oh.us/clerk

Delaware: Child Support Enforcement
800-490-9534; 740-833-2720

Delaware: Recorder
740-833-2460
www.co.delaware.oh.us/recorder

Delaware: Prosecutor
740-833-2690
www.co.delaware.oh.us/prosecutor

Delaware: Sheriff
740-833-2810
www.delawarecountysheriff.com

ERIE COUNTY

Erie: County Government
419-627-7672; 419-627-7682
www.erie-county-ohio.net

Erie: Courts
www.erie-county-ohio.net
(click "Elected Officials")

Erie: Clerk of Courts
419-627-7705
www.erie-county-ohio.net/ClerkofCourts

Erie: Child Support Enforcement
www.erie-county-ohio.net/jfs/Child_Support.htm

Erie: Recorder
419-627-7686
www.erie-county-ohio.net
(click "Elected Officials")

Erie: Prosecutor
419-627-7697
www.erie-county-ohio.net/Prosecutor

Erie: Public Defender
419-627-6620
opd.ohio.gov/pub/pub_cty.htm

Erie: Sheriff
416-627-7668
www.erie-county-ohio.net/Sheriff/sheriff.htm

FAIRFIELD COUNTY

Fairfield: County Government
740-687-7190
www.co.fairfield.oh.us

Fairfield: Court of Common Pleas
www.co.fairfield.oh.us/Commonpleas/index.htm

Fairfield: Clerk of Courts
740-687-7030
www.fairfieldcountyclerk.com

Fairfield: Child Support Enforcement
800-409-2732; 740-687-7155

Fairfield: Recorder
www.co.fairfield.oh.us
(click "Recorder" under "Agencies")

Fairfield: Prosecutor
www.co.fairfield.oh.us/prosecutor/index.htm

Fairfield: Sheriff
www.sheriff.fairfield.oh.us

FAYETTE COUNTY

Fayette: County Government
740-335-0720
www.fayette-co-oh.com

Fayette: Court of Common Pleas
740-335-4750
www.fayette-co-oh.com/Commplea/index.html

Fayette: Clerk of Courts
740-335-6371
www.fayette-co-oh.com/Clerkoct/index.html

Fayette: Child Support Enforcement
800-922-0745; 740-335-0745

Fayette: Recorder
740-335-1770
www.fayette-co-oh.com/Recorder/index.html

Fayette: Prosecutor
740-335-0888
www.fayette-co-oh.com/prosecutor/index.html

Fayette: Sheriff
740-335-6170
www.faycoso.com

FRANKLIN COUNTY

Franklin: County Government
614-462-3322
www.franklincountyohio.gov

Franklin: Court of Common Pleas
www.franklincountyohio.gov
(under "County Officials" select court entries)

Franklin: Clerk of Courts
614-462-3600
www.franklincountyohio.gov/clerk

Franklin: Child Support Enforcement
614-462-3275
www.franklincountyohio.gov/commissioners/csea

Franklin: Recorder
614-462-3930
www.franklincountyohio.gov/recorder

Franklin: Prosecutor
614-462-3555
www.franklincountyohio.gov/Prosecuting_Attorney

Franklin: Public Defender
614-462-3194
opd.ohio.gov/pub/pub_cty.htm

Franklin: Sheriff
614- 462-3360
www.sheriff.franklin.oh.us

FULTON COUNTY

Fulton: County Government
419-337-9255
www.fultoncountyoh.com

Fulton: Court of Common Pleas
www.fultoncountyoh.com
(click "Court" entries under "Elected Officials")

Fulton: Clerk of Courts
419-337-9230
www.fultoncountyoh.com/Clerkofcourts.htm

Fulton: Child Support Enforcement
800-344-3575; 419-337-0010

Fulton: Recorder
419-337-9232
www.fultoncountyoh.com
(click "recorder" entries under "Elected Officials")

Fulton: Prosecutor
419-337-9240
www.fultoncountyoh.com
(click "Prosecutor" under "Elected Officials")

Fulton: Sheriff
419-335-4010
www.fultoncountyoh.com/fcso/index.htm

GALLIA COUNTY

Gallia: County Government
740-446-4374
gallianet.net
gallianet.net/Gallia/index.htm
Gallia: Court of Common Pleas
gallianet.net/Gallia/common_pleas.htm

Gallia: Probate Court
740-446-4612 x289
gallianet.net/Gallia/probate_court.htm

Gallia: Clerk of Courts
614-446-4612
www.occaohio.com/County/gallia.htm

Gallia: Child Support Enforcement
800-871-5987; 740-446-0715

Gallia: Recorder
740-446-4612 x246
gallianet.net/Gallia/recorder.htm

Gallia: Prosecutor
gallianet.net/Gallia/prosecutor.htm

Gallia: Sheriff
740-446-1221
www.galliasheriff.org

GEAUGA COUNTY

Geauga: County Government
440-285-2222
www.co.geauga.oh.us

Geauga: Court of Common Pleas
440-285-2222
www.co.geauga.oh.us/departments/common_pleas.htm

Geauga: Clerk of Courts
440-285-2222 x2380
www.co.geauga.oh.us/officials.htm

Geauga: Child Support Enforcement
440-285-9141
www.co.geauga.oh.us/departments.htm
(click "Job & Family Services")

Geauga: Recorder
440-285-2222 x3680
www.co.geauga.oh.us/officials.htm

Geauga: Prosecutor
440-285-2222 x5760
www.co.geauga.oh.us/officials.htm

Geauga: Public Defender
440-285-2222 x5130

Geauga: Sheriff
440-286-4031
www.co.geauga.oh.us/officials/sheriff.htm

GREENE COUNTY

Greene: County Government
937-562-5006
www.co.greene.oh.us

Greene: Courts
www.co.greene.oh.us/CPC/

Greene: Clerk of Courts
937-562-5290
www.co.greene.oh.us/COC/clerk.htm

Greene: Child Support Enforcement
937-562-6000
www.co.greene.oh.us/job_family_serv.htm

Greene: Clerk-Recorder
937-562-5270
www.co.greene.oh.us/recorder.htm

Greene: Prosecutor
937-562-5250
www.co.greene.oh.us/prosecutor/default.htm

Greene: Public Defender
937-562-5041
opd.ohio.gov/pub/pub_cty.htm

Greene: Sheriff
937-562-4800
www.co.greene.oh.us/sheriff

GUERNSEY COUNTY

Guernsey: County Government
740-432-9200
www.guernseycounty.org

Guernsey: Courts
www.guernseycounty.org/Elected/elected.htm
(see "court entries" under "Elected Officials")

Guernsey: Clerk of Courts
740-432-9230
www.guernseycounty.org/Elected/clerk.htm

Guernsey: Child Support Enforcement
740-432-2381; 800-307-8422

Guernsey: Recorder
740-432-9275
www.guernseycounty.org/Elected/recorder.htm

Guernsey: Prosecutor
740-439-2082
www.guernseycounty.org/Elected/prosecutor.htm

Guernsey: Sheriff
740-432-4455
guernseysheriff.com

HAMILTON COUNTY

Hamilton: County Government
513-946-4400
www.hamilton-co.org

Hamilton: Courts
www.hamilton-co.org/hc/courts.asp

Hamilton: Clerk of Courts
www.courtclerk.org

Hamilton: Child Support Enforcement
513-946-7387; 800-315-7119
www.hcjfs.hamilton-co.org

Hamilton: Recorder
513-946-4570
recordersoffice.hamilton-co.org

Hamilton: Prosecutor
513-946-3000
www.hcpros.org

Hamilton: Public Defender
513-946-3700
www.hamilton-co.org/pub_def

Hamilton: Sheriff
www.hcso.org

HANCOCK COUNTY

Hancock: County Government
419-424-7044
www.co.hancock.oh.us

Hancock: Court
www.co.hancock.oh.us
(click "court" entries)

Hancock: Clerk of Courts
419-424-7037
co.hancock.oh.us/clerk

Hancock: Child Support Enforcement
419-424-1365; 800-228-2732

Hancock: Recorder
419-424-7091

Hancock: Prosecutor
419-424-7089
co.hancock.oh.us/prosecutor/prosecutor.htm

Hancock: Public Defender
419-242-7276; 419-242-7274
opd.ohio.gov/pub/pub_cty.htm

Hancock: Sheriff
www.hancocksheriff.org

HARDIN COUNTY

Hardin: Clerk of Courts
419-674-2205; 419-674-2278
www.occaohio.com/County/hardin.htm

Hardin: Child Support Enforcement
419-674-2269; 800-320-2148

Hardin: Auditor
419-674-2239
www.co.hardin.oh.us

Hardin: Recorder
419-674-2252
www.ohiorecorders.com/hardin.html

Hardin: Sheriff
419-673-1268
www.hardinsheriff.com

HARRISON COUNTY

Harrison: County Government
740-942-4623
www.harrisoncountyohio.org
(click "Government")

Harrison: Clerk of Courts
740-942-8863
www.occaohio.com/County/harrison.htm

Harrison: Child Support Enforcement
740-942-2900; 800-455-5355

Harrison: Recorder
740-942-8869
www.ohiorecorders.com/harrison.html

Harrison: Prosecutor
740-942-2621

Harrison: Public Defender
740-942-2010
opd.ohio.gov/pub/pub_cty.htm

Harrison: Sheriff
740-942-2197
pages.eohio.net/sheriff1

HENRY COUNTY

Henry: County Government
419-592-4876
www.henrycountyohio.com

Henry: Court of Common Pleas
419-592-5926
www.henrycountyohio.com/judgegeneralprobate.htm

Henry: Napoleon Municipal Court
419-592-2851
www.napoleonohio.cc/court.html

Henry: Clerk of Courts
419-592-5886
www.henrycountyohio.com/clerk.htm

Henry: Child Support Enforcement
419-592-4633; 800-592-4633
www.henrycountyohio.com/childsupport.htm

Henry: Clerk-Recorder
419-592-1766
www.henrycountyohio.com/recorder.htm

Henry: Prosecutor
419-599-1010
www.henrycountyohio.com/attorney.htm

Henry: Sheriff
419-592-8010
www.henrycountysheriff.com

HIGHLAND COUNTY

Highland: County Government
937-393-1911
www.co.highland.oh.us
homepages.rootsweb.com/~maggieoh/mhighland.html

Highland: Clerk of Courts
937-393-9957
www.occaohio.com/County/highland.htm

Highland: Child Support Enforcement
937-393-4278; 800-391-9631

Highland: Recorder
www.co.highland.oh.us

Highland: Prosecutor
937-393-1851

Highland: Sheriff
937-393-1421
www.highlandcoso.com

HOCKING COUNTY

Hocking: County Government
740-385-5195
www.co.hocking.oh.us

Hocking: Court of Common Pleas
740-385-4027

Hocking: Clerk of Courts
740-385-2616
www.occaohio.com/County/hocking.htm

Hocking: Child Support Enforcement
740-385-8905; 800-555-2480

Hocking: Recorder
740-385-2031
www.ohiorecorders.com/hocking.html

Hocking: Prosecutor
740-385-5343

Hocking: Sheriff
740-385-2131
www.hockingsheriff.org

HOLMES COUNTY

Holmes: County Government
330-674-0286
www.holmescounty.com/gov

Holmes: Court of Common Pleas
330-674-1876

Holmes: Clerk of Courts
330-674-1876
www.occaohio.com/County/holmes.htm

Holmes: Child Support Enforcement
330-674-1111; 800-971-7979
www.holmescountydjfs.com

Holmes: Recorder
330-674-5916
www.ohiorecorders.com/holmes.html

Holmes: Prosecutor
330-674-4841

Holmes: Sheriff
330-674-1936
www.holmescountysheriff.org

HURON COUNTY

Huron: County Government
419-668-3092
www.hccommissioners.com

Huron: Court of Common Pleas
419-668-6162
www.huroncountyclerk.com/html/common_pleas_court.html

Huron: Clerk of Courts
419-668-5113
www.huroncountyclerk.com

Huron: Child Support Enforcement
419-668-9152; 800-668-9152

Huron: Recorder
419-668-1916
www.ohiorecorders.com/huron.html

Huron: Prosecutor
419-668-8215

Huron: Public Defender
419-668-3702
opd.ohio.gov/pub/pub_cty.htm

Huron: Sheriff
419-668-6912
huron.ohiosheriffs.org

JACKSON COUNTY

Jackson: County Government
740-286-3301

Jackson: Court of Common Pleas
740-286-2006

Jackson: Clerk of Courts
740-286-2006
www.occaohio.com/County/jackson.htm

Jackson: Child Support Enforcement
740-286-4181; 800-588-7161

Jackson: Recorder
740-286-1919
www.ohiorecorders.com/jackson.html

Jackson: Prosecutor
740-286-5006

Jackson: Sheriff
jackson.ohiosheriffs.org

JEFFERSON COUNTY

Jefferson: County Government
740-283-8500
www.jeffersoncountyoh.com/cgi-bin/template.pl

Jefferson: Court of Common Pleas
740-283-8583
www.jeffersoncountyoh.com/cgi-bin/template.pl
(click "County Courts")

Jefferson: Clerk of Courts
740-283-8583
www.occaohio.com/County/jefferson.htm

Jefferson: Child Support Enforcement
740-282-0961; 800-353-2716
www.jcdjfs.com/cgi-bin/template.pl?child.html

Jefferson: Recorder
740-283-8566
www.ohiorecorders.com/jefferso.html

Jefferson: Sheriff
740-283-8600
www.jeffersoncountysheriff.com

KNOX COUNTY

Knox: County Government
740-393-6703
www.knoxcountyohio.org

Knox: Court of Common Pleas
740-393-6777
www.knoxcountyohio.org/offices/Court_Of_Common_Pleas.htm

Knox: Probate/Juvenile Court
740-393-6798
www.knoxcountyohio.org/offices/ProbateJuvenileCourt.htm

Knox: Clerk of Courts
740-393-6788
www.knoxcountyohio.org/offices/Clerk_Of_Courts.htm

Knox: Child Support Enforcement
740-397-7177 x1100; 800-298-2223
www.knoxcountyohio.org/offices/Child_Support_Agency.htm
www.knoxcountyohio.org/prosecutor/Child_Support.html

Knox: Recorder
740-393-6755
www.recorder.co.knox.oh.us/Resolution/default.asp

Knox: Prosecutor
740-393-6720
www.knoxcountyohio.org/prosecutor/index.html

Knox: Public Defender
740-393-6734
www.knoxcountyohio.org/offices/Public_Defender.htm

Knox: Sheriff
740-397-3333
knoxcountysheriff.com

LAKE COUNTY

Lake: County Government
440-350-2500; 440-350-2745
www.lakecountyohio.org

Lake: Court of Common Pleas
440-350-2662
www2.lakecountyohio.org/courts

Lake: Courts (other)
www.lakecountyohio.org
(click "court entries)

Lake: Clerk of Courts
440-350-2657
www.lakecountyohio.org/clerk2/contact.phtml

Lake: Child Support Enforcement
440-350-4000; 800-442-1955

Lake: Recorder
440-350-2510
www.lakecountyrecorder.org/recorders

Lake: Prosecutor
440-350-2683
www.lakecountyprosecutor.org

Lake: Public Defender
440-350-3200
opd.ohio.gov/pub/pub_cty.htm

Lake: Sheriff
440-350-5620
www.lakecountyohio.org/sheriff

LAWRENCE COUNTY

Lawrence: County Government
740-533-4300

Lawrence: Court of Common Pleas
740-533-4355

Lawrence: Clerk of Courts
www.lawrencecountyclkofcrt.org

Lawrence: Child Support Enforcement
740-533-4338; 800-510-4443

Lawrence: Recorder
740-533-4314
www.ohiorecorders.com/lawrence.html

Lawrence: Prosecutor
740-533-4360

Lawrence: Sheriff
740-534-5819
lcohiosheriff.com

LICKING COUNTY

Licking: County Government
740-349-6066; 740-670-5110
www.lcounty.com

Licking: Court of Common Pleas
740-349-1677

Licking: Municipal Court
67.141.197.6/connection/court

Licking: Clerk of Courts
740-670-5796
www.lcounty.com/clerkofcourts

Licking: Child Support Enforcement
740-670-5998; 800-513-1128
www.lcounty.com/csea

Licking: Recorder
740-670-5300
www.lcounty.com/rec

Licking: Prosecutor
740-349-6195

Licking: Sheriff
740-670-5551
www.lcounty.com/sheriff

LOGAN COUNTY

Logan: County Government
937-599-7283
www.co.logan.oh.us

Logan: Court of Common Pleas
937-599-7260
www.co.logan.oh.us/commonpleas

Logan: Courts (other)
www.co.logan.oh.us
(click "probate/juvenile court")

Logan: Clerk of Courts
937-599-7275
www.co.logan.oh.us/clerkofcourts

Logan: Child Support Enforcement
937-599-7232;800-599-7232
www.co.logan.oh.us/csea

Logan: Recorder
937-599-7201
www.co.logan.oh.us/recorder/index.html

Logan: Prosecutor
937-593-3755
www.co.logan.oh.us/prosecutor

Logan: Sheriff
937-592-5731
www.co.logan.oh.us/sheriff

LORAIN, CITY OF

Lorain: City Government
www.cityoflorain.org

Lorain Municipal Court
440-204-2140
www.lorainmunicourt.org

Lorain: Law Department
440-204-2250
www.cityoflorain.org/law/index.shtml

Lorain: City Police
440-204-2100
www.lorainpolice.com

LORAIN COUNTY

Lorain: County Government
440-329-5000
www.loraincounty.us/website/splash.asp

Lorain: Court of Common Pleas
www.loraincounty.com/clerk/

Lorain: Probate Court
440-329-5175
www.loraincounty.com/probate

Lorain: Municipal Courts
www.elyriamunicourt.org
www.lorainmunicourt.org
www.oberlinmunicipalcourt.org/

Lorain: Clerk of Courts
440-329-5536; 440-329-5538
www.loraincounty.com/clerk

Lorain: Child Support Enforcement
440-284-4500; 800-808-2991

Lorain: Recorder
440-244-6261; 440-329-5148
www.loraincounty.com/recorder

Lorain: Prosecutor
216-329-5375

Lorain: Sheriff
440-329-3709
www.loraincountysheriff.com

LUCAS COUNTY

Lucas: County Government
419-213-4000; 419-213-4500
www.co.lucas.oh.us

Lucas: Court of Common Pleas
419-213-4777
www.co.lucas.oh.us/commonpleas

Lucas: Courts (other)
www.co.lucas.oh.us/domesticrelations
www.co.lucas.oh.us/Juvenile
www.lucas-co-probate-ct.org
www.sylvaniacourt.com
www.toledomunicipalcourt.org
www.maumee.org/municipal/default.htm
www.ci.oregon.oh.us//ctydpt/court/court.htm
www.co.lucas.oh.us/Appeals

Lucas: Clerk of Courts
419-213-4484
www.co.lucas.oh.us/default.asp?RequestedAlias=clerk

Lucas: Child Support Enforcement
419-213-3000; 800-466-6396

Lucas: Recorder
419-213-3000; 800-466-6396
www.co.lucas.oh.us/default.asp?RequestedAlias=recorder

Lucas: Prosecutor
419-213-4700
www.co.lucas.oh.us/default.asp?RequestedAlias=prosecutor

Lucas: Public Defender
419-244-8351
opd.ohio.gov/pub/pub_cty.htm

Lucas: Sheriff
419-213-4784
www.co.lucas.oh.us/Sheriff

MADISON COUNTY

Madison: County Government
740-852-2972
www.co.madison.oh.us

Madison: Courts
www.co.madison.oh.us
(click the "Court"entries")

Madison: Clerk of Courts
740-852-9776
www.co.madison.oh.us/10185.html

Madison: Child Support Enforcement
740-852-4770; 800-852-0243

Madison: Recorder
740-852-1854
www.co.madison.oh.us/436/index.html

Madison: Prosecutor
740-852-2259
www.co.madison.oh.us/10269.html

Madison: Sheriff
740-852-1212
www.madisonsheriff.org

MAHONING COUNTY

Mahoning: County Government
330-740-2130
www.mahoningcountyoh.gov

Mahoning: Court of Common Pleas
330-740-2158
www.mahoningcountyoh.gov
(click "Judges")

Mahoning: Courts (other)
www.mahoningdrcourt.org
www.mahoningcountyprobate.org

Mahoning: Clerk of Courts
330-740-2104
www.mahoningcountyoh.gov
(click "Elected Officials")

Mahoning: Child Support Enforcement
330-740-2073; 800-528-9511

Mahoning: Recorder
330-740-2130
www.mahoningcountyoh.gov
(click "Elected Officials")

Mahoning: Prosecutor
330-740-2330
www.mahoningcountyoh.gov
(click "Elected Officials")

Mahoning: Sheriff
330-480-5000
www.mahoningsheriff.com

MARION COUNTY

Marion: County Government
740-223-4001
www.co.marion.oh.us

Marion: Court of Common Pleas
740-223-4270

Marion: Clerk of Courts
740-223-4270
www.occaohio.com/County/Marion.htm

Marion: Child Support Enforcement
740-387-6688; 800-960-5437
www.mcjfs.com/ChildSupport.html

Marion: Recorder
740-223-4100
recorder.co.marion.oh.us/resolution

Marion: Prosecutor
740-382-9242

Marion: Sheriff
740-382-8244
marion.ohiosheriffs.org

MEDINA COUNTY

Medina: County Government
330-722-9208
www.co.medina.oh.us

Medina: Court of Common Pleas
330-725-9722
www.medinacommonpleas.com

Medina: Courts (other)
www.medinadomesticrelations.org
www.medinamunicipalcourt.org
www.wadsworthmunicipalcourt.com/index.php

Medina: Clerk of Courts
330-725-9722
www.co.medina.oh.us/clerk/clrkhome.htm

Medina: Child Support Enforcement
330-722-9398; 800-706-2732

Medina: Recorder
www.recorder.co.medina.oh.us

Medina: Prosecutor
330-723-9536
www.co.medina.oh.us/prosecutor.htm

Medina: Sheriff
330-764-3635
www.medinasheriff.com

MEIGS COUNTY

Meigs: County Government
740-992-2895
www.dragonbbs.com/members/ww2186

Meigs: Court of Common Pleas
740-992-5290

Meigs: Clerk of Courts
740-992-5290
www.occaohio.com/County/meigs.htm

Meigs: Child Support Enforcement
740-992-2117/5031; 800-992-2608

Meigs: Recorder
740-992-3806
www.ohiorecorders.com/meigs.html

Meigs: Prosecutor
740-992-6371
www.ap.org/ohio/phones/prosecutors.html
www.ag.state.oh.us/victim/dir_county.asp?county=Meigs

Meigs: Sheriff
740-992-3371
www.buckeyesheriffs.org/Meigs/Meigs.htm

MERCER COUNTY

Mercer: County Government
419-586-3178
www.mercercountyohio.org

Mercer: Court of Common Pleas
419-586-5826

Mercer: Clerk of Courts
419-586-6461
www.mercercountyohio.org/clerk

Mercer: Child Support Enforcement
419-586-7961; 800-207-3597

Mercer: Recorder
419-586-4232
www.mercercountyohio.org/recorder

Mercer: Prosecutor
419-586-8677
www.mercercountyohio.org/prosecutor

Mercer: Sheriff
419-586-7724
www.mercercountysheriff.org

MIAMI COUNTY

Miami: County Government
937-332-7000; 937-440-5910
www.co.miami.oh.us

Miami: Courts
937-440-6010 (Court of Common Pleas)
937-440-5976 (Probate/Juvenile)
937-440-3933 (Municipal)

Miami: Clerk of Courts
937-440-6010
www.co.miami.oh.us
(click "Elected Officials")

Miami: Child Support Enforcement
937-440-3470: 800-308-0264
www.co.miami.oh.us/A55969/mcounty.nsf/JandF-child

Miami: Recorder
937-440-6040
www.co.miami.oh.us
(click "Elected Officials")

Miami: Prosecutor
937-440-5960
www.co.miami.oh.us
(click "Elected Officials")

Miami: Public Defender
937-440-3950
opd.ohio.gov/pub/pub_cty.htm

Miami: Sheriff
937-440-6085
www.co.miami.oh.us/sheriff

MONROE COUNTY

Monroe: County Government
740-472-1341
www.monroecountyohio.net

Monroe: Court of Common Pleas
740-472-0841; 740-472-0761

Monroe: County Court
740-472-5181

Monroe: Clerk of Courts
740-472-0761
www.occaohio.com/County/monroe.htm

Monroe: Child Support Enforcement
740-472-1602; 800-472-1602

Monroe: Recorder
740-472-5264
www.ohiorecorders.com/monroe.html

Monroe: Prosecutor
740-472-1158

Monroe: Public Defender
740-472-0703
opd.ohio.gov/pub/pub_cty.htm

Monroe: Sheriff
740-472-1612
monroe.ohiosheriffs.org

MONTGOMERY COUNTY

Montgomery: County Government
937-225-4690
www.co.montgomery.oh.us

Montgomery: Court of Common Pleas
www.montcourt.org

Montgomery: Clerk of Courts
937-496-7623
www.clerk.co.montgomery.oh.us

Montgomery: Child Support Enforcement
937-225-4600; 800-555-0430
www.mcsea.org

Montgomery: Recorder
937-255-4275
www.mcrecorder.org

Montgomery: Prosecutor
937-225-5757
www.mcpo.com

Montgomery: Public Defender
937-225-4652
opd.ohio.gov/pub/pub_cty.htm

Montgomery: Sheriff
937-225-4357
www.co.montgomery.oh.us/sheriff

MORGAN COUNTY

Morgan: County Government
740-962-3200; 740-962-3183
www.morgancounty.org/government.htm

Morgan: Clerk of Courts
740-962-4752
www.occaohio.com/County/morgan.htm

Morgan: Child Support Enforcement
740-962-3000; 800-564-9234

Morgan: Recorder
740-962-4051
www.ohiorecorders.com/morgan.html

Morgan: Prosecutor
740-962-6478

Morgan: Sheriff
740-962-4044
morgan.ohiosheriffs.org

MORROW COUNTY

Morrow: County Government
419-947-4085
www.morrowcounty.info

Morrow: Court of Common Pleas
419-947-4515

Morrow: Clerk of Courts
419-947-2085
www.occaohio.com/County/morrow.htm

Morrow: Child Support Enforcement
419-947-8075; 800-533-0353

Morrow: Recorder
419-947-3060
www.ohiorecorders.com/morrow.html

Morrow: Prosecutor
419-947-5515

Morrow: Sheriff
419-946-4444
morrow.ohiosheriffs.org

MUSKINGUM COUNTY

Muskingum: County Government
740-455-7100
www.muskingumcounty.org

Muskingum: Courts
www.muskingumcounty.org
(click "Court System")

Muskingum: Clerk of Courts
clerkofcourts.muskingumcounty.org

Muskingum: Child Support Enforcement
740-455-7146; 800-450-7146
www.jobandfamily.com/csea/cseaindex.htm

Muskingum: Recorder
740-455-7107
recorder.muskingumcounty.org

Muskingum: Prosecutor
prosecutor.muskingumcounty.org

Muskingum: Sheriff
740-452-3637
www.ohiomuskingumsheriff.org

NOBLE COUNTY

Noble: County Government
740-732-2969

Noble: Clerk of Courts
740-732-5604
www.occaohio.com/County/noble.htm

Noble: Child Support Enforcement
740-732-2392; 800-905-2732

Noble: Recorder
740-732-4319
www.ohiorecorders.com/noble.html

Noble: Prosecutor
740-732-5685

Noble: Sheriff
740-732-4158
noble.ohiosheriffs.org

OTTAWA COUNTY

Ottawa: County Government
419-734-6700
www.co.ottawa.oh.us

Ottawa County Court of Common Pleas
419-734-6755
www.ottawacocpcourt.com

Ottawa: Courts (other)
www.co.ottawa.oh.us
(click "court" entries)

Ottawa: Clerk of Courts
419-734-6755
www.occaohio.com/County/ottawa.htm

Ottawa: Child Support Enforcement
419-898-3688; 800-665-1677

Ottawa: Recorder
419-734-6730
www.ohiorecorders.com/ottawa.html

Ottawa: Sheriff
419-734-4404
www.ottawacountysheriff.org

PARMA, CITY OF

Parma: City Government
440-885-8000
www.cityofparma-oh.gov/cityhall/index.htm

Parma: Law Department
440-885-8132
www.cityofparma-oh.gov/cityhall/law.htm

Parma: City Police
www.cityofparma-oh.gov/cityhall/safety.htm

PAULDING COUNTY

Paulding: County Government
419-399-8215

Paulding: County Court
419-399-5370
www.pauldingcountycourt.com

Paulding: Clerk of Courts
419-399-8210
www.occaohio.com/County/paulding.htm

Paulding: Child Support Enforcement
419-399-8464; 800-399-2911

Paulding: Recorder
419-399-8275
www.ohiorecorders.com/paulding.html

Paulding: Sheriff
419-399-3791; 888-399-0171
www.pauldingohsheriff.com

PERRY COUNTY

Perry: County Government
740-342-2045
www.perrycountyohiocofc.com/Govnmentl.htm

Perry: Courts
740-342-1204 (Common Pleas)
740-342-3156 (County Court)
740-342-1118 (Juvenile Court)
740-342-1493 (Probate Court)

Perry: Clerk of Courts
740-342-1022

Perry: Child Support Enforcement
740-342-2278

Perry: Recorder
740-342-2494

Perry: Prosecutor
740-342-4582

Perry: Sheriff
740-342-4123

PICKAWAY COUNTY

Pickaway: County Government
740-74-6093
www.pickaway.org

Pickaway: Courts
www.pickaway.org
(click "court" entries)

Pickaway: Clerk of Courts
740-474-5231
www.occaohio.com/County/pickaway.htm

Pickaway: Child Support Enforcement
740-474-5437; 800-822-5437

Pickaway: Recorder
740-474-5826
www.ohiorecorders.com/pickaway.html

Pickaway: Sheriff
800-472-6033
www.pickawaysheriff.com

PIKE COUNTY

Pike: County Government
740-947-4817

Pike: Child Support Enforcement
800-646-2165; 740-947-2512

Pike: Recorder
740-947-2622
www.ohiorecorders.com/pike.html

Pike: Auditor
207.90.76.229/pikeweb/browser

Pike: Sheriff
740-947-2111 x28
www.pikecosheriff.com

PORTAGE COUNTY

Portage: County Government
330-297-3600
www.co.portage.oh.us

Portage: Courts
www.co.portage.oh.us/clerkofcourts.htm
(click "court" links)

Portage: Clerk of Courts
800-772-3799; 330-297-3644
www.co.portage.oh.us/clerkofcourts.htm

Portage: Child Support Enforcement
330-298-1105
www.co.portage.oh.us/jobandfamilyservices.htm

Portage: Recorder
330-297-3553
www.co.portage.oh.us/recorder.htm

Portage: Prosecutor
330-297-3850
www.co.portage.oh.us/prosecutor.htm

Portage: Public Defender
330-298-3665
opd.ohio.gov/pub/pub_cty.htm

Portage: Sheriff
330-297-3889
www.co.portage.oh.us/sheriff.htm

PREBLE COUNTY

Preble: County Government
937-456-8143
www.electionsonthe.net/oh/preble/electoff/county.htm

Preble: Eaton Municipal Court
www.eatonmunicipalcourt.com

Preble: Clerk of Courts
937-456-8160
www.occaohio.com/County/preble.htm

Preble: Child Support Enforcement
800-413-5899; 937-456-1499 x103

Preble: Recorder
937-456-8173
www.ohiorecorders.com/preble.html

Preble: Prosecutor
937-456-8156

Preble: Sheriff
937-456-6262

PUTNAM COUNTY

Putnam: County Government
419-523-3656

Putnam: Clerk of Courts
419-523-3110
www.occaohio.com/County/putnam.htm

Putnam: Child Support Enforcement
419-523-5586, 1-800-523-5799

Putnam: Recorder
419-523-6490
www.ohiorecorders.com/putnam.html

Putnam: Sheriff
866-788-2676
www.sheriffoff.com

RICHLAND COUNTY

Richland: County Government
419-774-5599
www.richlandcountyoh.us

Richland: Court of Common Pleas
419-774-5567
www.richlandcountyoh.us/cpc.htm

Richland: Clerk of Courts
www.richlandcountyoh.us/coc.htm

Richland: Child Support Enforcement
800-774-2552; 419-774-5700
www.richlandcountyoh.us/csea.htm

Richland: Recorder
www.richlandcountyoh.us/record.htm

Richland: Prosecutor
419-774-5676
www.richlandcountyoh.us/pros.htm

Richland: Sheriff
419-774-5881
www.richlandcountyoh.us/sheriff.htm

ROSS COUNTY

Ross: County Government
740-702-3085
www.co.ross.oh.us

Ross: Court of Common Pleas
www.rosscountycpcourt.org

Ross: Clerk of Courts
740-702-3010
co.ross.oh.us/ClerkOfCourts

Ross: Child Support Enforcement
800-413-3140; 740-773-2651

Ross: Recorder
www.co.ross.oh.us
(click "Recorder")

Ross: Public Defender
740-772-4772
opd.ohio.gov/pub/pub_cty.htm

Ross: Sheriff
740-773-1185
www.rosssheriff.com

SANDUSKY COUNTY

Sandusky: County Government
419-334-6100
www.sandusky-county.org

Sandusky: Courts
www.sandusky-county.org
(click "Courts")

Sandusky: Clerk of Courts
www.sandusky-county.org/Clerk/Clerk_of_Courts

Sandusky: Child Support Enforcement
419-334-2909
www.sanduskycountydjfs.org/cseainfo.htm

Sandusky: Recorder
419-334-6226
www.sandusky-county.org/County_Recorder.asp

Sandusky: Prosecutor
419-334-6222
www.sandusky-county.org/County_Prosecutor.asp

Sandusky: Sheriff
www.sandusky-county.org
(click "sheriff")

SCIOTO COUNTY

Scioto: County Government
740-355-8313
www.sciotocountyohio.com
www.sciotocountyohio.com/gov.htm

Scioto: Courts
www.sciotocountyohio.com/gov.htm
(click "court" entries")

Scioto: Clerk of Courts
740-335-8226
www.sciotocountyohio.com/clerk.htm

Scioto: Child Support Enforcement
800-354-6377; 740-355-8909

Scioto: Recorder
www.sciotocountyohio.com/recorder1.htm

SENECA COUNTY

Seneca: County Government
419-447-4550
www.senecacounty.com
www.bpsom.com/gov_officials_n_services/Directory.htm

Seneca: Courts
www.bpsom.com/co-govt.htm#Courts

Seneca: Clerk of Courts
419-447-0671

Seneca: Recorder
419-447-4434

Seneca: Prosecutor
419-448-4444

Seneca: Sheriff
419-447-3456
www.bpsom.com/co-govt.htm#Seneca%20County

SHELBY COUNTY

Shelby: County Government
937-498-7226
www.co.shelby.oh.us

Shelby: Court of Common Pleas
www.co.shelby.oh.us
(click "court" entries)

Shelby: Clerk of Courts
937-498-7221
www.co.shelby.oh.us/ClerkofCourts/index.asp

Shelby: Child Support Enforcement
800-339-0349; 330-451-8930

Shelby: Recorder
937-498-7270
www.co.shelby.oh.us/Recorder.asp

Shelby: Prosecutor
937-498-2101
www.co.shelby.oh.us/Prosecutor/index.asp

Shelby: Public Defender
937-498-1714
opd.ohio.gov/pub/pub_cty.htm

Shelby: Sheriff
937-498-1111
shelbycountysheriff.com

STARK COUNTY

Stark: County Government
330-451-7371
www.co.stark.oh.us

Stark: Courts
www.co.stark.oh.us
(under Elected Officials click "court" entries)

Stark: Clerk of Courts
www.starkclerk.org

Stark: Child Support Enforcement
330-451-8930
www.co.stark.oh.us
(click "Job & Family Services" "Child Support")

Stark: Recorder
330-451-7443
www.recorder.co.stark.oh.us

Stark: Prosecutor
www.prosecutor.co.stark.oh.us

Stark: Public Defender
330-451-7200
opd.ohio.gov/pub/pub_cty.htm

Stark: Sheriff
330-430-3800
www.sheriff.co.stark.oh.us

SUMMIT COUNTY

Summit: County Government
330-643-2510
www.co.summit.oh.us
www.co.summit.oh.us/brdsagncscomm.htm

Summit: Courts
www.co.summit.oh.us
(click entries under "courts")

Summit: Clerk of Courts
330-643-2212
www.co.summit.oh.us/clerkofcourts/index.htm

Summit: Child Support Enforcement
800-726-2765; 330-643-2765
www.co.summit.oh.us/prosecutor/childsupp.htm

Summit: Fiscal Officer
www.co.summit.oh.us/fiscaloffice

Summit: Prosecutor
330-643-2800
www.co.summit.oh.us/prosecutor/index.htm

Summit: Public Defender
330-434-3461
opd.ohio.gov/pub/pub_cty.htm

Summit: Sheriff
330-643-2181
www.co.summit.oh.us/sheriff/index.htm

TOLEDO, CITY OF

Toledo: City Government
www.ci.toledo.oh.us

Toledo: Department of Law
419-245-1020
www.ci.toledo.oh.us/index.cfm?Article=718

Toledo: City Police
419-245-3200
www.toledopolice.com

TRUMBULL COUNTY

Trumbull: County Government
330-675-2451
www.co.trumbull.oh.us

Trumbull: Courts
www.co.trumbull.oh.us
(click "Legal & Judicial")

Trumbull: Clerk of Courts
330-675-2557
clerk.co.trumbull.oh.us

Trumbull: Child Support Enforcement
330-675-2426
www.prosecutor.co.trumbull.oh.us/pr_childsupport.htm

Trumbull: Recorder
330-675-2401
www.tcrecorder.co.trumbull.oh.us/index.cfm

Trumbull: Prosecutor
330-675-2426
www.prosecutor.co.trumbull.oh.us

Trumbull: Public Defender
330-393-7727
opd.ohio.gov/pub/pub_cty.htm

Trumbull: Sheriff
330-675-2508
www.sheriff.co.trumbull.oh.us

TUSCARAWAS COUNTY

Tuscarawas: County Government
330-364-8811; 330-365-3240
www.co.tuscarawas.oh.us

Tuscarawas: Court of Common Pleas
330-365-3217
www.co.tuscarawas.oh.us/CommonPleasCourt/index.htm

Tuscarawas: Courts (other)
(Domestic Relations, Juvenile, Municipal)

Tuscarawas: Clerk of Courts
330-365-3243
www.co.tuscarawas.oh.us/ClerkofCourts/index.htm

Tuscarawas: Child Support Enforcement
800-685-2732; 330-343-0099
www.co.tuscarawas.oh.us/CSEA/index.htm

Tuscarawas: Recorder
330-365-3284
www.co.tuscarawas.oh.us/Recorder/index.htm

Tuscarawas: Public Defender
330-364-3523
opd.ohio.gov/pub/pub_cty.htm

Tuscarawas: Sheriff
330-339-2000
www.co.tuscarawas.oh.us/Sheriff/index.htm

UNION COUNTY

Union: County Government
937-645-3012
www.co.union.oh.us

Union: Court of Common Pleas
937-645-3015
www.co.union.oh.us/Common_Pleas/common_pleas.html

Union: Clerk of Courts
937-645-3006
www.co.union.oh.us/Clerk_of_Courts/clerk_of_courts.html

Union: Child Support Enforcement
800-248-2347; 937-644-1010
www.co.union.oh.us
(click "Child Support Agency")

Union: Recorder
937-645-3032
www.co.union.oh.us/Recorder/recorder.html

Union: Prosecutor
937-645-4190
www.co.union.oh.us/prosecutor

Union: Public Defender
937-642-5627; 937-644-3172
opd.ohio.gov/pub/pub_cty.htm

Union: Sheriff
937-645-4102
www.co.union.oh.us/sheriff

VAN WERT COUNTY

Van Wert: County Government
419-238-6159
www.vanwertcounty.org

Van Wert: Court of Common Pleas
419-238-6935
vwcommonpleas.org

Van Wert: Clerk of Courts
419-238-1022

Van Wert: Child Support Enforcement
800-830-0954; 419-238-9566

Van Wert: Recorder
419-238-2558
www.vanwertcounty.org/recorder

Van Wert: Public Defender
419-238-6621
opd.ohio.gov/pub/pub_cty.htm

Van Wert: Sheriff
419-238-3866
www.vanwertcountysheriff.com

VINTON COUNTY

Vinton: Courts
740-596-4571; 740-596-4319
www.co.vinton.oh.us/CommonPleasCourt.htm
www.co.vinton.oh.us/ProbateCourt.htm

Vinton: Clerk of Courts
740-596-3001
www.occaohio.com/County/vinton.htm

Vinton: Child Support Enforcement
800-679-8707; 740-596-2584

Vinton: Clerk-Recorder
740-596-4314
www.ohiorecorders.com/vinton.html

WARREN COUNTY

Warren: County Government
513-695-1250
www.co.warren.oh.us

Warren: County Court
513-695-1370
www.co.warren.oh.us/countycourt

Warren: Courts (other)
(Domestic Relations, Juvenile, Municipal)

Warren: Clerk of Courts
513-695-1120
www.co.warren.oh.us/clerkofcourt

Warren: Child Support Enforcement
800-644-2732
www.co.warren.oh.us/wcchildsupport

Warren: Recorder
513-695-1382
www.co.warren.oh.us/recorder

Warren: Prosecutor
513-695-1325
www.co.warren.oh.us/prosecutor

Warren: Public Defender
(court-appointed; no PD office)
opd.ohio.gov/pub/pub_cty.htm

Warren: Sheriff
513-695-1280
www.wcsooh.org/sheriff/index.asp

WASHINGTON COUNTY

Washington: County Government
740-373-6623
www.co.washington.oh.us

Washington: Courts
www.co.washington.oh.us/index-1.htm

Washington: Clerk of Courts
740-373-6623
www.co.washington.oh.us/cl-clerkofcourts.htm

Washington: Child Support Enforcement
800-888-2732; 740-373-9324

Washington: Recorder
740-373-6623
www.co.washington.oh.us/dept-recorder.htm

Washington: Prosecutor
740-373-7624
www.co.washington.oh.us/cl-Prosecutor.htm

Washington: Public Defender
740-373-1441
opd.ohio.gov/pub/pub_cty.htm

Washington: Sheriff
740-373-6623 x308
www.co.washington.oh.us/ps-sheriff.htm

WAYNE COUNTY

Wayne: County Government
330-287-5400
www.wayneohio.org
www.wayneohio.org/agencies.html

Wayne: Courts
www.wayneohio.org/officials.html

Wayne: Clerk of Courts
330-287-5590
www.waynecountyclerkofcourts.org

Wayne: Child Support Enforcement
800-216-6636; 330-294-5122

Wayne: Recorder
330-287-5460
www.wayneohio.org/officials.html

Wayne: Prosecutor
330-262-3030
www.wayneohio.org/officials.html

Wayne: Public Defender
330-287-5490
opd.ohio.gov/pub/pub_cty.htm

Wayne: Sheriff
330-287-5750
www.waynecountysheriff.com

WILLIAMS COUNTY

Williams: County Government
419-636-2059
www.co.williams.oh.us

Williams: Courts
www.co.williams.oh.us
(click "Common Pleas" "Probate/Juvenile")

Williams: Clerk of Courts
419-636-6910
www.occaohio.com/County/williams.htm

Williams: Child Support Enforcement
800-937-2732; 419-636-6725

Williams: Recorder
419-636-3259
www.co.williams.oh.us/Recorder/wms_co_recorder_home.htm

Williams: Prosecutor
www.co.williams.oh.us
(click "Prosecuting Attorney")

Williams: Public Defender
(court-appointed; no PD office)

Williams: Sheriff
419-636-3151
www.williamscosheriff.com

WOOD COUNTY

Wood: County Government
419-354-9100
www.co.wood.oh.us
www.co.wood.oh.us/deptdesc.htm

Wood: Courts
419-354-9230 (Probate)
www.probate-court.co.wood.oh.us

Wood: Clerk of Courts
419-354-9280
clerkofcourt.co.wood.oh.us

Wood: Child Support Enforcement
800-966-3543; 419-354-9270

Wood: Recorder
419-354-9140
recorder.co.wood.oh.us

Wood: Prosecutor
419-354-9250
woodcountyprosecutor.org

Wood: Public Defender
419-354-9244

Wood: Sheriff
419-354-9137
www.woodcountysheriff.com

WYANDOT COUNTY

Wyandot: County Government
419-294-3836
www.co.wyandot.oh.us

Wyandot: Court of Common Pleas
419-294-1727

Wyandot: Clerk of Courts
419-294-1432

Wyandot: Child Support Enforcement
800-320-5211; 419-294-5122

Wyandot: Recorder
419-294-1442

Wyandot: Prosecutor
419-294-2924

Wyandot: Sheriff
419-294-2362

C. More Information

County Auditors
www.caao.org

County Child Support Enforcement Agencies
jfs.ohio.gov/county/cntydir.stm

County Clerks of Court
www.fcmcclerk.com/links/clerks/clerks.htm

County Prosecutors
www.ap.org/ohio/phones/prosecutors.html
www.ohiopa.org/prosinfo.htm

County Public Defenders
opd.ohio.gov/pub/pub_cty.htm

County Recorders
www.ohiorecorders.com

County Sheriffs
www.usacops.com/oh/shrflist.html
www.megalaw.com/oh/ohenforce.php
www.buckeyesheriffs.org/Ohio%20Sheriffs.htm

Ohio Courts
www.sconet.state.oh.us/web_sites/courts
www.sconet.state.oh.us/District_Courts
www.oamcc.com/directry.htm
www.oamcc.com/links.htm
www.probatect.org/ohioprobatecourts/courtlinks.htm
www.sconet.state.oh.us/Web_Sites/courts
www.ncsconline.org/D_KIS/info_court_web_sites.html#ohio

D. Something to Check

1. Pick one kind of information pertaining to law and government (e.g., enforcement of the dog leash law). Find the address of where this information would be found in any ten Ohio counties or cities.
2. For any county you select, identify the kind of information available online about any aspect of real property in that county.

PART

5

Legal Research and Records Research

A. Introduction

In this section, we will answer the following question: Where can you find Ohio primary authority (e.g., cases, statutes) and secondary authority (e.g., legal encyclopedias and treatises) if you need to research an issue of Ohio law?

We will cover both traditional book sources as well as what is available online. For related material, see:

- state courts in Ohio, including links to their opinions (section 4.2)
- federal courts in Ohio, including links to their opinions (section 4.3)
- citing Ohio legal materials (section 5.2)
- research starters for 78 major Ohio topics (section 5.5)
- finding Ohio public records (section 5.7)
- finding law libraries in your area that have materials on Ohio law (section 5.8)
- finding continuing legal education resources in Ohio (section 1.6)

B. Finding Ohio State Law

Exhibit 5.1A presents an overview of Ohio law found in traditional and online sources.

C. Publishers of Materials on Ohio Law

Anderson Publishing
www.lexisnexis.com/Anderson

Casemaker
www.ohiobar.org/casemaker/?articleid=334

CaseClerk
www.caseclerk.com

Fastcase
www.fastcase.com

LexisNexis/Matthew Bender
www.lexisone.com
bender.lexisnexis.com

Loislaw
www.loislaw.com

Ohio State Bar Association Continuing Legal Education Institute
www.ohiobar.org/cle

TheLaw.net
thelaw.net

VersusLaw
www.versuslaw.com

West/Thomson
west.thomson.com/store/default.asp
west.thomson.com/store/CompleteList.aspx?Browseby=Jurisdictions

D. More Information

Online Portals to Ohio Law
www.megalaw.com/oh/oh.php
www.uakron.edu/law/library/olrlinks.php
www.romingerlegal.com/state/ohio.html
www.law.uc.edu/library/guideohlaw.html
www.utlaw.edu/students/lawlibrary/ohio.htm
www.ll.georgetown.edu/states/ohio.cfm
www.law.csuohio.edu/lawlibrary/stategov.html
www.clelaw.lib.oh.us/Public/Misc/REGUIDES/guide29.html
www.hg.org/usstates.html (click "Ohio")

E. Something to Check

1. Pick any legal issue (e.g., capital punishment, abortion, divorce). Using the free online materials referred to here, find and briefly summarize one case and one statute on your topic.
2. Use any of the sites to locate an Ohio legal form that can be used in a family law case.

A. Introduction

There are three major citation systems or manuals:

Citation System Explained:	Abbreviation Used Here:
Ohio Manual of Citations Internet Edition (1992) *Revisions to the Manual of Citations* (2002) (Reporter's Office for the State of Ohio)	Ohio Manual

(5.2 is continued on page 209)

EXHIBIT 5.1A Ohio Law on the Shelf and Online

CATEGORY	WHERE TO FIND IT ON THE SHELF	WHERE TO FIND IT ONLINE FOR A FEE	WHERE TO FIND IT ONLINE FOR FREE (complete, partial, or links)
Ohio Constitution	-*Page's Ohio Revised Code Annotated* (LexisNexis) -*Baldwin's Revised Code Annotated* (West) Note: The constitution is found within these codes.	-Lexis: *www.lexis.com* OHIO library OHCNST file -Westlaw: *www.westlaw.com* OH-ST-ANN database -Others: see addresses on page 206 for Casemaker, FastCase, Loislaw, TheLaw.Net, VersusLaw	-*www.legislature.state.oh.us/constitution.cfm* -*www.findlaw.com/11stategov/oh/laws.html* -*www.ohiohistory.org/onlinedoc/ohgovernment/constitution/cnst1851.html*
State Statutes (Ohio Codes)	-*Page's Ohio Revised Code Annotated* (LexisNexis) -*Baldwin's Revised Code Annotated* (West)	-Lexis: *www.lexis.com* OHIO library CODE file -Westlaw: *www.westlaw.com* OH-ST-ANN database OH-ST database -Others: see addresses on page 206 for Casemaker, FastCase, Loislaw, TheLaw.Net, VersusLaw	-*www.legislature.state.oh.us/laws.cfm* (click"Ohio Revised Code") -*onlinedocs.andersonpublishing.com/oh/lpExt.dll?f=templates&fn=main-h.htm&cp=PORC* -*www.findlaw.com/casecode* (click "Ohio") -*codes.ohio.gov*
State Statutes (session laws & advance services)	-*State of Ohio: Legislative Acts Passed and Joint Resolutions Adopted* -*Page's Ohio Legislative Bulletin* (LexisNexis) -*Baldwin's Ohio Legislative Service Annotated* (West)	-Lexis: *www.lexis.com* OHIO library OHALS file -Westlaw: *www.westlaw.com* OH-LEGIS database	-*www.legislature.state.oh.us/search.cfm#session_laws* -*www.legislature.state.oh.us/search.cfm* -*www.legislature.state.oh.us/acts.cfm*
Pending Bills/ Bill Tracking		-Lexis: *www.lexis.com* LEGIS library OHTRCK file OHIO library OHALS file -Westlaw: *www.westlaw.com* OH-BILLTRK database	-*www.legislature.state.oh.us/search.cfm*
Legislative History		-Westlaw: *www.westlaw.com* OH-LH database (*west.thomson.com/westlaw/statutesplus/OH.pdf*)	-*www.lsc.state.oh.us/membersonly/history.pdf* -*www.uakron.edu/law/library/ohlegisreseach.php* -*www.law.csuohio.edu/lawlibrary/lawpubs/ohio_research_guide.html#Legislative_History* -*library.osu.edu/sites/reference/govdocs/ohleghis.htm*
State Ballot Propositions			-*www.iandrinstitute.org/Ohio.htm* -*www.sos.state.oh.us*
State Administrative Regulations	-*Ohio Administrative Code* (West) -*Ohio Monthly Record* (West) -*Register of Ohio* (Ohio Legislative Service Commission)	-Lexis: *www.lexis.com* OHIO library OHADMN file -Westlaw: www.westlaw.com OH-ADC database -Others: see addresses on page 206 for FastCase, Loislaw, TheLaw.Net, VersusLaw	-*codes.ohio.gov* -*www.registerofohio.state.oh.us* -Overview of Administrative Rule-Making in Ohio (*www.lsc.state.oh.us/membersonly/126rulemakinginohio.pdf*)
State Administrative Decisions	-Many state administrative agencies publish their administrative decisions online. Example: Ohio Board of Tax Appeals (*bta.ohio.gov*). (See also Attorney General Opinions below.)	For Ohio Board of Tax Appeals: -Lexis: *www.lexis.com* OHIO library OHBDTA file -Westlaw: *www.westlaw.com* OHTAX database	-To check whether an Ohio administrative agency publishes its administrative decisions online, check the agency's site (*ohio.gov/contacts.stm*).
State Court Opinions of: **-Ohio Supreme Court** **-Ohio Court of Appeals**	-*Ohio State Reports* (Ohio St., Ohio St. 2d, Ohio St. 3d) -*Ohio Appellate Reports* (Ohio App., Ohio App.2d, Ohio App.3d) -*Ohio Miscellaneous* (Ohio Misc., Ohio Misc.2d) -*Ohio Opinions* (Ohio Op., Ohio Op.2d, Ohio Op.3d) -*North Eastern Reporter* (N.E., N.E.2d)	-Lexis: *www.lexis.com* OHIO library OHIO file OHIO library APP file -Westlaw: *www.westlaw.com* OH-CS database -Others: see addresses on page 206 for FastCase, Loislaw, The Law.Net, VersusLaw	-Supreme Court opinions (*www.sconet.state.oh.us*) -Courts of Appeals Opinions (*www.sconet.state.oh.us/web_sites/courts*) -*www.lexisone.com*
Ethics/Disciplinary opinions	-Advisory Opinions of the Board of Commissioners on Grievances and Discipline -Advisory Opinions of Ohio Ethics Commission	-Lexis: *www.lexis.com* OHIO library OHGRIE file OHIO library OHETHC file ETHICS library OHETOP file -Westlaw: *www.westlaw.com* OHETH-EO database OHETH-CS database OH-ETH database	-*www.sconet.state.oh.us/BOC/advisory_opinions* -*ethics.ohio.gov/ethicshome.html* -*www.ethics.ohio.gov/AdvisoryDigest.html* -*www.ll.georgetown.edu/states/ethics/ohio.cfm*

EXHIBIT 5.1A Ohio Law on the Shelf and Online—Continued

Ethics -Rules of Professional Conduct -Code of Professional Responsibility	-*Ohio Rules of Professional Conduct* -*Code of Professional Responsibility* -*Rules for the Government of the Bar of Ohio*	-Lexis: *www.lexis.com* OHIO library CODE file -Westlaw: *www.westlaw.com* OH-ST database Search: ci(cpr), ci(bar)	-*www.sconet.state.oh.us/Rules* -*www.sconet.state.oh.us/Rules/professional* -*www.sconet.state.oh.us/Rules/govbar* -*www.sconet.state.oh.us/Atty-Svcs/ProfConduct/default.asp* -*www.law.cornell.edu/ethics/oh/code* -*www.ll.georgetown.edu/states/ethics/ohio.cfm*
State Court Rules (Rules of Court)	-*Ohio Rules of Court: State and Federal* (West) -*Rules Governing the Courts of Ohio* (Anderson)	-Lexis: *www.lexis.com* OHIO library OHRULE file -Westlaw: *www.westlaw.com* OH-RULES database OH-TRIALRULES database -Others: see addresses on page 206 for Casemaker, FastCase, Loislaw, TheLaw.Net, VersusLaw	-Supreme Court Rules (*www.sconet.state.oh.us/Rules*) -Courts of Appeals Rules (*www.sconet.state.oh.us/web_sites/courts*) -*www.llrx.com/courtrules* (click "Ohio")
Citators	-*Shepard's Ohio Citations* -*Shepard's Ohio Unreported Appellate Decisions* -*Shepard's Northeastern Reporter Citations* -KeyCite (Westlaw) -Globalcite (Loislaw)	-Lexis: *www.lexis.com* OHIO Library -KeyCite: *www.westlaw.com* -Globalcite: Loislaw (see address on page 206)	
Digests of Ohio State Court Opinions	-*West's Ohio Digest 2d*	-Westlaw: *www.westlaw.com* Example of a digest search in the oh-cs database containing all Ohio state cases: di(murder)	
Ohio Attorney General Opinions	-*Ohio Attorney General Opinions*	-Lexis: *www.lexis.com* OHIO library OHAG file -Westlaw: *www.westlaw.com* OH-AG database -Other: see address on page 206 for Casemaker	-*www.ag.state.oh.us/legal/opinions*
Jury Instructions	-*Ohio Jury Instructions* (Anderson)	-Lexis: *www.lexis.com* OHIO library OHCVJI file OHIO library OHCRJI file -Westlaw: *www.westlaw.com* OH-JICIV database OH-JICRIM database	-Jury instructions for Casemaker (Ohio State Bar Association) (*www.ohiobar.org/pub/pr/index.asp?articleid=186*)
Local Government Laws (charters, codes, ordinances)	Links to municipal codes and other local law through the following county, city, and township sites: -*www.govengine.com/localgov/ohio.html* -*www.ccao.org/1008.htm* -*www.omunileague.org/ohiocities.htm*	-Westlaw: *www.westlaw.com* OHMUNL database CLEVE-MUN database	-*www.bpcnet.com/codes.htm* (*click "Ohio"*) -*www.amlegal.com/library* (*click "Ohio"*) -*www.conwaygreene.com/Municipal-Codes.htm* -*www.walterdrane.com/internet/index.htm* -*www.municode.com* (*click "Online Library" then "Ohio"*)
State Legal Encyclopedia	-*Ohio Jurisprudence 3d* (West)	-Lexis: *www.lexis.com* OHIO library OHJUR file -Westlaw: *www.westlaw.com* OHJUR database	
Legal Treatises on State Law	Examples: -*Ohio Forms of Pleading and Practice* (Matthew Bender) -*Baldwin's Ohio Practice-Civil Practice* (West)	-Lexis: *www.lexis.com* MATBEN library OHFPAP file -Westlaw: *www.westlaw.com* OHPRAC-CIV database	
Legal Research Manuals/Guides on Ohio Law	-Melanie Putnam and Susan Schaefgen, *Ohio Legal Research Guide* (Hein) -*Ohio Legal Resources: An Annotated Bibliography and Guide* (Ohio Library Council)		-See Online Portals to Ohio Law on page 206
Legal Newspapers	-*Akron Legal News* -*Central Ohio Source: The Daily Reporter* -*Cincinnati Court Index* -*Daily Legal News* -*Ohio Legal News*		-*www.akronlegalnews.com* -*www.sourcenews.com* -*www.courtindex.com* -*www.dln.com* -*www.ohiolegalnews.com*
Blogs on Ohio law	-Ohio Legal Research Blog -Ohio Law -Moritz Law Library Legal Information Blog -Cleveland Law Library Weblog		-*ohiolegalblog.blogspot.com* -*ohiocle.blogspot.com* -*ohiolawinfo.blogspot.com* -*moritzlegalinformation.blogspot.com* -*suealtmeyer.typepad.com/cleveland_law_library_web* -*www.uakron.edu/law/library/blawg.php#ohio*
Locating Ohio Attorneys	-*Martindale-Hubbell Law Directory*	-Lexis: *www.lexis.com* MARHUB library OHDIR file -Westlaw: *www.westlaw.com* WLD-OH database	-*www.sconet.state.oh.us/atty_reg/Public_AttorneyInformation.asp* -*www.martindale.com* -*lawyers.findlaw.com* -*lawyers.findlaw.com/lawyer/state/Ohio* -*www.ohiolegalservices.org/OSLSA/PublicWeb/LegalSvcs*

(5.2 Citation Examples, continued)

The Bluebook: A Uniform System of Citation (Columbia Law Review Ass'n et al. eds., 18th ed. 2005)	Bluebook
ALWD Citation Manual: A Professional System of Citation (2d ed. Aspen Publishers 2003) (Ass'n of Legal Writing Directors & Darby Dickerson)	ALWD

There is considerable similarity in how the three manuals cite laws and other categories of materials. Yet there are some important differences you should know about. In this section, we will give examples of citations using all three manuals. As you compare the examples, make careful note of large differences (e.g., how words are abbreviated and in what order they are used) as well as seemingly small ones (e.g., the use of spaces and commas).

B. Abbreviations

Within the Ohio Manual, the Bluebook, and ALWD, there is a list of abbreviations that each recommends or requires. For more information about abbreviations in citations, see section 5.3.

C. Comparison of Citation Formats

The following list presents the most commonly cited legal authority and the citation format adopted by the three legal citation manuals. The examples assume that the cite is being used in a document that will be submitted to an Ohio court.

Ohio Constitution

Ohio Manual: Section 2(B), Article IV, Ohio Constitution
Bluebook: Ohio Const. art. IV, § 2(B)
ALWD: Ohio Const. art. IV, § 2(B)

Ohio Statutes

Ohio Manual: R.C. 4511.19
Bluebook: Ohio Rev. Code Ann. § 4511.19 (LexisNexis 2003)
Ohio Rev. Code Ann. § 4511.19 (West 2003)
ALWD: Ohio Rev. Code Ann. § 4511.19 (Anderson 2003)
Ohio Rev. Code Ann. § 4511.19 (West 2003)

Ohio Administrative Code

Ohio Manual: Ohio Adm.Code 1501:9-3-01
Bluebook: Ohio Admin. Code 1501:9-3-01 (2004)
ALWD: Ohio Admin. Code 1501:9-3-01 (2004)

Ohio Cases

Note: Beginning May 1, 2002, WebCites are part of the official citations of opinions decided on or after May 1, 2002, and must be used for opinions decided on and after May 1, 2002.

Supreme Court of Ohio

Ohio Manual: *Walters v. Knox County Bd. of Revision* (1989), 47 Ohio St.3d 23, 546 N.E.2d 982
Bonacorsi v. Wheeling & Lake Erie Ry. Co., 95 Ohio St.3d 314, 2002-Ohio-2220, 767 N.E.2d 707
Bluebook: *Walters v. Knox County Bd. of Revision*, 546 N.E.2d 982 (Ohio 1989)
ALWD: *Walters v. Knox County Bd. of Revision*, 546 N.E.2d 982 (Ohio 1989)

Appellate Courts of Ohio

Ohio Manual: *State v. Crandall* (1983), 9 Ohio App.3d 291, 9 OBR 538, 460 N.E.2d 296
In re Reed, 147 Ohio App.3d 182, 2002-Ohio-43, 769 N.E.2d 412
Bluebook: *State v. Crandall*, 460 N.E.2d 296 (Ohio Ct. App. 1983)
ALWD: *State v. Crandall*, 460 N.E.2d 296 (Ohio App. 1st Dist. 1983)

Federal Court Opinions Applicable in Ohio

United States Supreme Court
Ohio Manual: *Miranda v. Arizona* (1966), 384 U.S. 436, 86 S.Ct. 1602, 16 L.Ed.2d 694
Bluebook: *Miranda v. Arizona*, 384 U.S. 436 (1966)
ALWD: *Miranda v. Arizona*, 384 U.S. 436 (1966)

United States Court of Appeals for the Sixth Circuit
Ohio Manual: *Scott v. Taylor* (C.A.6, 2005), 405 F.3d. 1251
Bluebook: *Scott v. Taylor*, 405 F.3d 1251 (6th Cir. 2005)
ALWD: *Scott v. Taylor*, 405 F.3d 1251 (6th Cir. 2005)

United States District Court in Ohio
Ohio Manual: *Foster v. Darby* (S.D.Ohio 1972), 390 F.Supp.2d 1084
Bluebook: *Foster v. Darby*, 390 F. Supp. 2d 1084 (S.D. Ohio 1972)
ALWD: *Foster v. Darby*, 390 F. Supp. 2d 1084 (S.D Ohio 1972)

Ohio Attorney General Opinions

Ohio Manual: 1999 Ohio Atty.Gen.Ops. No. 032
Bluebook: Ohio Att'y Gen. Op. No. 99-032 (May 25, 1999)
ALWD: Ohio Atty. Gen. Op. 032 (1999)

Ohio Rules

Ohio Manual: App.R. 9
Civ.R. 56
Crim.R. 11
Evid.R. 601

Bluebook: Ohio R. App. P. 9
Ohio R. Civ. P. 56
Ohio R. Crim. P. 11
Ohio R. Evid. 601

ALWD: Ohio R. App. P. 9
Ohio R. Civ. P. 56
Ohio R. Crim. P. 11
Ohio R. Evid. 601

Law Reviews

Ohio Manual: Pettys, Federal Habeas Relief and the New Tolerance for "Reasonably Erroneous" Applications of Federal Law (2002), 63 Ohio St.L.J. 731

Bluebook: Todd E. Pettys, *Federal Habeas Relief and the New Tolerance for "Reasonably Erroneous" Applications of Federal Law,* 63 Ohio St. L.J. 731 (2002)

ALWD: Todd E. Pettys, *Federal Habeas Relief and the New Tolerance for "Reasonably Erroneous" Applications of Federal Law,* 63 Ohio St. L.J. 731 (2002)

Encyclopedias

Ohio Manual: 32 Ohio Jurisprudence 3d (1997) 386, Decedents' Estates, Section 944

Bluebook: 32 Ohio Jur. 3d *Decedents' Estates* § 944 (1997)

ALWD: 32 Ohio Jur. 3d *Decedents' Estates* § 944 (1997)

Treatises

Single-Volume

Ohio Manual: Palmer, Ohio Courtroom Evidence (2 Ed.1988) 12-1

Bluebook: John W. Palmer, *Ohio Courtroom Evidence* 12-1 (2d ed., 1988)

ALWD: John W. Palmer, *Ohio Courtroom Evidence* 12-1 (2d ed., Michie 1988)

Multi-Volume

Ohio Manual: 2 McDermott, Ohio Real Property Law and Practice (3 Ed. 1966) 815 Section 17-41A

Bluebook: 2 Thomas J. McDermott, *Ohio Real Property Law and Practice* § 17-41A, p. 815 (3d ed. 1966)

ALWD: Thomas J. McDermott, *Ohio Real Property Law and Practice* vol. 2, § 17-41A, 815 (3d ed., A. Smith Co. 1966)

Dictionaries

Ohio Manual: Black's Law Dictionary (6 Ed.Rev.1990) 101

Bluebook: *Black's Law Dictionary* 101 (8th ed. 2004)

ALWD: *Black's Law Dictionary* 101 (Bryan A. Garner ed., 8th ed., West 2004)

D. More Information

Ohio Manual of Citations Internet Edition
(88 Ohio App.3d)
www.sconet.state.oh.us/ROD/pdf/MANCITEmain.pdf

Revisions to the Manual of Citations
www.sconet.state.oh.us/ROD
www.sconet.state.oh.us/ROD/pdf/Rev_Manual_Cit_02.pdf

Ohio Manual Quick Guide
people.sinclair.edu/mikebrigner
(click "Ohio Manual Quick Guide")

Sixth Circuit Electronic Citation
www.aallnet.org/committee/citation/rules_6th.html

Supreme Court of Ohio Rule on Citing Opinions
"Opinions shall be cited in accordance with the Manual of Citations adopted by the Supreme Court Reporter." Rules for Reporting Opinions, Rule 7(A)
www.sconet.state.oh.us/Rules/reporting/#rule7

Bluebook Citation
www.law.cornell.edu/citation
(for Ohio rules, click "Cross Reference Tables" then State-Specific Practices)

ALWD Citation
www.alwd.org
(for Ohio rules, click "ALWD Citation Manual" then "Appendices" then "Appendix 2")

Bluebook and ALWD Citation Comparisons
www.uchastings.edu/?pid=2527

Non-Legal Citation Guides
www.bluffton.edu/library/students/citeguide.html
www.lib.berkeley.edu/TeachingLib/Guides/Internet/Style.html
www.bgsu.edu/colleges/library/services/govdocs/citing.html

Citation and Style Manuals
www.bgsu.edu/colleges/library/services/govdocs/citing.html
exlibris.memphis.edu/resource/unclesam/citeweb.html

Cite-Checking
lib.law.washington.edu/ref/citecheck.html

E. Something to Check

Assume the following information about a citation. Re-write the cite, following the format given in the Ohio Manual of Citations, Bluebook, and ALWD.

1. Sec. 14 Art. 1 Constitution of the State of Ohio.
2. Ohio Constitution, art. XII, § 11.
3. Section 1321.84, West's Revised Code of Ohio, 2002.

4. Section 113:4-01 of the Administrative Code of Ohio, 2004.
5. Centerior Fuel Corporation versus Zaino, volume 90 of the third series of Ohio State Reports, beginning on page 540 and also published in volume 740 of the northeastern reporter 2d edition, starting on page 255, decided by the Ohio Supreme Court on January 17, 2001.
6. Borsick vs. State, 73 Ohio State third 258, 652 northeastern reporter 2nd 951 (Aug. 23, 1995).
7. Heid Thomann Tewardson, appellant versus appellee Michael J. Simon, 141 Ohio App. 3d 103, 750 n.e.2d 176 (9th Appellate Dist., Court of Appeals of Ohio, 1/3/01).
8. Richards et al v. C. Schmidt Company, 561 N.E.2d 569, 54 OH. APP. 3d 123 (First District Court of Appeals of Ohio, 9/20/89).
9. Opinion of Ohio Attorney General, 2001, number 96.
10. Rule 3 of the Ohio Rules of Appellate Procedure.
11. Ohio Rules of Civil Procedure, Rule 36.
12. Rule 3, Criminal Procedure, State of Ohio.
13. Evidence Rule, 401, State of Ohio.
14. Introduction of Biotech Foods to the Tort System: CREATING A NEW DUTY TO IDENTIFY, Summer, 2004, by Katharine Van Tassel, 72 Univ. of Cincin. Law Rev. 1645.
15. Sec. 3456, "DNA Testing, Criminal Law," Volume 29 Oh. Jur., p. 336 (2000).

5.3 Abbreviations in Citations

A. Introduction

As we saw in section 5.2, there are three major citation systems: The *Ohio Manual of Citations Internet Edition* and *Revisions to the Manual of Citations* (both referred to here as the Ohio Manual); *The Bluebook: A Uniform System of Citation* (Bluebook); and *ALWD Citation Manual: A Professional System of Citation* (ALWD).

One important citation concern is the abbreviation of words and phrases in legal writing. The three citation systems do not always agree on how something should be abbreviated or whether something should be abbreviated at all. In this section, we will compare how the three systems abbreviate important words and phrases. Our focus will be on those abbreviations that *differ* among any one of the three systems, although for major entries we will show the abbreviations even if all three systems agree. Note that often the only difference is whether a space is used between specific letters of the abbreviation.

B. Abbreviation Differences

	Ohio Manual	**Bluebook**	**ALWD**
Administrator	Admr.	Adm'r	Adminstr.
affirmed	affirmed	aff'd	aff'd
affirmed under the name of	affirmed sub nom.	aff'd sub nom.	aff'd sub nom.
affirming	affirming	aff'g	aff'g
Akron Law Review	Akron L.Rev.	Akron L. Rev.	Akron L. Rev.
American Jurisprudence	American Jurisprudence	Am. Jur.	Am. Jur.
American Jurisprudence Second	American Jurisprudence Second	Am. Jur. 2d	Am. Jur. 2d
American Law Reports Federal	A.L.R.Fed.	A.L.R. Fed.	A.L.R. Fed.
Association	Assn.	Ass'n	Assn.
California Reporter	Cal.Rptr.	Cal. Rptr.	Cal. Rptr.
Capital University Law Review	Cap. U.L.Rev.	Cap. U. L. Rev.	Cap. U. L. Rev.
chapter	chapter	ch.	ch.
Cleveland State Law Review	Cleve.St.L. Rev.	Clev. St. L. Rev.	Clev. St. L. Rev.
Commission	Comm.	Comm'n	Commn.
Committee	Commt.	Comm.	Comm.
County	Cty.	County	County
Court of Appeals	App.	Ct. App.	App.
Court of Claims of Ohio	Ct. of Cl.	Ct. Cl.	
Common Pleas	C.P.	Ct. Com. Pl.	Com. Pleas
doing business as	d.b.a	d/b/a	d/b/a
Education	Edn.	Educ.	Educ.

Engineering	Eng.	Eng'g	Engr.
Enterprise	Ent.	Enter.	Enter.
Executor	Exr.	Ex'r	
Federal Cases	F.Cas.	F. Cas.	F. Cas.
Federal Rules of Appellate Procedure	Fed.R.App.P.	Fed. R. App. P.	Fed. R. App. P.
Federal Rules of Civil Procedure	Fed.R.Civ.P.	Fed. R. Civ. P.	Fed. R. Civ. P.
Federal Rules of Criminal Procedure	Fed.R.Crim.P.	Fed. R. Crim. P.	Fed. R. Crim. P.
Federal Rules of Evidence	Fed.R.Evid.	Fed. E. Evid.	Fed. R. Evid.
Federal Rules Service	Fed.R.Serv.	Fed. R. Serv.	Fed. R. Serv.
Federal Supplement	F.Supp.	F. Supp.	F. Supp.
footnote	fn.	n.	n.
Federation	Fedn.	Fed'n	Fedn.
Government	Govt.	Gov't	Govt.
Harvard Law Review	Harv.L.Rev	Harv. L. Rev	Harv. L. Rev
Hawaii Reports	Hawaii	Haw.	Haw.
Illinois Appellate Reports	Ill.Rep.	Ill. Rep.	Ill. Rep.
Indemnity	Indemn.	Indem.	Indem.
Indiana Appellate Reports	Ind.App.	Ind. App.	Ind. App.
Investment	Invest.	Inv.	Inv.
Juvenile Court	J.C.	Juv. Ct.	Juv. Ct.
Lawyers Edition	L.Ed.	L. Ed.	L. Ed.
Lawyers Edition, Second	L.Ed.2d	L. Ed. 2d	L. Ed. 2d
Management	Mgt.	Mgmt.	Mgt.
Memorial	Mem.	Mem'l	Meml.
Michigan Appeals Reports	Mich.App.	Mich. App.	Mich. App.
Mortgage	Mtge.		Mortg.
Municipal Court	M.C.	Mun. Ct.	Mun. Ct.
National	Natl.	Nat'l	Natl.
Ohio Administrative Code	Ohio Adm.Code	Ohio Admin. Code	Ohio Admin. Code
Ohio Appellate Reports	Ohio App.	Ohio App.	Ohio App.
Ohio Appellate Reports, Second Series	Ohio App.2d	Ohio App. 2d	Ohio App. 2d
Ohio Appellate Reports, Third Series	Ohio App.2d	Ohio App. 3d	Ohio App. 3d
Ohio Bar Reports	OBR	Ohio B.	
Ohio Circuit Court Reports	Ohio C.C.	Ohio C.C.	
Ohio Circuit Court Reports, New Series	Ohio C.C.(N.S.)	Ohio C.C. (n.s.)	
Ohio Circuit Decisions	Ohio C.D.	Ohio Cir. Dec.	
Ohio Decisions	Ohio Dec.	Ohio Dec.	
Ohio Decisions Reprint	Ohio Dec.Rep.	Ohio Dec. Reprint	
Ohio Miscellaneous Reports	Ohio Misc.	Ohio Misc.	Ohio Misc.
Ohio Miscellaneous Reports, Second Series	Ohio Misc.2d	Ohio Misc. 2d	Ohio Misc. 2d
Ohio Monthly Record	Ohio Monthly Record	Ohio Monthly Rec.	Ohio Mthly. Rec.
Ohio Nisi Prius Reports	Ohio N.P.		
Ohio Nisi Prius Reports, New Series	Ohio N.P.(N.S.)	Ohio N.P. (n.s.)	
Ohio Northern University Law Review	Ohio N.U.L.Rev.	Ohio N.U. L. Rev.	Ohio N.U. L. Rev.
Ohio Reports	Ohio	Ohio	Ohio
Ohio Opinions	O.O.	Ohio Op.	Ohio
Ohio Opinions, Second Series	O.O.2d	Ohio Op. 2d	Ohio Op. 2d
Ohio Opinions, Third Series	O.O.3d	Ohio Op. 3d	Ohio Op. 3d
Ohio Revised Code	R.C.	Ohio Rev. Code Ann.	Ohio Rev. Code Ann.
Ohio Rules of Appellate Procedure	App.P.	Ohio R. App. P.	
Ohio Rules of Civil Procedure	Civ.P.	Ohio R. Civ. P.	Ohio R. Civ. P.
Ohio Rules of Evidence	Evid.R.	Ohio R. Evid.	Ohio R. Evid.
Ohio State Law Journal	Ohio St.L.J.	Ohio St. L.J.	Ohio St. L.J.
Ohio State Reports	Ohio St.	Ohio St.	Ohio St.
Ohio State Reports, Second Series	Ohio St.2d	Ohio St. 2d	Ohio St. 2d

Ohio State Reports, Third Series	Ohio St.3d	Ohio St. 3d	Ohio St. 3d
Pennsylvania Commonwealth Court Reports	Pa.Commw.	Pa. Commw.	Pa. Cmmw.
Pennsylvania District and County Reports	Pa.D.&C.	Pa. D. & C.	Pa. D. & C.
Pennsylvania Superior Court Reports	Pa.Super.	Pa. Super.	Pa. Super.
Probate Court	P.C.	Prob. Ct.	Prob. Ct.
Railroad	RR.	R.R.	R.R.
Secretary	Secy.	Sec'y	Sec.
Society	Soc.	Soc'y	Socy.
Southern Reporter, Second Series	So.2d	So. 2d	So. 2d
Supreme Court Reporter	S.Ct.	S. Ct.	S. Ct.
Tennessee Court of Appeals Reports	Tenn.App.	Tenn. App.	Tenn. App.
Tennessee Criminal Appeals Reports	Tenn.Crim.App.	Tenn. Crim. App.	Tenn. Crim. App.
title	title	tit.	tit.
University	Univ.	Univ.	U.
University of Dayton Law Review	U.Dayton L.Rev.	U. Dayton L. Rev.	U. Dayton L. Rev.
University of Cincinnati Law Review	U.Cin.L.Rev.	U. Cin. L. Rev.	U. Cin. L. Rev.
University of Toledo Law Review	U.Tol.L.Rev.	U. Tol. L. Rev.	U. Toledo L. Rev.
U.S. Bankruptcy Court Northern District	Bankr.Ct.N.D.Ohio	Bankr. N.D. Ohio	Bankr. N.D. Ohio
U.S. Bankruptcy Court Southern District	Bankr.Ct.S.D.Ohio	Bankr. S.D. Ohio	Bankr. S.D. Ohio
U.S. Court of Appeals, Sixth Circuit	C.A.6	6th Cir.	6th Cir.
U.S. District Court Northern District	N.D.Ohio	N.D. Ohio	N.D. Ohio
U.S. District Court Southern District	S.D.Ohio	S.D. Ohio	S.D. Ohio
West Virginia Reports	W.Va.	W. Va.	W. Va.

C. More Information

(See also the sources listed under More Information at the end of section 5.2 on citation examples.)

Ohio Manual of Citations Internet Edition
(88 Ohio App.3d)
www.sconet.state.oh.us/ROD/pdf/MANCITEmain.pdf

Revisions to the Manual of Citations
www.sconet.state.oh.us/ROD
www.sconet.state.oh.us/ROD/pdf/Rev_Manual_Cit_02.pdf

Ohio Manual Quick Guide
people.sinclair.edu/mikebrigner
(click "Ohio Manual Quick Guide")

Sixth Circuit Electronic Citation
www.aallnet.org/committee/citation/rules_6th.html

Association of Legal Writing Directors
www.alwd.org
(click "ALWD Citation Manual" then "appendices")

Miscellaneous
www.llrx.com/columns/reference37.htm
www.aallnet.org/sis/lisp/cite.htm
lib.law.washington.edu/pubs/acron.html
www.ulib.iupui.edu/subjectareas/gov/docs_abbrev.html
www.legalabbrevs.cardiff.ac.uk

D. Something to Check

Open any law book, e.g., a school textbook, a court reporter, or a statutory code. Find any ten abbreviations used in this book that do *not* conform with the Ohio Manual. Describe the discrepancies.

5.4 Abbreviations for Notetaking

A. Introduction

There are many settings in which paralegals must be able to write quickly. Examples include notetaking while:

- in class
- studying your textbooks
- conducting legal research
- receiving instructions from a supervisor

- interviewing a client or witness
- listening to a deposition witness give testimony
- listening to a trial witness give testimony

Using abbreviations in such settings can be helpful. This section presents some commonly used abbreviations in the law. Some entries have more than one abbreviation, e.g., c/a and coa for cause of action. When a choice is available, pick an abbreviation with which you are comfortable. The primary purpose of the abbreviations is to help you take notes that only you will read. Hence feel free to try out, adapt, and add to the following list.

These abbreviations are for use in notetaking, *not for use in citations or formal writing.* (For abbreviations in citations, see section 5.2 and section 5.3.)

B. Notetaking Abbreviations

A answer
a action
aa administrative agency
a/b appellate brief
a/c appellate court
acct account
acctg accounting
ad administrative decision
admr administrator
ADR alternative dispute resolution
aff affirmed
aka also known as
agt agent
alj administrative law judge
amt amount
And Anderson
ans answer
aplt appellant
aple appellee
app appeal
appnt appellant
appee appellee
apt apartment
ar administrative regulation
a/r assumption of the risk
assn association
atty attorney
b business
b/4 before
ba bar association
bankr bankruptcy
b/c because
bd board
b/k breach of contract
b/p burden of proof
bfp bona fide purchaser
bldg building
bus business
b/w breach of warranty
¢ complaint
© consideration
ca court of appeals
CA6 Sixth Circuit
c/a cause of action
CC Civil Code (or Circuit Court)
cc child custody
c/c counterclaim
c-dr creditor
c/e cross-examination
cert certiorari
cf compare
ch chapter
c/l common law
cle continuing legal education
coa cause of action
comm committee
commn commission
commr commissioner
compl complaint (or compliance)
conf conference
con law constitutional law
consv conservative
cont continued
corp corporation
cp community property
CP Common Pleas
cr criminal (or creditor)
cr-c criminal court
cs child support
ct court
cty county
cv civil
cy calendar year
cz cause
Δ defendant
d danger/dangerous
d. died, death
DA district attorney
dba doing business as
d/e direct examination
decrg decreasing
depo deposition
dept department
df defendant
dist district
dkt docket
dmg damages
dob date of birth
dod date of death
d-r debtor
dv domestic violence
= equals
e evidence
e/d eminent domain
ee employee
eg example
egs examples
emp employment
eng engineer (or engineering)
ent enterprise
eq equity
eqbl equitable
er employer
est estimate (or established or estate)
ev evidence
ex exhibit
exr executor
f fact
4cb foreseeable
fed federal
fn footnote
f-st federal statute
fy fiscal year
g govern
GA General Assembly
g/r general rule
gt government
gvt government
h husband
hb house bill
hdc holder in due course
HR House of Representatives
hrg hearing
i interest
ij injury
immig immigration
in interest
incrg increasing
indl individual
indp independent
info information
inj injunction
ins insurance
intl international
i-p in personam
i-r in rem
IRC Internal Revenue Code
IRS Internal Revenue Service
J judge, justice
JC Juvenile Court
j/d judgment for defendant
jp justice of the peace
j/p judgment for plaintiff
jj judges, justices
jt judgment (or joint)
jud judicial
jur jurisdiction
juv juvenile
jxn jurisdiction
K contract
l liable, liability
ll landlord
l/l limited liability
l/lc limited liability company
l/lp limited liability partnership
< less than; smaller than
lit litigation
lr legal research
ltd limited
LN Lexis-Nexis
LX Lexis
max maximum
mem memorial
mfr manufacturer
mfg manufacturing
misc miscellaneous
mj major

mgmt management
min minimum
mkt market
mo majority opinion
> more than; greater than
mtg mortgage (or meeting)
mtge mortgagee
mtgr mortgagor
mun municipal
MC Municipal Court
n/a irrelevant (not applicable)
natl national
neg negligence
negl negligence
number
nt nothing (or note or not)
ntry notary
O owner
o degree
OA Ohio Appellate
OAC Ohio Administrative Code
OAG Ohio Attorney General
OB Ohio Bar
obj object, objective
OC Ohio Constitution
OCA Ohio Court of Appeals
occ occupation
OCP Ohio Common Pleas
oee offeree
oer offeror
OG Ohio Governor
OGA Ohio General Assembly
OO Ohio Opinions
op opinion
ORC Ohio Revised Code
ord ordinance
OSC Ohio Supreme Court
OSL Ohio State Legislature
π plaintiff
p plaintiff
p. page
PC Penal Code
p/c proximate cause
pee promise
pet petition
petr petitioner
p/f prima facie
pg page
pj personal judgment
PL public law
pl plaintiff
pol practice of law
por promisor
pp public policy
p/r personal representative
priv private
pub public
pub-op public opinion
pvg privilege
pvt private
? question
?d questioned
Q equity (or equitable)
r regulation
RC Ohio Revised Code
® reasonable
re real estate (or regarding)
rec record
recd received
reg regulation
rel related to
rep representative (or representation)
rev reverse
revd reversed
r/o restraining order
roc rules of court
rogs interrogatories
rr railroad
rsb reasonable
s sum
S statute
$ suppose
sb Senate Bill
s/b should be
sc supreme court
secy secretary
s/f statute of frauds
Sh Shepard's Citations (or shepardize)
s-h self-help
Sh-z shepardize
6C Sixth Circuit
s/j summary judgment
sl strict liability
s/l statute of limitations
s-mj subject-matter jurisdiction
sn/b should not be
soc society
SOL statute of limitations
sos secretary of state
ss sections
s-st state statute
std standard
sub substantial
subj subject, subjective
t testimony
T tort
t/c trial court
tee trustee
test testimony
tp third party
tro temporary restraining order
tpr trespasser
u understanding
U university
UCC Uniform Commercial Code
ui unemployment insurance
USC United States Code
USSC United States Supreme Court
v versus, against
vs against; versus
w wife
wc workers' compensation
w/ with
w/i within
Wl Westlaw
w/o without
x cross
xe cross examination
© consideration
¢ complaint
Δ defendant
= equals
< less than; smaller than
> more than; greater than
number
π plaintiff
+ plus
? question
?d questioned
® reasonable
$ suppose
\ therefore

C. More Information

Taking Notes
www.nyls.edu/pages/3083.asp

Abbreviations
lib.law.washington.edu/pubs/acron.html
www.llrx.com/columns/reference37.htm

5.5 Research Starters for 78 Major Ohio Topics

A. Introduction
B. Abbreviations
C. Topics Covered
D. Research Starter Cites
E. More Information on Ohio Law
F. Something to Check

A. Introduction

Often in legal research, the first hurdle is finding your first lead. You need a starting point that will guide you into the various categories of case law, statutory law, administrative law, etc. You may also need a lead to a secondary authority, such as a legal treatise or legal encyclopedia, which will provide an overview of an area of the law that may be new to you. In this section, we provide you with such leads to 78 major topics of Ohio law. They are "starter cites," in the sense that they may lead you—directly or indirectly—to what you need.

B. Abbreviations

The starter cites use the following abbreviations for the legal materials covered, many of which are found online as well as on the shelves of moderate-sized law libraries:

AC: Administrative Code of Ohio

M-HLD: Martindale-Hubbell Law Digest

(The volume summarizes major laws of every state)

OD: Ohio Digest

(The OD will lead you to key numbers within the WestGroup digest system)

OJ: Ohio Jurisprudence 3d

(Ohio is one of the few states that has its own legal encyclopedia)

RC: Revised Code of Ohio

C. Topics Covered

Abortion
Administrative Law
Adoption
Affidavits
Agency
Alimony
Annulment
Appeal and Error
Arbitration
Attorney-Client Privilege
Attorneys
Banking
Child Custody
Child Support
Civil Procedure
Commercial Code
Constitutional Law
Consumer Protection
Contracts
Corporations
Courts in Ohio
Criminal Law
Damages
Deeds
Discovery
Divorce
Domestic Violence
Employment Discrimination
Enforcement of Judgment
Environment
Equity
Estates
Evidence
Family Law
Fraud
Garnishment
Government
Guardianship
Illegitimacy
Injunctions
Insurance
Intellectual Property
Labor Relations
Landlord and Tenant
Legal Separation
Limited Liability Companies
Marriage
Mediation
Medical Malpractice
Mineral, Water, and Fishing Rights
Minors
Mortgages
Motor Vehicles
Negligence
Notary Public
Paralegals
Partnerships
Pleading
Power of Attorney
Privacy
Privileged Communications
Products Liability
Property Division in Divorce
Real Property
Service of Process
Statute of Frauds
Statute of Limitations
Summary Judgment
Summons
Taxation
Torts
Traffic Laws
Trusts
Unemployment Insurance
Venue
Water Rights
Wills
Workers' Compensation

D. Research Starter Cites

ABORTION

Statutes: RC: §§ 124.85, 2151.85, 2317.56
Regulations: AC §§ 3701-47-02, 5101:3-17-01
Cases: OD: check Abortion and Birth Control, key numbers (⚿) 1ff
Encyclopedia: OJ: check Criminal Law § 805; Family Law § 1481; Health & Sanitation § 33; Physicians § 199; Public Welfare § 99
Internet:
megalaw.com/oh/top/ohfamily.php
www.womensmedcenter.com/laws/?ID=3
www.plannedparenthood.org

ADMINISTRATIVE LAW

Statutes: RC §§ 119.01ff
Regulations: AC §§ 173-2-05, 3333-1-06, 3770-1-02, 4901:2-7-13
Cases: OD: check Administrative Law and Procedure, key numbers (⚿) 1ff
Encyclopedia: OJ: check Administrative Law § 5ff
Internet:
www.law.csuohio.edu/lawlibrary/lawpubs/AdministrativeLaw.htm
megalaw.com/oh/top/ohcivpro.php
www.legislature.state.oh.us/laws.cfm
(click "Ohio Administrative Code")

ADOPTION

Statutes: RC §§ 3107.01ff
Regulations: AC §§ 5101:1-40-023, 5101:2-47-44, 5101:2-48-02,
Cases: OD: check Adoption, key numbers (⚿) 1ff
Encyclopedia: OJ: check Family Law §§ 900ff, 1191

Summary Overview: M-HLD: In the Ohio summary Family, check Adoption
Internet:
ohio.adoption.com
megalaw.com/oh/top/ohfamily.php
www.ohiobar.org/pub/lycu/index.asp?articleid=181
www.adoption.org/adopt/state-of-ohio-adoption-laws.php

AFFIDAVITS

Statutes: RC § 2319.03
Regulations: AC §§ 742-3-13, 4901:1-24-05, 4901:1-27-05
Cases: OD: check Affidavits, key numbers (⚿) 1ff
Encyclopedia: OJ: check Acknowledgements § 29ff
Summary Overview: M-HLD: In the Ohio summary under Documents and Records, check Affidavits
Internet:
www.findlaw.com/11stategov/oh/forms.html
www.alllaw.com/state_resources/ohio/forms

AGENCY

Statutes: RC § 4735.51
Cases: OD: check Principal and Agent, key numbers (⚿) 1ff
Encyclopedia: OJ: check Agency and Independent Contractors § 3ff
Summary Overview: M-HLD: In the Ohio summary under Business Organizations, check Agency

ALIMONY

Statutes: RC § 3105.18
Regulations: AC §§ 5101:1-29-06(A), 5101:2-16-34
Cases: OD: check Divorce, key numbers (⚿) 199ff
Encyclopedia: OJ: check Family Law § 351, Lis Pendens § 23
Summary Overview: M-HLD: In the Ohio summary under Family, check Alimony
Internet:
www.clelaw.lib.oh.us/Public/Misc/FAQs/SpousalSupport.html
megalaw.com/oh/top/ohfamily.php
www.divorcesource.com/OH/index.shtml
www.divorcenet.com/states/ohio/ohfaq05

ANNULMENT

Statutes: RC § 3105.31; Rules of Civil Procedure Rule 75
Regulations: AC §§ 3701-5-02 (Appendix N), 3701-5-11
Cases: OD: check Marriage, key numbers (⚿) 56ff
Encyclopedia: OJ: check Family Law § 8
Summary Overview: M-HLD: In the Ohio summary under Family, check Marriage (and Annulment under Marriage)
Internet:
www.ohiobar.org/pub/lycu/index.asp?articleid=199
megalaw.com/oh/top/ohfamily.php
www.clelaw.lib.oh.us/Public/Misc/FAQs/SpousalSupport.html

APPEAL AND ERROR

Statutes: RC §§ 2501.01ff, 2505.01ff
Cases: OD: check Appeal and Error, key numbers (⚿) 1ff
Encyclopedia: OJ: check Appellate Review § 1ff
Summary Overview: M-HLD: In the Ohio summary under Civil Actions and Procedure, check Appeal and Error
Internet:
megalaw.com/oh/top/ohcivpro.php
www.sconet.state.oh.us/Rules/civil/default.asp
www.law.csuohio.edu/lawlibrary/lawpubs/CivilProcedureResearchGuide.htm

ARBITRATION

Statutes: RC §§ 2711.01, 2711.03, 2712.01
Regulations: AC § 4901:1-26-04
Cases: OD: check Arbitration, key numbers (⚿) 1ff
Encyclopedia: OJ: check Alternative Dispute Resolution §§ 13, 210
Summary Overview: M-HLD: In the Ohio summary under Dispute Resolution, check Arbitration and Award
Internet:
www.sconet.state.oh.us/dispute_resolution/FAQ/default.asp

ATTORNEY-CLIENT PRIVILEGE

Statutes: RC §§ § 120.38, 2317.02; Evid. R. Rule 501; Code of Professional Resp., EC 4-4, DR 4-101
Regulations: AC Ohio Admin. Law Text § 8.11
Cases: OD: check Witnesses, key numbers (⚿) 198ff
Encyclopedia: OJ: check Evidence and Witnesses §§ 766ff
Summary Overview: M-HLD: In the Ohio summary under Civil Actions and Procedure, check Evidence (and Privileged Communications under Evidence)

ATTORNEYS

Statutes: RC § 4123.06; Const. Art. IV, § 2(B)(g)
Regulations: AC § §§
Cases: OD: check Attorneys, key numbers (⚿) 1ff
Encyclopedia: OJ: check Attorneys at Law §§ 2ff
Summary Overview: M-HLD: In the Ohio summary under Legal Profession, check Attorneys and Counselors
Internet:
www.ohiobar.org/pub/lawfacts
www.sconet.state.oh.us/BOC/faq/default.asp
www.ohiobar.org/pub/lawfacts/index.asp?articleid=9

BANKING

Statutes: RC §§ 1101.01ff
Regulations: AC §§ 1301:1-1-02ff
Cases: OD: check Banks and Banking, key numbers (⚿) 1ff

Encyclopedia: OJ: check Banks §§ 4ff
Summary Overview: M-HLD: In the Ohio summary under Business Regulation and Commerce, check Banks and Banking
Internet:
www.com.state.oh.us/ODOC/dfi
www.lawguru.com/ilawlib/316.htm

CHILD CUSTODY

Statutes: RC §§ 3105.21, 3127.23,
Regulations: AC § 5101:1-30-04
Cases: OD: check Child Custody, key numbers (🔑) 1ff
Encyclopedia: OJ: check Family Law § 369, 372, 658
Summary Overview: M-HLD: In the Ohio summary under Family, check Divorce (and Children under Divorce)
Internet:
megalaw.com/oh/top/ohfamily.php
www.divorcesource.com/info/divorcelaws/ohio.shtml
www.divorcelawinfo.com/states/ohio/ohio.htm

CHILD SUPPORT

Statutes: RC §§ 307.981, 2151.231, 3119.06
Regulations: AC §§ 4141-43-02, 5101:1-3-10, 5101:1-29-13
Cases: OD: check Child Support, key numbers (🔑) 1ff
Encyclopedia: OJ: check Family Law § 369, 373, 501, 572, 969
Summary Overview: M-HLD: In the Ohio summary Family, check Divorce (and Children under Divorce)
Internet:
jfs.ohio.gov/OCS
megalaw.com/oh/top/ohfamily.php
www.ohiobar.org/pub/lawfacts

CIVIL PROCEDURE

Statutes: RC §§ 2107.72, 2315.01ff, 3111.421; Rules of Civil Procedure Rule 1ff
Regulations: AC § 173-2-05
Cases: OD: check the vols. for Appeal and Error; Evidence; Pretrial Procedure; Trial; Witnesses, key numbers (🔑) 1ff
Encyclopedia: OJ: check Actions §§ 1ff, Appellate Review §§ 1ff; Alternative Dispute Resolution §§ 1ff, Discovery and Depositions §§ 1ff, Judgments §§ 1ff, Mandamus §§ 1ff, Parties §§ 1ff, Pleading §§ 1ff, Trial §§ 1ff, Venue §§ 1ff
Summary Overview: M-HLD: In the Ohio summary, check Civil Actions and Procedure
Internet:
megalaw.com/oh/top/ohcivpro.php
www.sconet.state.oh.us/Rules/civil/default.asp
www.law.csuohio.edu/lawlibrary/lawpubs/CivilProcedureResearchGuide.htm

COMMERCIAL CODE

Statutes: RC §§ 1301.01ff
Regulations: AC §§ 111-9-01
Cases: OD: check the vols. for Bills and Notes; Sales, key numbers (🔑) 1ff
Encyclopedia: OJ: check Assignments §§ 1ff, Banks §§ 1ff, Contracts § 25, Investment Securities §§ 1ff, Negotiable Instruments §§ 1ff, Sales and Exchanges of Personal Property §§ 1ff, Secured Transcations §§ 1ff
Summary Overview: M-HLD: In the Ohio summary under Business Regulation and Commerce, check Commercial Code
Internet:
www.sos.state.oh.us/sos/ucc/ucc.aspx
www.law.csuohio.edu/lawlibrary/ContractLawResourceGuide.htm

CONSTITUTIONAL LAW

Statutes: See index to Ohio Constitution within the Revised Code of Ohio
Cases: OD: check Constitutional Law, key numbers (🔑) 1ff
Encyclopedia: OJ: check Constitutional Law
Internet:
megalaw.com/oh/top/ohconstitution.php
www.law.csuohio.edu/lawlibrary/lawpubs/ConstitutionalLawResourceGuide.htm

CONSUMER PROTECTION

Statutes: RC §§ 1345.01, 1345.51
Regulations: AC § 109:4-1-06
Cases: OD: check Consumer Protection, key numbers (🔑) 1ff
Encyclopedia: OJ: check Actions § 49, Consumer and Borrower Protection §§ 1ff
Summary Overview: M-HLD: In the Ohio summary under Business Regulation and Commerce, check Consumer Protection
Internet:
www.pickocc.org
www.ohiolegalservices.org/OSLSA/PublicWeb/Library/Index/1090000

CONTRACTS

Statutes: RC §§ 1301.01ff, 1309.01ff
Cases: OD: check the vols. for Contracts; Sales, key numbers (🔑) 1ff
Encyclopedia: OJ: check Contracts §§ 1ff
Summary Overview: M-HLD: In the Ohio summary, check Business Regulation and Commerce
Internet:
www.law.csuohio.edu/lawlibrary/ContractLawResourceGuide.htm

downloads.ohiobar.org/conres/lawandyou/Law_and_You_6.pdf
www.law.csuohio.edu/lawlibrary/SecuredTransactionsResourceGuide.html

CORPORATIONS

Statutes: RC § 1701.04ff
Cases: OD: check the vols. for Corporations; Securities Regulation key numbers (🔑) 1ff
Encyclopedia: OJ: check Business Relationships § 6ff,
Summary Overview: M-HLD: In the Ohio summary under Business Organizations, check Corporations
Internet:
www.business.ohio.gov
www.sos.state.oh.us/sos/businessservices/corp.aspx
www.alllaw.com/state_resources/ohio/forms
www.law.csuohio.edu/lawlibrary/CorporationLawResources.htm

COURTS IN OHIO

Statutes: RC Const. Art. IV, §§ 1ff
Regulations: AC §§ 124-15-06
Cases: OD: check Courts, key numbers (🔑) 1ff
Encyclopedia: OJ: check Alternative Dispute Resolution §§ 1ff, Appellate Review §§ 1ff, Courts and Judges §§ 1ff
Summary Overview: M-HLD: In the Ohio summary, check Courts and Legislature
Internet:
www.cco.state.oh.us
www.sconet.state.oh.us
www.ohiobar.org/pub/lawfacts
megalaw.com/oh/top/ohcivpro.php
megalaw.com/oh/top/ohconstitution.php

CRIMINAL LAW

Statutes: RC §§ 2901.01ff
Cases: OD: check the vols. for Criminal Law; Sentencing and Punishment, key numbers (🔑) 1ff
Encyclopedia: OJ: check Criminal Law § 1ff
Summary Overview: M-HLD: In the Ohio summary, check Criminal Law
Internet:
www.ag.state.oh.us
megalaw.com/oh/top/ohconstitution.php
megalaw.com/oh/top/ohcriminal.php
www.law.csuohio.edu/lawlibrary/lawpubs/CriminalLawResourceGuide.htm

DAMAGES

Statutes: RC §§ 1302.84, 2125.02, 2315.18, 2315.20ff
Regulations: AC § 4112-6-02
Cases: OD: check Damages, key numbers (🔑) 1ff
Encyclopedia: OJ: check Damages §§ 1ff
Summary Overview: M-HLD: In the Ohio summary under Civil Actions and Procedure, check Damages
Internet:
megalaw.com/oh/top/ohcivpro.php

DEEDS

Statutes: RC §§ 317.19, 322.01, 1335.01, 2329.43, 5302.02, 5309.01
Cases: OD: check the vols. for Deeds; Property key numbers (🔑)1ff
Encyclopedia: OJ: check Abstracts and Land Titles §§ 1ff, Deeds §§1ff
Summary Overview: M-HLD: In the Ohio summary under Property, check Deeds
Internet:
www.ohiobar.org/pub/lycu/index.asp?articleid=191
www.law.csuohio.edu/lawlibrary/PropertyLawResourceGuide.htm

DISCOVERY

Statutes: RC Rules of Civil Procedure Rule 26
Regulations: AC §§ 101-7-10, 102-9-03, 1513-3-10
Cases: OD: check Pretrial Procedure, key numbers (🔑) 11ff
Encyclopedia: OJ: check Criminal Law § 366, Discovery and Depositions §§ 1ff
Summary Overview: M-HLD: In the Ohio summary under Civil Actions and Procedure, check Depositions and Discovery
Internet:
megalaw.com/oh/top/ohcivpro.php

DIVORCE

Statutes: RC §§ 3105.01ff, 3705.21; Rules of Civil Procedure Rule 75
Cases: OD: check the vols. for Divorce; Husband and Wife, key numbers (🔑) 1ff
Encyclopedia: OJ: check Family Law §§ 321, 651
Summary Overview: M-HLD: In the Ohio summary under Family, check Divorce
Internet:
megalaw.com/oh/top/ohfamily.php
www.ohiobar.org/pub/lawfacts
www.divorcelawinfo.com/states/ohio/ohio.htm
www.clelaw.lib.oh.us/Public/Misc/FAQs/SpousalSupport.html

DOMESTIC VIOLENCE

Statutes: RC §§ 2305.236, 2919.25, 2935.032
Regulations: AC § §§
Cases: OD: check Criminal Law, key numbers (🔑) 474.4(3)ff
Encyclopedia: OJ: check Criminal Law §§ 844, 1468
Internet:
megalaw.com/oh/top/ohcriminal.php
www.clelaw.lib.oh.us/Public/Misc/FAQs/Dom_Violence.html
www.ohiodvresources.org
www.odvn.org

EMPLOYMENT DISCRIMINATION

Statutes: RC §§ 153.59, 1513.39, 4112.14, 4111.17
Regulations: AC §§ 3342-4-01, 4112-5-08
Cases: OD: check Civil Rights, key numbers (⚷) 1101ff
Encyclopedia: OJ: check Civil Rights §§ 16ff
Summary Overview: M-HLD: In the Ohio summary under Employment, check Labor Relations (and Discrimination under Labor Relations)
Internet:
crc.ohio.gov
megalaw.com/oh/top/ohconstitution.php
megalaw.com/oh/top/ohlabor.php

ENFORCEMENT OF JUDGMENT

Statutes: RC §§ 1745.02, 1907.031, 2307.28, 2325.20, 2337.10, 5563.12; Rules of Civil Procedure Rule 62; Rules of Court of Claims Rule 8
Regulations: AC § §§
Cases: OD: check the vols. for Judgment; Execution key numbers (⚷) 1ff
Encyclopedia: OJ: check Creditors' Rights § 481, Enforcement of Judgments §§ 1ff
Summary Overview: M-HLD: In the Ohio summary under Civil Actions and Procedure, check Judgments
Internet:
megalaw.com/oh/top/ohcivpro.php

ENVIRONMENT

Statutes: RC §§ 3734.02, 3745.01ff
Regulations: AC §§ 3745-49-01ff
Cases: OD: check Environmental Law, key numbers (⚷) 1ff
Encyclopedia: OJ: check Environmental Protection §§ 1ff
Summary Overview: M-HLD: In the Ohio summary, check Environment
Internet:
www.epa.state.oh.us
www.dnr.state.oh.us
megalaw.com/oh/top/ohenvironmental.php
www.law.csuohio.edu/lawlibrary/lawpubs/EnvironmentalLawResourceGuide.htm

EQUITY

Statutes: RC §§ 1322.021, 1335.01, 1339.13, 1707.043, 1709.11, 1775.04, 2127.18, 2333.01, 3105.011, 3742.18, 3901.322
Regulations: AC § 1301:9-2-23
Cases: OD: check Equity, key numbers (⚷) 1ff
Encyclopedia: OJ: check Equity §§ 1ff
Summary Overview: M-HLD: In the Ohio summary under Civil Actions and Procedure, check Actions, Equity
Internet:
megalaw.com/oh/top/ohcivpro.php

ESTATES

Statutes: RC: Const. Art. XII, § 3; §§ 2101.01ff, 2117.01ff, 2131.07, 5301.02
Cases: OD: check the vols. for Estates in Property; Wills, key numbers (⚷) 1ff
Encyclopedia: OJ: check Abstracts and Land Titles §§ 1ff, Cotenancy and Partition §§ 1ff, Decedents' Estates §§ 1ff, Deeds §§ 1ff, Estates §§ 1ff
Summary Overview: M-HLD: In the Ohio summary, check Estates and Trusts
Internet:
megalaw.com/oh/top/ohprobate.php
www.ohiobar.org/pub/lawfacts
www.law.csuohio.edu/lawlibrary/EstatesTrustsResourceGuide.htm

EVIDENCE

Statutes: RC §§ 1306.12, 2317.01ff; Ohio Rules of Evidence Rule 101ff
Regulations: AC §§ 124-9-01, 4117-3-03, 4141-28-04
Cases: OD: check the vols. for Evidence; Trial; Witnesses, key numbers (⚷) 1ff
Encyclopedia: OJ: check Evidence and Witnesses §§ 1ff
Summary Overview: M-HLD: In the Ohio summary under Civil Actions and Procedure, check Evidence
Internet:
megalaw.com/oh/top/ohcivpro.php
www.law.csuohio.edu/lawlibrary/lawpubs/EvidenceResourceGuide.htm

FAMILY LAW

Statutes: RC §§ 307.981, 5101.22, 5101.821
Regulations: AC § 5101:1-1-01
Cases: OD: check the vols. for Child Custody; Child Support; Divorce; Husband and Wife; Marriage, key numbers (⚷) 1ff
Encyclopedia: OJ: check Family Law §§ 1ff
Summary Overview: M-HLD: In the Ohio summary, check Family
Internet:
megalaw.com/oh/top/ohfamily.php
www.ohiobar.org/pub/lawfacts
www.ohiofcf.org

FRAUD

Statutes: RC §§ 1302.95, 1305.08, 2305.09, 2307.65, 4165.01
Regulations: AC §§ 109:4-1-06, 5101:3-1-29
Cases: OD: check Fraud, key numbers (⚷) 1ff
Encyclopedia: OJ: check Actions § 121, Criminal Law § 1390, Fraud and Deceit §§ 1ff
Summary Overview: M-HLD: In the Ohio summary under Debtor and Creditor, check Fraudulent Sales and Conveyances

Internet:
www.pickocc.org

GARNISHMENT

Statutes: RC §§ 124.10, 2715.091, 2716.01, 2716.03, 2716.11, 5111.121
Cases: OD: check Garnishment, key numbers (🔑) 1ff
Encyclopedia: OJ: check Appellate Review § 96, Creditors' Rights § 170, 190, 255, 256, 461, Decedents' Estates § 1781, Enforcement of Judgments §§ 513, 521, Family Law § 1243, Unemployment Compensation § 64
Summary Overview: M-HLD: In the Ohio summary under Debtor and Creditor, check Garnishment
Internet:
www.ohiolegalservices.org/OSLSA/PublicWeb/Library/Index/1290000/1290050/index_html

GOVERNMENT

Cases: OD: check the vols. for Municipal Corporations; Officers and Public Employees; States, key numbers (🔑) 1ff
Encyclopedia: OJ: check Counties §§ 1ff; Government Tort Liability §§ 1ff; State of Ohio §§ 1ff
Summary Overview: M-HLD: In the Ohio summary under Courts and Legislature; under Introduction, check Government and Legal System
Internet:
www.ohio.gov
megalaw.com/oh/top/ohconstitution.php

GUARDIANSHIP

Statutes: RC §§ 2111.08, 2111.46, 2111.50, 5122.39; Sup. R. Rule 66
Regulations: AC §§ 145-1-63, 3307-7-01, 5123-15-01
Cases: OD: check Guardian and Ward, key numbers (🔑) 1ff
Encyclopedia: OJ: check Decedents' Estates § 241; Family Law § 1493; Guardian and Ward §§ 1ff
Summary Overview: M-HLD: In the Ohio summary under Family, check Guardian and Ward
Internet:
www.ohiobar.org/pub/lawfacts
www.ddc.ohio.gov/Pub/Guardianship.pdf

ILLEGITIMACY

Statutes: RC §§ 2105.17, 2919.21(A)(2)
Regulations: AC §§ 3301-80-01(C)(3), 5101:9-6-80(J)(2)
Cases: OD: check Children Out-of-Wedlock, key numbers (🔑) 1ff
Encyclopedia: OJ: check Death § 67, Decedents' Estates §§ 86ff, 527, Family Law § 1013
Summary Overview: M-HLD: In the Ohio summary under Estates and Trusts, check Descent and Distribution (and Illegitimate Children under Descent)
Internet:
megalaw.com/oh/top/ohfamily.php
downloads.ohiobar.org/conres/lawandyou/Law_and_You_10.pdf
www.ohiolegalservices.org/OSLSA/PublicWeb/Library/Index/1370100

INJUNCTIONS

Statutes: RC §§ 715.30, 1345.07, 2712.15, 2727.02, 2907.37, 3710.14
Regulations: AC § §§ 4703-3-06, 4703:1-3-05
Cases: OD: check Injunction, key numbers (🔑) 1ff
Encyclopedia: OJ: check Injunctions §§ 1ff
Summary Overview: M-HLD: In the Ohio summary under Civil Actions and Procedure, check Injunctions
Internet:
megalaw.com/oh/top/ohcivpro.php
acc.ohio.gov/470118.html

INSURANCE

Statutes: RC §§ 121.081, 3901.01
Regulations: AC §§ 3901-1-01ff
Cases: OD: check Insurance, key numbers (🔑) 1ff
Encyclopedia: OJ: check Automobiles and Other Vehicles § 210, Insurance §§ 1ff
Summary Overview: M-HLD: In the Ohio summary, check Insurance
Internet:
www.ohioinsurance.gov

INTELLECTUAL PROPERTY

Statutes: RC §§ 1329.01, 1329.54, 1333.52, 2913.34, 4165.01
Cases: OD: check Copyrights and Intellectual Property, key numbers (🔑) 1ff
Encyclopedia: OJ: check Business Relationships § 806, Literary Property § 1, Patents §§ 1ff, Records and Recording § 30, Trade Regulation § 65, Trade Secrets §§ 1ff
Summary Overview: M-HLD: In the Ohio summary under Intellectual Property
Internet:
www.sos.state.oh.us/sos/businessservices/trade.aspx

LABOR RELATIONS

Statutes: RC §§ 4101.11, 4111.02, 4117.01
Cases: OD: check Labor and Employment, key numbers (🔑) 1ff
Encyclopedia: OJ: check Employment Relations §§ ff
Summary Overview: M-HLD: In the Ohio summary under Employment, check Labor Relations
Internet:
www.serb.state.oh.us
megalaw.com/oh/top/ohlabor.php

LANDLORD AND TENANT

Statutes: RC §§ 5321.01ff
Regulations: AC § § 4901:1-10-25
Cases: OD: check Landlord and Tenant, key numbers (🔑) 1ff
Encyclopedia: OJ: check Landlord and Tenant §§ 3ff, Premises Liability §§ 1ff
Summary Overview: M-HLD: In the Ohio summary under Property, check Landlord and tenant
Internet:
megalaw.com/oh/top/ohlandlord.php
www.ohiobar.org/pub/lawfacts
www.ci.lakewood.oh.us/law_tenantlaw.html

LEGAL SEPARATION

Statutes: RC §§ 145.571, 742.462, 3105.17, 3305.21; Rules of Civil Procedure Rule 75
Cases: OD: check Divorce, key numbers (🔑) 155ff
Encyclopedia: OJ: check Family Law §§ 323, 329, 450, 579, 602, 660, 707, 713, 721,
Summary Overview: M-HLD: In the Ohio summary under Family, check Divorce (and Grounds for Legal Separation under Divorce)
Internet:
megalaw.com/oh/top/ohfamily.php

LIMITED LIABILITY COMPANIES

Statutes: RC §§ 1705.01ff
Regulations: AC § 4141-1-04
Cases: OD: check Limited Liability Companies, key numbers (🔑) 1ff
Encyclopedia: OJ: check Businesses and Occupations § 136; Business Relationships §§ 1401, 1410
Summary Overview: M-HLD: In the Ohio summary under Business Organizations, check Limited Liability Companies
Internet:
clevelandlawlibrary.org/Public/Misc/REGUIDES/guide24.html
www.alllaw.com/state_resources/ohio/forms

MARRIAGE

Statutes: RC Ohio Const. Art. XV, § 11; §§ 2101.27, 3101.01, 3103.06, 3105.12, 4757.30
Regulations: AC §§ 145-2-35, 3309-1-20
Cases: OD: check Marriage, key numbers (🔑) 1ff
Encyclopedia: OJ: check Family Law §§ 3ff
Summary Overview: M-HLD: In the Ohio summary under Family, check Marriage
Internet:
megalaw.com/oh/top/ohfamily.php
www.ohiobar.org/pub/lawfacts

MEDIATION

Statutes: RC §§ 2710.03, 3109.052
Regulations: AC §§ 901:3-4-10, 4117-9-04, 4901:1-26-03, 5717-1-21
Cases: OD: check Child Custody, key numbers (🔑) 419ff
Encyclopedia: OJ: check Alternative Dispute Resolution §§ 11ff; Employment Relations § 558
Summary Overview: M-HLD: In the Ohio summary under Dispute Resolution, check Alternative Dispute Resolution
Internet:
www.sconet.state.oh.us/dispute_resolution/FAQ/default.asp
www.ohiobar.org/pub/lawfacts
crc.ohio.gov/mediation.htm
megalaw.com/oh/top/ohcivpro.php
megalaw.com/oh/top/ohlabor.php

MEDICAL MALPRACTICE

Statutes: RC §§ 2305.113, 3929.682, 3937.28
Cases: OD: check Health, key numbers (🔑) 600ff
Encyclopedia: OJ: check Insurance § 161, Malpractice §§ 37, 210.4
Internet:
www.med.ohio.gov
www.ohioinsurance.gov/agent/MedMal.htm
www.mcandl.com/ohio.html

MINERAL, WATER, AND FISHING RIGHTS

Statutes: RC §§ 155.011, 715.08, 1505.07, 1517.14, 1533.32, 1561.03
Regulations: AC §§ 901:11-2-16, 1501-2-05, 1501:3-5-03, 1501:17-3-04
Cases: OD: check Environmental Law; Mines and Minerals; Water ad Water Courses, key numbers (🔑) 1ff
Encyclopedia: OJ: check Fish & Game §§ 1ff, Water §§ 1ff
Summary Overview: M-HLD: In the Ohio summary check Mineral, Water, and Fishing Rights
Internet:
megalaw.com/oh/top/ohenvironmental.php
www.dnr.state.oh.us
www.dnr.state.oh.us/wildlife/default.htm
www.owda.org
www.dnr.state.oh.us/parks

MINORS

Statutes: RC §§ 341.11, 1339.39, 2111.46, 4109.03
Regulations: AC § 4101:9-2-02
Cases: OD: check Infants, key numbers (🔑) 1ff
Encyclopedia: OJ: check Criminal Law § 612, Family Law § 816, Guardian and Ward § 16, Names § 15
Summary Overview: M-HLD: In the Ohio summary under Family, check Infants

Internet:
megalaw.com/oh/top/ohfamily.php
www.nowyoure18.org
www.ohiobar.org/pub/lycu/index.asp?articleid=362
www.ohiobar.org/pub/lycu/index.asp?articleid=300

MORTGAGES

Statutes: RC §§ 317.19, 1151.54, 1322.062, 2113.47, 2323.07, 5301.04ff
Regulations: AC § 1301:9-2-21
Cases: OD: check Mortgages, key numbers (🔑) 1ff
Encyclopedia: OJ: check Creditors' Rights § 135, Mortgages §§ 1ff
Summary Overview: M-HLD: In the Ohio summary, check Mortgages
Internet:
www.ohiobar.org/pub/lycu/index.asp?articleid=156

MOTOR VEHICLES

Statutes: RC §§ 5501.03ff, 2913.82, 4511.01ff
Regulations: AC §§ 1501:3-4-02, 5537-6-01
Cases: OD: check Automobiles, key numbers (🔑) 1ff
Encyclopedia: OJ: check Automobiles and Other Vehicles § 219
Summary Overview: M-HLD: In the Ohio summary under Transportation, check Motor Vehicles
Internet:
www.dot.state.oh.us
www.statepatrol.ohio.gov
www.clelaw.lib.oh.us/Public/Misc/FAQs/Traffic_Parking.html

NEGLIGENCE

Statutes: RC §§ 1303.49, 1547.34, 2305.09, 4113.07, 4171.10
Cases: OD: check Negligence; Torts, key numbers (🔑) 1ff
Encyclopedia: OJ: check Malpractice §§ 1ff, Negligence §§ 1ff, Premises Liability §§ 1ff, Products Liability §§ 1ff
Internet:
www.law.csuohio.edu/lawlibrary/Torts_Resource_Guide.htm
www.ohiobar.org/pub/lycu/index.asp?articleid=242
downloads.ohiobar.org/conres/lawandyou/Law_and_You_5.pdf
www.ohiobar.org/pub/?articleid=104
(click "Torts")

NOTARY PUBLIC

Statutes: RC §§ 147.01ff
Cases: OD: check Notaries, key numbers (🔑) 1ff
Encyclopedia: OJ: check Acknowledgements §§ 52; Discovery and Depositions § 187
Summary Overview: M-HLD: In the Ohio summary under Documents and Records, check Notaries Public
Internet:
www.sos.state.oh.us/sos/info/notaryCommission.aspx
www.akronbar.org/contentindex.asp?ID=48
www.sos.state.oh.us/LawsNT/Read.aspx?ID=1

PARALEGALS

Statutes: RC §§ 173.12(A)(5), 5311.18(A)(1)(b)
Regulations: AC § 123:1-7-21
Cases: OD: check the vols. for Costs, key number (🔑) 194.18; Prisons, key number (🔑) 4(11)
Encyclopedia: OJ: check Attorneys at Law §§ 67, 69
Internet:
www.capohio.org
www.pacoparalegals.org
www.cincinnatiparalegals.org

PARTNERSHIPS

Statutes: RC §§ 1775.05ff, 1782.02
Regulations: AC §§ 4123-17-07, 4141-1-03, 5703-7-03
Cases: OD: check Partnership, key numbers (🔑) 1ff
Encyclopedia: OJ: check Attorneys at Law § 11; Businesses and Occupations § 136; Business Relationships § 1108
Summary Overview: M-HLD: In the Ohio summary under Business Organizations, check Partnerships

PLEADING

Statutes: RC Rules of Civil Procedure Rules 7ff; RC §§ 2743.13, 2941.11ff
Regulations: AC §§ 1513-3-09, 3517-1-07, 3702-2-03, 4901-1-02ff
Cases: OD: check Pleading, key numbers (🔑) 1ff
Encyclopedia: OJ: check Actions §§ 1ff, Parties §§ 1ff, Pleading §§ 1ff, Venue §§ 1ff
Summary Overview: M-HLD: In the Ohio summary under Civil Action and Procedure, check Pleading
Internet:
megalaw.com/oh/top/ohcivpro.php

POWER OF ATTORNEY

Statutes: RC §§ 317.41, 1337.01, 1337.11, 3109.52
Regulations: AC §§ 145-1-63, 3701-62-10, 4901:2-11-06
Cases: OD: check Principal and Agent, key numbers (🔑) 10ff
Encyclopedia: OJ: check Agency and Independent Contractors § 42; Deeds § 34; Family Law § 1062.1; Guardian and Ward § 86.1; Mortgages § 98
Summary Overview: M-HLD: In the Ohio summary under Property, check Power of Attorney
Internet:
www.ohiobar.org/pub/lawfacts

PRIVACY

Statutes: RC §§ 109.571, 2907.08, 3904.22
Regulations: AC §§ 3301-2-12, 4123-16-03, 4501:1-12-02
Cases: OD: check Constitutional Law, key numbers (🔑) 82.7, 274(5); Torts, key number (🔑) 8.5
Encyclopedia: OJ: check Attorneys at Law § 54; Constitutional Law § 505.5; Criminal Law § 120; Defamation and Privacy §§ 1ff; Hospitals and Health Care Providers § 113; Injunctions § 101
Internet:
www.hipaadvisory.com/regs/StateLaws.htm
www.ccao.org/Handbook/hdbkchap129.htm

PRIVILEGED COMMUNICATIONS

Statutes: RC §§ 102.021, 2317.02ff, 2933.58, 4732.19, 4931.35
Cases: OD: check Witnesses, key numbers (🔑) 184ff
Encyclopedia: OJ: check Evidence and Witnesses §§ 398, 758; Workers' Compensation § 370
Summary Overview: M-HLD: In the Ohio summary under Civil Actions and Procedure, check Evidence (and Privileged Communications under Evidence)

PRODUCTS LIABILITY

Statutes: RC §§ 2125.02, 2305.10, 2307.71, 2315.18
Cases: OD: check the vols. for Negligence; Products Liability; Torts, key numbers (🔑) 1ff
Encyclopedia: OJ: check Products Liability §§ 1ff
Internet:
www.atra.org/states/OH
www.law.csuohio.edu/lawlibrary/Torts_Resource_Guide.htm

PROPERTY DIVISION IN DIVORCE

Statutes: RC § 3105.171
Cases: OD: check Divorce, key numbers (🔑) 248ff
Encyclopedia: OJ: check Family Law §§ 460, 471ff, 809, Trusts § 254
Summary Overview: M-HLD: In the Ohio summary under Divorce (and Division of Property under Divorce)
Internet:
megalaw.com/oh/top/ohfamily.php
www.clelaw.lib.oh.us/Public/Misc/FAQs/SpousalSupport.html

REAL PROPERTY

Statutes: RC §§ 322.01, 2305.04, 5309.01ff
Regulations: AC §§ 1301:5-1-06ff
Cases: OD: check the vols. for Estates in Property; Property, key numbers (🔑) 1ff
Encyclopedia: OJ: check Brokers §§ 5ff, Property §§ 7ff, Premises Liability §§ 1ff
Summary Overview: M-HLD: In the Ohio summary under Property, check Real Property
Internet:
megalaw.com/oh/top/ohlandlord.php
www.com.state.oh.us/ODOC/real
www.law.csuohio.edu/lawlibrary/PropertyLawResourceGuide.htm

SERVICE OF PROCESS

Statutes: RC Rules of Civil Procedure Rule 4
Regulations: AC § 5101:12-30-10
Cases: OD: check Process, key numbers (🔑) 48ff
Encyclopedia: OJ: check Process §§ 11ff
Summary Overview: M-HLD: In the Ohio summary under Civil Actions and Procedure, check Process
Internet:
megalaw.com/oh/top/ohcivpro.php

STATUTE OF FRAUDS

Statutes: RC §§ 1301.12, 1302.04, 1308.07, 1310.08, 1335.01
Cases: OD: check Frauds, Statute of, key numbers (🔑) 1ff
Encyclopedia: OJ: check Conflict of Laws § 55, Sales and Exchanges § 23, Specific Performance § 18, Frauds, Statute of §§ 1ff
Summary Overview: M-HLD: In the Ohio summary under Business Regulation and Commerce, check Frauds, Statute of
Internet:
www.sconet.state.oh.us/Rules/civil/default.asp

STATUTE OF LIMITATIONS

Statutes: RC §§ 718.12, 1302.98, 1303.16, 1304.09, 1305.14, 2305.16
Cases: OD: check Limitation of Actions, key numbers (🔑) 1ff
Encyclopedia: OJ: check Limitations and Laches §§ 1ff
Summary Overview: M-HLD: In the Ohio summary under Civil Actions and Procedure, check Limitation of Actions
Internet:
megalaw.com/oh/top/ohcivpro.php

SUMMARY JUDGMENT

Statutes: RC Rules of Civil Procedure Rule 56
Cases: OD: check Judgment, key numbers (🔑) 178ff
Encyclopedia: OJ: check Judgments §§ 406, 515, Pleading §§ 181, 293
Summary Overview: M-HLD: In the Ohio summary under Civil Actions and Procedure, check Judgments (and Summary Judgments under Judgment)
Internet:
megalaw.com/oh/top/ohcivpro.php

SUMMONS

Statutes: RC Rules of Civil Procedure Rule 4
Cases: OD: check Process, key numbers (⚷) 10ff
Encyclopedia: OJ: check Criminal Law § 1694, Process §§ 11ff
Summary Overview: M-HLD: In the Ohio summary under Civil Actions and Procedure, check Process
Internet:
megalaw.com/oh/top/ohcivpro.php

TAXATION

Statutes: RC §§ 5703.01ff
Regulations: AC §§ 5703-1-01ff
Cases: OD: check Taxation, key numbers (⚷) 1ff
Encyclopedia: OJ: check Taxation §§1ff
Summary Overview: M-HLD: In the Ohio summary, check Taxation
Internet:
www.tax.ohio.gov
www.bta.ohio.gov
www.alllaw.com/state_resources/ohio/forms
strp.tripod.com/ohio.html

TORTS

Statutes: RC §§ 1309.402, 2305.38, 2307.22, 2307.96, 2315.21, 3746.25
Cases: OD: check the vols. for Negligence; Products Liability; Torts, key numbers (⚷) 1ff
Encyclopedia: OJ: check Actions § 15; Government Tort Liability §§ 1ff; Malpractice §§ 1ff; Negligence §§ 1ff; Premises Liability §§ 1ff; Products Liability §§ 1ff
Internet:
www.law.csuohio.edu/lawlibrary/Torts_Resource_Guide.htm
www.ohiobar.org/pub/lycu/index.asp?articleid=242
downloads.ohiobar.org/conres/lawandyou/Law_and_You_5.pdf
www.ohiobar.org/pub/?articleid=104
(click "Torts")

TRAFFIC LAWS

Statutes: RC §§ 4511.01ff
Regulations: AC §§ 1501:3-4-02, 5537-6-01
Cases: OD: check Automobiles, key numbers (⚷) 5ff
Encyclopedia: OJ: check Automobiles and Other Vehicles § 219
Internet:
www.ohiobar.org/pub/lawfacts
www.statepatrol.ohio.gov
www.clelaw.lib.oh.us/Public/Misc/FAQs/Traffic_Parking.html

TRUSTS

Statutes: RC §§ 109.23, 1109.06, 1111.01, 1335.01, 2107.63
Regulations: AC §§ 109:1-1-09, 111-11-35
Cases: OD: check Trusts, key numbers (⚷) 1ff
Encyclopedia: OJ: check Banks § 159; Charities § 3; Fiduciaries § 30; Trusts §§ 1ff
Summary Overview: M-HLD: In the Ohio summary, check Estates and Trusts
Internet:
megalaw.com/oh/top/ohprobate.php
www.law.csuohio.edu/lawlibrary/EstatesTrustsResourceGuide.htm

UNEMPLOYMENT INSURANCE

Statutes: RC §§ 4141.01ff
Regulations: AC §§ 4141-11-28, 5101:1-30-79
Cases: OD: check Social Security and Public Welfare, key numbers (⚷) 251ff
Encyclopedia: OJ: check Unemployment Compensation §§ 1ff
Summary Overview: M-HLD: In the Ohio summary under Employment, check Labor Relations (and Unemployment under Labor Relations)
Internet:
jfs.ohio.gov/ouc
megalaw.com/oh/top/ohlabor.php
www.jfs.ohio.gov/ouc/ucBen/index.stm
www.odjfs.state.oh.us/forms/pdf/55213.pdf

VENUE

Statutes: RC §§ 2901.12, 2931.29, 3105.62, 3115.56, 4515.01; Rules of Civil Procedure Rules 3, 18
Cases: OD: check Venue, key numbers (⚷) 1ff
Encyclopedia: OJ: check Actions §§ 1ff, Pleading §§ 1ff, Trial §§ 1ff, Venue §§ 1ff
Summary Overview: M-HLD: In the Ohio summary under Civil Actions and Procedure, check Venue
Internet:
megalaw.com/oh/top/ohcivpro.php

WATER RIGHTS

Statutes: RC §§ 715.08, 971.14, 1517.14, 6101.24
Regulations: AC §§ 1501-2-05
Cases: OD: check Waters and Water Courses, key numbers (⚷) 1ff
Encyclopedia: OJ: check Agriculture and Crops § 17, Fish & Game §§ 1ff, Sanitary & Sewer Districts §§ 1ff, Water §§ 1ff
Summary Overview: M-HLD: In the Ohio summary, check Mineral, Water, and Fishing Rights
Internet:
megalaw.com/oh/top/ohenvironmental.php
www.dnr.state.oh.us
www.owda.org

WILLS

Statutes: RC §§ 2107.02ff
Cases: OD: check Wills, key numbers (🔑) 1ff
Encyclopedia: OJ: check Decedents' Estates §§ 52, 216
Summary Overview: M-HLD: In the Ohio summary under Estates and Trusts, check Wills
Internet:
megalaw.com/oh/top/ohprobate.php
www.ohiobar.org/pub/lawfacts
www.law.csuohio.edu/lawlibrary/EstatesTrusts ResourceGuide.htm

WORKERS' COMPENSATION

Statutes: RC §§ 4121.01, 4121.30, 4123.51
Regulations: AC §§ 4123-3-01, 4123-14-06
Cases: OD: check Workers' Compensation, key numbers (🔑) 1ff
Encyclopedia: OJ: check Employment Relations § 8
Summary Overview: M-HLD: In the Ohio summary under Employment, check Workers' Compensation
Internet:
megalaw.com/oh/top/ohlabor.php
www.ohiobwc.com/worker/programs/claiminfo
www.ohiobwc.com/basics/guidedtour/default.asp

E. More Information on Ohio Law

(See also section 5.1 on Ohio legal research.)
www.megalaw.com/oh/oh.php
www.uakron.edu/law/library/olrlinks.php
www.romingerlegal.com/state/ohio.html
www.law.uc.edu/library/guideohlaw.html
www.utlaw.edu/students/lawlibrary/ohio.htm
www.ll.georgetown.edu/states/ohio.cfm
www.law.csuohio.edu/lawlibrary/stategov.html
www.clelaw.lib.oh.us/Public/Misc/REGUIDES/guide29.html

F. Something to Check

One of the ways that law firms try to attract clients is to provide law summaries and overviews on their Web sites. Pick any two topics covered in this section (e.g., adoption, limited liability companies). For each topic, find three Ohio law firm Web sites that provide summaries or overviews of Ohio law on the topic. Compare the quality and quantity of what you learn about the law at each site. To locate the law firms, go to any search engine (e.g., *www.google.com*) and type in Ohio, law or lawyer, and your topic.

Examples:
Ohio law adoption
Ohio lawyer adoption

5.6 Self-Help Resources

A. Introduction

Where do Ohio citizens go when they are representing themselves but would still like some assistance? Such individuals are sometimes said to be engaged in "self-help." They are proceeding pro se, or acting on their own behalf. (Another meaning of self-help is to take steps to obtain redress outside the legal system.) It is useful to know about self-help resources for two main reasons. First, a law office will sometimes refer citizens to self-help materials when the office cannot provide representation. Second, self-help resources often provide excellent overviews of the law that everyone should know about. Even if people have attorney representation, they may sometimes consult self-help materials in order to be able to communicate with their attorneys more intelligently.

For related sections, see:

- 4.2 State Courts in Ohio
- 5.1 Ohio State Legal Research
- 5.5 Research Starters
- 5.7 Public Records Research
- 6.1 Timeline: Civil Case
- 6.4 Timeline: Criminal Case

B. A Caution from the Bar About Free Consumer Legal Information

A great deal of information about the law is available from many sources. The Ohio State Bar Association has issued the following caution about using such info:

> "General legal information does not replace an attorney's services. First, you can't assume the legal information you are getting is accurate and complete. A legal decision based upon inaccurate or incomplete information is unlikely to be a sound decision. Assuming the information is accurate, legal information

found...on Web sites can be very helpful, particularly in raising questions and providing background for legal issues consumers are likely to encounter. The more you understand about the law and the legal system, the better. However, the law is very complex and each situation is unique. Free legal information is necessarily general—'one size fits all.' By contrast, an attorney provides legal advice to a specific client with specific needs and wishes. While 'consumer' legal information you obtain may be accurate in general, it may not be accurate when applied to your particular case. However, if you have become somewhat knowledgeable about the area of law affecting your personal situation, your communications with your lawyer likely will be enhanced."

What You Should Know about the Value of "Free" Legal Information
(www.ohiobar.org/pub/lycu/index.asp?articleid=169).

C. General Resources

Self-Help Public Law Library
866-LAW OHIO (866-529-6446)
www.ohiolegalservices.org/OSLSA/PublicWeb/Library

Public Education on the Law
www.ohiobar.org/pub/lycu

Ohio State Bar Foundation: The Law and You
www.ohiobar.org/pub/?articleid=276

Self-Help: Representing Yourself in Court
www.ohiolegalservices.org/OSLSA/PublicWeb/Library/Index/2010000/2010004/index_html

D. Specific Areas of Ohio Law

Adoption Law Self-Help
www.ohiobar.org/pub/lycu/index.asp?articleid=181

Business Law Self-Help
downloads.ohiobar.org/conres/lawandyou/Law_and_You_7.pdf
www.ohiobar.org/pub/?articleid=104
(click "Business Organizations, Contracts and Bankruptcy")

Consumer Rights Self-Help
www.ohiolegalservices.org/OSLSA/PublicWeb/Library/Index/1090000

Contract Law Self-Help
downloads.ohiobar.org/conres/lawandyou/Law_and_You_6.pdf
www.ohiobar.org/pub/lycu/index.asp?articleid=218
www.ohiobar.org/pub/?articleid=104
(click "Business Organizations, Contracts and Bankruptcy")

Criminal Law and Records Self-Help
downloads.ohiobar.org/conres/lawandyou/Law_and_You_4.pdf
homepages.moeller.org/nowyoure18/criminal_charges.htm
www.ohiobar.org/pub/?articleid=104
(click "Criminal Law")

Disabilities Law Self-Help
olrs.ohio.gov/ASP/HomePage.asp
www.ohiobar.org/pub/lycu/index.asp?articleid=405

Discrimination Self-Help
www.ohiobar.org/pub/lycu/index.asp?articleid=310
www.ohiolegalservices.org/OSLSA/PublicWeb/Library/Index/1290000
(click "Discrimination")

Divorce, Custody, Support Self-Help
www.ohiobar.org/pub/?articleid=104
(click "Family Law")
downloads.ohiobar.org/conres/lawandyou/Law_and_You_10.pdf
www.divorcesource.com/OH/index.shtml
www.custodysource.com/oh~1.htm
www.divorcelawinfo.com/states/ohio/ohio.htm
homepages.moeller.org/nowyoure18/marriage.htm

Domestic Violence Self-Help
www.ohiodvresources.org
www.ohiolegalservices.org/OSLSA/PublicWeb/Library/Index/1370100

Education Law Self-Help
www.ohiobar.org/pub/lycu/index.asp?articleid=389
www.ohiolegalservices.org/OSLSA/PublicWeb/Library/Index/1110000

Employment Law Self-Help
downloads.ohiobar.org/conres/lawandyou/Law_and_You_11.pdf
www.ohiobar.org/pub/?articleid=104
(click "Workplace Law")
www.ohiolegalservices.org/OSLSA/PublicWeb/Library/Index/1290000

Estate Planning Self-Help
www.ohiobar.org/pub/lycu/index.asp?articleid=370
www.ohiobar.org/pub/lycu/index.asp?articleid=60
www.ohiolegalservices.org/OSLSA/PublicWeb/Library/Index/1950000

Family Law Self-Help
downloads.ohiobar.org/conres/lawandyou/Law_and_You_10.pdf

Foreclosure Law Self-Help
www.ohiobar.org/pub/lycu/index.asp?articleid=156
www.ohiobar.org/pub/lycu/index.asp?articleid=155
www.ohiolegalservices.org/OSLSA/PublicWeb/Library/Index/1690000

Healthcare, Nursing Care, and Medicaid Self-Help
www.ohiobar.org/pub/lycu/index.asp?articleid=279
www.ohiobar.org/pub/lycu/index.asp?articleid=393
www.ohiobar.org/pub/lycu/index.asp?articleid=78
www.ohiobar.org/pub/lycu/index.asp?articleid=216
www.ohiolegalservices.org/OSLSA/PublicWeb/Library/Index/1590000

Landlord-Tenant and Real Estate Law Self-Help
downloads.ohiobar.org/conres/lawandyou/Law_and_You_8.pdf
www.ci.lakewood.oh.us/law_tenantlaw.html
www.ohiolegalservices.org/OSLSA/PublicWeb/Library/Index/1690000
www.ohiobar.org/pub/lycu/index.asp?articleid=407
www.ohiobar.org/pub/lycu/index.asp?articleid=408
www.ohiolegalservices.org/OSLSA/PublicWeb/Library/Documents/1036684804.23/ProSeAnswer.pdf

Negligence and Other Torts
www.ohiobar.org/pub/lycu/index.asp?articleid=242
downloads.ohiobar.org/conres/lawandyou/Law_and_You_5.pdf
www.ohiobar.org/pub/?articleid=104
(click "Torts")

Probate Self-Help
downloads.ohiobar.org/conres/lawandyou/Law_and_You_9.pdf
www.ohiolegalservices.org/OSLSA/PublicWeb/Library/Index/1950000
www.ohiobar.org/pub/?articleid=104
(click "Probate Law")

Tax Law Self-Help
www.ohiobar.org/pub/lycu/index.asp?articleid=60
www.ohiolegalservices.org/OSLSA/PublicWeb/Library/Index/1290000
(click "Taxes, Social Security and Other Information")

Unemployment Compensation Self-Help
(see also section 1.9)
www.ohiobar.org/pub/lycu/index.asp?articleid=307
www.ohiolegalservices.org/OSLSA/PublicWeb/Library/Index/1710000
(click "Unemployment Compensation")

Utilities Law Self-Help
www.ohiobar.org/pub/lycu/index.asp?articleid=270
www.ohiobar.org/pub/lycu/index.asp?articleid=94
www.ohiolegalservices.org/OSLSA/PublicWeb/Library/Index/1690000
(click "Utilities")

Young Adults (Becoming 18) Self-Help
www.nowyoure18.org
www.ohiobar.org/pub/lycu/index.asp?articleid=362
www.ohiobar.org/pub/lycu/index.asp?articleid=300

"Welfare" (Government Benefits) Self-Help
www.ohiolegalservices.org/OSLSA/PublicWeb/Library/Index/1710000
Wills Self-Help
downloads.ohiobar.org/conres/lawandyou/Law_and_You_9.pdf
www.ohiolegalservices.org/OSLSA/PublicWeb/Library/Index/1950000
www.ohiobar.org/pub/lycu/index.asp?articleid=277
www.ohiobar.org/pub/?articleid=104
(click "Probate Law")

Workers' Compensation Self-Help Law
(see also section 1.10)
www.ohiobar.org/pub/lycu/index.asp?articleid=137
www.ohiobar.org/pub/lycu/index.asp?articleid=141

E. Links on Court and Law Library Web Sites

On a court's Web site you will often find court forms that can be used for particular kinds of cases. The sites will usually give you the online text of the local court rules that must be followed when proceeding pro se. Also check the information given on the FAQ (frequently asked questions) pages on a court's site.

Web Sites of Ohio Courts
(see also section 4.2)
www.sconet.state.oh.us/web_sites/courts

Ohio Court Web Sites with Pro Se Forms/Court Rules
www.ohiolegalservices.org/OSLSA/PublicWeb/Library/Index/2010000/2010004/index_html

Law library Web sites also frequently link to online information on Ohio law and procedure that is relevant to persons needing self-help resources. See, for example, the forms resources page on the site of the Cincinnati Law Library Association:
www.hamilton-co.org/cinlawlib/resources/forms.html

For a list of law libraries throughout Ohio, see section 5.8.

F. More Information

SelfHelp.Org
www.selfhelpsupport.org
www.selfhelpsupport.org/resourcesforselfrepresent378.cfm

ABA Legal Information Resources
www.abalawinfo.org
www.abanet.org/legalservices/findlegalhelp/main.cfm?id=OH

LawHelp.Org
www.lawhelp.org

Nolo Press Self-Help Law Center
www.nolo.com

Yahoo Self-Help Resources
dir.yahoo.com/Government/Law/Self_Help

Legal Information Law Institute
www.law.cornell.edu/index.html

FindForms
www.findforms.com
(type "ohio" in the search box)

City Legal Guide
www.citylegalguide.com
(click "Ohio" on the map)

Protecting Your Rights
www.atlanet.org/pressroom/Links.aspx

Guide to Self-Help Law Books
moritzlaw.osu.edu/library/assistance/selfhelp.pdf

G. Something to Check

1. Find online self-help information on collecting child support in Ohio.
2. Find online self-help information on suing your neighbor in Ohio for damage done to a common fence.

5.7 Public Records Research

A. Introduction

There are a large variety of public records that a law firm may seek to obtain. For example:

Business Records

Corporations	Sales Tax Registrations
Fictitious Names	Tax Liens
Limited Liability Companies	Trademarks and Service Marks
Partnerships	UCC Filings

Individual Records

Accident Reports	Divorce
Bankruptcies	Marriage
Birth	Occupational Licenses
Court Judgments (Civil)	Vehicle Ownership
Criminal Records	Workers' Compensation Claims
Death	

Access to these records varies. Some are available to the general public, while others are subject to substantial restrictions.

This section will provide starting points in finding out what is available. Some of the Internet sites and phone numbers in this section will give you complete access to the records involved. Others will simply help you can make inquiries about what might be available.

B. Search Resources

Accident Reports
(see also Repair Shop)
Department of Public Safety
614-752-1583
statepatrol.ohio.gov/crash.htm
crsweb.dps.state.oh.us/crashreports/index.asp

Accountants (license records)
614-466-4135
acc.ohio.gov/lookup.html
license.ohio.gov/lookup/default.asp
(under Division, select "Accountancy Board")

Acupuncturists (license records)
614-466-3934
www.med.ohio.gov
med.ohio.gov/ACUsubwebindex.htm
license.ohio.gov/lookup/default.asp
(under Division, select "Medical Board", under Profession/Institution, select "Acupuncturist")

Alcohol Beverage Control (license records)
Liquor Control Commission
877-464-6677
www.lcc.ohio.gov

Liquor Permit Holders
www.liquorcontrol.ohio.gov/liquor5.htm

Anesthesiologist Assistants (license records)
614-466-3934
www.med.ohio.gov
license.ohio.gov/lookup/default.asp
(under Division, select "Medical Board", under Profession, select "Anesthesiologist Assistant")

Appraisers (license records)
(see Land)

Architects (license records)
614-466-2316
Board of Examiners of Architects
www.arc.ohio.gov
license.ohio.gov/lookup/default.asp
(under Division, select "Architects Board")

Athletic Therapists (license records)
(see Physical Therapists)

Attorney General Opinions
www.ag.state.oh.us/sections/opinions/ag_opinions.htm

Attorneys (license records)
800-826-9010; 614-387-9000
www.sconet.state.oh.us
(click "Attorney Directory" under Attorney Information)

Audiologists (license records)
614-466-3145
slpaud.ohio.gov
slpaud.ohio.gov/lv.htm
license.ohio.gov/lookup/default.asp
(under Division, select "Speech Pathology & Audiology")

Audit Reports
Ohio Auditor of State
800-282-0370
www.auditor.state.oh.us
www.auditor.state.oh.us/Public/AuditSearch/default.aspx

Banks
(see Financial Institutions)

Barbers (license records)
614-466-5003
barber.ohio.gov
license.ohio.gov/lookup/default.asp
(under Division, select "Ohio State Barber Board")

Birth Records
Department of Health
614-466-2531
www.odh.state.oh.us/vitalstatistics/vitalstats.aspx
winslo.state.oh.us/services/genealogy/slogenebir.html
www.cdc.gov/nchs/howto/w2w/ohio.htm
www.vitalrec.com/oh.html

Brokers
(see Land)

Business Records (filings)
(Corporations, Limited Liability Companies, Limited Partnerships)
Secretary of State
614-466-2655
www.sos.state.oh.us/sos/businessservices/corp.aspx
www.sos.state.oh.us/sos/businessservices/corp.aspx?Section=104

Campaigns
See Elections

Cemetery Registration Records
614-466-4100
www.com.state.oh.us/odoc/real

Chiropractors (license records)
888-772-1384
chirobd.ohio.gov/mission.htm
license.ohio.gov/lookup/default.asp
(under Division, select "Chiropractic Board")

Contractors (license records)
614-644-3493
www.com.state.oh.us/dic
www.contractors-license.org/oh/Ohio.html

Corporations Records
Secretary of State
614-466-3910
www.sos.state.oh.us/sos/businessservices/corp.aspx

Cosmetic Therapists (license records)
614-466-3934
www.med.ohio.gov
license.ohio.gov/lookup/default.asp
(under Division, select "Medical Board", under Profession, select "Cosmetic Therapist")

Cosmetologists (license records)
Board of Cosmetology
614-466-3834
www.cos.ohio.gov
license.ohio.gov/lookup/default.asp
(under Division, select "Cosmetology Board")

Counselors (license records)
(see Social Workers)

County Profiles/Statistics
www.statelocalgov.net/state-oh.htm
www.epodunk.com/counties/oh_county.html
en.wikipedia.org/wiki/List_of_counties_in_Ohio

Courts (federal courts in Ohio)
(see also section 4.3)
www.ca6.uscourts.gov
www.uscourts.gov/courtlinks/index.cfm
(click the map of Ohio)

Courts (state)
(see also section 4.2)
www.sconet.state.oh.us
www.sconet.state.oh.us/Web_Sites/courts
www.govengine.com/stategov/ohio.html
www.sconet.state.oh.us/District_Courts

Court Opinions
www.sconet.state.oh.us/rod/newpdf

Credit Unions
See Financial Institutions

Crime Statistics
614-466-1830
www.crimestats.ohio.gov
www.ojp.usdoj.gov/bjs/sandlle.htm

Criminal Records/Civilian Background Checks
(see also Inmates, Sex offenders)
Bureau of Criminal Identification and Investigation
614-466-4320
www.ag.state.oh.us/sections/bci/identification_division.htm

Day Care Facilities, Licensed
gis1.odjfs.state.oh.us

Death Records
614-466-2531
www.odh.state.oh.us/vitalstatistics/vitalstats.aspx
winslo.state.oh.us/services/genealogy/slogenebir.html
www.cdc.gov/nchs/howto/w2w/ohio.htm
www.vitalrec.com/oh.html
www.funeral.ohio.gov/edrs.stm

Dentists; Dental Hygienists/Assistants (license records)
614-466-2580
Ohio State Dental Board
www.dental.ohio.gov
license.ohio.gov/lookup/default.asp
(under Division, select "Dental Board")

Dieticians (license records)
614-466-3291
dietetics.ohio.gov
license.ohio.gov/lookup/default.asp
(under Division, select "Ohio Board of Dietetics")

Divorce/Dissolution Records
www.odh.state.oh.us/vitalstatistics/mrgdiv.aspx
(contact the County Clerk of Court)
www.occaohio.com/clerkphonedir.htm

Doctors License and Discipline Records
(see also Dentists)
614-466-3934
www.med.ohio.gov
www.med.ohio.gov/consumers.htm#Section_14
license.ohio.gov/lookup/default.asp
(under Division, select "Medical Board")

Elections
County Boards of Election
www.sos.state.oh.us/sos/ElectionsVoter/OhioElections.aspx?Section=boeDir
Secretary of State; Election Results
www.sos.state.oh.us/sos/ElectionsVoter/electionResults.aspx
Ohio Elections Commission
614-466-3205
elc.ohio.gov

Embalmers
(see Funeral Directors)

Engineers (license records)
877-OHIO-ENG
www.ohiopeps.org/files/license_lookup.html

Family Therapists (license records)
(see Social Workers)

Fictitious Name Records
Secretary of State
877-767-6446
www.sos.state.oh.us/sos/businessservices/corp.aspx?Section=104

Financial Institutions
(banks, credit unions, savings and loan associations, small loan businesses)
Department of Commerce, Financial Institutions Division
614-728-8400; 866-278-0003
www.com.state.oh.us/dfi
www.com.state.oh.us/license.htm
www.com.state.oh.us/dfi/consumeraffairs.htm

Foreclosure Records
ffs.cc/state?state=OH&rsp=5610

Funeral Directors (license records)
Board of Embalmers and Funeral Directors
614-466-4252
www.funeral.ohio.gov

Government Records, Agency Retention Schedule
www.gsd.das.state.oh.us/rims/default/default.asp

Inmates and Offender Search
Ohio Department of Rehabilitation and Correction
www.brbpub.com/pubrecsitesStates.asp
www.drc.state.oh.us

Inmates on Death Row in Ohio
www.drc.state.oh.us/Public/deathrow.htm

Insurance
Ohio Department of Insurance
800-686-1526
www.ohioinsurance.gov
Authorized Insurance Companies
www.ohioinsurance.gov/company/authlist.asp

Insurance Agent/Agency Records
www.ohioinsurance.gov
(click "Agent/Agency Locator" and "Agent & Agency Services")

Labor Unions in Ohio
www.xpdnc.com/links/lousoh.html

Land
Landaccess
(documents in a county recorder's or clerk's office)
www.landaccess.com
Nonresident Alien Land Registration Records
www.sos.state.oh.us/sos/electionsvoter/nonResAlienLand.aspx#
Real Estate Agent License Records
Real Estate Appraiser License Records
Real Estate and Professional Licensing Division
614-466-4100
www.com.state.oh.us/odoc/real
www.com.state.oh.us/real/elicense.aspx

Legislature (bill information)
800-282-0253; 614-466-8842
www.legislature.state.oh.us/search.cfm

Limited Liability Company; Limited Partnership
(see Business)

Liquor
(see Alcohol)

Lobbyists, Registered
614-728-5100
Office of Legislative the Inspector General
www.jlec-olig.state.oh.us

Marriage Records
www.odh.state.oh.us/vitalstatistics/mrgdiv.aspx
(contact the county probate court)
www.franklincountyohio.gov/probate/ohio_judges.cfm

Mechanotherapists (license records)
614-466-3934
www.med.ohio.gov
license.ohio.gov/lookup/default.asp
(under Division, select "Medical Board", under Profession, select "Mecanotherapist")

Massage Therapists (license records)
614-466-3934
www.med.ohio.gov
license.ohio.gov/lookup/default.asp
(under Division, select "Medical Board", under Profession, select "Massage Therapist")

Ministers (license records)
(those authorized to perform marriages)
www.sos.state.oh.us/sos/ElectionsVoter/ministers.aspx

Mortgage Brokers, Licensed
866-278-0003; 614-728-8400
www.com.state.oh.us/ODOC/dfi

Motor Vehicle Records
(see Vehicles)

Nonprofit Organization Filings
www.sos.state.oh.us/sos/businessservices/nonprof.aspx

Notary Public Registration Records
614-644-4559
www.sos.state.oh.us/sos/info/notaryCommission.aspx

Nurses (license records)
Board of Nursing
614-466-3947
www.nursing.ohio.gov
www.nursing.ohio.gov/Verification.stm
license.ohio.gov/lookup/default.asp
(under Division, select "Ohio Board of Nursing")

Nursing Homes Inspection Reports
www.ltcohio.org/consumer/index.asp

Occupational Therapists (license records)
(see Physical Therapists)

Offenders
(see sex offender, inmates, and offenders)

Opticians (license records)
614-466-9709
optical.ohio.gov
license.ohio.gov/lookup/default.asp
(under Division, select "Optical Dispensers Board")

Optometrists (license records)
888-565-3044; 614-466-5115
optometry.ohio.gov
license.ohio.gov/lookup/default.asp
(under Division, select "Optometry Board")

Orthotists (license records)
(see Prosthetist)

Partnerships
(see Business)

Pedorthists (license records)
(see Prosthetist)

Pharmacists (license records)
Board of Pharmacy
641-466-4143
pharmacy.ohio.gov/index.htm

Physical Therapists (license records)
614-466-3774
otptat.ohio.gov
license.ohio.gov/lookup/default.asp
(under Division, select "Occ Therapy, Phys Therapy, & Athletic Trainers Board")

Physician
(see Dentists, Doctors)

Physician Assistants (license records)
614-466-3934
www.med.ohio.gov
license.ohio.gov/lookup/default.asp
(under Division, select "Medical Board", under Profession, select "Physician Assistant")

Police Departments
www.usacops.com/oh
www.the911site.com/911pd/ohio.shtml

Prisoners
(see Inmates)

Probate Courts
(see also Courts)
www.franklincountyohio.gov/probate/ohio_judges.cfm

Prosthetist (license records)
614-466-1157
www.opp.ohio.gov
license.ohio.gov/lookup/default.asp
(under Division, select "Orthotics, Prosthetics and Pedorthics Board")

Psychologists (license records)
614-466-8808
www.psychology.ohio.gov

license.ohio.gov/lookup/default.asp
(under Division, select "Psychology Board")

Putative Fathers Registry
888-313-3100
jfs.ohio.gov/pfr

Real Estate
(see Land)

Recorders, County
www.ohiorecorders.com

Religion
(see Ministers)

Repair Shop (Collision) (license records)
614-995-0714
www.collisionboard.ohio.gov
license.ohio.gov/lookup/default.asp
(under Division, select "Collision Repair Board")

Respiratory Care Practitioner (license records)
614-752-9218
respiratorycare.ohio.gov
license.ohio.gov/lookup/default.asp
(under Division, select "Respiratory Care Board")

Sanitarians (license records)
(environmental health workers)
614-466-1772
sanitarian.ohio.gov
license.ohio.gov/lookup/default.asp
(under Division, select "Sanitarian Board")

Savings & Loan Associations
(see Financial Institutions)

Secretary of State Records
614-466-2655
www.sos.state.oh.us

Securities Filings
614-644-7381
Department of Commerce, Securities Division
www.securities.state.oh.us
www.securities.state.oh.us/secu_apps/offering

Service Marks
(see Trademarks)

Sex Offender Records
866-40-OHLEG
Ohio's Electronic Sex Offender Registration and Notification (eSORN)
www.esorn.ag.state.oh.us/Secured/p1.aspx
www.esorn.ag.state.oh.us/Secured/p21_2.aspx
www.sexcriminals.com/registration-notification/us/ohio

Sheriff Offices (by county)
www.megalaw.com/oh/ohenforce.php
pickawaysheriff.com
(click "Ohio Sheriff's")

Social Worker (license records)
614-466-0912
www.cswmft.ohio.gov
license.ohio.gov/lookup/default.asp
(under Division, select "Counselor, Social Worker & Marriage & Family Therapist Bd")

Speech Language Pathologist (license records)
614-466-3145
slpaud.ohio.gov
slpaud.ohio.gov/lv.htm
license.ohio.gov/lookup/default.asp
(under Division, select "Speech Pathology and Audiology")

Surveyors (license records)
877-OHIO-ENG
www.ohiopeps.org/files/license_lookup.html

Therapists (license records)
(see Cosmetic Therapists, Massage Therapists, Mechanotherapists, Physical Therapists, Speech Language Pathologists)

Trademarks and Service Marks
www.sos.state.oh.us/sos/businessservices/trade.aspx

UCC
(see Uniform Commercial Code)

Unclaimed Property Records
Division of Unclaimed Funds
614-466-4433
www.com.state.oh.us/unfd
www.unclaimedfundstreasurehunt.ohio.gov

Uniform Commercial Code Filings
Secretary of State
614-466-3910
www.sos.state.oh.us/sos/ucc/UCC.aspx?Section=101

Vehicles
Bureau of Motor Vehicles
Driving Records
www.dmv.org/oh-ohio/driving-records.php

Motor Vehicle History Report
614-752-7500
ohiobmv.com
www.dmv.org/vehicle-history.php
www.dmv.org/vehicle-history-report.php

Vehicle and Watercraft Title Records
614-752-7671
www.dps.state.oh.us/atps

Vital Records
(see Birth, Death, Divorce, Marriage)
614-466-2531

Veterinarians (license records)
614-644-5281
ovmlb.ohio.gov

ovmlb.ohio.gov/licensing.htm
https://license.ohio.gov/lookup/default.asp
(under Division, select "Veterinary Medical Board")

Watercraft Title Records
(see Vehicles)

Workers' Compensation Records (look-ups)
800-OHIO-BWC
www.ohiobwc.com

C. More Information

State Archives
614-297-2510
www.ohiohistory.org/resource/archlib
www.ohiohistory.org/ar_tools.html

Provides access to the historic records of state government and some local governments. Records include older constitutions, legislative records, election records, case files and administrative records of the courts, etc. Genealogical resources provided for the following kinds of records:

Birth	Marriage
Census	Military
Death	Naturalization
Land Entry	

Ohio Public Records Act (PRA)
The PRA is similar to the federal Freedom of Information Act. The purpose of these acts is to give private citizens greater access to government information. With some exceptions, the PRA considers all records maintained by most state agencies to be public records, but also recognizes the right to individual privacy.
Revised Code § 149.43
www.ohiohistory.org/resource/lgr/databaseguidelines.html

Open Government Guide
www.rcfp.org/ogg/index.php
(click "Ohio")

Ohio Public Library Information Network
www.oplin.lib.oh.us

BP Free Access to Government Records
www.brbpub.com/pubrecsitesStates.asp
(click "Ohio")

Westlaw
www.westlaw.com

Examples of public records databases: People Finder-Person Tracker, Name Tracker, Telephone Tracker, Address Alert, Skip Tracer, Social Security Number Alert, Death Records, Professional Licenses; People Finder Plus Assets Library-Combined Asset Locator, Aircraft Registration Records, Watercraft Registration Records, Stock Locater Records, Motor Vehicle Registration Records, Real Property Assessor Records, Real Property Transactions; People Finder, Assets Plus Adverse Filings Library—Combined Adverse Filings, Bankruptcy Records, UCC, Liens/Civil Judgment Filings, Uniform Commercial Code Filings, Liens/Civil Judgment Filings; Public Records Library—U.S. Business Finder Records, Corporate and Limited Partnership Records, "Doing Business As" Records, Litigation Preparation Records, Executive Affiliation Records, Name Availability Records

Lexis, LexisNexis
www.lexis.com
www.lexisnexis.com

Examples of public records databases: Bankruptcy Filings, Business Locators, Corporate Filings (Business and Corporate Information, Limited Partnership Information, Fictitious Business Name Information, Franchise Index), Civil and Criminal Court Filings, Judgments and Liens (Including UCC and State Tax Liens), Jury Verdicts and Settlements, Professional Licenses Information, Person Locators (Military Locator, Voter Registration Record Information from 26 states, Social Security Death Records from 1962, Inmate Records from six states, Criminal History Records from 37 states), Personal Property Records (including Aircraft Registrations, Boat Registrations, Motor Vehicle Registrations from 20 states), Real Property Records (Deed Transfers, Tax Assessor Records, Mortgage Records).

Other Major Public Records Search Sites and Resources
www.brbpub.com
www.publicrecordfinder.com/states/ohio.html
www.50states.com/publicrecords/ohio.htm
www.netronline.com/frameset.asp?StateID=37
www.searchsystems.net
www.virtualchase.com/topics/introduction_public_records.shtml
www.oatis.com/publicrecords.htm
www.pretrieve.com
www.vitalchek.com

D. Something to Check

1. In the Yellow Pages, select three people or businesses in three different categories of services that probably require a license in Ohio (e.g., contractor, funeral home). Go to the Web site for each service.
   a. What kinds of information are available about that service?
   b. What information can you find about the three people or businesses you selected, e.g., were you able to verify that the person or business has a current valid license?
2. Go to a search site that allows you to find public records on individuals (e.g., *www.pretrieve.com*). Type in someone's name (e.g., your own) to find out what public records are available online.

A. Introduction

Elsewhere in this handbook we cover the extensive online availability of Ohio law (see section 5.1). In this section we present an overview of traditional bricks-and-mortar libraries where books are on shelves, often in addition to online materials. Here are some of the major options:

Federal Depository Libraries (FDL)

A federal depository library (FDL) is a public or private library that receives free federal government publications. The library must give the general public access to these publications, which include federal statutes, regulations, and court opinions. If the library is private, e.g., a private university library, the public's right of free access may be limited to those publications which the library receives from the federal government. The private library has the right to prevent the public from using the rest of its collection.

County Law Libraries (CLL)

There are many county law libraries (CLLs) in Ohio. Some are large facilities to which the general public has access, either without charge or by paying a membership fee. The use of others is limited to judges and attorneys of the county. Many county law libraries are relatively small and are stored in the offices of private attorneys.

State Depository Library (SDL)

A state depository library (SDL) is a library that receives legislative materials ("pamphlet laws") from the Ohio state legislature. These libraries sometimes also receive special reports from state administrative agencies. (For a list of Ohio depository libraries, see *winslo.state.oh.us/govinfo/govt_c.html.*) The goal of this distribution is to disseminate such materials among the general public.

Your Neighborhood Public Library

In the card or online catalog of your neighborhood public library, find out (1) what legal materials it has on its shelves, and (2) how current (up-to-date) any particular legal material is. In the catalog, check entries under Ohio law. Here are examples of what you *might* find:

Ohio Jurisprudence 3d

Page's Ohio Revised Code Annotated

Baldwin's Ohio Legislative Service Annotated

Ohio Administrative Code

Baldwin's Ohio Township Law: Text and Forms

The Ohio Basic Code: Code of Ordinances

Ohio Traffic Law Handbook

Ohio Planning and Zoning Law

Katz & Giannelli, Ohio Criminal Justice

Of course, not every local public library will have all of these sets of legal materials. Furthermore, those libraries that have them may not keep them current with the latest supplementary material. Nevertheless, it is worth checking what is available.

The remainder of this section contains contact information on law libraries in the state. As with any library, be sure to inquire about any restrictions on access to the materials on the shelves in the library. After the name of each library, you will find abbreviations that tell you whether the library is a:

- federal depository libraries (FDL)
- county law library (CLL)
- state depository library (SDL)

Some libraries fit into more than one category.

B. Library Listings by City and County

Adams County
Ada
Akron
Allen County
Alliance
Ashland
Ashtabula County
Athens
Auglaize County
Batavia
Bellefontaine
Belmont County
Bluffton
Bowling Green
Brown County
Bryan
Bucyrus
Butler County
Cadiz
Caldwell
Cambridge
Canton
Carrollton
Celina
Champaign County
Chardon
Chillicothe
Cincinnati
Circleville
Clark County
Clermont County
Cleveland
Clinton County
Columbiana County
Columbus
Coshocton
Crawford County
Cuyahoga County
Darke County
Dayton
Defiance
Delaware
Eaton
Elyria
Erie County
Fairfield County

Fayette County
Findlay
Franklin County
Fremont
Fulton County
Gallia County
Gallipolis
Gambier
Geauga County
Georgetown
Granville
Greene County
Greenville
Guernsey County
Hamilton
Hamilton County
Hancock County
Hardin County
Harrison County
Henry County
Highland County
Hillsboro
Hiram
Hocking County
Holmes County
Huron County
Ironton
Jackson
Jefferson
Jefferson County
Kent
Kenton
Knox County
Lake County
Lancaster
Lawrence County
Lebanon
Licking County
Lima
Lisbon
Logan
Logan County
London
Lorain County
Lucas County
Madison County
Mahoning County
Mansfield
Marietta
Marion
Marysville
McArthur
McConnellsville
Medina
Meigs County
Mercer County
Miami County
Millersburg
Monroe County
Montgomery County
Morgan County
Morrow County
Mount Gilead
Mount Vernon
Muskingum County
Napoleon
Newark
New Concord
New Lexington
New Philadelphia
Noble County
Norwalk
Oberlin
Ottawa
Ottawa County
Oxford
Painesville
Paulding
Perry County
Pickaway County
Pike County
Pomeroy
Portage County
Port Clinton
Portsmouth
Preble County
Putnam County
Ravenna
Richland County
Rio Grande
Ross County
Sandusky
Sandusky County
Scioto County
Seneca County
Shelby County
Sidney
Springfield
Stark County
St. Clairsville
Steubenville
Summit County
Tiffin
Toledo
Troy
Trumbull County
Tuscarawas County
Union County
University Heights
Upper Sandusky
Urbana
Van Wert
Vinton County
Youngstown
Wapakoneta
Warren
Warren County
Washington County
Wauseon
Wayne County
West Union
Washington Court House
Waverly
Westerville
Westlake
Williams County
Wilmington
Wood County
Woodsfield
Wooster
Worthington
Wyandot County
Xenia
Zanesville

AAA

Adams County
See West Union

Ada
Ohio Northern University Library (FDL) (SDL)
419-772-2254
www.law.onu.edu/govdocs/govdoc.htm

Akron
Akron Law Library Association
330-643-2804
www.akronlawlib.org

Akron-Summit County Public Library (FDL) (SDL)
330-643-9010
www.ascpl.lib.oh.us

University of Akron Library (FDL) (SDL)
330-972-8176
www3.uakron.edu/ul/subjects/govdocs.html

University of Akron Law Library (FDL)
330-972-7330
www.uakron.edu/law/library

Allen County
See Bluffton

Alliance
Mount Union College Library (FDL)
330-823-3795
www.muc.edu/library/library_collections/government_documents

Ashland
Ashland County Law Library Association (OCLL)
419-282-4219

Ashland University Library (FDL) (SDL)
419-289-5410
www.ashland.edu/library/depts/lgovern.html

Ashtabula County
See Jefferson

Athens
Athens County Law Library Association (OCLL)
740-593-8893

Ohio University Alden Library (FDL) (SDL)
740-593-2718
www.library.ohiou.edu/govdocs

Auglaize County
See Wapakoneta

BBB

Batavia
Clermont County Law Library (OCLL)
513-732-7109
www.clermontlawlibrary.org

Bellefontaine
Logan County Law Library (OCLL)
937-592-5846

Belmont County
See St. Clairsville

Bluffton
Bluffton College Musselman Library (FDL)
419-358-3450
www.bluffton.edu/library

Bowling Green
Bowling Green State University (FDL) (SDL)
419-372-2142
www.bgsu.edu/colleges/library/services/govdocs/index
Wood County Law Library (OCLL)
419-353-3921

Brown County
See Georgetown

Bryan
Williams County Law Library (OCLL)
419-636-4600

Bucyrus
Crawford County Law Library (OCLL)
419-562-7863
cclla.crawford-co.org

Butler County
See Hamilton, Oxford

CCC

Cadiz
Harrison County Law Library (OCLL)
740-942-0116

Caldwell
Noble County Law Library (OCLL)
740-732-4045

Cambridge
Guernsey County Law Library (OCLL)
740-432-9258

Canton
Malone College Library (FDL)
330-471-8324
www.malone.edu/1264
Stark County Law Library Association (OCLL)
330-451-7380
www.starklawlibrary.org

Carrollton
Carroll County Law Library Association (OCLL)
330-627-2450

Celina
Mercer County Law Library (OCLL)
419-586-5669

Champaign County
See Urbana

Chardon
Geauga County Library System (FDL)
216-285-7601
www.geauga.lib.oh.us/librariansfavorites7/Government.htm#Federal
Law Library Association of Geauga County (OCLL)
440-285-2222
www.co.geauga.oh.us/departments/law_library.htm

Chillicothe
Ross County Law Library (OCLL)
740-773-1075

Cincinnati
Cincinnati Law Library Association (OCLL)
513-946-5300
www.hamilton-co.org/cinlawlib
Public Library of Cincinnati and Hamilton County (FDL) (SDL)
513-369-6971
www.cincinnatilibrary.org/main/pd.asp
United States Court of Appeals, 6th Circuit Library (FDL)
513-564-7321
www.ca6.uscourts.gov/internet/library/library.htm
University of Cincinnati Langsam Library (FDL) (SDL)
513-556-1874
www.libraries.uc.edu/research/subject_resources/gov_docs/index.html
University of Cincinnati College of Law Library (FDL)
513-556-8078
www.law.uc.edu/library

Circleville
William Ammer Memorial Law Library Association (OCLL)
740-474-8376

Clermont County
See Batavia

Clark County
See Springfield

Cleveland
Case Western Reserve University Law Library (FDL)
216-368-5206
www.law.cwru.edu/tech_library/content.asp?id=301
Case Western Reserve University Smith Library (FDL)
216-368-6512
library.case.edu/ksl/govdocs
Cleveland Law Library Association (OCLL)
216-861-5070
clevelandlawlibrary.org
Cleveland Public Library (FDL) (SDL)
216-623-2870
www.cpl.org/sdi-government-documents.asp
Cleveland State University Law Library (FDL)
216-687-6877
www.law.csuohio.edu/lawlibrary/usgovernment
Cleveland State University Main Library (FDL) (SDL)
216-687-2487
www.law.csuohio.edu/lawlibrary/usgovernment
Municipal Reference Library (FDL)
216-664-2656

Clinton County
See Wilmington

Columbiana County
See Lisbon

Columbus
Capital University Blackmore Library (FDL)
614-236-6614
www.capital.edu/cc/library/index.shtml
Columbus Law Library Association (OCLL)
614-221-4181
www.columbuslawlib.org
Columbus Metropolitan Library (FDL) (SDL)
614-849-1249
www.cml.lib.oh.us
Ohio State University (FDL) (SDL)
614-292-6175 (Main Library)
614-292-9463 (Mortiz Law Library)
library.osu.edu/sites/reference/govdocs
State Library of Ohio (SDL)
800-686-1532; 614-644-7051
winslo.state.oh.us
winslo.state.oh.us/govinfo/slogovt.html
Supreme Court of Ohio Library (FDL)
614-387-9682
www.sconet.state.oh.us/LawLibrary

Coshocton
Coshocton County Law Library (OCLL)
740-622-6464

Crawford County
See Bucyrus

Cuyahoga County
See Cleveland, University Heights, Westlake

DDD

Darke County
See Greenville

Dayton
Dayton Law Library Association (OCLL)
937-225-4496
www.daylawlib.org
Dayton Metro Library (FDL) (SDL)
937-227-9500
University of Dayton Library (FDL)
937-229-4259
library.udayton.edu/basics/departments/govdocs.php
Wright State University Library (FDL) (SDL)
937-775-2533
www.libraries.wright.edu/find/gov

Defiance
Defiance County Law Library Association (OCLL)
419-782-1186

Delaware
Delaware County Law Library Association (OCLL)
740-833-2545
Ohio Wesleyan University Library (FDL)
740-368-3242
library.owu.edu/scrgov.htm

EEE

Eaton
Preble County Law Library Association (OCLL)
937-456-4727

Elyria
Lorain County Law Library (OCLL)
440-329-5567
www.lorainlawlib.org

Erie County
See Sandusky

FFF

Fairfield County
See Lancaster

Fayette County
See Washington Court House

Findlay
Hancock County Law Library (OCLL)
419-424-7077
www.co.hancock.oh.us/lawlibrary/lawlibrary.htm
University of Findlay Library (FDL) (SDL)
419-434-4700
www.findlay.edu/offices/resources/library/default.htm

Franklin County
See Columbus, Westerville, Worthington

Fremont
Sandusky County Law Library (OCLL)
419-334-6165

Fulton County
See Wauseon

GGG

Gallia County
See Gallipolis, Rio Grande

Gallipolis
Gallia County Law Library Association (OCLL)
740-446-7478

Gambier
Kenyon College Libraries (FDL)
740-427-5691
lbis.kenyon.edu/govdocs

Geauga County
See Chardon

Georgetown
Brown County Law Library (OCLL)
937-378-3101

Granville
Denison University Doane Library (FDL)
740-587-6682
www.denison.edu/library/about_lib/govdoccoll.html

Greene County
See Xenia

Greenville
Greenville Law Library Association
937-547-9741

Guernsey County
See Cambridge

HHH

Hamilton
Butler County Law Library Association (OCLL)
513-887-3455
www.bclawlib.org

Hamilton County
See Cincinnati

Hancock County
See Findlay

Hardin County
See Ada, Kenton

Harrison County
See Cadiz

Henry County
See Napoleon

Highland County
See Hillsboro

Hillsboro
Highland County Law Library (OCLL)
937-393-4863

Hiram
Hiram College Library (FDL) (SDL)
330-569-5358
library.hiram.edu/Gov_mainpage.htm

Hocking County
See Logan

Holmes County
See Millersburg

Huron County
See Norwalk

III

Ironton
Lawrence County Law Library (OCLL)
740-533-0582

JJJ

Jackson
Jackson County Law Library Association (OCLL)
740-286-8054

Jefferson
Ashtabula County Law Library Association (OCLL)
440-576-3690

Jefferson County
See Steubenville

KKK

Kent
Kent State University Library (FDL) (SDL)
330-672-3150
www.library.kent.edu/page/10357

Kenton
Hardin County Law Library (OCLL)
419-673-7219

Knox County
See Gambier, Mount Vernon

LLL

Lake County
See Painesville

Lancaster
Fairfield County Law Library (OCLL)
740-687-7116

Lawrence County
See Ironton

Lebanon
Warren County Law Library Association (OCLL)
513-695-1381

Licking County
See Granville, Newark

Lima
Allen County Law Library (OCLL)
419-223-1426
www.bright.net/~lawbooks/page3.htm

Lisbon
Columbiana County Law Library Association (OCLL)
330-420-3662
www.columbianacountylawlibrary.com

Logan
Hocking County Law Library Association (OCLL)
740-385-4968

Logan County
See Bellefontaine

London
Madison County Law Library (OCLL)
740-852-9515

Lorain County
See Elyria, Oberlin

Lucas County
See Toledo

MMM

Madison County
See London

Mahoning County
See Youngstown

Mansfield
Richland County Law Library Association (OCLL)
419-774-5595

Marietta
Marietta College Library (FDL) (SDL)
740-376-4543
library.marietta.edu/Government/home.html
Washington County Law Library (OCLL)
740-373-6623
www.co.washington.oh.us/cl-lawlibrary.htm

Marion
Marion County Law Library Association (OCLL)
740-223-4170
Marion Public Library (FDL)
740-387-0992
www.marion.lib.oh.us/Services/GovDocs.htm

Marysville
Union County Law Library (OCLL)
937-645-3000

McArthur
Vinton County Law Library Association (OCLL)
740-596-5291

McConnellsville
Morgan County Law Library (OCLL)
740-962-2262

Medina
Medina County Law Library (OCLL)
330-725-9744

Mercer County
See Celina

Meigs County
See Pomeroy

Miami County
See Troy

Millersburg
Holmes County Law Library (OCLL)
330-674-1876

Monroe County
See Woodsfield

Montgomery County
See Dayton

Morgan County
See McConnellsville

Morrow County
See Mount Gilead

Mount Gilead
Morrow County Law Library (OCLL)
419-946-6578

Mount Vernon
Knox County Law Library (OCLL)
740-397-4293

Muskingum County
See New Concord, Zanesville

NNN

Napoleon
Henry County Law Library Association (OCLL)
419-592-4451 (fax)

Newark
Licking County Law Library (OCLL)
740-349-6561

New Concord
Muskingum College Library (FDL) (SDL)
740-826-8152
muskingum.edu/home/library/find/govtdocs.html

New Lexington
Perry County Law Library (OCLL)
740-342-7211

New Philadelphia
Tuscarawas County Law Library (OCLL)
330-364-3703

Noble County
See Caldwell

Norwalk
Huron County Law Library Association (OCLL)
419-668-5127

OOO

Oberlin
Oberlin College Library (FDL) (SDL)
440-775-5129
www.oberlin.edu/library/research/gov.html

Ottawa
Putnam County Law Library (OCLL)
419-384-3238

Ottawa County
See Port Clinton

Oxford
Miami University Library (FDL) (SDL)
513-529-3340
www.lib.muohio.edu/libinfo/depts/documents

PPP

Painesville
Lake County Law Library Association (OCLL)
440-350-2899
www.lakecountyohio.org/lawlibrary

Paulding
Paulding County Law Library Association (OCLL)
419-399-2217

Perry County
See New Lexington

Pickaway County
See Circleville

Pike County
See Waverly

Pomeroy
Meigs County Law Library Association (OCLL)
740-992-4211

Portage County
See Hiram, Kent, Ravenna

Port Clinton
Ottawa County Law Library (OCLL)
419-734-6763

Portsmouth
Scioto County Law Library (OCLL)
740-355-8259

Shawnee State University Library (FDL)
740-351-3321
www.shawnee.edu/off/cml/index.html

Preble County
See Eaton

Putnam County
See Ottawa

RRR

Ravenna
Portage County Law Library (OCLL)
330-297-3661

Richland County
See Mansfield

Rio Grande
University of Rio Grande Library (FDL)
740-245-7344
library.rio.edu

Ross County
See Chillicothe

SSS

Sandusky
Sandusky Bay Law Library Association (OCLL)
419-626-4823

Sandusky County
See Fremont

Scioto County
See Portsmouth

Seneca County
See Tiffin

Shelby County
See Sidney

Sidney
Shelby County Law Library (OCLL)
937-492-2658

Springfield
Clark County Law Library (OCLL)
937-328-2477

Clark County Public Library (FDL) (SDL)
937-328-6903
www.ccpl.lib.oh.us

Stark County
See Alliance, Canton

St. Clairsville
Belmont County Law Library Association (OCLL)
740-695-2121

Steubenville
Jefferson County Law Library (OCLL)
740-283-8553

Public Library of Steubenville and Jefferson County (FDL) (SDL)
740-282-9782
www.steubenville.lib.oh.us

Summit County
See Akron

TTT

Tiffin
Heidelberg College Beeghly Library(FDL)
419-448-2104
www.heidelberg.edu/offices/library

Seneca County Law Library (OCLL)
567-230-0204

Toledo
Toledo Law Association (OCLL)
419-213-4747
www.toledolawlibrary.org

Toledo-Lucas County Public Library (FDL) (SDL)
419-259-5209
www.toledolibrary.org

University of Toledo Law Library (FDL)
419-530-2733
www.utlaw.edu/students/lawlibrary/government.htm

University of Toledo Carlson Library (FDL) (SDL)
419-530-2171
library.utoledo.edu/find/govinfo.html

Troy
Miami County Law Library (OCLL)
937-440-5994

Trumbull County
See Warren

Tuscarawas County
See New Philadelphia

UUU

Union County
See Marysville

Urbana
Champaign County Law Library Association (OCLL)
937-653-2709

University Heights
John Carroll University Library (FDL) (SDL)
216-397-4234
www.jcu.edu/library/connell/govhome.htm

Upper Sandusky
Wyandot County Law Library (OCLL)
419-294-4088

VVV

Van Wert
Van Wert County Law Library Association (OCLL)
419-238-6935

Vinton County
See McArthur

WWW

Wapakoneta
Auglaize County Law Library (OCLL)
419-738-3124
www.auglaizecounty.org/law.htm

Warren
Trumbull County Law Library Association (OCLL)
330-675-2525
www.tclla.org

Warren County
See Lebanon

Washington County
See Marietta

Washington Court House
Fayette County Law Library (OCLL)
740-335-3608

Wauseon
Fulton County Law Library Association (OCLL)
419-337-9260

Waverly
Pike County Law Library (OCLL)
740-947-2212

Wayne County
See Wooster

Westerville
Otterbein College Library (FDL)
614-823-1984
www.otterbein.edu/resources/library/libpages/docmain.htm

Westlake
Porter Public Library (FDL)
440-250-5460
www.westlakelibrary.org

West Union
Adams County Law Library (OCLL)
937-544-3331

Williams County
See Bryan

Wilmington
Clinton County Law Library Association (OCLL)
937-382-2428

Wilmington College Library (FDL)
937-382-6661
www.watsonlibrary.org

Wood County
See Bowling Green

Woodsfield
Monroe County Law Library (OCLL)
740-472-0841

Wooster
College of Wooster Libraries (FDL)
330-263-2522
www.wooster.edu/Library/Gov

Wayne County Law Library Association (OCLL)
330-262-5561
www.waynelawlibrary.org

Worthington
Worthington Libraries (FDL)
614-807-2626
www.worthingtonlibraries.org

Wyandot County
See Upper Sandusky

XYZ

Xenia
Greene County Law Library (OCLL)
937-562-5115

Youngstown
Mahoning Law Library Association (OCLL)
330-740-2295
www.mahoninglawlibrary.org

Public Library of Youngstown and Mahoning County (FDL) (SDL)
330-744-8636
www.maag.ysu.edu/17cd

Youngstown State University Library (FDL) (SDL)
330-941-3126
www.maag.ysu.edu

Zanesville
Muskingum County Law Library Association (OCLL)
740-455-7154

C. More Information

Federal Depository Libraries
www.gpoaccess.gov/libraries.html
www.bgsu.edu/colleges/library/services/govdocs/ohiodep.html

Ohio County Law Library Directory
www.tclla.org/index_files/page0006.htm

Ohio Regional Association of Law Libraries
www.orall.org
www.orall.org/ohweb.htm

Ohio State Depository Libraries
winslo.state.oh.us/govinfo/govt_c.html
www.wooster.edu/library/gov/ohgodort/ohiodepository.htm

Government Documents Roundtable of Ohio
www.wooster.edu/library/gov/ohgodort

Ohio Government Agency Libraries
winslo.state.oh.us/publib/agency_libs.html

Ohio Libraries (legal and general)
www.librarysites.info/states/oh.htm
e-guide.com/lists/vxOH13.htm
www.findthefun.com/lists/vxOH13.htm

Links to Ohio Library Systems
www.pcdl.lib.oh.us/mvl/links.htm

Ohio Web Library
www.ohioweblibrary.org

Ohio Public Library Information Network
www.oplin.org

D. Something to Check

1. Call a federal depository library (FDL) near you that is not fully public. An example would be a private university. Assume that you want to go to this library to use the Code of Federal Regulations (CFR) volumes on the shelves of this library. (You want to look at a "hard copy" of the CFR rather than examine it online.) Ask the library how to do this. Do you need a special pass? Are there any restrictions on your use of the rest of the library? In short, how do you gain admission to use the materials (like the CFR) that this private library receives under the federal depositary program? Repeat this assignment for any other federal depository library in the state and compare your answers for the two libraries.
2. Contact the nearest state depositary library (SDL) by phone or online. Find out what state legal materials it receives from the State Library of Ohio or from any state agency. Are there any restrictions on your access to these materials?
3. (a) What is the closest neighborhood public library to you that has Ohio Jurisprudence 3d, the legal encyclopedia on Ohio law? How current is this set of books? If the online catalog does not tell you, call or visit the library and ask about the date of the latest volumes and pocket-parts of this set.
   (b) What other legal materials are available at this library, and how current are they?

5.9 Hotline Resources and Complaint Directories

A. Introduction

On the job, you sometimes need quick access to the phone number or Web site of commonly used resources. This section provides many of them. See also section 4.5 for similar leads.

B. Hotline Resources

Abortion
800-230-7526
www.plannedparenthood.org
(click "OH" in pull-down menu)

Adoption
800-394-3366
www.childwelfare.gov/adoption/index.cfm

Adoption Registry
614-466-4784
www.odh.state.oh.us/vitalstatistics/legalinfo/adoption.aspx

Adult Abuse
(see Aging, Elder Abuse, Seniors)

Agencies of State Government
(see also section 4.5)
ohio.gov/contacts.stm

Aging, Ohio Department of
800-282-1206 (elder rights helpline)
www.goldenbuckeye.com

Agriculture (Ohio)
800-282-1955 (food safety)
www.ohioagriculture.gov

AIDS Hotline
800-332-2437; 800-342-AIDS

Alcohol and Drug Abuse
800-729-6686
ncadi.samhsa.gov

Alzheimers Helpline
800-272-3900
www.alz.org
(click "Search By State")

AMBER Alert
(see also Missing Children)
877-AMBER-OH
www.amberalert.gov

Attorney General (Ohio)
800-282-0515; 614-466-4320
866-AG-ELDER (senior fraud hotline)
www.ag.state.oh.us

Bar (State Bar Association)
(see also section 3.5)
614-487-2050; 800-232-7124 (membership)
www.ohiobar.org

Battered Women
(see Domestic Violence)

Better Business Bureau
800-759-2400
lookup.bbb.org
(type in an Ohio city)

Birth Records
(see also section 5.7)
614-466-2531
www.odh.state.oh.us/vitalstatistics/vitalstats.aspx
www.cdc.gov/nchs/howto/w2w/ohio.htm
www.vitalrec.com/oh.html

BMV (Bureau of Motor Vehicles)
800-589-TAGS; 614-752-7500
ohiobmv.com

Business (formation, assistance, taxation)
(see also Small Business Ombudsman)
800-248-4040 (one-stop business permit)
888-405-4089 (business taxation)
www.odod.state.oh.us/onestop/index.cfm
ohio.gov/business.stm
www.sos.state.oh.us/sos/businessservices/corp.aspx
tax.ohio.gov/channels/other/ohio_taxes.stm

Business Gateway
866-OHIO-GOV; 866-644-6468
obg.ohio.gov

Cancer Hotline
800-4-CANCER
www.cancer.gov/newscenter

CEB
(see Continuing Education of the Bar)

Child Abuse Hotline
800-4-A-CHILD; 888-PREVENT
www.childhelpusa.org
www.childwelfare.gov/pubs/reslist/tollfree.cfm

Children, Missing
(see Missing Children)

Children's Defense Fund—Ohio
614-221-2244
www.cdfohio.org

Child Support
800-686-1556 (hotline)
614-752-6561 (Ohio Office of Child Support)
jfs.ohio.gov/OCS

Child Support Agencies (by county)
jfs.ohio.gov/county/cntydir.stm

Chiropractic Board Consumer Hotline
888-772-1384
chirobd.ohio.gov/mission.htm

City Governments
www.govengine.com/localgov/ohio.html
www.odod.state.oh.us/CityandCountyLinks.cfm
www.megalaw.com/oh/ohcities.php
www.omunileague.org/ohiocities.htm

Civil Rights Commission
888-278-7101
crc.ohio.gov

Communicable Diseases Hotline
800-282-0546

Continuing Education of the Bar Requirements
614-387-9325
www.sconet.state.oh.us/CCLE

Congress
www.house.gov
202-225-3121
www.senate.gov
202-224-3121

Consumers' Counsel (utility issues)
877-PICKOCC (consumer complaint hotline)
www.pickocc.org

Consumer Product Safety Complaints
800-638-2772
www.cpsc.gov

Consumer Affairs
866-278-0003
com.state.oh.us/dfi/consumeraffairs.htm

Consumer Protection
800-282-0515
www.ag.state.oh.us/contact/hotline.asp
www.atlanet.org/pressroom/Links.aspx

Corporation
(see Business)

County Governments
www.ccao.org/1008.htm
www.govengine.com/localgov/ohio.html
www.oplin.org/page.php?Id=63-16

Courts (federal courts in Ohio)
(see also section 4.3)
www.ca6.uscourts.gov
www.uscourts.gov/courtlinks/index.cfm
(click the map of Ohio)

Courts (state)
(see also section 4.2)
www.sconet.state.oh.us
www.sconet.state.oh.us/Web_Sites/courts
www.govengine.com/stategov/ohio.html
www.sconet.state.oh.us/District_Courts

Crime Statistics
614-466-1830
www.crimestats.ohio.gov
www.ojp.usdoj.gov/bjs/sandlle.htm

Crime Victim Assistance
(see Victim)

Death Records
(see also section 5.7)
614-466-2531
www.odh.state.oh.us/vitalstatistics/vitalstats.aspx
www.cdc.gov/nchs/howto/w2w/ohio.htm
www.vitalrec.com/oh.html

Disability Rights
Ohio Legal Rights Service
800-282-9181
www.state.oh.us/olrs

Disability Services
(Ohio Rehabilitation Services Commission)
800-282-4536
rsc.ohio.gov

Discrimination
(see Civil Rights Commission, Housing)

Divorce/Dissolution Records
(see also section 5.7)
www.odh.state.oh.us/vitalstatistics/mrgdiv.aspx

Divorce Resources
www.divorcelawinfo.com/states/ohio/ohio.htm
www.divorcenet.com/states/ohio/index_html

Doctors
(see Medical Board)

Domestic Violence (county resources)
www.aardvarc.org/dv/states/ohdv.shtml

Domestic Violence Hotline
800-799-SAFE
www.ndvh.org

Drug and Alcohol Abuse
800-729-6686; 800-DRUGHELP
ncadi.samhsa.gov

Education, Department of
877-644-6338; 614-995-1545
www.ode.state.oh.us

Elder Abuse
866-AG-ELDER; 202-898-2586
www.elderabusecenter.org
www.proseniors.org
www.ag.state.oh.us/citizen/elderly/eatf.asp

Elections
Ohio Elections Commission
614-466-3205
elc.ohio.gov

Electric Choice Hotline
888-OEC-1314
www.ohioelectricchoice.com

Employment Discrimination
(see Civil Rights Commission)

Employment in Government
statejobs.ohio.gov/applicant/index.asp

Energy, Low-Income Energy Assistance
800-282-0880
www.odod.state.oh.us

Environmental Enforcement (Attorney General)
800-348-3248
www.ag.state.oh.us/contact/hotline.asp

Environmental Protection Agency (federal)
800-621-8431; 800-424-8802 (emergencies)
www.epa.gov

Environmental Protection Agency (Ohio)
614-644-3020; 800-282-9378(emergencies)
www.epa.state.oh.us

Equal Employment Opportunity
800-669-EEOC
www.eeoc.gov

Estate Taxes, Ohio
800-977-7711
tax.ohio.gov/divisions/estate/index.stm

Family Advocate
(Department of Mental Retardation)
614-466-8706
dmr.ohio.gov/families/moreinfo.htm

Federal Communications Commission
888-CALL-FCC
www.fcc.gov

Federal Government
800-FED-INFO; 800-333-4636
www.firstgov.gov

Federal Trade Commission
877-FTC-HELP; 202-326-2222
www.ftc.gov

Financial Institutions Hotline
866-278-0003
www.com.state.oh.us/dfi/consumeraffairs.htm

Fire Marshall, State
888-252-0803
www.com.state.oh.us/sfm

Fraud Hotline
(see also Postal Fraud, Insurance, Social Security)
800-876-7060
www.fraud.org

Gay and Lesbian Rights
(ACLU of Ohio)
216-472-2200
www.acluohio.org/issues/LGBT/default.asp

Gay and Lesbian Teen Hotline
800-347-TEEN
www.talkingwithkids.org/aids-resource-matrix.html

Golden Buckeye Card
866-301-6446
www.goldenbuckeye.com/contact.html

Government
614-466-2000 (information)
(see also Agencies, Ohio, City, County, Federal, Governor, Legislature)

Government Employment
statejobs.ohio.gov/applicant/index.asp

Governor
614-644-HELP
governor.ohio.gov

Health Plans Consumer Hotline
800-324-8680
jfs.ohio.gov

Highway Patrol
877-7-PATROL
800-GRAB-DUI (DUI hotline)
www.statepatrol.ohio.gov

Homeland Security—Ohio
614-466-2550
www.publicsafety.ohio.gov

Housing Discrimination
800-424-8590 (federal)
888-278-7101 (state)
crc.ohio.gov/cf_housing.htm
Housing Finance Agency
888-362-6432
www.ohiohome.org

Industrial Commission of Ohio
800-521-2691
www.ohioic.com

Identity Theft
877-ID-THEFT; 888-My-ID-4-ME
www.ftc.gov/bcp/edu/microsites/idtheft
www.ftc.gov
(click "File a Complaint" "Identity Theft Complaint Form")

IRS
(see Tax)

Insurance
800-686-1578 (Department of Insurance)
800-686-1526 (consumer hotline)

800-686-1527 (fraud hotline)
www.ins.state.oh.us
www.ohioinsurance.gov

Lawyer Referral Services
(county bar contacts)
www.ohiobar.org/pub/?articleid=72

Legal Services, Ohio
866-LAW-OHIO
www.oslsa.org/OSLSA

Legislature (State Senate and House)
614-466-4900
www.senate.state.oh.us
614-466-3357
www.house.state.oh.us

Legislature (bill information)
800-282-0253; 614-466-8842
www.legislature.state.oh.us/search.cfm

LexisNexis/Matthew Bender
800-223-1940; 800-356-6548
www.lexisone.com

Liquor Enforcement Hotline
800-282-3477
877-4-MINORS

Long-Term Care Ombudsman
800-282-1206

Marijuana Eradication
800-282-DRUG
www.ag.state.oh.us/contact/hotline.asp

Mediation Resources
614-752-9595
disputeresolution.ohio.gov
disputeresolution.ohio.gov/nfpmap.htm

Medical Board
800-554-7717; 614-466-3934
med.ohio.gov

Medicare and Medicaid Services
800-MEDICARE; 877-267-2323
www.cms.hhs.gov
www.cms.hhs.gov/RegionalOffices

Medicaid in Ohio
800-324-8680
jfs.ohio.gov/ohp

Mental Health Information Hotline
National Alliance for the Mentally Ill
800-950-6264
www.nami.org

Mental Health: Ohio Adult Recovery Network
800-991-1311
adultrecoverynetwork.org

Migrant Farmworker and Immigrant Worker Program
(Advocates for Basic Legal Equality)
800-837-0814

Missing Children Hotline
(see also AMBER Alert)
800-THE-LOST; 800-I-AM-LOST
www.missingkids.com
www.childwelfare.gov/pubs/reslist/tollfree.cfm

Mortgage Complaint Hotline
866-278-0003
www.com.state.oh.us/dfi/consumeraffairs.htm

Nursing Home Complaint Hotline
800-282-1206

Occupational Safety (Labor and Worker Safety)
800-282-1425; 614-644-2631
198.234.41.198/w3/webwh.nsf?Opendatabase

Ohio Business Gateway
866-OHIO-GOV; 866-644-6468
obg.ohio.gov

Ohio Citizen Action
888-777-7135
www.ohiocitizen.org

Ohio Government
614-466-2000
ohio.gov/index.stm

Ohio Legal Rights Service
(Disability Rights)
800-282-9181
www.state.oh.us/olrs

Patient Abuse
800-64A-BUSE
www.ag.state.oh.us/contact/hotline.asp

Poison Control Hotline
800-222-1222
www.poison.org
www.fasthealth.com/poison/oh.php

Police Departments
(see also Highway Patrol)
www.usacops.com/oh
www.the911site.com/911pd/ohio.shtml

Postal Fraud
800-372-8347
www.usps.com/postalinspectors

Public Defender (state)
800-686-1573; 614-466-5394
opd.ohio.gov
opd.ohio.gov/pub/pub_cty.htm

Public Utilities
800-686-PUCO
www.puco.ohio.gov

877-PICKOCC (consumer complaint hotline)
www.pickocc.org

Putative Fathers Hotline
888-313-3100
jfs.ohio.gov/pfr

Rape Hotline/Rape Crisis Centers
800-656-HOPE; 818-793-3385
www.rainn.org
www.aftertherain.com/help.html#ohio

Runaway Hotline
800-RUNAWAY
www.nrscrisisline.org

Secretary of State
614-466-2655
www.sos.state.oh.us

Senate
(see Legislature)

Senior Health Insurance Information
800-686-1578
www.ohioinsurance.gov

Seniors Legal Hotline
800-488-6070
www.proseniors.org/legal_services.html

Sex Offender Information
(Megan's Law)
866-40-OHLEG
www.esorn.ag.state.oh.us
www.drc.state.oh.us/cfdocs/inmate/search.htm
www.sexcriminals.com/registration-notification/us/ohio

Sexually Transmitted Diseases Hotline
800-227-8922

Sheriff Offices (by county)
www.megalaw.com/oh/ohenforce.php
pickawaysheriff.com
(click "Ohio Sheriff's")

Sixth Circuit
See Courts (federal)

Small Business Ombudsman
800-848-1300
www.odod.state.oh.us
(click "Small Business Ombudsman")

Social Security Information Hotline
800-772-1213 (information)
800-269-0271 (fraud hotline)
www.ssa.gov

STD Hotline
800-227-8922

Substance Abuse Information Hotline
(see also Drug and Alcohol Abuse)
800-662-HELP; 800-66-AYUDA

Suicide Prevention Hotline
800-273-TALK; 800-SUICIDE
www.suicidepreventionlifeline.org

Tax (federal income)
800-829-1040 (individuals)
800-829-4933 (businesses)
www.irs.gov
www.irs.gov/localcontacts
(click "Ohio")

Tax (state hotline numbers)
800-282-1782
tax.ohio.gov/channels/global/contact_us.stm

Telecommunication Resource & Action Center (TRAC)
800-344-8722
www.trac.org

Tourism in Ohio
800-BUCKEYE
www.discoverohio.com/home.asp

Tuition Trust Authority of Ohio
800-AFFORD-IT
www.collegeadvantage.com

Unclaimed Property
614-466-4433
www.com.state.oh.us/unfd
www.unclaimedfundstreasurehunt.ohio.gov

Unemployment Compensation
800-251-OBES (hotline)
877-644-6562 (claims)
jfs.ohio.gov/ouc

Veterans Services
800-253-4060
www.odjfs.state.oh.us/veterans

Vital Records
614-466-2531
www.vitalrec.com/oh.html
www.cdc.gov/nchs/howto/w2w/ohio.htm

Victim Compensation
800-582-CVSS
www.ag.state.oh.us
(click "Crime Victims Compensation" under Victim's Services)

Victim Identification and Notification Everyday (VINE)
800-770-0192
www.ag.state.oh.us/victim/pubs/vine_broch2004.pdf

Victim Resources (crime)
800-851-3420; 800-824-8263
ovc.ncjrs.org/findvictimservices
www.ojp.usdoj.gov/ovc

Victim Services
888-VICTIM4
www.drc.state.oh.us/web/victim.htm
West Group/Westlaw
800-328-4880; 800-WESTLAW
west.thomson.com

White House
202-456-1414
www.whitehouse.gov

Workers' Compensation
800-OHIO-BWC
www.ohiobwc.com

Youth Crisis Hotline
800-HITHOME
www.nrscrisisline.org
www.allaboutcounseling.com/crisis_hotlines.htm

C. More Information

www.house.state.oh.us/jsps/Hotlines.jsp
chuh.net/lwv/hotlines.html
www.uncg.edu/hrs/tollfree.htm
ohio.gov/resident.stm
www.genevaohio.com/links.htm
sandusky.osu.edu/gparent/page11.htm
library.osu.edu/sites/reference/govdocs/consumer.htm

D. Something to Check

What hotline resources might help a client concerned about the following circumstances?

1. stalking
2. insolvency
3. credit discrimination

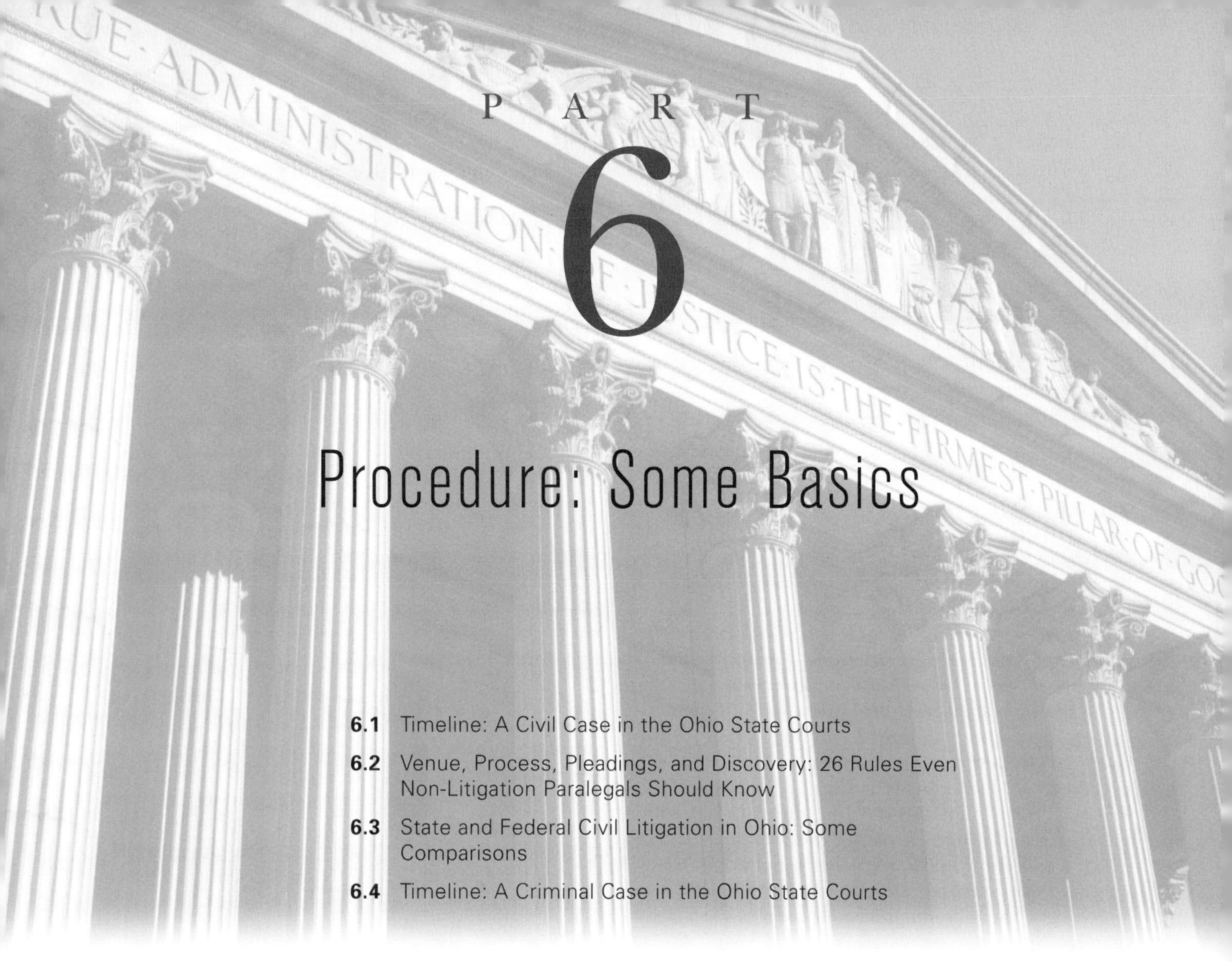

PART

6

Procedure: Some Basics

6.1 Timeline: A Civil Case in the Ohio State Courts

A. Introduction
B. Overview
C. More Information
D. Something to Check

A. Introduction

Our main focus in this section will be the litigation procedures followed in cases where one private party asserts a tort or contract cause of action against another private party. We will not cover criminal cases or civil claims against the state. Probate and domestic relations or family law cases are also civil matters, but they have their own specialized procedures.

The timeline in this section describes many of the major events in contested civil cases commonly filed in the state courts of Ohio. Keep in mind, however, that civil cases can vary a great deal in complexity, depending on the nature of the case, the magnitude of the issues involved, the amount of potential damages, the extent of contention between the parties, and the caliber of the attorneys. Also adding diversity and complexity are the local rules that apply only to the court in which a case is being litigated. Our timeline primarily covers rules of statewide applicability.

See also the following related sections:

- overview of Ohio state courts (section 4.2)
- venue, process, pleadings, and discovery (section 6.2)
- example of a civil complaint (section 7.1)
- timeline of a criminal case (section 6.4)
- self-help resources in Ohio (section 5.6)
- overview of federal courts sitting in Ohio (section 4.3)
- some comparisons between state and federal procedure (section 6.3)

B. Overview

Exhibit 6.1A presents an overview of many of the major events involved in the litigation of a relatively large contract or tort civil case in Ohio state courts.

Preliminary Considerations

Statute of limitations. The statute of limitations places time limits on filing a lawsuit. For example, an "action for breach of any contract for sale must be commenced within 4 years after the cause of action has accrued." (Revised Code § 1302.98(A)) If you do not bring suit within this time period, the suit is barred, meaning that you can no longer sue on that cause of action.

Subject-matter jurisdiction. To hear a case, a court must have power over that kind of case. This power is its subject-matter jurisdiction. Claims against the state, for example, are brought in the court of claims. Claims between private parties in which the amount in dispute is more than $15,000 are brought in a court of common pleas. A municipal court and a county court can hear claims up to $15,000. A small claims court can hear claims up to $3,000.

Personal jurisdiction. Personal jurisdiction is the court's power over a particular party. The main way in which this power is acquired is by serving the defendant with process in the state. The long-arm statute allows the state to acquire personal jurisdiction over an out-of-state defendant based upon certain contacts that the defendant has had within Ohio. An example of such contact would be marketing of a product in Ohio by an out-of-state manufacturer.

Venue. There may be more than one court that has subject-matter jurisdiction over a case as well as personal jurisdiction over the defendant. If so, the place of the trial is referred to as its venue. Most civil claims can be filed in the county in which the defendant resides or has a principal place of business, or in which the defendant engaged in the activity "that gave rise to" the plaintiff's claim for relief. (Rule 3(B), Ohio Rules of Civil Procedure) Claims involving real estate are generally brought in the county where the property is located.

Arbitration and mediation. Throughout the case, efforts to resolve the dispute without litigation are often made. This can include arbitration, mediation, and other methods of alternative dispute resolution (ADR). See the discussion of alternative dispute resolution below.

Commencement of the Case; Pleadings and Motions

Service of process. The defendant is given notice of the filing of a civil action by serving on (transmitting to) the defendant a complaint and a summons. These two documents are called process, and transmitting them is called service of process. A number of different methods of service can be authorized, such as certified or express mail addressed to the defendant, personal service by handing the complaint and summons to the defendant, leaving the documents at the place of business or residence of the defendant, or publication of a notice of the action in a newspaper of general circulation.

Complaint. The complaint is a pleading in which the plaintiff states a claim against the defendant. The plaintiff files this pleading with the court clerk. The complaint

EXHIBIT 6.1A Bringing and Defending a Civil Case in Ohio State Courts

(The following overview covers many of the major events in a relatively large contract or tort case filed in an Ohio state court; variations will depend on factors such the complexity of the case and the applicability of local rules.)

PRELIMINARY CONSIDERATIONS	**COMMENCEMENT OF THE CASE; PLEADINGS & MOTIONS**	**DISCOVERY**	**PRETRIAL CONFERENCES**	**SUMMARY JUDGMENT**	**ALTERNATIVE DISPUTE RESOLUTION (ADR)**	**TRIAL**	**APPEAL**
-Statute of limitations -Subject-matter jurisdiction -Personal jurisdiction -Venue -Arbitration and mediation	-Service of process -Complaint -Summons -Answer -Counterclaim -Reply to counter-claim -Cross-claim -Answer to cross-claim -Third-party complaint -Third-party answer -Motion to dismiss -Amendments to pleadings	-Deposition upon oral examination -Deposition upon written questions -Interrogatories -Request for production -Request for admissions -Physical or mental examination -Motion for order compelling discovery -Motion for protective order	Objectives: -Settlement discussions -Simplifying the issues -Itemizing expenses and special damages -Amending the pleadings -Exchange of reports and records -Avoiding unnecessary proof	-Motion for summary judgment	-Mediation -Arbitration -Early neutral evaluation -Fee-paid judge trial (private judging)	-Jury demand -Jury selection -Opening statements -Case in chief of plaintiff -Case in chief of defendant -Motion for a directed verdict -Closing statements -Instructions to jury -Verdict -Motion for a new trial -Motion for judgment notwithstanding the verdict -Final judgment	-Ohio Court of Appeals -Supreme Court of Ohio

identifies the plaintiff and the court in which the action is brought. It also contains "(1) a short and plain statement of the claim showing that the party is entitled to relief, and (2) a demand for judgment for the relief to which the party claims to be entitled." (Rule 8(A), Ohio Rules of Civil Procedure)

Summons. "Upon the filing of the complaint the clerk shall forthwith issue a summons for service upon each defendant." The summons is a document that notifies the defendant that a failure to file a response (called an answer) to the complaint within a designated number of days (usually 28) will result in a default judgment against the defendant. "The summons shall be signed by the clerk, contain the name and address of the court and the names and addresses of the parties, be directed to the defendant, state the name and address of the plaintiff's attorney, if any, otherwise the plaintiff's address, and the times within which these rules or any statutory provision require the defendant to appear and defend, and shall notify him that in case of his failure to do so, judgment by default will be rendered against him for the relief demanded in the complaint." (Rule 4, Ohio Rules of Civil Procedure)

Answer. To avoid a default judgment, the defendant must file an answer to the complaint within the time specified. The answer will either admit or deny the allegations in the complaint and may raise defenses (e.g., statute of limitations) that demonstrate why the plaintiff should not prevail. "Generally, the defendant shall serve his answer within 28 days after service of the summons and complaint upon him; if service of notice has been made by publication, he shall serve his answer within 28 days after the completion of service by publication." (Rule 12(A)(1), Ohio Rules of Civil Procedure) Alternatively the defendant may file a motion to dismiss the complaint (see below).

Counterclaim. If the defendant has a claim against the plaintiff, the defendant can state the claim (called a counterclaim) in his or her answer. The claim may or may not arise out of the transaction or occurrence that is the subject matter of the plaintiff's claim. An example of one that does arise out of the same occurrence is the defendant's claim that the plaintiff injured the defendant in the car collision that the plaintiff's complaint initially asserted was caused by the defendant.

Reply to counterclaim. The plaintiff must then reply to the counterclaim by admitting or denying the allegations in the counterclaim and raising any defenses the plaintiff may have.

"The plaintiff shall serve his reply to a counterclaim in the answer within 28 days after service of the answer." (Rule 12(A)(2), Ohio Rules of Civil Procedure)

Cross-claim. A cross-claim is a claim asserted by one defendant against another defendant when the plaintiff has sued more than one defendant in the same action. The defendant asserting the claim is the cross-claimant. "A pleading may state as a cross-claim any claim by one party against a co-party arising out of the transaction or occurrence that is the subject matter either of the original action . . . or relating to any property that is the subject matter of the original action. Such cross-claim may include a claim that the party against whom it is asserted is or may be liable to the cross-claimant for all or part of a claim asserted in the action against the cross-claimant." (Rule 13(G), Ohio Rules of Civil Procedure)

Answer to cross-claim. The co-party or co-defendant then answers the cross-claim.

Third-party complaint. A third-party complaint is a defendant's complaint against someone who is not now a party on the basis that the latter may be liable for all or part of what the plaintiff might recover from the defendant. The defendant filing this kind of complaint becomes known as a third-party plaintiff. "At any time after commencement of the action a defending party, as a third-party plaintiff, may cause a summons and complaint to be served upon a person not a party to the action who is or may be liable to him for all or part of the plaintiff's claim against him." (Rule 14(A), Ohio Rules of Civil Procedure) If, for example, Smith sues Jones for damaging Smith's fence, Jones may be able to assert a third-party complaint against the gardening company that Jones hired on the basis that the company caused the damage to the fence.

Third-party answer. The third party summoned into the action then prepares a third-party answer, which is its answer to the cross-party complaint.

Motion to dismiss. Another option in responding to a complaint is for the defendant to file a motion to dismiss the plaintiff's action. Grounds for such a motion include the court's lack of subject-matter jurisdiction, the failure of the plaintiff to acquire personal jurisdiction over the defendant, or the failure of the plaintiff to assert a valid legal claim even if the plaintiff is able to prove everything alleged in the complaint.

Amendments to pleadings. Once a party has filed a complaint or other pleading, he or she may wish to alter or amend it. "A party may amend his pleading once as a matter of course at any time before a responsive pleading is served or, if the pleading is one to which no responsive pleading is permitted and the action has not been placed upon the trial calendar, he may so amend it at any time within 28 days after it is served. Otherwise a party may amend his pleading only by leave of court or by written consent of the adverse party. Leave of court shall be freely given when justice so requires. A party shall plead in response to an amended pleading within the time remaining for response to the original pleading or within 14 days after service of the amended pleading, whichever period may be the longer, unless the court otherwise orders." (Rule 15(A), Ohio Rules of Civil Procedure)

Discovery

Before trial, the parties can use the discovery methods to obtain facts from an opponent in order to prepare for trial. "Parties may obtain discovery regarding any matter, not privileged, which is relevant to the subject matter involved in the pending action." (Rule 30(A), Ohio Rules of Civil Procedure)

Deposition upon oral examination. A deposition upon oral examination is the oral questioning of a witness under oath in the presence of a court reporter, who writes down or records the testimony of the deposition witness (called the deponent). Any party may take the oral deposition of any person who has information that may be pertinent to the case, including, of course, any party to the action. The questions are usually asked by the attorney of the party deposing the witness. "After commencement of the action, any party may take the testimony of any person, including a party, by deposition upon oral examination. The attendance of a witness deponent may be compelled by the use of subpoena." (Rule 30(B)(1), Ohio Rules of Civil Procedure) The parties can agree (or a court upon motion can order) that the deposition upon oral examination be taken by telephone.

Deposition upon written questions. A deposition upon written questions is the submission of written questions to a witness who answers them orally under oath in the presence of a court reporter, who writes down or records the testimony of the deposition witness (called the deponent). Any party may take the oral deposition of any person who has information that may be pertinent to the case, including a party to the action. The questions are usually written by the attorney of the party deposing the witness. "After commencement of the action, any party may take the testimony of any person, including a party, by deposition upon written questions." (Rule 30(A), Ohio Rules of Civil Procedure)

Interrogatories. Interrogatories are written questions posed to a party, requiring a written response. "Any party, without leave of court, may serve upon any other party up to forty written interrogatories to be answered by the party served. A party serving interrogatories shall provide the party served with both a printed and an electronic copy of the interrogatories. The electronic copy shall be provided on computer disk, by electronic mail, or by other means agreed to by the parties. A party who is unable to provide an electronic copy of the interrogatories may seek leave of court to be relieved of this requirement." The answers must be served "within a period designated by the party submitting the interrogatories, not less than 28 days after the service of the interrogatories or within such shorter or longer time as the court may allow." (Rule 33(A), Ohio Rules of Civil Procedure)

Request for production. A party may obtain discovery by serving "on any other party a request to produce and permit the party making the request, or someone acting on the requesting party's behalf (1) to inspect and copy any designated documents (including writings, drawings, graphs, charts, photographs, phonorecords, and other data compilations from which intelligence can be perceived, with or without the use of detection devices) that are in the possession, custody, or control of the party upon whom the request is served; (2) to inspect and copy, test, or sample any tangible things that are in the possession, custody, or control of the party upon whom the request is served; (3) to enter upon designated land or other property in the possession or control of the party upon whom the request is served for the purpose of inspection and measuring, surveying, photographing, testing, or sampling the property or any designated object or operation on the property." (Rule 34(A), Ohio Rules of Civil Procedure) "The party upon whom the request is served shall serve a written response within a period designated in the request that is not less than 28 days after the service of the request or within a shorter or longer time as the court may allow." (Rule 34(B), Ohio Rules of Civil Procedure)

Request for admissions. Requests for admissions are written requests from a party that any other party to the action admit the genuineness of specified documents, or the truth of specified matters of fact, opinion of fact, or application of law to fact. "The matter is admitted unless, within a period designated in the request, not less than 28 days after service thereof or within such shorter or longer time as the court may allow, the party to whom the request is directed serves upon the party requesting the admission a written answer or objection addressed to the matter, signed by the party or by the party's attorney." (Rule 36(A), Ohio Rules of Civil Procedure)

Physical or mental examination. Discovery can also include physical or mental examinations. "When the mental or physical condition (including the blood group) of a party, or of a person in the custody or under the legal control of a party, is in controversy, the court in which the action is pending may order the party to submit himself to a physical or mental examination or to produce for such examination the person in the party's custody or legal control. The order may be made only on motion for good cause shown and upon notice to the person to be examined and to all parties and shall specify the time, place, manner, conditions, and scope of the examination and the person or persons by whom it is to be made." (Rule 35(A), Ohio Rules of Civil Procedure)

Motion for order compelling discovery. Upon failure to comply with valid discovery requests (e.g., refusing to answer a deposition question or providing an evasive or incomplete answer), a party can ask the court to force compliance. "Upon reasonable notice to other parties and all persons affected thereby, a party may move for an order compelling discovery." (Rule 37(A), Ohio Rules of Civil Procedure)

Motion for a protective order. If a party is abusing the discovery process to harass the other side, or is demanding information that is privileged or otherwise protected from disclosure by law, the responding party may bring a motion for a protective order. "Upon motion by any party or by the person from whom discovery is sought, and for good cause shown, the court in which the action is pending may make any order that justice requires to protect a party or person from annoyance, embarrassment, oppression, or undue burden or expense." (Rule 26(C), Ohio Rules of Civil Procedure)

Pretrial Conferences

Before the trial begins, the court may schedule a number of pretrial or case management conferences with the parties or their attorneys to accomplish the following objectives:

- The possibility of settlement of the action;
- The simplification of the issues;
- Itemizations of expenses and special damages;
- The necessity of amendments to the pleadings;
- The exchange of reports of expert witnesses expected to be called by each party;
- The exchange of medical reports and hospital records;
- The limitation of the number of expert witnesses;
- The imposition of sanctions as authorized by Civ. R. 37;
- The possibility of obtaining: Admissions of fact; Admissions into evidence of documents and other exhibits that will avoid unnecessary proof; and
- Other matters as may aid in the disposition of the action.

(Rule 16, Ohio Rules of Civil Procedure)

Summary Judgment

Often a party will tell the court that a trial is not needed because a judgment can be rendered in its favor without a trial. This is done through a motion for a summary judgment.

Motion for summary judgment. A summary judgment is a judgment rendered without a full trial on all or part of a claim asserted by either party because of the absence of genuine conflict on any of the material facts involved. A motion for a summary judgment will be granted "if the pleadings, depositions, answers to interrogatories, written admissions, affidavits, transcripts of evidence, and written stipulations of fact, if any, timely filed in the action, show that there is no genuine issue as to any material fact and that the moving party is entitled to judgment as a matter of law." (Rule 56(C), Ohio Rules of Civil Procedure)

The motion can be made "at any time after the expiration of the time permitted under these rules for a responsive motion or pleading by the adverse party, or after service of a motion for summary judgment by the adverse party. If the action has been set for pretrial or trial, a motion for summary judgment may be made only with leave of court." (Rule 56(A), Ohio Rules of Civil Procedure)

Alternative Dispute Resolution (ADR)

Alternative dispute resolution (ADR) is a method of resolving a legal dispute without litigation. ADR can occur before or after a lawsuit is filed. Many types of ADR exist. Examples include direct settlement negotiation between the parties, conciliation, mediation, settlement conferences, neutral fact-finding, early neutral evaluation, mini-trials, summary jury trials, arbitration, and private judging. (*www.ohiobar.org/pub/lawfacts/index.asp?articleid=18*) Many Ohio courts encourage ADR and have programs and local rules on how they operate. Here, for example, is a typical list of ADR methods:

Mediation. A non-binding process involving a neutral mediator who acts as a facilitator to assist the parties to craft a mutually acceptable resolution for themselves.

Arbitration. A process by which a neutral person or persons decide the rights and obligations of the parties. The process may be consensual, mandatory, non-binding, or binding.

Early neutral evaluation. A process involving a neutral evaluator who meets with the parties early in the course of the litigation to help them focus on the issues, organize discovery, work expeditiously to prepare the case for trial, and, if possible, settle all or part of the case. The neutral evaluator provides the parties with an evaluation of the legal and factual issues, to the extent possible, at that early stage of the case.

Fee-paid judge trial (private judging). A process involving a retired judge who is paid by the parties (not the government) to adjudicate a jury or non-jury trial. (Stark County Common Pleas, General Rule 16)

Trial

Jury demand. In many cases, a party can demand a jury trial. "Any party may demand a trial by jury on any issue triable of right by a jury by serving upon the other parties a demand therefor at any time after the commencement of the action and not later than 14 days after the service of the last pleading directed to such issue." (Rule 38(B), Ohio Rules of Civil Procedure) Trials without a jury are called bench trials.

Jury selection. The process of selecting a jury is called voir dire. The judge (and, if allowed, opposing parties through their attorneys) ask questions of prospective jurors to assess whether any of them might have a bias for or against one of the parties. ("The court may permit the parties or their attorneys to conduct the examination of the prospective jurors or may itself conduct the examination." Rule 47(B), Ohio Rules of Civil Procedure.) All prospective jurors can be challenged for cause (e.g., they may not be impartial because they are related to one of the parties). A prospective juror can also be dismissed by a peremptory challenge from either side. No reason need be given for exercising a peremptory challenge. Each side has three peremptory challenges. Most juries consist of eight jurors and one or more alternates. (Rule 38(B), Ohio Rules of Civil Procedure)

Opening statements. Once the jury has been sworn in, the attorneys give their opening statements to the jury, usually with the plaintiff going first. The statement outlines what the party expects to prove during the trial.

Case in chief of plaintiff. The plaintiff presents its case by conducting a direct examination of the witnesses it calls and by offering physical evidence. The defendant can cross examine the plaintiff's witnesses. The plaintiff then rests.

Case in chief of defendant. The defendant presents its case by conducting a direct examination of the witnesses it calls and by offering physical evidence. The plaintiff can cross examine the defendant's witnesses. The plaintiff then rests.

Motion for a directed verdict. A directed verdict is a judge's decision not to allow the jury to deliberate because only one verdict is reasonable. "A motion for a directed verdict may be made on the opening statement of the opponent, at the close of the opponent's evidence or at the close of all the evidence." (Rule 50(A)(4), Ohio Rules of Civil Procedure) The motion will be granted if the trial court "after construing the evidence most strongly in favor of the party against whom the motion is directed, finds that upon any determinative issue reasonable minds could come to but one conclusion upon the evidence submitted and that conclusion is adverse to such party." (Rule 50(A)(1), Ohio Rules of Civil Procedure)

Closing statements. Assuming that directed verdicts have not been granted, the attorneys then make their closing arguments to the jury, summarizing what they believe the evidence has proven or failed to prove.

Instructions to jury. Jury instructions (also called the charge) are the trial judge's explanation to the jury of the law and the manner in which the jury should go about reaching a verdict. Each party is allowed to make a written request of any instructions it would like the court to use. "At the close of the evidence or at such earlier time during the trial as the court reasonably directs, any party may file written requests that the court instruct the jury on the law as set forth in the requests. . . . The court shall inform counsel of its proposed action on the requests prior to counsel's arguments to the jury and shall give the jury complete instructions after the arguments are completed. The court also may give some or all of its instructions to the jury prior to counsel's arguments. The court shall reduce its final instructions to writing or make an audio, electronic, or other recording of those instructions, provide at least one written copy or recording of those instructions to the jury for use during deliberations. . . ." (51(A), Ohio Rules of Civil Procedure)

Verdict. After receiving their instructions, the jury goes to the jury room to deliberate and reach a verdict. The moderator of their discussions is a foreperson whom they select from among the jurors. In most civil cases the jury must decide if the party with the burden of proof has proven its case by a preponderance of the evidence. Under this standard, the greater weight of the evidence must support every element of the party's claim. This means that the evidence on one side of the scale outweighs that on the other. Most verdicts are general verdicts, which simply state which side wins and the amount awarded, if the verdict includes an award of damages. At the request of a party, the jury can be asked to answer specific questions called written interrogatories (that are approved by the court) along with its general verdict. (49(A)(B), Ohio Rules of Civil Procedure)

Motion for a new trial. A motion for a new trial asks the trial court to order a new trial on all or part of the issues because of (1) irregularity in the proceedings that prevented a fair trial; (2) misconduct of the jury or prevailing party; (3) accident or surprise, which ordinary prudence could not have guarded against; (4) excessive or inadequate damages apparently due to passion or prejudice; (5) error in the amount of recovery; (6) the judgment is not sustained by the weight of the evidence; (7) the judgment is contrary to law; (8) newly discovered material evidence, which with reasonable diligence he could not have discovered and produced at trial; (9) error of law occurring at the trial and brought to the attention of the trial court; or (10) other good cause shown. (59(A), Ohio Rules of Civil Procedure)

Motion for a judgment notwithstanding the verdict. A motion for a judgment notwithstanding the verdict is a request that the trial court order a judgment that is contrary to the conclusion or verdict of the jury because no reasonable jury would have reached that verdict even when construing the evidence most strongly in favor of the party against whom the motion is directed. (50(B), Ohio Rules of Civil Procedure)

Final judgment. The trial court's final judgment embodies its rulings on these motions and the conclusions reached on the facts and law.

Appeals

Ohio Court of Appeals. The first level of appeal from judgments of a court of common pleas is one of the twelve district courts of appeals. In most cases, the dissatisfied party has 30 days from entry of the final judgment in which to file the appeal. The court of appeals decides (on the basis of oral arguments and appellate briefs) whether any errors of law were made below; the case is not retried in the court of appeals.

Supreme Court of Ohio. A party dissatisfied with the decision of the court of appeals can then request the Ohio Supreme Court to review the decision of the court of appeals. If the request is granted, the court decides (on the basis of oral arguments and appellate briefs) whether any errors of law were made below; the case is not retried in the Supreme Court of Ohio.

C. More Information

Overview of Ohio Civil Litigation
www.ohiobar.org/pub/?articleid=104
downloads.ohiobar.org/conres/lawandyou/Law_and_You_3.pdf
www.megalaw.com/oh/top/ohcivpro.php

Court Statistics
www.sconet.state.oh.us/publications/annrep/05OCS/default.asp
www.sconet.state.oh.us/publications/annrep/04OCS/default.asp
www.sconet.state.oh.us/publications/annrep/02OCS
www.ncsconline.org/D_Research/csp/2003_Files/2003_Civil.pdf

Web Sites of Ohio Trial Courts
www.ohiomagistrates.org/links.html
www.legaltrek.com/HELPSITE/States/State_Contents/Ohio.htm
www.ohiojudges.org
(under links click "Ohio Courts")

Alternative Dispute Resolution (ADR)
www.ohiobar.org/pub/lawfacts/index.asp?articleid=18
www.state.oh.us/cdr
disputeresolution.ohio.gov/nfpmap.htm

Ohio Rules of Civil Procedure, Evidence, Appellate Procedure
www.sconet.state.oh.us/Rules/civil/default.asp
www.sconet.state.oh.us/Rules

Local Court Rules
www.llrx.com/courtrules-gen/state-Ohio.html

D. Something to Check

1. Assume that an automobile accident occurs in the county where you live, work (or hope to work). The negligence case arising from the accident is eventually heard by the court of common pleas in that county, and appealed to the district court of appeals and the Ohio Supreme Court. The accident involves two private parties operating the cars that collided. Go to the Web site of the court of common pleas that will probably hear this case. (If this court does not have a Web site, pick a different county.) Also go to the Web site of the district court of appeals to which appeals of this court of common pleas will be filed and to the Web site of the Ohio Supreme Court. (See section 4.2 for Web addresses.) On these Web sites, identify each category of information that is likely to be relevant to the parties in this litigation. Give examples of each category and explain your selections. When needed, you can make additional assumptions about the facts of the accident.
2. Go to the online Ohio Rules of Civil Procedure (*www.sconet.state.oh.us/Rules/civil/default.asp*). Do a search of the word *privilege* in the rules. Summarize the context in which the word is used each time.

6.2 Venue, Process, Pleadings, and Discovery: 26 Rules Even Non-Litigation Paralegals Should Know

A. Introduction

Even if you do not work in litigation now, at some time in your career there is a good chance that you will. A majority of the paralegals you will meet at paralegal association gatherings work in some phase of litigation, either on the front lines or in indirect capacities. Attorneys and paralegals in transaction practices often have litigation on their mind—from the perspective of how to avoid it! In short, litigation dominates a large portion of the legal world. Knowing some of the essential rules of civil litigation in the Ohio courts will help you communicate intelligently with (and perhaps be better prepared one day to join) attorneys and paralegals in the world of litigation.

In this section, we introduce excerpts from 26 of the most important litigation rules in Ohio primarily in two areas where paralegals have their most prominent roles: pleadings and discovery. Because the rules are excerpted rather than presented in full, you of course will need to go to the codes or rules themselves to obtain the full text whenever working on a client's case.

Consider this recommendation: read through the excerpts at least once or twice a year. Each time you do, you will increase your "litigation literacy," and gain a richer context for many of the non-litigation tasks you perform.

For related material in this book, see:

- section 4.2 (state courts in Ohio)
- section 4.3 (federal courts in Ohio)
- section 6.1 (timeline: a civil case in the Ohio state courts)
- section 6.3 (state vs federal civil litigation in Ohio)
- section 7.1 (example of a civil complaint)

B. The Rules

Table of Contents

STATE COURTS

Art. IV, § 1. Ohio courts (Constitution of the State of Ohio)

Levels of Ohio Courts

The judicial power of the state is vested in a supreme court, courts of appeals, courts of common pleas and divisions thereof, and such other courts inferior to the supreme court as may from time to time be established by law.

VENUE

CIV. R. RULE 3. (Rules of Civil Procedure of Ohio)

Where Venue Can Lie

(B) Any action may be venued, commenced, and decided in any court in any county. When applied to county and municipal courts, "county," as used in this rule, shall be construed, where appropriate, as the territorial limits of those courts. Proper venue lies in any one or more of the following counties:

(1) The county in which the defendant resides;
(2) The county in which the defendant has his or her principal place of business;
(3) A county in which the defendant conducted activity that gave rise to the claim for relief;
(4) A county in which a public officer maintains his or her principal office if suit is brought against the officer in the officer's official capacity;
(5) A county in which the property, or any part of the property, is situated if the subject of the action is real property or tangible personal property;
(6) The county in which all or part of the claim for relief arose. . . .
(8) In an action against an executor, administrator, guardian, or trustee, in the county in which the executor, administrator, guardian, or trustee was appointed;
(9) In actions for divorce, annulment, or legal separation, in the county in which the plaintiff is and has been a resident for at least ninety days immediately preceding the filing of the complaint;
(10) In actions for a civil protection order, in the county in which the petitioner currently or temporarily resides;
(11) In tort actions involving asbestos claims, silicosis claims, or mixed dust disease claims, only in the county in which all of the exposed plaintiffs reside, a county where all of the exposed plaintiffs were exposed to asbestos, silica, or mixed dust, or the county in which the defendant has his or her principal place of business.

Catch-All Venue Rule

(12) If there is no available forum in divisions (B)(1) to (B)(10) of this rule, in the county in which plaintiff resides, has his or her principal place of business, or regularly and systematically conducts business activity;
(13) If there is no available forum in divisions (B)(1) to (B)(11) of this rule: (a) In a county in which defendant has property or debts owing to the defendant subject to attachment or garnishment; (b) In a county in which defendant has appointed an agent to receive service of process or in which an agent has been appointed by operation of law. . . .

SUMMONS

CIV. R. RULE 4. (Rules of Civil Procedure of Ohio)

(A) Summons: issuance

Upon the filing of the complaint the clerk shall forthwith issue a summons for service upon each defendant

Issuance of a Summons

listed in the caption. Upon request of the plaintiff separate or additional summons shall issue at any time against any defendant.

(B) Summons: form; copy of complaint

The summons shall be signed by the clerk, contain the name and address of the court and the names and addresses of the parties, be directed to the defendant, state the name and address of the plaintiff's attorney, if any, otherwise the plaintiff's address, and the times within which these rules or any statutory provision require the defendant to appear and defend, and shall notify him that in case of his failure to do so, judgment by default will be rendered against him for the relief demanded in the complaint. Where there are multiple plaintiffs or multiple defendants, or both, the summons may contain, in lieu of the names and addresses of all parties, the name of the first party on each side and the name and address of the party to be served. A copy of the complaint shall be attached to each summons. The plaintiff shall furnish the clerk with sufficient copies. . . .

Contents of the Summons

(E) Summons: time limit for service

If a service of the summons and complaint is not made upon a defendant within six months after the filing of the complaint and the party on whose behalf such service was required cannot show good cause why such service was not made within that period, the action shall be dismissed as to that defendant without prejudice upon the court's own initiative with notice to such party or upon motion. This division shall not apply to out-of-state service pursuant to Rule 4.3 or to service in a foreign country pursuant to Rule 4.5.

Failure to Serve within Six Months

SERVICE OF PROCESS

CIV. R. RULE 4.1. (Rules of Civil Procedure of Ohio)

Methods of service

All methods of service within this state, except service by publication as provided in Civ. R. 4.4(A), are described in this rule. Methods of out-of-state service and for service in a foreign country are described in Civ. R. 4.3 and 4.5.

(A) Service by certified or express mail

Evidenced by return receipt signed by any person, service of any process shall be by certified or express mail unless otherwise permitted by these rules. The clerk shall place a copy of the process and complaint or other document to be served in an envelope. The clerk shall address the envelope to the person to be served at the address set forth in the caption or at the address set forth in written instructions furnished to the clerk with instructions to forward. The clerk shall affix adequate postage and place the sealed envelope in the United States mail as certified or express mail return receipt requested with instructions to the delivering postal employee to show to whom delivered, date of delivery, and address where delivered.

Service by Mail

The clerk shall forthwith enter the fact of mailing on the appearance docket and make a similar entry when the return receipt is received. If the envelope is returned with an endorsement showing failure of delivery, the clerk shall forthwith notify, by mail, the attorney of record or, if there is no attorney of record, the party at whose instance process was issued and enter the fact of notification on the appearance docket. The clerk shall file the return receipt or returned envelope in the records of the action.

All postage shall be charged to costs. If the parties to be served by certified or express mail are numerous and the clerk determines there is insufficient security for costs, the clerk may require the party requesting service to advance an amount estimated by the clerk to be sufficient to pay the postage.

(B) Personal service

When the plaintiff files a written request with the clerk for personal service, service of process shall be made by that method.

Personal Service

When process issued from the Supreme Court, a court of appeals, a court of common pleas, or a county court is to be served personally, the clerk of the court shall deliver the process and sufficient copies of the process and complaint, or other document to be served, to the sheriff of the county in which the party to be served resides or may be found. When process issues from the municipal court, delivery shall be to the bailiff of the court for service on all defendants who reside or may be found within the county or counties in which that court has territorial jurisdiction and to the sheriff of any other county in this state for service upon a defendant who resides in or may be found in that other county. In the alternative, process issuing from any of these courts may be delivered by the clerk to any person not less than eighteen years of age, who is not a party and who has been designated by order of the court to make service of process. The person serving process shall locate the person to be served and shall tender a copy of the process and accompanying documents to the person to be served. When the copy of the process has been served, the person serving process shall endorse that fact on the process and return it to the clerk, who shall make the appropriate entry on the appearance docket.

When the person serving process is unable to serve a copy of the process within twenty-eight days, the person shall endorse that fact and the reasons therefor on the process and return the process and copies to the clerk who shall make the appropriate entry on the appearance docket. In the event of failure of service, the clerk shall follow the notification procedure set forth in division (A) of this rule. Failure to make service within the twenty-eight day period and failure to make proof of service do not affect the validity of the service.

(C) Residence service

When the plaintiff files a written request with the clerk for residence service, service of process shall be made by that method.

Request for Residence Service

Residence service shall be effected by leaving a copy of the process and the complaint, or other document to be served, at the usual place of residence of the person to be served with some person of suitable age and discretion then residing therein. The clerk of the court shall issue the process, and the process server shall return it, in the same manner as prescribed in division (B) of this rule. When the person serving process is unable to serve a copy of the process within twenty-eight days, the person shall endorse that fact and the reasons therefor on the process, and return the process and copies to the clerk, who shall make the appropriate entry on the appearance docket. In the event of failure of service, the clerk shall follow the notification procedure set forth in division (A) of this rule. Failure to make service within the twenty-eight-day period and failure to make proof of service do not affect the validity of service.

CIV. R. RULE 4.3. (Rules of Civil Procedure of Ohio)

Out-of-state service (long-arm jurisdiction)

(A) Service of process may be made outside of this state, as provided in this rule, in any action in this state, upon a person who, at the time of service of process, is a nonresident of this state or is a resident of this state who is absent from this state. "Person" includes an individual, an individual's executor, administrator, or other personal representative, or a corporation, partnership, association, or any other legal or commercial entity, who, acting directly or by an agent, has caused an event to occur out of which the claim that is the subject of the complaint arose, from the person's:

Out-of-State (Long-Arm) Service

(1) Transacting any business in this state;
(2) Contracting to supply services or goods in this state;
(3) Causing tortious injury by an act or omission in this state, including, but not limited to, actions arising out of the ownership, operation, or use of a motor vehicle or aircraft in this state;
(4) Causing tortious injury in this state by an act or omission outside this state if the person regularly does or solicits business, engages in any other persistent course of conduct, or derives substantial revenue from goods used or consumed or services rendered in this state;
(5) Causing injury in this state to any person by breach of warranty expressly or impliedly made in the sale of goods outside this state when the person to be served might reasonably have expected the person who was injured to use, consume, or be affected by the goods in this state, provided that the person to be served also regularly does or solicits business, engages in any other persistent course of conduct, or derives substantial revenue from goods used or consumed or services rendered in this state;
(6) Having an interest in, using, or possessing real property in this state;
(7) Contracting to insure any person, property, or risk located within this state at the time of contracting;
(8) Living in the marital relationship within this state notwithstanding subsequent departure from this state, as to all obligations arising for spousal support, custody, child support, or property settlement, if the other party to the marital relationship continues to reside in this state;
(9) Causing tortious injury in this state to any person by an act outside this state committed with the purpose of injuring persons, when the person to be served might reasonably have expected that some person would be injured by the act in this state;
(10) Causing tortious injury to any person by a criminal act, any element of which takes place in this state, that the person to be served commits or in the commission of which the person to be served is guilty of complicity. . . .

CIV. R. RULE 4.6. Rules of Civil Procedure of Ohio)

(C) Service refused

If service of process is refused, and the certified or express mail envelope is returned with an endorsement showing such refusal, or the return of the person serving process states that service of process has been refused, the clerk shall forthwith notify, by mail, the attorney of record or, if there is no attorney of record, the party at whose instance process was issued. If the attorney, or serving party, after notification by the clerk, files with the clerk

Service of Process that is Refused or Unclaimed

a written request for ordinary mail service, the clerk shall send by ordinary mail a copy of the summons and complaint or other document to be served to the defendant at the address set forth in the caption, or at the address set forth in written instructions furnished to the clerk. The mailing shall be evidenced by a certificate of mailing which shall be completed and filed by the clerk. Answer day shall be twenty-eight days after the date of mailing as evidenced by the certificate of mailing. The clerk shall endorse this answer date upon the summons which is sent by ordinary mail. Service shall be deemed complete when the fact of mailing is entered of record. Failure to claim certified or express mail service is not refusal of service within the meaning of division (C) of this rule.

(D) Service unclaimed

If a certified or express mail envelope is returned with an endorsement showing that the envelope was unclaimed, the clerk shall forthwith notify, by mail, the attorney of record or, if there is no attorney of record, the party at whose instance process was issued. If the attorney, or serving party, after notification by the clerk, files with the clerk a written request for ordinary mail service, the clerk shall send by ordinary mail a copy of the summons and complaint or other document to be served to the defendant at the address set forth in the caption, or at the address set forth in written instructions furnished to the clerk. The mailing shall be evidenced by a certificate of mailing which shall be completed and filed by the clerk. Answer day shall be twenty-eight days after the date of mailing as evidenced by the certificate of mailing. The clerk shall endorse this answer date upon the summons which is sent by ordinary mail. Service shall be deemed complete when the fact of mailing is entered of record, provided that the ordinary mail envelope is not returned by the postal authorities with an endorsement showing failure of delivery. If the ordinary mail envelope is returned undelivered, the clerk shall forthwith notify the attorney, or serving party, by mail. . . .

TIME

CIV. R. RULE 6. (Rules of Civil Procedure of Ohio)

(A) Computation of time

Computation of Time

In computing any period of time prescribed or allowed by these rules, by the local rules of any court, by order of court, or by any applicable statute, the date of the act, event, or default from which the designated period of time begins to run shall not be included. The last day of the period so computed shall be included, unless it is a Saturday, a Sunday, or a legal holiday, in which event the period runs until the end of the next day which is not a Saturday, a Sunday, or a legal holiday. When the period of time prescribed or allowed is less than seven days, intermediate Saturdays, Sundays, and legal holidays shall be excluded in the computation. When a public office in which an act, required by law, rule, or order of court, is to be performed is closed to the public for the entire day which constitutes the last day for doing such an act, or before its usual closing time on such day, then such act may be performed on the next succeeding day which is not a Saturday, a Sunday, or a legal holiday. . . .

(D) Time: motions

A written motion, other than one which may be heard ex parte, and notice of the hearing thereof shall be served not later than seven days before the time fixed for the hearing, unless a different period is fixed by these rules or by order of the court. Such an order may for cause shown be made on ex parte application. When a motion is supported by affidavit, the affidavit shall be served with the motion; and, except as otherwise provided in Rule 59(C), opposing affidavits may be served not later than one day before the hearing, unless the court permits them to be served at some other time.

(E) Time: additional time after service by mail

Whenever a party has the right or is required to do some act or take some proceedings within a prescribed period after the service of a notice or other paper upon him and the notice or paper is served upon him by mail, three days shall be added to the prescribed period. This subdivision does not apply to responses to service of summons under Rule 4 through Rule 4.6.

PLEADINGS

CIV. R. RULE 7. (Rules of Civil Procedure of Ohio)

(A) Pleadings

Complaints and Other Kinds of Pleadings in Ohio Courts

There shall be a complaint and an answer; a reply to a counterclaim denominated as such; an answer to a cross-claim, if the answer contains a cross-claim; a third-party complaint, if a person who was not an original party is summoned under the provisions of Rule 14; and a third-party answer, if a third-party complaint is served. No other pleading shall be allowed, except that the court may order a reply to an answer or a third-party answer.

(B) Motions

(1) An application to the court for an order shall be by motion which, unless made during a hearing or a trial, shall be made in writing. A motion, whether

Requirements for Motions

written or oral, shall state with particularity the grounds therefor, and shall set forth the relief or order sought. The requirement of writing is fulfilled if the motion is stated in a written notice of the hearing of the motion.

(2) To expedite its business, the court may make provision by rule or order for the submission and determination of motions without oral hearing upon brief written statements of reasons in support and opposition.

(3) The rules applicable to captions, signing, and other matters of form of pleading apply to all motions and other papers provided for by these rules.

(4) All motions shall be signed in accordance with Rule 11.

(C) Demurrers abolished

Demurrers shall not be used.

Civ. R. Rule 8. (Rules of Civil Procedure of Ohio)

General rules of pleading

(A) Claims for relief

A pleading that sets forth a claim for relief, whether an original claim, counterclaim, cross-claim, or third-party claim, shall contain (1) a short and plain statement of the claim showing that the party is entitled to relief, and (2) a demand for judgment for the relief to which the party claims to be entitled. If the party seeks more than twenty-five thousand dollars, the party shall so state in the pleading but shall not specify in the demand for judgment the amount of recovery sought, unless the claim is based upon an instrument required to be attached pursuant to Civ. R. 10. At any time after the pleading is filed and served, any party from whom monetary recovery is sought may request in writing that the party seeking recovery provide the requesting party a written statement of the amount of recovery sought. Upon motion, the court shall require the party to respond to the request. Relief in the alternative or of several different types may be demanded.

A "Short and Plain Statement of the Claim"

Statement of Damages

(B) Defenses; form of denials

A party shall state in short and plain terms the party's defenses to each claim asserted and shall admit or deny the averments upon which the adverse party relies. If the party is without knowledge or information sufficient to form a belief as to the truth of an averment, the party shall so state and this has the effect of a denial. Denials shall fairly meet the substance of the averments denied. When a pleader intends in good faith to deny only a part or a qualification of an averment, the pleader shall specify so much of it as is true and material and shall deny the remainder. Unless the pleader intends in good faith to controvert all the averments of the preceding pleading, the pleader may make the denials as specific denials or designated averments or paragraphs, or the pleader may generally deny all the averments except the designated averments or paragraphs as the pleader expressly admits; but, when the pleader does intend to controvert all its averments, including averments of the grounds upon which the court's jurisdiction depends, the pleader may do so by general denial subject to the obligations set forth in Civ. R. 11.

Statement of Defenses

(C) Affirmative defenses

In pleading to a preceding pleading, a party shall set forth affirmatively accord and satisfaction, arbitration and award, assumption of risk, contributory negligence, discharge in bankruptcy, duress, estoppel, failure of consideration, want of consideration for a negotiable instrument, fraud, illegality, injury by fellow servant, laches, license, payment, release, res judicata, statute of frauds, statute of limitations, waiver, and any other matter constituting an avoidance or affirmative defense. When a party has mistakenly designated a defense as a counterclaim or a counterclaim as a defense, the court, if justice so requires, shall treat the pleading as if there had been a proper designation.

Fraud and Other Affirmative Defenses

(D) Effect of failure to deny

Averments in a pleading to which a responsive pleading is required, other than those as to the amount of damage, are admitted when not denied in the responsive pleading. Averments in a pleading to which no responsive pleading is required or permitted shall be taken as denied or avoided.

(E) Pleading to be concise and direct; consistency

(1) Each averment of a pleading shall be simple, concise, and direct. No technical forms of pleading or motions are required.

(2) A party may set forth two or more statements of a claim or defense alternately or hypothetically, either in one count or defense or in separate counts or defenses. When two or more statements are made in the alternative and one of them if made independently would be sufficient, the pleading is not made insufficient by the insufficiency of one or more of the alternative statements. A party may also state as many separate claims or defenses as he has regardless of consistency and whether based on

legal or equitable grounds. All statements shall be made subject to the obligations set forth in Rule 11.

(F) Construction of pleadings

Substantial Justice

All pleadings shall be so construed as to do substantial justice. . . .

CIV. R. RULE 9 (Rules of Civil Procedure of Ohio)

Pleading special matters

(B) Fraud, mistake, condition of the mind

In all averments of fraud or mistake, the circumstances constituting fraud or mistake shall be stated with particularity. Malice, intent, knowledge, and other condition of mind of a person may be averred generally. . . .

Pleading Fraud, Mistake, Malice, Intent, or Knowledge

(G) Special damage

When items of special damage are claimed, they shall be specifically stated.

CIV. R. RULE 10. Form of pleadings

(A) Caption; names of parties

Every pleading shall contain a caption setting forth the name of the court, the title of the action, the case number, and a designation as in Rule 7(A). In the complaint the title of the action shall include the names and addresses of all the parties, but in other pleadings it is sufficient to state the name of the first party on each side with an appropriate indication of other parties.

Caption of Pleadings

(B) Paragraphs; separate statements

All averments of claim or defense shall be made in numbered paragraphs, the contents of each of which shall be limited as far as practicable to a statement of a single set of circumstances; and a paragraph may be referred to by number in all succeeding pleadings. Each claim founded upon a separate transaction or occurrence and each defense other than denials shall be stated in a separate count or defense whenever a separation facilitates the clear presentation of the matters set forth.

Numbered Paragraphs

(C) Adoption by reference; exhibits

Statements in a pleading may be adopted by reference in a different part of the same pleading or in another pleading or in any motion. A copy of any written instrument attached to a pleading is a part of the pleading for all purposes.

(D) Attachments to pleadings

(1) Account or written instrument. When any claim or defense is founded on an account or other written instrument, a copy of the account or written instrument must be attached to the pleading. If the account or written instrument is not attached, the reason for the omission must be stated in the pleading.

(2) Affidavit of merit; medical liability claim.

(a) Except as provided in division (D)(2)(b) of this rule, a complaint that contains a medical claim, dental claim, optometric claim, or chiropractic claim, as defined in section 2305.113 of the Revised Code, shall include an affidavit of merit relative to each defendant named in the complaint for whom expert testimony is necessary to establish liability. The affidavit of merit shall be provided by an expert witness pursuant to Rules 601(D) and 702 of the Ohio Rules of Evidence. The affidavit of merit shall include all of the following:

Medical Liability Cases

(i) A statement that the affiant has reviewed all medical records reasonably available to the plaintiff concerning the allegations contained in the complaint;

(ii) A statement that the affiant is familiar with the applicable standard of care;

(iii) The opinion of the affiant that the standard of care was breached by one or more of the defendants to the action and that the breach caused injury to the plaintiff.

(b) The plaintiff may file a motion to extend the period of time to file an affidavit of merit. The motion shall be filed by the plaintiff with the complaint. For good cause shown, the court shall grant the plaintiff a reasonable period of time to file an affidavit of merit.

(c) An affidavit of merit is required solely to establish the adequacy of the complaint and shall not otherwise be admissible as evidence or used for purposes of impeachment.

(E) Size of paper filed

All pleadings, motions, briefs, and other papers filed with the clerk, including those filed by electronic means, shall be on paper not exceeding 8 1/2 × 11 inches in size without backing or cover.

Size of Paper

CIV. R. RULE 11. Signatures (Rules of Civil Procedure of Ohio)

Every pleading, motion, or other document of a party represented by an attorney shall be signed by at least one attorney of record in the attorney's individual name, whose address, attorney registration number, telephone number, telefax number, if any, and business e-mail address, if any, shall be stated. A party who is not represented by an attorney shall sign the pleading, motion, or other document and state the party's address. Except when otherwise specifically provided by these rules, pleadings need not be verified or accompanied by affidavit. The signature of an attorney or *pro se* party constitutes a certificate by the attorney or party that the attorney or party has read the document; that to the best of the attorney's or party's knowledge, information, and belief there is good ground to support it; and that it is not interposed for delay. If a document is not signed or is signed with intent to defeat the purpose of this rule, it may be stricken as sham and false and the action may proceed as though the document had not been served. For a willful violation of this rule, an attorney or *pro se* party, upon motion of a party or upon the court's own motion, may be subjected to appropriate action, including an award to the opposing party of expenses and reasonable attorney fees incurred in bringing any motion under this rule. Similar action may be taken if scandalous or indecent matter is inserted.

Signing Pleadings

CIV. R. RULE 12. (Rules of Civil Procedure of Ohio)

Defenses and objections

(A) When answer presented

(1) *Generally.* The defendant shall serve his answer within twenty-eight days after service of the summons and complaint upon him; if service of notice has been made by publication, he shall serve his answer within twenty-eight days after the completion of service by publication.

Service of Answers

(2) *Other responses and motions.* A party served with a pleading stating a cross-claim against him shall serve an answer thereto within twenty-eight days after the service upon him. The plaintiff shall serve his reply to a counterclaim in the answer within twenty-eight days after service of the answer or, if a reply is ordered by the court, within twenty-eight days after service of the order, unless the order otherwise directs. . . .

(B) How presented

Every defense, in law or fact, to a claim for relief in any pleading, whether a claim, counterclaim, cross-claim, or third-party claim, shall be asserted in the responsive pleading thereto if one is required, except that the following defenses may at the option of the pleader be made by motion: (1) lack of jurisdiction over the subject matter, (2) lack of jurisdiction over the person, (3) improper venue, (4) insufficiency of process, (5) insufficiency of service of process, (6) failure to state a claim upon which relief can be granted, (7) failure to join a party under Rule 19 or Rule 19.1. . . .

Defenses Raised by Pleadings vs. by Motions

(C) Motion for judgment on the pleadings

After the pleadings are closed but within such time as not to delay the trial, any party may move for judgment on the pleadings.

(D) Preliminary hearings

The defenses specifically enumerated (1) to (7) in subdivision (B) of this rule, whether made in a pleading or by motion, and the motion for judgment mentioned in subdivision (C) of this rule shall be heard and determined before trial on application of any party.

(E) Motion for definite statement

If a pleading to which a responsive pleading is permitted is so vague or ambiguous that a party cannot reasonably be required to frame a responsive pleading, he may move for a definite statement before interposing his responsive pleading. The motion shall point out the defects complained of and the details desired. If the motion is granted and the order of the court is not obeyed within fourteen days after notice of the order or within such other time as the court may fix, the court may strike the pleading to which the motion was directed or make such order as it deems just.

Vague or Ambiguous Pleadings

(F) Motion to strike

Upon motion made by a party before responding to a pleading, or if no responsive pleading is permitted by these rules, upon motion made by a party within twenty-eight days after the service of the pleading upon him or upon the court's own initiative at any time, the court may order stricken from any pleading any insufficient claim or defense or any redundant, immaterial, impertinent or scandalous matter.

Redundant, Immaterial, Impertinent, or Scandalous Pleading

(G) Consolidation of defenses and objections

A party who makes a motion under this rule must join with it the other motions herein provided for and then available to him. If a party makes a motion under this rule and does not include therein all defenses and objections then available to him which this rule permits to be raised by motion, he shall not thereafter assert by motion or responsive pleading, any of the defenses or objections so omitted, except as provided in subdivision (H) of this rule.

(H) Waiver of defenses and objections

Waiver of Defenses

(1) A defense of lack of jurisdiction over the person, improper venue, insufficiency of process, or insufficiency of service of process is waived (A) if omitted from a motion in the circumstances described in subdivision (G), or (B) if it is neither made by motion under this rule nor included in a responsive pleading or an amendment thereof permitted by Rule 15(A) to be made as a matter of course.
(2) A defense of failure to state a claim upon which relief can be granted, a defense of failure to join a party indispensable under Rule 19, and an objection of failure to state a legal defense to a claim may be made in any pleading permitted or ordered under Rule 7(A), or by motion for judgment on the pleadings, or at the trial on the merits.
(3) Whenever it appears by suggestion of the parties or otherwise that the court lacks jurisdiction of the subject matter, the court shall dismiss the action.

CIV. R. RULE 13. (Rules of Civil Procedure of Ohio)

(A) Compulsory counterclaims

Counterclaims

A pleading shall state as a counterclaim any claim which at the time of serving the pleading the pleader has against any opposing party, if it arises out of the transaction or occurrence that is the subject matter of the opposing party's claim and does not require for its adjudication the presence of third parties of whom the court cannot acquire jurisdiction. But the pleader need not state the claim if (1) at the time the action was commenced the claim was the subject of another pending action, or (2) the opposing party brought suit upon his claim by attachment or other process by which the court did not acquire jurisdiction to render a personal judgment on that claim, and the pleader is not stating any counterclaim under this Rule 13.

(B) Permissive counterclaims

A pleading may state as a counterclaim any claim against an opposing party not arising out of the transaction or occurrence that is the subject matter of the opposing party's claim.

(C) Counterclaim exceeding opposing claim

A counterclaim may or may not diminish or defeat the recovery sought by the opposing party. It may claim relief exceeding in amount or different in kind from that sought in the pleading of the opposing party. . . .

PRETRIAL PROCEDURE

CIV. R. RULE 16. (Rules of Civil Procedure of Ohio)

Conferences before Trial

In any action, the court may schedule one or more conferences before trial to accomplish the following objectives:

(1) The possibility of settlement of the action;
(2) The simplification of the issues;
(3) Itemizations of expenses and special damages;
(4) The necessity of amendments to the pleadings;
(5) The exchange of reports of expert witnesses expected to be called by each party;
(6) The exchange of medical reports and hospital records;
(7) The limitation of the number of expert witnesses;
(8) The imposition of sanctions as authorized by Civ. R. 37;
(9) The possibility of obtaining: (a) Admissions of fact; (b) Admissions into evidence of documents and other exhibits that will avoid unnecessary proof;
(10) Other matters as may aid in the disposition of the action. . . .

CLASS ACTION

CIV. R. RULE 23. (Rules of Civil Procedure of Ohio)

(A) Prerequisites to a class action

Requirements for a Class Action

One or more members of a class may sue or be sued as representative parties on behalf of all only if (1) the class is so numerous that joinder of all members is impracticable, (2) there are questions of law or fact common to the class, (3) the claims or defenses of the representative parties are typical of the claims or defenses of the class, and (4) the representative parties will fairly and adequately protect the interests of the class.

(B) Class actions maintainable

An action may be maintained as a class action if the prerequisites of subdivision (A) are satisfied, and in addition:

(1) the prosecution of separate actions by or against individual members of the class would create a risk of (a) inconsistent or varying adjudications with respect to individual members of the class which would establish incompatible standards of conduct for the party opposing the class; or (b) adjudications with respect to individual members of the class which would as a practical matter be dispositive of the interests of the other members not parties to the adjudications or substantially impair or impede their ability to protect their interests; or

(2) the party opposing the class has acted or refused to act on grounds generally applicable to the class, thereby making appropriate final injunctive relief or corresponding declaratory relief with respect to the class as a whole; or

(3) the court finds that the questions of law or fact common to the members of the class predominate over any questions affecting only individual members, and that a class action is superior to other available methods for the fair and efficient adjudication of the controversy. The matters pertinent to the findings include: (a) the interest of members of the class in individually controlling the prosecution or defense of separate actions; (b) the extent and nature of any litigation concerning the controversy already commenced by or against members of the class; (c) the desirability or undesirability of concentrating the litigation of the claims in the particular forum; (d) the difficulties likely to be encountered in the management of a class action. . . .

DISCOVERY: OVERVIEW

CIV. R. RULE 26. (Rules of Civil Procedure of Ohio)

(A) Policy; discovery methods

Goals of Discovery

It is the policy of these rules (1) to preserve the right of attorneys to prepare cases for trial with that degree of privacy necessary to encourage them to prepare their cases thoroughly and to investigate not only the favorable but the unfavorable aspects of such cases and (2) to prevent an attorney from taking undue advantage of his adversary's industry or efforts.

Parties may obtain discovery by one or more of the following methods: deposition upon oral examination or written questions; written interrogatories; production of documents or things or permission to enter upon land or other property, for inspection and other purposes; physical and mental examinations; and requests for admission. Unless the court orders otherwise, the frequency of use of these methods is not limited.

(B) Scope of discovery

Scope of Discovery

Unless otherwise ordered by the court in accordance with these rules, the scope of discovery is as follows:

(1) *In general.* Parties may obtain discovery regarding any matter, not privileged, which is relevant to the subject matter involved in the pending action, whether it relates to the claim or defense of the party seeking discovery or to the claim or defense of any other party, including the existence, description, nature, custody, condition and location of any books, documents, or other tangible things and the identity and location of persons having knowledge of any discoverable matter. It is not ground for objection that the information sought will be inadmissible at the trial if the information sought appears reasonably calculated to lead to the discovery of admissible evidence.

Discovering the Existence of Insurance

(2) *Insurance agreements.* A party may obtain discovery of the existence and contents of any insurance agreement under which any person carrying on an insurance business may be liable to satisfy part or all of a judgment which may be entered in the action or to indemnify or reimburse for payments made to satisfy the judgment. Information concerning the insurance agreement is not by reason of disclosure subject to comment or admissible in evidence at trial.

Attorney Work-Product Rule

(3) *Trial preparation: materials.* Subject to the provisions of subdivision (B)(4) of this rule, a party may obtain discovery of documents and tangible things prepared in anticipation of litigation or for trial by or for another party or by or for that other party's representative (including his attorney, consultant, surety, indemnitor, insurer, or agent) only upon a showing of good cause therefor. A statement concerning the action or its subject matter previously given by the party seeking the statement may be obtained without showing good cause. A statement of a party is (a) a written statement signed or otherwise adopted or approved by the party, or (b) a stenographic, mechanical, electrical, or other recording, or a transcription thereof, which is a substantially verbatim recital of an oral statement which was made by the party and contemporaneously recorded.

(4) *Trial preparation: experts.*

Discovery of Opponent's Experts

(a) Subject to the provisions of subdivision (B)(4)(b) of this rule and Rule 35(B), a party may discover facts known or opinions held by an expert retained or specially employed by another party in anticipation of litigation or preparation for trial only upon a showing that the party seeking discovery is unable without undue hardship to obtain facts and opinions on the same subject by other means or upon a showing of other exceptional circumstances indicating that denial of discovery would cause manifest injustice.

(b) As an alternative or in addition to obtaining discovery under subdivision (B)(4)(a) of this rule, a party by means of interrogatories may require any other party (i) to identify each person whom the other party expects to call as an expert witness at trial, and (ii) to state the subject matter on which the expert is expected to testify. Thereafter, any party may discover from the expert or the other party facts known or opinions held by the expert which are relevant to the stated subject matter. Discovery of the expert's opinions and the grounds therefor is restricted to those previously given to the other party or those to be given on direct examination at trial.

(c) The court may require that the party seeking discovery under subdivision (B)(4)(b) of this rule pay the expert a reasonable fee for time spent in responding to discovery, and, with respect to discovery permitted under subdivision (B)(4)(a) of this rule, may require a party to pay another party a fair portion of the fees and expenses incurred by the latter party in obtaining facts and opinions from the expert.

(C) Protective orders

Annoyances, Excessive Costs, and Other Abuses of Discovery

Upon motion by any party or by the person from whom discovery is sought, and for good cause shown, the court in which the action is pending may make any order that justice requires to protect a party or person from annoyance, embarrassment, oppression, or undue burden or expense, including one or more of the following:

(1) that the discovery not be had; (2) that the discovery may be had only on specified terms and conditions, including a designation of the time or place; (3) that the discovery may be had only by a method of discovery other than that selected by the party seeking discovery; (4) that certain matters not be inquired into or that the scope of the discovery be limited to certain matters; (5) that discovery be conducted with no one present except persons designated by the court; (6) that a deposition after being sealed be opened only by order of the court; (7) that a trade secret or other confidential research, development, or commercial information not be disclosed or be disclosed only in a designated way; (8) that the parties simultaneously file specified documents or information enclosed in sealed envelopes to be opened as directed by the court.

Protective Orders

If the motion for a protective order is denied in whole or in part, the court, on terms and conditions as are just, may order that any party or person provide or permit discovery. The provisions of Civ. R. 37(A)(4) apply to the award of expenses incurred in relation to the motion.

Before any person moves for a protective order under this rule, that person shall make a reasonable effort to resolve the matter through discussion with the attorney or unrepresented party seeking discovery. A motion for a protective order shall be accompanied by a statement reciting the effort made to resolve the matter in accordance with this paragraph.

(D) Sequence and timing of discovery

Unless the court upon motion, for the convenience of parties and witnesses and in the interests of justice, orders otherwise, methods of discovery may be used in any sequence and the fact that a party is conducting discovery, whether by deposition or otherwise, shall not operate to delay any other party's discovery.

(E) Supplementation of responses

A party who has responded to a request for discovery with a response that was complete when made is under no duty to supplement his response to include information thereafter acquired, except as follows:

(1) A party is under a duty seasonably to supplement his response with respect to any question directly addressed to (a) the identity and location of persons having knowledge of discoverable matters, and (b) the identity of each person expected to be called as an expert witness at trial and the subject matter on which he is expected to testify.

Correcting Incorrect Discovery Responses

(2) A party who knows or later learns that his response is incorrect is under a duty seasonably to correct the response.

(3) A duty to supplement responses may be imposed by order of the court, agreement of the parties, or at any time prior to trial through requests for supplementation of prior responses.

DISCOVERY: DEPOSITIONS

CIV. R. RULE 28. (Rules of Civil Procedure of Ohio)

Persons before whom depositions may be taken

(A) Depositions within state

Depositions

Depositions may be taken in this state before: a person authorized to administer any oath by the laws of this state, a person appointed by the court in which the action is pending, or a person agreed upon by written stipulation of all the parties.

(B) Depositions outside state

Depositions may be taken outside this state before: a person authorized to administer oaths in the place where the deposition is taken, a person appointed by the court in which the action is pending, a person agreed upon by written stipulation of all the parties, or, in any foreign country, by any consular officer of the United States within his consular district. . . . [Note: Rule 29 allows the parties to stipulate modifications of this rule.]

CIV. R. RULE 30. Depositions upon oral examination

(A) When depositions may be taken

After commencement of the action, any party may take the testimony of any person, including a party, by deposition upon oral examination. The attendance of a witness deponent may be compelled by the use of subpoena as provided by Civ. R. 45. The attendance of a party deponent may be compelled by the use of notice of examination as provided by division (B) of this rule. . . .

(B) Notice of examination; general requirements; nonstenographic recording; production of documents and things; deposition of organization; deposition by telephone

(1) A party desiring to take the deposition of any person upon oral examination shall give reasonable notice in writing to every other party to the action. The notice shall state the time and place for taking the deposition and the name and address of each person to be examined, if known, and, if the name is not known, a general description sufficient to identify the person or the particular class or group to which the person belongs. If a subpoena duces tecum is to be served on the person to be examined, a designation of the materials to be produced shall be attached to or included in the notice.

(2) If any party shows that when the party was served with notice the party was unable, through the exercise of diligence, to obtain counsel to represent the party at the taking of the deposition, the deposition may not be used against the party.

(3) If a party taking a deposition wishes to have the testimony recorded by other than stenographic means, the notice shall specify the manner of recording, preserving, and filing the deposition. The court may require stenographic taking or make any other order to ensure that the recorded testimony will be accurate and trustworthy.

Recorded Discovery Testimony

(4) The notice to a party deponent may be accompanied by a request made in compliance with Civ. R. 34 for the production of documents and tangible things at the taking of the deposition.

(5) A party, in the party's notice, may name as the deponent a public or private corporation, a partnership, or an association and designate with reasonable particularity the matters on which examination is requested. The organization so named shall choose one or more of its proper employees, officers, agents, or other persons duly authorized to testify on its behalf. The persons so designated shall testify as to matters known or available to the organization. Division (B)(5) does not preclude taking a deposition by any other procedure authorized in these rules.

(6) The parties may stipulate in writing or the court may upon motion order that a deposition be taken by telephone. For purposes of this rule, Civ. R. 28, and Civ. R. 45(C), a deposition taken by telephone is taken in the county and at the place where the deponent is to answer questions propounded to the deponent.

(C) Examination and cross-examination; record of examination; oath; objections

Examination and cross-examination of witnesses may proceed as permitted at the trial. The officer before whom the deposition is to be taken shall put the witness on oath or affirmation and personally, or by someone acting under the officer's direction and in the officer's presence, shall record the testimony of the witness. The testimony shall be taken stenographically or recorded by any other means designated in accordance with division (B)(3) of this rule. If requested by one of the parties, the testimony shall be transcribed.

Examination and Cross-Examination of Deponent

All objections made at the time of the examination to the qualifications of the officer taking the deposition, or to the manner of taking it, or to the evidence presented, or to the conduct of any party, and any other objection to the proceedings, shall be noted by the officer upon the deposition. Evidence objected to shall be taken subject to the objections. In lieu of participating in the oral examination, parties may serve written questions on the party taking the deposition and require him to transmit them to the officer, who shall propound them to the witness and record the answers verbatim.

(D) Motion to terminate or limit examinations

At any time during the taking of the deposition, on motion of any party or of the deponent and upon a showing that the examination is being conducted in bad faith or in such manner as unreasonably to annoy, embarrass, or oppress the deponent or party, the court in which the action is pending may order the officer conducting the examination to cease forthwith from taking the deposition, or may limit the scope and manner of the taking of the deposition as provided in Civ. R. 26(C). If the order made terminates the examination, it shall be resumed thereafter only upon the order of the court in which the action is pending. Upon demand of the objecting party or deponent, the taking of the deposition shall be suspended for the time necessary to make a motion for an order. The provisions of Civ. R. 37 apply to the award of expenses incurred in relation to the motion.

(E) Submission to witness; changes; signing

When the testimony is fully transcribed, the deposition shall be submitted to the witness for examination and shall be read to or by the witness, unless examination and reading are waived by the witness and by the parties. Any changes in form or substance that the witness desires to make shall be entered upon the deposition by the officer with a statement of the reasons given by the witness for making them. The deposition shall then be signed by the witness, unless the parties by stipulation waive the signing or the witness is ill, cannot be found, or refuses to sign. If the deposition is not signed by the witness within seven days of its submission to the witness, or within such longer period, not exceeding twenty-eight days, to which the parties agree, the officer shall sign it and state on the record the fact of the waiver or of the illness or absence of the witness or the fact of the refusal to sign together with the reason, if any, given therefor; and the deposition may then be used as fully as though signed, unless on a motion to suppress the court holds that the reasons given for the refusal to sign require rejection of the deposition in whole or in part.

(F) Certification and filing by officer; exhibits; copies; notice of filing

(1) Upon request of any party or order of the court, the officer shall transcribe the deposition. Provided the officer has retained an archival-quality copy of the officer's notes, the officer shall have no duty to retain paper notes of the deposition testimony beyond five years from the date of the deposition. The officer shall certify on the transcribed deposition that the witness was fully sworn or affirmed by the officer and that the transcribed deposition is a true record of the testimony given by the witness. If any of the parties request or the court orders, the officer shall seal the transcribed deposition in an envelope endorsed with the title of the action and marked "Deposition of (here insert name of witness)" and, upon payment of the officer's fees, promptly shall file it with the court in which the action is pending or send it by certified or express mail to the clerk of the court for filing.

Transcription of Deposition Testimony

Unless objection is made to their production for inspection during the examination of the witness, documents and things shall be marked for identification and annexed to and returned with the deposition. The materials may be inspected and copied by any party, except that the person producing the materials may substitute copies to be marked for identification, if the person affords to all parties fair opportunity to verify the copies by comparison with the originals. If the person producing the materials requests their return, the officer shall mark them, give each party an opportunity to inspect and copy them, and return them to the person producing them, and the materials may then be used in the same manner as if annexed to and returned with the deposition.

(2) Upon payment, the officer shall furnish a copy of the deposition to any party or to the deponent.

(3) The party requesting the filing of the deposition shall forthwith give notice of its filing to all other parties.

(G) Failure to attend or to serve subpoena; expenses

(1) If the party giving the notice of the taking of a deposition fails to attend and proceed with the deposition and another party attends in person or by attorney pursuant to the notice, the court may order the party giving the notice to pay to the other party the amount of the reasonable expenses incurred by the other party and the other party's attorney in so attending, including reasonable attorney's fees.

(2) If the party giving the notice of the taking of a deposition of a witness fails to serve a subpoena upon the witness and the witness because of the failure does not attend, and another party attends in person or by attorney because the other party expects the deposition of that witness to be taken, the court may order the party giving the notice to pay to the other party the amount of the reasonable expenses incurred by the other party and the other party's attorney in so attending, including reasonable attorney's fees.

CIV. R. RULE 31. Depositions of witnesses upon written questions

(A) Serving questions; notice

After commencement of the action, any party may take the testimony of any person, including a party, by deposition upon written questions. The attendance of witnesses may be compelled by the use of subpoena as provided by Rule 45. . . . A party desiring to take a deposition upon written questions shall serve them upon every other party with a notice stating (1) the name and address of the person who is to answer them, if known, and if the name is not known, a general description sufficient to identify him or the particular class or group to which he belongs, and (2) the name or descriptive title and address of the officer before whom the deposition is to be taken. . . . Within twenty-one days after the notice and written questions are served, a party may serve cross questions upon all other parties. Within fourteen days after being served with cross questions, a party may serve redirect questions upon all other parties. Within fourteen days after being served with redirect questions, a party may serve

Deposition upon Written Questions

recross questions upon all other parties. The court may for cause shown enlarge or shorten the time.

(B) Officer to take responses and prepare record

A copy of the notice and copies of all questions served shall be delivered by the party taking the deposition to the officer designated in the notice, who shall proceed promptly, in the manner provided by Rule 30(C), (E), and (F), to take the testimony of the witness in response to the questions and to prepare, certify, and file or mail the deposition, attaching thereto the copy of the notice and the questions received by him. . . .

DISCOVERY: INTERROGATORIES

CIV. R. RULE 33. (Rules of Civil Procedure of Ohio)

Interrogatories to parties

(A) Availability; procedures for use

Interrogatories

Forty Interrogatories

Any party, without leave of court, may serve upon any other party up to forty written interrogatories to be answered by the party served. A party serving interrogatories shall provide the party served with both a printed and an electronic copy of the interrogatories. The electronic copy shall be provided on computer disk, by electronic mail, or by other means agreed to by the parties. A party who is unable to provide an electronic copy of the interrogatories may seek leave of court to be relieved of this requirement. A party shall not propound more than forty interrogatories to any other party without leave of court. Upon motion, and for good cause shown, the court may extend the number of interrogatories that a party may serve upon another party. For purposes of this rule, any subpart propounded under an interrogatory shall be considered a separate interrogatory.

If the party served is a public or private corporation or a partnership or association, the organization shall choose one or more of its proper employees, officers, or agents to answer the interrogatories, and the employee, officer, or agent shall furnish information as is known or available to the organization.

Interrogatories, without leave of court, may be served upon the plaintiff after commencement of the action and upon any other party with or after service of the summons and complaint upon the party.

Each interrogatory shall be answered separately and fully in writing under oath, unless it is objected to, in which event the reasons for objection shall be stated in lieu of an answer. The party upon whom the interrogatories have been served shall quote each interrogatory immediately preceding the corresponding answer or objection. When the number of interrogatories exceeds forty without leave of court, the party upon whom the interrogatories have been served need only answer or object to the first forty interrogatories. The answers are to be signed by the person making them, and the objections signed by the attorney making them. The party upon whom the interrogatories have been served shall serve a copy of the answers and objections within a period designated by the party submitting the interrogatories, not less than twenty-eight days after the service of the interrogatories or within such shorter or longer time as the court may allow. The party submitting the interrogatories may move for an order under Civ. R. 37 with respect to any objection to or other failure to answer an interrogatory.

(B) Scope and use at trial

Interrogatories may relate to any matters that can be inquired into under Civ. R. 26(B), and the answers may be used to the extent permitted by the rules of evidence.

The party calling for such examination shall not thereby be concluded but may rebut it by evidence.

An interrogatory otherwise proper is not objectionable merely because an answer to the interrogatory involves an opinion, contention, or legal conclusion, but the court may order that such an interrogatory be answered at a later time, or after designated discovery has been completed, or at a pretrial conference.

(C) Option to produce business records

Where the answer to an interrogatory may be derived or ascertained from the business records of the party upon whom the interrogatory has been served or from an examination, audit, or inspection of the business records, or from a compilation, abstract, or summary based on the business records, and the burden of deriving or ascertaining the answer is substantially the same for the party serving the interrogatory as for the party served, it is a sufficient answer to the interrogatory to specify the records from which the answer may be derived or ascertained and to afford to the party serving the interrogatory reasonable opportunity to examine, audit, or inspect the records and to make copies of the records or compilations, abstracts, or summaries from the records.

DISCOVERY: PRODUCTION OF DOCUMENTS AND THINGS

CIV. R. RULE 34. (Rules of Civil Procedure of Ohio)

Production of documents and things for inspection, copying, testing and entry upon land for inspection and other purposes

(A) Scope

Subject to the scope of discovery provisions of Civ. R. 26(B), any party may serve on any other party a request

Production of Documents and Things; Entry upon Land

to produce and permit the party making the request, or someone acting on the requesting party's behalf (1) to inspect and copy any designated documents (including writings, drawings, graphs, charts, photographs, phonorecords, and other data compilations from which intelligence can be perceived, with or without the use of detection devices) that are in the possession, custody, or control of the party upon whom the request is served; (2) to inspect and copy, test, or sample any tangible things that are in the possession, custody, or control of the party upon whom the request is served; (3) to enter upon designated land or other property in the possession or control of the party upon whom the request is served for the purpose of inspection and measuring, surveying, photographing, testing, or sampling the property or any designated object or operation on the property.

(B) Procedure

Without leave of court, the request may be served upon the plaintiff after commencement of the action and upon any other party with or after service of the summons and complaint upon that party. The request shall set forth the items to be inspected either by individual item or by category and describe each item and category with reasonable particularity. The request shall specify a reasonable time, place, and manner of making the inspection and performing the related acts.

The party upon whom the request is served shall serve a written response within a period designated in the request that is not less than twenty-eight days after the service of the request or within a shorter or longer time as the court may allow. With respect to each item or category, the response shall state that inspection and related activities will be permitted as requested, unless it is objected to, in which event the reasons for objection shall be stated. If objection is made to part of an item or category, the part shall be specified. The party submitting the request may move for an order under Civ. R. 37 with respect to any objection to or other failure to respond to the request or any part of the request, or any failure to permit inspection as requested.

A party who produces documents for inspection shall, at its option, produce them as they are kept in the usual course of business or organized and labeled to correspond with the categories in the request.

(C) Persons not parties

Subject to the scope of discovery provisions of Civ. R. 26(B) and 45(F), a person not a party to the action may be compelled to produce documents or tangible things or to submit to an inspection as provided in Civ. R. 45. . . .

Discovery: Physical or Mental Examination

CIV. R. RULE 35. (Rules of Civil Procedure of Ohio)

Physical and mental examination of persons

(A) Order for examination

When the mental or physical condition (including the blood group) of a party, or of a person in the custody or under the legal control of a party, is in controversy, the court in which the action is pending may order the party to submit himself to a physical or mental examination or to produce for such examination the person in the party's custody or legal control. The order may be made only on motion for good cause shown and upon notice to the person to be examined and to all parties and shall specify the time, place, manner, conditions, and scope of the examination and the person or persons by whom it is to be made.

Physical or Mental Examination

(B) Examiner's report

(1) If requested by the party against whom an order is made under Rule 35(A) or the person examined, the party causing the examination to be made shall deliver to such party or person a copy of the detailed written report submitted by the examiner to the party causing the examination to be made. The report shall set out the examiner's findings, including results of all tests made, diagnoses and conclusions, together with like reports of all earlier examinations of the same condition. After delivery, the party causing the examination shall be entitled upon request to receive from the party against whom the order is made a like report of any examination, previously or thereafter made, of the same condition, unless, in the case of a report of examination of a person not a party, the party shows that he is unable to obtain it. The court on motion may make an order against a party to require delivery of a report on such terms as are just. If an examiner fails or refuses to make a report, the court on motion may order, at the expense of the party causing the examination, the taking of the deposition of the examiner if his testimony is to be offered at trial.

(2) By requesting and obtaining a report of the examination so ordered or by taking the deposition of the examiner, the party examined waives any privilege he may have in that action or any other involving the same controversy, regarding the testimony of every other person who has examined or may thereafter examine him in respect of the same mental or physical condition.

(3) This subdivision, 35(B), applies to examinations made by agreement of the parties, unless the agreement expressly provides otherwise.

DISCOVERY: REQUESTS FOR ADMISSION

CIV. R. RULE 36. (Rules of Civil Procedure of Ohio)

Requests for admission

(A) Availability; procedures for use

A party may serve upon any other party a written request for the admission, for purposes of the pending action only, of the truth of any matters within the scope of Civ. R. 26(B) set forth in the request, that relate to statements or opinions of fact or of the application of law to fact, including the genuineness of any documents described in the request. Copies of documents shall be served with the request unless they have been or are otherwise furnished or made available for inspection and copying. The request may, without leave of court, be served upon the plaintiff after commencement of the action and upon any other party with or after service of the summons and complaint upon that party. A party serving a request for admission shall provide the party served with both a printed and an electronic copy of the request for admission. The electronic copy shall be provided on computer disk, by electronic mail, or by other means agreed to by the parties. A party who is unable to provide an electronic copy of a request for admission may seek leave of court to be relieved of this requirement.

Requests for Admission

Each matter of which an admission is requested shall be separately set forth. The party to whom the requests for admissions have been directed shall quote each request for admission immediately preceding the corresponding answer or objection. The matter is admitted unless, within a period designated in the request, not less than twenty-eight days after service thereof or within such shorter or longer time as the court may allow, the party to whom the request is directed serves upon the party requesting the admission a written answer or objection addressed to the matter, signed by the party or by the party's attorney. If objection is made, the reasons therefor shall be stated. The answer shall specifically deny the matter or set forth in detail the reasons why the answering party cannot truthfully admit or deny the matter. A denial shall fairly meet the substance of the requested admission, and when good faith requires that a party qualify his or her answer, or deny only a part of the matter of which an admission is requested, the party shall specify so much of it as is true and qualify or deny the remainder. An answering party may not give lack of information or knowledge as a reason for failure to admit or deny unless the party states that he or she has made reasonable inquiry and that the information known or readily obtainable by the party is insufficient to enable the party to admit or deny. A party who considers that a matter of which an admission has been requested presents a genuine issue for trial may not, on that ground alone, object to the request; the party may, subject to the provisions of Civ. R. 37(C), deny the matter or set forth reasons why the party cannot admit or deny it.

The party who has requested the admissions may move for an order with respect to the answers or objections. Unless the court determines that an objection is justified, it shall order that an answer be served. If the court determines that an answer does not comply with the requirements of this rule, it may order either that the matter is admitted or that an amended answer be served. The court may, in lieu of these orders, determine that final disposition of the request be made at a pretrial conference or at a designated time prior to trial. The provisions of Civ. R. 37(A)(4) apply to the award of expenses incurred in relation to the motion.

(B) Effect of admission

Any matter admitted under this rule is conclusively established unless the court on motion permits withdrawal or amendment of the admission. Subject to the provisions of Civ. R. 16 governing modification of a pretrial order, the court may permit withdrawal or amendment when the presentation of the merits of the action will be subserved thereby and the party who obtained the admission fails to satisfy the court that withdrawal or amendment will prejudice the party in maintaining his action or defense on the merits. Any admission made by a party under this rule is for the purpose of the pending action only and is not an admission by the party for any other purpose nor may it be used against the party in any other proceeding.

(C) Document containing request for admission

If a party includes a request for admission in a document containing any other form of discovery, the party shall include a caption on the document that indicates the document contains a request for admission. A party is not required to respond to requests for admission that are not made in compliance with this division.

Discovery: Sanctions

CIV. R. RULE 37 (Rules of Civil Procedure of Ohio)

Failure to make discovery: sanctions

(A) Motion for order compelling discovery

Upon reasonable notice to other parties and all persons affected thereby, a party may move for an order compelling discovery as follows:

Compelling Discovery; Sanctions for Abuse

(1) *Appropriate court.* A motion for an order to a party or a deponent shall be made to the court in which the action is pending.

(2) *Motion.* If a deponent fails to answer a question propounded or submitted under Rule 30 or Rule 31, or

a party fails to answer an interrogatory submitted under Rule 33, or if a party, in response to a request for inspection submitted under Rule 34, fails to respond that inspection will be permitted as requested or fails to permit inspection as requested, the discovering party may move for an order compelling an answer or an order compelling inspection in accordance with the request. On matters relating to a deposition on oral examination, the proponent of the question may complete or adjourn the examination before he applies for an order.

(3) *Evasive or incomplete answer.* For purposes of this subdivision an evasive or incomplete answer is a failure to answer.

(4) *Award of expenses of motion.* If the motion is granted, the court shall, after opportunity for hearing, require the party or deponent who opposed the motion or the party or attorney advising such conduct or both of them to pay to the moving party the reasonable expenses incurred in obtaining the order, including attorney's fees, unless the court finds that the opposition to the motion was substantially justified or that other circumstances make an award of expenses unjust.

If the motion is denied, the court shall, after opportunity for hearing, require the moving party or the attorney advising the motion or both of them to pay to the party or deponent who opposed the motion the reasonable expenses incurred in opposing the motion, including attorney's fees, unless the court finds that the making of the motion was substantially justified or that other circumstances make an award of expenses unjust.

If the motion is granted in part and denied in part, the court may apportion the reasonable expenses incurred in relation to the motion among the parties and persons in a just manner.

(B) Failure to comply with order

(1) If a deponent fails to be sworn or to answer a question after being directed to do so by the court, the failure may be considered a contempt of that court.

(2) If any party or an officer, director, or managing agent of a party or a person designated under Rule 30(B)(5) or Rule 31(A) to testify on behalf of a party fails to obey an order to provide or permit discovery, including an order made under subdivision (A) of this rule and Rule 35, the court in which the action is pending may make such orders in regard to the failure as are just, and among others the following:

(a) An order that the matters regarding which the order was made or any other designated facts shall be taken to be established for the purposes of the action in accordance with the claim of the party obtaining the order;

(b) An order refusing to allow the disobedient party to support or oppose designated claims or defenses, or prohibiting him from introducing designated matters in evidence;

(c) An order striking out pleadings or parts thereof, or staying further proceedings until the order is obeyed, or dismissing the action or proceeding or any part thereof, or rendering a judgment by default against the disobedient party;

(d) In lieu of any of the foregoing orders or in addition thereto, an order treating as a contempt of court the failure to obey any orders except an order to submit to a physical or mental examination;

(e) Where a party has failed to comply with an order under Rule 35(A) requiring him to produce another for examination, such orders as are listed in subsections (a), (b), and (c) of this subdivision, unless the party failing to comply shows that he is unable to produce such person for examination.

In lieu of any of the foregoing orders or in addition thereto, the court shall require the party failing to obey the order or the attorney advising him or both to pay the reasonable expenses, including attorney's fees, caused by the failure, unless the court expressly finds that the failure was substantially justified or that other circumstances make an award of expenses unjust.

(C) Expenses on failure to admit

If a party, after being served with a request for admission under Rule 36, fails to admit the genuineness of any documents or the truth of any matter as requested, and if the party requesting the admissions thereafter proves the genuineness of the document or the truth of the matter, he may apply to the court for an order requiring the other party to pay him the reasonable expenses incurred in making that proof, including reasonable attorney's fees. Unless the request had been held objectionable under Rule 36(A) or the court finds that there was good reason for the failure to admit or that the admission sought was of no substantial importance, the order shall be made.

(D) Failure of party to attend at own deposition or serve answers to interrogatories or respond to request for inspection

If a party or an officer, director, or a managing agent of a party or a person designated under Rule 30(B)(5) or Rule 3i(A) to testify on behalf of a party fails (1) to appear before the officer who is to take his deposition, after being served with a proper notice, or (2) to serve answers or objections to interrogatories submitted under Rule 33, after proper service of the interrogatories, or (3) to serve a written response to a request for inspection submitted under Rule 34, after proper service of the request, the court in which the action is pending on motion and notice may make such orders in regard to the failure as are just, and among others it may take any action authorized under subsections (a), (b), and (c) of subdivision (B)(2) of this rule. In lieu of any order or in addition thereto, the court shall require the party failing to act or the attorney advising him or both to pay the reasonable expenses, including attorney's fees, caused by the failure, unless the court expressly finds that the failure was substantially justified or that other circumstances make an award of expenses unjust.

The failure to act described in this subdivision may not be excused on the ground that the discovery sought is objectionable unless the party failing to act has applied for a protective order as provided by Rule 26(C).

(E) Before filing a motion authorized by this rule, the party shall make a reasonable effort to resolve the matter through discussion with the attorney, unrepresented party, or person from whom discovery is sought. The motion shall be accompanied by a statement reciting the efforts made to resolve the matter in accordance with this section.

ATTORNEY-CLIENT PRIVILEGE

Ohio Revised Code §2317.02

Privileged communications and acts

The following persons shall not testify in certain respects:

(A) An attorney, concerning a communication made to the attorney by a client in that relation or the attorney's advice to a client, except that the attorney may testify by express consent of the client or, if the client is deceased, by the express consent of the surviving spouse or the executor or administrator of the estate of the deceased client and except that, if the client voluntarily testifies or is deemed by section 2151.421 of the Revised Code to have waived any testimonial privilege under this division, the attorney may be compelled to testify on the same subject. . . .

Attorney-Client Privilege

C. More Information

Ohio Code of Civil Procedure
www.sconet.state.oh.us/Rules
www.sconet.state.oh.us/Rules/civil/default.asp
www.megalaw.com/oh/top/ohcivpro.php

Ohio Rules of Appellate Procedure
www.sconet.state.oh.us/Rules/appellate/default.asp

Ohio Rules of Evidence
www.sconet.state.oh.us/Rules/evidence/default.asp

General
www.law.csuohio.edu/lawlibrary/lawpubs/CivilProcedureResearchGuide.htm

D. Something to Check

1. Go to the site that contains the Code of Civil Procedure of Ohio (see More Information above). Do a search for any three topics covered in the statutes excerpted in this section. Look for *additional* statutes on these topics. Summarize what you find.
2. Go to the site that contains the Ohio Rules of Evidence (see More Information above). In these rules, what is the definition of hearsay?

6.3 State and Federal Civil Litigation in Ohio: Some Comparisons

A. Introduction

You will find overviews of state court jurisdiction and civil litigation in sections 4.2, 6.1, and 6.2. Federal courts sitting in Ohio are discussed in section 4.3. In this section, we will briefly outline some comparisons between litigating civil cases in Ohio courts and in the federal courts. Criminal cases are covered in sections 6.4 and 7.5.

Abbreviations

Civ.R. Rules of Civil Procedure of Ohio
FRCP: Federal Rules of Civil Procedure
R.C.: Revised Code of Ohio
USC: United States Code

B. Comparisons

Some comparisons between state and federal civil litigation are presented in Exhibit 6.3A.

EXHIBIT 6.3A State and Federal Civil Litigation: Some Points of Comparison

State Litigation	Federal Litigation
Major Courts Supreme Court of Ohio Ohio District Courts of Appeals Court of Claims of Ohio Courts of Common Pleas (General, Domestic Relations, Probate, and Juvenile Divisions) Municipal Courts (Small Claims Courts) County Courts (Small Claims Courts) Mayor's Courts	Major Courts Supreme Court of the United States United States Courts of Appeals United States District Courts United States Court of International Trade United States Court of Federal Claims United States Court of Appeals for the Armed Services United States Tax Court United States Court of Appeals for Veterans Claims Judicial Panel on Multidistrict Litigation
Subject-Matter Jurisdiction of Main Trial Court Court of Common Pleas (a court of general jurisdiction) -all felony cases -civil cases where the amount in controversy exceeds $500 (no upper limit) -appeals of administrative agency cases -exclusive mental health, estate, domestic relations, and juvenile jurisdiction (R.C. §§ 2305.01 et seq.)	Subject-Matter Jurisdiction of Main Trial Court United States District Court (a court of general jurisdiction) -federal questions -diversity cases (over $ 75,000) (28 USC §§ 1331; 1332)
Venue Examples: -county in which the defendant resides -county in which the defendant has his or her principal place of business -county in which the defendant conducted activity that gave rise to the claim for relief -county in which the property is situated if the subject of the action is real property or tangible personal property -county in which all or part of the claim for relief arose -county in which the plaintiff is and has been a resident for at least ninety days immediately preceding the filing of the complaint in actions for divorce, annulment, or legal separation (Civ.R. 3(B))	Venue Examples: -district where a substantial part of the events or omissions giving rise to the claim occurred or where the property in dispute is located -any district if the defendant is an alien (28 USC § 1391)
Forum Non Conveniens The doctrine of forum non conveniens permits a court to dismiss or transfer a case, despite the fact that venue is proper and it has jurisdiction, because there is a more appropriate forum in which the action may be heard. The doctrine permits a court to dismiss or transfer a case if it serves the administration of justice and the convenience of the parties, witnesses and the court. *Hughes v. Scaffide* (1978), 53 Ohio St.2d 85, 87, 372 N.E.2d 598, 600.	Forum Non Conveniens For the convenience of parties and witnesses, in the interest of justice, a district court may transfer any civil action to any other district or division where it might have been brought. (28 USC § 1404(a))
Joinder of Parties -Compulsory (Civ.R. 19) -Permissive (Civ.R. 20)	Joinder of Parties -Compulsory (FRCP 19) -Permissive (FRCP 20)
Complaint Notice pleading. A pleading that sets forth a claim for relief shall contain (1) a short and plain statement of the claim showing that the party is entitled to relief, and (2) a demand for judgment for the relief to which the party claims to be entitled. Relief in the alternative or of several different types may be demanded. (Civ.R. 8(A)) Each averment of a pleading shall be simple, concise, and direct. No technical forms of pleading or motions are required. (Civ.R. 8(E)(1))	Complaint Notice Pleading. A pleading which sets forth a claim for relief shall contain a short and plain statement of the claim showing that the pleader is entitled to relief, and a demand for judgment for the relief the pleader seeks. Relief in the alternative or of several different types may be demanded. (FRCP 8(a)) Each averment of a pleading shall be simple, concise, and direct. No technical forms of pleading or motions are required. (FRCP (8)(e)(1))
Special Damages When items of special damage are claimed, they shall be specifically stated. (Civ.R. 9(G))	Special Damages When items of special damage are claimed, they shall be specifically stated. (FRCP 9(g))
Subscription Every pleading, motion, or other document of a party represented by an attorney shall be signed by at least one attorney of record in the attorney's individual name, whose address, attorney registration number, telephone number, telefax number, if any, and business e-mail address, if any, shall be stated. A party who is not represented by an attorney shall sign the pleading, motion, or other document and state the party's address. (Civ.R. 11)	Subscription Every pleading, written motion, and other paper shall be signed by at least one attorney of record in the attorney's individual name, or, if the party is not represented by an attorney, shall be signed by the party. Each paper shall state the signer's address and telephone number, if any. (FRCP 11)
Time Limit for Service If a service of the summons and complaint is not made upon a defendant within six months after the filing of the complaint and the party on whose behalf such service was required cannot show good cause why such service was not made within that period, the action shall be dismissed as to that defendant without prejudice upon the court's own initiative with notice to such party or upon motion. (Civ.R. 4(E))	Time Limit for Service If service of the summons and complaint is not made upon a defendant within 120 days after the filing of the complaint, the court, upon motion or on its own initiative after notice to the plaintiff, shall dismiss the action without prejudice as to that defendant or direct that service be effected within a specified time. (FRCP 4(m))
Motion for Definite Statement If a pleading to which a responsive pleading is permitted is so vague or ambiguous that a party cannot reasonably be required to frame a responsive pleading, he may move for a definite statement before interposing his responsive pleading. The motion shall point out the defects complained of and the details desired. If the motion is granted and the order of the court is not obeyed within fourteen days after notice of the order or within such other time as the court may fix, the court may strike the pleading to which the motion was directed or make such order as it deems just. (Civ.R. 12(E))	Motion for a More Definite Statement If a pleading to which a responsive pleading is permitted is so vague or ambiguous that a party cannot reasonably be required to frame a responsive pleading, the party may move for a more definite statement before interposing a responsive pleading. The motion shall point out the defects complained of and the details desired. If the motion is granted and the order of the court is not obeyed within 10 days after notice of the order or within such other time as the court may fix, the court may strike the pleading to which the motion was directed or make such order as it deems just. (FRCP 12(e))
Answer A party shall state in short and plain terms the party's defenses to each claim asserted and shall admit or deny the averments upon which the adverse party relies. If the party is without knowledge or information sufficient to form a belief as to the truth of an averment, the party shall so state and this has the effect of a denial. (Civ.R. 8(B)) Each averment of a pleading shall be simple, concise, and direct. No technical forms of pleading or motions are required. (Civ.R. 8(E)(1))	Answer A party shall state in short and plain terms the party's defenses to each claim asserted and shall admit or deny the averments upon which the adverse party relies. If a party is without knowledge or information sufficient to form a belief as to the truth of an averment, the party shall so state and this has the effect of a denial. (FRCP 8(b)) Each averment of a pleading shall be simple, concise, and direct. No technical forms of pleading or motions are required. (FRCP (8)(e)(1))
Time Limit for Answer Generally. The defendant shall serve his answer within twenty-eight days after service of the summons and complaint upon him; if service of notice has been made by publication, he shall serve his answer within twenty-eight days after the completion of service by publication. (Civ.R. 12(A)(1))	Time Limit for Answer Unless a different time is prescribed in a statute of the United States, a defendant shall serve an answer within 20 days after being served with the summons and complaint. (FRCP 12(a)(1))
Amendments to Pleadings A party may amend his pleading once as a matter of course at any time before a responsive pleading is served or, if the pleading is one to which no responsive pleading is permitted and the action has not been placed upon the trial calendar, he may so amend it at any time within twenty-eight days after it is served. Otherwise a party may amend his pleading only by leave of court or by written consent of the adverse party. Leave of court shall be freely given when justice so requires. (Civ.R. 15(A))	Amendments to Pleadings A party may amend the party's pleading once as a matter of course at any time before a responsive pleading is served or, if the pleading is one to which no responsive pleading is permitted and the action has not been placed upon the trial calendar, the party may so amend it at any time within 20 days after it is served. Otherwise a party may amend the party's pleading only by leave of court or by written consent of the adverse party; and leave shall be freely given when justice so requires. (FRCP 15(a))
What Is Discoverable: Scope of Discovery Parties may obtain discovery regarding any matter, not privileged, which is relevant to the subject matter involved in the pending action, whether it relates to the claim or defense of the party seeking discovery or to the claim or defense of any other party, including the existence, description, nature, custody, condition and location of any books, documents, or other tangible things and the identity and location of persons having knowledge of any discoverable matter. It is not ground for objection that the information sought will be inadmissible at the trial if the information sought appears reasonably calculated to lead to the discovery of admissible evidence. (Civ.R. 26 (B)(1))	What Is Discoverable: Scope of Discovery Parties may obtain discovery regarding any matter, not privileged, that is relevant to the claim or defense of any party, including the existence, description, nature, custody, condition, and location of any books, documents, or other tangible things and the identity and location of persons having knowledge of any discoverable matter. For good cause, the court may order discovery of any matter relevant to the subject matter involved in the action. Relevant information need not be admissible at the trial if the discovery appears reasonably calculated to lead to the discovery of admissible evidence. (FRCP Rule 26(b))

Work-Product Rule A party may obtain discovery of documents and tangible things prepared in anticipation of litigation or for trial by or for another party or by or for that other party's representative (including his attorney, consultant, surety, indemnitor, insurer, or agent) only upon a showing of good cause therefor. (Civ.R. 26 (B)(3)) "The other type of work product is 'opinion work product,' which reflects the attorney's mental impressions, opinions, conclusions, judgments, or legal theories. . . . Because opinion work product concerns the mental processes of the attorney, not discoverable fact, opinion work product receives near absolute protection. . . . Notes made by the attorney or his agents that record the witness's statement, but that also convey the impressions of the interviewer, are protected as opinion work product, because such notes reveal the attorney's or agent's thoughts." *State v. Hoop* (1999) 134 Ohio App.3d 627, 642, 731 N.E.2d 1177, 1187-1188.	Work-Product Rule A party may obtain discovery of documents and tangible things otherwise discoverable under subdivision (b)(1) of this rule and prepared in anticipation of litigation or for trial by or for another party or by or for that other party's representative (including the other party's attorney, consultant, surety, indemnitor, insurer, or agent) only upon a showing that the party seeking discovery has substantial need of the materials in the preparation of the party's case and that the party is unable without undue hardship to obtain the substantial equivalent of the materials by other means. In ordering discovery of such materials when the required showing has been made, the court shall protect against disclosure of the mental impressions, conclusions, opinions, or legal theories of an attorney or other representative of a party concerning the litigation. (FRCP 26(b)(3))
Attorney-Client Privilege The following persons shall not testify in certain respects: (A) An attorney, concerning a communication made to the attorney by a client in that relation or the attorney's advice to a client, except that the attorney may testify by express consent of the client or, if the client is deceased, by the express consent of the surviving spouse or the executor or administrator of the estate of the deceased client and except that, if the client voluntarily testifies or is deemed by section 2151.421 of the Revised Code to have waived any testimonial privilege under this division, the attorney may be compelled to testify on the same subject. (R.C. $ 2317.02)	Attorney-Client Privilege Under the doctrine of attorney-client privilege, confidential communications between a client and an attorney for the purpose of obtaining legal advice are privileged. A court cannot compel revelation of these communications through discovery or testimony in civil or criminal matters. This doctrine is a common law privilege that can be explicitly or implicitly waived by the client and is subject to a number of restrictions and exceptions. The privilege is implicitly waived if the client communicates information to his attorney without the intent that that information remain confidential. *Denius v. Dunlap* 209 F.3d 944, 952 (7th Cir. 2000)
Methods of Discovery -Interrogatories (Civ.R. 33) -Deposition (Civ.R. 30) -Requests for admissions (Civ.R. 36) -Production of documents and things and entry on land for inspection and other purposes (Civ.R. 34) -Physical or mental examination (Civ.R. 35)	Methods of Discovery -Interrogatories (FRCP 33) -Deposition (FRCP 30) -Requests for admissions (FRCP 36) -Production of documents and things and entry on land for inspection and other purposes (FRCP 34) -Physical or mental examination (FRCP 35)
Summary Judgment A party may move for summary judgment at any time after the expiration of the time permitted under these rules for a responsive motion or pleading by the adverse party, or after service of a motion for summary judgment by the adverse party. If the action has been set for pretrial or trial, a motion for summary judgment may be made only with leave of court. (Civ.R. 56(A)) Summary judgment shall be rendered forthwith if the pleadings, depositions, answers to interrogatories, written admissions, affidavits, transcripts of evidence, and written stipulations of fact, if any, timely filed in the action, show that there is no genuine issue as to any material fact and that the moving party is entitled to judgment as a matter of law. A summary judgment may be rendered on the issue of liability alone although there is a genuine issue as to the amount of damages. (Civ.R. 56(C))	Summary Judgment A party may, at any time after the expiration of 20 days from the commencement of the action move for a summary judgment. The judgment sought shall be rendered forthwith if the pleadings, depositions, answers to interrogatories, and admissions on file, together with the affidavits, if any, show that there is no genuine issue as to any material fact and that the moving party is entitled to a judgment as a matter of law. A summary judgment may be rendered on the issue of liability alone although there is a genuine issue as to the amount of damages. (FRCP 56(a)(c))
Pretrial Planning Procedures -Pretrial procedures (Civ.R. 16(1-10))	Pretrial Planning Procedures -Pretrial conferences (FRCP 16(a-c)) -Final pretrial conferences (FRCP 16(d))
Alternate Dispute Resolution Many Ohio courts encourage ADR and have programs and local rules on how they operate within their courts. Examples include direct settlement negotiation between the parties, conciliation, mediation, settlement conferences, neutral fact-finding, early neutral evaluation, mini-trials, summary jury trials, arbitration, and private judging. Ohio State Bar Association (*www.ohiobar.org/pub/lawfacts/index.asp?articleid=18*) Ohio Commission on Dispute Resolution and Conflict Management (*disputeresolution.ohio.gov*)	Alternate Dispute Resolution An alternative dispute resolution process includes any process or procedure, other than an adjudication by a presiding judge, in which a neutral third party participates to assist in the resolution of issues in controversy, through processes such as early neutral evaluation, mediation, minitrial, and arbitration. Each United States district court shall authorize, by local rule the use of alternative dispute resolution processes in all civil actions. Each United States district court shall devise and implement its own alternative dispute resolution program to encourage and promote the use of alternative dispute resolution in its district. (28 USC § 651)

C. More Information

Ohio Code of Civil Procedure
www.sconet.state.oh.us/Rules/civil/default.asp

Overview of Ohio Civil Litigation
www.ohiobar.org/pub/?articleid=104
downloads.ohiobar.org/conres/lawandyou/Law_and_You_3.pdf
www.megalaw.com/oh/top/ohcivpro.php

Court Rules in Ohio Courts
www.llrx.com/courtrules-gen/state-Ohio.html

Alternative Dispute Resolution (ADR)
www.ohiobar.org/pub/lawfacts/index.asp?articleid=18
disputeresolution.ohio.gov/nfpmap.htm
www.mediate.com/ohio

Federal Rules of Civil Procedure
www.law.cornell.edu/rules/frcp/?
www.lectlaw.com/tcrf.htm

Federal Courts Overview
www.uscourts.gov/journalistguide/welcome.html

D. Something to Check

Using the online sites that give the text of state and federal statutes (see the sites under More Information), compare the state and federal rules on:

1. Interrogatories
2. Sanctions for failure to comply with discovery requests

6.4 Timeline: A Criminal Case in the Ohio State Courts

A. Introduction

In this section, we will focus on the major procedural steps involved in prosecuting serious criminal cases in the Ohio state courts. Over 80,000 felony cases are filed in Ohio state courts a year. (*www.ncsconline.org/D_Research/csp/2004_Files/EWCriminal_final_2.pdf*) Such cases can vary a great deal in complexity depending on the nature of the charge, the extent of contention between the state and the accused, and the caliber of attorneys representing both sides. With this qualification in mind, the overview presented here will apply to many serious criminal cases brought in the Ohio state courts. See also the following related sections:

- overview of Ohio state courts (section 4.2)
- overview of federal courts sitting in Ohio (section 4.3)
- example of a criminal complaint (section 7.6)

B. Overview of a Criminal Case

Exhibit 6.4A presents an overview of a typical criminal case in the Ohio state courts.

Crime Alleged

The categories of crimes that can be committed in Ohio are as follows:

Felony. In Ohio, a felony is an offense defined by law as a felony. (The general definition of felony is a crime punishable by death or imprisonment for a term exceeding a year; a crime more serious than a misdemeanor.)

Misdemeanor. In Ohio, a misdemeanor is an offense defined by law as a misdemeanor. (The general definition of misdemeanor is a crime punishable by fine or by detention in an institution other than a prison or penitentiary; a crime that is not as serious as a felony.)

Serious offense. Any felony, and any misdemeanor for which the penalty prescribed by law includes confinement for more than 6 months.

Petty offense. A misdemeanor other than serious offense.

Commencement of Case

Arrest with a warrant. A judge or other designated court official can issue a warrant that directs a police officer to arrest a person if satisfied that the latter probably violated the criminal law of Ohio.

Arrest without a warrant. A police office can arrest someone without a warrant (a) if the officer has probable cause to believe that the person has committed a felony, (b) if the person has committed a misdemeanor in the presence of the officer, of (c) if the officer has reasonable cause to believe that the person has committed designated misdemeanors such as theft, domestic violence, or public indecency.

Summons or citation in lieu of arrest. Instead of arresting someone, the officer can issue a summons or citation if convinced that an arrest is not needed to assure the accused's attendance in court. A citation serves the function of a complaint and summons by informing the accused of the alleged violation and when he or she must appear in court.

Citizen's arrest. A private citizen (someone who is not a police officer) can arrest someone if the citizen has reasonable cause to believe that the person has committed a felony.

Filing the complaint. A criminal case against a person formally begins in court when a complaint against that person is filed in court. A complaint is a written statement of the essential facts constituting the offense charged. It must state the numerical designation of the applicable statute or ordinance of the crime involved. It is made upon oath before any person authorized by law to administer oaths. (Rule 3, Ohio Rules of Criminal Procedure) If the accused was issued a citation, the citation itself is filed since it includes the complaint.

EXHIBIT 6.4A The Prosecution of a Criminal Case in Ohio State Courts

CRIME ALLEGED	COMMENCEMENT OF CASE	INITIAL APPEARANCE	PRELIMINARY HEARING & GRAND JURY	MOTIONS, DISCOVERY & PRETRIAL CONFERENCES	TRIAL	APPEAL & POST-CONVICTION RELIEF
-Felony -Misdemeanor -Serious Offense -Petty Offense	-Arrest with a warrant -Arrest without a warrant -Summons or citation in lieu of arrest -Citizen's arrest -Filing the complaint -Grand jury indictment prior to arrest -Bill of information	-Arraignment -Entering a plea -Plea bargaining -Setting Bail	-Preliminary hearing (dismissal; binding over) -Waiver -Grand jury (no bill; true bill)	-Bill of particulars -Motion to suppress -Other motions -Alibi defense -Discovery by the prosecution -Pretrial conferences	-Jury selection -Opening statements -Prosecution's case -Defense's case -Jury instructions -Verdict -Motion for a new trial -Motion for a judgment notwithstanding the verdict -Sentencing	-Appeal -Post-conviction relief

Grand jury indictment prior to arrest. Another way to begin a criminal case is for the grand jury to issue a formal accusation (called an indictment) against a person who has not been arrested or issued a summons or citation. In most cases, the grand jury becomes involved *after* arrest, but it is possible for the grand jury to indict someone who has not yet been arrested or involved in court proceedings.

Bill of information. A prosecutor can begin a case by filing a bill of information in court. Trying someone on a bill of information (rather than upon a grand jury indictment) is rare and in most cases requires the consent of the accused.

Initial Appearance

Arraignment. At the court proceeding called the arraignment, the judge makes sure that the accused understands (a) the nature of the charges (b) the right to hire counsel or to have counsel appointed, (c) the right to bail if charged with a bailable offense, (d) the right to remain silent, and (e) the rule that any statement the accused decides to make can be used against him or her by the state.

Entering a plea. The following pleas can be entered by the accused at any time such as during the arraignment: (a) guilty, (b) not guilty, (c) not guilty by reason of insanity because at the time the offense was committed the accused did not know the wrongfulness of the act due to a severe mental disease or defect, and (d) no contest if the accused admits the facts in the accusation but does not admit guilt.

Plea bargaining. The accused may be allowed to plead guilty to a less serious offense than the one charged. When this occurs, the record must contain the underlying facts involving the plea bargaining agreement.

Setting bail. Bail is the deposit of property (e.g., money) in court or a promise to pay or forfeit such property to the court if the accused fails to appear at all court proceedings or to comply with specified conditions such as travel restrictions and noncontact with the victim. In serious cases, bail is set at a court hearing. In some misdemeanor cases, however, a preset amount of bail can be paid by the accused at the police station without a court hearing. The forms of bail are (a) secured bail bond in which nonappearance results in forfeiture of a surety bond that the accused often buys from a bail bondsman, (b) unsecured bail bond in which nonappearance results in forfeiture of property not covered by security, (c) 10-percent bond in which nonappearance results in forfeiture of the minimum amount the accused was allowed to deposit in court, which was 10 percent of the full bond, and (d) personal recognizance in which nonappearance does not lead to forfeiture of any property since none was required. Personal recognizance is merely a promise to appear.

Preliminary Hearing and Grand Jury

Preliminary hearing. At a preliminary hearing in a felony case, a judge (or magistrate) of a municipal court or county court will examine the evidence to decide if credible evidence establishes probable cause that the accused committed the crime. If such evidence is found, a *bindover* occurs under which the court transfers the case to (binds the accused to) the grand jury. The case stays in the municipal or county court, however, if the court determines that there is probable cause the accused committed a misdemeanor rather than a felony.

Waiver. If the accused waives his or her right to a preliminary hearing, the case is automatically bound over to the grand jury.

Grand jury. After the grand jury examines the evidence presented by the county prosecutor, it will (a) return a *no bill* that dismisses the case if it finds insufficient evidence that the accused committed the crime, or (b) return a *true bill* leading to an indictment if it finds enough evidence that the accused committed a crime.

Motions, Discovery, and Pretrial Conferences

Bill of particulars. The accused can file a motion asking for a bill of particulars, which provides additional details on the facts constituting the criminal charges.

Motion to suppress. The accused can ask that certain evidence not be considered (i.e., that it be suppressed) on the ground that the evidence was obtained by an illegal search and seizure or other violation of the accused's constitutional rights.

Other motions. The accused may seek relief by filing other motions such as motions that address defects in the indictment or allegations.

Alibi defense. As a condition of raising the defense of alibi, the accused must summit a written notice to the court indicating where he or she claims to have been at the time the crime was committed.

Discovery by the accused. The accused has the option of seeking discovery by asking the prosecution to provide (a) statements made by the defendant or a co-defendant to the police; (b) the accused prior criminal record, if any; (c) documents and other tangible evidence that may be used during the trial; (d) reports of photographs, examinations, and tests; (e) the names and addresses of witnesses, if safe to disclose; and (f) evidence that is favorable to the accused.

Discovery by the prosecution. The deposition of the accused cannot be taken without the latter's consent. The prosecution cannot initiate discovery requests, but can make the kind of discovery requests that the accused makes.

Pretrial conferences. Pretrial conferences can be held to discuss dates for trial proceedings, anticipated problems of evidence, and plea negotiations.

Trial

Criminal trials are relatively rare. Most criminal cases are disposed of by pleas of guilty by the accused. When a trial is held, the steps are often as follows:

Jury selection. The jury consists of twelve jurors in felony cases and eight jurors in misdemeanor cases. Unless waived, defendants charged with most serious offenses automatically receive a jury trial. If the jury is waived in a capital case where the penalty can be death, a three-judge panel tries the case. In petty offense cases, the defendant must make a specific request for a jury. (No jury trial is allowed if the maximum sentence is a fine of $100 or less.)

When the trial begins, the bailiff asks everyone to stand when the judge enters the court. After the judge calls the case, the first step in a jury case is *voir dire,* the selection of the jury. Prospective jurors are questioned by the judge and the attorneys for each side. All prospective jurors can be challenged for cause (e.g., they may not be impartial because they are related to one of the parties). A prospective juror can also be dismissed by a peremptory challenge from either side. No reason need be given for exercising a peremptory challenge. If, however, the juror subject to a peremptory challenge by the prosecutor is of the same racial minority as the defendant, the prosecutor may be required to state an explanation that is not based on race. Each side has six peremptory challenges in capital cases, four in noncapital felony cases, and three in misdemeanor cases.

Opening statements. Once the jury has been sworn in, the attorneys give their opening statements to the jury, beginning with the prosecution. The statement outlines what the party expects to prove during the trial.

Prosecution's case. The prosecutor presents its case by conducting a direct examination of the witnesses it calls and by offering physical evidence. The defendant can cross-examine the state's witnesses. The prosecution then rests.

Defense's case. The defendant presents its case by conducting a direct examination of the witnesses it calls and by offering physical evidence. The prosecutor can cross-examine the defendant's witnesses. The defendant then rests.

Closing statements. The attorney for each side then presents to the jury its closing argument that summarizes and interprets the evidence that was presented. The prosecutor goes first, although he or she may use some of his or her allotted time for rebuttal after the defense attorney's closing argument.

Jury instructions. Finally, the judge gives the jury detailed legal instructions about the crimes and explains the deliberation process they should follow in reaching a verdict. This is called instructing or charging the jury. Before delivering the charge, the judge will decide whether to include any of the instructions the attorneys may have submitted as requests for instructions.

Verdict. The jurors then go to the jury room to deliberate and reach a verdict. The moderator of their discussion is a foreperson whom they select from among the jurors. The jury must decide by a unanimous verdict whether the state has proven the guilt of the defendant beyond a reasonable doubt. "'Reasonable doubt' is present when the jurors, after they have carefully considered and compared all the evidence, cannot say they are firmly convinced of the truth of the charge. It is a doubt based on reason and common sense. Reasonable doubt is not mere possible doubt, because everything relating to human affairs or depending on moral evidence is open to some possible or imaginary doubt." Proof beyond a reasonable doubt is "proof of such character that an ordinary person would be willing to rely and act upon it in the most important of his own affairs." Revised Code § 2901.05(D). When the verdict is announced, the attorneys can ask that the jurors be polled individually on whether each agreed with (voted for) the verdict.

Motion for a new trial. This motion will be granted (a) if the verdict is not sustained by sufficient evidence or is contrary to law, (b) if a serious error was committed that denied the defendant a fair trial, or (c) if the defendant provides newly discovered evidence that was unavailable at the trial and that probably would change the result.

Motion for a judgment notwithstanding the verdict. This motion asks the court to set aside the jury's guilty verdict. The motion will be granted if no reasonable person could find that the prosecution proved the charge beyond a reasonable doubt, even when the evidence is viewed in the light most favorable to the prosecution.

Sentencing. In minor cases, sentencing can occur immediately after a guilty verdict is announced. In more serious cases, sentencing is often delayed until the probation department prepares a pre-sentence investigation report. This report provides extensive biographical information about the defendant and other pertinent facts about the case in order to help the court impose an appropriate sentence under the guidelines established by the legislature and the courts.

Appeal and Post-Conviction Relief

Appeal. The defendant may appeal a conviction. In only limited situations, however, is the government allowed to appeal. In most cases, an appeal cannot be made until after the filing of the judgment journal entry imposing the sentence. The normal deadline for filing the appeal is 30 days from final judgment. In most felony cases, the defendant appeals to the court of appeals and then to the Ohio Supreme Court. If the death penalty is imposed, the defendant can appeal directly to the Ohio Supreme Court from the trial court.

Post-conviction relief. The defendant may file a petition for post-conviction relief in the court in which he or she was convicted on the ground that errors were made that do not appear in the record of the trial. In ruling on this petition, the court is not required to hold a hearing.

C. More Information

General
www.law.csuohio.edu/lawlibrary/lawpubs/CriminalLawResourceGuide.htm
www.ohiobar.org/pub/?articleid=104
www.ohiobar.org/pub/?articleid=276

Ohio Criminal Code
www.megalaw.com/oh/top/ohcriminal.php
www.law.cornell.edu/topics/state_statutes2.html

Ohio Rules of Criminal Procedure
www.sconet.state.oh.us/Rules/criminal/default.asp

Ohio Rules of Evidence
www.sconet.state.oh.us/Rules/evidence/default.asp

Crime Statistics in Ohio
www.crimestats.ohio.gov
www.disastercenter.com/crime/ohcrime.htm
www.crimestats.ohio.gov/crime%20by%20county%202003.pdf
columbusoh.areaconnect.com/crime1.htm

D. Something to Check

1. Go to the Web site for the state courts in your county (see sections 4.2 and 4.6). What information or assistance does it provide for defendants, witnesses, or jurors in criminal cases?
2. Select any three general search engines (e.g., *www.google.com*) and any three legal search engines or portals (e.g., *www.findlaw.com*). Run this search: "ohio criminal cases". What are the different categories of results you find? Compare the six sites you used for this search.

PART 7

Sample Documents

A. Introduction

This section presents an example of a civil complaint filed in an Ohio court of common pleas. The complaint seeks damages for injuries sustained from an allegedly defective product. Compare this complaint to the sample *federal* civil complaint printed in section 7.2. See also:

- section 4.2 for an overview of Ohio state courts
- section 6.3 on some of the distinctions between state and federal civil procedure
- section 6.2 for some of the major statutes covering pretrial procedures, including the drafting of complaints and other pleadings

B. A State Civil Complaint

Exhibit 7.1A contains a sample complaint filed in an Ohio state court.

C. More Information

Web Sites of Ohio Trial Courts
www.sconet.state.oh.us/web_sites/courts

Appendix of Forms
www.sconet.state.oh.us/Rules/civil/forms.pdf

Drafting and Self-Help Resources
moritzlaw.osu.edu/library/assistance/selfhelp.pdf
www.ohiolegalservices.org/OSLSA/PublicWeb
www.selfhelpsupport.org/index.cfm
dir.yahoo.com/Government/Law/Self_Help

Legal Forms
www.uslegalforms.com/Ohio.htm
www.findforms.com
(type "ohio" in the search box)

D. Something to Check

1. Find the Ohio Revised Code online. Go to *www.legislature.state.oh.us* (click "Laws, Acts, and Legislation" and then "Ohio Revised Code"). In the code, find each of the statutory sections referred to in the Boltuch complaint reprinted in Exhibit 7.1A. Quote the first clause of each section.
2. What information can you find online about the product that allegedly caused the injuries in the Boltuch complaint?
3. The complaint tells you what attorney and law firm represented the plaintiffs. Go to that law firm's Web site. Describe the kind of practice engaged in by this law firm. What associations does the attorney belong to?

A. Introduction

This section presents an example of a civil complaint filed in a United States District Court sitting in Ohio. The complaint alleges sexual harassment, employment discrimination, and violations of the Family and Medical Leave Act (FMLA). Compare this complaint to the sample state court civil complaint printed in section 7.1. See also section 6.3 covering some of the distinctions between state and federal civil procedure.

For more on federal courts in Ohio, see section 4.3.

B. A Federal Civil Complaint

Exhibit 7.2A contains a sample complaint filed in a federal court sitting in Ohio.

C. More Information

United States District Court Southern District of Ohio
www.ohsd.uscourts.gov/pdf/complnt.pdf
www.ohsd.uscourts.gov
(click "Forms" then "Complaint Form")

United States District Court Southern District of Ohio
www.ohsd.uscourts.gov
(click "Local Rules" then "Local Rules (PDF)" then click the binoculars in the Adobe menu bar and type "complaint" in the search box)

Attorneys Manual (Electronic Case Filing)
www.ohsd.uscourts.gov/pdf/ECFManual05.pdf
(see page 15: Filing a Civil Complaint)

United States District Court Northern District of Ohio
www.ohnd.uscourts.gov
(click "Rules" then "Local Rules" then "Civil Rules" then click the binoculars in the Adobe menu bar and type "complaint" in the search box)

EXHIBIT 7.1A Sample Complaint Filed in an Ohio State Court

IN THE COURT OF COMMON PLEAS, CUYAHOGA COUNTY, OHIO

Robert and Susan Boltuch, 32 Adams St. Cleveland, OH 44100 Plaintiffs, v. Electrolux NA, Inc., and Sears, Roebuck and Co. c/o statutory agent CT Corporation, and ABC Corporations I-V (names/addresses unknown), Defendants.	: : : : : : : : : : : :	Case No. 05-6834 June 9, 2005 Judge: Richard I. Cvans

COMPLAINT

(JURY DEMAND ENDORSED HEREON)

Now come Plaintiffs, and for their Complaint state as follows:

PARTIES

1. At all times relevant herein, Plaintiffs Robert and Susan Boltuch were husband and wife residing in the village of Gates Mills, Cuyahoga County, Ohio.

2. Upon information and belief, Defendant Electrolux North America, Inc. (Electrolux) is a corporation duly organized and existing under the laws of the State of Ohio and actively doing business in the State of Ohio.

3. Upon information and belief, Defendant Sears, Roebuck and Co. (Sears) is a corporation duly organized and existing under the laws of the State of New York and actively doing business in the State of Ohio.

4. Upon information and belief, Defendant ABC Corporations I-V are corporations or other legal entities whose real names and addresses are unknown. This Complaint will be amended to include their true names and addresses upon discovery of such information.

-1-

EXHIBIT 7.1A

FIRST CAUSE OF ACTION

5. Plaintiffs incorporate and re-aver all of the allegations set forth in Paragraphs 1–4 as though fully rewritten herein.

6. Defendant Electrolux is a manufacturer, pursuant to the provisions of Ohio Revised Code § 2307.71, which designed, developed, produced, created, made, constructed, and/or assembled a certain tractor, bearing Model No. 917.251522, under the brand name of American Yard Products.

7. At all times relevant herein, said tractor was defective in design, pursuant to the provisions of Ohio Revised Code § 2307.75.

8. At all times relevant herein, said tractor was defective due to inadequate warning and/or instruction, pursuant to the provisions of Ohio Revised Code § 2307.76.

9. At all times relevant herein, said tractor was defective by reason of its failure to conform to representations made by Defendant, pursuant to the provisions of Ohio Revised Code § 2307.77.

10. A defective aspect of said tractor, including but not limited to an unprotected and inadequate filler neck to the fuel tank which has the propensity to break when the tractor is used in a reasonably foreseeable manner, was a direct and proximate cause of the harm and loss for which Plaintiff seeks to recover compensatory damages.

11. On or about June 10, 2002, Plaintiff Robert Boltuch was using said tractor to push a post in the ground, in an attempt to loosen the base. Suddenly and unexpectedly, the front of the tractor lifted up on the pole, and the tractor tipped over backwards. As a direct and proximate result of the defective fuel tank and filler neck design, the filler neck broke, and gasoline poured from the tank, soaking Plaintiff's skin and clothing. The gasoline lit on fire, and caused extensive third degree burns to Plaintiff's body.

-2-

EXHIBIT 7.1A Sample Complaint Filed in an Ohio State Court

12. As a further direct and proximate result of the dangerous design of the tractor, Plaintiff incurred medical and other related expenses in excess of $400,000. He sustained great pain and suffering, has undergone extensive surgery and therapy, and has incurred lost wages and a diminution of his earning capacity. All of Plaintiff's injuries and losses are permanent, and his ability to carry on ordinary activities and enjoy life has been permanently and adversely affected.

<u>SECOND CAUSE OF ACTION</u>

13. Plaintiffs incorporate and re-aver all of the allegations set forth in Paragraphs 1–12 as though fully rewritten herein.

14. Defendant Sears is a supplier, pursuant to the provisions of Ohio Revised Code § 2307.71, which marketed, sold, maintained, and serviced the subject tractor to Plaintiff.

15. Defendant Sears was negligent in offering for sale, marketing, and servicing said tractor to Plaintiff, and in failing to provide adequate warnings or instruction to its customers, including the Plaintiff, with respect to the hazards and risks associated with the tractor.

16. As a direct and proximate result of Defendant Sears' negligence, Plaintiff suffered all of the injuries, damages and losses set forth herein above.

<u>THIRD CAUSE OF ACTION</u>

17. Plaintiffs incorporate and re-aver all of the allegations set forth in Paragraphs 1–16 as though fully rewritten herein.

18. At all times relevant herein, Defendant Sears is a manufacturer, pursuant to the provisions of Ohio Revised Code § 2307.78, which marketed and sold the aforementioned tractor, Model No. 917.251522, completely under the Craftsman brand name which is owned exclusively by Defendant Sears.

19. At all times relevant herein, said tractor was defective in design, pursuant to the provisions of Ohio Revised Code § 2307.75.

20. At all times relevant herein, said tractor was defective due to inadequate warning and/or instruction, pursuant to the provisions of Ohio Revised Code § 2307.76.

-3-

EXHIBIT 7.1A

21. At all times relevant herein, said tractor was defective by reason of its failure to conform to representations made by Defendant, pursuant to the provisions of Ohio Revised Code § 2307.77.

22. A defective aspect of said tractor, including but not limited to an unprotected and inadequate filler neck to the fuel tank which has the propensity to break when the tractor is used in a reasonably foreseeable manner, was a direct and proximate cause of the harm and loss for which Plaintiff seeks to recover compensatory damages.

23. On or about June 10, 2002, Plaintiff Robert Boltuch was using said tractor to push a post in the ground, in an attempt to loosen the base. Suddenly and unexpectedly, the front of the tractor lifted up on the pole, and the tractor tipped over backwards. As a direct and proximate result of the defective fuel tank and filler neck design, the filler neck broke, and gasoline poured from the tank, soaking Plaintiff's skin and clothing. The gasoline lit on fire, and caused extensive third degree burns to Plaintiff's body.

24. As a further direct and proximate result of the dangerous design of the tractor, Plaintiff suffered all of the injuries, damages, and losses set forth herein above.

<u>FOURTH CAUSE OF ACTION</u>

25. Plaintiffs incorporate and re-aver all of the allegations set forth in Paragraphs 1–24 as though fully rewritten herein.

26. At all times relevant herein, Defendants ABC Corporations I-V, whose real names and addresses are currently unknown, are manufacturers, pursuant to the provisions of Ohio Revised Code § 2307.71, which designed, produced, created, made, constructed, and/or assembled the subject tractor, Model No. 917.251522, and/or component parts of the tractor, including but not limited to the exhaust system, fuel tank, and filler neck to the fuel tank.

27. At all times relevant herein, said tractor and/or component parts were defective in design, pursuant to the provisions of Ohio Revised Code § 2307.75.

-4-

EXHIBIT 7.1A Sample Complaint Filed in an Ohio State Court

28. At all times relevant herein, said tractor and/or component parts were defective due to inadequate warning and/or instruction, pursuant to the provisions of Ohio Revised Code § 2307.76.

29. At all times relevant herein, said tractor and/or component parts were defective by reason of its failure to conform to representations made by Defendant, pursuant to the provisions of Ohio Revised Code § 2307.77.

30. A defective aspect of said tractor, including but not limited to an unprotected and inadequate filler neck to the fuel tank which has the propensity to break when the tractor is used in a reasonably foreseeable manner, was a direct and proximate cause of the harm and loss for which Plaintiff seeks to recover compensatory damages.

31. On or about June 10, 2002, Plaintiff Robert Boltuch was using said tractor to push a post in the ground, in an attempt to loosen the base. Suddenly and unexpectedly, the front of the tractor lifted up on the pole, and the tractor tipped over backwards. As a direct and proximate result of the defective fuel tank and filler neck design, the filler neck broke, and gasoline poured from the tank, soaking Plaintiff's skin and clothing. The gasoline lit on fire, and caused extensive third degree burns to Plaintiff's body.

32. As a further direct and proximate result of the dangerous design of the tractor, Plaintiff suffered all of the injuries, damages, and losses set forth herein above.

FIFTH CAUSE OF ACTION

33. Plaintiffs incorporate and re-aver all of the allegations set forth in Paragraphs 1–32 as though fully rewritten herein.

34. At all times relevant herein, Plaintiff Susan Boltuch was the wife of Plaintiff Robert Boltuch.

35. As a direct and proximate result of the injuries sustained by Plaintiff Robert Boltuch, Plaintiff Susan Boltuch sustained the loss of services, society, and companionship of her husband, and has suffered extreme emotional distress.

-5-

EXHIBIT 7.1A

WHEREFORE, Plaintiffs demand judgment against the Defendants, jointly and severally, individually and collectively, in an amount in excess of $25,000, together with the costs of this action and such further relief as the court deems proper.

JURY DEMAND

Plaintiffs demand a trial by jury herein.

____
Gregory S. Scott
Attorney for Plaintiffs

Respectfully submitted,
GREGORY S. SCOTT, (Reg. No. 0067255)
Lowe, Eklund, Wakefield & Mulvihill Co., L.P.A.
610 Skylight Office Tower
1660 West Second Street
Cleveland, Ohio 44114-1454
(216) 781-2600
(216) 781-2604 (fax)

-6-

EXHIBIT 7.2A Sample Federal Complaint Filed in a Federal Court in Ohio

IN THE UNITED STATES DISTRICT COURT

FOR THE SOUTHERN DISTRICT OF OHIO

Bridgette STAPLETON	)	
6745 Morning Sun Road	)	Case No. 1:05CV626
Oxford, OH 45056	)	Judge J. Black
(513) 917-1265	)	September 26, 2005.
Plaintiff	)	
v.	)	COMPLAINT FOR GENDER
CITY OF CINCINNATI	)	DISCRIMINATION, RETALIATION,
801 Plum Street	)	SEXUAL HARASSMENT, FMLA
Cincinnati, OH 45202	)	VIOLATION, AND ADA VIOLATION
(513) 451-4437	)	(Jury Demand Endorsed Hereon)
Defendant	)	

Plaintiff Bridgette Stapleton, complaining of Defendant City of Cincinnati, states as follows:

PARTIES

1. Plaintiff Bridgette Stapleton is a citizen and a resident of the State of Ohio.

2. Defendant City of Cincinnati is an employer within the meaning of federal and state law.

JURISDICTION AND VENUE

3. This Court has federal question jurisdiction to hear this case pursuant to 28 U.S.C. § 1331 as it arises under the laws of the United States. Plaintiff's Counts I, II and III arise under Title VII of the Civil Rights Act of 1964, as amended. Plaintiff's Count IV arises under the Family and Medical Leave Act ("FMLA"), 29 U.S.C. §2601, et seq., and Plaintiff's Count V arises under the Americans with Disabilities Act ("ADA"), 42 U.S.C. §12112, et seq.

4. This Court also has supplemental jurisdiction over Counts VI, VII, VIII and IX pursuant to 28 U.S.C. §1367 because they arise out of the same set of operative facts as those relevant to Counts I, II, III, IV and V so as to make them part of the same case in controversy.

5. Venue is proper in the Southern District of Ohio, Western Division, pursuant to 28 U.S.C. § 1391(b) because a substantial part of the events giving rise to these claims occurred in the Southern District of Ohio, Western Division.

6. Plaintiff received a Notice of Right to Sue from the Equal Employment Opportunity Commission less than 90 days ago.

-1-

EXHIBIT 7.2A

FACTUAL ALLEGATIONS

7. Plaintiff, a female, was employed by Defendant from April 1989 until her constructive termination on October 8, 2004.

8. Specifically, Plaintiff worked for the Cincinnati Recreation Commission ("CRC"), a department within the City of Cincinnati.

9. Throughout her employment with Defendant, Plaintiff was fully qualified for her position, performed the essential functions of her job within the reasonable expectations of Defendant, and was a loyal and dedicated employee.

10. Plaintiff was employed as a laborer in the maintenance department of CRC. As such, she reported directly to Larry Kalker, the Parks/Recreation Service Area Coordinator.

11. Kalker engaged in sexually inappropriate behavior in the workplace. This conduct included, but was not limited to, making sexual gestures and using sexual language on the worksite. This conduct was witnessed by other CRC employees.

12. Kalker treated Plaintiff less favorably than he treated similarly-situated male employees. For example, he responded to her concerns about workplace safety issues by treating her in a dismissive manner. By contrast, he treated her male counterparts more respectfully.

13. After enduring Kalker's treatment for a period of time, Plaintiff filed a complaint with Rodney Prince, Defendant's Human Resources Director, who communicated her concerns to CRC Director James Garges.

14. Garges responded to her complaints by stating that unhappy employees should stop complaining or leave.

15. Following Plaintiff's complaint, Kalker disciplined Plaintiff for attendance issues and sent her to counseling at Public Employees Assistance Program (PEAP).

16. Plaintiff's absences were related to her and her children's serious medical conditions.

17. Plaintiff resigned her employment on October 8, 2004, on advice of her physician, who felt that the stress of her work environment was contributing to her health problems.

-2-

EXHIBIT 7.2A Sample Federal Complaint Filed in a Federal Court in Ohio

COUNT I

(Gender Discrimination - Title VII of the Civil Rights Act of 1964, as amended, 42 U.S.C. §2000e, et sea.)

18. Plaintiff realleges the foregoing paragraphs as if fully rewritten herein.

19. Defendant intentionally, willfully, and wantonly discriminated against Plaintiff by treating her less favorably than male employees, in violation of Title VII of the Civil Rights Act of 1964, as amended.

20. As a direct and proximate result of Defendant's unlawful conduct, Plaintiff has suffered injuries and damages and is entitled to judgment against Defendant for all damages resulting from its unlawful discriminatory conduct in an amount to be proven at trial.

COUNT II

(Retaliation - Title VII of the Civil Rights Act of 1964, as amended, 42 U.S.C. §2000e, et sea.)

21. Plaintiff realleges the foregoing paragraphs as if fully rewritten herein.

22. Plaintiff engaged in protected conduct by complaining about sexual harassment and discrimination.

23. In response, Defendant intentionally, willfully, and wantonly retaliated against Plaintiff by disciplining Plaintiff for attendance issues and sending her to employee counseling in violation of Title VII of the Civil Rights Act of 1964, as amended.

24. As a direct and proximate result of Defendant's unlawful conduct, Plaintiff has suffered injuries and damages and is entitled to judgment against Defendant for all damages resulting from its unlawful discriminatory conduct in an amount to be proven at trial.

COUNT III

(Sexual Harassment - Title VII of the Civil Rights Act of 1964, as amended, 42 U.S.C. §2000e, et seq.)

25. Plaintiff realleges the foregoing paragraphs as if fully rewritten herein.

26. Plaintiff was subjected to comments and gestures of a sexual nature by her immediate supervisor.

-3-

EXHIBIT 7.2A

27. Plaintiff's complaints to Defendant about the work environment were unsuccessful.

28. Defendant intentionally, willfully, and wantonly discriminated against Plaintiff in violation of Title VII of the Civil Rights Act of 1964, as amended.

29. As a direct and proximate result of Defendant's unlawful conduct, Plaintiff has suffered injuries and damages and is entitled to judgment.

COUNT IV

(Family & Medical Leave Act ("FMLA") Violation, Retaliation and Harassment - 29 U.S.C. §2611, et se.)

30. Plaintiff realleges the foregoing paragraphs as if fully rewritten herein.

31. Plaintiff had a serious health condition.

32. Plaintiff availed herself of her right to FMLA leave because of her serious health condition by properly notifying Defendant of her need for medical leave and by taking medical leave.

33. Defendant disciplined and constructively terminated Plaintiff because she exercised her right to FMLA leave.

34. Defendant's actions were willful, wanton, malicious, and/or in reckless disregard of Plaintiff's rights.

35. As a direct and proximate result of Defendant's unlawful conduct, Plaintiff has been injured and is entitled to judgment and compensation pursuant to the FMLA. . . .

WHEREFORE, Plaintiff demands judgment against Defendant as follows:

(a) That Defendant be enjoined from further unlawful conduct as described in the Complaint;

(b) That Plaintiff be reinstated to her previous position;

(c) That Plaintiff be awarded all lost pay and benefits;

(d) That Plaintiff be awarded compensatory damages;

(e) That Plaintiff be awarded punitive damages;

-4-

EXHIBIT 7.2A Sample Federal Complaint Filed in a Federal Court in Ohio

(f) That Plaintiff be awarded pre-judgment interest;

(g) That Plaintiff be awarded reasonable attorneys' fees and costs; and

(h) That Plaintiff be awarded all other legal and equitable relief to which she may be entitled.

____

Respectfully Submitted
Randolph H. Freking (#0009158)
Trial Attorney for Plaintiff
FREKING & BETZ
215 East Ninth Street, Fifth Floor
Cincinnati, OH 45202
Phone: (513) 721-1975
Fax: (513) 661-2570

<u>JURY DEMAND</u>

Plaintiff hereby demands a jury trial on all issues so triable.

D. Something to Check

Go to the local rules of both of the United States District Courts in Ohio (see the Web sites listed in More Information on page 284).

1. For the Southern District, cite any rule on complaints.
2. For the Northern District, cite any rule on complaints.

7.3 A Sample Memorandum of Law Applying Ohio Law

A. Introduction

This section presents a sample memorandum of law that analyzes Ohio law. It is an internal memo (often called an office memo) in the sense that it will not be filed with the court nor shown to anyone outside the office. It is designed for discussion and analysis solely for members of the firm working on the case of a client. Hence the memo is *not* an advocacy document; it is not designed to convince a court or an opponent to take a particular position. Consequently, the memo does not hide or downplay the weaknesses in the client's position. It presents the strengths and weaknesses of the client's case.

All law firms do not use the same format for a memorandum of law. Most firms, however, have the same basic five components: facts, issues or questions, brief answers, analysis or discussion, and conclusion. Firms may package these components in different ways (and may add others), but all of the five basic components are often present.

The format selected for the sample memorandum of law has five parts presented in the following order:

I. Statement of Facts
II. Questions Presented
III. Brief Answers
IV. Discussion
V. Conclusion

B. Sample Memorandum of Law

MEMORANDUM OF LAW

TO: Adam Attorney

FROM: Peter Paralegal

DATE: February 23, 2007

RE: Negligent Infliction of Emotional Distress

Paula Patient v. Middle Medical Center

Case No. 07-1234

I. Statement of Facts

In 2002, Paula Patient had a mole excised from her left forearm. The mole was biopsied and found to be a malignant melanoma. She decided to have further testing to determine whether her melanoma had metastasized. The samples needed for further testing were taken by defendant. One procedure tested negative for metastasis. Another screening procedure for determining the metastasis involved shipping frozen lymph node samples to a research laboratory. This second screening procedure, consisting of frozen samples, is not often used for patients with melanoma, but was requested by plaintiff after further discussions with defendant. The samples, however, were lost for over three days. They had thawed by the time they arrived at the research laboratory, rendering them unusable for screening or further testing.

Plaintiff claims that the second screening procedure would have defined the probability of metastasis and her life expectancy, and that her quality of life is negatively affected by the extreme emotional distress caused by the uncertainty surrounding a recurrence of cancer.

II. Questions Presented

1. Does the tort of negligent infliction of emotional distress require a contemporaneous physical injury?
2. Can a fear of metastasis of cancer be the basis for a claim for negligent infliction of emotional distress?

III. Brief Answers

1. No. A contemporaneous physical injury is not required to maintain an action for negligent infliction of emotional distress.
2. No. Fear of metastasis of cancer that represents a nonexistent peril cannot be the basis for a claim of emotional distress.

IV. Discussion

The two major objections to Paula Patient's claim are that she did not suffer a contemporaneous physical injury and that there was no underlying injury or peril that can be the basis of a claim for negligent infliction of emotional distress.

Issue 1

Paula Patient suffered a physical injury in the form of cancer. This injury occurred before the alleged negligence of the defendant in handling the testing. The emotional distress she experienced, therefore, was not contemporaneous with the alleged negligence. Some states require such contemporaneity, primarily to help weed out frivolous claims in light of the ease with which a person can claim emotional distress. See, for example, *Payton v. Abbott Labs* (1982), 386 Mass. 540, 437 N.E.2d 171 and *Rodrigues v. State* (1970), 52 Hawaii 156, 472 P.2d 509. Ohio, however, does not have this requirement. In *Schultz v. Barberton Glass Co.* (1983), 4 Ohio St.3d 131, 447 N.E.2d 109, a sheet of glass fell off a truck and smashed into Schultz's windshield. Schultz was not physically injured, but nevertheless suffered serious emotional distress as a result of the accident. The Supreme Court of Ohio held that a "cause of action may be stated for the negligent infliction of serious emotional distress without a contemporaneous physical injury." *Id.* at 136, 447 N.E.2d at 113.

The court reinforced its *Schultz* holding in *Paugh v. Hanks* (1983), 6 Ohio St.3d 72, 451 N.E.2d 759. In *Paugh*, the court found an actionable claim for negligent infliction of emotional distress for a mother who alleged severe psychological harm due to three separate incidents in which a car crashed into her house or yard, causing her to fear for the lives of her children. There was no physical injury involved.

Issue 2

A more serious objection to Paula Patient's claim is that there was no physical injury that could be the basis of emotional distress. The negligence of the defendant in losing the samples did not cause or aggravate the cancer.

A similar situation in a case claiming negligent infliction of emotional distress arose in *Heiner v. Moretuzzo* (1995), 73 Ohio St.3d 80, 652 N.E.2d 664. In that case, plaintiff was incorrectly and repeatedly informed by health professionals that she had tested positive for HIV. After later discovering that she was in fact HIV negative, Heiner sued her physician, Akron General Medical Center, and the American Red Cross. She alleged that the false diagnosis was a result of the defendants' negligence, and sought recovery for negligent infliction of emotional distress. The court pointed out, however, that the plaintiff "neither witnessed nor was exposed to any real or impending physical calamity." *Heiner*, 73 Ohio St.3d at 85, 652 N.E.2d 664. The claimed negligent diagnosis never placed her or any other person in real physical peril, since she was, in fact, HIV negative. Thus, the court concluded that Ohio does not recognize a claim for negligent infliction of emotional distress where the distress is caused by the plaintiff's fear of a nonexistent peril.

Paula Patient was not diagnosed with cancer after the samples were lost. The loss of the samples did not cause or aggravate the condition of cancer. She is simply afraid that her previously diagnosed cancer may reoccur. This is similar to the fear of the plaintiff in *Heiner* that he might be HIV positive. Neither Paula Patient nor the plaintiff in *Heiner* have experienced an *actual* threat of physical harm caused by the alleged negligence. The fear of a recurrence of a physical harm (the cancer) does not constitute the basis for the claim of negligent infliction of emotional distress.

V. Conclusion

The tort of negligent infliction of emotional distress requires plaintiff to demonstrate a distress that results from a physical peril. Although the negligent infliction of emotional distress does not require a contemporaneous physical injury, a physical injury must exist. Even if Paula Patient genuinely fears a reoccurrence of cancer, such fear does not constitute a basis for relief under negligent infliction of emotional distress.

C. More Information

www.ualr.edu/cmbarger
(click "Format Guidelines")
www.alwd.org
(click "ALWD Citation Manual" then "appendices" then "Appendix 6")
users.ipfw.edu/vetterw/a339-research-sample-memo.htm

D. Something to Check

Find a memorandum of law online on any legal issue in any state. Compare its format or structure to the sample memorandum presented here in the products liability case involving the surgery stapler.

7.4 A Sample Appellate Brief Filed in the Ohio Supreme Court

A. Introduction

An appellate brief is a document submitted by a party to an appellate court and served on the opposing party, in which arguments are presented on why the appellate court should affirm (approve), reverse, or otherwise modify what a lower court has done. There are a number of roles that paralegals perform in this area of appellate practice. They might be asked to go through the transcript of the trial record to find references that the attorney wants to use in the brief. They might be asked to cite check the brief by making sure that

- all quotations are accurate
- all citations are in the format required by court rules
- the brief itself is in the format required by court rules
- all laws cited are still valid

The last role is performed by Shepardizing or KeyCiting each case, statute, or other law to make sure that it has not been overruled or changed since the time it was cited in the brief. Occasionally, an experienced paralegal will be asked to draft a portion of an appellate brief.

The main state courts in which appellate briefs are filed are the Ohio Supreme Court and the Ohio courts of appeals. In this section we concentrate on those filed in the Ohio Supreme Court, specifically the merit brief of the appellee.

B. Rules IV and VIII on Timing, Content, and Form of Appellate Briefs

Before examining a sample brief, review these excerpts from Rules VI and VIII of the Ohio Supreme Court on the timing, content, and form of appellate briefs.

Rules of Practice of the Supreme Court of Ohio

www.sconet.state.oh.us/Rules/practice/#rulevi

Rule VI. Briefs on the merits in appeals

Section 2. Appellant's Brief.

(A) In every [appeal other than one involving termination of parental rights or adoption of a minor child], the appellant shall file a merit brief within 40 days from the date the Clerk receives and files the record from the court of appeals or the administrative agency. . . .

(B) The appellant's brief shall contain all of the following:

(1) A table of contents listing the table of authorities cited, the statement of facts, the argument with proposition or propositions of law, and the appendix, with references to the pages of the brief where each appears.

(2) A table of the authorities cited, listing the citations for all cases or other authorities, arranged alphabetically; constitutional provisions; statutes; ordinances; and administrative rules or regulations upon which appellant relies, with references to the pages of the brief where each citation appears.

(3) A statement of the facts with page references, in parentheses, to supporting portions of both the original transcript of testimony and any supplement filed in the case pursuant to S. Ct. Prac. R. VII.

(4) An argument, headed by the proposition of law that appellant contends is applicable to the facts of the case and that could serve as a syllabus for the case if appellant prevails. See *Drake v. Bucher* (1966), 5 Ohio St. 2d 37, at 39. If several propositions of law are presented, the argument shall be divided with each proposition set forth as a subheading.

(5) An appendix containing copies of all of the following:

(a) The date-stamped notice of appeal to the Supreme Court;

(b) The judgment or order from which the appeal is taken;
(c) The opinion, if any, relating to the judgment or order being appealed;
(d) All judgments, orders, and opinions rendered by any court or agency in the case, if relevant to the issues on appeal;
(e) Any relevant rules or regulations of any department, board, commission, or any other agency, upon which appellant relies;
(f) Any constitutional provision, statute, or ordinance upon which appellant relies, to be construed, or otherwise involved in the case;
(g) In appeals from the Public Utilities Commission, the appellant's application for rehearing.

The pages of the appendix shall be numbered separately from the body of the brief.

(C) Except in appeals of right involving the death penalty, the appellant's brief shall not exceed 50 numbered pages, exclusive of the table of contents, the table of authorities cited, and the appendix.

Section 3. Appellee's Brief.

(A) In every [appeal other than one involving termination of parental rights or adoption of a minor child], the appellee shall file a merit brief within 30 days after the filing of appellant's brief. A statement of facts may be omitted from the appellee's brief if the appellee agrees with the statement of facts given in the appellant's merit brief. The appendix need not duplicate any materials provided in the appendix of the appellant's brief.

(B) Except in appeals of right involving the death penalty, the appellee's brief shall not exceed 50 numbered pages, exclusive of the table of contents, the table of authorities cited, and any appendix. . . .

Section 4. Appellant's Reply Brief.

(A) In every [appeal other than one involving termination of parental rights or adoption of a minor child], the appellant may file a reply brief within 20 days after the filing of appellee's brief. Except in appeals of right involving the death penalty, the reply brief shall not exceed 20 numbered pages, exclusive of the table of contents, the table of authorities cited, and any appendix. . . .

Rule VIII. Requirements as to form and number of documents filed

Section 1. Scope of Rule.

This rule sets forth the requirements as to the form and number of all documents filed in the Supreme Court.

Section 2. Cover Page.

Each document filed in the Supreme Court shall contain a cover page, which shall be white and shall contain only the following information:

(A) The case name and the case number assigned when the case was filed in the Supreme Court;

(B) The nature of the proceeding in the Supreme Court (e.g., appeal, original action in mandamus, etc.);

(C) If the proceeding is an appeal, the name of the court or the administrative agency from which the appeal is taken;

(D) The title of the document (e.g., notice of appeal, appellant's merit brief, memorandum in support of jurisdiction, etc.);

(E) An identification of the party on whose behalf the document is filed;

(F) The name, attorney registration number, address, telephone number, facsimile number, and e-mail address, if available, of each attorney who has filed an appearance in the case; an indication as to what party each attorney represents; and, where two or more attorneys represent a party, an indication of counsel of record. A party who is not represented by an attorney shall indicate his or her name, address, and telephone number.

Section 3. Signature.

The original of every pleading, memorandum, brief, or other document filed in the Supreme Court shall be signed by an attorney representing the party on whose behalf the document is filed. A party who is not represented by an attorney shall sign the document being filed.

Section 4. Mechanical Requirements.

(A) (1) Every original document filed with the Supreme Court shall be single-sided, shall be typewritten or prepared by word processor or other standard typographic process, and shall comply with the requirements of this rule. A medium weight, noncondensed Roman type style is preferred, and italic type style may be used only for case citations and emphasis. The Clerk may accept a handwritten document for filing only in an emergency, provided the document is clearly legible.

(2) All documents shall be on opaque, unglazed, 20 to 22 pound weight, white paper, $8\frac{1}{2}$ by 11 inches in size, and shall be firmly stapled or bound on the left margin. All margins shall be at least one inch, and the left margin shall be justified. Documents shall not be enclosed in notebooks or binders and shall not have plastic cover pages.

(3) The text of all documents shall be at least 12-point, double-spaced noncondensed type. As used in this provision, "noncondensed type" shall refer either to Times New Roman type or to another type that has no more than 80 characters to a line of text. Footnotes and quotations may be single-spaced.

(B) Whenever these rules require that a copy of the court or agency opinion or decision being appealed be attached to a document filed with the Supreme Court, the copy shall be either of the following:
(1) a photocopy of the opinion or decision issued directly by the court or agency;
(2) an electronically generated copy that meets the requirements of division (A)(3) of this section.

(C) Any supplement to the briefs filed pursuant to S. Ct. Prac. R. VII may be prepared and reproduced by photocopying the relevant documents in the record, even if those documents do not comply with the mechanical requirements of division (A) of this section, provided that the requirements as to paper size and paper type are met and each page of the supplement is clearly legible. Both sides of the paper may be used in preparing a supplement.

(D) Any document filed with the Supreme Court that exceeds two inches in thickness shall be bound and numbered in two or more parts, with each part containing a cover page.

Section 5. Number and Form of Copies.

(A) The original of a pleading, memorandum, brief, motion, or other document filed in the Supreme Court shall be accompanied by an appropriate number of copies as follows:
(1) Notice of appeal or cross-appeal—1;
(2) Praecipe filed in a death penalty appeal—1;
(3) Jurisdictional memorandum—10;
(4) Brief in an appeal or an original action—18;
(5) List of additional authorities filed pursuant to S. Ct. Prac. R. VI, Section 8, or S. Ct. Prac. R. IX, Section 7—18;
(6) Supplement to a merit brief filed pursuant to S. Ct. Prac. R. VII—2;
(7) Complaint in an original action—12, plus an additional copy for each respondent named in the complaint;
(8) Evidence in an original action—12;
(9) Request for extension of time or stipulation to an agreed extension of time to file a brief—none;
(10) Notices related to attorney representation under S. Ct. Prac. R. I—none;
(11) Any other pleading, memorandum, motion, or document—12.

(B) Any party wishing to receive a date-stamped copy of a document submitted for filing with the Clerk shall provide the Clerk with an extra copy of the document and a self-addressed, postage-paid envelope.

(C) Copies of documents shall be on opaque, unglazed, 20 to 22 pound weight, white paper, $8\frac{1}{2}$ by 11 inches in size, and shall be firmly stapled or bound on the left margin. Both sides of the paper may be used as long as the document is clearly legible. The use of recycled paper is encouraged. To facilitate recycling of paper after copies are disposed of by the Supreme Court, the parties shall use staples or other bindings that can be removed readily. Copies shall not be enclosed in notebooks or binders and shall not have plastic cover pages.

Section 6. Rejection of Noncomplying Originals and Copies.

The Clerk may reject the original and all copies of a document tendered for filing unless the original and each of the required number of copies are clearly legible and comply with the requirements of these rules.

Section 7. Corrections or Additions to Previously Filed Documents.

A party who wishes to make corrections or additions to a previously filed document shall file a revised document and copies that completely incorporate the corrections or additions. The revised document shall be filed within the time permitted by these rules for filing the original document, except that corrections or additions shall not be made to a motion if a memorandum opposing the motion has already been filed. Time permitted by these rules for filing any responsive document shall begin to run when the revised document is filed. The Clerk shall refuse to file a revised document that is not submitted in the form and within the deadlines prescribed by this rule.

C. Sample Appellate Brief Filed in the Ohio Supreme Court: Merit Brief of Apppellee

IN THE SUPREME COURT OF OHIO

John J. Jones, Natural Father & Next Friend of Johanna H. Jones	:	
Appellant,	:	Case No. 90-1234
v.	:	On Appeal from the Ottawa County Court of Appeals, Sixth Appellate District
David Dreary, M.D.	:	
Appellee.	:	

MERIT BRIEF OF APPELLEE DAVID DREARY

John Miller (123456)
Miller & Smith
100 South Street
Port Clinton, Ohio 43214
(419) 345-5341
Fax: (419) 346-2341
jmiller@worldlink.com

COUNSEL FOR APPELLANT

Janet Doe (121212)
90 East Fourth Street
Sandusky, Ohio 43234
(614) 222-1341
jdoe@pacbell.net

COUNSEL FOR APPELLEE

TABLE OF CONTENTS

TABLE OF AUTHORITIES

CASES:

Anderson v. St. Francis–St. George Hospital, Inc. (1966)
77 Ohio St.3d 82 2

Baker v. Cruz (Idaho 1984)
698 P.2d 315 3

Becker v. Schwartz (N.Y. 1978)
6 N.Y.2d 401, 413 N.Y.S.2d 895, 386 N.E.2d 807 3

Dumer v. St. Michael's Hospital (Wisc. 1975)
69 Wisc. 2d 766, 233 N.W.2d 372 3

Flanaga v. Williams (1993)
87 Ohio App.3d 768 1

Garrison v. Medical Inc. (Del. 1989)
581 A.2d 288 3

Greco v. United States (Nev. 1995)
893 P.2d 345 3

James v. Caserta (W.Va. 1985)
175 W.Va. 406, 332 S.E.2d 872 3

Reed v. Ampagnolo (Md. 1993)
810 F.Supp. 167 3

Siemieniec v. Lutheran Gen. Hospital (Ill. 1987)
512 N.E.2d 691 3

Smith v. Cote (N.H. 1986)
128 N.H. 231, 513 A.2d 341 3

Speck v. Finegold (Pa. 1981)
497 Pa. 77, 439 A.2d 110 4

Viccaro v. Milunsky (Mass. 1990)
406 Mass. 777, 551 N.E.2d 8 4

Walker by Pizano v. Mart (Ariz. 1990), 164 Ariz. 37,
790 P.2d 735 3

STATEMENT OF FACTS

Defendant David Dreary, M.D., provided obstetrical, gynecological, and prenatal care and treatment to Samantha Jones, during her pregnancy with Johanna H. Jones. (Supp. 38.) This included the administration of an alpha-fetoprotein (AFP) blood test and an amniocentesis. (Supp. 40.) Johanna H. Jones was born on July 8, 1994 with spina bifida, a genetic defect that occurred around the time of conception. (Supp. 29.)

This medical malpractice action was filed on April 5, 1995 by John J. and Samantha Jones, individually as the parents of, and on behalf of their daughter, Johanna Jones. (Supp. 40.) Plaintiff-appellant Johanna Jones alleges that the Defendant-appellee negligently failed to inform her parents that the AFP test was a positive indicator of birth defects. Mrs. Jones testified in deposition that had she been advised of the AFP results, the pregnancy would have been terminated by eugenic abortion. (Supp. 26.) By and through her father, Johanna seeks recovery of extraordinary expenses including all of the medical expenses, special educational costs, and all of the pain and suffering that she will incur as associated with her disabled life and related birth defects.

Pursuant to Defendant-appellee's Motion for Judgment on the Pleadings, the trial court dismissed Johanna Jones' damages claim for personal injuries and medical expenses based on *Flanaga v. Williams* (1993), 87 Ohio App.3d 768. (Supp. 50.) This judgment was affirmed on February 27, 2000, by the Ottawa County Court of Appeals, Sixth Appellate District, on the grounds that Ohio does not recognize a cause of action for "wrongful life." (Supp. 49.) Plaintiff-appellant filed a notice of appeal to the Ohio Supreme Court on April 5, 2000. (Supp. 32.)

-1-

ARGUMENT

Proposition of Law

Pursuant to Ohio common law, life is not a legally cognizable injury, and a cause of action for "wrongful life" or subsequent extraordinary damages related to a disabled life is not recognized. There is no basis in common or statutory law that recognizes or allows an individual to bring a cause of action based upon his or her life, whether normal or disabled, against health care providers for failure to furnish information that would have resulted in the termination of the individual's life before birth.

Spina bifida is a congenital anomaly that occurs around the time of conception, and it cannot be treated or cured during a mother's pregnancy. There is absolutely no causal connection between Appellant's genetic condition and the alleged negligence of Dr. Dreary for failure to inform Johanna Jones' parents of prenatal test results other than her life.

Johanna Jones' cause of action is premised upon the allegation that her parents did not terminate her life in utero and that as a result she was born with a congenital deformity. Nothing in the record indicates that Appellant was an unplanned or unwanted child as in the case of a failed sterilization; rather the Complaint and deposition testimony evidence that she became an unwanted child at the time of her birth when her parents learned that she was disabled.

Appellant's claim is not a matter of first impression relative to recovery on the basis of her life, as this Court in *Anderson* held that there is no cause of action for wrongful living and that life is not a compensable injury in Ohio. *Anderson v. St. Francis-St. George Hospital, Inc.* (1966), 77 Ohio St.3d 82. However, recognition of a cause of action upon the allegation that one's life was not terminated by abortion is a matter of first impression for this Court.

Several states have examined the issue of whether a child born with rubella syndrome has a cause of action for the physician's failure to properly diagnose and/or inform the mother of the possible effects of rubella in order to allow the termination of the pregnancy by abortion. Despite

-2-

the horrific impairments suffered by each child due to exposure to rubella, no wrongful life cause of action is recognized in Wisconsin, Idaho, New Hampshire or Arizona. *Dumer v. St. Michael's Hospital* (Wisc. 1975), 69 Wisc. 2d 766, 233 N.W.2d 372; *Baker v. Cruz* (Idaho 1984), 698 P.2d 315; *Smith v. Cote* (N.H. 1986), 128 N.H. 231, 513 A.2d 341; and *Walker by Pizano v. Mart* (Ariz. 1990), 164 Ariz. 37, 790 P.2d 735. As in Johanna Jones' case, several courts have refused to recognize the impaired child's wrongful life cause of action where the physician failed to properly detect or diagnose a genetic disorder, either by failure to offer or negligent performance of the diagnostic test, and to communicate the results to the mother in order to allow termination of the pregnancy. See *Greco v. United States* (Nev. 1995), 893 P.2d 345 (failure to detect severe birth defects); *Garrison v. Medical Inc.* (Del. 1989), 581 A.2d 288 (negligent reporting of prenatal chromosome study resulted in birth of child with Down's syndrome); *Becker v. Schwartz* (N.Y. 1978), 6 N.Y.2d 401, 413 N.Y.S.2d 895, 386 N.E.2d 807 (mother alleges never advised of availability of amniocentesis test, bore a child with Down's syndrome); *James v. Caserta* (W.Va. 1985), 175 W.Va. 406, 332 S.E.2d 872 (no wrongful life cause of action against physician for failure to perform amniocentesis to detect presence of Down's syndrome); *Siemieniec v. Lutheran Gen. Hospital* (Ill. 1987), 512 N.E.2d 691 (negligent post-conception assessment of risk of hemophilia); *Reed v. Ampagnolo* (Md. 1993), 810 F.Supp. 167 (no wrongful life cause of action recognized on behalf of child with spina bifida).

The courts have also refused to extend a "wrongful life" cause of action to negligent preconception conduct, as in the case of sterilization or genetic counseling. See e.g. *Speck v. Finegold* (Pa. 1981), 497 Pa. 77, 439 A.2d 110 (negligent vasectomy, coupled with failed abortion of child born with neurofibromatosis); *Viccaro v. Milunsky* (Mass. 1990), 406 Mass. 777, 551 N.E.2d 8 (negligent

-3-

preconception genetic counseling lead couple to conceive and have child with ectodermal dysplasia). Regardless of how it is defined, there is little merit to the term "wrongful life" if it is not a recognized cause of action. The overwhelming majority of jurisdictions have rejected wrongful life claims for relief brought by genetically or congenitally impaired children against health care professionals.

CONCLUSION

"Wrongful life" is a term that contradicts the sanctity of life and is inconsistent with the protected rights of all individuals to life, liberty and security of person regardless of genetic predisposition or physical or mental handicap. There is nothing in common law that supports a cause of action for life (disabled or not), and no basis to relate damages for a genetic disability to a life that was not terminated by abortion. Therefore, any expansion of the common law for a cause of action for "being" versus "nonbeing" is a matter appropriate for the Ohio Legislature, just as it addressed "wrongful death" in 1851.

Appellee respectfully requests that this Court uphold the lower court's denial of Johanna Jones' claim for wrongful life and related damages.

Respectfully submitted,

____

Janet Doe (121212)
Counsel for Appellee

Certificate of Service

I certify that a copy of this Merit Brief was sent by ordinary U.S. mail to counsel of record for appellant, John Miller, 100 South Street, Port Clinton, Ohio 43214 on May 21, 2000.

____

Janet Doe
Counsel for Appellee

-4-

D. More Information

Ohio Supreme Court Rules of Practice
www.sconet.state.oh.us/Rules

Sample Appellate Briefs
www.sconet.state.oh.us/Rules/practice/forms.pdf

Rules on Appellate Briefs to Courts of Appeals
www.sconet.state.oh.us/Rules/appellate/default.asp#rule16

Checklist for Briefs (6th Circuit)
www.ca6.uscourts.gov/internet/forms/briefs/checklistforbriefs.htm

Pro Se Appellate Briefs (6th Circuit)
www.ca6.uscourts.gov/internet/forms/briefs_appendices/prose_brief.pdf

Guide to Appellate Briefs Online
www.llrx.com/features/briefsonline.htm#free%20by%20jurisdiction
www.llrx.com/columns/reference43.htm
www.legaline.com/freebriefslinks.html
www.lawsource.com/also/usa.cgi?usb

E. Something to Check

Assume that you have been asked to cite check the merit brief of the appellee in the Jones v. Dreary case. Pick any three cases cited in the brief. Try to find them in a large law library or online. On finding cases online, check:
www.law.cornell.edu/states/listing.html
www.findlaw.com/casecode/#statelaw
www.lexisone.com
(click "Find Cases for Free")

For Ohio cases, see also section 5.1.

1. Check the accuracy of the location information in the citations by determining whether the three cases are found in the volumes and pages indicated in their citations.
2. Check the accuracy of what the brief says about the three cases (e.g., the brief says the *Anderson* case held that there is no cause of action for wrongful life in Ohio; read the *Andersen* case to determine if this is so).

7.5 A Sample Criminal Complaint Filed in an Ohio State Court

A. Introduction

This section presents an example of a criminal complaint filed in an Ohio state court. The case involves Elecia Battle, who made national news by claiming she had lost the $162,000,000 winning ticket in the Mega Millions Lottery.

See also section 4.2 on the state court system and section 6.4 for a timeline on the prosecution of a criminal case in state court.

B. A State Criminal Complaint

Exhibit 7.5A contains a sample criminal complaint filed in an Ohio state court.

C. More Information

Criminal Law in Ohio
www.megalaw.com/oh/top/ohcriminal.php
www.clelaw.lib.oh.us/Public/Misc/FAQs/Criminal.html
www.loc.gov/law/guide/us-oh.html
(click "Ohio Revised Code" then "Title XXIX")

Ohio State Attorney General
www.ag.state.oh.us

More Criminal Complaints
www.dol.gov/esa/regs/compliance/olms/USvsRichardson0404.htm
news.findlaw.com/cnn/docs/jacko/camj43004ind.html

D. Something to Check

1. Online, find the title on crimes-procedures in the Ohio Revised Code (see site listed above). Quote from the statute Elecia Battle was charged with violating.
2. The complaint charges the defendant with making a false statement. On the Internet, find more details of what she is alleged to have done.
3. Find online information about paralegals who work in criminal law offices in Ohio.

EXHIBIT 7.5A Sample Criminal Complaint Filed in an Ohio State Court

FILED

04 JAN -9 PM 2:16

SOUTH EUCLID MUNICIPAL COURT

SOUTH EUCLID MUNICIPAL COURT
SOUTH EUCLID, OHIO

State of Ohio)
vs.
Elecia Battle)
Name
4126 E. 150th Street)
Address Cleveland Ohio 44128

COMPLAINT

(Rule 4)

Complainant being duly sworn states that Elecia Battle
defendant
at city of South Euclid, Cuyahoga County, Ohio on or about January 2, 2004
place
did knowingly make a false statement when the statement was made with purpose to mislead a public official in performing his official function.

Said act was contrary to the statute in such case made and provided (Ohio Revised Code Section 2921.13(A)(3)) and against the peace and dignity of the State of Ohio.

ORC 2921.13 (A)(3) Misdemeanor - first degree
State the numerical designation of the applicable statute or ordinance.

[signature]
Complainant

Sworn to and subscribed before me by Det. Lt. Kevin Nietert on January 9, 2004.

[signature] Debra E. Roy
Judge / Clerk / Deputy Clerk /
South Euclid Municipal Court
or

Notary Public

County/State of Ohio
My commission expires ________

Source: *www.thesmokinggun.com/archive/eleciacharge1.html (see also elecia-battle.iqnaut.net)*

PART

8

A Comprehensive Legal Dictionary

(with selected Ohio-specific definitions)

A

AAA American Arbitration Association (*www.adr.org*).

AAfPE American Association for Paralegal Education (*www.aafpe.org*).

AALS Association of American Law Schools (*www.aals.org*).

a aver et tener To have and to hold. See habendem clause.

ABA See American Bar Association (*www.abanet.org*).

abaction Stealing animals, often by driving them off.

abandonee The person to whom something is abandoned or relinquished.

abandonment A total surrender of property, persons, or rights.

> In order for abandonment to exist, affirmative proof of intent to abandon coupled with acts or omissions implementing intent must be shown; therefore, occasional, infrequent or complete nonuse is not sufficient. *Hamilton*, 63 Ohio App.3d 27 (Ohio App., 1989)

abatable nuisance A nuisance that can be diminished or eliminated.

abatement 1. Termination or nullification. 2. A suspension of proceedings. 3. A reduction of testamentary legacies because estate assets are insufficient to pay debts and other legacies.

abatement of action A complete ending or quashing of a suit.

abator Someone who abates a nuisance.

abdication A voluntary renunciation of a privilege or office.

abduction The unlawful taking away of someone (e.g., child, wife, ward, servant) by force or trickery.

abet To encourage or assist another, often in criminal activity.

> Abet within aider and abettor statute means to counsel, to encourage, to incite or to assist in commission of criminal act. R.C. § 1.17. *State v. Trocodaro*, 36 Ohio App.2d 1 (Ohio App., 1973)

abettor A person who encourages another to commit a crime.

abeyance Suspension; not finally settled or vested.

ability The power or capacity to perform.

ab initio From the beginning.

abjuration Renunciation under oath, formally giving up rights.

abnormally dangerous Extrahazardous (ultrahazardous) even if reasonable care is used.

abode Dwelling place; residence.

abogado An advocate or lawyer (Spanish).

abolish To eliminate or cancel.

aboriginal Pertaining to inhabitants from earliest times.

abortifacient Causing abortion.

abortion 1. An induced termination of a pregnancy. 2. A miscarriage.

> As used in the Revised Code, abortion means the purposeful termination of a human pregnancy by any person, including the pregnant woman herself, with an intention other than to produce a live birth or to remove a dead fetus or embryo. Abortion is the practice of medicine or surgery for the purposes of section 4731.41 of the Revised Code. R.C. § 2919.11.

above 1. With a superior status. 2. Earlier or before.

abridge 1. To diminish. 2. To condense or shorten.

abrogate To annul, cancel, or destroy.

abscond To flee in order to avoid arrest or legal process.

absentee landlord A lessor who does not live on the leased premises.

absolute Unconditional; final.

absolute deed A deed that transfers land without encumbrances.

absolute law An immutable law of nature.

absolute liability See strict liability.

absolute nuisance A nuisance for which one is liable without regard to whether it occurred through negligence or other fault.

> The essence of absolute nuisance and nuisance per se is that no matter how careful one is, some activities are inherently injurious and cannot be conducted without damaging someone else's property or rights; they are based upon either intentional conduct or abnormally dangerous conditions and, as such, rule of absolute liability applies. *Brown*, 87 Ohio App.3d 704 (Ohio App., 1993)

absolution Release from an obligation or penalty.

absolutism A political system in which one person has total power.

absorption The assimilation of one entity or right into another.

abstain To refrain from; to refuse to use the jurisdiction that a court has.

abstention doctrine If a matter can be tried in federal or state court, a federal court can decline its jurisdiction to avoid unnecessary interference with the state.

abstract A summary or abridgment.

abstraction Taking something, often wrongfully with intent to defraud.

abstract of record Abbreviated history of court proceedings to date.

abstract of title A condensed history or summary of conveyances, interests, and encumbrances that affect title to land.

abuse 1. Improper use. 2. Physical or mental mistreatment.

abuse of discretion A decision that is manifestly unreasonable, depriving someone of a substantive right.

abuse of process A tort consisting of (a) the use of a civil or criminal process, (b) for a purpose for which the process is not designed, (c) resulting in actual damage.

> Abuse of process occurs where someone attempts to achieve through use of the court that which the court is itself powerless to order. *Robb*, 75 Ohio St.3d 264 (Ohio 1996)

abut To be next to or touch; to share a common border.

abutters Owners of property joined at a common border.

accede 1. To agree. 2. To attain an office.

accelerated depreciation Taking more depreciation deductions during the early years of the life of an asset.

acceleration Causing something to occur sooner, e.g., to pay an obligation, to enjoy a benefit.

acceleration clause A clause in a contract or instrument stating what will trigger an earlier payment schedule.

acceptance 1. Agreement (express or implied) with the terms of an offer. 2. The act of receiving a thing with the intention of retaining it. 3. The commitment to honor a draft or bill of exchange.

Acceptance means the drawee's signed agreement to pay the draft as presented. It must be written on the draft and may consist of his signature alone. R.C. § 1303.46

access Opportunity to enter, visit with, or be intimate with.

access easement See easement of access.

accession 1. An increase through addition. 2. A country's acceptance of a treaty. 3. The right to own what is added to land by improvements or natural growth.

accessory 1. One who, without being present, helps another commit or conceal a crime. 2. A subordinate part.

accessory after the fact One who knows a crime has been committed (although not present at the time) and who helps the offender escape.

accessory before the fact One who assists or encourages another to commit a crime, although not present at the time it is committed.

accident An unexpected misfortune whether or not caused by negligence or other fault.

The ordinary meaning of accident as used in liability insurance policies in which the term is undefined, refers to unintended and unexpected happenings. *Thomson*, 150 Ohio App.3d 352 (Ohio App., 2002)

accommodated party See accommodation party.

accommodation 1. A favor, e.g., making a loan, acting as a cosigner. 2. An adjustment or settlement. 3. Lodging.

accommodation indorser See accommodation party.

accommodation paper A promissory note or bill of exchange that is cosigned by a person (who does not receive payment or other consideration) in order to help someone else secure credit or a loan. The person signing is the accommodation party.

accommodation party Someone who signs a promissory note or other negotiable instrument in any capacity, e.g., as indorser, without receiving payment or other consideration, in order to act as surety for another party (called the accommodated party).

accomplice A person who participates with another in an offense before, during, or after its commission.

One who freely and voluntarily engages with another in the commission of a crime. *State v. Johnson*, 112 Ohio App. 124 (Ohio App., 1960)

accord 1. An agreement or contract to settle a dispute. 2. An agreement for the future discharge of an existing debt by a substituted performance. Also called executory accord. Once the debt is discharged, the arrangement is called an accord and satisfaction.

accord and satisfaction See accord (2).

account 1. A financial record of debts, credits, transactions, etc. 2. An action or suit to force the defendant to explain his or her handling of a fund in which the plaintiff has an interest. Also called accounting.

Any record, element, or summary in which financial transactions are identified and recorded as debit or credit transactions in order to summarize items of a similar nature or classification. R.C. § 131.01

accountable Responsible; liable.

accountant A person skilled in keeping financial records and accounts.

account debtor The person who has obligations on an account.

accounting 1. A bookkeeping system for recording financial transactions. 2. A settling of an account with a determination of what is owed. 3. See account (2).

accounting period The period of time, e.g., a year, used by a taxpayer for the determination of tax liability.

account payable A regular business debt not yet paid.

account receivable A regular business debt not yet collected.

account stated An agreement on the accuracy of an account, stating the balance due.

An agreement between parties, express or implied, based upon an account balanced and rendered. *Rudolph Bros.*, 187 N.E.2d 190 (Ohio App., 1961)

accredit 1. To acknowledge or recognize officially. 2. To accept the credentials of a foreign envoy.

accredited investor An investor who is financially sophisticated.

accretion Growth in size by gradual accumulation. An increase of land by natural forces, e.g., soil added to a shore.

accrual basis A method of accounting in which revenues are recorded when earned or due, even though not collected, and expenditures are recorded when liabilities are incurred, whether paid or not.

accrue To come into existence as a right; to vest.

accrued dividend A declared dividend yet to be paid.

accumulated earnings tax A penalty tax on a corporation that retains its earnings beyond the reasonable needs of the business.

accumulation trust A trust in which the trustee must invest trust income rather than pay it out to beneficiaries.

accumulative sentence See consecutive sentences.

accusation A charge that one has committed a crime or other wrong.

accusatory instrument A document charging someone with a crime, e.g., an indictment.

accused The person accused or formally charged with a crime.

acknowledgment 1. An affirmation that something is genuine. 2. A formal statement of a person executing an instrument that he or she is doing so as a free act. 3. An acceptance of responsibility.

The words "acknowledged before me" means that: (A) The person acknowledging appeared before the person taking the acknowledgment; (B) He acknowledged he executed the instrument; (C) In the case of: (1) A natural person, he executed the instrument for the purposes therein stated. R.C. § 147.541

acknowledgment of paternity A formal admission by a father that a child is his.

ACLU American Civil Liberties Union (*www.aclu.com*).

acquaintance rape Rape by someone the victim knows.

acquest Property acquired by a means other than inheritance.

acquiesce To consent passively; to comply without protest.

acquire To obtain; to gain ownership of.

acquit 1. To release someone from an obligation. 2. To declare that the accused is innocent of the crime.

acquittal 1. A discharge or release from an obligation. 2. A formal declaration of innocence of a crime.

acquittance A written discharge from an obligation.

ACRS Accelerated cost-recovery system.

act 1. Something done voluntarily; an external manifestation of the will. 2. A law passed by the legislature.

acting Temporarily functioning as or substituting for.

actio A right or claim.

action 1. A civil or criminal court proceeding. 2. Conduct.

Action in the sense of a judicial proceeding includes recoupment, counterclaim, set-off, suit in equity, and any other proceedings in which rights are determined. R.C. § 1301.01(A)

actionable Pertaining to that which can become the basis of a lawsuit.

actionable per se Pertaining to words that on their face and without the aid of extrinsic proof are defamatory. They are called actionable words.

actionable words See actionable per se.

action at law An action in a court of law, not in a court of equity.

action on the case An action to recover for damages caused indirectly rather than directly or immediately. Also called trespass on the case.

active trust See special trust.

act of bankruptcy Debtor's conduct that could trigger involuntary bankruptcy.

act of God A force of nature; an unusual force of nature.

For an event to be an *act of God,* it must not be foreseeable by the exercise of reasonable foresight and prudence. *Helton,* 123 Ohio App.3d 158 (Ohio App., 1997)

act of state doctrine Courts of one country should not judge the validity of an act of another country that occurs within the latter.

actual Real; existing in fact.

actual authority The authority a principal intentionally confers on an agent or permits the agent to believe has been conferred.

actual cash value 1. Fair market value. 2. Replacement cost less depreciation.

actual damages Damages that compensate for an actual or proven loss.

actual fraud See positive fraud.

actual loss Amounts paid or payable as a result of a substantial loss.

actual malice 1. Conscious wrongdoing; intent to injure. Also called malice in fact. 2. Knowledge of the falsity of a defamatory statement or a reckless disregard as to truth or falsity.

Either that state of mind under which a person's conduct is characterized by hatred, ill will, or a spirit of revenge; or a conscious disregard for the rights and safety of other persons that has a great probability of causing substantial harm. *UZ Engineered Products,* 147 Ohio App.3d 382 (Ohio App., 2001)

actual notice Notice given to a person directly and personally. Also called express notice.

actual value Fair market value.

actuary One skilled in statistics for risk and premium calculations.

actus reus The physical deed or act that is wrongful.

ADA Americans with Disabilities Act (*www.eeoc.gov/ada*).

ad damnum clause A clause stating the damages claimed.

addict A habitual user of something, e.g., a drug.

additur A practice by which a judge offers a defendant the choice between a new trial and accepting a damage award higher than what the jury awarded.

adduce To present or introduce.

ADEA Age Discrimination in Employment Act (*www.eeoc.gov/policy/adea.html*).

adeem To take away; to revoke a bequest.

ademption The extinction of a specific bequest or devise because of the disappearance of or disposition of the subject matter of the gift from the estate of the testator in his or her lifetime.

adequate consideration Fair and reasonable consideration.

adequate remedy at law A legal remedy, e.g., damages, that is complete, practical, and efficient.

An adequate remedy at law precluding equitable jurisdiction is one that affords relief with reference to the matter in controversy and is appropriate to the particular circumstances of the case. *Discover Bank,* 129 Ohio Misc.2d 71 (Ohio Mun., 2004)

adhesion contract A standard contract offered on a take-it-or-leave-it basis to a consumer who has no meaningful choice as to its terms.

ad hoc For this special purpose only.

ad hominem Appealing to emotions or personal matters, not to reason.

ad idem On the same matter.

ad interim Temporarily.

adjacent Lying near or close by; next to.

adjective law Procedural law, rules of practice.

adjoining Touching; contiguous.

adjourn To postpone or suspend until another time.

adjournment Postponing a session until another time.

Adjournment in constitutional provision that if a bill is not returned by the governor within ten days after being presented to him it becomes law unless the General Assembly by adjournment prevents its return, in which case it becomes law unless within ten days after adjournment it is filed, with objections, in office of Secretary of State refers to an adjournment sine die and not to a weekend adjournment. Ohio Const. Art. 2, § 16. *State ex rel. Gilmore,* 6 Ohio St.3d 39 (Ohio 1983)

adjudge To decide judicially.

adjudicate To judge; to resolve a dispute judicially.

adjudication A determination or judgment by a court of law.

adjudicative facts Facts concerning the who, what, when, where, and how pertaining to a particular case.

adjunction Adding or attaching one thing to another.

adjure To request solemnly.

adjust 1. To assess and determine what will be paid under an insurance policy. 2. To set a new payment plan for debts.

adjustable-rate mortgage (ARM) A mortgage with a fluctuating interest rate tied to a market index. Also called variable-rate mortgage (VRM).

adjusted basis The cost or other original basis of an asset reduced by deductions for depreciation and increased by capital improvements.

adjusted gross income (AGI) Gross income less allowable deductions.

adjuster One who determines (or settles) the amount of a claim.

ad litem For the suit, for purposes of this litigation.

administration 1. The persons or entities managing an estate, a government agency, or other organization. 2. The management and settlement of the estate of a decedent. administrative agency See agency (2).

administrative discretion An administrative agency's power to use judgment in choosing among available alternatives.

administrative law The laws governing and created by administrative agencies.

Administrative Law Judge (ALJ) A hearing officer within an administrative agency. Also called hearing examiner.

Administrative Procedure Act (APA) A federal or state statute on rulemaking and hearing procedures before administrative agencies.

> Administrative procedure in the Revised Code. R.C. §§ 119.12 et seq

administrative remedy Relief granted by an administrative agency.

administrator 1. A manager. 2. A person appointed by the court to manage the estate of someone who dies without a will (i.e., intestate) or who dies with a will that does not name a functioning executor.

administrator ad litem An administrator appointed by the court to represent an estate of a decedent in a court proceeding.

administrator cum testamento annexo (CTA) See cum testamento annexo.

administrator de bonis non (DBN) See de bonis non.

administratrix A woman who administers the estate of the deceased.

admiralty The law that applies to maritime disputes or offenses involving ships and navigation. Also called maritime law.

admissible Allowed into court to determine its truth or believability.

admission 1. An assertion of the truth of a fact. 2. An official acknowledgement of someone's right to practice law.

> An admission is merely a statement by the accused, direct or implied, of facts pertinent to the issue and tending to show his guilt; a confession is an acknowledgement of guilt. *City of Middletown*, 120 N.E.2d 903 (Ohio Mun., 1954)

admission against interest A statement by a party that is harmful to a position he or she is taking in the litigation.

admit To accept as true or valid.

admonition 1. A reprimand. 2. A warning from a judge to a jury.

adopt To go through a formal process of establishing a relationship of parent and child between persons.

adoptee The person adopted.

ADR See alternative dispute resolution.

ad testificandum To or for testifying.

adult A person who has reached the age of majority (e.g., 21, 18).

adulterate To contaminate by adding something inferior.

> A drug or device is adulterated . . . if . . . (A) It consists, in whole or in part, of any filthy, putrid, or decomposed substance. (B) It has been produced, processed, prepared, packed, or held under unsanitary conditions . . . R.C. § 3715.63

adultery Sexual relations between a married person and someone other than his or her spouse.

ad valorem tax A tax based on a percentage of the value of property.

advance To lend; to pay or supply something before it is due.

advance directive A statement of one's wishes regarding medical treatment upon becoming incompetent. Also called living will or healthcare proxy.

advancement A gift in advance, usually by a parent to a child. The amount or value of the gift is deducted from what the recipient eventually receives when the giver dies intestate (i.e., without a valid will).

advance sheet A pamphlet containing laws (e.g., court opinions) that comes out before a later volume of the same set.

adventure A risky business venture, e.g., a shipment of goods at sea.

adversary An opponent.

adversary proceeding A hearing in which the opponents are present.

adversary system A method of resolving a legal dispute whereby the parties argue their conflicting claims before a neutral decision-maker.

adverse Having opposite interests, against.

adverse interest Goals or claims of one person that are different from or opposed to those of another.

adverse parties Parties in a suit with conflicting interests.

adverse possession A method of obtaining title to the land of another by using the land under a claim of right in a way that is open, exclusive, hostile to the current owner, and continuous.

> To acquire title by *adverse possession* for 21 years or over, the possession must be actual, open and notorious, hostile and under claim of right, continuous and exclusive. *Wilberforce University*, 86 Ohio App. 121 (Ohio App., 1948)

adverse witness See hostile witness.

advice 1. An opinion offered as guidance. 2. Notice that a draft has been drawn.

advice and consent The U.S. Senate's approval power on treaties and major presidential appointments. U.S. Const. art. II, § 2.

advisement Careful consideration.

advisory jury A jury whose verdict is not binding on the court.

advisory opinion An opinion of a court that is not binding.

> An advisory opinion is merely an opinion of a judge or judges of a court that adjudicates nothing and is binding on no one. R.C. § 2721.03. *Cincinnati Metropolitan Housing Authority*, 22 Ohio App.2d 39 (Ohio App., 1969)

advocacy Arguing for or against something; pleading.

advocate One who argues or pleads for another.

AFDC See Aid to Families with Dependent Children.

aff'd Affirmed.

affect To act on (upon); to influence.

affected class 1. Persons who suffered job discrimination. 2. Persons who constitute a class for bringing a class action.

affecting commerce Involving commerce or trade.

aff'g Affirming.

affiant Someone who makes an affidavit.

affidavit A written or printed statement of facts made under oath before a person with authority to administer the oath.

In order for a declaration to be considered an affidavit, it must be sworn in the presence of a notary or other person authorized to administer oaths. *Pollock,* 130 Ohio App.3d 505 (Ohio App., 1998)

affidavit of service A sworn statement that a document (e.g., summons) has been delivered (served) to a designated person.

affiliate A subsidiary; one corporation controlled by another.

affiliation order An order determining paternity.

affinity Relationship by marriage, not by blood.

affirm 1. To declare that a judgment is valid. 2. To assert formally, but not under oath. The noun is affirmance.

affirmance See affirm.

affirmation A solemn declaration, often a substitute for an oath.

affirmative action Steps designed to eliminate existing and continuing discrimination, to remedy the effects of past discrimination, and to create systems to prevent future discrimination.

affirmative charge An instruction that removes an issue from the jury.

affirmative defense A defense raising new facts that will defeat the plaintiff's claim even if the plaintiff's fact allegations are proven.

(1) A defensive matter admitting the plaintiff has a claim, but asserting a legal reason why the plaintiff cannot have any recovery on that claim. *Kraft Constr.,* 128 Ohio App.3d 33 (Ohio App., 1998). (2) A defense expressly designated as affirmative or a defense involving an excuse or justification peculiarly within the knowledge of the accused, on which he can fairly be required to adduce supporting evidence. R.C. § 2901.05

affirmative easement An easement that forces the landowner to allow the easement holder to do specific acts on the land.

affirmative relief Relief (e.g., damages) a defendant could have sought in his or her own suit, but instead is sought in a counterclaim or cross-claim.

affirmative warranty An insurance warranty that asserts the existence of a fact at the time the policy is entered into.

affix To attach; to add to permanently.

affray Fighting in a public place so as to cause terror in the public.

affreightment A contract to transport goods by ship.

aforementioned See aforesaid.

aforesaid Mentioned earlier in the document.

aforethought Thought of beforehand; premeditated.

a fortiori With greater force; all the more so.

after-acquired property Property acquired after a particular event, e.g., after making a will, after giving a security interest.

after-acquired title rule When a seller does not obtain title to an asset until after attempting to sell it, title automatically vests in the buyer the moment the seller obtained it.

after-born child A child born after the execution of a will.

age discrimination Discrimination on the basis of one's age.

agency 1. A relationship in which one person acts for and can bind another. 2. A governmental body, other than a court or legislature, that carries out the law.

A contract, express or implied, by which one of the parties confides to the other the management of some business to be transacted in his name, or on his account, by which the other, who is the agent, assumes to do the business and to render an account of it. *Case,* 103 Ohio Misc.2d 1 (Ohio Ct.Cl., 1998)

agency shop A business or other entity that collects union dues from all employees, even those who decided not to join the union.

agent 1. A person authorized to act for another. 2. A power or force that produces an effect.

age of consent The age at which one can marry without parental consent or have sexual intercourse without the partner committing statutory rape.

age of majority The age at which a person has the right to vote, enter a contract that cannot be disaffirmed, make a will, etc. Also called full age.

All persons of the age of eighteen years or more, who are under no legal disability, are capable of contracting and are of full age for all purposes. R.C. § 3109.01

age of reason The age at which a child is deemed capable of making reasoned judgments and, therefore, can commit a crime or tort.

aggravated assault A more serious crime of assault for reasons such as the defendant's intent to cause serious bodily harm.

aggravation Circumstances that increase the enormity of a crime or tort, e.g., using a weapon.

aggregate Combined into a whole.

aggregation The unpatentability of an invention because its parts lack a composite integrated mechanism.

aggregation doctrine To reach the jurisdictional amount in a federal diversity case, the total of all the claims cannot be added.

aggrieved party One whose legal rights have been invaded.

A party entitled to resort to a remedy. R.C. § 1301.01

AGI See adjusted gross income.

agio Money paid to convert one kind of money into another.

agreed case Facts agreed upon by the parties, allowing a court to limit itself to deciding the questions of law on those facts. Also called case agreed, case stated.

agreement Mutual assent by the parties; a meeting of the minds.

Agreement means the bargain of the parties in fact, as found in their language or inferred from other circumstances and from rules, regulations, and procedures given the effect of agreements under laws otherwise applicable to a particular transaction. R.C. § 304.01

aid and abet Assist or encourage someone to commit a crime.

aider by verdict A jury verdict cures technical pleading defects.

Aid to Families with Dependent Children (AFDC) Federal public assistance replaced by TANF (Temporary Assistance for Needy Families).

airbill A bill of lading used in a shipment of goods by air.

air rights The right of a landowner to use all or part of the airspace above his or her land.

air piracy Using force or threats to seize or hijack an aircraft.

aka Also known as.

alderman A member of the local legislative body.

aleatory Depending on uncertain circumstances or contingencies.

aleatory contract A contract in which performance depends on uncertain events, e.g., an insurance contract.

ALI See American Law Institute (*www.ali.org*).

***Alford* plea** A defendant pleads guilty, but does not admit guilt. *NC v. Alford*, 96 S. Ct. 160 (1970).

alias Otherwise known as; an assumed name.

alias summons; alias writ A new summons or writ given when the original one was issued without effect.

alibi A defense alleging absence from the scene of the crime.

> Defense of alibi means the defendant claims he was at some place other than the scene of the crime at the time the crime was taking place and hence could not have taken part. *State v. Payne*, 104 Ohio App. 410 (Ohio App., 1957)

alien One who is not a citizen of the country where he or she resides.

alienable Legally transferable to the ownership of another.

alienage The condition or status of an alien.

alienate To transfer; to transfer title.

alienation clause A clause in an insurance policy that voids the policy if the property being insured is sold or transferred.

alienation of affections The tort of causing a diminishment of the marital relationship between the plaintiff and his or her spouse.

> Defendant wrongfully, maliciously and intentionally enticed, induced, persuaded and caused plaintiff's spouse to lose affection for plaintiff and that defendant intended to bring about the alienation. *Singh*, 81 Ohio App.3d 376 (Ohio App., 1992)

alienee A person to whom property is conveyed or transferred.

alieni juris Under another's power.

alienor A person who transfers or conveys property.

alimony A court-ordered payment of money or other property by one spouse to another for support after divorce or separation. Also called spousal support.

> Property-division alimony and sustenance alimony are both types of alimony. *Pacht*, 13 Ohio App.3d 363 (Ohio App., 1983). Alimony consists of two components: division of marital assets and liabilities, and periodic payments for sustenance and support. R.C. § 3105.18. *Kunkle*, 51 Ohio St.3d 64, (Ohio 1990)

alimony in gross Alimony in the form of a single definite sum that cannot be modified. Also called lump-sum alimony.

alimony pendente lite See temporary alimony.

aliquot An exact division or fractional part.

aliunde rule Jury deliberations may not be scrutinized, unless there is evidence from a source other than a juror to impeach the jury verdict.

ALJ See administrative law judge.

allegation A statement of fact that one expects to prove.

alleged Asserted as true, but not yet proven.

allegiance Loyalty owed to a government.

Allen charge A supplementary instruction given to a deadlocked jury to encourage it to reach a verdict. Also called dynamite charge. *Allen v. U.S.*, 17 S. Ct. 154 (1896).

all faults A sale of goods "as is," in their present condition.

all fours See on all fours.

allocation A setting aside or designation for a purpose.

> A portion of an appropriation which is designated for expenditure by specific organizational units or for special purposes, activities, or objects that do not relate to a period of time. R.C. § 131.01(D)

allocatur It is allowed. In Pennsylvania, the permission to appeal.

allocution 1. The judge asks a convicted defendant if he or she has anything to say before sentence is imposed. 2. The defendant's right to make such a statement.

allodial Owned absolutely, free and clear.

allograph A writing or signature made by one person for another.

allonge A slip of paper attached to a negotiable instrument to provide space for more indorsements.

allotment A share, e.g., the land awarded to an individual American Indian.

allotment certificate A document stating the number of shares of a security to be purchased, payment terms, etc.

allowance 1. Portion assigned or bestowed. 2. Deduction or discount.

alluvion The washing up of sand or soil so as to form firm ground.

alteration Making something different, e.g., modifying real property, changing the language or meaning of a document.

> Alteration means (1) an unauthorized change in an instrument that purports to modify in any respect the obligation of a party; or (2) an unauthorized addition of words or numbers or other change to an incomplete instrument relating to the obligation of a party. R.C. § 1303.50(A)

alter ego rule Personal liability can be imposed on shareholders who use the corporation for personal business.

alternate valuation The value of assets 6 months after death.

alternative contract A contract that gives options for performance.

alternative dispute resolution (ADR) Arbitration, mediation, and similar methods of resolving a dispute without litigation.

alternative minimum tax (AMT) A tax imposed to assure that enough income tax is paid by persons with large deductions, credits, or exclusions.

alternative pleading Alleging facts or claims in a complaint or other pleading that are not necessarily consistent.

alternative relief Inconsistent relief sought on the same claim.

alternative writ A writ requiring a person to do a specified thing or to show cause why he or she should not be compelled to do it.

amalgamation Consolidation, e.g., two corporations into a new one.

ambassador An officer of high diplomatic rank representing a country.

ambit Boundary; the limits of a power.

ambulance chasing Soliciting injury victims by or for an attorney.

ambulatory 1. Revocable. 2. Able to walk.

ameliorating waste Waste by a tenant that in fact improves the land.

amenable Subject to answer to the law; legally accountable.

amendment A formal change (e.g., addition, subtraction, correction) made in the text of a document (e.g., statute, legislative bill, pleading, contract).

amercement A fine or punishment imposed (e.g., on a public official) at the court's discretion.

American Law Institute (ALI) An organization of scholars that writes model acts and restatements of the law (*www.ali.org*).

American Association for Paralegal Education (AAfPE) A national association of paralegal schools (*www.aafpe.org*).

American Bar Association (ABA) A national voluntary association of attorneys (*www.abanet.org*).

American rule Each side in litigation pays its own attorney fees and court costs unless a statute provides otherwise. Under the English rule, also called loser-pays, the losing party may be required to pay the attorney fees and court costs incurred by the winning side.

> Ohio has adopted the American Rule, by which each party to a lawsuit must pay his or her own attorney fees. *Keal*, 2005 WL 2679643 (Ohio App., 2005)

amicable action An action brought by mutual consent of the parties to seek a ruling on facts they do not dispute.

amicus curiae Friend of the court. A nonparty who obtains court permission to file a brief with its views on the case.

amnesty A pardon for crimes, often granted to a group.

amortization 1. The gradual elimination of a debt, often by making regular payments toward principal along with interest payments. 2. Writing off the cost of an intangible asset over its useful life.

amotion Removing or turning someone out.

amount in controversy The amount sued for. The amount needed (over $75,000) to establish diversity jurisdiction in federal court. Also called jurisdictional amount (28 U.S.C. 1332(a)).

analogous 1. Sufficiently similar to lend support. 2. Involving facts and rules that are similar to those now under consideration.

anarchist One who believes government should not exist.

anarchy The absence of political authority or order.

ancestor A person from whom one is descended; a forebear.

ancient documents Deeds and other writings 20 or more years old that are presumed to be genuine if kept in proper custody.

> Ancient documents or data compilation. Evidence that a document or data compilation, in any form, (a) is in such condition as to create no suspicion concerning its authenticity, (b) was in a place where it, if authentic, would likely be, and (c) has been in existence twenty years or more at the time it is offered. Evid. R. Rule 901 (B)(8)

ancient lights rule Windows with outside light for a period of time (e.g., 20 years) cannot be blocked off by an adjoining landowner.

ancillary Supplementary; subsidiary.

ancillary administration An administrator appointed by the court for property or the decedent located in a different jurisdiction.

ancillary jurisdiction Authority of a court to hear claims that otherwise would not be within its jurisdiction if these claims are sufficiently related to the case properly before the court.

and his heirs Words giving transferee a fee simple absolute.

animo With the intention.

animus 1. Intention, e.g., animus furandi (intent to steal), animun testandi (intent to make a will). 2. Animosity; ill will.

> Animus within R.C. § 2941.25(B) is intended to mean "purpose" or, more properly, "immediate motive". *State v. Logan*, 60 Ohio St.2d 126 (Ohio 1979)

annexation 1. Merging or attaching one thing to another. 2. The formal takeover or appropriation of something (e.g., territory).

annotated statutes A collection of statutes that include research references such as case summaries interpreting the statutes.

annotation A remark or note on a law, e.g., a summary of a case.

annual exclusion The amount one can give away each year gift-tax free.

annual percentage rate (APR) The true cost of borrowing money expressed as an annual interest rate.

annual report A corporation's annual financial report to stockholders.

annuitant A beneficiary of an annuity.

annuity A fixed sum payable periodically to a person for life or a specific period of time.

annuity certain An annuity that continues paying for a set period even if the annuitant dies within the period.

annuity due An annuity payable at the start of each pay period.

annul To obliterate or nullify.

annulment 1. A nullification or voiding. 2. A declaration that a valid marriage never existed or that an attempted marriage is invalid.

answer 1. The first pleading of the defendant that responds to the plaintiff's claims. 2. To assume someone else's liability.

> The pleading by which issue is taken with averments of claims for relief, or confesses and avoids them by new matter. Rules Civ.Proc., Rule 8(B). *Gordon Food Service*, 76 Ohio App.3d 105 (Ohio App., 1991)

ante Before, prior to.

ante litem motam Before the suit began or arose.

antecedent Preexisting.

antecedent debt A debt that preexists an event, e.g., filing for bankruptcy. A prior debt may be consideration for a new promise to pay.

antedate 1. To backdate; to place a date on a document that is earlier than the date the document was written. 2. To precede.

antenuptial Occurring before marriage. See premarital agreement.

antichresis An agreement giving the creditor the income from and possession of the property pledged, instead of interest.

anticipation 1. Doing something before its scheduled time. 2. Prior disclosure or use of an invention, jeopardizing its patentability.

anticipatory breach A repudiation of a contract duty before the time fixed in the contract for the performance of that duty.

> A repudiation by the promisor of a contractual duty before the time fixed for performance has arrived. *McDonald*, 59 Ohio App.3d 38 (Ohio App., 1989)

anticipatory search warrant A search warrant usable only on a future date, not upon issuance.

antidumping law A law against selling imported goods at less than their fair price if the imports hurt comparable domestic products.

antilapse A gift in a will goes to the heirs of the beneficiary to prevent the gift from failing because the beneficiary predeceases the testator.

antinomy A contradiction between two laws or propositions.

anti-racketeering See RICO.

antitrust law Laws against price fixing, monopolies, and other anticompetitive practices and restraints of trade.

APA See Administrative Procedure Act.

apostille A certificate authenticating foreign documents.

apparent 1. Capable of being seen; visible. 2. Seeming.

apparent authority An agent's authority that the principal reasonably leads another to believe the agent has. Also called ostensible authority.

> Apparent authority an of insurance agent is such authority as the insurance company knowingly permits the agent to assume, or such authority as a reasonably prudent person, using diligence and discretion, would naturally suppose that the agent possessed in view of company's conduct. *Randall*, 38 Ohio App.3d 87 (Ohio App., 1987)

apparent defects Defects observable upon reasonable inspection. Also called patent defects.

apparent heir An heir who will inherit unless he or she predeceases the ancestor or is disinherited by will. Also called heir apparent.

app. Appellate; appeal.

appeal Asking a higher tribunal to review or reconsider the decision of an inferior tribunal.

> The procedure by which a person, aggrieved by a finding, decision, order, or adjudication of any agency, invokes the jurisdiction of a court. R.C. § 119.01(H)

appealable Sufficiently final so that it can be appealed.

appeal bond A bond of a party filing an appeal to cover the opponent's costs if the appeal is later deemed to have been not genuine.

appearance Formally coming before a tribunal as a party or as a representative of a party.

> An appearance is ordinarily made when a party comes into court by some overt act of that party that submits a presentation to the court. *Medina Supply Co.*, 2002 WL 500340 (Ohio App., 2002)

appellant The person or party who brings the appeal.

appellate Concerning appeals or an appellate court.

appellate brief See brief (1).

appellate jurisdiction The power of an appellate court to review and correct the decisions of a lower tribunal.

appellee The person against whom an appeal is brought. Respondent.

append To attach.

appoint To give someone a power or authority.

appointee The person selected.

apportionment 1. A proportional division. 2. The process of allocating legislators among several political subdivisions.

appraisal Estimation of value or worth.

appraisal remedy A shareholder's right to have its shares bought back by the corporation due to dissent with an extraordinary corporate decision.

appraiser Someone who impartially evaluates (appraises) property.

appreciation Increase in property value, often due to inflation.

apprehension 1. Knowledge. 2. Fear. 3. Seizure or arrest.

appropriation 1. Taking control or possession. 2. An invasion-of-privacy tort committed by the use of a person's name, likeness, or personality for commercial gain without authorization. 3. The legislature's setting aside of money for a specific purpose.

approval sale See sale on approval.

appurtenance A thing or right belonging or attached to something else.

appurtenant Belonging to; incident to the principal property.

> Things pass as incidents to or appurtenances of realty when they are attached thereto and are essential to its use, or, in other words, when they are "fixtures." *Szilagy*, 63 Ohio App. 105 (Ohio App., 1939)

appurtenant easement See easement appurtenant.

APR See annual percentage rate.

a priori Deductively; derived from logic or self-evident propositions, without reference to observed experience.

arbiter A referee or judge, someone who can resolve a dispute.

arbitrage Simultaneous matched purchase and sale of identical or equivalent securities in order to profit from price discrepancies.

arbitrament 1. The decision of an arbitrator. 2. The act of deciding.

arbitrary Capricious, subjective. Biased individual preferences.

> For purposes of determining whether abuse of discretion has occurred, arbitrary means without adequate determining principle, and unreasonable means irrational. *Detelich*, 90 Ohio App.3d 793 (Ohio App., 1993)

arbitration The submission of a dispute to an impartial third person for a binding decision as an alternative to litigation.

arbitration clause A contract clause providing for compulsory arbitration of disputes under the contract.

arbitrator The person rendering the decision in arbitration.

arguendo In arguing; for the sake of argument.

argument A presentation of reasons for a legal position.

argumentative Containing conclusions as well as facts; contentious.

arise 1. To stem from or originate. 2. To come into notice.

aristocracy A government ruled by a superior or privileged class.

ARM See adjustable-rate mortgage.

armed robbery Robbery committed while armed with a dangerous weapon.

arm's length As between two strangers who are looking out for their own self-interests.

arraignment A court proceeding in which the accused is formally charged with a crime and enters a plea of guilty, not guilty, etc. The verb is arraign.

> The proceeding that is had after indictment is rendered in a court of common pleas. *State v. Bayer*, 102 Ohio App.3d 172 (Ohio App., 1995)

arrangement with creditors A plan whereby the debtor settles with his or her creditors or obtains more time to repay debts.

array A group of persons summoned to be considered for jury duty.

arrearages, arrears Unpaid debts; overdue debts.

arrest Taking someone into custody to answer a criminal charge.

> Arrest is a term of art and signifies the apprehension or detention of the person of another in order that he may be forthcoming to answer an alleged crime. *State v. Long*, 127 Ohio App.3d 328 (Ohio App., 1998)

arrest of judgment A court's staying of a judgment because of errors.

arrest record 1. A form filled out when the police arrest someone. 2. A list of a person's prior arrests.

arrest warrant A written order of a judge or magistrate that a person be arrested and brought before the court.

arrogation Claiming or seizing something without authority or right.

arson The willful and malicious burning of property.

art 1. Applying knowledge and skill to produce a desired result. 2. A process or method to produce a useful result. 3. See terms of act.

art. Article.

artful pleading An attempt to phrase a federal claim as a state claim.

article A part or subdivision of a law or document.

Article I court A federal court created by legislation. Also called legislative courts.

Article III court A federal court created by the United States Constitution in article III. Also called constitutional court.

articled clerk In England, one apprenticed to a solicitor.

Articles of Confederation The governing document for the thirteen original states.

articles of impeachment Formal accusations against a public official asserted as grounds for removing him or her from office.

articles of incorporation The document that establishes (incorporates) a corporation and identifies its basic functions and rules.

artifice Contrivance, trick, or fraud.

artificial person A legal person. An entity, such as a corporation, created under the laws of the state and treated in some respects as a human being. Also called fictitious person, juristic person.

artisan's lien See mechanic's lien.

ascendant An ancestor, e.g., grandparent.

as is In its present condition; no warranty given.

> "As is" sales place the buyer of secondhand or used property on notice that he buys at his own risk, should acquaint himself with the whole situation, and is not entitled to rescission of sale contract except for fraud, imposition, or other like reasons. *Regula*, 70 N.E.2d 662 (Ohio Com.Pl., 1946)

asportation Carrying away for purposes of larceny.

assailant One who attacks or assaults another.

assault 1. As a tort, assault is an act intended to cause harmful or offensive contact with another or an imminent apprehension of such contact and the other is thereby placed in such imminent apprehension. 2. As a crime, assault may require an intent to cause physical harm and actual contact with the victim.

> An "assault" in tort is the willful threat or attempt to harm or touch another offensively, which threat or attempt reasonably places the other in fear of such contact. *Vandiver*, 126 Ohio App.3d 634 (Ohio App., 1998)

assault and battery The crime of battery.

assay An examination to test the quality and quantity of metals.

assembly 1. A gathering of people for a common goal. 2. One of the houses of the legislature in many states.

assent Agreement, approval.

assert To declare; to state as true.

> As used in the hearsay rule, Ohio Rules of Evid., Rule 801(A), the verb "to assert" means simply to say that something is so. *State v. Saunders*, 23 Ohio App.3d 69 (Ohio App., 1984)

assessable stock Stock that subjects the holder to an additional assessment or contribution.

assessment 1. A determination of the value of something, often for purposes of taxation. 2. A determination of the share that is due from someone; an amount assessed. 3. The requirement of an additional payment to a business.

assessed ratio The ratio of assessed value to fair market value.

assessment work Labor on a mining claim each year to maintain the claim.

assessor A technical expert or adviser, e.g., on making assessments.

asset Anything of value; tangible or intangible property.

asset depreciation range IRS's range of depreciable lives of assets.

asseveration A solemn declaration.

assign 1. To transfer or convey property or rights. 2. To point out or specify, e.g., errors. 3. See assigns.

assigned counsel A court-appointed attorney for a poor person.

assigned risk A person an insurance company is required to insure.

assignee The person to whom property or rights are transferred.

assignment The transfer of ownership or rights.

> A transfer of property or of some right or interest from one person to another, which causes to vest in another his or her right of property or interest in property. *Cincinnati ex rel. Ritter*, 150 Ohio App.3d 728 (Ohio App., 2002)

assignment for benefit of creditors A transfer of the debtor's property to a trustee, with authority to liquidate the debtor's affairs and distribute the proceeds equitably to creditors.

assignment of errors A party's list of errors claimed to have been made by a trial court submitted to an appellate court on appeal.

assignor The person who transfers property or rights.

assigns Assignees; persons to whom property or rights are transferred.

assise; assize An old English court, law, or writ.

assistance of counsel See effective assistance of counsel.

associate An attorney employee who hopes one day to be promoted to partner.

associate justice An appellate court judge who is not the chief justice.

association 1. An organization of people joined for a common purpose. 2. An unincorporated company or other organization.

assume 1. To take upon oneself. 2. To suppose without proof.

assumpsit 1. A promise. 2. An action to breach of contract.

assumption 1. The act of taking something upon oneself. 2. Something taken for granted without proof.

assumption of mortgage A property buyer's agreement to be personally liable for payment of an already existing mortgage.

assumption of the risk The knowing and voluntary acceptance of the risk of being harmed by someone's negligence or other conduct.

> Assumption of risk is (1) consent or acquiescence in (2) an appreciated or known (3) risk. *Westray*, 133 Ohio App.3d 426 (Ohio App., 1999)

assurance 1. A statement tending to inspire confidence. 2. Insurance. 3. A pledge or guarantee. 4. The act (and the document) that conveys real property.

assured A person who has been insured.

asylum 1. A sanctuary or hiding place. 2. A government's protection given to a political refugee from another country. Also called political asylum.

at bar Currently before the court.

at issue In dispute.

at large 1. Free. 2. An entire area rather than one of its districts.

at law Pertaining to a court of law as opposed to a court of equity.

at risk Pertaining to an investment that could lead to actual loss.

attaché A person in a diplomatic office with a specific specialty.

attachment The act or process of taking, apprehending, or seizing persons or property, by virtue of writ, summons, or other judicial order, and bringing same into custody of the law.

attachment bond A bond given by one whose property has been attached in order to reclaim it and provide protection to the party who attached it.

attainder The loss of civil rights upon receiving a death sentence or being designated as an outlaw.

attaint 1. To disgrace or condemn to attainder. 2. To accuse a jury of giving a false verdict.

attempt An overt act or conduct (beyond mere preparation) performed with the intent to commit a crime that was not completed.

> Attempt occurs if the defendant takes a substantial step in a course of conduct planned to culminate in the commission of the crime. R.C. § 2923.02(A). *In re Phillips*, 2002 WL 501147 (Ohio App., 2002)

attendant circumstances Relevant facts surrounding an event.

attenuation Illegally obtained evidence might be admissible if the link between the illegal conduct and the evidence is so attenuated as to dissipate the taint.

attest To affirm to be true or genuine; to bear witness.

> To certify to the verity of a copy of a public document formally by signature; an attested copy of a document is one which has been examined and compared with the original, with a certificate or memorandum of its correctness, signed by the persons who have examined it. *State ex rel. Steele*, 103 Ohio St.3d 355 (Ohio 2004)

attestation clause A clause stating that you saw (witnessed) someone sign a document or perform other tasks related to the validity of the document.

attorn 1. To transfer something to another. 2. To acknowledge being the tenant of a new landlord.

attorney 1. One licensed to practice law. A lawyer. Also called attorney at law. 2. One authorized to act in place of or for another. Also called attorney-in-fact.

attorney at law See attorney (1).

attorney-client privilege A client and an attorney can refuse to disclose communications between them if their purpose was to facilitate the provision of legal services to the client.

> The following persons shall not testify in certain respects: (A) An attorney, concerning a communication made to the attorney by a client in that relation or the attorney's advice to a client, except that the attorney may testify by express consent of the client or, if the client is deceased, by the express consent of the surviving spouse or the executor or administrator of the estate of the deceased client. R.C. § 2317.02

attorney general The chief attorney for the government.

attorney in fact See attorney (2).

attorney of record The attorney noted in the court files as the attorney representing a particular party.

attorney's lien The right of an attorney to retain possession of money or property of a client until his or her proper fees have been paid.

attorney work product See work product rule.

attornment See attorn.

attractive nuisance doctrine A duty of reasonable care is owed to prevent injury to a trespassing child unable to appreciate the danger from an artificial condition or activity on land to which the child can be expected to be attracted. Also called turntable doctrine.

attribution Assigning one taxpayer's ownership interest to another.

at-will employee An employee with no contract protection. An employee who can quit or be terminated at any time and for any reason.

auction A public sale of assets to the highest bidder.

audit An examination of records to verify financial or other data.

> Audit means (1) Any examination, analysis, or inspection of the state's or a public office's financial statements or reports; (2) Any examination, analysis, or inspection of records, documents, books, or any other evidence relating to . . . (a) The collection, receipt, accounting, use, or expenditure of public money by a public office or by a private institution, association, board, or corporation . . . R.C. § 117.01(G)

auditor Someone who performs audits, often an accountant.

augmented estate A decedent's estate with adjustments keyed to the length of marriage and gifts decedent made shortly before death.

authentication Evidence that a writing or other physical item is genuine and is what it purports to be.

author An originator of a work in various media (e.g., print, film) plus other participants with copyright protection, e.g., translators.

authority 1. The power or right to act. 2. A source relied upon.

authorize To give power or permission; to approve.

> Authorized person means a parent, guardian, or other person authorized to act on behalf of an enrollee with respect to health care decisions. R.C. § 1751.77(C)

authorized stock See capital stock (1).

automobile guest statute See guest statute.

autopsy An examination of a cadaver to identify the cause of death. Also called postmortem.

autoptic evidence See demonstrative evidence.

autrefois acquit A plea that one has already been acquitted of the offense.

autre vie Another's life.

aver To assert or allege.

average 1. Usual, ordinary, norm. 2. Mean, median. 3. Partial loss or damage.

averment A positive allegation or assertion of fact.

avoid 1. To annul or cancel. 2. To escape.

avoidable consequences See mitigation of damages.

avoidance Escaping; invalidating. See also confession and avoidance.

avowal 1. An offer to prove. 2. An acknowledgement.

avulsion The sudden loss or addition to land caused by flood or by a shift in the bed or course of a stream.

award What a court or other tribunal gives or grants via its decision.

axiom An established or self-evident principle.

AWOL Absent without leave or permission. See also desertion.

B

baby act A minor's defense of infancy in a breach of contract action.

BAC See blood alcohol concentration.

bachelor of laws See LL.B.

back To assume financial responsibility for; to indorse.

bad 1. Defective. 2. Void or invalid.

bad check A check dishonored for insufficient funds.

bad debt An uncollectible debt.

bad faith 1. Dishonest purpose. Also called mala fides. 2. The absence of a reasonable basis to delay or deny an insurance claim.

> Bad faith generally implies something more than bad judgment or negligence; it imports a dishonest purpose, moral obliquity, conscious wrongdoing, breach of a known duty through some ulterior motive, or ill will partaking of the nature of fraud, and it also embraces actual intent to mislead or deceive another. *State v. Miller,* 161 Ohio App.3d 145 (Ohio 2005)

badge of fraud Factors from which an inference of fraud can be drawn.

bad law 1. A court opinion that fails to follow precedent or statutes. 2. A court opinion whose broader implications are unfortunate even though probably accurate for the narrow facts before the court.

bad title Title that is so defective as to be unmarketable.

bail 1. Money or other property deposited with the court as security to ensure that the defendant will reappear at designated times. Failure to appear forfeits the security. 2. Release of the defendant upon posting this security. 3. The one providing this security.

> Bail means cash, a check, a money order, a credit card, or any other form of money that is posted by or for an offender pursuant to sections 2937.22 to 2937.46 of the Revised Code, Criminal Rule 46, or Traffic Rule 4 to prevent the offender from being placed or held in a detention facility, as defined in section 2921.01 of the Revised Code. R.C. § 2743.70

bailable offense An offense for which an accused is eligible for bail.

bail bond A surety contract under which the surety will pay the state the amount of the bond if the accused fails to appear in court.

bailee One to whom property is entrusted under a contract of bailment.

bailiff A court officer with duties in court, e.g., keep order.

bail jumping See jump bail.

bailment A delivery of personal property by one person to another under an express or implied contract whereby the property will be redelivered when the purpose of the contract is completed.

bailment for hire A bailment under which the bailee is paid.

bailor One who delivers property to another under a contract of bailment.

bailout 1. Financial help to one in need of rescue. 2. Seeking alternative tax treatment of income.

bait and switch Using a low-priced item to lure a customer to a merchant who then pressures the customer to buy another item at a higher price.

balance 1. To calculate the difference between what has been paid and what is due. 2. To check to ensure that debits and credits are equal. 3. The equality of debits and credits. 4. See balancing test.

balance sheet A dated statement showing assets, liabilities, and owners' investment.

balancing test Weighing competing interests or values in order to resolve a legal issue.

balloon note A note on a loan calling for a large final payment and smaller intervening periodic payments.

ballot A paper or other media on which to vote; a list of candidates.

> The official election presentation of offices and candidates, including write-in candidates, and of questions and issues, and the means by which votes are recorded. R.C. § 3506.01

ban 1. To prohibit. 2. An announcement.

banc Bench. See also en banc.

banish See exile.

bank A financial institution that receives money on deposit, exchanges money, makes loans, and performs similar functions.

> A corporation that solicits, receives, or accepts money or its equivalent for deposit as a business, whether the deposit is made by check or is evidenced by a certificate of deposit, passbook, note, receipt, ledger card, or otherwise. R.C. § 1101.01(B)

bank bill See bank note.

bank credit Money a bank allows a customer to borrow.

bank draft A check that one bank writes on its account with another bank.

banker's lien The right of a bank to seize property of a depositor in the bank's possession to satisfy a customer's debt to the bank.

bank note A promissory note issued by a bank payable to bearer on demand and usable as cash. Also called bank bill.

bankrupt 1. Unable to pay debts as they are due. 2. A debtor undergoing a bankruptcy proceeding.

bankruptcy 1. The federal process by which a bankruptcy court gives a debtor relief by liquidating some or all of the unsecured debts or by otherwise rearranging debts and payment schedules. 2. Insolvency.

bankruptcy estate Assets of a debtor when bankruptcy is filed.

bankruptcy trustee See trustee in bankruptcy.

bar 1. The court or court system. 2. The courtroom partition behind which spectators sit. 3. All the attorneys licensed to practice in a jurisdiction. 4. The examination taken by attorneys to become licensed to practice law. 5. An impediment or barrier to bringing or doing something.

bar association An association of members of the legal profession.

bar examination See bar (4).

bare licensee One who enters the land for his or her own purposes, but with the express or implied consent of the occupier. Also called naked licensee.

> The claimant was a bare licensee on the premises of the owners, by sufferance only for his own convenience. *Elliman*, 86 Ohio App. 352 (Ohio App., 1949)

bareboat charter A document under which one who charters or leases a boat becomes for the period of the charter the owner for all practical purposes. Also called demise charter.

bargain 1. To negotiate the terms of a contract. 2. An agreement establishing the obligations of the parties.

bargain and sale deed A deed of conveyance without covenants.

bargaining agent A union bargaining on behalf of its members.

bargaining unit A group of employees allowed to conduct collective bargaining for other employees.

barratry 1. Persistently instigating or stirring up lawsuits. 2. Fraud or other misconduct by a captain or crew that harms the ship owner.

barrister An attorney in England and other Commonwealth countries who is allowed to try cases in specific courts.

barter To exchange goods or services without the use of money.

basis 1. The foundation; the underlying principle. 2. The cost or other amount assigned to an asset for income tax purposes.

bastard A child born before its parents were married or born from those who never married. An illegitimate child.

bastardy proceeding See paternity suit.

battered child syndrome A diagnosis that a child's injury or injuries are not accidental and are presumed to have been caused by someone of mature strength, such as an adult caregiver.

battered woman syndrome Psychological helplessness because of a woman's financial dependence, loneliness, guilt, shame, and fear of reprisal from her husband or boyfriend who has repeatedly battered her in the past.

> When raising the defense of self-defense, the person may introduce expert testimony of the battered woman syndrome. R.C. § 2901.06. Although the Ohio Supreme Court did not specifically state what evidence is necessary to establish that a defendant is a battered woman, it did quote the following language from a New Jersey case: "[I]n order to be classified as a battered woman, the couple must go through the battering cycle at least twice. Any woman may find herself in an abusive relationship with a man once. If it occurs a second time, and she remains in the situation, she is defined as a battered woman." *State v. Donner*, 96 Ohio App.3d 486 (Ohio App., 1994)

battery An intentional touching of the person of another that is harmful or offensive. Battery can be a tort and a crime.

> Battery results when an individual acts intending to cause harmful or offensive contact, and harmful contact results. *Retterer*, 111 Ohio App.3d 847 (Ohio App., 1996)

bear 1. To produce or yield. 2. To carry.

bearer One who holds or possesses a negotiable instrument that is payable to bearer or to cash.

> The person in possession of an instrument, document of title, or certificated security payable to bearer or endorsed in blank. R.C. § 1301.01

bearer paper Commercial paper payable to one who holds or possesses it.

belief The mind's acceptance that something is probably true or certain.

belief-action There are no unconstitutional beliefs, but a person's actions can violate constitutional rights.

belligerent A country at war or in armed conflict.

below 1. Pertaining to a lower court in the judicial system. 2. Later in the document.

bench The court, the judge's seat, or the judiciary.

bench conference A meeting at the judge's bench between the judge and the attorneys out of the hearing of the jury. Also called a sidebar conference.

bench memo A memorandum of law by a party's attorney for a trial judge or by a law clerk for a judge.

bench trial A trial without a jury. Also called nonjury trial.

bench warrant A judge's direct order for the arrest of a person.

beneficial Tending to the benefit of a person.

beneficial interest A right to a benefit from property or an estate as opposed to the legal ownership of that property or estate.

> Beneficial interest means: (1) The interest of a person as a beneficiary under a trust in which the trustee holds title to personal or real property; (2) The interest of a person as a beneficiary under any other trust arrangement under which any other person holds title to personal or real property for the benefit of such person; (3) The interest of a person under any other form of express fiduciary arrangement under which any other person holds title to personal or real property for the benefit of such person. R.C. § 2923.31(B)

beneficial owner See equitable owner.

beneficial use A right to the benefits of property when legal title to the property may be held by others.

beneficiary 1. A person whom a trust was created to benefit. 2. A person entitled to insurance benefits. 3. One who receives a benefit.

benefit Assistance, advantage, profit, or privilege; payment or gift.

benefit of clergy 1. A former right of clerics not to be tried in secular courts. 2. The approval or blessing given by a religious rite.

benefit of the bargain rule 1. In a fraud action, the damages should be the value as represented less the value actually received. 2. In a contract action, the damages should be what would place the victim in the position he or she would have been in if the contract had not been breached. Also called loss of bargain rule.

bequeath To give property (sometimes only personal property) by will.

bequest Property (sometimes only personal property) given in a will.

> The term bequest, in addition to its meaning at common law or under any other section or sections of the Revised Code, includes any testamentary disposition of real property and any testamentary disposition of a vendor's interest in a land installment contract. R.C. § 2107.011(B)

best efforts Diligence more exacting than the duty of good faith.

best evidence rule When a factual dispute arises about a writing, painting, photograph, or recording, the original should be produced unless it is unavailable. Also called original document rule.

> To prove the content of a writing, recording, or photograph, the original writing, recording, or photograph is required, except as otherwise provided in these rules or by statute enacted by the General Assembly not in conflict with a rule of the Supreme Court of Ohio. Evid. R. Rule 1002

bestiality Sexual relations between a human and an animal.

bestow To give or convey.

best use See highest and best use.

betterment A property improvement beyond mere repairs.

beyond a reasonable doubt See reasonable doubt.

BFOQ See bona fide occupational qualification.

BFP See bona fide purchaser.

BIA Bureau of Indian Affairs (*www.doi.gov/bureau-indian-affairs.html*).

biannual 1. Twice a year. 2. Every 2 years.

bias A tendency or inclination to think and to act in a certain way. A danger of prejudgment. Prejudice.

bicameral Having two chambers or houses in the legislature.

bid 1. An offer to perform a contract for a designated price. 2. An offer to pay a designated price for property, e.g., auction bid.

bid and asked Price ranges quoted for securities in an over-the-counter market.

bid bond A bond to protect the government if a bidder fails to enter the contract according to its bid.

bid in A bid on property by its owner to set a floor auction price.

bid shopping A general contractor's use of a low subcontractor's bid as a tool to negotiate lower bids from other subcontractors.

biennial 1. Occurring every 2 years. 2. Lasting 2 years.

biennium A 2-year period.

bifurcated trial A case in which certain issues are tried separately (e.g., guilt and punishment; liability and damages).

bigamy Marrying while still in a valid marriage with someone else.

bilateral contract A contract of mutual promises between the parties.

bilateral mistake See mutual mistake.

bill 1. A proposed statute. Legislation under consideration for enactment by a legislature. 2. The statute that has been enacted. 3. A statement of money owed. 4. Paper money. 5. A pleading that states a claim in equity. Also called bill in equity. 6. A list of specifics or particulars. 7. A draft. See bill of exchange.

billable Pertaining to tasks for which an attorney, paralegal, or other timekeeper can charge a client fees.

bill in equity See bill (5).

bill of attainder An act of the legislature that imposes punishment (e.g., death) on a specific person or group without a trial.

> A law that (1) inflicts punishment, (2) without a judicial trial, (3) upon an identifiable individual. *State v. Williams*, 88 Ohio St.3d 513 (Ohio 2000)

bill of exchange See draft (1).

bill of health A certificate on the health of a ship's cargo and crew.

bill of indictment A document asking the grand jury to determine whether enough evidence exists to bring a formal criminal charge against the accused.

bill of lading A document from a carrier that lists (and acknowledges receipt of) the goods to be transported and the terms of their delivery.

A document evidencing the receipt of goods for shipment issued by a person engaged in the business of transporting or forwarding goods, and includes an airbill. R.C. § 1301.01(F)

bill of pains and penalties An act of the legislature that imposes punishment (other than death) on a specific person or group without a trial.

bill of particulars A more detailed statement of the civil claims or criminal charges brought against another.

bill of review A request that a court of equity revise a decree.

bill of rights A list of fundamental rights, e.g., the first ten amendments to the U.S. Constitution.

bill of sale A document that conveys title to personal property from seller to buyer.

bind To place under a legal duty.

binder 1. A contract giving temporary protection to the insured until a formal policy is issued. 2. A statement (and often a deposit) to secure the right to purchase property.

A temporary policy of insurance that is effective until the issuance of a formal policy. *Midland Ent.*, 139 Ohio App.3d 650 (Ohio App., 2000)

binding instruction See mandatory instruction.

bind over 1. To hold or transfer for further court proceedings. 2. To place under an obligation.

blackacre A fictitious name for a parcel of land. Also, whiteacre.

black code Laws of southern states regulating slavery.

black letter law A statement of a fundamental or basic principle of law. Also called hornbook law.

blackmail Unlawful demand of money or property under threat of bodily harm, property damage, accusation of crime, or exposure. Extortion.

black market Illegal avenues for buying and selling.

blanket bond 1. A bond protecting against loss from employee dishonesty. 2. A bond covering a group rather than named persons.

blank indorsement An indorsement without naming a person to whom the instrument is to be paid.

An indorsement that is made by the holder of the instrument and that is not a special indorsement. When an instrument is indorsed in blank, the instrument becomes payable to bearer and may be negotiated by transfer of possession alone until specially indorsed. R.C. § 1303.25(B)

blasphemy Language or acts showing contempt for God or sacred matters.

blind trust A trust with a trustee who acts without control or influence by the owner or settlor to avoid a conflict of interest.

blockage rule A tax rule allowing a lower value for a large block of shares than the sum of their individual values.

blockbusting Persuading homeowners to sell by asserting that minority newcomers will lower property values.

blood alcohol concentration (BAC) The percentage of alcohol in a person's blood.

blotter A book recording daily events, e.g., arrests.

bluebook 1. Popular name of *A Uniform System of Citation*, a citation guidebook. 2. A directory of government offices and employees.

blue chip Pertaining to a high-quality investment stock.

blue flu Police officers call in sick as a labor protest.

blue laws Laws regulating Sunday commerce.

blue ribbon jury A jury with members having special skills.

blue sky laws State securities laws to prevent fraud.

board 1. A group of persons with authority to manage or advise. 2. Regular meals.

boarder One to whom meals are supplied, often with a room.

board of aldermen A local legislative body, e.g., city council.

board of directors Individuals elected by shareholders to hire officers and set policy.

board of education A government body that manages local public schools.

board of equalization A government agency with responsibility for ensuring that the tax burden is distributed fairly in a particular state or district.

board of pardons A government agency with the power to issue pardons.

board of parole See parole board.

board of supervisors The body that governs a county.

board of trade 1. An organization of businesses that promote common business interests. 2. The governing body of a commodities exchange.

bodily harm Physical damage to the body, including injury, illness, and pain.

bodily heir See heir of the body.

bodily injury Physical harm or damage to the body. Also called physical injury.

body 1. A collection or laws. 2. The main section(s) of a document. 3. A person, group, or entity.

body corporate Another term for corporation.

body execution Taking a person into custody by order of the court.

body of the crime See corpus delicti.

body politic The people of a nation or state as a political group.

The state of Ohio is a "body politic" within the meaning of the statute providing that money of a debtor in the possession of any person, or "body politic" or corporate, shall be subject to the payment of the judgment. *Wiesenthal*, 64 Ohio App. 124 (Ohio App., 1940)

bogus Counterfeit, sham.

boilerplate Standard language commonly used in some documents.

boiler room sale A high-pressure phone sale of goods and services, e.g., securities.

bona fide In good faith; sincere.

bona fide occupational qualification (BFOQ) Sex or other discrimination that is reasonably necessary for the operation of a particular business.

bona fide purchaser (BFP) One who has purchased property for value without notice of defects in the title of seller or of any claims in the property by others. Also called good faith purchaser, innocent purchaser.

A bona fide purchaser of real property is one who takes property: (1) for valuable consideration; (2) in good faith; and (3) absent notice of any adverse claims. *Groza-Vance*, 162 Ohio App.3d 510 (Ohio App., 2005)

bona immobilia Immovable property such as land.

bond 1. A certificate that is evidence of a debt in which the entity that issues the bond (a company or a governmental body) promises (a) to pay the bondholders a specified amount of interest for a specified amount of time and (b) to repay the loan on the expiration date. 2. An obligation to perform an act (e.g., payment of a sum of money) upon the occurrence or nonoccurrence of a designated condition. 3. A promise or binding agreement.

bond discount An amount that is lower than the face value of the bond.

bonded Placed under or secured by a bond.

bonded debt A debt that has the added backing or security of a bond.

bonded warehouse A private warehouse that stores imported goods subject to special taxes or custom duties.

bondholder One who holds a government, corporate, or commercial bond.

bond issue Bonds offered for sale at the same time.

bond premium An amount that is higher than the face value of the bond.

bondsman A surety; a person or business that guarantees a bond.

bonification A forgiveness of taxes, usually on exports.

bonus Extra; a consideration paid in addition to what is strictly due.

book 1. To enter charges against someone on a police register. The process is called booking. 2. To engage the services of someone. 3. Books: original financial or accounting records. Also called books of account. See also shop-book rule.

The books of a corporation, which are generally regarded as the accounting records of such corporation and are kept in the ordinary course of the business of the corporation in accordance with any sound and generally recognized and approved accounting system. R.C. §§ 5733.03(H), 5733.05(A) (1996). *Goodyear Tire*, 85 Ohio St.3d 615 (Ohio 1999)

book entry 1. A note in a financial ledger or book. 2. A statement acknowledging ownership of securities.

booking See book (1).

bookkeeper One who records financial accounts and transactions.

bookmaking Taking or placing or offering to take or place a bet for another.

Bookmaking means the business of receiving or paying off bets. R.C. § 2915.01(B)

bookie One engaged in bookmaking.

books; books of account See book (3).

book value 1. The value at which an asset is carried on a balance sheet. 2. Net worth.

Boolean search A computer search that allows words to be included or excluded by using operatives such as AND, OR, and NOT in the query.

boot 1. The taxable component in a transaction that is otherwise not taxable. 2. An additional payment or consideration.

bootlegger One who deals in (e.g., copies, sells) products illegally.

bootstrap sale Using the future earnings of a business to acquire that business.

border search A search upon entering the country, usually at the border.

borough A political subdivision of a state with self-governing powers.

borrowed servant rule See loaned servant doctrine.

bottomry A contract by which the owner of a ship borrows money for a voyage, giving the ship as security for the loan.

bought and sold notes Written confirmations of a sale from a broker to the buyer and seller.

bound 1. To identify the boundary. 2. Obligated. See also bind.

bound over See bind over.

bounty 1. A reward. 2. Generosity.

boycott A concerted refusal to work or do business with a particular person or business in order to obtain concessions or to express displcasurc with ccrtain practices of the person or business.

The refusal to work for, purchase from or handle products of an employer. *C. Comella, Inc.*, 33 Ohio App.2d 61 (Ohio App., 1972)

***Brady* material** Evidence known by the prosecution to be favorable to the defense must be disclosed to the defendant. *Brady v. Maryland*, 83 S. Ct. 1194 (1963).

brain death Irreversible cessation of circulatory and respiratory functions, or irreversible cessation of all functions of the entire brain, including the brain stem. Also called legal death.

branch A subdivision, member, or department.

Brandeis brief An appellate brief in which economic and social studies are included along with legal principles.

breach The breaking or violation of a legal duty, or law.

breach of contract The failure to perform a contract obligation.

Breach of contract occurs when a party demonstrates: (1) the existence of a binding contract or agreement, (2) that the non-breaching party performed its contractual obligations, (3) that the other party failed to fulfill its contractual obligations without legal excuse, and (4) that the non-breaching party suffered damages as a result of the breach. *Laurent*, 146 Ohio App.3d 392 (Ohio App., 2001)

breach of promise to marry Breaking an engagement (promise) to marry.

breach of the peace A violation or disturbance of the public tranquility and order. Disorderly conduct.

breach of trust Violation of a fiduciary obligation by a trustee.

breach of warranty Breaking an express or implied warranty.

breaking a close Trespassing on land.

breaking and entering See burglary.

breaking bulk Unlawfully opening by a bailee of a container entrusted to his or her care and stealing the contents.

breathalyzer A device to measure blood alcohol concentration.

breve A writ.

bribe An offer, acceptance, or solicitation of an unlawful payment with the understanding that it will corruptly affect the official action of the recipient.

bridge loan A short-term loan given until other funding is arranged.

brief 1. Shorthand for appellate brief, which is a document submitted by a party to an appellate court in which arguments are presented on why the appellate court should affirm (approve), reverse, or otherwise modify what a lower court has done. 2. A document submitted to a trial court in support of a particular position. 3. A summary of the main or essential parts of a court opinion. 4. Shorthand for a trial brief, which is an attorney's personal notes on how to conduct a trial.

bright-line rule A clear-cut (but sometimes overly simple) legal principle that resolves a dispute.

bring an action To sue someone.

broad interpretation See liberal construction.

broker An agent who arranges or negotiates contracts for others.

> A person who acts as an intermediary or agent in finding, arranging, or negotiating loans, and charges or receives a fee for these services. R.C. § 1321.51(J)

brokerage 1. The business or occupation of a broker. 2. The wages or commissions of a broker.

broker-dealer A firm that buys and sells securities as an agent for others and as a principal, buying or selling in its own name.

brutum fulmen 1. An empty threat. 2. An invalid judgment.

bubble An extravagant commercial project based on deception.

bucket shop A fraudulent business that pretends to be engaged in securities transactions.

buggery Sodomy or bestiality.

building code Laws that provide standards for constructing buildings.

> Ohio building code means the rules and regulations adopted by the board of building standards under Chapter 3781. of the Revised Code. R.C. § 3783.01

building line Distances from the ends and sides of the lot beyond which construction may not extend.

bulk goods Goods not divided into parts or packaged in separate units.

bulk sale or transfer The sale of all or a large part of a seller's inventory, not in the ordinary course of the seller's business.

bulletin An ongoing or periodic publication.

bull market A stock market climate of persistent rising prices.

bumping 1. Depriving someone of a reserved seat due to overbooking. 2. Replacing a worker with someone more senior.

burden 1. A duty or responsibility. 2. A limitation or hindrance.

burden of going forward The obligation to produce some evidence tending to prove (not necessarily conclusive evidence) its case. Also called burden of producing evidence, burden of production.

burden of persuasion The obligation to convince the trier of fact (judge or jury) that the party has introduced enough evidence on the truth of its version of the facts to meet the standard of proof, e.g., preponderance of the evidence. Also called risk of nonpersuasion.

burden of producing evidence See burden of going forward.

burden of production See burden of going forward.

burden of proof The obligation of proving the facts of one's claim. This obligation is met by meeting the burden of going forward and the burden of persuasion.

> The burden of proof is a composite burden usually requiring the party on whom it rests to "go forward" with the evidence, which is "burden of production," and to convince the trier of fact by some quantum of evidence, which is the "burden of persuasion." *Chari*, 91 Ohio St.3d 323 (Ohio 2001)

***Burford* abstention** To avoid unnecessary federal-state friction, a federal court can refuse to review a state court's decision involving complex state regulations or sensitive state policies. *Burford v. Sun Oil Co.*, 63 S. Ct. 1098 (1943).

burglary 1. Entering a building of another with the intent to commit a felony therein. 2. Breaking and entering the dwelling house of another in the nighttime with the intent to commit a felony therein.

> The word burglary connotes the entering of a building in the night season with intent to commit a felony or with intent to steal property of value. *Herman*, 116 N.E.2d 311 (Ohio App., 1951)

burgle To commit burglary; to burglarize.

bursar Someone in charge of funds, especially at a college.

business agent 1. One selected by union members to represent them. 2. A manager of another's business affairs.

business compulsion Exerting improper economic coercion on a business in a weak or vulnerable position. Also called economic duress.

business entry ruie An exception to the hearsay rule allowing the introduction into evidence of entries (records) made in the ordinary course of business. Also called the business records exception.

business expense An amount paid for goods or services used in operating a taxpayer's business or trade.

business invitee Someone who has been expressly or impliedly invited to be present or to remain on the premises, primarily for a purpose directly or indirectly connected with business dealings between them. Also called business guest, business visitor.

business judgment rule Courts will defer to good-faith decisions made by boards of directors in business dealings and presume the decisions were made in the best interests of the company.

> A rebuttable presumption that directors are better equipped than the courts to make business judgments, and that the directors acted without self-dealing or personal interest, exercised reasonable diligence, and acted in good faith. *Marsalis*, 149 Ohio App.3d 637 (Ohio App., 2002)

business records exception See business entry rule.

business trust An unincorporated business in which a trustee manages its property for the benefit and use of the trust beneficiaries. Also called common law trust, Massachusetts trust.

business visitor See business invitee.

but-for test A test for causation: an event (e.g., injury) would not have happened without the act or omission of the defendant.

buy and sell agreement An arrangement under which there is a right or duty of one or more owners of an entity to buy another owner's interest upon the occurrence of certain events, e.g., an owner dies or withdraws.

buyer in the ordinary course of business One who buys goods in good faith, without knowledge that the sale violates the rights of another person in the goods, and in the ordinary course from a person (other than a pawnbroker) in the business of selling goods of that kind. UCC 1–201(b)(9)

by-bidding Planting someone to make fictitious auction bids. Also called puffing.

bylaws Rules governing internal affairs of an organization.

by operation of law See operation of law.

bypass trust A trust designed to take full advantage of the unified credit against estate taxes by reducing the surviving spouse's estate.

by the entirety See tenancy by the entirety.

C

c Copyright, often printed as ©.

CA Court of Appeals.

cabinet An advisory board or council of a chief executive.

caduary Subject to forfeiture.

c.a.f. See Cost and freight.

calendar A list of cases awaiting court action or bills awaiting legislative action.

calendar call A hearing to determine the status of, and establish court dates for, cases on the court calendar.

call 1. A demand for payment. 2. A demand to present bonds or other securities for redemption before maturity. 3. A property boundary landmark. 4. See call option.

callable Subject to be called and paid for before maturity.

callable bonds See redeemable bond.

call option The right to buy something at a fixed price.

call premium The added charge paid to redeem a bond prior to maturity.

calumny A false and malicious accusation.

camera See in camera.

cancellation 1. Striking or crossing out. 2. Invalidation, termination.

> Cancellation occurs when either party puts an end to the contract for breach by the other and its effect is the same as that of "termination" except that the cancelling party also retains any remedy for breach of the whole contract or any unperformed balance. R.C. § 1302.01(A)(14)

c&f See cost and freight.

cannabis The plant from which marijuana is prepared.

canon A rule, law, or principle.

canonical disability An impediment justifying a church annulment.

canon law Ecclesiastical law; Roman church jurisprudence.

canons of construction Rules for interpreting statutes and contracts.

canvass 1. To examine carefully, e.g., the votes cast. 2. To solicit votes, contributions, opinions, etc.

capacity 1. Legal qualification or competency to do something. 2. The ability to understand the nature of one's acts. 3. Occupation, function, or role.

> Impaired earning capacity connotes not what claimant did earn but what he or she could have earned. R.C. § 4123.57 (1985). *State ex rel. Backus*, 91 Ohio St.3d 251 (Ohio 2001)

capias A writ requiring that someone be taken into custody.

capias ad respondendum A writ commanding the sheriff to bring the defendant to court to answer the claims of the plaintiff.

capias ad satisfaciendum A writ commanding the sheriff to hold a judgment debtor until the latter satisfies its judgment debt.

capias pro fine A writ commanding the sheriff to arrest someone who has not paid a fine.

capita Head, person. See also per capita.

capital 1. Assets available for generating more wealth. 2. Assets less liabilities; net worth. 3. Relating to the death penalty.

capital asset See fixed assets.

capital budget Projected spending to buy long-term or fixed assets.

capital gains tax A tax on the sale or exchange of a capital asset.

capital goods Assets (e.g., tools) used to produce goods and services.

capitalization 1. The total value of stocks and other securities used for long-term financing. 2. See capitalize.

capitalize 1. To treat an asset as capital; to classify an expenditure as a long-term investment. 2. To provide with investment funds. 3. To determine current value of cash flow.

capital loss Loss realized on the sale or exchange of a capital asset.

capital market The market for long-term securities.

capital punishment A death sentence.

capital stock 1. All of the stock a corporation is authorized to issue. Also called authorized stock. 2. The total par value of stock a corporation is authorized to issue.

capital surplus Surplus other than retained earnings. Funds owners pay over par value.

capitation tax See poll tax.

capitulary A collection or code of laws.

capricious Impulsive; not based on evidence, law, or reason.

> All actions that are arbitrary and capricious necessarily also are unreasonable. *Broad-Miami Co.*, 185 N.E.2d 76 (Ohio Com.Pl., 1959)

caption 1. The heading or introductory part of a pleading, court opinion, memo, or other document that identifies what it is, the names of the parties, the court involved, etc. 2. Arresting someone.

care 1. Caution in avoiding harm. 2. Heed. 3. Supervision or comfort.

Care as used in statute of limitations requiring action upon medical claim to be commenced within one year and defining medical claim as claim arising out of medical care means prevention or alleviation of physical or mental defect or illness. *Browning v. Burt*, 66 Ohio St.3d 544, 613 N.E.2d 993 (Ohio 1993)

career criminal See habitual criminal.

careless Absence of reasonable care; negligent.

carjacking Using violence or threats to take a vehicle from the driver.

carnal knowledge Sexual intercourse.

carrier 1. A person or company engaged in transporting passengers or goods for hire. See also common carrier. 2. An insurance company.

Carrier means any sickness and accident insurance company or health insuring corporation authorized to issue health benefit plans in this state. R.C. § 3924.01(D)

carrier's lien The legal right of a carrier to hold cargo until its owner pays the agreed shipping costs.

carry 1. To transport. 2. To bear the burden of. 3. To have in stock. 4. To list on one's accounts as a debt.

carryback Applying a loss or deduction from 1 year to a prior year.

carrying charge 1. Charges of a creditor, in addition to interest, for providing credit. 2. Costs involved in owning land, e.g., taxes.

carryover Applying a loss or deduction from 1 year to a later year.

carryover basis When property is transferred in a certain way (e.g., by gift) the basis of the property in the transferee is the same as (is carried over from) the transferor's basis.

cartel 1. An association of producers or sellers of any product joined together to control the production, sale, or price of the product. 2. An agreement between enemies while at war.

carve out To separate income from the property that generates it.

CASA Court appointed special advocate (*www.nationalcasa.org*).

case 1. A court's written explanation of how it applied the law to the facts to resolve a legal dispute. See also opinion. 2. A pending matter on a court calendar. 3. A client matter handled by a law office. 4. A statement of arguments and evidence. See also action on the case.

case agreed See agreed case.

casebook A law school textbook containing many edited court opinions.

caselaw (case law) The law found within court opinions. See also common law.

case method Learning law by studying court opinions.

case of first impression See first impression.

case-in-chief The presentation of evidence by one side, not including the evidence it introduces to counter the other side.

case or controversy For a federal court to hear a case, the plaintiff must have suffered a definite and concrete injury.

case reports See reporter (3).

case stated See agreed case.

cash basis Reporting or recognizing revenue only when actually received and expenses only when actually paid out.

cash dividend A dividend paid by a corporation in money.

cash flow 1. Cash from income-producing property. 2. Income less expenses over a designated period of time.

cashier's check A check drawn by a bank on its own funds, signed by a bank officer, and payable to a third party named by a customer.

Cashier's check means a draft with respect to which the drawer and drawee are the same bank or branches of the same bank. R.C. § 1303.03(G)

cash out To receive cash for one's total ownership interest.

cash price A lower price if paid in cash rather than with credit.

Cash price means the price measured in dollars, agreed upon in good faith by the parties as the price at which the specific goods which are the subject matter of any retail installment sale would be sold if such sale were a sale for cash to be paid upon delivery instead of a retail installment sale. R.C. § 1317.01(K)

cash sale A sale in which the buyer and seller exchange goods and full payment in cash at same time.

cash surrender value Cash available upon surrender of an insurance policy before it becomes payable in the normal course (e.g., at death). Also called surrender value.

cash value See fair market value.

castle doctrine See retreat rule.

casual 1. Unexpected. 2. Occasional. 3. Without formality.

casual ejector A fictitious defendant who casually enters the land to eject the person lawfully in possession of it.

casualty 1. A serious accident. 2. A person injured or killed.

casualty insurance Insurance against loss from accident. (Covers many different kinds of insurance.)

casualty loss Damage to property due to an event that is sudden, unexpected, and unusual in nature.

catching bargain An unconscionable purchase from one who has an estate in reversion or expectancy.

caucus A meeting of the members of a particular group, e.g., a political party.

Caucus means all of the members of either house of the general assembly who are members of the same political party. R.C. § 101.15(A)(1)

causa A cause; what produces an effect.

causa causans The predominating effective cause.

causa mortis In contemplation of approaching death. Also phrased mortis causa.

causa proxima The immediate cause.

causa sine qua non "But-for" cause. Without (but-for) the act or omission, the event in question would not have occurred.

causation Bringing something about. Producing an effect.

cause 1. Bringing something about. Producing an effect. 2. A reason, justification, or ground. 3. A lawsuit.

cause of action The facts that give a person a right to judicial relief. A legally acceptable reason for suing.

A cause of action embraces the facts which it is necessary to establish in order to sustain a claim for judicial relief. *McGuire*, 92 Ohio App. 445 (Ohio App., 1952)

cautionary instruction A judge's caution or warning to the jury to avoid outside contact about the case, to ignore certain evidence, or to consider the evidence for a limited purpose.

caveat 1. A warning or admonition. 2. A party's notice filed in court asking that the case be stopped.

caveat actor Let the doer (the actor) beware.

caveatee The person being challenged by someone who files a caveat. The latter is the caveator.

caveat emptor Let the buyer beware. A buyer should examine and judge the product on his or her own.

Caveat emptor precludes recovery where (1) a defect is discoverable upon reasonable inspection, (2) the purchaser had an unimpeded opportunity to inspect the premises and (3) the vendor did not commit fraud. *Padgett*, 130 Ohio App.3d 117 (Ohio App., 1998)

CC Circuit Court; County Court; Civil Code.

C corporation A corporation whose income is taxed at the corporate level; it has not chosen S corporation status. Also called subchapter C corporation.

CD Certificate of deposit.

cease and desist order A court or agency order prohibiting the continuation of a course of conduct.

cede 1. To surrender or yield. 2. To assign or transfer.

cedent A person who transfers something. One who cedes.

censor A person who examines material in order to identify and remove what is objectionable.

censure 1. An official reprimand. 2. To express formal disapproval.

census An official counting of a population.

center of gravity doctrine In conflict-of-law cases, courts apply the law of the place that has the most significant contacts or relationship with the matter in dispute.

ceremonial marriage A marriage entered in compliance with statutory requirements, e.g., obtaining a marriage license.

cert. See certiorari.

certificated Having met the qualifications for certification from a school or training program.

certificate A document that asserts the truth of something or that something has been done, e.g., that requirements have been met.

certificate of acknowledgement The confirmation that the signature on a document was made by a person who is who he or she claimed to be.

certificate of convenience and necessity An authorization from a regulatory agency that a company can operate a public utility.

certificate of deposit (CD) A document from a bank confirming that a named person has a designated amount of money in the bank, usually for a fixed term earning a fixed rate of interest. A time deposit.

An instrument containing an acknowledgment by a bank that a sum of money has been received by the bank and a promise by the bank to repay the sum of money. A certificate of deposit is a note of the bank. R.C. § 1303.03(J)

certificate of incorporation A document issued by the state to a company that grants its status as a corporation.

certificate of occupancy A document confirming that the premises comply with building codes regulations.

certificate of title A document confirming who owns designated property, including who holds encumbrances such as liens.

Certificate of title means a certificate of title with respect to which a statute provides for the security interest in question to be indicated on the certificate as a condition or result of the security interest's obtaining priority over the rights of a lien creditor with respect to the collateral. R.C. § 1309.102(A)(10)

certification 1. The act of affirming the truth or authenticity of something. 2. A request by a federal court that a state court resolve a state issue relevant to a case in the federal court. 3. The process by which a nongovernmental organization grants recognition to a person who has met the qualifications established by that organization.

certification mark Any word, name, symbol, or device used to certify some aspect of goods or services, e.g., their origin.

Certification mark means a mark used in connection with the goods or services of a person other than the certifier to indicate geographic origin, material, mode of manufacture, quality, accuracy, or other characteristics of the goods or services or to indicate that the work or labor on the goods or services was performed by members of a union or other organization. R.C. § 4165.01(A)

certified Having complied with the qualifications for certification.

certified check A check drawn on funds in a depositor's account whose payment is guaranteed by the bank on which it is drawn.

Certified check means a check accepted by the bank on which it is drawn. R.C. § 1303.46(D)

certified copy A duplicate of an original document, certified as an exact reproduction. Also called exemplified copy.

Certified Legal Assistant (CLA) The credential bestowed by the National Association of Legal Assistants (NALA) (*www.nala.org*) for meeting its criteria such as passing a national, entry-level certification exam.

Certified Public Accountant (CPA) An accountant who has met the requirements to be certified as a public accountant (*www.aicpa.org*).

certiorari (cert.) An order (or writ) by a higher court that a lower court send up the record of a case because the higher court has decided to use its discretion to review that case.

cession A surrender or yielding up.

cestui ("he who") One who benefits, a beneficiary.

cestui que trust Beneficiary of a trust. See also trust.

cf. Compare.

CFI Cost, freight, and insurance.

CFR See Code of Federal Regulations (*www.gpoaccess.gov/cfr*).

Ch. Chancellor; chancery; chapter.

chain of causation The sequence of actions and omissions that led to or resulted in the harm or other event in question.

chain of custody A list of places an item of physical evidence has been in and the name of anyone who has possessed it over a period of time.

> Chain of custody means a record or other evidence that tracks a subject sample of biological material from the time the biological material was first obtained until the time it currently exists in its place of storage. R.C. § 2953.71(C)

chain of title The history of ownership of land from the original title holder to the present holder.

challenge 1. A formal objection to the selection of a particular prospective juror. 2. A protest or calling into question.

challenge for cause An objection to selecting a prospective juror because of specified causes or reasons, e.g., bias.

challenge to the array A formal protest to the manner in which the entire pool or panel of prospective jurors has been selected.

chamber 1. A room, e.g., a judge's office. 2. A legislative body.

champerty Conduct by an individual (called the champertor) who promotes or supports someone else's litigation, often by helping to finance the litigation in exchange for a share in the recovery.

> Champerty is a form of maintenance in which a nonparty undertakes to further another's interest in a suit in exchange for a part of the litigated matter if a favorable result ensues. *Rancman*, 99 Ohio St.3d 121 (Ohio 2003)

chancellor 1. Judge in a court of equity. 2. An officer of high rank.

chancery 1. Equity jurisprudence. 2. A court of equity.

change of venue The transfer of a suit begun in one court to another court in the same judicial system.

chapter 1. A subdivision of a code. 2. A division of an organization.

Chapter 11 A category of bankruptcy (found in chapter 11 of the bankruptcy act) in which the debtor is allowed to postpone payment of debts in order to reorganize the capital structure of his or her business.

character evidence Evidence of a person's habits, personality traits, and moral qualities.

charge 1. To instruct a jury, particularly on the law pertaining to the verdict it must reach. 2. A jury instruction. 3. To accuse someone of a crime. 4. To impose a burden or obligation; to assign a duty. 5. To defer payment. 6. A person (e.g., a child) entrusted to the care of another. 7. Price.

chargé d'affaires A diplomatic officer of a lower rank.

charge off To treat or report as a loss.

charitable Having the character or purpose of the public good; philanthropic, eleemosynary.

> Gifts for relief of poverty, and for assistance to the aged, the infirm, the poor, the indigent and the afflicted are charitable. *Edgeter*, 136 N.E.2d 630 (Ohio Prob., 1955)

charitable contribution A gift of money or other property to a charitable organization.

charitable deduction An income tax deduction taken for gifts to a qualified tax-exempt charitable organization.

charitable remainder annuity trust A trust that pays designated amounts to beneficiaries for a period of time after which the trust property goes to a charity.

charitable trust A trust established to serve a purpose that is beneficial to a community. Also called public trust.

> Charitable trust means any fiduciary relationship with respect to property arising under the law of this state or of another jurisdiction as a result of a manifestation of intention to create it, and subjecting the person by whom the property is held to fiduciary duties to deal with the property within this state for any charitable, religious, or educational purpose. R.C. § 109.23(A)

charter 1. The fundamental law governing a municipality or other local unit of government, authorizing it to perform designated functions. 2. A document creating an organization that states its fundamental purposes and powers. 3. The legal authorization to conduct business 4. To rent for temporary use.

chattel Personal property.

chattel mortgage A mortgage or lien on personal property as security for a debt.

chattel paper A document that is evidence of both a monetary obligation and a security interest in specific goods.

> Chattel paper means a record that evidences both a monetary obligation and a security interest in specific goods, a security interest in specific goods and software used in the goods, a security interest in specific goods and license of software used in the goods, a lease of specific goods, or a lease of specific goods and license of software used in the goods. R.C. § 1309.102(A)(11)(a)

check 1. A written order instructing a bank to pay on demand a certain amount of money from the check writer's account to the person named on the check (the payee). See also negotiable instrument. 2. To control; to hold within bounds. 3. To examine for accuracy; to investigate. 4. To deposit for safekeeping.

check kiting A form of bank fraud in which the kiter opens accounts at two or more banks, writes checks on insufficient funds on one account, and then, taking advantage of bank processing delays, covers the overdraft by depositing a check on insufficient funds from the other account. Also called kiting.

checkoff An employer's deduction of union dues from employee wages and turning the dues over to the union.

checks and balances An allocation of powers among the three branches of government (legislative, executive, and judicial) whereby one branch can block, check, or review what another branch wants to do (or has done) in order to maintain a balance of power among the branches.

chief justice The presiding judge (called a justice) in a higher court. In a lower court, he or she is often called the chief judge.

child 1. A son or daughter. 2. A person under the age of majority.

child abuse Physically or emotionally harming a child, intentionally or by neglect.

> An act that inflicts serious physical harm or creates a substantial risk of serious harm to the physical health or safety of the child. *State v. Burdine-Justice*, 125 Ohio App.3d 707 (Ohio App., 1998)

child abuse report law A law that requires designated individuals (e.g., teachers) to report suspected child abuse to the state.

child molestation Subjecting a child to sexual advances, contact, or activity.

child neglect The failure to provide a child with support, medical care, education, moral example, discipline, and other necessaries.

child pornography Visual portrayal of a person under 18 engaged in sexual activity, actual or simulated.

child support The obligation of a parent to pay a child's basic living expenses.

chilling effect Being hindered or inhibited from exercising a constitutional right, e.g., free speech.

Chinese wall Steps taken in an office to prevent a tainted employee from having any contact with a particular case in order to avoid a disqualification of the office from the case. The employee is tainted because he or she has a conflict of interest in that case.

> Chinese wall is a procedure that permits an attorney involved in an earlier adverse role to be screened from other attorneys in the firm, so as to prevent disqualification of entire law firm simply because one member of firm previously represented a client who is now an adversary of a client currently represented by firm. *Kala*, 81 Ohio St.3d 1 (Ohio 1998)

chit 1. A voucher for food and drinks. 2. A short letter or note.

choate Complete; perfected or ripened.

choate lien A perfected lien, enforceable without further steps.

choice of evils Acts otherwise criminal may be justifiable if performed under extraordinary circumstances out of some immediate necessity to prevent a greater harm from occurring. Also called necessity.

choice of law Deciding which jurisdiction's law should govern when an event involves the law of more than one jurisdiction.

chose Chattel; a thing.

chose in action 1. A right to recover something in a lawsuit, e.g., money. 2. The thing itself that embodies the right to sue. Also called thing in action.

churning A broker's excess trading in a customer's account to benefit the broker (via commissions), not the client.

CIF See cost, insurance, and freight.

circuit 1. One of the 13 appellate subdivisions in the federal judicial system. 2. Pertaining to a court that has jurisdiction in several counties or areas. 3. A district traveled by a judge.

circular note See letter of credit.

circumstantial evidence Evidence of a fact that is not based on personal knowledge or observation from which another fact might be inferred. Also called indirect evidence.

> By circumstantial evidence is meant the proof of certain facts and circumstances in a given case from which a jury may reasonably, logically and directly infer other connected facts and circumstances that usually and reasonably follow, according to the common experience of mankind. *State v. Butler*, 94 N.E.2d 457 (Ohio App., 1950)

citation; cite 1. A reference to any legal authority printed on paper or stored in a computer database. 2. An order to appear in court to answer a charge. 3. An official notice of a violation.

citator A book, CD-ROM, or online service with lists of citations that can help assess the current validity of an opinion, statute, or other authority and give leads to additional relevant material.

cite checking Examining citations in a document to assess whether the format of the citation is correct, whether quoted material is accurate, and whether the law cited is still valid.

citizen A person born or naturalized in a country to which he or she owes allegiance and who is entitled to full civil rights.

citizen's arrest A private person making an arrest for a crime that is a breach of the peace committed in his or her presence or for reasonably believing the person arrested has committed a felony.

civil Pertaining to (a) private rights, (b) noncriminal cases, (c) the state or citizenship, (d) public order and peace, and (e) legal systems of Western Europe other than England.

civil action A lawsuit to enforce private rights.

> Civil action or proceeding means any civil litigation that must be determined by judgment entry. R.C. § 1907.24(B)(2)(b)

civil arrest The arrest of the defendant until he or she satisfies the judgment.

civil assault The tort of assault.

civil code 1. A collection of statutes governing noncriminal matters. 2. The code containing the civil law of France, from which the civil code of Louisiana is derived.

civil commitment Noncriminal confinement of those who because of incompetence or addiction cannot care for themselves or who pose a danger to themselves or to society. Also called involuntary commitment.

civil conspiracy A combination of two or more persons acting in concert to commit an unlawful act and an overt act that results in damages.

civil contempt The refusal of the party to comply with a court order, resulting in punishment that can be avoided by compliance.

> A civil contempt is one in which the court imposes an indefinite sanction until the contemnor purges himself by performing the act ordered by the court, with the sentence either immediately carried out or deferred pending compliance; its purpose is remedial, to coerce the contemnor to perform, for the benefit of the opposing party. *In re Contemnor Caron*, 110 Ohio Misc.2d 58 (Ohio Com.Pl., 2000)

civil court A court that hears noncriminal cases.

civil damage law See Dram Shop Act.

civil death The status of a person who has lost civil rights (e.g., to vote) because of a conviction of certain crimes. Also called legal death.

civil disabilities Civil rights that are lost when a person is convicted of a serious crime (e.g., to drive a car).

civil disobedience Breaking the law (without using violence) to show the injustice or unfairness of the law.

civilian One who is not a police officer or in the military.

civil law 1. The law governing civil disputes. Any law other than criminal law. 2. The statutory or code law applicable in Louisiana and many Western European countries other than England.

civil liability Damages or other noncriminal responsibility.

civil liberties Basic individual rights that should not be unduly restricted by the state (e.g., freedom of speech).

> Natural rights that appertain originally and essentially to each person as human being and are inherent in his nature; such rights, which are constitutionally protected, are not actually rights but are immunities, or restraints on government. R.C. §§ 4112.01–4112.08, 4112.99. *Sowers*, 20 Ohio Misc. 115 (Ohio Com.Pl., 1969)

civil penalty A fine or assessment for violating a statute or administrative regulation.

civil procedure Laws governing the mechanics of resolving a civil (noncriminal) dispute in a court or administrative agency.

civil rights Basic individual rights (e.g., to vote) guaranteed by the United States Constitution and special statutes.

> Civil rights includes, without limitation, the rights to contract, hold a professional, occupational, or motor vehicle driver's or commercial driver's license, marry or obtain a divorce, annulment, or dissolution of marriage, make a will, vote, and sue and be sued. R.C. § 5122.301

civil service Nonmilitary government employment, often obtained through merit and competitive exams.

civil union A same-sex relationship with the same *state* benefits and responsibilities the state grants spouses in a marriage.

CLA See Certified Legal Assistant (*www.nala.org*).

Claflin trust A trust that cannot be terminated by a beneficiary. Also called indestructible trust.

claim 1. A right to sue. 2. To demand as one's own or as one's right. 3. To assert something.

claim and delivery A suit to recover personal property that was wrongfully taken or kept.

claimant One who makes a demand or asserts a right or claim.

claim jumping Asserting a mining claim that infringes on the claim of another.

claim of right 1. A good-faith assertion that one was entitled to do something. 2. If a taxpayer receives income (without restrictions) that he or she claimed the right to have, it must be reported in the year received even if it may have to be returned in a later year.

claim preclusion See res judicata.

claims court A court in which a party seeks to resolve claims against the government, e.g., United States Court of Federal Claims.

claims-made policy Insurance that covers only claims actually filed (i.e., made) during the period in which the policy is in effect.

> Claims made policy provides coverage for claims brought against insured only during life of policy, as opposed to occurrence policy, that provides coverage for acts performed during policy period regardless of when the claim is brought. *C.V. Perry & Co.*, 110 Ohio App.3d 23 (Ohio App., 1996)

class A group with common characteristics, e.g., persons injured by the same product.

class action A lawsuit in which one or more members of a class sue (or are sued) as representative parties on behalf of everyone in the class, all of whom do not have to be joined in the lawsuit. Also called representative action.

class gift A gift to a group containing an unknown number of persons at the time the gift is made.

> A gift of aggregate sums to be divided among group of persons, uncertain in number and specific identification at the time of the gift, but which can be ascertained at future time, with amount of each share depending on the ultimate number of persons included in class. *Central Trust Co.*, 50 Ohio St.3d 133 (Ohio 1990)

clause A subdivision of a sentence in a law or other document.

Clayton Act A federal antitrust statute prohibiting price discrimination and other monopolistic practices. 15 USC § 12.

CLE See Continuing Legal Education.

clean bill A proposed statute (bill) that has been substantially revised and introduced to the legislature as a new bill.

clean bill of lading A bill of lading without qualifications.

clean hands doctrine A party may not be allowed to assert an equitable claim or defense if his or her conduct has been unfair or in bad faith. Also called unclean hands doctrine.

clear 1. Free from encumbrance. 2. To vindicate or acquit. 3. To pay a check according to the instructions of the maker. 4. To pass through a clearinghouse. 5. Obvious, unambiguous.

clearance card A letter from an employer given to a departing employee stating facts such as the duration of the latter's employment.

clear and convincing evidence Evidence demonstrating that the existence of a disputed fact is much more probable than its nonexistence. This standard is stronger than preponderance of the evidence but not as strong as beyond a reasonable doubt.

clear and present danger Imminent risk of severe harm, the test used to help determine whether the state can restrict First Amendment freedoms.

clearing 1. The process by which checks are exchanged and pass through the banking system. 2. A ship leaving port in compliance with laws.

clearinghouse A place where banks exchange checks and drafts drawn on each other and reconcile accounts.

> Clearing house means an association of banks or other payors regularly clearing items. R.C. § 1304.01(A)(4)

clearly erroneous The definite and firm conviction of an appellate court that a mistake has been made by a lower court.

clear title 1. Title that is free of reasonable doubt as to its validity. Marketable title. 2. Title that is free of encumbrances.

clemency Leniency from the president or a governor to a criminal, e.g., a pardon or reduction in sentence. Also called executive clemency.

clergy-penitent privilege A privilege preventing spiritual advisors from disclosing confessions or religious confidences made to them. Also called priest-penitent privilege.

clerical error A copying error or other minor mistake.

clerk 1. An official who manages records and files and performs other administrative duties, e.g., a court clerk.

2. A law student or recent law school graduate who works for a law office or judge, usually for a short period of time. 3. One who performs general office duties.

clerkship Employment as a clerk in a legal office. See clerk (2).

client One who hires or receives services from a professional, e.g., an attorney.

Client means a person, firm, partnership, corporation, or other association that, directly or through any representative, consults an attorney for the purpose of retaining the attorney or securing legal service or advice from him in his professional capacity, or consults an attorney employee for legal service or advice, and who communicates, either directly or through an agent, employee, or other representative, with such attorney. R.C. § 2317.021

client security fund A fund (often run by the bar association) used to compensate victims of attorney misconduct.

client trust account An attorney's bank account that contains client funds that may not be used for office operating expenses. Also called trust account.

Clifford trust A fixed-term trust in which the principal is returned to the grantor after a period of time.

close 1. Land that is enclosed. 2. To bring to completion.

close corporation; closed corporation; closely held corporation A corporation whose shares are held by a small group, e.g., a family.

Corporation was close corporation where corporation had few shareholders, its shares were not generally traded on national exchange, were rarely bought and sold, and there was identity of management and ownership. *Gigax*, 83 Ohio App.3d 615 (Ohio App., 1992)

closed-end mortgage A mortgage loan whose principal cannot be increased during the life of the loan and cannot be prepaid.

closed shop A business whose employees must be members of a union as a condition of employment.

closing The meeting in which a transaction is finalized. Also called settlement.

closing argument The final statements by opposing trial attorneys to the jury (or to the trial judge if there is no jury) summarizing the evidence and requesting a favorable decision. Also called final argument, summation, summing up.

closing costs Expenses incurred in the sale of real estate in addition to the purchase price.

cloture A legislative procedure to end debate and allow a vote.

cloud on title A claim or encumbrance on land, which, if valid, would affect or impair the title rights of the owner.

cluster zoning Modifications in zoning restrictions in exchange for other land being set aside for public needs, e.g., a park.

coaching Telling a witness how to give testimony on the stand.

COBRA See Consolidated Omnibus Budget Reconciliation Act.

coconspirator One who engages in a conspiracy with another. Under the conspirator exception to the hearsay rule, statements of one coconspirator can be admitted against another coconspirator if made in furtherance of the conspiracy.

COD Collect on delivery.

code A systematic collection of laws, rules, or guidelines, usually organized by subject matter.

code civil The code containing the civil law of France. Also called the Code Napoléon.

codefendant One of two or more defendants sued in the same civil case or prosecuted in the same criminal case.

Defendant's co-conspirators in commission of murder were not within the definition of "co-defendant," for purposes of the rule allowing discovery of co-defendant's grand jury testimony, where defendant was the only person charged in the indictment with having caused the victim's death. Rules Crim.Proc., Rule 16(B)(1)(a)(iii). *State v. Stojetz*, 84 Ohio St.3d 452 (Ohio 1999)

Code Napoléon See code civil.

code pleading See fact pleading.

codicil A supplement that adds to or changes a will.

codification Collecting and systematically arranging laws or rules by subject matter.

coercion Compelling something by force or threats. Overpowering another's free will by force or undue influence.

Coercion, for purposes of offense of coercing a political contribution, does not require that the person being coerced take or refrain from action because of the coercive conduct; rather, coercion occurs when a person, among other things, threatens another with the purpose of coercing the other into taking or refraining from action, irrespective of how the person threatened responds to the threat. R.C. § 2921.43(C). *State v. Conese*, 102 Ohio St.3d 435 (Ohio, 2004)

cognizable 1. Pertaining to what can be heard and resolved by a court. 2. Capable of being known.

cognizance 1. The power of a court to hear and resolve a particular dispute. 2. Judicial notice. 3. Awareness or recognition.

cognovit A written statement that acknowledges liability or the validity of a debt. The statement confesses judgment. A cognovit note (also called judgment note) is a promissory note containing a cognovit.

cohabitation Living together as a couple or in a sexual relationship.

Essential elements of cohabitation, for purposes of a domestic violence charge, are the sharing of familial responsibilities and consortium. R.C. § 2919.25(E)(2). *Cleveland*, 111 Ohio Misc.2d 16 (Ohio Mun., 2001)

coheir One of several persons to whom an inheritance passes or descends. A joint heir.

coif A ceremonial cap or other headpiece. See also Order of the Coif.

coinsurance A sharing of the risks between two or more insurers or between the insurer and the insured.

COLA Cost of living adjustment.

cold blood Premeditated killing.

collapsible corporation A corporation set up to be sold or liquidated before it earns substantial income.

collateral 1. Property pledged as security for the satisfaction of a debt. 2. Not in the direct line of descent. 3. Not directly relevant. 4. Accompanying but of secondary importance.

collateral attack A challenge or attack against the validity of a judgment that is not raised in a direct appeal from the court that rendered the judgment.

> An attempt to avoid, defeat, or evade judgment, or to deny its force and effect, in some judicial proceeding not provided by law for the express purpose of reviewing it. *Hall*, 161 Ohio App.3d 245 (Ohio App., 2005)

collateral estoppel When parties have litigated and resolved an issue in one case, they cannot relitigate the issue in another case against each other even if the two cases raise different claims or causes of action. Also called direct estoppel, estoppel by judgment, estoppel by record, issue preclusion.

> When a valid, final judgment has determined an issue of ultimate fact, the same parties cannot relitigate that issue. *In re Burton*, 160 Ohio App.3d 750 (Ohio App., 2005)

collateral fraud Deception by one party that does not pertain to the actual issues that were resolved in a trial but which prevented the other party from presenting its case fairly. Also called extrinsic fraud.

collateral heir One who is not of the direct line of the deceased, but comes from a collateral line, as a brother, aunt, or a cousin of the deceased. Also called heir collateral.

collateral order doctrine An appeal of a nonfinal order will be allowed if the order conclusively determines the disputed question, resolves an important issue that is completely separate from the merits of the dispute, and is effectively unreviewable on appeal from a final judgment.

collateral source rule The amount of damages caused by the tortfeasor shall not be reduced by any injury-related funds received by the plaintiff from sources independent of the tortfeasor such as a health insurance policy of the plaintiff.

> Under the collateral source rule, a plaintiff's recovery cannot be reduced by payments or benefits from other sources. *Robinson*, 160 Ohio App.3d 668 (Ohio App., 2005)

collateral warranty A warranty of title given by someone other than the seller.

collation 1. A comparison of a copy with the original to determine the correctness of the copy. 2. Taking into account property already given to some heirs as an advancement.

collecting bank A bank handling a check for collection other than the payor bank.

collective bargaining Negotiations between an employer and representatives of its employees on working conditions.

collective mark A mark used by members of an organization (e.g., a union) to indicate membership or to identify what it offers.

> Collective mark means a mark used by members of a cooperative, association, or other collective group or organization to identify goods or services and distinguish them from those of others, or to indicate membership in the collective group or organization. R.C. § 4165.01(B)

colloquium Extrinsic facts showing that a defamatory statement was of and concerning the plaintiff. A complaint alleging such facts.

colloquy A formal discussion, e.g., between the judge and the defendant to determine if the defendant's plea is informed.

collusion 1. An agreement to commit fraud. 2. An agreement between a husband and wife that one or both will lie to the court to facilitate the obtaining of their divorce.

colorable 1. Plausible. Having at least some factual or legal support. 2. Deceptively appearing to be valid.

color of law 1. Acting or pretending to act in an official, governmental capacity. 2. The pretense of law.

color of office Asserted official or governmental authority.

> Color of office means actually, purportedly, or allegedly done under any law, ordinance, resolution, order, or other pretension to official right, power, or authority. R.C. § 117.01(A)

color of title A false appearance of having title to property.

comaker See cosigner.

combination The union or association of two or more persons or entities to achieve a common end. See also conspiracy, restraint of trade.

combination in restraint of trade An agreement among businesses to create a monopoly or otherwise stifle competition.

combination patent A combination of known elements which, when combined, accomplish a patentable function or result.

coming and going rule See going and coming rule.

comity Giving effect to the laws of another state, not as a requirement, but rather out of deference or respect.

> Comity refers to an Ohio court's recognition of a foreign decree and is a matter of courtesy rather than of right. *Kalia*, 151 Ohio App.3d 145 (Ohio App., 2002)

commerce Buying, selling, or exchanging goods or services.

Commerce Clause The clause in the U.S. Constitution (art. I, § 8, cl. 3) giving Congress the power to regulate commerce among the states, with foreign nations, and with Indian tribes.

commercial bank A bank with a variety of services such as providing loans, checking accounts, and safety deposit boxes.

commercial bribery The advantage secured over a competitor by corrupt dealings with agents of prospective purchasers.

commercial frustration An excuse not to perform a contract due to an unforeseen event not under the control of either party.

commercial impracticability See impracticability.

commercial law The law governing commercial transactions such as the sale and financing of goods and services.

commercial paper 1. A negotiable instrument (e.g., a draft, a promissory note) used in commerce. 2. A short-term, unsecured negotiable note, often sold to meet immediate cash needs.

commercial speech Expression related solely to the economic interests of the speaker and its audience.

commercial unit Goods considered a single whole for purposes of sale, the value of which would be materially impaired if divided into parts.

> A unit of goods as by commercial usage is a single whole for purposes of sale and division of which materially impairs its character or value on the market or in use. A commercial unit may be a single article (as a machine) or a set of articles (as a suite of furniture or an assortment of sizes) or a quantity (as a bale, gross, or carload) or any other unit treated in use or in the relevant market as a single whole. R.C. § 1302.01(A)(10)

commingling Mixing what should be kept separate, e.g., depositing client funds in a single account with general law firm funds or an attorney's personal funds.

commission 1. The granting of powers to carry out a task. 2. A government body granted power to carry out a task. 3. Compensation, often a percentage of the value of the transaction. 4. The act of committing something, usually a crime.

commitment 1. An agreement or pledge to do something. 2. The act of institutionalizing someone as to a prison or mental hospital.

commitment fee A fee paid by a loan applicant for a lender's promise to lend money at a defined rate on a specified date.

committee 1. A group appointed to perform a function on behalf of a larger group. 2. A special guardian appointed to protect the interests of an incompetent person.

committee of the whole A special committee consisting of the entire membership of a deliberative body.

commodity Something useful; an article of commerce.

common 1. The legal right to use another's land or waters. 2. Land set apart for use by the general public. 3. Shared.

common carrier A company that holds itself out to the general public as engaged in transporting people or goods for a fee.

> Common carrier includes any carrier that seeks the privilege of transporting for hire goods of the public. *Pennant Moldings*, 11 Ohio App.3d 248 (Ohio App., 1983)

common disaster An event causing the death of two or more persons with shared interests, without clear evidence of who died first.

common enemy doctrine Landowners can fend off surface waters (e.g., rain) as needed, without liability to other landowners.

common law 1. Judge-made law in the absence of controlling statutory law or other higher law. Law derived from court opinions. 2. Law based on the legal system of England.

> Common law is all the statutory and case law background of England and the American colonies before the American revolution. *In re Estate of Pulford*, 122 Ohio App.3d 92 (Ohio App., 1997)

common law action An action based on the common law. See also action at law.

common law copyright The author's proprietary interest in his or her creation before it has been made available to the pubic.

common law marriage A marriage entered without license or ceremony by persons who have agreed to marry, have lived together as husband and wife, and have held themselves out as such.

> Common-law marriage is marital joinder of man and woman without benefit of formal papers or procedures. *Fitzgerald*, 66 Ohio App.3d 298 (Ohio App., 1990)

common law trust See business trust.

common nuisance See public nuisance.

Common Pleas The name of a trial court in some states (e.g., Ohio) and an intermediate appellate court in others.

common situs picketing Picketing an entire construction project even though the labor grievance is with only one subcontractor.

common stock Stock in a corporation with voting rights and the right to dividends after preferred stockholders have been paid.

commonwealth 1. A nation or state as a political entity. (In the United States, four states are officially designated commonwealths: KY, MA, PA, and VA.) 2. A political unit that is voluntarily united with the United States but is self-governing, e.g., Northern Mariana Islands.

community 1. A section or neighborhood in a city or town. 2. A group of people with common interests. 3. The marital entity that shares or owns community property.

community notification law See Megan's law.

community property Property in which each spouse has a one-half interest because it was acquired during the marriage (by a method other than gift or inheritance to one spouse only) regardless of who earned it.

community trust An entity that operates a charitable trust.

commutation 1. A change of punishment to one that is less severe. 2. An exchange or substitution.

> Commutation or commutation of sentence means the substitution by the governor of a lesser for a greater punishment. R.C. § 2967.01(C)

commutative contract A contract in which what each party promises or exchanges is considered equal in value.

commutative justice A system of justice in which the goal is fundamental fairness in transactions among the parties.

commuted value The present value of a future interest or payment.

compact An agreement, often between states or nations.

company An association of persons who are engaged in a business.

company union An employer-controlled union of employees in a single company.

comparable worth Jobs requiring the same levels of skill should receive equal pay whether performed by men or women.

comparative negligence In a negligence action, the plaintiff's damages will be reduced in proportion to the plaintiff's negligence in causing his or her own injury.

comparative rectitude When both spouses have grounds for a divorce, it will be granted to the spouse least at fault.

compelling state interest A substantial need for the state to act that justifies the resulting restriction on the constitutional right claimed by the person challenging the state's action.

compensating balance The minimum balance a bank requires one of its borrowers to have on deposit.

compensation 1. Payment of wages or benefits for services rendered. 2. Payment for a loss incurred. Indemnification.

compensatory damages Money to restore an injured party to his or her position prior to the injury or wrong. Actual damages.

> Damages that measure actual loss and are allowed as amends therefor. *Fantozzi*, 64 Ohio St.3d 601 (Ohio 1992)

competency proceeding A hearing to determine if someone has the mental capacity to do something, e.g., to stand trial.

competent 1. Having the knowledge and skill reasonably necessary to represent a particular client. 2. Having sufficient understanding to be allowed to give testimony as a witness. 3. Having the ability to understand the criminal proceedings, to consult with one's attorney, and to assist in one's own defense. 4. Having the capacity to manage one's own affairs.

competent evidence Evidence that is relevant and admissible.

compilation 1. A collection of laws, usually statutes. 2. An original work formed by the collection and assembling of preexisting works.

complainant One who files a complaint to initiate a civil lawsuit or who alleges that someone has committed a crime.

complaint 1. A plaintiff's first pleading, stating a claim against the defendant. Also called petition. 2. A formal criminal charge.

completion bond A bond given as insurance to guarantee that a contract will be completed within the agreed-upon time. Also called performance bond, surety bond.

complex trust See discretionary trust.

composition An agreement between a debtor and two or more creditors on what will be accepted as full payment.

compos mentis Of sound mind; competent.

compound 1. To adjust or settle a debt or other claim by paying a lesser amount. 2. To accept an illegal payment in exchange for not prosecuting a crime. 3. To calculate interest on both the principal and on interest already accrued. 4. A mixture of parts.

compound interest See compound (3).

compounding a crime Receiving something of value in exchange for an agreement to interfere with a prosecution or not to prosecute.

compromise To settle a dispute through mutual concessions.

> Compromise and offers to compromise. Evidence of (1) furnishing or offering or promising to furnish, or (2) accepting or offering or promising to accept, a valuable consideration in compromising or attempting to compromise a claim which was disputed as to either validity or amount, is not admissible to prove liability for or invalidity of the claim or its amount. Ohio Evid. R. Rule 408

compromise verdict A verdict that results when jurors resolve their inability to reach unanimity by conceding some issues to entice agreement on others.

comptroller A fiscal officer of an organization appointed to examine accounts, issue financial reports, and perform other accounting duties. Also spelled controller.

compulsion 1. Forcing someone to do or refrain from doing something. 2. An irresistible impulse.

compulsory arbitration Arbitration that parties are required to undergo to resolve their dispute.

compulsory counterclaim A claim that arises out of the same subject matter as the opposing party's claim.

compulsory joinder Someone who must be joined as a party if his or her absence means that complete relief is not possible for the parties already in the lawsuit or that one or more of the parties may be subject to inconsistent or multiple liability.

> Compulsory joinder. (A) Persons to be joined. A person who is subject to service of process shall be joined as a party in the action, except as provided in division (B) of this rule, if the person has an interest in or a claim arising out of the following situations: (1) Personal injury or property damage to the person or property of the decedent which survives the decedent's death and a claim for wrongful death to the same decedent if caused by the same wrongful act . . . Ohio Civ. R. Rule 19.1

compulsory process A summons or writ that compels a witness to appear in court, usually by subpoena or arrest.

compurgator Someone called to give testimony for the defendant.

computer crime The use of a computer to commit an illegal act, e.g., accessing or damaging computer data without authorization.

concealed weapon A weapon carried on a person in such a manner as to conceal it from the ordinary sight of another.

concerted Planned or accomplished together. Concerted activity is the conduct of employees who have joined together to achieve common goals on conditions of employment.

> Any action by two or more employees may constitute concerted activity protected under the NLRA if it relates to group action in the interest of employees. *Woodell*, 156 Ohio App.3d 602 (Ohio App., 2004)

concert of action 1. A person cannot be prosecuted for both a substantive offense and a conspiracy to commit that offense where an agreement between two or more persons is a necessary element of the substantive offense. Also called Wharton's rule. 2. Concerted action—conduct planned by persons—results in liability for each other's acts.

conciliation 1. Conduct taken to restore trust in an effort to resolve a dispute. 2. Settlement of a conflict without undue pressure or coercion.

conclusion of fact An inference of fact drawn from evidence of another fact. See also finding of fact.

conclusion of law The result of applying the law to the facts. See also holding.

conclusive 1. Decisive. 2. Supported by substantial evidence.

conclusive presumption An inference of fact that the fact finder must find despite any evidence to the contrary. Also called irrebuttable presumption.

conclusory Pertaining to an argument that states a conclusion without providing the underlying facts to support the conclusion.

concur 1. To agree. 2. To accept a conclusion but for different reasons. See also concurring opinion.

concurrent 1. At the same time. 2. With the same authority.

concurrent cause A cause that acts together (simultaneously) with another cause to produce an injury or other result.

concurrent condition A condition that one party must fulfill at the same time that another party must fulfill a mutual condition.

concurrent covenants Two covenants that must be performed or ready to be performed simultaneously.

concurrent jurisdiction The power of two or more courts to resolve the same dispute. Also called coordinate jurisdiction.

concurrent negligence Negligence by two or more persons who, though not working in concert, combine to produce a single injury.

Concurrent negligence consists of the negligence of two or more persons concurring, not necessarily in point of time, but in point of consequence, in producing a single indivisible injury. *Am. States Ins. Co.*, 126 Ohio App.3d 401 (Ohio App., 1998)

concurrent power A legislative power that can be exercised by the federal or state government, or by both.

concurrent resolution A measure adopted by both houses of the legislature but does not have the force of law.

concurrent sentence A sentence served simultaneously, in whole or in part, with another sentence.

concurring opinion A court opinion in which a judge agrees with the result of the majority opinion but for different reasons.

condemn 1. To set apart or expropriate (take) property for public use in exercise of the power of eminent domain. 2. To judge someone to be guilty. 3. To declare to be unfit.

When used in connection with real property, condemn ordinarily refers to appropriation of property in eminent domain proceedings. *Carroll Weir*, 2 Ohio St.2d 189 (Ohio 1965)

condemnee A person whose property is taken for public use.

condition 1. An uncertain future event upon which a legal result (e.g., a duty to pay) is dependant. 2. A prerequisite.

conditional Depending on or containing a condition.

conditional bequest A gift in a will that will be effective only if a specific event (condition) occurs or fails to occur.

conditional contract An executory (i.e., unperformed) contract whose existence and performance depends on a contingency.

conditional fee 1. See contingent fee. 2. See fee simple conditional.

conditional privilege A right to do or say something that can be lost if done or said with malice. Also called a qualified privilege.

conditional sale A sale in which the buyer does not receive title until making full payment.

conditional use Permitted land use upon compliance with specified conditions. Also called special exception, special use.

condition of employment A job requirement.

condition precedent An act or event (other than a lapse of time) that must occur before performance becomes due.

A condition precedent calls for the performance of some act or the happening of some event after the contract is entered into, and upon the performance or happening of which its obligation is made to depend. *Sweeney*, 146 Ohio App.3d 380 (Ohio App., 2001)

condition subsequent An act or event that will, if it occurs, render an obligation invalid.

A condition in the contract the happening of which will defeat a note given pursuant thereto is a condition subsequent. *Maurer*, 96 Ohio App. 471 (Ohio App., 1954)

condominium A real estate interest that combines two forms of ownership: exclusive ownership of an individual unit of a multi-unit project and common ownership of the common project areas.

condonation Overlooking or forgiving, e.g., one spouse's express or implied forgiveness of the marital fault of the other.

conference committee A committee consisting of members of both houses of the legislature that seeks to reach a compromise on two versions of the same bill the houses passed.

confession A statement acknowledging guilt.

confession and avoidance A plea that admits some facts but avoids their legal effect by alleging new facts.

confession of judgment See cognovit.

confidence game Obtaining money or other property by gaining a victim's trust through deception.

confidential communication An exchange of information that is privileged—the exchange cannot be disclosed against the will of the parties involved.

confidential relationship 1. See fiduciary relationship. 2. A relationship that requires non-disclosure of certain facts.

Confidential relationship, which may support existence of de facto fiduciary relationship, arises when one person comes to rely on and trust another in important affairs and relations that are not necessarily legal, but may be moral, social, domestic or merely personal, but there must be mutual understanding that one party has reposed special confidence in the other. *Applegate*, 70 Ohio App.3d 813 (Ohio App., 1990)

confirmation 1. Giving formal approval. 2. Corroboration. 3. Rendering enforceable something that is voidable.

confiscation Seizing private property under a claim of authority.

conflict of interest Divided loyalty that actually or potentially harms someone who is owed undivided loyalty.

Possible conflict of interest exists where interests of defendants may diverge at some point so as to place attorney under inconsistent duties, and actual conflict of interest exists if, during course of representation, defendants' interests do diverge with respect to material factual or legal issue or to course of action. *State v. Gillard*, 78 Ohio St.3d 548 (Ohio 1997)

conflict of laws Differences in the laws of two coequal legal systems (e.g., two states) involved in a legal dispute. The choice of which law to apply in such disputes.

conformed copy An exact copy of a document with notations of what could not be copied.

conforming In compliance with the contract or the law.

Conforming goods or performance under a lease contract means goods or performance that are in accordance with the obligations under the lease contract. R.C. § 1310.01(A)(4)

conforming use A use of land that complies with zoning laws.

confrontation Being present when others give evidence against you and having the opportunity to question them.

confusion of goods The mixing of like things belonging to different owners so that sorting out what each originally owned is no longer possible. Also called intermixture of goods.

conglomerate A corporation that has diversified its operations, usually by acquiring enterprises in widely different industries.

Congress 1. The national legislature of the United States. 2. A formal meeting of representatives of different groups (congress).

Congressional Record (Cong. Rec.) The official record of the day-to-day proceedings of Congress.

conjoint Joined together; having a joint interest.

conjugal Pertaining to marriage or spouses, e.g., the rights that one spouse has in the other's companionship, services, support, and sexual relations.

connecting-up Evidence demonstrating the relevance of prior evidence.

connivance A willingness or a consent by one spouse that a marital wrong be committed by the other spouse.

consanguinity Relationship by blood or a common ancestor.

conscience of the court The court's power to apply equitable principles.

conscientious objector A person who for religious or moral reasons is sincerely opposed to war in any form.

conscious parallelism A process, not in itself unlawful, by which firms in a concentrated market might share monopoly power.

consecutive sentences Sentences that are served one after the other—in sequence. Also called accumulative sentences, cumulative sentences.

consensus ad idem A meeting of the minds; agreement.

consent Voluntary agreement or permission, express or implied.

consent decree A court decree agreed upon by the parties.

> A consent decree is essentially a contract between the parties; however, it also is similar to a judgment, and is enforced as one. *Ohio State Medical Bd.*, 59 Ohio App.2d 133 (Ohio App., 1978)

consent judgment An agreement by the parties (embodied in a court order) settling their dispute.

consent search A search consented to by the person affected who has the authority to give the consent.

consequential damages Losses or injuries that do not flow directly from a party's action, but only from some of the consequences or results of such action.

conservator A person appointed by the court to manage the affairs of someone, usually an incompetent. A guardian.

consideration A bargained-for promise, act, or forbearance. Something of value exchanged between the parties.

> Consideration, for purposes of the requirement that the purchaser takes the real property for valuable consideration, as element for status as bona fide purchaser, consists of a bargained-for benefit to the vendor or a detriment to the purchaser. *Groza-Vance,* 162 Ohio App.3d 510 (Ohio App., 2005)

consignment Transferring goods to someone, usually for sale by the latter. The one transferring the goods is the consignor; the person receiving them is the consignee.

consignee, consignor See consignment.

consolidated appeal An appeal from two or more parties who file a joint notice of appeal and proceed as a single appellant.

Consolidated Omnibus Budget Reconciliation Act (COBRA). A federal statute that gives workers limited rights to keep their health insurance policy when they leave a job.

consolidation 1. A joining together or merger. 2. Combining two or more corporations that dissolve into a new corporate entity. 3. Uniting the trial of several actions into one court action.

consolidation loan A new loan that pays the balances owed on previous loans that are then extinguished.

consortium 1. The benefits that one spouse is entitled to receive from the other, e.g., companionship, cooperation, services, affection, and sexual relations. 2. The companionship and affection a parent is entitled to receive from a child and that a child is entitled to receive from a parent. 3. An association or coalition of businesses or other organizations.

> Consortium refers to benefits that one spouse is entitled to receive from the other or that a child is entitled to receive from his or her parent, including companionship, cooperation, aid, affection, and, between spouses, sexual relations. *Thomson*, 150 Ohio App.3d 352 (Ohio App., 2002)

conspiracy An agreement between two or more persons to commit a criminal or other unlawful act or to perform a lawful act by unlawful means. Also called criminal conspiracy.

constable A peace officer whose duties (e.g., serving writs) are similar to (but not as extensive as) those of a sheriff.

constitution The fundamental law that creates the branches of government, allocates power among them, and defines some basic rights of individuals.

constitutional Pertaining to or consistent with the constitution.

constitutional court See Article III court.

constitutional fact A fact whose determination is decisive of constitutional rights.

constitutional law The body of law found in and interpreting the constitution.

constitutional right A right guaranteed by a constitution.

construction An interpretation of a law or other document. The verb is construe.

constructive True legally even if not factually.

constructive bailment An obligation imposed by law on a person holding chattels to deliver them to another.

constructive contempt See indirect contempt.

constructive contract See implied in law contract.

constructive delivery Acts that are the equivalent of the actual delivery of something.

constructive desertion The misconduct of the spouse who stayed home that justified the other spouse's departure from the home.

constructive discharge Acts by an employer that make working conditions so intolerable that an employee quits.

> Constructive discharge exists if employee's working conditions are so difficult or unpleasant that reasonable person would feel compelled to resign. *Scandinavian Health Spa*, 64 Ohio App.3d 480 (Ohio App., 1990)

constructive eviction A landlord's causing or allowing premises to become so uninhabitable that a tenant leaves.

constructive fraud A breach of a duty that violates a fiduciary relationship. Also called legal fraud.

constructive knowledge What one does not actually know, but should know or has reason to know and, therefore, is treated as knowing.

constructive notice Information the law assumes one has because he or she could have discovered it by proper diligence and had a duty to inquire into it.

Notice the law regards as sufficient to give notice and is regarded as a substitute for actual notice. *Imburgia,* 114 Ohio Misc.2d 38 (Ohio Ct.Cl., 1999)

constructive possession Control or dominion one rightfully has over property that he or she does not actually possess.

constructive receipt of income Having control over income without substantial restriction even though not actually received.

constructive service See substituted service.

constructive trust A trust implied as an equitable remedy to prevent unjust enrichment by one who has obtained the legal right to property by wrongdoing. Also called implied trust, involuntary trust, trust de son tort, trust ex delicto, trust ex maleficio.

A constructive trust is a trust by operation of law which arises contrary to intention and in invitum, against one who, by fraud, actual or constructive, by duress or abuse of confidence, by commission of wrong, or by any form of unconscionable conduct, artifice, concealment, or questionable means, or who in any way against equity and good conscience, either has obtained or holds the legal right to property which he ought not, in equity and good conscience, hold and enjoy. *Groza-Vance,* 162 Ohio App.3d 510 (Ohio App., 2005)

construe See construction.

consul An official in a foreign country who promotes the commercial and other interests of his or her own country.

consumer A buyer of goods and services for personal use rather than for resale or manufacturing.

consumer credit Credit to buy goods or services for personal use.

consumer goods Products used or bought for personal, family, or household use.

Consumer goods or services means goods or services purchased, leased, or rented primarily for personal, family, or household purposes, including courses or instruction or training regardless of the purpose for which they are taken. R.C. § 1345.21(E)

consumer lease A lease of personal property for personal, family, or household use.

consumer price index (CPI) A measurement by the Bureau of Labor Statistics of average monthly changes in prices of basic goods and services bought by consumers (*www.bls.gov/cpi*).

consummate 1. To complete or bring to fruition. 2. To engage in the first act of sexual intercourse after marriage.

contemner (contemnor) One who commits contempt.

contemplation of death The thought of death as a primary motive for making a transfer of property.

contemporaneous Existing or occurring in the same period of time.

contempt Disobedience of or disrespect for the authority of a court or legislature.

A person guilty of any of the following acts may be punished as for a contempt: (A) Disobedience of, or resistance to, a lawful writ, process, order, rule, judgment, or command of a court or officer; (B) Misbehavior of an officer of the court in the performance of official duties, or in official transactions; (C) A failure to obey a subpoena duly served, or a refusal to be sworn or to answer as a witness, when lawfully required. . . . R.C. § 2705.02

contest To challenge; to raise a defense against a claim.

contested Challenged; litigated.

contingency 1. A possible event. 2. Uncertainty. 3. A contingent fee.

contingent 1. Uncertain; pertaining to what may or may not happen. 2. Dependent; conditional.

contingent annuity An annuity whose commencement or exact terms of payment depend on an uncertain future event.

contingent beneficiary A person who receives a gift or insurance proceeds if a condition occurs.

contingent estate An estate that will become a present or vested estate if an event occurs or condition is met.

contingent fee A fee that a paid only if the case is successfully resolved by litigation or settlement. Also called conditional fee.

contingent interest An interest whose enjoyment is dependent on an uncertain event.

One in which there is no present fixed right of present or future enjoyment, but in which a fixed right will arise in the future under specified contingencies. *Cleveland Trust Co.,* 106 Ohio App. 237 (Ohio App., 1957)

contingent liability Liability that depends on an uncertain event.

contingent remainder A remainder that is limited to take effect either to an uncertain person or upon an uncertain event. Also called executory remainder.

continuance An adjournment or postponement of a session.

continuing jurisdiction A court's power (by retaining jurisdiction) to modify its orders after entering judgment.

continuing legal education (CLE) Training in the law (often short term) received after completing one's formal legal training.

continuing offense An offense involving a prolonged course of conduct.

continuing trespass Allowing a structure or other permanent invasion on another's land.

Tortious activity is ongoing, perpetually creating fresh violations of the plaintiff's property rights. *Reith,* 2005-Ohio-4852 (Ohio App., 2005)

contra Against; in opposition to.

contraband Property that is unlawful to possess, import, export, or trade.

contract A legally enforceable agreement. A promise that, if breached, will entitle the aggrieved to a remedy.

The total legal obligation that results from the parties' agreement. R.C. § 1301.01(K)

contract carrier A private company that transports passengers or property under individual contracts, not for the general public.

Contract Clause A clause in the U.S. Constitution (art. I, § 10, cl. 1) providing that no state shall pass a law impairing the obligation of contracts.

contract for deed An agreement to sell property in which the seller retains title or possession until full payment has been made. Also called land sales contract.

contract implied in fact See implied in fact contract.

contract implied in law See implied in law contract.

contract of adhesion See adhesion contract.

contract under seal A signed contract that has the waxed seal of the signer attached. Consideration was not needed. Also called special contract, specialty.

contractor A person or company that enters contracts to supply materials or labor to perform a job.

Contractor means an individual who provides services to an employer as an independent contractor for compensation that is reported as income other than wages and who is an individual, the sole shareholder of a corporation, or the sole member of a limited liability company. R.C. § 3121.89(A)

contributing to the delinquency of a minor Conduct by an adult that is likely to lead to illegal or immoral behavior by a minor.

contribution 1. The right of one tortfeasor who has paid a judgment to be proportionately reimbursed by other tortfeasors who have not paid their share of the damages caused by all the tortfeasors. 2. The right of one debtor who has paid a common debt to be proportionately reimbursed by the other debtors.

contributory 1. Helping to bring something about. 2 Pertaining to one who pays into a common fund or benefit plan.

contributory negligence Unreasonableness by the plaintiff that helps cause his or her own injury or loss.

Contributory fault means contributory negligence, other contributory tortious conduct, or, except as provided with respect to product liability claims in section 2307.711 of the Revised Code, express or implied assumption of the risk. R.C. § 2307.011(B)

controlled substance A drug whose possession or use is prohibited or otherwise strictly regulated.

controller See comptroller.

controlling interest Ownership of enough of the stock of a company to be able to control it.

controversy A dispute that a court can resolve; a justiciable dispute. An actual rather than a hypothetical dispute.

For a controversy to exist, there must be a genuine dispute between parties having adverse legal interests of sufficient immediacy and reality to warrant the issuance of a declaratory judgment. R.C. § 2721.01 et seq. *R.A.S. Entertainment*, 130 Ohio App.3d 125 (Ohio App., 1998)

contumacy Refusal to obey a court order. Contempt.

convenience and necessity See certificate of convenience and necessity.

convention 1. An agreement or treaty. 2. A special assembly.

conventional 1. Customary. 2. Based on agreement rather than law.

conventional mortgage A mortgage that is not government insured.

conversation See criminal conversation.

conversion 1. An intentional interference with personal property that is serious enough to force the wrongdoer to pay its full value. An action for conversion is called trover. 2. Changing the nature of property.

Any exercise or control wrongfully exerted over the personal property of another in denial of, or under a claim inconsistent with, his rights. *Bono*, 159 Ohio App.3d 571 (Ohio App., 2005)

convertible security One kind of security (e.g., bond) that can be exchanged for another kind (e.g., stock).

conveyance A transfer of an interest in land. A transfer of title.

conveyancer One skilled in transferring interests in land.

convict 1. To find a person guilty of a crime. 2. A prisoner.

A person who has been convicted of a felony under the laws of this state, whether or not actually confined in a state correctional institution, unless the person has been pardoned or has served the person's sentence or prison term. R.C. § 2967.01(G)

conviction 1. A finding of guilty of a crime. 2. A firm belief.

cooling off period 1. A period of time during which neither side can take any further action. 2. The time given to a buyer to cancel the purchase.

cooperative 1. A business owned by customers that use its goods and services. 2. A multiunit building owned by a corporation that leases units to individual shareholders of the corporation.

Housing cooperative means a housing complex of at least two hundred fifty units that is owned and operated by a nonprofit corporation that issues a share of the corporation's stock to an individual, entitling the individual to live in a unit of the complex, and collects a monthly maintenance fee from the individual to maintain, operate, and pay the taxes of the complex. R.C. § 323.151(F)

coordinate jurisdiction See concurrent jurisdiction.

coparcenary An estate that arises when several persons inherit property from the same ancestor to share equally as if they were one person or one heir. Also called estate in coparcenary, parcenary.

coparcener A concurrent or joint heir through coparcenary. Also called parcener.

copyhold Tenure as laid out in a copy of the court roll (an old form of land tenure).

copyright (©) The exclusive right for a fixed number of years to print, copy, sell, or perform original works. 17 U.S.C. § 101.

coram nobis ("before us") An old remedy allowing a trial judge (via a writ of error) to vacate its own judgment because of factual errors. If the request to vacate is made to an appellate court, the remedy was called coram vobis ("before you").

Coram nobis is a procedural writ that is used to correct errors of fact. However, it is not part of Ohio law. *Lutz*, 2002 WL 973099 (Ohio App., 2002)

coram vobis See coram nobis.

core proceeding A proceeding that invokes a substantive bankruptcy right. 28 U.S.C.A. § 157(b).

corespondent 1. The person who allegedly had sexual intercourse with a defendant charged with adultery. 2. A joint respondent.

corner Dominance over the supply of a particular commodity.

coroner A public official who inquires into suspicious deaths.

corporal punishment Punishment inflicted on the physical body.

corporate-opportunity doctrine Corporate directors and officers must not take personal advantage of business opportunities they learn about in their corporate role if the corporation itself could pursue those opportunities.

corporate veil Legitimate corporate actions are not treated as shareholder actions. See piercing the corporate veil.

corporation An organization that is an artificial person or legal entity that has limited liability and can have an indefinite existence separate from its shareholders.

An artificial person, created by the General Assembly and deriving its power, authority and capacity from the statutes. *Worthington,* 85 Ohio St.3d 156 (Ohio 1999)

corporation counsel A city's salaried attorney.

corporeal Tangible; pertaining to the body.

corporeal hereditament Anything tangible that can be inherited, e.g., land.

corpus 1. Assets in a trust. Also called res, trust estate, trust fund. 2. Principal as opposed to interest or income. 3. A collection of writings. 4. The main part of a body (anatomy).

corpus delicti ("body of the crime") The fact that a loss or injury has occurred as a result of the criminal conduct of someone.

Corpus delicti is the body or substance of a crime, and is made up of two elements: (1) the act itself; and (2) the criminal agency of the act. *State v. Tolliver,* 146 Ohio App.3d 186 (Ohio App., 2001)

corpus juris A collection or body of laws.

correction 1. The system of imposing punishment and treatment on offenders. 2. Removing an error. 3. A market adjustment.

correspondent An intermediary for an organization that needs access to a particular market.

corroborating evidence Supplemental or supporting evidence.

corruption of blood Punishment by taking away the right to inherit or transfer property to blood relatives.

corrupt practices act A statute regulating campaign contributions, spending, and disclosure.

cosigner One who signs a document along with another, often to help the latter secure a loan. The cosigner can have repayment obligations upon default of the other. Also called comaker.

cost and freight (c&f)(c.a.f.) The price includes the cost of the goods and of transporting them.

cost basis The acquisition costs of purchasing property.

cost, insurance, and freight (CIF) The price includes the cost of purchasing, insuring, and transporting the goods.

cost-of-living clause A clause providing an automatic wage or benefit increase tied to cost-of-living rises as measured by indicators such as the Consumer Price Index.

costs Court-imposed charges or fees directly related to litigation in that court, e.g., filing fees. (Usually does not include attorney fees.) Also called court costs.

Costs are generally defined as the statutory fees to which officers, witnesses, jurors, and others are entitled for their services in an action and which the statutes authorize to be taxed and included in the judgment. *Cave,* 94 Ohio St.3d 299 (Ohio 2002)

costs to abide the event Court costs that will be awarded to the prevailing party at the conclusion of the case.

cotenancy An interest in property whereby two or more owners have an undivided right to possession.

cotrustees Two or more persons who administer a trust together.

council An assembly or body that meets to advise or to legislate.

counsel 1. An attorney. A client's lawyer. Also called counselor, counselor at law. 2. Advice. 3. To give advice, to advise.

counselor See counsel (1).

count In pleading, a separate claim (cause of action) or charge.

counterclaim An independent claim by one side in a case filed in response to a claim asserted by an opponent.

Under both the Ohio and federal civil rules, the concept of counterclaim is broad and encompasses both setoff and recoupment. *Laventhol,* 62 Ohio Misc.2d 718 (Ohio Mun., 1991)

counterfeit To copy without authority in order to deceive by passing off the copy as genuine; fraudulent imitation, forgery.

countermand To change or revoke instructions previously given.

counteroffer A response by someone to whom an offer is made that constitutes a new offer, thereby rejecting the other's offer.

counterpart A corresponding part or a duplicate of a document.

countersign To sign in addition to the signature of another in order to verify the identity of the other signer.

county The largest territorial and governmental division within most states.

county commissioners Officers who manage county government.

coupon An interest or dividend certificate attached to a bond or other instrument that can be detached and presented for payment.

course of business What is usually and normally done in a business. Also called ordinary or regular course of business.

course of dealing A pattern of prior conduct between the parties.

course of employment Conduct of an employee that fulfills his or her employment duties.

Phrase "in course of," in statute providing that injury must have occurred in course of and arising out of employment to be compensable by workers' compensation, relates to time, place, and circumstances of injury. R.C. § 4123.01(C). *Carrick,* 115 Ohio App.3d 573 (Ohio App., 1996)

course of performance Repeated occasions for performing a contract in the past by either party with knowledge of the nature of the performance and opportunities for objection to it.

court 1. A unit of the judicial branch of government that applies the law to disputes and administers justice. 2. A judge or group of judges on the same tribunal.

court costs See costs.

court en banc See en banc.

court-martial A military court for trying members of the armed services for offenses violating military law.

court of appeals The middle appeals court in most judicial systems and the highest appellate court in a few.

court of chancery See chancery (2), equity (1).

court of claims A court that hears claims against the government for which sovereign immunity has been waived.

court of common pleas (C.P.) 1. A trial court in several states, e.g., Ohio, Pennsylvania. 2. An appellate court in some states.

court of equity See court of law, equity (1).

court of law 1. A court that applied the common law as opposed to a court of equity that applied equitable principles.

court reporter See reporter.

covenant A promise or contract, e.g., a promise made in a deed or other legal instrument.

covenantee One to whom a promise by covenant is made.

covenant for quiet enjoyment A grantor's promise that the grantee's possession will not be disturbed by any other claimant with a superior lawful title.

covenant marriage A form of marriage that requires proof of premarital counseling, a promise to seek marital counseling when needed during the marriage, and proof of marital fault to dissolve.

covenant not to compete A promise in an employment contract or contract for the sale of a business not to engage in competitive activities, usually within a specified geographic area and for limited time. Also called restrictive covenant.

covenant of seisin An assurance that the grantor has the very estate in quantity and quality that he or she purports to convey to the grantee. Also called right-to-convey covenant.

covenant of warranty An assurance that the grantee has been given good title and a promise to provide compensation if the title is attacked.

covenantor One who makes a promise by covenant to another.

covenant running with the land A covenant whose benefits or duties bind all later purchasers of the land.

cover The right of a buyer, after breach by the seller, to purchase goods in substitution for those due from the seller.

> After a breach within the preceding section, the buyer may "cover" by making in good faith and without unreasonable delay any reasonable purchase of or contract to purchase goods in substitution for those due from the seller. R.C. § 1302.86(A)

coverage The amount and extent of risk included in insurance.

coverture The legal status of a married woman whereby her civil existence for many purposes merged with that of her husband.

craft union A labor union whose members do the same kind of work (e.g., plumbing) across different industries. Also called horizontal union.

credibility Believability; the extent to which something is worthy of belief.

> The quality in a witness that renders his or her evidence worthy of belief. *State v. Schecter*, 47 Ohio App.2d 113 (Ohio App., 1974). Ohio Evid. R. Rule 806

credit 1. The ability to acquire goods or services before payment. 2. Funds loaned. 3. An accounting entry for a sum received. 4. A deduction from the amount owed.

credit bureau A business that collects financial information on the creditworthiness of potential customers of businesses.

credit insurance Insurance against the risk of a debtor's nonpayment due to insolvency or other cause.

> (A) Consumer credit insurance means credit life insurance and credit accident and health insurance. (B) Credit life insurance means insurance on the life of a debtor pursuant to or in connection with a specific loan or other credit transaction. (C) Credit accident and health insurance means insurance on a debtor to provide indemnity for payments becoming due on a specific loan or other credit transaction while the debtor is disabled as defined in the policy. R.C. § 3918.02

credit line See line of credit.

creditor One to whom a debt is owed.

creditor beneficiary A third person who is to receive the benefit of the performance of a contract (of which he or she is not a direct party) in satisfaction of a legal duty owed to him or her by one of the parties of that contract.

creditor's bill An equitable proceeding brought by a judgment creditor to enforce the judgment out of the judgment debtor's property that cannot be reached by ordinary legal process.

credit rating An assessment of one's ability to repay debts.

crime Conduct defined as criminal by the government.

> Crime means any of the following: (1) A felony; (2) A violation of section 2903.05, 2903.06, 2903.13, 2903.21, 2903.211, 2903.22, 2907.06, 2919.25, or 2921.04 of the Revised Code, a violation of section 2903.07 of the Revised Code as it existed prior to the effective date of this amendment, or a violation of a substantially equivalent municipal ordinance. R.C. § 2930.01(A)

crime against humanity Conduct prohibited by international law that is knowingly committed as part of a widespread or systematic attack against any civilian population.

crime against nature See sodomy.

crimen falsi A crime involving false statements, e.g., perjury.

crime of passion A crime committed in the heat of an emotionally charged moment.

criminal 1. One who has committed or been convicted of a crime. 2. Pertaining to crimes.

criminal action A prosecution for a crime.

criminal assault See assault.

criminal attempt See attempt.

criminal conspiracy See conspiracy.

criminal contempt An act directed against the authority of the court that obstructs the administration of justice and tends to bring the court into disrepute.

> A criminal contempt is one in which the court imposes a definite punitive sentence, for the purpose of punishing the contemnor for defying the court's authority; its purpose is punitive, to uphold the authority of the court and vindicate the law. *In re Contemnor Caron*, 110 Ohio Misc.2d 58 (Ohio Com.Pl., 2000)

criminal conversation (crim. con.) A tort that is committed when the defendant has sexual relations with the plaintiff's spouse.

criminal forfeiture An action against a defendant convicted of a crime to seize his or her property as part of the punishment.

criminalize To declare that specific conduct will constitute a crime.

criminal law Laws defining crimes, punishments, and procedures for investigation and prosecution. Also called penal law.

criminal mischief See malicious mischief.

criminal negligence Conduct that is such a gross deviation from the standard of reasonable care that it is punishable as a crime.

> The line between ordinary and criminal negligence is to be distinguished by the trier of fact by considering the surrounding circumstances. Reasonable inferences can be drawn to find a criminally negligent culpable mental state. *In re Tiber,* 154 Ohio App.3d 360 (Ohio App., 2003)

criminal procedure The law governing the investigation and prosecution of crimes, including sentencing and appeal.

criminal syndicalism Advocacy of crime or other unlawful methods of achieving industrial or political change.

criminal trespass Knowingly entering or remaining on land with notice that this is forbidden.

> (A) No person, without privilege to do so, shall do any of the following: (1) Knowingly enter or remain on the land or premises of another; . . . (D) Whoever violates this section is guilty of criminal trespass, a misdemeanor of the fourth degree. R.C. § 2911.21

criminology The study of the causes, punishment, and prevention of crime.

critical legal studies (CLS) The theory that law is not neutral but exists to perpetuate the interests of those who are rich and powerful. *Critical race theory* emphasizes the disadvantages imposed on racial minorities under this theory.

critical stage A step in a criminal investigation or proceeding that holds significant consequences for the accused, at which time the right to counsel applies.

cross action 1. A claim brought by the defendant against the plaintiff in the same action. Sometimes called a counterclaim. 2. A claim brought by one defendant against another defendant or by one plaintiff against another plaintiff in the same action. Also called a cross-claim.

cross appeal An appeal by the appellee in the case that the appellant has appealed.

cross bill An equitable claim brought by the defendant against the plaintiff or another defendant in the same suit.

cross-claim See cross action (2).

cross collateral 1. Pooling collateral among participants. 2. Collateral used to secure additional loans or accounts.

cross-complaint 1. A claim by the defendant against another party in the same case. 2. A claim by the defendant against someone not now a party in the case that is related to the claim already filed against the defendant.

cross-examination Questioning a witness by an opponent after the other side called and questioned that witness.

> The term cross-examination does not strictly import anything more than a leading and searching inquiry of the witness for further disclosure touching the particular matters detailed by him in his examination in chief. *Aluminum Industries,* 61 Ohio App. 111 (Ohio App., 1938)

crown cases A criminal case brought in England.

cruel and unusual punishment Degrading or disproportionate punishment, shocking the conscience and offending human dignity.

cruelty The intentional or malicious infliction of serious mental or physical suffering on another.

> The term extreme cruelty is not limited in scope to acts of physical violence or reasonable apprehension thereof, but is sufficiently broad to encompass acts and conduct, effect of which is calculated to permanently destroy peace of mind and happiness of one of the parties to the marriage and thereby render marital relationship intolerable. R.C. § 3105.01. *Verplatse,* 17 Ohio App.3d 99 (Ohio App., 1984)

CTA See cum testamento annexo.

culpable At fault; blameworthy.

cum Together with, along with.

cum testamento annexo (CTA) Concerning administration of an estate where no executor is named in the will, or where one is named but is unable to serve. Administration with the will annexed.

cumulative That which repeats earlier material and consolidates it with new material. Added and combined into one unit.

cumulative dividend A dividend that, if not paid in one period, is added to dividends to be paid in the next period.

cumulative evidence Additional evidence tending to prove the same point as other evidence already given.

> Additional evidence of the same kind to the same point. *Blake,* 116 N.E.2d 827 (Ohio App., 1951)

cumulative legacy An additional gift of personal property in the same will (or its codicil) to the same person.

cumulative sentences See consecutive sentences.

cumulative voting A type of voting in which a voter is given as many votes are there are positions to fill and can use the votes for one candidate or spread them among several candidates.

curative Tending to correct or cure a mistake or error.

curator A guardian or custodian of another's affairs.

cure 1. To remove a legal defect or error. 2. The seller's right, after delivering defective goods, to redeliver conforming goods.

current asset Property that can readily be converted into cash.

current liabilities A debt that is likely to be paid within the current business cycle, usually a year.

curtesy A husband's right to lifetime use of land his deceased wife owned during the marriage if a child was born alive to them.

> The estate by the curtesy is abolished. R.C. § 2103.09

curtilage The land (often enclosed) immediately surrounding and associated with a dwelling house.

custodial interrogation Questioning by law enforcement officers after a person is taken into custody or otherwise deprived of his or her freedom in any significant way.

custodian One with responsibility for the care and custody of property, a person, papers, etc.

custody The protective care and control of a thing or person.

custom 1. An established practice that has acquired the force of law. 2. A tax (duty) on the importation and exportation of goods.

> Custom or usage, in context of the "under color of state law" requirement of § 1983, is that which has become common

law, such that it must have the force of law by virtue of the persistent practices of state officials. *Peoples Rights Org.*, 142 Ohio App.3d 443 (Ohio App., 2001)

cy-pres As near as possible. The intention of the author of an instrument (e.g., will, trust) will be carried out as closely as possible if carrying it out literally is impossible.

D

DA 1. District Attorney. 2. Deposit account.

dactylography The study of identification through fingerprints.

damage An injury or loss to person, property, or rights.

damages Monetary compensation a court can award for wrongful injury or loss to person or property.

"Damages," absent a restrictive modifier like "compensatory," "actual," "consequential" or "punitive," is an inclusive term when used in a statute, embracing the panoply of legally recognized pecuniary relief. *Rice*, 84 Ohio St.3d 417 (Ohio 1999)

damnum absque injuria A loss that cannot be the basis of a lawsuit because it was not caused by a wrongful act.

dangerous instrumentality An object or condition that in its normal operation is an implement of destruction or involves grave danger.

date of issue The date fixed or agreed upon as the beginning or effective date of a security or document in a series (e.g., bonds).

date rape Rape committed by the victim's social escort.

day in court The right to assert your claim or defense in court.

daybook A book on which daily business transactions are recorded.

dba (d/b/a) Doing business as. A trade name; an assumed name.

dbn See de bonus non.

DC District Court; District of Columbia.

dead freight The amount paid for the portion of a ship's cargo space that is contracted for but not used.

deadlock 1. A standstill due to a refusal of the parties to compromise. 2. The threatened destruction of a business that results when contending shareholders owning an equal number of shares cannot agree.

deadly force Force that is likely or intended to cause death or great bodily harm.

Any force that carries a substantial risk that it will proximately result in the death of any person. R.C. § 2901.01(A)(2)

deadly weapon A weapon or other instrument intended to be used or likely to be used to cause death or great bodily harm. Also called lethal weapon.

dead man's statute A rule making some statements of a dead person inadmissible when offered to support claims against the estate of the dead person.

dealer 1. One who buys goods for resale to others. 2. One who buys and sells securities on his or her own account rather than as an agent.

death Permanent cessation of all vital functions and signs.

deathbed declaration See dying declaration.

death certificate An official record of someone's death, often including vital information such as the date and cause of death.

death knell exception A nonfinal order is appealable if delaying the appeal will cause a party to lose substantial rights.

death penalty Capital punishment; a death sentence.

death qualified rule In a death penalty case, prospective jurors who oppose the death penalty should not be selected.

death tax See estate tax, inheritance tax.

death warrant A court order to carry out a death sentence.

debar To prohibit someone from possessing or doing something.

de bene esse Conditionally allowed for now.

debenture A bond or other debt backed by the general credit of a corporation and not secured by a lien on any specific property.

de bonis non (dbn) Of the goods not administered. An administrator de bonis non is an administrator appointed (in place of a former administrator or executor) to administer the remainder of an estate.

debit A sum owed; an entry made on the left side of an account.

debt An amount of money that is due; an enforceable obligation.

A debt for which State Constitution prohibited imprisonment is a voluntary consensual contract obligation and arises out of promises and consideration between debtor and creditor. Ohio Const. art. 1, § 15. *City of Cincinnati v. De Golyer*, 26 Ohio App.2d 178 (Ohio App., 1971)

debt capital Money raised by issuing bonds rather than stock.

debtor One who owes a debt, usually money.

debtor in possession A debtor in bankruptcy while still running its business.

debt service Payments to be made to a lender, including interest, principal, and fees.

deceased A dead person.

decedent A dead person.

Decedent means a deceased individual and includes a stillborn infant or fetus. R.C. § 2108.01(B)

decedent's estate Property (real and personal) in which a person has an interest at the time of his or her death.

deceit Willfully or recklessly misrepresenting or suppressing material facts with the intent to mislead someone.

decertify 1. To withdraw or revoke certification. 2. To declare that a union can no linger represent a group of employees.

decision A determination of a court or administrative agency applying the law to the facts to resolve a conflict.

decisional law Case law; the law found in court opinions.

declarant A person who makes a declaration or statement.

A declarant is a person who makes a statement. Ohio Evid. R. Rule 801(B)

declaration 1. A formal or explicit statement. 2. An unsworn statement. 3. The first pleading of the plaintiff in an action at law.

declaration against interest A statement made by a nonparty that is against his or her own interest. The statement can be admitted as an exception to the hearsay rule if it was made by someone with personal knowledge who is now not available as a witness.

declaration of trust The establishment of a trust by one who declares that he or she holds the legal title to property in trust for another.

declaratory judgment A binding judgment that declares rights, status, or other legal relationships without ordering anything to be done.

> Declaratory judgment is a binding adjudication of contested rights of litigants, whereas advisory opinion is merely an opinion of a judge of a court that adjudicates nothing and is binding on no one. *Village of Moscow*, 29 Ohio Misc.2d 15 (Ohio Com.Pl., 1984)

declaratory statute A statute passed to remove doubt about the meaning of an earlier statute. Also called expository statute.

decree 1. A court order. 2. The decision of a court of equity.

decree nisi A decree that will become absolute unless a party convinces the court that it should not be. Also called order nisi, rule nisi.

decretal Pertaining to a decree.

decriminalization A law making legal what was once criminal.

dedication A gift of private land (or an easement) for public use.

deductible 1. What can be taken away or subtracted. 2. The amount of a loss the insured must bear before insurance payments begin.

deduction The part taken away, e.g., an amount that can be subtracted from gross income when calculating adjusted gross income.

deed 1. A document transferring (conveying) an interest in land. 2. An act; something that is done or carried out.

> Deed means any deed, instrument, or writing by which any real property or any interest in real property is granted, assigned, transferred, or otherwise conveyed. R.C. § 322.01(D)

deed of trust A security instrument (similar to a mortgage) in which title to real property is given to a trustee as security until the debt is paid Also called trust deed, trust indenture.

deem To treat as if; to regard something as true or present even if this is not actually so.

deep pocket An individual, business, or other organization with resources to pay a potential judgment. The opposite of shallow pocket.

Deep Rock doctrine A controlling shareholder's loan to its own company that is undercapitalized may, in fairness, be subordinated in bankruptcy to other loan claims.

deface To mar or destroy the physical appearance of something.

de facto 1. In fact. 2. Functioning or existing even if not formally or officially encouraged or authorized.

> The phrase de facto with respect to adoption proceedings is used in contradistinction to the phrase de jure and the former means arising out of or founded in fact, in contrast with de jure, meaning of right, legitimate, lawful, or by right and just title. *Logan*, 111 Ohio App. 534 (Ohio App., 1960)

de facto corporation An enterprise that attempts to exercise corporate powers even though it was not properly incorporated in a state where it could have incorporated and where it made a good faith effort to do so.

de facto government A government that has assumed the exercise of sovereignty over a nation, often by illegal or extralegal means.

de facto segregation Segregation caused by social, economic, or other factors rather than by state action or active government assistance.

defalcation 1. A fiduciary's failure to account for funds entrusted to it. Misappropriation; embezzlement. 2. The failure to comply with an obligation.

defamation The publication of a written (or gestured) defamatory statement (libel) or an oral one (slander) of and concerning the plaintiff that harms the plaintiff's reputation.

> A false statement published by a defendant acting with the required degree of fault, that injures a person's reputation, exposes the person to public hatred, contempt, ridicule, shame or disgrace, or adversely affects the person's profession. *Burns*, 157 Ohio App.3d 620 (Ohio App., 2004)

default 1. The failure to carry out a duty. 2. The failure to appear.

default judgment A judgment against a party for failure to file a required pleading or otherwise respond to the opponent's claim.

defeasance 1. The act of rendering something null and void. 2. An instrument that defeats the force or operation of an estate or deed upon the fulfillment of a condition.

defeasible Subject to being revoked or avoided.

defeasible fee See fee simple defeasible.

defeat To prevent, frustrate, or circumvent; to render void.

defect A shortcoming; the lack of something required.

defective Lacking in some particular that is essential to completeness, safety, or legal sufficiency.

defend 1. To protect or represent someone. 2. To contest or oppose.

defendant One against whom a civil action or criminal prosecution is brought.

defender 1. One who raises defenses. 2. One who represents another.

defense 1. An allegation of fact or a legal theory offered to offset or defeat a claim or demand. 2. The defendant and his or her attorney.

> A right possessed by a defendant, arising from facts alleged in his pleadings, which defeats plaintiff's cause of action or claim for remedy demanded by his action. *Eagle*, 71 Ohio App. 485 (Ohio App., 1942)

deferred annuity An annuity that begins payment at a future date.

deferred compensation Work income set aside for payment in the future.

deferred income Income to be received in the future, after it was earned.

deficiency 1. A shortage or insufficiency. 2. The amount still owed.

deficiency judgment A judgment for an unpaid balance after the creditor has taken the secured property of the debtor.

deficit 1. An excess of outlays over revenues. 2. An insufficiency.

defined benefit plan A pension plan where the amount of the benefit is fixed but the amount of the contribution is not.

defined contribution plan A pension plan where the amount of the contribution is generally fixed but the amount of the benefit is not.

definite failure of issue See failure of issue.

definite sentence See determinate sentence.

definitive Complete; settling the matter.

defraud To use deception to obtain something or harm someone.

> To knowingly obtain, by deception, some benefit for oneself or another, or to knowingly cause, by deception, some detriment to another. R.C. § 2913.01(B)

degree 1. The measure or scope of the seriousness of something; a grade or level of wrongdoing. 2. One of the steps in a process. 3. A step in the line of descent.

degree of care The standard of care that is required.

degree of proof The level of believability or persuasiveness that one's evidence must meet.

dehors Beyond the scope, outside of.

de jure Sanctioned by law; in compliance with the law.

de jure segregation Segregation allowed or mandated by the law.

del credere agent A business agent or factor who guarantees the solvency and performance of the purchaser.

delectus personae The right of a partner to exercise his or her preference on the admission of new partners.

delegable duty A responsibility that one can ask another to perform.

delegate 1. To appoint a representative. 2. A representative.

delegation 1. The granting of authority to act for another. 2. The persons authorized to act as representatives.

> Nursing delegation means the process . . . under which a registered nurse or licensed practical nurse acting at the direction of a registered nurse transfers the performance of a particular nursing activity or task to another person who is not otherwise authorized to perform the activity or task. R.C. § 5123.41(J)

deliberate 1. To weigh or examine carefully. 2. Intentional.

deliberative process privilege The government can maintain secrecy when needed to ensure the free exchange of ideas in the making of policy.

delict, delictum A tort or offense; a violation of the law.

delinquency 1. A violation of duty. 2. The failure to pay a debt. 3. Misconduct, unruly, or immoral behavior by a minor.

delinquent 1. Pertaining to that which is still due; in arrears. 2. Failing to abide by the law or to conform to moral standards. 3. A minor who has committed an offense or other serious misconduct.

> Delinquent child includes any of the following: (1) Any child, except a juvenile traffic offender, who violates any law of this state or the United States, or any ordinance of a political subdivision of the state, that would be an offense if committed by an adult; . . . (4) Any child who is a habitual truant and who previously has been adjudicated an unruly child for being a habitual truant; (5) Any child who is a chronic truant. R.C. § 2152.02(F)

delisting Removing a security from the list of what can be traded on an exchange.

delivery 1. The act by which something is placed in the possession or control of another. 2. That which is delivered.

demand 1. To claim as one's due or right. 2. The assertion of a right.

demand deposit Any bank deposit that the depositor may withdraw (demand) at any time without notice.

demand loan A loan without a set maturity date that the lender can demand payment of at any time. A call loan.

demand note A note that must be paid whenever the lender requests (demands) payment.

demeanor Outward or physical appearance or behavior; deportment.

demesne 1. Domain 2. Land a person holds in his or her own right.

de minimis Very small; not significant enough to change the result.

demise 1. A lease. A conveyance of land to another for a term. 2. The document that creates a lease. 3. To convey or create an estate or lease. 4. To transfer property by descent or by will. 5. Death.

demise charter See bareboat charter.

democracy A system of government controlled by the people directly or through elected representatives.

demonstrative bequest; demonstrative legacy A gift by will payable out of a specific fund.

> A pecuniary gift to be paid out of a specified fund. *In re Estate of Oberstar*, 126 Ohio App.3d 30 (Ohio App., 1998)

demonstrative evidence Evidence (other than testimony) addressed to the senses. Physical evidence offered for illumination and explanation, but otherwise unrelated to the case. Also called autopic evidence.

demur 1. To state a demurrer. 2. To take exception.

demurrer A pleading that admits, for the sale of argument, the allegations of fact made by the other party in order to show that even if they are true, they are do not entitle this party to relief.

denial 1. A declaration that something the other side alleges is not true. 2. Rejection; refusing to do something.

de novo Anew; as if for the first time. See trial de novo.

depecage Under conflicts of law principles, a court can apply the laws of different jurisdictions to different disputes in the same case.

dependency 1. A geographically separate territory under the jurisdiction of another country or sovereign. 2. A relationship in which one person relies on another for society or a standard of living.

> Chemical dependency means either of the following: (a) The chronic and habitual use of alcoholic beverages to the extent that the user no longer can control the use of alcohol or endangers the user's health, safety, or welfare or that of others; (b) The use of a drug of abuse to the extent that the user becomes physically or psychologically dependent on the drug or endangers the user's health, safety, or welfare or that of others. R.C. § 2151.3514(A)(2)

dependent 1. One who derives his or her main support from another. 2. A person who can be claimed as a personal exemption by a taxpayer.

dependent covenant A party's agreement or promise whose performance is conditioned on and subject to prior performance by the other party.

dependent relative revocation The revocation of an earlier will was intended to give effect to a later will, so if the later will is inoperative, the earlier will shall take effect.

depletion An exhausting or reduction during the taxable year of oil, gas, or other mineral deposits and reserves.

deponent One who gives testimony at a deposition.

deport To banish or exile someone to a foreign country.

depose 1. To question a witness in a deposition. 2. To give testimony. 3. To remove from office or power.

deposit 1. To place for safekeeping. 2. An asset placed for safekeeping. 3. Money given as security or earnest money for the performance of a contract. Also called security deposit.

Deposit means to place money in the custody of a financial organization for the purpose of establishing an income-bearing account by purchase or otherwise. R.C. § 169.01(I)

depositary A person or institution (e.g., bank) that receives an asset for safekeeping.

depositary bank The first bank to which checks or other deposits are taken for collection.

deposition A method of discovery by which parties or their prospective witnesses are questioned outside the courtroom before trial.

deposition de bene esse A deposition of a witness who will not be able to testify at trial, taken in order to preserve his or her testimony.

depository The place where an asset is placed and kept for safekeeping.

depreciable life The period over which an asset may reasonably be expected to be useful in a trade or business. Also called useful life.

depreciation A gradual decline in the value of property caused by use, deterioration, time, or obsolescence.

Depreciation means a reduction in value due to wear, tear, decay, corrosion, or gradual obsolescence of a fixed asset having a useful life of more than one year. R.C. § 1340.83(A)

deputy One duly authorized to act on behalf of another.

deregulate To lessen government control over an industry or business.

derelict 1. Abandoned property. 2. Delinquent in a duty.

dereliction 1. A wrongful or shameful neglect or abandonment of one's duty. 2. The gaining of land from the water as a result of a shrinking back of the sea or river below the usual watermark.

derivative 1. Coming from another; secondary. 2. A financial instrument whose value is dependent on another asset or investment.

A derivative claim or action is a lawsuit resulting from an injury to another person, such as one spouse's action for loss of consortium arising from an injury to the other spouse caused by a third person. *Thomson*, 150 Ohio App.3d 352 (Ohio App., 2002)

derivative action 1. A suit by a shareholder to enforce a corporate cause of action. Also called a derivative suit, representative action. 2. An action to recover for a loss that is dependent on an underlying tort or wrong committed against someone else.

derivative evidence Evidence that is inadmissible because it is derived or spawned from other evidence that was illegally obtained.

derivative suit See derivative action (1).

derivative work A translation or other transformation of a preexisting work.

derogation 1. A partial repeal or abolishing of a law, as by a subsequent act that limits its scope or force. 2. Disparaging or belittling, or undermining something or someone.

descend To be transferred to persons entitled to receive a deceased's assets by intestate succession. To pass by inheritance.

descendant Offspring; persons in the bloodline of an ancestor.

Synonyms "descendant," "issue," and "offspring" are ordinarily used to refer to those who have issued from individual and include his children, grandchildren and their children to the remotest degree; no distinction is ordinarily made between "heir" and "next of kin." *First Nat. Bank of Cincinnati*, 15 Ohio Misc. 109 (Ohio Prob., 1967)

descent A transfer to persons entitled to receive a deceased's assets by intestate succession. Passing by inheritance.

descent and distribution 1. See intestate succession. 2. The passing of a decedent's assets by intestacy or will.

desecrate To violate something that is sacred; to defile.

desegregation The elimination of policies and laws that led to racial segregation.

desertion 1. The voluntary, unjustified leaving of one's spouse for an uninterrupted period of time with the intent not to return to resume marital cohabitation. 2. The willful failure to fulfill a support obligation. 3. Remaining absent (without authority) from one's military place of duty with the intent to remain away permanently.

design defect A flaw rendering a product unreasonably dangerous because of the way in which it was designed or conceived.

designer drug A synthetic substitute for an existing controlled substance or drug, often made to avoid anti-drug laws.

destination contract A contract in which the risk of loss passes to the buyer when the seller tenders the goods at the destination.

destructibility of contingent remainders A contingent remainder must vest before or at the end of the preceding estate, or it fails (is destroyed).

desuetude 1. Discontinuation of use. 2. The equivalent of a repeal of a law by reason of its long and continued nonuse.

detainer 1. Withholding possession of land or goods from another. Keeping someone or something in your custody. See also unlawful detainer. 2. A request or writ that an institution continue keeping someone in custody.

A detainer is a warrant filed against a person already in custody with the purpose of insuring that he will be available to the authority which has placed the detainer or a notification filed with the institution in which a prisoner is serving a sentence, advising that he is wanted to face pending criminal charges in another jurisdiction. *State v. Brown*, 152 Ohio App.3d 8 (Ohio App., 2003)

detention Holding in custody; confinement.

determinable 1. Capable of coming to an end (terminable) upon the occurrence of a contingency. 2. Susceptible of being determined, ascertained, or settled.

determinable fee See fee simple determinable.

determinate sentence A sentence to confinement for a fixed period. Also called definite sentence.

determination 1. The final decision of a court or administrative agency. 2. The ending of an estate or property interest.

detinue An action for the recovery of personal property held (detained) wrongfully by another.

detraction Transferring property to another state upon a transfer of the title to it by will or inheritance.

detriment 1. Any loss or harm to person or property. 2. A legal right that a promisee gives up. Also called legal detriment.

Detriment comprising consideration necessary to support contract may consist of some forbearance, loss, or responsibility given, suffered, or undertaken by promisee. *Crocker,* 113 Ohio App.3d 478 (Ohio App., 1996)

detrimental reliance A loss, disadvantage, or change in one's position for the worse because of one's reliance on another's promise.

devaluation A reduction in the value of a currency in relation to other currencies.

devastavit An act of omission, negligence, or misconduct of an administrator or other legal representative of an estate.

devest See divest.

deviation Departure from established or usual conduct or ideology.

deviation doctrine A variation in the terms of a will or trust will be allowed to avoid defeating the purposes of the document.

Under doctrine of deviation, a court can direct or permit deviation from terms of trust where compliance is impossible or illegal, or where owing to circumstances not known to settlor and not anticipated by him compliance would defeat or substantially impair accomplishment of purposes of trust. *Daloia,* 79 Ohio St.3d 98 (Ohio 1997)

device 1. A mechanical or electronic invention or gadget. 2. A scheme.

devise The gift of property (sometimes only real property) by a will.

devisee The person to whom property is devised or given in a will.

devisor The person who devises or gives property in a will.

devolution The transfer or transition of a right, title, estate, or office to another or to a lower level. The verb is devolve.

devolve See devolution.

dicta See dictum, which is the singular form of dicta.

dictum 1. An observation made by a judge in an opinion that is not essential to resolve the issues before the court; comments that go beyond the facts before the court. Also called obiter dictum. 2. An authoritative, formal statement or announcement.

dies A day; days, e.g., dies non juridicus: A day on which courts are not open for business.

diet The name of the legislature in some countries.

digest An organized summary or abridgment. A set of volumes that contain brief summaries of court opinions, arranged by subject matter and by court or jurisdiction.

dilatory plea A plea raising a procedural matter, not on the merits.

diligence 1. Persistent activity. 2. Prudence, carefulness.

dilution Diminishing the strength or value of something, e.g., voting strength by increasing the number of shares issued, uniqueness of a trademark by using it on too many different products.

diminished capacity or **responsibility** A mental disorder not amounting to insanity that impairs or negates the defendant's ability to form the culpable mental state to commit the crime. Also called partial insanity.

Doctrine of diminished capacity does not attempt to distinguish sane from the insane, but rather, attempts to ascertain whether particular person who does not meet insanity test could have formed specific intent to commit the crime of which he or she is accused. *State v. Wong,* 95 Ohio App.3d 39 (Ohio App., 1994)

diminution in value As a measure of damages, the difference between the fair market value of the property with and without the damage.

diplomatic immunity A diplomat's exemption from most laws of the host country.

direct 1. To command, regulate, or manage. 2. To aim or cause to move in a certain direction. 3. Without interruption; immediate. 4. In a straight line of descent, as opposed to a collateral line.

direct attack An attempt to have a judgment changed in the same case or proceeding that rendered the judgment, e.g., an appeal.

direct cause See proximate cause.

direct contempt A contempt committed in the presence of the court or so near the court as to interrupt its proceedings.

Direct contempt occurs in the presence of the court, while indirect contempt occurs outside its immediate presence. R.C. §2705.02. *Adkins,* 2002 WL 1070693 (Ohio App., 2002)

direct damages See general damages.

directed verdict A judge's decision not to allow the jury to deliberate because only one verdict is reasonable. In federal court, the verdict is called a *judgment as a matter of law* (see this phrase).

direct estoppel See collateral estoppel.

direct evidence Evidence that, if believed, proves a fact without using inferences or presumptions; evidence based on what one personally saw, heard, or touched. Also called positive evidence.

direct examination The first questioning of a witness by the party who has called the witness. Also called examination in chief.

direct line A line of descent traced through those persons who are related to each other directly as descendants or ascendants.

director 1. One who directs or guides a department, organization, or activity. 2. A member of the board that oversees and controls the managers or officers of an entity such as a corporation.

directory Nonmandatory. Pertaining to a clause or provision in a statute or contract that is advisory rather than involving the essence of the statute or contract.

A mandatory statutory provision is one which, if not followed, renders the proceeding to which it relates illegal and void, while a directory provision is one the observance of which is not necessary to the validity of the proceeding. *Woodmansee,* 115 Ohio App. 409 (Ohio App., 1961)

directory trust A trust whose details will by filled out by later instructions.

direct tax A tax imposed directly on property rather than on the transfer of property or on some other right connected with property.

disability 1. Legal incapacity to perform an act. 2. A physical or mental condition that limits one's ability to participate in a major life activity such as employment. Also called incapacity.

disaffirm To repudiate; to cancel or revoke consent.

disallow To refuse to allow; to deny or reject.

disavow To repudiate; to disclaim knowledge of or responsibility for.

disbar To expel an attorney or revoke his or her license to practice law.

disbursement Paying out money; an out-of-pocket expenditure.

discharge 1. To relieve of an obligation. 2. To fulfill an obligation. 3. To release or let go. 4. To cancel a court order. 5. To shoot. 6. To release from employment or service.

In civil service law a discharge refers to removal of employee from his position and not to elimination of position itself. *Durbin*, 120 Ohio App. 366 (Ohio App., 1964)

discharge in bankruptcy The release of a bankrupt from all nonexcepted debts in a bankruptcy proceeding.

disciplinary rule (DR) A rule stating the minimum conduct below which no attorney should fall without being subject to discipline.

disclaimer The repudiation of a one's own or another's claim, right, or obligation.

disclosure 1. The act of revealing that which is secret or not known. 2. Complying with a legal duty to provide specified information.

discontinuance 1. The plaintiff's withdrawal or termination of his or her suit. 2. In zoning, the abandonment of a use.

discount 1. An allowance or deduction from the original price or debt. 2. The amount by which interest is reduced from the face value of a note or other financial instrument at the outset of the loan. 3. The amount by which the price paid for a security is less than its face value.

Discount refers to that step in lending transaction where interest on loan is taken in advance by deducting amount therefor for term of loan, giving borrower face value of obligation less interest. *Russell*, 27 Ohio Misc. 171 (Ohio Com.Pl., 1966)

discounting Converting future cash flows into a present value.

discount rate 1. A percentage of the face amount of commercial paper (e.g., note) that an issuer pays when transferring the paper to a financial institution. 2. The interest rate charged by the Federal Reserve to member banks.

discoverable Pertaining to information or other materials an opponent can obtain through a deposition or other discovery device.

discovered peril doctrine See last clear chance doctrine.

discovery Compulsory exchanges of information between parties in litigation. Pretrial devices (e.g., interrogatories) to obtain information about a suit from the other side.

discredit To cast doubt on the credibility of a person, an idea, or evidence.

discretion 1. The power or right to act by the dictates of one's own judgment and conscience. 2. The freedom to decide among options. 3. Good judgment; prudence.

Judicial discretion is the option that a judge may exercise between the doing and not doing of a thing that cannot be demanded as absolute legal right, guided by the spirit, principles and analogies of law, and founded upon reason and conscience of judge, to a just result in light of particular circumstances of case. *In re Judicial Campaign Complaint Against Carr*, 74 Ohio Misc.2d 81 (Ohio Comm. of Judges 1995)

discretionary review An appeal that an appellate court agrees to hear when it has the option of refusing to hear it.

discretionary trust A trust giving the trustee discretion to decide when a beneficiary will receive income or principal and how much. Also called complex trust.

discrimination 1. Differential imposition of burdens or granting of benefits. 2. Unreasonably granting or denying privileges on the basis of sex, age, race, nationality, religion, or handicap.

Discrimination means act of making a distinction in favor of or against a person or thing based on the group, class or category to which that person or thing belongs, rather than on individual merit. *Cortner*, 25 Ohio Misc. 156 (Ohio Com.Pl., 1970)

disenfranchise To deprive someone of a right or privilege, e.g., the right to vote. Also called disfranchise.

disfranchise See disenfranchise.

disgorge To surrender unwillingly.

dishonor To refuse to accept or pay a draft or other negotiable instrument when duly presented.

disinheritance Taking steps to prevent someone from inheriting property.

disinterested Objective; without bias; having nothing to gain or lose.

Free from bias, prejudice, or partiality. *State ex rel. Pontillo*, 98 Ohio St.3d 500 (Ohio 2003)

disintermediation The withdrawal by depositors of funds from low-yielding bank accounts for use in higher-yielding investments.

disjunctive allegations Assertions pleaded in the alternative, e.g., he stole the car or caused it to be stolen.

dismissal 1. An order that ends an action or motion without additional court proceedings. 2. A discharge; an order to go away.

dismissal without prejudice Termination of the action that is not on the merits, meaning that the party can return later with the same claim.

dismissal with prejudice Termination of the action that is the equivalent of an adjudication on the merits, meaning that the party is barred from returning later with the same claim.

disorderly conduct Behavior that tends to disturb the peace, endanger the health of the community, or shock the public sense of morality.

disorderly house A dwelling where acts are performed that tend to corrupt morals, promote breaches of the peace, or create a nuisance.

disparagement The intentional and false discrediting of the plaintiff's product or business (sometimes called trade libel when written or slander of goods when spoken) or the plaintiff's title to property (sometimes called slander of title) resulting in specific monetary loss.

> The dissemination to the public in any manner of any false information that a perishable agricultural or aquacultural food product is not safe for human consumption. R.C. § 2307.81(B)(1)

disparate impact Conduct that appears neutral on its face but that disproportionately and negatively impacts members of one race, sex, age, disability, or other protected group.

disparate treatment Intentionally treating some people less favorably than others because of sex, age, race, nationality, religion, or disability.

dispensation An exemption from a duty, burden, penalty, or law.

disposition 1. The act of distributing or transferring assets. 2. The final ruling or decision of a tribunal. 3. An arrangement or settlement. 4. Temperament or characteristics.

dispossess To evict from land; to deprive of possession.

disputable presumption See rebuttable presumption.

dispute 1. A controversy. 2. The conflict leading to litigation.

> Dispute resolution and conflict management includes any process that assists persons with a dispute or a conflict to resolve their differences without further litigation, prosecution, civil unrest, economic disruption, or violence. R.C. § 179.01(A)

disqualification That which renders something ineligible or unfit.

disseisin Wrongful dispossession of another from property.

dissent 1. A judge's vote against the result reached by the judges in the majority on a case. 2. A dissenting opinion.

dissipation 1. Wasting, squandering, or destroying. 2. The use of marital property by a spouse for a personal purpose.

dissolution 1. Cancellation. 2. The act or process of terminating a legal relationship or organization. 3. A divorce.

dist. ct. District court.

distinguish To point out an essential difference; to demonstrate that a particular court opinion is inapplicable to the current legal dispute.

distrain To take and hold the personal property of another until the latter performs an obligation.

distrainee A person who is distrained.

distrainer or **distrainor** One who seizes property under a distress.

distraint Property seized to enforce an obligation.

distress Seizing property to enforce an obligation, e.g., a landlord seizes a tenant's property to secure payment of delinquent rent.

distress sale 1. A foreclosure sale; a forced sale to pay a debt. 2. A sale at below market rates because of a pressure to sell.

distributee One who shares in the distribution of an estate. An heir.

distribution 1. The apportionment and division of something. 2. The transfer of property under the law of intestate succession after estate taxes and other debts are paid.

distributive finding A jury's finding in part for the plaintiff and in part for the defendant.

distributive justice A system of justice where the goal is the fair allocation of available goods, services, and burdens.

district A geographic division for judicial, political, electoral, or administrative purposes.

> The word district, with reference to, among other things, elections, describes a special geographical area over which specific authority, executive, legislative or judicial is exercised by properly constituted officers. *Hammond*, 117 N.E.2d 227 (Ohio Com.Pl., 1953)

district attorney A prosecutor representing the government in criminal cases in an area or district. Also called prosecuting attorney or state attorney.

district court A trial court in the federal and some state judicial systems.

disturbance of the peace See breach of the peace.

divers Various, several.

diversion 1. Turning aside or altering the natural course or route of a thing. 2. An alternative to criminal prosecution leading to the dismissal of the charges if the accused completes a program of rehabilitation. Also called diversion program, pretrial diversion, pretrial intervention.

> Diversion means a withdrawal of water resources from either the Lake Erie or Ohio river drainage basin and transfer to another basin without return. Diversion does not include evaporative loss within the basin of withdrawal. R.C. § 1501.30(A)(2)

diversity of citizenship The disputing parties are citizens of different states. This fact gives jurisdiction (called diversity jurisdiction) to a United States District Court when the amount in controversy exceeds $75,000.

divest To dispose of or be deprived of rights, duties, or possessions. Also spelled devest.

divestiture 1. The selling, spinning off, or surrender of business assets. 2. The requirement that specific property, securities, or other assets be disposed of, often to avoid a restraint of trade.

divided custody A custody arrangement in which the parents alternate having full custody (legal and physical) of a child.

dividend A share of corporate profits given pro rata to stockholders.

divisible Capable of being divided.

divisible contract A contract with parts that can be enforced separately so that the failure to perform one part does not bar recovery for performance of another.

divisible divorce A divorce decree that dissolves the marriage in one proceeding but that resolves other marital issues, such as property division and child custody, in a separate proceeding.

divorce A declaration by a court that a validly entered marriage is dissolved.

divorce a mensa et thoro See legal separation.

divorce a vinculo matrimonii An absolute divorce that terminates the marital relationship.

DNA fingerprinting The process of identifying the genetic makeup of an individual based on the uniqueness of his or her DNA pattern. Deoxyribonucleic acid (DNA) is the carrier of genetic information in living organisms.

DNR Do not resuscitate (a notice concerning terminally ill persons).

dock 1. The space in a criminal court where prisoners stand when brought in for trial. 2. A landing place for boats.

docket 1. A list of pending court cases. 2. A record containing brief notations on the proceedings that have occurred in a court case.

docket number A consecutive number assigned to a case by the court and used on all documents filed with the court during the litigation of that case.

doctor of jurisprudence See juris doctor.

doctor-patient privilege. A patient and doctor can refuse to disclose communications between them concerning diagnosis or treatment. Also called physician-patient privilege.

> The following persons shall not testify in certain respects: . . . (B)(1) A physician or a dentist concerning a communication made to the physician or dentist by a patient in that relation or the physician's or dentist's advice to a patient, except as otherwise provided in this division, division (B)(2), and division (B)(3) of this section, and except that, if the patient is deemed by section 2151.421 of the Revised Code to have waived any testimonial privilege under this division, the physician may be compelled to testify on the same subject. R.C. § 2317.02(B)(1)

doctrine A rule or legal principle.

document 1. Any physical or electronic embodiment of words or ideas (e.g., letter, X-ray plate). 2. To support with documentary evidence or with authorities. 3. To create a written record.

documentary evidence Evidence in the form of something written.

document of title A document giving its holder the right to receive and dispose of goods covered by the document (e.g., a bill of lading).

doing business Carrying on or conducting a business.

doli capax Capable of having the intent to commit a crime.

dolus Fraud; deceitfulness.

domain 1. Land that is owned; an estate in land. 2. Absolute ownership and control. 3. The territory governed by a ruler.

***Dombrowski* doctrine** To protect First Amendment rights, a federal court can enjoin state criminal proceedings based on a vague statute. *Dombrowski v. Pfister*, 85 S. Ct. 1116 (1965).

domestic Concerning one's own country, state, jurisdiction, or family.

domestic corporation A corporation established in a particular state.

domestic partners Persons in a same-sex (or unmarried opposite-sex) relationship who are emotionally and financially interdependent and who register with the government to receive marriage-like benefits.

domestic relations Family law (e.g., the law on adoption and divorce).

domestic violence Actual or threatened physical injury or abuse by one member of a family or household on another member.

> Threats of violence constitute domestic violence for the purpose of a civil protection order (CPO) if the fear resulting from those threats is reasonable; the reasonableness of the fear should be determined with reference to the history between the petitioner and the defendant. R.C. § 3113.31. *Wardeh*, 158 Ohio App.3d 325 (Ohio App., 2004)

domicile 1. The place where someone has physically been present with the intention to make that place a permanent home; the place to which one would intend to return when away. 2. The place where a business has its headquarters or principal place of business. 3. The legal residence of a person or business. (Residence and domicile are sometimes used interchangeably.)

> Domicile has two components: an actual residence in a particular jurisdiction, and an intention to make a permanent home in the jurisdiction. *In re Protest of Brooks*, 155 Ohio App.3d 384 (Ohio App., 2003)

domiciliary Someone who has established a domicile in a place.

domiciliary administration The administration of an estate in the state where the decedent was domiciled at the time of death.

dominant estate The parcel of land that is benefited from an easement. Also called dominant tenement.

dominant tenement See dominant estate.

dominion Ownership or sovereignty; control over something.

donated surplus Assets contributed by shareholders to a corporation.

donatio A gift or donation.

donative intent The donor's intent that title and control of the subject matter of the gift be irrevocably and presently transferred.

donee One to whom a gift or power of appointment is given.

donee beneficiary A nonparty to a contract who receives the benefit of the contract as a gift.

donor One who makes a gift, confers a power, or creates a trust.

> Donor means a man who supplies semen for a non-spousal artificial insemination. R.C. § 3111.88(B)

dormant In abeyance, suspended; temporarily inactive.

dormant judgment An unsatisfied judgment that has remained unexecuted for so long that it needs to be revived before it can be executed.

dormant partner A partner who receives financial benefits from a business, but does not run it and may be unknown to the public. Also called a silent partner, sleeping partner.

double hearsay A hearsay statement contained within another hearsay statement.

double indemnity Twice the benefit for losses from specified causes.

double insurance Overlapping insurance whereby an insured has two or more policies on the same subject and against same the risks.

double jeopardy A second prosecution for the same offense after acquittal or conviction; multiple punishments for the same offense.

double taxation Taxing the same thing twice for the same purpose by the same taxing authority during identical taxing periods.

double will See mutual wills (1).

doubt Uncertainty of mind. See also reasonable doubt.

doubtful title Title that raises serious doubts as to its validity.

dower A wife's right to a life estate in one-third of the land her deceased husband owned in fee at any time during the marriage.

During the lifetime of both spouses, dower is a contingent inchoate right that becomes vested in the surviving spouse only upon the death of the other spouse. *Ogan,* 122 Ohio App.3d 580 (Ohio App., 1997)

down payment An amount of money paid by the buyer to the seller at the time of sale, which represents only a part of the total cost.

dowry Property that a woman brings to her husband upon marriage.

DR See disciplinary rule.

draft 1. An unconditional written order (e.g., a check) by the first party (called the drawer) instructing a second party (called the drawee or payor, e.g., a bank) to pay a specified sum on demand or at a specified time to a third party (called the payee) or to bearer. Also called bill of exchange. 2. A preliminary version of a plan, drawing, memo, or other writing. 3. Compulsory selection; conscription.

Dram Shop Act A law imposing civil liability on a seller of liquor to one whose intoxication causes injury to a third person. Also called civil damage law.

draw 1. To prepare a legal document. 2. To withdraw money. 3. To make and sign (e.g., draw a check to pay the bill). 4. To pick a jury. 5. An advance against profits or amounts owed.

drawee The bank or other entity ordered to pay the amount on a draft.

drawer One who makes and signs a draft for the payment of money.

Dred Scott case The U.S. Supreme Court case holding that slaves and former slaves were not citizens even if they lived in states where slavery was not legal. *Scott v. Sanford,* 60 U.S. 393 (1867).

driving under the influence (DUI); driving while intoxicated (DWI) The offense of operating a motor vehicle while impaired due to alcohol or drugs. States may treat DWI as more serious than or the same as DUI.

droit A legal right; a body of law.

drug-free zone Geographic areas (e.g., near schools) where conviction of a drug offense will lead to increased punishment.

dry 1. Without duties. 2. Prohibiting the sale or use of liquor.

dry trust See passive trust.

dual capacity doctrine An employer may be liable in tort to its employee if it occupies, in addition to its capacity as employer, a second capacity that confers on it obligations independent of those imposed on an employer.

Dual capacity doctrine is a legal theory or vehicle by which workers' compensation laws are sidestepped to allow presentation of common-law negligence or malpractice claims against the employer. *McGee,* 103 Ohio App.3d 236 (Ohio App., 1995)

dual citizenship The status of a person who is a citizen of the United States and of another country at the same time.

dual contract Two contracts by the same parties for the same matter or transaction, something entered to mislead others.

dual-purpose doctrine An employee injured on a trip serving both business and personal purposes is covered under workers' compensation if the trip would have been made for the employer even if there was no personal purpose.

dubitante Having doubt.

duces tecum Bring with you. See also subpoena duces tecum.

due 1. Payable now or on demand; owing. 2. Proper, reasonable.

due-bill An acknowledgement of indebtedness; an IOU.

due care See reasonable care.

due course See holder in due course.

due diligence Reasonable prudence and effort in carrying out an obligation.

due notice Notice likely to reach its target; legally prescribed notice.

due process of law Fundamental fairness in having a dispute resolved according to established procedures and rules, e.g., notice, hearing.

Due process of law assures to every person his day in court; it requires some legal procedure in which the person proceeded against, if he is to be concluded thereby, shall have an opportunity to defend himself, and the open-courts provision in the Ohio Constitution makes similar assurances, although litigants are not assured any particular process. Const. Art. 1, § 16. *Johns,* 101 Ohio St.3d 234 (Ohio 2004)

DUI See driving under the influence.

duly In due and proper form or manner.

dummy 1. One who buys property and holds the legal title for someone else, usually to conceal the identity of the real owner. 2. Sham.

dummy corporation A corporation formed to avoid personal liability or conceal the owner's identity, not to conduct a legitimate business.

dumping 1. Selling in quantity at a very low price. 2. Selling goods abroad at less than their fair market price at home. 3. Shifting a nonpaying patient onto another health care provider.

dun To make a demand for payment.

duplicate A copy or replacement of the original.

duplicity 1. Deception. 2. Improperly uniting two or more causes of action in one count or two or more grounds of defense in one plea. 3. Improperly charging two or more offenses in a single count of an indictment.

duress 1. Coercion; the unlawful use of force or threat of force. 2. Wrongful confinement or imprisonment.

Duress consists of any conduct which overpowers a person's will and coerces or constrains his performance of an act which he otherwise would not have performed. *State v. Grinnell,* 112 Ohio App.3d 124 (Ohio App., 1996)

duress of goods A tort of seizing or detaining another's personal property and wrongfully requiring some act before it is returned.

***Durham* rule** See insanity (3).

duty 1. A legal or moral obligation that another has a right to have performed. 2. The obligation to conform to a standard of conduct prescribed by law or by contract. Also called legal duty. 3. A function or task expected to be performed in one's calling. 4. A tax on imports or exports.

> Duty, as used in tort law, refers to the relationship between the plaintiff and the defendant from which arises an obligation on the part of the defendant to exercise due care toward the plaintiff. *Childs*, 129 Ohio Misc.2d 50 (Ohio Com.Pl., 2004)

duty of tonnage See tonnage (2).

dwelling house The building that is one's residence or abode.

DWI See driving while intoxicated.

dying declaration A statement of fact by one conscious of imminent death about the cause or circumstances of his or her death. An exception to the hearsay rule. Also called deathbed declaration.

dynamite instruction See *Allen* charge.

E

E&O See errors and omissions insurance.

earmarking To set aside or reserve for a designated purpose.

earned income Income (e.g., wages) derived from labor and services.

earned income credit A refundable tax credit on earned income for low income workers who have dependent children and who maintain a household.

earned premium The portion of an insurance premium that has been used thus far during the term of a policy.

earned surplus The surplus a corporation accumulates from profits after dividends are paid. Also called retained earnings.

earnest money Part of the purchase price paid by a buyer when entering a contract to show the intent and ability to carry out the contract.

earnings report A company report showing revenues, expenses, and losses over a given period and the net result. Also called an income statement, profit-and-loss statement.

easement A property interest in another's land that authorizes limited use of the land, e.g., a right-of-way across private property.

> A property interest in the land of another which entitles the owner of the easement to a limited use of the land in which the interest exists. *State ex rel. Butler Twp.*, 162 Ohio App.3d 394 (Ohio App., 2005)

easement appurtenant An easement interest that attaches to the land and passes with it when conveyed.

easement by implication See implied easement.

easement by prescription See prescriptive easement.

easement in gross A personal right to use the land of another that usually ends with the death of the person possessing this right. An easement that does not benefit a particular piece of land.

easement of access The right to travel over the land of another to reach a road or other location.

eavesdrop To listen to another's private conversation without consent.

ecclesiastical Pertaining to the church. See also canon law.

economic duress See business compulsion.

economic realities test The totality of commercial circumstances that a court will examine to determine the nature of a relationship.

economic strike A strike one over wages, hours, working conditions, or other conditions of employment, not over an unfair labor practice.

edict A formal decree, command, law, or proclamation.

EEOC Equal Employment Opportunity Commission (*www.eeoc.gov*).

effect 1. That which is produced. 2. To bring about or cause.

effective assistance of counsel Representation provided by an attorney using the skill, knowledge, time, and resources of a reasonably competent attorney in criminal cases.

effective date The date a law, treaty, or contract goes into effect and becomes binding or enforceable.

effective tax rate The percentage of total income actually paid for taxes.

effects Personal property; goods.

efficient cause See proximate cause.

efficient intervening cause See intervening cause.

efficient market A market in which material information on a company is widely available and accurately reflected in the value of the stock.

eggshell skull An unusually high vulnerability to injury.

egress The means or right to leave a place. The act of leaving.

ejectment An action for the recovery of the possession of land and for damages for the wrongful dispossession.

ejusdem generis Where general words follow a list of particular words, the general words will be interpreted as applying only to things of the same class or category as the particular words in the list.

> Where general words follow enumeration of particular classes of things, general words will be construed as applying only to things of same general class as those enumerated; if legislature meant general words to be applied without restriction, it would have only used general terms, rather than specifically enumerating certain subjects, objects or persons followed by general terminology. *Brooks*, 111 Ohio App.3d 342 (Ohio App., 1996)

election A selection among available persons, conduct, rights, etc.

election by spouse The right of a widow or widower to choose between what a deceased spouse gives the surviving spouse by will or the share of the decedent's estate designated by statute.

election of remedies A choice by a party between two inconsistent remedies for the same wrong.

elective share The statutory share a surviving spouse chooses over what the will of his or her deceased spouse provides.

elector 1. A voter. 2. A member of the electoral college.

electoral college A body of electors chosen to elect the president and vice-president based on the popular vote in each individual state.

eleemosynary Having to do with charity.

element 1. A constituent part of something. 2. A portion of a rule that is a precondition of the applicability of the entire rule.

elisor A person appointed by the court to perform duties of a disqualified sheriff or coroner.

eloign To remove something in order to conceal it from the court.

emancipation 1. Setting free. 2. The express or implied consent of a parent to relinquish his or her control and authority over a child.

> Emancipation is the entire surrender by parent of right to care, custody, and earnings of minor child as well as renunciation of parental duties. *Swanson*, 109 Ohio App.3d 231 (Ohio 1996)

embargo A government prohibition of ships into or out of its waters or of the exchange of goods and services to or from a particular country.

embezzlement Fraudulently taking personal property of another, which was initially acquired lawfully because of a position of trust.

> An intentional conversion by embezzler to his own use of property entrusted to him. *State v. Kearns*, 129 N.E.2d 547 (Ohio Com.Pl., 1955)

emblements The crops produced by the labor of a tenant.

embracery The crime of corruptly trying to influence a jury by promises, entertainments, etc. Also called jury tampering.

emend To correct or revise.

emergency doctrine 1. One will not be liable for ordinary negligence when confronted with an emergency situation he or she did not aid in creating. Also called imminent peril doctrine, sudden emergency doctrine. 2. A warrantless search is allowed if the police have an objectively reasonable belief that an emergency has occurred and that someone within the residence is in need of immediate assistance. 3. In an emergency, consent to medical treatment for a child or unconscious adult will be implied if no one is available to give express consent.

eminent domain The power of government to take private property for public use upon the payment of just compensation. The exercise of eminent domain is called *condemnation*.

> The power of the state to take private property for necessary public use without owner's consent upon payment of just compensation. Ohio Const. Art. 1, § 19. *State v. Penrod*, 81 Ohio App.3d 654 (Ohio App., 1992)

emolument Payment or other benefit for an occupation or office.

emotional distress Mental or emotional suffering or pain, e.g., depression, shame, worry. Also called mental anguish, mental distress, mental suffering.

empanel See impanel.

employee One hired by another who has the right to control the employee in the material details of how the work is performed.

Employee Retirement Income Security Act (ERISA) A federal statute creating the Pension Benefit Guarantee Corporation to regulate private pension plans (29 USC § 1001) (*www.pbgc.gov*).

employee stock ownership plan (ESOP) An employee benefits plan that primarily invests in the shares of stock of the employer creating the plan.

employers' liability See workers' compensation.

employment at will See at-will employee.

emptor A buyer or purchaser. See also caveat emptor.

enabling statute The statute that allows (enables) an administrative agency to carry out specified delegated powers.

enact To make into a law, particularly by a legislative body.

enacting clause A clause in a statute (often in the preamble) that states the authority by which it is made (e.g., "Be it enacted . . .").

enactment 1. The method or process by which a bill in a legislature becomes a law. 2. A statute.

en banc or **in banc** By the full membership of a court as opposed to one of its smaller groupings or panels. Also called by the full bench or full court.

encroach To trespass, interfere with, or infringe on another's property or rights. Also spelled incroach.

encumbrance Every right to, interest in, or claim on land that diminishes the value of land, e.g., a mortgage or easement. Also spelled incumbrance.

> A right or interest in land that subsists in third persons to the diminution of value of land but which is nonetheless consistent with passing of the fee by conveyance. *Tenbusch*, 107 Ohio App. 133 (Ohio App., 1958)

encumbrancer Someone who holds an encumbrance (e.g., a lien) against land.

endorsee See indorsee.

endorsement 1. See indorsement. 2. A modification to an insurance policy. An insurance policy rider.

endorser See indorser.

endowment 1. A special gift or fund for an institution. 2. An endowment insurance policy will pay the insured a stated sum at the end of a definite period, or, if the insured dies before such period, to pay the amount to the person designated as beneficiary.

enfeoff To invest someone with a freehold estate. See also feoffment.

enforcement Forcing someone to comply with a law or other obligation.

enfranchisement 1. Giving a right or franchise, e.g., the right to vote. 2. Freeing someone from bondage.

engage 1. To hire or employ. 2. To participate.

English rule See American rule.

engrossment 1. Copying or drafting a document (e.g., a bill) for its final execution or passage. 2. Preparing a deed for execution. 3. Buying up or securing enough of a commodity in order to obtain a monopoly.

engrossed bill The version of a bill passed by one of the chambers of the legislature after incorporating amendments or other changes.

enjoin 1. To require a person to perform or to abstain from some act. 2. To issue an injunction.

enjoyment 1. The ability to exercise a right or privilege. 2. Deriving benefit from possession.

enlarge To make or become bigger. To allow more time.

Enoch Arden doctrine The presumption that a spouse is dead after being missing without explanation for a designated number of years.

enroll To register or record officially.

enrolled agent An attorney or nonattorney authorized to represent taxpayers at the Internal Revenue Service.

enrolled bill A bill that is ready to be sent to the chief executive after both chambers of the legislature have passed it.

entail To impose a limitation on who can inherit real property; it does not pass to all the heirs of the owner.

enter 1. To place anything before a court or on the court record. 2. To go into or onto. 3. To become part of or party to.

enterprise 1. A venture or undertaking, often involving a financial commitment. 2. Any individual, partnership, corporation, association, or other legal entity, and any union or group of individuals associated in fact although not a legal entity. 18 USC § 1961(4). See also RICO.

enterprise liability theory Liability for harm caused by a product is spread over the entire industry or enterprise that made the product.

enticement 1. The tort of wrongfully (a) encouraging a wife to leave or stay away from her husband or (b) forcing or encouraging a child to leave or stay away from his or her parent. 2. The crime of luring a child to an area for sexual contact.

entire Whole, without division; indivisible.

entirety The undivided whole; the entire amount or extent. See also tenancy by the entirety.

> For an estate by the entireties to exist at common law, the tenants must be husband and wife and have equal interest which was acquired by same conveyance, commenced at same time and held by same undivided possession. *Koster*, 11 Ohio App.3d 1 (Ohio App., 1982)

entitlement 1. The right to benefits, income, or other property. 2. The right to receive a government benefit that cannot be abridged without due process.

entity An organization that has a legally independent existence that is separate from its members.

entrapment Conduct by a government official that instigates or induces the commission of a crime by someone not ready and willing to commit it in order to prosecute him or her for that crime.

> An affirmative defense that is established where the criminal design originates with the officials of the government, and they implant in the mind of an innocent person the disposition to commit the alleged offense and induce its commission in order to prosecute; it is not established when government officials merely afford opportunities or facilities for the commission of the offense and it is shown that the accused was predisposed to commit the offense. *State v. Turner*, 156 Ohio App.3d 177 (Ohio App., 2004)

entry 1. The act of making a notation or record; the notation or record itself. 2. The act of presenting something before the court for or on the record. 3. The right or act of going into or onto real property. 4. Entering a building with one's whole body, a part of the body, or a physical object under one's control (for purposes of burglary).

enumerated Specifically or expressly listed or mentioned (e.g., the enumerated powers of Congress in the U.S. Constitution).

enure See inure.

en ventre sa mere In its mother's womb; an unborn child. Also spelled in ventre sa mere.

environmental impact statement (EIS) A detailed report on the potential positive and negative environmental effects of a proposed project or law.

envoy A diplomat of the rank of minister or ambassador.

EO See executive order

eo die On that day.

eo instanti At that instant.

eo nomine By that name

Equal Employment Opportunity Commission (EEOC) The federal regulatory agency that enforces antidiscrimination laws (*www.eeoc.gov*).

equality The status of being equal in rights, privileges, immunities, opportunities, and duties.

equalization 1. The act or process of making equal; bringing about uniformity or conformity to a common standard. 2. Adjusting tax assessments to achieve fairness.

equal protection of the law A constitutional guarantee that the government will not deny a person or class of persons the same treatment it gives other persons or other classes under like circumstances. 14th Amendment, U.S. Constitution.

> No person or class of persons shall be denied same protection of law which is enjoyed by other persons or other classes in same place and under like circumstances. *Cahill*, 79 Ohio App.3d 109 (Ohio App., 1992)

Equal Rights Amendment A proposed amendment to the U.S. Constitution that did not pass. ("Equality of rights under the law shall not be denied or abridged by the United States or by any State on account of sex.")

equipment Implements needed for designated purposes or activities, including goods that do not qualify as consumer goods, farm products, or inventory.

equitable 1. Just; conformable to the principles of what is right. 2. Available or sustainable in equity or under the principles of equity.

> With respect to division of property, equitable does not imply equal. R.C. § 3105.171(C, D). *Guziak*, 80 Ohio App.3d 805 (Ohio App., 1992)

equitable adoption A child will be considered the adopted child of a person who agreed to adopt the child but failed to go through the formal adoption procedures.

equitable abstention doctrine Where an order of a state agency predominantly affects local matters, a federal court should refuse to exercise its equity powers to restrain enforcement of the order if adequate state judicial relief is available to the aggrieved party.

equitable action An action seeking equitable remedy relief (e.g., an injunction) rather than damages.

equitable assignment An assignment that, though invalid at law, will be enforced in equity.

equitable defense A defense (e.g., unclean hands, laches) that was once recognized only by courts of equity but is now recognized by all courts.

equitable distribution The fair, but not necessarily equal, division of all marital property upon divorce in a common law property state.

equitable election An obligation to choose between two inconsistent or alternative rights or claims (e.g., a party cannot accept the benefits of a will and also refuse to recognize the validity of the will in other respects).

equitable estate An estate recognized by courts of equity.

equitable estoppel The voluntary conduct of a person will preclude him or her from asserting rights against another who justifiably relied on the conduct and who would suffer damage or injury if the person is now allowed to repudiate the conduct. Also called estoppel in pais.

> Equitable estoppel precludes a party from asserting certain facts where by his conduct the party has induced another to change his position in good faith reliance upon that conduct. *Gullatte*, 145 Ohio App.3d 620 (Ohio App., 2000)

equitable lien A restitution right enforceable in equity to have a fund or specific property, or its proceeds, applied in whole or part to the payment of a particular debt or class of debts.

equitable mortgage Any agreement to post certain property as security before the security agreement is formulized.

equitable owner The person who is recognized in equity as the owner of the property even though bare legal title to the property is in someone else. Also called beneficial owner.

equitable recoupment Using a claim barred by the statute of limitations as a defense to offset or diminish another party's related claim.

equitable relief An equitable remedy (e.g., injunction, specific performance) that is available when remedies at law (e.g., damages) are not adequate.

equitable restraint doctrine A federal court will not intervene to enjoin a pending state criminal prosecution without a strong showing of bad faith and irreparable injury. Also called *Younger* abstention. *Younger v. Harris*, 91 S. Ct. 746 (1971).

equitable servitude See restrictive covenant (1).

equitable title 1. The right (enforceable against the trustee) to the beneficial enjoyment of the trust property or corpus under the terms of the trust. 2. The right of the person holding equitable title to have legal title transferred to him or her upon the performance of specified conditions.

> A beneficiary's interest in trust, sometimes called equitable title, consists of right to beneficial enjoyment of corpus enforceable against trustee. *Goralsky*, 59 Ohio St.3d 197 (Ohio 1991)

equitable tolling A litigant may sue after the statute of limitations has expired if, despite due diligence, he or she was prevented from suing due to inequitable circumstances, e.g., wrongful concealment of vital information by the other party.

equity 1. Justice administered according to fairness in a particular case, as contrasted with strictly formalized rules once followed by common-law courts. 2. Fairness, justice, and impartiality. 3. The monetary value of property in excess of what is owed on it. Net worth. 4. Shares of stock in a corporation.

equity capital The investment of owners in exchange for stock.

equity court A court with the power to apply equitable principles.

equity financing Raising capital by issuing stock, as opposed to bonds.

equity loan A loan to a homeowner that is secured by the amount of equity in the home at the time of the loan. A home equity loan.

equity of redemption Before foreclosure is finalized, the defaulting debtor-mortgagor can recover (redeem) the property upon payment of the debt plus interest and costs. Also called right of redemption.

> The mortgagor's equity of redemption is typically cut off once a mortgagee seeks and is granted a decree of foreclosure. Generally, a common pleas court grants the mortgagor a three-day grace period to exercise the equity of redemption, which consists of paying the debt, interest and court costs, to prevent the sale of the property. *Hausman*, 73 Ohio St.3d 671 (Ohio 1995)

equivalent 1. Equal in value or effect; essentially equal. 2. Under the doctrine of equivalents, an accused patent infringer cannot avoid liability for infringement by changing only minor or insubstantial details of the claimed invention while retaining the invention's essential identity.

ERA See Equal Rights Amendment.

erase 1. To wipe out or obliterate written words or marks. 2. To seal from public access.

ergo Therefore; consequently.

***Erie* doctrine** Federal courts in diversity cases will apply the substantive law of the state in which the federal court is situated, except as to matters governed by the U.S. Constitution and acts of Congress. *Erie v. Tompkins*, 58 S. Ct. 817 (1938).

ERISA See Employee Retirement Income Security Act.

erroneous Involving error, although not necessarily illegal.

error A mistaken judgment or incorrect belief as to the existence or the consequences of a fact; a false application of the law.

errors and omissions insurance (E&O) Insurance against liability for negligence, omissions, and errors in the practice of a particular profession or business. A form of malpractice insurance for nonintentional wrongdoing.

escalator clause A clause in a contract or lease providing that a payment obligation will increase or decrease depending on a measurable standard such as changing income or the cost-of-living index. Also called fluctuating clause.

escape clause A provision in a contract or other document allowing a party to avoid liability or performance under defined conditions.

escheat A reversion of property to the state upon the death of the owner when no one is available to claim it by will or inheritance.

> When, under Chapter 2105. of the Revised Code, personal property escheats to the state, the prosecuting attorney of the county in which letters of administration are granted upon such estate shall collect and pay it over to the county treasurer. R.C. § 2105.07

***Escobedo* rule** Statements of a suspect in custody who is the focus of a police investigation are inadmissible if not told of his or her right to counsel and to remain silent. *Escobedo v. Illinois*, 84 S. Ct. 1758 (1964).

escrow Property (e.g., money, a deed) delivered to a neutral person (e.g., bank, escrow agent) to be held until a specified condition occurs, at which time it is to delivered to a designated person.

> A written instrument which by its terms imports a legal obligation and which is deposited by the grantor with a third party to be kept by the depositary until performance of a condition or happening of a certain event and then to be delivered to the grantee. *McGriff*, 74 N.E.2d 619 (Ohio App., 1947)

ESOP See employee stock ownership plan.

espionage Spying to obtain secret information about the activities or plans of a foreign government or rival company.

Esq. See esquire.

esquire (Esq.) A courtesy title given to an attorney.

essence 1. The gist or substance of something. 2. That which is indispensable. See also time is of the essence.

establish 1. To make or institute. 2. To prove. 3. To make secure.

establishment 1. A business or institution. 2. The act of creating, building or establishing. 3. Providing governmental sponsorship, aid, or preference. 4. The people or institutions that dominate a society.

Establishment Clause Government cannot establish an official religion, become excessively entangled with religion, nor endorse one form of religion over another. U.S. Constitution, 1st Amendment.

estate 1. An interest in real or personal property. 2. The extent and nature of one's interest in real or personal property. 3. All of the assets and liabilities of a decedent after he or she dies. 4. All of the property of whatever kind owned by a person. 5. Land.

estate at sufferance The interest that someone has in land he or she continues to possess after the permission or right to possess it has ended. Also called holdover tenancy, tenancy at sufferance.

estate at will See tenancy at will.

estate by the entirety See tenancy by the entirety.

estate for years An estate whose duration is known at the time it begins. A tenancy for a term.

estate from year to year See periodic tenancy.

estate in common See tenancy in common.

estate in expectancy See future interest.

estate of inheritance An estate that may be inherited.

estate per autre vie See life estate pur autre vie.

estate planning Presenting proposals on how a person can have assets distributed at death in a way that will achieve his or her goals while taking maximum advantage of tax and other laws.

estate tail See fee tail.

estate tax A tax on the transfer property at death; the tax is based on the value of what passes by will or intestacy. Also called death tax.

> An estate tax is a tax upon transmission of property by a deceased person and tax is a charge upon decedent's whole estate, regardless of manner in which it is distributed. R.C. §§ 5731.01–5731.56, 5731.13. *In re Smith's Estate*, 188 N.E.2d 650 (Ohio Prob., 1962)

estimated tax The current year's anticipated tax that is paid quarterly on income not subject to withholding.

estop To stop or prevent something by estoppel.

estoppel 1. Stopping a party from denying something he or she previously said or did, especially if the denial would harm someone who reasonably relied on it. 2. Stopping a party from relitigating an issue.

> A bar that precludes a person from denying a fact that has become settled by an act of the person himself. *Mark-It Place Foods, Inc.*, 156 Ohio App.3d 65 (Ohio App., 2004)

estoppel by deed A party to a deed will be stopped from denying the truth of a fact stated in a deed (e.g., that the party owns the land being transferred) as against someone induced to rely on the deed.

estoppel by judgment See collateral estoppel.

estoppel by laches Denial of relief to a litigant who unreasonably delayed enforcing his or her claim.

estoppel by record See collateral estoppel.

estoppel by silence Estoppel against a person who had a duty to speak, but refrained from doing so and thereby misled another.

estoppel certificate A signed statement certifying that certain facts are correct (e.g., that mortgage payments are current) as of the date of the statement and can be relied upon by third parties.

estoppel in pais See equitable estoppel.

estover 1. The right to use, during a lease, any timber on the leased premises to promote good resource management. 2. Support or alimony.

et al. And others.

ethical 1. Conforming to minimum standards of professional conduct. 2. Pertaining to moral principles or obligations.

> Ethical drug means a prescription drug that is prescribed or dispensed by a physician or any other person who is legally authorized to prescribe or dispense a prescription drug. R.C. § 2307.71(A)(4)

ethics 1. Rules that embody the minimum standards of behavior to which members of an organization are expected to conform. 2. Standards of professional conduct.

et seq. And following. When used after a page or section number, the reference is to several pages or sections after the one mentioned.

et ux. And wife.

et vir. And husband.

Euclidian zoning Comprehensive zoning in which every square foot of the community is within some fixed zone and is subject to the predetermined set of land use restrictions applicable to that zone. Zoning by district.

eurodollar A U.S. dollar on deposit in a bank outside the United States, especially in Europe.

euthanasia The act of painlessly putting to death those persons who are suffering from incurable diseases or conditions. Also called mercy killing.

evasion 1. The act of avoiding something, usually by artifice. 2. The illegal reduction of tax liability, e.g., by underreporting income.

evasive answer An answer that neither admits nor denies a matter.

evergreen agreement A contract that automatically renews itself.

eviction 1. The use of legal process to dispossess a land occupier. 2. Depriving one of land or rental property he or she has held or leased.

> Actual eviction involves expulsion of exclusion from demised premises, and constructive eviction involves surrender of possession by tenant on justifiable grounds. *Liberal Sav. & Loan Co.*, 137 Ohio St. 489 (Ohio 1940)

evidence Anything that could be offered to prove or disprove an alleged fact. Examples: testimony, documents, fingerprints.

evidence aliunde See extrinsic evidence.

evidentiary fact 1. A Subsidiary fact required to prove an ultimate fact. 2. A fact that is evidence of another fact.

evidentiary harpoon Deliberately introducing inadmissible evidence in order to prejudice the jury against the accused.

ex; Ex. without, from, example; Exchequer.

ex aequo et bono According to dictates of equity and what is good.

examination 1. Questioning someone under oath. 2. An inspection.

examination in chief See direct examination.

examined copy A copy of a record or other document that has been compared with the original and often sworn to be a true copy.

examiner One authorized to conduct an examination; one appointed by the court to take testimony of witnesses.

except 1. To leave out. 2. Other than.

exception 1. An objection to an order or ruling of a hearing officer or judge. 2. The act of excluding or separating something out (e.g., a judge excludes something from an order; a grantor retains an interest in property transferred). 3. That which is excluded.

excess Pertaining to an act, amount, or degree that is beyond what is usual, proper, or necessary.

excess insurance Supplemental insurance coverage available once the policy limits of the other insurance policies are exhausted.

> Excess insurance or stop-loss insurance means an insurance policy purchased by a multiple employer welfare arrangement under which it receives reimbursement for benefits it pays in excess of a preset deductible or limit. R.C. § 1739.01(B)

excessive Greater than what is usual, proper, or necessary.

excessive bail A sum that is disproportionate to the offense charged and beyond what is reasonably needed to deter evasion by flight.

excess of jurisdiction Action taken by a court or other tribunal that is not within its authority or powers.

excessive verdict A verdict that is clearly exorbitant and shocking.

exchange 1. A transaction (not using money) in which one piece of property is given in return for another piece of property. 2. Swapping things of value. 3. The conversion of the money of one country for that of another. The price of doing so is the rate of exchange. 4. Payment using a bill of exchange or credits. 5. An organization bringing together buyers and sellers of securities or commodities, e.g., New York Stock Exchange.

Exchequer The treasury department in England.

excise A tax that is not directly imposed on persons or property but rather on performing an act (e.g., manufacturing, selling, using), on engaging in an occupation, or on the enjoyment of a privilege.

excited utterance A statement relating to a startling event or condition, made while under the stress of excitement caused by the event or condition. An exception to the hearsay rule.

> An excited utterance admissible under exception to hearsay rule is one in which the declarant was under the excitement of a startling event, so that the statement therefore was not the product of reflection. Rules of Evid., Rule 803(2). *State v. Baker*, 137 Ohio App.3d 628 (Ohio App., 2000)

exclusion 1. Denial of entry, admittance, or admission. 2. A person, event, condition, or loss not covered by an insurance policy. 3. Income that does not need to be included in gross income.

exclusionary rule Evidence obtained in violation of the constitution (e.g., an illegal search and seizure), will be inadmissible.

exclusive Not allowing others to participate; restricted; belonging to one person or group.

exclusive agency An agreement in which the owner grants a broker the right to sell property to the exclusion of other brokers, but allows the owner to sell the property through his or her own efforts.

exclusive jurisdiction The power of a court to hear a particular kind of case to the exclusion of all other courts.

> Exclusive jurisdiction is a court's power to adjudicate an action or class of actions to the exclusion of all other courts. *Johns*, 101 Ohio St.3d 234 (Ohio 2004)

exclusive listing An agreement giving only one broker the right sell the owner's property for a defined period. Also called exclusive agency listing.

ex contractu Arising from or out of a contract.

exculpate To free from guilt or blame.

exculpatory clause A clause in a lease or other contract relieving a party from liability for injury or damages he or she may wrongfully cause.

exculpatory evidence Any evidence tending to show excuse or innocence.

exculpatory-no doctrine An individual who merely supplies a negative and exculpatory response to an investigator's questions cannot be prosecuted for making a false statement to a government agency even if the response is false. The doctrine preserves the individual's self-incrimination protection.

ex curia Out of or away from court.

excusable neglect The failure to take the proper step (e.g., to file an answer) at the proper time that will be excused (forgiven) because the failure was not due to carelessness, inattention, or recklessness but rather was due to (a) an unexpected or unavoidable hindrance or accident, (b) reliance on the care and vigilance of one's attorney, or (c) reliance on promises made by an adverse party.

> On motion and upon such terms as are just, the court may relieve a party or his legal representative from a final judgment, order or proceeding for the following reasons: (1) mistake, inadvertence, surprise or excusable neglect. . . . Ohio Civ. R. Rule 60 (B)

excuse A reason one should be relieved of a duty or not be convicted.

ex delicto Arising from a tort, fault, crime, or malfeasance.

ex dividend (x)(xd) Without dividend. Upon purchase of shares ex dividend, the seller, not the buyer, receives the next dividend.

execute 1. To complete, perform, or carry into effect. 2. To sign and do whatever else is needed to finalize a contract or other instrument to make it legal. 3. To enforce a judgment. 4. To put to death.

executed contract 1. A contract that has been carried out according to its terms. 2. See execute (2).

An executed contract is one in which the object of the agreement is performed and everything that was to be done is done and remains in force until disaffirmed. *Cassella*, 150 Ohio St. 27 (Ohio 1948)

executed trust A trust in which nothing remains to be done for it to be carried out.

execution 1. Carrying out or performing some act to its completion. 2. Signing and doing whatever else is needed to finalize a document and make it legal. 3. The process of carrying into effect the decisions in a judgment. A command (via a writ) to a court officer (e.g., sheriff) to seize and sell the property of the losing litigant in order to satisfy the judgment debt. Also called general execution, writ of execution. 4. Implementing a death sentence.

execution sale See forced sale.

executive 1. Pertaining to that branch of government that is charged with carrying out or enforcing the laws. 2. A managing official.

executive agreement An agreement between the United States and another country that does not require the approval of the Senate.

executive clemency See clemency.

executive order (EO) An order issued by the chief executive pursuant to specific statutory authority or to the executive's inherent authority to direct the operation of government agencies and officials.

Executive order means an order of the president of the United States or the chief executive officer of a state that has the force of law and that is promulgated in accordance with applicable law. R.C. § 109.571(11)

executive privilege The privilege, based on the separation of powers, that exempts the executive branch from disclosing information in order to protect national security and also to protect confidential advisory and deliberative communications among government officials.

executive session A meeting of a board or governmental unit that is closed to the general public.

executor A person appointed by someone writing a will (a testator) to carry out the provisions of the will.

executory Yet to be executed or performed; remaining to be carried into operation or effect; dependent on a future performance or event.

executory contract A contract that is wholly unperformed or in which substantial duties remain to be performed by both sides.

Executory contract is one in which a party binds himself to do or not to do a particular thing and which requires affirmative action for its establishment, *Cassella*, 150 Ohio St. 27 (Ohio 1948)

executory interest A future interest created in one other than the grantor, which is not a remainder and vests upon the happening of a condition or event and in derogation of a vested freehold interest.

executory trust A trust that cannot be carried out until a further conveyance is made. Also called imperfect trust.

executrix A woman appointed by a will to carry it out. A female executor.

exemplar 1. Nontestimonial identification evidence, e.g., fingerprints, blood sample. 2. A typical example; a model.

exemplary damages See punitive damages.

exemplification An official copy of a public record, ready for use as evidence.

exemplified copy See certified copy.

exempt Relieved of a duty others still owe.

exemption 1. Release or freedom from a duty, liability, service, or tax. 2. A right of a debtor to retain a portion of his or her property free from the claims of creditors. 3. A deduction from adjusted gross income.

As applied to taxation, exemption is freedom from burden of enforced contributions to expenses and maintenance of government, or an immunity from the general tax. *Kroger Co.*, 9 Ohio St.2d 80 (Ohio 1967)

exercise 1. To make use of. 2. To fulfill or perform; to execute.

ex facie On its face; apparently.

ex gratia As a matter of grace; as a favor rather than as required.

exhaustion of remedies Using available dispute-solving avenues (remedies) in an administrative agency before asking a court to review what the agency did.

exhibit 1. A document, chart, or other object offered or introduced into evidence. 2. An attachment to a pleading, instrument, or other document.

exigency (exigence) An urgent need, requiring an immediate response.

exigent circumstances 1. An emergency justifying the bypassing of normal procedures. 2. An emergency requiring swift action to prevent imminent threat to life or property, escape, or destruction of evidence.

Entry and search by the state without a warrant is permissible under the exigent circumstances exception, which applies when police have a reasonable basis to believe that someone inside the premises needs immediate aid. *State v. Taylor*, 144 Ohio App.3d 255 (Ohio 2001)

exile 1. Banishment from the country. 2. A person banished.

ex officio Because of or by virtue of one's position or office.

exonerate To free or release from guilt or blame; responsibility or duty.

exoneration 1. Releasing one from a burden, charge, blame, responsibility, or duty. 2. The right to be reimbursed by reason of having paid what another should be compelled to pay. 3. A surety's right, after the principal's debt has matured, to compel the principal to honor its obligation to the creditor.

ex parte With only one side present; involving one party only.

ex parte order A court order requested by one party and issued without notice to the other party.

expatriation 1. The abandonment of one's country and becoming a citizen or subject of another. 2. Sending someone into exile.

expectancy 1. The bare hope (but more than wishful thinking) of receiving a property interest of another, such as may be entertained by an heir apparent. 2. A reversion or remainder.

expectation damages The cost of restoring the non-breaching party to the position in which it would have been if the contract not been breached. Also called expectancy damages.

> Damages awarded for breach of contract should place injured party in as good a position as it would have been in but for the breach; such compensatory damages, often termed expectation damages, are limited to actual loss, which loss must be established with reasonable certainty. *Textron Fin. Corp.*, 115 Ohio App.3d 137 (Ohio App., 1996)

expectation of privacy The belief that one's activities and property would be private and free from government intrusion.

expenditure 1. The act of spending or paying out money. 2. An amount spent. An expense.

expense 1. What is spent for goods and services. 2. To treat (write off) as an expense for tax and accounting purposes.

experience rating A method of determining insurance rates by using the loss record (experience) of the insured over a period of time.

expert One who is knowledgeable, through experience or education, in a specialized field.

expert witness A person qualified by scientific, technical, or other specialized knowledge or experience to give an expert opinion relevant to a fact in dispute.

> To qualify a witness as an expert, the court should consider the witness's knowledge, skill, experience, training, or education; an expert must only possess knowledge that will aid the trier of fact in assessing the evidence, and the expert need not possess special education, certification, or complete knowledge of the field in question. Ohio Rules of Evid., Rule 702. *State v. Rangel*, 140 Ohio App.3d 291 (Ohio App., 2000)

export 1. To carry or send abroad. 2. A commodity that is exported.

expository statute See declaratory statute.

ex post facto After the fact; operating retroactively.

ex post facto law A law that punishes as a crime an act that was innocent when done, that makes punishment more burdensome after its commission, or that deprives one of a defense that was available when the act was committed.

exposure The financial or legal risk one has assumed or could assume.

express Definite; unambiguous and not left to inference. Direct.

express agency The actual agency created when words of the principal specifically authorize the agent to take certain actions.

express authority Authority that the principal explicitly grants the agent to act in the principal's name.

express condition A condition agreed to by the parties themselves rather than imposed by law.

express contract An oral or written agreement whose terms were stated by the parties rather than implied or imposed by law.

> In an express contract, the parties assent to the terms as actually expressed through the offer and acceptance. *Vargo v. Clark* 128 Ohio App.3d 589, 716 N.E.2d 238 (Ohio App. 4 Dist., 1998)

expressio unius est exclusio alterius A canon of interpretation that when an author (e.g., the legislature) expressly mentions one thing, we can assume it intended to exclude what it does not mention.

express malice 1. Ill will, the intent to harm. Actual malice; malice in fact. 2. Harming someone with a deliberate mind or formed design.

express notice See actual notice.

express power A power that is specifically listed or mentioned.

express repeal An overt statement in a statute that it repeals an earlier statute.

express trust A trust created or declared in explicit terms for specific purposes, usually in writing.

express waiver Oral or written statements intentionally and voluntarily relinquishing a known right or privilege.

express warranty A seller's affirmation of fact, description, or specific promise concerning a product that becomes part of the basis of the transaction or bargain.

> An affirmation of fact by the seller as to a product or commodity to induce the purchase thereof, on which affirmation the buyer relies in making the purchase. *Wagner*, 85 Ohio St.3d 457 (Ohio 1999)

expropriation The government's taking of private property for public purposes. See also eminent domain.

expulsion A putting or driving out; a permanent cutting off from the privileges of an institution or society.

expunge To erase or eliminate.

> Expunge means: (1) The removal and destruction of court files and records, originals and copies, and the deletion of all index references; . . . R.C. § 5122.01(R)

expungement of record The process by which the record of a criminal conviction, an arrest, or an adjudication of delinquency is destroyed or sealed after the expiration of a designated period of time.

ex rel. **(ex relatione)** Upon relation or information. A suit ex rel is brought by the government in the name of the real party in interest (called the realtor).

ex rights **(x)(xr)** Without certain rights, e.g., to buy additional securities.

extension 1. An increase in the length of time allowed. 2. An addition or enlargement to a structure.

extenuating circumstances See mitigating circumstances.

exterritoriality An exemption from a foreign country's local laws, enjoyed by diplomats when living in that country.

extinguishment The destruction or cancellation of a right, power, contract, or estate.

extort To compel or coerce; to obtain by force, threats, or other wrongful methods.

> Extortionate means is any means that involves the use, or an express or implicit threat of use, of violence or other criminal means to cause harm to the person or property of the debtor or any member of his family. R.C. § 2905.21(G)

extortion 1. Obtaining property from another through the wrongful use of actual or threatened force, violence, or fear. 2. The use of an actual or apparent official right (i.e., color of office) to obtain a benefit to which one is not entitled. See also blackmail.

extra 1. Additional. 2. Beyond or outside of.

extradition The surrender by one state (or country) to another of an individual who has been accused or convicted of an offense in the state (or country) demanding the surrender.

extrajudicial Outside of court and litigation. Done or given outside the course of regular judicial proceedings.

extralegal Not governed, regulated, or sanctioned by law.

extraneous evidence See extrinsic evidence.

extraordinary remedy A remedy (e.g., habeas corpus, writ of mandamus) allowed by a court when more traditional remedies are not adequate.

extraordinary session A session of the legislature called to address a matter that cannot wait till the next regular session. Also called special session.

extraordinary writ A special writ (e.g., habeas corpus) using a court's discretionary or unusual power. Also called prerogative writ.

extraterritoriality The application of a country's jurisdiction and laws to occurrences outside that country's borders.

extrinsic evidence External evidence; evidence that is not contained in the body of an agreement or other document; evidence outside of the writing. Also called extraneous evidence, evidence aliunde.

> Extrinsic evidence, within meaning of rule generally prohibiting proof by extrinsic evidence of specific instances of witness' conduct for purpose of attacking or supporting witness' credibility, is evidence offered other than during testimony of witness sought to be impeached. Ohio Rules of Evid., Rule 608(B). *State v. Hamilton*, 77 Ohio App.3d 293 (Ohio App., 1991)

extrinsic fraud See collateral fraud.

ex warrants (x)(xw) Without warrants. See also warrant (3).

eyewitness A person who saw or experienced the act, fact, or transaction about which he or she is giving testimony.

F

fabricated evidence Evidence that is manufactured or made up with the intent to mislead.

face 1. That which is apparent to a spectator; outward appearance. 2. The front of a document.

face amount 1. The amount of coverage on an insurance policy. 2. See par value.

face value See par value.

facial Pertaining to what is apparent in a document—the words themselves—as opposed to their interpretation.

facilitation Aiding; making it easier for another to commit a crime.

> Automobile was subject to forfeiture as having been used "to facilitate the commission" of narcotics offense, where defendant admittedly drove vehicle to the place from which he obtained marijuana for sale to undercover police officers, even though vehicle was not used to transport any drugs or drug money. R.C. § 2925.43(A). *State v. Garcia*, 89 Ohio App.3d 161 (Ohio App., 1993)

facility of payment clause A provision in an insurance policy permitting the insurer to pay the death benefits to a third person on behalf of the beneficiary.

facsimile 1. An exact copy of the original. 2. Transmitting printed text or pictures by electronic means. Fax.

fact A real occurrence. An event, thing, or state of mind that actually exists or that is alleged to exist, as opposed to its legal consequences.

fact-finder The person or body with the duty of determining the facts. If there is a jury, it is the fact-finder; if not, it is the judge or hearing officer. Also called trier of fact.

fact-finding The determination of the facts relevant to a dispute by examining evidence.

factor 1. One of the circumstances or considerations that will be weighed in making a decision, no one of which is usually conclusive. 2. A circumstance or influence that brings about or contributes to a result. 3. An agent who is given possession or control of property of the principal and who sells it for a commission. 4. A purchaser of accounts receivable at a discount.

factoring The purchase of accounts receivable at a discounted price.

factor's act A statute that protects good-faith buyers of goods from factors or agents who did not have authority to sell.

fact pleading Pleading those alleged facts that fit within the scope of a legally recognized cause of action. Also called code pleading.

> Under Civ.R. 8, Ohio has abandoned the practice of fact pleading and has embraced notice pleading. *Vinicky*, 163 Ohio App.3d 508 (Ohio App., 2005)

fact question See issue of fact.

factual impossibility Facts unknown by or beyond the control of the actor that prevent the consummation of the crime he or she intends to commit.

factum 1. A fact, deed, or act, e.g., the execution of a will. 2. A statement of facts.

factum probandum The fact to be proved.

factum probans The evidence on the fact to be proved; an evidentiary fact.

failure 1. The lack of success. 2. An omission or neglect of something expected or required. Deficiency.

failure of consideration Failure of performance. The neglect, refusal or failure of one of the contracting parties to perform or furnish the agreed upon consideration.

> Failure of consideration exists when promise has been made to support contract, but promise has not been performed. *Rhodes*, 71 Ohio App.3d 797 (Ohio App., 1991)

failure of issue Dying without children or other descendants who can inherit. Also called definite failure of issue.

failure to prosecute A litigant's lack of due diligence (e.g., failure to appear) in pursuing a case in court. Want of prosecution.

faint pleader Pleading in a misleading or collusive way.

fair Free from prejudice and favoritism, evenhanded; equitable.

fair comment The honest expression of opinion on a matter of legitimate public interest.

fair hearing A hearing that is conducted according to fundamental principles of procedural justice (due process), including the rights to an impartial decision maker, to present evidence, and to have the decision based on the evidence presented.

fair market value The amount at which property would change hands between a willing buyer and a willing seller, neither being under any compulsion to buy or sell and both having reasonable knowledge of the relevant facts. Also called cash value, market value, true value.

> The amount of money that could be obtained on the open market at a voluntary sale of property; it is amount that a purchaser who is willing, but not required to buy, would pay, and that a seller who is willing, but not required to sell, would accept, when both are fully aware and informed of all circumstances involving value and use of the property. *Masheter*, 38 Ohio App.2d 49 (Ohio App., 1973)

fairness doctrine A former rule of the Federal Communications Commission that a broadcaster must provide coverage of issues of public importance that is adequate and that fairly reflects differing viewpoints. Replaced by the equal-time doctrine.

fair preponderance of the evidence See preponderance of the evidence.

fair trade laws Statutes that permitted manufacturers or distributors of brand goods to fix minimum retail prices.

fair trial A trial in which the accused's legal rights are safeguarded, e.g., the procedures are impartial.

fair use The privilege of limited use of copyrighted material without permission of the copyright holder.

fair warning A due process requirement that a criminal statute be sufficiently definite to notify persons of reasonable intelligence that their planned conduct is criminal.

faith 1. Confidence. 2. Reliance or trust in a person, idea, or thing.

false 1. Knowingly, negligently, or innocently untrue. 2. Not genuine.

> Wholly or partially untrue or deceptive. R.C. § 2913.48(E)(1)

false advertising A misdescription or deceptive representation of the specific characteristics of products being advertised.

false arrest An arrest made without privilege or legal authority.

false impersonation See false personation.

false imprisonment The intentional confinement of someone within fixed boundaries set by the defendant where the victim was conscious of the confinement or was harmed by it.

> Claim for false imprisonment requires plaintiff to demonstrate that he was intentionally confined without lawful privilege and against his consent within a limited area for any appreciable time, however short. *Tucker*, 133 Ohio App.3d 140 (Ohio App., 1999)

false light An invasion-of-privacy tort committed by unreasonably offensive publicity that places another in a false light.

false personation The crime of falsely representing yourself as someone else for purposes of fraud or deception. Also called false impersonation.

false pretenses Obtaining money or other property by using knowingly false statements of fact with the intent to defraud.

false representation See misrepresentation.

false return 1. A false statement filed by a process server, e.g., falsely stating that he or she served process. 2. An incorrect tax return. A tax return that is knowingly incorrect.

false statement 1. A falsehood. 2. Knowingly stating what is not true. Covering up or concealing a fact.

false swearing See perjury.

false verdict A verdict that is substantially unjust or incorrect.

falsi crimen See crimen falsi.

falsify To forge or alter something in order to deceive. To counterfeit.

> Materially falsify means to alter or conceal in a manner that would impair the ability of a recipient of an electronic mail message . . . or a law enforcement agency to identify, locate, or respond to the person. . . . R.C. § 2913.421(A)(11)

family 1. A group of people related by blood, adoption, marriage, or domestic partnership. 2. A group of persons who live in one house and under one head or management.

family car See family purpose.

family court A special court with subject matter jurisdiction over family law matters such as adoption, paternity, and divorce.

family farmer A farmer whose farm has income and debts that qualify it for Chapter 12 bankruptcy relief. 11 USA § 101(18).

family law The body of law that defines relationships, rights, and duties in the formation, existence, and dissolution of marriage and other family units.

family purpose (automobile/car) doctrine The owner of a car who makes it available for family use will be liable for injuries that result from negligent operation of the car by a family member.

> Negligence is not imputed solely because of the husband-wife relationship or because a bailment existed. Ohio has not adopted the family purpose doctrine for imputing negligence. *West American Ins. Co.*, 65 Ohio App.2d 188 (Ohio App., 1979)

Fannie Mae Federal National Mortgage Association (FNMA) (*www.fanniemae.com*).

FAS See free alongside ship.

fascism A system of government characterized by nationalism, totalitarianism, central control, and often, racism.

fatal Pertaining to or causing death or invalidity.

fatal error See prejudicial error.

fatal variance A variance between the indictment and the evidence at trial that deprives the defendant of the due process guarantee of notice of the charges or exposes him or her to double jeopardy.

***Fatico* hearing** A proceeding to hear arguments on a proposed sentence for the defendant. *Fatico v. U.S.*, 603 F.2d 1053 (2d Cir. 1979).

fault An error or defect in someone's judgment or conduct to which blame and culpability attaches. The wrongful breach of a duty.

> Fault means wrongful act, omission, or breach. R.C. § 1301.01(P)

favored beneficiary A beneficiary in a will who is suspected of exerting undue influence on the decedent in view of the relative size of what this beneficiary receives under the will.

FBI Federal Bureau of Investigation (*www.fbi.gov*).

FCC Federal Communications Commission (*www.fcc.gov*).

FDA Food and Drug Administration (*www.fda.gov*).

FDIC Federal Deposit Insurance Corporation (*www.fdic.gov*).

fealty Allegiance of a feudal tenant (vassal) to a lord.

feasance The performance of an act or duty.

featherbedding Requiring a company to hire more workers than needed.

Fed 1. Federal. 2. Federal Reserve System (*www.federalreserve.gov*).

federal United States; pertaining to the national government of the United States.

Federal Circuit Court of Appeals for the Federal Circuit (*www.fedcir.gov*), one of the thirteen federal courts of appeal.

federal common law Judge-made law created by federal courts when resolving federal questions.

federal courts Courts with federal jurisdiction created by the U.S. Constitution under Article III or by Congress under Article I. The main federal courts are the U.S. district courts (trial courts), the U.S. courts of appeals, and the United States Supreme Court.

federalism The division of powers between the United States (federal) government and the state governments.

federal magistrate See magistrate.

federal preemption See preemption.

federal question A legal issue based on the U.S. Constitution, a statute of Congress, a treaty, or a federal administrative law.

Federal Register (Fed. Reg.) The official daily publication for rules, proposed rules, and notices of federal agencies and organizations, as well as executive orders and other presidential documents (*www.gpoaccess.gov/fr*).

federal rules Rules of procedure that apply in federal courts (*www.uscourts.gov/rules/newrules4.html*).

Federal Torts Claims Act (FTCA) The federal statute that specifies the torts for which the federal government can be sued because it waives sovereign immunity for those torts (28 USC §§ 1346, 2671).

federation An association or joining together of states, nations, or organizations into a league.

fee 1. Payment for labor or a service. 2. An estate in land that can be passed on by inheritance.

fee simple An estate over which the owner's power of disposition is without condition or limitation, until he or she dies without heirs. Also called fee simple absolute.

> Fee simple is highest right, title and interest that one can have in land; it is full and absolute estate in all that can be granted. *Wray*, 77 Ohio App.3d 122 (Ohio App., 1991)

fee simple absolute See fee simple.

fee simple conditional A fee that is limited or restrained to particular heirs, exclusive of others. Also called conditional fee.

fee simple defeasible A fee that is subject to termination upon the happening of an event or condition.

fee simple determinable A fee subject to the limitation that the property automatically reverts to the grantor upon the occurrence of a specified event.

fee splitting A single bill to a client covering the fee of two or more attorneys who are not in the same law firm.

> For those who share office space, fee-splitting is permissible as long as the office-sharing attorneys obtain the prior consent of the client and the division of fees is in proportion to the work performed. *Duff*, 87 Ohio App.3d 558 (Ohio App., 1993)

fee tail An estate that can be inherited by the lineal heirs, e.g., children (not the collateral heirs) of the first holder of the fee tail. Also called estate tail. If the estate is limited to female lineal heirs, it is a fee tail female; if it is limited to male lineal heirs, it is a fee tail male.

> A fee tail is an estate of inheritance wherein issue take by descent from preceding donees in tail rather than by purchase. *Casey*, 11 Ohio St.2d 42 (Ohio 1967)

fee tail female; fee tail male See fee tail.

fellow servant rule An employer will not be liable for injuries to an employee caused by the negligence of another employee (a fellow servant). This rule has been changed by workers' compensation law.

felon Someone convicted of a felony.

felonious 1. Malicious. Done with the intent to commit a serious crime. 2. Concerning a felony.

felonious assault A criminal assault that amounts to a felony.

felonious homicide Killing another without justification or excuse.

felony Any offense punishable by death or imprisonment for a term exceeding a year; a crime more serious than a misdemeanor.

> Felony means an offense defined by law as a felony. Ohio Crim. R. Rule 2(A)

felony murder rule An unintended death resulting from the commission or attempted commission of certain felonies is murder.

feme covert A married woman.

feme sole An unmarried woman.

fence 1. A receiver of stolen property. 2. To sell stolen property to a fence. 3. An enclosure or boundary about a field or other space.

feoffee One to whom a feoffment is conveyed. A feoffor conveys it.

feoffment The grant of land as a fee simple (i.e., full ownership of an estate). The grant of a freehold estate.

ferae naturae Of a wild nature; untamed, undomesticated.

***Feres* doctrine** The federal government is not liable under the Federal Tort Claims Act for injuries to members of the armed services where the injuries arise incident to military service. *Feres v. U.S.*, 71 S. Ct. 153 (1950).

fertile octogenarian rule A person is conclusively presumed to be able to have children (and therefore heirs) at any age.

feudalism A social and political system in medieval Europe in which laborers (serfs) were bound to and granted the use of land in return for services provided to their lords.

FHA Federal Housing Administration (*www.hud.gov/offices/hsg/fhahistory.cfm*).

fiat 1. An authoritative order or decree. 2. An arbitrary command.

FICA Federal Insurance Contributions Act (a statute on social security payroll taxes).

fiction of law See legal fiction.

fictitious 1. Based on a legal fiction. 2. False; imaginary.

fictitious name 1. The name to be used by a business. A d/b/a (doing business as) name. 2. An alias.

Fictitious name means a name used in business or trade that is fictitious and that the user has not registered or is not entitled to register as a trade name. R.C. § 1329.01(A)(2)

fictitious payee A payee on a check named by the drawer or maker without intending this payee to have any right to its proceeds.

fictitious person See artificial person.

fidelity bond or **insurance** A contract whereby the insurer agrees to indemnify the insured against loss resulting from the dishonesty of an employee or other person holding a position of trust.

fides faith, honesty, veracity.

fiduciary One whose duty is to act in the interests of another with a high standard of care. Someone in whom another has a right to place great trust and to expect great loyalty.

fiduciary bond A bond that a court requires of fiduciaries (e.g., trustees, executors) to guarantee the performance of their duties.

fiduciary duty A duty to act with the highest standard of care and loyalty for another's benefit, always subordinating one's own personal interests.

fiduciary relationship A relationship in which one owes a fiduciary duty (see this phrase) to another, e.g., attorney-client relationship. Also called confidential relationship.

A relationship is one in which special confidence and trust is reposed in the integrity and fidelity of another and there is a resulting position of superiority or influence, acquired by virtue of this special trust. *Tucker*, 123 Ohio Misc.2d 88 (Ohio Mun., 2003)

fiduciary shield doctrine A person's business in a state solely as a corporate officer does not create personal jurisdiction over that person.

field warehousing Financing by pledging inventory under the control of the lender or a warehouser working on behalf of the lender.

fieri facias (fi. fa.) A writ or order to a sheriff to seize and sell the debtor's property to enforce (satisfy) a judgment.

fi. fa. See fieri facias.

FIFO First in, first out. An inventory flow assumption by which the first goods purchased are assumed to be the first goods used or sold.

Fifth Amendment The amendment to the U.S. Constitution that provides rights pertaining to grand juries, double jeopardy, self-incrimination, due process of law, and just compensation for the taking of private property.

fighting words Words likely to provoke a violent reaction when heard by an ordinary citizen and consequently may not have free-speech protection.

Words that by their very utterance inflict injury or tend to incite an immediate breach of the peace. *State v. Thompson*, 95 Ohio St.3d 264 (Ohio 2002)

file 1. To deliver a document to a court officer so that it can become part of the official collection of documents in a case. To deliver a document to a government agency. 2. To commence a lawsuit. 3. A law firm's collection of documents for a current or closed case.

file wrapper The entire record of the proceedings on an application in the U.S. Patent and Trademark Office. Also called prosecution history.

file wrapper estoppel One cannot recapture in an infringement action the breadth of a patent previously surrendered in the patent office.

filiation 1. The relationship between parent and child. 2. A court determination of paternity.

filiation proceeding A judicial proceeding to establish paternity.

filibuster A tactic to delay or obstruct proposed legislation, e.g., engaging in prolonged speeches on the floor of the legislature.

filing A document delivered to a court or government agency.

filius nullius ("son of nobody") An illegitimate child.

final 1. Not requiring further judicial or official action. 2. Conclusive. 3. Last.

final argument See closing argument.

final judgment; final decree A judgment or decree that resolves all issues in a case, leaving nothing for future determination other than the execution or enforcement of the judgment.

Final decree is one that determines the whole case, or distinct branch thereof, and reserves nothing for future determination, so that it will not be necessary to bring cause before the court for further proceedings. *Renner's Welding*, 117 Ohio App.3d 61 (Ohio App., 1996)

final submission Completing the presentation (including arguments) of everything a litigating party has to offer on the facts and law.

finance 1. To supply with funds; to provide with capital or loan money to. 2. The management of money, credit, investments, etc.

finance charge The extra cost (e.g., interest) imposed for the privilege of deferring payment of the purchase price.

finance company A company engaged in the business of making loans.

Financing agency means a bank, finance company, or other person who in the ordinary course of business make[s] advances against goods or documents of title or who by arrangement with either the seller or the buyer intervenes in ordinary course to make or collect payment due or claimed under the contract for sale, as by purchasing or paying the seller's draft or making advances against it or by merely taking it for collection whether or not documents of title accompany the draft. R.C. § 1302.01(A)(6)

financial institution A bank, trust company, credit union, savings and loan association, or similar institution engaged in financial transactions with the public such as receiving, holding, investing, or lending money.

financial responsibility law A law requiring owners of motor vehicles to prove (through personal assets or insurance) that they can satisfy judgments against them involving the operation of the vehicles.

financial statement A report summarizing the financial condition of an organization or individual on or for a certain date or period.

financing statement A document filed as a public record to notify third parties, e.g., prospective buyers or lenders, that there may be an enforceable security interest in specific property.

find To make a determination of what the facts are.

finder Someone who finds or locates something for another. An intermediary who brings parties together (e.g., someone who secures mortgage financing for a borrower).

finder of fact See fact-finder.

finder's fee A fee paid to someone for finding something or for bringing parties together for a business transaction.

finding of fact The determination of a fact. A conclusion, after considering evidence, on the existence or nonexistence of a fact.

fine 1. To order someone to pay a sum of money to the state as a criminal or civil penalty. 2. The money so paid.

> A fine is a financial punishment for committing a wrong and is for public benefit. *In re Howard's Estate*, 68 N.E.2d 820 (Ohio Prob., 1946)

fine print The part of an agreement or other document containing exceptions, disclaimers, or other details, often difficult to read.

fingerprint The unique pattern of lines on a person's fingertip that can be made into an impression, often for purposes of identification.

firefighter's rule Negligence in causing a fire or other dangerous situation furnishes no basis for liability to a firefighter, police officer, or other professional who is injured while responding to the danger.

firm 1. A business or professional entity. 2. Fixed, binding.

firm offer An offer that remains open and binding (irrevocable) for a period of time until accepted or rejected.

First Amendment The amendment to the U.S. Constitution that provides rights pertaining to the establishment and free exercise of religion, freedom of speech and press, peaceful assembly, and petitioning the government.

first degree The most serious level of an offense.

first-degree murder Killing another with premeditation, with extreme cruelty or atrocity, or while committing another designated felony.

first impression Concerning an issue being addressed for the first time.

first in, first out See FIFO.

first lien; first mortgage A lien or mortgage with priority that must be satisfied before other liens or mortgages on the same property.

first offender A person convicted of a crime for the first time and, therefore, may be entitled to more lenient sentencing or treatment.

> Anyone who has been convicted of an offense in this state or any other jurisdiction and who previously or subsequently has not been convicted of the same or a different offense in this state or any other jurisdiction. R.C. § 2953.31(A)

first refusal See right of first refusal.

fiscal Pertaining to financial matters, e.g., revenue, debt, expenses.

fiscal year Any 12 consecutive months chosen by a business as its accounting period (e.g., 7/01/08 to 6/30/09).

fishing expedition Unfocused questioning or investigation. Improper discovery undertaken with the purpose of finding an issue.

fitness for a particular purpose See warranty of fitness for a particular purpose.

fix 1. To determine or establish something, e.g., price, rate. 2. To prearrange something dishonestly. 3. To fasten or repair. 4. An injection or dose of heroin or other illegal drug.

fixed assets An asset (e.g., machinery, land) held long-term and used to produce goods and services. Also called capital assets.

fixed capital Fixed assets. Money invested in fixed assets.

fixed charges Expenses or costs that must be paid regardless of the condition of the business (e.g., tax payments, overhead).

fixed income Income that does not fluctuate (e.g., interest on a bond).

fixed liability 1. A debt that is certain as to obligation and amount. 2. A debt that will not mature soon; a long-term debt.

fixed rate An interest rate that does not vary for the term of the loan.

fixture Something that is so attached to land as to be deemed a part of it. An item of personal property that is now so connected to the land that it cannot be removed without substantial injury to itself or the land.

> To be a fixture, the item must be actually affixed to or next to realty; generally, this means that chattel must be so attached that it loses its identity as chattel or that it cannot be removed without injury to itself or to freehold. *Rose*, 68 Ohio Misc.2d 9 (Ohio Com.Pl., 1994)

flagrante delicto See in flagrante delicto.

flat rate A fixed payment regardless of how much of a service is used.

flight Fleeing to avoid arrest or detention.

float 1. The time between the writing of a check and the withdrawal of the funds that will cover it. 2. The total amount representing checks in the process of collection. 3. To allow a given currency to freely establish its own value as against other currencies in response to supply and demand.

floater policy An insurance policy that is issued to cover items that have no fixed location (e.g., jewelry that is worn).

floating capital Funds available for current needs; capital in circulation.

floating debt Short-term debt for current needs.

floating interest rate A rate of interest that is not fixed; the rate may fluctuate by market conditions or be pegged to an index.

> Floating rate interest structure means provisions in the bond proceedings whereby the interest rate or rates payable on the bonds, or upon successive series of commercial paper, vary from time to time pursuant to or in relation to an index provided by an indexing agent or otherwise established, a formula, base, publicly announced rate, yields on other obligations, determinations of an agent, or any one or combination of the foregoing, with or without approval or consent of the absolute obligor or issuer as provided in the bond proceedings. R.C. § 9.98(I)

floating lien A lien on present and after-acquired assets of the debtor during the period of the loan.

floating zone A special detailed use district of undetermined location; it "floats" over the area where it may be established.

floor 1. The minimum or lowest limit. 2. Where legislators sit and cast their votes. 3. The right of someone to address the assembly.

floor plan financing A loan secured by the items for sale and paid off as the items are sold.

flotsam Goods that float on the sea when cast overboard or abandoned.

FLSA Fair Labor Standards Act (29 USC § 201) (*www.dol.gov/esa/whd/flsa*).

FNC See forum non conveniens.

FOB See free on board.

FOIA See Freedom of Information Act.

follow 1. To accept as authority. 2. To go or come after.

forbearance Deciding not to take action, e.g., to collect a debt.

for cause For a reason relevant to one's ability and fitness to perform a duty as a juror, employee, fiduciary, etc.

force Strength or pressure directed to an end; physical coercion.

> Force may properly be defined as effort rather than violence. *State v. Muniz*, 162 Ohio App.3d 198 (Ohio App., 2005)

forced heir A person who by law must receive a portion of a testator's estate even if the latter tries to disinherit that person.

forced sale 1. A court-ordered sale of property to satisfy a judgment. Also called execution sale. 2. A sale one is pressured to make.

force majeure An unexpected event; an irresistible and superior force that could not have been foreseen or avoided.

forcible detainer 1. Unlawfully (and often by force) keeping possession of land to which one is no longer entitled. 2. See forcible entry and detainer.

forcible entry Taking possession of land with force or threats of violence. Using physical force to enter land or gain entry into a building.

forcible entry and detainer 1. A summary, speedy, and adequate remedy to obtain the return of possession of land to which one is entitled. Also called forcible detainer. 2. Using physical force or threats of violence to obtain and keep possession of land unlawfully.

> Action of forcible entry and detainer is an action at law based upon contract, i.e., action to obtain possession or repossession of real property which had been transferred from one to another pursuant to contract, and such proceeding is not an action to determine ownership of title to property. *Behrle*, 6 Ohio St.3d 41 (Ohio 1983)

foreclosure The procedure to terminate the rights of a defaulting mortgagor in property that secured the mortgagor's debt. The lender-mortgagee can then sell the property to satisfy the remaining debt.

foreign Pertaining to another country or to one of the 50 states of the United States other than the state you are in.

> Foreign judgment, defined as the judgment of a state or federal court located outside of Ohio. *Kemper Securities*, 107 Ohio App.3d 258 (Ohio App., 1995)

foreign administrator A person appointed in another state or jurisdiction to manage the estate of the deceased.

foreign commerce Trade involving more than one nation.

foreign corporation A corporation chartered or incorporated in one state or country but doing business in another state or country.

foreign exchange 1. The currency of another country. 2. Buying, selling, or converting one country's currency for that of another.

foreman 1. The presiding member and spokesperson of a jury. 2. A superintendent or supervisor of other workers. Also called foreperson.

forensic 1. Belonging to or suitable in courts of law. 2. Pertaining to the use of scientific techniques to discover and examine evidence. 3. Concerning argumentation. 4. Forensics: ballistics or firearms evidence.

forensic medicine The science of applying medical knowledge and techniques in court proceedings to discover and interpret evidence.

foreperson See foreman.

foreseeability The extent to which something can be known in advance; reasonable anticipation of something.

> Foreseeability, as applicable to determination of proximate cause necessary to conviction for involuntary manslaughter, is likened to where consequences of conduct are direct, normal, and reasonably inevitable when viewed in light of ordinary experience. *State v. Voland*, 99 Ohio Misc.2d 61 (Ohio Com.Pl., 1999)

forestalling the market Buying products on their way to market in order to resell them at a higher price.

forfeiture The loss of property, rights, or privileges because of penalty, breach of duty, or the failure to make a timely claim of them.

forgery 1. Making a false document or altering a real one with the intent to commit a fraud. 2. The document or thing that is forged.

form 1. Technical matters of style, structure, and format not involving the merits or substance of something. 2. A document, usually preprinted as a model, to be filled in and adapted to one's needs. 3. See forms of action.

> Form means any document, device, or item used to convey information, regardless of medium, that has blank spaces for the insertion of information and that may have a predetermined format and data elements to guide the entry, interpretation, and use of the information. R.C. § 125.91(B)

formal 1. Following accepted procedures or customs. 2. Pertaining to matters of form as opposed to content or substance. 3. Ceremonial.

formal contract 1. A contract under seal or other contract that complies with prescribed formalities. 2. A contract in writing.

forma pauperis See in forma pauperis.

former adjudication See collateral estoppel and res judicata on when a former adjudication (prior judgment) on the merits will prevent relitigating issues and claims.

former jeopardy, defense of A person cannot be tried or prosecuted for the same offense more than once. See also double jeopardy.

forms of action The procedural devices or actions (e.g., trespass on the case) that are used to take advantage of common-law theories of liability.

fornication Sexual relations between unmarried persons or between married persons who are not married to each other.

forswear 1. To give up something completely. To renounce something under oath. 2. To swear falsely; to commit perjury.

forthwith Without delay; immediately.

Forthwith, as used in provision of State Constitution which requires city charter amendment to be submitted to election forthwith upon petition by ten percent of electors, means immediately. Const. Art. 18, §§ 8, 9. *State ex rel. Committee for Charter Amendment Petition*, 81 Ohio St.3d 590 (Ohio 1998)

fortiori See a fortiori.

fortuitous Happening by chance or accident rather than by design.

forum 1. The court; the court where the litigation is brought. 2. A setting or place for public discussion.

forum domicilii The court in the jurisdiction where a party is domiciled.

forum non conveniens (FNC) The discretionary power of a court to decline the exercise of the jurisdiction it has when the convenience of the parties and the ends of justice would be better served if the action were brought and tried in another forum that also has jurisdiction.

Doctrine of forum non conveniens permits trial court to deny plaintiff use of its jurisdiction as otherwise proper venue to further the ends of justice and promote convenience of the parties, but doctrine is not available to transfer case from one proper Ohio venue to another, as that is not provided for in the rule governing changes of venue. Rules Civ.Proc., Rule 3(C). *Soloman*, 14 Ohio App.3d 20 (Ohio App., 1996)

forum rei The court in the jurisdiction where the defendant is domiciled or the subject matter of the case is located.

forum selection clause A contract clause stating that any future litigation between the parties will be conducted in a specified forum (jurisdiction).

forum shopping Choosing a court or jurisdiction where you are most likely to win.

forward contract An agreement to buy or sell goods at a specified time in the future at a price established when the contract is entered. The agreement is not traded on an exchange.

foster home A home that provides shelter and substitute family care temporarily or for extended periods when a child's own family cannot properly care for him or her, often due to neglect or delinquency.

foundation 1. A fund for charitable, educational, religious, or other benevolent purpose. 2. The underlying basis or support for something. Evidence that shows the relevance of other evidence.

founder One who establishes something, e.g., an institution or trust fund.

founding father A leader in establishing a country or organization.

four corners The contents of a written document; what is written on the surface or face of a document.

four corner's rule 1. The intention of the parties to a contract or other instrument is to be ascertained from the document as a whole and not from isolated parts thereof. 2. If a contract is clear on its face, no evidence outside the contract may be considered to contradict its terms.

Four corners of insurance policy include liability coverage section and exclusions section, and proper construction of policy cannot be accomplished by relying on one provision to exclusion of the others. *Natl. Union Fire Ins. Co. of Pittsburgh*, 78 Ohio App.3d 765 (Ohio App., 1992)

frame 1. To formulate or draft. 2. To produce false evidence that causes an innocent person to appear guilty.

franchise 1. The right to vote. 2. A contract that allows a business (the franchisee) the sole right to use the intellectual property and brand identity, marketing experience, and operational methods of another business (the franchisor) in a certain area. 3. A government authorization to engage in a specified commercial endeavor or to incorporate.

franchisee The person or entity granted a franchise.

franchise tax A tax on the privilege of engaging in a business.

A tax on the privilege of doing business within the state; it is not a tax on property of the paying entity. *Mutual Holding Co.*, 71 Ohio St.3d 59 (Ohio 1994)

franchisor The person or entity that grants a franchise.

franking privilege The privilege of sending certain matter through the mail without paying postage. Also called frank.

fraternal benefit association or **society** A nonprofit association of persons of similar calling or background who aid and assist one another and promote worthy causes.

fratricide The killing of a brother or sister.

fraud A false statement of material fact made with the intent to mislead by having the victim rely on the statement. A tort is committed if the victim suffers actual damage due to justifiable reliance on the statement.

The elements of fraudulent misrepresentation are: (1) a false representation, actual or implied, or the concealment of a matter of fact, material to the transaction, made falsely; (2) knowledge of the falsity, or statements made with such utter disregard and recklessness that knowledge is inferred; (3) intent to mislead another into relying on the representation; (4) reliance with a right to rely; and (5) injury as a consequence of that reliance. *Westfield Ins. Co.*, 128 Ohio App.3d 270 (Ohio App., 1998)

fraud in fact See positive fraud.

fraud in law Constructive or presumed fraud.

fraud in the factum A misrepresentation about the essential nature or existence of the document itself.

fraud in the inducement Misrepresentation as to the terms other aspects of a contractual relation, venture, or other transaction that leads (induces) a person to agree to enter into the transaction with a false impression or understanding of the risks or obligations he or she has undertaken.

fraud on the market theory When false information artificially inflates the value of a stock, it is presumed that purchasers on the open market relied on that information to their detriment.

frauds, statute of See statute of frauds.

fraudulent Involving fraud.

fraudulent concealment 1. Taking affirmative steps to hide or suppress a material fact that one is legally or morally bound to disclose. 2. An equitable doctrine that estops a defendant who concealed his or her wrongful conduct from asserting the statute of limitations.

fraudulent conveyance Transferring property without fair consideration in order to place the property beyond the reach of creditors.

> Fraudulent conveyance occurs either when debtor transfers assets without receiving adequate consideration, when debtor transfers assets during insolvency or resulting in insolvency, or when debtor transfers assets for purpose of delaying or defrauding creditors. *Link*, 79 Ohio App.3d 735 (Ohio App., 1992)

fraudulent misrepresentation See fraud.

FRCP Federal Rules of Civil Procedure. See federal rules.

free 1. Not subject to the legal constraint of another. 2. Not subject to a burden. 3. Having political rights. 4. To liberate. 5. Without cost.

free alongside ship (FAS) The quoted price includes the cost of delivering the goods to a designated point alongside of the ship. The risk of loss is with the seller up to this point.

free and clear Not subject to liens or other encumbrances.

freedom of association The right protected in the First Amendment to join with others for lawful purposes.

freedom of contract The right of parties to enter a bargain of their choice subject to reasonable government regulation in the interest of public health, safety, and morals.

freedom of expression The rights protected in the First Amendment concerning freedom of speech, press, and religion.

Freedom of Information Act (FOIA) A federal statute making information held by federal agencies available to the public unless the information is exempt from public disclosure (5 USC § 552). Many states have equivalent statutes for state agencies.

freedom of religion The right protected in the First Amendment to believe and practice one's form of religion or to believe in no religion. In addition, the right to be free of governmental promotion of religion or interference with one's practice of religion.

freedom of speech The right protected in the First Amendment to express one's ideas without government restrictions subject to the right of the government to protect public safety and to provide a remedy for defamation.

freedom of the press The First Amendment prohibition against government restrictions that abridge the freedom of the press such as imposing prior restraint or censorship.

freedom of the seas The right of ships to travel without restriction in the sea beyond the territorial waters of any nation.

free exercise clause The clause in the First Amendment stating that "Congress shall make no law . . . prohibiting the free exercise" of religion.

freehold An estate in land for life, in fee simple, or in fee tail. An estate in real property of uncertain or unlimited duration, unlike a leasehold, which is for a definite period of time.

> A freeholder is an owner of an interest in land, the duration of which is not fixed by a specified or certain period of time. *Citizens for Choice*, 143 Ohio App.3d 823 (Ohio App., 2001)

freelance paralegal See independent paralegal.

free on board (FOB) In a sales price quotation, the seller assumes all responsibilities and costs up to the point of delivery on board.

freeze To hold something (e.g., wages, prices) at a fixed level; to immobilize or maintain the status quo.

freeze-out Action by major shareholders or a board of directors to eliminate minority shareholders or to marginalize their power.

fresh Prompt; without material interval.

fresh complaint rule A victim's complaint of sexual assault made to another person soon after the event is admissible.

fresh pursuit 1. A police officer, engaged in a continuous and uninterrupted pursuit, can cross geographic or jurisdictional lines to arrest a felon even if the officer does not have a warrant. 2. A victim of property theft can use reasonable force to obtain it back just after it is taken. Also called hot pursuit.

> Fresh pursuit includes fresh pursuit as defined by the common law. . . . Fresh pursuit does not necessarily imply instant pursuit, but pursuit without unreasonable delay. R.C. § 2935.29(A)

friendly Pertaining to someone who is favorably disposed; not hostile.

friendly suit A suit brought by agreement between the parties to obtain the opinion of the court on their dispute.

friend of the court See amicus curiae.

friendly takeover The acquisition of one company by another that is approved by the boards of directors of both companies.

fringe benefits Benefits provided by an employer that are in addition to the employee's regular compensation (e.g., vacation).

frisk To conduct a pat-down search of a suspect in order to find concealed weapons.

frivolous 1. Involving a legal position that cannot be supported by a good-faith argument based on existing law or on the need for a change in the law. 2. Clearly insufficient on its face.

> A frivolous claim . . . is a claim that is not supported by facts in which the complainant has a good-faith belief, and which is not grounded in any legitimate theory of law or argument for future modification of the law. R.C. § 2323.51. *Mason*, 140 Ohio App.3d 474 (Ohio App., 2000)

frivolous appeal An appeal that is devoid of merit or one that has no reasonable chance of succeeding.

frolic Employee conduct outside the scope of employment because it is personal rather than primarily for the employer's business.

front A person or organization acting as a cover for illegal activities or to disguise the identity of the real owner or principal.

frontage The land between a building and the street; the front part of property.

> Frontage includes streets on which a lot fronts breadthwise but does not include a street on which such lot abuts lengthwise. *State ex rel. Gulf Refining Co.*, 89 Ohio App. 1 (Ohio App., 1950)

front-end load A sales fee or commission (the load) levied at the time of making a stock or mutual fund purchase.

frozen assets Nonliquid assets. Assets that cannot be easily converted into cash.

fructus The fruit or produce of land.

fruit 1. The effect, consequence, or product of something. 2. Evidence resulting from an activity.

fruit and tree doctrine One cannot avoid taxation on income simply by assigning it to someone else.

fruit of the poisonous tree doctrine Evidence derived directly or indirectly from illegal governmental activity (e.g., an illegal search and seizure), is inadmissible as trial evidence.

> An exclusionary rule that reaches not only primary evidence obtained as a direct result of an illegal search or seizure but also evidence later discovered and found to be derivative of an illegality, or fruit of the poisonous tree. *State v. Smith*, 163 Ohio App.3d 567 (Ohio App., 2005)

fruits of crime Stolen goods or other products of criminal conduct.

frustration Preventing something from occurring. Rendering something ineffectual.

frustration of contract or **purpose** See commercial frustration.

FTC Federal Trade Commission (*www.ftc.gov*).

fugitive One who flees in order to avoid arrest, prosecution, prison, service of process, or subpoena to testify (18 USC § 1073).

> Fugitive felon means an individual who is fleeing to avoid prosecution, or custody or confinement after conviction, under the laws of the place from which the individual is fleeing, for a crime or an attempt to commit a crime that is a felony under the laws of the place from which the individual is fleeing or, in the case of New Jersey, a high misdemeanor, regardless of whether the individual has departed from the individual's usual place of residence. R.C. § 5101.26(B)

full age See age of majority.

full bench; full court See en banc.

full coverage Insurance with no exclusions or deductibles.

full faith and credit A state must recognize and enforce (give full faith and credit to) the legislative acts, public records, and judicial decisions of sister states. U.S. Constitution, art. IV, § 1.

full settlement An adjustment of all pending matters and the mutual release of all prior obligations existing between the parties.

full warranty A warranty that covers labor and parts for all defects.

functus officio Without further official authority once the authorized task is complete.

fund 1. Money or other resources available for a specific purpose. 2. A group or organization that administers or manages money. 3. To convert into fixed-interest, long-term debt.

fundamental Serving as an essential component; basic.

fundamental error See plain error.

fundamental law Constitutional law; the law establishing basic rights and governing principles.

fundamental right A basic right that is either explicitly or implicitly guaranteed by the constitution.

funded debt 1. A debt that has resources earmarked for the payment of interest and principal as they become due. 2. Long-term debt that has replaced short-term debt.

fungible Interchangeable; substitutable; able to be replaced by other assets of the same kind. Examples: grain, sugar, oil.

future advances Funds advanced by a lender after creation of, but still secured by, the mortgage or other security agreement.

future damages Sums awarded for future pain and suffering, impairment of earning capacity, future medical expenses, and other future losses.

> Future damages means damages that result from an injury or loss to person or property that is a subject of a tort action and that will accrue after the verdict or determination of liability by the trier of fact is rendered in that tort action. R.C. § 2317.62(A)(2)

future earnings Income that a party is no longer able to earn because of injury or loss of employment.

future estate See future interest.

future interest An interest in real or personal property in which possession, use, or other enjoyment is future rather than present. Also called estate in expectancy, future estate.

futures Commodities or securities sold or bought for delivery in the future.

futures contract A contract for the sale or purchase of a commodity or security at a specified price and quantity for future delivery.

FY Fiscal year.

G

GAAP Generally Accepted Accounting Principles.

gag order 1. A court order to stop attorneys, witnesses, or media from discussing a current case. 2. An order by the court to bind and gag a disruptive defendant during his or her trial.

gain 1. Profit; excess of receipts over costs. 2. Increments of value.

gainful employment Available work for pay.

gambling Risking money or other property for the possibility—chance—of a reward. Also called gaming.

> Gambling device means any of the following: (1) A book, totalizer, or other equipment for recording bets; (2) A ticket, token, or other device representing a chance, share, or interest in a scheme of chance or evidencing a bet; (3) A deck of cards, dice, gaming table, roulette wheel, slot machine, or other apparatus designed for use in connection with a game of chance; (4) Any equipment, device, apparatus, or paraphernalia specially designed for gambling purposes; (5) Bingo supplies sold or otherwise provided, or used, in violation of this chapter. R.C. § 2915.01(F)

game laws Laws regulating the hunting of wild animals and birds.

gaming See gambling.

GAO General Accountability Office (*www.gao.gov*).

gaol A place of detention for temporary or short-term confinement; jail.

garnishee; garnishnor (garnisher) A garnishee is the person or entity in possession of a debtor's property that is being reached or attached (via garnishment) by a creditor of the debtor. The creditor is the garnishor (garnisher).

garnishment A court proceeding by a creditor to force a third party in possession of the debtor's property (e.g., wages) to turn the property over to the creditor to satisfy the debt.

Meaning of garnishment is that person who owes or holds money belonging to another is warned by order of court not to make payment to his immediate creditor, but to third person who has obtained or may obtain final judgment against that creditor. *Sheahan,* 44 Ohio App.2d 393 (Ohio App., 1974)

gavelkind A feudal system under which all sons shared land equally upon the death of their father.

gender discrimination Discrimination based on one's sex or gender.

GBMI Guilty but mentally ill. See also insanity.

general administrator A person given a grant of authority to administer the entire estate of a decedent who dies without a will.

general agent An agent authorized to conduct all of the principal's business affairs, usually involving a continuity of service.

general appearance Acts of a party from which it can reasonably be inferred that the party submits (consents) to the full jurisdiction of the court.

general assembly A legislative body in some states.

general assignment A transfer of a debtor's property for the benefit of all creditors. See also assignment for benefit of creditors.

general average contribution rule When one engaged in a maritime venture voluntarily incurs a loss (e.g., discards part of the cargo) to avert a larger loss of ship or cargo, the loss incurred is shared by all who participated in the venture.

general bequest A gift in a will payable out of the general assets of the estate. A gift in a will of a designated quantity or value of property.

A pecuniary gift of a specified amount to be paid out of the general estate funds, as opposed to a specific bequest, which is a gift of a particular, identifiable item to be given to the beneficiary. *In re Estate of Oberstar,* 126 Ohio App.3d 30 (Ohio App., 1998)

general contractor One who contracts to construct an entire building or project rather than a portion of it; a prime contractor who hires subcontractors, coordinates the work, etc. Also called original contractor, prime contractor.

general counsel The chief attorney or law firm that represents a company or other organization in most of its legal matters.

General Court The name of the legislature in Massachusetts and in New Hampshire.

general creditor See unsecured creditor.

general court marshal A military trial court consisting of five members and one military judge, which can impose any punishment.

general damages Damages that naturally, directly, and frequently result from a wrong. The law implies general damages to exist; they do not have to be specifically alleged. Also called direct damages.

General damages, which are those which flow as conclusion of law from injury suffered, are presumed by the injury and need not be pleaded or proved. *Robb,* 114 Ohio App.3d 595 (Ohio App., 1996)

general demurrer A demurrer challenging whether an opponent has stated a cause of action or attacking a petition in its entirety. See also demurrer.

general denial A response by a party that controverts all of the allegations in the preceding pleading, usually the complaint.

general deposit Placing money in a bank to be repaid upon demand or to be drawn upon from time to time in the usual course of banking business.

general devise A gift in a will to be satisfied out of testator's estate generally; it is not charged upon any specific property or fund.

general election A regularly scheduled election.

general execution See execution (3).

general finding A finding in favor of one party and against the other.

general jurisdiction The power of a court to hear any kind of case, with limited exceptions.

general intent The state of mind in which a person is conscious of the act he or she is committing without necessarily understanding or desiring the consequences of that action.

general law A law that applies to everyone within the class regulated by the law.

Subject of a statute is general, for purposes of state constitution's requirement that all general laws operate uniformly, if the subject does or may exist in, and affect the people of, every county, in the state. Ohio Const. Art. 2, § 26. *Simmons-Harris,* 86 Ohio St.3d 1 (Ohio 1999)

general legacy A gift of personal property in a will that may be satisfied out of the general assets of the testator's estate.

general lien A lien that attaches to all the goods of the debtor, not just the goods that causes the debt.

general partner A business co-owner who can participate in the management of the business and is personally liable for its debts.

general partnership A partnership in which all the partners are general partners, have no restrictions on running the business, and have unlimited liability for the debts of the business. An association of two or more persons to carry on as co-owners of a business for profit.

general power of appointment A power of appointment exercisable in favor of any person that the donee (i.e., the person given the power) may select, including the donee him or herself.

General power of appointment means a power which is exercisable in favor of the decedent, his estate, his creditors, or the creditors of his estate. R.C. § 5731.11(B). General power of appointment means a power that is exercisable in favor of the individual possessing the power, the person's estate, the person's creditors, or the creditors of the person's estate. R.C. § 2131.09(C)

general power of attorney A grant of broad powers by a principal to an agent.

general statute A statute that operates equally upon all persons and things within the scope of the statute. A statute that applies to persons or things as a class. A statute that affects the general public.

general strike Cessation of work by employees throughout an entire industry or country.

general verdict A verdict for one party or the other, as opposed to a verdict that answers specific questions.

general warrant A blanket warrant that does not specify the items to be searched for or the persons to be arrested.

general warranty deed See warranty deed.

General Welfare Clause The clause in the federal constitution giving Congress the power to impose taxes and spend for defense and the general welfare. U.S. Constitution, art. I, § 8, cl. 1.

generation-skipping transfer A transfer of assets to a family member who is more than one generation below the transferor, e.g., from grandparent to grandchild.

generation-skipping trust Any trust having younger generation beneficiaries of more than one generation in the same trust. A trust that makes a generation-skipping transfer.

generic 1. Relating to or characteristic of an entire group or class. 2. Not having a brand name. Identified by its nonproprietary name.

generic drug A drug not protected by trademark that is the same as a brand name drug in safety, strength, quality, intended use, etc.

genetic markers Separate genes or complexes of genes identified as a result of genetic tests. In paternity cases, such tests may exclude a man as the biological father, or may show how probable it is that he is the father.

> Genetic tests and genetic testing mean either of the following: (a) Tissue or blood tests, including tests that identify the presence or absence of common blood group antigens, the red blood cell antigens, human lymphocyte antigens, serum enzymes, serum proteins, or genetic markers; (b) Deoxyribonucleic acid typing of blood or buccal cell samples. Genetic test and genetic testing may include the typing and comparison of deoxyribonucleic acid derived from the blood of one individual and buccal cells of another. R.C. § 3111.09(E)(1)

Geneva Conventions International agreements on the conduct of nations at war, e.g., protection of civilians, treatment of prisoners of war.

genocide Acts committed with intent to destroy, in whole or in part, a national, ethnic, racial, or religious group, e.g., killing members of the group, causing them serious mental harm, or imposing measures designed to prevent births within the group.

gentleman's agreement An agreement, usually unwritten, based on trust and honor. It is not an enforceable contract.

genuine Authentic; being what it purports to be; having what it says it has.

germane Relevant; on point.

gerrymander Dividing a geographic area into voting districts in order to provide an unfair advantage to one political party or group by diluting the voting strength of another party or group.

gestational surrogacy The sperm and egg of a couple are fertilized in vitro in a laboratory; the resulting embryo is then implanted in a surrogate mother who gives birth to a child with whom she has no genetic relationship.

gift A transfer of property to another without payment or consideration. To be irrevocable, (a) there must be a delivery of the property; (b) the transfer must be voluntary; (c) the donor must have legal capacity to make a gift; (d) the donor must intend to divest him or herself of title and control of what is given; (e) the donor must intend that the gift take effect immediately; (f) there must be no consideration (e.g., payment) from the donee; (g) the donee must accept the gift.

> A gift, by its very nature, is gratuitous, and is defined as the voluntary transfer of property to another made without compensation. *Bobo*, 162 Ohio App.3d 565 (Ohio App., 2005)

gift causa mortis A gift made in contemplation of imminent death subject to the implied condition that if the donor recovers or the donee dies first, the gift shall be void.

gift in contemplation of death See gift causa mortis.

gift inter vivos See inter vivos gift.

gift over A gift of property that takes effect when a preceding estate in the property ends or fails.

gifts to minors act The Uniform Transfers to Minors Act covering adult management of gifts to minors, custodial accounts for minors, etc.

gift tax A tax on the transfer of property by gift, usually paid by the donor, although a few states tax the donee.

gilt-edged 1. Of the highest quality. 2. Pertaining to a very safe investment.

Ginnie Mae (GNMA) Government National Mortgage Association (*www.ginniemae.gov*).

gist The central idea or foundation of a legal action or matter.

give To make a gratuitous transfer of property. See also gift.

giveback A reduction in wages or other benefits agreed to by a union during labor bargaining.

gloss A brief explanatory note. An interpretation of a text.

GNP See gross national product.

go bare To engage in an occupation or profession without malpractice insurance.

go forward 1. To proceed with one's case. 2. To introduce evidence.

going and coming rule The scope of employment usually does not include the time when an employee is going to or coming from work. Respondeat superior during such times does not apply.

> Pursuant to the coming and going rule, a fixed-situs employee is generally not entitled to participate in the workers' compensation fund when he is injured during a commute, because a causal connection does not exist between his injury and his employment to satisfy the "arising out of" requirement of workers' compensation statute. R.C. § 4123.01(C). *Barber*, 146 Ohio App.3d 262 (Ohio App., 2001)

going concern An existing solvent business operating in its ordinary and regular manner with no plans to go out of business.

going-concern value What a willing purchaser, in an arm's length transaction, would offer for a company as an operating business as opposed to as one contemplating liquidation.

going private Delisting equity securities from a securities exchange. Going from a publicly owned corporation to a close corporation.

going public Issuing stock for public purchase for the first time; becoming a public corporation.

golden parachute Very high payments and other economic benefits made to an employee upon his or her termination.

golden rule 1. A guideline of statutory interpretation in which we presume that the legislature did not intend an interpretation that would lead to absurd or ridiculous consequences. 2. Urging jurors to place themselves in the position of the injured party or victim.

good 1. Sufficient in law; enforceable. 2. Valid. 3. Reliable.

good behavior Law-abiding. Following the rules. A standard used to grant inmates early release.

good cause A cause that affords a legal excuse; a legally sufficient ground or reason. Also called just cause, sufficient cause.

good consideration Consideration based on blood relationship or natural love and affection. Also called moral consideration.

good faith A state of mind indicating honesty and lawfulness of purpose; the absence of an intent to seek an undue advantage; a belief that known circumstances do not require further investigation.

> Good faith in the case of a merchant means honesty in fact and the observance of reasonable commercial standards of fair dealing in the trade. R.C. § 1302.01 (A)(2)

good faith bargaining Going to the bargaining table with an open mind and a sincere desire to reach agreement.

good faith exception Evidence is admissible (in an exception to the exclusionary rule) if the police reasonably rely on a warrant that is later invalidated because of the lack of probable cause.

good faith purchaser See bona fide purchaser.

goods 1. Movable things other than money or intangible rights. 2. Any personal property.

> All things, including specially manufactured goods but not including the money in which the price is to be paid or things in action, that satisfy both of the following: (a) They are movable at the time of identification for sale or identification to the contract for sale; (b) They are purchased primarily for personal, family, or household purposes. R.C. § 1317.01(C)(1)

Good Samaritan Someone who comes to the assistance of another without a legal obligation to do so. Under good-samaritan laws of most states, a person aiding another in an emergency will not be liable for ordinary negligence in providing this aid.

goods and chattels 1. Personal property. 2. Tangible personal property.

good time Credit for an inmate's good conduct that reduces prison time.

good title A valid title; a title that a reasonably prudent purchaser would accept. Marketable title.

goodwill The reputation of a business that causes it to generate additional customers. The advantages a business has over its competitors due to its name, location, and owner's reputation.

govern 1. To direct or control by authority; to rule. 2. To be a precedent or controlling law.

government 1. The process of governing. 2. The framework of political institutions by which the executive, legislative, and judicial functions of the state are carried on. 3. The sovereign power of a state.

governmental function 1. An activity of government authorized by law for the general public good. 2. A function that can be performed adequately only by the government. An essential function of government.

> Governmental function means a function of a political subdivision that is specified in division (C)(2) of this section or that satisfies any of the following: (a) A function that is imposed upon the state as an obligation of sovereignty and that is performed by a political subdivision voluntarily or pursuant to legislative requirement; (b) A function that is for the common good of all citizens of the state; (c) A function that promotes or preserves the public peace, health, safety, or welfare; that involves activities that are not engaged in or not customarily engaged in by nongovernmental persons; and that is not specified in division (G)(2) of this section as a proprietary function. R.C. § 2744.01(C)(1)

governmental immunity See sovereign immunity.

government contract A contract in which at least one of the parties is a government agency or branch.

government corporation A government-owned corporation that is a mixture of a corporation and a government agency created to serve a predominantly business function in the public interest.

government security A security (e.g., a treasury bill) issued by the government or a government entity.

governor A chief executive official of a state of the United States.

grace period Extra time past a due date given to avoid a penalty (e.g., cancellation) that would otherwise apply to the missed date.

graded offense A crime that can be committed in different categories or classes of severity, resulting in different punishments.

graduated lease A lease for which the rent will vary depending on factors such as the amount of gross income produced.

graduated payment mortgage (GPM) A mortgage that begins with lower payments and that increase over the term of the loan.

graduated tax See progressive tax.

graft Money or personal gain unlawfully received because of one's position of public trust.

grandfather clause A special exemption for those already doing what will now be prohibited or otherwise restricted for others.

grand jury A jury of inquiry that receives accusations in criminal cases, hears the evidence of the prosecutor, and issues indictments when satisfied that a trial should be held.

grand larceny Unlawfully taking and carrying away another's personal property valued in excess of a statutorily set amount (e.g., $100).

grant 1. To give property or a right to another with or without compensation. 2. To transfer real property by deed or other instrument. 3. Something given or transferred.

grantee The person to whom a grant is made or property is conveyed.

grant-in-aid Funds given by the government to a person or institution for a specific purpose, e.g., education or research.

granting clause That portion of a deed or instrument of conveyance that contains the words of transfer of an interest.

grantor The person who makes the grant or conveys property.

Grantor is a person who creates a trust R.C. § 5111.151(B)(3)

grantor-grantee index A master index by grantor name to all recorded instruments (e.g., deeds, mortgages) allowing you to trace the names of sellers and buyers of land up to the present owner.

grantor trust A trust in which the grantor is taxed on its income because of his or her control over the income or corpus.

gratis Without reward or consideration. Free.

gratuitous 1. Given or granted free, without consideration. 2. Unwarranted; unjustified.

gratuitous bailment A bailment in which the care and custody of the bailor's property by the bailee is without charge or expectation of payment.

gratuitous promise A promise made by one who has received no consideration for it.

gravamen The essence of a grievance; the gist of a charge.

gray market A market where goods are legally sold at lower prices than the manufacturer would want or that are imported bearing a valid United States trademark, but without consent of the trademark holder.

great bodily injury A significant or substantial injury or damage; a serious physical impairment. Also called serious bodily harm.

great care The amount of care used by reasonable persons when involved in very important matters. Also called utmost care.

Great Charter See Magna Carta.

Great Writ See habeas corpus.

green card The government-issued registration card indicating the permanent resident status of an alien.

greenmail Inflated payments to buy back the stock of a shareholder (a raider) who has threatened a corporate takeover.

Green River ordinance An ordinance that prohibits door-to-door commercial solicitations without prior consent.

grievance 1. An injury or wrong that can be the basis for an action or complaint. 2. A charge or complaint. 3. A complaint about working conditions or about a violation of a union agreement.

The term grievance as used in a collective bargaining agreement, is not a term of art, having a meaning separate and apart from its meaning in ordinary use. *Gillam,* 1 Ohio App.2d 548 (Ohio App., 1965)

grievance procedure Formal steps established to resolve disputes arising under a collective bargaining agreement.

gross 1. Glaring, obvious. 2. Reprehensible. 3. Total; before or without diminution or deduction.

gross estate The total assets of a person at his or her death before deductions are taken.

gross income All income from whatever source before exemptions, deductions, credits, or other adjustments.

gross lease A lease in which the tenant pays only rent; the landlord pays everything else, e.g., taxes, utilities, insurance, etc.

gross national product (GNP) The total value of all goods and services produced in a given period.

gross negligence 1. The intentional failure to perform a manifest duty in reckless disregard of the consequences to the life or property of another. 2. The failure to use even slight care and diligence. Also called willful negligence.

Gross negligence is evidenced by willful and wanton conduct, and exists where actor does an act or intentionally fails to do an act which it is his duty to do, knowing or having reason to know of facts which would lead reasonable man to realize not only that his conduct creates unreasonable risk of physical harm to another but also that such risk is substantially greater than that which is necessary to make his conduct negligent. *Harsh,* 111 Ohio App.3d 113 (Ohio App., 1996)

gross receipts The total amount of money (and any other consideration) received from selling goods or services.

ground 1. Foundation; points relied on. 2. A reason that is legally sufficient to obtain a remedy or other result.

ground rent 1. Rent paid to the owner for the use of undeveloped land, usually to construct a building on it. 2. A perpetual rent reserved to the grantor (and his or her heirs) from land conveyed in fee simple.

group annuity A policy that provides annuities to a group of people under a single master contract.

group boycott Agreements among competitors within the same market tier not to deal with other competitors or market participants.

group insurance A single insurance policy covering a group of individuals, e.g., employees of a particular company.

group legal services A form of legal insurance in which members of a group make a periodic payment for future legal services.

growth stock The stock in a company that is expected to have higher than average growth, particularly in the value of the stock.

GSA General Services Administration (*www.gsa.gov*).

guarantee 1. An assurance that a particular outcome will occur, e.g., a product will perform as stated or will be repaired at no cost. Also called guaranty. 2. A promise to fulfill the obligation of another if the latter fails to do so. 3. To give security. 4. Security given.

A guaranty or guarantee does not always import a guaranty contract, but may mean a promise or agreement importing an original obligation. *West,* 134 N.E.2d 185 (Ohio Com.Pl., 1956)

guaranteed stock The stock of one corporation whose dividends are guaranteed by another corporation, e.g., by a parent corporation.

guarantor One who makes a guaranty; one who becomes secondarily liable for another's debt or performance.

guaranty 1. A promise to fulfill the obligation of another if the latter fails to do so. 2. See guarantee (1).

guardian A person who lawfully has the power and duty to care for the person, property, or rights of another who is incapable of managing his or her affairs (e.g., a minor, an insane person).

guardian ad litem (GAL) A special guardian appointed by the court to represent the interests of another (e.g., a minor) in court. See also ad litem.

guardianship 1. The office, duty, or authority of a guardian. 2. The fiduciary relationship that exists between guardian and ward.

guest 1. A passenger in a motor vehicle who is offered a ride by someone who receives no benefits from the passenger other than hospitality, goodwill, and the like. 2. One who pays for the services of a restaurant or place of lodging. 3. A recipient of one's hospitality, especially at home.

guest statute A statute providing that drivers of motor vehicles will not be liable for injuries caused by their ordinary negligence to nonpaying guest passengers.

> Where the transportation is furnished for mutual business or material interests of both rider and driver, the rider is passenger and not guest within the meaning of the guest statute. R.C. § 4515.02. *Roberts*, 41 Ohio Misc. 23 (Ohio Com.Pl., 1974)

guilty 1. A defendant's plea that accepts (or does not contest) the criminal charge against him or her. 2. A determination by a jury or court that the defendant has committed the crime charged. 3. Responsible for criminal or civil wrongdoing.

H

habeas corpus ("you have the body") A writ designed to bring a party before a court in order to test the legality of his or her detention or imprisonment. Also called the Great Writ.

> A writ of habeas corpus is an extraordinary remedy available where there is an unlawful restraint of a person's liberty and no adequate remedy at law. *Pratts*, 102 Ohio St.3d 81 (Ohio 2004)

habeas corpus ad faciendum et recipiendum A writ to move a civil case (and the body of the defendant) from a lower to a higher court.

habeas corpus ad prosequendum A writ issued for the purpose of indicting, prosecuting, and sentencing a defendant already confined within another jurisdiction.

habeas corpus ad testificandum A writ used to bring in a prisoner detained in a jail or prison to give evidence before the court.

> A writ of habeas corpus ad testificandum does not inquire into lawfulness of restraint; it merely addresses discretion of court to permit person detained to appear as witness. *In re Colburn*, 30 Ohio St.3d 141 (Ohio 1987)

habendum clause The portion of a deed (often using the words, "to have and to hold") that describes the ownership rights being transferred (i.e., the estate or interest being granted).

habitability The condition of a building that allows it to be enjoyed because it is free from substantial defects that endanger health or safety.

habitable Suitable or fit for living.

habitation 1. Place of abode; one's dwelling or residence. 2. Occupancy.

habitual Customary, usual, regular.

habitual criminal A repeat offender. Also called career criminal, recidivist.

> Habitual sex offender includes any person who is convicted two or more times, in separate criminal actions, for commission of any of the sex offenses set forth in division (B) of this section. R.C. § 2950.01(A)

half blood (half brother, half sister) The relationship between persons who have the same father or the same mother, but not both.

halfway house A house in the community that helps individuals make the adjustment from prison or other institutionalization to normal life.

hand down To announce or file an opinion by a court.

handicap A physical or mental impairment or disability that substantially limits one or more of a person's major life activities.

harassment Intrusive or unwanted acts, words, or gestures (often persistent and continuing) that have a substantial adverse effect on the safety, security, or privacy of another and that serve no legitimate purpose.

harbor To shelter or protect, often clandestinely and illegally.

hard cases Cases in which a court sometimes overlooks fixed legal principles when they are opposed to persuasive equities.

hard labor Forced physical labor required of an inmate.

harm 1. Loss or detriment to a person. 2. To injure.

harmless Not causing any damage.

harmless error An error that did not prejudice the substantial rights of the party alleging it. Also called technical error.

> Harmless error is one which does not affect substantial right of parties. Ohio Rules Civ.Proc., Rule 61. *Knor*, 73 Ohio App.3d 177 (Ohio App., 1991)

Hatch Act A federal statute that prohibits federal employees from engaging in certain types of political activities (5 USC § 1501).

hate crime A crime motivated by hatred, bias, or prejudice, based on race, color, religion, national origin, ethnicity, gender, or sexual orientation of another individual or group of individuals.

have and hold See habendum clause.

hazard 1. A risk or danger of harm or loss. The chance of suffering a loss. 2. Danger, peril.

hazardous Exposed to or involving danger. Risky.

> Hazardous substance means any substance or mixture of substances which is toxic, corrosive, an irritant, strong sensitizer, flammable, or which generates pressure through decomposition, heat, or other means, if such substance or mixture of substances may cause substantial personal injury or illness during any customary or reasonably anticipated handling or use. R.C. § 3716.01(D)

H.B. House Bill. A proposed statute considered by the House of Representatives.

headnote A short-paragraph summary of a portion of a court opinion printed before the opinion begins. Also called syllabus.

head of household 1. The primary income earner in a household. 2. An unmarried taxpayer (or married if living and filing separately) who maintains a home that for more than one-half of the taxable year is the principal place of abode of certain dependents, such as an unmarried child.

head tax See poll tax.

healthcare proxy See advance directive.

health maintenance organization (HMO) A prepaid health insurance plan consisting of a network of doctors and healthcare institutions that provide medical services to subscribers.

hearing 1. A proceeding designed to resolve issues of fact or law. Usually, an impartial officer presides, evidence is presented, etc. The hearing is *ex parte* if only one party is present; it is *adversarial* if both parties are present. 2. A meeting of a legislative committee to consider proposed legislation or other legislative matters. 3. A meeting in which one is allowed to argue a position.

hearing officer; hearing examiner See administrative law judge.

hearsay 1. What one learns from another rather than from first-hand knowledge. 2. An out-of-court statement offered to prove the truth of the matter asserted in the statement. A "statement, other than one made by the declarant while testifying at the trial or hearing, offered in evidence to prove the truth of the matter asserted." Federal Rule of Evidence 801(c).

> Hearsay is a statement, other than one made by the declarant while testifying at the trial or hearing, offered in evidence to prove the truth of the matter asserted. Ohio Evid. R. Rule 801(B)

heart balm statute A law abolishing heart balm actions, which are actions based on a broken heart or loss of love (e.g., breach of promise to marry, alienation of affections, criminal conversation).

heat of passion Fear, rage, or resentment in which a person loses self-control due to provocation. Also called hot blood, sudden heat of passion.

hedge To safeguard oneself from loss on a bet, bargain, or speculation by making compensatory arrangements on the other side. To reduce risk by entering a transaction that will offset an existing position.

hedge fund A special investment fund that uses aggressive (higher risk) strategies such as short selling and using derivatives.

hedonic damages Damages that cover the victim's loss of pleasure or enjoyment of life.

heinous Shockingly odious or evil.

heir 1. One designated by state law to receive all or part of the estate of a person who dies without leaving a valid will (intestate). Also called heir at law, legal heir. 2. One who inherits (or is in line to inherit) by intestacy or by will.

> In a technical sense, term "heir" refers to anyone who would take estate of intestate under statute of descent and distribution. *Varns*, 81 Ohio App.3d 26 (Ohio App., 1991)

heir apparent See apparent heir.

heir at law See heir (1).

heir collateral See collateral heir.

heir of the blood One who inherits because of a blood relationship with the decedent in the ascending or descending line.

heir of the body A blood relative in the direct line of descent, e.g., children, grandchildren (excluding adopted children).

heir presumptive See presumptive heir.

heirs and assigns Words used to convey a fee simple estate.

held Decided. See also hold.

henceforth From this (or that) time on.

hereafter 1. From now on. 2. At some time in the future.

hereditament 1. Property, rights, or anything that can be inherited. 2. Real property.

hereditary Capable of being inherited. Pertaining to inheritance.

hereditary succession See intestate succession.

herein In this section; in the document you are now reading.

hereto To this (document or matter).

heretofore Before now; up to now.

hereunder 1. By the terms of or in accordance with this document. 2. Later in the document.

herewith With this or in this document.

heritable Capable of being inherited.

hermeneutics The science or art of interpreting documents.

hidden asset Property of a company that is either not stated on its books or is stated at an undervalued price.

hidden defect A deficiency in property that could not be discovered by reasonable and customary observation or inspection and for which a lessor or seller is generally liable if such defect causes harm. Also called inherent defect, latent defect.

> A latent defect may be defined as a hidden defect or blemish in the article sold, either known or unknown to the seller, but not apparent to the purchaser, and which could not be discovered by observation and inspection provided for in the contract. *Chesapeake & O. Ry. Co.*, 21 Ohio App. 373 (Ohio App., 1926)

high crime A major offense that is a serious abuse of governmental power. Can be the basis of impeachment and removal from office.

highest and best use The use of property that will most likely produce the highest market value, greatest financial return, or the most profit.

> Market value is determined by most valuable and best use to which property could reasonably, practically and lawfully be adapted, referred to as "highest and best use." R.C. § 163.01 et seq. *Masheter*, 38 Ohio App.2d 49 (Ohio App., 1973)

high-low agreement A compromise agreement under which the parties set a minimum (floor) and maximum (ceiling) for damages. The defendant will pay at least the floor (if the jury awards less than this amount) but no more than the ceiling (if the jury awards over that amount).

high seas That portion of the ocean or seas that is beyond the territorial jurisdiction of any country.

high-water line or mark The line on the shore to which high tide rises under normal weather conditions.

hijack To seize possession of a vehicle from another; to seize a vehicle and force it to go in another direction.

HIPAA Health Insurance Portability and Accountability Act. A federal statute providing protections such as maintaining the privacy of personal health information (*www.hhs.gov/ocr/hipaa*).

hire 1. To purchase the temporary use of a thing. 2. To engage the services of another for a fee.

Typically, the word "hire," as used in automobile insurance policy provision affording insured status to one making permissive use of vehicle "hired" by named insured, does not involve physical possession of vehicle hired, but rather suggests remuneration for its use. *Davis*, 102 Ohio App.3d 82 (Ohio App., 1995)

hiring hall An agency or office operated by a union (or by both union and management) to place applicants for work.

hit and run The crime of leaving the scene of an accident without being identified.

HMO See health maintenance organization.

hoard To accumulate assets beyond one's reasonable needs, often anticipating an increase in their market price.

Hobbs Act A federal anti-racketeering act that makes it illegal to obstruct, delay, or affect interstate commerce or attempt to conspire to do so by robbery, physical violence, or extortion (18 USC § 1951).

hobby losses A nondeductible loss suffered when engaged in an activity that is not pursued for profit.

hodgepodge See hotchpot.

hold 1. To possess something by virtue of lawful authority or title. 2. To reach a legal conclusion; to resolve a legal dispute. 3. To restrain or control; to keep in custody. 4. To preside at.

holder 1. One who has possession of something, e.g., a check, bond, document of title. 2. One who has legally acquired possession of a negotiable instrument (e.g., a check, a promissory note) and who is entitled to receive payment on the instrument.

holder for value Someone who has given something of value for a promissory note or other negotiable instrument.

holder in due course (HDC; HIDC) One who gives value for a negotiable instrument in good faith, without any apparent defects, and without notice that it is overdue, has been dishonored, or is subject to any claim or defense.

Holder in due course means the holder of an instrument if both of the following apply: (1) The instrument when issued or negotiated to the holder does not bear evidence of forgery or alteration that is so apparent, or is not otherwise so irregular or incomplete as to call into question its authenticity; (2) The holder took the instrument under all of the following circumstances: (a) For value; (b) In good faith; (c) Without notice that the instrument is overdue or has been dishonored or that there is an uncured default with respect to payment of another instrument issued as part of the same series; (d) Without notice that the instrument contains an unauthorized signature or has been altered; (e) Without notice of any claim to the instrument as described in section 1303.36 of the Revised Code; (f) Without notice that any party has a defense or claim in recoupment described in division (A) of section 1303.35 of the Revised Code. R.C. § 1303.32(A)

hold harmless To assume any liability in a transaction thereby relieving another from responsibility or loss. Also called save harmless.

holding 1. A court's answer to or resolution of a legal issue before it. 2. A court ruling. 3. Property owned by someone.

holding company A company that owns stock in and supervises the management of other companies.

holding period The length of time a taxpayer owns a capital asset, which determines whether a gain or loss will be short term or long term.

holdover tenancy See estate at sufferance.

holdover tenant A tenant who retains possession of the premises after the expiration of a lease or after a tenancy at will has been ended.

holograph A handwritten document.

holographic will A will written entirely by the testator in his or her own handwriting, often without witnesses.

home equity conversion mortgage A first mortgage that provides for future payments to a homeowner based on accumulated equity.

homeowner's policy A multiperil insurance policy covering damage to a residence and liability claims based on home ownership.

Homeowners insurance means insurance on owner-occupied dwellings providing personal multi-peril property and liability coverages commonly known as homeowners insurance, and is subject to such reasonable underwriting standards, exclusions, deductibles, rates, and conditions as are customarily used by member insurers for similar coverages. R.C. § 3929.42(B)

homeowner's warranty (HOW) A warranty and insurance protection program offered by many home builders, providing protection for 10 years against major structural defects. A construction warranty.

home port doctrine A vessel engaged in interstate and foreign commerce is taxable only at its home port (e.g., where it is registered).

home rule A designated amount of self-government granted to local cities and towns.

homestead The dwelling house and adjoining land where the owner or his or her family lives.

Homestead means either of the following: (1) A dwelling, including a unit in a multiple-unit dwelling and a manufactured home or mobile home taxed as real property pursuant to division (B) of section 4503.06 of the Revised Code, owned and occupied as a home by an individual whose domicile is in this state and who has not acquired ownership from a person, other than the individual's spouse, related by consanguinity or affinity for the purpose of qualifying for the real property tax reduction provided in section 323.152 of the Revised Code. (2) A unit in a housing cooperative that is occupied as a home, but not owned, by an individual whose domicile is in this state. R.C. § 323.151(A)

homestead exemption laws Laws that allow a householder or head of a family to designate a residence and adjoining land as his or her homestead that, in whole or part, is exempt from execution or attachment for designated general debts.

homicide The killing of one human being by another. Whether the killing is a crime depends on factors such as intent.

homologate To approve; to confirm officially.

Hon. Honorable.

honor To accept or pay a check or other negotiable instrument when presented for acceptance or payment.

honorable discharge A declaration by the government that a member of the military left the service in good standing.

honorarium A fee for services when no fee was required.

honorary trust A trust that may not be enforceable because it has no beneficiary to enforce it. Example: a trust for the care of a pet.

horizontal agreement An agreement between companies that directly compete at the same level of distribution, often in restraint of trade.

horizontal merger The acquisition of one company by another company producing the same or a similar product and selling it in the same geographic market. A merger of corporate competitors.

horizontal price fixing An agreement by competitors at the same market level to fix or control prices they will charge for their goods or services.

horizontal privity The relationship between a supplier and a nonpurchasing party affected by the product, such as a relative of the buyer or a bystander.

horizontal property acts A statute on condominiums or cooperatives.

horizontal restraint See horizontal agreement.

horizontal union See craft union.

hornbook A book summarizing the basics or fundamentals of a topic.

hornbook law See black letter law.

hostile environment sexual harassment A work setting in which severe and pervasive conduct of a sexual nature creates a hostile or offensive working environment.

> Hostile environment harassment where the relationship results in unreasonable interference with the employee's work performance or creates an intimidating or hostile work environment. *Western-Southern Life Ins. Co.*, 69 Ohio App.3d 190 (Ohio App., 1990)

hostile fire 1. A fire that breaks out or spreads to an unexpected area. 2. Gunfire from an enemy.

> Where fire is serving purpose intended, it is a "friendly fire", but when it gets beyond control it loses its original innocent character, and becomes a "hostile fire" so as to bring the resulting loss within the terms of a fire policy. *Stillpass*, 71 Ohio App. 197 (Ohio App., 1942)

hostile possession Possession asserted to be superior to or incompatible with anyone else's claim to possession.

hostile witness A witness who manifests bias or prejudice, who appears aligned with the other side, or who refuses to answer questions. Also called adverse witness.

hot blood See heat of passion.

hot cargo 1. Goods produced or handled by an employer with whom a union has a dispute. 2. Stolen goods.

hotchpot Mixing or blending all property, however acquired, in order to divide it more equally. Also called hodgepodge.

hot pursuit See fresh pursuit.

house 1. Living quarters; a home. 2. One of the chambers of a legislature (e.g., United States House of Representatives, Ohio House of Representatives, Maryland House of Delegates).

house bill (H.B.)(H.) Proposed legislation considered by the House of Representatives.

housebreaking Breaking and entering a dwelling-house with the intent to commit any felony therein. Also called burglary.

house counsel An attorney who is an employee of a business or organization, usually on salary. Also called in-house counsel.

household 1. Belonging or pertaining to the house and family. 2. A group of persons living together.

> Plain and ordinary meaning of undefined term "household," as used in homeowners' policy providing coverage for relatives who were residents of insured's household, includes those who dwell under same roof and compose family; social unit composed of those living together in same dwelling; inmates of house collectively; organized family, including servants or attendants, dwelling in house; domestic establishment. *Am. States Ins. Co.*, 108 Ohio App.3d 547 (Ohio App., 1996)

House of Representatives (H.R.) See house (2).

H.R. See House of Representatives.

H. Res. House resolution. See also concurrent resolution.

H.R. 10 plan See Keogh plan.

humanitarian doctrine See last clear chance doctrine.

hung jury A jury so irreconcilably divided in opinion that a verdict cannot be agreed upon.

husband-wife immunity See interspousal immunity.

husband-wife privilege See marital communications privilege.

hybrid security A security that combines the features of a debt instrument and an equity instrument.

hypothecate To pledge property as security or collateral for a debt without transferring title or possession.

hypothesis An assumption or theory to be proven or disproven.

hypothetical 1. Based on conjecture; not actual or real, but presented for purposes of discussion and analysis. 2. A set of assumed facts presented for the sake or argument and illustration.

hypothetical question A question in which the person being interviewed (e.g., an expert witness) is asked to give an opinion on a set of facts that are assumed to be true for purposes of the question.

> A question that assumes the facts the evidence tends to show and calls for an opinion based on the hypothesis. *Strizak*, 159 Ohio St. 475 (Ohio 1953)

I

ibid. In the same place; in the work previously cited or mentioned.

ICJ See International Court of Justice (*www.icj-cij.org*).

id. The same. (Id. refers to the case or other authority cited immediately above or before in the text or footnotes.)

idem sonans Sounding the same. A misspelled signature can be effective if the misspelled name sounds the same as the correct spelling.

> The names Esterly and Easterly are so nearly alike that under the principle of "idem sonans" the marketability of a title to real estate taken in the former name and divested under the latter name was not impaired by such difference. *Horton*, 72 Ohio App. 187 (Ohio App., 1943)

identify 1. To establish the identity of someone or something. 2. To associate or be associated with. 3. To specify the subject of a contract.

identity of interests Two persons being so closely related that suing one acts as notice to the other. Being only nominally separate.

identity of parties Two persons being so closely related that a judgment against one will bar (via res judicata) a later suit against the other.

identity theft Knowingly transferring or using a means of identification of another person with the intent to commit any unlawful activity.

i.e. That is; in other words.

IFP See in forma pauperis.

ignoramus We do not know. (A notation by a grand jury indicating a rejection of the indictment.)

ignorance The absence of knowledge.

ignorantia juris non excusat Ignorance of the law excuses no one.

illegal Against the law; prohibited by law.

illegal entry 1. Unauthorized entry with intent to commit a crime. 2. Entry into a country by an alien at the wrong time or place or by fraud; or eluding immigration officers when here.

illegality That which is contrary to law.

illegally obtained evidence Evidence collected in violation of a suspect's statutory or constitutional rights.

> In prosecution for operating vehicle while under the influence of alcohol, any objection to admission of results of breath alcohol test based on failure to comply with regulations of Department of Health must be raised before trial; such objections amount to attempts to suppress evidence "on the ground that it was illegally obtained," within meaning of Rule of Criminal Procedure addressing pretrial motions. R.C. § 4511.19(A)(1–4); Rules Crim.Proc., Rule 12(B)(3). *State v. French*, 72 Ohio St.3d 446 (Ohio 1995)

illegitimate 1. Born out of wedlock. 2. Contrary to law.

illicit Not permitted, illegal; improper.

illicit cohabitation Two unmarried persons living together as man and wife.

Illinois Land Trust See land trust.

illusory Deceptive, based on false appearances; not real.

illusory contract An agreement in which one party's consideration is so insignificant that a contract obligation cannot be imposed.

illusory promise An apparent promise that leaves the promisor's performance entirely within the discretion of the promisor.

imbecility Severe mental retardation or cognitive disfunction.

imitation Substantial duplication; resembling something enough to cause confusion with the genuine article.

immaterial Not material. Tending to prove something not in issue.

immaterial variance A discrepancy between the pleading and the proof that is so slight that it misleads no one.

immediate annuity An annuity bought with a lump sum that starts making payments soon after its purchase.

immediate cause The last of a series or chain of events that produced the occurrence or result; a cause immediate in time to what occurred.

immemorial Beyond human memory. Exceptionally old.

immigrant A foreigner who comes into a country with the intention to live there permanently.

imminent Near at hand; about to occur.

> Imminent meaning near at hand or impending. *City of Cincinnati v. Baarlaer*, 115 Ohio App.3d 521 (Ohio App., 1996)

imminent peril doctrine See emergency doctrine.

immoral Contrary to good morals; inimical to public welfare according to the standards of a given community.

immovables Land and those things so firmly attached to it as to be regarded as part of it; property that cannot be moved.

immunity 1. Exemption or freedom from a duty, penalty, or liability. 2. A complete defense to a tort claim whether or not the defendant committed the tort. 3. The right not to be subjected to civil or criminal prosecution.

> The "immunity" that may be granted pursuant to statute providing for the granting to a witness of immunity from prosecution, other than for perjury, is a "use" immunity not a "transaction" immunity and is not immunity from prosecution for a crime. R.C. § 2945.44. *State v. Broady*, 41 Ohio App.2d 17 (Ohio App., 1974)

immunize To grant immunity to; to render immune.

impact rule A party may recover emotional distress damages in a negligence action only if he or she suffered accompanying physical injury or contact.

impair To cause something to lose some or all of its quality or value.

impair the obligation of contracts To nullify or materially change existing contract obligations. See also Contract Clause.

impanel To enlist or enroll. To enroll or swear in (a list of jurors) for a particular case. Also spelled empanel.

imparl 1. To delay a case in an attempt to settle. 2. To seek a continuance for more time to answer and pursue settlement options.

impartial Favoring neither side; unbiased.

impasse A deadlock in negotiations. The absence of hope of agreement.

impeach To attack; to accuse of wrongdoing; to challenge the credibility of.

impeachment 1. An attack or challenge because of impropriety, bias, or lack of veracity. 2. A procedure against a public officer before a quasi-political court (e.g., a legislative body), instituted by written accusations called articles of impeachment that seek his or her removal from office.

impediment A legal obstacle that prevents the formation of a valid marriage or other contract.

imperfect Missing an essential legal requirement. Unenforceable.

imperfect trust See executory trust.

impersonation Pretending or representing oneself to be another.

impertinent Irrelevant or not responsive to the issues in the case.

implead To bring a new party into the lawsuit on the ground that the new party may be liable for all or part of the current claim. The procedure is called impleader or third-party practice.

implied Expressed by implication; suggested by the circumstances.

implied acquittal A guilty verdict on a lesser included offense is an implied acquittal of the greater offense about which the jury was silent.

implied agency An actual agency established through circumstantial evidence.

implied authority Authority that is necessary, usual, and proper to perform the express authority delegated to the agent by the principal.

Implied authority is agent's power to do that which is reasonably necessary to carry into effect power actually conferred, except as expressly limited by principal. *Young,* 114 Ohio App.3d 499 (Ohio App., 1996)

implied consent Consent inferred from the surrounding circumstances.

implied consent law A law providing that a person who drives a motor vehicle in the state is deemed to have given consent to a test that determines the alcoholic or drug content of that person's blood.

implied contract An implied in fact contract or an implied in law contract (see these terms.)

An implied contract is a contract inferred by a court from the circumstances surrounding the transaction, making a reasonable or necessary assumption that a contract exists between the parties by tacit understanding. *Hollis Towing,* 155 Ohio App.3d 300 (Ohio App., 2003)

implied in fact Inferred from the facts and circumstances.

implied in fact contract An actual contract whose existence and the parties' intentions are inferred from facts rather than by express agreement.

implied in law Imposed by law; arising by operation of law.

implied in law contract An obligation created by the law to avoid unjust enrichment. Also called constructive contract, quasi contract.

Implied-in-law contract is a legal fiction also called quasi-contract because it is not characterized by a meeting of the minds but rather is based upon unjust enrichment. *Staffilino Chevrolet,* 158 Ohio App.3d 1 (Ohio App., 2004)

implied easement An easement created by law when land is conveyed that does not contain an express easement, but one is implied as an intended part of the transaction. Also called easement by implication, way of necessity.

implied malice Malice that is inferred from conduct, e.g., reckless disregard for human life. Also called legal malice, malice in law.

implied notice Knowledge implied from surrounding facts so that the law will treat one as knowing what could have been discovered by ordinary care.

implied powers Powers presumed to have been granted because they are necessary to carry into effect expressly granted powers.

implied promise A fictional promise created by law to impose a contract liability, and thereby avoid fraud or unjust enrichment.

implied trust See constructive trust, resulting trust.

implied warranty A warranty imposed by operation of law regardless of the parties' intent. See also warranty of fitness for a particular purpose, warranty of habitability, warranty of merchantability.

"Implied warranty in tort" is a common-law cause of action that imposes liability upon a manufacturer or a seller for breach of an implied representation that a product is of good and merchantable quality, fit and safe for its ordinary intended use. *White,* 129 Ohio App.3d 472 (Ohio App., 1998)

imply 1. To suggest; to state something indirectly. 2. To impose or declare something by law.

import To bring goods into a country from a foreign country.

impossibility That which no person in the course of nature or the law can do or perform; that which cannot exist.

impossibility of performance doctrine A defense to a breach of contract when performance becomes objectively impossible, not due to anyone's fault.

imposts A duty that is levied. An import tax.

impotence The inability to perform the act of sexual intercourse.

imposter One who deceives by pretending to be someone else.

impound To seize and take into custody of the law.

impoundment 1. Seizing and taking something into custody of the law. 2. Refusing to spend money appropriated by the legislature.

impracticability 1. A defense to breach of contract when performance can be undertaken only at an excessive and unreasonable cost. 2. Difficulty or inconvenience of joining all parties because of their large number.

impracticable Excessively burdensome to perform.

impress 1. To force someone into public service, e.g., military service. 2. To impose a constructive trust. The noun is impressment.

impression See first impression.

imprimatur ("let it be printed") Official approval to publish a book.

imprison To put in prison; to place in confinement.

improper 1. Not in accord with proper procedure or taste. 2. Wrongful.

improved land Land that has been developed, e.g., by adding roads.

improvement An addition to or betterment of land (usually permanent) that enhances its capital value. Something beyond mere repairs.

In determining whether an item is "improvement to real property" under ten-year statute of real property for actions to recover damages arising out of defective improvement to real property based on designing, planning, or constructing improvement, court must look to enhanced value created when item is put to its intended use, level of integration of item within any manufacturing system, whether item is essential component of system, and item's permanence. R.C. § 2305.131. *Brennaman,* 70 Ohio St.3d 460 (Ohio 1994)

improvident Lacking in care and foresight. Ill-considered.

impulse A sudden urge or thrusting force within a person.

impunity Exemption or protection from penalty or punishment.

impute To credit or assign to; to ascribe. To attribute to another or to make another responsible because of a relationship that exists.

imputed disqualification If one attorney or employee in a firm has a conflict of interest with a client, the entire firm is ineligible to represent that client. Also called vicarious disqualification.

imputed income A monetary value assigned to certain property, transactions, or situations for tax purposes (e.g., the value of a home provided by an employer for an employee).

imputed knowledge Information that a person does not actually know, but should know or has reason to know and, therefore, is deemed to know.

imputed negligence Negligence of one person that is attributed to another solely because of a special relationship between them.

in absentia In the absence of.

inadequate remedy at law An ineffective legal remedy, e.g., damages, justifying a request for an equitable remedy, e.g., injunction.

inadmissible Cannot be received and considered.

inadvertence An oversight; a consequence of carelessness, not planning.

inalienable Incapable of being bought, sold, transferred, or assigned. Also called unalienable.

> Word "inalienable" as used in statute providing that aid to dependent children shall be "inalienable" means that such aid cannot be transferred from one for whom it is intended. R.C. § 5107.12. *Goodyear Service Store,* 48 Ohio App.2d 115 (Ohio App., 1976)

in banc See en banc.

in being In existence; existing in life.

in blank Not identifying a particular indorsee. Not filled in.

Inc. Incorporated.

in camera In private with the judge; in chambers; without spectators.

incapacity 1. The existence of a legal impediment preventing action or completion. 2. Physical or mental inability. 3. See disability (2).

incarcerate To imprison or confine in jail.

incendiary 1. A bomb or other device designed to causes fire. 2. One who maliciously and willfully sets fire to property.

incest Sexual intercourse between a man and woman who are related to each other within prohibited degrees (e.g., brother and sister).

in chief 1. Main or principal. 2. See case-in-chief.

inchoate Begun but not completed; partial.

inchoate crime A crime in its early stage, constituting another crime. The inchoate crimes are attempt, conspiracy, and solicitation.

inchoate dower A wife's interest in the land of her husband during his life; a possibility of acquiring dower.

inchoate lien A lien in which the amount, exact identity of the lienor, and time of attachment must await future determination.

incident 1. Connected with, inherent in, or arising out of something else. 2. A dependent or subordinate part. 3. An occurrence.

incidental Depending upon and secondary to something else.

incidental beneficiary One who will be benefited by performance of a promise but who is neither a promisee nor an intended beneficiary.

> An "intended beneficiary" is one who has enforceable rights under the contract, in contrast to an "incidental beneficiary," who has no rights of enforcement. *Berge,* 136 Ohio App.3d 281 (Ohio App., 1999)

incidental damages 1. The additional expenses reasonably incurred because of a breach of contract. 2. In class actions, those damages that flow directly from liability to the class as a whole on claims forming the basis of the injunctive or declaratory relief.

incident of ownership An ownership right retained in an insurance policy, e.g., the right to change beneficiaries.

incite To urge, persuade, stir up, or provoke another.

included offense See lesser included offense.

income Money or other financial gain derived from one's business, labor, investments, and other sources.

> Income is not synonymous with "earnings" or "wages", for purposes of calculating workers' compensation claimant's average weekly wage; rather, "income" is a much broader term. R.C. § 4123.61. *State ex rel. McDulin,* 89 Ohio St.3d 390 (Ohio 2000)

income in respect of a decedent (IRD) The right to income earned by a decedent at death that was not included in his or her final income tax return.

income splitting Seeking a lower total tax by allocating income from persons in higher tax brackets to those in lower tax brackets.

income statement See earnings report.

income tax A tax on the net income of an individual or entity.

in common Shared together equally.

incompatibility Such discord between a husband and wife that it is impossible for them to live together in a normal marital relationship

incompetent 1. Failing to meet legal requirements; unqualified. 2. Not having the skills needed. Physically or mentally impaired.

> "Incompetent" means any person who is so mentally impaired as a result of a mental or physical illness or disability, or mental retardation, or as a result of chronic substance abuse, that the person is incapable of taking proper care of the person's self or property or fails to provide for the person's family or other persons for whom the person is charged by law to provide, or any person confined to a correctional institution within this state. R.C. § 2111.01(D)

incompetent evidence Evidence that is not admissible.

inconsistent Not compatible. Mutually repugnant; the acceptance of one fact, position, or claim implies the abandonment of the other.

in contemplation of death With a view toward death. See contemplation of death.

incontestability clause An insurance policy clause providing that after a period of time (e.g., 2 years), the insurer cannot contest it on the basis of fraud, mistake, or statements made in the application.

inconvenient forum See forum non conveniens.

incorporate 1. To form a corporation. 2. To combine or include within.

incorporation by reference Making one document a part of another document by stating that the former shall be considered part of the latter.

incorporation doctrine See selective incorporation.

incorporator A person who is one of the original founders (formers) of a corporation.

> "Incorporator" means a person who signed the original articles of incorporation. R.C. § 1701.01(E)

incorporeal Not having a physical nature; intangible.

incorporeal hereditament An intangible land right that is inheritable.

incorrigible incapable of being corrected or reformed. Unmanageable.

increment An increase or addition in amount or quality.

incriminate 1. To charge with a crime; to accuse someone. 2. To show involvement in the possibility of crime or other wrongdoing.

incriminating Tending to demonstrate criminal conduct.

incriminating statement A statement that tends to establish a person's guilt.

incriminatory Charging or showing involvement with a crime.

incroach See encroach.

inculpatory Tending to show involvement with crime.

incumbent 1. One presently holding an office. 2. Obligatory.

incumbrance See encumbrance.

incur To become liable or subject to; to bring down upon oneself.

indebitatus assumpsit An action based on undertaking a debt.

indecent Sexually vulgar, but not necessarily obscene.

indecent assault Unconsented sexual contact with another.

indecent exposure Displaying one's self in public (especially one's genitals) in such manner as to be offensive to common decency.

> Indecent exposure refers to exhibition of those private parts which instinctive modesty, human decency or self-respect require shall be kept covered in presence of others; exposure of person becomes indecent when it occurs at such time and place where reasonable man knows or should know his act will be open to observation of others. R.C. § 2905.30. *State v. Borchard*, 24 Ohio App.2d 95 (Ohio App., 1970)

indecent speech Vulgar or offensive (but not necessarily obscene) speech concerning sexual or excretory activities and organs.

indefeasible Not capable of being defeated, revoked, or made void.

indefinite Not definite or fixed; lacking fixed boundaries.

indefinite failure of issue A failure of issue (dying without descendants who can inherit) whenever it occurs.

indefinite sentence See indeterminate sentence.

indemnify To compensate or promise to compensate someone for a specified loss or liability that has resulted or that might result.

indemnitee A person who is indemnified by another.

indemnitor A person who indemnifies another.

indemnity 1. The duty of one person to pay for another's loss, damage, or liability. 2. A right to receive compensation to make one person whole from a loss that has already been sustained but which in justice ought to be sustained by the person from whom indemnity is sought.

> Indemnity is the right, arising out of an implied contract, of a person who has been compelled to pay what another should pay, to obtain complete reimbursement. *USX Corp.*, 137 Ohio App.3d 19 (Ohio App., 2000)

indemnity insurance Insurance covering losses to the insured's person or to his or her own property. Also called first-party insurance.

indenture 1. A deed with the top of the parchment having an irregular (indented) edge. 2. A written agreement under which bonds and debentures are issued; the agreement sets forth terms such as the maturity date and the interest rate. 3. An apprenticeship agreement.

independent 1. Not subject to control or limitation from an outside source. 2. Not affiliated; autonomous.

independent agency A government board, commission, or other agency that is not subject to the policy supervision of the chief executive.

independent contractor One who operates his or her own business and contracts to do work for others who do not control the method or administrative details of how the work is performed.

> An "independent contractor" is defined as one who in the exercise of an independent employment contracts to do a piece of work according to his own methods, and without being subject to the control of the employer except as to the product or result of his work. *Amerifirst Savings Bank of Xenia*, 136 Ohio App.3d 468 (Ohio App., 1999)

independent counsel 1. An outside attorney hired to conduct an investigation or perform other special tasks. 2. Counsel chosen by an insured or with the approval of the insured, but paid by the insurer.

independent covenant An obligation that is not conditioned on performance by the other party.

independent paralegal An independent contractor (a) who sells his or her paralegal services to, and works under the supervision of, one or more attorneys or (b) who sells his or her paralegal services directly to the public without attorney supervision. Also called freelance paralegal or legal technician. Note, however, that in some states, (e.g., California), the paralegal and legal assistant titles are limited to those who work under attorney supervision.

independent source rule Illegally obtained evidence will be admitted if the government shows that it is also obtained through sources wholly independent of the illegal search or other constitutional violation.

> "Independent-source rule" provides that if the government can prove that evidence to be used at trial is derived from sources "wholly independent" of immunized testimony, then that evidence will not be suppressed. *State v. Sess*, 136 Ohio App.3d 689 (Ohio App., 1999)

indestructible trust See Claflin trust.

indeterminate Not designated with particularity; not definite.

indeterminate sentence A prison sentence that is not fixed by the court but is left to the determination of penal authorities within minimum and maximum time limits set by the court. Also called indefinite sentence.

index fund A mutual fund that seeks to match the results of a stock market index, e.g., the S&P 500.

indexing 1. Adjusting wages or other payments to account for inflation. 2. Tracking investments to an index, e.g., the S&P 500.

Indian reservation Land set apart for tribal use of Native Americans (American Indians).

indicia Signs or indications of something; identifying marks.

indict To bring or issue an indictment.

indictable Subject or liable to being indicted.

indictable offense A crime that must be prosecuted by indictment.

indictment A formal accusation of crime made by a grand jury.

indigent 1. Impoverished. 2. Without funds to hire a private attorney.

> Indigent means a person or persons whose income is not greater than one hundred twenty-five per cent of the current poverty threshold established by the United States office of management and budget. R.C. § 120.51(B)

indignity Humiliating, degrading treatment of another.

indirect contempt Behavior outside the presence of the judge that defies the authority or dignity of the court. Also called constructive contempt.

indirect evidence See circumstantial evidence.

indirect tax A tax upon some right, privilege, or franchise.

indispensable evidence Evidence essential to prove a particular fact.

indispensable party A party so essential to a suit that no final decision can be rendered without his or her joinder. The case cannot be decided on its merits without prejudicing the rights of such a party.

> An "indispensable party," within procedural rule, is one whose absence seriously prejudices any party to the action or prevents the court from rendering any effective judgment between the parties or whose interests would be adversely affected or jeopardized by the judgment rendered between the parties to the action; mere avoidance of multiple litigation is not a sufficient basis to render one an indispensable party. Ohio Civ.R. 12(H). *Layne*, 43 Ohio App.2d 53 (Ohio App., 1974)

individual retirement account (IRA) A special account in which qualified persons can set aside a certain amount of tax-deferred income each year for savings or investment. The amount is subject to income tax upon withdrawal at the appropriate time.

indorse To place a signature on a check or other negotiable instrument to make it payable to someone other than the payee or to accept responsibility for paying it. Also spelled endorse.

indorsee The person to whom a check or other negotiable instrument is transferred by indorsement. Also spelled endorsee.

indorsement 1. Signing a check or other negotiable instrument to transfer or guarantee the instrument or to acknowledge payment. 2. The signature itself. Also spelled endorsement.

> "Indorsement" means a signature, other than that of a signer as maker, drawer, or acceptor, that alone or accompanied by other words is made on an instrument for any of the following purposes: (a) To negotiate the instrument; (b) To restrict payment of the instrument; (c) To incur the indorser's liability on the instrument. R.C. § 1303.24(A)(1)

indorser One who transfers a check or other negotiable instrument by indorsement.

inducement 1. The benefit or advantage that motivates a promisor to enter a contract. 2. An introductory statement in a pleading, e.g., alleging extrinsic facts that show a defamatory meaning in a libel or slander case. 3. Persuading or influencing someone to do something.

industrial relations The relationship between employer and employees on matters such as collective bargaining and job safety.

industrial union A labor union with members in the same industry (e.g., textiles) irrespective of their skills or craft. Also called vertical union.

industry An occupation or business that is a distinct branch of manufacture and trade, e.g., the steel industry.

inebriated Intoxicated; drunk.

ineffective assistance of counsel See effective assistance of counsel.

in equity Pertaining to (or in a court applying) equitable principles.

inescapable Being helpless to avoid a result by oneself; inevitable.

in esse In being, actually existing.

in evidence Before the court, having been declared admissible.

inevitable accident See unavoidable accident.

inevitable discovery doctrine Illegally obtained evidence is admissible if it inevitably would have been discovered by lawful means.

infamous 1. Having a notorious reputation; shameful. 2. Denied certain civil rights due to conviction of a crime.

infamous crime A crime punishable by imprisonment or the loss of some civil rights.

> An "infamous crime" is one which is determined by the nature of the punishment and not by the character of the crime, and any offense is infamous that is punishable by death or by imprisonment in the penitentiary. *City of Cleveland v. Betts*, 168 Ohio St. 386 (Ohio 1958)

infancy 1. See minority (1). 2. Childhood at its earliest stage.

infanticide The murder or killing of an infant soon after its birth.

inference 1. A process of reasoning by which a fact to be established is deduced from other facts. Reaching logical conclusions from evidence. 2. A deduction or conclusion reached by this process.

inferior court Any court that is subordinate to the highest court within its judicial system. Also called lower court.

infeudation Granting legal possession of land in feudal times.

infirm Lacking health; weak or feeble.

infirmative Tending to weaken a criminal charge.

infirmity Physical or mental weakness; frailty due to old age.

in flagrante delicto In the act of committing an offense.

infliction of emotional distress See intentional infliction of emotional distress.

in force In effect; legally operative.

informal Not following formal or normal procedures or forms.

informal contract 1. An oral contract. 2. A binding contract that is not under seal.

informal proceedings Proceedings that are less formal (particularly in applying the rules of evidence) than a court trial.

informant See informer.

in forma pauperis (IFP) With permission (as a poor person) to proceed without paying filing fees or other court costs.

information A formal accusation of a criminal offense from the prosecutor rather than from a grand jury indictment.

"Information" means data, text, images, sounds, codes, computer programs, software, databases, or the like. R.C. § 304.01(F)

information and belief Good faith belief as to the truth of an allegation, not based on firsthand knowledge.

informed consent Agreement to let something happen based on having a reasonable understanding of the benefits and risks involved.

"Informed consent" means consent voluntarily given by a person after a sufficient explanation and disclosure of the subject matter involved to enable that person to have a general understanding of the nature, purpose, and goal of the treatment or procedures, including the substantial risks and hazards inherent in the proposed treatment or procedures and any alternative treatment or procedures, and to make a knowing health care decision without coercion or undue influence. R.C. § 2135.01(J)

informed intermediary A skilled and knowledgeable individual (e.g., a doctor) in the chain of distribution between the manufacturer of a product and the ultimate consumer. Also called learned intermediary.

informer A person who informs against another; one who brings an accusation against another on the basis of a suspicion that the latter has committed a crime. Also called informant.

informer's privilege The government's limited privilege to withhold the identity of persons who provide information of possible violations of law.

infra Below; later in the text.

infraction A violation (often minor) of a law, agreement, or duty.

infringement An invasion of a right; a violation of a law or duty.

infringement of copyright The unauthorized use of copyrighted material (17 USC § 106).

infringement of patent An unauthorized making, using, offering for sale, selling, or importing an invention protected by patent (35 USC § 271(a)).

infringement of trademark The unauthorized use or imitation of a registered trademark on goods of a similar class likely to confuse or deceive (15 USC § 1114).

in futuro At a future time.

ingress The act or right of entering.

in gross In a large sum or quantity; undivided.

in haec verba In these words; verbatim.

inherent Existing as a permanent or essential component.

inherently dangerous Being susceptible to harm or injury in the nature of the product, service, or activity itself. Requiring great caution.

inherent defect See hidden defect.

inherent power A power that must necessarily exist in the nature of the organization or person, even if not explicitly granted.

inherent right A fundamental, nontransferable right that is basic to the existence of a person or organization. An inalienable right.

inherit 1. To take by inheritance. 2. To take by will.

inheritance 1. Property received by an heir when an ancestor dies without leaving a valid will (i.e., intestate). 2. Property received through the will of a decedent.

The term "inheritance," in addition to its meaning at common law or under any other section or sections of the Revised Code, includes any change of title to real property by reason of the death of the owner of that real property, regardless of whether the owner died testate or intestate. R.C. § 2107.011(A)

inheritance tax A tax on the right to receive property by descent (intestate succession) or by will. Also called death tax, succession tax.

in hoc In this regard.

in-house counsel See house counsel.

in invitum Against an unwilling party.

initial appearance The first criminal court appearance by the accused during which the court informs him or her of the charges, makes a decision on bail, and determines the date of the next proceeding.

initiative The electorate's power to propose and directly enact a statute or change in the constitution or to force the legislature to vote on the proposal.

injunction A court order requiring a person or organization to do or to refrain from doing something.

"Injunction" is extraordinary equitable remedy which is available if there is no adequate remedy at law; its purpose is to prevent future wrongdoing that law cannot. *Abraham*, 107 Ohio App.3d 773 (Ohio App., 1995)

injuria absque damno A legal wrong, from which no loss or damage results, will not sustain a lawsuit for damages.

injurious falsehood 1. The publication of a false statement that causes special damages. 2. The publication of a false statement that is derogatory to plaintiff's business of a kind calculated to prevent others from dealing with the business or otherwise to interfere with its relations with others, to its detriment. Sometimes called disparagement.

Injurious falsehood, defined, for our purposes, as a false statement which does harm to the pecuniary interests of another and causes pecuniary loss. *Village of Grafton*, 70 Ohio App.2d 205 (Ohio App., 1980)

injury 1. Any harm or damage to another or oneself. 2. An invasion of a legally protected interest of another.

in kind 1. Of the same species or category. 2. In goods or services rather than money.

in lieu of In place of.

in limine At the outset. Preliminarily. See also motion in limine.

in loco parentis In the place of a parent; assuming the duties of a parent without adoption.

inmate A person confined in a prison, hospital, or other institution.

innocence 1. The absence of guilt. 2. The lack of cunning or deceit.

innocent Free from guilt; untainted by wrongdoing.

innocent agent One who engages in illegal conduct on behalf of the principal wrongdoer without knowing of its illegality.

innocent construction rule If words can be interpreted as harmless or defamatory, the harmless interpretation will be adopted.

If a statement is reasonably susceptible of both a defamatory and an innocent meaning, the innocent meaning is to be adopted as a matter of law. *Holley*, 149 Ohio App.3d 22 (Ohio App., 2002)

innocent party 1. One who has not knowingly or negligently participated in wrongdoing. 2. One without actual or constructive knowledge of any limitations or defects.

innocent purchaser See bona fide purchaser.

innocent spouse A spouse who did not know or have reason to know that the other spouse understated the taxes due on their joint tax return.

innocent trespasser One who enters the land of another under the mistaken belief that it is permissible to do so.

inn of court An association or society of the main trial attorneys (called barristers) in England that has a large role in their legal training and admission to practice.

innominate Belonging to no specific class.

innuendo 1. The portion of a complaint that explains a statement's defamatory meaning when this is not clear on its face. 2. An indirect derogatory comment or suggestion.

inoperative No longer in force or effective.

in pais Done informally or without legal proceedings.

in pari delicto In equal fault; equally culpable.

in pari materia Upon or involving the same matter or subject. Statutes in pari materia are to be interpreted together to try to resolve any ambiguity or inconsistency in them.

Where ambiguity exists in wording of statute, or significance of terms of statute are doubtful, "in pari materia" rule of construction is applicable, pursuant to which statutes or sections of statutes which cover same subject matter must be read in pari materia and construed so as to give force and affect to each and all of statutes or sections. *McAtee*, 111 Ohio App.3d 812 (Ohio App., 1996)

in perpetuity Forever.

in personam Against the person. See also personal judgment.

in personam jurisdiction See personal jurisdiction.

in posse Capable of being; not yet in actual being or existence.

in praesenti At the present time; now.

in propria persona (in pro per) In one's own person. See pro se.

inquest An inquiry by a coroner or medical examiner to determine the cause of death of a person who appears to have died suddenly or by violence.

inquiry 1. A careful examination or investigation. 2. A question.

inquiry notice Knowledge of facts that would lead a reasonably cautious person to inquire further.

inquisitorial system The fact-finding system in some civil law countries in which the judge has a more active role in questioning the witnesses and in conducting the trial than in an adversary system.

in re In the matter of. A way of designating a court case in which there are no adversary parties in the traditional sense.

in rem (against the res or thing) Pertaining to a proceeding or action binding the whole world in which the court resolves the status of a specific property or thing. The action is not against a person.

An "in personam criminal forfeiture" is an action against a person whereas an "in rem forfeiture" is an action against the property itself. *State v. Bybee*, 134 Ohio App.3d 395 (Ohio App., 1999)

in rem jurisdiction The court's power over a particular res, which is a thing within the territory over which the court has authority.

INS Immigration and Naturalization Service (*www.uscis.gov*).

insane delusion An irrational, persistent belief in nonexistent facts.

insanity 1. That degree of mental illness that negates an individual's legal responsibility or capacity to perform certain legal actions. Also called lunacy. 2. Model Penal Code test: As a result of a mental disease or defect, the accused lacks substantial capacity to appreciate the criminality of his or her conduct or to conform the conduct to the law. Also called substantial capacity test. 3. *Durham* test: The unlawful act was the product of mental disease or mental defect. 4. *M'Naghten* test: Laboring under such a defect of reason, from disease of the mind, as not to know the nature and quality of the act the accused was doing, or if the accused did know it, he or she did not know that it was wrong. Also spelled *McNaghten*. Also called right-and-wrong test. 5. Irresistible impulse test: An urge to commit an act induced by a mental disease so that the person is unable to resist the impulse to commit the act even if he or she knows that the act was wrong.

A person is "not guilty by reason of insanity" relative to a charge of an offense only if the person proves, in the manner specified in section 2901.05 of the Revised Code, that at the time of the commission of the offense, the person did not know, as a result of a severe mental disease or defect, the wrongfulness of the person's acts. R.C. § 2901.01(A)(14)

inscription Entering, enrolling, or registering a fact or name on a list or record.

in se In and of itself. See malum in se.

insecurity clause A clause stating that a party may accelerate payment or performance or require collateral (or additional collateral) when he or she feels insecure because of a danger of default.

insider 1. One with knowledge of facts not available to the general public. 2. An officer or director of a corporation or anyone who owns more than 10 percent of its shares.

insider trading Conduct by corporate employees (or others who owe a fiduciary duty to the corporation) who trade in their company's stock based on material, nonpublic information, or who tip others about confidential corporate information. Trading in securities based on material, nonpublic information acquired in violation of a duty of confidence owed to the source of the information.

insolvency The condition of being unable to pay one's debts as they mature or fall due in the usual course of one's trade and business.

in specie In kind; in the same or like form.

inspection An examination of the quality or fitness of something.

installment A part of a debt payable in stages or successive periods.

installment contract A contract that requires or authorizes the delivery of goods in separate lots to be separately accepted or paid for. UCC 2–612.

An "installment contract" is one which requires or authorizes the delivery of goods in separate lots to be separately accepted, even though the contract contains a clause "each delivery is a separate contract" or its equivalent. R.C. § 1302.70(A)

installment credit A commercial arrangement in which the buyer pays for goods or services in more than one payment (often at regular intervals), for which a finance charge may be imposed.

installment loan A loan to be repaid in specified (often equal) amounts over a designated period.

installment note See serial note.

installment sale A commercial arrangement in which a buyer makes an initial down payment and agrees to pay the balance in installments over a period of time. The seller may keep title or take a security interest in the goods sold until full payment is made.

instance 1. Bringing of a law suit. 2. Occurrence. 3. Urgent insistence.

instant 1. Now under consideration. 2. The present.

instanter At once.

in statu quo In the same condition in which it was.

instigate To stimulate or goad someone to act; to incite.

in stirpes See per stirpes.

institute 1. To inaugurate or begin. 2. An organization that studies or promotes a particular area. 3. Legal treatise or textbooks.

institution 1. The commencement of something. 2. An enduring or established organization. 3. A place for the treatment of those with special needs. 4. A basic practice or custom, e.g., marriage.

instruction See charge (1).

instrument 1. A formal written document that gives expression to or embodies a legal act or agreement, e.g., contract, will. 2. See negotiable instrument. 3. A means by which something is achieved.

(a) "Instrument" means a negotiable instrument or any other writing that evidences a right to the payment of a monetary obligation, is not itself a security agreement or lease, and is of a type that in ordinary course of business is transferred by delivery with any necessary indorsement or assignment. (b) "Instrument" does not include (i) investment property, (ii) letters of credit, or (iii) writings that evidence a right to payment arising out of the use of a credit or charge card or information contained on or for use with the card. R.C. § 1309.102(A)(47)

instrumentality A means or agency by which something is done.

insubordination Intentional disregard of instructions. Disobedience.

insufficient evidence Evidence that cannot support a finding of fact.

insurable Capable of being insured against loss.

insurable interest Any actual, legal, and substantial economic interest in the safety or preservation of the subject of the insurance.

Whenever there is a real interest to protect and a person is so situated with respect to the subject of the insurance that its destruction would or might reasonably be expected to impair the value of that interest, such person has an "insurable interest." *Stauder*, 105 Ohio App. 105 (Ohio App., 1957)

insurance A contract to provide compensation for loss or liability that may occur by or to a specified subject by specified risks.

insurance adjuster A person who investigates, values, and tries to settle insurance claims.

insurance broker An intermediary or middleman between the public and an insurer on insurance matters such as the sale of an insurance policy. A broker is not tied to a particular insurance company.

insurance policy An instrument in writing by which one party (insurer) engages for the consideration of a premium to indemnify another (insured) against a contingent loss by providing compensation if a designated event occurs, resulting in the loss.

insurance trust A trust containing insurance policies and proceeds for distribution under the terms of the trust.

insure 1. To obtain insurance. 2. To issue a policy of insurance.

insured The person covered or protected by insurance.

insurer The underwriter or insurance company that issues insurance.

insurgent One in revolt against government or political authority.

insurrection A rising of citizens or subjects in revolt against civil authority. Using violence to overthrow a government.

intangible 1. Without physical form. 2. Property or an asset that is a "right" (e.g., copyright, option) rather than a physical object even though the right may be evidenced by something physical such as a written contract.

"Intangible property" means patents, copyrights, secret processes, formulas, services, good will, promotion and organization fees and expenses, trademarks, trade brands, trade names, licenses, franchises, any other assets treated as intangible according to generally accepted accounting principles, and securities, accounts receivable, or contract rights having no readily determinable value. R.C. § 1707.01(L)(1)

intangible asset; intangible property See intangible (2).

integrated bar A bar association to which all lawyers must belong if they want to practice law. Also called unified bar.

integrated contract A contract that represents the complete and final understanding of the parties' agreement.

integration 1. Bringing together different groups, e.g., different races. 2. Making something whole or entire. Combining into one.

integration clause A contract clause stating that the writing is meant to represent the parties' entire and final agreement. Also called merger clause.

intellectual property Intangible property rights that can have commercial value (e.g., patents, copyrights, trademarks, trade names, trade secrets) derived from creative or original activity of the mind or intellect.

intend 1. To have in mind as a goal; to plan. 2. To mean or signify. See also intent.

intended use doctrine Manufacturers must design their products so that they are reasonably safe for their intended users.

intendment The true meaning or intention of something.

intent 1. One's state of mind while performing an act. 2. The design or purpose of a person in acting. The desire to cause the consequences of one's acts or the knowledge with substantial certainty that the consequences will follow from what one does.

> Intent is a subjective fact seldom susceptible of proof by direct evidence, and ordinarily it must be ascertained by a consideration of the objective facts and the inferences fairly to be drawn therefrom. *Serrer*, 74 N.E.2d 841 (Ohio Com.Pl., 1946)

intention 1. The purpose or design with which an act is done. Goal. See also intent. 2. Determination or willingness to do something.

intentional Deliberately done; desiring the consequences of an act or knowing with substantial certainty that they will result.

intentional infliction of emotional distress (IIED) The tort of intentionally or recklessly causing severe emotional distress by an act of extreme or outrageous conduct. Also called outrage.

> Intentional infliction of emotional distress occurs when one, by extreme and outrageous conduct, intentionally or recklessly causes serious emotional distress. *Blevins*, 68 Ohio App.3d 665 (Ohio App. 12 Dist., 1990)

inter alia Among other things.

intercept 1. To seize benefits owed to a parent to cover delinquent child support obligations. 2. To covertly acquire the contents of a communication via an electronic or other device. To wiretap.

interdict 1. To forbid, prevent, restrict. 2. To intercept and seize. 3. An injunction or prohibition. 4. One incapacitated by an infirmity.

interest 1. A right, claim, title, or legal share in something; a right to have the advantage accruing from something. 2. A charge that is paid to borrow money or for a delay in its return when due.

> "Interest" means all charges payable directly or indirectly by a borrower to a registrant as a condition to a loan or an application for a loan, however denominated, but does not include default charges, deferment charges, insurance charges or premiums, court costs, loan origination charges, check collection charges, credit line charges, points, prepayment penalties, or other fees and charges specifically authorized by law. R.C. § 1321.51(E)

interested Involved, nonobjective; having a stake in the outcome.

Interest on Lawyers' Trust Accounts (IOLTA) A program in which designated client funds held by an attorney are deposited in a bank account, the interest from which can be used (often through a foundation) to help finance legal services for low-income persons.

interference 1. Hindering or obstructing something. 2. Meddling. 3. A patent proceeding to determine who has priority in an invention.

interference with prospective advantage The tort of intentionally interfering with a reasonable expectation of an economic advantage, usually a commercial or business advantage.

> One who without privilege to do so, induces or otherwise purposely causes a third person not to perform a contract with another or enter into or continue a business relation with another is liable to the other for the harm caused thereby. *Reichman*, 89 Ohio App. 222 (Ohio App., 1951)

interim 1. Intervening time; meantime. 2. Temporary.

interim order A temporary order that applies until another order is issued.

interlineation Writing between the lines of an existing document.

interlocking director A member of the board of directors of more than one corporation at the same time.

interlocutory Not final; interim.

interlocutory appeal An appeal before the trial court reaches its final judgment.

interlocutory decree An intermediate decree or judgment that resolves a preliminary matter or issue.

interlocutory injunction See preliminary injunction.

interlocutory order An order made before final judgment on an incidental or ancillary matter. Also called intermediate order.

interloper One who meddles in the affairs of others.

intermeddler See officious intermeddler.

intermediary A go-between or mediator who tries to resolve conflicts.

intermediary bank Any bank (other than a depositary or payor bank) to which an item is transferred in the course of collection.

> "Intermediary bank" means a bank to which an item is transferred in course of collection except the depositary or payor bank. R.C. § 1304.01(B)(4)

intermediate In the middle position.

intermediate court An appellate court below the court of last resort.

intermediate order See interlocutory order.

intermittent easement An easement that is used only occasionally.

intermixture of goods See confusion of goods.

intern 1. To restrict or confine a person or group. 2. A student obtaining practical experience and training outside the classroom.

internal law The law within a state or country; local law.

internal revenue Tax revenue from internal (not foreign) sources.

Internal Revenue Code (IRC) The federal statute in title 26 of the U.S. Code that codifies federal tax laws.

Internal Revenue Service (IRS) The federal agency responsible for enforcing most federal tax laws (*www.irs.gov*).

internal security Laws and government activity to counter threats from subversive activities.

international agreements Contracts (e.g., treaties) among countries.

International Court of Justice (ICJ) The judicial arm of the United Nations that renders advisory opinions and resolves disputes submitted to it by nations (*www.icj-cij.org*).

international law The legal principles and laws governing relations between nations. Also called law of nations, public international law.

International Paralegal Management Association (IPMA) An association of paralegal managers at law firms and corporations (*www.paralegalmanagement.org*).

internment The confinement of persons suspected of disloyalty.

interplead 1. To file an interpleader. 2. To assert your claim or position on an issue in a case already before the court.

interpleader A remedy or suit to determine a right to property held by a disinterested third party (called the stakeholder) who is in doubt about ownership and who, therefore, deposits the property with the trial court to permit interested parties to litigate ownership.

> Persons having claims against the plaintiff may be joined as defendants and required to interplead when their claims are such that the plaintiff is or may be exposed to double or multiple liability. It is not ground for objection to the joinder that the claims of the several claimants or the titles on which their claims depend do not have a common origin or are not identical but are adverse to and independent of one another, or that the plaintiff avers that he is not liable in whole or in part to any or all of the claimants. Ohio Civ. R. Rule 22

Interpol International Criminal Police Organization; a coordinating group for international law enforcement (*www.interpol.int*).

interpolation Inserting words in a document to change or clarify it.

interpose To submit or introduce something, especially a defense.

interpret To explain the meaning of language or conduct. To construe.

interpretive rule The rule of an administrative agency that explains or clarifies the meaning of existing statutes and regulations.

interrogation A methodical questioning of someone, e.g., a suspect.

interrogatories A discovery device consisting of written questions about a lawsuit submitted by one party to another.

in terrorem clause A clause with a threat, e.g., a clause in a will stating that a gift to a beneficiary will be forfeited if he or she contests the validity of the will. Also called a no-contest clause.

inter se; inter sese Among or between themselves.

interspousal Relating to or between husband and wife.

interspousal immunity Spouses cannot sue each other for personal torts, e.g., battery. Also called husband-wife immunity.

> Interspousal tort immunity is abolished. *Shearer*, 18 Ohio St.3d 94, 480 N.E.2d 388 (Ohio 1985)

interstate Involving two or more states.

interstate commerce The exchange of goods or services (commerce) between two or more states of the United States (including a U.S. territory or the District of Columbia).

interstate compact An agreement between two or more states (and approved by Congress) that is designed to meet common problems.

interval ownership See time-sharing.

intervening Coming or occurring between two times or events.

intervening cause A new and independent force that breaks the causal connection between the original wrong and the injury; a later cause that so interrupts the chain of events as to become the proximate cause of the injury. Also called efficient intervening cause.

intervenor A person with an interest in real or personal property who applies to be made a party to an existing lawsuit involving that property.

intervention The procedure by which a third person, not originally a party but claiming an interest in the subject matter of the suit, is allowed to come into the case to protect his or her own interests.

inter vivos Between or pertaining to the living.

inter vivos gift A gift that takes effect when the donor is living.

inter vivos trust A trust that takes effect when its creator (the settler) is living. Also called living trust.

> "Inter vivos trust" is a trust that is created and becomes effective during the lifetime of the settlor. *In re Guardianship of Lombardo*, 86 Ohio St.3d 600 (Ohio 1999)

intestacy Dying without a valid will.

intestate 1. Without making a valid will. 2. The person who dies without making a valid will.

intestate succession The transfer of property to the relatives of a decedent who dies without leaving a valid will. Also called descent and distribution, hereditary succession.

> A "testate succession" is one which depends at least in part on provisions of will. An "intestate succession" is one which depends entirely upon provisions of law alone. *Bauman*, 160 Ohio St. 296, 116 N.E.2d 439 (Ohio 1953)

in testimonium In witness; in evidence whereof.

in the matter of See in re.

intimidate To coerce unlawfully.

in toto In total; completely.

intoxication A significantly lessened physical or mental ability to function normally, caused by alcohol or drugs.

> "Acute alcohol intoxication" means a heavy consumption of alcohol over a relatively short period of time, resulting in dysfunction of the brain centers controlling behavior, speech, and memory and causing characteristic withdrawal symptoms. R.C. § 2935.33(D)(2)

intra Within.

intrastate commerce Commerce that occurs exclusively within one state.

intra vires Within the power; within the scope of lawful authority.

intrinsic Pertaining to the essential nature of a thing.

intrinsic evidence The evidence found within the writing or document itself.

intrinsic fraud Fraud that goes to the existence of a cause of action or an issue in the case, e.g., perjured testimony.

intrinsic value The true, inherent, and essential value of a thing, not depending on externals, but the same everywhere and to everyone.

intrusion 1. Wrongfully entering upon or taking something. 2. See invasion of privacy (1)(c).

inure 1. To take effect. 2. To habituate. Also spelled enure.

in utero In the uterus.

invalid 1. Having no legal effect. 2. A disabled person.

invasion 1. An encroachment on the rights of others. 2. Making payments from the principal of a trust rather than from its income.

invasion of privacy 1. Four separate torts. (a) Appropriation: The use of a person's name, likeness, or personality for commercial gain without authorization. (b) False light: Unreasonably offensive publicity that places another in a false light. (c) Intrusion: An unreasonably offensive encroachment or invasion into someone's private affairs or concerns (d) Public disclosure of a private fact: Unreasonably offensive publicity concerning the private life of a person. 2. A constitutional prohibition of unreasonable governmental interferences with one's private affairs or effects.

> Actionable "invasion of privacy" is unwarranted appropriation or exploitation of one's personality, publicizing of one's private affairs with which public has no legitimate concern, or wrongful intrusion into one's private activities in such manner as to outrage or cause mental suffering, shame, or humiliation to person of ordinary sensibilities. *Cook*, 79 Ohio App.3d 328 (Ohio App., 1992)

invention The creation of a potentially patentable process or device through independent effort. The discovery of a new process or product.

inventory 1. A detailed list of property or assets. 2. Goods in stock held for sale or lease or under contracts of service, raw materials, works in process, or materials used or consumed in a business.

in ventre sa mere See en ventre sa mere.

inverse condemnation A cause of action for the taking of private property for public use without proper condemnation proceedings.

> "Inverse condemnation" is a shorthand description of manner in which landowner recovers just compensation for a taking of his property when condemnation proceedings have not been instituted. *City of Cincinnati v. Chavez Properties*, 117 Ohio App.3d 269 (Ohio App., 1996)

inverse order of alienation doctrine One seeking to collect on a lien or mortgage on land sold off in successive parcels must collect first from any land still with the original owner; if this land is insufficient to satisfy the debt, he or she must resort to the parcel last sold, and then to the next to the last, and so on until the debt is satisfied.

invest 1. To use money to acquire assets in order to produce revenue. 2. To give power or authority to. 3. To devote to a task; to commit.

investment advisor One who, for compensation, engages in the business of advising others (directly or through publications) on the value of securities or the advisability of investing in, purchasing, or selling securities, or who, as a part of a regular business, publishes reports about securities.

> "Investment adviser" means any person who, for compensation, engages in the business of advising others, either directly or through publications or writings, as to the value of securities or as to the advisability of investing in, purchasing, or selling securities, or who, for compensation and as a part of regular business, issues or promulgates analyses or reports concerning securities. R.C. § 1707.01(X)(1)

investment bank A financial institution engaged in underwriting, selling securities, raising capital, and giving advice on mergers and acquisitions.

investment company A company in the business of investing, reinvesting, or trading in securities (15 USC § 80a-3). A company that sells shares and invests in securities of other companies. Also called an investment trust.

investment contract A contract in which money is invested in a common enterprise with profits to come solely from the efforts of others.

investment income Income from investment capital rather than income resulting from labor. Also called unearned income.

investment securities Instruments such as stocks, bonds, and options used for investment.

investment trust See investment company.

investment tax credit A credit against taxes, consisting of a percentage of the purchase price of capital goods and equipment.

invidious discrimination An arbitrary classification that is not reasonably related to a legitimate purpose. Offensively unequal treatment.

invited error rule On appeal, a party cannot complain about an error for which he or she is responsible, such as an erroneous ruling that he or she prompted or invited the trial court to make.

> Under the "invited-error doctrine," a party may not take advantage of an error that he induced or invited. *State v. Deters*, 163 Ohio App.3d 157 (Ohio App., 2005)

invitee One who enters land upon the express or implied invitation of the occupier of the land to use the land for the purpose for which it is held open to the public or to pursue the business of the occupier.

invocation 1. Calling upon for assistance or authority. 2. The enforcement of something. The verb is invoke.

invoice A document giving the price and other details of a sale of goods or services.

involuntary 1. Not under the control of the will. 2. Compulsory.

involuntary bailment A bailment arising by an accidental, nonnegligent leaving of personal property in the possession of another.

involuntary bankruptcy Bankruptcy forced on a debtor by creditors.

involuntary commitment See civil commitment.

involuntary confession A confession obtained by threats, improper promises, or other unlawful pressure from someone in law enforcement.

involuntary conversion The loss or destruction of property through theft, casualty, or condemnation.

involuntary dismissal A dismissal of an action for failure to prosecute the action or to comply with a court rule or order.

involuntary dissolution The forced termination of the existence of a corporation or other legal entity.

involuntary intoxication Intoxication resulting when one does not knowingly and willingly ingest an intoxicating substance.

involuntary manslaughter The unintentional killing of another without malice while engaged in an unlawful activity that is not a felony and does not naturally tend to cause death or great bodily harm or while engaged in a lawful activity with a reckless disregard for the safety of others.

"Involuntary manslaughter" is unintentional killing while in commission of unlawful act. R.C. §§ 2901.01, 2901.05, 2901.06. *Wadsworth,* 23 Ohio Misc. 112 (Ohio Prob., 1970)

involuntary nonsuit The dismissal of an action when the plaintiff fails to appear, gives no evidence on which a jury could find a verdict, or receives an adverse ruling that precludes recovery.

involuntary servitude The condition of being compelled to labor for another (with or without compensation) by force or imprisonment.

involuntary trust See constructive trust.

IOLTA See Interest on Lawyers' Trust Accounts.

IPMA See International Paralegal Management Association (*www.paralegalmanagement.org*).

ipse dixit An unproven or unsupported assertion made by a person.

ipso facto By that very fact; in and of itself.

ipso jure By the law itself; by the mere operation of law.

IRA See individual retirement account.

IRC See Internal Revenue Code.

irrational Illogical, not guided by a fair assessment of the facts.

irrebuttable presumption See conclusive presumption.

irreconcilable differences A no-fault ground of divorce that exists when persistent, unresolvable disagreements between the spouses lead to an irremediable breakdown of the marriage.

irrecusable Cannot be challenged or rejected.

irregular Not according to rule, proper procedure, or the norm.

irrelevant Not tending to prove or disprove any issue in the case.

irremediable breakdown See irretrievable breakdown.

irreparable Not capable of being repaired or restored.

irreparable injury Harm that cannot be adequately redressed by an award of monetary damages. An injunction, therefore, is possible.

An injury is "irreparable," as element for granting injunctive relief, when there could be no plain, adequate, and complete remedy at law for its occurrence and when any attempt at monetary restitution would be impossible, difficult, or incomplete. *Sequoia Voting Sys., Inc.,* 125 Ohio Misc.2d 7 (Ohio Ct.Cl., 2003)

irresistible impulse See insanity (5).

irretrievable breakdown A no-fault ground of divorce that exists when there is such discord and incompatibility between the spouses that the legitimate objects of matrimony have been destroyed and there is no reasonable possibility of resolution. Also called irremediable breakdown.

irrevocable Not capable of being revoked or recalled.

irrevocable trust A trust that cannot be terminated by its creator.

IRS See Internal Revenue Service (*www.irs.gov*).

issuable 1. Open to debate or litigation. 2. Allowed or authorized for issue or sale. 3. Possible.

issue 1. To send forth, announce, or promulgate. 2. A legal question. A point or matter in controversy or dispute. 3. Offspring; lineal descendants, e.g., child, grandchild. 4. A group or class of securities offered for sale in a block or at the same time. Also called stock issue. 5. The first delivery of a negotiable instrument.

Synonyms "descendant", "issue" and "offspring" are ordinarily used to refer to those who have issued from individual and include his children, grandchildren and their children to the remotest degree; no distinction is ordinarily made between "heir" and "next of kin". *First Nat. Bank of Cincinnati,* 15 Ohio Misc. 109 (Ohio Prob., 1967)

issue of fact A dispute over the existence or nonexistence of an alleged fact. The controversy that exists when one party asserts a fact that is disputed by the other side. Also called question of fact or fact question.

issue of law A question of what the law is, what the law means, or how the law applies to a set of established, assumed, or agreed-upon facts. Also called legal question, question of law.

issue preclusion See collateral estoppel.

item 1. An instrument or a promise or order to pay money handled by a bank for collection or payment. 2. An entry on an account. 3. A part of something.

itemized deduction A payment that is allowed as a deduction from adjusted gross income on a tax return.

J

J Judge; justice.

jactitation False boasting; false claims causing harm.

JAG See Judge Advocate General.

jail A place of confinement, usually for persons awaiting trial or serving sentences for misdemeanors or minor crimes.

Jail means a jail, workhouse, minimum security jail, or other residential facility used for the confinement of alleged or convicted offenders that is operated by a political subdivision or a combination of political subdivisions of this state. R.C. § 2929.01(T)

jailhouse lawyer An inmate who is allowed to give legal assistance and advice to other prisoners if the institution provides no alternatives.

Jane Doe; Jane Roe A fictitious name for a female party in legal proceedings if the real name is unknown or is being kept confidential.

***Jason* clause** A clause in a bill of lading requiring a general average contribution (see this phrase). *The Jason,* 32 S. Ct. 560 (1912).

jaywalking Failure to use crosswalks or to comply with other regulations for crossing the street.

J.D. See Juris Doctor.

***Jencks* rule** After a witness called by the federal prosecutor has testified on direct examination, the court shall, on motion of the defendant, order the prosecution to produce any statement of the witness in the possession of the prosecution that relates to the subject matter of the testimony to aid the defendant in the cross-examination of this witness. 18 USC § 3500(b); *Jencks v. U.S.,* 77 S. Ct. 1007 (1957).

jeopardy The risk of conviction and punishment once a criminal defendant has been placed on trial. Legal jeopardy.

Jeopardy means exposure to danger. A person is in legal jeopardy when he is put on trial before a court of competent jurisdiction, on an indictment or information which is sufficient in form and substance to sustain a conviction, and a jury has been charged with his deliverance. (Quoting 21 Am Jur 2d 236) *State v. Clark*, 1979 WL 207917 (Ohio App., 1979)

jeopardy assessment If the collection of a tax appears to be in question, the IRS may assess and collect the tax immediately without going through the usual formalities.

jetsam Goods that the owner voluntarily throws overboard in an emergency in order to lighten the ship.

jettison To discard or throw overboard in order to lighten the load of a ship in danger. Goods thrown overboard for this purpose.

Jim Crow law A law that intentionally discriminates against blacks.

JJ Judges; justices.

JNOV See judgment notwithstanding the verdict.

jobber 1. One who buys goods from manufacturers and sells them to retailers. A wholesaler. 2. One who does odd jobs or piecework.

John Doe; Richard Roe A fictitious name for a male party in legal proceedings if the real name is unknown or is being kept confidential.

joinder Uniting two or more parties as plaintiffs, two or more parties as defendants, or two or more claims into a single lawsuit.

Joinder test, whereby state is not required to meet stricter other acts admissibility test but instead is only required to show that evidence of each crime joined at trial is simple and direct. Ohio Rules Crim.Proc., Rule 14; Rules of Evid., Rule 404(B). *State v. Miller*, 105 Ohio App.3d 679 (Ohio App., 1995)

joinder of issue The assertion of a fact by a party in a pleading and its denial by the opposing party. The point in litigation when opponents take opposite positions on a matter of law or fact.

joint 1. Shared by or between two or more. 2. United or coupled together in interest or liability.

joint account An account of two or more persons containing assets that each can withdraw in full, and, upon the death of one of them, is payable to the others rather than to the heirs or beneficiaries of the decedent.

joint adventure See joint venture.

joint and mutual will A single will executed by two or more persons disposing of property owned individually or together that shows that the devises or dispositions were made in consideration of one another.

joint and several Together as well as individually or separately.

joint and several liability Legally responsible together and individually. Each wrongdoer is individually responsible for the *entire* judgment; the plaintiff can choose to collect from one wrongdoer or from all of them until the judgment is satisfied.

If damages are caused by joint acts of two or more persons, each defendant may be held liable for damages incurred jointly or severally so that judgment can be taken against any joint tort-feasor for entire amount and apportionment applies to contribution among various tort-feasors and not to individual joint tort-feasor's liability to plaintiff. *Shoemaker*, 78 Ohio App.3d 53 (Ohio App., 1991)

joint and survivor annuity An annuity with two beneficiaries (e.g., husband and wife) that continues to make payments until both beneficiaries die.

joint annuity An annuity with two beneficiaries that stops making payments when either dies.

joint bank account See joint account.

joint committee A legislative committee whose membership is from both houses of the legislature.

joint custody This phrase can mean (a) joint legal custody in which both parents share the right to make the major decisions on raising their child, who may reside primarily with one parent, (b) joint physical custody in which the child resides with each parent individually for alternating, although not necessarily equal, periods of time, or (c) both joint legal custody and joint physical custody.

As used in this section, "joint custody" and "joint care, custody, and control" have the same meaning as "shared parenting." R.C. § 3109.041(C)

joint enterprise See joint venture.

joint estate A form of joint ownership, e.g., joint tenancy, tenancy in common, tenancy by the entirety.

joint legal custody See joint custody.

joint liability Two or more parties together have an obligation or liability to a third party. Liability that is owed to a third party by two or more parties together.

joint lives The duration of an estate lasting until either one of two named persons dies.

joint obligation An obligation incurred by two or more debtors to a single performance to one creditor.

joint ownership Two or more persons who jointly hold title to, or have an interest in, property.

joint physical custody See joint custody.

joint resolution A resolution passed by both houses of a legislative body.

joint return A federal, state, or local tax return filed by a husband and wife together regardless of who earned the income.

joint stock company An unincorporated association of individuals who hold shares of the common capital they contribute. Also called stock association.

joint tenancy Property that is owned equally by two or more persons (called joint tenants) with the right of survivorship. Joint tenants have one and the same interest; accruing by one and the same conveyance, instrument, or act; commencing at one and the same time; with one and the same undivided possession.

joint tortfeasors Two or more persons who together commit a tort. One or more persons jointly or severally liable in tort for the same loss to person or property.

Joint tortfeasor is one who actively participates, cooperates in, requests, aids, encourages, ratifies, or adopts wrongdoer's actions in pursuance of common plan or design to commit a tortious act. *Clevecon, Inc.*, 90 Ohio App.3d 215 (Ohio App., 1993)

jointure A widow's freehold estate in lands (in lieu of dower) to take effect on the death of her husband and to continue during her life.

joint venture An association of persons who jointly undertake some commercial enterprise in which they share profits. An agreement among members of a group to carry out a common purpose, in which each has an equal voice in the control and direction of the enterprise. Also called joint adventure, joint enterprise.

A joint venture is a contractual association in which the parties intend to carry out a common business purpose. *Nilavar,* 127 Ohio App.3d 1 (Ohio App., 1998)

joint will A single testamentary instrument (will) executed by more than one person. It can dispose of property owned individually and jointly.

joint work A work prepared by two or more authors with the intention that their contributions be merged into inseparable or interdependent parts of a unitary whole (17 USC § 101).

Jones Act The federal statute that provides a remedy to seamen injured in the course of employment due to negligence (46 App. USC § 688).

journal 1. A book in which entries are made, often on a regular basis. 2. A periodical or magazine.

journalist's privilege 1. The privilege of a journalist not to disclose information obtained while gathering news, including the identity of sources. Also called reporter's privilege. 2. The qualified privilege of the media (asserted in defamation actions) to make fair comment about public figures on matters of public concern.

journeyman A person who has progressed through an apprenticeship in a craft or trade and is now qualified to work for another.

joyriding Driving an automobile without authorization but without the intent to steal it.

J.P. See justice of the peace.

J.S.D. Doctor of Juridical Science.

judge 1. A public officer appointed or elected to preside over and to administer the law in a court of justice or similar tribunal. 2. To resolve a dispute authoritatively.

"Judge" means judge of the court of common pleas, juvenile court, municipal court, or county court, or the mayor or mayor's court magistrate of a municipal corporation having a mayor's court. Ohio Crim. R. Rule 2(E)

judge advocate A legal officer or adviser in the military. A legal officer on the staff of the Judge Advocate General.

Judge Advocate General (JAG) The senior legal officer in the army, navy, or air force (see e.g., *www.jag.navy.mil*).

judge-made law 1. Law created by judges in court opinions. Law derived from judicial precedents rather than from statutes. 2. A court decision that fails to apply the intent of the legislature. Also called judicial legislation.

judgment The final conclusion of a court that resolves a legal dispute or that specifies what further proceedings are needed to resolve it.

Mere oral pronouncement of the court is not a "judgment," for purposes of court rule under which a judgment is effective only when entered on the journal by the clerk. Rules Crim.Proc., Rule 32(B). *State v. Jackson,* 123 Ohio App.3d 22 (Ohio App., 1997)

judgment as a matter of law A judgment on an issue in a federal jury trial (and in some state jury trials) ordered by the judge against a party because there is no legally sufficient evidentiary basis for a reasonable jury to find for that party on that issue. The judgment may be rendered before or after the verdict. In some state courts, the judgment is called a *directed verdict* if it is rendered before the jury reaches a verdict and a *judgment notwithstanding the verdict* (JNOV or judgment n.o.v.) if it is rendered after the jury reaches a verdict.

judgment by default See default judgment.

judgment book The book or docket in which the clerk enters the judgments that are rendered.

judgment creditor A person in whose favor a money judgment (damages) is entered or who becomes entitled to enforce it.

judgment debtor A person ordered to pay a money judgment (damages) rendered against him or her.

judgment in personam See personal judgment.

judgment in rem A judgment concerning the status or condition of property. The judgment is against or on the property, not a person. See also in rem.

A "judgment in rem" binds property subjected to court's jurisdiction, but when it has converted such property, it is functus officio and without further vitality for any purpose. *Falk,* 69 Ohio App. 550 (Ohio App., 1942)

judgment lien A lien on property of a judgment debtor giving the judgment creditor the right to levy on it to satisfy the judgment.

judgment nisi ("a judgment unless") A judgment that will stand unless the party affected by it appears and shows cause against it.

judgment non obstante veredicto See judgment notwithstanding the verdict.

judgment note See cognovit.

judgment notwithstanding the verdict (JNOV) A court judgment that is opposite to the verdict reached by the jury. Also called judgment non obstante veredicto or judgment n.o.v. In federal court, it is called a judgment as a matter of law (see this phrase).

Motion for judgment notwithstanding the verdict. Whether or not a motion to direct a verdict has been made or overruled and not later than fourteen days after entry of judgment, a party may move to have the verdict and any judgment entered thereon set aside and to have judgment entered in accordance with his motion. . . . Ohio Civ. R. Rule 50(B)

judgment n.o.v. See judgment notwithstanding the verdict.

judgment on the merits A judgment, rendered after evidentiary inquiry and argument, determining which party is in the right, as opposed to a judgment based solely on a technical point or procedural error.

judgment on the pleadings A judgment based solely on the facts alleged in the complaint, answer, and other pleadings.

judgment proof A person without assets to satisfy a judgment.

judgment quasi in rem A judgment determining a particular person's interest in specific property within the court's jurisdiction. See also quasi in rem.

judicature 1. The judiciary. 2. The administration of justice. 3. The jurisdiction or authority of a judge.

judicial Pertaining to the courts, the office of a judge, or judgments.

judicial act A decision or other exercise of power by a court.

judicial activism Writing court decisions that invalidate arguably valid statutes, fail to follow precedent, or that inject the court's political or social philosophy. Sometimes called judicial legislation.

judicial admission A deliberate, clear statement of a party on a concrete fact within the party's peculiar knowledge that is conclusive upon the party making it, thereby relieving the opposing party from presenting any evidence on it.

judicial bonds Generic term for bonds required by a court for appeals, costs, attachment, injunction, etc.

judicial discretion The ability or power of a court (when it is not bound to decide an issue one way or another) to choose between two or more courses of action. Also called legal discretion.

> Judicial discretion is the option which a judge may exercise between the doing and not doing of a thing which cannot be demanded as an absolute legal right, guided by the spirit, principles and analogies of the law, and founded upon the reason and conscience of the judge, to a just result in the light of the particular circumstances of the case. *Cleveland Bd. of Educ.*, 22 Ohio Misc.2d 18 (Ohio Com.Pl., 1985)

judicial economy Efficiency in the use of the courts' resources.

judicial immunity The exemption of judges from civil liability arising out of the discharge of judicial functions.

judicial legislation 1. Statutes creating or involving the courts. 2. See judge-made law (2), judicial activism.

judicial lien A lien that arises by judgment, sequestration, or other legal or equitable process or proceeding (11 USC § 101).

judicial notice A court's acceptance of a well-known fact without requiring proof of that fact.

> Proof by evidence may be dispensed with where the court is justified by general considerations in declaring truth of proposition without requiring evidence from the party, which is the process most commonly meant by the term "judicial notice". *First Nat. Bank of Cincinnati*, 7 Ohio Misc. 130 (Ohio Prob., 1966)

judicial power The power of the court to decide and pronounce a judgment and carry it into effect between parties in the case.

judicial question A question that is proper for the courts to resolve.

judicial restraint Courts should resolve issues before them without reaching other issues that do not have to be resolved, follow precedent closely without injecting personal views and philosophies, and defer to the right of the legislature to make policy.

judicial review 1. The power of a court to interpret statutes and administrative laws to determine their constitutionality. 2. The power of a court to examine the legal and factual conclusions of a lower court or administrative agency to determine whether errors were made.

judicial sale A sale based on a court decree ordering the sale.

judicial separation See legal separation.

judiciary The branch of government vested with the judicial power; the system of courts in a country; the body of judges; the bench.

jump bail To fail to appear at the next scheduled court appearance after having been released on bail.

junior Subordinate; lower in rank or priority.

> Shares of a class are "junior" to shares of another class when any of their dividend or distribution rights are subordinate to, or dependent or contingent upon, any right of, or dividend on, or distribution to, shares of such other class. R.C. § 1701.01(J)

junior bond A bond that has a lower payment priority than other bonds.

junior lien A lien that has a lower priority than other liens on the same property.

junk science Unreliable, potentially misleading scientific evidence.

jura Rights; laws.

jural Pertaining to law, justice, rights, and legal obligations.

jurat A certificate of a person before whom a writing was sworn. A certification by a notary public that the person signing the writing (e.g., an affidavit) appeared before the notary and swore that the assertions in the writing were true.

jure By the law; by right.

juridical Relating to the law or the administration of justice.

juris Of law; of right.

jurisdiction 1. The power of a court to decide a matter in controversy. 2. The geographic area over which a particular court has authority. 3. The scope of power or authority that a person or entity can exercise. See also personal jurisdiction, in rem jurisdiction, quasi in rem jurisdiction, and subject-matter jurisdiction.

> Jurisdiction means the courts' statutory or constitutional power to adjudicate the case; the term encompasses jurisdiction over the subject matter and over the person. *Pratts*, 102 Ohio St.3d 81 (Ohio 2004)

jurisdictional amount See amount in controversy.

jurisdictional dispute Competing claims by different unions that their members are entitled to perform certain work.

jurisdictional facts Those facts that must exist before the court can properly take jurisdiction of the particular case.

jurisdiction in personam See personal jurisdiction.

jurisdiction in rem See in rem jurisdiction.

jurisdiction of the subject matter See subject-matter jurisdiction.

jurisdiction quasi in rem See quasi in rem jurisdiction.

Juris Doctor (J.D.) Doctor of law. The standard degree received upon completion of law school. Also called doctor of jurisprudence.

jurisprudence The philosophy of law; a science that ascertains the principles on which legal rules are based. The system of laws.

jurist A legal scholar; a judge.

juristic person See artificial person.

juror A member of a jury.

jury A group of persons selected to resolve disputes of fact and to return a verdict based on the evidence presented to them.

jury box The courtroom location where the jury observes the trial.

jury charge See charge (1).

jury commissioner An official in charge of prospective jurors.

jury instructions See charge (1).

jury list A list of citizens who could be called for jury duty.

jury nullification A jury's refusal to apply a law perceived to be unjust or unpopular by acquitting a defendant in spite of proof of guilt.

jury panel A list or group of prospective jurors. Also called venire.

jury tampering See embracery.

jury trial The trial of a matter before a judge and jury as opposed to a trial solely before a judge. The jury decides the factual issues.

> The right of trial by jury shall be inviolate, except that, in civil cases, laws may be passed to authorize the rendering of a verdict by the concurrence of not less than three-fourths of the jury. Ohio Const. Art. I, § 5

jury wheel A system for the storage and random selection of the names or identifying numbers of prospective jurors.

jus (**jura** plural) Law; system of law; right; power; principle.

jus accrescendi The right of survivorship or accrual.

jus cogens A rule or legal principle that the parties cannot change.

jus gentium The law of nations; international law.

jus publicum 1. Public law. 2. State ownership of land.

just Conforming to what is legal or equitable.

just cause See good cause.

just compensation Compensation that is fair to both the owner and the public when the owner's property is taken for public use through eminent domain.

> Just compensation means the payment of compensation by a public agency that orders the removal of an advertising device, in the same manner as it would for other property acquired pursuant to this chapter. R.C. § 163.31(C)

jus tertii The right of a third person or party.

justice 1. A judge, usually of a higher court. 2. The proper administration of the law; the fair resolution of legal disputes.

justice court A lower court (e.g., a justice of the peace court) that can hear minor civil or criminal matters.

justice of the peace (J.P.) A judicial magistrate of inferior rank with limited jurisdiction over minor civil or criminal cases.

justiciable Appropriate for court resolution.

justifiable Warranted or sanctioned by law. Defensible.

justifiable homicide Killing another when permitted by law (e.g., in self-defense).

justification A just or lawful reason to act or to fail to act.

> A proceeding is substantially justified if it had a reasonable basis in law or fact at the time that it was initiated. R.C. § 3916.11(G)(3)

juvenile One under 18 (or other age designated by law) and, therefore, not subject to be treated as an adult for purposes of the criminal law.

juvenile court A special court with jurisdiction over minors alleged to be neglected or juvenile delinquents.

juvenile delinquent A minor (e.g., someone under 18) who has committed an act that would be a crime if committed by an adult. Also called youthful offender.

K

k Contract.

kangaroo court A sham legal proceeding in which a person's rights are disregarded and the result is a foregone conclusion due to bias.

K.B. See King's Bench.

keeper A person or entity that has the custody or management of something or someone.

Keogh plan A retirement plan for self-employed taxpayers, the contributions to which are tax deductible. Also called H.R. 10 plan.

KeyCite The citator on Westlaw that allows online checking of the subsequent history of cases, statutes, and other laws.

key number A number assigned to a topic by West Group in its indexing or classification system of case law.

key man insurance Life insurance on employees who are crucial to a company. The company pays for the insurance and is the beneficiary.

kickback A payment made by a seller of a portion of the purchase price to the buyer or to a public official in order to induce the purchase or to influence future business transactions.

kiddie tax A popular term used for the tax paid by parents at their rate for the investment (unearned) income of their children.

kidnapping Taking and carrying away a human being by force, fraud, or threats against the victim's will and without lawful authority.

> Kidnapping. (A) No person, by force, threat, or deception, or, in the case of a victim under the age of thirteen or mentally incompetent, by any means, shall remove another from the place where the other person is found or restrain the liberty of the other person, for any of the following purposes: (1) To hold for ransom, or as a shield or hostage; (2) To facilitate the commission of any felony or flight thereafter; (3) To terrorize, or to inflict serious physical harm on the victim or another; (4) To engage in sexual activity, as defined in section 2907.01 of the Revised Code, with the victim against the victim's will; (5) To hinder, impede, or obstruct a function of government, or to force any action or concession on the part of governmental authority. R.C. § 2905.01(A)

kin One's relatives; family, kindred.

kind Generic class; type. See also in kind.

kindred Family, relatives.

King's Bench (K.B.) One of the superior courts of common law in England. If the monarch is a queen, the court is called Queen's Bench.

kiting See check kiting.

knock-and-announce rule Police must announce their presence before forcibly entering premises to be searched. An exception (called the useless-gesture exception) exists if the occupants already know why the police are there.

knock down Final acceptance of a bid by an auctioneer.

knowingly With awareness or understanding; conscious or deliberate; intentionally.

knowledge Acquaintance with fact or truth. Understanding obtained by experience or study. Awareness.

> A person knows or has knowledge of the fact when the person has actual knowledge of it. Discover or learn or a word

or phrase of similar import refers to knowledge rather than to reason to know. R.C. § 1301.01(Y)(3)

L

labor Mental or physical exertion or work, usually for a wage.

labor contract A collective bargaining agreement between a union and an employer covering wages, conditions of labor, and related matters.

laborer's lien A lien on property of someone responsible for paying for the work of a laborer on that property.

Labor-Management Relations Act The federal statute that covers procedures to settle strikes involving national emergencies, protects employees who do not want to join the union, and imposes other restrictions on unions (29 USC § 141). Also called Taft-Hartley Act.

labor organization A union.

labor union See union.

laches A party's unreasonable delay in asserting a legal or equitable right and another's detrimental good-faith change in position because of the delay.

> An equitable defense that bars an action as a result of an unexcused delay in bringing the action that prejudices the defendant. *Jefferson Regional Water Auth.*, 161 Ohio App.3d 310 (Ohio App., 2005)

lading See bill of lading.

LAMA See International Paralegal Management Association (*www.paralegalmanagement.org*).

lame duck 1. An elected official still in office who has not been or cannot be reelected. 2. A member of a stock exchange who has overbought and cannot meet his or her obligations.

lame duck session A legislative session conducted after the election of new members but before they are installed.

land 1. The surface of the earth, anything growing or permanently attached to it, the airspace above the earth, and what exists beneath the surface. 2. An interest in real property.

> Earth, sand, and gravel are part of the soil and are "land" within meaning of section of statute of frauds governing contracts for the sale of interests in lands, and oral contract for the sale of such material is within the statute. R.C. § 1335.05. *DePugh*, 79 Ohio App.3d 503 (Ohio App., 1992)

land bank A federally created bank under the Federal Farm Loan Act organized to make loans on farm land at low interest rates.

land grant A gift or donation of public land by the government to an individual, corporation, or other government.

landlord The owner who leases land, buildings, or apartments to another. Also called lessor.

landlord's lien The right of a landlord to levy upon goods of a tenant in satisfaction of unpaid rents or property damage.

landmark 1. A monument or other marker set up on the boundary line of two adjoining estates to fix such boundary. 2. Historically important. A landmark case establishes new and significant legal principles.

land sales contract See contract for deed.

land trust A trust that gives legal and equitable title of real property to a trustee but management and control of the property to the trust beneficiary. Also called Illinois Land Trust.

land use planning The use of zoning laws, environmental impact studies, and coordination efforts to develop the interrelated aspects of a community's physical environment and its social and economic activities.

lapping Theft of cash receipts from a customer that is covered up by crediting someone else's receipts to that customer.

lapse 1. To end because of a failure to use or a failure to fulfill a condition. 2. To fail to vest because of the death of the prospective beneficiary before the death of the donor. 3. A slip, mistake, or error. 4. A period of time.

> Lapse means falling from the original condition, and generally refers to a legacy or devise which would have taken effect if testator had died the instant after he executed his will, but which fails because the devisee or legatee has in some way become incapable of taking under the will between the time the will was made and the time the testator died. *Kammer*, 96 N.E.2d 439 (Ohio Prob., 1950)

lapsed Expired; no longer effective.

larcenous Having the character of or contemplating larceny.

larceny The wrongful taking and carrying away of another's personal property with the intention to deprive the possessor of it permanently.

larceny by trick Larceny by using fraud or false pretenses to induce the victim to give up possession (but not title) to personal property.

lascivious Tending to incite lust; obscene.

last antecedent rule Qualifying words will be applied only to the word or phrase immediately preceding unless the qualifying words were clearly intended to apply to other language in the document as well.

last clear chance doctrine A plaintiff who has been contributorily negligent in placing himself or herself in peril can still recover if the negligent defendant had the last opportunity (clear chance) to avoid the accident and failed to exercise reasonable care to do so. Also called discovered peril doctrine, humanitarian doctrine, supervening negligence.

> Last clear chance doctrine is applicable in those situations where plaintiff placed himself in perilous position, through his own negligence, but can still recover if defendant, after becoming aware of plaintiff's perilous position, could have avoided injuring plaintiff, in exercise of ordinary care, and failed to do so. *Patterson*, 112 N.E.2d 65 (Ohio App., 1952)

last in, first out (LIFO) An accounting assumption that the last goods purchased are the first ones sold or used.

last resort The end of the appeal process, referring to a court from which there is no further appeal.

last will The testator's most recent will before dying.

latent Concealed; dormant or not active.

latent ambiguity A lack of clarity in otherwise clear language that arises when some extrinsic evidence creates a necessity for interpretation.

> A latent ambiguity is a defect that does not appear on the face of language used or an instrument being considered; it arises when language is clear and intelligible and suggests but a single meaning, but some intrinsic fact or some extraneous evidence creates a necessity for interpretation or a choice between two or more possible meanings. *Conkle*, 31 Ohio App.2d 44 (Ohio App., 1972)

latent defect See hidden defect.

lateral support right The right to have land in its natural state supported by adjoining land.

laundering Concealing or disguising the source or origin of something (e.g., money) that was obtained illegally.

law 1. A rule of action or conduct prescribed by a controlling authority and having binding force. 2. The aggregate body of rules governing society. 3. The legal profession.

law clerk 1. An attorney's employee who is in law school studying to be an attorney or is waiting to pass the bar examination. 2. One who provides research and writing assistance to a judge.

law day 1. The date on which a mortgagor can avoid foreclosure by paying the debt on the mortgaged property. 2. May 1st, the date each year set aside to honor our legal system.

law enforcement officer Someone empowered by law to investigate crime, make arrests for violations of the criminal law, and preserve the peace.

> Law enforcement officer means a sheriff, deputy sheriff, constable, municipal police officer, marshal, deputy marshal, or state highway patrolman, and also means any officer, agent, or employee of the state or of any of its agencies, instrumentalities, or political subdivisions, upon whom, by statute, the authority to arrest violators is conferred, when the officer, agent, or employee is acting within the limits of statutory authority. Ohio Crim. R. Rule 2(J)

lawful Legal, authorized by law.

law journal A legal periodical of a law school or bar association. See also law review.

law list A list or directory of attorneys containing brief information relevant to their practice.

law merchant The practices and customs of those engaged in commerce that developed into what is known today as commercial law.

law of nations See international law.

law of nature See natural law.

law of the case doctrine An appellate court's determination of a legal issue binds both the trial court and the court on appeal in any subsequent appeal involving the same case and substantially the same facts.

> The law-of-the-case doctrine provides that the decision of a reviewing court in a case remains the law of that case on the legal questions involved for all subsequent proceedings in the case at both the trial and reviewing levels. *Wright*, 159 Ohio App.3d 154 (Ohio App., 2004)

law of the land 1. The law that applies in a country, state or region. 2. Due process of law and related constitutional protections.

law of the road Traffic laws.

law reports, law reporters See reporter (3), report (2).

law review (L. Rev.) A legal periodical (usually student-edited) published by a law school. Also called law journal.

Law School Admission Test (LSAT) A standardized aptitude test used by many law schools in making decisions on admission.

lawsuit A court proceeding that asserts a legal claim or dispute. Also called a suit.

lawyer See attorney (1).

lay 1. Nonprofessional; not having expertise. 2. Nonecclesiastical; not belonging to the clergy. 3. To state or allege in a pleading.

layaway A seller's agreement with a consumer to hold goods for sale at a later date at a specified price.

> "Layaway price" means the price at which the specific goods which are the subject of a layaway arrangement are offered for sale at retail by the seller if such sale were a sale for cash to be paid in full upon delivery on the date the layaway arrangement was entered into instead of pursuant to a layaway arrangement. R.C. § 1317.01(T)

layoff A temporary or permanent termination of employment at the will of the employer.

lay witness A person giving only fact or lay (not expert) opinion testimony.

LBO See leveraged buyout.

lead counsel The attorney managing the case of a client with several attorneys. The primary attorney in a class action.

leading case An opinion that has had an important influence in the development of the law on a particular point.

leading question A question to someone being interviewed or examined that suggests the answer within the question.

learned intermediary See informed intermediary.

lease 1. A contract for the use or possession of real or personal property for a designated rent or other consideration. Ownership of the property is not transferred. 2. To let or rent.

> A "lease" is a species of contract for the possession and profits of lands and tenements either for life, or a certain period of time, or during pleasure of the parties. *Cook*, 207 N.E.2d 405 (Ohio Com.Pl., 1965)

leaseback The sale of property to a buyer who gives the seller the right to lease the property from the buyer. Also called sale and leaseback.

leasehold An estate in real property held by a tenant/lessee under a lease; property held by a lease.

leave 1. To give in a will; to bequeath. 2. To withdraw or depart. 3. Permission to do something, e.g., to be absent from work or military service.

ledger A book used to record business transactions.

legacy 1. Any gift in a will. 2. A gift of personal property in a will. 3. Something handed down from an ancestor.

legal 1. Authorized, required, permitted, or involving the law. 2. Pertaining to law rather than to equity.

legal age See age of consent, age of majority, age of reason.

legal aid A system (often government-funded) of providing legal services to people who cannot afford counsel.

> Legal aid society means a nonprofit corporation that satisfies all of the following: (1) It is chartered to provide general legal services to the poor, it is incorporated and operated exclusively in this state, its primary purpose or function is to provide civil legal services, without charge, to indigents, and, in addition to providing civil legal services to indigents, it may provide legal training or legal technical assistance to other legal aid societies in this state. (2) It has a board of trustees, a majority of its board of trustees are attorneys, and at least one-third of its board of trustees, when selected, are eligible to receive legal services from the legal aid society. (3) It receives funding from the legal

services corporation or otherwise provides civil legal services to indigents. R.C. § 120.51(A)

legal assistant See paralegal.

legal cap Long, ruled paper in tablet form.

legal capital The par or stated value of outstanding stock. Also called stated capital.

legal cause See proximate cause.

legal certainty test A court will find federal diversity jurisdiction on the basis of the plaintiff's complaint unless it appears to a legal certainty that the claim is for less than the jurisdictional amount.

legal conclusion A statement of legal consequences, often without including the facts from which the consequences arise. See also conclusion of law.

> A particular statement which would be considered a statement of fact in everyday conversation might, nevertheless, be considered a "legal conclusion" when used in connection with a legal proceeding if the truth of the fact stated is one of the ultimate issues to be determined in such proceeding. *Cortner*, 25 Ohio Misc. 156 (Ohio Com.Pl., 1970)

legal consideration See valuable consideration.

legal custody 1. The right and duty to make decisions about raising a child. 2. The detention of someone by the government.

legal death See brain death, civil death.

legal description A description of real property by various methods (e.g., by metes and bounds), including a description of portions subject to any easements or other restrictions.

> "Legal description" means a description of the property by metes and bounds or lot numbers of a recorded plat including a description of any portion of the property subject to an easement or reservation, if any. R.C. § 5313.01(E)

legal detriment See detriment.

legal discretion See judicial discretion.

legal duty See duty (2).

legal entity An artificial person (e.g., a corporation) that functions in some ways as a natural person (e.g., it can sue and be sued).

legalese Technical language or jargon used by attorneys.

legal ethics Rules that embody the minimum standards of behavior to which members of the legal profession are expected to conform.

legal fiction An assumption of fact made by a court in order to dispose of a matter with justice even though the fact may not be true.

legal fraud See constructive fraud.

legal heir See heir (1).

legal holiday A day designated as a holiday by the legislature. A day on which court proceedings and service of process cannot occur.

legal impossibility A defense asserting that the defendant's intended acts, even if completed, would not amount to a crime.

legal injury An invasion of a person's legally protected interest.

legal interest 1. A legally protected right or claim. A legal share of something. 2. A rate of interest authorized by law.

legal investments Those investments, sometimes called legal lists, in which banks and other financial institutions may invest.

legal issue A legal question. See also issue of law.

legality 1. Lawfulness; the state of being in accordance with law. 2. A technical legal requirement.

legalize To declare or make legal that which was once illegal.

legal list See legal investments.

legal malice 1. Pertaining to wrongful conduct committed or continued with a willful or reckless disregard for another's rights. 2. Malice that is inferred. Also called implied malice.

> Legal malice is that state of mind under which person acts with disregard and lack of consideration for just rights of others. *Trainor*, 22 Ohio App.2d 135 (Ohio App.,1969)

legal malpractice The failure of an attorney to use such skill, prudence, and diligence as reasonable attorneys of ordinary skill and capacity commonly possess and exercise under the same circumstances. Professional misconduct or wrongdoing by attorneys.

> Legal malpractice requires an attorney-client relationship giving rise to a duty, breach of that duty, and damages caused by breach. *Am. Express Travel Related Serv. Co.*, 111 Ohio App.3d 160 (Ohio App., 1996)

legal name The designation of a person or entity recognized by the law.

legal notice Notification of something in a manner prescribed by law.

legal opinion An attorney's interpretation (often in writing) of how the law applies to facts in a client's case.

legal positivism The legal theory that the validity of laws is based, not on natural law or morality, but on being duly enacted or decreed by the three branches of government and accepted by society.

legal proceedings Formal actions in court or administrative tribunals to establish legal rights or resolve legal disputes.

legal question See issue of law.

legal realism The legal theory that the development of law in court opinions is based on public policy and social science considerations rather than on a pure or rigid legal analysis of rules.

legal representative One who represents the legal interests of another, e.g., one who is incapacitated.

legal reserve Assets that a business (e.g., insurance company, bank) must set aside to be available to meet the demands of its customers.

legal residence The residence required by law for legal purposes, e.g., receipt of process. See also domicile (3).

> "Residence" and "legal residence" have the same meaning as "legal settlement," which is acquired by residing in Ohio for a period of one year without receiving general assistance prior to July 17, 1995. . . . R.C. § 5123.01(T)

legal separation A court order allowing spouses to live separately and establishing their rights and duties while separated, but still married. Also called divorce a mensa et thoro, judicial separation, limited divorce.

> The court of common pleas may grant legal separation on a complaint or counterclaim, regardless of whether the parties are living separately at the time the complaint or counterclaim is filed, for the following causes: (1) Either

party had a husband or wife living at the time of the marriage from which legal separation is sought; (2) Willful absence of the adverse party for one year; (3) Adultery; (4) Extreme cruelty. . . . R.C. § 3105.17(A)

legal technician See independent paralegal.

legal tender Coins and currencies that can be used to pay debts.

legal title 1. A title that is recognizable and enforceable in a court of law. 2. A title that provides the right of ownership but no beneficial interest in the property. See also beneficial interest.

legatee The person to whom personal property (and sometimes real property) is given by will.

legation A diplomatic mission; the staff and premises of such a mission.

legislate To enact laws through legislation. To make or pass a law.

legislation 1. The enactment of laws by a legislative body. 2. Law or laws passed by a legislature. 3. A statute; a body of statutes.

legislative Pertaining to the enactment of laws by a legislative body.

If action of legislative body creates a law, the action is "legislative," but if the action consists of executing or administrating an existing law, the action is "administrative." *State ex rel. Srovnal*, 46 Ohio St.2d 207 (Ohio 1976)

legislative council A body that plans legislative strategy, primarily between sessions of the legislature.

legislative counsel The person or office that assists legislators by conducting research and drafting proposed legislation.

legislative court See Article I court.

legislative history Hearings, debates, reports, and all other events that occur in the legislature before a bill is enacted into a statute.

legislative immunity An immunity from civil suit enjoyed by a member of the legislature while engaged in legislative functions.

legislative intent The design, aim, end, or plan of the legislature in passing a particular statute.

legislative rule A rule of an administrative agency based on its quasi-legislative power. An administrative rule that creates rights or assigns duties rather than merely interprets a governing statute. Also called substantive rule.

legislative veto A legislative method of rejecting administrative action. The agency's action (e.g., a rule) would be valid unless nullified by resolutions of the legislature. On the unconstitutionality of such vetoes, see *INS v. Chadha*, 103 S. Ct. 2764 (1983).

legislator A member of a legislative body.

legislature The assembly or body of persons that makes statutory laws for a state or nation.

legitimacy 1. The condition of being born within a marriage or acquiring this condition through steps provided by law. 2. The condition of being in compliance with the law or with established standards.

legitimate 1. Lawful, valid, or genuine. 2. Born to married parents or to parents who have legitimated the child.

legitimation 1. Making legitimate or lawful. 2. The procedure of legalizing (legitimating) the status of an illegitimate child.

legitime A portion of decedent's estate that must be reserved for a forced heir such as a child. See also forced heir.

lemon law A law giving a buyer of a new car with major defects the right to a refund or to have it replaced.

lend 1. To provide money to another for a period of time, often for an interest charge. 2. To give something of value to another for a fixed or indefinite time, with or without compensation, with the expectation that it will be returned.

lese majesty A crime against the sovereign, e.g., treason. Also spelled leze majesty.

lessee A person who rents or leases property from another. A tenant.

lesser included offense A crime composed solely of some but not all of the elements of a greater crime so that it would be impossible to commit the greater offense without committing the lesser. Also called included offense.

Offense may be "lesser included offense" of charged offense if offense carries lesser penalty than charged offense, charged offense cannot ever be committed without lesser offense also being committed, and some element of charged offense is not required to prove commission of lesser offense. R.C. § 2945.74; Rules Crim.Proc., Rule 31(C). *State v. Wong*, 95 Ohio App.3d 39 (Ohio App., 1994)

lessor A person who rents or leases property to another. A landlord.

let 1. To allow. 2. To lease or rent. 3. To award a contract to one of the bidders.

lethal weapon See deadly weapon.

letter A writing that grants a power, authority, or right.

letter of attornment A letter to a tenant stating that the premises have been sold and that rent should be paid to the new owner.

letter of credit (LOC) An engagement by a bank or other issuer (made at the request of a customer) to honor demands for payment by a third party upon compliance with conditions stated in the letter. Also called circular note.

"Letter of credit" means a definite undertaking that satisfies the requirements of section 1305.03 of the Revised Code by an issuer to a beneficiary at the request or for the account of an applicant or, in the case of a financial institution, to itself or for its own account, to honor a documentary presentation by payment or delivery of an item of value. R.C. § 1305.01(A)10)

letter of intent (LOI) A nonbinding writing that states preliminary understandings of one or both parties to a possible future contract.

letter rogatory A court's request to a court in a foreign jurisdiction for assistance in a pending case, e.g., to take the testimony of a witness in the other jurisdiction.

letter ruling A written statement issued to a taxpayer by the IRS that interprets and applies the tax laws to a specific set of facts.

letters of administration The court document that authorizes a person to manage the estate of someone who has died without a valid will.

letters of marque A government authorization to a private citizen to seize assets of a foreign country.

letters patent A public document issued by the government that grants a right, e.g., a right to the sole use of an invention.

letters testamentary A formal document issued by a court that empowers a person to act as an executor of a will.

letter stock See restricted security.

levari facias A writ of execution to satisfy a party's judgment debt out of his or her profits and other assets.

leverage 1. The use of credit or debt to increase profits and purchasing power. The use of a smaller investment to generate a larger rate of return through borrowing. 2. Added power or influence.

leveraged buyout (LBO) Taking over a company by using borrowed funds for a substantial part of the purchase. The sale of a corporation in which at least part of the purchase price is obtained through debt assumed by the corporation.

levy 1. To assess or impose a tax, charge, or fine. 2. To seize assets in order to satisfy a claim. 3. To conscript into the military. 4. To wage or carry on. 5. A tax, charge, or fine.

lewd Indecent, obscene; inciting to lustful desire.

> "Lewd," within meaning of statute governing nuisance, is a word of common usage, meaning sexually unchaste or licentious, lascivious, inciting to sensual desire or imagination. R.C. § 3767.01(C)(2). *State ex rel. Nasal*, 127 Ohio Misc.2d 101 (Ohio Com.Pl., 2003)

lex law or a collection of laws.

lex fori The law of the forum where the suit is brought.

LexisNexis A fee-based legal research computer service.

lex loci contractus The law of the place where the contract was formed or will be performed.

lex loci delicti The law of the place where the wrong (e.g., the tort) took place.

leze majesty See lese majesty.

liability 1. The condition of being legally responsible for a loss, penalty, debt, or other obligation. 2. The obligation owed.

liability insurance Insurance in which an insurer pays covered damages the insured is obligated to pay a third person.

liability without fault See strict liability.

liable Obligated in law; legally responsible.

libel 1. A defamatory statement expressed in writing or other graphic or visual form such as by pictures or signs. See also defamation. 2. A plaintiff's pleading in an admiralty or ecclesiastical court.

> Libel is generally defined as a false written publication made with some degree of fault, reflecting injuriously on a person's reputation, or exposing a person to public hatred, contempt, ridicule, shame, or disgrace or affecting a person adversely in his trade, business, or profession. *Wilson*, 2005 WL 2807253, 2005-Ohio-5722 (Ohio App., 2005)

libelant The complainant in an admiralty or ecclesiastical court.

libelee The defendant in an admiralty or ecclesiastical court.

libelous Defamatory; constituting or involving libel.

libel per quod A writing that requires extrinsic facts to understand its defamatory meaning. Libel that requires proof of special damages.

libel per se A written defamatory statement that is actionable without proof that the plaintiff suffered special damages. Libel that is defamatory on its face.

liberal construction An expansive or broad interpretation of the meaning of a statute or other law to include facts or cases that are within the spirit and reason of the law.

liberty 1. Freedom from excessive or oppressive restrictions imposed by the state or other authority. 2. A basic right or privilege.

license 1. Permission to do what would otherwise be illegal or a tort. 2. The document that evidences this permission.

licensee 1. One who enters land for his or her own purposes or benefit, but with the express or implied consent of the owner or occupier of the land. 2. One who has a license.

> A licensee, for purposes of determining an owner's duty of care to such person, is a person who enters an owner's premises, with permission or acquiescence, for personal benefit. *Dodson*, 782 N.E.2d 190 (Ohio Ct.Cl., 2002)

licensor One who gives or grants a license.

licentious Without moral restraint. Disregarding sexual morality.

licit Permitted by law, legal.

lie 1. A deliberately or intentionally false statement. 2. To make a false statement intentionally. 3. To be sustainable in law.

lie detector See polygraph.

lien A charge, security, or encumbrance on property; a creditor's claim or charge on property for the payment of a debt.

> Generally, a lien is a charge upon property to secure the performance of an obligation such as the payment of a debt, while an "easement" is a right of an owner of land to use the land of another for a specific purpose. *Ross*, 139 Ohio St. 395 (Ohio 1942)

lien creditor One whose claim is secured by a lien on particular property of the debtor.

lienee One whose property is subject to a lien.

lienholder; lienor One who has a lien on the property of another.

life annuity An annuity that guarantees payments for the life of the annuitant.

life-care contract A contract (often with a nursing care facility) to provide designated health services and living care for the remainder of a person's life in exchange for an up-front payment.

life estate An estate in property whose duration is limited to the life of an individual. Also called estate for life, life tenancy.

life estate pur autre vie A life estate whose duration is measured by the life of someone other than the possessor of the estate. Also called estate pur autre vie.

life expectancy The number of years a person of a given age and sex is expected to live according to statistics.

life in being The remaining length of time in the life of a person who is in existence at the time that a future interest is created.

life insurance A contract for the payment of a specified amount to a designated beneficiary upon the death of the person insured.

In a policy of "life insurance," death is the contingency insured against, and if it be the result of an accident, the accident is but an incidental factor, while in an "accidental death policy" the accident causing death is the thing insured against, and death is but one of the incidents creating liability. *Oglesby-Barnitz Bank & Trust Co.*, 112 Ohio App. 31 (Ohio App., 1959)

life interest An interest in property whose duration is limited to the life of the party holding the interest or of some other person.

life tenant One who possesses a life estate. A tenant for life.

LIFO See last in, first out.

lift To rescind or stop.

like-kind exchange The exchange of property held for productive use in a trade or business or for investment on which no gain or loss shall be recognized if such property is exchanged solely for property of like kind or character that is to be held either for productive use in a trade or business or for investment (26 USC § 1031).

limine See in limine, motion in limine.

limitation 1. Restriction. 2. The time allowed by statute for bringing an action at the risk of losing it. See also statute of limitations.

limited (Ltd.) 1. Restricted in duration or scope. 2. A designation indicating that a business is a company with limited liability.

limited admissibility Allowing evidence to be considered for isolated or restricted purposes.

limited divorce See legal separation.

limited jurisdiction The power of a court to hear only certain kinds of cases. Also called special jurisdiction.

limited liability Restricted liability; liability that can be satisfied out of business assets, not out of personal assets.

limited-liability company (L.L.C.) A hybrid business entity with features of a corporation and a partnership. The company has a legal existence separate from its members/owners who can participate in the management of the company and have limited liability.

"Limited liability company" means a limited liability company formed under Chapter 1705. of the Revised Code or under the laws of another state. R.C. § 718.14(A)(1)

limited-liability partnership (L.L.P.) A type of partnership in which a partner has unlimited liability for his or her wrongdoing but not for the wrongdoing of other partners.

limited partner A partner who takes no part in running the business and who incurs no liability for partnership obligations beyond the contribution he or she invested in the partnership.

limited partnership (L.P.) A type of partnership consisting of one or more general partners who manage the business and who are personally liable for partnership debts, and one or more limited partners who take no part in running the business and who incur no liability for partnership obligations beyond the contribution they invested in the partnership.

limited power of appointment A power of appointment that restricts who can receive property under the power or under what conditions anyone can receive it. Also called special power of appointment.

limited publication The distribution of a work to a selected group for a limited purpose, and without the right of reproduction, distribution, or sale.

limited purpose public figure See public figure.

limited warranty A warranty that does not cover all defects or does not cover the full cost of repair.

lineage Line of descent from a common ancestor.

lineal Proceeding in a direct or unbroken line; from a common ancestor.

lineal heir One who inherits in a line either ascending or descending from a common source, as distinguished from a collateral heir.

line item veto The chief executive's rejection of part of a bill passed by the legislature, allowing the rest to become law with his or her signature.

line of credit The maximum amount of money that can be borrowed or goods that can be purchased on credit. Also called credit line.

lineup A group of people, including the suspect, shown at one time to a witness, who is asked if he or she can identify the person who committed the crime. The procedure is called a showup if the witness is shown only one person.

link-in-chain principle The privilege against self-incrimination covers questions that could indirectly connect (link) someone to a crime.

liquid Consisting of cash or what can easily be converted into cash.

liquidate 1. To pay and settle a debt. 2. To wind up the affairs of a business or estate by identifying assets, converting them into cash, and paying off liabilities.

liquidated claim A claim as to which the parties have already agreed what the damages will be or what method will be used to calculate the damages that will be paid.

Term "liquidated claim," supporting award of prejudgment interest, means one that can be determined with exactness from agreement between parties or by application of definite rules of law. *Dixon*, 695 N.E.2d 284 (Ohio App., 1997)

liquidated damages An amount the parties agree will be the damages if a breach of contract occurs. Also called stipulated damages.

liquidity The condition of being readily convertible into cash.

lis pendens 1. A pending lawsuit. 2. A recorded notice that an action has been filed affecting the title to or right to possession of the real property described in the notice. Also called notice of pendency. 3. Jurisdiction or control that courts acquire over property involved in a pending lawsuit.

Doctrine of "lis pendens" means that the filing of a lawsuit concerning specific property gives notice to others of the claim alleged in the lawsuit, and that a purchaser of the property may take the property subject to the outcome of the lawsuit. *Cincinnati ex rel. Ritter*, 150 Ohio App.3d 728 (Ohio App., 2002)

list 1. A court's case docket. 2. A series or registry of names. 3. See listing.

listed security A security that is bought or sold on an exchange.

listing 1. A contract between an owner of real property and a real estate agent authorizing the latter to find a buyer or tenant in return for a fee or commission. 2. A contract between a firm and a stock exchange, covering the trading of that firm's securities on the stock exchange. 3. Making a schedule or inventory.

list price The published or advertised retail price of goods.

literal construction See strict construction.

literary property 1. The corporal or physical embodiment (e.g., a book) of an intellectual production. 2. The exclusive right of an owner to possess, use, and dispose of his or her intellectual productions.

literary works Under copyright law, works, "expressed in words, numbers, or other verbal or numerical symbols or indicia, regardless of the nature of the material objects, such as books, periodicals, manuscripts, phonorecords, film, tapes, disks, or cards, in which they are embodied." Audiovisual works are not included. (17 USC § 101).

litigant A party in litigation.

litigate To resolve a dispute or seek relief in a court of law.

litigation 1. The formal process of resolving a legal dispute through the courts. 2. A lawsuit.

litigious Prone to engage in disputes and litigation.

littoral Concerning or belonging to the shore or coast.

> "Littoral rights" are those ownership rights of property owner whose land abuts lake to the use and enjoyment of waters of and land underlying lake. *Lemley*, 104 Ohio App.3d 126 (Ohio App., 1995)

livery of seisin A ceremony to transfer legal title of land (e.g., deliver a twig, as a symbol of the whole land).

living apart As a ground for divorce, the spouses live separately for a designated period of consecutive time with no present intention of resuming marital relations.

> Where wife suffered a stroke and was admitted to a hospital and was later transferred to a nursing home, then to a health center, and had not returned to the marital premises for over two years, wife's conduct did not constitute "living separate and apart without cohabitation" within meaning of divorce statute, since before separation can be used as a ground for divorce, separation must have been voluntary. R.C. § 3105.01(K). *Dailey*, 11 Ohio App.3d 121 (Ohio App., 1983)

living trust See inter vivos trust.

living will A formal document that expresses a person's desire not to be kept alive through artificial or extraordinary means if in the future he or she suffers from a terminal condition.

LL.B.; LL.M.; LL.D. Law degrees: bachelor of laws (LL.B.), master of laws (LL.M.), doctor of laws (LL.D.). See also Juris Doctor.

LKA Last known address.

L.L.C. See limited-liability company.

L.L.P. See limited-liability partnership.

load The charge added to the cost of insurance or securities to cover commissions and administrative expenses. See also no-load.

loan 1. Anything furnished for temporary use. 2. The act of lending.

loan commitment An enforceable promise to make a loan for a specified amount on specified terms.

loaned servant doctrine When an employer lends its employee to another employer for some special service, the employee becomes (for purposes of respondeat superior liability) the employee of the party to whom he or she has been loaned with respect to that service.

> The "loaned servant doctrine" provides that, when one employer lends his employee to another for a particular employment, the employee, for anything done in that employment, must be dealt with as the employee of the one to whom he has been lent, although he remains the general employee of the loaning employer. *Ferguson*, 149 Ohio App.3d 380 (Ohio App., 2002)

loan for consumption A contract in which a lender delivers to a borrower goods that are consumed by use, with the understanding that the borrower will return to the lender goods of the same kind, quantity, and quality.

loan for use A loan of personal property for normal use and then returned.

loan ratio The ratio, expressed as a percentage, of the amount of a loan to the value of the real property that is security for the loan.

loansharking Lending money at excessive rates with the threat or actual use of force to obtain repayment.

loan value The maximum amount one is allowed to borrow on a life insurance policy or other property.

lobbying Attempts to influence the policy decisions of a public official, particularly a legislator.

lobbyist One in the business of lobbying.

local action An action that must be brought in a particular state or county, e.g., where the land in dispute is located.

local agent A person who takes care of a company's business in a particular area or district.

local assessment A tax upon property in a limited area for improvements (e.g., sidewalk repair) that will benefit property within that area.

local law 1. A law that is limited to a specific geographic region of the state. 2. The law of one jurisdiction, usually referring to a jurisdiction other than the one where a case is in litigation.

local option The right of a city or other local government to accept or reject a particular policy, e.g., Sunday liquor sales.

local union A unit or branch of a larger labor union.

lockdown The confinement of inmates to their cells or dorms, usually as a security measure.

lockout Withholding work from employees or temporarily closing a business due to a labor dispute.

> A "lockout" occurs for unemployment benefits purposes when the conduct of the employer in laying down terms must lead to unemployment inevitably in the sense that the employees could not reasonably be expected to accept the terms and, in reason, there was no alternative for them but to leave their work. R.C. § 4141.29(D). *Abrams-Rodkey*, 163 Ohio App.3d 1 (Ohio App., 2005)

lockup A place of detention in a police station, court, or other facility while awaiting further official action. A holding cell.

loco parentis See in loco parentis.

locus A locality. The place where a thing occurs or exists.

locus contractus The place where the last act is performed that makes an agreement a binding contract.

locus delicti The place of the wrong. The place where the last event occurred that was necessary to make the party liable.

locus in quo The place or scene of the occurrence or event.

locus poenitentiae The last opportunity to reconsider and withdraw before legal consequences (civil or criminal) occur.

locus sigilli (L.S.) The place where a document's seal is placed.

lodestar A method of calculating an award of attorney fees authorized by statute. The number of reasonable hours spent on a case is multiplied by a reasonable hourly rate. Sometimes considered above the lodestar are the quality of representation and the risk that there would be no fee.

> "Lodestar" is determined by multiplying reasonable hours expended on litigation by reasonable hourly rate for attorneys or paraprofessionals; however, in calculating lodestar court should exclude any hours which were unreasonably expended. *Gibney*, 73 Ohio App.3d 99 (Ohio App. 6, 1991)

lodger One who uses a dwelling without acquiring exclusive possession or a property interest, e.g., one who lives in a spare room of a house.

logrolling Trading political votes or favors.

LOI See letter of intent.

loitering Remaining idle in essentially one place. Walking about aimlessly.

> As used in defining offense of loitering for purpose of engaging in drug-related activity, term "loitering" means remaining idle in essentially one place and includes concepts of spending time idly, loafing, or walking about aimlessly. *Akron*, 62 Ohio Misc.2d 218 (Ohio Mun., 1992)

long Holding securities or commodities in the hope that prices will rise.

long-arm statute A statutory method of obtaining personal jurisdiction by substituted service of process over a nonresident defendant who has sufficient purposeful contact with a state.

long-term capital gain The gain (profit) realized on the sale or exchange of a capital asset held for the required period of time.

lookout 1. Keeping careful watch. 2. One who keeps careful watch.

Lord Campbell's Act A statute giving certain relatives of a decedent a wrongful-death claim for a tort that caused the death of the decedent.

Lord Mansfield's rule Testimony of either spouse is inadmissible on whether the husband had access to the wife at the time of conception if such evidence would tend to declare the child to be illegitimate.

loser-pays See American rule.

loss 1. Damage, detriment, or disadvantage to person or property. 2. The amount by which expenses exceed revenues. 3. The amount by which the basis of property exceeds what is received for it.

loss leader An item sold by a merchant at a low price (e.g., below cost) in order to entice people to come into the store.

loss of bargain rule See benefit of the bargain rule.

loss of consortium Interference with the companionship, services, affection, and sexual relations one spouse receives from another.

> A "loss of consortium" refers to a loss of the benefits that one spouse is entitled to receive from the other or that a child is entitled to receive from his or her parent, including companionship, cooperation, aid, affection, and, between spouses, sexual relations. *Thomson*, 150 Ohio App.3d 352 (Ohio App., 2002)

loss payable clause An insurance clause designating someone other than the insured to receive insurance proceeds.

loss ratio The ratio between claims paid out and premiums received by an insurance company.

lost property Property that the owner has parted with through neglect or inadvertence and the whereabouts of which is unknown to the owner.

lost volume seller A seller who, upon a buyer's breach, resells to a second buyer who would have bought the same kind of goods from the seller even if the first buyer had not breached.

lost will A decedent's executed will that cannot be located.

lot 1. One of several parcels into which real property is divided. 2. A number of associated persons or things taken collectively. 3. A number of units of something offered for sale or traded as one item. 4. The shares purchased in one transaction.

> "Lot" means a parcel or a single article which is the subject matter of a separate sale or delivery, whether or not it is sufficient to perform the contract. R.C. § 1302.01 (A) (9)

lottery A scheme for the distribution of prizes by chance for which a participant pays something of value to enter.

lower court See inferior court.

L. Rev. See law review.

L.P. See Limited partnership.

LSAT See Law School Admission Test.

Ltd. See limited.

lucid interval A temporary restoration to sanity, during which an insane person has sufficient intelligence to enter a contract.

lucrative title Title acquired without giving consideration.

lucri causa The intent to derive profit. For the sake of gain.

lump-sum alimony See alimony in gross.

lump-sum payment A single amount paid at one time.

> "Lump sum payment" means a payment of accumulated contributions standing to a participant's credit under sections 742.01 to 742.61 or Chapter 145., 3307., 3309., or 5505 of the Revised Code. R.C. § 3105.80(B)

lunacy See insanity (1).

luxury tax An excise tax on expensive, nonessential goods.

lying in wait Waiting and watching for an opportune time to inflict bodily harm on another by surprise.

lynch law Seizing persons suspected of crimes and summarily punishing them without legal trial or authority.

M

MACRS See Modified Accelerated Cost Recovery System.

magistrate 1. A judicial officer who has some but not all the powers of a judge. Also called referee. In federal court, the duties of a United States Magistrate were once performed by a United States Commissioner. 2. A public civic officer with executive power.

> Magistrate means any person appointed by a court pursuant to Crim. R. 19. "Magistrate" does not include an official

included within the definition of magistrate contained in section 2931.01 of the Revised Code, or a mayor's court magistrate appointed pursuant to section 1905.05 of the Revised Code. Ohio Crim. R. Rule 2(F)

magistrate court An inferior court with limited jurisdiction over minor civil or criminal matters. Also called police court.

Magna Carta The Great Charter of 1215, considered the foundation of constitutional liberty in England.

mail box rule 1. The proper and timely mailing of a document raises a rebuttable presumption that the document has been received by the addressee in the usual time. 2. A prisoner's court papers are deemed filed when given to the proper prison authorities. 3. A contract is formed upon the act of mailing where the use of the mail is authorized by both parties.

mail fraud The use of the U.S. Postal Service to obtain money by false pretenses or to commit other acts of fraud (18 USC § 1341).

mail-order divorce Obtaining a divorce from a state or country with no jurisdiction to award it, because, for example, neither spouse was domiciled there.

maim The infliction of a serious (and often disabling) bodily injury.

main purpose rule Under the statute of frauds, contracts to answer for the debt of another must be in writing *unless* the main purpose of the promisor's undertaking is his or her own benefit or protection.

Under the "main purpose doctrine," a contract must be construed as a whole and the intent of the parties must be determined from the entire instrument and not from detached parts. *Tri-State Group*, 151 Ohio App.3d 1 (Ohio App., 2002)

maintain 1. To make repairs or perform upkeep tasks. 2. To bear the expenses for the support of. 3. To declare or affirm. 4. To continue or carry forward. 5. To involve oneself or meddle in another's lawsuit.

maintenance 1. Support or assistance. See also separate maintenance. 2. Keeping something in working order. 3. Becoming involved or meddling in someone else's lawsuit.

major dispute A dispute under the Railway Labor Act that relates to the formation or alteration of a collective bargaining agreement (45 USC § 155).

major federal action Projects that require an environmental impact statement because of their significant environmental effects.

majority 1. The age at which a person is entitled to the management of his or her own affairs and to the enjoyment of adult civil rights. 2. Greater than half of any total.

majority opinion The opinion in which more than half of the voting judges on the court joined.

make To formalize the creation of an instrument; to execute.

make law 1. To enact a law. To legislate. 2. To establish or expand upon a prior legal principle or rule in a court opinion.

maker One who signs a promissory note or other negotiable instrument.

make–whole rule An insurer cannot enforce subrogation rights against settlement funds until the insured is fully compensated (made whole). An insured who settles with a third-party tortfeasor is liable to the insurer-subrogee only for any excess received over the total amount of the insured's loss.

mala fides See bad faith (1).

mala in se See malum in se.

mala prohibita See malum prohibitum.

malefactor One who is guilty of a crime or offense. A wrongdoer.

malfeasance Wrongdoing, usually by a public official.

"Nonfeasance," for purposes of statute allowing the removal of a public official for misconduct in office, is the omission of an act which a person ought to do, "misfeasance" is the improper doing of an act which a person might lawfully do, and "malfeasance" is the doing of an act which a person ought not to do at all. R.C. § 3.07. *In re Removal of Kuehnle*, 161 Ohio App.3d 399 (Ohio App., 2005)

malice 1. The intentional doing of a wrongful act without just cause or excuse. 2. The intent to inflict injury; ill will. 3. Reckless or wanton disregard.

malice aforethought 1. A fixed purpose or design to do some physical harm to another. 2. In a murder charge, the intention to kill, actual or implied, under circumstances that do not constitute excuse (e.g., insanity) or justification (e.g., self-defense) or mitigate the degree of the offense to manslaughter.

malice in fact See actual malice (1).

malice in law See implied malice.

malicious 1. Doing a wrongful act intentionally and without just cause or excuse. 2. Pertaining to conduct that is certain or almost certain to cause harm.

malicious mischief Intentional, wanton, or reckless damage or destruction of another's property. Also called criminal mischief.

malicious prosecution A tort with the following elements: (a) To initiate or procure the initiation of civil or criminal legal proceedings; (b) without probable cause; (c) with malice or an improper purpose; (d) the proceedings terminate in favor of the person against whom the proceedings were brought.

Elements of tort of "malicious prosecution" are (1) malice in instituting or continuing prosecution; (2) lack of probable cause, and (3) termination of prosecution in favor of accused. *Garza*, 119 Ohio App.3d 478 (Ohio App., 1997)

malpractice 1. The failure of a professional to exercise the degree of skill commonly applied under the circumstances by an ordinary, prudent, and reputable member of the profession in good standing. 2. Professional misconduct.

malum in se A wrong in itself; an act that is inherently and essentially evil and immoral in its nature (plural: mala in se).

malum prohibitum An act that is wrong because laws prohibit it; the act is not wrong in itself (plural: mala prohibita).

manager One who administers an organization or project.

managing agent A person given general powers to exercise judgment and discretion in dealing with matters entrusted to him or her.

mandamus A court order or writ to a public official to compel the performance of a ministerial act or a mandatory duty.

mandate 1. A court order, especially to a lower court. 2. To require. 3. An authorization to act.

mandatory Compulsory, obligatory.

> A mandatory statutory provision is one which, if not followed, renders the proceeding to which it relates illegal and void, while a directory provision is one the observance of which is not necessary to the validity of the proceeding. *Woodmansee,* 115 Ohio App. 409 (Ohio App., 1961)

mandatory injunction An injunction that requires an affirmative act or course of conduct.

mandatory instruction An instruction to the jury that if it finds that a certain set of facts (laid out by the judge) exists, then it must reach a verdict for one party and against the other. Also called binding instruction.

mandatory sentence A sentence of incarceration that, by statute, must be served; the judge has no discretion to order alternatives.

manifest 1. Evident to the senses, especially to sight. 2. A list of a vehicle's cargo or passengers.

manifest necessity Extraordinary circumstances requiring a mistrial; a retrial can occur without violating principles of double jeopardy.

manifesto A formal, public statement declaring policies or intentions.

manifest weight of the evidence, against the As a standard of review, an opposite finding is clearly called for; the verdict is unreasonable, arbitrary, or not based on the evidence.

> Finding of fact is not "against the manifest weight of the evidence" if finding is supported by some competent credible evidence. Rules App.Proc., Rule 12(C). *Allen Twp. Bd. of Trustees,* 97 Ohio App.3d 250 (Ohio App., 1994)

manipulation Activity designed to deceive investors by controlling or artificially affecting the price of securities, e.g., creating a misleading appearance of active trading. Also called stock manipulation.

Mann Act A federal statute making it a crime to transport someone in interstate or foreign commerce for prostitution or other sexually immoral purpose (18 US. § 2421).

manslaughter The unlawful killing of another without malice.

> Manslaughter," is an unintentional killing in commission of an unlawful act which is the proximate cause of the ensuing death. R.C. § 2901.06. *State v. Kotowski,* 183 N.E.2d 262 (Ohio Com.Pl., 1962)

manual 1. Made or performed with the hands. 2. A book with basic practical information or procedures.

manumission The act of liberating a slave from bondage.

***Mapp* hearing** A hearing in a criminal case to determine whether seized evidence is admissible. *Mapp v. Ohio,* 81 S. Ct. 1684 (1961).

Marbury v. Madison The United States Supreme Court case that ruled that the courts can determine whether an act of Congress is constitutional. 5 U.S. 137 (1803).

margin 1. The edge or border. 2. An amount available beyond what is needed. 3. The difference between the cost and the selling price of a security. 4. An amount a buyer on credit must give to a securities broker to cover the broker's risk of loss. 5. The difference between the value of collateral securing a loan and the amount of the loan.

margin account An account allowing a client to borrow money from a securities broker in order to buy more stock, using the stock as collateral.

margin call A demand by a broker that a customer deposit additional collateral to cover broker-financed purchases of securities.

marijuana or **marihuana** A drug prepared from cannabis plant leaves.

marine insurance Insurance that covers hazards encountered in maritime transportation, including risks of river and inland navigation.

marital agreement 1. A contract between spouses. See also postnuptial agreement, separation agreement. 2. See premarital agreement.

marital communications privilege A spouse has a privilege to refuse to disclose and to prevent others from disclosing private or confidential communications between the spouses during the marriage. Also called husband-wife privilege, spousal privilege.

> Every person is competent to be a witness except: . . . (B) A spouse testifying against the other spouse charged with a crime except when either of the following applies: (1) a crime against the testifying spouse or a child of either spouse is charged; (2) the testifying spouse elects to testify. Ohio Evid. R. Rule 601 ()

marital deduction The amount of the federal estate and gift tax deduction allowed for transfers of property from one spouse to another (26 USC § 2056).

marital portion The part of a deceased spouse's estate that must be received by a surviving spouse.

marital property Property acquired by either spouse during the marriage that does not constitute separate property, plus any appreciation of separate property that occurs during the marriage. See also separate property.

maritime Pertaining to the sea, navigable waters, and commerce thereon.

maritime contract A contract on ships, commerce or navigation on navigable waters, transportation by sea, or maritime employment.

maritime law See admiralty.

mark 1. Language or symbols used to identify or distinguish one's product or service. Short for servicemark and trademark. 2. A substitute for the signature.

> "Mark" means a word, name, symbol, device, or combination of a word, name, symbol, or device in any form or arrangement. R.C. § 4165.01(C)

market 1. The place or geographic area where goods and services are bought and sold. 2. An exchange where securities or commodities are traded. 3. The geographical or economic extent of commercial demand.

marketable Capable of attracting buyers; fit to offer for sale.

marketable title A title that a reasonably prudent buyer, knowing all the facts, would be willing to accept.

market-maker Any "dealer who, with respect to a security, holds himself out (by entering quotations in an inter-dealer communications system or otherwise) as being willing to buy and sell such security for his own account on a regular or continuous basis." 15 USC § 78c(a)(38).

market order An order to buy or sell securities at the best price currently obtainable.

market price The prevailing price in a given market. The last reported price.

market share The percentage of total industry sales made by a particular company.

market value See fair market value.

mark up 1. The process by which a legislative committee puts a bill in its final form. 2. An increase in price, usually to derive profit.

marriage 1. The legal union of one man and one woman as husband and wife. 2. The status of being a married couple.

> Marriage is status created by operation of law, and legal relationship that parties may not by contract alter. R.C. § 3103.06. *Langer*, 123 Ohio App.3d 348 (Ohio App., 1997). Any marriage between persons of the same sex is against the strong public policy of this state. Any marriage between persons of the same sex shall have no legal force or effect in this state and, if attempted to be entered into in this state, is void ab initio and shall not be recognized by this state. R.C. § 3101.01(C)(1)

marriage certificate The document filed by the person performing a marriage ceremony containing evidence that the ceremony took place.

marriage license The document (issued by the government) giving a couple authorization to be married.

marriage settlement See premarital agreement, separation agreement.

marshal 1. A federal judicial officer (U.S. Marshal) who executes court orders, helps maintain security, and performs other duties for the court. 2. A local police or fire department official.

marshaling 1. Arranging, ranking by priority, or disposing in order. 2. An equitable principle compelling a senior creditor to attempt to collect its claim first from another source that is unavailable to a junior creditor.

> Doctrine of "marshaling of assets" holds that where a debtor gives his creditor two mortgages, each being on separate parcels not of the same tract, a subsequent mortgagee of one tract can insist that the first mortgage be satisfied, as far as possible, from the other lots. *St. Clair Sav. Assn.*, 40 Ohio App.2d 211 (Ohio App., 1974)

martial law Rule (or rules) imposed by military authorities over civilian matters.

Martindale-Hubbell Law Directory A set of books that contain a state-by-state list of attorneys and a digest of state and foreign laws.

***Mary Carter* agreement** A contract in which one or more defendants (a) agree to remain in the case, (b) guarantee the plaintiff a certain minimum monetary recovery regardless of the outcome of the lawsuit, and (c) have their liability reduced in direct proportion to the increase in the liability of the nonagreeing defendants. *Booth v. Mary Carter Paint Co.*, 202 So. 2d 8 (Fla.Dist.Ct.App., 1967).

mass picketing Picketing in large numbers, usually obstructing the ingress and egress of the target's employees, customers, or suppliers.

Massachusetts trust See business trust.

master 1. An employer. A principal who hires others and who controls or has the right to control their physical conduct in the performance of their service. 2. An officer appointed by the court to assist it in specific judicial duties (e.g., take testimony). Also called special master. 3. One who has reached the summit of his or her trade, and who has the right to hire apprentices and journeymen. 4. Main or central.

master agreement A labor agreement at one company that becomes the pattern for agreements in an entire industry.

master and servant An employer-employee relationship in which the employer reserves the right to control the manner or means of doing the work.

> "Master and servant" or "employer and employee" relationship exists when one person employs another to do certain work and has right of control over performance of work to extent of prescribing manner in which it is to be executed. *L. C. Dortch, Inc.*, 200 N.E.2d 828 (Ohio Mun., 1964)

master deed The major condominium document that will govern individual condominium units within a condominium complex.

master in chancery An officer in a court of equity who acts as an assistant to the judge in tasks such as taking testimony.

master limited partnership A limited partnership whose ownership interest is publicly traded.

master of laws (LL.M.) An advanced law degree earned after obtaining a Juris Doctor (J.D.) degree.

master plan A comprehensive land-use plan for the development of an area.

master policy An insurance policy that covers a group of persons, e.g. health or life insurance written as group insurance.

material 1. Essential, important, or relevant; having influence or effect. 2. Pertaining to concrete, physical matter.

> For purposes of ruling on a motion for summary judgment, a dispute of fact is "material" if it affects the outcome of the litigation. OhioRules of Civil Procedure., Rule 56(C). *Moskowitz*, 128 Ohio Misc.2d 10 (Ohio Com.Pl., 2004)

material allegation An allegation that is essential to a claim or defense.

material alteration A change in a document or instrument that alters its meaning or effect.

material breach A failure to perform a substantial part of a contract, justifying rescission or other remedy.

material evidence Relevant evidence a reasonable mind might accept.

material fact An influential fact; a fact that will affect the result.

material issue An important issue the parties need to resolve.

materialman One who furnishes materials (supplies) for construction or repair work.

> "Materialman" or "material supplier" includes any person by whom any materials are furnished in furtherance of an improvement. R.C. § 1311.01(B)

material witness A witness who can give testimony on a fact affecting the merits of the case.

maternal Pertaining to, belonging to, or coming from the mother.

matricide The killing of one's mother.

matrimonial action A divorce proceeding or other action pertaining to the status of a marriage.

matter 1. A case or dispute; the subject for which representation is sought. 2. Something that a tribunal can examine or establish.

matter in controversy 1. The subject of litigation. 2. The amount of damages sought.

matter of See in re.

matter of fact A subject involving the truth or falsity of a fact.

matter of law A subject involving the interpretation or application of the law. See also judgment as a matter of law.

matter of record Pertaining to a subject that is part of or within an official record.

mature Due or ripe for payment, owing; developed, complete.

maxim A principle; a general statement of a rule or a truth.

mayhem The crime of depriving another of a limb or of disabling, disfiguring, or rendering it useless, especially for self-defense.

> At common-law, an injury to member of body did not amount to "mayhem" or "maim," if it did not permanently affect injured person's physical ability to defend himself or annoy his adversary. *State v. Kuchmak*, 159 Ohio St. 363 (Ohio 1953)

MBE Multistate bar examination.

***McNabb-Mallory* rule** Confessions or incriminating statements can be excluded from evidence if obtained during a period of unnecessary delay in taking the accused before a magistrate. *McNabb*, 63 S. Ct. 608 (1943); *Mallory*, 77 S. Ct. 1356 (1957).

***McNaghten* rule** See insanity (4).

M.D. 1. Middle District. 2. Doctor of medicine.

MDL See multidistrict litigation.

MDP See multidisciplinary practice.

mean high tide The average height of all the high waters (tides) over a complete or regular tidal cycle of 18.6 years.

means 1. That which is used to attain an end. A cause. 2. Assets or available resources.

means test The determination of eligibility for a public benefit based on one's financial resources.

mechanic's lien A right or interest in real or personal property (in the nature of an encumbrance) that secures payment for the performance of labor or the supply of materials to maintain or improve the property. Also called artisan's lien.

> Every person who performs work or labor upon or furnishes material in furtherance of any improvement undertaken by virtue of a contract, express or implied, with the owner, part owner, or lessee of any interest in real estate, or his authorized agent, and every person who as a subcontractor, laborer, or materialman, performs any labor or work or furnishes any material to an original contractor or any subcontractor, in carrying forward, performing, or completing any improvement, has a lien to secure the payment therefor upon the improvement and all interests that the owner, part owner, or lessee may have or subsequently acquire in the land or leasehold to which the improvement was made or removed. R.C. § 1311.02

mediation A method of alternate dispute resolution (ADR) in which the parties submit a dispute to a neutral third person (the mediator) who helps the parties resolve their dispute; he or she does not render a decision resolving it for them.

mediator See mediation.

Medicaid A federal-state public assistance program that furnishes health care to people who cannot afford it.

medical examiner A public officer who conducts autopsies and otherwise helps in the investigation and prosecution of death cases.

Medicare A federal program of medical insurance for the elderly.

meeting of creditors A bankruptcy hearing or meeting in which creditors can examine the debtor.

meeting of the minds Mutual agreement and assent of the parties to the substance and terms of their contract.

Megan's law A state law (named in honor of a victim) requiring the registration of sex offenders and a method of notifying the community when they move into an area. Also called community notification law.

memorandum 1. A written statement or note that is often brief and informal. 2. A brief record of a transaction or occurrence. 3. A written analysis of how the law applies to a given set of facts.

memorandum decision (mem.) The decision of a court with few or no supporting reasons, often because it follows established principles. Also called memorandum opinion.

memorandum of points and authorities A document submitted to a trial court that makes arguments with supporting authorities for something a party wishes to do, e.g., have a motion granted.

memorial 1. A statement of facts in a petition or demand to the legislature or to the executive. 2. A summary or abstract of a record.

mensa et thoro Bed and board. See also legal separation.

mens rea A guilty mind that produces the act. The unlawful intent or recklessness that must be proved for crimes that are not strict liability offenses.

mental anguish See emotional distress.

mental cruelty Conduct causing distress that endangers the mental and physical health of a spouse (a fault ground for divorce).

mental defect or disease See insanity (2) and (3).

mental distress; mental suffering See emotional distress.

mercantile Commercial; involving the business of merchants.

merchant A person in the business of purchasing and selling goods.

> "Merchant" means a person who deals in goods of the kind or otherwise by the person's occupation holds the person out as having knowledge or skill peculiar to the practices or goods involved in the transaction or to whom such knowledge or skill may be attributed by the person's employment of an agent or broker or other intermediary who by the agent's, broker's, or other intermediary's occupation holds the person out as having such knowledge or skill. R.C. § 1302.01(A)(5)

merchantable Fit for the ordinary purposes for which the goods are used. The noun is merchantability.

mercy killing See euthanasia.

meretricious Involving vulgarity, unlawful sexual relations, or insincerity.

merger 1. The fusion or absorption of one duty, right, claim, offense, estate, or property into another. 2. The absorption of one company by another. The absorbed company ceases to exist as a separate entity.

Merger includes consolidation and the purchase of substantially all of the assets and assumption of liabilities of another institution. R.C. § 1151.60(F)(2)

merger clause See integration clause.

meritorious Legally plausible. Having merit; not frivolous.

merits See on the merits.

mesne Intermediate; occurring between two periods or ranks.

mesne process Any writ or process issued between commencement of the action and execution of the judgment.

mesne profits Profits accruing between two periods while held by one in wrongful possession.

messuage A dwelling house, its outbuildings, and surrounding land.

metes and bounds A system of describing the boundary lines of land with their terminal points and angles on the natural landscape.

metropolitan Pertaining to a city and its suburbs.

Mexican divorce A divorce granted by a court in Mexico by mail order or when neither spouse was domiciled there.

migratory divorce A divorce obtained in a state to which one or both spouses briefly traveled before returning to their original state.

military commission A military court for violations of martial law.

military government A government in which civil or political power is under the control of the military.

military jurisdiction Jurisdiction of the military in the areas of military law, military government, and martial law.

military law A system of laws governing the armed forces.

military will; military testament A will that may be valid even if it does not comply with required formalities when made by someone in military service. Also called sailor's will, seaman's will, soldier's will.

militia A citizen military force not part of the regular military.

Organized militia means the Ohio national guard, the Ohio naval militia, and the Ohio military reserve. R.C. § 5924.01(A)

mill One-tenth of one cent.

mineral A lifeless substance formed or deposited through natural processes and found either in or upon the soil or in the rocks beneath the soil.

Minerals means sand, gravel, clay, shale, gypsum, halite, limestone, dolomite, sandstone, other stone, metalliferous or nonmetalliferous ore, or other material or substance of commercial value excavated in a solid state from natural deposits on or in the earth, but does not include coal or peat. R.C. § 1514.01(B)

mineral lease A contract or other form of authorization to explore, develop, or remove deposits of oil, gas, or other minerals. A mining lease allows such activity in a mine or mining claim.

mineral right The right to explore for and remove minerals, with or without ownership of the surface of the land.

miner's inch A unit for measuring water flow through a hole one-inch square in a miner's box (about 9 gallons a minute).

minimal diversity A plaintiff is a citizen of one state and at least one of the defendants is a citizen of another state.

minimum contacts Purposely availing oneself of the privilege of conducting activities within a state, thus invoking the benefits and protections of its laws. (Basis of personal jurisdiction over a nonresident.)

For purposes of specific jurisdiction, "minimum contacts" exist when the nonresident defendant's purposeful and related contacts create a substantial connection with the forum state. *Joffe*, 163 Ohio App.3d 479 (Ohio App., 2005)

minimum-fee schedule A bar association list of the lowest fees an attorney can charge for designated legal services. Such lists violate antitrust law.

minimum wage The lowest allowable wage certain employers may pay.

mining lease See mineral lease.

minister 1. An agent; one acting on behalf of another. 2. An administrator in charge of a government department. 3. A diplomatic representative or officer.

ministerial Involving a duty that is to be performed in a prescribed manner without the exercise of judgment or discretion.

ministry The duties or functions of a religious minister.

minitrial An abbreviated presentation of each side's case that the parties agree to make to each other and to a private, neutral third party, followed by discussions that seek a negotiated settlement. An example of alternate dispute resolution.

minor A person under the legal age, often 18. One who has not reached the age of majority.

minority 1. The status of being below the minimum age to enter a desired relationship (e.g., marriage) or perform a particular task. Also called infancy, nonage. 2. The smaller number. 3. A group of persons of the same race, gender, or other trait that differs from the dominant or majority group in society and that is often the victim of discrimination.

As used in sections 184.171, 184.172, and 184.173 of the Revised Code, "minority" means an individual who is a United States citizen and who is a member of one of the following economically disadvantaged groups: Blacks or African Americans, American Indians, Hispanics or Latinos, and Asians. R.C. § 184.17

minority opinion An opinion of one or more justices that disagrees with the majority opinion. It is often a dissenting opinion.

minority shareholder Any shareholder who does not own or control more than 50 percent of the voting shares of a corporation.

minute book The book maintained by the court clerk containing a record (the minutes) of court proceedings.

minutes A record of what occurred at a meeting.

Miranda warnings Prior to any custodial interrogation, a person must be warned that: (a) he or she has a right to remain silent, (b) any statement made can be used as evidence against him or her, (c) he or she has the right to his or her own attorney or one provided at government expense. *Miranda v. Arizona*, 86 S. Ct. 1602 (1966).

Mirandize To give a suspect the Miranda warnings.

misadventure An accident or misfortune (e.g., killing), often occurring while performing a lawful act.

misapplication The wrongful use of legally possessed assets.

misappropriate To take wrongfully; to use someone else's property to one's own advantage without permission. See also appropriation (2).

misbranding The use of a label that is false or misleading.

miscarriage of justice A fundamentally unfair result.

miscegenation Marriage between persons of different races.

mischarge An erroneous charge to a jury.

mischief 1. Conduct that causes discomfort, hardship, or harm. 2. The evil or danger that a statute is intended to cure or avoid.

misconduct Wrongdoing; a breach of one's duty.

misdelivery Delivery of mail or goods to someone other than the specified or authorized recipient.

misdemeanant A person convicted of a misdemeanor.

misdemeanor A crime, not as serious as a felony, punishable by fine or by detention in an institution other than a prison or penitentiary.

> "Misdemeanor" means an offense defined by law as a misdemeanor. Ohio Crim. R. Rule 2(B)

misdemeanor-manslaughter The unintentional killing of a human being while committing a misdemeanor.

misfeasance Improper performance of an otherwise lawful act.

misjoinder Improper joining of parties, causes of action, or offenses.

mislay To forget where you placed something you intended to retrieve.

misleading Leading one astray or into error, often intentionally.

misprision 1. Nonperformance of a duty by a public official. 2. A nonparticipant's concealment or failure to disclose a crime. Misprision of felony occurs when the crime involved is a felony.

misrepresentation 1. Any untrue statement of fact. 2. A false statement of fact made with the intent to deceive. Also called false representation. See also fraud.

mistake An unintentional act, omission, or error arising from ignorance, surprise, imposition, or misplaced confidence.

> So far as reformation of instrument is concerned, "mistake" exists only when instrument, in its terms or legal effect, is different from what parties believed it to be at time of its execution. *Snyder*, 110 Ohio App.3d 443 (Ohio App., 1996)

mistake of fact 1. An unconscious ignorance or forgetfulness of the existence or nonexistence of a material fact, past or present. 2. An honest and reasonable belief in the existence of circumstances, which, if true, would make the act for which the person is indicted an innocent act.

mistake of law A misunderstanding about legal requirements or consequences.

mistrial A trial terminated before its normal conclusion because of unusual circumstances, misconduct, procedural error, or jury deadlock.

mitigate To render less painful or severe.

mitigating circumstances Facts that can be considered as reducing the severity or degree of moral culpability of an act, but do not excuse or justify it. Also called extenuating circumstances.

mitigation-of-damages rule An injured party has a duty to use reasonable diligence to try to minimize his or her damages after the wrong has been inflicted. Also called avoidable consequences.

> "Mitigation" of damages, or "avoidable consequences," means that one injured by tort of another is not entitled to recover damages for any harm that he could have avoided by use of reasonable effort or expenditure after commission of tort. *Schafer*, 138 Ohio App.3d 244 (Ohio App., 2000)

mittimus 1. An order commanding that a person be detailed or conveyed to a prison. 2. An order for the transfer of records between courts.

mixed nuisance A nuisance that injures the public at large and also does some special damage to an individual or class of individuals.

mixed question of law and fact An issue involving the application of the law to the facts when the facts and the legal standards are not in dispute.

***M'Naghten* rule** See insanity (4).

MO See modus operandi

model act A statute proposed to all state legislatures for adoption.

Model Penal Code A proposed criminal law code proposed by the American Law Institute. For its test for insanity, see insanity (2).

Model Rules of Professional Conduct The current ethical rules for attorneys recommended to the states by the American Bar Association.

modification An alteration or change; a new qualification.

Modified Accelerated Cost Recovery System (MACRS) A method to calculate the depreciation tax deduction over a shorter period.

modus Manner or method.

modus operandi (MO) A method of doing things, e.g., a criminal's MO.

moiety 1. One-half. 2. A portion or part.

molest 1. To abuse sexually. 2. To disturb or harass.

money 1. Coins and paper currency or other legal medium of exchange. 2. Assets that are readily convertible into cash.

> "Money" means United States currency, or a check, draft, or cashier's check for United States currency, payable on demand and drawn on a bank. R.C. § 122.15(K)

money demand A claim for a specific dollar amount.

money had and received An action to prevent unjust enrichment when one person obtains money that in good conscience belongs to another.

money judgment The part of a judgment that requires paying money (damages).

money laundering See laundering.

money market The financial market for dealing in short-term financial obligations such as commercial paper and treasury bills.

money order A type of negotiable draft purchased from an organization such as the Postal Service and used as a substitute for a check.

money supply The total amount of money circulating and on deposit in the economy.

monition 1. A summons to appear in an admiralty case. 2. A warning.

monopoly A market where there is a concentration of a product or service in the hands of a few, thereby controlling prices or limiting competition. A power to control prices or exclude competition.

> The Valentine Act was formulated to prevent "monopoly," which, in general, means concentration of business in hands of a few or a combination for purpose of raising or controlling prices. R.C. § 1331.01 et seq. *Schweizer*, 108 Ohio App.3d 539 (Ohio App., 1996)

month to month tenancy A lease without a fixed duration that can be terminated on short notice, e.g., a month. See also periodic tenancy.

monument Natural or artificial boundary markers or objects on land.

moot 1. Pertaining to a nonexistent controversy where the issues have ceased to exist from a practical point of view. 2. Subject to debate.

moot case A case that seeks to resolve an abstract question that does not rest upon existing facts.

moot court A simulated court where law students argue a hypothetical case for purposes of learning and competition.

moral 1. Pertaining to conscience or to general principles of right conduct. 2. Pertaining to a duty binding in conscience but not in law. 3. Demonstrating correct character or behavior.

moral certainty A very high degree of probability although not demonstrable to an absolute certainty. Beyond a reasonable doubt.

moral consideration See good consideration.

moral evidence Evidence based on belief or the general observations of people rather than on what is absolutely demonstrable.

moral hazard The risk or probability that an insured will destroy the insured property or permit it to be destroyed to collect on the insurance.

moral right A right of integrity enjoyed by the creator of a work even if someone else now owns the copyright. Examples include the right to be acknowledged as the creator and to insist that the work not be distorted.

moral turpitude Conduct that is dishonest or contrary to moral rules.

> Acts of "moral turpitude," although not subject to exact definition in context of attorney disciplinary proceeding, are characterized by baseness, vileness, or depravity in private and social duties which man owes to fellow man, or to society in general. Code of Prof.Resp., DR 1–102(A)(3). *Disciplinary Counsel v. Burkhart*, 75 Ohio St.3d 188 (Ohio 1996)

moratorium Temporary suspension. A period of delay.

more or less An approximation; slightly larger or smaller.

morgue A place where dead persons are kept for identification or until burial arrangements are made.

mortality tables A guide used to predict life expectancy based on factors such as a person's age and sex.

mortgage An interest in property created by a written instrument providing security for the performance of a duty or the payment of a debt. A lien or claim against property given by the buyer to the lender as security for the money borrowed.

> "Mortgage" means a consensual interest in real property, including fixtures, that secures payment or performance of an obligation. R.C. § 1309.102(A)(55)

mortgage bond A bond for which real estate or personal property is pledged as security that the bond will be paid as stated in its terms.

mortgage certificate Document evidencing one's ownership share in a mortgage.

mortgage commitment A written notice from a lending institution that it will advance mortgage funds for the purchase of specified property.

mortgage company A company that makes mortgage loans, which it then sells to investors.

mortgagee A lender to whom property is mortgaged.

mortgage market The existing supply and demand for mortgages, including their resale. Rates and terms being offered by competing mortgagees.

mortgagor The debtor who mortgages his or her property; one who gives legal title or a lien to the mortgagee to secure the mortgage loan.

mortis causa See causa mortis.

mortmain statute A statute that restricts one's right to transfer property to institutions such as churches that would hold it forever.

most favored nation clause (MFN) A treaty promise that each side will grant to the other the broadest rights that it gives any other nation.

motion An application for an order or ruling from a court or other decision-making body.

motion for a more definite statement A request that the court order the other side to make its pleading more definite, since it is so vague or ambiguous that one cannot frame a responsive pleading.

motion in limine A request for a ruling on the admissibility of evidence prior to or during trial but before the evidence has been offered.

> A "motion in limine" is a pretrial motion requesting the court to prohibit opposing counsel from referring to or offering evidence on matters so highly prejudicial to the moving party that curative instructions cannot prevent predispositional effect on the jury. *Tucker*, 107 Ohio Misc.2d 38 (Ohio Com.Pl., 1999)

motion to dismiss A request, usually made before the trial begins, that the judge dismiss the case because of lack of jurisdiction, insufficiency of the pleadings, or the reaching of a settlement.

motion to strike A request that the court remove specific statements, claims, or evidence from the pleadings or the record.

motion to suppress A request that the court eliminate from a criminal trial any illegally secured evidence.

motive A cause or reason that moves the will and induces action or inaction.

> Proof of motive is to be distinguished from intent. Motive is a mental state which may induce an act. It is not an element of the crime, but rather a circumstantial fact used to strengthen an inference, drawn from other evidence, that

an act was done. *State v. Young,* 7 Ohio App.2d 194 (Ohio App., 1966)

movables Things that can be carried from one place to another. Personal property.

movant One who makes a motion or applies for a ruling or order.

move To make an application or request for an order or ruling.

moving papers Papers or documents submitted in support of a motion.

mug 1. To criminally assault someone, often with the intent to rob. 2. A human face. A mug shot is a photograph of a suspect's face.

mulct 1. A penalty or punishment such as a fine. 2. To defraud a person of something.

mulier 1. A woman; a wife. 2. A son who is legitimate.

multidisciplinary practice (MDP) A partnership of attorneys and nonattorney professionals that offers legal and nonlegal services.

multidistrict litigation (MDL) Civil actions with common questions of fact pending in different federal district courts that are transferred to one district solely for consolidated pretrial proceedings under a single judge before returning to their original district courts.

multifarious 1. Improperly joined claims, instructions, or parties. 2. Diverse.

multilateral agreement An agreement among three or more parties.

multiple access The defense in a paternity case that more than one lover had access to the mother during the time of conception.

multiple listing An arrangement among real estate agents whereby any member agent can sell property listed by another agent. The latter shares the fee or commission with the broker who made the sale.

multiplicity 1. A large number or variety of matters or particulars. 2. The improper charging of a single offense in several counts.

multiplicity of actions Several attempts to litigate the same right or issue against the same defendant.

For double jeopardy purposes, "multiplicity" occurs when one offense is stated in several counts of indictment. *State v. Worsencroft,* 100 Ohio App.3d 255 (Ohio App., 1995)

municipal 1. Pertaining to a city, town, or other local unit of government. 2. Pertaining to a state or nation.

municipal bond A bond or other debt instrument issued by a state or local unit of government to fund public projects. Also called municipal security.

municipal corporation A city, county, village, town or other local governmental body established to run all or part of local government. Also called municipality.

"Municipal corporation" means all municipal corporations, including those that have adopted a charter under Article XVIII, Ohio Constitution. R.C. § 5705.01(B)

municipal court An inferior court with jurisdiction over relatively small claims or offenses arising within the local area where it sits.

municipal ordinance See ordinance.

municipality 1. The body of officials elected or appointed to administer a local government. 2. See municipal corporation.

municipal securities See municipal bond.

muniments Documents used to defend one's title or other claim.

murder The unlawful, premeditated killing of a human being.

mutatis mutandis With the necessary changes in any of the details.

mutilate 1. To maim, to dismember, to disfigure someone. 2. To alter or deface a document by cutting, tearing, burning, or erasing, without totally destroying it.

mutiny An insurrection or uprising of seamen or soldiers against the authority of their commanders.

mutual Reciprocal, common to both parties. In the same relationship to each other.

mutual company A company owned by its clients or customers.

mutual fund An investment company with a pool of assets, consisting primarily of portfolio securities, and belonging to the individual investors holding shares in the fund.

mutual insurance company An insurance company that has no capital stock and in which the policyholders are the owners.

mutuality An action by each of two parties; reciprocation; both sides being bound.

mutuality of contract; mutuality of obligation 1. Liability or obligation imposed on both parties under the terms of the agreement. 2. Unless both sides are bound, neither is bound.

mutual mistake A mistake common to both parties wherein each labors under a misconception respecting the terms of the agreement. Both contracting parties misunderstand the fundamental subject matter or term of the contract. Mistake of both parties on the same fact. Also called bilateral mistake.

For purposes of mutual mistake as to material part of contract as grounds for rescission of contract, "mutual mistake of fact" is present where mistake by both parties as to basic assumption on which contract was made has material effect on agreed exchange of performances. *Pharmacia Hepar, Inc.,* 111 Ohio App.3d 468 (Ohio App., 1996)

mutual wills 1. Separate wills made by two persons, which are reciprocal in their provisions and by which each testator makes testamentary disposition in favor of the other. Also called double will, reciprocal will. 2. Wills executed pursuant to an agreement between testators to dispose of their property in a particular manner, each in consideration of the other.

N

naked licensee See bare licensee.

naked power A mere authority to act, not accompanied by any interest of the holder of the power in the subject-matter of the power.

naked trust See passive trust.

NALA See National Association of Legal Assistants (*www.nala.org*).

NALS See National Association of Legal Secretaries, now called NALS the Association for Legal Professionals (*www.nals.org*).

named insured The person specifically mentioned in an insurance policy as the one protected by the insurance.

Automobile policyholder's wife was not a "named insured" where she was not listed on the declaration page and was not the party who contracted with the insurer, and where the policy language, particularly the definitions of "you" and "your," could not reasonably be interpreted as making her a "named insured" by virtue of her spousal status. *Stacy*, 125 Ohio App.3d 658 (Ohio App., 1998)

Napoleonic Code See code civil.

narcotic Any addictive drug that dulls the senses or induces sleep.

National Association of Legal Assistants (NALA) A national association of paralegals (*www.nala.org*).

National Association of Legal Secretaries A national association of legal secretaries and paralegals, now called NALS the Association for Legal Professionals (*www.nals.org*).

national bank A bank incorporated under federal law.

National Federation of Paralegal Associations (NFPA) A national association of paralegals (*www.paralegals.org*).

nationality The status that arises as a result of a person's belonging to a nation because of birth or naturalization.

nationalization The acquisition and control of privately owned businesses by the government.

Native American A member of the indigenous peoples of North, South, and Central America.

natural affection The affection that naturally exists between parent and child and among other close relatives.

natural death Death not caused by accidental or intentional injury.

natural heirs Next of kin by blood (consanguinity) as distinguished from collateral heirs or those related by adoption.

naturalization The process by which a person acquires citizenship after birth.

natural law A system of rules and principles (not created by human authority) discoverable by our rational intelligence as growing out of and conforming to human nature.

natural monument Boundary markers or objects on land that are not artificial.

natural object of bounty Descendants, surviving spouse, and other close relatives who are assumed to become recipients of the estate of a decedent.

natural person A human being. See also artificial person.

natural right A right based on natural law.

navigable water A body of water over which commerce can be carried on.

"Navigable waters" means waters that come under the jurisdiction of the department of the army of the United States and any waterways within or adjacent to this state, except inland lakes having neither a navigable inlet nor outlet. R.C. § 1547.01(B)(10)

navigation The art, science, or business of traveling the sea or other navigable waters in ships or vessels.

N.B. (nota bene) Note well, take notice, attention.

necessaries 1. The basic items needed by family members to maintain a standard of living. 2. Food, medicine, clothing, shelter, or personal services usually considered reasonably essential for preservation and enjoyment of life. 3. Goods or services reasonably needed in a ship's business for a vessel's continued operation.

necessary 1. Essential. 2. Logically true.

Necessary and Proper Clause The clause in the U.S. Constitution (art. I, § 8, cl. 18) giving Congress the power to enact laws that are needed to carry out its enumerated powers.

necessary party A party with a legal or beneficial interest in the subject matter of the lawsuit and who should be joined if feasible.

necessity 1. A privilege to make reasonable use of someone's property to prevent immediate harm or damage to person or property. 2. See choice of evils. 3. Something necessary or indispensable.

Contracts for necessities are contracts for food, medicine, clothes, shelter, or personal services usually considered reasonably essential for preservation and enjoyment of life. *Muller*, 161 Ohio App.3d 771 (Ohio App., 2005)

ne exeat A writ that forbids a person from leaving the country, state, or jurisdiction of the court.

negative act Not acting when a duty to act exists.

negative averment An allegation of a fact that must be proved by the alleging party even though the allegation is phrased in the negative.

negative covenant A promise not to do or perform some act.

negative easement An easement that precludes the owner of land subject to the easement (the servient estate) from doing an act which would otherwise be lawful.

negative evidence Testimony or other evidence about what did not happen or does not exist.

negative pregnant A negative statement that also implies an affirmative statement or admission (e.g., "I deny that I owe $500" may be an admission that at least some amount is owed).

neglect 1. The failure to perform an act one has a duty to perform. 2. Carelessness. See also child neglect.

negligence Harm or damage caused by not doing what a reasonably prudent person would have done under like circumstances. A tort with the following elements: (a) a duty of reasonable care, (b) a breach of this duty, (c) proximate cause, (d) actual damages.

Negligence is the failure to exercise that degree of care which persons of ordinary care and prudence are accustomed to use under the same or similar circumstances, in order to bring the enterprise engaged in to a safe and successful termination, having due regard for the rights of others and the object to be accomplished. *Paulson*, 145 N.E.2d 364 (Ohio Mun., 1957)

negligence per se Negligence as a matter of law when violating a statute that defines the standard of care.

negligent Unreasonably careless. See also neglect, negligence.

negligent entrustment Creating an unreasonable risk of harm by carelessly allowing someone to use a dangerous object, e.g., a car.

negligent homicide Death due to the failure to perceive a substantial and unjustifiable risk that one's conduct will cause the death of another person.

negligent infliction of emotional distress (NIED) Carelessly causing someone to suffer substantial emotional distress.

Negligent infliction of emotional distress is a claim based upon the negligence of one party creating actionable emotional distress in another. *Nadel,* 119 Ohio App.3d 578 (Ohio App., 1997)

negotiability words Words that make an instrument negotiable, e.g., "to the order of."

negotiable 1. Legally capable of being transferred by indorsement or delivery. See also negotiation (1). 2. Open to compromise.

negotiable bill of lading A bill of lading that requires delivery of goods to the bearer of the bill or, if to the order of a named person, to that person.

negotiable instrument Any writing (a) signed by the maker or drawer; (b) containing an unconditional promise or order to pay a sum certain in money; (c) is payable on demand or at a definite time; and (d) is payable to order or to bearer. UCC § 3–104(a).

Negotiable instrument means an unconditional promise or order to pay a fixed amount of money, with or without interest or other charges described in the promise or order, if it meets all of the following requirements: (1) It is payable to bearer or to order at the time it is issued or first comes into possession of a holder. (2) It is payable on demand or at a definite time. (3) It does not state any other undertaking or instruction by the person promising or ordering payment to do any act in addition to the payment of money, but the promise or order may contain any of the following: . . . R.C. § 1303.03(A)

negotiate 1. To bargain with another concerning a sale, settlement, or matter in contention. 2. To transfer by delivery or indorsement. See also negotiation (1).

negotiated plea See plea bargaining.

negotiation 1. The transfer of an instrument through delivery (if the instrument is payable to bearer), or through indorsement and delivery (if it is payable to order) in such form that the transferee becomes a holder. 2. The process of submitting and considering offers.

nemo est supra leges No one is above the law.

nepotism Granting privileges or patronage to one's relatives.

net The amount that remains after all allowable deductions.

net assets See net worth.

net asset value (NAV) The per share value of a company or mutual fund measured by its assets less debts divided by the number of shares.

net estate The portion of a probate estate remaining after all allowable deductions and adjustments.

Term "net estate," as used in statute concerning right of a spouse to elect to take against deceased spouse's will is that portion of estate remaining after satisfaction of all indebtedness of decedent and obligations of the estate. R.C. § 2107.39. *Winkelfoos,* 16 Ohio App.3d 266 (Ohio App., 1984)

net income Income subject to taxation after allowable deductions and exemptions have been subtracted from gross or total income.

net lease A lease in which the tenant pays not only rent, but also items such as taxes, insurance, and maintenance charges.

net listing A listing in which the amount of real estate commission is the difference between the selling price of the property and a minimum price set by the seller.

net operating loss (NOL) The excess of allowable deductions over gross income.

net premium 1. The amount of an insurance premium less expenses such as commission. 2. The amount required by an insurer to cover the expected cost of paying benefits.

net weight The weight of an article after deducting the weight of the box or other wrapping.

net worth The total assets of a person or business less the total liabilities. Also called net assets.

net worth method To reconstruct the income of a taxpayer, the IRS compares his or her net worth at the beginning and end of the tax year and makes adjustments for personal expenses and allowable deductions.

neutral Not taking an active part with either of the contending sides; disinterested, unbiased.

Under "neutral reportage privilege," report of defamatory accusation is privileged if accusation is made by responsible, prominent organization or individual, accusation concerns matter of public interest, and report accurately and disinterestedly republishes accusation without espousing or concurring in charges made by others or deliberately distorting statements to launch personal attack on plaintiff. *April,* 46 Ohio App.3d 95 (Ohio App., 1988)

neutrality laws Acts of Congress that forbid military assistance to either of two belligerent powers with which we are at peace.

ne varietur It must not be altered (a notary's inscription).

new and useful For an invention to be patented, it must be novel and provide some practical benefit.

newly discovered evidence Evidence discovered after the trial and not discoverable before the trial by the exercise of due diligence.

new matter A fact not previously alleged by either party in the pleadings.

newsman's privilege See journalist's privilege, neutral.

new trial Another trial of all or some of the same issues that were resolved by judgment in a prior trial.

A new trial is a reexamination of an issue of fact in same court after a trial. Ohio Civ.R. 52, 59; R.C. § 2321.17. *Rippel,* 328 N.E.2d 816 (Ohio App., 1974)

new value Newly given money or money's worth in goods, services, new credit, or release by a transferee of property previously transferred (11 USC § 547(a)(2)).

next friend Someone specially appointed by the court to look after the interests of a person who cannot act on his or her own (e.g., a minor). Also called prochein ami.

next of kin 1. The nearest blood relatives of the decedent. 2. Those who would inherit from the decedent if he or she died intestate.

Any person who would be entitled to inherit from a ward under Chapter 2105 of the Revised Code if the ward dies intestate. R.C. § 2111.01(E)

nexus A causal or other connection or link.

NFPA See National Federation of Paralegal Associations (*www.paralegals.org*).

NGO Nongovernmental organization.

NGRI Not guilty by reason of insanity.

nighttime 1. The period between sunset and sunrise when there is not enough daylight to discern a person's face. 2. Thirty minutes after sunset to 30 minutes before sunrise.

nihil dicit ("he says nothing") The name of the judgment against a defendant who omits to plead or answer the plaintiff.

nihil est ("there is nothing") A form of return made by a sheriff when he or she has been unable to serve a writ.

nil (nihil) Nothing.

nisi Unless. Refers to the rule that something will remain or be valid unless an opponent comes forward to demonstrate otherwise.

nisi prius (n.p.) ("unless before") A civil trial court with a jury (in New York and Oklahoma).

NLRB National Labor Relations Board (*www.nlrb.gov*).

no action letter A letter from a government agency that no action will be taken against a person based on the facts before the agency.

no bill A grand jury statement that the evidence is insufficient to justify a formal charge or indictment. Also called not found.

> No bill means a report by the foreperson or deputy foreperson of a grand jury that an indictment is not found by the grand jury against a person who has been held to answer before the grand jury for the commission of an offense. R.C. § 2953.51(A)

no contest 1. See nolo contendere. 2. See in terrorem clause.

no evidence A challenge to the legal sufficiency of the evidence to support a particular fact finding.

no eyewitness rule If there is no direct evidence (e.g., eyewitness testimony) of what decedent did or failed to do immediately before an injury, the trier of facts may infer that decedent was using ordinary care for his or her own safety.

no fault Pertaining to legal consequences (e.g., granting a divorce, paying insurance benefits) that will occur regardless of who was at fault or to blame.

no-knock search warrant A warrant that authorizes the police to enter the premises without first announcing themselves.

nolle prosequi (nol-pros) A formal notice by the government that a criminal prosecution will not be pursued.

no-load Sold without a commission.

nolo contendere ("I will not contest it") A plea in a criminal case in which the defendant does not admit or deny the charges. The effect of the plea, however, is similar to a plea of guilty in that the defendant can be sentenced to prison, fined, etc. Also called no contest, non vult contendere.

nol-pros See nolle prosequi.

nominal 1. In name only; not real or substantial. 2. Trifling.

nominal consideration Consideration so small as to bear no relation to the real value of what is received.

nominal damages A trifling sum (e.g., $1) awarded to the plaintiff because there was no significant loss or injury suffered, although a technical invasion of rights did occur.

> Damages recoverable where a legal right is to be vindicated against an invasion thereof which has produced no actual loss of any kind, or where, from nature of case, some injury has been done, the extent of which evidence fails to show, and are limited to some small or nominal amount in terms of money. *Lacey*, 166 Ohio St. 12 (Ohio 1956)

nominal party A party who has no interest in the result of the suit or no actual interest or control over the subject matter of the litigation but is present to satisfy a technical rule of practice.

nominal trust See passive trust.

nominee 1. One who has been nominated or proposed for an office or appointment. 2. One designated to act for another. An agent.

nominee trust 1. A trust in which the trustee lacks power to deal with the trust property except as directed by the trust beneficiaries. 2. A trust in which property is held for undisclosed beneficiaries.

nonaccess A paternity defense in which the alleged father asserts the absence of opportunities for sexual intercourse with the mother.

nonage See minority (1).

non assumpsit A plea in an assumpsit action that the undertaking was not made as alleged.

non compos mentis Not sound of mind. Mentally incompetent.

nonconforming use A use of land that is permitted because the use was lawful prior to a change in the zoning law even though the new law would make the use illegal.

> A nonconforming use of land is a use that was lawful before the enactment of a zoning amendment, but one which, although no longer valid under the current zoning rules, may be lawfully continued. *Wooster*, 158 Ohio App.3d 161 (Ohio App., 2004)

noncore proceeding A nonbankruptcy proceeding related to the debtor's estate that, in the absence of a petition in bankruptcy, could have been brought in a state court.

nondelegable duty An affirmative duty that cannot be escaped by entrusting it to a third party such as an independent contractor.

nonexclusive listing See open listing.

nonfeasance The failure to perform a legal duty.

> Nonfeasance, for purposes of statute allowing the removal of a public official for misconduct in office, is the omission of an act which a person ought to do, "misfeasance" is the improper doing of an act which a person might lawfully do, and "malfeasance" is the doing of an act which a person ought not to do at all. R.C. § 3.07. *In re Removal of Kuehnle*, 161 Ohio App.3d 399 (Ohio App., 2005)

nonintervention will A will providing that the executor shall not be required to account to any court or person.

nonjoinder The failure to join a necessary person to a suit.

nonjury trial See bench trial.

nonjusticiable Inappropriate or improper for judicial resolution.

nonmailable Pertaining to what cannot be transported by U.S. mail because of size, obscene content, etc.

nonnegotiable 1. Not capable of transfer by indorsement or delivery. 2. Fixed; pertaining to what will not be bargained.

non obstante veredicto Notwithstanding the verdict. See judgment notwithstanding the verdict.

nonperformance The failure or refusal to perform an obligation.

nonprofit corporation A corporation whose purpose is not to make a profit. Also called not-for-profit corporation.

A domestic or foreign corporation that is formed otherwise than for the pecuniary gain or profit of, and whose net earnings or any part of them is not distributable to, its members, directors, officers, or other private persons, except that the payment of reasonable compensation for services rendered and the distribution of assets on dissolution as permitted by section 1702.49 of the Revised Code is not pecuniary gain or profit or distribution of net earnings. In a corporation all of whose members are nonprofit corporations, distribution to members does not deprive it of the status of a nonprofit corporation. R.C. § 1702.01(C)

non prosequitur ("he does not prosecute") A judgment against a plaintiff who fails to pursue his or her action.

nonrecourse creditor A creditor who can look only to its collateral for satisfaction of its debt, not to the debtor's other assets.

nonresident alien One who is neither a citizen nor a resident of the country he or she is presently in.

nonstock corporation A corporation whose ownership is not determined by shares of stock.

nonsuit A termination or dismissal of an action by a plaintiff who is unable to prove his or her case, defaults, fails to prosecute, etc.

nonsupport The failure to provide food, clothing, and other support needed for living to someone to whom an obligation of support is owed.

nonuse The failure to exercise a right or claim.

non vult contendere He will not contest. See also nolo contendere.

no par stock Stock issued without a value stated on the stock certificate.

noscitur a sociis ("it is known by its associates") A word with multiple meanings is often best interpreted with regard to the words surrounding it.

no-strike clause A commitment by a labor union not to strike during the period covered by the collective bargaining agreement.

nota bene See N.B.

notarial Performed or taken by a notary public.

Notarial acts means acts which the laws and regulations of this state authorize notaries public of this state to perform, including the administration of oaths and affirmations, taking proof of execution and acknowledgment of instruments, and attesting documents. R.C. § 147.51

notarize To certify or attest, e.g., the authenticity of a signature.

notary public One authorized to perform notarial acts such as administering oaths, taking proof of execution and acknowledgment of instruments, and attesting the authenticity of signatures.

note See promissory note.

not-for-profit corporation See nonprofit corporation.

not found See no bill.

not guilty 1. A jury verdict acquitting the accused. 2. A plea entered by the accused that denies guilt for a criminal charge.

not guilty by reason of insanity (NGRI) A verdict of not guilty because of a finding of insanity. See also insanity.

A person is "not guilty by reason of insanity" relative to a charge of an offense only if the person proves, in the manner specified in section 2901.05 of the Revised Code, that at the time of the commission of the offense, the person did not know, as a result of a severe mental disease or defect, the wrongfulness of the person's acts. R.C. § 2901.01(A)(14)

notice 1. Information or knowledge about something. 2. Formal notification. 3. Knowledge of facts that would naturally lead an honest and prudent person to make inquiry.

A person has "notice" of a fact when any of the following applies: (1) The person has actual knowledge of it. (2) The person has received a notice or notification of it. (3) From all the facts and circumstances known to the person at the time in question, the person has reason to know that it exists. R.C. § 1301.01(Y)(3)

notice by publication Notice given through a broad medium such as a general circulation newspaper.

notice of appeal Notice given to a court (through filing) and to the opposing party (through service) of an intention to appeal.

notice of appearance A formal notification to a court by an attorney that he or she is representing a party in the litigation.

notice of pendency See lis pendens (2).

notice pleading Pleading by giving a short and plain statement of a claim that shows the pleader is entitled to relief.

notice to quit A landlord's written notice to a tenant that the landlord wishes to repossess the leased premises and end the tenancy.

notorious 1. Well-known for something undesirable. 2. Conspicuous.

notorious possession Occupation or possession of property that is conspicuous or generally known. Also called open possession.

NOV See judgment notwithstanding the verdict.

novation The substitution by mutual agreement of one debtor for another or of one creditor for another, whereby the old debt is extinguished, or the substitution of a new debt or obligation for an existing one.

novelty That which has not been known or used before. Innovation.

NOW account An interest-bearing savings account on which checks can be written. NOW means negotiable order of withdrawal.

nude Lacking something essential.

nudum pactum ("a bare agreement") A promise or undertaking made without any consideration.

nugatory Without force; invalid.

nuisance A substantial interference with the reasonable use and enjoyment of private land (private nuisance); an unreasonable interference with a right that is common to the general public (public nuisance).

Any activity by a person on his own land that produces material annoyance, inconvenience, and discomfort to another person. *Portage Cty. Bd. of Commrs.*, 156 Ohio App.3d 657 (Ohio App., 2004)

nuisance per se An act, occurrence, or structure that is a nuisance at all times and under all circumstances.

null; null and void Having no legal effect; binding no one.

nulla bona "No goods" on which a writ of execution can be levied.

nullification 1. The state or condition of being void or without legal effect. 2. The process of rendering something void.

nullify To invalidate; to render void.

nullity Having absolutely no legal effect. Something that is void.

nullius filius ("the son of no one") An illegitimate child.

nul tiel record ("no such" record) A plea asserting that the record relied upon in the opponent's claim does not exist.

nunc pro tunc ("now for then") With retroactive effect. As if it were done as of the time that it should have been done.

> Appointment of counsel "nunc pro tunc" is common device used by all courts to make record of proceedings accord with what actually occurred; phrase means "now for then," and signifies that counsel was actually present at proceedings prior to his or her appointment and participated therein on behalf of party he or she is being appointed to represent. *State v. Murnahan*, 117 Ohio App.3d 71 (Ohio App., 1996)

nuncupative will An oral will declared or dictated in anticipation of imminent death.

NYSE New York Stock Exchange (*www.nyse.com*).

O

oath 1. A solemn declaration. 2. A formal pledge to be truthful.

obiter dictum See dictum (1).

object 1. To express disapproval; to consider something improper or illegal and ask the court to take action accordingly. 2. The end aimed at; the thing sought to be accomplished.

objection 1. A formal disagreement or statement of opposition. 2. The act of objecting.

objective 1. Real in the external world; existing outside one's subjective mind. 2. Unbiased 3. Goal.

obligation 1. Any duty imposed by law, contract, or morals. 2. A binding agreement to do something, e.g., to pay a certain sum.

> "Obligations" means bonds, notes, or other evidences of obligation, including interest coupons pertaining thereto. R.C. § 152.09(A)(1)

obligee The person to whom an obligation is owed; a promisee or creditor.

obligor The person under an obligation; a promisor or debtor.

obliterate To destroy; to erase or wipe out.

obloquy Abusive language; disgrace due to defamatory criticism.

obscene Material that enjoys no free-speech protection if: (a) the average person, applying contemporary community standards, finds that the work, taken as a whole, appeals to the prurient interest in sex; (b) the work depicts or describes, in a patently offensive way, sexual conduct specifically defined by the applicable state law; and (c) the work, taken as a whole, lacks serious literary, artistic, political, or scientific value.

> When considered as a whole, and judged with reference to ordinary adults or, if it is designed for sexual deviates or other specially susceptible group, judged with reference to that group, any material or performance is "obscene" if any of the following apply: (1) Its dominant appeal is to prurient interest; (2) Its dominant tendency is to arouse lust by displaying or depicting sexual activity. . . . R.C. § 2907.01(F)

obscenity 1. See obscene. 2. Conduct tending to corrupt the public morals by its indecency or lewdness.

obsolescence Diminution in value caused by changes in taste or new technology, rendering the property less desirable on the market; the condition or process of falling into disuse.

obstruction of justice Conduct that impedes or interferes with the administration of justice (e.g., hindering a witness from appearing).

obvious Easily discovered or readily apparent.

occupancy 1. Obtaining possession of real property for dwelling or lodging purposes. 2. The period during which one is in actual possession of land.

occupation 1. Conduct in which one is engaged. 2. One's regular employment or source of livelihood. 3. Conquest or seizure of land.

> Occupation means any occupation, service, trade, business, industry, or branch or group of industries or employment or class of employment in which individuals are employed. R.C. § 4111.01(E)

occupational disease A disease resulting from exposure during employment to conditions or substances detrimental to health.

Occupational Safety and Health Administration (OSHA) A federal agency that develops workplace health and safety standards, and conducts investigations to enforce compliance (*www.osha.gov*).

occupation tax A tax imposed for the privilege of carrying on a business or occupation.

occupying the field A form of preemption (see this term) where a federal rule is so pervasive that no room is left for states to supplement it.

occurrence policy Insurance that covers all losses from events that occur during the period the policy is in effect, even if the claim is not actually filed until after the policy expires.

> An occurrence policy provides liability coverage when allegedly wrongful acts occur during the policy period without regard to when a claim is presented or a suit is filed. *Buckeye Ranch, Inc.*, 134 Ohio Misc.2d 10 (Ohio Com.Pl., 2005)

odd lot An irregular or nonstandard amount for a trade, e.g., less than 100.

odd lot doctrine For workers' compensation, permanent total disability may be found in the case of workers who, while not altogether incapacitated for work, are so handicapped that they will not be employed regularly in any well-known branch of the labor market.

odium Contempt or intense dislike. Held in disgrace.

of age See adult, majority (1).

of counsel 1. An attorney who is semiretired or has some other special status in the law firm other than regular member or employee. 2. An attorney who assists the principal attorney in a case.

offender One who has committed a crime or offense.

offense A crime or violation of law for which a penalty can be imposed.

offensive 1. Disagreeable, objectionable, displeasing. 2. Offending the personal dignity of an ordinary person who is not unduly sensitive.

offer 1. A proposal presented for acceptance or rejection. 2. To request that the court admit an exhibit into evidence.

> An offer is the manifestation of willingness to enter into a bargain, so made as to justify another person in understanding that his assent to that bargain is invited and will conclude it. *Reedy,* 143 Ohio App.3d 516 (Ohio App., 2001)

offeree The person to whom an offer is made.

offering The sale or offer for sale of an issue of securities.

offer of compromise An offer to settle a case.

offer of proof Telling the court what evidence a party proposes to present after the judge has ruled it inadmissible so that a record will be made for a later appeal of this ruling.

offeror The party who makes an offer.

office 1. A position of trust and authority. 2. A place where everyday administrative business is conducted. 3. A unit or subdivision of government.

> Office includes all state and local offices, the powers and duties of which are defined by the constitution, statutes, charters, and ordinances. R.C. § 161.01(C)

officer A person holding a position of trust, command, or authority in organizations.

officer of the court A person who has a responsibility in carrying out or assisting in the administration of justice in the courts, such as judges, bailiffs, court clerks, and attorneys.

official 1. An elected or appointed holder of a public office. An officer. 2. Concerning that which is authorized. 3. Proceeding from, sanctioned by, or pertaining to an officer.

Official Gazette Publication of the U.S. Patent and Trademark Office.

official immunity The immunity of government employees from personal liability for torts they commit while performing discretionary acts within the scope of their employment.

official notice The equivalent of judicial notice when taken by an administrative law judge or examiner.

official report or **official reporter** A collection of court opinions whose printing is authorized by the government.

officious intermeddler One who interferes in the affairs of another without justification (or invitation) and is generally not entitled to restitution for any benefit he or she confers. Also called intermeddler.

offset A deduction; that which compensates for or counters something else. See also setoff.

Old Age, Survivors, and Disability Insurance A federal program providing financial benefits for retirement and disability. Also called Social Security.

oligarchy Government power in the hands of a few persons.

oligopoly A market structure in which a few sellers dominate sales of a product, resulting in high prices.

ombudsman One who investigates and helps resolve grievances that people have within or against an organization, often employed by the organization.

> Abuse of Mentally Retarded Adult. There is hereby created within the legal rights service the ombudsman section. R.C. § 5123.601(B)

omission 1. The intentional or unintentional failure to act. 2. Something left out or neglected.

omnibus bill 1. A legislative bill that includes different subjects in one measure. 2. A legislative bill covering many aspects of one subject.

omnibus clause 1. A clause in an instrument (e.g., a will) that covers all property not specifically mentioned or known at the time. 2. A clause extending liability insurance coverage to persons using the car with the permission of the named insured.

on all fours Pertaining to facts that are exactly the same, or almost so; being a very close precedent.

on demand Upon request; when demanded.

onerous Unreasonably burdensome or one-sided.

on information and belief See information and belief.

on its face Whatever is readily observable, e.g., the language of a document. See also face.

on or about Approximately.

one man (person), one vote The equal protection requirement that each qualified voter be given an equal opportunity to participate in an election.

on point 1. Germane, relevant. 2. Covering or raising the same issue (in a case, law review article, etc.) as the one before you.

on the brief Helped to research or write the appellate brief.

on the merits Pertaining to a court decision that is based on the facts and on the substance of the claim, rather than on a procedural ground.

on the pleadings Pertaining to a ruling based on the allegations in the pleadings rather than on evidence presented in a hearing.

on the record Noted or recorded in the official record of the proceeding.

open 1. Visible, apparent, exposed. 2. Still available or active. 3. Not restricted. 4. Not resolved or settled.

open account 1. A type of credit from a seller that permits a buyer to make purchases on an ongoing basis without security. 2. An unpaid account.

open and notorious Conspicuous, generally recognized, or commonly known.

> Under open and obvious doctrine, owner or occupier of property owes no duty to warn invitees entering property of open and obvious dangers on property. *Anderson,* 100 Ohio App.3d 601 (Ohio App., 1995)

open court A court in session to which the general public may or may not be invited.

open end 1. Without a defined time or monetary limit. 2. Allowing further additions or other changes.

open-end mortgage A mortgage that allows the debtor to borrow additional funds without providing additional collateral.

> One that secures unpaid balances of loan advances made after mortgage is delivered for record to extent that total

unpaid loan indebtedness exclusive of interest does not exceed maximum amount of loan indebtedness stated on mortgage. R.C. § 5301.232(A). *Jones*, 39 Ohio App.3d 73 (Ohio App., 1987)

open field doctrine No violation of one's constitutional right to privacy occurs when the police search an open field without a warrant.

opening statement An attorney's statement to the jury made before presenting evidence that summarizes the case he or she intends to try to establish during the trial.

open listing A listing available to more than one agent in which the owner agrees to pay a commission to any agent who produces a ready, willing, and able purchaser. Also called nonexclusive listing.

open market An unrestricted competitive market in which any buyer and purchaser is free to participate.

open order An order placed with a broker that remains viable (open) until filled or the client cancels the order.

open policy See unvalued policy.

open possession See notorious possession.

open price The amount to be paid has yet to be determined or settled.

open shop A business in which union membership is not a condition of employment.

operating lease A short-term lease that expires before the end of the useful life of the leased property.

operating loss See net operating loss.

operation of law The means by which legal consequences are imposed by law, regardless of the intent of the parties involved.

opinion 1. A court's written explanation of how it applied the law to the facts to resolve a legal dispute. 2. A belief or conclusion expressing a value judgment that is not objectively verifiable.

opinion evidence Beliefs or inferences concerning facts in issue.

Opinion and reputation evidence of character. The credibility of a witness may be attacked or supported by evidence in the form of opinion or reputation. Ohio Evid. R. Rule 608(A)

opinion of the attorney general Formal legal advice from the chief law officer of the government to another government official or agency.

opportunity cost Benefits a business foregoes by choosing one course of action (e.g., an investment) over another.

opportunity to be heard A due process requirement of being allowed to present objections to proposed government action that would deprive one of a right.

oppression 1. An act of cruelty; conduct intended to frighten or harm. 2. Excessive and unjust use of authority. 3. Substantial inequality of bargaining power of the parties to the contract and an absence of real negotiation or a meaningful choice on the part of the weaker party.

option 1. An agreement that gives the person to whom the option is granted (the optionee) the right within a limited time to accept an offer. The right to buy or sell a stated quantity of securities or other goods at a set price within a defined time. 2. An opportunity to choose.

An option is a privilege existing in one person, for which he has paid money, which gives him the right to buy certain commodities or certain specified securities from another person, if he chooses, at any time within an agreed period, at a fixed price, or to sell such commodities or securities to such other person at an agreed price and time. *Blanchard Valley Farmers Coop.*, 143 Ohio App.3d 795 (Ohio App., 2001)

option contract A unilateral agreement to hold an offer open. See option (1).

optionee The person to whom an option is granted.

OR Own recognizance. See also personal recognizance.

oral Spoken, not written.

oral argument A spoken presentation to the court on a legal issue, e.g., telling an appellate court why the rulings of a lower tribunal were valid or were in error.

oral contract See parol contract.

oral trust A trust established by its creator (the settler) by spoken words rather than in writing.

oral will See nuncupative will.

ordeal An ancient form of trial in which the innocence of an accused person was determined by his or her ability to come away from an endurance test (e.g., hold a red-hot iron in the hand) unharmed.

order 1. A command or instruction from a judge or other official. 2. An instruction to buy or sell something. 3. The language on a check (or other draft) directing or ordering the payment or delivery of money or other property to a designated person.

Order means a written instruction to pay money signed by the person giving the instruction. R.C. § 1303.01(A)(8)

order bill of lading A negotiable instrument, issued by a carrier to a shipper at the time goods are loaded aboard ship, that serves as a receipt that the carrier has received the goods for shipment, as a contract of carriage for those goods, and as documentary evidence of title to those goods.

ordered liberty The constitutional balance between respect for the liberty of the individual and the demands of organized society.

order nisi See decree nisi.

Order of the Coif An honorary organization of law students whose membership is based on excellence.

order paper A negotiable instrument payable to a specific person or to his or her designee (it is payable to order, not to bearer).

order to show cause See show cause order.

ordinance 1. A law passed by the local legislative branch of government (e.g., city council) that declares, commands, or prohibits something. Also called municipal ordinance. 2. A law or decree.

ordinary Usual; regularly occurring.

ordinary care Reasonable care under the circumstances.

ordinary course of business See course of business.

ordinary income Wages, dividends, commissions, interest earned on savings, and similar kinds of income; income other than capital gains.

ordinary life insurance See whole life insurance.

ordinary negligence The failure to use reasonable care (often involving inadvertence) that does not constitute gross negligence or recklessness. Sometimes called simple negligence.

Ordinary negligence as been defined as ordinary care and diligence. Payne, 103 Ohio St. 59 (Ohio 1921)

ordinary prudent person See reasonable man (person).

organic Inherent, integral, or basic.

organic law The fundamental law or constitution of a state or nation; laws that establish and define the organization of government.

organization A society or group of persons joined in a common purpose.

organize To induce persons to join an organization, e.g., a union.

organized crime A continuing conspiracy among highly organized and disciplined groups to engage in supplying illegal goods and services.

organized labor Employees in labor unions.

original 1. The first form, from which copies are made. 2. New and unusual.

original contractor See general contractor.

original document rule See best evidence rule.

original intent The meaning understood by the framers or drafters of the U.S. Constitution, a statute, a contract, or other document.

original jurisdiction The power of a court to be the first to hear and resolve a case before it is reviewed by another court.

A court's power to hear and decide a matter before any other court can review the matter. *Johns*, 101 Ohio St.3d 234 (Ohio 2004)

original package doctrine Goods imported into a state cannot be taxed by that state if they are in their original packaging when shipped.

original promise A promise, made for the benefit of the promisor, to pay or guarantee the debt of another.

Under the "original promise rule," the statute of frauds does not apply to a promisor's oral agreement to become liable on another's debt if the agreement makes the promisor primarily liable and the original debtor has been discharged; in essence, the promisor is no longer answering for the debt of another and a new contract with new consideration has been formed. R.C. § 1335.05. *Trans-Gear, Inc.*, 128 Ohio App.3d 504 (Ohio App., 1998)

original writ The first process or initial step in bringing or prosecuting a suit.

origination fee A fee charged by the lender for preparing the loan documents and processing the loan.

orphan's court See probate court.

OSHA See Occupational Safety and Health Administration (*www.osha.gov*).

ostensible Apparent; appearing to be accurate or true.

ostensible agency An agency that arises when the principal's conduct allows others to believe that the agent possesses authority, which in fact does not exist.

ostensible authority The authority a principal intentionally or by lack of ordinary care allows a third person to believe the agent possesses. See also apparent authority.

Apparent and ostensible authority is such authority as a principal intentionally or by want of ordinary care causes or allows a third person to believe that the agent possesses. *Luken*, 77 Ohio App. 451 (Ohio App., 1945)

OTC See over-the-counter.

our federalism Federal courts must refrain from hearing constitutional challenges to state action when federal action is regarded as an improper intrusion on the right of a state to enforce its own laws in its own courts.

oust To remove; to deprive of possession or of a right.

ouster Turning out (or keeping excluded) someone entitled to possession of property. Wrongful dispossession.

outlaw 1. To prohibit or make illegal. 2. A person excluded from the benefits and protection of the law. 3. A fugitive.

out-of-court Not part of a court proceeding.

out-of-court settlement The resolution or settlement of a legal dispute without the participation of the court.

out-of-pocket expenses Expenditures made out of one's own funds.

out-of-pocket rule The damages awarded will be the difference between the purchase price and the real or actual value of the property received.

output contract A contract in which one party agrees to sell its entire output, which the other party agrees to buy during a designated period.

outrage See intentional infliction of emotional distress.

outrageous Shocking; beyond the bounds of human decency.

outside director A member of a board of directors who is not an officer or employee of the corporation.

outstanding 1. Uncollected, unpaid. 2. Publicly issued and sold.

Outstanding checks and travelers checks means any checks and travelers checks sold in the United States, reports of which have been received by a licensee from its agents and subagents, but which have not yet been paid. R.C. § 1315.01(F)

over Passing or taking effect after a prior estate or interest ends or is terminated.

overbreadth doctrine A law is invalid, though designed to prohibit legitimately regulated conduct, if it is so broad that it includes within its prohibitions constitutionally protected freedoms.

overdraft 1. A check written on an account with less funds than the amount of the check. 2. The act of overdrawing a bank account.

overhead The operating expenses of a business (e.g., rent, utilities) for which customers or clients are not charged a separate fee.

overissue To issue shares in an excessive or unauthorized quantity.

overreaching Taking unfair advantage of another's naiveté or other vulnerability, especially by deceptive means.

override 1. To set aside, supersede, or nullify. 2. A commission paid to managers on sales made by subordinates. 3. A commission paid to a real estate agent when a landowner makes a sale on his or her own (after the listing agreement expires) to a purchaser who was found by the agent.

overrule 1. To decide against or deny. 2. To reject or cancel an earlier opinion as precedent by rendering an opposite decision on the same question of law.

overt act 1. An act that reasonably appears to be about to inflict great bodily harm, justifying the use of self-defense. 2. An outward act from which criminality may be implied. 3. An outward objective action performed by one of the members of a conspiracy.

An "overt act" is simply an act that meets the substantial step criterion for an attempt offense. R.C. § 2923.02(A). *State v. Group*, 98 Ohio St.3d 248 (Ohio 2002)

over-the-counter (OTC) 1. Sold or transferred independent of a securities exchange. 2. Sold without the need of a prescription.

owelty Money paid to equalize a disproportionate division of property.

ownership The right to possess, control, and use property, and to convey it to others. Having rightful title to property.

oyer Reading a document aloud in court or a petition to have such a reading.

oyer and terminer A special court with jurisdiction to hear treason and other criminal cases. A judge's commission to hear such cases.

oyez Hear ye; a call announcing the beginning of a court proceeding or a proclamation.

P

P.A. See professional association.

PAC See political action committee.

PACE See Paralegal Advanced Competency Exam (*www.paralegals.org*).

PACER See Public Access to Court Electronic Records (*pacer.psc.uscourts.gov*).

pack 1. To assemble with an improper purpose. 2. To fill or arrange.

pact 1. A bargain. 2. An agreement between two or more nations or states.

pactum An agreement. See also nudum pactum.

paid-in capital Money or property paid to a corporation by its owners for its capital stock.

Paid-in capital means the aggregate par value of all of a bank's outstanding shares of all classes. R.C. § 1101.01(L)

paid-in surplus That portion of the surplus of a corporation not generated by profits but contributed by the stockholders. Surplus accumulated by the sale of stock at more than par value.

pain Physical discomfort and distress.

pain and suffering Physical discomfort or emotional distress; a disagreeable mental or emotional experience.

Pain and suffering is used not only to describe physical discomfort and distress, but also to describe the mental and emotional trauma that are recoverable as elements of compensatory damages. *Volz*, 115 Ohio Misc.2d 63 (Ohio Mun., 2001)

pains and penalties See bill of pains and penalties.

pais See in pais.

palimony Support payments ordered after the end of a nonmarital relationship if the party seeking support was induced to sustain or initiate the relationship by a promise of support or if support is otherwise equitable.

palming off Misrepresenting one's own goods or services as those of another. Also called passing off.

***Palsgraf* rule** Negligence liability is limited to reasonably foreseeable harm. *Palsgraf v. Long Island R. Co.*, 162 N.E. 99 (NY 1928).

pander To engage in pandering. A panderer is one who panders.

pandering The recruitment of prostitutes. Acting as a go-between to cater to the lust or base desires of another.

panel 1. A group of judges, usually three, who decide a case in a court with a larger number of judges. 2. A list of persons summoned to be examined for jury duty or to serve on a particular jury. 3. A group of attorneys available in a group legal services plan.

paper A written or printed document that is evidence of a debt. Commercial paper; a negotiable instrument.

A retail installment contract usually consists of a promissory note and a chattel mortgage and is referred to as "paper". R.C. § 1317.01. *Teegardin*, 166 Ohio St. 449 (Ohio 1957)

paper loss; paper profit An unrealized loss or gain on a security or other investment that is still held. Loss or profit that will not become actual until the asset is sold or closed out.

papers Pleadings, motions, and other litigation documents filed in court.

paper title The title listed or described on public records after the deed is recorded. Also called record title.

par 1. An acceptable average or standard. 2. See par value.

paralegal A person with legal skills who works under the supervision of an attorney or who is otherwise authorized by law to use his or her skills; this person performs substantive tasks that do not require all the skills of an attorney and that most secretaries are not trained to perform. Also called legal assistant.

Paralegal Advanced Competency Exam (PACE) The certification exam of the National Federation of Paralegal Associations for experienced paralegals (*www.paralegals.org*).

parallel citation A citation to an additional reporter where you can read the same court opinion.

paramount title Superior title as among competing claims to title.

paraphernalia 1. Property kept by a married woman on her husband's death in addition to her dower. 2. Equipment used for an activity.

As used in this section, drug paraphernalia means any equipment, product, or material of any kind that is used by the offender, intended by the offender for use, or designed for use, in propagating, cultivating, growing, harvesting, manufacturing, compounding, converting, producing, processing, preparing, testing, analyzing, packaging, repackaging, storing, containing, concealing, injecting, ingesting, inhaling, or otherwise introducing into the human body, a controlled substance in violation of this chapter. R.C. § 2925.14(A)

parcel 1. To divide into portions and distribute. 2. A small package or wrapped bundle. 3. A part or portion of land.

parcenary See coparcenary.

parcener See coparcener.

pardon An act of government exempting an individual from punishment for crime and from any resulting civil disabilities.

Pardon means the remission of penalty by the governor in accordance with the power vested in the governor by the constitution. R.C. § 2967.01(B)

parens patriae The state's power to protect and act as guardian of persons who suffer disabilities (e.g., minors, insane persons).

parent A biological or adoptive mother or father of another.

Cohabiting, unmarried female same-sex partner of children's biological and adoptive mother was not children's "parent" for purposes of entering into shared parenting agreement. R.C. §§ 3109.04(A)(2), 3111.01(A). *In re Bonfield*, 97 Ohio St.3d 387 (Ohio 2002)

parental kidnapping A parent's taking and removing his or her child from the custody of a person with legal custody without the latter's consent with the intent of defeating the custody jurisdiction of the court that currently has such jurisdiction.

parental liability law A law that makes parents liable (up to a limited dollar amount) for torts committed by their minor children.

parental rights The rights of a parent to raise his or her children, receive their services, and control their income and property.

parent corporation A corporation that controls another corporation (called the subsidiary corporation) through stock ownership.

"Parent corporation" or "parent" means a domestic or foreign corporation that owns and holds of record shares of another corporation, domestic or foreign, entitling the holder of the shares at the time to exercise a majority of the voting power in the election of the directors of the other corporation without regard to voting power that may thereafter exist upon a default, failure, or other contingency. R.C. § 1701.01(P)

pari delicto See in pari delicto.

pari materia See in pari materia.

parish 1. A territorial government division in Louisiana. 2. An ecclesiastical division of a city or town administered by a pastor.

parity Equality in amount, status, or value.

parliament A legislative body of a country, e.g., England.

parliamentarian An expert who provides advice on parliamentary law.

parliamentary Pertaining to the parliament or to its rules.

parliamentary law Rules of procedure to be followed by legislatures and other formal organizations.

parol 1. Spoken rather than in writing. 2. An oral statement.

parol contract A contract that is not in writing. Also called oral contract.

parole Allowing a prisoner to leave confinement before the end of his or her sentence.

parole board A government agency that decides if and under what conditions inmates can be released before completing their sentences.

parolee An ex-prisoner who has been placed on parole.

Parolee means any inmate who has been released from confinement on parole by order of the adult parole authority or conditionally pardoned, who is under supervision of the adult parole authority and has not been granted a final release, and who has not been declared in violation of the inmate's parole by the authority or is performing the prescribed conditions of a conditional pardon. R.C. § 2967.01(I)

parol evidence rule Prior or contemporaneous oral statements cannot be used to vary or contradict a written contract the parties intended to be final.

parole officer A government official who supervises persons on parole.

partial average See particular average.

partial breach A nonmaterial breach of contract that entitles a party to a remedy but not the right to consider the contract terminated.

partial disability A worker's inability to perform jobs he or she could perform before a work injury, even though still able to perform other gainful jobs subject to the disability.

"Partial disability" for purposes of disability and pension fund for fire fighters and police implies that person would be able to perform other gainful employment, notwithstanding inability to return to former position as fire fighter. R.C. § 742.01(F). *Kinsey*, 49 Ohio St.3d 224 (Ohio 1990)

partial insanity See diminished capacity.

partial verdict A verdict that is not the same on all the counts charged or on all the defendants in the trial.

particeps criminis A participant in a crime; an accomplice or accessory.

participation loan A loan issued or owned by more than one lender.

particular average An accidental partial loss of goods at sea by one who must bear the loss alone. Also called partial average.

particular estate An estate less than a fee simple, e.g., life estate.

particular lien A right to hold property as security for labor or funds expended on that specific property. Also called special lien.

particulars The details. See also bill of particulars.

partition The dividing of land held by co-owners into distinct portions, resulting in individual ownership.

partner 1. One who has united with others to form a partnership. 2. Two or more persons engaged in a jointly owned business.

partnership A voluntary association of two or more persons to place their resources in a jointly owned business or enterprise, with a proportional sharing of profits and losses.

A "partnership" exists where there is (1) an express or implied partnership contract between the parties; (2) the sharing of profits and losses; (3) mutuality of agency; (4) mutuality of control; and (5) co-ownership of the business and of the property used for partnership purposes or acquired with partnership funds. *Grendell*, 146 Ohio App.3d 1 (Ohio App., 2001)

partnership association A hybrid type of business with characteristics of a close corporation and a limited partnership.

part performance rule When an oral agreement fails to meet the requirements of the statute of frauds, the agreement may sometimes still be enforced when a relying party has partly performed the agreement.

party 1. One who brings a lawsuit or against whom a lawsuit is brought. 2. One who is concerned with, has an interest in, or takes part in the performance of an act. 3. A formal political association.

party aggrieved See aggrieved party.

party in interest See real party in interest.

party to be charged One against whom another seeks to enforce a contract.

par value An amount stated in a security, policy, or other instrument as its value. Also called face amount, face value, par, stated value.

> "Par value" means a number, expressed in dollars, points, or as a percentage or fraction, attached to a unit by the declaration. R.C. § 5311.01(Y)

pass 1. To utter or pronounce. 2. To transfer. 3. To enact into law by a legislative body. 4. To approve. 5. To forego.

passage Enactment into law by a legislative body.

passbook A bank document that records a customer's account activities.

passenger Any occupant of a motor vehicle other than the operator.

passim Here and there; in various places throughout.

passing off See palming off.

passion Any strong emotion that often interferes with cool reflection of the mind. See also heat of passion.

passive 1. Submitting without active involvement. 2. Inactive.

> "Passive income" means income acquired other than as a result of the labor, monetary, or in-kind contribution of either spouse. R.C. § 3105.171(A)(4)

passive negligence The unreasonable failure to do something; carelessly permitting defects to exist.

passive trust A trust whose trustee has no active duties. Also called dry trust, naked trust, nominal trust, simple trust.

passport A document that identifies a citizen, constitutes permission to travel to foreign countries, and acts as a request to foreign powers that the citizen be allowed to pass freely and safely.

past consideration An earlier benefit or detriment that was not exchanged for a new promise.

past recollection recorded A written record of a matter about which a witness now has insufficient memory. The record may be read into evidence if it was made or adopted by the witness when the matter was fresh in his or her memory. Fed. R. Evid. 803(5). An exception to the hearsay rule. Also called recorded recollection.

> The following are not excluded by the hearsay rule, even though the declarant is available as a witness: . . . (5) Recorded recollection. A memorandum or record concerning a matter about which a witness once had knowledge but now has insufficient recollection to enable him to testify fully and accurately, shown by the testimony of the witness to have been made or adopted when the matter was fresh in his memory and to reflect that knowledge correctly. If admitted, the memorandum or record may be read into evidence but may not itself be received as an exhibit unless offered by an adverse party. Ohio Evid. R. Rule 803

patent 1. A grant of a privilege or authority by the government. 2. A grant made by the government to an inventor for the exclusive right to make, use, and sell an invention for a term of years.

patentable Suitable to be patented because the device or process is novel, useful, and nonobvious.

patent defect See apparent defects.

patentee A person to whom a patent is granted; the holder of a patent.

patent infringement See infringement of patent.

patent medicine Packaged medicines or drugs sold over the counter under a trademark or other trade symbol.

paternity The state or condition of being a father.

paternity suit A court action to determine whether a person is the father of a child for whom support is owed. Also called bastardy proceeding.

patient-physician privilege See doctor-patient privilege.

pat. pend. Patent (application is) pending.

patricide 1. Killing one's father. 2. One who has killed his or her father.

patrimony 1. Heritage from one's ancestors. 2. That which is inherited from a father. 3. The total value of a person's rights and obligations.

patronage 1. The power to offer political jobs or other privileges. 2. Assistance received from a patron. 3. The customers of a business.

pattern 1. A reliable sample of observable features. 2. A model.

> "Pattern of conduct" means two or more actions or incidents closely related in time, whether or not there has been a prior conviction based on any of those actions or incidents. R.C. § 2903.211(B)(1)

pauper A person so poor that he or she needs public assistance.

pawn To deliver personal property to another as security for a loan.

pawnbroker A person in the business of lending money upon the deposit of personal property as security.

payable 1. Able to be paid. 2. Money or a balance owed.

payable to bearer Payable to whoever holds or possesses the instrument.

> A promise or order is "payable on demand" if it states that it is payable on demand or at sight or otherwise indicates that it is payable at the will of the holder, or if it does not state any time of payment. R.C. § 1303.07(A)

payable to order Payable to a named person, the payee.

payee One to whom or to whose order a check or other negotiable instrument is made payable. One who receives money.

payer or **payor** One who makes or should make payment, particularly on a check or other negotiable instrument.

payment 1. The partial or full performance of an obligation by tendering money or other consideration. 2. An amount paid.

> "Payment" in its narrow sense is the transfer of money or property or something of value in discharge of an existing obligation. *Dorn*, 133 Ohio St. 375 (Ohio 1938)

payment bond A guarantee from a surety that laborers and material suppliers will be paid if the general contractor defaults.

payment in due course Payment made in good faith at or after maturity to the holder without notice that his or her title is defective.

payment into court Property deposited into court for eventual distribution by court order.

payor See payer.

payroll tax 1. A tax on employees based on their wages. 2. A tax on employers as a percentage of wages paid to employees.

P.C. See professional corporation.

PCR See postconviction relief.

P.D. 1. See public defender. 2. Police department.

peace Orderly behavior in the community. Public tranquility.

peaceable 1. Without force or violence. 2. Gentle, calm.

peaceable possession 1. Possession that is continuous and not interrupted by adverse claims or attempts to dispossess. 2. Peaceful enjoyment.

peace bond A bond required of one who threatens to breach the peace.

peace officers A person designated by public authority to keep the peace and to arrest persons suspected of crime.

> "Peace officer" includes a sheriff, deputy sheriff, marshal, deputy marshal, chief of police and member of a municipal or township police department, chief of police and member of a township police district police force, chief of police of a university or college police department, state university law enforcement officer . . . state highway patrol trooper, and employee of the department of natural resources who is a natural resources law enforcement staff officer, park officer, forest officer, preserve officer, wildlife officer, or state watercraft officer. R.C. § 109.802(D)(1)

peculation Misappropriation of money or goods. Embezzlement.

pecuniary Relating to money.

pecuniary interest A financial interest, e.g., the opportunity, directly or indirectly, to share in the profit (or loss) derived from a transaction.

pederasty Sexual relations (oral or anal) between a man and boy.

penal Concerning or containing a penalty.

penal action 1. A civil action based on a statute that subjects a wrongdoer to liability in favor of the person wronged as a punishment for the wrongful act. 2. A criminal prosecution.

penal bond A bond obligating the payment of a specified penalty (called the penal sum) upon nonperformance of a condition.

penal code A compilation of statutes on criminal law.

penal institution See penitentiary.

penal law See criminal law.

penal statute A statute that defines a crime and its punishment.

> For purposes of statutory construction, "penal statute" is one which imposes penalty or creates forfeiture, while "remedial statute" is enacted to correct past defects, to redress existing wrong, or to promote public good. *Wright*, 69 Ohio App.3d 775 (Ohio App., 1990)

penal sum See penal bond.

penalty 1. Punishment for a criminal or civil wrong. 2. An extra charge imposed if a stated condition (e.g., late payment) occurs.

penalty clause A contract clause imposing a stated penalty (rather than actual damages) for nonperformance.

pendency While waiting; while still undecided.

pendent Undecided; pending.

pendente lite During the progress of the suit; pending the litigation.

pendent jurisdiction The power of a court to hear a claim over which it has no independent subject-matter jurisdiction if the facts of the claim are closely enough related on the facts of a main claim over which it does have such jurisdiction.

pending Under consideration; begun but not yet completed.

> Action is "pending" until final judgment is rendered in trial court, but not while in reviewing court. *P. B. Realty Co.*, 93 N.E.2d 603 (Ohio App., 1950)

penetration An intrusion, however slight, of any object or any part of the defendant's body into the genital or anal openings of the victim's body.

penitentiary A place of confinement for persons convicted of crime, usually serious crimes. Also called penal institution, prison.

***Pennoyer* rule** A personal judgment requires personal jurisdiction. *Pennoyer v. Neff*, 95 U.S. 714 (1877).

penny stocks High-risk equity securities, often selling at less than $1 a share and usually not traded on an approved securities exchange.

penology The study of prisons and the rehabilitation of criminals.

pen register A device that records the numbers dialed on a telephone but not the conversations themselves.

pension Regularly paid funds as a retirement or other benefit.

> Pension is a periodic allowance to an individual, or to his family, given because of some meritorious work or when certain conditions, as age, length of service, and the like, have been fulfilled, and it is sometimes referred to as deferred compensation for services rendered. *Murrell*, 16 Ohio Misc. 1 (Ohio Com.Pl., 1968)

pension plan A plan of an employer, primarily to pay determinable retirement benefits to its employees or their beneficiaries.

penumbra doctrine Implied constitutional rights, e.g., the right of privacy, exist on the periphery of explicit constitutional rights.

peonage Illegally compelling one to perform labor to pay off a debt.

people The prosecution in a criminal case representing the citizenry.

peppercorn A small amount; nominal consideration.

per By; for each.

per annum Annually.

per autre vie See pur autre vie.

per capita 1. For each person. 2. Divided equally among each person.

percentage depletion A method of taking a depletion deduction based on a percentage of gross income from an oil or gas well.

percentage lease A lease in which the rent is a percentage of gross or net sales, often with a minimum required payment.

per curiam opinion (an opinion "by the court" as a whole) A court opinion, usually a short one, that does not name the judge who wrote it.

per diem By the day; an allowance or amount of so much per day.

peremptory 1. Conclusive; final. 2. Without need for explanation.

peremptory challenge The right to challenge and remove a prospective juror without giving any reasons. Such challenges, however, cannot be used to discriminate against a protected minority.

> If there is one defendant, each party peremptorily may challenge three prospective jurors in misdemeanor cases, four prospective jurors in felony cases other than capital cases, and six prospective jurors in capital cases. Crim. R. Rule 24(D)

peremptory instruction An instruction by the judge to the jury that it must obey. (The equivalent of a directed verdict.)

perfect 1. Complete, executed. 2. To follow all procedures needed to complete or put in final form so that it is legally enforceable.

perfected Completed, executed; legally enforceable.

perfect tender rule Exact (perfect) performance by the seller of its obligations can be a condition of the enforceability of the contract.

performance The fulfillment of an obligation according to its terms.

performance bond See completion bond.

peril That which may cause damage or injury; exposure to danger.

peril of the sea A peril peculiar to the sea that cannot be guarded against by ordinary human skill and prudence.

periodic Happening at fixed intervals; recurring now and then.

periodic alimony Alimony paid indefinitely at scheduled intervals. Also called permanent alimony.

periodic tenancy A tenancy that continues indefinitely for successive periods (e.g., month to month, year to year) unless terminated by the parties.

> "Periodic tenancy" is one where duration of lease is for express or implied periods of time, for example month-to-month. *Steiner*, 72 Ohio App.3d 754 (Ohio App., 1991)

perjury Making a false statement under oath concerning a material matter with the intent to provide false testimony. Also called false swearing.

perks See perquisites.

permanent Continuing indefinitely.

> A "permanent nuisance" occurs when the wrongdoer's tortious act has been completed, but the plaintiff continues to experience injury in the absence of any further activity by the defendant. A "continuing nuisance" arises when the wrongdoer's tortious conduct is ongoing, perpetually generating new violations. *Haas*, 132 Ohio App.3d 875 (Ohio App., 1999)

permanent alimony See periodic alimony.

permanent injunction An injunction issued after a court hearing on the merits of the underling issues. Also called perpetual injunction.

permissive 1. Allowable; optional. 2. Lenient.

permissive counterclaim A counterclaim that does not arise out of the same transaction or occurrence that is basis of the plaintiff's claim.

permissive joinder The joinder of a party that is allowed (but not required) if the claims involved arise out of the same occurrence and there are questions of law or fact that will be common to all the parties.

permissive presumption A presumption that allows (but does not require) the fact finder to infer the presumed fact.

> "Permissive presumption" is one which allows, but does not require, trier of fact to infer elemental fact from proof by prosecutor of basic one, and which places no burden of any kind on defendant. *State v. Scott*, 8 Ohio App.3d 1 (Ohio App., 1983)

permissive use A use expressly or impliedly within the scope of permission.

permissive waste A tenant's failure to use ordinary care to preserve and protect the property, such as allowing deterioration for lack of repair.

permit 1. To expressly agree to the doing of an act. 2. A formal document granting the right to do something. A license.

perp (slang) Perpetrator of a crime.

perpetrate To commit or carry out an act, often criminal in nature.

perpetrator A person who commits a crime or other serious wrong.

perpetual injunction See permanent injunction.

perpetual lease A lease of land with no termination date.

perpetual succession The uninterrupted (perpetual) existence of a corporation even though its owners (shareholders) change.

perpetuation of testimony Procedures to ensure that the testimony of a deposition witness will be available for trial.

> "Perpetuation of testimony" is procedural instrument to assist in just disposition of litigation by informing one party or another in advance of filing of lawsuit as to true value of his claim. *Evans*, 12 Ohio Misc. 108 (Ohio Com.Pl., 1964)

perpetuity 1. Continuing forever. 2. A future interest that will not vest within the period prescribed by law.

perquisites (perks) Incidental benefits in addition to salary.

per quod Needing additional facts or proof of special damages.

per se In itself; inherently. Without needing additional facts.

persecution The offensive infliction of suffering or harm upon those who differ in race, religion, sexual orientation, or beliefs.

person A natural person, plus legal entities such as corporations that the law endows with some of the rights and duties of natural persons.

personal Pertaining to a person or to personal property.

personal bond A bail bond with no sureties.

personal chattel Tangible or intangible personal property.

personal effects Articles intimately or closely associated with the person (e.g., clothing, jewelry, wallet).

> Phrase "personal effects" as used in statute providing guidelines for valuation of property stolen is not intended to include all items of tangible property having some personal

use but is limited to articles having intimate association with owner, and phrase did not encompass batteries, radiators or other equipment removed from owner's automobile. R.C. § 2913.61(D)(2). *State v. Chaney*, 11 Ohio St.3d 208 (Ohio 1984)

personal exemption A deduction from adjusted gross income for an individual and qualified dependents.

personal injury (PI) Injury, damage, or invasion of one's body or personal rights. Harm to personal (as opposed to property) interests.

personality The legal status of being a person.

personal judgment A judgment against the person (over whom the court had personal jurisdiction) that may be satisfied out of any property of that person. Also called judgment in personam.

personal jurisdiction A court's power over a person to adjudicate his or her personal rights. Also called in personam jurisdiction. More limited kinds of jurisdiction include the court's power over a person's interest in specific property (quasi in rem jurisdiction) or over the property itself (in rem jurisdiction).

personal knowledge Firsthand knowledge rather than what others say.

"Personal knowledge" which can be the basis of an affidavit to defeat a motion for summary judgment is defined as knowledge of the truth in regard to a particular factor or allegation which is original and does not depend on information or hearsay. Rules Civ.Proc., Rule 56(C). *Suleiman*, 146 Ohio App.3d 41 (Ohio App., 2001)

personal liability An obligation that one can be forced to pay or satisfy out of personal (not just business) assets.

personal notice Information communicated directly to a person.

personal property Everything, other than real property, that can be owned, e.g., a car, a stock option.

personal recognizance Pretrial release of a defendant in a criminal case without posting a bond, based solely on a promise to appear. Release on own recognizance (ROR).

personal representative A person appointed to administer the estate and legal affairs of someone who has died or who is incapacitated.

"Personal representative" includes an executor, administrator, successor personal representative, special administrator, and persons who perform substantially the same function under the law governing their status. R.C. § 1709.01(E)

personal right A right that inheres in the status of an individual as opposed to his or her property rights.

personal service Handing a copy of a notice or summons to the defendant.

personalty Personal property.

personam See in personam, personal judgment.

per stirpes Taking the share a deceased ancestor would have been entitled to (had he or she lived) rather than taking as individuals in their own right. Taking by right of representation. Also called in stirpes.

The term "per stirpes" as used by a testator means simply that his devise or bequest is to be divided into as many equal shares as there are members of the root generation, counting both living and deceased members leaving lineal descendants, with an equal share being distributed to each living member of such generation and the share of each deceased member of such generation being divided and subdivided, in turn, per stirpes, among his lineal descendants. *Kraemer*, 168 Ohio St. 221 (Ohio 1958)

persuasive authority Any source a court relies on in reaching its decision that it is not required to rely on.

pertinent Relevant to an issue.

petit Lesser, minor.

petition 1. A formal written request. 2. A complaint.

petitioner One who presents a petition or complaint to a tribunal.

petit jury An ordinary jury called and sworn in (impaneled) to try a particular civil or criminal case. Also called petty jury, trial jury. See also grand jury.

petition in bankruptcy A formal application from a debtor to a bankruptcy court to file for bankruptcy.

pettifogger 1. One who quibbles over trivia. 2. An incompetent, ill-prepared attorney who sometimes engages in questionable practices.

petty Of less importance or merit.

petty jury See petit jury.

petty larceny The larceny or stealing of personal property with a value below a statutorily set amount (e.g., $200).

petty offense A minor violation of the law, e.g., a traffic violation.

"Petty offense" means a misdemeanor other than serious offense. Ohio Crim. R. Rule 2(D)

p.h.v. See pro hac vice.

physical Pertaining to the body or other material (non-mental) things.

physical evidence See real evidence (1).

physical fact A thing or action that can be perceived by the senses.

physical-fact rule The testimony of a witness that is positively contradicted by physical facts can be disregarded.

physical injury See bodily injury.

physician-patient privilege See doctor-patient privilege.

PI See personal injury.

picket To patrol or demonstrate outside a business or other organization in order to protest something it is doing or proposing and thereby pressure it to change.

pickpocket One who secretly steals something from another's person.

piecework Work for which one is paid by the number of units produced.

piercing the corporate veil A process by which a court disregards the limited liability normally afforded corporations and instead imposes personal liability on officers, directors, and shareholders.

"Piercing the corporate veil" means any and all common law doctrines by which a holder may be liable for an obligation or liability of a covered entity on the basis that the holder controlled the covered entity, the holder is or was the alter ego of the covered entity, or the covered entity has been used for the purpose of actual or constructive fraud or as a sham to perpetrate a fraud or any other common law doctrine by which the covered entity is disregarded for purposes of imposing liability on a holder for the debts or obligations of that covered entity. R.C. § 2307.902(H)(5)

pilferage Stealing; petty larceny.

pillage Using force or violence to rob someone, often in times of war.

pimp One who solicits customers for prostitutes.

pioneer patent A patent concerning a function or advance never before performed or one of major novelty and importance.

piracy 1. Robbery or seizure of a ship at sea or airplane in motion. See also hijack. 2. Copying in violation of intellectual property laws.

P.J. Presiding judge.

P.L. See public law.

place of abode One's residence or domicile.

placer claim A mining claim to loose minerals in sand or gravel.

plagiarism Using another's original ideas or expressions as one's own.

plain error An obvious, prejudicial error an appellate court will hear even if it was not raised at trial. Also called fundamental error.

> "Plain error" is obvious and prejudicial error, neither objected to nor affirmatively waived, that, if permitted, would have a material adverse effect on the character and public confidence in judicial proceedings. *Hinkle*, 159 Ohio App.3d 351 (Ohio App., 2004)

plain meaning The usual and ordinary meaning given to words by reasonable persons at the time and place of their use.

plaintiff The person who initiates a civil action in court.

plaintiff in error The appellant; the party bringing the appeal.

plain view doctrine An officer can seize objects without a warrant if they can plainly be seen, there is probable cause they are connected to a crime, and the officer is lawfully present.

planned unit development (PUD) Development of land areas where standard zoning rules are suspended to achieve mixed-use flexibility.

plant patent A patent granted to someone who invents or discovers and asexually reproduces any distinct and new variety of plant.

plat 1. A map showing streets, easements, etc. 2. A small land area.

plea 1. The first pleading of the defendant in a civil case. 2. The defendant's formal response to a criminal charge, e.g., not guilty.

plea bargaining Negotiations whereby an accused pleads guilty to a lesser included offense or to one of multiple charges in exchange for the prosecution's agreement to support a dismissal of some charges or a lighter sentence. Also called negotiated plea.

plead To file a pleading, enter a plea, or argue a case in court.

pleadings Formal litigation documents (e.g., a complaint, an answer) filed by parties that state or respond to claims or defenses of other parties.

> There shall be a complaint and an answer; a reply to a counterclaim denominated as such; an answer to a cross-claim, if the answer contains a cross-claim; a third-party complaint, if a person who was not an original party is summoned under the provisions of Rule 14; and a third-party answer, if a third-party complaint is served. No other pleading shall be allowed, except that the court may order a reply to an answer or a third-party answer. Ohio Civ. R. Rule 7(A)

plea in abatement A plea objecting to the timing or other defect in the plaintiff's claim without challenging its merits.

plea in bar A plea that seeks a total rejection of a claim or charge.

plebiscite A vote of the people on a proposed law or policy.

pledge 1. Delivering personal property as security for the payment of a debt or other obligation. A bailment for this purpose. 2. A solemn promise or agreement to do or forbear something.

> "Pledged revenues" means net revenues, moneys and investments, and earnings on those investments, in the applicable bond service fund and any other special funds, and the proceeds of any bonds issued for the purpose of refunding prior bonds, all as lawfully available and by resolution of the district committed for application as pledged revenues to the payment of bond service charges on particular issues of bonds. R.C. § 5540.01(N)

pledgee The person to whom something is delivered in pledge.

pledgor The person who pledges; the one who delivers goods in pledge.

plenary 1. Complete, unlimited. 2. Involving all members.

plenary jurisdiction A court's unlimited judicial power over the parties and subject matter of a legal dispute.

plenipotentiary Someone (e.g., a diplomat) with full powers to act.

PLI Practicing Law Institute (*www.pli.edu*).

plottage The additional value of adjacent, undeveloped lots when combined into a single tract.

PLS See professional legal secretary (*www.nals.org*).

plurality The largest number of votes received even though this number is not more than half of all votes cast or that could have been cast.

plurality opinion The controlling opinion that is joined by the largest number of judges on the bench short of a majority.

pluries Process (e.g., a writ) that issues in the third (or later) instance, after earlier ones have been ineffectual.

PMI See private mortgage insurance.

pocket part A pamphlet inserted into a small pocket built into the inside back (and occasionally front) cover of a book. The pamphlet contains text that supplements or updates the material in the book.

pocket veto The President's "silent" or indirect rejection of a bill by not acting on it within 10 weekdays of receiving it if the legislature adjourns during this period.

POD account Pay-on-death account. An account payable to the owner during his or her life, and upon death, to a designated beneficiary.

point 1. A distinct legal position or issue. 2. A fee or service charge equal to one percent of the principal amount of the loan. 3. A unit for measuring the price or value of stocks or other securities.

"Point" means a charge equal to one per cent of either of the following: (1) The principal amount of a precomputed loan or interest-bearing loan; (2) The original credit line of an open-end loan. R.C. § 1321.51(L)

point of error A lower court error asserted as a ground for appeal.

point reserved An issue on which the trial judge will rule later in the trial, allowing the case to proceed. Also called reserved point.

points and authorities See memorandum of points and authorities.

poisonous tree doctrine See fruit of the poisonous tree doctrine.

poison pill Steps by a corporation to discourage a hostile takeover, e.g., issuing new shares that would increase the takeover costs.

police A unit of the government charged with maintaining public order primarily through the prevention and investigation of crime.

police court See magistrate court.

police power The power of the state to enact laws, within constitutional limits, to promote public safety, health, morals, and convenience.

To constitute valid exercise of "police power," legislation must directly promote general health, safety, welfare or morals and must be reasonable, the means adopted to accomplish the legislative purpose must be suitable to the end in view, must be impartial in operation, must have real and substantial relation to such purpose and must not interfere with private rights beyond the necessities of the situation. Ohio Const. art. 1, §§ 16. *Nolden*, 12 Ohio Misc. 205 (Ohio Com.Pl., 1966)

policy 1. The principles by which an organization is managed. 2. An insurance contract. 3. A lottery-type numbers game.

policyholder An owner of an insurance policy, usually the insured.

political action committee (PAC) An organization (other than a political party or candidate committee) that uses fundraising or contributions to advocate the election or defeat of a clearly identified candidate for office or the victory or defeat of a public question.

political asylum See asylum (2).

political offense Crimes against a state or political order, e.g., treason.

political question A question that a court should not resolve because it concerns policy choices that are constitutionally committed for resolution to the legislative or executive branches or because of the absence of judicially discoverable and manageable standards for resolving it.

poll the jury To ask each juror how he or she voted on the verdict.

poll tax A tax imposed on each individual regardless of income. Also called capitation tax, head tax.

polyandry Having more than one husband at the same time.

polygamy Having more than one spouse at the same time.

polygraph An instrument to record physiological processes, e.g., blood pressure, to detect lying. Also called lie detector.

Ponzi scheme A fraudulent investment scheme whereby returns to investors are financed, not through the success of an underlying business venture, but from the funds of newly attracted investors.

A Ponzi scheme is perpetrated with fabricated investment deals in which investors are paid not with actual dividends and principal, but with money on loan from another source, usually new investors. *Disciplinary Counsel v. Ulinski*, 106 Ohio St.3d 53 (Ohio 2005)

pool 1. To combine for a common purpose. 2. A combination or agreement by persons or companies to carry out a joint purpose. 3. A sum of money made up of stakes contributed by bettors in a game of chance.

popular Pertaining to the general public.

pornography The portrayal of erotic behavior designed to cause sexual excitement. The portrayal is protected unless it is obscene.

port authority A government agency that plans and regulates traffic through a port by sea vessels, airplanes, public transportation, etc.

portfolio All the investments held by one person or institution.

port of entry The port where goods and travelers from abroad may enter the country. The port containing a station for customs officials.

positive evidence See direct evidence.

positive fraud Fraud that is actual or intentional rather than implied or constructive. Also called actual fraud, fraud in fact.

Positive fraud, i.e., fraud of commission rather than omission, such as fraudulent misrepresentation or fraudulent concealment. *Jacobs*, 105 Ohio App.3d 1 (Ohio App., 1995)

positive law Law actually and specifically enacted by a proper authority, usually a legislative body.

positivism See legal positivism.

posse See in posse.

posse comitatus ("the power or force of the county") Citizens called by the sheriff for special purposes, e.g., to help keep the peace.

possession 1. The actual custody or control of something. 2. That which one holds, occupies, or controls. 3. That which one owns.

"Possess" or "possession" means having control over a thing or substance but may not be inferred solely from mere access to the thing or substance through ownership or occupation of the premises upon which the thing or substance is found. R.C. § 2925.01(L)

possession is nine-tenths of the law A false adage that nevertheless reflects the truth that the law does not always make it easy for a rightful property owner to oust someone in wrongful possession.

possessor One who has possession or custody of property.

possessory Relating to, founded on, or claiming possession.

possessory action An action to assert the right to keep or maintain possession of property.

possessory interest The right to exert control over specific property to the exclusion of others whether or not the right is based on title.

possibility of reverter The interest remaining in a grantor who conveys a fee simple determinable or a fee simple conditional. Any reversionary interest that is subject to a condition precedent. Also called reverter.

> In Ohio, "possibility of reverter" denominates future interest remaining in transferor of a qualified fee and this interest is not an estate but only possibility of having an estate at a future time; estate is vested in grantee subject to divestment at a future time. *Long*, 45 Ohio St.2d 165 (Ohio 1976)

post To send by mail. See also posting.

post-conviction relief (PCR) A remedy sought by a prisoner to challenge the legality of his or her conviction or sentence. A prisoner's collateral attack of his or her final judgment.

postdate To insert a date that is later than the actual date.

posterity 1. All descendants of a person. 2. Future generations.

posthumous Referring to events occurring after the death of a person.

posting 1. A form of substituted service of process by placing process in a prominent place (e.g., the front door of the defendant's residence). 2. The transfer of an original entry of debits or credits to a ledger. 3. The steps followed by a bank in paying a check. 4. Making something available on the Internet. 5. Making payment.

postmortem 1. Pertaining to what occurs after death. 2. See autopsy.

postnuptial agreement An agreement between spouses on the division of their property in the event of death or divorce.

postpone 1. To put off. 2. To subordinate or give a lower priority.

post-trial discovery Discovery procedures (e.g., deposition) conducted after judgment to help enforce (e.g., collect) a judgment.

pourover trust A trust that receives property from a will.

pourover will A will that transfers property to a trust.

poverty affidavit A written declaration of one's finances for purposes of qualifying for free legal services or other public benefit.

power 1. The right, ability, or authority to do something. 2. The right of a person to produce a change in a given legal relation by doing or not doing a given act. 3. Control over another.

power coupled with an interest A right or power to do some act, together with an interest in the subject matter on which the power is to be executed.

power of acceptance The right of an offeree to create a contract by accepting the terms of the offer.

power of appointment A power created when one person (the donor) grants another (the donee) authority to designate beneficiaries of the donor's property.

power of attorney A document that authorizes another to act as one's agent or attorney-in-fact.

> "Power of attorney" is written instrument authorizing agent to perform specific acts on behalf of his principal. *Testa*, 44 Ohio App.3d 161 (Ohio App., 1988)

power of sale The right to sell property, e.g., the right of a trustee or mortgagee to sell the real property mortgaged in the event of a default.

pp. Pages.

PPO Preferred provider organization, a group of health care providers.

practice 1. A repeated or customary action; habitual performance. 2. The rules, forms, and methods used in a court or administrative tribunal. 3. The exercise of a profession or occupation.

practice of law Using legal skills to assist a specific person resolve his or her specific legal problem. The work of a lawyer in counseling and representing clients on legal matters.

> The "practice of law" is not limited to appearances in court, but also includes giving legal advice and counsel and the preparation of legal instruments and contracts by which legal rights are preserved. R.C. § 4705.01. *Miami Cty. Bar Assn.*, 107 Ohio St.3d 259 (Ohio 2005)

praecipe 1. A formal request that a court take some action. 2. A writ ordering an action or a statement of why it should not be taken.

praedial See predial.

praesenti See in praesenti.

prayer for relief The portion of a complaint or other pleading that sets forth the requested relief (e.g., damages) sought from the court.

> The "prayer" of the petition is that part of a pleading which designates or asks for relief sought. *Spang*, 134 N.E.2d 586 (Ohio Com.Pl., 1956)

preamble A clause at the beginning of a law (e.g., statute) or instrument (e.g., contract) setting out its objectives.

precarious Uncertain; at the whim or discretion of someone.

precatory Embodying a recommendation, hope, or advice rather than a positive command or direction; pertaining to a wish.

precedent A prior decision that can be used as a standard or guide in a later similar case.

precept 1. A rule imposing a standard of conduct or action. 2. A warrant, writ, or order.

precinct A subdivision or other geographical unit of local government.

preclusion order An order preventing a party from introducing specific evidence, usually because of a violation of discovery rules.

precognition A pretrial questioning of a potential witness.

precontract A contract designed to prevent a person from entering another contract of the same nature with someone else.

predatory pricing A company's artificially low prices designed to drive out competition so that it can reap monopoly profits at a later time.

predecessor One who goes or who has gone before. A prior holder.

predial Pertaining or attached to land. Also spelled praedial.

predisposition A defendant's tendency or inclination to engage in certain conduct, e.g., illegal activity.

preemption 1. Under the Supremacy Clause, federal laws take precedence over (preempts) state laws when Congress (a) expressly mandates the preemption, (b) regulates an area so pervasively that an intent to preempt the entire field may be inferred, or (c) enacts a law that directly conflicts with state law. 2. The right of first purchase.

preemptive right The right of a stockholder to maintain a proportionate share of ownership by purchasing a proportionate share of any new stock issues. Also called subscription right.

> If the plan of conversion provides for consideration in the form of stock and if the initial issue of stock of the new company exceeds the number of shares to which the policyholders are entitled in the aggregate, each policyholder is also entitled to preemptive rights in subscribing to his proportionate number of shares of such excess. R.C. § 3913.12(A)

pre-existing duty rule When a contracting party does or promises something that it is already legally obligated to do, there is no adequate consideration because the party has not incurred a detriment.

prefer 1. To submit for consideration; to file or prosecute. 2. To give advantage, priority, or privilege.

preference 1. Making a payment or a transfer by an insolvent debtor to one of the creditors, to the detriment of the other creditors. 2. The choice of one over another; the choice made.

preferential shop A job site in which union members are given priority or advantage over non-union members in hiring, promotion, etc.

preferred dividend A dividend payable to preferred shareholders, which has priority over dividends payable to common shareholders.

preferred risk An insurance classification of people who statistically have fewer accidents or have better health records and who, therefore, are often eligible for a reduced rate.

preferred stock Stock in a corporation that has a claim to income (dividends) or liquidation assets ahead of holders of common stock.

prejudice 1. Bias. A leaning toward or against one side of a cause for a reason other than merit. 2. Detriment or harm to one's legal rights.

prejudicial error An error justifying a reversal because it probably affected the outcome and was harmful to the substantial rights of the party objecting to the error. Also called fatal error, reversible error.

preliminary Introductory; prior to the main body or theme.

preliminary examination See preliminary hearing.

preliminary hearing A pretrial hearing on whether probable cause exists that the defendant committed a crime. Also called preliminary examination, probable cause hearing.

preliminary injunction A temporary order to preserve the status quo and prevent irreparable loss of rights prior to a trial on the merits. Also called interlocutory injunction, temporary injunction.

> The purpose of a "preliminary" or "temporary injunction" or "restraining order" is to preserve the status quo of the parties and their rights pending final adjudication of the cause upon the merits. *City of Cleveland v. Division 268 of Amalgamated Ass'n of St. Elec. Ry. & Motor Coach Emp. of America*, 84 Ohio App. 43 (Ohio App., 1948)

premarital agreement A contract made by two persons about to be married that covers spousal support, property division, and related matters in the event of the separation of the parties, the death of one of them, or the dissolution of the marriage by divorce or annulment. Also called antenuptial agreement, marriage settlement, prenuptial agreement.

premeditated Considered, deliberated, or planned beforehand.

premise A statement that is a basis of an inference or conclusion.

premises 1. Land, its buildings, and surrounding grounds. 2. The part of a deed describing the interest transferred and related information, e.g., why the deed is being made. 3. The foregoing statements.

> As used in this section, "land or premises" includes any land, building, structure, or place belonging to, controlled by, or in custody of another, and any separate enclosure or room, or portion thereof. R.C. § 2911.21(E)

premium 1. An extra payment or bonus. 2. The payment to an insurance company to keep the policy. 3. The amount by which the market value of a bond or other security exceeds its par or face value.

prenuptial agreement See premarital agreement.

prepackaged bankruptcy (prepack) A plan negotiated between debtor and creditors prior to filing for bankruptcy.

prepaid legal services A plan by which a person pays premiums to cover future legal services. Also called legal plan, group legal services.

prepayment penalty An extra payment imposed when a promissory note or other loan is paid in full before it is due.

preponderance of evidence The burden of proof that is met when the evidence establishes that it is more likely than not that the facts are as alleged. Also called fair preponderance of the evidence.

> "Preponderance of the evidence" means the greater weight of the evidence. *Dawson*, 121 Ohio App.3d 9 (Ohio App., 1997)

prerogative An exclusive right or privilege of a person or office.

prerogative writ See extraordinary writ.

prescription 1. A method of acquiring ownership or title to property or rights by reason of continuous usage over a designated period of time. 2. An order for drugs issued by a licensed health professional. 3. A direction; a practice or course or action that is ordered. 4. The laying down or establishing of rules or directions.

prescriptive easement An easement created by an open, adverse, continuous use of another's land under claim of right over a designated period of time.

presence 1. Being physically present. 2. Being in physical proximity to or with something, including a sensory awareness of it.

present 1. Currently happening. 2. In attendance. 3. Under examination.

present danger See clear and present danger.

presentence report A probation report on the background of a convicted offender to assist the judge in imposing a sentence.

present estate An interest in property that can be possessed and enjoyed now, not just in the future. Also called present interest.

presenting bank Any bank (other than the payor bank) that presents an item.

"Presenting bank" means a bank presenting an item except a payor bank. R.C. § 1304.01(B)(6)

present interest See present estate.

present memory refreshed See present recollection refreshed.

presentment 1. A grand jury's accusation of crime that is not based on a prosecutor's request for an indictment. 2. Producing a check or other negotiable instrument for acceptance or payment.

present recollection refreshed A use by witnesses of writings or other objects to refresh their memory so that testimony can be given about past events from present recollection. Also called present memory refreshed, present recollection revived, refreshing memory or recollection.

presents This document being considered; the present instrument.

present sense impression A statement describing or explaining an event or condition made while perceiving it or immediately thereafter.

The following [is] not excluded by the hearsay rule, even though the declarant is available as a witness: (1) Present sense impression. A statement describing or explaining an event or condition made while the declarant was perceiving the event or condition, or immediately thereafter unless circumstances indicate lack of trustworthiness. Ohio Evid. R. Rule 803

present value The amount of money you would have to be given now in order to produce or generate, with compound interest, a certain amount of money in a designated period of time. Also called present worth.

preside To be the person in authority; to direct the proceedings.

president The chief executive officer of an organization or country.

presidential elector See electoral college.

president judge The presiding or chief judge on some courts.

presume To take for granted as true before establishing it as such.

presumption An assumption or inference that a certain fact is true once another fact is established.

A presumption is a deduction based on acceptable standards and/or practices, without having to offer proof of facts or reasons to justify the conclusion. State v. Vannata, 8 Ohio Misc.2d 22 (Ohio Mun., 1983). "Presumption" or "presumed" means that the trier of fact must find the existence of the fact presumed unless and until evidence is introduced that would support a finding of its nonexistence. R.C. § 1301.01(EE)

presumption of death A presumption that a person is no longer alive after being missing without explanation for a set period of time.

presumption of fact An inference; a logical inference or conclusion that the trier of the facts is at liberty to draw or refuse to draw.

presumption of innocence An accused cannot be convicted of a crime unless the government proves guilt beyond a reasonable doubt. The accused does not have the burden of proving his or her innocence.

presumption of law A particular conclusion the court must reach in absence of evidence to the contrary.

presumption of paternity; presumption of legitimacy A man is presumed to be the natural father of a child if he and the child's natural mother are married to each other and the child is conceived or born during the marriage. The presumption also applies if he receives the child into his home and holds the child out as his natural child.

presumption of survivorship In a common disaster involving multiple victims, a younger, healthier victim is presumed to have died after the others in the absence of evidence to the contrary.

presumptive 1. Providing a logical basis to believe; probable. 2. Created by or arising out of a presumption.

presumptive evidence Evidence sufficient to establish a given fact and which, if not rebutted or contradicted, will remain sufficient.

presumptive heir A person who can inherit if a closer relative is not born before the ancestor dies. Also called heir presumptive.

presumptive trust See resulting trust.

pretermit To pass by, omit, or disregard.

pretermitted heir A child or spouse omitted in a will by a testator.

If, after making a last will and testament, a testator has a child born alive, or adopts a child, . . . or if a child or designated heir who is absent and reported to be dead proves to be alive, and no provision has been made in such will or by settlement for such pretermitted child or heir, or for the issue thereof, the will shall not be revoked; but unless it appears by such will that it was the intention of the testator to disinherit such pretermitted child or heir, the devises and legacies granted by such will, except those to a surviving spouse, shall be abated proportionately, or in such other manner as is necessary to give effect to the intention of the testator as shown by the will, so that such pretermitted child or heir will receive a share equal to that which such person would have been entitled to receive out of the estate if such testator had died intestate with no surviving spouse. . . . R.C. § 2107.34

pretext arrest A valid arrest for an improper reason, e.g., to investigate a different offense for which an arrest is not valid.

pretrial conference A meeting of the attorneys and the judge (or magistrate) before the trial to attempt to narrow the issues, to secure stipulations, and to make a final effort to settle the case without a trial.

pretrial detention Keeping someone in custody before trial.

pretrial discovery Devices parties can use to uncover facts that will help them prepare for trial (e.g., depositions, interrogatories).

pretrial diversion; pretrial intervention See diversion (2).

pretrial order A judge's order before a trial stating the issues to be tried and any stipulations of the parties.

prevail 1. To be in general use or practice. 2. To succeed.

prevailing party The party winning the judgment.

preventive detention Detaining someone before trial to prevent fleeing, future antisocial behavior, or self-inflicted harm.

preventive justice Restraining orders, peace bonds, and other remedies designed to keep the peace and prevent future wrongdoing.

price discrimination A difference in price a seller charges different customers for the same product or one of like quality.

price fixing An agreement on prices that otherwise would be set by market forces. Any means calculated to eliminate competition and manipulate price.

price supports Devices (e.g., government subsidies) to keep prices from falling below a set level.

priest-penitent privilege See clergy-penitent privilege.

prima facie 1. On the face of it, at first sight. 2. Sufficient.

prima facie case A case as presented that will prevail until contradicted and overcome by contrary evidence.

> "Prima facie tests" are mechanisms by which courts may readily dispose of cases that cannot sustain a particular cause of action; to say that a plaintiff has established a prima facie case is simply to say that he has produced sufficient evidence to present his case to the jury, i.e., he has avoided a directed verdict. *Coryell*, 101 Ohio St.3d 175 (Ohio 2004)

prima facie evidence Sufficient evidence of a fact unless rebutted.

prima facie tort The intentional infliction of harm without justification, resulting in special damages.

primary activity A strike, picketing, or other action directed against an employer with whom a union has a labor dispute.

primary authority Any law (e.g., case, statute) that a court could rely on in reaching a decision.

primary boycott Action by a union to urge its members and the public not to patronize a firm with which the union has a labor dispute.

primary election An election by a party's voters to select (nominate) candidates to run in a general election.

primary evidence The best or highest quality evidence available.

primary jurisdiction doctrine Although a case is properly before a court, if there are issues requiring administrative expertise, the court can refrain from acting until the administrative agency acts.

> The "primary jurisdiction doctrine" comes into play if the use of administrative proceedings will contribute to a meaningful resolution of the lawsuit; if it will, the trial court should defer any action until that determination is made by the agency. *Lazarus*, 144 Ohio App.3d 716 (Ohio App., 2001)

primary liability Liability for which one is directly responsible, rather than secondarily after someone else fails to pay or perform.

primary market 1. The market where new issues of securities are first sold. 2. The main target of an initial offering of goods and services.

prime contractor See general contractor.

prime rate The lowest rate of interest charged by a bank to its best (most creditworthy) customers for short-term loans.

primogeniture 1. The status of being the first-born of siblings. 2. The right of the oldest son to inherit the entire estate.

principal 1. The amount of debt not including interest. 2. The initial sum invested. 3. A perpetrator of a crime. 4. One who permits an agent to act on his or her behalf. 5. One with prime responsibility for an obligation. 6. See corpus (2).

prior 1. Before in time or preference. 2. An earlier conviction.

prior art Any relevant knowledge, acts, and descriptions that pertain to, but predate, the invention in question.

prior consistent statement An earlier statement made by a witness that supports what he or she is now saying at the trial.

prior inconsistent statement An earlier statement made by a witness that conflicts what he or she is now saying at the trial.

priority A legal preference or precedence, e.g., the right to be paid first.

> Under "rule of priority," when there are courts of common jurisdiction, court that first obtains in personam jurisdiction has jurisdiction to proceed to judgment to the exclusion of all other courts. *Adams Robinson Ent.*, 111 Ohio App.3d 426 (Ohio App., 1996)

prior lien A lien with rights superior to other liens.

prior restraint A judicial or other government restriction on a publication before it is published.

prison See penitentiary.

prisoner A person in police custody serving a prison sentence.

> "Prisoner" means a person who is in actual confinement in a state correctional institution. R.C. § 2967.01(H)

privacy The absence of unwanted attention into one's private concerns or affairs. Being left alone. See also invasion of privacy.

private 1. Pertaining to individual or personal matters as opposed to public or official ones. 2. Restricted in use to designated persons or groups. 3. Confidential. 4. Not sold or offered to the general public.

private act See private law (2).

private bill A proposal for a private law. See private law (2).

private corporation A corporation established by private individuals for a nongovernmental or nonpublic purpose.

private foundation A charitable organization whose main source of funds is not the general public.

privateer A privately owned ship authorized by the government to attack enemy ships.

private international law Conflict of laws involving different states or countries. See also international law.

private investigator Someone other than a police officer who is licensed to do detective work or to conduct investigations.

> (A) "Private investigator" means any person who engages in the business of private investigation. (B) "Business of private investigation" means, except when performed by one excluded under division (H) of this section, the conducting, for hire, in person or through a partner or employees, of any investigation relevant to any crime or wrong done or threatened, or to obtain information on the identity, habits, conduct, movements, whereabouts, affiliations, transactions, reputation, credibility, or character of any person, or to locate and recover lost or stolen property, or to determine the cause of or responsibility for any libel or slander, or any fire, accident, or damage to property, or to secure evidence for use in any legislative, administrative, or judicial investigation or proceeding. R.C. § 4749.01

private law 1. The law governing private persons and their interelationships. 2. A law that applies to specifically named persons or groups and has little or no permanence or general interest. A special law.

private mortgage insurance (PMI) Insurance to protect the lender if the debtor dies or defaults.

private necessity A privilege to make reasonable use of another's property to prevent an immediate threat of harm or damage to one's private property.

private nuisance A substantial interference with the reasonable use and enjoyment of private land.

> A "private nuisance" is an act that wrongfully interferes with another's interest, use, or enjoyment of land; it can also be anything that obstructs the reasonable and comfortable use of property. *Abraham,* 149 Ohio App.3d 471 (Ohio App., 2002)

private offering A sale of an issue of securities to a limited number of persons. Also called private placement.

private person One who is not a public official, public figure, or member of the military.

private placement 1. The placement of a child for adoption by the parents or their intermediaries rather than by a state agency. 2. See private offering.

private sale A sale that was not open to the public through advertising, auction, or real estate agents.

private statute See private law (2).

privatize Convert from government control or ownership to the private sector.

privies See privy.

privilege 1. A special legal benefit, right, immunity, or protection. 2. A defense that authorizes conduct that would otherwise be wrongful.

> "Privilege" means an immunity, license, or right conferred by law, bestowed by express or implied grant, arising out of status, position, office, or relationship, or growing out of necessity. R.C. § 2901.01 (A)(12)

privilege against self-incrimination 1. A criminal defendant cannot be compelled to testify. 2. The right not to answer incriminating questions by the government that could directly or indirectly connect oneself to the commission of a crime.

privileged Protected by a privilege, e.g., does not have to be disclosed.

privileged communication A communication that does not have to be disclosed. A statement protected by privilege.

Privileges and Immunities Clause The clause in the U.S. Constitution (art. IV, § 2) that "citizens of each state shall be entitled to all Privileges and Immunities of citizens" in every other state. A state cannot discriminate within its borders against citizens of other states.

privity A relationship that persons share in property, a transaction, or a right. Mutuality of interest.

> "Privity" exists if the interest of the client is concurrent with the interest of the third person. *Sayyah,* 143 Ohio App.3d 102 (Ohio App., 2001)

privity of contract The relationship that exists between persons who enter a contract with each other.

privity of estate A mutual or successive relationship to the same rights in property.

privy A person who is in privity with another; someone so connected with another as to be identified with him or her in interest (plural: privies).

prize 1. A reward given to a winner. 2. A vessel seized during war.

pro For.

probable cause 1. A reasonable belief that a specific crime has been committed and that the defendant committed the crime. Also called sufficient cause. 2. A reasonable belief that evidence of a crime will be found in a particular place. 3. A reasonable ground for a belief in the existence of supporting facts.

> In search warrant context, "probable cause" means the existence of evidence less than the evidence that would justify condemnation, such as proof beyond a reasonable doubt or by a preponderance; in other words, probable cause is the existence of circumstances that warrant suspicion. Ohio Const. Art. 1, § 14. *State v. Young,* 146 Ohio App.3d 245 (Ohio App., 2001)

probable cause hearing See preliminary hearing.

probate 1. A court procedure to establish the validly of a will and to oversee the administration of the estate. 2. To establish the validity of a will.

probate court A court for probating wills, supervising the administration of estates, and handling related family law issues. Also called orphan's court, surrogate's court.

probate estate Assets owned by the decedent at death plus assets later acquired by the decedent's estate.

probation 1. The conditional release of a person convicted of a crime in lieu of a prison sentence. Conditions can include attending drug counseling and remedial training. 2. A trial or test period for a new employee to determine competence and suitability for the job.

probationer A convicted offender on probation.

probation officer A government employee who supervises probationers.

probative Furnishing proof; tending to prove or disprove.

probative evidence Evidence that contributes toward proof.

> For purposes of finding that reliable, probative, and substantial evidence supports agency order on appeal, "probative evidence" is relevant evidence that tends to prove the issue in question. R.C. § 119.12. *Reed,* 162 Ohio App.3d 429 (Ohio App., 2005)

probative fact A fact from which an ultimate or decisive fact may be inferred or proven.

probative value The extent to which evidence tends to establish whatever it is offered to prove.

pro bono Concerning or involving legal services that are provided for the public good (pro bono publico) without fee or compensation. Sometimes also applied to services given at a reduced rate. Shortened to pro bono.

procedendo A writ ordering a lower court to proceed to judgment.

procedural due process Minimum requirements of procedure (e.g., notice and the opportunity to be heard) that are constitutionally mandated before the government deprives a person of life, liberty, or property.

> In its most fundamental form, "procedural due process" demands that prior to state action, an individual must receive adequate and timely notice of proposed action and meaningful opportunity to be heard; encompassed in this is concept that, in order for procedure to be meaningful, governmental activity must be fundamentally fair. *Abraham,* 107 Ohio App.3d 773 (Ohio App., 1995)

procedural law A law that governs the steps or mechanics of resolving a dispute in a court or administrative agency.

procedure A method or process by which something is done, e.g., to resolve a legal dispute in court or in an administrative agency.

proceeding 1. A part or step in a lawsuit, e.g., a hearing. 2. A sequence of events. 3. Going forward or conducting something.

proceeds Money derived from some possession, sale, or other transaction. The yield.

process 1. A summons, writ, or court order, e.g., to appear incourt. 2. Procedures or proceedings in an action or prosecution.

Word "process," in statute defining an action, means method taken by law to compel a defendant to appear in court after initiating the action. R.C. § 2307.01. *Thomas,* 283 N.E.2d 456 (Ohio Com.Pl., 1970)

process server Someone with the authority to serve or deliver process.

prochein ami See next friend.

proclamation An official and public declaration.

pro confesso As having accepted responsibility or confessed.

proctor One who manages the affairs of another. A supervisor.

procuration The appointment of an agent. A power of attorney.

procurement 1. Obtaining or acquiring something. 2. The persuasion of another to engage in improper sexual conduct.

procurement contract A government contract to acquire goods or services.

procuring cause 1. See proximate cause. 2. The chief means by which a sale of property was effected, entitling the broker to a commission.

prodition Treason.

produce 1. To bring forth or yield. 2. Products of agriculture.

producing cause See proximate cause.

product Something produced by physical labor, intellectual effort, or natural processes. A commercial item that is used or consumed.

production of documents See request for production.

products liability A general term that covers different causes of action (e.g., negligence, strict liability in tort, and breach of warranty) based on defective products that cause harm.

"Product liability claim" means a claim that is asserted in a civil action pursuant to sections 2307.71 to 2307.80 of the Revised Code and that seeks to recover compensatory damages from a manufacturer or supplier for death, physical injury to person, emotional distress, or physical damage to property other than the product in question, that allegedly arose from any of the following: (a) The design, formulation, production, construction, creation, assembly, rebuilding, testing, or marketing of that product; (b) Any warning or instruction, or lack of warning or instruction, associated with that product; (c) Any failure of that product to conform to any relevant representation or warranty. R.C. § 2307.71(A)(13)

profert The document relied on in the pleading is produced in court.

professional association (P.A.) 1. Two or more professionals (e.g., doctors) who practice together. 2. A group of professionals organized for a common purpose, e.g., continuing education, lobbying.

professional conduct See Model Rules of Professional Conduct.

professional corporation (P.C.) A corporation of persons performing services that require a professional license, e.g., attorneys.

professional legal secretary (PLS) A certification credential of NALS, the Association for Legal Professionals (*www.nals.org*).

professional responsibility Ethical conduct of professionals.

proffer To tender or offer.

profiling Targeting, suspecting, or selecting out individuals based on group characteristics, e.g., race.

profit The gross proceeds of a business transaction less the costs of the transaction; excess of revenue over expenses. Gain.

Profit is gain realized from business or investment which is over and above expenditures. *Hunter,* 100 Ohio App.3d 532 (Ohio App., 1995)

profit-and-loss (P&L) statement See earnings report.

profit à prendre The right to enter another's land and remove something of value from the soil or the products of the soil. Also called right of common.

profiteering Making excessive profits through unfair advantage.

profit sharing A company plan in which employees can share profits.

pro forma 1. Perfunctorily; as a formality. 2. Provided in advance for purposes of description or projection.

progressive tax A type of graduated tax that applies higher tax rates as one's income range increases. Also called graduated tax.

pro hac vice (p.h.v.) ("for this particular occasion") Pertaining to permission given to an out-of-state attorney to practice law in the jurisdiction for this case only.

prohibited degree A relationship too close to be allowed to marry.

prohibition 1. Suppression or interdiction; an order forbidding something. 2. A law preventing the manufacture, sale, or transportation of intoxicating liquors. 3. See writ of prohibition.

"Prohibition" is an extraordinary writ issued by a higher court to a lower court or tribunal to prevent usurpation or exercise of judicial powers or functions for which the lower court or tribunal lacks jurisdiction. *Dental Care Plus, Inc.,* 135 Ohio App.3d 574 (Ohio App., 1999)

prohibitory injunction A court order that a person refrain from doing a specific act. An injunction that maintains the status quo.

prolixity Superfluous statements of fact in a pleading or as evidence.

promise 1. A manifestation of an intention to act or to refrain from acting in a specified way so as to justify the promisee in understanding that a commitment has been made. 2. To make a commitment.

promisee The person to whom a promise has been made.

promisor The person who makes a promise.

promissory estoppel The rule that a promise (not supported by consideration) will be binding if (a) the promisor makes a promise he or she should reasonably expect will induce action or forbearance by the promisee, (b) the promise does induce such action or forbearance, and (c) injustice can be avoided only by enforcement of the promise.

Doctrine of "promissory estoppel" seeks to prevent harm from reasonable and detrimental reliance of one party on false representations of another. *Landskroner*, 154 Ohio App.3d 471 (Ohio App., 2003)

promissory note A written promise to pay. An unconditional promise in writing made by one person to another, signed by the maker, engaging to pay on demand, or at a fixed or determinable future time, a certain sum of money, to order or to bearer. Also called note.

"Promissory note" means an instrument that evidences a promise to pay a monetary obligation, does not evidence an order to pay, and does not contain an acknowledgment by a bank that the bank has received for deposit a sum of money or funds. R.C. § 1309.102(A)(65)

promissory warranty A commitment by the insured that certain facts will continue or remain true after the insurance policy takes effect.

promoter 1. One who promotes or furthers some venture. 2. One who takes preliminary steps in the organization of a corporation or business.

promulgate 1. To announce officially. 2. To put into effect.

pronounce To declare formally.

proof 1. The effect of being persuaded by evidence that a fact has been established or refuted. 2. Evidence that establishes something.

proof beyond a reasonable doubt See reasonable doubt.

proof of claim A written statement a creditor files with the bankruptcy court showing the amount and character of the debt owed to the creditor.

proof of loss Providing an insurer with the information and evidence needed to determine its liability under an insurance policy.

proof of service Evidence that a summons or other process has been served on a party in an action. Also called certificate of service, return of service.

proof to a moral certainty See moral certainty.

pro per See in propria persona, pro se.

proper lookout The duty of a driver to see what is clearly visible or what in the exercise of due care would be visible.

proper party A person whose interest may be affected by the action and, therefore, may be joined, but whose presence is not essential for the court to adjudicate the rights of others.

property 1. That which one can possess, enjoy, or own. 2. The right of ownership. 3. The quality or characteristic of a thing.

property settlement An agreement dividing marital property between spouses upon separation or divorce. A court judgment on this division.

property tax A tax on real or personal property that one owns, the amount often dependent on the value of the property.

prophylactic Acting to prevent something.

proponent An advocate; one who presents or offers an argument, proposal, or instrument.

proposal An offer or plan.

propound To offer or propose for analysis or acceptance.

proprietary 1. Owned by a private person or company. 2. Pertaining to ownership.

proprietary drug A drug that has the protection of a patent.

proprietary function A function of a municipality that (a) traditionally or principally has been performed by private enterprise, or (b) is conducted primarily to produce a profit or benefit for the government rather than for the public at large.

Proprietary function means a function of a political subdivision that is specified in division (G)(2) of this section or that satisfies both of the following: (a) The function is not one described in division (C)(1)(a) or (b) of this section and is not one specified in division (C)(2) of this section; (b) The function is one that promotes or preserves the public peace, health, safety, or welfare and that involves activities that are customarily engaged in by nongovernmental persons. R.C. § 2744.01(G)(1)

proprietary interest One's right or share based on property ownership.

proprietary lease A lease in a cooperative apartment between the owner-cooperative and a tenant-stockholder.

proprietor The owner of property, e.g., a business. See also sole proprietorship.

pro rata Proportionately; according to a certain rate or factor.

pro rata clause A clause in an insurance policy that the insurer will be liable only for the proportion of the loss represented by the ratio between its policy limits and the total limits of all available insurance.

prorate To divide, calculate, or distribute proportionally.

proscription A prohibition or restriction.

pro se (on one's own behalf) Appearing for or representing oneself. Also called in propria persona, pro per.

prosecute To initiate and pursue a civil case or a criminal case.

prosecuting attorney See district attorney, prosecutor (1).

prosecuting witness The person (often the victim) who instigates a criminal charge and gives evidence.

prosecution 1. Court proceedings to determine the guilt or innocence of a person accused of a crime. 2. The prosecuting attorney or the government in a criminal case. 3. Pursuing a lawsuit.

prosecution history See file wrapper.

prosecutor 1. The representative of the government in a criminal case. 2. One who instigates a prosecution or files a complaint.

"Prosecuting attorney" means the attorney general of this state, the prosecuting attorney of a county, the law director, city solicitor, or other officer who prosecutes a criminal case on behalf of the state or a city, village, township, or other political subdivision, and the assistant or assistants of any of them. As used in Crim. R. 6, "prosecuting attorney" means the attorney general of this state, the prosecuting attorney of a county, and the assistant or assistants of either of them. Ohio Crim. R. Rule 2(G)

prosecutorial discretion The right of prosecutors to decide whether to charge someone for a crime, whether to plea bargain, and whether to ask for a particular sentence.

prosecutory Involving or relating to a prosecution.

prospective Pertaining to or applicable in the future; expected.

prospective law A law applicable to cases or events arising after its enactment.

prospectus A document containing facts on a company designed to help a prospective investor decide whether to invest in the company.

prostitution Engaging in sexual activities for hire.

> "Prostitute" means a male or female who promiscuously engages in sexual activity for hire, regardless of whether the hire is paid to the prostitute or to another. R.C. § 2907.01(D)

pro tanto For so much; to the extent of.

protected class A group of people (e.g., members of a minority race) given special statutory protection against discrimination.

protection Defending or shielding from harm; coverage.

protection order See restraining order.

protective custody Being held under force of law for one's own protection or that of the public.

protective order 1. A court order designed to protect a person from harassment during litigation. 2. See restraining order.

protective trust A trust designed to protect trust assets from the spendthrift tendencies of the beneficiary.

pro tem (pro tempore) For the time being; temporarily.

protest 1. A formal declaration of dissent or disapproval. 2. A written declaration (often by a notary public) that a check or other negotiable instrument was presented but not paid or accepted. 3. A disagreement that a debt is owed but paying it while disputing it.

prothonotary A chief clerk of court.

protocol 1. The etiquette of diplomacy. 2. A brief summary of a document, e.g., a treaty. 3. The first copy or draft of a treaty; an amendment of a treaty. 4. The formal record or minutes of a meeting.

prove To establish a fact or position by sufficient evidence.

province 1. A division of the state or country. 2. A sphere of expertise or authority.

provision 1. A section or part of a legal document. 2. A stipulation.

provisional remedy A temporary remedy, pending final court action.

> "Provisional remedy" means a proceeding ancillary to an action, including, but not limited to, a proceeding for a preliminary injunction, attachment, discovery of privileged matter, suppression of evidence, a prima-facie showing pursuant to section 2307.85 or 2307.86 of the Revised Code, a prima-facie showing pursuant to section 2307.92 of the Revised Code, or a finding made pursuant to division (A)(3) of section 2307.93 of the Revised Code. R.C. § 2505.02(A)(3)

proviso A condition, exception, or stipulation in a law or document.

provocation Inciting another to do a particular deed.

proximate Nearest or closest; close in causal connection.

proximate cause The legally sufficient cause of an event when (a) the defendant is the cause in fact of the event, (b) the event was the foreseeable consequence of the original risk created by the defendant, and (c) there is no policy reason why the defendant should not be liable for what he or she caused in fact. Also called direct cause, efficient cause, legal cause, procuring cause, producing cause.

> Proximate cause of an event is that which in a natural and continuous sequence, unbroken by any new, independent cause, produces that event and without which that event would not have occurred. *Click*, 152 Ohio App.3d 560 (Ohio App., 2003)

proxy 1. An agent; one authorized to act for another. 2. The authorization to act for another.

proxy marriage The performance of a valid marriage ceremony through agents because one or both of the prospective spouses are absent.

proxy statement A document mailed to shareholders giving information on matters for which the company is seeking proxy votes.

prudent Cautious; careful in adapting means to ends.

prudent investor rule A trustee must use such diligence and prudence in managing and investing a trust fund as a reasonable person would use.

prurient Pertaining to a shameful or morbid interest in sex.

P.S.; **p.s.** 1. Public Statute (P.S.). See public law (1). 2. Postscript (p.s.).

psychotherapist-patient privilege A patient can refuse to disclose, and can prevent others from disclosing, confidential communications between patient and psychotherapist involving the patient's diagnosis or treatment.

public 1. The community at large. 2. Open for use by everyone. 3. Traded on the open market.

Public Access to Court Electronic Records (PACER) An electronic public access service that allows subscribers to obtain case and docket information from federal courts via the Internet (*pacer.psc.uscourts.gov*).

public accommodation A business or place that is open to, accepts, or solicits the patronage of the general public.

> "Place of public accommodation" means any inn, restaurant, eating house, barbershop, public conveyance by air, land, or water, theater, store, other place for the sale of merchandise, or any other place of public accommodation or amusement of which the accommodations, advantages, facilities, or privileges are available to the public. R.C. § 4112.01(A)(9)

public act See public law (1).

public administrator Someone appointed by the court to administer an intestate estate when relatives or associates of the decedent are not available to do so.

publication 1. Making something known to people. 2. Communication of a statement to someone other than the plaintiff.

public bill A legislative proposal for a public law.

public contract A contract (often with a private person or business) in which a government buys goods or services for a public need.

public convenience and necessity Reasonably meeting the needs of the public, justifying the grant of public funds or a license for a project or service.

public corporation 1. A company whose shares are traded on the open market. Also called publicly held corporation. 2. A corporation owned by the government and managed under special laws in the public interest.

> "Public corporations" are instrumentalities created by state, formed and owned by it in public interest, supported in whole or part by public funds, and governed by managers deriving their authority from state. *Sharon Realty Co.*, 188 N.E.2d 318 (Ohio Com.Pl., 1961)

public defender (P.D.) An attorney appointed by a court and paid by the government to represent indigent defendants in criminal cases.

public domain 1. Work product or other property that is not protected by copyright or patent. A status that allows access to anyone without fee. 2. Government-owned land.

public duty doctrine The government is not liable for a public official's negligent conduct unless it is shown that the official breached a duty owed to the injured person as an individual as opposed the breach of an obligation owed to the public in general.

public easement An easement for the benefit of the general public.

public figure A person who has assumed special prominence in the affairs of society. A public figure for a limited purpose is a person who has voluntarily become involved in a controversy of interest to the general public.

> A person whose position or activities thrust him into the center of an important public controversy. *Kassouf*, 142 Ohio App.3d 413 (Ohio App., 2001)

public forum Settings or places traditionally available for public expression and debate, such as public streets and the radio.

public hearing A hearing open to the general public.

publici juris ("of public right") Being owned by the public and subject to use by anyone.

public interest 1. A matter of health or welfare that concerns the general public. 2. The well-being of the public.

public interest law Law involving broad societal issues.

public international law See international law.

public land Government-owned land.

public law (P.L.; Pub.L.) 1. A statute that applies to the general public or to a segment of the public and has permanence or general interest. Also called public act, public statute. 2. Laws governing the operation of government or relationships between government and private persons. The major examples are constitutional law, administrative law, and criminal law.

publicly held corporation See public corporation (1).

public necessity The privilege to make a reasonable use of someone's property to prevent an immediate threat of harm or damage to the public.

public nuisance Unreasonably interfering with a right of the general public. An act that adversely affects the safety, health, morals, or convenience of the public. Also called common nuisance.

> "Public nuisance" is unreasonable interference with right common to general public; it affects public at large or such of them as may come in contact with it, by injuriously affecting safety or health of public, or working some substantial annoyance, inconvenience, or injury to public. *Crown Property Dev.*, 113 Ohio App.3d 647 (Ohio App., 1996)

public offering A sale of stock to the public on the open market.

public office A position created by law by which an individual is given power to perform a public function for a given period.

> Public office means any state agency, public institution, political subdivision, other [FN1] organized body, office, agency, institution, or entity established by the laws of this state for the exercise of any function of government. R.C. § 117.01(D)

public official An elected or appointed holder of a public office.

> Public official means any officer, employee, or duly authorized representative or agent of a public office. R.C. § 117.01(E)

public policy Principles inherent in customs and societal values that are embodied in a law.

public property Government-owned property.

public purpose Benefit to or welfare of the public as a goal of government action.

public record A record the government must keep that may or may not be open to the public.

> "Public record" means records kept by any public office, including, but not limited to, state, county, city, village, township, and school district units, and records pertaining to the delivery of educational services by an alternative school in Ohio kept by a nonprofit or for profit entity operating such alternative school pursuant to section 3313.533 of the Revised Code. "Public record" does not mean any of the following: (a) Medical records; (b) Records pertaining to probation and parole proceedings or to proceedings related to the imposition of community control sanctions and post-release control sanctions; . . . R.C. § 149.43(A)(1)

public records exception Some written statements that would normally be excluded as hearsay may be admitted into evidence if they qualify as public records and reports (Federal Rules of Evidence Rule 803(8)).

> The following are not excluded by the hearsay rule, even though the declarant is available as a witness: . . . (8) Public records and reports. Records, reports, statements, or data compilations, in any form, of public offices or agencies, setting forth (a) the activities of the office or agency, or (b) matters observed pursuant to duty imposed by law as to which matters there was a duty to report, excluding, however, in criminal cases matters observed by police officers and other law enforcement personnel, unless offered by defendant, unless the sources of information or other circumstances indicate lack of trustworthiness. Evid. R. Rule 803(8)

public sale A sale in which members of the public are invited to become buyers.

public security Bonds, notes, certificates of indebtedness, and other instruments evidencing government debt.

public service commission A government commission that supervises or regulates public utilities.

public statute (P.S.) See public law (1).

public trial A trial that the general public can observe.

public trust See charitable trust.

public use 1. A use that confers some benefit or advantage to the public. A use affecting the public generally, or any number thereof, as distinguished from particular individuals. 2. A use of an invention by one under no restriction or obligation of secrecy to the inventor.

> "Public use" within rule that private property may not be taken except for public use means a use which is beneficial to the public and actual use by the public is not required. *State ex rel. Allerton Parking Corp.*, 4 Ohio App.2d 57 (Ohio App., 1965)

public utility A company or business that regularly supplies the public with some commodity or service that is of public consequence and need (e.g., electricity).

public works Construction, demolition, installation, or repair work on roads, dams, and similar structures done under contract with public funds.

public wrong An offense against the state or the general community, e.g., a crime, public nuisance, or breach of a public contract.

publish To make known, to make public; to distribute or disseminate.

puffing 1. A seller's opinion consisting of an exaggeration of quality or overstatement of value. 2. See by-bidding.

puisne Subordinate in rank.

***Pullman* abstention** Federal courts can refrain or postpone the exercise of federal jurisdiction when a federal constitutional issue might be mooted or presented in a different posture by a state court determination of pertinent state law. *Railroad Comm'n v. Pullman*, 61 S. Ct. 643 (1941).

punishment Any fine, penalty, confinement, or other sanction imposed by law for a crime, offense, or breach of a duty.

punitive damages Damages that are added to actual or compensatory damages in order to punish outrageous or egregious conduct and to deter similar conduct in the future. Also called exemplary damages, smart money, vindictive damages.

> "Punitive damages" are damages given in enhancement of compensatory damages on account of wanton, reckless, malicious, or oppressive character of acts complained of. *Robb*, 114 Ohio App.3d 595 (Ohio App., 1996)

pur autre vie For or during the life of another. Also spelled per autre vie.

purchase Acquisition by buying; receiving title to property by a means other than descent, inheritance, or gift.

purchase money mortgage A mortgage taken back when purchasing property to secure payment of the balance of the purchase price.

purchase money resulting trust A trust imposed when title to property is transferred to one person, but the entire purchase price is paid by another.

> "Purchase-money resulting trust" arises when property is acquired under circumstances indicating that beneficial interest is not intended to be enjoyed by holder of legal estate; central to inquiry are issues of who paid for purchase and who was intended to beneficially enjoy property. *Cayten*, 103 Ohio App.3d 354 (Ohio App., 1995)

purchase money security interest (PMSI) A security interest taken or retained by a seller to secure all or part of the price of the collateral, or a security interest taken by one who gives value that is used by the debtor to acquire the collateral.

purchaser One who acquires property by buying it for a consideration.

pure accident See unavoidable accident.

pure plea A plea stating matters not in the bill to defeat the claim.

pure race statute See race statute.

purge To clear or exonerate from a charge or of guilt.

purloin To steal.

purport 1. To appear to be; to claim or seem to be. 2. Meaning.

purpose Goal or objective.

purposely Intentionally; with a specific purpose.

purpresture An encroachment on public rights or the appropriation to private use of that which belongs to the public.

pursuant to In accordance with; under.

pursuit of happiness The phrase in the Declaration of Independence interpreted to mean the right to be free in the enjoyment of our faculties, subject to restraints that are necessary for the common welfare.

purview The body, scope, or extent of a something, e.g., a statute or other law.

putative Generally regarded or reputed, believed.

putative father A man reputed or alleged to be the biological father of a child born out of wedlock.

> "Putative father" means a man, including one under age eighteen, who may be a child's father and to whom all of the following apply: (1) He is not married to the child's mother at the time of the child's conception or birth; (2) He has not adopted the child; (3) He has not been determined, prior to the date a petition to adopt the child is filed, to have a parent and child relationship with the child by a court proceeding pursuant to sections 3111.01 to 3111.18 of the Revised Code, a court proceeding in another state, an administrative agency proceeding pursuant to sections 3111.38 to 3111.54 of the Revised Code, or an administrative agency proceeding in another state; (4) He has not acknowledged paternity of the child pursuant to sections 3111.21 to 3111.35 of the Revised Code. R.C. § 3107.01(H)

putative marriage A marriage that has been solemnized in proper form and celebrated in good faith by one or both parties, but which, by reason of some legal infirmity, is either void or voidable.

put option The right to sell a specified security or commodity at a specified price. See also call option.

pyramid scheme A sales device or plan in which participants are recruited to pay the person who recruited them, hoping to receive payments from the persons they recruit. A pyramid scheme rewards participants for inducing other people to join the program, whereas a Ponzi scheme operates strictly by paying earlier investors with money tendered by later investors.

> "Pyramid sales plan or program" means any scheme, whether or not for the disposal or distribution of property, whereby a person pays a consideration for the chance or opportunity to receive compensation, regardless of whether he also receives other rights or property, under

either of the following circumstances: (1) For introducing one or more persons into participation in the plan or program; (2) When another participant has introduced a person into participation in the plan or program. R.C. § 1333.91(A)

pyramiding Speculating on stocks or commodities by using unrealized (paper) profits as margin for more purchases.

Q

Q.B. Queen's Bench. See King's Bench.

QDRO See qualified domestic relations order.

QTIP Qualified terminable interest property.

qua As; in the character or capacity of.

quaere Ask, question; a query.

qualification 1. A quality or circumstance that is legally or inherently necessary to perform a function. 2. A restriction or modification in a document or transaction.

qualified 1. Eligible; possessing legal power or capacity. 2. Restricted or imperfect.

qualified acceptance A counteroffer; an acceptance that modifies the offer.

qualified disclaimer An irrevocable and unqualified refusal by a person to accept an interest in property (26 USC § 2518).

qualified domestic relations order (QDRO) A court order that allows a nonemployee to reach retirement benefits of an employee or former employee in order to satisfy a support or other marital obligation to the nonemployee.

> To qualify as qualified domestic relations order (QDRO) excepted from ERISA's antialienation provision, order must relate to provision of child support, alimony payments or marital property rights of spouse, former spouse, child or other dependent of participant, and must be made pursuant to state domestic relations law. *Albertson*, 85 Ohio App.3d 765 (Ohio App., 1993)

qualified immunity A government official's immunity from liability for civil damages when performing discretionary functions if his or her conduct does not violate clearly established statutory or constitutional rights of which a reasonable person would have known.

qualified indorsement An indorsement that limits the liability of the indorser of a negotiable instrument.

qualified privilege See conditional privilege.

qualify 1. To make oneself fit or prepared. 2. To limit or restrict.

quantum meruit ("as much as he deserves") 1. An equitable theory of recovery based upon an implied agreement to pay for benefits or goods received. 2. The measure of damages imposed when a party prevails on the equitable claim of unjust enrichment.

> An equitable doctrine based upon the concept that a party should not be unjustly enriched at the expense of another; to prevent such unjust enrichment, the law implies a promise to pay for the reasonable value of services rendered in the absence of a contract for such services. *Blue Ribbon Remodeling Co.*, 97 Ohio Misc.2d 8 (Ohio Mun., 1999)

quantum valebant An action seeking payment for goods sold and delivered based on an implied promise to pay as much as the goods are reasonably worth.

quarantine Isolation of persons, animals, goods, or vehicles suspected of carrying a contagious disease.

quare clausum fregit See trespass quare clausum fregit.

quash To vacate or annul; to suppress completely.

quasi Somewhat the same, but different; resembling.

quasi contract See implied in law contract.

quasi corporation A body or entity (often part of the government) that has some of the characteristics of a corporation but is not a corporation in the full sense.

quasi estoppel A party should be precluded from asserting, to another's disadvantage, a right or claim that is inconsistent with a position previously taken by the party.

quasi in rem jurisdiction A court's power over a person, but restricted to his or her specific interest in property within the territory over which the court has authority.

quasi judicial Pertaining to the power of an administrative agency (or official in the executive branch) to hear and determine controversies between the public and individuals in a manner that resembles a judicial trial.

> Quasi-judicial proceeding appealable to the courts is one that requires notice and a hearing, and the opportunity for the introduction of evidence. R.C. § 2506.01. *Cincinnati v. Jenkins*, 146 Ohio App.3d 27 (Ohio App., 2001)

quasi legislative Pertaining to the power of an administrative agency (or official in the executive branch) to write rules and regulations in a manner that resembles the legislature.

quasi-suspect classification A classification such as one based on gender or illegitimacy that will receive intermediate scrutiny by the court to determine its constitutionality.

Queen's Bench (Q.B.) See King's Bench.

question 1. An issue to be resolved. 2. Something asked; a query.

question of fact; question of law See issue of fact; issue of law.

quia emptores A 1290 English statute that had the effect of facilitating the alienation of fee-simple tenants.

quia timet An equitable remedy to be protected from anticipated future injury where it cannot be avoided by a present action at law.

quick assets Cash and assets readily convertible into cash (other than inventory).

quid pro quo Something for something; giving one thing for another.

> Quid pro quo sexual harassment exists where employer conditions employment benefit upon sexual favors. *Brewer*, 122 Ohio App.3d 378 (Ohio App., 1997)

quiet 1. Free from interference or adverse claims. 2. To make secure.

quiet enjoyment Possession of land that is not disturbed by superior ownership rights asserted by a third person.

quiet title action An action to resolve conflicting claims to land. An action asserting an interest in land and calling on others to set forth their claims.

quit 1. To surrender possession. 2. To cease.

qui tam action An action in which a private plaintiff is allowed to sue under a statute that awards part of any penalty recovered to the plaintiff and the remainder to the government.

quitclaim 1. To transfer the extent of one's interest. 2. To surrender a claim.

quitclaim deed A deed that transfers any interest or claim the grantor may have, without warranting that the title is valid.

quittance A release from debt.

quod vide (q.v.) A reference directing the reader elsewhere in the text for more information.

quorum The minimum number of members who must be present in a deliberative body before business may be transacted.

quota 1. An assigned goal; the minimum sought. 2. A proportional part or allotment.

quotation 1. A word-for-word reproduction of text from another source. 2. A statement of current price.

quotient verdict A verdict on damages reached when the jurors agree to average the figures each juror states as his or her individual verdict.

quo warranto A court inquiry (by writ) to determine whether someone exercising government power is legally entitled to do so.

> Quo warranto is limited action designed to prevent continued exercise of unlawfully asserted authority. R.C. § 2733.01. *State ex rel. DeMint*, 76 Ohio App.3d 315 (Ohio App., 1991)

q.v. See quod vide.

R

® The symbol indicating registration of a trademark or service mark with the U.S. Patent and Trademark Office.

race The historical division of humanity by physical characteristics. A grouping based on ancestry or ethnic characteristics.

race notice statute A recording law giving priority to the first party to record, unless this person had notice of an unrecorded prior claim.

race statute A recording law giving priority to the first party to record, even if this person had notice of another's unrecorded prior claim. Also called pure race statute.

racial discrimination Discrimination based on one's race.

racketeer One who commits racketeering.

Racketeer Influenced and Corrupt Organizations Act (RICO) A federal statute imposing civil and criminal penalties for racketeering offenses such as engaging in a pattern of fraud, bribery, extortion, and other acts enumerated in the statute (18 USC § 1961). Some states have enacted similar statutes.

racketeering Crime engaged in as a business or organized enterprise, often involving illegal activity such as extortion, bribery, gambling, prostitution, and drug sales.

raid 1. An effort to entice personnel or customers away from a competitor. 2. A hostile attempt to take over a corporation by share purchases. 3. A sudden attack or forcible entry by law enforcement.

railroad To rush someone through without due care or due process.

rainmaker An attorney who brings fee-generating cases into the office due to his or her contacts or reputation.

raise 1. To increase. 2. To invoke or put forward. 3. To gather or collect. 4. To create or establish.

raise a check To increase the face amount of a check fraudulently.

rake-off A share of profits, often taken as a payoff or bribe.

RAM See reverse annuity mortgage.

ransom Money or other payment sought for the return of illegally detained persons or property.

rape Nonconsensual sexual intercourse.

> No person shall engage in sexual conduct with another when the offender purposely compels the other person to submit by force or threat of force. R.C. § 2907.02(A)(2)

rape shield law A law imposing limits on defendant's use of evidence of the prior sexual experiences of an alleged rape victim.

rap sheet The arrest and conviction record of someone.

rasure Erasing part of a document by scraping.

ratable 1. Able to be evaluated or apportioned. 2. Taxable. 3. Proportionate.

rate 1. Relative value. A measure or degree in relationship to another measure. 2. Cost or price.

> "Rate" means any rate, classification, fare, toll, rental, or charge of a public utility. R.C. § 121.24(A)(7)

rate base The fair value of the property of a utility (or other entity) upon which a reasonable return is allowed.

rate of exchange See exchange (3).

rate of return Earnings or profit as a percentage of an investment.

ratification 1. An adoption or confirmation of a prior act or transaction, making one bound by it. 2. Formal approval.

ratio decidendi The ground, reason, principle, or rule of law that is the basis of a court's decision.

rational basis test A law will be upheld as constitutional if it rationally furthers a legitimate government objective.

> Under a rational basis analysis, a statute will be declared invalid on equal protection grounds only if it bears no rational relation to a legitimate state interest, and no grounds can be conceived to justify it. *Hitch*, 114 Ohio App.3d 229 (Ohio App., 1996)

ravish 1. To rape. 2. To seize and carry away by force.

re In the matter of; concerning or regarding.

reacquired stock See treasury securities (1).

ready, willing, and able Having sufficient funds, capacity, and desire to complete the transaction.

reaffirmation 1. A confirmation or approval of something already agreed to. 2. An agreement by a debtor to pay an otherwise dischargeable debt.

real 1. Pertaining to stationary or fixed property such as land. 2. True or genuine.

real chattel A real property interest that is less than a freehold or fee interest. An example is a lease of land.

real defense A defense such as duress and fraud in the factum that is good against everyone, including a holder in due course.

real estate See real property.

real estate broker An agent or intermediary who negotiates or arranges agreements pertaining to the sale and lease of real property.

"Real estate broker" includes any person, partnership, association, limited liability company, limited liability partnership, or corporation, foreign or domestic, who for another, whether pursuant to a power of attorney or otherwise, and who for a fee, commission, or other valuable consideration, or with the intention, or in the expectation, or upon the promise of receiving or collecting a fee, commission, or other valuable consideration does any of the following: (1) Sells, exchanges, purchases, rents, or leases, or negotiates the sale, exchange, purchase, rental, or leasing of any real estate; . . . R.C. § 4735.01(A)

real estate investment trust (REIT) A business that invests in real estate on behalf of its shareholders.

Real Estate Settlement Procedures Act (RESPA) A federal law on disclosure of settlement costs in the sale of residential property financed by a federally insured lender (12 USC § 2601).

real evidence 1. Evidence that was actually involved in the incident being considered by the court. Also called physical evidence. 2. Evidence produced for inspection at trial.

realization 1. Conversion of an asset into cash. 2. The receipt by a taxpayer of actual economic gain or loss from the disposition of property.

realized gain or loss The difference between the amount realized on the disposition of property and the adjusted basis of the property.

real party in interest The person who benefits from or is harmed by the outcome of the case and who by substantive law has the legal right to enforce the claim in question. Also called party in interest.

real property Land and anything permanently attached or affixed to the land such as buildings, fences, and trees. Also called real estate, realty.

"Real property" includes all lands, including improvements and fixtures thereon, and property of any nature appurtenant thereto, or used in connection therewith, and every estate, interest, right, and use, legal or equitable, therein, including terms for years and liens by way of judgment, mortgage, or otherwise. R.C. § 303.26(J)

realtor A real estate broker or agent, often a member of the National Association of Realtors (*www.realtor.org*).

realty See real property.

reapportionment Redrawing boundaries of a political subdivision to reflect population changes, leading to a reallocation of legislative seats. Also called redistricting.

reargument Another presentation of arguments before the same court.

reason 1. An inducement, motive, or ground for action. 2. The faculty of the mind to form judgments based on logic.

reasonable Sensible and proper under the circumstances. Fair.

reasonable care The degree of care a person of ordinary prudence and intelligence would use under the same or similar circumstances to avoid injury or damage. Also called due care, ordinary care.

reasonable diligence The care and persistence of an ordinarily prudent person under the same or similar circumstances.

reasonable doubt Doubt that would cause prudent people to hesitate before acting in matters of importance to themselves. The standard of proof needed to convict someone of a crime is proof beyond a reasonable doubt.

"Reasonable doubt" is present when the jurors, after they have carefully considered and compared all the evidence, cannot say they are firmly convinced of the truth of the charge. It is a doubt based on reason and common sense. Reasonable doubt is not mere possible doubt, because everything relating to human affairs or depending on moral evidence is open to some possible or imaginary doubt. R.C. § 2901.05(D)

reasonable force Force that an average person of ordinary intelligence in like circumstances would deem necessary.

reasonable man (person) A person who uses ordinary prudence under the circumstances to avoid injury or damage. (A legal guide or standard.) Also called ordinary prudent person.

reasonable suspicion A particularized and objective reason based on specific and articulable facts for suspecting someone of criminal activity.

"Reasonable suspicion" is more than an ill-defined hunch; it must be based upon a particularized and objective basis for suspecting the particular person of criminal activity. *State v. Hunter*, 151 Ohio App.3d 276 (Ohio App., 2002)

reasonable time As much time as is needed, under the particular circumstances involved, to do what a contract or duty requires to be done.

reasonable use A use of one's property that is consistent with zoning rules and does not interfere with the lawful use of surrounding property.

reasonable woman test A female plaintiff states a prima facie case of hostile environment sexual harassment when she alleges conduct that a reasonable woman would consider sufficiently severe or pervasive to alter the conditions of employment and create an abusive working environment.

rebate A reduction or return of part to the price.

rebellion Organized and open resistance, by force and arms, to a government or ruler committed by a subject.

rebut To refute, oppose, or repel.

rebuttable presumption An inference of fact that can be overcome by sufficient contrary evidence. Also called disputable presumption.

rebuttal Arguments or evidence given in reply to explain or counter an opponent..

Rebuttal evidence is that given to explain, refute, or disprove new facts introduced into evidence by the adverse party; it becomes relevant only to challenge the evidence offered by the opponent, and its scope is limited by such evidence. *Sidenstricker*, 158 Ohio App.3d 356 (Ohio App., 2004)

recall 1. Removing a public official from office before the end of his or her term by a vote of the people. 2. A request by the manufacturer to return a defective product. 3. Revocation of a judgment.

recant To repudiate or retract something formally.

recapitalization A change or adjustment in the capital structure (stock, bonds, or other securities) of a corporation.

recaption Retaking chattels once in your possession or custody.

recapture 1. To retake or recover. 2. The recalculation of tax liability in order to remove improperly taken deductions or credits.

receipt 1. Written acknowledgment of receiving something. 2. Taking physical possession of something. 3. Receipts: income, money received.

"Receipt" of goods means taking physical possession of them. R.C. § 1302.01(A)(3)

receivable 1. Awaiting collection. 2. The amount still owed.

receiver A person appointed by the court to manage property in litigation or in the process of bankruptcy.

receivership The condition of a company or individual over whom a receiver has been appointed. See receiver.

receiving stolen property Receiving or controlling stolen movable property of another, knowing that it has been stolen.

recess An interval when business is suspended without adjourning.

recidivism The tendency to return to a life of crime.

recidivist Repeat offender; habitual criminal.

reciprocal 1. Given or owed to each other. 2. Done in return.

reciprocal negative easement When an owner sells a portion of land with a restrictive covenant that benefits the land retained by the owner, the restriction becomes mutual.

"Reciprocal negative easement" doctrine is that, where owner sells a portion of a tract or lots, and conveyances contain restrictive covenants which would be beneficial to land retained by owner, servitude becomes mutual, and during period of restraint owner of lot or tract retained can do nothing forbidden to owner of lot or tract sold. *King*, 88 Ohio App. 213 (Ohio App., 1950)

reciprocal wills See mutual wills (1).

reciprocity A mutual exchange of the same benefits or treatment.

recision See rescission.

recital The formal setting forth of facts or reasons.

reckless Consciously failing to exercise due care but without intending the consequences; wantonly disregarding risks.

reckless disregard Conscious indifference to consequences.

reckless endangerment Creating a substantial risk of major injury or death.

recklessness Knowing but disregarding a substantial risk that an injury or wrongful act may occur.

"Recklessness" is not same as "negligence"; "negligence" consists of mere inadvertence, incompetence, unskillfulness, or failure to take precautions to enable actor adequately to cope with possible or probable future emergency; on other hand, conduct is in reckless disregard of safety of another if actor does act or intentionally fails to do act which it is his duty to other to do, knowing or having reason to know of facts which would lead reasonable man to realize, not only that his conduct creates unreasonable risk of physical harm to another, but also that such risk is substantially greater than that which is necessary to make his conduct negligent. *Ickes*, 110 Ohio App.3d 438 (Ohio App., 1996)

reclamation 1. Converting unusable land into land that is usable. 2. A seller's right to recover possession of goods from an insolvent buyer.

recognition 1. A formal acknowledgment or confirmation. 2. The point at which a tax on gain or loss is accounted for.

recognizance An obligation recorded in court to do some act required by law, e.g., to appear at all court proceedings.

recollection The act of recalling or remembering.

reconciliation 1. The voluntary resumption of full marital relations. 2. The bringing of financial accounts into consistency or agreement.

reconduction 1. Renewing a lease. 2. The forcible return of illegal aliens.

reconsideration A review or reevaluation of a matter.

reconstruction 1. Rebuilding. 2. Re-creating an event.

reconveyance A transfer back. The return of something, e.g., title.

record 1. To make an official note of; to enter in a document. 2. A formal account of some act or event, e.g., a trial. 3. The facts that have been inscribed or stored.

recordation The formal recording of an instrument (e.g., a deed) with a county clerk or other public registry.

record date A date by which a shareholder must officially own shares in order to be entitled to a dividend or to vote.

recorded recollection See past recollection recorded.

recorder 1. An officer appointed to maintain public records, e.g., recorder of deeds. 2. A magistrate or judge with limited jurisdiction in some states.

recorder's court A court with limited criminal jurisdiction.

recording act; recording statute A law on recording deeds and other property instruments in order to establish priority among claims.

record owner Anyone recorded in a public registry as the owner.

record title See paper title.

recoupment 1. The defendant's right to a deduction from the plaintiff's damages due to plaintiff's breach of duty arising from the same contract. 2. An equitable remedy that permits the offset of mutual debts based on the same transaction or occurrence. 3. A reimbursement or recovery.

A "recoupment" is generally defined as a demand arising from the same transaction as the plaintiff's claim. *Akron Nat. Bank & Trust Co.*, 60 Ohio App.2d 13 (Ohio App., 1978)

recourse 1. Turning or appealing for help; a way to enforce a right. 2. The right of a holder of a negotiable instrument to recover against an indorser or other party who is secondarily liable. 3. The right to reach other assets of the debtor if the collateral is insufficient.

recover 1. To obtain by court judgment or legal process. 2. To have restored; to regain possession.

recovery 1. That which is awarded by court judgment or legal process. 2. Restoration.

recrimination 1. A charge by the accused against the accuser. 2. An accusation that the party seeking the divorce has committed a serious marital wrong that in itself is a ground for divorce.

recross-examination Another cross-examination of a witness after redirect examination.

recusal A judge's (or other decision-maker's) removal of him or herself from a matter because of a conflict of interest. Also called recusation. The verb is recuse.

redaction Revising or editing a text. Removing confidential or inappropriate parts of a text.

reddendum A provision in a deed in which the grantor reserves something out of what had been granted (e.g., rent).

redeemable bond A bond that the issuer may call back for payment before its maturity date. Also called callable bond.

redemption 1. Buying back; reclaiming or regaining possession by paying a specific price. Recovering what was mortgaged. 2. The repurchase of a security by the issuing corporation. 3. Converting shares into cash.

> "Redemption" of a security is merely a repurchase by the issuing corporation. *Dunbar*, 100 Ohio Misc.2d 1 (Ohio Com.Pl., 1998)

red herring 1. A diversion from the main issue; an irrelevant issue. 2. A preliminary prospectus.

redhibition Avoiding a sale due to a major defect in the thing sold.

redirect examination Another direct examination of a witness after he or she was cross-examined.

rediscount rate The rate the Federal Reserve System charges a member bank on a loan secured by paper the bank has already resold.

redistricting See reapportionment.

redlining 1. The discriminatory practice of denying credit or insurance to geographic areas due to the income, race, or ethnicity of its residents. 2. Showing the portions of a earlier draft of a text that have been stricken out.

redraft A second note or bill drafted by the original drawer after the first draft has been dishonored.

redress Damages, equitable relief, or other remedy.

reductio ad absurdum Disproving an argument by showing that it leads to an absurd consequence or conclusion.

reduction to practice The point in time at which an invention is sufficiently tested to demonstrate it will work for its intended purpose.

redundancy Needless repetition; superfluous matter in a pleading.

reentry Retaking possession of land.

reexchange The expenses incurred due to a dishonor of a bill of exchange in a foreign country.

refer To send for further consideration or action.

referee A person to whom a judge refers a case for specific tasks, e.g., to take testimony and to file a report with the court.

referee in bankruptcy A court-appointed officer who performs administrative and judicial functions in bankruptcy cases.

reference 1. The act of referring or sending a case for further consideration or action. 2. A source of information. 3. A citation in a document.

referendum The electorate's power to give final approval to an existing provision of the constitution or statute of the legislature.

refinance To replace one loan for another on different terms.

reformation An equitable remedy to correct a writing so that it embodies the actual intent of the parties.

> Reformation is the modification of an instrument to express the actual intent of the parties. *Butler Cty. Bd. of Commrs.*, 145 Ohio App.3d 454 (Ohio App., 2001)

reformatory A correctional institution for youthful offenders.

refreshing memory or recollection See present recollection refreshed.

refugee One seeking refuge in one country after being unwilling or unable to return to another.

refund 1. The return of an overpayment. 2. The return of the price paid for the returned product. 3. To finance again; to refinance.

refunding Refinancing a debt. Replacing a bond with a new bond issue.

reg. See regulation.

regent 1. A member of the governing board of a school. 2. A governor or ruler.

regime 1. A system of rules. 2. The current government.

register 1. To record formally. 2. To enroll. 3. A book containing official facts. 4. One who keeps official records. 5. A probate judge.

> The "Register of Ohio" is an electronic publication that functions as a gazette to which members of the public may readily resort for notice of and information about rule-making processes. The director of the legislative service commission shall publish the register. R.C. § 103.051

registered bond See registered security.

registered check A check guaranteed by a bank for a customer who provides funds for its payment.

registered mail Mail that is numbered and tracked by the U.S. Postal Service to monitor a safe delivery.

registered representative A representative who meets the requirements of the Securities and Exchange Commission to sell securities to the public.

registered security 1. A stock, bond, or other security whose owner is recorded (registered) by the issuer. 2. A security for sale for which a registration statement has been filed.

register of ships A customs list containing data on vessels, e.g., their owner and country of registration.

registrar The official in charge of keeping records.

registration Inserting something in an official record; formally applying or enrolling. The process by which persons or institutions list their names on an official roster.

registration statement A statement disclosing relevant financial and management data to potential investors in the securities of a company.

registry 1. A book or list kept for recording or registering documents or facts, e.g., a deed, the nationality of a ship. 2. A probate judge.

regressive tax A tax whose rate decreases as the tax base increases.

regs. See regulation.

regular course of business See course of business.

regular session One of the meetings scheduled at fixed times.

regulate To adjust or control by rule, method, or principle.

regulation (reg.) 1. A rule governing conduct; the management of conduct by rules. 2. An administrative agency's rule or order that carries out statutes or executive orders that govern the agency.

Regulation D A regulation of the Securities and Exchange Commission governing the limited offer and sale of unregistered securities.

regulatory agency A government agency that regulates an area of public concern and that can implement statutes by issuing regulations.

regulatory offense 1. A crime created by statute. 2. A minor offense.

regulatory taking Government regulation that deprives a private owner of all or substantially all practical uses of his or her property.

Regulatory taking refers to situations in which government exercises its "police powers" to restrict use of land or other forms of property. *City of Cincinnati v. Chavez Properties*, 117 Ohio App.3d 2691 (Ohio App., 1996)

rehabilitation 1. Restoration of credibility to an impeached witness. 2. Improving the character of an offender to prevent recidivism. 3. A reorganizing of debts in bankruptcy.

rehearing An additional hearing to correct an error or oversight.

reimburse 1. To pay back. 2. To indemnify.

reinstate To restore; to place again in a former condition or office.

reinsurance A contract by which one insurer (called the reinsurer) insures all or part of the risks of another insurer; insurance for insurers.

REIT See real estate investment trust.

rejection A refusal to accept something, e.g., an offer, performance.

rejoinder Defendant's response to a plaintiff's reply or replication.

relation back The rule that an act done at one time is considered by a fiction of the law to have been done at a prior time.

relative A person related by blood or marriage.

relator 1. See ex rel. 2. An informer. 3. One who applies for a writ.

release 1. To set free from custody. 2. To discharge or relinquish a claim against another. 3. To allow something to be communicated or published. 4. The giving up of a right, claim, interest, or privilege.

release on own recognizance (ROR) See personal recognizance.

relevance Logically connected to the matter at hand. Being relevant.

relevant Logically tending to establish or disprove a fact. Pertinent.

Relevant evidence is evidence which has any tendency to make existence of any fact more or less probable; all relevant evidence is admissible, unless specifically excluded. Ohio Rules of Evid., Rules 401, 402. *In re Dukes*, 81 Ohio App.3d 145 (Ohio App., 1991)

reliance Faith or trust felt by someone; dependence on someone.

relict A widow or widower.

reliction The gradual alteration of land by withdrawing water.

relief 1. Redress sought from a court. 2. Assistance to the poor.

religion A belief system of faith and worship, often involving a supernatural being or power.

rem See in rem.

remainder 1. A future estate or interest arising in someone other than the grantor or transferor (or the heirs of either) that will take effect upon the natural termination of the prior estate. 2. That which is left over; the remaining portions not otherwise disposed of.

A "remainder" is a future interest created in some person other than the grantor or transferor. *Folden*, 188 N.E.2d 193 (Ohio App., 1962)

remainderman One who holds or is entitled to a remainder.

remand 1. To send back for further action. 2. To return to custody.

remediable Capable of being remedied.

remedial 1. Intended to correct wrongs and abuses. 2. Providing an avenue of redress.

remedial action 1. Action to solve long-term environmental damage. 2. Action to redress an individual wrong.

remedial statute 1. A statute that provides a remedy or means to enforce a right. 2. A statute designed to correct an existing law.

remedy 1. The means by which a right is enforced or the violation of a right is prevented or redressed. 2. To correct.

remise To give up or release.

remission 1. Canceling or relinquishing a debt or claim. 2. Pardon or forgiveness.

remit 1. To send or forward. 2. To transmit (money). 3. To refer for further action. 4. To cancel or excuse; to pardon. 5. To mitigate.

remittance Money sent (or the sending of money) as payment.

remitter 1. A person who purchases an instrument from its issuer if the instrument is payable to an identified person other than the purchaser. 2. The relation back of a later defective title to an earlier valid one. 3. Sending a case back to a lower court. 4. One who sends payment to another.

remittitur The power of the court to order a new trial unless a party agrees to reduce the jury verdict in its favor by a stated amount.

Remittitur is a device whereby a trial court may reduce an excessive jury award. *Burke*, 123 Ohio App.3d 98 (Ohio App., 1997)

remonstrance A statement of grievances or reasons against something.

remote 1. Removed in relation, space, or time. 2. Minor or slight.

remote cause 1. A cause too removed in time from the event. 2. A cause that some independent force took advantage of to produce what was not the probable or natural effect of the original act.

removal The transfer of a person or thing from one place to another, e.g., transfer of a case from one court to another.

render To pronounce or deliver. To report formally.

rendition 1. Returning a fugitive to a state where he or she is wanted. 2. Making or delivering a formal decision.

renewal A reestablishment of a legal duty or relationship.

renounce To repudiate or abandon.

rent Cash or other consideration (often paid at intervals) for the use of property.

"Gross rents" means the actual sum of money or other consideration payable for the use or possession of property. R.C. § 5733.056(A)(9)

rent-a-judging A method of alternate dispute resolution in which the parties hire a private person (e.g., a retired judge) to resolve their dispute.

rental 1. Something rented. 2. Rent to be paid.

rent strike An organized effort by tenants to withhold rent until grievances are resolved, e.g., repair of defective conditions.

renunciation The abandonment or waiver of a right or venture.

renvoi The doctrine under which the court of the forum, in resorting to a foreign law, adopts the rules of the foreign law as to conflict of laws, which rules may in turn refer the court back to the law of the forum.

reopen To allow new evidence to be introduced in a trial that was completed. To review a closed case.

reorganization A financial restructuring of a corporation for purposes of achieving bankruptcy protection, tax benefits, or efficiency.

reorganization plan A corporation's proposal to a bankruptcy court for restructuring under Chapter 11.

rep. See report, reporter, representative, republic.

reparable injury An injury for which money compensation is adequate.

reparation Compensation for an injury or wrong. Expiation.

repeal The express or implied abrogation of a law by a legislative body. Rescind.

repeat offender Someone convicted of a crime more than once.

replacement cost The current cost of creating a substantially equivalent structure or other asset.

replevin An action to recover possession of personal property wrongfully held or detained and damages incidental to the detention.

> Writ of replevin enforces legal right of immediate possession of specified property, which is granted to one who has right to that immediate possession against another who is holding property wrongfully or unlawfully. *State ex rel. Jividen*, 112 Ohio App.3d 458 (Ohio App., 1996)

replevin bond A bond posted by the plaintiff when seeking replevin.

replevy To regain possession of personal property through replevin.

replication A plaintiff's response to the defendant's plea or answer.

reply A plaintiff's response to the defendant's counterclaim, plea, or answer.

reply brief The appellate brief filed by the appellant in response to the appellee's brief. A brief responding to an opponent's brief.

repo 1. An agreement to buy back a security. 2. See repossession.

report (rep.) 1. A written account of a court decision. 2. A volume (or set of volumes) of court opinions. Also called reports. 3. A volume (or set of volumes) of administrative decisions. 4. A formal account or descriptive statement.

reporter (rep.) 1. The person in charge of reporting the decisions of a court. 2. The person who takes down and transcribes proceedings. 3. A volume (or set of volumes) of court opinions. Also called case reports.

reporter's privilege See journalist's privilege (1).

reports See report (2).

repose See statute of repose.

repossession (repo) The taking back of property, e.g., a creditor's seizure of property bought on credit by a debtor in default.

representation 1. The act of representing or acting on behalf of another. 2. A statement of fact expressed by words or conduct, often made to induce another's conduct. 3. See also per stirps.

representative (rep.) 1. One who acts on behalf of another. 2. A legislator. 3. Serving as an example.

representative action See derivative action; class action.

reprieve A stay or postponement in carrying out a sentence.

> "Reprieve" means the temporary suspension by the governor of the execution of a sentence or prison term. The governor may grant a reprieve without the consent of and against the will of the convict. R.C. § 2967.01(D)

reprimand An official declaration that an attorney's conduct was unethical. The declaration does not affect the attorney's right to practice law. A *private reprimand* is not disclosed to the public; a *public reprimand* is.

reprisal Action taken in retaliation.

reproductive rights Rights pertaining to one's reproductive and sexual life, e.g., using contraceptives, access to abortion.

republic Government in which supreme authority lies with the voters who act through elected representatives. A republican form of government.

republication 1. Repetition of a statement already published or communicated once. 2. Steps that reestablish a revoked will, e.g., adding a codicil to it.

repudiation 1. Denial or rejection. 2. Declaring a refusal to perform.

repugnant Incompatible; irreconcilably inconsistent.

reputation The views or esteem others have of a person.

request for admission A method of pretrial discovery in which one party asks another to admit or deny the substance of a statement, e.g., a statement of fact.

request for instructions A party's request that the trial judge provide the jury with the instructions stated in the request.

request for production A method of pretrial discovery consisting of a demand that the other side make available documents and other tangible things for inspection, copying, and testing.

> Production of documents and things for inspection, copying, testing and entry upon land for inspection and other purposes. Ohio Civ. R. Rule 34

requirements contract A contract in which the buyer agrees to buy all of its goods and services from a seller, which agrees to fill these needs during the period of the contract.

requisition 1. A formal request or demand. 2. The seizure of property by the state.

res 1. The subject matter of a trust or will. 2. A thing or object, a status.

res adjudicata See res judicata.

resale A sale of goods after another buyer of those goods breaches its contract to buy them.

resale price maintenance A form of vertical price-fixing by which a manufacturer sets the price at which its buyers resell to others.

rescind 1. To annul or repeal. 2. To cancel a contract.

rescission A party's cancellation of a contract because of a material breach by the other party or by mutual agreement. Also spelled recision.

rescript 1. A direction from a court to a clerk on how to dispose of a case. 2. The decision of the appellate court sent to the trial court.

rescue doctrine An injured rescuer can recover from the original tortfeasor who negligently caused the event that precipitated the rescue.

> Under rescue doctrine, one injured in an attempt to rescue a person in danger may recover from the party negligently causing the danger to the same extent as the person being rescued, and recovery is precluded if the rescue is attempted in a rash or reckless manner. *Moore*, 118 Ohio Misc.2d 112 (Ohio Com.Pl., 1998)

reservation 1. A right or interest created for the grantor in land granted to the grantee. 2. A tract of land to which a Native American tribe retains the original title or which is set aside for its use. 3. A condition through a limitation, qualification, or exception.

reserve 1. To keep back or retain. 2. A fund set aside to cover future expenses, losses, or claims.

reserve banks Member banks of the Federal Reserve System.

reserve clause A contract clause giving club owners a continuing and exclusive right to the services of a professional athlete.

reserved point See point reserved.

reserved powers Powers not delegated to the federal government by the U.S. Constitution nor prohibited by it to the states and hence are reserved to the states or to the people. (U.S. Const. amend. X.)

reserve price The minimum auction price a seller will accept.

res gestae declarations Spontaneous or unfiltered statements made in the surrounding circumstances of an event (e.g., excited utterances) are sometimes admissible as exceptions to the hearsay rule.

residence 1. Living or remaining in a particular locality for more than a transitory period but without the intent to stay there indefinitely. If this intent existed, the place would be a domicile. Sometimes, however, residence and domicile are treated as synonyms. 2. A fixed abode or house.

> Term "residence," as used in statute providing that divorce action can be instituted only by resident of state, requires both actual residence within state and intention to make state permanent home. R.C. § 3105.03. *Hager*, 79 Ohio App.3d 239 (Ohio App., 1992)

residency The place where one has a residence.

resident One who occupies a dwelling and has an ongoing physical presence therein. This person may or may not be a domiciliary.

resident agent One authorized to accept service of process for another.

resident alien A noncitizen who legally establishes a long-term residence or domicile in this country.

residual 1. Pertaining to that which is left over or what lingers. 2. Payment for reuse of a protected work.

residuary What is left over. See also residuary estate.

residuary bequest A bequest of the residuary estate.

> A "residuary bequest" is a gift of the remainder of the estate after all debts, expenses, and bequests are satisfied. *In re Estate of Oberstar*, 126 Ohio App.3d 30 (Ohio App., 1998)

residuary clause A clause in a will disposing of the residuary estate.

residuary devise A devise of the residuary estate.

residuary estate The remainder of an estate after all debts and claims are paid and after all specific bequests (gifts) are satisfied. Also called residuary, residue, residuum.

residuary legacy A legacy of the residuary estate.

residuary legatee The person who receives the residuary estate.

residue What is left over. See also residuary estate.

residuum What is left over. See also residuary estate.

res inter alios acta ("a thing done among others") A person cannot be affected by the words or acts of others with whom he or she is in no way connected, and for whose words or acts he or she is not legally responsible.

res ipsa loquitur ("the thing speaks for itself") An inference of the defendant's negligence arises when the event producing the harm (a) was of a kind that ordinarily does not occur in the absence of someone's negligence, (b) was caused by an agency or instrumentality within the defendant's exclusive control, and (c) was not due to any voluntary action or contribution on the part of the plaintiff.

> Doctrine of "res ipsa loquitur" permits the jury to draw an inference of negligence where (1) the instrumentality causing the injury was under the exclusive control of the defendant, and (2) the injury occurred under such circumstances that in the ordinary course of events it would not have occurred if ordinary care had been observed. *Brokamp*, 132 Ohio App.3d 850 (Ohio App., 1999)

resisting arrest Intentionally preventing a peace officer from effecting a lawful arrest.

res judicata ("a thing adjudicated") A final judgment on the merits will preclude the same parties from later relitigating the same claim and any other claim based on the same facts or transaction that could have been raised in the first suit but was not. Also called claim preclusion.

res nova A question the courts have not yet addressed.

resolution 1. An expression of the opinion or will of an assembly or group. 2. A decision or authorization. The verb is to resolve.

resort A place or destination to obtain redress or assistance.

RESPA See Real Estate Settlement Procedures Act.

respite A delay, e.g., a temporary suspension of the execution of a sentence, additional time to pay a debt.

respondeat superior ("let the master answer") An employer or principal is responsible (liable) for the wrongs committed by an employee or agent within the scope of employment or agency.

> The doctrine of "respondeat superior" holds an employer liable for its employee's torts committed in the scope of employment. *Groob*, 155 Ohio App.3d 510 (Ohio App., 2003)

respondent 1. The party against whom a claim, petition, or bill is filed. 2. The party against whom an appeal is brought; the appellee.

responsibility 1. Being accountable, liable, or at fault. 2. A duty.

responsible bidder An experienced, solvent, available contract bidder.

responsive Constituting an answer or response; nonevasive.

responsive pleading A pleading that replies to a prior pleading of an opponent.

rest To indicate to the court that a party has presented all of the evidence he or she intends to submit at this time.

Restatements Treatises of the American Law Institute (e.g., Restatement of Torts 2d) that state the law and indicate changes in the law that the Institute would like to see implemented (*www.ali.org*).

restitution 1. Making good or giving an equivalent value for any loss, damage, or injury. 2. An equitable remedy to prevent unjust enrichment.

restraining order A court order not to do a threatened act, e.g., to harass someone, to transfer assets. Also called protection order, protective order.

> The purpose of a "preliminary" or "temporary injunction" or "restraining order" is to preserve the status quo of the parties and their rights pending final adjudication of the cause upon the merits. *City of Cleveland v. Division 268 of Amalgamated Ass'n of St. Elec. Ry.*, 84 Ohio App. 43 (Ohio App., 1948)

restraint Restriction, prohibition; confinement.

restraint of marriage An inducement or obligation not to marry that results from a condition attached to a gift.

restraint of trade Contracts or combinations that tend to or are designed to eliminate competition, artificially set prices, or otherwise hamper a free market in commerce.

restraint on alienation A provision in an instrument (e.g., a deed) that prohibits or restricts transfers of the property by the grantee.

restricted security Stock whose sale to the public is restricted. The stock is not registered with the Securities and Exchange Commission. Also called letter stock.

restrictive covenant 1. A restriction created by covenant or agreement (e.g., in a deed) on the use of land. Also called equitable servitude. 2. See covenant not to compete.

> Restrictive covenant means any specification limiting the transfer, rental, lease, or other use of any housing accommodations because of race, color, religion, sex, familial status, national origin, disability, or ancestry, or any limitation based upon affiliation with or approval by any person, directly or indirectly, employing race, color, religion, sex, familial status, national origin, disability, or ancestry as a condition of affiliation or approval. R.C. § 4112.01(A)(11)

restrictive indorsement An indorsement that limits or conditions the further negotiability of the instrument.

resulting trust A remedy used when a person makes a disposition of property under circumstances that raise the inference that he or she did not intend to transfer a beneficial interest to the person taking or holding the property. Also called implied trust, presumptive trust.

resulting use An implied use remaining with the grantor in a conveyance without consideration.

retailer A business that sells goods to the ultimate consumer.

retain 1. To engage the services of or employ. 2. To hold.

retainage A portion of the contract price withheld to assure that the contractor will satisfy its obligations and complete the project.

retained earnings See earned surplus.

retainer 1. The act of hiring or engaging the services of someone, usually a professional. 2. An amount of money (or other property) a client pays a professional as a deposit or advance against future fees, costs, and expenses of providing services.

retaliatory eviction An eviction because the tenant has complained about the leased premises.

> Landlord's seeking to evict tenant for failure to provide landlord with a passkey for a lock installed by the tenant is a "retaliatory eviction." R.C. § 5321.02. *Spencer*, 22 Ohio Misc.2d 52 (Ohio Mun., 1985)

retirement 1. Voluntarily withdrawing from one's occupation or career. 2. Taking out of circulation.

retirement plans Pension or other benefit plans for retirement.

retraction Withdrawing a declaration, accusation, or promise. Recanting.

retraxit Voluntary withdrawal of a lawsuit that cannot be rebrought.

retreat rule Before using deadly force in self-defense against a deadly attack, there is a duty to withdraw or retreat if this is a safe alternative, unless (under the castle doctrine) the attack occurs in one's home or business.

retrial A new trial of a previously tried case.

retribution Punishment that is deserved.

retroactive Applying or extending to a time prior to enactment or issuance. Also called retrospective.

retrocession Ceding back something, e.g., title, jurisdiction.

retrospective See retroactive.

return 1. A report of a court officer on what he or she did with a writ or other court instrument. 2. Profit. 3. See tax return.

return day The day on which a litigation event must occur, e.g., file an answer, appear in court.

> Return day as used in statute providing for substituted service of process in automobile accident cases and requiring that copy of summons be left at secretary of state's office at least 15 days before return day thereof is the day set forth in summons on which process is returnable and not day on which return may actually be made. R.C. §§ 2703.05, 2703.20. *George*, 4 Ohio App.2d 116 (Ohio App., 1964)

return of service See proof of service.

rev'd See reversed.

revenue Gross income; total receipts.

revenue bond A government bond payable by public funds.

Revenue Procedure The position of the Internal Revenue Service on procedural requirements for matters before it.

Revenue Ruling (Rev. Rul.) The opinion of the Internal Revenue Service of how the tax law applies to a specific transaction.

revenue stamp A stamp used to certify that a tax has been paid.

reversal An appellate court's setting aside of a lower court decision.

reverse annuity mortgage (RAM) A mortgage on a residence in which the borrower receives periodic income and the loan is repaid when the property is sold or the borrower dies. Also called reverse mortgage.

reversed (rev'd) Overturned on appeal.

reverse discrimination Discrimination against members of a majority group, usually because of affirmative action for a minority group.

reverse mortgage See reverse annuity mortgage.

reverse stock split Calling in all outstanding shares and reissuing fewer shares with greater value.

reversible error See prejudicial error.

reversion The undisposed portion of an estate remaining in a grantor when he or she conveys less than his or her whole estate and, therefore, retains a portion of the title. The residue of the estate left with the grantor.

A reversion is the residue of an estate left in grantor or other transferor, to commence in possession after determination of some particular estate transferred by him; reversion operates only by operation of law and is a vested right. *Long*, 45 Ohio St.2d 165 (Ohio 1976)

reversionary interest The interest that a person has in the reversion of property. See reversion. Any future interest left in a transferor.

reversioner A person who is entitled to an estate in reversion.

revert To turn back; to return to.

reverter See possibility of reverter.

revest To vest again with a power or interest.

rev'g Reversing.

review 1. To examine or go over a matter again. 2. The power of a court to examine the correctness of what a lower tribunal has done. Short for judicial review (see this phrase).

Revised Statutes (R.S.)(Rev. Stat.) A collection of statutes that have been revised, rearranged, or reenacted as a whole.

revival Renewing the legal force or effectiveness of something.

revocable Susceptible of being withdrawn, canceled, or invalidated.

revocable trust A trust that the maker (settlor) can cancel or revoke.

Revocable trust is a trust that can be revoked by the grantor or the beneficiary. R.C. § 5111.151(B)(9)

revocation Canceling, voiding, recalling, or destroying something.

revolving credit An extension of credit to customers who may use it as desired up to a specified dollar limit.

Rev. Rul. See Revenue Ruling.

Rev. Stat. See Revised Statutes.

RFP Request for production; request for proposals.

Richard Roe See John Doe.

RICO See Racketeer Influenced and Corrupt Organizations Act.

rider An amendment or addition attached to a legislative bill, insurance policy, or other document.

right 1. Morally, ethically, or legally proper. 2. A legal power, privilege, immunity, or protected interest one can claim.

right-and-wrong test See insanity (4).

right of action The right to bring a suit. A right that can be enforced.

right of common See profit à pendre.

right of election See election by spouse.

right of first refusal A right to equal the terms of another offer.

Right of first refusal is a preemptive right requiring the owner to offer the property first to the holder of the right; it differs from an "option" because the grantee of a right of first refusal cannot compel the owner to sell the property as the grantee can with an option. *Beder*, 129 Ohio App.3d 188 (Ohio App., 1998)

right of privacy See invasion of privacy.

right of redemption 1. A mortgagor's right to redeem property after it has been foreclosed. 2. See equity of redemption.

right of re-entry The estate that the grantor may acquire again upon breach of a condition under which it was granted.

right of survivorship A joint tenant's right to receive the entire estate upon the death of the other joint tenant.

Co-owners with right of survivorship includes joint tenants, tenants by the entireties, and other co-owners of real or personal property, insurance or other policies, or bank or other accounts held under circumstances that entitle one or more persons to the whole of the property or account on the death of the other person or persons. R.C. § 2105.31(A)

right of way 1. The right to pass over the land of another. 2. The right in traffic to pass or proceed first.

right to bear arms The Second Amendment right "to keep and bear arms."

right-to-convey covenant See covenant of seisin.

right to counsel A constitutional right to an appointed attorney in some criminal and juvenile delinquency cases when the accused cannot afford private counsel.

right to die A right of a competent, terminally ill adult to refuse medical treatment.

right to travel A constitutional right to travel freely between states.

right-to-work law A state law declaring that employees are not required to join a union as a condition of receiving or retaining a job.

rigor mortis Muscular rigidity or stiffening shortly after death.

riot Three or more persons assembled together for a common purpose and disturbing the peace by acting in a violent or tumultuous manner.

riparian right The right of owners of land adjoining a waterway to make reasonable use of the water, e.g., for ingress, egress, and fishing.

ripeness doctrine A court will decline to address a claim unless the case presents definite and concrete issues, a real and substantial controversy exists, and there is a present need for adjudication. See also justiciable.

risk The danger or hazard of a loss or injury occurring.

Risk means a significant possibility, as contrasted with a remote possibility, that a certain result may occur or that certain circumstances may exist. R.C. § 2901.01(A)(7)

risk capital An investment of money or property in a business, often a new venture involving high risk. See also venture capital.

risk of loss Responsibility for loss, particularly during transfer of goods. The danger of bearing this responsibility.

risk of nonpersuasion See burden of persuasion.

robbery Unlawfully taking property from the person of another (or in his or her presence) by the use of violence or threats.

> Whoever by force or violence or by putting in fear steals and takes from the person of another anything of value is guilty of robbery. *State v. Rogers*, 64 Ohio App. 39 (Ohio App., 1938)

Robert's Rules of Order Rules for conducting meetings. A parliamentary manual.

rogatory letters See letter rogatory.

roll 1. The record of official proceedings. 2. An official list.

rollover 1. Refinancing or renewing a short-term loan. 2. Reinvesting funds in a plan that qualifies for the same tax treatment.

Roman Law The legal system and laws of ancient Rome that is the foundation of civil law in some European countries.

root of title The recorded conveyance that begins a chain-of-title search on specific real property.

> "Root of title" means that conveyance or other title transaction in the chain of title of a person, purporting to create the interest claimed by such person, upon which he relies as a basis for the marketability of his title, and which was the most recent to be recorded as of a date forty years prior to the time when marketability is being determined. R.C. § 5301.47(E)

ROR Release on own recognizance. See personal recognizance.

ROTH IRA An individual retirement account with nondeductible contributions but tax-free distributions after age 59½.

round lot The unit of trading securities, e.g., 100 shares.

royalty 1. Payment for each use of a work protected by copyright or patent. 2. Payment for the right to extract natural resources.

R.S. See Revised Statutes.

rubric 1. The title of a statute. 2. A rule. 3. A category. 4. A preface.

rule 1. An established standard, guide, or regulation. 2. A court procedure. 3. The controlling authority. 4. To decide a point of law.

rule against accumulations Limits on a trust's accumulation of income.

rule against perpetuities No interest is valid unless it must vest, if at all, within 21 years (plus a period of gestation) after the death of some life or lives in being (i.e., alive) at the time the interest was created.

rule in Shelley's case When in the deed or other instrument an estate of freehold is given to a person and a remainder to his or her heirs in fee or in tail, that person takes the entire estate—a fee simple absolute.

> When lands, tenements, or hereditaments are given by deed or will to a person for his life, and after his death to his heirs in fee, the conveyance shall vest an estate for life only in such first taker and a remainder in fee simple in his heirs. If the remainder is given to the heirs of the body of the life tenant, the conveyance shall vest an estate for life only in such first taker and a remainder in fee simple in the heirs of his body. The rule in Shelley's case is abolished by this section and shall not be given effect. R.C. § 2107.49

rule in Wild's case If X devises land to Y and Y's children, the devise is a fee tail (if Y has no children at the time of the devise) but a joint tenancy (if Y has children at that time).

rulemaking The process and power of an administrative agency to make rules and regulations.

rule nisi See decree nisi.

rule of completeness A party may introduce the whole of a statement if any part is introduced by the opposing party.

rule of four The United States Supreme Court will accept a case on certiorari if at least four justices vote to do so.

rule of law 1. A legal principle or ruling. 2. Supremacy of law.

rule of lenity When there is ambiguity in a criminal statute, particularly as to punishment, doubts are resolved in favor of the defendant.

> Except as otherwise provided in division (C) or (D) of this section, sections of the Revised Code defining offenses or penalties shall be strictly construed against the state, and liberally construed in favor of the accused. R.C. § 2901.04(A)

rule of reason 1. In antitrust cases, the issue is whether the restraint's anticompetitive effects substantially outweigh the procompetitive effects for which the restraint is reasonably necessary. 2. A requirement to consider pertinent evidence and reasonable alternatives in decision making.

rules committee A legislative committee establishing agendas and procedures for considering proposed legislation.

rules of professional conduct See Model Rules of Professional Conduct.

ruling A judicial or administrative decision.

run 1. To apply or be effective. 2. To expire because of elapsed time. 3. To accompany or go with a conveyance.

runaway shop An employer who relocates or transfers work for antiunion reasons.

runner 1. One who solicits business, especially accident cases. 2. An employee who delivers and files papers.

running account A continuous record kept to show all the transactions (charges and payments) between a debtor and creditor.

running with the land See covenant running with the land.

S

sabotage Willful destruction of property or interference with normal operations of a government or employer.

safe harbor Protection from liability if acting in good faith

said Before mentioned; aforementioned.

sailor's will See military will.

salable Fit to be offered for sale. Merchantable.

salary Compensation for services paid at regular intervals.

> A fixed compensation which is paid at stated times for services rendered. *Pleasants*, 27 Ohio App.2d 191 (Ohio App., 1971)

sale The transfer of title to property for a consideration or price. A contract for this transfer.

sale and leaseback See leaseback.

sale by sample A sale of goods in quantity or bulk with the understanding that they will conform in quality with a sample.

sale in gross A sale of land in which the boundaries are identified but the quantity of land is unspecified or deemed to be immaterial.

sale on approval A conditional sale that is absolute only if the buyer is satisfied with the goods, whether or not they are defective.

sale or return A sale to a merchant buyer who can return any unsold goods (even if not defective) if they were received for resale.

sales tax A tax on the sale of goods and services, computed as a percentage of the purchase price.

> The "sales tax" is an excise tax levied on each retail sale made in Ohio. R.C. §§ 5739.01–5739.31. *Ellwood*, 98 Ohio St.3d 424 (Ohio 2003)

salvage 1. Property saved or remaining after a casualty. 2. Rescue of assets from loss. 3. Payment for saving a ship or its cargo.

salvage value An asset's value after its useful life for the owner has ended.

same evidence test When the same acts violate two distinct statutory provisions, the double-jeopardy test of whether there are two offenses or one is whether each provision requires proof of a fact the other does not.

sanction 1. A penalty for a violation. 2. Approval or authorization.

S&L See savings and loan association.

sane Of sound mind; able to distinguish right from wrong.

sanitary Pertaining to health and hygiene.

sanity The condition of having a sound mind.

sanity hearing A hearing to determine fitness to stand trial or whether institutionalization is needed.

satisfaction The discharge or performance of a legal obligation.

> Satisfaction is a technical term in its application to judgment and means payment of money due and all things come by judgment. *Dorger*, 4 Ohio App.2d 106 (Ohio App., 1965)

satisfaction contract A contract in which the stated standard of performance is the satisfaction of one of the parties (e.g., a contract giving an employer sole discretion to decide if an employee should be terminated for unacceptable work).

satisfaction of judgment 1. Full payment or compliance with a judgment. 2. A document so stating.

satisfaction piece A statement by the parties that the obligation between them has been paid or satisfied.

save harmless See hold harmless.

saving clause 1. A clause in a statute that preserves certain rights, remedies, privileges, or claims. 2. See severability clause. 3. See saving-to-suitors clause.

savings and loan association (S&L) A financial institution that specializes in making mortgage loans for private homes.

saving-to-suitors clause A statutory clause allowing certain admiralty claims to be brought in nonadmiralty courts. (28 USC § 1333) Also called saving clause.

savings bank trust See Totten trust.

savings bond A United States government bond that cannot be traded.

S.B. See senate bill.

scab A worker who crosses a picket line to work or otherwise acts in disregard of positions or demands of a union. Also called strikebreaker.

scalper One who resells something at an inflated price for a quick profit.

scandalous matter Irrelevant matter in a pleading that casts a derogatory light on someone's moral character or uses repulsive language.

scènes à faire General themes that cannot be copyrighted.

schedule A written list or plan. An inventory.

> "Schedule" means the basic child support schedule set forth in section 3119.021 of the Revised Code. R.C. § 3119.01(B)(12)

scheduled property A list of properties with their values.

scheme A plan of action, often involving deception.

scienter 1. Intent to deceive or mislead. 2. Knowingly done.

> The indictment specifically alleges "scienter" (knowledge). *State v. Lisbon Sales Book Co.*, 176 Ohio St. 482 (Ohio 1964)

sci. fa. See scire facias.

scintilla A minute amount; a trace.

scire facias (sci. fa.) 1. A writ ordering one to appear on a matter of record and show cause why another should not be able to take advantage of that record. 2. The procedure by which a lienholder prosecutes a lien to judgment.

scope of authority An agent's express or implied authorization to act for the principal.

scope of employment That which is foreseeably done by an employee for an employer under the latter's specific or general control.

> For an intentional act committed by an employee to be within the scope of employment, the act must be calculated to facilitate or promote the business for which the servant was employed. *Gebhart*, 106 Ohio App.3d 1 (Ohio App., 1995)

S corporation A corporation whose shareholders are taxed on the income of the corporation. Also called subchapter S corporation.

scrip 1. A substitute for money. 2. A document entitling one to a benefit. 3. A document representing a fraction of a share.

scrip dividend A dividend in the form of the right to receive future issues of stock.

script 1. Handwriting. 2. The original document.

scrivener One who prepares documents. A professional copyist or drafter.

seal An impression or sign to attest the execution of an instrument or to authenticate the document.

sealed bid A bid that is not revealed until all bids are submitted.

sealed records Publicly filed documents that are kept confidential.

> "Sealed record information" means both of the following: (A) With respect to adults, that portion of a record that is not available for criminal justice uses, not supported by fingerprints or other accepted means of positive identification,

or subject to restrictions on dissemination for noncriminal justice purposes pursuant to a court order related to a particular subject or pursuant to a federal or state statute that requires action on a sealing petition filed by a particular record subject; (B) With respect to juveniles, whatever each state determines is a sealed record under its own law and procedure. R.C. § 109.571(21)

sealed verdict A jury verdict not yet officially given to the court.

seaman's will See military will.

search An examination by police of private areas (e.g., one's person, premises, or vehicle) in an attempt to discover evidence of a crime.

search and seizure See unreasonable search.

search warrant A court order allowing a law enforcement officer to search designated areas and to seize evidence of crime found there.

seasonable Within the agreed-upon time; timely; at a reasonable time.

seaworthy Properly constructed and equipped for a sea voyage.

secession The act of withdrawing.

secondary Subordinate; inferior.

secondary authority Any nonlaw a court can rely on in its decision. Writings that describe or explain, but do not constitute, the law.

secondary boycott A boycott of customers or suppliers with whom the union has no labor dispute to induce them to stop dealing with a business with whom the union does have a labor dispute. The boycott can include picketing.

secondary easement An incident to an easement that allows those things necessary to the full enjoyment of the easement.

secondary evidence Evidence that is not the stronger or best evidence.

secondary liability Liability that applies only if the wronged party cannot obtain satisfaction from the person with primary liability.

Secondary liability on part of party seeking indemnification, which will allow implied indemnification, arises in situations where, like vicarious liability, relationship exists between tort-feasors such that one tort-feasor may be held liable for the other's actions, while "primary liability" exists when one is actively negligent or has actual knowledge of dangerous situation and acquiesces in continuance thereof. *Whitney*, 112 Ohio App.3d 511 (Ohio App., 1996)

secondary market A market for previously available goods or services.

secondary meaning Public awareness that a common or descriptive name or symbol identifies the source of a particular product or service.

secondary picketing See secondary boycott.

second-degree murder The unlawful taking of human life without premeditation or other facts that make the crime first-degree murder.

second-look See wait and see.

second mortgage A mortgage with a ranking in priority that is immediately below a first mortgage on the same property.

secretary The corporate officer in charge of keeping official records.

secret partner A partner whose identity is not known by the public.

secta 1. Followers. 2. A lawsuit.

section 1. A subdivision of a law or document. 2. A square mile area.

secundum 1. Second. 2. According to.

secured Backed by collateral, a mortgage, or other security.

secured creditor; secured party A creditor who can reach collateral of the debtor if the latter fails to pay the debt.

"Secured party" means: (a) A person in whose favor a security interest is created or provided for under a security agreement, whether or not any obligation to be secured is outstanding. . . . R.C. § 1309.102(A)(72)

secured transaction A contract in which the seller or lender is a secured creditor.

securities See also security (2).

securities broker One in the business of buying and selling securities for others.

securitize To convert an asset into a security offered for sale.

security 1. Collateral that guarantees a debt or other obligation. 2. A financial instrument that is evidence of a debt interest (e.g., a bond), an ownership/equity interest, (e.g., a stock) or other specially defined rights (e.g., a futures contract). 3. Surety. 4. The state of being secure.

security agreement An agreement that creates or provides for a security interest.

security deposit See deposit (3).

security interest A property interest that secures a payment or the performance of an obligation.

"Security interest" means an interest in personal property or fixtures that secures payment or performance of an obligation. "Security interest" also includes any interest of a consignor and a buyer of accounts, chattel paper, a payment intangible, or a promissory note in a transaction that is subject to Chapter 1309. of the Revised Code. R.C. § 1301.01(KK)(1)

sedition Communicating, agreeing to, or advocating lawlessness, treason, commotions, or revolt against legitimate authority.

seditious libel Libelous statements designed to incite sedition.

seduction Wrongfully inducing another, without the use of force, to engage in sexual relations.

segregation The unconstitutional separation of people based on categories such as race, religion, or nationality.

seise To hold in fee simple.

seisin or **seizin** Possession of land under a claim of freehold estate.

A covenant of "seisin" in a deed is a covenant for title, the word being used as synonymous with "right". *Shewell*, 88 Ohio App. 1 (Ohio App., 1950)

seize To take possession forcibly.

seizure Taking possession of person or property.

select committee A committee set up for a limited or special task.

selective enforcement Enforcing the law primarily against a member of certain groups or classes of people, often arbitrarily.

selective incorporation The process of making only some of the Bill of Rights applicable to the states through the

Fourteenth Amendment. Total incorporation makes all of them applicable.

Selective Service System A federal agency in charge of military registration and, if needed, a draft (*www.sss.gov*).

selectman An elected municipal officer in some towns.

self-authenticating Not needing extrinsic proof of authenticity.

self-dealing Acting to benefit oneself when one should be acting in the interest of another to whom a fiduciary duty is owed.

self-defense The use of force to repel threatened danger to one's person or property.

Self-defense is an affirmative defense that a defendant claims justifies his conduct and "exempts him from liability even if it is conceded that the facts claimed by the prosecution are true." *State v. Robinson*, 132 Ohio App.3d 830 (Ohio App., 1999)

self-employment tax Social security tax on the self-employed.

self-executing Immediately or automatically having legal effect.

self-help Acting to redress a wrong without using the courts.

self-incrimination Acts or declarations by which one implicates oneself in a crime; exposing oneself to criminal prosecution.

self-insurance Funds set aside by a business to cover any loss.

self-proving Not requiring proof outside of the documents themselves.

self-serving declaration An out-of-court statement benefiting the person making it.

sell To transfer an asset by sale.

seller One who sells enters a contract to sell.

"Seller" means a person who sells or contracts to sell goods. R.C. § 1302.01(A)(4)

semble It would appear.

senate The upper chamber of a two-house (bicameral) legislature.

senate bill (S.B.)(S.) A bill pending or before passage in the senate.

senior Higher in age, rank, preference, or priority.

senior interest An interest that is higher in precedence or priority.

seniority Greater rights than others based on length of service.

senior judge A judge with the longest tenure or who is semi-retired.

senior lien A lien on property that has priority over other liens.

senior mortgage A mortgage that has priority over other mortgages.

sentence Punishment imposed by the court on one convicted of a crime.

"Sentence" means the sanction or combination of sanctions imposed by the sentencing court on an offender who is convicted of or pleads guilty to an offense. R.C. § 2929.01(FF)

SEP See simplified employee pension plan.

separability clause See severability clause.

separable Capable of being separated.

separable controversy A dispute that is part of the entire controversy, yet by its nature is independent and can be severed from the whole.

separate Distinct, not joined.

separate but equal Segregated with equal opportunities and facilities.

separate maintenance Support by one spouse to another while separated.

separate property Property acquired by one spouse alone (a) before marriage, (b) during marriage by gift, will, or intestate succession, or (c) during marriage but after separating from the other spouse.

"Separate property" means all real and personal property and any interest in real or personal property that is found by the court to be any of the following: (i) An inheritance by one spouse by bequest, devise, or descent during the course of the marriage; (ii) Any real or personal property or interest in real or personal property that was acquired by one spouse prior to the date of the marriage; . . . (v) Any real or personal property or interest in real or personal property that is excluded by a valid antenuptial agreement. . . . R.C. § 3105.171(6)(a)

separate trial An individual (separate) trial of one of the defendants jointly accused of a crime or of one of the issues in any case.

separation Living separately while still married.

separation agreement A contract between spouses who have separated or who are about to separate in which the terms of their separation (e.g., child custody, property division) are spelled out.

separation of powers The division of government into judicial, legislative, and executive branches with the requirement that each branch refrain from encroaching on the authority of the other two.

sequester 1. To separate or isolate a jury or witness. 2. To seize or take and hold funds or other property. Sometimes called sequestrate.

sequestrate See sequester.

sequestrator One who carries out an order or writ of sequestration.

sergeant at arms An officer who keeps order in a court or legislature.

serial bonds A number of bonds issued at the same time but with different maturity dates.

serial note A promissory note payable in regular installments. Also called installment note.

seriatim One by one in a series; one following after another.

series bonds Groups of bonds usually issued at different times and with different maturity dates but under the same indenture.

serious bodily harm See great bodily injury.

servant One employed to perform service, whose performance is controlled by or subject to the control of the master or employer.

One submitting to directions of an employer as to the details of work and means of accomplishment is a "servant," not an independent contractor. *Snodgrass*, 31 Ohio App. 470 (Ohio App., 1929)

serve To deliver a legal notice or process.

service 1. Delivery of a legal notice or process. 2. Tasks performed for others. 3. To pay interest on.

service by publication Publishing a notice in a newspaper or other media as service of process upon an absent or nonresident defendant.

service charge An added cost or fee for administration or handling.

servicemark (SM) See mark (1).

service of process A formal delivery of notice to a defendant that a suit has been initiated to which he or she must respond.

servient estate; servient tenement The track of land on which an easement is imposed or burdened. Also called servient tenement.

servitude 1. An easement or similar right to use another's land. 2. The condition of forced labor or slavery.

session 1. A continuous sitting of a court, legislature, council, etc. 2. Any time in the day during which such a body sits.

session laws (S.L.; sess.) Uncodified statutes enacted by a legislature during a session, printed chronologically.

set aside 1. To vacate a judgment, order, etc. 2. Set-aside: Something reserved for a special reason.

setback The distance that buildings are set back from property lines.

setoff 1. A defendant's claim against the plaintiff that is independent of the plaintiff's claim. 2. A debtor's right to reduce a debt by what the creditor owes the debtor.

> The "setoff" rule allows parties that owe mutual debts to state the accounts between them, subtract one from the other, and pay only the balance. *Covington*, 149 Ohio App.3d 479 (Ohio App. 10 Dist., 2002)

settlement 1. An agreement resolving a dispute without full litigation. 2. Payment or satisfactory adjustment of an account. 3. Distributing the assets and paying the debts of an estate. 4. See closing.

settlement option Choices available to pay life insurance benefits.

settlor One who makes a settlement of property (e.g., one who creates a trust). Also called trustor.

severability clause A clause in a statute or contract providing that if parts of it are declared invalid, the remaining parts shall continue to be effective. Also called saving clause, separability clause.

several 1. A few. 2. Distinct or separate, e.g., a person's several liability is distinct from (and can be enforced independently of) someone else's liability.

severally Apart from others, separately.

severalty The condition of being separate or distinct.

severance 1. Separating claims or parties. 2. Removing; cutting off.

> "Severance" means the extraction or other removal of a natural resource from the soil or water of this state. R.C. § 5749.01(F)

severance tax A tax on natural resources removed from the land.

sewer service Falsely claiming to have served process.

sex discrimination Discrimination that is gender based.

sexual abuse; sexual assault Rape or other unlawful sexual contact with another.

sexual harassment Unwelcome conduct of a sexual nature on the job.

sexual predator A person with a propensity to commit sexual assault.

> "Sexual predator" means a person to whom either of the following applies: (1) The person has been convicted of or pleaded guilty to committing a sexually oriented offense that is not a registration-exempt sexually oriented offense and is likely to engage in the future in one or more sexually oriented offenses. (2) The person has been adjudicated a delinquent child for committing a sexually oriented offense that is not a registration-exempt sexually oriented offense, was fourteen years of age or older at the time of committing the offense, was classified a juvenile offender registrant based on that adjudication, and is likely to engage in the future in one or more sexually oriented offenses. R.C. § 2950.01(E)

shadow jurors Persons hired by one side to observe a trial as members of the general audience and, as the trial progresses, to give feedback to a jury consultant hired by the attorney of one of the parties, who will use the feedback to assess strategy for the remainder of the trial.

shall 1. Is required to, must. 2. Should. 3. May.

sham Counterfeit, a hoax; frivolous, without substance.

sham transaction Conduct with no business purpose other than tax avoidance.

share 1. The part or portion that you contribute or own. 2. An ownership interest in a corporation. A unit of stock.

share and share alike To divide equally.

shareholder One who owns a share in a corporation. Also called stockholder.

> "Shareholder" means a person whose name appears on the books of the corporation as the owner of shares of such corporation. Unless the articles, the regulations, or the contract of subscription otherwise provides, "shareholder" includes a subscriber to shares. R.C. § 1701.01(F)

shareholder's derivative action See derivative action (1).

shelf registration Registration with the Securities and Exchange Commission involving a delayed stock sale.

shell corporation A corporation with no assets or active business.

Shelley's Case See rule in Shelley's Case.

shelter An investment or other device to reduce or defer taxes.

shepardize To use *Shepard's Citations* to find data on the history and currentness of cases, statutes, and other legal materials. See also citator.

sheriff's deed A deed given a buyer at a sheriff's sale.

sheriff's sale A forced sale based on a court order.

shield law 1. A law to protect journalists from being required to divulge confidential sources. 2. See rape shield law.

shifting income Transferring income to someone in a lower tax bracket.

shifting the burden Transferring the burden of proof (or the burden to produce evidence) from one party to another during a trial.

shipment contract A sale in which the risk of loss passes to the buyer when the seller duly delivers the goods to the carrier.

shop A place of business or employment.

shop-book rule A rule allowing regularly kept original business records into evidence as an exception to the hearsay rule.

shoplifting The theft of goods displayed for sale.

> A merchant, or an employee or agent of a merchant, who has probable cause to believe that items offered for sale by a mercantile establishment have been unlawfully taken by a person, may, for the purposes set forth in division (C) of this section, detain the person in a reasonable manner for a reasonable length of time within the mercantile establishment or its immediate vicinity. R.C. § 2935.041(A)

shop steward A union official who helps enforce the union contract.

short sale A sale of a security the seller does not own that is made by the delivery of a security borrowed by, or for the account of, the seller.

short summons A summons with a shorter-than-usual response time.

short-swing profit Profit earned on stock by a corporate insider within 6 months of purchase or sale.

short-term capital gain Gain from the sale or exchange of a capital asset held for less than a year or other designated short term.

show To establish or prove.

show cause order A court order to appear and explain why the court should not take a proposed action to provide relief.

shower One who takes the jury to a scene involved in the case.

showup See lineup.

shut-in royalty A payment by a lessee to continue holding a functioning well that is not being currently utilized due to a weak oil or gas market.

shyster Slang for an unscrupulous attorney.

sic A signal alerting the reader that you are quoting exactly, including the error in the quote.

sidebar conference See bench conference.

sight draft A draft payable on demand when shown.

sign 1. To affix one's signature (or mark substitute). 2. To indicate agreement.

signing statement An announcement by the president upon signing a bill into law that states the president's objections, interpretation, or intention in implementing the law.

signatory The person or nation signing a document.

signature One's name written by oneself. A word, mark, or symbol indicating identity or intended to authenticate a document.

> "Electronic signature" means an electronic sound, symbol, or process attached to or logically associated with a record and executed or adopted by a person with the intent to sign the record. R.C. § 304.01(E)

silent partner See dormant partner.

silent witness theory Evidence such as photographs may be admitted without testimony of a witness if there is sufficient proof of the reliability of the process that produced the evidence.

silver platter doctrine The former rule that evidence obtained illegally by state police is admissible in federal court if no federal officer participated in the violation of the defendant's rights.

simple 1. Not aggravated. 2. Uncomplicated. 3. Not under seal.

simple assault; simple battery An assault or battery not accompanied by aggravating circumstances.

> (A) No person shall knowingly cause or attempt to cause physical harm to another or to another's unborn. (B) No person shall recklessly cause serious physical harm to another or to another's unborn. R.C. § 2903.13. [Comment of Legislative Service Commission: "This section prohibits simple assault and simple battery in the traditional sense."]

simple interest Interest on the principal only, not on any interest earned on the principal.

simple negligence See ordinary negligence.

simple trust 1. A trust requiring the distribution of all trust income to the beneficiaries. 2. See passive trust.

simpliciter Simply; unconditionally.

simplified employee pension plan (SEP) An employee benefit plan consisting of an annuity or an individual retirement account.

simulated sale A sham sale in which no consideration was exchanged.

Simultaneous Death Act A statute providing that when two people die together but without evidence of who died first, the property of each may be disposed of as if each survived the other.

sine die ("without day") With no day being designated.

sine prole (s.p.) Without issue.

sine qua non An essential condition.

single-juror charge A jury instruction stating that if a single juror is not reasonably satisfied with the plaintiff's evidence, the jury cannot find for the plaintiff.

single-publication rule Only one defamation cause of action exists for the same communication, even if it was heard or read by many.

sinking fund Regular deposits and interest accrued thereon set aside to pay long-term debts.

> "Mandatory sinking fund requirements" means amounts required by proceedings to be deposited in a year or fiscal year in a bond retirement fund for the purpose of paying the principal of securities that is due and payable in a subsequent year or fiscal year. R.C. § 133.01(W)

SIPC Securities Investor Protection Corporation (*www.sipc.org*).

sister corporations Corporations controlled by the same shareholders.

sistren Sisters. Female colleagues.

sit 1. To hold a session. 2. To occupy an office.

sit-down strike Employees' refusal to work while at the work site.

sitting In session.

situs Position. The place where a thing happened or is located.

S.J.D. Doctor of Juridical Science.

skip person A recipient of assets in a generation-skipping transfer.

skiptracing Efforts to locate persons (e.g., debtors) or assets.

S.L. See session laws.

slander Defamation that is oral or gestured.

slander of goods; slander of title See disparagement.

slander per se Slander that accuses a person of unchastity or sexual misconduct, of committing a crime of moral turpitude, of engaging in business or professional misconduct, or of having a loathsome disease.

> This court has previously held that slander *per se* means that the slander is accomplished by the very words spoken. When a claim of slander *per se* is established, damages will be presumed. *Leal*, 123 Ohio App.3d 51 (Ohio App., 1998)

SLAPP See Strategic Lawsuit Against Public Participation.

slavery A status or system of enforced labor and bondage.

sleeping partner See dormant partner.

slight care More than the absence of care but less than ordinary care.

slight negligence The failure to exercise great care.

slip law One act of the legislature printed in a single pamphlet.

slip opinion The first printing of a single court opinion.

slowdown Causing production to decrease as a union or labor protest.

SM Servicemark. See mark (1).

small-claims court A court that uses more informal procedures to resolve smaller claims—those under a designated amount.

small loan acts Laws on interest-rate limits for small consumer loans.

smart money 1. See punitive damages. 2. Funds of a shrewd investor.

smuggle To import or export goods illegally without paying duties.

social guest One invited to enter or remain on another's property to enjoy private hospitality, not for a business purpose.

> A "social guest," for purposes of negligence liability, is one who does not come as a member of the public upon premises held open to the public for that purpose, nor does he enter for purpose directly or indirectly connected to business dealings with possessor; use of the premises is extended to him merely as a personal favor. *Doelker*, 61 Ohio Misc.2d 69 (Ohio Ct.Cl., 1990)

society 1. An association of persons united for a common purpose. 2. Companionship and love among family members.

sodomy Oral sex or anal intercourse between humans, or between humans and animals. Also called unnatural offense.

soil bank A federal program paying farmers not to grow certain crops.

soldier's will See military will.

sole actor doctrine The knowledge of an agent is treated as the knowledge of his or her principal.

sole custody Only one parent makes all child-rearing decisions.

sole proprietorship A form of business that does not have a separate legal identity apart from the one person who owns all assets and assumes all debts and liabilities.

solicitation 1. A request for something. 2. Enticing or urging someone to commit a crime. 3. An appeal or request for clients or business.

> Solicit is defined as to entice, urge, lure or ask. *State v. Swann*, 142 Ohio App.3d 88 (Ohio App., 2001)

solicitor 1. One who solicits. 2. A lawyer for a city or government agency. 3. A British lawyer who prepares documents and gives clients legal advice but (unlike a barrister) does not do extensive trial work.

solicitor general A high-ranking government litigator.

solvent Able to meet one's financial obligations.

Son of Sam law A law against criminals earning income by selling the story of their crime to the media.

sound 1. Healthy; able. 2. Marketable. 3. Well-founded. 4. To be actionable.

source of law The authority for court opinions or statutes, e.g., constitutions, other court opinions and statutes, and custom.

sovereign 1. Having supreme power. 2. The ruler or head of state.

sovereign immunity The sovereign (i.e., the state) cannot be sued in its courts without its consent. Also called governmental immunity.

sovereignty Supreme political authority.

s.p. 1. Same principle. 2. See sine prole.

speaker The chairperson or presiding officer of an assembly.

speaking demurrer A demurrer that alleges facts that are not in the pleadings. See also demurrer.

special act See private law (2).

special administrator An estate administrator with limited duties.

special agent An agent delegated to do a specific act.

special appearance Appearing solely to challenge the court's jurisdiction.

special assessment An additional tax on land that benefits from a public improvement.

> A "special assessment" is not a tax as such, but is an assessment against realty based on proposition that, due to a public improvement of some nature, such realty has received a benefit, and such assessment is levied only against property benefited by the improvement. *State v. Carney*, 166 Ohio St. 81 (Ohio 1956)

special contract 1. An express contract with explicit terms. 2. See contract under seal.

special counsel An attorney hired by the government for a particular matter.

special court-martial An intermediate level of court-martial.

special damages Actual and provable economic losses, e.g., lost wages.

> Special damages are damages of such a nature that they do not follow as a necessary consequence of the injury complained of. *Stokes*, 111 Ohio App.3d 176 (Ohio App., 1996)

special demurrer A challenge to the form of a pleading.

special deposit A deposit in a bank made for safekeeping or for some special application or purpose.

special exception 1. A challenge to the form of a claim. 2. See conditional use.

special-facts rule A duty of disclosure exists when special circumstances make it inequitable for a corporate director or officer to withhold information from a stockholder.

special finding A finding of essential facts to support a judgment.

special grand jury A grand jury called for a limited or special task.

special guaranty A guarantee enforceable only by designated persons.

special indorsement An indorsement that specifies the person to whom the instrument is payable or to whom the goods are to be delivered.

A "special indorsement" means an indorsement that is made by the holder of an instrument, whether payable to an identified person or payable to the bearer, and that identifies a person to whom it makes the instrument payable. An instrument, when specially indorsed, becomes payable to the identified person and may be negotiated only by the indorsement of that person. R.C. § 1303.25(A)

special interrogatory A separate question a jury is asked to answer.

specialist One possessing special expertise, often certified as such.

special jurisdiction See limited jurisdiction.

special jury A jury chosen for its special expertise or for a case of special importance. Also called struck jury.

special law See private law (2).

special lien See particular lien.

special master See master (2).

special meeting A nonregular meeting called for a special purpose.

special power of appointment See limited power of appointment.

special power of attorney A power of attorney with limited authority.

special prosecutor An attorney appointed to conduct a criminal investigation of a matter.

special session See extraordinary session.

special trust A trust whose trustee has management duties other than merely giving trust assets to beneficiaries. Also called active trust.

specialty See contract under seal.

special use See conditional use.

special use valuation Real property valued on its actual current use rather than on its best possible use.

special verdict A jury's fact findings on fact questions given to it by the judge, who then states the legal consequences of the findings.

A special verdict is a statement by the jury of facts it has found; based on those facts, the court determines which party is to have judgment. *Leavers*, 156 Ohio App.3d 286 (Ohio App., 2004)

special warranty deed 1. A deed in which the grantor warrants title only against those claiming by or under the grantor. 2. A quitclaim deed.

specie 1. See in specie. 2. Coined money.

specification 1. A list of contract requirements or details. 2. A statement of charges. 3. Invention details in a patent application.

specific bequest A gift of specific or unique property in a will.

specific denial A denial of particular allegations in a claim.

specific devise A devise of a specific property.

specific intent Desiring (intending) the precise criminal consequences that follow one's act.

specific legacy A gift of specific or unique property in a will.

A specific legacy or a bequest of specific property is a bequest of some particular thing or portion of a testator's estate which is so described in the will as to be distinguished from other articles of the same general nature in the estate. *In re Radu's Estate*, 35 Ohio App.2d 187 (Ohio App., 1973)

specific performance An equitable remedy directing the performance of a contract according to the precise terms agreed upon by the parties.

spectograph A machine used for voiceprint analysis.

speculation 1. Seeking profits through investments that can be risky. 2. Theorizing in the absence of sufficient evidence and knowledge.

speculative damages Damages that are not reasonably certain; damages that are too conjectural to be awarded.

speech Spoken communication.

Speech or Debate Clause The clause in the U.S. Constitution (art. I, § 6, cl. 1) giving members of Congress immunity for what they say during their legislative work.

speedy trial A trial that begins after reasonable preparation by the prosecution and is conducted with reasonable dispatch.

spendthrift One who spends money irresponsibly.

spendthrift trust A trust whose assets are protected against the beneficiary's improvidence and are beyond the reach of his or her creditors.

A trust that imposes a restraint on the voluntary and involuntary transfer of the beneficiary's interest in the trust property. *Scott*, 62 Ohio St.3d 39 (Ohio 1991)

spin-off A new and independent corporation that was once part of another corporation whose shareholders will own the new corporation.

spirit of the law The underlying meaning or purpose of the law.

split See stock split.

split gift A gift from a spouse to a nonspouse that is treated as having been given one-half by each spouse.

split-off A new corporation formed by an existing corporation, giving shares of the new corporation to the existing corporation's stockholders in exchange for some of their shares in the existing corporation.

split sentence A sentence served in part in an institution and suspended in part or served on probation for the remainder.

splitting a cause of action Suing on only part of a cause of action now and on another part later.

split-up Dividing a corporation into two or more new corporations.

spoliation Intentionally destroying, altering, or concealing evidence.

"Spoliation" is the doing of some act manifest on face of a will, by someone other than the testator. R.C. § 2107.26. *In re Downie's Estate*, 6 Ohio Misc. 36 (Ohio Prob., 1966)

sponsor 1. One who makes a promise or gives security for another. 2. A legislator who proposes a bill.

spontaneous declaration An out-of-court statement or utterance (made with little time to reflect or fabricate) about a perceived event. An exception to the hearsay rule.

> The following are not excluded by the hearsay rule, even though the declarant is available as a witness: . . . (2) Excited utterance. A statement relating to a startling event or condition made while the declarant was under the stress of excitement caused by the event or condition. Ohio Evid. R. Rule 803

spot zoning Singling out a lot or small area for different zoning treatment than similar surrounding land.

spousal abuse Physical, sexual, or emotional abuse of one's spouse.

spousal privilege See marital communications privilege.

spousal support See alimony.

spread The difference between two amounts, e.g., the buyer's bid price and the seller's asked price for a security.

springing use A use that is dependent or contingent on a future event.

sprinkling trust A trust that spreads income among different beneficiaries at the discretion of the trustee.

spurious Counterfeit or synthetic; false.

squatter One who settles on land without legal title or authority.

squeeze-out An attempt to eliminate or weaken the interest of an owner, e.g., a minority shareholder.

ss. 1. Sections. 2. Sometimes used to abbreviate scilicet, meaning to wit.

SSI See Supplemental Security Income.

stake 1. A deposit to be held until its ownership is resolved. 2. A land boundary marker. 3. A bet. 4. An interest in a business.

stakeholder See interpleader.

stale No longer effective due to the passage of time.

stalking Repeatedly following or harassing someone, who is thereby placed in reasonable fear of harm.

stamp tax The cost of stamps affixed to legal documents such as deeds.

stand See witness stand.

standard 1. A yardstick or criterion. 2. Customary.

standard deduction A fixed deduction from adjusted gross income, used by taxpayers who do not itemize their deductions.

standard mortgage clause A mortgage clause stating that the interest of the mortgagee will not be invalidated by specified acts of the mortgagor.

> Loss payable clause in automobile policy constituted "standard mortgage clause" that served as separate contract between insurer and secured creditor, where clause provided, in essence, that coverage to creditor would not be invalidated by fraudulent acts or omissions of insured, other than insured's conversion, embezzlement or secretion of vehicle. *Pittsburgh Natl. Bank v. Motorists Mut. Ins. Co.*, 87 Ohio App.3d 82 (Ohio App., 1993)

standard of care The degree of care the law requires in a particular case, e.g., reasonable care in a negligence case.

standard of need A level of need qualifying one for public benefits.

standard of proof The degree to which the evidence of something must be convincing before a fact finder can accept it as true.

standing A person's right to seek relief from a court.

standing committee An ongoing committee.

standing mute A defendant refusing to answer or plead to the charge.

standing orders Rules adopted by a court governing practice before it.

Star Chamber 1. An early English court that known for arbitrariness. 2. A term used to describe an arbitrary or secret tribunal or proceeding.

stare decisis ("stand by things decided") Courts should decide similar cases in the same way. Precedent should be followed.

stat. Statute.

state 1. A sovereign government. 2. A body of people in a defined territory organized under one government.

> "State" means this state, a county, city, village, township, other political subdivision, or any other entity of this state that may prosecute a criminal action. Ohio Crim. R. Rule 2(H)

state action 1. Conduct of a government. 2. Court proceedings made available to protect or enforce conduct of a private person or entity.

state bank A bank chartered by a state.

stated account See account stated.

stated capital See legal capital.

stated value See par value.

statement 1. An assertion of fact or opinion. 2. An organized recitation of facts.

> A statement is (1) an oral or written assertion or (2) nonverbal conduct of a person, if it is intended by him as an assertion. Ohio Evid. R. Rule 801(A)

statement of affairs A list of assets and debts.

state of mind 1. One's reasons and motives for acting or failing to act. 2. See mens rea. 3. The condition or capacity of a mind.

state-of-mind exception An out-of-court declaration of an existing motive or reason is admissible as an exception to the hearsay rule.

> The following are not excluded by the hearsay rule, even though the declarant is available as a witness: . . . A statement of the declarant's then existing state of mind, emotion, sensation, or physical condition (such as intent, plan, motive, design, mental feeling, pain, and bodily health), but not including a statement of memory or belief to prove the fact remembered or believed unless it relates to the execution, revocation, identification, or terms of declarant's will. Ohio Evid. R. Rule 803(3)

state's attorney The prosecutor or district attorney.

state secrets Government information that would threaten national security or compromise diplomacy if disclosed to the public.

state's evidence Testimony of one criminal defendant against another.

states' rights 1. The political philosophy that favors increased powers for state governments as opposed to expanding the powers of the federal government. 2. Powers not granted to the federal government and not forbidden to the states "are reserved to the states" and the people. U.S. Const. amend. X.

status crime; status offense 1. A crime that consists of having a certain personal status, condition, or character. Example: vagrancy. 2. Conduct by a minor that, if engaged in by an adult, would not be legally prohibited.

status quo The existing state of things.

statute 1. A law passed by the state or federal legislature that declares, commands, or prohibits something. 2. A law passed by any legislative body.

statute of frauds A law requiring some contracts (e.g., one that cannot be performed within a year of its making) to be in writing and signed by the party to be charged by the contract.

> Except as otherwise provided in this section a contract for the sale of goods for the price of five hundred dollars or more is not enforceable by way of action or defense unless there is some writing sufficient to indicate that a contract for sale has been made between the parties and signed by the party against whom enforcement is sought or by his authorized agent or broker. A writing is not insufficient because it omits or incorrectly states a term agreed upon but the contract is not enforceable under this division beyond the quantity of goods shown in such writing. R.C. § 1302.04(A)

statute of limitations A law stating that civil or criminal actions are barred if not brought within a specified period of time.

statute of repose A law barring actions unless brought within a designated time after an act of the defendant. The law extinguishes the cause of action after a fixed period of time, regardless of when the cause of action accrued.

statute of uses An old English statute that converted certain equitable titles into legal ones.

Statutes at Large The United States Statutes at Large is the official chronological collection of the acts and resolutions of a session of Congress.

statutory Pertaining to or required by a statute.

statutory construction The interpretation of statutes.

statutory employer An employer of a worker covered by workers' compensation.

statutory foreclosure A nonjudicial foreclosure of a mortgage.

statutory lien A lien created by statute.

statutory rape Sexual intercourse with a person under a designated age (e.g., 16) even if the latter consents.

> (A)(1) No person shall engage in sexual conduct with another who is not the spouse of the offender or who is the spouse of the offender but is living separate and apart from the offender, when any of the following applies: . . . (b) The other person is less than thirteen years of age, whether or not the offender knows the age of the other person. R.C. § 2907.02

stay The suspension of a judgment or proceeding.

stealing Unlawfully taking and keeping the property of another.

stenographic record The transcript of a trial or deposition.

step-up basis The tax basis of inherited property, which is its value on the date the donor died or on the alternate valuation date.

step transaction doctrine For tax purposes, a series of formally separate steps are treated as a single transaction.

stet ("let it stand") 1. Leave the text unchanged (usually meaning undo the last correction). 2. A stay.

steward See shop steward.

sting An undercover operation to catch criminals.

stipulated damages See liquidated damages.

stipulation 1. An agreement between parties on a matter, often so that it need not be argued or proven at trial. 2. A requirement or condition.

> "Stipulation" may be defined as a voluntary agreement, admission, or concession, made in a judicial proceeding by the parties or their attorneys concerning disposition of some relevant point so as to eliminate the need for proof or to narrow the range of issues to be litigated. *State v. Small*, 162 Ohio App.3d 375 (Ohio App., 2005)

stirpes See per stirpes.

stock 1. An ownership interest or share in a corporation. 2. The capital raised by a corporation, e.g., through the sale of shares. 3. Goods to be sold by a merchant.

stock association See joint stock company.

stockbroker One who buys or sells stock on behalf of others.

stock certificate Documentary evidence of title to shares of stock.

> "Stock certificate" is evidence of written contract between shareholder and corporation subject to State and Federal Constitutions, applicable statutes, corporate records, and provisions of charter or articles of corporation in effect at time corporation is created. *Bitonte*, 65 Ohio App.3d 734 (Ohio App., 1989)

stock corporation A corporation whose capital is divided into shares.

stock dividend A dividend paid in additional shares of stock.

stock exchange The place at which shares of stock are bought and sold.

stockholder See shareholder.

stockholder's derivative action See derivative action (1).

stock in trade 1. Inventory for sale. 2. Equipment used in business.

stock issue See issue (4).

stock manipulation See manipulation.

stock market See market (2).

stock option A right to buy or sell stock at a set price within a specified period of time.

stock right A shareholder's right to purchase new stock issues before the public can make such purchases.

stock split Each individual share is split into a larger number of shares without changing the total number of shareholders.

stock warrant See warrant (3).

stolen property Property taken by theft or embezzlement.

> No person shall receive, retain, or dispose of property of another knowing or having reasonable cause to believe that the property has been obtained through commission of a theft offense. R.C. § 2913.51(A)

stop and frisk Temporary detention, questioning, and "patting down" of a person whom the police reasonably believe has committed or is about to commit a crime and may have a weapon. Also called Terry stop.

stop-loss order An order to buy or sell securities when they reach a particular price. Also called stop order.

stop order 1. An instruction of a customer who has written a check that his or her bank should not honor it. A stop-payment order. 2. See stop-loss order.

stoppage in transit (*in transitu*) A seller's right to repossess goods from a carrier before they reach the buyer when payment by the later is in doubt.

stop-payment order See stop order (1).

straddle The option to purchase or sell the same asset.

straight bill of lading A bill of lading that names a specific person to whom the goods are to be delivered.

straight life insurance See whole life insurance.

straight-line depreciation Depreciation computed by dividing the purchase price of an asset (less its salvage value) by its estimated useful life.

stranger Someone not a participant or party to a transaction.

Strategic Lawsuit Against Public Participation (SLAPP) A meritless suit brought primarily to chill the free speech of the defendant.

straw man 1. A cover or front. 2. A fictitious person or argument.

street name A broker's name on a security, not that of its owner.

strict construction A narrow construction; nothing is taken as intended that is not clearly expressed in the literal language of the law or document. Also called literal construction.

> While the rule of strict interpretation of an insurance policy is a fundamental principle in insurance law, it is tempered by other canons of construction that seek to bring balance and reason to the analysis. *Felton*, 163 Ohio App.3d 436 (Ohio App., 2005)

strict foreclosure A transfer of title (to the mortgaged property) to the mortgagee without a foreclosure sale upon the mortgagor's default.

stricti juris According to a strict or narrow construction of the law.

strict liability Legal responsibility even if one used reasonable care and did not intend harm. Also called absolute liability, liability without fault.

strict scrutiny The standard requiring a government to show its law is the least restrictive way to further a compelling state interest.

> A law restricting speech on the basis of content is subject to "strict scrutiny" under First Amendment, which requires that the law be necessary to serve a compelling state interest, and narrowly tailored to achieve that end. *Regal Cinemas, Inc.*, 137 Ohio App.3d 61 (Ohio App., 2000)

strike 1. An organized work stoppage or slowdown by workers in order to press demands. 2. To remove something.

strikebreaker See scab.

strike suit A shareholder derivative action that is baseless.

striking a jury Selecting a jury for a particular or special case.

struck jury 1. A jury chosen by a process that allows the parties to take turns striking names from a large panel of prospective jurors until a sufficient number exists for a jury. 2. See special jury.

style The title or name of a case.

suable Capable of being sued.

sua sponte On one's own motion; voluntarily.

sub Under; secondary.

subagent Someone used by an agent to perform a duty for the principal.

subchapter C corporation See C corporation.

subchapter S corporation See S corporation.

subcontract A contract that performs all or part of another contract.

subcontractor One who performs under a subcontract.

subdivision 1. The division of something into smaller parts. 2. A portion of land within a development.

subinfeudation A feudal system of vassals creating vassals of their own.

subjacent support The support of land by land that lies beneath it.

subject 1. A citizen or resident under another; one governed by the laws of a sovereign. 2. A theme or topic acted upon.

subject-matter jurisdiction The power of the court to resolve a particular category of dispute.

> "Subject-matter jurisdiction" of a court connotes the power to hear and decide a case upon its merits. *Internatl. Bhd. of Elec. Workers,*, 133 Ohio Misc.2d 1 (Ohio Com.Pl., 2005)

sub judice Under judicial consideration; before a court.

sublease A lease of leased premises. A lease (called a sublease, subtenancy, or underlease) granted by an existing lessee (called a sublessor) to another (called a sublessee, subtenant, or undertenant) of all or part of the leased premises for a portion of the sublessor's original term.

> "Sublease" means a lease of goods the right to possession and use of which was acquired by the lessor as a lessee under an existing lease. R.C. § 1310.01(A)(23)

sublessee; sublessor See sublease.

subletting The granting of a sublease.

submission 1. Yielding to authority. 2. An argument to be considered.

sub modo Within limits; subject to qualifications.

sub nominee (sub nom.) Under the name or title.

subordinate 1. One who works under another's authority. 2. To place in a lower priority or rank.

subordination agreement An agreement to accept a lower priority than would otherwise be due.

suborn To induce another to commit an illegal act, e.g., perjury.

subornation of perjury Instigating another to commit perjury.

subpoena A command to appear in a court, agency, or other tribunal.

subpoena ad testificandum A command to appear to give testimony.

subpoena duces tecum A command to appear and bring specified things, e.g., records.

subrogation The substitution of one party (called the subrogee) in place of another party (called the subrogor), along with any claim, demand, or right the latter party had.

"Subrogation" is the substitution of one person in the place of another with reference to a lawful claim or right. *Physicians Ins. Co. of Ohio,* 146 Ohio App.3d 685 (Ohio App., 2001)

subrogee; subrogor See subrogation.

subscription 1. A signature; the act of writing one's name on a document. 2. An agreement to purchase new securities of a corporation.

subscription right See preemptive right.

subsequent Occurring or coming later.

subsidiary 1. Under another's control. 2. A branch or affiliate.

"Subsidiary" means, with respect to a specified company, a company that is controlled by the specified company. R.C. § 1109.53(G)

subsidiary corporation A corporation owned or controlled by another corporation.

sub silentio Under silence; without specific reference or notice.

substance 1. The material or essential part of a thing. 2. A drug.

substantial 1. Not imaginary. 2. Considerable in amount or degree.

substantial capacity test See insanity (2).

substantial compliance Compliance with the essential requirements.

substantial evidence Relevant evidence a reasonable mind might accept as adequate to support a conclusion.

substantial justice A fair proceeding or trial even if minor procedural errors are made.

substantial performance Performance of the essential terms.

substantiate To establish by supporting evidence. To support with proof.

substantive due process The constitutional requirement (based on the 5th and 14th Amendments) that legislation be rationally related to a legitimate government purpose.

substantive evidence Evidence offered to support a fact in issue.

"Substantial" evidence, within meaning of statute providing that administrative order may be affirmed on review if it is supported by reliable, probative, and substantial evidence, is evidence with some weight, importance, and value. R.C. § 119.12. *Fire,* 163 Ohio App.3d 392 (Ohio App., 2005)

substantive law Nonprocedural laws that define or govern rights and duties.

substantive rule See legislative rule.

substituted basis The basis of property in the hands of the transferor becomes the transferee's basis of that property.

substituted service Service by an authorized method (e.g., by mail) other than personal service. Also called constructive service.

substitution Taking the place of another.

subtenancy; subtenant See sublease.

subversive Pertaining to the overthrow or undermining of a government.

succession 1. Obtaining property or interests by inheritance rather than by deed or contract. The acquisition of rights upon the death of another. 2. Taking over or continuing the rights of another entity.

Succession being defined as passing of property in possession or in enjoyment, present or future. *In re Smith's Estate,* 188 N.E.2d 650 (Ohio Prob., 1962)

succession tax See inheritance tax.

successor A person or entity that takes the place of or follows another.

successor in interest One who follows another in ownership or control of property.

sudden emergency doctrine See emergency doctrine (1).

sudden heat of passion See heat of passion.

sue To commence a lawsuit.

sue out To ask a court for an order.

suffer 1. To feel physical or emotional pain. 2. To allow or admit.

sufferance The absence of rejection; passive consent.

sufficient Adequate for the legal purpose involved.

sufficient cause See good cause, probable cause (1).

sufficient consideration Consideration that creates a binding contract.

suffrage The right to vote.

suicide The voluntary termination of one's life.

"Assist suicide" or "assisting suicide" means knowingly doing either of the following, with the purpose of helping another person to commit or attempt suicide: (1) Providing the physical means by which the person commits or attempts to commit suicide; (2) Participating in a physical act by which the person commits or attempts to commit suicide. R.C. § 3795.01(A)

sui generis ("of its own kind") Unique.

sui juris ("of one's own right") Possessing full civil rights.

suit See lawsuit.

suitor A plaintiff, one who sues.

sum certain An exact amount.

summary 1. Not following usual procedures. 2. Done quickly. 3. Short or concise.

summary court-martial The lowest-level court-martial.

summary judgment A judgment on a claim or defense rendered without a full trial because of the absence of genuine conflict on any of the material facts involved.

"Summary judgment" is a procedural device designed to terminate litigation and to avoid a formal trial where there is no genuine issue of material fact to be tried and the moving party is entitled to judgment as a matter of law. Ohio Rules Civ.Proc., Rule 56. *Westfield Ins. Co.,* 128 Ohio App.3d 270 (Ohio App., 1998)

summary jury trial A nonbinding trial argued before a mock jury as a case evaluation technique and an incentive to settle.

summary proceeding A nonjury proceeding that seeks to achieve a relatively prompt resolution.

summary process A special procedure that provides an expeditious remedy.

summation; summing up See closing argument.

summons 1. A notice directing the defendant to appear in court and answer the plaintiff's complaint or face a default judgment. 2. A notice directing a witness or juror to appear in court.

"Summons" includes a subpoena, order, or other notice requiring the appearance of a witness. R.C. § 2939.25(C)

sumptuary Regulating personal expenditures; restricting immorality.

Sunday closing laws See blue laws.

sunset law A law that automatically terminates a program unless it is affirmatively renewed.

sunshine law A law requiring increased public access to government meetings and records.

suo nomine In one's own name.

Superfund A government fund for hazardous-waste cleanup.

superior Having a higher rank, authority, or interest.

superior court A trial court in most states.

supermajority Two-thirds, 60 percent, or any other voting requirement of greater than half plus one.

supersede To supplant; to annul by replacing.

supersedeas A writ or bond to stay the enforcement of a judgment.

superseding cause An intervening cause that is beyond the foreseeable risk originally created by the defendant's unreasonable acts or omissions and thereby cuts off the defendant's liability.

Intervening act of third person which relieves one of liability for his negligence is referred to as a "superseding cause." *McRoberts*, 143 Ohio App.3d 304 (Ohio App., 2001)

supervening cause A superseding cause.

supervening negligence See last clear chance doctrine.

supplemental jurisdiction Jurisdiction over a claim that is part of the same controversy over which the court already has jurisdiction.

supplemental pleading A pleading that adds facts to or corrects an earlier pleading.

Supplemental Security Income (SSI) A government income benefit program (part of social security) for the aged, blind, or disabled.

supplementary proceeding A new proceeding that supplements another, e.g., to help collect a judgment.

support 1. Provide a standard of living. 2. Maintenance with necessities. 3. Foundation.

suppress To stop or prevent.

suppression hearing A pretrial criminal hearing to decide if evidence was seized illegally and should be inadmissible (i.e., suppressed).

Motion to suppress is defined as device used to eliminate from trial of criminal case evidence which has been secured illegally, generally in violation of Fourth, Fifth, or Sixth Amendment of United States Constitution; thus motion to suppress is proper vehicle for raising constitutional challenges based on the exclusionary rule. *State v. French*, 72 Ohio St.3d 446 (Ohio 1995)

suppression of evidence 1. A prosecutor's failure to disclose exculpatory evidence to the defense. 2. Evidence held inadmissible at a suppression hearing.

supra Above; mentioned earlier in the document.

supremacy Being in a higher or the highest position of power.

Supremacy Clause The clause in the U.S. Constitution (art. VI, cl. 2) that has been interpreted to mean that when valid federal law and state law conflict, federal law controls.

supreme court 1. The highest court in the federal and in most state judicial systems. 2. In New York, it is a trial court with some appellate jurisdiction. 3. The Supreme Court of Appeals is the highest state court in West Virginia. 4. The Supreme Judicial Court is the highest state court in Maine and Massachusetts.

surcharge 1. An added charge or tax. 2. A charge imposed on a fiduciary for misconduct.

surety One who becomes liable for the payment of another's debt or the performance of another's contractual obligation. The surety generally becomes primarily and jointly liable with the other, the principal.

surety bond See completion bond.

suretyship The contractual relation whereby one person (the surety) agrees to answer for the debt, default, or miscarriage of another (the principal), with the surety generally being primarily and jointly liable with the principal.

"Suretyship" is contractual relation whereby one person (the surety) agrees to answer for debt, default or miscarriage of another (the principal), with the surety generally being primarily and jointly liable with the principal. *Solon Family Physicians, Inc.*, 96 Ohio App.3d 460 (Ohio App., 1994)

surplus What is left over. The amount remaining after the purpose of a fund or venture has been accomplished.

"Surplus" means the total of amounts paid for shares in excess of their respective par values, amounts contributed other than for shares, and amounts transferred from undivided profits, less amounts transferred to stated capital. R.C. § 1101.01(R)

surplusage Extraneous matter or words in a statute, pleading, or instrument that do not add meaning.

surprise Something unexpected, often unfairly so.

surrebuttal A rebuttal to a rebuttal.

surrejoinder An answer of the defendant to a rejoinder.

surrender 1. To return a power, claim, or estate. 2. To release.

surrender value See cash surrender value.

surrogacy The status or act of being a substitute for another.

surrogate 1. A substitute for another. 2. A probate judge.

surrogate mother A woman who gestates an embryo and bears a child for another person. The surrogate relinquishes her parental rights.

surrogate's court See probate court.

surtax 1. An additional tax added to something already taxed. 2. A tax levied on a tax.

surveillance Close and continual observation of a person or place.

survey 1. A map that measures boundaries, elevations, and structures on land. 2. A study or poll.

survival action An action brought on behalf of a decedent to recover damages the decedent suffered up to the time of his or her death. The action seeks what the decedent would have sought if he or she had not died.

survivorship See right of survivorship.

survivorship annuity An annuity that continues paying benefits to the survivor of the annuitant after the latter's death.

suspect classification A classification in a statute whose constitutional validity (under the Equal Protection Clause) will be measured by the standard of strict scrutiny. An example would be a preference in a statute on the basis of on race, alienage, or national origin.

> A suspect class is one saddled with such disabilities, or subjected to such a history of purposeful unequal treatment, or relegated to such a position of political powerlessness as to command extraordinary protection from the majoritarian political process. *State v. Williams*, 88 Ohio St.3d 513 (Ohio 2000)

suspended sentence A sentence that is imposed but postponed, allowing the defendant to avoid prison if he or she meets specified conditions.

suspension A temporary delay or interruption, e.g., the removal of the right to practice law for a specified period.

suspicion A belief that someone has or may have committed wrongdoing but without proof.

sustain 1. To uphold or agree with. 2. To support or encourage. 3. To endure, withstand, or suffer.

swear 1. To take or administer an oath. 2. To talk obscenely.

sweating Questioning an accused through harassment or threats.

sweetheart deal An arrangement providing beneficial treatment that is illegal or ethically questionable.

syllabus 1. A brief summary or outline. 2. See headnote.

symbolic delivery The constructive delivery of property by delivering something that represents the property, e.g., a key to a building.

symbolic speech Nonverbal activity or conduct that expresses a message or thought, e.g., the hood worn by the KKK; expressive conduct.

sympathy strike A strike against an employer with whom the workers do not have a labor dispute in order to show support for other workers on strike.

synallagmatic Reciprocal, bilateral.

syndicalism A movement advocating control of industry by labor unions. Criminal syndicalism is an act or plan intended to accomplish change in industrial ownership or government by means of unlawful force, violence, or terrorism.

syndicate A group formed to promote a common interest.

synopsis A brief summary.

T

tacit Understood without being openly stated; implied by silence.

tacking 1. One claiming adverse possession adds its period of possession to that of a previous possessor to meet the statutory period. 2. Gaining priority for a lien by joining it to a superior lien.

tail Limitation in the right of inheritance. See fee tail.

tail female Limitation to female heirs. See fee tail.

tail male Limitation to male heirs. See fee tail.

taint 1. A defect or contamination. 2. A felony conviction.

tainted evidence Illegally obtained evidence.

take 1. To seize or obtain possession. 2. To acquire by eminent domain.

takeover Obtaining control, management, or ownership.

taking See take.

talesman A prospective juror. A bystander called to serve on a jury.

tamper To meddle or change something without authorization.

TANF See Temporary Assistance to Needy Families.

tangible Having physical form. Capable of being touched or seen.

> All property other than intangible property and includes securities, accounts receivable, and contract rights, when the securities, accounts receivable, or contract rights have a readily determinable value. R.C. § 1707.01(L)(2)

target corporation A corporation that someone wants to take over.

tariff 1. A tax paid on categories of imported or exported goods. 2. A list of rates or fees charged for services.

tax Compulsory monetary payments to support the government.

taxable Subject to taxation.

taxable estate A decedent's gross estate less allowable deductions.

taxable gift See gift tax.

taxable income Gross income less deductions and exemptions.

taxable year; tax year A calendar year or a taxpayer's fiscal year.

> The corresponding tax reporting period as prescribed for the taxpayer under the Internal Revenue Code. R.C. § 718.01(A)(9)

tax avoidance Using lawful tax-reducing steps and strategies.

tax benefit rule When already deducted losses and expenses are recovered in a later year, the recovery is listed as income in the later year.

tax bracket The range of income to which the same tax rate is applied.

tax certificate An instrument issued to the buyer of property at a tax sale entitling him or her to the property after the redemption period.

tax court A court that hears appeals involving tax disputes.

tax credit A subtraction from the tax owed rather than from income.

tax deduction A subtraction from income to arrive at taxable income.

tax deed A deed given to the purchaser by the government to property purchased at a tax sale.

> A tax deed of registered land, or an interest therein, issued in pursuance of any sale for a tax, assessment, or other imposition, shall have only the effect of an agreement for the transfer of the title upon the register. R.C. § 5309.60

tax deferred Not taxable until later.

tax evasion; tax fraud See evasion (2).

tax exempt; tax free Not subject to taxation.

tax home One's principal place of employment or business.

taxing power A government's power to impose taxes.

tax lien A government's lien on property for nonpayment of taxes.

tax preference items Regular deductions that must be factored back in when calculating the alternative minimum tax.

tax rate The percentage used to calculate one's tax.

tax refund An overpayment of taxes that can be returned or credited.

tax return The form used to report income and other tax information.

tax roll A government list of taxable assets and taxpayers.

tax sale The forced sale of property for nonpayment of taxes.

tax shelter An investment or other device to reduce or defer taxes.

tax title The title obtained by a buyer of property at a tax sale.

technical error See harmless error.

teller 1. A bank employee who receives and pays out money. 2. A vote counter at an election.

temporary Lasting for a limited time; transitory.

> "Temporary protection order" means a protection order issued under section 2903.213 or 2919.26 of the Revised Code. R.C. § 2923.124(J)

temporary alimony An interim order of spousal support pending the final outcome of the action for divorce or legal separation. Also called alimony pendente lite.

Temporary Assistance to Needy Families (TANF) The welfare program that replaced Aid to Families with Dependent Children (AFDC).

temporary injunction See preliminary injunction.

temporary restraining order (TRO) An order maintaining the status quo pending a hearing on the application for a permanent injunction.

tenancy 1. The possession or holding of real or personal property by right or title. 2. Possession or occupancy of land under a lease.

tenancy at sufferance See estate at sufferance.

tenancy at will A lease with no fixed term or duration. Also called estate at will.

tenancy by the entirety A form of joint tenancy for a married couple. Co-ownership of property by spouses with a right of survivorship. Also called estate by the entirety.

> For an "estate by the entireties" to exist at common law, the tenants must be husband and wife and have equal interest which was acquired by same conveyance, commenced at same time and held by same undivided possession. *Koster*, 11 Ohio App.3d 1 (Ohio App., 1982)

tenancy for years A tenancy for any predetermined time period, not just for years. Also called tenancy for a term.

tenancy from year to year See periodic tenancy.

tenancy in common Ownership of property by two or more persons in shares that may or may not be equal, each person having an equal right to possess the whole property but without the right of survivorship. Also called estate in common.

tenant 1. One who pays rent to possess another's land or apartment for a temporary period. 2. One who holds a tenancy.

> "Tenant" means a person who is entitled under a rental agreement to the use or occupancy of premises, other than premises located in a manufactured home park, to the exclusion of others. R.C. § 1923.01(A)(1)

tenantable Habitable, fit for occupancy.

tenant for life One who holds a life estate.

tender 1. To offer payment or other performance. 2. An offer.

tender of delivery An offer of conforming goods by the seller.

> Tender of delivery requires that the seller put and hold conforming goods at the buyer's disposition and give the buyer any notification reasonably necessary to enable him to take delivery. R.C. § 1302.47(A)

tender offer An offer to purchase shares at a fixed price in an attempt to obtain a controlling interest in a company.

tender years doctrine In custody disputes, very young children should go to the mother unless she is unfit.

tenement 1. An apartment or other residence. 2. An estate of land.

ten-K (10-K) A company's annual financial report filed with the SEC.

tentative trust See Totten trust.

tenure 1. The right to permanent employment subject to termination for cause in compliance with procedural safeguards. 2. The right to hold land subordinate to a superior.

term 1. A fixed period. 2. A word or phrase. 3. A contract provision.

terminable interest An interest that ends upon a given time or condition.

termination 1. The end of something. 2. Discontinuation.

term life insurance Life insurance for a specified or limited time.

term loan A loan that must be paid within a specified date.

terms of art Words or phrases with a special or technical meaning. Also called words of art.

territorial Pertaining to a particular area or land.

territorial court A court in a United States territory, e.g., Guam.

territorial waters Inland and surrounding bodies of water controlled by a nation, including water extending 3 miles offshore.

territory 1. A geographical area. 2. A part of the United States with its own branches of government but not part of or within any state.

terrorem clause A condition in a will that voids gifts to any beneficiary who contests the will. Also called no-contest clause.

terrorism Politically motivated violence against noncombatants. Using or threatening violence to intimidate for political or ideological goals.

> "Terrorism" means any activity to which all of the following apply: (1) The activity involves a violent act or an act that is dangerous to human life. (2) The act described in division

(R)(1) of this section is committed within the territorial jurisdiction of the United States and is a violation of the criminal laws of the United States, this state, or any other state or the act described in division (R)(1) of this section is committed outside the territorial jurisdiction of the United States and would be a violation of the criminal laws of the United States, this state, or any other state if committed within the territorial jurisdiction of the United States. (3) The activity appears to be intended to do any of the following: (a) Intimidate or coerce a civilian population; (b) Influence the policy of any government by intimidation or coercion; (c) Affect the conduct of any government by assassination or kidnapping. R.C. § 2743.51(R)

***Terry* stop** See stop and frisk.

testament A will.

testamentary Pertaining to a will.

testamentary capacity Sufficient mental ability to make a will. Knowing the nature of a will, the extent of one's property, and the natural objects of one's bounty.

testamentary class A group of beneficiaries under a will whose number is not known when the will is made.

testamentary disposition A transfer of assets to another by will.

testamentary gift A gift made in a will.

testamentary intent The intent to make a revocable disposition of property that takes effect after the testator's death.

testamentary trust A trust created in a will and effective on the death of the creator.

"Testamentary trust" is a trust that is established by a will and does not take effect until after the death of the person who created the trust. R.C. § 5111.151(B)(13)

testate 1. Having died leaving a valid will. 2. See testator.

testate succession Acquiring assets by will.

testator One who has died leaving a valid will. Also called testate.

testatrix A female testator.

test case Litigation brought to create a new legal principle or right.

teste The clause in a document that names the witness.

testify To give evidence as a witness. To submit testimony under oath.

testimonium clause A clause in the instrument giving the date on which the instrument was executed and by whom.

testimony Evidence given by a witness under oath.

test oath An oath of allegiance and fidelity to the government.

theft Taking personal property with the intent to deprive the owner of it permanently. Larceny.

Undefined term "theft" within policy drafted by insurer includes any wrongful deprivation of property of another without claim or color of right. *Munchick*, 2 Ohio St.2d 303 (Ohio 1965)

theory of the case The application of the law to the facts to support the judgment you are seeking.

***Thibodaux* abstention** A federal court can abstain from exercising its federal jurisdiction when facing difficult and unresolved state law issues involving policy. *Louisiana Power v. Thibodaux*, 79 S. Ct. 1070 (1959).

thief One who commits larceny or theft.

thing in action See chose in action.

third degree Overly aggressive or abusive interrogation techniques.

third party A nonparty or nonparticipant who is involved in a transaction in some way.

third-party beneficiary One for whose benefit a contract is made but who is not a party to the contract.

A "third-party beneficiary" is one for whose benefit a promise is made, but who is not a party to the contract encompassing the promise. *Bobb Forest Products, Inc.*, 151 Ohio App.3d 63 (Ohio App., 2002)

third-party complaint A defendant's complaint against someone who is not now a party on the basis that the latter may be liable for all or part of what the plaintiff might recover from the defendant.

third-party plaintiff A defendant who files a third-party complaint.

third-party practice See implead.

threat An expression of an intent to inflict pain or damage.

three-judge court A panel of three judges hearing a case.

three-strikes law A statute imposing harsher sentences for persons convicted of their third felony.

through bill of lading A contract covering the transport of cargo from origin to destination, including the use of additional carriers.

ticket 1. A paper giving the holder a right. 2. A traffic citation.

tideland Land covered and uncovered each day by the action of tides.

tie-in See tying arrangement.

time-barred Pertaining to a claim barred by a statute of limitations.

time bill See time draft.

time deposit A bank deposit that remains in the account for a specified time and is not payable on demand before that time without penalty.

time draft A draft payable on a specified date. Also called time bill.

time immemorial Time beyond the reach of memory or records.

time is of the essence The failure to do what is required by the time specified will be considered a breach of the contract.

The phrase "time is of the essence of a contract" means in equity that performance by one party at a time or within a period specified in the agreement is essential to enable him to require performance by the other party or is so material that failure to perform at the time prescribed will deprive the other party of some part of the benefits of the agreement. *Bouse*, 135 N.E.2d 274 (Ohio App., 1956)

timely Within the time set by contract or law.

time note A note payable only at a definite time.

time, place, or manner restriction The government can restrict the time, place, or manner of speech and assembly, but not their content.

time-sharing Joint ownership of property that is used or occupied for limited alternating time periods. Also called interval ownership.

tippee One who receives material inside information about a company. See also insider trading.

title The legal right to control, possess, and dispose of property. All ownership rights in property.

title company A company that issues title insurance.

title insurance Insurance for losses incurred due to defects in the title to real property.

"Title insurance" means insuring, guaranteeing, or indemnifying owners of real property or others interested in real property against loss or damage suffered by reason of liens or encumbrances upon, defect in, or the unmarketability of the title to the real property, guaranteeing, warranting, or otherwise insuring by a title insurance company the correctness of searches relating to the title to real property, or doing any business in substance equivalent to any of the foregoing. R.C. § 3953.01(A)

title search A determination of whether defects in the title to real property exist by examining relevant public records.

title state See title theory.

title theory The theory that a mortgagee has title to land until the mortgage debt is paid. States that so provide are called title states.

TM See trademark.

to have and to hold See habendum clause.

toll 1. Payment for the use of something. 2. To stop the running of.

tombstone ad An advertisement (sometimes printed in a black-border box) for a public securities offering.

tonnage 1. The weight carrying capacity of ships. 2. A duty on ships.

tontine A financial arrangement among a group in which the last survivor receives the entire fund.

Torrens title system A system for land registration under which a court issues a binding certificate of title.

tort A civil wrong (other than a breach of contract) for which the courts will provide a remedy such as damages.

A "tort" is a legal wrong committed on the person or property of another, either a direct invasion, infraction of public duty or violation of private obligation by reason of which damages accrue. *Hammond*, 164 N.E.2d 919 (Ohio Com.Pl., 1959)

tortfeasor A person who has committed a tort.

tortious Pertaining to conduct that can lead to tort liability.

tortious interference with prospective advantage See interference with prospective advantage.

total breach A breach that so substantially impairs the value of the contract to the injured party at the time of the breach that it is just in the circumstances to allow recovery of damages based on all the injured party's remaining rights to performance.

total disability Inability to engage in any gainful occupation.

"Total disability" means inability to perform the duties of any gainful occupation for which the insured is reasonably fitted by training, experience, and accomplishment. R.C. § 3923.011(A)

total incorporation See selective incorporation.

total loss Damage beyond physical repair; complete destruction.

Totten trust A trust created by a deposit of funds in a bank account in trust for a beneficiary. The trustee is the depositor, who retains the power to revoke the trust. Also called savings bank trust, tentative trust.

to wit That is to say, namely.

township 1. A political subdivision, usually part of a county. 2. A square tract that is six miles on each side.

tract index A publicly kept index of parcels (tracts) of land.

trade Commerce. Buying, selling, or bartering goods or services.

trade acceptance A bill of exchange drawn by a seller on the buyer of goods for the amount of the purchase, and accepted for payment by the buyer at a set time.

trade association An organization of businesses in an industry that promotes the interests of the industry.

trade dress The total image or overall appearance of a product.

trade fixture Personal property affixed to the realty by a tenant who uses it in its business and has the right to remove it.

trade libel See disparagement.

trademark (TM) A distinctive word, mark, or emblem that serves to identify a product with a specific producer and to distinguish it from others. See also infringement.

"Trademark" means any word, name, symbol, device, or combination of any word, name, symbol, or device, that is adopted and used by a person to identify and distinguish the goods of that person, including a unique product, from the goods of other persons, and to indicate the source of the goods, even if that source is unknown. R.C. § 1329.54(A)

trade name A name or symbol that identifies and distinguishes a business.

"Trade name" means a name used in business or trade to designate the business of the user and to which the user asserts a right to exclusive use. R.C. § 1329.01(A)(1)

trade secret A business formula, pattern, device, or compilation of information known only by certain individuals in the business and used for competitive advantage.

trade union A union or workers in the same trade or craft.

trade usage A practice or method of dealing having such regularity of observance in a place, vocation, or trade as to justify an expectation that it will be observed in the transaction in question.

traffic 1. Commerce or trade. 2. Transportation of people or things.

tranche A slice or portion of a bond offering or other investment.

transact To have dealings; to carry on.

transaction 1. The act of conducting something. 2. A business deal.

transactional immunity Immunity from prosecution for any matter about which a witness testifies.

transcript A word-for-word account. A written copy of oral testimony.

transfer To deliver or convey an interest. To place with another.

"Transfer" means every direct or indirect, absolute or conditional, and voluntary or involuntary method of disposing of or parting with an asset or an interest in an asset, and includes payment of money, release, lease, and creation of a lien or other encumbrance. R.C. § 1336.01(L)

transfer agent An agent appointed by a corporation to keep records on registered shareholders, handle transfers of shares, etc.

transferee One to whom an interest is conveyed.

transfer payments Payments made by the government to individuals for which no services or goods are rendered in return.

transferred-intent rule The defendant may be held responsible for a wrong committed against the plaintiff even if the defendant intended a different wrong against a different person.

transfer tax A tax imposed on the transfer of property by will, inheritance, or gift.

transitory action An action that can be tried wherever the defendant can be personally served.

transmit To send or transfer something (e.g., an interest, a message) to another person or place.

transmutation The voluntary change of separate property into marital property or vice versa.

traveler's check A cashier's check that requires the purchaser's signature when purchased and countersigned when cashed.

> "Travelers check" means an instrument identified as a traveler's check on its face or commonly recognized as a travelers check and issued in a money multiple of United States or foreign currency with a provision for a specimen signature of the purchaser to be completed at the time of purchase and a countersignature of the purchaser to be completed at the time of negotiation. R.C. § 1315.51(N)

traverse A formal denial of material facts stated in an opponent's pleading.

treason An attempt by overt acts to overthrow the government of the state to which one owes allegiance or to give aid and comfort to its foreign enemies.

treasurer An officer with responsibility over the receipt, custody, and disbursement of moneys or funds. The chief financial officer.

treasure trove Valuable property found hidden in a private place and whose owner is unknown.

treasury 1. The funds of an organization. 2. The place where such funds are stored.

Treasury bill (T-bill) A short-term debt security of the U.S. government that matures in a year or less.

Treasury bond (T-bond) A long-term debt security of the U.S. government that matures in more than 10 years.

treasury certificate An obligation of the U.S. government with a 1-year maturity and interest paid by coupon.

Treasury note (T-note) An intermediate-term debt security of the U.S. government that matures in more than 1 year but not more than 10 years.

treasury securities 1. A corporation's stock that it reacquires. Also called treasury stock. 2. Debt instruments of the U.S. government.

> "Treasury shares" means shares belonging to the corporation and not retired that have been either issued and thereafter acquired by the corporation or paid as a dividend or distribution in shares of the corporation on treasury shares of the same class. R.C. § 1701.01(K)

treatise A book that gives an overview of a topic.

treaty A formal agreement between two or more nations. Senate approval is required for U.S. treaties.

treble damages Three times the amount of damages found to be owed.

trespass A wrongful interference with another's person or property.

trespass de bonis asportatis Wrongfully taking and carrying away the goods of another.

trespasser A wrongdoer who commits a trespass.

trespass on the case See action on the case.

trespass quare clausum fregit Wrongfully entering the enclosed land of another.

trespass to chattels An intentional interference with another's personal property, resulting in dispossession or intermeddling.

trespass to land A wrongful entry on another's land.

trespass vi et armis A wrongful interference with another's person or property through force.

trial A judicial proceeding that applies the law to evidence in order to resolve conflicting legal claims.

trial brief 1. An attorney's presentation to a trial court of the legal issues and positions of his or her client. 2. An attorney's strategy notes for trial. Also called trial book, trial manual.

trial by ordeal See ordeal.

trial court The first court that provides a complete forum to hear evidence and arguments on a legal claim. A court of original jurisdiction. Also called court of first instance.

trial de novo A new trial as if a prior one had not taken place.

> The appeal to the common pleas court is not a trial *de novo* because the court is limited to an examination of the record of the hearing before the administrative agency and such additional evidence as the court, in its discretion, may allow to be presented upon the theory that it is newly discovered. *Asad*, 79 Ohio App.3d 143 (Ohio App., 1992)

trial jury See petit jury.

tribal land Reservation land held by a tribe for its community.

tribunal A court or other body that adjudicates disputes.

trier of fact See fact-finder.

TRO See temporary restraining order.

trover See conversion (1).

true bill A grand jury's notation on a bill of indictment that there is enough evidence for a criminal trial. A grand jury indictment.

true value See fair market value.

trust A device or arrangement by which its creator (the settlor or trustor) transfers property (the corpus) to a person (the trustee) who holds legal title for the benefit of another (the beneficiary or cestui que trust).

> A trust may be defined as the right, enforceable in equity, to the beneficial enjoyment of property, the legal title to which is in another. *In re Guardianship of Lombardo*, 86 Ohio St.3d 600 (Ohio 1999)

trust account See client trust account.

trust company A company or bank that serves as a trustee for trusts. A trust officer is the employee in charge of a trust.

trust deed 1. The document setting up a trust. 2. See deed of trust.

trust de son tort See constructive trust.

trustee The person or company holding legal title to property for the benefit of another.

Trustee is a person who manages a trust's principal and income for the benefit of the beneficiaries. R.C. § 5111.151(B)(5)

trustee in bankruptcy A person appointed or elected to administer the estate of a debtor in bankruptcy.

trust estate See corpus (1).

trust ex delicto See constructive trust.

trust ex maleficio See constructive trust.

trust fund See corpus (1).

trust fund doctrine An insolvent corporation's assets are held in trust for its creditors.

trust indenture 1. The document specifying the terms of a trust. 2. See deed of trust.

trust instrument The document setting up a trust.

trust officer See trust company.

trustor See settlor.

trust receipt A document stating that a dealer/borrower is holding goods in trust for the benefit of the lender.

trust territory A territory placed under the administration of a country by the United Nations.

trusty A trusted prisoner given special privileges and duties.

truth-in-lending Required disclosure of credit terms.

try 1. To litigate. 2. To decide a legal dispute in court.

turnkey contract A contract in which the builder agrees to complete the work of building and installation to the point of readiness for occupancy.

turnover order A court order that the losing litigant transfer property to the winning litigant.

turntable doctrine See attractive nuisance doctrine.

turpitude Depravity.

twisting Deception to induce an insured to switch insurance policies.

two-dismissal rule A voluntary dismissal of a second action operates as a dismissal on the merits if the plaintiff has previously dismissed an action involving the same claim.

two-issue rule A jury verdict involving two or more issues will not be set aside if the verdict is supported as to at least one of the issues.

Under the "two-issue rule," where there are two causes of action, or two defenses, thereby raising separate and distinct issues, and a general verdict has been returned, and the mental processes of the jury have not been tested by special interrogatories to indicate which of the issues was resolved in favor of the successful party, it will be presumed that all issues were so determined; where a single determinative issue has been tried free from error, error in presenting another issue will be disregarded. *Hampel*, 89 Ohio St.3d 169 (Ohio 2000)

two-witness rule In a perjury or treason case, proof of falsity of the testimony cannot be established by the uncorroborated testimony of a single witness.

tying arrangement A seller conditions the sale of one product or service on the buyer's purchase of a separate product or service.

U

uberrima fides Highest degree of good faith.

ubi Where.

UCC See Uniform Commercial Code.

UCCC Uniform Consumer Credit Code.

UCMJ Uniform Code of Military Justice.

UFTA Uniform Fraudulent Transfer Act.

ukase An official decree or proclamation.

ultimate facts Facts essential to a cause of action or a defense.

ultrahazardous See abnormally dangerous.

ultra vires Beyond the scope of corporate powers; unauthorized.

umbrella policy An insurance policy that covers risks not covered by homeowners, automobile, or other standard liability policies.

umpire A neutral person asked to resolve or help resolve a dispute.

unalienable See inalienable.

unanimous opinion An opinion in which all judges or justices are in full agreement.

unauthorized practice of law (UPL) Engaging in acts that require either a license to practice law or other special authorization by a person who does not have the license or special authorization.

A layperson rendering legal services, including the management of actions and proceedings on behalf of clients before courts of law and the preparation of legal pleadings and other papers by a layperson without the supervision of a licensed attorney. *Stark Cty. Bar Assn.*, 107 Ohio St.3d 29 (Ohio 2005)

unavoidable accident An accident that could not have been prevented by ordinary care. Also called inevitable accident, pure accident.

uncertificated security A security not represented by an instrument, the transfer of which is registered on the issuer's books.

unclean hands doctrine See clean hands doctrine.

unconditional Without contingencies or conditions.

unconscionable So one-sided as to be oppressive and grossly unfair.

An unconscionable contract clause is one in which there is an absence of meaningful choice for the contracting parties, coupled with draconian contract terms unreasonably favorable to the other party. *Featherstone*, 159 Ohio App.3d 27 (Ohio App., 2004)

unconstitutional Contrary to or inconsistent with the constitution.

uncontested Unopposed; without opposition.

uncontrollable impulse An impulse or urge that cannot be resisted.

undercapitalized Insufficient capital to run a profitable business.

under color of law See color of law.

underlease See sublease.

under protest Waiving no rights; to be challenged later, but paid now.

undersigned The person signing at the end of the document or page.

understanding 1. A meeting of the minds; agreement. 2. Interpretation.

undertaking 1. A promise or guaranty. 2. A bail bond. 3. A task.

undertenant See sublease.

under the influence See driving under the influence.

underwriting 1. Assuming a risk by insuring it. The process of deciding whether to insure a risk. 2. An agreement to buy the shares of a new issue of securities not purchased by the public.

undisclosed principal A principal whose existence and identity are not revealed by the agent to a third party.

undivided interest; undivided right; undivided title The interest of each individual in the entire or whole property rather than in a particular part of it.

undivided profits Accrued profit a corporation has not distributed.

> Undivided profits means the cumulative undistributed amount of a bank's net income not otherwise allocated. R.C. § 1101.01(T)

undue influence Improper persuasion, coercion, force, or deception that substitutes the will of one person for the free will of another.

unearned income 1. Income that has been received but not yet earned, e.g., prepaid rent. 2. See investment income.

unemployment compensation Temporary income from the government to persons who have lost their jobs (for reasons other than misconduct) and are looking for work.

unethical In violation of standards of practice or an ethical code.

unfair competition Passing off one's goods or services as those of another. Trade practices that unfairly undermine competition.

unfair labor practice Acts by workers, employers, or unions that are illegal under laws on labor-management relations.

> The city's refusal to bargain, culminating in its enactment of residency ordinance, was unfair labor practice under Ohio Public Employees' Collective Bargaining Act. R.C. § 4117.11(A)(1, 5). *St. Bernard*, 74 Ohio App.3d 3 (Ohio App., 1991)

unicameral Having one house or chamber in the legislature.

unified bar See integrated bar.

unified transfer tax A single or unified federal tax on property transfers during one's life and at death.

uniform Without change or variation; the same in all cases.

Uniform Commercial Code (UCC) A law adopted in all states (with some variations) on commercial transactions (e.g., sale of goods, negotiable instruments).

Uniform Code of Military Justice (UCMJ) The rules governing discipline in the armed forces.

uniform laws Laws proposed by the National Conference of Commissioners on Uniform State Laws to state legislatures, which may adopt, modify, or reject them (*www.nccusl.org*).

unilateral Affecting only one side; obligating only one side.

unilateral contract A contract in which only one party makes a promise and the other party completes the contract by rendering performance.

unilateral mistake A mistake by only one of the parties to a contract.

> A unilateral mistake generally occurs when one party recognizes the true effect of an agreement while the other does not. *Marshall*, 143 Ohio App.3d 432 (Ohio App., 2001)

unincorporated association A group of persons formed (but not incorporated) to promote a common enterprise or objective.

uninsured motorist coverage Insurance protection when injured by motorists without liability insurance.

union An association that negotiates with employers on labor issues.

union certification A government declaration that a particular union is the bargaining representative of a group of workers.

union shop A business where all workers must join the union.

United States (U.S.) The federal government.

United States Attorney An attorney who represents the federal government.

United States Code (USC) An official codification of permanent and public federal statutes organized by subject matter.

United States Commissioner See magistrate (1).

United States courts The federal courts (*www.uscourts.gov*).

United States Marshal See marshal (1).

United States Magistrate See magistrate (1).

United States Reports (U.S.) The official collection of opinions of the U.S. Supreme Court.

United States Statutes at Large See Statutes at Large.

unit investment trust A trust investing in a portfolio of securities.

unit rule Valuing shares by multiplying the sale price of one share on a stock exchange by the total number of shares.

unity The four elements of a joint tenancy: (1) *unity of interest* (the interests of all the joint tenants have the same nature, extent, and duration); (2) *unity of title* (all the joint tenants had their estate created by the same instrument); (3) *unity of time* (the interests of all the joint tenants vested at the same time); and (4) *unity of possession* (all the joint tenants have the right to possess the whole property).

universal agent An agent with full powers to act for the principal.

unjust enrichment Receiving a benefit that in justice and in equity belongs to another.

> Unjust enrichment is an equitable doctrine to justify a quasi-contractual remedy that operates in the absence of an express contract or a contract implied in fact to prevent a party from retaining money or benefits that in justice and equity belong to another *Beatley*, 160 Ohio App.3d 600 (Ohio App., 2005)

unlawful Contrary to the law; illegal.

unlawful arrest An arrest without a warrant or probable cause.

unlawful assembly Three or more persons who meet to do an unlawful act or a lawful act in a violent, boisterous, or tumultuous manner.

unlawful detainer Remaining in possession of real property unlawfully by one whose original possession was lawful.

unlawful entry 1. A trespass on real property. 2. Entering a country illegally.

unlawful force The wrongful use of force against another.

unliquidated Not determined or specified; not ascertained in amount.

unlisted security A security not registered with a stock exchange.

unmarketable title A title an ordinary prudent buyer would not accept.

unnatural offense See sodomy.

unnecessary hardship Ground for a variance from a zoning regulation based on the unreasonableness of its application.

> To amount to unnecessary hardship and thus justify use variance, there must be showing that all permitted uses are not economically feasible or cannot be efficiently continued. R.C. § 519.14(B). *Warner*, 63 Ohio Misc.2d 385 (Ohio Com.Pl., 1993)

unprofessional conduct Conduct that violates the ethical code.

unrealized Pertaining to a gain or loss on paper. See realization (2).

unreasonable Irrational; arbitrary or capricious.

> Unreasonable means that which is not in accordance with reason, or that which has no factual foundation. *Waste Mgt. of Ohio*, 159 Ohio App.3d 806 (Ohio App., 2005)

unreasonable restraint of trade A restraint of trade whose anticompetitive effects outweigh its procompetitive effects.

unreasonable search A search conducted without probable cause or consent, or that is otherwise illegal.

unrelated business income Income of a non-profit organization that is taxable because it is not substantially related to the organization's purpose.

unrelated offenses Crimes that are separate and independent.

unresponsive Not answering the question or charge; irrelevant.

unreviewable Not ripe or suitable for review by a court or other body.

unsecured creditor A creditor unprotected by a lien or other security in any property of the debtor. Also called general creditor.

unsound 1. Unhealthy 2. Not based on sufficient evidence or analysis.

unsworn Not given under oath.

untenantable Unfit for the purpose leased.

untimely Too soon or too late.

unvalued policy An insurance policy in which the value of the thing insured is not agreed upon and stated in the policy. Also called open policy.

unwritten law Law derived from custom. Law not formally promulgated but collected from court opinions and learned treatises.

UPA Uniform Partnership Act.

UPC Uniform Probate Code.

UPL See unauthorized practice of law.

upset price The lowest action price a seller will accept.

U.S. See United States.

usage A custom or practice that is widely known or established.

> Practice or method of dealing qualifies as usage of trade, upon which court can rely in interpreting parties' contract, if it has such regularity of observance in place, vocation or trade as to justify an expectation that it will be observed with respect to transaction in question. *Abram*, 88 Ohio App.3d 253 (Ohio App., 1993)

USC See United States Code.

USCA United States Code Annotated.

U.S.D.C. United States District Court.

use 1. Taking, employing, or applying something. 2. The value of something. 3. The profit or benefit of land. 4. A purpose.

useful Having practical utility.

useful life See depreciable life.

use immunity Compelled statements cannot be used in a later criminal trial.

useless-gesture exception See knock-and-announce rule.

use tax A tax on goods bought outside the state.

usufruct A right to use another's property without damaging it.

usurious Pertaining to usury.

usury Lending money at an interest rate above what is authorized by law.

utility 1. Usefulness, providing a benefit. 2. See public utility.

UTMA Uniform Transfers to Minors Act.

utmost care See great care.

utter 1. To place or send into circulation. 2. To say or publish. See also excited utterance.

> To issue, publish, transfer, use, put or send into circulation, delivery, or display. R.C. § 2913.01 (H)

ux. (**uxor**) Wife.

V

v. Versus; volume.

VA Veterans Administration, now the Department of Veterans Affairs (*www.va.gov*).

vacant succession Succession when no one claims it, when all the heirs are unknown, or when all the known heirs to it have renounced it.

vacate 1. To cancel or set aside. 2. To surrender possession.

vacation 1. Cancellation or setting aside. 2. A period of time between sessions or terms.

vacatur ("it is annulled") Setting aside.

vagrancy Wandering without a home or lawful means of support.

vague, vagueness Unclear or imprecise. Not giving fair warning of what is commanded or prohibited.

> A vague statute is one that either forbids or requires the doing of an act in terms so vague that persons of common intelligence must necessarily guess at its meaning and differ

as to its application. *Lesiak*, 128 Ohio App.3d 743 (Ohio App., 1998)

valid Having the force of law; legally sufficient. Meritorious.

valuable consideration A benefit to the promisor or detriment to the promisee. Any valid consideration. Also called legal consideration.

valuation 1. Determining the value of something. 2. The appraised price.

value 1. Monetary worth. 2. Usefulness; desirability. 3. Consideration.

Value as used in statute authorizing court to allow alimony upon consideration of, among other things, value of real and personal estate of either at time of decree, means reasonable or fair market value at time of decree. R.C. § 3105.18. *Roberts*, 113 Ohio App. 33 (Ohio App., 1961)

value-added tax (VAT) A tax on whatever additional value is added at the various stages of production.

valued policy An insurance policy in which the value of the thing insured is agreed upon and stated in the policy as the amount to be paid in the event of a loss.

vandalism Willful or malicious destruction of property.

variable annuity An annuity in which benefit payments fluctuate with the performance of the fund's earnings.

variable-rate mortgage (VRM) See adjustable-rate mortgage.

variance 1. Permission not to follow a zoning requirement. 2. An inconsistency between two allegations, positions, or provisions.

VAT See value-added tax.

vehicular homicide Killing while operating a motor vehicle illegally, particularly with gross negligence.

vel non Or not; or without it.

vendee A buyer.

vendor A seller.

vendor's lien A seller's lien securing the unpaid purchase price.

venire See jury panel.

venire facias A writ requiring the sheriff to summon a jury.

venireman, veniremember, venireperson A prospective member of a jury.

venture A business enterprise or other undertaking that often has an element of risk and speculation.

venture capital An investment in a business, often involving potentially high risks and gains. Also called risk capital.

venue The proper county or geographical area in which a court with jurisdiction may hear a case. The place of the trial.

Venue commonly refers to appropriate place of trial for a dispute, it being assumed that court has subject matter or territorial jurisdiction. *State v. Kushlan*, 10 Ohio Misc.2d 13 (Ohio Mun., 1984)

veracity Accuracy, truthfulness.

verbal Concerned with words; expressed orally.

verbal act An utterance to which the law attaches duties and liabilities.

verdict The jury's decision on the fact questions it was asked to resolve.

verification 1. Confirmation of correctness. 2. A declaration (often sworn) of the authenticity or truth of something.

Verification of a petition for writ of habeas corpus means a formal declaration made in the presence of an authorized officer, such as a notary public, by which one swears to the truth of the statements in the document. R.C. § 2725.04. *Chari*, 91 Ohio St.3d 323 (Ohio 2001)

versus (vs.)(v.) Against (e.g., Smith vs. Jones).

vertical integration The performance within one business of two or more steps in the chain of production and distribution.

vertical merger A merger between two businesses with a buyer-seller relationship with each other.

vertical price fixing An attempt by someone in the chain of distribution to set prices that someone lower on that chain will charge. An attempt by a supplier to fix the prices charged by those who resell its products.

vertical union See industrial union.

vest To give an immediate, fixed right of present or future enjoyment. To confer ownership or title.

vested Fixed; absolute, not subject to be defeated by a condition.

vested estate; vested interest An estate or interest in which there is a present fixed right either of present or of future enjoyment.

vested remainder An estate in land that presently exists unconditionally in a definite or ascertained person, but the actual enjoyment of it is deferred until the termination of a previous estate.

vested right A right that cannot be infringed upon or taken away.

A vested right is one which it is proper for the state to recognize and protect and which an individual cannot be deprived of arbitrarily without injustice. *State v. Muqdady*, 110 Ohio Misc.2d 51 (Ohio Mun., 2000)

veto A chief executive's rejection of a bill passed by the legislature.

vexatious Without reasonable or just cause; annoying.

viable 1. Able to live outside the womb. 2. Practicable.

viatical settlement A contract of a terminally ill person to sell his or her life insurance policy, allowing the buyer to collect the death benefits.

vicarious Experienced, endured, or substituting for another.

vicarious disqualification See imputed disqualification.

vicarious liability Liability imposed on one party for the conduct of another, based solely upon the status of the relationship between the two.

vice 1. In substitution for; in place of. 2. Immoral; illegal; defect.

vicinage Vicinity; the area or locale where the crime was committed from which prospective jurors will be drawn.

victim impact statement Comments made during sentencing by a victim on the impact of the crime on his or her life.

In all criminal cases in which a person is convicted of or pleads guilty to a felony, if the offender, in committing the offense, caused, attempted to cause, threatened to cause, or created a risk of physical harm to the victim of the offense, the court, prior to sentencing the offender, shall order the preparation of a victim impact statement by the department of probation of the county in which the victim of the offense resides, by the court's own regular probation officer, or by a victim assistance program that is operated by the state, any county or municipal corporation, or any other governmental entity. R.C. § 2947.051(A)

victimless crime A crime with a consenting victim or without a direct victim, e.g., drug use or possession.

victualer One who serves food prepared for eating on the premises.

videlicet See viz.

vi et armis With force and arms.

vinculo matrimonii Marriage bond. See divorce a vinculo matrimonii.

vindictive damages See punitive damages.

violation 1. Breaching a law or rule. 2. Rape or sexual assault.

violent Involving great or extreme physical or emotional force.

vir 1. A man. 2. A husband.

virtual representation doctrine A person may be bound by a judgment even though not a party if one of actual parties in the suit is so closely aligned with that person's interests as to be his or her virtual representative.

vis (power) Force; disturbance.

visa An authorization on a passport giving the holder permission to enter or leave a country.

visitation Time allowed someone without custody to spend with a child.

vis major An irresistible force or natural disaster; a loss caused by nature that was not preventable by reasonable care.

> If the *vis major* is so unusual and overwhelming as to do the damage by its own power, without reference to and independently of any negligence by defendant, there is no liability.
> *Lytle*, 91 Ohio App. 232 (Ohio App., 1951)

vital statistics Public records on births, deaths, marriages, diseases, etc.

vitiate To impair or destroy the legal efficacy of something.

viva voce By word of mouth, orally.

viz (abbreviation for videlicet) Namely, in other words.

void 1. Having no legal force or binding effect. 2. To invalidate.

void ab initio Invalid from its inception or beginning.

voidable Valid but subject to being annulled or declared void.

voidable preference A debtor's transfer of assets to a creditor (before filing for bankruptcy) that constitutes an advantage over other bankruptcy creditors.

void for vagueness A law that is so obscure that a reasonable person could not determine what the law purports to command or prohibit.

> Void for vagueness doctrine generally requires that penal statute define criminal offense with sufficient definiteness that ordinary people can understand what conduct is prohibited and in such manner that it does not encourage either arbitrary or discriminatory enforcement. *State v. Gaines*, 64 Ohio App.3d 230 (Ohio App., 1990)

voir dire ("to speak the truth") A preliminary examination (a) of prospective jurors for the purpose of selecting persons qualified to sit on a jury or (b) of prospective witnesses to determine their competence to testify.

volenti non fit injuria ("to a willing person it is not wrong") There is no cause of action for injury or harm to which one consented.

voluntary 1. By choice; proceeding from a free and unconstrained will. 2. Intentional. 3. Without consideration; gratuitous.

voluntary bankruptcy A petition for bankruptcy filed by the debtor.

voluntary bar A bar association that attorneys are not required to join.

voluntary commitment Civil commitment or institutionalization with the consent of the person committed or institutionalized.

voluntary dismissal A dismissal of a suit at the plaintiff's request.

voluntary manslaughter The intentional, unlawful killing of someone without malice or premeditation. Murder reduced to manslaughter.

> (A) No person, while under the influence of sudden passion or in a sudden fit of rage, either of which is brought on by serious provocation occasioned by the victim that is reasonably sufficient to incite the person into using deadly force, shall knowingly cause the death of another or the unlawful termination of another's pregnancy. (B) Whoever violates this section is guilty of voluntary manslaughter, a felony of the first degree. R.C. § 2903.03

voluntary trust 1. A trust created by express agreement. 2. A trust created as a gift.

voluntary waste Harm to real property committed by a tenant intentionally or negligently.

volunteer 1. One who voluntarily performs an act (e.g., pays someone's debt) without a duty to do so. 2. One who acts without coercion.

vote A formal expression of one's choice for a candidate or position.

voter One who votes or who has the qualifications to vote.

voting stock Stock entitling a holder to vote, e.g., for directors.

voting trust An agreement between stockholders and a trustee whereby the rights to vote the stock are transferred to the trustee.

vouch To give a personal assurance or to serve as a guarantee.

voucher 1. A receipt for payment. 2. An authorization to pay.

> Voucher means the document used to transmit a claim for payment and evidentiary matter related to the claim. R.C. § 131.01(R)

vouching-in A mechanism whereby a defendant in a proceeding may notify a non-party, the vouchee, that a suit is pending against the defendant and that, if liability is found, the defendant will look to the vouchee for indemnity and hold it to the findings in that suit.

VRM See adjustable-rate mortgage.

vs. See versus.

W

***Wade* hearing** A pretrial hearing on the admissibility of lineup or other identification evidence. *United States v. Wade*, 87 S. Ct. 1926 (1967).

wage Payments made to a hired person for his or her labor or services.

Wages means remuneration paid to an employee by each of the employee's employers with respect to employment. R.C. § 4141.01(G)(1)

wage and hour laws Statutes on minimum wages and maximum work hours.

wage assignment 1. A court order to withhold someone's wages in order to satisfy a debt. An attachment by a creditor of a debtor's wages. 2. A contract transferring the right to receive wages.

wage earner's plan A new payment schedule or plan for the payment of all or a portion of a debtor's debts in a Chapter 13 bankruptcy when the debtor still has regular income.

wager policy An insurance policy to one with no insurable interest in the risks covered by the policy.

wait and see Basing the rule against perpetuities on vesting that actually occurs rather than what might occur. Also called second look.

waiting period The time that must elapse before the next legal step can occur or a right can be exercised.

waiver The express or implied voluntary relinquishment of a right, claim, or benefit.

The voluntary surrender or relinquishment of a known legal right or the intentionally doing of an act inconsistent with claiming it; mere silence will not amount to waiver where one is not bound to speak. *Baughman*, 160 Ohio App.3d 642 (Ohio App., 2005)

walkout A labor strike or departure in protest.

want of consideration A total lack of consideration for a contract.

wanton A conscious disregard of consequences. Malicious.

war Armed conflict between nations, states, or groups.

war crimes Conduct in violation of international laws governing wars.

ward 1. A person (e.g., minor) placed by the court under the care or protection of a guardian. 2. A division of a city or town.

warden A superintendent or person in charge.

warehouseman; warehouser Someone in the business of offering storage facilities.

warehouseman's lien A lien of a warehouseman in goods it is storing that provides security for unpaid storage charges.

warehouse receipt A receipt issued by a person engaged in the business of storing goods for hire. The receipt is a document of title.

A written or electronic receipt issued by a person engaged in the business of storing goods for hire. R.C. § 1301.01(SS)

warrant 1. A court order commanding or authorizing a specific act, e.g., to arrest someone, to search an area. 2. A document providing authorization, e.g., to receive goods or make payment. 3. A long-term option to purchase stock at a given price. Also called stock warrant. 4. To guarantee or provide a warranty.

warrantless arrest An arrest made without a warrant. The arrest is proper if a misdemeanor is committed in the officer's presence or if the officer has probable cause to believe that a felony has been committed.

warranty 1. A commitment imposed by contract or law that a product or service will meet a specified standard. 2. A guarantee in a deed that assures the conveyance of a good and clear title.

"Express warranty" and "warranty" mean the written warranty of the manufacturer or distributor of a new motor vehicle concerning the condition and fitness for use of the vehicle, including any terms or conditions precedent to the enforcement of obligations under that warranty. R.C. § 1345.71(C)

warranty deed A deed in which the grantor promises to convey a specified title to property that is free and clear of all encumbrances. Also called general warranty deed.

warranty of fitness for a particular purpose An implied warranty that goods will meet a buyer's special need when the seller knows the buyer is relying on the seller's expertise for such need.

warranty of habitability An implied promise by a landlord that the premises are free of serious defects that endanger health or safety.

warranty of merchantability An implied promise that the goods are fit for the ordinary purposes for which they are used.

warranty of title A seller's warranty that he or she owns what is being sold and that there are no undisclosed encumbrances on it.

wash sale A deceptive transaction involving the sale and purchase of securities that does not change beneficial ownership.

waste 1. Serious harm done to real property that affects the rights of holders of future interests in the property. 2. Refuse.

wasting asset An asset with a limited life or subject to depletion.

wasting trust A trust, the res of which consists of property that is gradually being depleted by payments to the beneficiaries.

watered stock 1. Stock issued at less than par value. 2. Stock issued at an inflated price.

water rights Rights to use water in its natural state, e.g., a lake.

waybill The non-negotiable document containing details of a carrier's contract for the transport of goods and acknowledging their receipt.

way of necessity See implied easement.

ways and means Methods and sources for raising government revenue.

weapon An instrument used for combat or to inflict great bodily harm.

weight of the evidence The inclination of the evidence to support one side over another; the persuasiveness of the evidence presented.

Weight of the evidence concerns the inclination of the greater amount of credible evidence, offered in a trial, to support one side of the issue rather than the other; it indicates clearly to the jury that the party having the burden of proof will be entitled to their verdict, if, on weighing the evidence in their minds, they shall find the greater amount of credible evidence sustains the issue which is to be established before them. *In re D.M.*, 158 Ohio App.3d 780 (Ohio App., 2004)

welfare 1. The well-being and the common blessings of life. 2. Public assistance; government aid to those in need.

well-pleaded complaint rule Federal-question jurisdiction exists only when a federal issue is presented on the face of the plaintiff's complaint.

Westlaw (WL) West Group's system of computer-assisted legal research.

Wharton rule See concert of action.

whereas 1. That being the case; since. 2. Although.

whereby By means of which; through which.

whiplash Injury to the cervical spine (neck) due to a sudden jerking of the head.

whistleblower One who discloses wrongdoing. A worker who reports employer wrongdoing to a public body.

Employees to report violations of state or federal law; retaliatory conduct prohibited. R.C. § 4113.52

whiteacre See blackacre.

white-collar crime A nonviolent crime, often involving a business.

white knight One who helps prevent a hostile takeover of a target corporation.

white slavery Forced prostitution.

whole law All the law in a jurisdiction, including choice of law rules.

whole life insurance Insurance covering the insured's entire life, not just for a term. Also called ordinary life insurance, straight life insurance.

wholesale Selling goods to one who is in the business of reselling them.

widow's (or **widower's**) **allowance** Part of a decedent's estate set aside by law for the surviving spouse, which most creditors cannot reach.

widow's (or **widower's**) **election** See election by spouse.

wildcat strike A strike called without authorization from the union.

Wild's case See rule in Wild's case.

will 1. An instrument that a person makes to dispose of his or her property upon his or her death. 2. Desire or choice.

will contest A challenge to the validity of a will.

willful Voluntary, intentional, deliberate.

Willful conduct under parental liability statute means intentional doing of act which occasions injury and resulting damage; there must be intent to cause injury. R.C. § 3109.09(A). *State Auto. Mut. Ins. Co.*, 65 Ohio Misc.2d 23 (Ohio Mun., 1994)

willful negligence See gross negligence.

will substitute An alternative method or device (e.g., life insurance) that is used to achieve all or part of what a decedent's will is designed to accomplish.

wind up To settle the accounts and liquidate the assets of a business about to be dissolved.

wire fraud A scheme to defraud using interstate electronic communication.

wiretapping Connecting a listening device to a telephone line to overhear conversations. Electronic eavesdropping.

with all faults As is; no warranty given.

withdraw 1. To remove, take back, or retract. 2. To take (funds) out of.

withholding tax Income taxes taken from one's salary or other income.

without prejudice With no loss or waiver of rights or privileges.

Term "without prejudice" essentially means that the party may refile the action at a later date. *McCann*, 95 Ohio App.3d 226 (Ohio App., 1994)

without recourse Disclaiming liability to subsequent holders in the event of non-payment.

with prejudice Ending all further rights; ending the controversy.

witness 1. To see, hear, or experience something. 2. A person who gives testimony, often under oath.

witness stand The place in court where a witness gives testimony.

wobbler An offense that could be charged as a felony or a misdemeanor.

words actionable in themselves Words that constitute libel per se or slander per se.

words of art See terms of art.

words of limitation In a conveyance or will, words that describe the duration or quality of an estate being transferred.

words of negotiability See negotiability words.

words of purchase Words designating the recipients of a grant.

work The physical or mental exertion of oneself for a purpose. Labor.

workers' compensation A no-fault system of benefits for workers injured on the job. Also called employers' liability.

work for hire An employee-authored work whose copyright is owned by the employer.

workhouse A jail for persons convicted of lesser offenses.

working capital Current assets of a business less its current liabilities.

working papers A permit certifying one's right to work.

workout A restructuring of the payment and other terms of a debt.

work product rule Material prepared by or for an attorney in anticipation of litigation is not discoverable, absent a showing of substantial need.

Trial preparation: materials. Subject to the provisions of subdivision (B)(4) of this rule, a party may obtain discovery of documents and tangible things prepared in anticipation of litigation or for trial by or for another party or by or for that other party's representative (including his attorney, consultant, surety, indemnitor, insurer, or agent) only upon a showing of good cause therefor. Ohio Civ. R. Rule 26(B)(3)

work release program A program allowing inmates to leave the institution for employment during part of the day.

work stoppage A cessation of work, often due to a labor dispute.

work-to-rule A slowdown due to excessive compliance with work rules.

World Court The International Court of Justice (*www.icj-cij.org*).

worth 1. The monetary or emotional value of something. 2. Wealth.

worthier title doctrine A person who receives by will what he or she would have inherited as an heir by intestacy, takes as an heir.

wraparound mortgage A second mortgage in which the lender of additional funds assumes the payments on the first mortgage.

wreck The cast-aside wreckage of a ship or its cargo.

writ A written court order to do or refrain from doing an act.

write-down; write-up A reduction (write-down) or an increase (write-up) in the value of an asset as noted in an accounting record.

write-off Removing a worthless asset from the books of account.

writ of assistance A writ to transfer possession of land after a court has determined the validity of its title.

writ of capias See capias.

writ of certiorari See certiorari.

writ of coram nobis See coram nobis.

writ of error An appellate court's writ that the record of a lower court proceeding be delivered for review.

writ of error coram nobis See coram nobis.

writ of execution See execution (3).

writ of habeas corpus See habeas corpus.

writ of mandamus See mandamus.

writ of ne exeat See ne exeat.

writ of possession A writ to repossess real property.

writ of prohibition A writ to correct or prevent judicial proceedings that lack jurisdiction.

writ of quo warranto See quo warranto.

writ of replevin See replevin.

writ of right A writ issued as a matter of course or right.

writ of supersedeas See supersedeas.

wrong A violation of the right of another. A breach of duty.

wrongdoer One who does what is illegal.

wrongful birth action An action by parents of an unwanted impaired child for negligence in failing to warn them of the risks that the child would be born with birth defects. The parents seek their own damages.

wrongful conception See wrongful pregnancy action.

wrongful death action An action by a decedent's next of kin for their damages resulting from a wrongful injury that killed the decedent.

> When the death of a person is caused by wrongful act, neglect, or default which would have entitled the party injured to maintain an action and recover damages if death had not ensued, the person who would have been liable if death had not ensued, or the administrator or executor of the estate of such person, as such administrator or executor, shall be liable to an action for damages. R.C. § 2125.01

wrongful discharge Terminating employment for a reason that violates a contract, the law, or public policy.

wrongful life An action by or on behalf of an unwanted impaired child for negligence that precluded an informed parental decision to avoid the child's conception or birth. The child seeks its own damages.

wrongful pregnancy action An action by parents of an unwanted healthy child for negligence in performing a sterilization procedure. Also called wrongful conception.

> A suit by a parent for damages arising from the birth of a child subsequent to the doctor's failure to properly perform a sterilization procedure. *Johnson*, 44 Ohio St.3d 49 (Ohio 1989)

X

x 1. The mark used as the signature of someone who is illiterate. 2. See ex dividend. 3. See ex rights. 4. See ex warrants.

Y

year-and-a-day rule Death occurring more than 1 year and a day after the alleged criminal act cannot be a homicide, e.g., murder, manslaughter.

yellow-dog contract A contract forbidding union membership.

yield 1. To relinquish or surrender. 2. Profit stated as an annual rate of return on an investment.

***Younger* abstention** See equitable restraint doctrine.

youthful offender See juvenile delinquent.

Z

z-bond A bond payable upon satisfaction of all prior bond classes.

zealous witness A witness overly eager or anxious to help one side.

zero coupon bond A bond that does not pay interest.

zipper clause A contract clause that closes out bargaining during the contract term, making the written contract the exclusive statement of the parties' rights and obligations.

> A contract provision that limits agreement between parties solely to those matters included in collective bargaining agreement. *Portsmouth*, 141 Ohio App.3d 423 (Ohio App., 2001)

zone An area set aside or that has distinctive characteristics.

zone of danger test To recover for negligent infliction of emotional distress, the plaintiff must have been frightened due to actual personal physical danger caused by defendant's negligence.

zone of employment The place of employment and the area thereabout, including the means of ingress and egress under control of the employer.

zone of privacy Activities and areas of a person given constitutional protection against unreasonable intrusion or interference.

zoning Geographic divisions within which regulations impose land use requirements covering permissible uses for buildings, lot size limitations, etc.

> Zoning and planning are not synonymous; zoning is concerned chiefly with use and regulation of buildings and structures, whereas planning is of broader scope and significance and embraces the systematic and orderly development of a community with particular regard for streets, parks, industrial and commercial undertakings, civic beauty and other kindred matters properly included within police power. *State ex rel. Kearns*, 163 Ohio St. 451 (Ohio 1955)

Index